# 1 MONTH OF
# FREE
# READING

## at

## www.ForgottenBooks.com

By purchasing this book you are
eligible for one month membership to
ForgottenBooks.com, giving you
unlimited access to our entire
collection of over 1,000,000 titles via
our web site and mobile apps.

To claim your free month visit:

www.forgottenbooks.com/free1086703

ISBN 978-0-331-48205-8

PIBN 11086703

# INDEX

## TO THE

# CHARTERS AND ROLLS

### IN THE

## DEPARTMENT OF MANUSCRIPTS

# BRITISH MUSEUM.

EDITED BY

### HENRY J. ELLIS AND FRANCIS B. BICKLEY,

SENIOR ASSISTANTS IN THE DEPARTMENT OF MSS.

VOLUME I.

*INDEX LOCORUM.*

## PRINTED BY ORDER OF THE TRUSTEES.

*SOLD AT THE BRITISH MUSEUM;*

AND BY

LONGMANS & Co., 39 Paternoster Row; BERNARD QUARITCH, 15 Piccadilly;
Asher & Co., 13 Bedford Street, Covent Garden;
KEGAN PAUL, TRENCH, TRÜBNER & Co., Paternoster House, Charing Cross Road
and HENRY FROWDE, Oxford University Press Warehouse, Amen Corner,
London.

1900.

LONDON:
PRINTED BY WILLIAM CLOWES AND SONS, Limited,
STAMFORD STREET AND CHARING CROSS

# NOTICE.

This Index embraces all the various collections of deeds in the Department, namely, the Royal, Cotton, Harley, Sloane, Campbell, Lansdowne, Topham and Wolley Charters, together with the Additional and Egerton Charters acquired up to the year 1882 and a special series of Church Briefs. The Stowe Charters, acquired in 1883, have already been indexed in the *Catalogue of the Stowe MSS.*, 1895–1896; and an index to Charters before the Norman Conquest will be found in Vol. IV. of *Facsimiles of Ancient Charters in the British Museum*, 1873–1878. The more important entries, however, in the latter have also been inserted here. The present volume is confined to the topography of the Charters relating to the British Isles only, reserving for the present all Foreign documents. Headings of personal names, Religious Houses, and subjects will be dealt with in future volumes. A list of the contractions employed is subjoined.

One of the chief points of interest and value of this Index lies in the evolution of modern place-names from the early forms found in the oldest documents, which have all been carefully traced by means of full cross-references. At the end will be found an Index to places collected under their respective Counties, and additions and corrections to the whole Index which were overlooked during the passage of the sheets through the press.

The original compilation of the slips from the descriptions of Charters was the work of the Department generally; but the labour of final revision and collation has devolved upon Mr. Ellis and Mr. Bickley, two of the Senior Assistants, under the direction of Mr. Warner, Assistant Keeper of MSS.

EDWARD J. L. SCOTT,

*Keeper of the MSS.*

1 *February*, 1900.

# CONTRACTIONS.

| | | | | |
|---|---|---|---|---|
| Add. | . | . | . | . = Additional. |
| Campb. | . | . | . | . = Campbell. |
| Cott. | . | . | . | . = Cotton. |
| Eg. | . | . | . | . = Egerton. |
| Harl. | . | . | . | . = Harley. |
| Lansd. | . | . | . | . = Lansdowne. |
| Slo. | . | . | . | . = Sloane. |
| Toph. | . | . | . | . = Topham. |
| Woll. | . | . | . | . = Wolley. |

| | | | | |
|---|---|---|---|---|
| Ch. | . | . | . | . = Charter. |
| Conf. | . | . | . | . = Confirmation. |
| Exemplif. | . | . | . | . = Exemplification. |
| Inspex. | . | . | . | . = Inspeximus. |
| Notif. | . | . | . | . = Notification. |
| Ref. | . | . | . | . = Reference. |

# INDEX LOCORUM

## TO

# CHARTERS AND ROLLS

### IN THE

# BRITISH MUSEUM.

## A

**Abbandun.** *v.* Abingdon, *co. Berks.*

**Abbas Hall Manor.** *v. sub* Cornard, Gt., *co. Suff.*

**Abbenay, Abbeney.** *v.* Abney, *in Hope, co. Derb.*

**Abberton,** *co. Essex.* Power to take seisin in, 1364 (Adburton). Harl. 55 E. 6.

**Abberton,** *co. Worc.* Conf. of grants at, to Pershore Abbey, 972 (in Eadbrihtincgtune). Cott. MS. Aug. ii. 6.

**Abbot, Newton.** *v.* Newton Abbot, *co. Devon.*

**Abbot's Manor.** *v. sub* Denham, *co. Suff.*

**Abbot's Anne.** *v.* Anne, Abbot's, *co. Southt.*

**Abbot's Court Manor.** *v. sub* Boro Regis, *co. Dors.*

**Abbot's Hall Manor.** *v. sub* Brent Eleigh, *co. Suff.*

——— *v. sub* Pettaugh, *co. Suff.*

**Abbot's Langley.** *v.* Langley, Abbot's, *co. Hertf.*

**Abbot's Ripton.** *v.* Ripton, Abbot's, *co. Hunt.*

**Abbotsbury,** *co. Dors.* Briefs conc. fires at, 1764, 1789. Ch. Br. B. iv. 12, xxix. 1.

**Abbotstoke.** *v.* Stoke Abbas, *co. Dors.*

**Aben.** *v.* Avon, *River, co. Glouc.*

**Aberafon (Avene),** *co. Glam.* Grants, etc., in Avon Marsh nr., to Margam Abbey, 1205. Harl. 75 B. 30 ;—early 13 cent. Harl. 75 C. 36 ;—*t. Hen. III.* Harl. 75 C. 21, 75 D. 21.

——— Grant nr., to Margam Abbey, to mine coal, early 13 cent. Harl. 75 B. 4.

——— Grant in, 1350. Harl. 75 B. 5 *a.*

——— Appropriation of the rectory by Margam Abbey, 1385. Harl. 75 A. 33.

——— Suit conc. tithes, betw. Margam Abbey and the Bp. of Llandaff, 1413. Harl. 75 A. 3.

——— Brief for rebuilding the church, 1766. Ch. Br. B. vi. 9.

——— *Dominus.* Joh. de Auene, 1328. Harl. 75 C. 25.

——— *Senescallus.* Joh. Louel, 1328. Harl. 75 C. 25 ;—1350. Harl. 75 B. 5 *a.*

——— *Bedellus.* Jeuan ap Gourgent, 1350. Harl. 75 B. 5 *a.*

——— *Capellanus.* Worgan, early 13 cent. Harl. 75 C. 36.

——— *Clerici.* Eneas, Mauricius, *c.* 1200. Harl. 75 B. 4.

——— *Clericus.* Walt. Lokyngton, 1385. Harl. 75 A. 33.

——— *Rector.* Thomas, 1350. Harl. 75 B. 5 *a.*

**Aberdare,** *co. Glam.* Settlement of suit conc. lands nr., betw. Margam and Caerleon Abbeys, 1203 (Aberdar). Harl. 75 A. 32.

Æscmere, nr. Buttermere, co. Wilts (?). Bequest of land at, c. 950. Cott. viii. 16.

Aeste. v. Ashtead, co. Surr.

Ævintona. v. Evington, co. Leic.

Afan hamme. v. Offenham, co. Worc.

Afene. v. Avon, co. Wilts.

Afon, River, co. Glam. Release of lands betw., and river Kenfig, to Margam Abbey, late 12 cent. (Avene). Harl. 75 B. 11.

Afon Marsh, co. Glam. Grant for the defence of the sea-walls in, by Margam Abbey, 1349 (Avene). Harl. 75 A. 44.

Agardsley, in Hanbury, co. Staff. Fine of the manor, 1638 (Agardesley). Woll. xi. 29.

Agetorp, Aghthorpe, Agthorp. v. Authorpe, co. Linc.

Aghaloo, co. Tyrone. Decree restoring lands in, 1663. Eg. 315.

Aghene Manor. v. sub Romney, Old, co. Kent.

Aghton. v. Aughton, co. York.

Agmodesham. v. Amersham, co. Buck.

Ahys. v. Ash Bocking, co. Suff.
—— v. Campsey Ash, co. Suff.

Aigatorp. v. Authorpe, co. Linc.

Aighton, in Milton, co. Linc. Brief conc. a fire in, 1813. Ch. Br. B. liv. 6.

Aihum. v. Eyam, co. Derb.

Aikering. v. Eakring, co. Notts.

Aikton, co. Cumb. Grant, etc., in, 1484 (Ayktone). Harl. 112 G. 29;— 1572 (Acton). Harl. 77 H. 37.

Ailberton. v. Elberton, co. Glouc.

Ailby (Alebi, Aleby, etc.), nr. Rigsby, co. Linc. Grants, etc., in, to Greenfield Priory, t. Hen. II. Harl. 45 B. 38, 39, 45 C. 3, 5, 47 I. 34, 55 D. 12;—late Hen. II. or late 12 cent. Harl. 45 B. 41-43, 45 C. 1. 2, 4, 6, 7;— early 13 cent.-t. Hen. III. Harl. 45 B. 40, 44-55, 45 E. 41, 47 G. 44, 45, 48 C. 4 b, 55 D. 14, 57 B. 5;—late 13 cent. or t. Edw. I. Harl. 51 A. 22, 52 A 24;—1392. Cott. xxvii. 5, Harl. 43 E. 36.

—— Conf. by Hen. II. of grants in, to Greenfield Priory, [1175?]. Harl. 43 C. 21.

Ailby (Alebi, Aleby, etc.), nr. Rigsby, co. Linc. (continued). Grants of "Drihil" or "Dribehil" in, to same, late 12 cent. Harl. 54 B. 23;—early 13 cent. Harl. 54 B. 21.

—— Grant in, from same, early 13 cent. Harl. 44 D. 59.

—— Grants in "Derewen hil" and "Craketheit" in, to same, early 13 cent. Harl. 54 B. 42.

—— Exch. in "le Pinkeldic" and "Depker" in, by same, c. 1260. Harl. 44 D. 61.

—— Release "ultra Trentesic" in or nr., to same, late Hen. III. Harl. 54 B. 31.

—— Bequest in, to same, "ad augmentacionem cervisie," 1267. Harl. 57 G. 1, 2.

—— Grants, etc., in, t. Hen. III. Harl. 45 C. 8, 51 A. 21, 23;—early Edw. I. Harl. 52 A. 25;—1301. Harl. 44 E. 2;—1346. Harl. 52 I. 9;— 1474. Harl. 50 C. 27.

Ailesham. v. Aylsham, co. Norf.

Aileton. v. Elton, co. Hunt.

Aillesforth. v. Aylesford, co. Kent.

Ailmundestre. v. Elmstree, co. Glouc.

Ailricheseia. v. Arlsey, co. Bedf.

Ailsham. v. sub Well, in Ickham, co. Kent.

Ainreker. v. sub Saleby, co. Linc.

Ainstable, co. Cumb. Lease in, 1572. Harl. 77 H. 37.

Airdrie, in Crail, co. Fife. Conf. of a grant in, by William, King of Scotland, late 12 cent. (Ardaria). Campb. xxx. 5.

Airton, co. York. Sale of the manor, 1530 (Ayrton in Malhomdales). Add. 5797.

Aisby (Aseby, etc.), in Haydor, co. Linc. Grants, etc., in, early Hen. III. (Husebia). Add. 6370;—t. Hen. III. Add. 6371, 6373, 6374;—late 13 cent. Add. 6376;—1306-1577. Add. 6378-6387, 6389, 6391-6400, 6402-6404, 6406, 6408, 6409, 6414-6422, 6425-6431;—1528 (Aesby). Add. 6441;— 1564 (Aysby). Add. 6446.

—— Release of the manor, 1563 (Aysby). Add. 6427.

—— Fines in, 1564, 1577. Add. 6447, 6450.

**Aldburgh,** *in Masham. co. York.* Conf. of a grant in. to Fountains Abbey, *t.* Hen. II. Add. 7491.

**Aldbury,** *co. Hertf.* Grant of an annuity from Pendeley manor in, 1547. Harl. 84 C. 28.

**Aldebergh.** *v.* Alburgh, *co. Norf.*

**Aldebi.** *v.* Aldeby, *co. Norf.*

**Aldebur.** *v.* Oldbury on the Hill, *co. Glouc.*

**Aldebury.** *v.* Albury, *co. Surr.*

—— *v.* Oldbury, *co. Salop.*

**Aldebury** [Aldborough, *co. York?*]. Grant in, 1357. Add. 5750.

**Aldeby,** *co. Norf.* Grants, etc., in, early 13th cent. Harl. 57 F. 7 (Aldebi);—1361. Harl. 52 B. 11;—1386. Harl. 56 G. 21:—1417. Harl. 46 D. 34;—1422. Harl. 50 F. 36.

—— *Fines* in, 1310. Harl. 46 D. 32:—1419. Harl. 51 E. 53;—1462. Harl. 54 I. 19.

**Aldefeld.** *v. sub* Faldingworth, *co Linc.*

—— *v. sub* Yarnfield, *co. Som.*

**Aldeham.** *v.* Aldenham, *co. Hertf.*

—— *v.* Yaldham, *in Wrotham, co. Kent.*

**Aldelond.** *v. sub* Bitton, *co. Glouc.*

**Aidelose Manor.** *v. sub* Hastingleigh, *co. Kent.*

**Aldelyme.** *v.* Audlem, *co. Chest.*

**Aldenham,** *co. Hertf.* Conf. by Edw. the Confessor of a grant in, to Westminster Abbey, 1066 [*sc.* 1065] (Ealdenham). Cott. vi. 2 (*copy*).

—— *Custumary,* early Hen. III. (Aldeham). Add. 8139.

—— *Sales* in, 1477. Harl. 58 F. 29;—1577. Add. 1599, 1600.

**Aldenneby.** *v.* Holdenby, *co. Northt.*

**Aldensheles.** *v.* Aydon Shields, *in Hexham, co. Northumb.*

**Aldeport.** *v.* Alport, *in Youlgreave, co. Derb.*

**Aldercar Park,** *in Heanor, co. Derb.* Inspex. of a grant of the custody of, with order for salary of keeper, 1459. Woll. iv. 31.

**Alderfordde Mill.** *v. sub* Horsham St. Faith, *co. Norf.*

**Alderide,** *in Hawthorpe, co. Linc.* Grant in, to Sempringham Priory, early 13 cent. Add. 20604.

**Alderley,** *co. Chest.* Crown leases of the manor, 1536. Harl. 84 C. 25 (Alderlegh);—1545. Harl. 83 H. 10 (Alderleigh).

**Alderman's Haw,** *in Charnwood Forest, co. Leic.* Papal conf. of grant in, to Ulvescroft Priory, 1174. Harl. 111 A. 6 (*copy*).

**Aldermaston,** *co. Berks.* Lease in, 1698. Add. 19238.

—— *Vicarius. Dom.* Willelmus, 1242. Add. 20372.

**Aldershaw,** *nr. Lichfield, co. Staff.* Grant nr., *t.* Hen. III. Campb. iv. 14 (Alresawe).

**Alderton,** *co. Glouc.* Parson. Joh. Carter, *t.* Hen. VII.-VIII. Add. 18549.

**Alderton,** *co. Northt.* Grants, etc., in, [1215-26]. Harl. 57 E. 28 (Aldrinton);—early Edw. III. Add. 21514 (Aldrynglona);—1393. Harl. 57 E. 22.

**Alderton,** *co. Suff.* Lease of Howes-and Erle-Alderton manors in, 1537. Add. 909.

—— *Recovery* in, 1544. Add. 1384.

—— *Rental* of Howes in Alderton and Alderton Comitis manors in, 1685. Add. 910.

—— *Sale* of Alderton Hall, Nawton, Bovils and Peches manors in, 1714. Add. 911.

—— *Persona.* Joh. de Pishale *al.* Pysale, 1368. Harl. 47 B. 2;—1369. Harl. 54 G. 50.

**Alderton,** *co. Wilts.* Bond by M. Lungespe for a rent from the manor, 1261 (Audinton). Harl. 53 B. 13.

—— *Grants* in, *t.* Edw. I. Add. 1535 (Aldrynton), 7064 (Aldrintone).

—— *Grant* of the manor, 1458 (Aldryngton). Add. 1536.

—— *Grant* of an annuity in, 1675. Add. 18445 (Aldrington).

**Alderwas.** *v.* Alrewas, *co. Staff.*

**Alderwasley** (Alderwaslegh, etc.), *in Wirksworth, co. Derb.* Grants, etc., in, 1503. Woll. iii. 19;—1566. Woll. iii. 20;—1598. Woll. iii. 86;—1613. Woll. xi. 87 (Aldernsley);—1624. Woll. xi. 119;—1640. Woll. xi. 121.

—— *Extracts* from Court-rolls, 1598. Woll. iii. 86;—1633. Woll. iii. 87;—1639. Woll. iii. 88.

—— *Lease* to give seisin of Milnhay common in, 1684. Woll. xi. 125.

**Aldworth**, *co. Berks. Rector.* Will. de Rutherewyke, 1267. Add. 19627.

**Aldyngton.** *v.* Aldington, *co. Kent.*

—— *v.* Allington, *in S. Stoneham, co. Southt.*

**Alebi, Aleby, Alesbia.** *v.* Ailby, *nr. Rigsby, co. Linc.*

**Aleburne.** *v.* Albourne, *co. Suss.*

**Alesbi.** *v.* Aylesby, *co. Linc.*

**Alestre**, *co. Derb.* Grant iu, 1424. Harl. 84 A. 49.

**Alewardby.** *v.* Audby, *co. Linc.*

**Aleweshey.** *v. sub* Richard's Castle, *co. Heref.*

**Aleweston.** *v.* Alveston, *co. Glouc.*

**Alewoldeston.** *v.* Alvaston, *co. Derb.*

**Alferton.** *v.* Alfreton, *co. Derb.*

**Alfestun.** *v.* Alveston, *co. Warw.*

**Alfeton.** *v.* Alpheton, *co. Suff.*

**Alfewelond e la Dune**, [*co. Essex or Suff.?*] Grant of, late 12 cent. Harl. 54 A. 16.

**Alfhameston.** *v.* Alphamstone, *co. Essex.*

**Alfold**, *cos. Surr. and Suss.* Grants, etc., in, 1304–5. Add. 8811 ;—1313. Add. 5585 ;—1315. Add. 5586.

—— Mortgage nr. Monkenhook in, 1325. Add. 26762.

—— Conveyance of Wildwood (Wyldewoole) manor in, 1439. Add. 5618.

—— Precipe conc. Iford manor, etc., in, 1592. Add. 25542.

**Alford** (Auford), *co. Linc.* Settlement of tithes upon the church, 1220. Harl. 57 F. 51.

—— Grants and leases in, 1355. Harl. 57 G. 11 ;—[1361-8]. Harl. 55 B. 24 ; —1478. Lansd. 648 ;—1479. Lansd. 649, 650.

—— Court-rolls, 1425, 1426, 1479. Lansd. 647, 649.

—— *Capellanus.* Thomas, early 13 cent. Harl. 44 D. 59, 45 B. 40, 45 E. 41.

—— *Clericus.* Alanus, *t.* Hen. II. Harl. 45 B. 38, 39, 45 C. 2, 5, 51 B. 4, 5, 55 D. 13.

—— —— Willelmus, *t.* Hen. III. Harl. 45 C. 19, 45 E. 46.

—— *Sacerdos.* Rogerus, early Hen. II. Harl. 45 B. 38, 39.

**Alford** (Auford), *co. Linc. (continued). Sacerdos (continued).* J—, early Hen. III. Cott. xxvii. 51.

—— *Vicarius.* Joh. Cayfas, early 13 cent. Harl. 45 C. 36.

—— —— Johannes, *t.* Hen. III. Cott. xxix. 72.

—— —— Walterus, *t.* Hen. III. Harl. 45 C. 19.

—— —— Thomas, early Edw. I. Harl. 52 A. 25.

**Alfreton** (Alferton), *co. Derb.* Lease, etc.. in, 1284. Woll. i. 21 ;—1542. Woll. xii. 136 ;—1623. Woll. xi. 84.

**Alfrichespihtel**, [*nr. Pulloxhill?*], *co. Bedf.* Grant in, early Hen. III. Add. 5954.

**Alfrick**, *co. Worc.* Exchange in, 1523 (Aufurwcke). Slo. xxxiii. 79.

**Alfriston**, *co. Suss.* Precipe on a covenant conc. land in, 1588. Add. 25524.

**Algarkirk**, *co. Linc.* Grant of the advowson, 1341 (Dalgerkirke). Harl. 46 A. 49.

—— Grants, etc., in, 1380. Add. 8400 (Algerkyrke) ; — 1412. Add. 20803 ;—1424. Add. 8402 ;—1461. Add. 8403.

—— Fine in, 1432. Add. 24914.

—— *Rector.* Dom. Maur. de Bermyngham, 1341. Harl. 46 A. 49.

**Alhampton**, *in Ditcheat, co. Som.* Grant of the manor, 1365 (Alamtone). Harl. 111 F. 51.

**Alisford.** *v.* Alresford, *co. Essex.*

**Alkborough**, *co. Linc.* Power to take seisin of the manor, 1339 (Alkebarwe). Harl. 56 D. 27.

**Alkesbourne.** *v.* Albourne, *co. Suss.*

**Alkham**, *co. Kent.* Evidence conc. tithes, etc., from. to St. Radegund's Abbey. Dover, 1326. Add. 26837.

**Alkintona.** *v.* Elkington, *co. Linc.*

**Alkmonton**, *in Longford, co. Derb.* Lease of the manor, 1746 (Alkmanton). Woll. xi. 117.

**Aller**, *co. Som.* Decl. of homage for the manor, 1408. Add. 25886.

—— *Persona.* Joh. Kirchill, 1397. Harl. 44 H. 46.

**Allerdale**, *co. Cumb.* Conf. of grants in, to St. Bees Priory, early Hen. II. Cott. xi. 13.

—— Partition of the forest of, *c.* 1250 (Alredal). Harl. 58 H. 8 (*copy*).

**Allerton.** *v.* Ollerton, *co. Nott.*

**Allerton,** *nr. Badgworth, co. Som.* Grant in, 1381 (Alwerton). Harl. 48 A. 24.

—— Bond conc. the manor, 1458. Add. 5469.

—— *Dominus.* Ric. Calweton, 1363. Add. 6504.

**Allerton,** *nr. Bradford, co. York.* Conff. of grants, etc., in, to Byland Abbey, *post* 1194. Add. 7477 (*copy*); —[1232–40]. Add. 7465 (*copy*);—*ante* 1298. Add. 7438.

**Allerton Bywater,** *in Kippax, co. York.* Fine of the manor, 1638. Woll. xi. 29.

**Allerton, Chapel,** *nr. Leeds, co. York. v.* Bentley, *in Chapel Allerton, co. York.*

**Allerton, North,** *co. York.* Grants, etc., in, late 13 cent. Add. 5730, 5731 (Alverton);—1382. Cott. xxviii. 84 (Aluertone).

**Allesford.** *v.* Alresford, *co. Southt.*

**Allesley,** *co. York.* Grant, etc., in, 1396. Harl. 111 D. 27, 111 G. 40, 41.

**Alleweston.** *v.* Alveston, *co. Glouc.*

**Allexton** (Alakestona, etc.), *co. Leic.* Grants in, late 12 cent. Harl. 46 F. 39;—early Hen. III. Harl. 45 F. 24.

—— Descent of the manor from P. de Nevyll, *t.* Rich. II. Add. 26912.

—— *Capellanus.* Willelmus, late 12 cent. (Halak.). Harl. 46 F. 39.

**Allington.** *v.* Athelington, *co. Suff.*

**Allington,** *co. Denb.* Grants, etc., in, 1347. Add. 8632 (Alunton);—1391. Add. 8633–8635 (Alynton);—1464. Add. 8643;—1546. Add. 8649 (Alinton);—1551. Add. 8528 (Alyngton).

**Allington,** *co. Kent.* Lease in, 1613 (Aldington). Harl. 79 G. 17.

—— Mortgage of Bockhurst wood in, 1643. Harl. 79 F. 8.

**Allington** (Athelington, etc.), *co. Linc.* Grants, etc., in, *t.* Edw. I. (Athelinton). Add. 5491;—1304. Add. 5495; —1316. Add. 5496;—1317. Add. 5497.

—— Grant of the manor, 1345 (Westathelyngton). Harl. 83 G. 54.

**Allington,** *in S. Stoneham, co. Southt.* Covenant conc. the mill and fishery of, betw. St. Mary's Church and St. Denis' Priory, Southampton, 1258 (Aldinton). Add. 20212.

—— Precipe on a covenant conc. the manor, 1422 (Aldyngton). Add. 25219.

—— (?) Grant in, 1429 (Alyngton). Add. 17431.

**Allington,** *nr. Lewes, co. Suss.* Assignment of the manor to Edw. II., 1316 (Alington). Harl. 57 E. 33.

**Allington,** *nr. Amesbury, co. Wilts.* Bond on land in, 1560 (Ablington). Harl. 78 I. 16.

**Allington,** *nr. Chippenham, co. Wilts.* License for Farley Priory to acquire land in, 1397 (Alyngtone juxta Chipenham). Cott. ii. 22.

**Allington, South,** *in Chivelstone, co. Devon.* Conveyance, etc., of the manor, 1312 (Alynton). Add. 13013;—1414 (South Alyngton). Harl. 48 I. 25.

**Allington, West.** *v.* Alvington, West, *co. Devon.*

**Allithwaite, Lower,** *co. Lanc.* Brief conc. a fire at, 1824. Ch. Br. C. v. 7.

**Allmer,** *nr. Gresford, co. Denb.* Recovery in, 1551. Add. 8528.

**Allonby,** *in Bromfield, co. Cumb.* Leases, etc., in, 1668. Add. 17178, 17179, 17181;—1690. Add. 17180, 17183.

**Allt,** *in Berriew, co. Montgom.* Lease in, 1638. Add. 1039.

**Alltbough,** *nr. Lit. Dewchurch, co. Heref.* Grants, etc., in, 1474. Add. 1331, 1332 (Altebogh);—1534. Add. 1346 (Haltbough):—1548. Add. 1353; —1565. Add. 1831 (Halteboughe).

**Almanebir.** *v.* Almondbury, *co. York.*

**Almeley,** *co. Heref.* Defeasance of bond conc. the rectory, 1610 (Allmeley). Harl. 75 G. 56.

**Almodington,** *co. Suss.* Assignment in, 1501 (Almodyton). Add. 18790.

**Almondbury,** *co. York.* Release of dower in, 1270 (Almanebir). Harl. 52 H. 43 b.

—— Brief conc. an inundation in, 1778. Ch. Br. B. xviii. 1.

**Almondsbury**, *co. Glouc.* Lease in Saltmarsh (Salsus Mariscus) nr. (?), 1248. Harl. 75 D. 13.

———— Conf. of grants in Saltmarsh nr. (?), to Margam Abbey, [1234–64]. Harl. 75 D. 19.

**Almsworthy**, *in Exford, co. Som.* Court-roll, 1461 (Almondesworth Blwet). Add. 7671.

**Alne**, *co. York.* Grant in, 1324. Add. 20543.

———— Brief for rebuilding the church, 1765. Ch. Br. B. v. 9.

———— Brief conc. a fire at, 1802. Ch. Br. B. xlii. 1.

**Alne, Little**, *co. Warw.* Grants, etc., in, *t.* Edw. I. Add. 9215 ;—1322-1513. Add. 8436-8442.

———— Release in, to Studley Priory, 1482. Add. 8435.

**Alnwick**, *co. Northumb.* Grant in the manor of, 1295 (Alnewyck). Harl. 57 C. 34.

———— Grant of the constableship of, to Sir R. Ogle, 1461. Cott. xvii. 17.

———— Decl. conc. settlement of lands in, etc., 1617, 1618. Harl. 79 G. 8, 9.

———— Sale in, 1655. Add. 17214.

**Alphamstone**, *co. Essex.* Grants in, to Colne Priory, *t.* Hen. III. ? (Alfhameston). Add. 26405 (4, 5) (*copies*).

———— Grant, etc., in, *t.* Edw. I. Harl. 54 F. 50 (Alfelmeston) ;—1359. Lansd. 123.

———— Precipes on covenants conc. lands in, 1593. Add. 25025, 25044.

**Alpheton** (Alfeton, etc.), *co Suff.* Grants, etc. in, 1283. Harl. 46 D. 9 a ; —1316. Harl. 47 E. 7 ;—1318. Harl. 54 C. 27 ;—1364. Cott. xii. 45, Harl. 53 C. 4, 5 ;—1367. Harl. 53 C. 32, 33 ;—1371. Harl. 51 D. 12 ;—1375. Harl. 50 H. 30 (Alfton) ;—1375, 1377, 1378. Harl. Roll O. 27 ;—1381. Harl. 53 C. 34 ;—1382. Harl. 48 D. 3, 4 ;—1407. Harl. 48 D. 12, 54 A. 22 ;—1421. Harl. 48 D. 15 (Alphton) ; —1583. Harl. 57 H. 18 ;—1634. Harl. 45 G. 7.

———— Assignm. of a mortgage of "Mansers," etc., in, 1634. Harl. 112 D. 24.

**Alphington**, *co. Devon.* Rector, late. Rob. Wiseman, 1507. Harl. 51 F. 33.

**Alport**, *in Youlgrave and Bakewell, co. Derb.* Lease and grant in, 1347. Harl. 83 F. 6 (Aldeport) ;—1349. Harl. 84 A. 47 (Aldport).

———— Ref. to claim on the mill of, 1446. Woll. vi. 5.

———— Release of suit to the mill, etc., 1484 (Aldeport). Woll. ii. 31-33.

———— License to grind at "Hovershull" mill in, *n. d.* (Aldeport). Woll. ii. 5 (*copy*).

**Alre.** *v. sub* Buckfastleigh, *co. Devon.*

**Alredal.** *v.* Allerdale, *co. Cumb.*

**Alrenemor.** *v. sub* Wilmarston, *co. Heref.*

**Alresawe.** *v.* Aldershaw, *nr. Lichfield, co. Staff.*

**Alresford**, *co. Essex.* Bequest of land at, *post* 991 (æt Ælesforda). Harl. 43 C. 4.

———— Release in, 1310 (Alysford). Harl. 54 H. 15.

———— Power to give seisin of the manor and advowson, 1388 (Alisford). Harl. 48 E. 52.

**Alresford**, *co. Southt.* A boundary mark, 909 (Alres forda). Harl. 43 C. 1.

————, **New and Old.** Grant in, to Newark Priory, *t.* Hen. III. (Allesford). Harl. 47 B. 51.

———— Grants, etc., in, 1362. Harl. 51 G. 40 ;—1390. Harl. 49 D. 48 ;—1410. Harl. 57 G. 33 ;—1525-6. Add. 13313. ———— Precipes conc. lands in, 1593. Add. 25235, 25242.

———— *Prepositi.* Joh. atte Rugge, Tho. Meriwedir, 1382. Harl. 46 F. 9.

**Alretona, Alretun.** *v.* Ollerton, *co. Nott.*

**Alrewas**, *co. Staff.* Grants, etc., in, *t.* Edw. I. Campb. xi. 8 ;—1573. Add. 13565 (Alderwas) ;— 1585. Add. 13568 - 13571 (do.) ; — 1586. Add. 13573 ;—1589. Add. 13578.

———— Grant, etc., of the manor, 1305. Campb. xi. 16, xxix. 7.

———— Rental, 1509. Add. 15883.

———— *Prepositus.* Radulfus, *t.* Edw. I. Campb. xi. 8.

**Alricheseya.** *v.* Arlsey, *co. Bedf.*

**Alrington**, *co. Devon.* Grant, etc., of dower in, to A. de Traci, *c.* 1200 (Alureton). Cott. xxix. 83, 84.

**Alsiest., Alsistona.** *v.* Alciston, *co. Suss.*

**Alson.** *v. sub* Chardstock, *co. Dors.*

**Alsop le Dale,** *co. Derb.* Grant, etc., in, 1613. Woll. xi. 87 ;—1628. Woll. xi. 123.

**Alspath,** *in Meriden, on. Warw.* Grants, etc., in, 1348. Add. 8398 ;— 1441. Harl. 86 F. 25.

—— Precipe on a covenant conc. land in, 1592. Add. 25552.

*v. also* Meriden, *co. Warw.*

**Alstanewich.** *v.* Elsternwick, *nr. Hull, co. York.*

**Alston,** *nr. Badgworth, co. Som.* Grant in, 1381 (Alleston). Harl. 48 A. 24.

**Alston,** *co. Staff.* Grant of free warren in, 1267 (Alureston). Add. 15773.

**Alston,** *co. Worc.* Lease at, 969 (Ælfsigestun). Add. 19792.

**Alstonfield,** *co. Staff.* Extract from roll of Court at, 1440. Woll. iii. 9.

**Alstonlegh.** *v. sub* Combs, *in Chapel en le Frith, co. Derb.*

**Alstrey.** *v.* Anstrey, *co. Warw.*

**Alswick,** *in Layston, co. Hertf.* Grant of the chapel to H. Trinity Priory, Aldgate, [1162–70]; with conff., *t.* Hen. II.–*t.* John (Alswike). Cott. xiii. 18 (6–10) (*copies*).

**Altebogh.** *v.* Alltbough, *nr. Little Dewchurch, co. Heref.*

**Altegwynt.** *v.* Altwent, *nr. Little Dewchurch, co. Heref.*

**Altestone,** *co.* ——?. Acquittance for a fine for the advowson of, 1355. Cott. xxvii. 152.

**Altham,** *in Whalley, co. Lanc.* Conf. of the chapel of, to Whalley Abbey, 1344 (Aluetham). Add. 1060.

**Althorpe,** *co. Northt.* Testimony conc. bequest of the manor, 1486 (Olthorp). Add. 16172.

—— *Persona.* Joh. de Holt, 1347. Add. 6030.

**Altofts,** *in Normanton, co. York.* Grants in, 1359. Add. 16819 ;—1485. Add. 16966.

—— Grants, etc., of the manor, 1401. Add. 16887–16890, 16892–16894 ;— 1423. Add. 16904 ; — 1424. Add. 16909 ;—1427. Add. 16913.

**Altofts,** *in Normanton, co. York (continued).* Land in, held by Rob. Calverley, *c.* 1450. Add. 16954.

—— Crown lease in, 1555. Harl. 84 C. 32.

**Alton,** *co. Southt.* Lease of the George Inn at, 1637. Add. 1942.

**Alton,** *co. Wilts.* Conf. of the church to St. Cross Hosp., Winchester, 1189 (Aulton). Harl. 43 C. 28.

**[Alton Pancras],** *co. Dors.* Grant of wardship of a third of Holcombe Manor in, etc., *t.* Edw. VI. Cott. MS. Vesp. F. xiii., art. 222.

**Alton Westbrooke,** *co. Southt.* Extract from Court-roll, 1622. Add. 8514.

**Altunia.** *v.* Halton, East, *co. Linc.*

**Altus Peccus.** *v.* Peak, The, *co. Derb.*

**Altwent,** *nr. Little Dewchurch, co. Heref.* Grants in, 1409. Add. 1323 (Alztgweynte) ; — 1419. Add. 1326, 1327 (Altegwynt).

**Aluen.** *v.* Avon, *River.*

**Aluertone.** *v.* Allerton, North, *co. York.*

**Aluiuelegha.** *v.* Alveley, *co. Salop.*

**Alunton.** *v.* Allington, *co. Denb.*

**Alureston.** *v.* Alston, *co. Staff.*

**Alureton.** *v.* Alrington, *co. Devon.*

**Alvaston,** *co. Derb.* Grant in, to Derby Priory, early Hen. III. (Alewoldeston). Woll. viii. 62.

—— Release in, to Durley Abbey, 1282 (Alwaston). Add. 5237.

—— Acquittance for rent of the manor, 1289. Harl. 86 I. 3.

—— Grant of a moiety of the manor, 1322 (Ayllewaston). Add. 6106 (1).

—— *Presbyter.* Herbertus, *t.* Hen. II. (Aluualdest ona). Add. 7213.

**Alvechurch,** *co. Worc.* Conff. of grants of " Osemercslcia " in, to Bordesley Abbey, [1138 ?]. Add. 20419 ; —[1157?]. Cott. MS. Nero C. iii., f. 176.

**Alvediston,** *co. Wilts.* Court-rolls, 1558-9. Add. 24440 ;—1567. Add. 24441.

**Alveley,** *co. Essex.* Entail and sale of the Queen's Arms Inn in, 1616. Harl 111 F. 33 ;—1626. Harl. 111 F. 35.

**Alveley,** *co. Salop.* Grant of, by Hen. II., [1155] (Aluiuelegha). Cott. xi. 14.

—— Brief for rebuilding the church, 1763. Ch. Br. B. iii. 5.

**Alveneley,** *co. Suff.* Grants of the manor, 1298. Harl. 45 I. 32 (Alwyneleye), 33 (Alwynleye).

**Alverd's Manor.** *v. sub* Ipswich, *co. Suff.*

**Alverstoke,** *co. Southt.* Grant in, 1405 (Ailwardstoke). Harl. 111 E. 30.

**Alverton,** *co. Nott.* Grant in, 1340. Add. 5397.

**Alvertun.** *v.* Allerton, North, *co. York.*

**Alvescott,** *co. Oxon.* Grant of the manor and rectory, by Hen. VIII., 1540. Add. 26022.

**Alveston,** *co. Glouc.* Grants, etc., in, early Hen. III. Harl. 50 C. 15 (Aluest.);—1316. Add. 7719 (Allwestone);—1317. Add. 7718 (Alleweston);—1342. Add. 20402 (Aleweston).

—— Grant in "Grava" in the manor of, 1282. Add. 7717.

—— Grant in Earthcott, etc., in, 1299. Add. 26759.

—— Fine in, 1346. Add. 25876.

**Alveston,** *co. Warw.* Grant of, to Worcester Priory, 1089 (Alfestun). Cott. xi. 51.

**Alvetham.** *v.* Altham, *in Whalley, co. Lanc.*

**Alvington** *al.* **Allington, West.** *co. Devon.* Grant in Woolstone (Wolsaton) in, 1312. Add. 13013.

**Alwalton,** *co. Hunt.* Inspex. of grant by Hen. III. of a market in the manor of, 1314. Harl. 58 I. 52 (*copy*).

**Alwerton.** *v.* Allerton, *nr. Badgworth, co. Som.*

**Alwyneleye.** *v.* Alveneley, *co. Suff.*

**Alyeteston.** *v.* Alaxton, *in Lidney, co. Glouc.*

**Alyncestre Hundred.** *v.* Alcester Liberty, *in Shaftesbury, co. Dors.*

**Alyngton.** *v.* Athelington, *co. Suff.*

—— *v.* Elton, *co. Hunts.*

**Alynton.** *v.* Allington, South, *co. Devon.*

**Alysheys.** *v. sub* Combe Rawleigh, *co. Devon.*

**Alztgweynte.** *v.* Altwent, *nr. Little Dewchurch, co. Heref.*

**Amber,** *River.* Grants of land nr. in Ashover, *co.* Derb., 1461, 1556 (Ambur). Woll. vii. 6, 7.

**Amberley,** *co. Heref.* Leases in, 1593. Add. 1867; — 1597. Add. 1871; — 1600. Add. 1879; —1605. Add. 1888; —1614. Add. 1906;—1621. Add. 1920, 1921;—1635. Add. 1938;— 1648. Add. 1948;—1679. Add. 1968; —1698. Add. 1972, 1973.

**Amberley.** *co. Surr.* Capellanus. Robertus, 12–13 cent. (Amberle). Harl. 77 E. 43.

**Ambleston,** *co. Pembr.* Crown-lease of the rectory, etc., 1586 (Amlaston). Harl. 83 H. 16.

**Ambringehale.** *v.* Arminghall, *co. Norf.*

**Ambrosden,** *co. Oxon. Persona.* Willelmus, *t.* John. Harl. 86 D. 49.

**Ambur.** *v.* Amber, *River.*

**Amersham,** *co. Buck.* Conf. by Edw. the Confessor of a grant in, to Westminster Abbey, 1066 [*sc.* 1065] (Agmodesham). Cott. vi. 2 (*copy*).

—— Grants, etc., in, *t.* Hen. III. Harl. 49 D. 49 (Augmodesham);— Harl. 49 I. 12 (Aucomodesham);— 1275. Harl. 46 F. 45 (Aumodsham); —1471. Add. 17385 (Agmondesham); —1546. Add. 17386.

—— Covenant for recovery of Tomlyn's manor, etc., in, 1591. Add. 19544.

**Ametun.** *v.* Ampton, *co. Suff.*

**Amington,** *nr. Tamworth, co. Warw.* Grants and release of the mill, *t.* John. Cott. xxiv. 19 (Aminthon), 20 (Aminton), Cott. xxv. 26 (Amintuna).

—— Grant in, 1321 (Amyntona). Add. 21443.

—— Grant of the manor, 1356 (Amyntona). Add. 21444.

—— Sale in, 1540 (Grete and Lyttell Amyntone). Cott. ii. 15.

**Amlaston.** *v.* Ambleston, *co. Pembr.*

**Amounderness Hundred,** *co. Lanc.* Settlement of the office of Bailiff of, 1392. Add. 20511.

**Amport,** *co. Southt.* Grants, etc., of the manor, 1306. Add. 23834 (Anne Port);—1325. Add. 23835 (Aune de Port);—1375. Add. 23837.

**Amport,** *co. Southt. (continued).* Covenant conc. the manor, water-mill, etc., 1328 (Anne de Port). Add. 23836.

—— *Rector.* Elias le Blounte, 1375. Add. 23837.

**Ampton,** *co. Suff.* Grants, etc., in, late 13 cent. Add. 18582 (Ametun); —1310. Add. 18602 (Ametone);— 1331. Add. 9101, 18624;—1341. Add. 18636;—1349. Add. 18643 (Amton); —1367. Add. 18647;—1396. Add. 18684.

—— Court-roll, 1363. Add. 9111.

—— Entail of the manor, 1380. Add. 18667.

—— Grant of the manor and advowson, 1404. Add. 15537.

**Amredene.** *v.* Hamperden, *nr. Debden, co. Essex.*

**Amwell, Great,** *co. Hertf.* Compotus rolls of the manor, 1289–90. Add. 26827;—1397–8. Add. 26829.

—— Grant in, 1368. Campb. viii. 16.

—— Rentals of the manor, 1374 (?). Add. 26828;—1591. Add. 26830.

—— Assignment of a lease of the manor, 1566. Harl. 80 F. 26.

—— Fine of the manor, 1608. Add. 13582.

**Anand.** *v.* Annan, *co. Dumfries.*

**Ancaster.** *co. Linc.* Attestation "coram militibus in decem wapentachiis aput Hanecastre," early 13 cent. Eg. 438.

—— Settlement in, 1524. Add. 21156.

—— *Clericus.* Martinus, 1262 (Hancastre). Eg. 444.

—— *Vicarius.* Joh. Taillour, 1524. Add. 21156.

**Ancholm,** *co. Linc.* (?). Grant in, to Beverley College, co. York, early 13 cent. Lansd. 413.

**Ancholme,** *River, co. Linc.* Conf. by Hen. II. of a grant nr., to Newhouse Abbey, [1156–7] (Ancolne). Harl. 51 H. 1.

—— Grants, etc., on, nr. Hibaldstow, to Bullington Priory, early Hen. II. Harl. 48 I. 36 (Ancolna), 50 C. 1;— *t.* Hen. II. Harl. 48 I. 38, 51, 57 D. 20.

—— Grant of a fishery in, to Bullington Priory, late Hen. II. (Ancolne.) Harl. 54 B. 26.

**Anderby** (Andrebi, etc.), *co. Linc.* Grants, etc., in, to Greenfield Priory, early 13 cent. Harl. 45 C. 36;—*t.* Hen. III. Harl. 44 G. 5 (Andirby), 46 A. 30, 58 A. 35.

—— Grants in, 1311. Harl. 52 H. 29;—1333. Harl. 47 I. 26;—1355. Harl. 57 G. 11.

—— Bond of Greenfield Priory for a feoffment in, 1371. Harl. 44 E. 9.

—— Brief to rebuild the church, 1759. Ch. Br. A. v. 6.

—— *Capellanus.* Lambertus, early Hen. III. Harl. 47 F. 22.

—— —— M—, early 13 cent. Harl. 45 C. 36.

—— —— Moyses, early 13 cent. Harl. 45 B. 44.

—— *Persona.* Robertus, early 13 cent. Harl. 51 G. 44;—*t.* Hen. III. Harl. 46 A. 30 b, 47 F. 22, 56 G. 20.

—— —— Will. de Synythwayt, 1346. Harl. 54 E. 14.

—— —— Ric. de Anderby, 1355. Harl. 57 G. 11.

**Andeswrth.** *v.* Handsworth, *co. York.*

**Andover,** *co. Southt.* Grant, etc., in, 1280 (Andevere). Add. 7735;—1438. Add. 6202.

—— Precipe on a covenant conc. land in, 1578. Add. 25220.

—— Lease of fishing, etc., at, 1601 (Andever). Add. 686.

—— *Ballivi.* Philip le Power, Edm. Osward, 1355. Add. 24696.

**Andred,** *Forest of, co. Kent.* Grants of wood in, 833. Cott. MS. Aug. ii. 102;— 973. Cott. viii. 33.

**Anecote.** *v.* Onecote, *co. Staff.*

**Anelori.** *v.* Anlore, *co. Monaghan* (?).

**Anesaker.** *v. sub* Bradfield, *co. York.*

**Anestelay.** *v.* Ansley, *co. Warw.*

**Angenlabeshaam,** *co. Essex.* Grant of, to Barking Abbey, 692–3. Cott. MS. Aug. ii. 29.

**Angerhall,** *co. Suff.* (?). *Clericus.* Walterus, early 13 cent. Harl. 48 H. 50.

**Angle** (Angulus), *co. Pembr.* Settlement, etc., in, 1273. Slo. xxxii. 14*; —1299. Slo. xxxii. 14.

**Angmering**, *co. Suss.* Feoffment in Ham (Hamme) in, 1485. Add. 20075.
—— Settlement in, 1605. Add. 18899.
—— *Capellanus cantarie B. Marie de Estangemerynge.* Will. atte Gate, 1359. Lansd. 124.
—— *Vicarius eccl. de Westangemerynge.* Joh. de Weston, 1359. Lansd. 124.

**Angodestorp.** *v.* Osgathorpe, *co. Leic.*

**Angre, Alta.** *v.* Ongar, High, *co. Essex.*

**Anhus.** *v.* Onehouse, *co. Suff.*

**Anke,** *in Clist Hydon, co Devon.* Courtrolls, 1407-10 (Aunke). Add. 7673, 7674.

**Anlaby,** *co. York.* Grant, etc., in, 1321. Lansd. 417;—1431. Harl. 54 L 15.
—— Release of the manor, 1430. Harl. 43 E. 19, 45 L 12.

**Anlore,** *co. Monaghan* (?). Grant of the church to Neddrum Priory, 1194 (Anelori). Cott. xiii. 21 (3) (*copy*).

**Anmer,** *co. Norf.* Release in, 1607. Add. 19382.

**Annan,** *co. Dumfries.* Conf. of grant of the church to Gisburne Priory, *t.* Edw. I. (Anand). Cott. xi. 58, Harl. 43 B. 12.

**Annandale,** *co. Dumfries.* Grant of, to R. de Brus, *c.* 1125 (Estrahanent). Cott. xviii. 45.

**Anne, Abbot's,** *co. Southt.* Mortgage of the manor, 1572. Add. 16153.

**Anne de Port, Anne Port.** *v.* Amport, *co. Southt.*

**Anne Savage,** *nr. Amport, co. Southt.* Grant in, 1325. Add. 23835.

**Annesley,** *co. Nott.* Covenant conc. Wandesley Manor in, 1421. Cott. xii. 41.

**Anninga Dune.** *v.* Annington, *co. Suss.*

**Annington,** *co. Suss.* Grant at, 956 (æt Anninga dune). Cott. MS. Aug. ii. 45.

**Ansedelee.** *v.* Anslow, *in Rolleston, co. Staff.*

**Ansley,** *co. Warw.* Grants, etc., of Ansley and Monewode manors, 1426. Harl. 76 G. 45 (Ansteley);—1429. Harl. 76 G. 49 (Ancstelay);—1434. Harl. 77 F. 14 (Anseley);—1536. Harl. Roll V. 3 (Anselc);—1542. Harl. 76 A. 31.

**Ansley,** *co. Warw.* (*continued*). Sale, etc., in, 1544. Harl. 76 H. 46, 79 A. 42;—1549. Harl. 76 H. 53.

**Anslow, *in Rolleston, co. Staff.*** Grant in, 1303 (Aunsedeleye). Woll. ix. 27.
—— License to empark a chace in, 1300 (Ansedelee). Campb. xi. 18.

**Anstey,** *co. Hertf.* License to endow Fotheringhay College, *co.* Northt., with the manor and advowson, 1415. Campb. x. 6.

**Anstey,** *co. Warw.* Persona. Philippus, 1232. Harl. 83 A. 32.

**Anstey Manor.** *v. sub* Waltham Holy Cross, *co. Essex.*

**Anston, North** (N. Anston), *co. York.* Grants, etc., in, late 13 cent. Harl. 112 H. 27;—1312. Harl. 112 G. 47;—1391. Harl. 84 A. 23.

**Anston, South,** *co. York.* Grants, etc., in, *t.* Edw. I. Harl. 112 G. 46 (Anstan);—1316. Cott. xxvi. 31 (Suthanstan);—1548. Harl. 112 L 11;—1391. Harl. 84 A. 23.

**Anstrey,** *co. Warw.* Sale of the reversion of the manor, 1540 (Anstrey *al.* Alstrey). Cott. ii. 15.

**Antidona.** *v.* Eatington (?), *co. Warw.*

**Antingham,** *co. Norf.* Regrant of the manor, etc., 1346 (Antyngham). Add. 22565.
—— Inspex., in 1454, of feoffment of the advowson, 1422. Add. 17243.

**Antiokes Manor.** *v. sub* Stalbridge, *co. Dors.*

**Antrim, *County of, in Ireland.*** Compotus of H. de Maundeville, as Custos, 1261-2 (Twescard in Ultonia). Add. 26515 (3).
—— Grant in, 1571. Add. 15574.
—— Petition from Protestants of, on the Act of Resumption, 1702. Add. 19537.

**Anutwalda,** *co. Kent.* Grant of five "denn" in, 862. Cott. viii. 32.

**Apelby.** *v.* Appleby, Gt., *co. Leic.*

**Apeldre.** *v.* Applodore, *co. Kent.*

**Apeldreham.** *v.* Appledram, *co. Suss.*

**Apeltona.** *v.* Appleton Roebuck, *co. York.*

**Apesdown.** *v.* Apse Down, *I. of Wight.*

**Apilknoll.** *v.* Apperknowl, *in Unstone, co. Derb.*

**Apley**, *co. Linc.* Grants *of* Wivedale and West woods nr., to Bullington Priory, *c.* 1175. Harl. 52 G. 28;—late 13 cent. Harl. 52 H. 7.

—— Lease of fishery at, to Barlings Abbey, 1452 (Appley). Harl. 44 B. 15.

**Apley**, *nr. Wellington, co. Salop.* Grant of the manor, 1384 (Appeleye). Cott. v. 8.

**Apley**, *nr. Ashbrittle, co. Som.* Power to take seisin in, 1501 (Appelegh). Add. 13074.

**Aplr.** *v.* Appledore, *co. Kent.*

**Appeldoreford.** *v.* Appleford, *I. of Wight.*

**Apperknowl**, *in Unstone, co. Derb.* Grant in, in the fee of Wingerworth, 1319 (Apilknoll). Woll. viii. 50.

—— Grants, etc., in, 1418. Woll. viii. 47 (Appulknoll);—1440. Woll. viii. 43 (Apulknol);—1441. Woll. viii. 44.

**Appincg lond**, *in Rainham, co. Kent.* Grant of, 811. Cott. MS. Aug. ii. 10.

**Appleby**, *co. Derb. Rector.* Tho. Chesshyre, 1509 (Appulbe). Woll. x. 31.

**Appleby**, *co. Westm.* Grant in, 1444 (Appilby). Harl. 83 F. 3, 4.

**Appleby, Great**, *co. Leic.* Settlement in, 1290 (Appelby). Harl. 47 B. 24.

—— Terrier of lands in, 15 cent. Slo. xxxi. 9.

—— Recovery of presentation to the church of, against Lythom Priory, 1502. Add. 26921.

—— *Capellanus Parochialis.* Willelmus, 1361. Add. 26916.

—— *Persona. Sire* Will. de Berforde, 1343. Cott. xvi. 60.

—— *Rector. Dom.* Tho. de Andevill, *t.* Hen. III. (Apelby). Add. 5992.

—— —— Joh. Helperly, 1493. Add. 26920.

**Appleby, Little**, *co. Leic.* Grants, etc., in, early Hen. III. Add. 26913 (Appelb.), 26914 (do.), 26915 (Appelby);—1361. Add. 26916 (Appulby), 26917 (Appelby);—1458. Add. 26918 (Appulby parva), 26919 (do.).

—— Inq. p. m. of the manor, 1566. Add. 7252.

**Appledore.** *v. sub* Farway, *co. Devon.*

**Appledore**, *co. Kent.* Conf. of a covenant conc. a marsh in (?), betw. Christ Church, Canterbury, and Robertsbridge Abbey, [1170–83]. Campb. xxii. 5.

—— Grant, etc., in, to Christ Church, Canterbury, *t.* Hen. III. Add. 16343 (Apuldr.);—late 13 cent. Add. 16340 (Aplr.).

—— Grants, etc., in, *t.* Hen. III. Add. 16337 (Apeldere), 16338;—1261. Add. 16341 (Apeldre);—1410. Add. 8553 (Apuldre);—1419. Add. 16345 (Apuldr.);— 1551. Harl. 78 G. 31 (Apuldore).

—— Covenant conc. services in the church of, 1306 (Appuldr.). Add. 16342.

—— *Perpet. vicarius.* Joh. de Graucourt, 1306. Add. 16342.

**Appledram**, *co. Suss.* Conf. of the manor, by Hen. I., to Battle Abbey, in exch. for Reading, co. Berks., *c.* 1121 (Apeldreham). Campb. xvi. 13.

**Appleford, West**, *I. of Wight.* Grant of manors in, late 13 cent. (W. Appeldoreford). Harl. 112 A. 32.

**Applesham**, *co. Suss.* Sale in, 1620. Add. 18927.

**Appleton le Street** (?), *in Rydale Wap., co. York.* Exchequer acquittance for a fine for the rectory, 1595. Add. 25716.

**Appleton Roebuck**, *co. York.* Conff. of grants in, to Nun Appleton Priory, *c.* 1150–60. Cott. xii. 46 (Apeltun);—early Hen. II. Harl. 50 A. 37 (Apeltona).

—— Brief conc. a fire in, 1802. Ch. Br. B. xlii. 1.

**Appleton upon Wiske**, *co. York.* Brief for rebuilding the church, 1773. Ch. Br. B. xiii. 7.

**Appletree Hundred**, *co. Derb.* Acquittance for subsidy in, 1489 (Appultre). Woll. viii. 69.

—— Warrant to the freeholders of, 1611. Woll. iii. 96.

**Appley.** *v.* Apley, *co. Linc.*

**Appley Wood**, *co. Bedf.* Grant of, to Chicksand Priory, *c.* 1150 (Appeleia). Harl. 45 I. 7.

**Appulbe.** *v.* Appleby, *co. Derb.*

**Appulknoll, Apulknol.** *v.* Apperknowl, *co. Derb.*

**Arlicheseie.** *v.* Arlsey, *co. Bedf.*

**Arlincumbe,** *co. Som. Persona.* Philip, [1192-1205]. Add. 19066.

**Arlingham,** *co. Glouc.* Grant in, to St. Augustine's Abbey, Bristol, 1251 (Erlingham). Add. 8445.

**Arlington,** *in Bibury, co. Glouc.* Livery of the manor to R. Westwood, 1561. Add. 19542.

**Arlington,** *co. Suss.* Grant in, 1395 (Erlyntone). Add. 21939.

—— Precipe on a covenant in, 1382 (Erlyngton). Add. 18089.

**Arlsey,** *co. Bedf.* Grants, etc., in, to Waltham Abbey, 1206. Add. 26731 (Ailricheseys);—*t.* John. Add. 26732; —*t.* Hen. III. Add. 17639, 17642 (Alricheseya), 17645, 17646, 17648, 17651, 17654, 18203, 26740, 26741.

—— Grants in Holmesburne, Shiteyham, etc., in, to Waltham Abbey, early 13 cent. Add. 26730, Eg. 407.

—— Release of the church from visitation, *c.* 1228 (Ailricheseia). Add. 18198.

—— Grants in, nr. St. Andrew's Chapel, to Waltham Abbey, *t.* Hen. III. Add. 17644 (Alricheseia), 17648.

—— Grant at Lullesfordehiderande in or nr., *t.* Hen. III. Eg. 411.

—— Grant to the men of, to make a free road in, *t.* Hen. III. (Aurich.). Add. 17647.

—— Grant in, to Wymondley Priory, *t.* Hen. III. (Arlicheseie). Add. 17649.

—— Suit for tithes, betw. Waltham Abbey and Chepstow Priory, 1251. Eg. 409 (Alricheseye);—1254. Add. 17653 (Aylricheseia).

—— Inquisition with Waltham Abbey, "super incrementis Cambrii" in, 1255 (Haurich.). Add. 24329.

—— Grant, etc., in. from Waltham Abbey, [1263-9] (Alriches.). Add. 26742.

—— Grants, etc., in, *t.* Hen. III. Add. 17640 (Ailrichesheihe), 17641 (Auricheseya), 17643 (Alricheseya), 17650 (Arlicheseie), 18200, 26733—26739 (Aurich., etc.);—1300. Add. 49 I. 2;—1338. Add. 17657 (Arlicheseye);—1388. Add. 17662 (Alrychesey);—1402. Harl. 49 D. 20;—1424. Add. 17663;—1443. Add. 17664.

—— Court-roll, 1386 (Arlechey). Harl. Roll A. 4.

**Arlsey,** *co. Bedf.* (*continued*). Compotus-rolls, 1402-3. Harl. Roll A. 37 (Arlycheseye);—1438-9. Harl. Roll R. 24 (Erleshey).

—— Conveyance of the manor, 1531 (Arlessey). Harl. 55 F. 38.

—— *Vicarius.* David, 1255. Add. 24329;—*t.* Hen. III. Add. 17641, 17652.

—— Ricardus, late Hen. III. Add. 18203.

**Armagh,** *County of.* Address to Will. III. against the Pretender, 1702. Add. 19529.

**Armin,** *in Snaith, co. York.* Lease in, 1314 (Hayrminne). Add. 20558.

**Arminghall** (Ambringehale), *co. Norf.* Grant of, with conf., to Norwich Priory, [1103-6?]. Cott. MS. Aug. ii. 103 (*copy*);—[1136-45]. Cott. ii. 1, Cott. ii. 21 (9) (*copy*).

**Armitage,** *co. Staff.* Lease, etc., in, 1520. Harl. 55 F. 19 (Armytage);—1540. Add. 13558.

**Armston** (Armeston), *co. Northt.* Grants in, 1424, 1437. Add. 738 a, b.

**Armthorpe,** *co. York.* Release in, *t.* Hen. III. (Arnestorp). Add. 5725.

**Armyston.** *v.* Harmston, *co. Linc.*

**Arnale.** *v.* Arnold, *in Long Riston, co. York.*

**Arncliffe,** *co. York.* Brief for rebuilding the church, 1797. Ch. Br. B. xxxvii. 3.

**Arneforth,** *co. York.* Grant of tithes of, to Bolton Priory, 1303 (Arneford). Add. 15648.

**Arnold,** *co. Nott.* Grant in, *t.* Edw. I. (Arnehal). Add. 8115.

—— Lease of the manor, 1316. Add. 15251.

**Arnold,** *in Long Riston, co. York.* Release in, to Beverley College, *t.* Hen. III. (Arnale). Lansd. 391.

—— Grant in, 1441 (Arnall). Harl. 55 A. 43.

**Arnsby,** *co. Leic.* Release in, by Sulby Abbey, *c.* 1260-76 (Ernesby). Add. 21202.

**Arnyngton.** *v.* Arrington, *co. Camb.*

**Arreton,** *I. of Wight.* Grant of free warren in, to Quarr Abbey, 1284 (Aretone). Add. 15701.

**Arreton,** *I. of Wight (continued).* Sales and leases in, *t.* Hen. VIII. Add. 9199 (Atherton);—1531. Harl. 112 F. 5 (Adderton);—1584. Add. 8469;—1591. Add. 18871.

—— Crown-appointments of a bailiff and steward of the manor, 1571. Harl. 75 E. 38, 40.

**Arrington,** *co. Camb.* Lease in, 1316 (Arnyngton). Harl. 83 A. 39.

**Arthington,** *co. York.* Grant in, *t.* Hen. III. Add. 976.

**Arthingworth,** *co. Northt.* Fines in, 1326. Add. 22154;—1330. Add. 6049.

—— Settlement of the manor, 1347 (Arthyngworthe). Cott. xxvi. 38.

—— Grants, etc., in, 1353. Add. 22177;—1359. Add. 22179;—1360. Add. 22180;—1361. Add. 22185, 22186;—1378. Add. 5364;—1501. Add. 709.

—— *Capellanus.* Randulfus, early 13 cent. Add. 20524.

—— *Persona.* Rog. Basset, [1339]. Slo. xxxi. 4 (46, 54).

**Artington,** *in Guildford, co. Surr.* Grants, etc., in, *t.* Hen. III. (Ertedon, Ertendone). Add. 24582-24584.

—— Return to the Hundred court, 1484. Add. 26892.

**Arundel,** *co. Suss.* Grant in, from the Knights Hospitallers, 1190. Add. 7208.

—— Grant in, *t.* Edw. I. Lansd. 86.

—— —— Fines in, 1313 (?). Add. 24885; —1487. Add. 15213.

—— *Castellanus.* Joscelinus, *frater Regine, c.* 1180. Add. 19603, 19604.

**Arundel,** *Honour of.* Notif. to the men of, from William, Earl of Sussex, *ante* 1220. Harl. 45 B. 29.

**Asby, [Great (?)],** *co. Westm.* Grant in, 1316 (Eskhilby). Harl. 51 D. 53.

**Ascerton,** *in Sidmouth, co. Devon.* Release in, 1420 (Aserton). Add. 13039.

**Aschebi.** *v.* Ashby, *co. Linc.*

**Aschedon.** *v.* Ashdon, *co. Essex.*

**Aschefeld.** *v.* Ashfield, Great, *co. Suff.*

**Aschene.** *v.* Ashton, *co. Northt.*

**Aschover.** *v.* Ashover, *co. Derb.*

**Ascote,** *in Pattishall, co. Northt.* Mortgage in, 1277 (Acheskot). Harl. 57 F. 24.

—— Release and mortgage, etc., of the manor, *c.* 1278. Add. 21519 (Auescote);—1342. Cott. xxiii. 27 (do.);— 1386. Add. 21520 (do.).

**Ascote Chapel,** *co. Warw.* Power for seisin in, to J. de Catesby, 1405 (Ascote). Cott. xii. 8.

**Ascott,** *in Gt. Milton, co. Oxon.* Precipe on a covenant conc. the manor, etc., 1593. Add. 25217.

**Ascott d'Oyley,** *co. Oxon.* Pension to R. de Waterton from the manor, 1423 (Ascotedoly). Harl. 43 E. 40.

**Ascpatric.** *v.* Aspatric, *co. Cumb.*

**Aseby.** *v.* Aisby, *in Haydor, co. Linc.*

**Asedeby.** *v.* Haceby (?), *nr. Haydor, co. Linc.*

**Asenawe, Boscus de.** *v. sub* Wickham Skeith, *co. Suff.*

**Asewordeby.** *v.* Aswarby, *co. Linc.*

**Asfordby.** *v.* Asserby (?), *nr. Alford, co. Linc.*

**Asgarby,** *nr. Horncastle, co. Linc.* Grant in, 1332 (Askerby). Harl. 58 B. 49, 50.

**Ash (Essha, etc.),** *nr. Sandwich, co. Kent.* Grant in "Opedune" in, 1280. Harl. 75 G. 20.

—— Grant in Cotmanton in, 1280. Harl. 78 D. 24.

—— Grants, etc., in Goldstone (Goldstanestone) in, 1294. Harl. 76 E. 55, 56;—1296. Harl. 80 A. 43;—c. 1294-6. Harl. 80 A. 53, 57.

—— Grant "in tenura de Ulmis" in, 1299. Harl. 77 D. 51.

—— Grants, etc., in, 1299. Harl. 78 I. 40;—1313. Harl. 78 D. 25;—1319. Harl. 77 E. 45;—1325. Harl. 80 G. 37;—1327. Harl. 80 G. 38;—1328. Harl. 56 D. 13;—1340. Harl. 79 E. 29;—1342. Harl. 76 C. 54, 78 D. 29-31;—1549. Add. 4607.

—— Release of lands held of Goldstone Manor, Fleet Court and Hills Court in, 1313. Harl. 78 I. 41.

—— Grant, etc., at "Garebregge" in, 1330. Harl. 77 G. 15, 80 G. 43.

—— Grant in "Hellis" in, 1337. Harl. 80 C. 23.

—— Release of a third part of Goldstone Manor in, 1347. Harl. 78 D. 32.

Ashbourne (Asseburn, Ascheburn, etc.), co. Derb. (continued). v. also Offcote, in Ashbourne.

v. also Underwood, in Ashbourne.

v. also Yeldersley, in Ashbourne.

Ashbrittle, co. Som. Power to take seisin in, 1501 (Aysbrytell). Add. 13074.

Ashburnham, co. Suss. Grants, etc., in, 1344. Add. 20158 (Esbornhamme); —1412. Add. 20064 (Asscheburne-ham);—1475. Add. 23800 (Aysshe-burham).

Ashburton, co. Devon. Grant in, 1618. Add. 7891.

Ashbury, co. Berks. Grant at, 956 (Æscesburuh). Cott. MS. Aug. ii. 40.

Ashby, nr. Spilsby, co. Linc. Fines in, 1259. Harl. 58 A. 36 (Askeby);— 1302. Harl. 45 H. 18 (Askeby juxta Partenay).

—— Clericus. Rogerus, late 12 cent. (Aschebi). Harl. 45 C. 4.

Ashby, co. Suff. Rector. Will. Smyth, 1483. Add. 10456.

Ashby, Castle, co. Northt. Grant of remainder in the castle and manor, 1392 (Assheby). Harl. 47 B. 11.

—— Dominus. Will. de La Pole, Miles, 1359. Cott. xii. 1.

—— Persona. Johannes, 1349. Harl. 57 C. 27, 28.

—— Rector. Rad. de Wlvernebam-ton, 1296. Add. 22357.

———— Dom. Joh. Drewell, 1422. Harl. 47 B. 17.

Ashby, Cold (Coldesseby, etc.), co. Northt. Grants, etc., in, to Pipewell Abbey, c. 1150. Add. 21685 (Caldcs-sebi);—c. 1230. Add. 21684;—1230. Add. 21686;—1232. Add. 21687;— 1242. Add. 21518.

—— Grants, etc., in, to Sulby Abbey, early Hen. III. Add. 22510 (Chald Asseby);—[1248-50]. Add. 21517.

—— Release of rents in, by Sulby Abbey, late Hen. III. (Esseby). Add. 21515.

—— Grant in trust of the reversion of the manor, 1415 (Coldeasshby). Add. 22410.

—— Sales, etc., in, 1650. Add. 6127;—1685. Add. 5375, 5376.

—— Dominus. Walterus, c. 1320. Add. 22403.

—— Diaconus. Jordanus, t. Hen. III. Harl. 45 B. 21.

Ashby, Cold (Coldesseby, etc.), co. Northt. (continued). Sacerdos. Ri-cardus, [1160-70]. Add. 22539.

—— Vicarius. Herbertus (?), 1242. Add. 21518.

———— Jac. de Hascho, 1514. Add. 22457.

Ashby de la Zouche, co. Leic. Grants of an oven in, 1357 (Essebya la Zouche). Add. 24209, 24210.

Ashby Folville, co. Leic. Lease in, 1721. Add. 19050.

Ashby, Great (Magna Esseby), co. Leic. Grant in, to Catesby Priory, t. Hen. III. Harl. 49 H. 31.

—— Vicarius. Rob. de Cotis, t. Hen. III. Harl. 49 H. 30, 31, Add. 5885.

Ashby, Little, co. Leic. Fines in, [1175-6] (Essebi parva). Slo. xxxi. 4 (34) (copy);—[1321-5]. Add. 24207.

Ashby Mears, co. Northt. Covenant conc. tithes of, betw. Aunay Abbey and Northampton Priory, 1176 (Ais-sebi). Harl. 44 A. 1.

—— Grant in (?), from R. de Humez, ante 1181 (Hessebi). Harl. 83 A. 6.

—— Grant in, 1415 (Asscheby Mars). Add. 6051.

—— Precipe on a covenant conc. land in, 1578 (Meeres Asshebye). Add. 25151.

Ashby Puerorum, co. Linc. Fine and release in, 1302. Harl. 45 H. 18 (Askeby juxta Horncastre);—1351. Campb. v. 13 (Askeby Puerorum).

—— Vicarius. Henricus, 1351. Campb. v. 13.

Ashby St. Legers (Essebi, etc.), co. Northt. Covenant for a marriage settlement on L. de Diva in, late Hen. II. (Assebi). Add. 21516.

—— Grants in, to Catesby Priory, t. John. Add. 7524;—t. Hen. III. Add. 7521.

Ashcoombe, co. Devon. Court-rolls, 1610-13. Add. 25985 a, b.

Ashdon (Asshedon, etc.), co. Essex. Reservation of rights to the church of, by R., Abbat of Battle, [1218-35] (Eston). Add. 20076.

—— Grant, etc., in Newnham (Newenham) in, 1303. Harl. 52 H. 48 (Essendon);—1327. Harl. 52 H. 47.

Ashford (Esshetesford, etc.), co. *Kent.* Grant at Northbrook (Northebrook) in (?), early 13 cent. Harl. 79 C. 55.

—— Conf. of denns free from service to the Court of Ripton (Rapetun) in, to Combwell Priory, 1231. Harl. 77 F. 23.

—— Fine in, 1294. Harl. 78 F. 20.

—— Grants, etc., in, 1377. Harl. 46 D. 14 (Essheforde);—1397. Harl. 56 D. 46;—1482. Add. 20013;—1492. Add. 20015;—1638. Harl. 85 H. 53 (Eshetisford).

—— Settlement of lands in, on divorce of Marg. de Valoignes, 1326. Harl. 80 H. 4.

—— Lease of the manor, etc., to St. Stephen's Chapel, Westminster, 1382 (Asshattesford). Harl. 43 E. 16.

—— Title in, *post* 1439. Harl. 78 F. 40, 41.

—— Lease of the mill, etc., 1620 (Essheforde). Harl. 80 D. 37.

—— Lease of East Stour (Eastowre) manor in, 1638. Harl. 85 H. 53.

—— Lease of the Saracen's Head and Swan Inns in, 1640. Harl. 85 H. 11.

—— *Rector.* Salomon Russel, 1383. Add. 8548.

Ashford Jones, co. *Heref.* Grant in, 1350 (Ouerahsforde). Add. 4599.

Ashford, Upper (?), co. *Salop.* Conf. by Hen. II. of land in, to Bromfield Priory, [1155] (Esseford). Cott. xvii. 4.

Ashfordby, co. *Leic.* Conf. of grant of the manor to Leicester Abbey, [1190–1204] (Esfordebi). Slo. xxxii. 22.

—— Power to take seisin in, 1518. Add. 9265.

Ashill, co. *Som.* Release in, 1438 (Asshhilyate). Harl. 50 E. 6.

Ashingdon (Assendon, etc.), co. *Essex.* Grants, etc., in, *ante* 1253. Harl. 54 H. 54;—1269. Harl. 55 B. 15, 55 C. 3;—1273. Harl. 48 G. 4 (Assindon).

—— Grant in Katherine's land in, *t.* Hen. III. (Ayssebedon). Harl. 48 B. 32.

Ashley, co. *Camb.* Grants, etc., in, 1303. Harl. 53 D. 41 (Assele);—1319. Harl. 48 C. 47 (Asshelee);—1360. Harl. 48 C. 52 (Asschele).

—— Precipe on a covenant conc. lands in, 1555 (Assheley). Add. 24920.

—— Award conc. lands in, held of Cheveley manor, 1582. Add. 19259.

Ashley, co. *Norf.* Transfer of service in the manor of, 1403 (Asshele). Add. 15561.

Ashley, co. *Northt.* Conf., by King John, of grant in, 1208 (Essele). Add. 6014.

—— Grants, etc., in, 13–14 cent. (Assele). *Copies.* Slo. xxxi. 4 (50–52).

—— Fines for the manor, 1339, 1357. *Copies.* Slo. xxxi. 4 (56, 45).

—— Compotus conc. sale of the manor, 1391 (Asshle). Harl. 48 E. 53.

—— Compotus-rolls of the manor, 1402–3. Harl. Roll A. 37 (Asshele);—1438–9. Harl. Roll K. 24 (Asshelee).

—— Sale, etc., of the manor, 1403. Harl. 47 B. 15 (Asahele);—1424. Harl. 48 F. 25 (do.);—1548. Add. 6066;—1552. Add. 6122;—1570. Add. 6136;—c. 1620. Add. 6124.

—— Sale of the advowson, 1552 (Assheley). Add. 6122.

Ashley, co. *Staff.* Brief to rebuild the church, 1778. Ch. Br. B. xviii. 5.

Ashley, in *Box,* co. *Wilts.* Conf. of grants in, to Farleigh Priory, *t.* Hen. III. (Hasseleye, Asseleye). Harl. 46 I. 61.

Ashley, co. *Wilts.* Fine of the manor and advowson, 1341 (Asshesleghe). Harl. 58 G. 5.

Ashley Green, in *Chesham,* co. *Buck.* Warranty of lands in, *t.* Hen. III. (Esseleya). Harl. 46 F. 43.

—— Conveyance in, 1468 (Assheley grene). Harl. 58 E. 39.

—— Extract from Court-roll, 1521 (Ayssheley grene). Harl. 58 E. 4.

Ashley, North, co. *Southt.* Grant of the manor, 1390 (Northascheley). Add. 15852.

Ashleyhay, in *Wirksworth,* co. *Derb.* Grants, etc., in, 1566. Woll. iii. 20 (Ashelehe);—1598. Woll. iii. 86 (Asshelehey);—1612. Woll. xi. 87;—1624. Woll. xi. 119;—1633. Woll. iii. 87;—1639. Woll. iii. 88.

—— Fine in, 1606. Woll. xi. 76.

Ashmanhaugh, co. *Norf.* Appropriation of the church to Hulme Abbey, [1146–74]. *Copy.* Cott. iv. 57 (17).

Ashmore, co. *Dors.* Attornment of two parts of Fifhyde St. Quintyn manor in, 1351. Harl. 48 B. 5.

Ashop, *nr. Hope,* co. *Derb.* Grant in, 1424 (Asahcoppe). Harl. 84 A. 49.

Ashorn, *nr. Newbold Pacy,* co. *Warw.* Feoffment of the manor, 1370 (Asshorne). Add. 20422.

**Ashton under Lyne,** *co. Lanc.*
*Rector.* Rob. Parker (late), 1619.
Add. 1794.

—— —— Hen. Fairfax, 1619. Add.
1794;—1633. Add. 1796.

**Ashurst,** *co. Kent.* Grant in, 1310
(Asscheherst). Add. 16459.

**Ashurst,** *co. Suss.* Feoffment, etc., in,
1474. Add. 18767;—1492. Add. 8909
(Asshehurst); — 1587. Add. 8959
(Assherste).

**Ashwater,** *co. Devon.* Title of Alice
de Beauvyle to the manor, 1332 (Asshe-
water). Harl. Roll N. 34.

**Ashwell,** *in Finchingfield, co. Essex.*
Conf. of tithes in, to Dunmow Priory,
1221 (Essewell). Cott. xxi. 15.

**Ashwell,** *co. Hertf.* Grant in, by Edw.
the Confessor, to Westminster Abbey,
1066 [sc. 1065] (Æscepelle). Cott. vi.
2 (copy).

—— Custumary, early Hen. III.
(Essewell). Add. 8139.

—— Release in, 1622. Add. 5273.

—— Brief conc. a fire in, 1796. Ch.
Br. B. xxxvi. 3.

**Ashwelthorpe,** *co. Norf.* Power to
take seisin in, 1586 (Thorpe). Add.
14686.

**Askeby.** *v.* Ashby, *co. Linc.*

**Askham,** *co. Westm.* Brief conc. a fire
at, 1793. Ch. Br. B. xxxiii. 6.

**Askham Bryan,** *co. York.* Grant of
the manor, 1510 (Brian Askam). Roy.
Roll 14 B. xviii.

**Askwith,** *co. York.* Power to give seisin
in, etc., 1320. Add. 16770;—1321.
Add. 16773.

—— Sale of the manor, 1637. Add.
1797.

**Aslackby** (Aslakby), *co. Linc.* Grants,
etc., in, 1397. Harl. 54 G. 35 b;—
1438. Add. 6407; — 1447. Add.
6409.

—— Precipe on a covenant conc. land
in, 1578. Add. 25094.

**Aslacoe,** *co. Linc.* Charter witnessed
by decanal chapter of, 1242 (Aslachow).
Harl. 44 E. 49.

**Aslo.** *v.* Hadlow (?), *co. Kent.*

**Aspall** (Aspale, etc.), *co. Suff.* Grants,
etc., in, late 12 cent. Harl. 50 H. 19
(Aspaleshage);—1348. Harl. 55 F.
44;—1409. Harl. 46 G. 52;—1480 (?).
Add. 16567; — 1621. Add. 10484
(Aspell, Aspehall).

—— Acquittance for fines for the
manor, 1355 (Asphale). Cott. xxvii.
152.

—— Grant of the manor, 1375. Harl.
51 E. 10.

—— Compotus-roll, 1404-5 (Aspale-
hall). Harl. Roll G. 29.

**Aspatric,** *co. Cumb.* Conf. of grants of
salmon, etc., to St. Bees Priory, early
Hen. III. (Ascpatric). Cott. xi. 13.

**Aspley,** *co. Bedf.* Grant in, 909
(Æpslea). Add. 19793.

**Aspley Guise,** *co. Bedf.* Leases, etc.,
in, 1573. Add. 24108, 24109;—1608.
Add. 24118;—1649. Add. 24079;—
1655. Add. 24122;—1661. Add.
24080;—1678. Add. 24081.

**Ass.** *v.* Ashfield, Great, *co. Suff.*

**Assch.** *v.* Ash Bocking, *co. Suff.*

**Asscheburne.** *v.* Ashbourne, *co. Derb.*

**Asschedone.** *v.* Ashdon, *co. Essex.*

**Asscheherst.** *v.* Ashurst, *co. Kent.*

**Asschfeld Parva.** *v.* Ashfield, Lea, al.
Little, *co. Suff.*

**Assebi.** *v.* Ashby St. Legers, *co.
Northt.*

**Asseburn.** *v.* Ashbourne, *co. Derb.*

**Assedenne.** *v. sub* Pembury, *co. Kent.*

**Asselby,** *in Howden, co. York.* Grant
in, 1519 (Astilby). Lansd. 456.

**Assele.** *v.* Ashley, *co. Camb.*

**Assenton,** *co. Oxon.* Sale in, 1614.
Harl. 79 G. 5.

**Asserby,** *co. Linc.* Lease in, 1566.
Harl. 46 D. 13.

**Asserby** (?), *nr. Alford, co. Linc.* Clericus de Asfordby. Eudo, 1263. Cott.
xxiii. 10.

**Asserton.** *v.* Ascerton, *in Sidmouth,
co. Devon.*

**Asserton,** *in Winterbourne Stoke, co.
Wilts.* Order for an extent of the
manor, 1301 (Wynterburne Asterton).
Add. 19302.

—— Fines of the manor, 1577, 1596,
1600. Add. 15117.

**Aston,** *co. Heref.* Exch. by B. de Bromton for lands in, early Hen. III. (Eyston). Slo. xxxii. 18.

**Aston,** *co. Hertf.* Conff. of the manor to Reading Abbey by W. de Albini and Hen. II., [1138] (Estona). Add. 19586 ;—[1157] (Eston). Add. 19593.

—— Release of Shephall, co. Hertf., from subjection to the church of, [1151–4] (Estuna). Add. 19590.

—— Conf. to Reading Abbey by H., Bp. of Lincoln, of a pension from the church of, 1403. Add. 19647.

—— Compotus-rolls of the manor, 1472 (Heston). Harl. Rolls A. 15, H. 13.

**Aston,** *co. Salop.* Briefs for rebuilding the church, 1793, 1800, 1824. Ch. Br. B. xxxiii. 7, xl. 9, C. v. 6.

**Aston,** *nr. Stone, co. Staff.* Suit and covenant in, with Stone Priory, [1155?] (Estona). Copy. Cott. xiii. 6 (5).

**Aston,** *co. Worc.* Leases at, 904. Add. 19791 (Easttun) ;—1033–38. Add. 19797 (East tune).

**Aston,** *with Aughton, co. York.* Grants, etc., in, 1316. Harl. 83 D. 21 ;—1343. Harl. 112 F. 51 ;—1345. Harl. 83 D. 14 ;—1376 (Asston). Harl. 84 A. 40.

—— *Constabularius.* Matheus, late 13 cent. Harl. 83 D. 5, 112 F. 48.

—— *Persona.* Joh. Danyell, 1377. Harl. 57 A. 16.

     v. also Aughton, co. York.

**Aston, Blank** *al. Cold, co. Glouc.* Grant in, by Little Malvern Priory, 1275 (Estona frigida). Slo. xxxiii. 14.

**Aston Botterell,** *co. Salop.* Releases in, 1316. Cott. xxiv. 13 (Astone Boterel) ;—1377. Cott. xxiii. 6 (Astone).

**Aston Cantlow,** *co. Warw.* Appropriation of the church to Maxstoke Priory, 1345. Add. 21418.

—— Decree, etc., in a suit betw. Maxstoke and Studley Priories for the church of, 1404. Add. 21419, 21420.

—— Grants in, 1410. Add. 8440 (Aston Canntelowe) ;—1460. Add. 8441 ;—1513. Add. 8442.

—— Release in, to Studley Priory, 1482. Add. 8435.

—— Sale of the manor, 1540. Harl. 47 A. 53 (Aston Cantloo).

**Aston Clinton,** *co. Buck.* Grant in, early 14 cent. Add. 5994.

**Aston, Coal,** *co. Derb.* Fine in, 1541 (Haston). Woll. ii. 71.

—— Land late held in, by Beauchief Abbey, 1547 (Cold Aston). Woll. iv. 52.

**Aston le Walls,** *co. Northt.* Grant in, [1485–7]. Harl. 49 F. 48.

—— Suit conc. lands in West Wardon, etc., in, with Wardon Abbey, 1502 (Aston in the Wallys). Add. 6121.

**Aston Sandford,** *co. Buck.* Grant of the manor, 1466 (Aston Samford). Harl. 57 C. 14.

**Aston, Steeple** (?), *co. Oxon.* Grants in, to Biddlesdon Abbey, early 13 cent. (Eston). Harl. 86 D. 20, 22.

—— Exch. for lands in, with the same, early Hen. III. Harl. 84 D. 30.

—— *Dominus.* Math. de Romeli, early 13 cent. Harl. 86 D. 22.

—— *Capellanus.* Willelmus, early 13 cent. Harl. 86 D. 22.

—— *Clericus.* Willelmus, early 13 cent. Harl. 86 D. 22.

**Aston, Street,** *co. Warw.* Defeasance of bond for a marriage settlement in, 1409. Add. 24216.

**Aston sub edge,** *co. Glouc.* Sale in, 1587. Harl. 75 H. 27.

**Aston Tirrold** (Astone, etc.), *co. Berks.* Release of the manor, etc., to W. de Wykeham, 1381. Add. 20282.

—— Release of the manor to New College, Oxford, 1384. Add. 24322.

—— Power to give seisin of the manor, etc., as held of New College, 1392. Add. 20284.

—— Feoffment in, 1432 (Aston Thorald). Add. 20241.

—— Dispensation to R. Scrope, as Rector, to hold Sherrington rectory, co. Wilts., 1772. Add. 18463.

**Aston, Upper** (?) or **Lower** (?), *nr. Church Stoke, co. Montgom.* Power from T. Bp. of Hereford to give seisin in, 1344. Add. 20445.

**Aston Wheaton,** *co. Staff.* Brief conc. a fire there, 1777. Ch. Br. B. xvii. 10.

**Astona.** *v.* Ashton, *nr. Oundle, co. Northt.*

**Astorp.** *v.* Aisthorpe, *co. Linc.*

**Astran.** Council held at, by K. Ethelwulf, 839. Cott. MS. Aug. ii. 20, 37.

**Astrat.** v. Ystrad, nr. Denbigh, co. Denb.

**Astwell.** v. sub Wappenham, co. Northt.

**Astwick** (Estwyk, Astwyke), co. Bedf. Grant, etc., in, ante 1260. Harl. 45 I. 18;—1349. Add. 24055.

**Astwick,** in Evenly, co. Northt. Grants in, 1396 (Astwyk). Add. 854, 855.

**Astwood** (Estwode, Astwode), co. Buck. Grants, etc., in, late 13 cent. Add. 23872;—1304. Add. 23902:—1306. Add. 23873, 23874;—1370. Add. 23875;—1391. Add. 23876;—1412. Add. 23877;—1428. Add. 23878;—1436. Add. 23926;—1449. Add. 23879;—1463. Add. 23928;—1550. Add. 23881;—1552. Add. 23880;—1558. Add. 23882;—1580. Add. 23883;—1591. Add. 23884;—1595. Add. 23886, 23887;—1712. Add. 23968;—1717. Add. 23892;—1718. Add. 23970.

—— Fines in, 1575. Add. 23893, 23894;—1591. Add. 23885;—1602. Add. 23888-23890; — 1612. Add. 23891.

—— Vicarius. Joh. Cook, 1412. Add. 23877.

**Astwood,** in Feckenham, co. Worc. Covenant for settlement of the manor, etc., 1598. Harl. 79 F. 6.

**Aswarby,** co. Linc. Rector. Johannes, t. Edw. I. (Asewordeby). Add. 6377.

**Atforton.** v. Adferton, co. Heref.

**Athboy,** co. Meath. Release in, 1431. Eg. 102.

**Athelington.** v. Allington, co. Linc.

**Athelington** al. Allington, co. Suff. Release in, 1477 (Alyngton). Harl. 57 B. 35.

—— Precipes conc. lands in, 1588. Add. 25389;—1593. Add. 25448.

**Athelstanford,** co. Haddington. Covenant betw. St. Andrew's Priory and the nuns of Haddington conc. tithes of, 1245 (Helstanford). Cott. xviii. 28, 30.

**Athelyngflet.** v. Adlingfleet, co. York.

**Atherston,** co. Warw. Court-roll, [1399?]. Add. 17358.

—— Petition from the Abbat of Merevale for the Lordship of, [1485?]. Harl. 44 G. 14.

**Atherton.** v. Arreton, I. of Wight.

**Athescompe.** v. Addiscombe, in Croydon, co. Surr.

**Athorp.** v. Authorpe, co. Linc.

**Athwyke.** v. Adwick, co. York.

**Atlant,** [in Boxford?], co. Suff. Grant in, early 13 cent. Harl. 55 C. 13.

**Atleburgh.** v. Attleborough, co. Norf.

**Atlingworth,** co. Suss. License to alienate the manor, etc., 1564. Add. 8949;—1590. Add. 18868.

**Atram.** v. Stoke Atram, in Whitchurch Canonicorum, co. Dors.

**Attenestona.** v. Adstone, co. Northt.

**Attercliffe,** in Sheffield, co. York. Fine in, 1541 (Atterclyff). Woll. ii. 71.

**Attilburgh.** v. Attleborough, co. Norf.

**Attilton,** in Wickhambrook, co. Suff. Grant, etc., in, t. Edw. I. Harl. 52 I. 10 (Attelthon);—1382. Harl. 48 D. 3, 4.

**Attingewic.** v. Atwick, E. R., co. York.

**Attleborough,** co. Norf. Grant of fairs in the manor, 1310 (Atleburgh). Harl. 58 I. 47 (copy).

—— Grants in, 1445. Add. 14840 (Attilburgh);—1504. Add. 14845 (Attilburgh).

—— Persona duarum parcium eccl. de Attylburgh. Pet. Leverych, 1428. Add. 14637.

**Attlebridge** (Attlebrige, etc.), co. Norf. Grants in, t. Hen. III. Harl. 51 E. 43;—1335. Add. 9960.

—— Sale of a swannery in Brodishe al. Brokedishe manor in, 1609. Add. 14666.

—— Persona. Walt. de Caune, t. Hen. III. Harl. 51 E. 43.

**Attona.** v. Aughton, co. York.

**Atwick** (Atwyk, etc.), E. R., co. York. Conf. of a grant of the church to Bridlington Priory, [1128-32] (Attingewic). Cott. MS. Aug. ii. 56.

—— Grants, etc., in, 1491. Add. 5774 (Attwyk);—1511. Add. 5777;—1513. Add. 5778;—1514. Add. 5781, 5782;—1515. Add. 5780, 5784 (Atweke).

**Auchencrieff,** in Kirkmahoe, co. Dumfries. Conf. of grant of, to Melrose Abbey, 1237 (Hauchycref). Cott. xviii. 11.

**Auchincruiff,** co. Ayr. Conf. of a settlement, in 1626, of the Barony, etc., 1632. Add. 26691.

Auckland St. Helen, co. Durh. Grant, etc., in, 1689. Add. 19430, 19431;—1695. Add. 19433.

Audby, in Hawerby, co. Linc. Conf. of the church to Beauport Abbey, 1204 (Alewardby). Add. 15238.

Audebyre. v. Oldbury, co. Glouc.

Audeham. v. Yaldham, in Wrotham, co. Kent.

Audewerk. v. Aldwark, in Bradborne, co. Derb.

Audinton. v. Alderton, co. Wilts.

Audlem, co. Chester. Grant of the church to St. Thomas' Priory, Stafford, [1282–7?] (Aldelyme). Add. 875–877.

—— Briefs for rebuilding the church, 1809, 1816. Ch. Br. B. xlix. 10, lvi. 10.

Auecheston, co. —— (?). Releases in, 1329. Harl. 49 I. 50;—1339. Harl. 50 D. 55.

Auene. v. Aberafon, co. Glam.

Auene, Aqua de. v. Afon, River, co. Glam.

Auerigge. v. Havering atte Bower, co. Essex.

Auerthorpe, Auetorp. v. Hawthorpe, in Irnham, co. Linc.

Auescote. v. Ascote, in Pattishall, co. Northt.

Auford. v. Alford, co. Linc.

Aufurweke. v. Alfrick, co. Worc.

Aughnacloy, co. Tyrone. Royal grant of a market, etc., in, 1633 (Lurgybawen). Add. 26020.

Aughton, in Lonsdale, co. Lanc. Marr. settlement in, 1670. Add. 19547.

Aughton (Actona, etc.), in Aston, co. York. Grants at "le Staubrige" and "le Westedie" in, t. Hen. III. Harl. 83 D. 5, 6.

—— Grants, etc, in, t. Hen. III. Harl. 83 D. 12;—late 13 cent. Harl. 84 B. 36 (Attona), 112 F. 48, 49;—t. Edw. I. Harl. 83 D. 31 (Attona), 112 F. 47;—1302. Harl. 112 I. 57;—1304. Harl. 112 I. 8;—t. Edw. II. Harl. 112 F. 57 (Hactona);—1312. Harl. 83 E. 47;—1316. Harl. 83 D. 7, 8, 112 H. 3 (Hactona);—1318. Harl. 83 E. 18;—1323. Harl. 112 F. 50;—1328. Harl. 112 G. 61 (Acthona);—1345. Harl. 83 D. 14 (Aghton);—1359. Harl. 83 E. 48;—1374. Harl. 112 G. 59;—

1399. Harl. 84 A. 15 (Ayghton);—1528. Add. 17963;—1617. Add. 18050.

—— Fine in, 1604. Add. 18009.

Ault Hucknall. v. Hucknall, Ault, co. Derb.

Aulton. v. Alton, co. Wilts.

Aumodsham. v. Amersham, co. Buck.

Aungre. v. Ongar Hundred, co. Essex.

Aungre ad Castrum. v. Ongar, Chipping, co. Essex.

Aungre, Alta. v. Ongar, High, co. Essex.

Aunsby, co. Linc. Grant in, 1296 (Onnesbye). Harl. 83 A. 9.

Aunsedeleye. v. Anslow, in Rolleston, co. Staff.

Aurell Knolle, in Farway (?), co. Devon. Grant in, 1564. Add. 13811.

Aurich., Auricheseya. v. Arlsey, co. Bedf.

Aust, co. Glouc. Grant of a windmill, ferry, etc., in, t. Hen. III (Hauste). Add. 6231.

—— Conveyance of the manor, etc., 1389. Harl. 46 G. 20.

Austeleye, co. —— (?). Vicarius. Joh. Margery, 1361. Add. 26916.

Austen Sernelles, co. Surr. Excheq. acquittance for the rent of, 1616. Add. 25665.

Austewyke, co. York (?). Compotus-roll of the manor, 1514–15. Add. 24451.

Authenby. v. Owmby, co. Linc.

Authorpe, co. Linc. Grants, etc., in, early Hen. II. Harl. 51 D. 22 (Agetorp), 54 E. 6 (do.);—1309. Cott. xxix. 81 (Athorp);—1325. Cott. xxvii. 34 (Aghthorpe);—t. Edw. II. Harl. 52 H. 4 (Augthorp), 52 H. 6 (Hauthorp).

—— Conf. of grant in, to Burwell Priory, late 12 cent. (Haghethorp). Harl. 51 D. 20.

—— Grant of the manor, c. 1292 (Agthorp). Harl. 51 D. 31.

—— Capellanus. Hugo, ante 1254. Cott. xxvii. 40 (Aigatorp).

—— Rector. Willelmus, t. Hen. III. Cott. v. 35, Harl. 50 F. 50.

**Auton** *al.* **Aveton, Black,** *co. Devon.* Grant, etc., in, 1516. Add. 26184 (Blakeaveton);—1522. Add. 26186; —1541. Add. 26189.

———— Admission to lands of Norden in the manor of, 1567. Add. 26191.

**Autun.** *v.* Holton Beckering (?), *co. Linc.*

**Auvelers.** *v.* Aveley, *co. Essex.*

**Aveley,** *co. Essex.* Grants, etc., in, *t.* Edw. I. Add. 24546 (Auvelers);— 1323. Add. 24495 (Alvithele), 24496; —1594. Harl. 51 H. 30 (Aveligh).

———— Suit in, 1594 (Alvethley). Harl. 57 A. 7.

———— Sale of Barnards in, 1614 (Avethley). Harl. 78 I. 33.

**Avenbury,** *co. Heref.* Grant in, 1496. Add. 13966.

**Avene.** *v.* Aberafon, *co. Glam.*

**Averham,** *co. Nott.* Covenant with Rufford Abbey conc. tithes of, [1195-1205] (Egrum). Harl. 83 C. 27, 28.

———— Papal conf. of covenant betw. Rufford Abbey and the rector conc. tithes, 1231 (Egrum). Harl. 111 A. 11.

———— Assignment of life interest of Qu. Catharine in land in, 1680. Harl. 111 H. 11.

———— *Persona.* Ric. f. Ric. de Marcham, *t.* Hen. III. Harl. 112 F. 33.

**Avethley.** *v.* Aveley, *co. Essex.*

**Aveton Giffard,** *co. Devon.* Grant of Bornatone in, by Plympton Priory, 1326. Add. 24240.

———— Grants, etc., in, 1380. Harl. 86 C. 12;—1384. Harl. 86 F. 47;—1391. Harl. 86 G. 4;—1398. Harl. 86 E. 28;—1402. Harl. 85 F. 44;—1459. Harl. 84 I. 3;—1479. Harl. 86 F. 24.

———— *Prepositus.* Sim. Hyndeston, 1479. Harl. 86 F. 24.

———— *Rector.* Joh. Julyate, 1402. Harl. 85 F. 44.

**Avintone.** *v.* Evington, *co. Leic.*

**Avon, River.** Grant at Westbury, *co.* Glouc., nr., 793-796 (Aben). Add. 19790.

———— Grants of fishery in, betw. Barford and Wasperton, *co.* Warw., to Thelesford Priory, *t.* Edw. II. Add. 21407, 21408;—1332. Add. 21410.

———— Grant in Bristol "super pontem Abbone," 1387. Harl. 46 G. 17.

**Avon,** *River (continued).* Reservation of fishing rights in, at Hannam Abbot's, *co.* Glouc, 1657. Add. 15840.

**Avon,** *co. Wilts.* Grant at (?), 962 (æt Afene). Cott. viii. 28.

**Avon Dasset.** *v.* Dasset, Avon *al.* Little, *co. Warw.*

**Avon, Nether,** *co. Wilts.* Power to take seisin of the manor, 1368 (Netheranene). Cott. xxiv. 11.

**Axbridge** (Axebrygge, Axebrugge), *co. Som.* Grants, etc., in, 13-14 cent. Add. 12949;—early 14 cent. Add. 12948, 12950, 12951;—1320. Add. 12952;—1325. Add. 12953;—1363. Add. 12954;—1410. Add. 12955;— 1431. Harl. 112 C. 18;—1439. Harl. 111 D. 5;—1499. Harl. 49 I. 38.

———— *Prepositus.* Elyas de Deyghare, early 14 cent. Add. 12950.

———— ———— Joh. Wilteschire, 1363. Add. 12954.

———— ———— Joh. Spryng, 1431. Harl. 112 C. 18.

———— *Ballivus.* Joh. Fytz, 1431. Harl. 112 C. 18.

**Axholme, Isle of,** *co. Linc.* Grant in, by R. de Molbrai, to the Knts. Hospitallers, *t.* Steph. (Insula). Add. 19816.

———— Grant of pasturage in, by N. de Molbrai, [1180-90?] (Insula). Add. 20607.

———— Conf. of grant in, by N. de Mulbrai, to Monks Kirby Priory, *ante* 1191 (?) (Axiholm). Harl. 53 G. 55.

———— Grants of nativi and lands in, to Sulby Abbey, early 13 cent. Add. 19822, 21530;—1255. Add. 20608 (Ins. de Haxyholm);—c. 1255. Add. 20609;—t. Edw. I. Add. 22437.

———— Grants, etc., in, early 13 cent. Add. 21180;—c. 1230-40. Cott. xxiv. 49;—1385. Add. 22568.

**Axminster,** *co. Devon.* Grants, etc., in, 1299. Add. 25894 (Axem.);—1386. Harl. 53 C. 12 (Axmystre);—1409. Harl. 46 G. 49 (Axemynstre);—1636. Add. 13985.

———— Feoffment of Chepmanhegh and Capehegh nr., 1402. Harl. 57 B. 52.

———— Fine in, 1403 (Axmystre). Harl. 58 G. 37.

*v. also* Weycroft, *co. Devon.*

**Axmouth**, *co. Devon.* Fine in Bruckland (Brokelond) in, 1403. Harl. 58 G. 37.

—— Enquiry conc. disturbances at, 1427. Harl. 58 C. 37.

**Axton**, *co. Flint.* Grant in, 1528 (Axtawne). Add. 7034.

**Aycliffe**, *co. Durh.* Sale of church lands in, 1650. Add. 12628.

**Aydon Shields**, *in Hexham, co. Northumb.* Grant of free warren in, 1341 (Aldensheles). Cott. xvii. 13.

**Ayghton.** *v.* Aughton, co. York.

**Aykring.** *v.* Eakring, co. Nott.

**Aylesbury**, *co. Buck.* Recovery in, 1497. Add. 13929.

—— Rental of the manor, 1627. Cott. i. 4.

**Aylesbury Hundred**, *co. Buck.* Exchequer acquittance to collector of subsidies in, 1596. Add. 25569.

**Aylesby**, *co. Linc.* Grants, etc., in, to Newhouse Abbey, c. 1150–60. Harl. 43 H. 16 (Halesbi), 17 (Alesbi);—[1156–7]. Harl. 51 H. 1 (Alcabi);—early 13 cent. Harl. 50 I. 3.

—— Grants of the church to Beauport Abbey, 1202. Harl. 45 B. 23 (Alewardebi);—1204. Add. 15238.

—— Compotus of the manor, 1482–3 (Alesby). Campb. ix. 6.

—— Crown lease in (?), 1562 (Alesby). Harl. 75 E. 35.

**Aylesford** (Aylisford, etc.), *co. Kent.* Grants, etc., of Cosington (Cosynton, Cosyngton magna) manor in, 1364. Harl. 48 H. 23, 24;—1369. Harl. 54 H. 27;—1374. Harl. 48 H. 25, 28.

—— Grants, etc., in, 1531. Add. 941, 942;—1556. Harl. 57 H. 11;—1617. Add. 943;—1628. Add. 944.

—— Particulars of forfeited lands of Sir T. Wyatt in, 1554 (Aillesforth). Harl. Roll CC. 20.

**Aylestone**, *co. Leic.* Lease in, 1436. Campb. xix. 13.

**Ayllewaston.** *v.* Elvaston (?), co. Derb.

**Aylmerton**, *co. Norf.* Power to give seisin in, 1379. Add. 14521.

**Aylrichessia.** *v.* Arlsey, co. Bedf.

**Aylsham**, *co. Norf.* Grant of the manor by Edw. III. to John, his son, 1372 (Ailesham). Cott. xv. 1.

—— Sale in, 1538 (Aylesham). Harl. 55 H. 44.

—— Foundation of scholarships at Cambridge for the Grammar School of, 1567. Add. 26723.

—— Fine of the manor, 1638 (Ailesham). Woll. xi. 29.

**Aylstone**, *co. Leic.* Inquest of the manor, 1566. Add. 7252.

**Aylswythorp.** *v.* Gaytonthorpe, co. Norf.

**Aylwarton**, *in Stone.* *v. sub* Stone next Faversham, co. Kent.

**Aylworth**, *in Naunton, co. Glouc.* Settlement in, 1412 (Eyleworths). Slo. xxxiii. 59.

**Ayly.** *v.* Yellow, *in Stogumber, co. Som.*

**Aylyngton**, **Aileton.** *v.* Elton, co. Hunt.

**Aylysham.** *v. sub* Nonington, co. Kent.

**Aymestrey**, *co. Heref.* Sale of Gateley park, etc., in, 1566. Harl. 79 G. 21.

—— *Vicarius.* Gaufridus, 1399. Cott. xxvi. 5;—1402. Cott. xxiii. 39, 40. —— Will. Michell, 1659. Add. 6229.

**Ayott St. Lawrence**, *co. Hertf.* Conf., by Edw. the Confessor, of grant in, to Westminster Abbey, 1066 [sc. 1065] (Ægete). Cott. vi. 2 (copy).

—— Compotus-roll of the manor, 1470–71. Harl. Roll A. 15.

—— Release of the manor, 1572. Add. 1994.

—— Brief for rebuilding the church, 1772. Ch. Br. B. xiii. 1.

**Ayott St. Peter**, *co. Hertf.* Grant of the manor and advowson, *ante* 1302 (Hayete Munfichet). Lansd. 93.

**Ayr**, *River, co. Ayr.* Conf. of grants on banks of, to Melrose Abbey, 1264 (Flumen de Ar). Campb. xxx. 8.

**Ayrton.** *v.* Airton, co. York.

**Aysbrytell.** *v.* Ashbrittle, co. Som.

**Aysfeld.** *v.* Ashfield, Great, co. Suff.

**Aysfeld parva.** *v.* Ashfield Lea, co. Suff.

**Ayshe Regny.** *v.* Ash Reigny, co. Devon.

Aysah, Aysah juxta Wytnesham. *v.* Ash Bocking, *co. Suf.*

Aysahedon. *v.* Ashingdon, *co. Essex.*

Aysahen. *v.* Ashen, *co. Essex.*

Ayston. *v.* Ashton, *co. Northt.*

Ayton, *in Seamer, nr. Scarborough, co. York.* Grant in, 1555. Add. 13099.

## B

Babbeton, Babeton. *v.* Bapton, *in Fisherton Delamere, co. Wilts.*

Babbeuurde. *v.* Babworth, *co. Nott.*

Babbing þyrnan. *v.* Bobbingworth, *co. Essex.*

Baberhays (Babereaheys, etc.), *co. Dors.* Grants, etc., in, 1410. Harl. 51 F. 40, 41;—1438. Harl. 50 E. 6.

Babinge, *in Waltham, co. Kent.* Grant in, 1260-1. Harl. 78 E. 11.

Babraham, *co. Camb.* Papal conff. of "Coppelawe" Grange in, to Sawtrey Abbey, [1164]. Cott. MS. Aug. ii. 116;—1176. Cott. MS. Aug. ii. 125 (Baburgeham);—1195. Cott. MS. Aug. ii. 115 (Badburgham).

—— Papal conf. of the church to the same, 1195 (do.). Cott. MS. Aug. ii. 115.

Babworth (Babbeuurde, etc.), *co. Nott.* Grants in Morton in, to Rufford Abbey, late 12-early 13 centt. Cott. xxvii. 166, 167, Harl. 112 B. 44, 112 H. 34.

—— Papal conf. of Morton Grange in, to Rufford Abbey, [1171-80]. Harl. 111 A. 4.

—— *Presbiter.* Ricardus, late 12-early 13 cent. Cott. xxvii. 166, Harl. 112 B. 44.

Bache, *nr. Llangollen, co. Denb.* Demise in, 1577 (Baghey). Add. 8487.

Bache, *co. Salop.* Grants in, late 13 cent. (La Bache). Add. 8330, 8332.

—— *Dominus.* Rog. fil. dni. Hen. de Bradelegh, late 13 cent. Add. 8330.

Backnoe, *co. Bedf.* Grant in the manor of, 1549 (Bakenhoe). Add. 4607.

—— Exemplif. of fine in, 1589 (Bakenhoe). Add. 5156.

—— Sale of the manor, 1596. Add. 5157.

Backwell, *co. Som. Persona.* Will. de Pyggealegh, 1337. Add. 5453, 5454;—*as Rector,* (Will. de Pykeale), 1340. Add. 25891.

—— —— Joh. Sypyzete *al.* Sypizete, 1371. Harl. 48 I. 9, 49 F. 31.

Baconsthorpe (Baconesthorp), *co. Norf.* Grants, etc., in, late 12 cent. Add. 22571;—1370. Add. 14867;—1408. Harl. 52 O. 17;—1416. Add. 14820;—1417. Add. 14821;—1659, 1674. Add. 19266.

Bacton (Baketon, Bakton, etc.), *co. Norf.* Grants, etc., in, 1281. Toph. 54 *dors;—t.* Edw. I. Add. 14511 (Baketune);—1330. Add. 14709;—1382. Add. 14512;—1432. Add. 14513;—1463. Add. 14514.

—— Grants of the manor, 1313. Harl. 52 A. 36;—1354. Add. 14767.

—— Fines, etc., in Keswick (Casewyk), etc., in, 1381. Harl. 54 C. 28, 56 B. 35;—1403. Harl. 49 G. 45;—1405. Harl. 58 B. 19;—1449. Harl. 58 E. 37.

—— Release, etc., in, from Hulme Abbey, 1422. Toph. 4, 24.

—— Grant in, from Bromholm Priory, 1422. Toph. 54.

—— Covenant conc. the manor betw. Lord Suffolk and Bromholm Priory, [1436]. Add. 14570.

—— Surrender in, to Bromholm Priory, 1444. Add. 14571.

—— *Perpet. Vicarius.* Joh. Tryce, 1382. Add. 14512.

Bacton (Baketon), *co. Suf.* Grant, etc., in, 1418. Harl. 58 D. 12;—1442. Cott. xxix. 30.

—— Report on a tithe-suit conc., 1515. Cott. ii. 13.

—— Precipes on covenants conc. lands in, 1578. Add. 25337, 25338.

—— *Rector.* Will. Soper, 1515. Cott. ii. 13.

Badburgham. *v.* Babraham, *co. Camb.*

Badby, *co. Northt.* Grant at, 944 (æt Baddan byrig). Cott. MS. Aug. ii. 63.

Baddeley, *in Norton on the Moors, co. Staff.* Grants in, 1344, 1347 (Baddelegha, Baddeleye). Add. 22574, 22575.

Baddeshulle. *v. sub* Tudeley, *co. Kent.*

Baddiley, *co. Chest.* Briefs for rebuilding the church, 1808, 1812. Ch. Br. B. xlix. 1, liii. 4.

D

**Baddington.** *v.* Bainton, *co. Northt.*

**Baddoowelle.** *v. sub* Newsham, *co. Linc.*

**Baddow, Great,** *co. Essex.* Settlement of, in marriage, on Matilda, daughter of Hugh, Earl of Chester, [1189?] (Badewenna). Cott. xxiv. 15 (*copy*).

—— Conf. of the church of, by Earl David, to Repton Priory, *c.* 1190 (?) (B[a]dewen). Campb. xxx. 4.

—— Release in, 1555. Add. 5263.

—— Sale of lands in, late bel. to Coggeshall chantry in the church of, 1564. Harl. 79 G. 20.

—— Precipe on a covenant conc. land in, 1593. Add. 25033.

—— *Vicarius. Dom.* Robertus, 1301. Harl. 58 C. 7.

**Baddow, Little,** *co. Essex.* Grant in, *c.* 1250 (Parva Badewe). Add. 18575.

—— License for a tavern in, 1596. Harl. 57 H. 23.

**Badechewell.** *v.* Bakewell, *co. Derb.*

**Badeherste.** *v.* Bathurst, *nr. Battle, co. Suss.*

**Badekneche,** *nr. Shobdon, co. Heref.* Conf. by Wigmore Abbey of a grant in, 1281. Cott. xxi. 43.

**Badelee.** *v.* Badley, *co. Suff.*

**Badelesdonia.** *v.* Battlesden, *co. Bedf.*

**Badewelle Asfelde.** *v.* Badwell Ash, *co. Suff.*

**Badewenna.** *v.* Baddow, Gt., *co. Essex.*

**Badgeworth,** *co. Glouc.* Inspex. in 1330 of grant of the church to Usk Priory, *c.* 1150 (Begewordia). Add. 5342.

—— Presentation of Dom. W. Dylowe to the vicarage, by Usk Priory, 1434 (Beggeworth). Harl. 49 G. 10.

**Badgworth,** *co. Som.* Grants, etc., in, 1308. Add. 6501 (Bageworth);— 1363. Add. 6504 (Northebageworth); —1375. Add. 6505 (Beggeworth);— 1381. Harl. 48 A. 24;—1398. Add. 6507 (Nethyrbaggeworth); — 1428. Add. 6509, 6510;—1440. Add. 6511; —1518. Add. 6513;—1533. Add. 6514, 6515.

—— Court-rolls, 1602-4. Add. 26507.

—— *Persona.* Will. atte Forde, 1375. Add. 6505.

**Badgworth,** *co. Som.* (*continued*). *Rector.* Joh. Penvin, 1589. Add. 6516.

**Badilande, Badilonde.** *v. sub* Ewhurst, *co. Suss.*

**Badimyncgtun.** *v.* Badminton, *co. Glouc.*

**Badingham** (Badyngham), *co. Suff.* Conf. of a grant in, to Campsey Priory, 1321. Cott. v. 5.

—— Inspex., in 1454, of a feoffment of the manor, 1422 (Badyngham). Add. 17243.

—— Sale of messuages called "Wolseys," etc., in, 1542. Add. 5518.

—— Precipes on covenants conc. lands in, 1564. Add. 25314;—1588. Add. 25382.

—— Presentation to the rectory, 1630. Add. 5523.

—— Forfeiture of Colson Hall manor in, for recusancy, 1635. Add. 5522.

—— *Rector.* Tho. Bartone, 1415. Add. 10059.

—— —— Simon Sumpter, 1630. Add. 5523;—1640. Add. 5524, 5525.

**Badingherst, Denna de,** *nr. Bethersden, co. Kent.* Grant in, 1342. Add. 19992.

**Badlesmere,** *co. Kent.* Bequest to the church, 1344. Add. 948.

—— *Rector.* Hugo, 1344. Add. 948.

**Badley,** *co. Suff.* Inspex., in 1454, of a feoffment in, 1422 (Badelee). Add. 17243.

—— Precipe on a covenant conc. land in, 1558. Add. 25286.

**Badlingham** (Badlyngham), *co. Camb.* Grants, etc., in, 1312. Add. 22581;—1409. Add. 9200;—1476. Add. 18768, 18769.

—— Lease of pasture in the manor, 1332. Harl. 45 G. 35.

—— Lease of a moiety of the manor, 1402. Add. 18690.

**Badminton,** *co. Glouc.* Conf. of grants at, to Pershore Abbey, 972 (Badimyncgtun). Cott. MS. Aug. ii. 6.

—— Surrender, etc., in, by Pershore Abbey, [1198 - 1203] (Badmintun). Campb. xviii. 10.

**Badricheseye, Badrigesee.** *v.* Battersea, *co. Surr.*

**Badshill** *al.* **Badsell,** *co. Kent.* Ref. to, as a boundary in Brenchley, [1227-35] (Badeshull). Campb. xiv. 3.

Badshill Manor. *v. sub* Tudeley, *co. Kent.*

Badwell, *co. Suf.* Release from mortuary dues to Ixworth Priory, 1528. Add. 18813.

—— Award conc. a lease of Schakerlonde manor, etc., in, 1533. Add. 18816.

Badwell Ash *al.* Little Badwell (Badewelle Asfelde), *co. Suf.* Grants in, late 13 cent. Add. 18569;—1319. Add. 9099.

—— Precipes on covenants conc. lands in, 1564. Add. 25326;—1589. Add. 25391.

Badyalton. *v.* Bathealton, *co. Som.*

Badyngton. *v.* Bainton, *co. Northt.*

Bag Enderby. *v.* Enderby, Bag, *co. Linc.*

Bagborough, West (Baggebere. Westbaggeburgh, etc.), *co. Som.* Grants, etc., in, *t.* Hen. III. Add. 15483 (Baggeburþe);—1311. Add. 25874; —1570. Add. 6136.

—— Grants, etc., of the manor and advowson, 1268. Harl. 55 C. 45 (Bageber);—*c.* 1268. Harl. 55 B. 42;—1338. Cott. xxvii. 95;—1345. Harl. 45 H. 54;—1363. Add. 25877;—1364. Harl. 45 E. 66;—1366. Harl. 46 F. 33;— 1370. Cott. xxvii. 108, Harl. 47 D. 26; —1371. Harl. 48 I. 9, 49 F. 31;— 1407. Harl. 46 G. 46;—1413. Harl. 55 B. 20;—1421. Harl. 56 H. 32;— 1438. Harl. 50 E. 6;—1458. Add. 6144.

—— Covenant on a suit for waste on the Quantock Hills, bel. to the manor of, 1314 (Westbaggborgh). Add. 25875.

—— Fine for the manor, church, etc., 1346 (Westbaggebirgh). Add. 25876.

—— Court-roll, 1458 (Westbaggeborough). Harl. Roll N. 16.

—— *Persona.* Tho. de Reygni, *t.* Hen. III. Add. 15483.

—— —— Will Drapere, 1370. Cott. xxvii. 108;—*ante* 1371. Harl. 49 F. 31.

—— —— Joh. Smok, 1458. Add. 6144.

Bagby, *co. York.* Grants in, *t.* John (Baggebi). Harl. 83 G. 53;—1278 (Baggeby). Add. 6194.

Bageworth, Baggeworth. *v.* Badgworth, *co. Som.*

Baggebirgh. *v.* Bagborough, *co. Som.*

Baggehurst. *v.* Baughurst, *co. Southt.*

Baggethorpp. *v.* Bagthorpe, *in Brampton, co. Derb.*

Baghey. *v.* Bache, *nr. Llangollen, co. Denb.*

Bagley, *co. York.* Release in, 1509. Add. 17001.

Bagnall, *in Stoke upon Trent, co. Staf.* Briefs for rebuilding the chapel, 1782, 1813, 1820. Ch. Br. B. xxii. 7, liii. 7, C. l. 9.

Bagottys Marsh, [*in Rochford, co. Essex ?*]. Fine of, 1541. Add. 15868.

Bagshot, *co. Surr.* Grant in, 1513. Harl. 56 I. 6.

Bagthorpe, *in Brampton, co. Derb.* Grants, etc., in, 1477. Woll. iii. 58 (Baggethorpp);—1491. Woll. iii. 77; —1501. Woll. iii. 66;—1536. Woll. iii. 63;—1552. Woll. iii. 65;—1555. Woll. iii. 70, 71;—1584. Woll. ii. 72.

—— Admissions to lands in, by the Knts. Hospitallers, 1535. Woll. iii. 68, 69.

Baihalle, Le. *v. sub* Pembury, *co. Kent.*

Baildon (Bayldon), *co. York.* Grants in, 1265. Add. 15646;—1374. Harl. 83 C. 15.

—— *Ballivus.* Will. de Ottelay, 1265. Add. 15646.

—— *Decanus de Baildon.* Henricus, 1265. Add. 15646.

Bailey, *in Milton, co. Lanc.* Brief conc. a fire in, 1813. Ch. Br. B. liv. 6.

Bainflete. *v.* Benfleet, S., *co. Essex.*

Bainton, *co. Northt.* Grant and sale in, 1482. Add. 6467 (Badyngton);— 1579. Add. 9272 (Baddington, Baynton).

Bainton, *co. York* (?). *Persona al. Rector.* Will. fil. Rob. de Welton *al.* Welleton, *de Broclesby,* [*co. Linc.*], 1335. Harl. 44 H. 23, 49 C. 48, 51 H. 3, 4, 57 G. 24, 25.

—— *Rector, quondam.* Will. de Broclesby, *ante* 1376. Harl. 56 E. 6.

Bakchilde. *v.* Bapchild, *co. Kent.*

Bakesbourne. *v.* Beaksbourne, *co. Kent.*

Baketon, Baketune. *v.* Bacton, *co. Norf.*

D 2

**Bakewell,** *co. Derb.* Grants, etc., in, *t.* Edw. I. Harl. 83 D. 57 (Bathe-quell);—1337. Woll. vii. 19 (Bauque-well);—1347. Harl. 83 F. 6 (Bauke-well);—1394. Woll. ii. 73;—1400. Woll. vii. 46 (Bawkwell); — 1490. Woll. vii. 48;—1556. Woll. xii. 32; —1623. Woll. xii. 76.

—— Grant in Catteclyf in (?), *t.* Edw. I. Woll. viii. 11.

—— Surrender, etc., of the manor, 1325. Harl. 50 G. 28 (Baukwell);—1480. Woll. x. 67.

—— Lease in Birobill (Birchulles) in, 1347. Harl. 83 F. 6.

—— Acquittance from the Receiver of Lichfield Chapter at, 1438. Woll. iii. 24.

—— Ref. to a claim on Harthill manor in, 1446. Woll. vi. 5.

—— Grant in Cowdale in, 1598. Woll. ii. 84.

—— Rent due to the Hospital of St. John in, 1606. Woll. xi. 46.

—— Exchequer acquittance for tenths of, 1615. Add. 25690.

—— Exemplif. of decree in suit conc. tithes of lead ore in, 1730. Woll. xii. 144.

—— *Clericus.* Thomas, *t.* Hen. II. (Badechewell). Woll. vi. 3.

—— *Vicarius.* Will. Brome, 1438. Woll. iii. 24.

—— —— Ric. Crichelowe, 1472. Woll. ii. 30.

—— —— Joh. Rowlandson, 1615. Add. 25690.

—— *v. also* Calver, *co. Derb.*

—— —— Chelmorton, *co. Derb.*

—— —— Longstone, Gt. and Lit., *co. Derb.*

**Bakewell Hall Manor.** *v. sub* London, St. Michael Bassishaw par.

**Bakton.** *v.* Bacton, *co. Norf.*

**Balbuthie,** *co. Fife.* Conf. of a grant in, by Will., King of Scotland, late 12 cent. (Ballebutlia). Campb. xxx. 5.

**Balcholm, Balcolm.** *v.* Balkholme, *in Howden, co. York.*

**Balcombe,** *co. Surr.* *Parson.* Sir Will. Mawdesleye, 1558. Add. 6234.

**Baldac.** *v.* Baldock, *co. Hertf.*

**Balderston,** *in Blackburn, co. Lanc.* Brief for re-building the chapel, 1815. Ch. Br. B. lv. 8.

**Balderton,** *co. Nott.* Lease of the parsonage, 1543. Harl. 111 C. 35.

—— Assignment of life interest of Qu. Catharine of Braganza in the manor of, 1680. Harl. 111 H. 11.

—— *Capellanus.* Thomas, *t.* John. Harl. 83 F. 45.

—— *Parson.* Ric. Benese, *Canon of Lincoln,* 1543. Harl. 111 C. 35.

—— *Vicarius.* Rob. Bolour, 1392. Harl. 46 F. 17.

**Balderton,** *co. Salop.* Power to give seisin in, 1536. Add. 9372.

**Baldesey.** *v.* Bawdsey, *co. Suff.*

**Baldeswelle.** *v.* Bawdeswell, *co. Norf.*

**Baldingham.** *v.* Ballingham, *co. Heref.*

**Baldock,** *co. Hertf.* Grants in, to Clothall Hospital, early 13 cent. (Baldac). Harl. 112 C. 14;—1301. Harl. 111 D. 4.

—— Grant in, with a rent to be paid to the Templars, etc., *t.* Hen. III. (Baudak). Harl. 111 D. 24.

**Baldon, Marsh,** *co. Oxon.* Release in, 1312 (Mersbaldyndone). Add. 20289.

**Baldon St. Lawrence,** *co. Oxon.* Release in, 1312 (Baldyndone S. Laurentii). Add. 20289.

—— License to alienate lands in, late bel. to Littlemore Priory, 1548. Add. 20366.

**Baldon, Toot,** *co. Oxon.* Release in, 1312 (Totbaldyndone). Add. 20289.

**Baldoyle,** *co. Dublin.* Exemplif., in 1491, of grant of wreck in the manor, 1478 (Baldowill). Add. 1974.

**Baldreseia.** *v.* Bawdsey, *co. Suff.*

**Balichatlan,** *nr. Ballidargan, co. Down.* Grant in, to Neddrum Priory, c. 1190. Cott. xiii. 21 (4) (copy).

**Baliden.** *v.* Ballidon, *co. Derb.*

**Balikaruell,** *in Ireland.* Grant of the mill and lands of, [1219–31]. Add. 8411.

**Balimackille.** *v.* Ballynakill, *nr. Waterford.*

**Balingeiam.** *v.* Ballingham, *co. Heref.*

**Balkholme (Balcholm, Balcolm, etc.),** *in Howden, co. York.* Grants, etc., in, *t.* Hen. III.–*t.* Edw. I. Add. 26109-26112;—1322. Add. 26113, 26114;—1331. Add. 26115;—1338. Add. 26116;

**Bamford** (Baumford, Baumforth), co. *Derb.* (*continued*). Fine in, 1704. Add. 18065.

**Bampton**, co. *Devon.* Appointment of procurator in suit betw. J. Michel, rector of, and the chapels of Petton and Dupeford in, 1368 (Baunton). Harl. 44 H. 51.

*v. also* Petton, co. *Devon.*

**Bampton**, co. *Oxon.* Restoration of, by K. John, to Reg. de Danmartin, 1212 (Bamton). Add. 11239 (copy).

**Bampton**, co. *Westm.* Brief conc. a fire at, 1799. Ch. Br. B. xxxix. 1.

**Bampton Hundred**, co. *Oxon.* Grant of liberties in, to Oseney Abbey, 1266. Add. 20290.

**Banbury**, co. *Oxon.* Release in, 1353 (Bannebury). Harl. 56 E. 3.

—— (?) Grant of a rent in Beverley, co. York, to Joh. Heton, " magister scolarum de Bannebury," 1400. Lansd. 349.

—— Rental of the lordship of, held by the see of Lincoln, 1441. Lansd. Roll 32.

—— Precipe on a covenant conc. land in, 1593. Add. 25211.

**Bandale** [Burton-Bandals ?], in *Prestwold*, co. *Leic.* Exch. in, with Bullington Priory, late 13 cent. Cott. v. 56.

**Bandon** (Bandone, Bandune, etc.), in *Beddington*, co. *Surr.* Grants, etc., in, early Hen. III.-t. Edw. I. Add. 22727, 22728, 22730, 22735 - 22738, 22740, 22741, 22743-22754, 22756, 22758, 22759, 22762, 22768, 22770-22773, 22775 - 22798, 22800 - 22803, 22805, 22806, 22808 - 22821, 22827, 22920, 22965, 22966;—1271. Add. 22818;—1273. Add. 22708;—c. 1273. Add. 22709;—1274. Add. 22711, 22714;—c. 1274. Add. 22712, 22713;—1275. Add. 22715;—1276. Add. 22716, 22925;—1277. Add. 22717, 22720;—c. 1277. Add. 22718, 22719, 22721, 22722;—1281. Add. 22927;—1291. Add. 22729;—1292. Add. 22726;—1295. Add. 22731;—1296. Add. 22931;—1297. Add. 22934;—1299. Add. 22732-22734;— 1302. Add. 23025;— 1303. Add. 22822, 22823;—1304. Add. 23027;—1305. Add. 22824, 23028;— 1306. Add. 22825, 22826;—1309. Add. 22828;—1312. Add. 22829, 22830, 23037;—1313. Add. 22831, 23039;— 1315.

Add. 22832-22834, 22836, 23040 :—1316. Add. 22837, 22838, 23053;—1317. Add. 23054; — 1319. Add. 22840, 22841;—1320. Add. 23058;—1321. Add. 22842, 23060;— 1322. Add. 23063;—1323. Add. 22725, 22843, 22844;— 1324. Add. 22845;—1325. Add. 23071;— 1326. Add. 22846, 22847;—1327. Add. 22848;—1328. Add. 22849;—1332. Add. 22850, 22851;—1334. Add. 22852;—1335. Add. 22853-22855; — 1337. Add. 22856-22858; — 1338. Add. 22859;—1339. Add. 22860;—1341. Add. 22861;—1343. Add. 22862;—1344. Add. 23094;—1345. Add. 22863;—1348. Add. 23108;—1349. Add. 22864, 22865, 23109;— 1351. Add. 22867, 22868;—1359. Add. 22869;—1360. Add. 22870;— 1370. Add. 22872;—1378. Add. 23145, 23146;—1379. Add. 22873;—1386. Add. 22874;—1388. Add. 22875;—1393. Add. 23157;—1404. Add. 22878;—1406. Add. 22876;—1409. Add. 22877;—1438. Add. 22879;—1455. Add. 22881, 22882;— 1459. Add. 22880;—1464. Add. 22883;— 1466. Add. 22884;—1530. Add. 22888;—1571. Add. 22890;— 1613. Add. 22893;—1646. Add. 22895, 22896.

—— Grants, etc., in, to St. Thomas's Hosp., Southwark. t. Hen. III.-t. Edw. I. Add. 22710, 22739, 22742, 22755, 22757, 22761, 22799;—1316. Add. 22837;—1318. Add. 22839.

—— Leases, etc., in, from St. Thomas's Hosp., t. Hen. III. Add. 22769;—1342. Add. 23090;—1349. Add. 22866.

—— Grants, etc., of the manor, 1410. Add. 23170;—1431. Add. 23176;—1457. Add. 23187; — 1468. Add. 22805;—c. 1495. Add. 23198;—1497. Add. 22886, 23195;—1593. Add. 23232, 23234;—1605. Add. 22892.

—— Leases of the mill in, reserving the "troute" fishing, 1515. Add. 22887;—1536. Add. 22889;—1592. Add. 22891.

—— Extr. from Court-roll, 1644. Add. 22894.

*v. also* Beddington.

**Banested.** *v.* Banstead, co. *Surr.*

**Banham**, co. *Norf.* Grant of the church to St. Mary's Abbey, York, [1239-41]. Campb. ix. 9 (2) (copy).

—— Acknowledgment of services due from the rector to St. Mary's Abbey and to Rumburgh Priory, *n. d.*, 1244. Campb. ix. 9 (8-10) (*copies*).

—— Inq. conc. right of presentation to tl e rectory, 1253. Campb. ix. 9 (11).

—— Grant in, 1362. Add. 14515.

—— *Capellanus.* Gilbertus, 1253. Campb. ix. 9 (11).

—— *Rector. Mag.* Lamb. de Beverlaco, *n. d.* Campb. ix. 9 (8).

—— —— Joh. de Longocampo, *n. d.* Campb. ix. 9 (9)

—— —— *Mag.* Will. de Horham, 1244. Campb. ix. 9 (10).

**Banhunta.** *v.* Bonhunt, Wicken, *co. Essex.*

**Banker's Manor.** *v. sub* Lee, *co. Kent.*

**Bannagh,** *co. Donegal.* Release in the barony of, 1632. Add. 7051.

**Banstead,** *co. Surr.* Grant in, from N. de Moubrai to Southwark Priory, *c.* 1180-90. Cott. xvi. 41.

—— Lease, etc., in Suthmeresfelde *al.* Suthmeresfeld in, to Southwark Priory, 1181. Cott. MS. Nero C. iii., f. 197;—1203. Campb. xvi. 2;— *t.* Hen. III. Campb. xvi. 3.

—— Fines in, with Southwark Priory, 1198. Harl. 56 B. 16 (Sumeresfeld); —1199. Cott. MS. Nero C. iii., f. 197 (Bensted).

—— Precept of Galf. f. Petri in a suit in, with Southwark Priory, [1199?] (Bennestede). Cott. MS. Nero C. iii., f. 197.

—— Acquittance, etc., to Southwark Priory for rents, etc., in, 1261 (Bansted). Harl. 47 E. 34.

—— Grant in, to Southwark Priory, *c.* 1269 (Banstede). Cott. xvi. 45.

—— Release to Southwark Priory of all services for the manor, 1269 (Bansted). Harl. 47 E. 35.

—— Extent of the manor, 1325 (Banstede). Add. 16532.

—— Grants, etc., in, 1345 (Benstede). Add. 22897;—1424. Add. 23174;— 1440. Add. 23730;—1451. Add. 23656.

—— Lease of the manor from Qu. Katharine, 1514. Add. 22629.

—— Notif. by Qu. Katharine of her rights in the manor, 1522. Add. 22898.

—— Lease of Westborough and Preston Manors in, 1553. Add. 22899.

**Banstead,** *co. Surr.* (*continued*). Sale and lease in, 1577. Add. 22900;— 1582. Add. 22902.

—— Accompts of rents of Courts of the manor, 1587. Add. 22903.

—— Feoffment of the manor, with revocation, 1593, 1597. Add. 23232, 23234.

—— Acquittances for fines for the manor, 1613-1642. Add. 23242-23268.

—— Fine in, 1615. Add. 23718, 23719.

—— Pipe-roll acquittances for fees from the manor, 1619-1630. Add. 22906, 22907, 22909, 22911-22916.

—— Lease of part of the Olde Parke in, 1623. Add. 22910.

—— Action for ejectment from the manor, 1728. Add. 23519.

—— Appointment of a gamekeeper over the manor, 1757. Add. 22917.

—— Suit for trespass in, 1759. Add. 22918, 22919.

**Banwell** (Banewell), *co. Som.* Release, etc., in, 1343. Harl. 54 D. 26;—1489. Harl. 111 D. 5.

**Bapchild** (Bakchilde, etc.), *co. Kent.* Enquiry conc. presentation of Walt. de Micheldevere to the chapel of St. Mary of Radfield (Rodefeld) in, 1314. Harl. 43 G. 28.

—— Grant of the advowson of Radfield (Rodefeld) chapel in, 1345. Harl. 45 C. 24.

—— Grants, etc., in Radfield, etc., in, 1361. Harl. 48 E. 21 (Bakchild);— 1405. Harl. 78 H. 28;—1406. Harl. 78 B. 53;—1407. Harl. 79 C. 16;— 1505. Lansd. 174;—1572. Add. 912 (Babchilde).

—— Sale of the parsonage, etc., late bel. to Chichester Cathedral, 1540. Harl. 76 H. 23.

**Bapton,** *in Fisherton Delamere, co. Wilts.* Grant, etc., in, 1362. Add. 24873 (Babeton);—1413. Add. 26777 (Babbeton).

**Barawa.** *v.* Barrow, *co. Linc.*

**Barbour's Manor.** *v. sub* Middleton, *co. Essex.*

**Barbury,** *in Ogbourne St. George, co. Wilts.* Covenant conc. tithes of, betw. Bec and Boscherville Abbeys, 1252 (Berebyre). Campb. xxii. 11.

**Barby,** *co. Northt.* Grant in, to H. Trinity Hospital, Kingsthorpe, *t.* John (Bergebi). Add. 21531.

**Barby,** *co. Northt. (continued).* Grant in, *t.* Edw. I. (Beruby). Campb. viii. 10.

—— Covenant betw. the rector and H. Trinity Hospital conc. an annuity from the church of, 1293 (Berubi). Add. 22382.

—— Covenant conc. an annuity from the manor, 1430 (Berughby). Add. 21871.

—— *Clericus.* Willelmus, c. 1200 (Berheby). Add. 21890.

—— *Persona al. Decanus.* Willelmus, early Hen. III. (Becueby, Bergebi). Add. 21893, 21895.

—— *Rector.* Baldw. Daraynes, 1293. Add. 22382.

**Barcheword, Barchewrhe, Barcworð,** etc. *v.* Barkwith, *co. Linc.*

**Barcombe,** *co. Suss.* Sale, etc., of the manor, 1433. Add. 20055 (Bercompe); —1572. Add. 23796, 23797.

—— Court-roll, 1672. Add. 24650.

**Barcroft,** *in Pudsey, co. York.* Grants in, early 13 cent. Add. 16582 (Berecroft), 16585;—*t.* Edw. I. Add. 16698; —1372. Add. 16829 (Bercroft).

**Barden., Bardenay, Bardenei,** etc. *v.* Bardney, *co. Linc.*

**Bardfield,** *co. Essex.* Grant in, *t.* Hen. III. Add. 5946.

—— Compotus of the manor, 1320-21 (Berdefeld). Add. 26816.

—— *Rector.* Will. Wygox, 1398. Harl. 58 C. 34.

**Bardfield Saling.** *v.* Saling, Lit., *co. Essex.*

**Bardney,** *co. Linc.* Grant by Bardney Abbey of St. Andrew's Chapel for masses for R. de Millay and his family, [1266-79] (Barden.). Harl. 44 A. 7.

—— Grant of a moiety of the advowson of St. Andrew's Chapel, *t.* Edw. I. (Bartheney). Harl. 48 G. 3.

—— Suit conc. fishery in the Witham at, 1369 (Bardenay). Harl. 43 E. 5.

—— *Capellanus.* Walterus, *ante* 1155. Harl. 43 B. 45;—*c.* 1156. Cott. xvi. 37;—1158. Harl. 49 A. 1;—*c.* 1160. Harl. 50 B. 18;—1162. Harl. 45 H. 7; —1163. Harl. 44 E. 55.

—— Symon, early Hen. III. (Bardenei). Harl. 52 D. 3.

—— *Clericus.* Ricardus, *t.* Hen. III. Harl. 45 H. 12.

**Bardolfes al. Whitefoots Manor.** *v. sub* Feltborpe, *co. Norf.*

**Bardwell** (Berdewell), *co. Suff.* Release of scutage in, *c.* 1200. Harl. 58 A. 30.

—— Grant of Wykes manor in, with the advowson, etc., *c.* 1230-40 (Berdenuelle). Add. 15520.

—— Grant of the mill, *t.* Hen. III. Harl. 56 H. 44.

—— Grants, etc., in, *t.* Hen. III.—late 13 cent. Harl. 45 I. 17. 47 D. 39, 56 I. 24, 26, Add. 5923;—1293. Harl. 56 B. 36;—1300. Harl. 54 D. 5;— 1310. Harl. 56 E. 15;—1313. Harl. 51 D. 41;—1337. Add. 19634;— 1350. Harl. 54 F. 6;—1376. Harl. 50 B. 11;—1387. Harl. 58 G. 43 a; —1422. Harl. 51 F. 1.

—— Appointment of a bailiff in, 1332. Harl. 57 G. 27.

—— Conveyance, etc., of Wykene al. Wykes manor in, 1404. Add. 15537; —1422. Harl. 51 F. 1.

—— Acquittance for payment for Wyken wood in, 1412. Harl. 49 B. 26.

—— Covenant for annuity from Wicken al. Wiggen manor in, 1560. Harl. 57 H. 18.

—— *Persona.* Joh. de Cove, 1376. Harl. 50 B. 11.

**Barentun.** *v.* Barrington, *co. Camb.*

**Bareselle,** *co. Suss.* Conf. by Hen. I. to Battle Abbey of freedom from service for, as a member of Alciston Manor, *ante* 1123. Harl. 43 C. 12.

**Bareswrd, Bareswrth.** *v.* Bosworth, Husband's, *co. Leic.*

**Barford,** *co. Bedf.* (?). Power to give seisin in, 1872 (Bereford). Add. 22609.

**Barford** (Bereford), *co. Warw.* Grants, etc., of the church and lands in, to Thelesford Priory, [1200-1212]. Add. 21406;—*t.* Edw. I. Add. 21407, 21408; —*t.* Edw. II.-III. Add. 21409.

—— Grants and sales in, *t.* Hen. III. Harl. 46 A. 30;—1335. Add. 21411; —1591. Harl. 79 F. 18, 19.

—— Lease of a fishery in the Avon at, to Thelesford Priory, 1332. Add. 21410.

**Barford, Great,** *co. Bedf.* Marriage settlement in, 1300 (Berford). Harl. 111 D. 57.

—— Grant in Langenho nr., 1328. Harl. 47 G. 55.

**Barford, Great,** *co. Bedf.* (*continued*). Sale of the manor, etc., 1509 (Barkford). Slo. xxxiii. 76*.

—— Covenant conc. the manor, 1581 (Berkeforde). Harl. 78 A. 48.

**Barford, Great,** *al.* **Barford St. Michael,** *co. Oxon.* Grant of, late Hen. II. (Bereford). Add. 21405.

—— Letter conc. a suit for the manor, *t.* Edw. II. (Berford). Add. 20301.

—— Grants, etc., of the manor, 1336. Add. 22163 (Bereford S. Michaelis); —1383, 1385. Add. 22213-22216;— —1422. Add. 22263, 22264;—*ante* 1437. Add. 21265;—1437. Add. 20303-20305;—1441. Add. 22274;— 1464. Add. 20306.

—— Lease in, 1378 (Berford S. Michaelis). Add. 20302.

—— Letter conc. claims by the parson to pasture in, 1397 (Bereford). Add. 21412.

—— *Persona.* Ric. de Wardyngton, [1338]. Add. 21412.

—— —— *Sire* Tho. de Strattone, 1397. Add. 21412.

**Barford, Little,** *co. Bedf.* Grant nr., *t.* Hen. III (Bereford). Harl. 56 B. 11.

**Barford Oluff** (Bereford Olof, Oloof, Oluff), *in Gt. Barford, co. Oxon.* Grants, etc., in, 1336. Add. 22163;— *ante* 1437. Add. 21265;—1437. Add. 20303-20305;—1464-5. Add. 22292; —1470. Add. 22296;—1473. Add. 20307, 20308.

**Barford St. Martin,** *co. Wilts.* Claim to lands in, early Edw. III. Add. 15149 (*copy*).

—— Grant in, 1559. Add. 15106.

**Barfotesmede,** *nr. Wilden*(?), *co. Bedf.* Grant of, *t.* Edw. I. Harl. 54 E. 37.

**Bargh** *al.* **Barugh,** *co. York.* Grants, etc., in. *t.* Edw. I. Add. 8211 (Bergh); —*c.* 1300. Add. 8242 (do.);—1518. Harl. 55 A. 44 (Mykle Baurghe).

—— *Clericus.* Ricardus, *t.* Hen. III. (Berk). Harl. 112 I. 10.

**Bargham,** *in Seaford, co. Suss.* Foundation of the chapel, with St. James's Hospital, as a prebend of Chichester Cathedral, 1524. Cott. xii. 80.

—— *Rector.* Will. Potter, 1454. Add. 8894.

**Bargothow** *al.* **Bargoythou.** *v. sub* St. Stephen in Brannel, *co. Cornw.*

**Barham,** *nr. Linton, co. Camb.* Grant in, to Warden Abbey, early 13 cent. Add. 15722 (Berhhom).

**Barham,** *co. Kent.* Grant nr., 805 (Beoraham). Cott. MS. Aug. ii. 55.

—— Grant in Walterchine in, 1278-9. Add. 17820 (Berham).

—— Conveyance, etc., in, 1445. Harl. 80 E. 35 (Berham);—1533. Harl. 79 B. 49;—1541. Harl. 75 H. 3;—1548. Harl. 76 I. 38;—1551. Harl. 80 C. 15;—1557. Harl. 76 I. 27, 34;—1599. Add. 7889;—1650. Add. 17827.

—— Lease of Sa-lvyng manor in (?), 1462. Harl. 78 F. 38.

—— Settlement by H. Oxenden of household stuff, etc., in, 1668. Add. 17828.

—— *Rector.* Ric. Wolvyn, 1365. Add. 24664.

**Barham,** *co. Suff.* Conff. in, by Bps. of Ely, to Ely Abbey, [1109-31, 1133-69] (Bercham). Harl. 43 H. 4, 5 (*copies*).

—— Release, etc., in, *t.* Edw. I. (Braham). Add. 8363;—1367 (Bergham). Add. 8378.

—— *Rector.* Mag. Galf. de Fresingfeuld, 1316. Add. 9579.

**Barholme,** *co. Linc.* Grants, etc., in, 1335. Add. 6457 (Berham);—1348. Add. 6466;—1482. Add. 6467 (Barham);—1491. Add. 6468 (Bargham).

—— Particulars of lands of Edw., Earl of Warwick (*ob.* 1499), in, 16 cent. (Barholme cum Stowe). Harl. Roll CC. 14.

—— Fine in, 1577 (Barham). Add. 6469.

**Barkby** (Barkeby), *co. Leic.* Grants in, to Langley Priory, *t.* Hen. III. or Edw. I. Harl. 55 E. 27.

—— Release to Langley Priory from coming to view of frank-pledge in, 1312. Harl. 55 E. 19.

**Barkby Thorpe,** *co. Leic.* Grant in, to Langley Priory, *t.* Henry III. or Edw. I. Harl. 55 E. 27.

**Barkeswell.** *v.* Berkeswell, *co. Warw.*

**Barkford.** *v.* Barford, Gt., *co. Bedf.*

**Barkham.** *co. Berks.* Lease in, 1635. Add. 19216.

**Barking** (Berking, Berkyng, etc.), *co. Essex.* Grants, etc., in, *t.* Hen. III. Harl. 55 G. 30;—1379. Add. 19972; —1385. Add. 19973;—1472. Add. 19406.

**Barking** (Berking, Berkyng. etc.). *co. Essex (continued)*. Grant of " Benes in Berkyng Clay " in, 1480. Harl. 77 G. 22.

—— Brief of conveyances, etc., of **Gaysham Hall** manor, etc., in, 1545–1605. Harl. 57 H. 39.

—— Sale in Ripple Marsh in, 1585. Harl. 77 F. 38.

—— Mortgage of lease of Clayhall manor in, 1594. Harl. 57 H. 22.

—— Exchequer acquittance for a fine on land in Chadwell in, 1596. Add. 25718 b.

—— Sale in Sparkswood, etc., in, 1611. Add. 19966.

—— *Seneschallus*. Ric. Rikyld, 1385. Add. 19973.

**Barking**, *co. Suff.* Grant in, 1520 (Berkyng). Add. 19409.

**Barklowe.** *v.* Bartlow, *co. Essex.*

**Barkstone**, *co. Linc.* Fine in the manor of, 1655. Add. 6456.

—— *Clerici.* Robertus, Willelmus, *t.* Hen. III. (Bracston). Eg. 449.

**Barkway**, *co. Hertf.* Dispute conc. right of presentation to the vicarage, [1181–4] (Bercheweie). Harl. 75 A. 13.

—— Demise of lands in Newsells manor in, 1509. Add. 16572.

—— *Clerici.* Martin. de Colecestria, Walt. de Bercheweie, [1181–4.] Harl. 75 A. 13.

**Barkwith, East and West,** *co. Linc.* Bond of services in, with Bullington Priory, *t.* Hen. II. (Barcheword). Add. 20082.

—— Grant nr. Thinhou in, to Bullington Priory, late Hen. II. (Barchewrhe). Harl. 45 F. 49.

—— Grant in, to Bullington Priory, late Hen. II. (Est Barkeworth). Harl. 54 I. 31.

—— Grant in, from Bullington Priory, *t.* Hen. III. (Estbarkewurth). Harl. 44 A. 50.

—— Precipe on a covenant conc. the manor, 1555 (Est Barkworthe). Add. 25056.

—— *Clericus.* Robertus, late Hen. II. (Barcwor̄). Harl. 45 F. 49.

—— —— Robertus, *t.* Hen. III. Harl. 44 A. 50.

—— *Sacerdos.* Rudulphus, 1165. Cott. xxvii. 195.

**Barkwith, East and West,** *co. Linc. (continued). Rector of West B.* Will. Byrdall, 1495. Harl. 51 G. 27.

**Barlaston** (Berlestone), *co. Staff.* Grant, etc., of the manor, 1332. Harl. 48 G. 50;—1350. Harl. 54 D. 28.

—— Brief for rebuilding the church, 1762. Ch. Br. B. ii. 8.

**Barlborough,** *co. Derb.* Payment to be made to the parson of, on account of lands in Unstone, etc., co. Derb., 1440 (Barlburgh). Woll. viii. 43.

—— Grant in, 1462 (Barleburgh). Woll. ii. 58.

—— Exemplif. of plea conc. rights in, 1631. Woll. xii. 1.

—— *Capellanus.* Johannes, 1345. Harl. 112 G. 45.

—— *Persona.* Johannes, *t.* Edw. I. Woll. vii. 78.

**Barleia.** *v.* Barlow, *co. Derb.*

**Barley,** *co. Hertf.* Feoffment in, 1435 (Burleye). Add. 23178.

—— *Capellanus.* Ric. Frensch, 1394. Add. 15192.

—— *Persona.* Mag. Joh. Dunwych, 1379. Add. 25943.

**Barley** *al.* **Barlow,** *co. York.* Rentals of tenants " infra dominium ville," 1510, 1512. Add. 24184 a, b.

—— Sale of a third part of the manor, 1520 (Baile). Add. 24168.

**Barley Hall Manor.** *v. sub* Stradbrooke, *co. Suff.*

**Barlings,** *co. Linc.* Grants, etc., in Newbold nr., to Bullington Priory, c. 1175. Harl. 52 G. 28;—c. 1205. Harl. 52 A. 18, 54 A. 45;—late Hen. III. Cott. xxviii. 7, Harl. 50 D. 47, 57 E. 17.

—— Grant of Barlings Bank, 1565. Harl. 80 F. 25.

**Barlow** *al.* **Barley,** *in Staveley,* *co. Derb.* Lease in, to the Knts. Hospitallers, [1207] (Barleia). Harl. 86 G. 46.

—— Sales, etc., in, 1577. Woll. xii. 97;—1628. Woll. xii. 98;—1641. Woll. xii. 99.

—— Brief for rebuilding the church, 1784. Ch. Br. B. xxiv. 6.

**Barlow Woodseats,** *in Dronfield,* *co. Derb.* Descent of lands in, 1635 (Barley Woodseates). Woll. xi. 39.

**Barmby on the Marsh,** *co. York.* Grant in, 1519. Lansd. 456.

Barnetby le Wold (Bernetebi), *co.*
*Linc.* (*continued*). *Persona.* Alanus,
*c.* 1150. Harl. 55 D. 5.
—— *Sacerdos.* Walterus, [1143–7].
Harl. 51 B. 50.
—— *Vicarius.* Ricardus, 1349. Harl.
43 H. 48.

Barnetun. *v.* Barrington, *co. Camb.*

Barnfield, East, Hundred, *co. Kent.*
Leases, etc., of, 1555. Harl. 75 E. 31 ;
—1556. Harl. 75 H. 23 ;—1574. Harl.
77 H. 35.

Barnham (Bernham), *co. Suff.* Cove-
nant conc. possession of the manor,
1354. Harl. 51 E. 5.
—— Surrender in, 1360. Harl. 49
G. 42.
—— Precipe on a covenant conc.
Baggott's manor and advowson of
St. Gregory's in, 1589. Add. 25417.

Barnham Broom (Bernham), *co. Norf.*
Release at Gore Gap in, early Edw. I.
Add. 19289.
—— Declaration conc. reversion of
Hauteyns hall manor in, 1363. Add.
14547.
—— Feoffment of above manor, etc.,
in, 1372. Add. 14548, 14549.
—— *Persona.* Hugo [Brandon], 1372.
Add. 14548, 14549.

Barnhorn, *nr. Bexhill, co. Suss.* Court-
rolls, 1593, 1600 (Bernhorn). Add.
14048, 14050.

Barningham, *co. Suff.* Conveyance,
etc., in, 1490. Add. 14550 (Bernyngham) ;—1606. Add. 13560.
—— Precipe on a covenant conc. land
in, 1578. Add. 25340.
—— Precipe on a covenant conc.
Sintclers and Netherhall manors in,
1578. Add. 25341.

Barningham, Great *al.* Winter, *co.*
*Norf.* Surrender, etc., in, 1370. Add.
14867 (Townebernyngham) ; — 1416.
Add. 14820 ;—1417. Add. 14821
(Toun Bernyngham).

Barningham, Little. (Bernyngham
Parva), *co. Norf.* Surrender, etc., in,
1370. Add. 14867 ;—1416. Add.
14820 ;—1417. Add. 14821.
—— *Persona.* Willelmus, 1409. Add.
14128.

Barningham Norwood, *co. Norf.*
Grant, etc., in, 1416. Add. 14820
(Bernyngham Northwode) ; — 1417.
Add. 14821 (Northwode Bernyngham).

Barnoldby le Beck, *co. Linc.* Grant
of the church, with conf., to Beauport
Abbey, 1202. Harl. 45 B. 23 (Ber-
nolesbi) ;—1204. Add. 15238 (Ber-
noloby).
—— Grants in, 1326. Harl. 112 H.
15 (Barnolby) ;—1393. Harl. 112 G.
60 (Barnolby).

Barnoldswick, *co. York.* Inquisition
conc. claims of Kirkstall Abbey to the
manor, 1333 (Bernolveswik). Add.
20548.
—— Fine of the manor, 1638. Woll.
xi. 29.

Barns Hagwood, *co. Linc.* Conf. of
grant of, to Kirkstead Abbey, *c.* 1295
(Berneshag). Harl. 45 H. 14.

Barnsley, *in Wimborne Minster, co.*
*Dors.* Extract from court-roll, 1550
(Bernerdisley). Harl. 80 I. 94.
—— Release in, 1595. Harl. 80 B.
39.

Barnsley, *co. Worc.* Conf. of grants
at (?), to Pershore Abbey, 972 (Beo-
nothes leah). Cott. MS. Aug. ii. 6.

Barnsley (Berneslay, Bernislay), *W. R.,*
*co. York.* Grants, etc., in, *t.* Edw. I.
–*t.* Edw. II. Add. 8153, 8167, 8172,
8195, 8198, 8209, 8211, 8218, 8229,
8231, 8232, 8234, 8248, 8250, 8251,
8266, 8271 ;—1334. Harl. 49 D. 1.
—— *Ballivus.* Thomas, *t.* Edw. I. or
II. Add. 8153, 8172, 8248.
*v. also* Keresforth, *co. York.*

Barnsole, *in Woodnesborough, co. Kent.*
Exemption of rents in, from lease by
the prior of Christ Church, Canterbury, 1467 (Bernesole). Harl. 75 F.
48.

Barnstaple, *co. Devon.* Fine, conveyance, etc., of the Honour, Castle, etc.,
1653. Harl. 86 I. 59 ;—1655. Harl.
111 E. 35 ;—1656. Harl. 83 H. 40 ;—
1660. Harl. 85 H. 59, 111 E. 36.
—— Grants in, 1674. Harl. 83 H.
24 a, 37.
—— *Mayor.* Rob. Eade, 1571. Add.
13087.
—— *Aldermen.* Joh. Darte, Will.
Dawkins, 1571. Add. 13087.

Barnston (Berneston), *co. Essex.* Conf.
of tithes in, to Dunmow Priory, 1221.
Cott. xxi. 15.
—— Fine in, 1227. Harl. 50 B. 27.
—— Conf. of grant in, 1273. Harl.
48 G. 4.

**Barnston** (Berneston), co. *Essex* (*continued*). Inquisition p. m. of lands of J. de Cokham in, 1275. Harl. 46 D. 1.

—— *Capellanus.* Samuel, *t.* Edw. I. Lansd. 95.

**Barnstone** (Berneston), *co. Nott.* Bond for fine of the manor, 1286. Harl. 43 G. 50.

—— Grant in, 1347. Add. 45 C. 27.

**Barnwell** (Bernewell), *co. Camb.* Grant of a fair at, to Barnwell Priory, 1229. Harl. 58 H. 41 (*copy*).

—— Papal commission to the precentor of, etc., conc. tithes of Charwelton, co. Northt., 1253. Harl. 84 F. 45.

—— Crown grant in, 1549. Add. 7060.

**Barnwell All Saints**, *co. Northt.* Release in, 1336 (Bernewelle Regis). Add. 21534.

**Barnwell St. Andrew's**, *co. Northt.* Grant, etc., in, *t.* Hen. II. Add. 21533 (Bernewelle):—1336. Add. 21534 (Bernewelle Moigne).

**Barnwood Forest.** *v.* Bernwood Forest, *co. Buck.*

**Baron Wood**, *nr. Ainstable, co. Cumb.* Lease of, 1572 (Barron). Harl. 77 H. 37.

**Baroua.** *v.* Barrow on Soar, *co. Leic.*

**Barowcote.** *v.* Borowcote, *in Crich, co. Derb.*

**Barr, Gt. and Lit.**, *co. Staff.* Recovery of seisin in, 1570. Harl. 84 C. 35.

**Barraway**, *co. Camb.* Grant in, 1337 (Berwey). Lansd. 108.

**Barretts**, *Barony of, co. Cork.* Lease of Greenagh and other lands in, 1709. Add. 24473.

**Barreys Goseford.** *v. sub* Odcombe, *co. Som.*

**Barrington**, *co. Camb.* Grants in, *t.* Hen. III. Harl. 53 E. 16 (Barenton); —*ante* 1302. Lansd. 93 (Barentun); —1334. Harl. 76 E. 37 (Barnetun).

—— Grant of "Edmundes Chauntery," etc., in, 1549. Add. 7060.

**Barrington**, *co. Glouc.* Court-rolls, 1505–6 (Beruynton). Add. 26826.

**Barrmoor**, *in Kyle, co. Ayr.* Conf. of grant of, to Melrose Abbey, 1266 (Barmor). Cott. xviii. 3.

**Barroc Scire.** *v.* Berks, *County of.*

**Barrow** (Barua, Barwe, etc.), *co. Linc.* Grants, etc., in, to Newhouse Abbey, [1143–7]. Harl. 43 H. 10;—[c. 1150]. Harl. 43 H. 14 (Barawa);—[c. 1150]. Harl. 45 F. 19, 50 H. 58;—[1152–75]. Harl. 47 I. 33;—early 13 cent. Harl. 45 G. 17.

—— Grants in, from Newhouse Abbey, *t.* Hen. III. Harl. 44 G. 33, 39.

—— Exch. in, betw. Thornton Abbey and Elsham Priory, 1269 (Baruue). Harl. 45 A. 12.

—— Rental in, 1699. Add. 13595.

**Barrow**, *co. Som.* (?). Feoffment in, 1304 (La Barwe). Add. 5306.

**Barrow**, *co. Suff.* Release in, *t.* Edw. I. (Barewe). Harl. 52 I. 49.

**Barrow on Soar**, *co. Leic.* Grant in, 1395 (Burowe). Add. 24215.

—— Lease in, from Leicester Abbey, 1534. Add. 13315.

—— *Capellanus. Mag.* Johannes, [1214–26] (Baroua). Add. 20397.

—— *Clericus.* Willelmus, early Hen. II. (Barwa). Add. 22572.

—— *Vicarius.* 'Dom. Tho. de Prestwold, *t.* Hen. III.–Edw. I. Cott. xxiii. 2.

**Barrowby**, *co. Linc.* Lease of Craxton manor or farm in, 1633. Harl. 112 C. 54.

**Barrowcote.** *v.* Borowcote, *in Crich, co. Derb.*

**Barrowden**, *co. Rutl.* Release in, to Fineshed Priory, *t.* Hen. III. (Beruedon). Add. 21532.

—— Valor of Crown lands in, *t.* Hen. VIII. Harl. Roll Y. 1.

**Barrys.** *v. sub* Farway, *co. Devon.*

**Barsby**, *co. Leic.* Lease in, 1721. Add. 19050.

**Barsham**, *co. Suff.* Grants, etc., in, early 14 cent. Harl. 48 G. 13;—1375. Harl. 53 E. 45;—1422. Harl. 50 F. 36.

—— Settlement, etc., of the manor, 1435. Cott. v. 3, 22;—1436. Harl. 50 F. 37, 38.

—— Release of Barsham Hall manor in, 1476. Add. 10074.

—— Precipes on covenants conc. lands in, 1564. Add. 25315, 25316; —1578. Add. 25342.

1210. Harl. 84 D. 20 (Berton);—
c. 1210. Harl. 84 H. 13 (Berthon),
33 (Berton), 34 (do.).

—— Surrender in, by the same,
[1199]. Harl. 84 D. 14.

—— Grant of the manor, 1420. Add.
1984.

**Barton in the Beans**, co. Leic. Inquisition of the manor, 1566 (Bartone
juxta Maylstone). Add. 7252.

**Barton in the Clay**, co. Bedf.
Grants, etc., in, 1370. Add. 219;—
1378. Add. 220;—1462. Add. 223;
—1495. Add. 224.

**Barton, Little**, co. Suff. Grant, etc., in,
t. Hen. III. Add. 14517 (Bertun);—
1514. Add. 18797.

—— Precipe on a covenant conc. land
in, 1589. Add. 25392.

—— Rector. Rob. Lute, 1466. Add.
18763;—1468. Add. 9102;—1476.
Add. 18768, 18769.

**Barton on Humber** (Barton), co.
Linc. Grant in, by Earl Symon, c.
1140. Add. 20613.

—— Papal conff. of grants in, to
Rufford Abbey, 1156. Harl. 111 A.
2;—1160. Harl. 111 A. 5.

—— Conff. in S. Ferriby of the Fee
of, to Bullington Priory, t. Hen. II.
Harl. 54 E. 7, 10;—[1215–19?]. Harl.
54 E. 11.

—— Acquittance from Jews to the
men of, for £10, [1181 or 2]. Add.
1250.

—— Grants, etc., in, to Rufford
Abbey, c. 1200. Harl. 83 E. 53;—
early 13 cent. Harl. 112 G. 32;—t.
Hen. III. Harl. 112 I. 49.

—— Grant in, from Rufford Abbey,
t. Hen. III. Harl. 112 F. 36.

—— Grant in, from Thornton Abbey
to Elsham Priory, 1269. Harl. 45 A.
12.

—— Precipe on a covenant conc. land
in, 1578. Add. 25107.

—— Rents late held in, by Ormsby
Priory, 1589. Add. 8490.

—— Rental in, 1699. Add. 13595.

—— Clericus. Jacobus, c. 1200.
Harl. 112 G. 32.

—— Presbiter. Wido, t. Hen. II.
Harl. 52 C. 50.

—— Vicarius. Johannes, t. Hen. III
Harl. 49 A. 7.

**Barton St. David**, co. Som. Grant
in, 1330. Add. 5449.

**Barton Segrave** al. B. Hanred, co.
Northt. Release of a nativus in, to
Sulby Abbey, early Hen. III. Add.
22427.

—— Grant, etc., in, 1295. Harl. 47
C. 1 (Bartone):—t. Edw. I. Harl. 47
D. 37;—t. Edw. II. Harl. 83 D. 34.

**Barton, Steeple** al. Great, co.
Oxon. Grant of the church to Oseney
Abbey, end 12 cent. (Bertona). Add.
20291.

—— Covenant conc. an annuity from
the manor, 1360 (Barton). Harl. 53
B. 33.

—— Grant of the manor, 1371 (Barton
Seint John). Harl. 43 I. 42.

—— Precipe on a covenant conc. land
in, 1593. Add. 25213.

**Barton under Needwood** (Barton
sub al. juxta Nedwode), co. Staff.
Grant, etc., in, t. Hen. III. Add.
4881;—late 13 cent. Add. 4880.

—— Clericus. Henricus, t. Hen. III.
Harl. 45 F. 24.

—— —— Ricardus, 1305. Campb.
xi. 16.

**Barua, Barue, Baruue, Barwa.**
v. Barrow, co. Linc.

**Barwe, La.** v. Barrow, co. Som. (?).

—— v. Berrow, co. Worc.

**Barwick in Elmett**, co. York. License for a mill nr., early 13 cent.
(Berewic). Harl. 52 H. 42.

—— Fine of Barwick and Roundhay
manors, 1638. Woll. xi. 29.

**Baschurch**, co. Salop. Brief for rebuilding the church, 1790. Ch.
Br. B. xxx. 4.

**Bascote**, co. Warw. Grant of the
manor, t. Hen. III. Harl. 53 H. 30
(copy).

**Bascumbe.** v. Boscombe, co. Wilts.

**Basford** (Baseford), co. Nott. Grant
of the manor, 1369. Woll. x. 48.

—— Fine in, 1412. Woll. x. 53.

—— Release, etc., in, 1412. Woll. x.
54;—1424. Woll. x. 56.

—— Vicarius. Joh. Brown, 1415.
Add. 21173.

**Bashall**, co. York. Settlement of the
manor, etc., 1649. Add. 19546.

**Basildon**, co. Berks. Release in, 1365
(Bascildene). Cott. xxvii. 22.

Basildon, *co. Berks. (continued).* Sales, etc., of the manor, 1368. Harl. 55 F. 52 (Basteld<sup>n</sup>);—1543. Add. 19180;—1544. Add. 19187. 19188; —1605. Add. 19199-19202;—1619. Add. 19212;—1622. Add. 19219.

—— Marriage settlement in, 1615. Add. 19209.

—— *Rector. Dom.* Ranulphus, 1368. Harl. 55 F. 52.

—— *Vicarius. Dom.* Adam, 1368. Harl. 55 F. 52.

Basildon, *co. Essex.* Precipe on a covenant conc. lands in, 1561 (Bartelesdon). Add. 24937.

Basingebi. *v.* Bessingby, *co. York.*

Basingham. *v.* Bassingham, *co. Linc.*

—— *v.* Bessingham, *co. Norf.*

Basingstoke, *co. Southt.* Rental of lands of R. Pexhall in, 1549. Add. 26560.

—— Rental of lands of Lady Savage in, 1590. Add. 26579.

—— Precipe on a covenant conc. land in, 1593. Add. 25236.

Baslow, *in Bakewell, co. Derb.* Bonds conc. lands in, 1485 (Baslaue). Woll. iii. 72, 76.

—— Lease in, 1640. Woll. xi. 80.

Basset Houses, *in Normanton Turville, co. Leic.* Grant, etc., of the manor, 1371. Add. 26922, 26923;— 1444. Add. 26924-26927.

Bassingbourne (Bassyngborne, etc.), *co. Camb.* Grants, etc., in, 1368. Add. 25939;—1410. Add. 25952, 25953;— 1457. Add. 25956;—1549. Add. 7060.

—— Court-rolls of Bassingbourne Rectory manor, 1457-8. Harl. Roll R. 29;—1533. Harl. Roll R. 30;— 1567. Harl. Roll R. 32;—1575. Harl. Roll R. 34.

—— Extracts of court-rolls of the same manor, 1567. Harl. Roll R. 31; —1575. Harl. Roll R. 33;—1588. Cott. xxi. 1, Harl. Roll R. 35;—1591. Harl. Roll R. 36.

—— *Rector.* Rogerus, 1373. Harl. 78 A. 3, 4.

Bassingfield, *in Holme Pierrepoint, co. Nott.* Covenant to convey land in, 1571 (Basingefeild). Woll. xi. 51.

Bassingham, *co. Linc.* Grants, etc., of Raudemilne *al.* Routhemilne in, to Newhouse Abbey, *c.* 1150-60.

Harl. 50 B. 44;—*c.* 1231. Harl. 52 C. 5.

—— Lease of Routhemilne in, by Newhouse Abbey, with covenant conc. the chapel, 1230. Harl. 44 G. 19.

—— Surrender to Newhouse Abbey of Rugemolyn manor in, 1299. Harl. 52 C. 6.

—— License to Newhouse Abbey for service in the oratory of Rouchemolyn manor, 1344. Harl. 43 H. 42 (Basyngham).

—— *Clericus.* Willelmus, *c.* 1230-40. Cott. xxiv. 49.

—— *Presbiter.* Osbertus, *c.* 1150-60. Harl. 50 B. 44.

—— *Vicarius.* Rogerus, *c.* 1150-60. Harl. 50 B. 44.

—— —— Willelmus, 1230 (Basingham). Harl. 44 G. 19.

Bassyngborne. *v.* Bassingbourne, *co. Camb.*

Bastead (Berstede), *in Wrotham, co. Kent.* Grants, etc., of the manor, 1397, 1399. Harl. Roll V. 9;—1420. Harl. 80 D. 39;—1444. Harl. 78 G. 14.

Bastelden. *v.* Basildon, *co. Berks.*

Baston, *co. Linc.* Patent of conf. to the guild of St. Mary at, 1442. Add. 5309.

—— Sale of Fateland water-mill in, 1552. Add. 26416.

—— *Vicarius.* Johannes, *t.* Hen. IV. Add. 5309.

Bastwick, *co. Norf.* Appropriation of the church to Hulme Abbey, *c.* 1150. Cott. iv. 57 (12) (*copy*).

—— Conf. of grant in, to St. Giles' Hospital, Norwich, 1279 (Bastwyk). Add. 14781.

Basyngham. *v.* Bassingham, *co. Linc.*

—— *v.* Bessingham, *co. Norf.*

Batenhale. *v.* Battenhall, *in Worcester, co. Worc.*

Baterton. *v.* Betterton, *co. Berks.*

Batesford. *v.* Battisford, *co. Suf.*

Bath, *co. Som.* Charter of King Edgar dated at, [972 or 973?] (Civitas scha manni). Cott. MS. Aug. ii. 67 (*copy*).

—— Fine for the advowson of St. Mary's "juxta Northgate" in, 1329. Eg. 260.

E

Battlesden, *co. Bedf.* Grant of, by Hugh Talbot, [1179] (Badelesdonia). Harl. 111 G. 50.

Baudak. *v.* Baldock, *co. Hertf.*

Baugburg. *v.* Bawburgh, *co. Norf.*

Baughurst, *co. Southt.* Conf. of the chapel to St. Cross Hospital, Winchester, 1189 (Baggehurst). Harl. 43 C. 28.

Baukewell, Bauquewell. *v.* Bakewell, *co. Derb.*

Baumford, Baumforth. *v.* Bamford, *co. Derb.*

Baunton. *v.* Bampton, *co. Devon.*

Baurghe, Mykle. *v.* Bargh, *co. York.*

Bawburgh, *co. Norf.* Grant of tithes in. to Rumburgh Priory, [1121-87] (Bauburg). Campb. ix. 9 (7).

—— Conf. of the church to Norwich Priory, 1241. Cott. ii. 21 (5).

—— Grant in, 1447. Add. 6500.

—— *Rector.* Mag. Will. le Puygur, 1241. Cott. ii. 21 (5).

Bawdeswell (Baldeswell), *co. Norf.* Grant, etc., in, 1418. Campb. xii. 8; —1461. Add. 2007.

—— *Persona.* Ric. de Walsham, 1396. Add. 14665.

Bawdon. *v. sub* Chapel en le Frith, *co. Derb.*

Bawdrip, *co. Som.* Livery, etc., of the manor, 1613. Add. 5714;—1634. Add. 9282.

Bawdsey, *co. Suff.* Conf. in, to Ely Abbey, from H., Bp. of Ely, [1109-31] (Baldreseia). Harl. 43 H. 4 (copy).

—— Grants, etc., of the manor, 1400. Harl. 54 H. 2 (Baudeseye);—1429. Harl. 58 B. 17;—1431. Harl. 57 A. 1 (Bawdesey);—1434. Harl. 47 C. 44 (Bawdesay).

—— Lease, etc., in, 1537. Add. 909; —1544. Add. 1384 (Baldesey);—1640. Add. 10580.

Bawkwell. *v.* Bakewell, *co. Derb.*

Bawtry, *cos. York and Nott.* Grants, etc., in, 1316. Harl. 112 F. 58 (Bautre); —1359. Harl. 112 G. 14 (do.);—1414. Harl. 112 A. 15 (Bawtre);—1575. Harl 112 I. 1.

Baycliffe, *in Hill Deverill, co. Wilts.* Grant in, early Hen. III. (Baylecliue). Harl. 57 F. 6.

Bayhall Manor. *v. sub* Pembury, *co. Kent.*

Bayldon. *v.* Baildon, *co. York.*

Bayleclive. *v.* Baycliffe, *in Hill Deverill, co. Wilts.*

Baylham, *co. Suff.* Precipe on a covenant conc. land in, 1592. Add. 25423.

—— Warranty of a sale of the manor, 1626. Harl. 112 E. 51.

Baynard's Manor. *v. sub* Spexhall, *co. Suff.*

Baynard's *al.* Knipsho Manor. *v. sub* Mayland, *co. Essex.*

Baynard's *al.* Mauncelhall Manor. *v. sub* St. Lawrence, *co. Essex.*

Baynton. *v.* Bainton, *co. Northt.*

—— *v.* Bainton, *co. York* (?).

Baysham, *nr. Ross, co. Heref.* Release and grant in, t. Hen. III. Harl. 112 B. 42 (Beysaam);—1374. Add. 1319.

Beachampton, *co. Buck. Capellanus.* Thomas, *t.* Hen. III. Harl. 86 E. 85-87.

Beaconsfield (Bekenesfeld, etc.), *co. Buck.* Grants, etc., in, late 13 cent. or *t.* Edw. I. Cott. xxv. 37, Campb. iv. 12, Harl. 53 A. 18;—1322. Harl. 49 D. 27, Campb. vi. 15;—1331. Harl. 47 G. 38;—1350. Harl. 53 B. 36;— 1362. Harl. 52 A. 32;—1375. Harl. 46 D. 18;—1376. Harl. 45 E. 57;— 1381. Harl. 49 D. 45;—1384. Harl. 49 D. 30;—1386. Harl. 45 H. 27;— *c.* 1386. Harl. 50 I. 29;—1410. Add. 5160;—1415. Add. 5161.

—— Release in Dernedene in, late 13 cent. Harl. 58 C. 28.

—— Notif. of a grant in Dernedene in, by Medmenham Abbey, 1318. Campb. x. 8.

—— Grant in, by Bisham Priory, 1345 (Bokenesfeld). Harl. 44 B. 40.

—— Feoffment, etc., of Hyde manor and lands in, 1416. Add. 5162;—1569. Add. 5163.

—— Sale of timber at Holmelond in, 1420. Harl. 78 F. 32.

—— Compotus of the manor, 1420-23. Harl. Roll S. 1.

—— Fine in, 1571 (Beckensfeld). Harl. 75 G. 44.

Beaddingtun. *v.* Beddington, *co. Surr.*

Beadlam, *nr. Helmsley, co. York.* Power to give seisin in, 1463 (Budlome). Harl. 86 H. 45.

—— Grant of the manor, 1650 (Budlome *al.* Budlowe). Add. 1800.

**Beadlow,** *sr. Clophill, co. Bedf.* Pardon for alienation of the manor, 1578 (Bedlowe, Bedloe, Beawlowe). Add. 9271.

—— Exemplif. of record of suit in, 1590 (Bedlow). Add. 9274.

**Beaford,** *co. Devon.* Brief for rebuilding the church, 1798. Ch. Br. B. xxxviii. 9.

**Beahalle.** *v. sub* Pembury, *co. Kent.*

**Beaksbourne** (Bekysbourne, etc.), *co. Kent.* Returns of service due for the manor of, by serjeantry, *t.* Hen. III. (Burn, Burnes). Harl. 75 D. 64.

—— Grants, etc., in, 1279–80. Harl. 76 E. 2 (Bekesborne);—1298–9. Harl. 78 H. 38 (Lyvingesburne);—1301. Harl. 79 D. 56, 57;—1315. Harl. 80 G. 21 (Bekesburne);—1325. Add. 13999 (Lyvyngesburne);—1340. Harl. 76 B. 47;—1345. Harl. 45 C. 24 (Bakesbourne);—1405. Harl. 76 D. 48 (Levyngesbourne), 49, 50 (Bekesborne);—1434. Harl. 80 I. 68;—1438. Harl. 79 D. 9;—1541. Harl. 76 H. 37; —1548. Harl. 75 E. 22 (Bekysburne); —1551. Harl. 75 E. 28;—1557. Harl. 76 I. 27, 34.

—— Rentals of the manor, *c.* 1320–30. Harl. Roll S. 7 (Bekesbourne);—15 cent. Harl. Rolls S. 2–4;—1510–11. Harl. Roll Z. 7 (Lyvyngesbourne);— 1518. Harl. Roll Z. 8; —16 cent. Harl. Roll S. 10.

—— Acquittance from the Bailiff of Hastings for service due to the Crown from the manor of, 1345. Harl. 80 I. 98.

—— Mem. of sale of the manor, *t.* Edw. III. (Bourne). Harl. Roll S. 23.

—— Compotus-rolls of the manor, 1365–6. Harl. Roll Z. 5 (Lyvyngesbourne);—1383–4. Harl. Roll S. 24 *b* (Burne);—[*c.* 1383–4 ?]. Harl. Roll S. 6 (Bekesborne);—1384. Harl. Roll Z. 2 (Lyvyngesbourne);—1391–2. Harl. Roll Z. 3;—1396–7. Harl. Roll S. 4;—*t.* Ric. II. Harl. Roll S. 22;— 1401. Harl. Roll Z. 6;—early 15 cent. Harl. Roll S. 5;—1434–6. Harl. Roll S. 11.

—— Court-rolls, 1370–71. Harl. Roll Z. 1 (Lyvyngesbourne); — 1385 - 6. Harl. Roll S. 24 *a* (Borne Cobeham); —1459–62. Harl. Roll S. 13 (Bekysbourne); — 1499–1505. Harl. Roll S. 12.

—— Acquittance for stock, etc., of the manor, 1389. Harl. 80 C. 8.

**Beaksbourne** (Bekysbourne, etc.), *co. Kent (continued).* Extent of the manor, *t.* Hen. IV. Harl. Roll S. 8.

—— Inquisition on grant of, by Card. Beaufort, to Christ Church, Canterbury, 1442–3. Harl. Roll S. 14.

—— Terrier of the manor, 15 cent. Harl. Roll S. 9.

—— Copies of deeds conc. conveyance and covenants for amortization of the manor, 15 cent. Harl. Roll S. 15 *b*.

—— Fines inflicted in the manor courts of, 1451–2. Harl. Roll S 15 *a*.

—— Bill of quit-rent due to the manor from Ospringe Hospital, 1452. Harl. 76 A. 25.

—— Lease of the manor, by Christ Church, Canterbury, 1467. Harl. 75 F. 48.

—— Covenant botw. the farmer of the manor and Christ Church Priory, 1506. Harl. Roll S. 33.

—— Acquittance for a subsidy from the manor, as a member of the port of Hastings, 1513. Harl. 76 E. 10.

—— Valor of Crown lands in, late held by Christ Church Priory, *t.* Hen. VIII. Harl. Rolls S. 34, 35.

—— Sale of the manor, by the Crown, 1541. Harl. 75 H. 3.

—— Appointment of a steward of the manor, 1541 (Lyvyngisbourn). Harl. 76 H. 38.

—— Fine in, 1548. Harl. 75 H. 4, 76 H. 50.

—— *Perpet. Vicarius.* Will. Paryce, 1405. Harl. 76 D. 48, 49.

**Bealings, Great,** *co. Suff.* Release in, *t.* Edw. I. Add. 5492 (Beling);—1415. Campb. i. 27 (Bolyngges Magna).

—— *Persona.* Dom. Ric. de Westhorpe, 1334 (Belyngges Magna). Add. 10306.

—— Ric. Larwood, 1593. Add. 26353.

**Bealings, Little,** *co. Suff.* Grant in, *t.* Hen. III. (Parva Belinges). Add. 10178.

**Beamfleote.** *v.* Benfleet, S., *co. Essex.*

**Beamsley,** *co. York.* Lease of pasture in, *t.* Hen. III. (Bimsleia). Harl. 52 I. 44.

**Beansetas,** *co. Worc.* (?). Accord conc. land at, 836. Cott. MS. Aug. ii. 9.

**Beanstede** [Bunstead, *nr. Hursley* ?], *co. Southt.* A boundary mark, 909. Harl. 43 C. 1.

E 2

Beardinga leag, *nr. Chart Sutton, co. Kent.* Grant at, 814. Harl. 83 A. 1.

Beare. *v. Beer, co. Som.*

Bearley, *co. Warw.* Conf. and release at Edstone in, to Bordesley Abbey, late Hen. III. (Burlega). Add. 21428.

—— Release in, to same, late 13 cent. (Burleia). Add. 20421.

—— Releases of the manor, 1430 (Burley). Harl. 43 E. 19, 45 I. 12.

Bearwardcote, *in Etwall, co. Derb.* Grant in, to Derby Priory, *t.* Hen. III. (Bervardecote). Woll. ix. 33.

—— Grants in, [1290]. Woll. ix. 34 (Berewardcote);—1476. Woll. ix. 42 (Berwardcote).

Beatrisden. *v. Betheraden, co. Kent.*

Beauchampes Manor. *v. sub Dullingham, co. Camb.*

Beauchampes Manor. *v. sub Bloxham, co. Oxon.*

Beaudesert, *co. Warw.* Grant of the castle and manor, 1376 (Beudesert). Cott. xi. 70.

—— Inquest conc. descent of same, 1412. Cott. xxiii. 12.

—— Petition for restitution of the manor, *c.* 1490. Add. 5836.

—— *Persona. Dom.* Johannes, 1285. Add. 5995.

Beaugham, Beaughom. *v.* Bewholme, *co. York.*

Beaumanor, *co. Leic.* Exchequer acquittance on a purchase of free warren in the manor of, 1616. Add. 25614.

Beaumaris, *co. Angl.* Garrison establishment of the castle, 1369 (Beaumarreys). Harl. Roll E. 7.

Beaumeis Manor, *nr. Shinfield, cos. Wilts. and Berks.* Grant of a third part of, 1365 (Beaumys). Add. 20239.

Beaumont, *co. Essex.* Conveyance of the manor and advowson, 1393. Add. 15602.

Beaurepaire Manor. *v. sub* Sherborne St. John, *co. Southt.*

Beaureper. *v.* Belper, *co. Derb.*

Beausale, *in Hatton, co. Warw.* Grant of the "vivarium" of, to Wroxhall Priory, 12-13 cent. (Beausala). Add. 21450.

—— Grant of the manor, *post* 1250 (Beusalo). Cott. xii. 12.

Beausfeld. *v. Whitfield al. Bewsfield, co. Kent.*

Beawlowe. *v.* Beadlow, *nr. Clophill, co. Bedf.*

Beccles, *in Chalk, co. Kent.* Grant of reversion of the manor, 1345 (Bekkele). Harl. 45 C. 24.

Beccles, *co. Suff.* Grants, etc., in, 1296, 1297. Harl. 48 G. 13, 15-17;—1375. Harl. 53 E. 45 (Becclys);—1386. Harl. 56 G. 21 (Beclys);—1396. Harl. 48 I. 39 (Beklis);—1422. Harl. 50 F. 36 (Becklys);—1483. Add. 7564.

—— Fine in, 1539 (Bicolys). Harl. 58 H. 13.

—— Precipes on covenants in, 1555. Add. 25287;—1564. Add. 25323, 25324;—1588. Add. 25386.

—— *Persona.* Edmundus *al.* Esmon de Wello, 1378. Add. 10376;—*c.* 1378. Add. 14664.

Becham. *v.* Beckham, E. and W., *co. Norf.*

Bechansted. *v.* Berkhampstead, *co. Hertf.*

Bechegate. *v. sub* Waltham, *co. Kent.*

Becheleya. *v.* Beckley, *co. Suss.*

Bechewelle [Buckwell(?)], *in Wye Manor, co. Kent.* Conf. of tithes of, to Battle Abbey, [1114-22]. Harl. 43 G. 18.

Becheworth, Bechesworth. *v.* Betchworth, *co. Surr.*

Bechyngton. *v. sub* Friston, *co. Suss.*

Beckeberri. *v. sub* Harbledown, *co. Kent.*

Beckenham, *co. Kent.* A boundary mark, 862 (Biohahhema mearo). Cott. viii. 32;—973. Cott. viii. 33;—987 (Beohhæma mearc). Cott. viii. 14.

—— Ref. to a suit before Hen. I. [in 1131-3] at, [1155?] (Beccheham). Cott. xiii. 6 (5) (*copy*).

—— (Beghenham, Bekenham, etc.). Grants, etc., in, *t.* Hen. III.–*t.* Edw. I. Harl. 111 C. 69, 111 D. 9 (Bechenham), 11, 111 E. 46 (Bheuenham), 47, 111 G. 35, 45 (Behhenham), 52, 112 A. 2, 16, 112 B. 10, 40 (Bheuenham), 112 C. 16, 112 E. 36, 54, 59 (Bheuhenham), 60, 61;—1289-90. Harl. 111 G. 9 (Bechenham);—1292. Harl. 111 F. 60, 112 C. 20 (Behenham);—1293. Harl. 111 D. 36, 112 B. 34, 112 D. 46 (Bechenham);—1295. Harl. 46 E. 35 (Bekeham);—*c.* 1300. Harl. 111

D. 50, 51;—1308. Harl. 111 D. 52, 111 G. 23 (Beyghenham); — 1309. Harl. 112 A. 23, 112 B. 35, 112 E. 55; —1316. Harl. 112 D. 16;—1317. Harl. 112 F. 3;—1318. Harl. 112 F. 4;—1322. Harl. 111 C. 63, 112 A. 44, 112 D. 17;—post 1322. Harl. 112 B. 39;—1324. Harl. 111 C. 64, 111 E. 38, 49;—1328. Harl. 111 B. 50, 111 F. 52, 112 A. 25;—1331. Harl. 111 E. 53, 54;—1348. Harl. 112 E. 53;—1350. Harl. 111 F. 14;—1376. Harl. 111 D. 49, 111 E. 57;—1384. Harl. 112 E. 45;—1385. Harl. 112 E. 46;—1391. Harl. 111 D. 60;—1407. Harl. 111 D. 43;—1408. Harl. 47 D. 23;—1411. Harl. 112 A. 36, 112 E. 13;—1424. Harl. 111 G. 55 (Bekynham);—1433. Harl. 111 G. 27;—1500. Harl. 112 A. 9;—1533. Harl. 112 F. 16;—1536. Harl. 112 A. 41;—1587. Harl. 112 D. 31;—1589. Harl. 112 D. 30;—1612. Harl. 111 C. 65;—1619. Harl. 112 A. 49;—1629. Harl. 112 A. 50.

—— Grant in, in the fee of Westminster Abbey, bounded by "fovea que appellatur marc de Cancia." etc., t. Hen. III. (Bekeham). Harl. 111 G. 46.

—— Grants in Bledindon in, t. Hen. III. Harl. 112 C. 26 (Bekeham), 112 D. 44 (Bekenham), 45, 112 B. 33 (Beckeham).

—— Grant at Scaldeford in, t. Hen. III. (Bekeham). Harl. 112 C. 15.

—— Grant nr. Langley Park in, late 13 cent. (Bekenham). Harl. 112 B. 58.

—— Release of La Hoke in, 1302 (Bekenham). Harl. 112 F. 20.

—— Releases, etc., of Kent house in, 1329. Harl. 111 E. 40 (Beghenham); —1331. Harl. 111 E. 50 (Begenham); —1429. Harl. 112 C. 2 (Bekenham).

—— Bequests of lands in, etc., 1481. Harl. 112 E. 35;—1549, 1602. Harl. 112 A. 47, 48.

—— Fines in, 1597. Harl. 111 H. 6; —1618. Harl. 111 E. 33.

—— Bedellus (?). Ric. de Langeleye, sen., 1308. Harl. 111 D. 52.

—— Clericus. Ricardus, t. Hen. III. Harl. 112 A. 16.

—— Persona. Joh. Martham, 1407. Harl. 111 D. 43.

Beckensfeld. v. Beaconsfield, co. Buck.

Beckering (Bekering, Bekeryng), in Holton, co. Linc. Bond of services in, with Bullington Priory, t. Hen. II. (Bechering). Add. 20682.

—— Grants in, to Bullington Priory, 1165. Cott. xxvii. 195;—late 12 cent. Harl. 45 H. 29, 58 G. 38 a (copy);—early 13 cent. Harl. 45 H. 30, 31;—1349. Harl. 45 H. 33, 34.

—— Lease in, from Bullington Priory, 1237. Cott. xii. 16.

—— Grant, etc., in, 1335. Harl. 54 G. 21;—1375. Cott. xxvii. 204.

Becketwessell. v. sub Salehurst, co. Suss.

Beckford, co. Glouc. Covenant with Tewkesbury Abbey conc. tithes to the church of, in Didcot, and release of Washbourne chapel, 1177 (Bekef.). Add. 7013.

—— Appointment of a steward in, by Fotheringhay College, 1467 (Bekford). Slo. xxxiii. 72.

—— Pardon for alienation in Grafton in, 1590. Eg. 369.

—— [Persona ?]. Mag. Silvester, 1177. Add. 7013.

Beckham, co. Norf. Grant in, t. Rich. I.-John (Becham). Add. 14520.

—— East (Est Bekham, Est Becham), co. Norf. Grants, etc., of the manor, 1379. Add. 14521;—1380. Add. 14522; — 1409. Add. 19325; — 1415. Add. 14523;—1442. Add. 14524;—1445. Add. 14525; — 1469. Add. 14526;—1503. Add. 17743.

—— West, co. Norf. Grants in, to Norwich Priory, [1101]. Cott. MS. Aug. ii. 103 (Becham) (copy);—[1121-35]. Cott. ii. 21 (8) (copy).

—— Grants of the manor, 1300. Add. 19298 (W. Becham);—1347. Add. 14761 (W. Becham).

—— Grant, etc., in, 1306. Add. 19304 (W. Becham), 19305;—1379. Add. 14521 (W. Bckham); — 1409. Add. 19325.

—— Lease in, to Nutley Abbey, 1331. Add. 14519.

Beckhurst, in Allington, co. Kent. Mortgage of a Crown lease of the wood of, 1643. Harl. 79 F. 8.

Beckingham, co. Linc. Grant in, to Rufford Abbey, late 12 cent. (Beghingham). Harl. 83 E. 43.

Beckingham, co. Nott. Grant in, t. Hen. III. (Beghenham). Harl. 111 D. 32.

**Beckington** (Bekyngton, etc.), co. *Som.* Grants, etc., in, 1334. Harl. 44 G. 8; —1335. Add. 7810 (Bekynton):— 1393. Add. 7848:—1444. Add. 7867; —1469. Add. 7874.

**Beckley**, co. *Suss.* Grant in Smalewede in, 1253 (Bocheleya). Eg. 254.

—— Grant in, " de feofo de Grestlingeu," 1299-1300 (Beckele). Add. 20153.

—— Grants, etc., in, *t.* Edw. I. Add. 20045 (Beckele), 20046, 20018 (copy); —1363. Add. 971 :—1427. Add. 20047 (Beckeley):—1458. Add. 16158 (Bokle):—1496. Add. 23803 :—1541. Add. 5675 (Bekele); — 1578. Add. 25830.

**Beckling** (Beklyng), *in Snape, co. Suff.* Grants, etc., of the manor, 1408. Harl. 54 I. 7:—1430. Harl. 43 E. 19, 54 I. 10;—1431. Harl. 45 I. 12, 50 H. 27, 28, 54 I. 15.

—— Extract from Court-roll, 1609. Add. 26361.

**Beckling Manor.** *v. sub* Friston, co. *Suff.*

**Becton.** *v.* Beighton, co. *Derb.*

**Becueby.** *v.* Barby, co. *Northt.*

**Beddesburie.** *v. sub* Goudhurst, co. *Kent.*

**Beddington,** co. *Surr.* Land at (?), to be restored to the see of Winchester, 900 (Bradalintun). Harl. 43 C. 1.

—— (Bedinton, etc.). Grants, etc., in, *t.* Hen. III.-*t.* Edw. I. Add. 22706, 22957, 22960 - 22963, 22966 - 22969, 22974-22977. 22979, 22980, 22982 - 22983, 22995, 22997 - 23004, 23006, 23159 :—1262. Add. 22921, 22922:— *c.* 1280-90. Add. 22936:—1291. Add. 22929:—1292. Add. 22930:—1296. Add. 22932, 22933; — 1298. Add. 22935:—1301. Add. 23024 (Bedinthon), 23026:—1305. Add. 23029:— 1308. Add. 23030, 23031:— *c.* 1310. Add. 22994:—1310. Add. 23035:— 1314. A· d. 23041, 23042:—1315. Add. 23049;—1316. Add. 23050, 23052;—1317. Add. 23055:—1318. Add. 23056;—1320. Add. 23058:— 1321. Add. 23061;—1323. Add. 23068, 23070;—1324. Add. 23069:— 1327. Add. 23072, 23073:—1336. Add. 23080 - 23082; — 1337. Add. 23083;—1338. Add. 23085:—1340. Add. 23087:—1341. Add. 23089:— 1342. Add. 23091;—1344. Add.

23093;—1346. Add. 23096:—1347. Add. 23099;—1348. Add. 23100- 23102, 23107, 23108;—1351. Add. 23114 - 23119 ;—1352. Add. 23121, 23122;—1353. Add. 23124;—1354. Add. 23382 ;—1357. Add. 23444 ;— 1359. Add. 23127; — 1360. Add. 23381 —1363. Add. 23128, 23129 :— 1365. Add. 23134; — 1367. Add. 23135 ;—1372. Add. 23136 (Benyngton);— 1375. Add. 23138 ;— 1377. Add. 23140, 23394, 23446:—1378. Add. 23141 - 23144 ;—1379. Add. 23147 :— 1380. Add. 23148 ;— 1383. Add. 23149 ;—1387. Add. 23155 :— 1388. Add. 23398 ;—1390. Add. 23150;— 1398. Add. 23158 ;— 1400. Add. 23160 ;—1401. Add. 23161-23164 :— 1402. Add. 23165, 23166, 23402 :— 1404. Add. 23167 - 23169 ; — 1416. Add. 23171 :—1420. Add. 23172 :— 1424. Add. 23174 ; — 1427. Add. 23175 ;—1441. Add. 23179 ;—1444. Add. 23180 ;—1449. Add. 23181 ;— 1455. Add. 23182, 23183 ; — 1457. Add. 23184, 23185 ; — 1458. Add. 23188 ;—1461. Add. 23191 ;—1463. Add. 23192 ;—1466. Add. 23194 :— 1507. Add. 23410 ;—1515. Add. 23200, 23201 ;—1517. Add. 23202 :— 1572. Add. 23228, 23224 ; — 1578. Add. 23228 ;—1610. Add. 23239 :— 1617. Add. 23274; — 1619. Add. 23276, 23279 ;—1632. Add. 23303 :— 1646. Add. 23313 ;—1668. Add. 23318 ;—1670. Add. 23317 ;—1676. Add. 23319 ;—1688. Add. 23320 ;— 1709. Add. 23321.

—— Grants, etc., in, to St. Thomas's Hospital, Southwark, early Hen. III. Add. 22774 ;—*post* 1228. Add. 23007, 23008, 23010, 23011, 23016-23018 ;—*t.* Hen. III. Add. 23009, 23015, 23019, 23022 ;—late Hen. III. Add. 22973, 23732 ;—1268-9. Add. 23014 ;—1284. Add. 22928 ;—*t.* Edw. I. Add. 22785, 22964, 23013 ;—1311. Add. 23036 ; —1341. Add. 23086 ;—1350. Add. 23113.

—— Assignment to Merton Priory of rent in, due from St. Thomas's Hospital, *post* 1228 (Bedintun). Add. 23012.

—— Covenant conc. custody of deeds of lands in, by St. Thomas's Hospital, 1275. Add. 22924.

—— Release of wardship of E. and A. Morin in, early Edw. I. Add. 22636.

—— Rental of Tho. Huscarl's manor of, *t.* Edw. I. Add. 22971.

**Beddington**, *co. Surr. (continued).*
Notif. to tenants to pay service in, 1310. Add. 23034.

—— Rolls of deeds conc. lands in, granted to St. Thomas's Hospital by Dom. W. de Huntingfield, c. 1311. Add. 22970, 22972.

—— Court-rolls, 1325. Add. 23070; —1418. Add. 22638.

—— Grants, etc., of the manor, 1338. Add. 23084; — 1420. Add. 23632, 23633;—1429. Add. 23540:—1435. Add. 23178;—1452. Add. 23173;— 1457. Add. 23187; — 1497. Add. 23195;—1593. Add. 23232;—1597. Add. 23234.

—— Leases in, from St. Thomas's Hospital, 1340. Add. 23088;—1365. Add. 23133.

—— Fine in, 1346. Add. 23653.

—— Acquittance in, from Merton Priory to St. Thomas's Hospital, 1359. Add. 22869.

—— Valor of the manor, [1440]. Add. 23023.

—— Claims for dower in, by Mercye Carru, c. 1440. Add. 23408.

—— Privy seal conc. a suit for the manor, c. 1495. Add. 23198.

—— Covenant to convey the manor as security for a loan to Sir R. Carew, 1518. Add. 23204.

—— Covenant conc. dower of Lady Darcie in, 1558. Add. 23214.

—— Bond not to kill deer, etc., in the park, 1572. Add. 23225.

—— Order conc. lands in Horley held of the manor of, 1598. Add. 23515.

—— Fines of the manor, 1613-1642. Add. 23242-23268.

—— Security conc. dower of Rebecca Carew in, 1645. Add. 23312.

—— *Capellanus.* Rogerus, early Hen. III. Add. 22774.

—— *Rector.* Dom. Joh. Blund, late Hen. III. Add. 22636, 22710, 22739, 22770, 22796, 22805, 22806, 22960, 22966.

—— —— *(porcionis eccl.).* Rogerus, late Hen. III. Add. 22945.

—— —— *Dom.* Hugo Poinaunt, t. Hen. III. or Edw. I. Add. 22756.

—— —— *(porcionarius eccl.).* Mag. Will. de Carreu, 1351. Add. 23118, 23119;—1353. Add. 23124; — 1354. Add. 23125.

**Beddington**, *co. Surr. (continued).*
*Rector (continued).* Will. Wotton, 1400. Add. 23160.

—— —— Hugo Gaynesburgh, 1441. Add. 23179.

—— —— Ric. Tanner, 1473. Add. 23547.

*v. also* Bandon, *co. Surr.*
Wallington, *co. Surr.*
Woodcote, *co. Surr.*

**Bedefons.** *v.* Bedfont, *co. Midd.*

**Bederesden.** *v.* Betheraden, *co. Kent.*

**Bedewinde.** *v.* Bedwin, *co. Wilts.*

**Bedfield**, *co. Suff.* Conveyance of the manor, 1434 (Beadfeld). Harl. 47 C. 44.

**Bedfont**, *co. Midd.* Grants in, to Southwark Priory, t. Steph. or Hen. II. (Bedefons). Cott. v. 11, Harl. 50 B. 23.

—— Release in, to Newark Priory, co. Surr., 1281 (Bedefunte). Harl. 50 F. 47.

—— Exemplif. of recovery in, 1624. Cott. xxx. 10.

**Bedfont, West**, *co. Midd.* Conf. of a grant of, [1189-1212] (Westbedefont). Harl. 45 G. 67.

**Bedford.** *v.* Bideford, *co. Devon.*

**Bedford,** *County of.* Compotus of the Earl of Surrey's Receiver in, 1509-10. Add. 16560.

—— Appointment of an escheator for, 1545. Harl. 84 C. 27.

—— Conveyance, etc., of a third part of the barony of Bedford in, 1610, 1611. Add. 994-996.

—— Commission to Sir N. Carew as Deputy-Lieutenant for, 1715. Add. 24078.

—— *Sheriff.* Joh. Cheyne, 1426. Add. 656.

—— —— Sir Rob. Peckham, 1556. Harl. 84 C. 33.

—— —— Tho. Pycott, 1557. Harl. 84 C. 33.

—— —— Sir Geo. Peckham, 1573. Harl. 84 C. 37.

—— —— Ralph Astrey, 1574. Harl. 84 C. 38.

—— —— Tho. Anscell, 1610. Add. 995.

**Bedford** (Bedef., Bedeford), *co. Bedf.* Grants in, in prebenda Sti. Pauli, t. Hen. III. Harl. 55 E. 43;—1303. Harl. 45 F. 57;—1305. Harl. 45 F.

58;—1316. Harl. 48 G. 28;—1326. Harl. 47 I. 2.

—— Lease, etc., in, 1448. Add. 9708; —1451. Add. 15726.

—— Compotus of the castle, 1457-8. Add. 657.

—— Reasons for refounding St. John's Hospital at, as not being a parish church, t. Jas. I. Cott. xxi. 2.

**Bedford Level al. Great Level, in the Fens.** Award of 95000 acres in, to the Earl of Bedford, 1636. Cott. iii. 15.

—— Act for draining, 1645. Cott. iii. 3.

**Bedgbury, co. Kent.** Grant at, 814 (Begœbyra). Harl. 83 A. 1.
        v. sub Goudhurst, co. Kent.

**Bedgrove, in Weston Turville, co. Buck.** Rental of the manor, 1627 (Belgrove). Cott. i. 4.

**Bedingfield, co. Suff.** Grants, etc., in and nr., late 12 cent. (?). Harl. 45 G. 70 (Bedingefeld); — early 13 cent. Harl. 49 B. 21;—t. Hen. III. Harl. 50 G. 55 (Bedingefeud);—1299. Harl. 5½ H. 48 (Bedingfeld);—1303. Harl. 4⁷ A. 15.

—— Conveyance of wardship in, 1317 (Bedingfeld). Harl. 57 G. 41.

—— Grant, etc., of the manor, 1348. Harl. 55 F. 44;—1381. Harl. 48 A. 42 (Bedyngfeld).

—— Precipe on a covenant conc. land in, 1588. Add. 25389.

**Bedingham** (Bedyngham, etc.), co. Norf. Grants, etc., in, 1293. Add. 14527;—1296. Add. 14528;—1312. Add. 14529 (Bedighum);—1316. Add. 14530;—1334. Add. 14531;—1355. Add. 14532;—1357. Add. 14533;—1359. Add. 14534;—1382. Add. 14535;—1387. Harl. 50 I. 2, 6. 1391. Add. 14537;—1439. Add. 14538;—1476. Add. 14539;—1506. Add. 14540;—1549. Add. 14541;—1551. Add. 14542;—1559. Add. 14544;—1675. Add. 14546.

—— Vicarius. Willelmus, 1334. Add. 14958.

—— —— (perpetuus). Johannes, 1382. Add. 14535.

—— —— Will. Bret, 1506. Add. 14540.

**Bedlow.** v. Beadlow, nr. Clophill, co. Bedf.

**Bedminster, co. Som.** Grants, etc., in, 12-13 cent. Add. 7764 (Bedmunstria); —late Hen. III. Add. 7766 (Bedministria);—1381. Add. 6506 (Bedmynstre);—1524. Add. 6363 (Bedmyster), 6544.

—— Quo warranto conc. the tenure of the manor, [1280] (Bemynstre). Add. 7791.

—— Lease of the manor, 1337 (Bedministre). Add. 7183.

—— Capellanus. Philippus, 12-13 cent. Add. 7764.

**Bedminster Hundred, co. Som.** Grant of, c. 1148 (Bedmunistre). Add. 7760.

**Bedwardine, co. Worc.** Fine in, 1501 (Bedwardyn). Harl. 43 I. 6.

**Bedwas, co. Monm.** Precipe on a covenant conc. land in, 1592. Add. 25118.

**Bedwin, co. Wilts.** Grant at, by Cynewulf of Wessex, 778 (Bedewinde). Cott. viii. 4.

**Bedwin, Great, co. Wilts.** Compotusrolls of, bel. to the Duke of Buckingham, 1499-1500, 1511-12. Add. 26873, 26874.

**Bedyng.** v. Beeding, co. Suss.

**Beechamwell, co. Norf.** Inquest of lands in, 1276-7 (Bychamwelle). Harl. Roll K. 6.

—— Grant in, 1377 (Bychamwell). Harl. 52 B. 43.

—— Rental in, t. Hen. IV. (?) (Bichamwellys, Parva Bicham). Harl. Roll A. 10.

**Beeding** (Bedyng), co. Suss. Feoffment, etc., of the manor, 1474. Add. 7619;—1475. Add. 7629.

**Beeford, co. York.** Grants in, to Newhouse Abbey, t. Hen. III. Harl. 46 D. 37 (Biford), 40, 47 F. 18 (Byford); —1303. Harl. 50 I. 2, 6.

—— Grants in, t. Hen. III. Harl. 46 D. 39 (Biford):—late 13 cent. Harl. 45 H. 2 (Beford).

—— Capellanus. Alexander, t. Hen. III. Harl. 46 D. 39.

**Beeley, in Bakewell, co. Derb.** Grant of Harwood (Harewda) grange, etc., in, to Beauchief Abbey, early 13 cent. Woll. i. 13.

—— Grants in the Greaves in, etc., t. Hen. III. Woll. ii. 43 (Beytley), 43 a, 44;—1303. Woll. ii. 52 (Beyleye) (copy);—early 14 cent. Woll. ii.

Beesthorpe (Bestorp), co. *Nott.* Grant with conf. in, [1203–4]. Harl. 83 G. 18;—c. 1203–4. Harl. 112 G. 53.

—— Assignment of life-interest of Qu. Catharine of Braganza in the fishery, etc., of, 1680. Harl. 111 H. 11.

Beeston, co. *Norf.* Covenant conc. rent of the manor due to the ward of Dover Castle, late Hen. III. Harl. 47 E. 33.

Beeston Regis, co. *Norf.* Power to give seisin in, 1379 (Bestone). Add. 14521.

Beeston St. Andrew's, co. *Norf.* Grant in, 1320 (Bestone). Add. 15189, 15190.

Beetham, co. *Westm.* Grant of the church to St. Mary's Abbey, York, t. John (Biethum). Add. 17153.

Beford. v. Beeford, co. *York.*

**Begewordia, Beggeworth.** v. **Badgeworth.** co. *Glouc.*

Beggary, in *Eaton Socon,* co. *Bedf.* Grants, etc., in, 1351 (Begerie). Harl. 48 H. 29;—1366 (Beggeria). Harl. 54 E. 41;—1374 (Beggaria). Harl. 46 I. 56, 57.

**Beggebery, Beggere.** v. *sub* Goudhurst, co. *Kent.*

Beghalle. v. *sub* Pembury, co. *Kent.*

Beghenham. v. Beckenham, co. *Kent.*
—— r. Beckingham, co. *Nott.*

Beghingham. v. Beckingham, co. *Linc.*

Beghley. v. Beeley, co. *Derb.*

Beghton. v. Beighton, co. *Derb.*

Begvyles Manor. v. *sub* Tatterset, co. *Norf.*

Behhenham. v. Beckenham, co. *Kent.*

Behtmeswelle. v. Bitteswell, co. *Leic.*

Beighton, co. *Derb.* Grant of the manor, t. Edw. I. (Becton). Campb. iv. 11.
—— Grants in, 1328 (Beothon). Campb. v. 16; — 1330 (Beghton). Campb. i. 1.
—— Lease at Walterthorpe in, 1328 (Beethon). Campb. viii. 17.
—— Fine in, 1541 (Beghton). Woll. ii. 71.
—— *Dominus.* Rob. de Fornaus, *miles,* 1328. Campb. v. 16, viii. 17.
—— *Clericus.* Galfridus, t. Hen. III. Harl. 83 G. 47.

Beighton, co. *Derb.* (*continued*). *Clericus* (*continued*). Radulphus, t. Hen. III. Harl. 83 G. 47.
—— Willelmus, t. Hen. III. Harl. 83 G. 48.

Beighton, co. *Norf.* Rental, 1638. Add. 14288.

Beighton, co. *Suff.* Recovery in, 1495 (Beketon). Add. 1382.

Beinflete. v. Benfleet, South, co. *Essex.*

Bek, in *Isleham* and *Freckenham,* cos. *Camb.* and *Suff.* Release of the manor, 1349. Harl. 48 D. 9.

Bekef. v. Beckford, co. *Glouc.*

Bekeham. v. Beckenham, co. *Kent.*

Bekenesfeld. v. Beaconsfield, co. *Buck.*

Bekenore. v. Bicknor, co. *Kent.*

Bekering. v. Beckering, in *Holton,* co. *Linc.*

Bekerton, in *Stow, Wayland Hund.,* co. *Norf.* Certificate as to seisin of the manor, 1448 (Bekyrton). Add. 14902.

**Bekesbourne, Bekysbourne.** v. Beaksbourne, co. *Kent.*

Beketon. v. Beighton, co. *Suff.*

Bekham. v. Beckham, co. *Norf.*

Bekkele. v. Beccles, co. *Kent.*

Bekle, Bekele. v. Beckley, co. *Suss.*

**Bekwesell, Bekwesill.** v. *sub* Salehurst, co. *Suss.*

Bekyngton. v. Beckington, co. *Som.*

Bela, co. *Camb.* Conff. of, by Bps. of Ely, to Ely Abbey [1103–31, 1133–69]. Harl. 43 H. 4, 5 (*copies*).

Belaugh, co. *Norf.* Demise in, 1398 (Bilawe). Harl. 45 D. 28.

Belaugh, co. *York.* Sale in, 1535. Add. 26790.

Belay. v. Beeley, co. *Derb.*

Belbroughton, co. *Worc.* Covenant as to descent of the manor and advowson, 1496. Add. 5684.
—— Recovery of the manor and advowson, 1500. Add. 5685 b.

Belby, in *Howden,* co. *York.* Grants in, t. Edw. III. Lansd. 419 (Belleby); —1519. Lansd. 456.

Belchamp Otton, co. *Essex.* Release in, 1341 (Beuchamp Ottonis). Add. 15595.

**Belton** (Beltona, etc.), *in Isle of Axholme, co. Linc.* Grant in, to Sulby Abbey, *ante* 1222 (Beltuna). Add. 20615.

—— Grants, etc., in, early 13 cent.— *t.* Hen. III. Add. 19819, 20616, Cott. xxiv. 49;—1385. Add. 22568.

—— Grants in, from Sulby Abbey, *t.* Hen. III. Add. 20614;—early Edw. I. Add. 20617.

—— Conf. of the church to Esholt Priory, 1486. Add. 17126.

—— Admission in, as of Epworth manor, 1666. Harl. 111 C. 57.

—— *Persona.* Rob. fil. Hugon. de Beltoft, early 13 cent. Add. 19822;— (as Robertus), early 13 cent.—*t.* Hen. III. Add. 19819, 21875, Cott. xxiv. 49.

—— —— Hugo, 1255. Add. 20608.

**Belton,** *nr. Grantham, co. Linc.* Release in, 1663. Harl. 111 H. 31.

**Belton,** *co. Rutl.* Lease, etc., in, 1325. Add. 5435, 5436.

**Belton,** *co. Suff.* Grant in, 1538. Add. 10225.

**Belvoir,** *co. Leic. or co. Linc.* Treaty conc. the castle of, betw. the Earls of Chester and Leicester, [1151–2] (Belveeir). Cott. MS. Nero C. iii., f. 178.

—— Treaty of Henry, Duke of Normandy, conc., with the Earl of Chester, [1153] (Belvarium). Cott. xvii. 2.

—— Lands in Kirkby Underwood, co. Linc., held of the Fee or Honour of, c. 1150–60. Add. 20865 (Feudum de Bauveer);—*t.* Hen. II. Add. 20868 (Honor de Balveir).

—— Release to Langley Abbey from suits of court at, for lands in Barkby Thorpe, co. Leic., *t.* Hen. III. or Edw. I. (Beauver). Harl. 55 E. 27.

**Belyngdone.** *v.* Billington, *co. Bedf.*

**Belyngges Magna.** *v.* Bealings, Gt., *co. Suff.*

**Bemerton,** *co. Wilts.* Fines of the manor. 1585. Add. 15150;—1609. Add. 15151;—1611. Add. 15152;— 1615. Add. 15153;—1627. Add. 15123.

—— Acquittance for rent of the manor, 1586. Add. 15154.

—— Acquittance on a covenant conc. the manor, 1613. Add. 15155.

**Bemerton,** *co. Wilts.* (*continued*). Extent of the manor, *t.* Jas. I. Add. 15156.

—— Sale of the manor, 1661. Add. 15124.

**Bempton,** *co. York.* Conf. by Hen. I. of a grant in, to Bridlington Priory, [1128–32] (Bemtona). Cott. MS. Aug. ii. 5g.

—— Excheq. acquittance for rent of the manor, 1623. Add. 25723.

**Bemynstre.** *v.* Bedminster, *co. Som.*

**Benchesham.** *v.* Bensham, *in Croydon, co. Surr.*

**Benclolle.** *v.* Bincknoll, *co. Wilts.*

**Bendish,** *in Radwinter, co. Essex.* Grant of tithes in, to H. Trinity Priory, Aldgate, *t.* Steph. (Benedissh). Cott. xiii. 18 (26) (*copy*).

—— Conf. of above, 1206 (Benedis). Cott. xiii. 18 (22) (*copy*).

—— Rental of Bendish Hall manor, 1642. Harl. Roll S. 16.

**Beneacre.** *v.* Binacre, *co. Suff.*

**Benefeld.** *v.* Binfield, *in Shiplake, co. Oxon.*

**Benefield,** *co. Northt.* Power to give seisin in, 1364 (Benyfeld). Harl. 57 E. 18.

—— Warrant for payment for works on the king's lodge in, 1386 (Benefeld). Add. 10650.

—— (?) *Persona.* Simon, 1219 (Beinivilla). Harl. 50 A. 41.

—— *Rector.* Mag. Joh. la Zouche, 1348. Harl. 45 G. 36.

**Beneford.** *v.* Blandford, *co. Dors.*

**Benehale.** *v.* Benhall, *co. Suff.*

**Beneitleye.** *v.* Bentley, *co. Suff.*

**Benenden** (Benyndenne, etc.), *co. Kent.* Fine of the advowson to Combwell Priory, 1227 (Benindenne). Harl. 79 B. 44.

—— Grants, etc., in, 1333. Add. 16346;—1394. Add. 16347;—1432. Campb. vii. 17;—1548. Harl. 76 H. 51;—1551. Harl. 78 G. 81;— 1648. Add. 9424;—1760. Add. 5977.

—— Declaration conc. patronage of St. George's church in, 14 cent. (Benynden). Harl. Roll V. 13.

—— Lease in, from Combwell Priory, 1496. Harl. 75 G. 3.

—— Acquittances from Leeds Priory for aids to the King from the vicarage of, 1512–16. Harl. 44 F. 14, 15, 17, 18.

**Benniworth,** *co. Linc.* (*continued*). Grant in, *t.* Hen. III. (Benigwrð). Harl. 45 I. 51.

—— Release to Bullington Priory of payment for a chantry at, 1392 (Benyngworth). Harl. 49 F. 22.

—— Sale of the manor, 1572 (Benyngworth). Harl. 77 F. 55.

—— *Capellanus.* Benedictus, 1221. Harl. 43 I. 45; —early 13 cent.-*t.* Hen. III. Harl. 46 A. 3, 6, 34.

—— *Clericus.* Walterus, *c.* 1162. Harl. 44 E. 53.

—— *Persona.* Willelmus. early 13 cent. Harl. 45 I. 55, 46 A. 3, 10.

**Bennyngton.** *v.* Binnington, *co. York.*

**Bensham** (Benchesham, etc.), *in Croydon, co. Surr.* Covenant for warranty, and release of quit-rent, of the manor, 1230. Add. 23326; —*t.* Hen. III. Add. 23323.

—— Rental and court-roll of Hugo de Nevyle for the manor of, 1296, 1300, *n. d.* Add. 23324 (N. Benchesham), 23325 (N. Bunchesham).

—— Compotus of the manor, [1299?]. Add. 23441.

—— License from S., Bp. of London, to hold lands in, 1328 (N. Bynchesham). Add. 23327.

—— Grants, etc., in, 1357. Add. 23328; —1358. Add. 23329; —1359. Add. 23330; —1360. Add. 23331 (N. Bynchysham): —1361. Add. 23445 (N. Benchesham); — 1384. Add. 23447; —1385. Add. 23332.

*v. also* Croydon, *co. Surr.*

**Bensherne.** *v. sub* Harbledown, *co. Kent.*

**Bensinget., Bensinton.** *v.* Bilsington, *co. Kent.*

**Bensington,** *co. Oxon.* Conveyance, etc., in, 1416. Harl. 54 I. 34 (Bensyngton); —1440. Harl. 45 A. 26 (do.).

**Bensted.** *v.* Binstead, *co. Southt.*

**Benstede,** *in Cheveley, co. Camb.* Award conc. the manor, as held of Cheveley manor, 1582. Add. 19259.

—— Sale of the manor, 1620. Add. 19261.

**Benston,** *nr. Holt. co. Denb.* (?). Admission to lands in, 1450. Add. 8640.

**Bentcliff,** *in Eccles, co. Lanc.* Sale of annuity from the manor, 1571. Harl. 111 H. 15.

**Bentclyffe,** *nr. Bradford, co. York.* Surrender in, 1485. Add. 16925.

**Bentham,** *nr. Gloucester, co. Glouc.* Certificate concerning tenure of the manor, 1492. Add. 23845.

**Bentley,** *co. Southt.* Grants, etc., in, *t.* Edw. II. Add. 17401 (Benetlegh); —1326. Add. 17398-17400 (Benetlygh):—1333. Add. 17403 (Benetlexh), 17404 (Bentle):—1337. Add. 17405:—1350. Add. 17413 (Benetlie):—1417. Add. 17428 (Bentele); —1501, 1502. Add. 17436-17439.

—— Grant in Mere in, 1317. Add. 17393.

—— Grants in Coldrey in, 1323. Add. 10662; —1439. Add. 17432.

—— Power to give seisin of Purye [Bury?] manor in, 1447. Add. 17434.

**Bentley** (Benetlebe, Benetleye, Benteleye, etc.), *co. Suff.* Grants, etc., in, 1246. Add. 9485; —1256. Add. 9480, 9486; —1269. Add. 9487; —*t.* Hen. III. —1441. Add. 9466, 9467, 9469 (Bentel.), 9471 (Bentlebe), 9473 (Benethleye), 9474, 9476, 9478, 9479, 9481 (Benetl.), 9482, 9489 (Benetlegba), 9490 (Bunentleye), 9492-9502, 9504-9508, 9510, 9513-9516, 9520, 9521, 9524, 9528, 9534, 9538, 9540, 9545, 9548, 9551, 9553, 9555-9557, 9560, 9562, 9566-9571, 9573, 9574, 9576, 9579, 9589, 9591-9595, 9598-9600, 9602, 9603, 9605, 9606, 9610-9613, 9616, 9622, 9627-9629, 9634-9640, 9643, 9645, 9650, 9652, 9654, 9656-9658, 9667, 9671, 9674, 9675, 9677, 9681, 9683, 9688-9690, 9693, 9701, 9706;—1307. Add. 9872:—1359. Add. 8377;—1361. Add. 24246;—1371. Add. 10570;—1383. Add. 10201;— 1464. Harl. 55 C. 43 (Bentlegh).

—— Grant of rents from Buxton (Bugestune) mill, etc., in, to the Knights Hospitallers, late Hen. III. Add. 9472.

—— Lease of the manor, 1396 (Benteleye). Add. 9671.

—— Receipts of Tho. Fyncham at, 14 cent. Add. 9588.

—— Suit concerning the manors of Bentleyhowes, etc., 1456. Add. 17244.

—— Petition for restoration to lands in, [1461]. Harl. 55 H. 29.

—— *Clericus.* Radulfus, *t.* Edw. I. Add. 9493, 9495.

—— *Vicarius.* Rogerus, 1276. Add. 9517.

Bentley, *co. Suff. (continued). Vicarius (perpetuus) (continued).* Thomas *al.* Tho. Werri, 1348. Add. 9610–9612;— 1358. Add. 9629.

——— Henricus, 1400. Add. 10048.

*v. also* Dodnash, *co. Suff.*

Bentley, *in Shustoke, co. Warw.* Grant in, 1323 (Benttleye). Add. 1503.

——— Sale of the parsonage, 1540. Harl. 47 A. 53.

Bentley, *in Arksey, co. York.* Grants, etc., early Hen. III. Harl. 111 D. 29 (Benetlai);—late Hen. III. Cott. xxix. 61 (Bentlay):—1382. Add. 20606 (Bentelay);—1463. Harl. 112 B. 24; —1478. Harl. 50 C. 28.

——— Fine of the manor, 1391. Add. 19221.

Bentley, *in Chapel Allerton, co. York.* Grants, etc., of Headdingley mill in, etc., *t.* Edw. I. or II. Add. 16750, 16765 (Bentelay in Allerton);—1322. Add. 16792 (Bentlay in Allerton);— 1323. Add. 16776 (do.), 16777, 16793.

Bentley, *in Emley. v. sub* Emley, *co. York.*

Bentley (Bentele), *in Rowley, co. York.* Grants, etc., in, *t.* Edw. I. Lansd. 420, 421;—1321. Lansd. 422; —1349. Lansd. 423;—1354. Lansd. 437.

——— Sale of " vestura bladi " on land in, 1356. Lansd. 424.

——— Grant for endowment of a chantry in Beverley from the manor of, 1371. Lansd. 425.

——— Lease of recusants' land in, 1635. Add. 6273.

Bentley, Fenny *al.* Hungry, *co. Derb.* Grants, etc., in, *c.* 1160–70. Harl. 45 F. 23 (Benethleia);—1377. Woll. iii. 4 (Benteleye);—1380. Woll. iii. 6;—1382. Woll. iii. 5.

——— Lease of the manor, 1746 (Hungary Bentley). Woll. xi. 117.

Bentley, Great, *co. Essex.* Precipe on a covenant in, 1578. Add. 24958.

Bentley, Little, *co. Essex. Rector.* Walt. le Gros, 1340. Harl. 51 A. 3.

Bentworth, *co. Southt.* Precipe on a covenant conc. land in, 1593. Add. 25233.

Benyndenne. *v.* Benenden, *co. Kent.*

Benynghoo. *v.* Bengeo, *co. Hertf.*

Benyngton. *v.* Beddington, *co. Surr.*

Benyngworth. *v.* Benniworth, *co. Linc.*

Beohhæma Mearc. *v.* Beckenham, *co. Kent.*

Beoley, *co. Worc.* Conf. of grants in, to Pershore Abbey, 972 (Beoleah). Cott. MS Aug. ii. 6.

Beoraham. *v.* Barham, *co. Kent.*

Beorgan stede. *v.* Bersted, *co. Suss.*

Beornothes leah. *v.* Barnsley, *co. Worc.*

Berbald, *co.* ———. License from the Knts. Hospitallers to appoint a chaplain in St. Mary's Chapel, *c.* 1240. Add. 15521 (*copy*).

Bercamsted, Berch., Berchamested. *v.* Berkhampstead, *co. Hertf.*

Bercham. *v.* Barham, *co. Suff.*

Berchelaia. *v.* Berkeley, *co. Glouc.*

Bercheweie. *v.* Barkway, *co. Hertf.*

Bercholt. *v.* Bergholt, West, *co. Essex.*

Bercompe. *v.* Barcombe, *co. Suss.*

Bercroft. *v.* Barcroft, *in Pudsey, co. York.*

Berdefeld. *v.* Bardfield, *co. Essex.*

Berdefeld Salyngg, Berdfeld Salyng. *v.* Saling, Lit., *co. Essex.*

Berdewell. *v.* Bardwell, *co. Suff.*

Bere. *v. sub* Waltham, *co. Kent.*

Bere, *in Shilling Okeford, co. Dors.* Conveyance of the manor, etc., 1453. Harl. 53 A. 24, 54 D. 19;—1498. Harl. 53 C. 13.

Bere, *co. Worc.* (?). Conf. of a grant of a mill at, to Bordesley Abbey, [1138 ?]. Add. 20419.

Bere Forest, *co. Southt.* Sale of timber in, to Winchester Priory, 1298–9. Add. 19292 (3).

——— Grant of custody of game in, 1669. Add. 19001.

Bere Craucombe. *v.* Beer Crocombe, *co. Som.*

Bere Hackett, *co. Dors. Persona.* Hugo, *t.* Edw. I. (Bere). Campb. vi. 8.

Bere Regis, *co. Dors.* Release to Bec Herlouin Abbey from suits of court at, for lands in Milborne Stileham in, 1340 (Ber). Toph. 29.

**Bere Regis**, co. Dors. (continued). Writ to give seisin in, 1477 (Kyngesbyre). Harl. 53 G. 49.

—— Grant of custody of a third part of Abbot's Court (Abesoourte) manor, etc., in, [1550–53] (Kingesbere). Cott. MS. Vesp. F. xiii. Art. 222.

—— Grant of the advowson, 1578 (Beere). Harl. 77 G. 1.

—— Dominus. Ric. de Turbervill, miles, 1310. Toph. 29.

**Bereacre**, in Bridge, co. Kent. Grant of the manor, etc., 1507. Harl. 79 B. 3;—1508. Harl. 78 E. 20.

**Berebyre**. v. Barbury, co. Wilts.

**Berecroft**. v. Barcroft, in Pudsey, co. York.

**Berefeld**. v. Burghfield, co. Berks.

**Bereford**. v. Barford, co. Bedf. (?).

—— v. Barford, co. Warw.

—— v. Barford, Great al. St. Michael, co. Oxon.

**Bereford Olof, Bereford Oloof**. v. Barford Oluff, co. Oxon.

**Beres Manor**. v. sub Geldeston, co. Norf.

**Bereton**. v. Bierton al. Burton, nr. Aylesbury, co. Buck.

**Bereueg**. v. Berwick (?), co. Kent.

**Berewardcote**. v. Bearwardcote, in Etwall, co. Derb.

**Berewe**, co. ——. Grant in, "apud Keysende," 1423. Add. 8452.

**Berewell**, v. sub Petworth, co. Suss.

**Bereweremersche**. v. Burmarsh, co. Kent.

**Berewic**. v. Barwick in Elmett, co. York.

**Berewich, Berewyk**. v. Berwick on Tweed, co. Berw.

**Berewyc**. v. Berwick Basset, co. Wilts.

**Berewyc, Berewyke**. v. Berwick Prior (?), co. Oxon.

**Berewyke**. v. Berwick St. James, co. Wilts.

—— v. Berwick St. John, co. Wilts.

**Berford**. v. Barford, Great al. St. Michael, co. Oxon.

**Berford Oloof**. v. Barford Oluff, co. Oxon.

**Berfyld**. v. Burghfield, co. Berks.

**Berg., Bergen**. v. Abergavenny, co. Monm.

**Berga**. v. Berrow, co. Worc.

**Bergebi**. v. Barby, co. Northt.

**Bergh**. v. Bargh, co. York.

**Bergham**. v. Barham, co. Suff.

**Bergholt, East**, co. Suff. Grants, etc., in, 1292. Harl. 56 H. 8 (Berkholte); —1319. Add. 10584;—1324. Add. 9920;—1346. Add. 9608, 9609;— 1349. Add. 9615;—1381. Add. 9653 (Berholte).

**Bergholt, West**, co. Essex. Grants, etc., in, 1273. Harl. 56 C. 24;—1289. Harl. 45 D. 14 (Bercholt);—t. Edw. I. Harl. 46 A. 48 (Barkholte);—early 14 cent. Harl. 46 A. 38;—1433. Add. 5253.

**Berham**. v. Barham, co. Kent.

—— v. Barholme, co. Linc.

**Berheby**. v. Barby, co. Northt.

**Berhhom**. v. Burham, nr. Linton, co. Camb.

**Berk**. v. Bargh, co. York.

**Berkamested**. v. Berkhampstead, co. Hertf.

**Berkeford**, co. Suff. (?). Exch. in, t. Edw. I. Add. 9492.

**Berkeforde**. v. Barford, Great, co. Bedf.

**Berkeley**, co. Glouc. Conf. by Hen. II. of the church of, to Reading Abbey, 1157 (Berchelais). Add. 19591.

—— Grants in, 1308. Add. 5274 (Berkelaye);—1397. Add. 9244;— 1405. Add. 9245;—1425. Add. 9248.

**Berkelowe**. v. Bartlow, co. Camb.

**Berkeswell**, co. Warw. Precipe on a covenant in, 1592 (Barkeswell). Add. 25546.

**Berkhampstead**, co. Hertf. Grants of, to Odo and Alberic de Dammartin, [1141–53?] (terra de Bechansted). Add. 11233 (5);—t. Hen. II. (terra de Bichchamestede). Add. 11233 (6).

—— Release to Biddlesdon Abbey from ward to, for lands in Charwelton, co. Northt., [1198–9?] (Berchamested). Harl. 85 A. 58.

—— Grants, etc., in the honour, halimote, liberty and town of, early 13 cent. Harl. 50 H. 39, 85 C. 10 (Berkamested), 85 E. 50 (Berchamested), 86 B. 5 (do.);—t. Hen. III. Cott. xxvii. 38

**Berks,** *County of (continued).* *Vice-comes (continued).* Joh. Archer, 1693. Add. 19235.

—— *Coronator Dni. Regis.* Edm. Le Budon, 1381. Add. 13031.

**Berley,** *nr. Blithfield, co. Staff.* Release in, 1388. Cott. xxviii. 104.

**Berling, Berlinges.** *v.* Birling, *co. Kent.*

**Bermancherch, S. Martinus de.** *v.* London, St. Martin Vintry parish.

**Bermondsey** (Bermundesey, etc.), *co. Surr.* Grants, etc., in the parish of St. Mary Magdalen in, 1381. Harl. 76 C. 52;—1384. Harl. 76 G. 2;—1385. Harl. 76 C. 49;—1386. Harl. 76 C. 47;—1396. Harl. 76 C. 50;—1398. Harl. 76 C. 51;—1399. Harl. 76 C. 48;—1400. Harl. 78 A. 15, 78 B. 50;—1412. Harl. 79 B. 22;—1432. Harl. 77 D. 56;—1436. Harl. 76 C. 31;—1443. Harl. 77 F. 1;—1457. Harl. 76 G. 31, 32;—1467. Harl. 80 I. 82;—1472. Harl. 80 I. 83;—1510. Harl. 78 E. 30 (Barmondesry);—1597. Harl. 48 C. 4a (Barmondsey);—1599. Harl. 51 H. 32;—1684. Eg. 325, 326;—1697. Eg. 330.

—— Conveyance of St. Saviour's mill in, 1617 (Barmsey). Harl. 58 H. 28 (*draft*).

—— *Rector (nuper).* Joh. Lorkys, 1384. Harl. 76 G. 2.

—— —— Joh. Andever, 1467. Harl. 80 I. 82.

—— —— Joh. Paget, 1718. Add. 26396.

**Bernak, Berneche.** *v.* Barnack, *co. Northt.*

**Bernecestria.** *v.* Bicester, *co. Oxon.*

**Bernemerss,** *nr. Cricksea, co. Essex.* Compotus-roll of, 1365-6. Lansd. 630.

**Bernerdisley.** *v.* Barnsley, *in Wimborne Minster, co. Dors.*

**Berners Roothing.** *v.* Roothing, Berners, *co. Essex.*

**Berneshag Wood.** *v.* Barns Hagwood, *co. Linc.*

**Bernesole.** *v.* Barnsole, *in Woodnesborough, co. Kent.*

**Berneston.** *v.* Barnston, *co. Essex.*

—— *v.* Barnstone, *co. Nott.*

**Bernet Manor,** *co. Kent.* Grant of, 1407. Harl. 76 G. 39.

**Bernetebi.** *v.* Barnetby le Wold, *co. Linc.*

**Bernewell.** *v.* Barnwell, *co. Camb.*

**Bernewelle** *al.* **Bernewelle Moigne.** *v.* Barnwell St. Andrew's, *co. Northt.*

**Bernewelle Regis.** *v.* Barnwell All Saints, *co. Northt.*

**Bernham.** *v.* Barnham, *co. Suff.*

—— *v.* Barnham Broom, *co. Norf.*

**Bernhorn.** *v.* Barnhorn, *co. Suss.*

**Bernislay.** *v.* Barnsley, *co. York.*

**Bernolby.** *v.* Barnoldby le Beck, *co. Linc.*

**Bernolveswik.** *v.* Barnoldswick, *co. York.*

**Bernwood** *al.* **Barnwood Forest,** *co. Buck.* Covenant for a fine of the keepership, etc., of, 1547. Harl. 79 G. 13.

—— Excheq. acquittance for rent of herbage, etc., in, 1576. Add. 25641.

**Bernyngham.** *v.* Barningham, *co. Suff.*

**Berriew,** *co. Montgom.* Lease in, 1638 (Berryw). Add. 1038.

—— Briefs for rebuilding the church, 1794, 1801. Ch. Br. B. xxxiv. 3, xli. 7.

**Berrington,** *co. Glouc.* Release in, 1362 (Beruyngton). Harl. 58 D. 45.

**Berrow,** *co. Worc.* Grants, etc., in, t. Edw. I. Add. 24750, Slo. xxxiii. 7 (La Berwe), 10 (Berga);—1304. Slo. xxxiii. 16 (Berga); — 1431. Slo. xxxiii. 65 (Berewe).

—— Feoffment in (?), 1304 (La Barwe). Add. 5306.

—— *Clericus.* Robertus, t. Edw. I. Add. 24750.

**Berry Down,** *nr. Combe Martin, co. Devon.* Lease of "le Tvychyn" in, 1450 (Byrydowne). Add. 13059.

**Bersham,** *co. Denb.* Grant, etc., in, 1470. Add. 8644 (Borasham hous);—1484. Add. 8645.

—— Fines in, 1618. Add. 8657, 8658.

**Bersted, North and South,** *co. Suss.* Grant at, to Bp. Wilfrid. 680 (*sic*) (Beorgan stede). Cott. MS. Aug. ii. 86.

**Bersted, North,** *co. Suss.* Fine in, 1457 (Northberstede). Add. 24902.

**Berys Manor.** *v. sub* Geldeston, co. *Norf.*

**Besacre.** *v.* Bessacarr, *in Cantley*, co. *York.*

**Besby, Besebi, Beseby, Besibi.** *v.* Beesby, co. *Linc.*

**Besford,** co. *Worc.* Conf. of grants in, to Pershore Abbey, 972 (in Bettesforda). Cott. MS. Aug. ii. 6.

—— *Clericus.* Alexander, *t.* Edw. I. Harl. 83 A. 37 (*copy*).

**Bessacarr,** *in Cantley*, co. *York.* Grant in, to Newhouse Abbey, *t.* Hen. III. (Besacre). Harl. 46 D. 22.

**Bessehegh, Besshehey.** *v. sub* Holditch, co. *Devon.*

**Bessingby,** co. *York.* Conf. by Hen. I. of grants in, to Bridlington Priory. [1128–32] (Basingebi). Cott. MS. Aug. ii. 56.

—— Excheq. acquittance for a fine in, 1596. Add. 25719.

**Bessingham** (Basingham, Basyngham), co. *Norf.* Customary roll of the manor, *t.* Hen. III. or Edw. I. Add. 688.*

—— Grants, etc., of the manor, 1343. Add. 14518;—1370. Add. 14867;—1434. Add. 17738;—1435. Add. 17739.

—— Bequests to the church, etc., 1482. Add. 17253.

**Besthorpe,** co. *Norf.* Declar. of uses of a fine in, 1687. Add. 19100.

**Bestone.** *v.* Beeston St. Andrew's, co. *Norf.*

**Bestorp.** *v.* Beesthorpe, co. *Nott.*

**Bestwood Park,** co. *Nott.* Conf. of grant of the keepership of, to Lord Cromwell. 1437. Cott. MS. Vesp. F. xiii. art. 72.

—— Leases in, 1681. Add. 15862, 15864.

**Beswick** (Beswyk), co. *York.* Grants, etc., in, 1371. Add. 5756; — 1407. Add. 5759;—1415. Add. 904;—1521. Add. 5791, 5792;—1524. Add. 5795.

**Betchworth,** co. *Surr.* Grant in Cotstedele nr., early Hen. III. Add. 8794.

—— Conf. by J. de Warenne of a grant in, 1254 (Estbecheworth). Add. 24551, 24552.

—— Assignm. of the manor to Edw. II., 1316 (Becheworth). Harl. 57 E. 33.

**Betchworth,** co. *Surr.* (*continued*). Title to lands in, late 15 cent. (Becheworth). Add. 9043.

**Betelesd., Betlesdena, Bettlesdena, Bethlesdena, etc.** *v.* Biddlesdon, co. *Buck.*

**Betelesford,** co. *Suss.* Battle Abbey freed from services for, [1100–23]. Harl. 43 C. 12.

**Bethersden,** co. *Kent.* Grants, etc., in, 1291–2. Add. 16394 (Bederesden); —1346. Add. 19993 (Beteresdenn); —1607. Harl. 79 F. 42.

—— Grant in Runsell (Rynsole) dene, Chillardindene, etc., in, 1342 (Beterchesdenne). Add. 19992.

—— Feoffment of Etchden (Hacchesden) manor, etc., in, 1410 (Beatrisden). Add. 16372.

—— Title to lands in, *post* 1439 (Beterisden). Harl. 78 F. 40, 41.

—— Fine in, 1548. Harl. 75 H. 4, 76 H. 50.

**Bethnal Green,** co. *Midd.* Grant in trust of houses in, 1642. Add. 4891.

**Betmeswell.** *v.* Bitteswell, co. *Leic.*

**Betreton.** *v.* Betterton, co. *Berks.*

**Betshanger,** co. *Kent.* Grant in, 1349 (Betlishangre). Cott. xxvii. 27.

**Betterton,** co. *Berks.* Covenant conc. service in, due by Poughley Priory, 1244 (Westbatorton). Add. 10604.

—— Release of above service to Bicester Priory, *post* 1244 (Betreton). Add. 10603.

**Bettesforda.** *v.* Besford, co. *Worc.*

**Bettiscombe,** co. *Dors.* *Rector.* Adam Cotheleston *al.* Codelstone, 1409. Harl. 47 H. 10;—1426. Harl. 48 F. 44.

**Bettws Gwerfil Goch,** co. *Merion.* Brief for rebuilding the church, 1776. Ch. Br. B. xvi. 1.

**Bettws Newydd,** co. *Monm.* Releases in, 1452. Add. 5344 (Bethouse Newithe);—1547. Add. 5347 (Bettous Newith).

**Beuchamp Ottonis.** *v.* Belchamp Otton, co. *Essex.*

**Beuchamp Wauter.** *v.* Belchamp Walter, co. *Essex.*

**Beudeford.** *v.* Belchford, co. *Linc.*

**Beudesert.** *v.* Beaudesert, co. *Warw.*

**Beumarreys.** *v.* Beaumaris, co. *Angl.*

Beverley (Beverlacum, etc.), co. *York*
(*continued*). *Ballivus* (*continued*). Ric.
Roce, 1323. Lansd. 256; — 1328.
Lansd. 263, 264.

—— —— Jac. Lyouns, 1368.
Lansd. 321.

—— *Ballivus Archiepiscopi Ebor. de
Beverlaco.* Joh. Tikhill, 1414. Lansd.
457.

—— *Custodes sive gubernatores.*
     Rog. Rolleston.
     Joh. Brompton.
     Tho. Skypwith.
     Tho. Yole.
     Tho. White.
     Joh. Sleforth.
     Tho. Lovirsal.
     Tho. Lyndlowe.
     Will. Syxhill.
     Tho. Dene.
     Rob. Wartyr.
     Rob. Bevine.
1425. Add. 15888.

—— *Servientes Burgi.* Joh. le Boteler,
Alex. le Caretter, late 13 cent. Lansd.
224.

—— *Clericus communitatis ville.* Joh.
Thorn, 1449. Lansd. 370.

Beverley Manor. *v. sub* Harbledown,
*co. Kent.*

Bewholme (Beaugham), co. *York.*
Release of the manor, etc., 1430. Harl.
43 E. 19;—1431. Harl. 45 I. 12, 54 I.
15 (Beaughom);—1435. Add. 2016.

Bewick, *nr. Aldborough,* co. *York.*
Conf. by Hen. II. of the exchange of,
for Meaux, [1163–6] (Bewich). Cott.
xi. 27.

Bewsfield *al.* Whitfield. *v.* Whitfield, *co. Kent.*

Bexhill, *co. Suss.* Conf. of tithes of
Buckholt (Boccholte) in, to Battle
Abbey, [1121–5]. Cott. MS. Nero
C. iii. f. 189.

—— Lease of Buckholt (Bocholte)
manor, etc., in, 1281. Add. 16182.

Bexington, *co. Dors.* Conf. of a grant
of the manor to Bindon Abbey, 1234
(Bixinton). Harl. 58 H. 45 (*copy*).

—— Grant of the manor and advowson, 1545. Add. 18827.

—— Recovery of the manor, 1587.
Add. 9189.

Bexley. *v.* Bixley, *co. Norf.*

Bexley, *co. Kent.* Grant at, 814
(Byxlea). Cott. MS. Aug. ii. 77.

—— Feoffment of the church and
vicarage, 1476. Add. 23733.

Bexley, *co. Kent* (*continued*). *Vicarius
perpetuus.* Joh. Selby, 1476. Add.
23733.

Beyardregg, *in Wye Manor, co. Kent.*
Conf. of a grant of tithes of, to Battle
Abbey, [1114–22]. Harl. 43 G. 18.

Beyeley, Beyleye. *v.* Beeley, *co.
Derb.*

Beyhalle, Le. *v. sub* Pembury, *co.
Kent.*

Beysbroke, *co. Wilts.* Pipe-roll acquittance for dues from the manor,
1536–7. Add. 18280.

Beyssam. *v.* Baysham, *nr. Ross, co.
Heref.*

Beytley. *v.* Beeley, *co. Derb.*

Bheuhenham. *v.* Beckenham, *co.
Kent.*

Biars Park. *v. sub* Hartleyburn, *co.
Northumb.*

Bibleham Manor. *v. sub* Mayfield,
*co. Suss.*

Bibsworth, *in Kimpton, co. Hertf.*
Grant in, to Hertford Priory, late Hen.
II. (Bibewrthia). Campb. x. 12.

—— *Clericus.* Robertus, late Hen. II.
Campb. x. 12.

Bibury, *co. Glouc.* Livery of the
manor, etc., 1561. Add. 19542.

Bicester (Berneccstria, Berencestria,
Burencestria, Burnecestria, etc.), *co.
Oxon.* Grants, etc., in, to Bicester
Priory, [1182]. Add. 10593, 10595,
10616, 10617; — [1205 – 15]. Add.
10605;—early Hen. III. Add. 10612;
—c. 1250. Add. 10614;—1286. Add.
10624;—1323. Add. 10630.

—— Grant of Gravenhull and Cub-
rugge in, to the same, [1205–15]. Add.
10601.

—— Grants, etc., in. [1205–15]. Add.
10607;—4. Hen. III. Add. 10599;—
c. 1270–80. Add. 10606;—1295. Add.
10625;—1316. Add. 10628;—1318.
Add. 10629;—1332. Add. 10631,
10632;—1337 (Burncestre). Add.
10633.

—— Suit for tithes in, betw. Bicester
Priory and Oseney Abbey, 1300 (Buren-
cestre). Add. 10627.

—— Power to distrain on the manor,
1334. Add. 21417.

—— *Clericus.* Robertus, early Edw. I.
Add. 10606, 10615, 10618.

—— —— Robertus, 1316. Add.
10628.

Biddlesdon (Betlesden, Bethlesdena, etc.), co. *Buck.* (*continued*). Royal and other conff. of grants in, to the abbey, c. 1147. Harl. 84 H. 18;—1150-51. Harl. 84 C. 2, 41 (Bettesdena). 47, 48, 85 G. 48;—[1153?]. Harl. 84 C. 3;—[1155?]. Harl. 84 C. 4. 5;—*ante* 1166. Harl. 84 D. 1 (Betelsad.);—late 12 cent. Harl. 84 H. 52;—1251. Harl. 84 D. 6 (Bettlesdena);— 1265-6. Harl. 84 C. 40 (Bytlesden).

—— Covenants betw. Biddlesdon and St. Mary de Pré Abbeys conc. tithes in, etc., c. 1150-60. Harl. 84 D. 12;—1209. Harl. 84 D. 19;—1382. Harl. 84 F. 7.

—— Bond to Biddlesdon Abbey of rent in Water Stratford, co. Buck., "ad fabricam ecclesie de Bethlesden," late 13 cent. Harl. 85 A. 23.

—— Grants in, from Biddlesdon Abbey, 1317. Harl. 84 E. 54 (Byttlesden);—1392. Harl. 84 F. 10 (Buttullusden).

—— License to the abbey to enclose a roadway in, 1385. Harl. 84 C. 18.

—— Crown acquittance for service for the manor, 1559 (Bytlesden). Harl. 86 B. 19.

—— Release in, 1575 (Beddlesden). Harl. 86 B. 2.

Bideford, co. *Devon.* Grant of a market and fair in the manor of, 1272. Harl. 58 I. 31 (copy).

—— Award conc. land in, 1499. Add. 5148.

—— Return of the yearly value of the manor, etc., 1572 (Bedford). Cott. xvii. 22.

Bidford, co. *Warw.* Grants, etc., of, with royal conff. to Bordesley Abbey, [1138?]. Harl. 45 I. 30 (Budefurdia). Add. 20419 (Budifordia);—[1141?]. Harl. 43 C. 13 (Bideford);—[1141-2]. Add. 20420;—[1157?]. Cott. MS. Nero C. iii. f. 176.

—— Grant of the manor in dower, c. 1222 (Budiford). Cott. xxiv. 17.

—— Recovery in, 1608. Add. 7040.

Bidminden, boscus de. *v. sub* Farleigh, E., co. *Kent.*

Bidynden. *v.* Biddenden, co. *Kent.*

Bierley (Byrille), *in* Bradford, co. *York.* Grant, etc., at "Le Parkhous" in, 1465. Add. 16955;—1466. Add. 16956.

Bierlyng. *v.* Birling, co. *Kent.*

Bierton *al.* Burton, *nr.* Aylesbury, co. *Buck.* Recovery in, 1497 (Bereton). Add. 13929.

—— Rental of Bierton and Broughton Abbots Manors, 1627 (Beerton). Cott. i. 4.

Biethum. *v.* Beetham, co. *Westm.*

Bifeld, Biffeld. *v.* Byfield, co. *Northt.*

Biflet. *v.* Byfleet, co. *Surr.*

Biford. *v.* Beeford, co. *York.*

Bigberry. *v. sub* Harbledown, co. *Kent.*

Bigbury, co. *Devon.* Award conc. land in, 1499 (Bikbery). Add. 5148.

Bigbury, *Isle of Wight.* Grant of free warren in, to Quarr Abbey, 1284 (Bykebergh). Add. 15701.

Biggin Manor. *v. sub* Wirksworth, co. *Derb.*

Biggins *al.* Byggyng Manor. *v. sub* Mitcham, co. *Surr.*

Biggleswade, co. *Bedf.* Grant in, 1386 (Bykeleswade). Harl. 46 D. 50.

Bighton, co. *Southt.* Rector. Johannes, 1382. Harl. 46 F. 9.

Bigod's Manor. *v. sub* Tofts, West, co. *Norf.*

Bigrave. *v.* Bygrave, co. *Hertf.*

Bikemers. *v.* Bickmarsh, co. *Warw.*

Bikenhulle. *v.* Bickenhill, co. *Warw.*

Bikenore. *v.* Bicknor, co. *Kent.*

Bikenore Galeys. *v.* Bicknor, Welsh, co. *Heref.*

Biketun. *v.* Bicton, co. *Pembr.*

Bikir. *v.* Bicker, co. *Linc.*

Bikirwude in Macwrh. *v. sub* Mackworth, co. *Derb.*

Bilawe. *v.* Belaugh, co. *Norf.*

Bilawe Manor, co. *Suff.* (*sic*). Claim for arrears of a rent in, 1434. Harl. Roll C. 30.

Bilbrough, co. *York.* Grant, etc., in, t. Edw. I. Harl. 53 E. 42 (Bilburg);—1641. Add. 1798.

—— Sale of the manor, 1637. Add. 1797.

Bilchangr. *v.* Birchanger, co. *Essex.*

Bildeston. *v.* Bilston, co. *Leic.*

Bildeston, co. *Suff.* Bequests at (?), to Stoke Monastery, late 10 cent. (at Byliges dyne, etc.). Harl. 43 C. 4.

Bingham, *co. Nott. (continued).* Precipe on a covenant conc. lands in, 1578 (Byngham in Le Vale). Add. 25191.

—— *Rector.* Ricardus, 1345. Woll. ii. 25.

Bingham Hundred, *co. Nott.* Exchequer acquittance for a subsidy from, 1576. Add. 25635.

Bingley (Byngley), *co. York.* Grants in, 1485. Add. 16966;—1547. Add. 17010, 17011.

—— *Vicarius.* Joh. Hunte, 1454. Add. 16946.

Binnebroc. *v.* Binbrook, *co. Linc.*

Binningham, *nr. Occold, co. Suff.* Grants, etc., in, *t.* Hen. III. Harl. 50 C. 33 (Benigham);—1308. Harl. 47 A. 15 (Beningham).

Binnington, *co. York.* Grant in, 1555 (Benington *al.* Bennyngton). Add. 13099.

Binscomb, *in Godalming, co. Surr.* Sale in, 1587 (Bynscombe). Add. 13577.

Binstead, *co. Suss.* Exchequer acquittance for farm of land in, 1595. Add. 25671.

Binsted (Bensted, etc.), *co. Southt.* Lease in Isington (Esedentone) in, by Waverley Abbey, *post* 1286. Add. 26611.

—— Grants in S. Hay and Week, etc., in, 1302. Add. 26612, 26613;— 1305. Add. 26615;— 1309. Add. 26617;—1313. Add. 26620, 26621;—1322. Add. 26622;—1323. Add. 26623;—1332. Add. 26624;—1333. Add. 26625 (Bynstede);—1336. Add. 26627;— 1338. Add. 20214 (Byenstede), 20215;—1352. Add. 26630;—1357. Add. 17414;—1370. Add. 26635;—1400. Add. 26638, 26639;—1447. Add. 17434;—1471. Add. 26667, 26668.

—— Lands late bought in Wheatley (Whately) in, from Waverley Abbey, 1406. Add. 26611.

—— Precipe on a covenant conc. land in, 1593. Add. 25237.

—— Sales in, 1610, 1611. Add. 8503, 8504.

—— Fines in, 1610. Add. 8501, 8502;—1622. Add. 8514.

Binton, *co. Warw.* Release in, 1325 (Bunynton). Add. 24759.

Bintree, *co. Norf.* Grant in, 1380 (Byntre). Add. 15498.

Binweston, *in Worthin, co. Salop.* Covenant conc. reversion of the manor, 1315. Add. 20438.

Biohahhema mearc. *v.* Beckenham, *co. Kent.*

Birch, Great (Magna Brich, Brych), *co. Essex.* Grants, etc., in, *t.* Hen. III. Harl. 46 F. 18, 50 G. 20, 22;—1316. Harl. 46 F. 19, Lansd. 102;—1375. Harl. 54 A. 42;—1398. Harl. 57 B. 30;—1453. Harl. 47 D. 24.

—— Precipe on a covenant conc. lands in, 1592. Add. 24996.

—— Precipe on a covenant conc. Will. a Birches manor, etc., in, 1593. Add. 25027.

Birch, Little, *co. Essex.* Grant in, 1357 (Parva Briche). Harl. 51 F. 17.

Birch, Much and Little, *co. Heref.* Grant in, 1654. Add. 1953.

Birchanger, *co. Essex.* Grant in, by Tremhall Priory, *c.* 1200 (Bilchangr.). Harl. 45 A. 8.

Birchett. *v. sub* Dronfield, *co. Derb.*

Birchill. *v. sub* Bakewell, *co. Derb.*

Birchover (Birchouer, Bircheouere, etc.), *in Youlgreave, co. Derb.* Grant, etc., of the mill or lands in, *t.* Edw. I. Woll. ii. 7, 11, 29;—1345. Woll. ii. 64;—1349. Woll. ii. 24, 67;—1351. Woll. ii. 17;—1379. Woll. ii. 28;—1502. Woll. ii. 68 (Birchore);—1549. Woll. xi. 67 (Byrcheover);— 1550. Woll. xi. 78 (Byrcheor);—1602. Woll. xi. 79.

—— Grant of the manor, 1336. Woll. ii. 66.

—— Lease of tithes in, from Leicester Abbey, 1535 (Burchore). Woll. xi. 74.

—— Lease of the lordship of, 1541 (Byrcheover). Woll. xi. 66.

—— Exemplif. of recovery of part of the manor, 1647 (Bircher). Woll. xii. 141.

—— *Lord of.* Tho. Kenylmarch, 1502. Woll. ii. 68.

*v. also* Youlgreave, *co. Derb.*

Birchwood (Birchewude), *co. Nott.* Grant with conf. in, [1203–4]. Harl. 83 G. 18;—*c.* 1203–4. Harl. 112 G. 53.

**Birdbrook,** *co. Essex.* Precipe conc. land in, 1561 (Byrdebroke). Add. 24934.

—— Estreats of courts of Birdbrook and Harsted (Hersted) manors, 1577 (Byrdbrok). Add. 1276.

**Birdham,** *co. Suss.* Assignment of lands in, 1501 (Byrdeham). Add. 18790.

—— Fine in, 1561 (Bridham). Add. 24906.

—— Award in, 1579 (Bordham). Eg. 298.

**Birdsall,** *co. York.* Release in, to Watton priory, 1322 (Bridsal). Harl. 55 E. 23.

**Birgham,** *in Eccles, co. Berwick.* Appointment of a Deputy to hold "jours de marches" at, 1394 (Brigehamhalgh). Woll. v. 7.

**Birkby,** *co. York.* Brief for rebuilding the church, 1773. Ch. Br. B. xiii. 7.

**Birkdale,** *co. Lanc.* *Rector.* Hen. Wright, 1626 (?). Add. 1688.

**Birling,** *co. Kent.* Inspex. in 1280, and conf. of grant of a mill at, to Fontevrault Abbey, 1200 (Berlinges). Harl. 58 I. 34 (copy).

—— Grants, etc., in, 1345. Harl. 45 C. 24 (Berling);—1367. Harl. 48 E. 24 (Bierlyng);—1381. Harl. 48 E. 36 (Bierling).

—— Bond and fine in, 1538. Harl. 51 C. 48 (Byrlyng);—1539. Harl. 46 I. 18, 19.

—— Mortgage and lease of the manor, 1578, 1582. Add. 23798, 23799.

**Birlingham,** *co. Worc.* Conf. of grants in, to Pershore Abbey, 972 (in Byrlingahamme). Cott. MS. Aug. ii. 6.

**Birlingham, North.** *v.* Burlingham St. Andrew, *co. Norf.*

**Birmingham,** *co. Warw.* Assignment of dower in the manor, 1387 (Burmyngham). Harl. 47 C. 15.

—— Grant, etc., in, 1489. Add. 16189 (Birmycham) (copy);—1519. Add. 16190 (Brymmycham).

—— *Bailiff.* Rog. Foxall, 1519. Add. 16190.

—— *Constable.* Will. Niccols al. Merch, 1519. Add. 16190.

**Birstall,** *co. Leic.* Release in, 1519 (Bristale). Add. 7173.

**Birstall** (Byrstal, etc.), *co. York.* Grants, etc., in, late 13 cent. or t.

Edw. I. Add. 8205, 8274;—1293. Add. 12633 (Berstal);—1305. Add. 8284;—early 14 cent. Add. 8236 (Bristall) (copy), 8262;—t. Edw. III. Add. 8212;—1331. Add. 12636;—1342. Add. 12639;—1373. Add. 8313;—1413. Add. 8321;—1415. Add. 8322, 12643;—1438. Add. 8326.

—— *Rector.* Tho. de Dalton, late 13 cent. Add. 8274.

—— *Vicarius.* Dom. Rob. Davy al. David, 1381. Add. 15660;—1401. Add. 16891.

—— —— Ric. Lyversege, 1405. Add. 8319.

—— —— Tho. Gudale, 1452. Add. 8327.

—— —— Joh. Kent, 1483. Add. 19345.

**Birston.** *v.* Burston, *co. Norf.*

**Birstowe.** *v.* Burstow, *co. Surr.*

**·Birtham Sands,** *co. Linc.* Note of a wreck at, 1500. Harl. 48 I. 30.

**Birthorpe,** *in Sempringham, co. Linc.* Grant in. to Croyland Abbey, *t.* Hen. III. (Burthorpe). Campb. iii. 13.

**Birtley** (Birteley), *co. Northumb.* Warrant of Edw. I. to give seisin of the manor, 1303. Harl. 43 D. 8.

—— Settlement of the manor, *t.* Edw. II. Harl. 58 G. 22.

**Bisbiche.** *v. sub* Marden, *co. Kent.*

**Bisbrooke,** *co. Rutl.* Restoration of the church to Daventry Priory, [1147?] (Bitlesbroc). Add. 21204.

—— Inquisition conc. land in, 1302 (Bittelesbrook). Add. 737.

—— Lease in, 1358 (Bytlesbrok). Add. 21184.

—— *Vicarius.* Johannes, 1358. Add. 21184.

**Biscathorpe,** *co. Linc.* Exchange in, with Kirkstead Abbey, 1162 (Biscoptorp). Harl. 45 H. 7.

—— Conf. of grants in, to the same, c. 1295 (Byscopthorpe). Harl. 45 H. 14.

—— Lease in, *t.* Edw. I. (Biscopthorpe). Add. 20549.

—— Fine in, 1302 (Bysshopestthorp). Harl. 45 H. 18.

—— Precipe on a covenant conc. the manor, 1555 (Byscopthrope). Add. 25056.

Blackwall, co. *Midd.* Lease of store-houses in the E. India Dock, 1654, 1655. Add. 13716, 13718, 13719.

—— Covenant conc. the E. India Dock, 1677. Add. 26388, 26389.

Blackwell, *nr. Alfreton, co. Derb.* Exchange of lands in, early 13 cent. (Blacwelle). Harl. 54 E. 12.

—— Grants, etc., of the manor, 1369. Woll. x. 48 (Blacwelle), 51;—1412. Woll. x. 53 (Blakwell), 54;—1424. Woll. x. 56 (Blakewell).

—— Grant of a rent charge on the manor, 1431 (?). Woll. xi. 47.

—— Brief for rebuilding the church, 1825. Ch. Br. C. vi. 6.

—— *Vicarius.* Johannes, *t.* Hen. III. Woll. x. 63.

Blacoluysle. *v.* Blakesley, co. *Northt.*

Bladbean Manor. *v. sub* Elham, co. *Kent.*

Blædeue, [*River?*], *nr. Daylesford, co. Worc.* A boundary, 949. Cott. viii. 6 (*copy*).

Blaen Malwg, *in Margam, co. Glam.* Grant in, from Margam Abbey, 1525 (Blayn Maluke). Harl. 75 A. 48.

Blafelda. *v.* Blofield Hundred, co. *Norf.*

Blagdon (Blakedon), co. *Som.* Power to give seisin of the manor, *t.* Edw. III. Harl. 45 E. 38.

—— Conveyance of W. Aldwick (Westaldewyke) in, 1384. Harl. 48 A. 30.

—— Power to give seisin of St. Cross "infra dominium de," 1421. Harl. 112 D. 32.

—— *Persona. Dom.* Hewe, *t.* Edw. III. Harl. 45 E. 38.

Blagrave. *v.* Blackgrove, *in Waddesdon,* co. *Buck.*

Blainslee, co. *Roxburgh.* Grant in, to Melrose Abbey, *ante* 1196 (Bleineslei). Cott. xviii. 15.

Blair [Gowrie?], co. *Perth.* Covenant by Cupar Abbey for lighting the church, *c.* 1210 (Blare). Cott. xviii. 33, 34.

Blakeaveton. *v.* Auton, Black, co. *Devon.*

Blakedon. *v.* Blagdon, co. *Som.*

Blakeham. *v. sub* Hawkhurst, co. *Kent.*

Blakeham, *in Astwell. v. sub* Wappenham, co. *Northt.*

Blakelond. *v.* Blackland, co. *Dors.*

Blakemannestone. *v.* Blackmanstone, co. *Kent.*

Blakemere. *v. sub* Chesham, co. *Bucks.*

Blakemora, terra de. *v. sub* Cannington, co. *Som.*

Blakeney [*olim* Snitterley], co. *Norf.* Surrender of the advowson, etc., 1323 (Snetirle). Add. 9915.

Blakenham, Great, co. *Suff.* Grants, etc., in, late 13 cent. Add. 9816;—1332. Add. 9952;—1417. Add. 10061.

Blakenham, Little, co. *Suff.* Grant, etc., in, 1313. Add. 9883;—1417. Add. 10061.

Blakenottele. *v.* Notley, Black, co. *Essex.*

Blakerewe. *v.* Blackrow, co. *Dors.*

Blake's Manor. *v. sub* Melford, Long, co. *Suff.*

Blakesley, co. *Northt.* Grant in, *t.* Edw. II.-III. (Blacoluysle). Add. 19923.

—— Acquittance for homage in, 1409 (Blacolueslee). Harl. 58 D. 49.

—— License to alienate in, 1623. Add. 24709.

Blanckenay. *v.* Blankney, co. *Linc.*

Blandford, co. *Dors.* Inspex., in 1280, of a conf. by King John of rents in the manor to Font-vrault Abbey, 1200 (Beneford). Harl. 58 I. 34 (*copy*).

—— Inspex., in 1231, of a Papal conf. of the same rents to the same, 1201 (Bleinefort). Add. 17861.

Blandford Forum, co. *Dors.* Settlement of lands in, 1661. Add. 5984.

Blank Aston. *v.* Aston, Blank *al.* Cold, co. *Glouc.*

Blankney, co. *Linc.* Conf. by Hen. II. of grants in, to Kirkstead Abbey, [1155?] (Blankenie). Harl. 43 C. 17.

—— Grant in, *t.* Hen. III. (Blankenay). Harl. 45 E. 59.

—— Grants in, to Bullington Priory, *t.* Hen. III. Harl. 45 E. 60 (Blankensy), 61, 46 E. 21 (Blanckenay).

—— Marriage settlement of the manor, 1343 (Blaunkenay). Harl. 57 G. 9.

—— Sale in, 1617. Harl. 75 H. 42.

—— *Rector.* Rog. de Scaccario, *t.* Hen. III. Harl. 45 E. 59-61.

—1467. Add. 24550 (Blechynglegh);
—1529. Harl. 112 F. 23 (Blechyng-leghe).

—— Grant in Chivington in, 1318.
Add. 24548.

—— Covenant conc. timber-cutting,
etc., in, 1357. Add. 20035 (Bletching-lighe).

—— Precipe on a covenant conc. land
in, 1545 (Blechynglye). Add. 25500.

—— Covenant to levy a fine of Hec-stalls, al. Park Place, manor in, 1575.
Add. 23334.

—— Settlement of the advowson,
1642. Add. 5638.

—— Exemplif. of suit conc. the manor,
1709. Add. 15893.

—— *Persona*. Tho. de Sekyndon,
1381. Harl. 84 F. 6.

**Bletchley**, *co. Buck*. Grant in Water
Eaton (Eton) in, 1469. Add. 8128.

**Blethewode**. *v. sub* Hereford, Lit., *co.
Heref*.

**Bletsoe** (Bletnesho), *co. Bedf. Dominus
Manerii*. Will. de Pateshall, .1354,
1355. Harl. 86 B. 8-10.

—— *Persona*. Florus, late 13 cent.
Harl. 111 D. 45.

**Blewberry** (Bleberia), *co. Berks*. Grant
of, by Matilda, the Empress, to Read-ing Abbey, [1144-7]. Add. 19577,
19579.

—— Grant of, by K. Stephen, to the
same, [1142-8]. Add. 19581.

—— Conf. of, by Hen. II., to the same,
[1157 ?]. Add. 19591.

**Bleweham**. *v*. Blunham, *co. Bedf*.

**Blewhenston**. *v*. Bluehenstone, *nr.
Lit. Drewchurch, co. Heref*.

**Blickling**, *co. Norf*. Grant of tithes
in, to St. Paul's Hosp., Norwich, [1121-30]. Cott. ii. 19 (1) (copy).

**Blidworth**, *co. Nott*. Lease nr., 1598
(Blodworth). Woll. xi. 77.

**Blie**. *v*. Blyth, *Honour of, cos. Nott. and
York*.

**Blintesfield**, *in Shaftesbury, co. Dors*.
Grant of, to Alcester Abbey, *c*. 1140
(tota terra de Blingesfelda). Add.
21494.

**Blisland**, *co. Cornw*. Fine in Westrose
in the manor of, 1432 (Blyston). Add.
15356.

**Blisworth**, *co. Northt*. Grant in (?),
to H. Trinity Hosp., Kingsthorpe,
early 13 cent. Add. 22379.

**Blisworth**, *co. Northt. (continued)*.
Grant in, 1348 (Blythesworthe). Add.
17376.

—— Grant of the manor, 1354 (Blise-worthe). Cott. xxx. 6.

—— Release of the manor and advow-son, 1437 (Blysseworth). Add. 21543.

—— *Persona*. Joh. de Langeton, 1354.
Cott. xxx. 6.

**Blithefield**, *co. Staff*. Release in, 1388
(Blithefeld). Cott. xxviii. 104.

**Blockesham**. *v*. Bloxham, *co. Oxon*.

**Blodbeine Manor**. *v. sub* Elham, *co.
Kent*.

**Blodhall Manor**. *v. sub* Debenham,
*co. Suff*.

**Blodworth**. *v*. Blidworth, *co. Nott*.

**Blofield**, *co. Norf*. Grant nr. Brant-hueid in or nr. (?), late 12 cent. Harl.
46 E. 23.

—— Settlement of lands in, 1621
(Blowfeild). Add. 14584.

**Blofield Hundred**, *co. Norf*. Grant
by Hen. I. of rent from, *c*. 1129-33
(Blafelda). Cott. ii. 4.

—— Riots in, 1452 (Blofeld). Add.
16545.

**Blofield Manor**. *v. sub* Trimley St.
Mary, *co. Suff*.

**Blondelesheye, Blontyshaye,
Bloundelshay, Bloundesheyes**. *v.
sub* Whitchurch Canonicorum, *co. Dors*.

**Blondeston Sci. Andree**. *v*. Bluns-don St. Andrew, *co. Wilts*.

**Blossom Hall Manor**. *v. sub* Kirton,
*co. Linc*.

**Blossomville Newton**. *v*. Newton
Blossomville, *co. Buck*.

**Bloungham, Blounham**. *v*. Blun-ham, *co. Bedf*.

**Blount's Manor**. *v. sub* Wratting,
Lit., *co. Suff*.

**Blowfeild**. *v*. Blofield, *co. Norf*.

**Blownham**. *v*. Blunham, *co. Bedf*.

**Bloxham**, *co. Oxon*. Grant of the
church, etc., by Will. I. to Westminster
Abbey, 1067 (Blockesham). Cott. vi.
3 (copy).

—— Extracts from court - rolls of
Beauchamps manor, 1479, 1499, 1505.
Harl. 58 E. 9, 11, 12 :—1513. Harl.
Roll A. 24.

Bobbingworth, *co. Essex (continued)*. Fine in, 1437 (Bobyngworthe). Harl. 54 E. 55.

Bobingseata, *co. Kent.* Exchange of land called, 798. Cott. MS. Aug. ii. 97.

Boccholte. *v. sub* Bexhill, *co. Suss.*

Bocherst. *v. sub* Woodford, *co. Essex.*

Bochilde, terra de, *co. Southt.* (?). Papal conf. of grant of, to Waverley Abbey, 1147. Lansd. 27.

Bochlant. *v.* Buckland, *in Woodhall, co. Linc.*

Bochnal, *in Treglastan, co. Cornw.* Grant in, early Hen. III. Harl. 53 B. 42.

Bocholt. *v.* Bookholt, *co. Kent.*

Bocholte. *v. sub* Bexhill, *co. Suss.*

Bockhampton, *in Lambourn, co. Berks.* Grant in, 1427 (Bochampton). Harl. 49 C. 16.

Bockhampton, *nr. Christchurch, co. Southt.* Grants, etc., in, late 13 cent. Harl. 50 H. 53 (Northbocamtone); —1295. Harl. 50 H. 54 (Bochamton); —1299. Harl. 50 H. 55.

Bockholt, *in Petham, co. Kent.* Grant at, to Abp. Wulfred, 805 (Bocholt). Cott. MS. Aug. ii. 87.

Bocking (Bokkingg, Bockyngg, etc.), *co. Essex.* Grants, etc., in, 1355. Add. 6190;—1381. Add. 13544;—1419. Add. 13546;—1548. Add. 6188.

—— Power from Christ Church, Canterbury, for seisin of lands in, 1418. Cott. xxi. 11.

—— Foundation of a hospital in, 1455. Add. 13551.

—— Rental of manors in, 15 cent. Add. 13596.

—— Settlement of the park, 1539. Add. 6191.

—— Precipes on covenants conc. lands in, 1561. Add. 24938;—1578. Add. 24954;—1587. Add. 24990.

—— Bequest to the poor of, by J. Smith, 1601. Cott. i. 7.

Bocking Hall Manor. *v. sub* Helmingham, *co. Suff.*

Bockingfold Manor. *v. sub* Brenchley, *co. Kent.*

—— *v. sub* Goudhurst, *co. Kent.*

—— *v. sub* Yalding, *co. Kent.*

Bocland. *v.* Buckland, *in Woodhall, co. Linc.*

Bocstede. *v.* Buxted, *co. Suss.*

Bocstepe. *v. sub* Warbleton, *co. Suss.*

Bocton subtus le Blen. *v.* Boughton under Blean, *co. Kent.*

Boctone Alulph. *v.* Boughton Aluph, *co. Kent.*

Boctone Munchensy. *v.* Boughton Monchelsea, *co. Kent.*

Bodcarn. *v.* Boscarne, *co. Cornw.*

Boddington, *co. Glouc.* Grants, etc., in Heydon in, late Hen. III. Add. 8393;—1353. Slo. xxxiii. 38 *a, b.*

—— Settlement of Withybrigge and Heydon manors in, 1419. Harl. 76 F. 14.

Boddington, Upper, *co. Northt.* Conf. of grant of a manor in, [1276-83] (Superior Botindon). Add. 26755.

Bodecton. *v.* Burton, *co. Suss.*

Bodemeakil. *v.* Bottomsall, *co. Nott.*

Bodenham (Bodeham, etc.), *co. Heref.* Grant, etc., in, *t.* Hen. III. Add. 8072;—1317. Eg. 353.

—— Grant in Rowbury, Maund Rous, Whitechurch Maund and Moor in, late Hen. III. Eg. 349.

—— Feoffment of Bradefeld Ryffeyn manor in, 1377. Add. 8399.

—— Re-feoffment in Upper Broadfield (Bradefeld Superior), Brockington, Hackley, etc., in, 1378. Harl. 112 D. 43.

—— Grant of reversion in Whitechurch Maund, etc., in, 1419. Harl. 112 B. 46.

—— Release in [Brian's Maund ?] in, 1446. Harl. 112 B. 4.

—— Conveyance of Brian's Maund, Fearne, etc., manors in, 1654. Add. 1953.

Bodeton, *in South Hilne, co. Devon.* Grant in, 1318. Add. 9223.

Bodiam *al.* Bodyham, *co. Suss.* Release nr. the bridge of, late 13 cent. (Bodihamme). Eg. 392.

—— Settlements, etc., of the manor and castle. 1347. Cott. xxvi. 38;—1408. Add. 20049;—1473. Add. 20050;—1583. Add. 8792.

Bodillick (Bodelek, etc.), *co. Cornw.* Grants, etc., in, *t.* Edw. II. or III. Harl. 57 A. 37;—1332. Harl. 57 A. 38;—1337. Harl. 50 C. 34;—1513 (Bodelleck). Harl. 50 C. 41.

Bodkonan, *co. Cornw.* Grant, etc., in, 1331. Harl. 51 E. 2.

Bodley's. *v. sub* Chertsey, *co. Surr.*

Bodmescombe, *nr. Sheldon, co. Devon. Magister de Bothenescome.* Fr. Hugo, *t. Edw. I.* Add. 12940.

Bodmeshil. *v.* Bottomsall, *co. Nott.*

Bodmin (Bodmyn), *co. Cornw.* Grants, etc., in, 1422. Add. 12976, 12977 ;— 1425. Add. 12980 - 12982 ;—1480. Add. 13051 ;—1487. Add. 15364 ;— 1513. Harl. 50 C. 41, 42.

———— Award in suit with Bodmin Priory conc. Ruthern moor nr., 1518. Harl. 44 A. 20.

———— Release of Lancarffe Holton al. Holton Bosnyves manor in, etc., 1566. Lansd. 187.

———— *Major.* Joh. Nicolle, 1412. Harl. 50 C. 40.

———— Joh. Nicoll, 1430. Add. 13051.

———— Tho. Moyle, 1434. Harl. 57 A. 35.

———— Tho. Lucombe, 1439. Add. 15358.

———— Tho. Lanhergy, 1444. Harl. 51 F. 26.

———— Joh. Wattys, 1487. Add. 15364.

———— Joh. Lavedwen, 1513. Harl. 50 C. 42, 43.

———— Tho. Opy, 1542. Harl. 50 H. 6, 7.

———— *Prepositus.* Tho. Lanhergy, 1439. Add. 15358.

———— Joh. Cobbe, 1444. Harl. 51 F. 26.

———— *v. also* Ruthern, *nr. Bodmin, co. Cornw.*

Bodney (Bodeneye), *co. Norf.* Grants, etc., in, *t.* Hen. III.-late 13 cent. Harl. 46 E. 51, 48 I. 31 ;—1291. Harl. 46 E. 52.

Bodrede Wydesore, *in St. Germans, co. Cornw.* Grant in, 1460. Add. 13060.

Bodrugan, *in Gorran, co. Cornw.* Grant of annuity from the manor of, 1521. Add. 23846.

Bodwideo. *v.* Bowithick, *nr. Davidstow, co. Cornw.*

Boebi. *v.* Boothby Pagnel, *co. Linc.*

Bogelegh. *v. sub* Warminster, *co. Wilts.*

Bogeton. *v.* Buckden. *co. Hunt.*

Bognor, *co. Suss.* Grant at, to Bp. Wilfrid, 680 (*sic*) (Bucgan ora). Cott. MS. Aug. ii. 86.

———— Feoffment in, 1549. Add. 18828.

Boilistona. *v.* Boylstone, *co. Derb.*

Bokeham. *v.* Buckenham, Lit., *co. Norf.*

Bokeland, Bokland. *v.* Buckland, *in Woodhall, co. Linc.*

Bokele. *v. sub* Warminster, *co. Wilts.*

Bokelond. *v.* Buckland, *co. Surr.*

Bokenesfeld. *v.* Beaconsfield, *co. Buck.*

Bokenham Ferye. *v.* Buckenham Ferry, *co. Norf.*

Bokenham Nova. *v.* Buckenham, New, *co. Norf.*

Bokenhulle. *v.* Bucknall, *cos. Salop and Heref.*

———— *v. sub* Woolhope, *co. Heref.*

Bokesworth. *v.* Boxworth, *co. Camb.*

Bokingham. *v.* Buckingham, *co. Buck.*

Bokkynge Assh. *v.* Ash Bocking, *co. Suff.*

Bokkynghalle. *v. sub* Helmingham, *co. Suff.*

Boklond. *v.* Buckland, *co. Buck.*

———— *v.* Buckland, *co. Linc.*

———— *v. sub* Luddesdown, *co. Kent.*

Bokstede. *v.* Buxted, *co. Suss.*

Bokyllysham. *v.* Bucklesham, *co. Suff.*

Bokyngfold. *v. sub* Brenchley, *co. Kent.*

Bolam (Belom), *co. Durh.* Releases of the manor, 1430. Harl. 43 E.19 ;— 1431. Harl. 45 I. 12.

———— *Persona.* Johannes, [1186-8]· Cott. v. 75.

Bolam, *co. Northumb.* Grant by Hen. II. of Harewood wood in the fee of, *c.* 1155 (Bolum). Campb. ii. 2.

Bold, The, *nr. Aston Botterell, co. Salop.* Release in, 1316 (La Bolde). Cott. xxiv. 13.

———— Recovery of dower in the manor of, 1381 (Boold). Cott. xxvi. 4.

Boldre, *co. Southt.* Grant by Hen. III. of woodlands in, to Breamore Priory, 1236 (Bolre). Add. 15695.

———— Briefs conc. fires in, 1760, 1806. Ch. Br. A. vi. 9, B. xlvii. 2.

**Bole,** *co. Nott.* Precipe on a covenant in, 1555 (Bolle). Add. 25188.

**Bole Hall.** *v. sub* Tamworth, *cos. Warw. and Staff.*

**Bolebi.** *v.* Bulby, *in Irnham, co. Linc.*

**Bolebroke,** *in Hartfield. co. Suss.* Refeoffment in the manor of, 1408 (Bolbrok). Add. 20049.

**Boleham Marsh.** *v. sub* Shorne, *co. Kent.*

**Bolehurst.** *v.* Bolnhurst, *co. Bedf.*

**Boles Manor.** *v. sub* Yaxley, *co. Suff.*

**Bolestrode.** *v.* Bulstrode, *co. Buck.*

**Bolewik.** *v.* Bulwick, *co. Northt.*

**Bolham.** *v.* Bollam, *co. Nott.*

**Bolingbroke,** *co. Linc.* Grant in the soke of, by W., Earl of Lincoln, *c.* 1145 (Bullinbroca). Harl. 55 E. 10.

—— Rent to be paid by Newhouse Abbey to the Lord of, for lands in Habrough, *t.* Hen. III. (Bolingbroc). Harl. 48 H. 32, 33.

—— The Duke of Orleans a prisoner in the castle, 1423. Add. 311, 313;—1427. Add. 3613.

—— *Præpositus.* Willelmus, *t.* Hen. III. (Bulingbroc). Harl. 48 C. 9.

**Bollam** *al.* **Bolham** (Bolum), *in Clareborough, co. Nott.* Acquittance for tithes in, to the chapel of the B. Mary and H. Angels *al.* St. Sepulchre, York, 1335. Harl. 83 C. 37.

—— Grant in, 1361. Cott. xxvii. 96.

**Bollebrichill, Bollebrikhelle.** *v.* Brickhill, Bow, *co. Buck.*

**Bolleby.** *v.* Boulby, *co. York.*

**Bolney,** *co. Suss.* Fines in, 1426. Add. 15211;—1673. Add. 19014.

**Bolnhurst,** *co. Bedf.* Grants, etc., in, late 12 cent. Cott. xxvii. 209 (Bolehurst);—early Hen. III. Harl. 56 E. 23 (do.);—*t.* Edw. I. Harl. 56 E. 25 (Bolhurst).

—— Grant of church lands in Greensbury, etc., in, 1549. Add. 4607.

—— Exemplif. of fine in, 1589. Add. 5156.

—— Sale in, 1596 (Bonehurst *al.* Bolenhurste). Add. 5157.

**Bolouthow,** *co. Cornw.* Grant in, 1516. Add. 13078.

**Bolre.** *v.* Boldre, *co. Southt.*

**Bolsover,** *co. Derb.* Covenant to convey in, 1571. Woll. xi. 51.

**Bolsover,** *co. Derb. (continued).* Award in a suit of, with Lord Shrewsbury, 1578. Add. 13938.

**Bolsterstone,** *co. York.* Brief for rebuilding the chapel, 1787. Ch. Br. B. xxvii. 4.

**Bolston,** *co. Heref.* Bond conc. land in, 1583. Add. 1853.

**Bolstrode.** *v.* Bulstrode, *co. Buck.*

**Boltby,** *co. York.* Release of common in. to Byland Abbey, 1330. Add. 8660.

—— Assignment of land in, 1404. Add. 22391.

—— Brief for rebuilding the chapel, 1797. Ch. Br. B. xxxvii. 4.

**Boltishayne.** *v. sub* Colyton, *co. Devon.*

**Bolton.** *v.* Boulton, *nr. Derby, co. Derb.*

**Bolton,** *co. Lanc.* (?). *Rector.* Steph. Elis, 1520. Harl. 112 B. 48.

**Bolton,** *co. Northumb. Capellanus.* Nicholaus, *t.* Edw. III. (Bolitun). Lansd. 614.

**Bolton,** *co. Westm.* Lease of tithes in, 1572. Harl. 77 H. 37.

—— Brief conc. a fire in, 1776. Ch. Br. B. xvi. 8.

**Bolton,** *nr. Bradford, co. York.* Grant in, 1328 (Boulton). Add. 16788.

**Bolton le Moors,** *co. Lanc.* Power to take seisin of the manor, 1411. Add. 20515.

**Bolton on Dearne,** *co. York.* Grants in, *t.* Edw. I. Campb. vi. 18 (Boulton), 19 (Bohilton):—1309. Campb. vi. 2 (Boulton super Dyrne):—1321. Harl. 112 G. 27 (do.).

—— Grant in, to Monk Bretton Priory, to endow a chantry in the church of, for Hen. de Laci, etc., 1328 (Boulton). Campb. vii. 14.

—— Surrender of the manor to J. de Bellew, 1341. Add. 17962 (9).

—— Covenant for marriage settlement of the manor, 1437. Add. 20542.

—— Grant in, from Monk Bretton Priory, 1496. Campb. v. 18.

—— *Capellanus.* Hamo, *t.* Edw. I. Campb. vi. 18, 19.

**Bolton Percy,** *co. York.* Bond to the Bp. of Durham for warranty of the manor, 1299 (Boulton). Harl. 54 G. 19.

**Bolum.** *v.* Bollam, *co. Nott.*

**Bolwyk.** *v.* Bulwick, *co. Northt.*

**Bolys Manor.** *v. sub* Yaxley, *co. Suff.*

**Bonavilla.** *v.* Bonvilston, *co. Glam.*

**Bonbusk.** *v. sub* Cuckney, *co. Nott.*

**Bonby** *al.* **Bondeby,** *co. Linc.* Exchange in, betw. Thornton Abbey and Elsham Priory, 1269 (Bondeby). Harl. 45 A. 12.

—— Grant in, to Philip, Vicar of, 1295. Harl. 44 D. 32.

—— Sale in, 1594. Add. 5312.

**Bondesale, Bonesale.** *v.* Bonsall, *co. Derb.*

**Bonevileston.** *v.* Bonvilston, *co. Glam.*

**Bongey.** *v.* Bungay, *co. Suff.*

**Bonham,** *co. Som., in Stourton par., co. Wilts.* Release, etc., of the manor, 1356. Add. 17754;—1449. Add. 15089, 15090.

**Bonhunt, Wicken,** *co. Essex.* Grant in, by Matilda the Empress, [1141] (Banhunta). Cott. xvi. 27.

**Bonnington,** *co. Kent.* Settlement in, on divorce of Marg. de Valoignes, 1326 (Bonynton). Harl. 80 H. 4.

**Bonsall,** *co. Derb.* Fine in, 1541. Woll. ii. 71.

—— Sale in, 1618. Woll. xi. 92.

—— *Persona.* Will. de Monyasche, 1390 (Bondesale). Woll. vi. 26.

—— —— Jon. Dethyk, 1442 (Bonsale). Woll. ii. 37.

—— *Rector.* Hen. de Mapulton, 1427 (Bonesale). Woll. i. 4.

**Bonthorpe (?).** *v.* Brunthorpe, *co. Linc.*

**Bontyngford.** *v.* Buntingford, *co. Hertf.*

**Bonvilston** (Bonavilla, Bonevileston, etc.), *co. Glam.* Grants in, late 12 cent. Harl. 75 B. 12;—early 13 cent. Harl. 75 B. 13, 18;—*t.* Hen. III. Harl. 75 C. 54.

—— Grants, etc., in, to Margam Abbey, early 13 cent. — early Hen. III. Harl. 75 B. 14–17, 35, 36;—*c.* 1230. Harl. 75 B. 19, 20;—1230. Harl. 75 A. 35;—1237. Harl. 75 B. 21;—*t.* Hen. III. Harl. 75 C. 22;—1302. Harl. 75 B. 22.

—— Settlement of suit in, with Margam Abbey, [1262–95]. Harl. 75 A. 36, 75 C. 38.

**Bonvilston** (Bonavilla, Bonevileston, etc.), *co. Glam. (continued).* Exchanges in, by Margam Abbey, 1292. Harl. 76 A. 42;—1308. Harl. 75 A. 43.

—— Lease in the fee of, by Margam Abbey, 1376. Harl. 75 A. 45.

—— *Sacerdos al. Presbyter.* Ricardus, [1186–91]. Harl. 75 D. 25;—late 12 cent.—early 13 cent. Harl. 75 B. 12, 15–17, 36, 75 D. 9.

**Bookham, Great,** *co. Surr.* Grants, etc., in, 1273. Add. 5569 (Bokham Magna);—1303. Add. 5580 (Bocham Magna);—1335. Add. 5596 (do.);—1364. Add. 18658 (Magna Bokham); —1394. Add. 5609;—1401. Add. 5612;—1415. Add. 5616 (Bocham Magna);—1418. Add. 9064 (Bokham);—1434. Add. 9067 (Bokeham).

—— Grant in Preston in, *t.* Edw. I. or II. (Major Bocham). Add. 5568.

—— Feoffment of Eastwick (Estwyk) manor in, 1439. Add. 5618.

**Bookham, Little,** *co. Surr.* Suit conc. the manor, 1307 (Parva Bokham). Add. 20036.

—— *Persona.* Joh. Roweberue, 1394. Add. 5609.

**Bootham, nr. York, co. York.** Warrant of Edw. III. for custody of, during disputes with St. Mary's Abbey conc., 1350 (Bouthom). Harl. 43 D. 46.

**Boothby, nr. Welton, Candleshoe Wap., co. Linc.** Release in, late 13 cent. (Botheby). Cott. xxx. 14.

**Boothby Graffo,** *co. Linc.* Fine in, 1302 (Botheby in Kesteven). Harl. 45 H. 18.

—— Fine of Somerton manor in, 1638. Woll. xi. 29.

**Boothby Pagnel,** *co. Linc. Clericus.* Osbertus, [1167–74?]. Add. 20624 (Boebi), 20626 (do.).

—— *Capellanus.* Alexander, end of 12 cent. (Bobi). Add. 20580.

**Booton** (Boton, etc.), *co. Norf.* Sale in, with advowson of St. Michael's church, 1528. Add. 14205.

—— Rental of the manor, 16 cent. Add. 9369.

—— Defeasance on a mortgage in, 1584. Add. 14256.

—— *Persona.* Roger Shirreve, 1415–16. Add. 9329.

—— *Rector.* Robertus, 1270 (Bothone). Toph. 50.

**Borasham hous.** *v.* Bersham, *co. Denb.*

**Borden**, *co. Kent.* Grant in, 1580. Add. 957.

—— Suit in, 1626. Harl. 75 H. 22.

**Bordeshowe, Bordyshawe Manor.** *v. sub* Sproughton, *co. Suf.*

**Bordesley** (Bordesleia, etc.), *co. Worc.* Grant of, to Bordesley Abbey. [1138?]. Add. 20419.

—— Notif. of above to S., Bp. of Worcester, 1138. Harl. 45 I. 30.

—— Conff. of, to the same, by Kings Stephen and Hen. II., [1141?]. Harl. 43 C. 13;—[1157?]. Cott. MS. Nero C. iii., f. 176 (Bordeslegha).

—— Grant of annuity from the manor, 1542. Lansd. 181.

**Bordewode, Bordwode.** *v.* Borthwood, *I. of Wight.*

**Bordham.** *v.* Birdham, *co. Suss.*

**Boreham** (Borham), *co. Essex.* Grants, etc., in, *t.* Hen. III. Harl. 46 L 40;—1483. Add. 24072;—1501. Add. 24073.

—— Grant of the profits of Newhall manor in, 1650. Add. 1800.

—— *Vicarius.* Hug. de Wodeston, 1301. Harl. 58 C. 7.

**Boreham**, *in Wartling, co. Suss.* Grant in, *t.* Hen. III. or Edw. I. Add. 23820.

**Borehams.** *v. sub* Hackington, *co. Kent.*

**Boresclive**, *in Cold Hiendley*(?). *v. sub* Hiendley, Cold, *co. York.*

**Boresforde.** *v. sub* Brampton Bryan, *co. Heref.*

**Borewaremersh.** *v.* Burmarsh, *co. Kent.*

**Borewell.** *v.* Burwell, *co. Linc.*

**Borewerdescote.** *v.* Buscot, *co. Berks.*

**Borgemera.** *v.* Burgemere, *co. Suss.*

**Borgyersache.** *v.* Burwash, *co. Suss.*

**Boriswrthe.** *v.* Bosworth, Husband's, *co. Leic.*

**Borley**, *co. Essex.* Lease of tithes in the manor of, 1336 (Borlee). Add. 15593.

—— Exemplif. of recovery in, etc., 1510. Harl. 43 F. 28;—1517. Harl. 47 C. 6.

**Borley**, *co. Essex (continued).* Extract from Court-roll of Borley Hall Manor, 1510. Harl. 58 E. 8.

**Borley, Little,** *co. Essex.* Award conc. tithes in, 1249 (Parva Borle). Add. 15586.

**Bornatone.** *v. sub* Aveton Giffard, *co. Devon.*

**Borne Cobeham Manor.** *v. sub* Beaksbourne, *co. Kent.*

**Boroughbridge,** *co. York.* Grant of, by Hen. II. to W. de Stutevill, *c.* 1177 (Burg). Add. 5719.

**Borowoote** *al.* **Borrowoote** (Barowoote, etc.), *in Crich, co. Derb.* Grants, etc., in, 1546. Woll. x. 68;—1547. Woll. iv. 52;—1590. Woll. iv. 55;—1604. Woll. iv. 56.

**Borraton.** *v.* Burrington, *in Weston Peverell, co. Devon.*

**Borstal.** *v. sub* Rochester, *co. Kent.*

**Borstall.** *v.* Boarstall, *co. Buck.*

**Borstall**, *in Minster* (?), *co. Kent.* Settlement of the manor, 1441. Harl. 79 A. 8.

**Borstowe.** *v.* Burstow, *co. Surr.*

**Borthelby**, *in E. Harlsey, co. York.* Power to give seisin of the manor, 1366. Lansd. 411.

**Borthwood, *I. of Wight.*** Grant in Witefeld in, *t.* Edw. I. (Bordwode). Harl. 111 F. 30.

—— Compotus of the manor, 1488–9 (Bordewode). Harl. Roll A. 38.

**Borton.** *v.* Bourton, *nr. Buckingham, co. Buck.*

**Borueleye.** *v.* Burleigh, *in Knebworth, co. Herts.*

**Borwell.** *v.* Burwell, *co. Linc.*

**Bosbury,** *co. Heref.* Lease in, 1651. Eg. 313.

**Boscarne,** *co. Cornw.* Grants, etc., in, 1392. Harl. 50 C. 37 (Bodcarn);—1394. Harl. 51 E. 16 (do.);—1513. Harl. 50 C. 41, 42, 43 (Parva Boscarn, Bocarn mur).

—— Suit in, with Bodmin Priory, 1432. Harl. 43 E. 41 (Boskarn parva);—1434. Harl. 57 A. 35.

—— Lease of the barton of, 1504. Harl. 50 C. 48.

Boscastle, co. *Cornw.* Grant of a market, etc., in, 1312 (Chastelboterel). Harl. 58 I. 49.

Boscawen Woon, co. *Cornw.* Grant in, 1518. Eg. 276.

Boscobel House, co. *Salop.* Resettlement of, on F. Cotton, 1632. Cott. iv. 13 (1–4).

Boscombe, co. *Wilts.* Papal conf. of the church to St. Neot's Priory, [1180?] (Bascumbe). Harl. 43 A. 21.

Bosegete, Bosezate, Bosgieta, Bosiet. *v.* Bozeat, co. *Northt.*

Boselee. *v.* Bosley, co. *Chest.*

Bosford Hall Manor. *v. sub* Sproughton, co. *Suff.*

Bosham, co. *Suss.* Fine in, 1334. Add. 15208.

Bosindenne Wood. *v. sub* Blean, co. *Kent.*

Boskarn. *v.* Boscarne, co. *Cornw.*

Boskenvewe, [*nr. the Lizard?*], co. *Cornw.* Power to give seisin in, 1481. Add. 15363.

Bosley (Boselee, etc.), co. *Chest.* Attornment for the manor of, to W., Earl of Salisbury, 1337. Harl. 43 D. 26.

—— Conf. by Edw. III. of an exchange of the manor, 1338. Cott. xi. 61.

—— Scire facias, etc., conc. the manor of, *c.* 1400 (Boslee). Add. 662.

—— Brief for rebuilding the chapel, 1771. Ch. Br. B. xi. 8.

Bosmere and Claydon Hundred, co. *Suff.* Assessment of subsidy in, t. Eliz. Add. 10099.

Bosomhall. *v. sub* Kirton, co. *Linc.*

Bossehaugh al. Bosshall Manor. *v. sub* Sproughton, co. *Suff.*

Bossoghan al. Bosoghen, Bosoghan, co. *Cornw.* Grants, etc., in, 1366. Harl. 50 C. 36;—1394. Harl. 50 C. 37;—1513. Harl. 50 C. 41.

Bossulyan (Bussulyan, etc.), *nr. Grampound,* co. *Cornw.* Grants, etc., in, 1400. Add. 12974, 12975, 12978;—1422. Add. 12976, 12977;—1425–1438. Add. 12979–12996, 13046.

Boston (S. Botulphus, S. Botulfus, villa S. Botulphi), co. *Linc.* Conf. of grants in, to Kirkstead Abbey, [1160–70]. Harl. 48 G. 41.

—— Fine for land "in feria S. Botulfi," 1183. Harl. 49 A. 3.

Boston (S. Botulphus, S. Botulfus, villa S. Botulphi), co. *Linc.* (*continued*). Grants to Bullington Priory for purchases of "Camisie," etc., "in nundinis S. Botulfi," 1235. Harl. 44 I. 14;—1263. Harl. 44 I. 17;—1311. Harl. 44 I. 21.

—— Fines, etc., in, 1302. Harl. 45 H. 18;—1306. Harl. 52 A. 7, 55 G. 2;—1355. Harl. 57 G. 11;—1388. Add. 24911;—1391. Add. 4789;—1393. Harl. 57 E. 22;—1431. Harl. 51 H. 6;—1438. Harl. 57 F. 12.

—— Grant to J. de Chalons of an annuity on the customs of the port of, 1347. Add. 11307.

—— Release in Fenn nr., 1387. Harl. 53 C. 38.

—— Sir R. Rochefort seneschal of, for Hen. IV., 1412. Add. 12652.

—— Admission of Sir Mark Lowe to the Guild of St. Mary in St. Botolph's Church, *post* 1511. *Printed.* Woll. iii. 94.

—— Precipes on covenants conc. lands in, 1529. Add. 25051;—1555. Add. 25055;—1578. Add. 25067.

—— Inquiry conc. trespass on lands in Rippingale, co. Linc., held by St. Mary's Guild, 1534. Add. 21118.

Bosvisack. *v.* Busvisack, co. *Cornw.*

Bosvorvegh wartha, co. *Cornw.* Grants, etc., in, 1302 (Bosuoruet wartha). Add. 15347;—1417. Add. 15354;—1439. Add. 15358;—1459. Add. 15361.

Bosworth, Husband's, co. *Leic.* Grants, etc., in, to Sulby Abbey, early -late Hen. III. Harl. 48 F. 30 (Bareswrth), Add. 5871 (Bareswrd), 5872 (Bareswrth), 21189 (Barisword), 21190 (Barsword), 21192 (Bariswrthe), 22338 (Bareswrdia);—[1275-8]. Add. 21188 (Barisworthe);—1344. Add. 21193.

—— Grant of rent from the mill to a chapel in Marston Trussel church, co. Northt., early Hen. III. (Boriswrthe). Harl. 57 A. 53.

—— Assignment of rents in, due from Sulby Abbey, late Hen. III. (Bareswrthe). Add. 21191.

—— Grants, etc., in, t. Edw. I. Add. 20434 (Bareswith);— 1446. Add. 24220 (Barisworth).

—— *Capellanus Nicholai persone.* Jordanus, early Hen. II. Add. 21512.

**Bosworth, Husband's,** *co. Leic.* (*continued*). *Clericus.* Ricardus, early Hen. III. Add. 5871.

—— —— Simon, *t.* Hen. III. Add. 5873, 22463.

—— —— Alexander, late Hen. III. Add. 21192.

—— *Persona.* Nicholaus, early Hen. II. (Bareaw.). Add. 21512.

**Bosworth, Market,** *co. Leic.* Settlement of the manor, 1507. Harl. 111 F. 55.

—— Brief for rebuilding the church, 1768. Ch. Br. B. viii. 7.

**Botelers Manor.** *v. sub* Shopland, *co. Essex.*

**Boteleryswandeatre.** *v.* Wanstrow, Buller's, *co. Som.*

**Boterlegh.** *v.* Butterleigh, *in Silverton, co. Devon.*

**Boterley.** *v.* Butterley, *co. Derb.*

**Botermere.** *v.* Buttermere, *co. Wilts.*

**Botesdale,** *co. Suff.* Covenant conc. Facon's Hall manor in, 1501. Add. 16570, 16571.

**Botheby.** *v.* Boothby, *nr. Welton, co. Linc.*

**Botheby in Kesteven.** *v.* Boothby Graffo, *co. Linc.*

**Bothenescome.** *v.* Bodmescombe, *co. Devon.*

**Bothone.** *v.* Booton, *co. Norf.*

**Bothwell,** *co. Lanark.* Crailing manor, co. Roxburgh, held as a member of, 1801 (Bothouill). Harl. 43 D. 7.

**Botindon, Superior.** *v.* Boddington, Upper, *co. Northt.*

**Botley,** *co. Southt.* Mortgage in, 1572. Add. 16153.

**Botley's.** *v. sub* Chertsey, *co. Surr.*

**Botmeshil.** *v.* Bottomsall, *co. Nott.*

**Botolphs,** *nr. Steyning, co. Suss.* Sale in, 1620. Add. 18927.

**Boton.** *v.* Booton, *co. Norf.*

**Botrewyk.** *v.* Butterwick, *co. Linc.*

**Bottesford,** *co. Leic.* *Persona.* Joh. de Codyngton, 1355. Harl. 57 D. 1;—1359. Cott. xii. 1.

**Bottle Cleidon.** *v.* Claydon St. Botulph, *co. Buck.*

**Bottomsall,** *co. Nott.* Papal conf. of grant in, to Rufford Abbey. [1171–80] (Bolemeskil). Harl. 111 A. 4.

**Bottomsall,** *co. Nott.* (*continued*). Reservation of rights in Murton, co. Nott., to the lords of, against Rufford Abbey, late 12 cent. Cott. xxvii. 166 (Bodmeshil), 167;—early 13 cent. Harl. 112 B. 44 (Botmeshil).

**Botulfuspir., Botyllesperye.** *v.* Buttabury, *co. Essex.*

**Botwell,** *nr. Hayes, co. Midd.* Grant of, to Abp. Wulfred, 831 (Botewalle). Cott. MS. Aug. ii. 94.

**Boudon.** *v.* Bowden, *co. Leic.*

**Bouedich, Bouedych, Boudeche.** *v. sub* Chardstock, *co. Dors.*

**Boughton.** *v.* Boulton, *nr. Derby, co. Derb.*

**Boughton,** *co. Norf.* Grant in, "super Gunetun," to W. Dercham Abbey, early Hen. III. (Buketun). Add. 10643.

—— Compotus of the manor, 1515–16 (Bukton). Harl. Roll S. 28.

—— Court-roll, 1529 (Bukton). Harl. Roll S. 29.

**Boughton,** *co. Northt.* Covenant for sale of the manor, etc., 1717. Add. 26395.

**Boughton,** *co. Nott.* Grant in, to Rufford Abbey, early 13 cent. (Buketon). Harl. 83 D. 49.

—— Grants, etc., in, 1318. Harl. 84 B. 25 (Bucton);—1377. Harl. 83 E. 44 (Bughton);—1520. Add. 24168;—1571. Woll. xi. 51.

**Boughton Aluph,** *co. Kent.* Grant at Igelonde in (?), 1343. Add. 20022.

—— Grants "in tenura de," etc., 1366. Harl. 48 I. 18 (Boctone Alulph);—1414. Add. 19994 (B. Allulph);—1560. Add. 19995;—1583. Add. 19996, 19997;—1594. Add. 19998, 19999.

—— Grant of Barton and Buckwell (Bucwell) manors in, to St. Stephen's Chapel, Westminster, 1382. Harl. 43 E. 16.

—— Fine of Seaton's manor etc., in, 1548. Harl. 75 H. 4, 76 H. 50.

—— License for alienation of, and covenants conc., Seaton's manor, etc., in, 1548. Harl. 75 E. 22;—1551. Harl. 75 E. 28;—1554. Harl. 79 D. 18, 79 G. 2;—1581. Harl. 79 F. 24.

**Boughton Malherb,** *co. Kent.* Grant of reversion of Colbrigge manor in, to St. Stephen's Chapel, Westminster, 1382. Harl. 43 E. 16.

**Boughton Monchelsea,** *co. Kent.* Grant in, rent being paid at Wierton (Wertyng) in, *t.* Edw. I. Add. 16388.

—— Grant in, 1544 (Boughton Mountchesey). Harl. 83 H. 25.

—— *Vicarius.* Alan Styword, 1383 (Boctone Munchensy). Add. 8548.

**Boughton under Blean** (Bocton subtus le Blen, etc.), *co. Kent.* Grants, etc., in, 1339. Harl. 79 B. 13 ;—1167. Add. 946;—1515. Add. 953;—1555. Harl. 77 H. 21 :—1582. Harl. 75 F. 1:—1589. Harl. 77 H. 46.

—— Fines in, 1548. Harl. 75 H. 4, 76 H. 50.

—— Suit conc. Hookwood in, 1555–8. Harl. 76 I. 15.

—— Covenants for fines and fine of Brendley *al.* Butler's manor, etc., in, 1587. Harl. 76 A. 34 (Bowghton Blene), 35, 78 A. 33 ;—1570. Harl. 79 B. 27, 28.

—— *Vicarius.* Joh. Langhwathe, *ante* 1367. Harl. 76 D. 28.

**Bouinton.** *v.* Boynton, *E. R., co. York.*

**Boulby,** *co. York.* Grant in, [1262] (Bulleby). Eg. 410.

**Boulge,** *co. Suff.* Extract from Court-roll, 1646. Add. 10251.

**Boultham** (Bultham), *co. Linc.* Grants of a mill, etc., in, to St. Sepulchre's Hospital, Lincoln, *t.* Hen. III. Harl. 47 B. 36, 47 C. 9.

**Boulton** (Bolton, etc.), *nr. Derby, co. Derb.* Grants, etc., in, to Darley Abbey, *post* 1250. Add. 5236;—1282. Add. 5237;—1287. Add. 5238.

—— Grants, etc., in, 1294. Harl. 86 G. 43 ;—1344. Add. 5240;—1580. Woll. xi. 122 (Boughton *al.* Bolton); —1598. Woll. ii. 77.

**Bourgersshe.** *v.* Burwash, *co. Suss.*

**Bourghmerssh.** *v.* Burmarsh, *co. Kent.*

**Bourn,** *co. Camb.* Grants, etc., in, to Sawtrey Abbey, *t.* Hen. II. Harl. 83 B. 49 (Brunne, Brune) ;—late 13 cent. Harl. 83 B. 46, 47.

—— Papal conf. of grants in, to Sawtrey Abbey, 1176 (Bronna). Cott. MS. Aug. ii. 125.

—— Lease in, from Sawtrey Abbey, *t.* Edw. I. (Brunna). Harl. 83 A. 38.

**Bourne.** *v.* Beaksbourne, *co. Kent.*

—— *v. sub* Bishopsbourne, *co. Kent.*

—— *v.* Eastbourne, *co. Suss.*

**Bourne,** *co. Linc.* Grant of Oustirby in, nr. Thurlby, etc., 1354. Add. 20680 (Brunne) ;—1549. Add. 13561 (Burne).

—— Precipe on a covenant conc. lands in, 1578. Add. 25065.

—— *Prepositus.* Rodbertus, *t.* Steph. Harl. 50 A. 9.

**Bournham.** *v.* Burnham, *co. Buck.*

**Bourton.** *v.* Burton, *co. Denb.*

**Bourton** (Burton, etc.), *nr. Buckingham, co. Buck.* Grants, etc., in, early 13 cent.–*t.* Hen. III. Harl. 84 I. 24, 85 C. 49 ;—1239–40. Harl. 85 E. 60 ;— 1358. Lansd. 566 ;—1403. Lansd. 569 (Borton), 570, 571 ;—1486. Lansd. 575 (Bouretun).

—— Grants in, to Biddlesdon Abbey, *t.* Hen. III. Harl. 85 C. 20 (Burthou), 85 C. 50, 86 A. 19 (Borton).

—— Lease in, from the same, 1325. Harl. 84 E. 52.

**Bourton,** *co. Warw. Persona.* Ricardus, *ante* 1182. Add. 21458.

**Bourton, Black,** *co. Oxon.* Grant of the chapel to Oseney Abbey, end of 12 cent. (Burton). Add. 20292.

—— Grant for enclosure in, to Oseney Abbey, 1266. Add. 20290.

**Bourton, Gt. and Lit.,** *co. Oxon.* Grants, etc., in, to Chacombe Priory, *co.* Northt., *t.* Hen. III. Add. 7518 (Borton), 7519 (Burton), 7543 (Burthou).

**Bourton on the Water,** *co. Glouc.* Grant of land nr. (?), 779 (Sulmonnesburg). Cott. MS. Aug. ii. 4.

—— Grant in, 949 (Burgtune). Cott. viii. 6 (*copy*).

—— Settlement in Nethercote, etc in, 1412 (Burton). Slo. xxxiii. 59.

—— Grant by Jas. I. of Nethercote manor in, 1612. Cott. xiii. 35.

**Bouthom.** *v.* Bootham, *co. York.*

**Bouwode.** *v. sub* Netherbury, *co. Dors.*

**Bovedon,** *co. Som.* Release, etc., of the manor, 1468. Harl. 52 A. 41 ;— 1469. Harl. 54 D. 20.

**Bovehatch.** *v. sub* Chartham, *co. Kent.*

**Boveney,** *in Burnham, co. Buck.* Recovery in, 1537. Harl. 86 O. 30.

Bovey, North, *co. Devon.* Suit in, 1340 (Northbouy). Harl. 53 C. 47.

Bovey Tracy, *co. Devon.* Lease in, 1504. Add. 14037.

------ Brief conc. a fire at Chapple in, 1823. Ch. Br. C. iv. 1.

Bovil's Manor. *v. sub* Alderton, *co. Suff.*

Bovingdon, *co. Hertf.* Conf. of a grant in, *t.* Hen. III. (Buuendon). Harl. 111 G. 8.

Bow Brickhill. *v.* Brickhill, Bow, *co. Buck.*

Bowcombe, *Isle of Wight.* Compotus of the manor, 1488–9. Harl. Roll A. 38.

Bowden, *co. Roxburgh.* Covenant betw. Melrose and Kelso Abbeys conc. bounds in, [1208?] (Bowlden). Cott. xviii. 17.

Bowden, Great, *co. Leic.* Extent, etc., 1494 (Boudon Magna). Add. 6108.

------ *Persona.* Nicholaus, late Hen. II. (Bugedune). Add. 22519.

------------ Will. Huse *al.* Heuse, 1414. Add. 21819, 21822.

Bowden, Little, *co. Northt.* Conf. by King John of grant in, 1208 (Bugedon). Add. 6014.

------ Release in, early 13 cent. (Budune). Add. 6040.

------ Plea for view of frank-pledge, etc., in, 1329 (Parva Boudon). Slo. xxxi. 12.

------ Pardon for alienation in, 1598. Add. 6070.

------ *Rector.* Herbert. de Karleton, late Hen. III. Add. 26958, 26959.

Bowditch. *v. sub* Chardstook, *co. Dors.*

Bowdon. *v. sub* Buckfastleigh, *co. Devon.*

------ *v. sub* Chapel en le Frith, *co. Derb.*

------ *v. sub* Sherford, *co. Devon.*

Bower, East, *in Bridgwater, co. Som.* Grant in, 1391 (Estboure). Add. 13030.

Bowers Gifford, *co. Essex.* Grant, etc., in, late Hen. III. Cott. xxvii. 97 (Burea); — 1345. Add. 15459 (Burys).

------ Release of the manor, 1281 (Bures). Add. 5251.

Bowes, *co. York.* Surrender of a lease of the castle and manor, 1395. Add. 20582.

------ Court-roll, 1441. Harl. Roll G. 23.

Bowghton Blene. *v.* Boughton under Blean, *co. Kent.*

Bowithick, *nr. Davidstow, co. Cornw.* Grant, etc., in, early Hen. III. (Bodwideo). Harl. 53 B. 42.

Bowithick, in ------ (?), *co. Cornw.* Grant in, 1437 (Moobel Bodwhidek). Eg. 265.

Bowkers. *v. sub* Grinstead, West, *co. Suss.*

Bowland with Leagram, *cos. Lanc. and York.* Lease of Leagram Park in, for disparking, 1556. Campb. ix. 7.

------ Fine in, 1638. Woll. xi. 29.

Bowlden. *v.* Bowden, *co. Roxburgh.*

Bowmford. *v.* Bamford, *co. Derb.*

Bowness, *in Kendal, co. Westm.* (?) *Persona.* Rob. Avenell, 1411. Add. 20515.

Bownest, *co. Bedf.* Acquittances for fines for the manor (?), 1627-1632. Add. 24082–24089.

Bowood, N. and S. *v. sub* Netherbury, *co. Dors.*

Bowthorpe (Buthorp, Butorp, etc.), *co. Norf.* Grants, etc., in, early 13 cent. Add. 14554; — *t.* Hen. III. Add. 14557; —1523. Add. 17746.

------ Grants, etc., in, to Langley Abbey, *t.* Hen. III.—late 13 cent. Add. 7367, 14555, 14556, 14558–14562.

------ *Persona.* Willelmus, *t.* Hen. III. Add. 14555, 14560.

------ *Sacerdos al. Capellanus.* Stephanus, early 13 cent.—*t.* Hen. III. Add. 14554, 14555.

Box, *co. Wilts.* Exchange in Slade in (?), *t.* Hen. II. Campb. xxiii. 4.

------ Grant, etc., of the mill and advowson to Farley Priory, *t.* Hen. III. (Boxa). Harl. 46 I. 61.

------ Court-rolls, 1390-1419. Add. 26903–26905.

------ *Persona.* Ricardus, late 12 cent. (La boxa). Campb. xiii. 11.

------ *Vicarius.* Johannes, *t.* Hen. III. Harl. 46 I. 61.

Boxford, *co. Berks.* Grant at, 960 (Boxoran). Cott. MS. Aug. ii. 40.

**Boyton,** co. *Wilts.* Grant of the manor, 1348. Harl. 83 D. 44.

—— Sale of Chiltern and Chicklade Ridge woods in, 1639. Add. 15189.

—— *Rector.* Joh. Fakenham, 1362. Add. 24873.

**Boyton Hall Manor.** *v. sub* Monks Eleigh, co. *Suf.*

**Bozeat,** co. *Northt.* Grant of the church to St. James's Abbey, Northampton, c. 1150–60 (Bosegete). Harl. 52 C. 4.

—— Covenant of Dryburgh Abbey to lease the church of, to St. James's Abbey, late Hen. II. (Bougieta). Cott. xxi. 13.

—— Grant, etc., in, 12–13 cent. Harl. 86 F. 46 (Bosiet);—*t.* Hen. III. Harl. 49 I. 18 (Boseghate).

—— Grant of Stanway wood in, with tithes, etc., to St. James's Abbey, early 13 cent. Harl. 53 C. 39 (Bose_ate) (copy);—1292. Harl. 54 D. 13.

—— Lease in, to the same, 1255 (Bosynte). Harl. 56 F. 1.

**Bozedon,** nr. *Buckfastleigh,* co. *Devon.* Grants in or nr. 1317. Add. 9221, 9222:—1344. Add. 9230.

**Bozenham.** *v. sub* Hartwell, co. *Northt.*

**Bozonhalle.** *v. sub* Kirton, co. *Linc.*

**Brabourn,** co. *Kent.* Release, etc., in, late Hen. III. (Braburne). Add. 20001:—1551. Harl. 75 H. 6.

**Braceborough,** co. *Linc.* Grant, etc., in, 1491 (Brassingburgh). Add. 6468;—1564. Harl. 77 F. 52 (Braseborowe).

**Bracebridge,** co. *Linc.* Conf. of lands in, to St. Sepulchre's Hospital, Lincoln, [1203–13] (Bracebrige). Harl. 57 D. 27.

**Bracell, Brachal.** *v.* Brackley, co. *Northt.*

**Brackele,** co. *Kent* (?). *Perpet. vicarius.* Johannes, early 13 cent. Harl. 78 A. 50.

**Bracken,** co. *York.* Release in, to Watton Priory, 1322 (Brackyn). Harl. 55 E. 23.

**Brackenfield,** in *Morton,* co. *Derb.* Lease in, 1480 (Brakynwhith). Lansd. 168.

—— Covenant conc. a sale of timber in, 1552 (Brakynthwayte). Harl. 112 F. 61.

**Bracklesham,** co. *Suss.* Grant of the manor, 1363 (Brakelesham). Add. 20086.

**Brackley** (Brackele, etc.), co. *Northt.* Reservation of tithe in Whitfield, co. *Northt.,* to the mother church of, c. 1150–58 (Brachal). Harl. 84 D. 12.

—— Covenant betw. Biddlesdon and St. Mary de Pré Abbeys conc. tithes to the church of, 1209 (Brakele). Harl. 84 D. 19.

—— Grant in, to Biddlesdon Abbey, t. Hen. III. (Brakele). Harl. 85 E. 51.

—— Mandamus to the dean of, in tithe-suits of Biddlesdon Abbey, c. 1250. Harl. 84 F. 44:—1252. Harl. 84 F. 35.

—— Grants, etc., in the castle fields, etc., in, t. Hen. III. Harl. 85 F. 18, 85 G. 29, 86 E. 23;—late 13 cent. Harl. 85 C. 3, 86 E. 3, 86 F. 34;— 1299. Harl. 86 E. 46;—1301. Harl. 86 F. 52;—1316. Harl. 86 D. 34, 86 G. 7;—1326. Harl. 84 I. 17, 86 E. 57, 58;—1332. Harl. 86 C. 60;— 1344. Harl. 85 A. 3 (Brakkele);—1347. Harl. 86 E. 54;—1348. Harl. 84 H. 24; —1349. Harl. 85 C. 51;—1366. Harl. 86 E. 8;—1367. Harl. 86 D. 58, 59, 86 F. 53;—1396. Add. 854 (Brakkele), 855;—1430. Harl. 84 H. 40.

—— Bequests to St. Peter's Church and St. James's Chapel, and to the Vicar, 1474. Harl. 86 F. 36.

—— Lease of the parsonage, etc., 1540 (Brakley). Harl. 112 C. 45.

—— *Ballivus Domini.* Ric. le Wyse, 1316. Harl. 86 D. 34.

—— *Persona.* Thomas, t. Rich. I.- John. Harl. 84 I. 21 (Brak.):—early 13 cent. Harl. 86 D. 23 (Bracell.).

**Braconash,** co. *Norf.* Grant in, to St. Giles's Hospital, Norwich, c. 1249–70 (Braken.). Toph. 30.

—— Release of the manor, 1614. Add. 14284.

**Bracondale,** nr. *Norwich,* co. *Norf.* Conf. of grant of St. Nicholas Church at, to Norwich Priory, [1136–45] (Brakendale). Cott. ii. 1.

**Bracston.** *v.* Barkstone, co. *Linc.*

**Brad. in Pecco.** *v.* Bradborne, co. *Derb.*

**Brada, Feodum de.** License to rebuild Clothall Hospital, co. *Hertf.,* in, 1305. Harl. 112 A 3.

**Bradanfelda.** *v.* Bradfield, co. *Berks.*

Bradanwege. *v.* Broadway, *co. Worc.*

Bradborne, *co. Derb.* Conf. of grant in (?), *t.* John. Campb. xi. 9.

—— Award conc. tithes in, betw. Dunstable Priory and Dale Abbey, 1286 (Brad. in Pecco). Woll. x. 33.

*v. also* Aldwark, *co. Derb.*
Brassington, *co. Derb.*

Bradbury, *co. Durh.* Releases of the manor, 1430. Harl. 43 E. 19;—1431. Harl. 45 I. 12.

Bradcarhall Manor. *v. sub* Shropham, *co. Norf.*

Bradcroft, *nr. Stamford, co. Linc.* Conf. of a grant in, to St. Michael's Nunnery, Stamford, [1180–1200] (Bradecrofd). Add. 20242.

—— Grant in, to Southwick Priory, [1180–1200] (Bradecroft). Harl. 52 A. 22.

Brad dene [Bramdean?], *co. Southt.* A boundary mark, 909. Harl. 43 C. 1.

Bradden, *co. Northt.* Power to give seisin of the manor and advowson, 1489. Cott. xxx. 34.

Bradcote. *v.* Bredicot, *co. Worc.*

Bradefeld, Bradefeud. *v.* Bradfield, *co. Berks.*

—— *v.* Bradfield, *co. Norf.*

—— *v.* Bradfield, *co. Suff.*

—— *v. sub* Totham, Gt., *co. Essex.*

Bradefeld Ryffeyn, B. Superior. *v. sub* Bodenham, *co. Heref.*

Bradegat. *v. sub* Ingham, *co. Linc.*

Bradeham. *v.* Bradenham, East, *co. Norf.*

Bradel., Bradelege, Bradeley. *v.* Bradley, *co. Derb.*

Bradelay. *v. sub* Denby, *co. York.*

Bradelegh. *v.* Bradley, Maiden, *co. Wilts.*

Brademare, *in Hatfield Chase, co. York.* Order to the "marerii" of Earl Warren in, for eels for Roche Abbey, *c.* 1147. Cott. xxx. 17 (*copy*).

Brademora, *in Kington, co. Heref.* Grant in, to Clifford Priory, *t.* Hen. III. Harl. 48 C. 28.

Braden, *co. Wilts.* Royal license to impark wood in the forest of, 1230. Harl. 43 C. 38.

Bradenham, *co. Buck.* Rector. Dom. Johannes, 1406, 1414. Add. 20351–20354.

Bradenham, East, *co. Norf.* Grant in, *post* 1245 (Bradeham). Campb. v. 4.

—— Inquisition on lands in, 1612. Add. 9276.

Bradenham, West, *co. Norf.* Grant of the manor, 1476. Harl. 52 F. 48.

Bradenhop. *v.* Bradnop, Over, *co. Staff.*

Bradenstoke, *co. Wilts.* Rental of lands of R. Pexhall in, 1549. Add. 26560.

—— Rental of lands of Lady Savage in, 1590. Add. 26579.

Bradeston, *co. Norf.* Inspex., in 1454, of a feoffment of the manor, etc., 1422 (Breydeston). Add. 17243.

—— Court-rolls, 1423–1461. Add. 26849.

—— *Rector.* Martinus, 1318. Add. 14579.

Bradetun. *v.* Bradington, *co. Glam.*

Bradewater. *v.* Broadwater, *co. Suss.*

Bradewerde, Mariscus de North. *v. sub* Fobbing, *co. Essex.*

Bradewerde, Mariscus de Sud. *v. sub* Horndon on the Hill, *co. Essex.*

Bradeweye. *v.* Broadway, *co. Worc.*

Bradewrdin. *v.* Bredwardine, *co. Heref.*

Bradfield. *v.* Broadfield, *co. Wilts.*

Bradfield, *co. Berks.* Suit conc. land in, 990–994 (æt Bradanfeldu). Cott. MS. Aug. ii. 15.

—— The manor in custody of A. de Valence, 1277 (Bradefeud). Add. 20253.

—— Fine in, 1727. Add. 19245.

—— *Clericus.* Galfridus, early Hen. III. Add. 7363 (Bradefeld);—*c.* 1230–40. Add. 20267 (Bradef.).

Bradfield, *co. Norf.* Re-grant in, 1346 (Bradefeld). Add. 22565.

Bradfield, *co. York.* Grants in Walderself (Walderself, Waldershelf) and Whitwell in, 1227. Add. 8166; —1350. Add. 8306;—1382. Add. 8316;—1403. Cott. xxvii. 182;— 1408. Harl. 112 F. 31;—1431. Add. 8324.

—— Grants, etc., in Ughill (Ughil, Uggil, Ughul, Hughil, Wggyl) in, *t.* Hen. III.—*t.* Edw. II. Add. 8159, 8161, 8166, 8168, 8179, 8181, 8221, 8228, 8246, 8253, 8257.

Bradfield, *co. York (continued).* Grants, etc., in Wormll (Wyrhale, Werall, Wirale) in, *t.* Hen. III.-4. Edw. I. Add. 7492, 8199 ; — 1350. Add. 8304, 8305 ; — 1356. Add. 8309 ; — 1421. Add. 19328 ;—1568. Harl. 112 I. 48.

—— Grants, etc., in or nr. Dwaraden (Dueridene) and Westemondhath *al.* Westmondhalgh in, *t.* Edw. I. Add. 8258 ;—1303. Add. 8278 ;—early 14 cent. Add. 8226;—1351. Add. 8308.

—— Grants, etc., in Onesacre (Anesaker, Onysacker) in, *t.* Edw. I.-*t.* Edw. II. Add. 8244, 8249, 8264 ;— 1323. Add. 8286.

—— Grant at Thornessete in, 1322. Add. 8284.

—— Grants in Wadsley (Waddesley) in, 1356. Add. 8309 ;—1409. Add. 8320 ;—1568. Harl. 112 I. 48.

—— Covenant conc. an annuity charged on, 1367 (Braidefeld). Woll. v. 32.

—— Grants in Wigtwizle (Wygtwysill) in, 1421. Add. 19329.

—— Fine in, 1541. Woll. ii. 71.

—— Admission to lands in, 1714. Add. 18009.

Bradfield, *co. Suff.* Grant, etc., in, 1317 (Bradef.). Add. 24501 ;—1319 (Bradefeld). Add. 24502.

—— *Rector.* Will. de Gelham, 1319. Add. 24502.

Bradfield St. Clare, *co. Suff.* Grant in, 1316 (Bradefelde Seyncler). Harl. 48 F. 48.

—— *Rector.* Edm. Tilney, 1471. Add. 8431.

Bradford, *co. Chest.* Writ on a claim to lands in, 1420. Add. 6278.

Bradford, *co. Dors.* Fine in, for a chantry in Shaftesbury Abbey, 1282. Add. 5250.

—— Inquisition conc. charges on the manor, 1386. Add. 6087.

Bradford, *in Bocking, co. Essex.* Release in, 1419 (Bredeford). Add. 13546.

Bradford, *co. Som.* Bond of warranty for the manor, *c.* 1250. Add. 23840.

Bradford, *in Kingsbury, co. Warw.* Grant in, *t.* Hen. I. (Bradeford). Cott. xxii. 3.

Bradford, *co. Wilts.* Exchange nr., *t.* Hen. II. Campb. xxiii. 4.

Bradford, *co. Wilts (continued).* Grant in, to Farley Priory, *t.* Hen. III. (Bradeford). Campb. xiii. 13.

—— Lease in, nr. Barton Grange, 1436. Campb. ii. 13.

—— Sale in, 1551. Add. 5702.

—— *Ballivus.* Will. de Wancy, *t.* Hen. III. Campb. xiii. 13.

Bradford, *co. York.* Grant, etc., in, 1428 (Bradforth). Add. 16915 ;— 1435. Add. 16925.

—— Grant, etc., in Bierley (Byrille) in, 1465. Add. 16955 ;—1466. Add. 16956.

—— Release in Gt. Horton in, 1585. Add. 26130.

—— Fine of the manor, 1638. Woll. xi. 29.

—— Certificate of tenancy in the manor, 1691. Add. 15011.

—— Brief conc. a hail-storm in, 1769. Ch. Br. B. ix. 5.

—— *Prepositus.* Alexander, *t.* Hen. III. Add. 16598.

—— *Persona.* Sire Rob. de Toynton, 1310. Add. 7677, 20568.

—— *Vicarius.* Hen. Gelles, 1465. Add. 16955.

*v. also* Wilsden, *co. York.*

Bradford Bridge. *v. sub* Hampton in Arden, *co. Warw.*

Bradford, Villula de. *v. sub* Leominster, *co. Heref.*

Bradgar. *v.* Bredgar, *co. Kent.*

Brading, *Isle of Wight.* Conveyance in, 1360 (Brerding). Harl. 50 H. 3.

—— Compotus of the manor, 1488-9. (Brethdyng). Harl. Roll A. 38.

Bradington, *co. Glam.* Grants, etc., of "terra de," to Margam Abbey, [1190]. Harl. 75 A. 17 (Bradetun); —[1199]. Harl. 75 A. 18 (Bradinctune), 75 C. 24 (do.);—1217. Harl. 75 D. 14 (Bradington); — [1219-30]. Harl. 75 D. 16 (Bradingtun).

Bradker hall Manor. *v. sub* Shropham, *co. Norf.*

Bradleigh, *nr. Newton Bushel, co. Devon.* Grant of fairs in the manor of, 1309 (Bradelegh). Harl. 58 I. 46 (copy).

Bradley, *in Malpas, co. Chest.* Exchequer acquittance for rent in, 1615. Add. 25574.

Bradwater. *v.* Broadwater, *co. Suss.*

Bradway. *v. sub* Norton, *co. Derb.*

Bradwell, *co. Derb.* Grant in, *t.* Edw. I. (Bradewell). Add. 7267.

—— Fine in, 1376 (Bradwall). Woll. ii. 75.

Bradwell, *nr. Coggeshall, co. Essex. Persona. Dom.* Tho. Pake, 1347. Cott. xxviii. 52.

Bradwell, *co. Suff.* Grants in Gapton, etc., in, n.d., 1343. Add. 691 (1, 2) (copies).

—— Grant of Gapton Hall manor in, 1538 (Bredwell). Add. 10225.

—— Precipes on covenants in, 1589. Add. 25404;—1593. Add. 25451.

Bradwell on Sea, *co. Essex.* Grants, etc., in, *t.* Hen. III. Harl. 45 I. 44; —1376. Add. 7284 (Bradwall);— 1462. Harl. 53 D. 9 (Bradewell);— 1485. Add. 9262.

—— Fine in, 1545. Add. 15610.

—— Precipes on covenants in, 1578. Add. 24951;—1592. Add. 25019.

Braghyngg. *v.* Braughin, *co. Hertf.*

Braham. *v.* Brantham, *co. Suff.*

Braibroc. *v.* Braybrooke, *co. Northt.*

Braidefald. *v.* Bradfield, *co. York.*

Braidewell. *v.* Braithwell, *co. York.*

Braifald. *v.* Brayfield, *co. Northt.*

Brailes, *co. Warw.* Grant in, 1326 (Braylies). Cott. xxvii. 137.

—— Brief conc. a hail-storm in, 1768. Ch. Br. B. viii. 3.

Brailsford, *in Appletree Hundred, co. Derb.* Covenant conc. lands in Ednaston in, with Tutbury Priory, *c.* 1230. Woll. ix. 76.

—— *Parson.* Will. Greaves, 1619. Woll. xi. 63.

Brailsford, *nr. N. Wingfield, co. Derb.* Grant in, 1356 (Braylesford juxta Tupton). Woll. vi. 65.

Braintree, *co. Essex.* Release in, 1419 (Branketre). Add. 13546.

—— Precipes on covenants in, 1561 (Braynktrye). Add. 24938;—1578 (Branktre). Add. 24968;—1593 (Braintrie). Add. 25035.

Braiseworth, *co. Suff.* Release in, 1375 (Brieseworth). Harl. 56 A. 47.

Braithwell, *co. York.* Grants, etc., in, *t.* Hen. III. Harl. 83 E. 88 (Braidewell);—1321. Harl. 112 F. 59.

—— License to endow Fotheringhay College, *co.* Northt., with the manor of, 1415 (Braiwell). Campb. x. 5.

—— *Clericus.* Willelmus, *t.* Hen. III. Harl. 83 E. 38.

—— *Vicarius.* Willelmus, *c.* 1240-50. Add. 21268.

—— —— Hugo, 1389. Add. 16864, 16865.

Brakanhill. *v. sub* Normanton, *co. York.*

Brakelond. *v. sub* Coney Weston, *co. Suff.*

Braken. *v.* Braconash, *co. Norf.*

Braken Wood, *nr. Kirkstead, co. Linc.* Release in, to Kirkstead Abbey, [1196-8] (Braken). Harl. 58 B. 44.

Brakkele. *v.* Brackley, *co. Northt.*

Brakynthwayte, Brakynwhith. *v.* Brackenfield, *in Morton, co. Derb.*

Bramber (Brembre), *co. Suss.* Land in Henfield, *co. Suss.*, held by Lewes Priory, "faciendo clausuram castelli de," [1255-68]. Cott. MS. Nero C. iii., f. 214.

—— Court-roll, 1383. Harl. Roll S. 27.

—— Release in, 1626. Add. 18932.

Brambletye, *nr. E. Grinstead, co. Suss.* Lease of the water-mill of, 1291 (Brambeltye.) Harl. 51 A. 47.

—— Power to give seisin in, 1554. Add. 18837.

Brambridge, *co. Southt.* A boundary-mark, 909 (at Brombrigce). Harl. 43 C. 1.

Bramcote, *in Bulkington, co. Warw.* Grants, etc., in, late Hen. III. Add. 17360 (Brancot);—1262. Add. 17361 (Bromcote);—1301. Add. 17366 (Bramkote);—1337. Add. 17378;— 1359. Add. 17377-17380 (Brompcote); —1390. Add. 17382 (Brampkote).

Bramfield (Bromfeld, etc.), *co. Suff.* Grants, etc., in, 1317. Harl. 47 C. 35, 47 D. 13 (Bromfild);—1330. Add. 10367;—1336. Add. 10368 (Brounfeld), 10369;—1353. Add. 10373;— 1375. Harl. 49 C. 7 (Braunfeld).

Bramford (Bromford, Braunford, etc.), *co. Suff.* Grants, etc., in, *t.* Hen. III. -*t.* Edw. I. Add. 9800-9809, 9819-9821;—1259. Add. 9813;—1286-7.

**Brampton Bryan** (Brompton, Brompton Brian, etc.), *co. Heref.* (*continued*). *Rector* (*continued*). *Dom.* Joh. Davyes, 1524. Cott. xxiv. 35.
*v. also* Pedwardine, *co. Heref.*

**Brampton, Chapel** *al.* **Little** (Parva Brampton, etc.), *co. Northt.* Grants, etc., in, 1262. Add. 21576, 21577;— 1280-90. Add. 21621, 21622;—1287. Add. 21623;—1307. Add. 21624;— 1316. Add. 21625, 21626;—1322. Add. 21627;—1324. Add. 21628;— 1346. Add. 21631;—1356. Add. 21632;—1388. Add. 21633;—1391. Add. 21634 - 21637;—1395. Add. 21638;—1414. Add. 21640, 21641;— 1421. Add. 21613, 21614; — 1435. Add. 21618, 21642; — 1474. Add. 21562 (Chapell Brampton).

—— Acquittance for an aid in, 1333. Add. 21883.

—— Settlements of the manor, etc., 1334. Add. 21629; — 1409. Add. 21639;—1427. Add. 21555, 21615.

—— Inquisition of lands of Hen. de Dyve in, 1336. Add. 21630.

—— Sub-lease of the Queen's water fishery, etc., in, 1568. Add. 21572.

**Brampton, Church** *al.* **Great** (Chirche Brampton, Magna Brampton, etc.), *co. Northt.* Bond for a hen rent in, late Hen. III. (Bromptona). Add. 21620 (*copy*).

—— Grants, etc., in, *c.* 1280. Add. 21579;—1285. Add. 21581; — 1288. Add. 22312;—*c.* 1290. Add. 21574, 21578, 21580;—1297. Add. 21585;— 1303. Add. 21587; — 1305. Add. 22313;—1306. Add. 21548;—1307. Add. 21546, 21547;—1312. Add. 21907;—1314. Add. 21549, 21589, 21590;—1315. Add. 22314;—1317. Add. 21550;—1320. Add. 21591;— *post* 1330. Add. 21588;—1337. Add. 21592-21594, 21916;—1341. Add. 21595;—1342. Add. 21596, 21598, 21599;—1343. Add. 21601;—1344. Add. 21551 (Schyrchebramptona); —1351. Add. 21602;—1354. Add. 21603, 21604;—1361. Add. 21605, 21606;—1366. Add. 21552;—1371. Add. 21608;—1390. Add. 21936;— 1395. Add. 21939;—1403. Add. 21609, 21941;—1414. Add. 21945;— 1416. Add. 21946;—1421. Add. 21613, 21614;—1432. Add. 21556, 21954, 21955;—1455. Add. 21557; —1456. Add. 21558, 21956;—1463. Add. 21559-21561, 21957 - 21959;—

1478. Add. 21961;—1505. Add. 21563;—1506. Add. 21970;—1508. Add. 21564, 21565;—1511. Add. 21971;—1520. Add. 21981, 21982;— 1522. Add. 21566-21568, 21617;— 1544. Add. 21569;—1546. Add. 21570;—1548. Add. 21571;—1576. Add. 21996;—1580. Add. 21573;— 1594. Add. 21997.

—— Lease at Storkesnest, etc., in, by St. James's Abbey, Northampton, 1298. Add. 21586.

—— Grants, etc., of the manor, 1367. Add. 21607;—1375. Add. 21553, 21554;—1427. Add. 21555.

—— *Persona.* Johannes, 1337. Add. 21594.

**Brampton en le Morthen** (Bramton, Brampton in Morthing, etc.), *in Treeton, co. York.* Grants, etc., in, late Hen. III. Harl. 47 A. 38;—*t.* Edw. I.–II. Add. 21575, Woll. v. 23–25;—1336. Harl. 45 E. 2;—1442. Woll. v. 29;—1485. Woll. v. 28 (*copy*); —1528. Add. 17963.

**Bramshall,** *co. Staff.* Grant in le Okiruding in, *t.* Hen III. (Bromsulf). Cott. xxiii. 36.

**Bramshill,** *co. Southt.* Covenant conc. St. Peter's Chapel at, 1313 (Bromeshulle). Add. 6713.

**Bramshot,** *co. Southt.* Release in, 1465. Add. 26567.

—— Court - rolls, 1605, 1609, 1611, 1616, 1625, 1647, 1711. Add. 24820- 24824.

**Bramston.** *v.* Brandistone, *co. Norf.*

**Brancepeth,** *co. Durh.* Grant of the advowson by Edw. III. to John his son, 1372 (Braunspathe). Cott. xv. 1.

**Branch.** *v. sub* Frome, *co. Som.*

**Brancroft.** *v. sub* Rossington, *co. York.*

**Brandesburton.** *v.* Brandsburton, *co. York.*

**Brandeston.** *v. sub* Waldingfield, Great, *co. Suff.*

**Brandeston,** *co. Suff.* Grant in, to the Lepers' Hospital, Dunwich, 12-13 cent. (?) (Brantost.). Add. 15262 (*copy*).

—— Grants, etc., in, 1314. Add. 10272 (Brandiston); — 1418. Add. 10282;—1440. Add. 10205.

—— *Persona.* Heute, 12-13 cent. (?). Add. 15262 (*copy*).

Brandistone (Brandeston, etc.), co.
Norf. Grants, etc., in, 1320. Add.
15188;—1321. . Add. 15191;—1409.
Add. 14128;—1414. Add. 14181;—
1425. Add. 15193;—1449. Add.
14148;—1450. Add. 14150;—1468.
Add. 15195;—1473. Add. 14162;—
1492. Add. 15197;—1496. Add.
14178;—1516. Add. 14197;—1528.
Add. 14205;—1551. Add. 14222;—
1553. Add. 14563 (Bramston);—
1569. Add. 14242 (Branston);—1584.
Add. 14256 (do.).

—— Fine in, 1587. Add. 9398-9401.

—— Extracts from Court-rolls of
Guton Hall manor in, 1603, 1613,
1632. Add. 14354, 14356, 14358.

—— Settlement to uses of the manor,
etc., 1646. Add. 19160.

—— Rector. Rich. Huys, 1553. Add.
14563.

Brandon, co. Norf. Rental in, 14 cent.
Add. 17224.

Brandon (Braundon), co. Warw.
Grants, etc., of the manor, etc., 1397.
Harl. 45 C. 50;—1406. Harl. 49 I.
30;—1415. Harl. 45 C. 55;—1439.
Harl. 55 G. 5;—1510. Cott. v. 16, Harl.
58 B. 25.

Brandon Ferry, co. Suff. Precipe on
a covenant conc. "the Bull," etc., in,
1545. Add. 25270.

—— Precipes on covenants conc. lands
in, 1561. Add. 25312;—1578. Add.
25343;—1589. Add. 25395.

Brandsburton (Brandesburton, etc.),
co. York. Grants, etc., in, t. Hen. III.
Add. 5729;—1341. Add. 5745;—1369.
Add. 5754, 5755;—1404. Add. 5758
(Braynes Burton);—1457. Add. 5766;
—1458. Lansd. 427, 428;—1475. Add.
5772.

—— Exemplif. of fine in Burshill
(Brustell), etc., in, 1579. Add. 905.

—— Clericus. Robertus, t. Hen. III.
Add. 5729.

—— Rector. Mag. Will. de Melton,
1369. Add. 5754.

—— —— Will. Cok, 1458. Lansd.
427, 428.

Branfeld (?). v. Brayfield, co. Northt.

Branfold, Brangewold, Brangil-
fold, Brangynfold, Den of. v. sub
Goudhurst, co. Kent.

Branketre. v. Braintree, co. Essex.

Branleis. v. Brynllys, co. Brecon.

Bransby, co. York. Brief for rebuilding the church, 1766. Ch. Br. B.
vi. 1.

—— Persona. Radulfus, t. Hen. III.
(Braudesby). Harl. 112 D. 42.

Branscombe, co. Devon. Release in
Littlecomb in, 1420. Add. 13089.

Bransholm. v. sub Sutton, in Holderness, co. York.

Branston, co. Linc. List of deeds
conc. lands of Kirksteud Abbey in,
early 18 cent. (Branston). Harl. Roll
O. 5.

Branteston. v. Braunston, co. Northt.

Branteston, Brantestun. v. sub
Waldingfield, Gt., co. Suff.

Brantham (Braham, etc.), co. Suff.
Grants, etc., in, t. Hen. III. Add.
9470;—t. Edw. I. Add. 9490, 9492,
9503; — 1294. Add. 9530; — 1298.
Add. 9543; — 1301. Add. 9548; —
1302. Add. 9550; — 1313. Add.
9882; — 1331. Add. 9591-9595;—
1336. Add. 9602; — 1348. Add.
9610-9612; — 1359. Add. 8377;—
1361. Add. 24246;—1363-1380. Add.
9634, 9635, 9637, 9639, 9640, 9643,
9645, 9652.

—— Grant nr. Cattiwade bridge in,
t. Edw. I. Add. 9511.

—— Rental of J. de Braham in, 1302-
3. Add. 9552.

—— Rector. Dom. Nic. de Sparcke-
forde, t. Edw. I. Add. 22566.

Branthingessorpe, Brantinges-
torp. v. Bruntingthorpe, co. Leic.

Brantingham, co. York. Release in,
1309. Harl. 83 E. 58.

Brantleys. v. Brynllys, co. Brecon.

Brantons. v. Brampton, co. Derb.

Bransthoft. v. sub Killingholme, co.
Linc.

Branston. v. Branston, co. Linc.

Braseborowe. v. Braceborough, co.
Linc.

Brassington, in Bradborne, co. Derb.
Settlement of suit conc. rights in the
chapel, 1286 (Bracinton). Woll. x. 33.

—— Fine in, 1638. Woll. xi. 29.

—— Extract from court-roll, 1640.
Woll. xi. 86.

—— Capellanus. Will. Bagger, 1410.
Woll. vii. 17.

Brayfield, Cold, co. *Buck.* Lease, etc., of Waterhall, Old Layton and Cold Brayfield manors or farms in, 1630. Cott. xxiii. 29 *b*, xxviii. 70.

Brayleaford. *v.* Brailsford, co. *Derb.*

Braytoft (Braitoft), co. *Linc.* Conff. of grants in, to Bullington Priory, 1256. Harl. 52 H. 28 ;—*t.* Edw. I. or II. Harl. 52 H. 5 ;—*c.* 1322. Harl. 52 H. 27.

—— Grants, etc., in, 1292. Harl. 54 D. 12 ;—1355. Harl. 57 G. 11.

—— Fine in, 1302. Harl. 45 H. 18.

—— *Persona.* Will. de Scraithefeld *al.* Scrayfeld, 1395. Harl. 58 B. 11 ; —1396. Cott. v. 21, Harl. 58 B. 4 ;— 1401. Cott. xxvii. 6.

Brasenhill, *in Haughton,* co. *Staff.* Brief conc. a fire at, 1823. Ch. Br. C. v. 7.

Breadalbane, co. *Perth.* Crown lease of, to the Earl of Argyle, 1542. Add. 1373.

Breadsall, co. *Derb.* Fine in, 1694 (Bradsall). Woll. xi. 111.

—— *Persona.* Joh. Forest, 1401 (Braydeshall). Woll. iv. 72.

Bream, co. *Glouc.* Brief for rebuilding the chapel, 1820. Ch. Br. C. i. 8.

Breamore, co. *Southt.* Conf. of grant in, by B. de Redvers, *ante* 1245 (Brummor). Slo. xxxiii. 1.

Brearton, co. *Durh.* Grant of the manor, 1444 (Brereton). Harl. 83 F. 3, 4.

Breaston, co. *Derb.* Loan payable at, 1282 (Breydistone). Lansd. 590–592.

Brech, La. *v. sub* Corscomb, co. *Dors.*

Brechefieta. *v. sub* Erith, co. *Kent.*

Brechfa, *nr. Brynllys,* co. *Brecknock.* Grant of rent from, to Clifford Priory, [1222–31] (Breofa). Harl. 48 C. 29.

Breckles, co. *Norf.* Grant in, 1353 (?) (Magna Brecles). Harl. 76 E. 6.

Brecknock *al.* Brecon, *County of.* Protection to tenants of Margam Abbey against the men of, early 13 cent. (Brechineoch). Harl. 75 C. 19.

Brecknock, co. *Brecknock.* Grant of liberties in, to Clifford Priory, [1143–54] (Brakenau). Harl. 55 D. 44.

—— Grants, etc., in, 1387. Harl. 111 B. 20 (Brechon) ;—1400. Harl. 111 B. 30 ;—1493. Harl. 111 B. 31 ;—

1506. Harl. 111 B. 17 ;—1517. Harl. 111 B. 38.

—— Certificate of birth of Edw. Duke of Buckingham at the Castle of, 1514. Add. 19868.

—— Lease of Trallong Prebend bel. to Christ's College at, 1573. Add. 1837.

—— Valor of Crown lands in, 1590. Harl. Roll 8. 26.

—— Extracts from Court-rolls of the manor, 1632 - 1659. Add. 24452– 24470.

—— *Ballivus.* Lewis Havard, 1490. Harl. 111 B. 30.

—— —— Will. Herbert, 1493. Harl. 111 B. 31.

—— —— Tho. Walter, 1517. Harl. 111 B. 38.

Brecton. *v. sub* Stanbridge, Gt., co. *Essex.*

Brede, co. *Suss.* Grant nr. the bridge of "Hednesbroc" in, by Fécamp Abbey, [1192 -1219]. Add. 19273.

—— Grants, etc., in Witefiet *al.* Hwitefiet, etc., and Gadeburgh marshes in or nr., *t.* Hen. III.—*t.* Edw. I. Add. 960, 963, 966–968 ;— 1302. Add. 959 ;—1319. Add. 961, 962 ;—1331. Add. 969 ;—1333. Add. 970 ;—1419. Add. 972.

—— Grants, etc., in, *t.* Edw. I. Add. 965 ;—1331. Add. 964 ;—1340. Add. 24844 ;—1354. Add. 20056 ;—1366. Add. 20191 ;—1368. Add. 20057 ;— 1378. Harl. 76 D. 46 ;—1388. Add. 20059 ;—1410. Add. 24852 ;—1421. Add. 20060 ;—1431. Add. 20061, 20062 ; — 1450. Add. 973 ; — 1453. Add. 24855 ;—1457. Add. 24856 ;— 1473. Add. 24857.

—— Grants in, in Burga de Smegle, 1340. Add. 24849 ;—1431. Add. 24854.

—— Sale of a house in, to be rebuilt in Rye, 1374. Add. 20058.

—— Grants of, or in, "Potesterf" *al.* "Pasterves" in, 1374. Add. 24850 ; —1394. Add. 24851 ;—1426. Add. 24853 ;—1431. Add. 24854.

—— Fines in, 1405. Add. 24892 ; —1507. Add. 24910.

—— Precipe on a covenant in, 1592. Add. 15232.

Bredeford. *v.* Bradford, *in Bocking,* co. *Essex.*

Bredele. *v.* Bradley, co. *Linc.*

Brembresooc, *co. Sux.* Battle Abbey freed from service for, as part of Alciston Manor, [1100–23]. Harl. 43 C. 12.

Brembridge. *v. sub* Westbury, *co. Wilts.*

Bremyngton. *v.* Brimington, *co. Derb.*

Brenchley (Brencheale, etc.), *co. Kent.* Grant of the church to Tonbridge Priory, with tithes of Witherinden (Westguterindenne) in, [1227–35] (Brenchealeg). Campb. xiv. 3.

—— Grants, etc., in, *t.* Hen. III. Harl. 77 F. 50, 80 E. 30;—1391. —Harl. 80 I. 93;—1407. Harl. 76 G. 39;—1444. Harl. 76 G. 53;—1448. Harl. 80 E. 32;—1531. Harl. 80 G. 2, 3;—1559. . Harl. 76 I. 44, 77 G. 24;—1599. Harl. 111 E. 48;—1648. Harl. 79 G. 14.

—— Covenant conc. tithes of, betw. the Vicar and Tonbridge Priory, 1351. Campb. xiv. 2.

—— Bond to Combwell Priory conc. rents in, 1484. Harl. 76 E. 44.

—— Sale of Stokeshyll and Stodmerhyll manors in, 1545. Harl. 76 H. 48.

—— Sale, etc., of, or in, Bockingfold manor in, 1556. Harl. 77 H. 25;—1557. Harl. 76 I. 30;—1558. Harl. 77 E. 55;—1559. Harl. 76 I. 44, 77 G. 24 (Bokyngfold);—1560. Harl. 76 I. 37;—1561. Harl. 77 A. 4.

—— Rents of Lady Packington's manor of Bockingfold in, c. 1600. Cott. ix. 10 (1).

—— Survey of Lady Packington's lands in Bockingfold in, 1619. Cott. xxix. 51.

—— Rental of Cnowles manor in, 1626. Cott. xv. 50.

—— *Rector de Bokyngfold.* Dom. Will. atte Wealde, 1370. Harl. 80 B. 29.

—— *Vicarius.* Adam Partriche, 1351. Campb. xiv. 2.

—— *Perpet. vicarius.* Elias, 1365. Add. 16178.

Brendewenham, Brenewenham. *v.* Wenham, Gt., *co. Suff.*

Brendfen Manor. *v. sub* Middleton, *co. Suff.*

Brendhall Manor. *v. sub* Clopton, *co. Suff.*

Brendley Manor. *v. sub* Boughton under Blean, *co. Kent.*

Brenles. *v.* Brynllys, *co. Brecon.*

Brensete. *v.* Brenzett, *co. Kent.*

Brensindenn, *nr. Goudhurst* (?), *co. Kent.* Conf. of, to Combwell Priory, 1231. Harl. 77 F. 23.

—— Covenant for recovery and fine in, 1559. Harl. 76 I. 44 (Breseden), 77 G. 24 (Bressenden).

Brent Hundred, *co. Som. Ballivus.* Rob de S. Barba, *t.* Hen. III.–Edw. I. Add. 24299.

Brent Eleigh. *v.* Eleigh, Brent, *co. Suff.*

Brent, South, *co. Som.* Order to give seisin in, *t.* Hen. III.–Edw. I. (Subrente). Add. 24299.

—— Covenant for settlement of lands in, 1408. Add. 5467.

Brentfen Manor. *v. sub* Middleton, *co. Suff.*

Brentford, *co. Midd.* Meeting at, conc. disputes betw. Wessex and Essex, 705 (Breguntford). Cott. MS. Aug. ii. 18.

—— Admissions in, as of Ealing manor, 1548. Add. 24829 (Olde Braynford);—1701. Add. 19106.

—— Recovery in, 1624 (West, New and East, Brayneford). Cott. xxx. 10.

—— Brief for rebuilding the chapel, 1762. Ch. Br. B. ii. 5.

Brentles. *v.* Brynllys, *co. Brecon.*

Brentwood, *co. Essex.* Grant in, 1372 (Brendewode). Harl. 49 H. 14.

Brentyngthorpe. *v.* Bruntingthorpe, *co. Leic.*

Brensett, *co. Kent.* Grant in, by a canon of St. Mary's, Hastings, *t.* Rich. I. (Bretsete). Campb. xvi. 17.

—— Grant, etc., in, [1271]. Harl. 58 C. 14 (Brensete) (*copy*);—1509. Add. 8596 (Branset).

—— Suit in, 1626. Harl. 75 H. 22.

Breoduninga gemære. *v.* Breden, *co. Worc.*

Brerdewordin. *v.* Bredwardine, *co. Heref.*

Brerding. *v.* Brading, *I. of Wight.*

Brerdtuisil, Breretuisel, Breretwisill, Breretwysil, etc. *v.* Brierstwistle, *co. York.*

Brereton. *v.* Brearton, *co. Durh.*

Bricklehampton, *co. Worc.* Conf. of grants in, to Pershore Abbey, 972 (Brihtulfingtune). Cott. MS. Aug. ii. 6.

Briclesworth. *v.* Brixworth, *co. Northt.*

Bricthicesfel. *v.* Brushfield, *in Bakewell, co. Derb.*

Bricthwella. *v.* Brightwell, *co. Suff.*

Briddlesford, *Isle of Wight.* Grant in, 13–14 cent. (Bridlesforde). Harl. 51 G. 26.

Bride, *Isle of Man. Rector eccl. S. Brigidi.* Patricius, 1408. Add. 8482.

Bridecote. *v.* Burcot, *in Dorchester, co. Oxon.*

Bridell [Brill, *co. Buck.* ?]. Power to give seisin in, 1372. Add. 22609.

Bridetuna. *v.* Burton Bradstock, *co. Dors.*

Bridge (Bregge, etc.), *co. Kent.* Grant of Blackmansbury (Blakemannesbery) manor in, 1266. Harl. 78 G. 22.

—— Resignation to St. Augustine's Abbey, Canterbury, of homage for same manor, 1266. Harl. 78 G. 23, 24.

—— Leases, etc., in, 1315. Harl. 80 G. 21 :—1472. Harl. 76 B. 16 :—1488. Harl. 76 C. 45 :—1507. Harl. 79 B. 3 :—1508. Harl. 78 E. 29 :—1529. Harl. 76 D. 15 :—1530. Harl. 76 D. 16 :—1541. Harl. 75 H. 3 (Brigge) ; — 1548. Harl. 76 I. 28 (Brege) : — 1551. Harl. 80 C. 15 (do.) ;—1557. Harl. 76 I. 27, 34.

Bridge, *nr. Dunwich* (?), *co. Suff.* Feoffm., etc., in, 1441. Cott. xii. 42 (Bregge) ; — 1473. Harl. 51 F. 3 (Bregge).

Bridge Hundred, *co. Kent.* Grant, etc., in, 1313. Harl. 78 F. 22 ;—1415. Harl. 76 C. 9.

Bridge Sollars, *co. Heref.* Grant in, with : the advowson, to Acornbury Priory, late Hen. III. (Bruges). Harl. 48 C. 32.

Bridgeford, *co. Nott.* Grant by K. John of a market and fair at, 1203 (Brigiford). Harl. 43 C. 34.

Bridgeford, East, *co. Nott.* Grant of the manor, 1345 (Estbryggeford). Harl. 83 G. 54.

—— Brief for rebuilding the church, 1770. Ch. Br. B. xi. 2.

—— *Rector.* Nic. Culcheth, 1499. Add. 17700.

Bridgers. *v. sub* Sevenoaks, *co. Kent.*

Bridghampton, *co. Som.* Bond conc. the manor of, 1316 (Brigghamptom). Harl. 50 B. 16.

Bridgnorth, *co. Salop.* Grant in, late Hen. III. (Brugia). Add. 13286.

—— Crown-grant in, 1612. Cott. xiii. 35.

—— Certificate of burgess-ship to W. White, 1724. Add. 19411.

—— Briefs for rebuilding St. Mary Magdalen's Church, 1791, 1796. Ch. Br. B. xxxi. 4, xxxvi. 2.

—— *Prepositi.* Hen. Cuynterel, Rob. Tinctor, late Hen. III. Add. 13286.

—— *Ballivi.* Jos. Mason, Tho. Corser, 1724. Add. 19411.

Bridgwater, *co. Som.* Grant in East Bower and Horsey in, 1391. Add. 13030.

—— Grant in, 1420 (Briggewater). Add. 13976.

—— Lease of the castle, etc., to Rich., Duke of York, c. 1433 (?) (Bruggewater). Harl. 53 H. 17.

—— Crown appointment of a steward over the castle manor, 1574. Harl. 75 E. 42.

—— Presentment conc. debts to the Crown in, 1602. Add. 24438.

Bridhurst. *v.* Bredhurst, *co. Kent.*

Briditaua. *v.* Burton Bradstock, *co. Dors.*

Bridlesforde. *v.* Briddlesford, *Isle of Wight.*

Bridlington, *co. York.* Conf. by Hen. I. of grants in, to Bridlington Priory, [1128–32] (Brellintona). Cott. MS. Aug. ii. 56.

—— Exemplif. of fine in, 1687. Add. 890.

Bridport, *co. Dors.* Conff. of the church to Fontenelle Abbey, *t.* Hen. L. [1142–80]. Add. 8071 (6, 7) (*copies*).

Bridsal. *v.* Birdsall, *co. York.*

Bridstow, *co. Heref.* Grant in, 1654. Add. 1953.

Briestwistle, *in Whitley, co. York.* Grants, etc., in, to Byland Abbey, *post* 1194. Add. 7477 (Breretwysil) ; —[1203]. Add. 7445 (Brerituisil) ;— c. 1203. Add. 7409 (Brertwisil), 7411 (Breretuisel), 7422, 7424, 7425 (Brerdtuisil) ;—*t.* John. Add. 7433, 7439 ;—[1232–40]. Add. 7465 (Breretwisill) ;—*ante* 1298. Add. 7438.

*v. also* Whitley, *co. York.*

Brikleswurth. *v.* Brixworth, co. Northt.

Brill, co. Buck. Power to give seisin in (?), 1372 (Bridell). Add. 22609.

—— Covenant for fine of the manor, etc., 1547. Harl. 79 G. 13.

Brimeshope, Brimhope. *v.* Brinsop, co. Heref.

Brimfield, co. Heref. Conf. of rights of burial to the chapel of, c. 1173-80 (Brunfeld). Add. 19585.

Brimington, co. Derb. Grants in Tapton, etc., in, t. Hen. III. Woll. vii. 11 (Briminton):—1347. Harl. 112 G. 37 (Brymyngton).

—— Fine in, 1541 (Bremyngton). Woll. ii. 71.

—— Senescallus. Petrus, t. Hen. III. Harl. 112 G. 39.

Brimmage. *v. sub* Cornwood, co. Devon.

Brimpsfield, co. Glouc. Lease of the manor, c. 1433 (?) (Brymmesfeld). Harl. 53 H. 17.

Brimpton, co. Berks. Grant, etc., in, 1316. Add. 19177; — 1463. Add. 19179.

Brimsnorton. *v.* Norton Brize, co. Oxon.

Brindle, co. Lanc. Rector. Joh. Kyrke, 1480 (Brynhill). Harl. 78 I. 47.

Bringhurst, co. Leic. Vicar. Sire Rich. de Overton, 1364 (Bryngehurst). Harl. 57 E. 18.

Brington, co. Northt. Grant, etc., in, 1448. Add. 21662 (Chirchebryngtone):—1520. Add. 21663 (Brynton).

—— Terrier, 1511 (Bryngtone Magna). Add. 1978.

Bringwine. *v.* Bryngwyn, co. Radnor.

Briningham (Brynyngham), co. Norf. Court-rolls, 1386-1383. Add. 19070; —1422-1455. Add. 19076.

—— Recovery of the manor, 1540 (Byrnyngham). Add. 14871.

Brinkburn, in Felton, co. Northumb. Brief for rebuilding the chapel, 1766. Ch. Br. B. vi. 7.

Brinkworth, co. Wilts. Brief conc. a fire at, 1758. Ch. Br. A. iv. 6.

Brinsop, co. Heref. Grants, etc., in, late 13 cent. Add. 4582 (Brimhope), 4583 (Broneshope), 4587 (Brimeshope), 4588 (Ouerebrymeshope), 4589 (Bruns-

hop), 7025 (Broneshope), 7026 (Brunneshope), 7030 (Brunshope):—1295-6. Add. 4584 (Bruneshop):—1297. Add. 4585 (Brunsope):—1323. Add. 4591 (Brunshope).

—— Powers to give seisin of the manor, 1440. Add. 4608 (Brynishope):—1446. Harl. 111 E. 2 (Brynshope).

—— Entail in, 1459. Add. 4605 (Brynshope).

Brisingham. *v.* Bressingham, co. Norf.

Brisley, co. Norf. Writ for conf. of lands, etc., in, to the Bp. of Norwich, [1100-7] (Bruselea). Cott. ii. 6.

Brislington, co. Som. Sale of a Crown lease of the rectory, 1588. Harl. 79 F. 16.

Bristale. *v.* Birstall, co. Leic.

Bristall. *v.* Birstall, co. York.

Bristol, co. Glouc. Notif. to the "prepositus" of, for immunity to Farley Priory from tolls, t. Hen. II. (Bristou). Harl. 43 C. 16.

—— Papal conf. of grants in, to Margam Abbey, 1186 (Bristowe). Harl. 75 A. 1.

—— Ref. to a recovery at, by H. de Hunteneford, against Pershore Abbey, [1198-1203] (Bristollum). Campb. xviii. 10.

—— Willelmus, Capellanus de Radecl[iva], a witness, 12-13 cent. Add. 7764.

—— Grant in, from Nuneaton Priory, early 13 cent. (Bristoll). Harl. 75 A. 31.

—— Warrants to distrain on Jews at, [1217-21]. Add. 7179.

—— Roll of Irs. of D., Abbat of St. Augustine's at, c. 1220. Cott. iv. 58.

—— Grants, etc., in, [1235?]. Add. 6518, 6519, 25881:—[1240?]. Add. 26420, 26421:—early Edw. I. Harl. 56 A. 38:—1273. Add. 15203:—1284-1288. Add. 26422-26429:—[1285?]. Add. 25882:—1295. Add. 16204:—1298. Harl. 53 D. 39:—early 14 cent. Harl. 47 G. 32, 58 D. 21:—1311. Harl. 53 B. 10:—1314. Harl. 47 G. 12:—1319. Add. 26432:—1321. Harl. 52 I. 11:—1324. Add. 26433:—1331. Harl. 47 G. 5:—1332. Harl. 47 C. 51:—1338. Harl. 53 D. 42:—1342. Harl. 45 E. 67, 55 B. 9:—1348. Harl. 52 I. 13:—1349. Harl. 51 F. 38, 52 I. 14:—1361. Harl. 45 B. 8:—1362.

Bristol, co. *Glouc.* (*continued*). **Major** (*continued*). Roger Tortle, 1324. Add. 26433.

———— Joh. de Axobrugg, 1331. Harl. 47 G. 5.

———— Hugo de Langebrugge, 1332. Harl. 47 C. 51.

———— Steph. le Spicer, 1338. Harl. 53 D. 42.

———— Everard. le Fraunceis, 1342. Harl. 45 E. 67, 55 B. 9.

———— Joh. Godereat, 1348, 1349. Harl. 52 I. 13, 14.

———— Joh. Spicer, 1349. Harl. 51 F. 38.

———— Ric. Spicer, 1361. Harl. 45 B. 8, 45 I. 20.

———— Ric. de Brompton, 1363. Add. 7837.

———— Joh. Stoke, 1368. Add. 15206.

———— Walt. Derby, 1369. Harl. 56 D. 37.

———— Joh. Bathe, 1370. Harl. 49 D. 12.

———— Will. Canynges, 1374. Harl. 56 D. 12.

———— Joh. Stoke, 1380. Harl. 48 A. 22, 23.

———— Elias Spelly, 1383. Harl. 48 A. 25, 26.

———— Tho. Beaupyne, 1383. Harl. 48 A. 27.

———— Joh. Somerwelle, 1393, 1394. Harl. 46 G. 25, 26.

———— Will. Frome, 1394, 1395. Harl. 46 G. 27, 28.

———— Tho. Knap, 1396. Harl. 46 G. 30.

———— Joh. Bannebury, 1397. Harl. 46 G. 33.

———— Joh. Barstaple, 1402. Harl. 46 G. 37.

———— Tho. Knap, 1404. Harl. 46 G. 39.

———— Rob. Dudbrook, 1405. Harl. 46 G. 42.

———— Joh. Fisshere, 1409. Harl. 46 G. 50.

———— Joh. Droys, 1410. Harl. 46 G. 51, 53 ;—1414. Add. 26469.

———— Joh. Sherp, 1416. Harl. 46 H. 2.

———— Jac. Cokkys, 1420. Harl. 47 G. 54.

———— Marc. William, 1423. Add. 26476 (6).

———— Joh. Clyve, 1426. Add. 26476 (7).

Bristol, co. *Glouc.* (*continued*). **Major** (*continued*). Joh. Stanley, 1444. Add. 26471, 26472.

———— Will. Canynges, 1449. Harl. 112 D. 40.

———— Philip Meede, 1459. Add. 26474.

———— Will. Rogent, 1496. Add. 26476.

———— Joh. Jay, 1518. Add. 26487.

———— Rob. Adams, [1545]. Add. 26500.

———— Will. Chester, 1553. Add. 26500.

———— Joh. Whitsone, 1616. Harl. 58 E. 15.

———— Geo. Harrington, 1617. Harl. 111 C. 54 ;—1618. Harl. 58 E. 18.

———— Joh. Guy, 1618. Harl. 58 E. 19.

———— *Prepositi al. Ballivi.* Will. de Bellomonte, Rob. de Kilmeynan, [1240 ?]. Add. 26420, 26421.

———— Will. de la Marine, 1273. Add. 15203.

———— Simon Adrian, Ric. Draper, *jun.*, early Edw. I. Add. 15205.

———— Symon Adrian, Will. de la Marine, early Edw. I. Harl. 56 A. 38.

———— Walt. le Franceys, Ric. le repere, [1284 ?] Add. 16205.

———— Will. de la Marine, Johannes, *clericus*, [c. 1285]. Add. 26423–26425.

———— Will. de la Marine, Galfr. Godeshalf, [1285 ?]. Add. 25882.

———— Will. de la Marine, Tho. de Weston. [1286 ?], 1286. Add. 26422, 26426, 26428.

———— Galfr. Agodeshalf, Symon de Boritone, 1288. Add. 26429.

———— Tho. de la Grave, Will. Randalph, 1295. Add. 16204.

———— Tho. le Spocer, Rob. Randalf, 1311. Harl. 53 B. 10.

———— Will. de Clyve, Gilb. Pokerel, 1314. Harl. 47 G. 12.

———— Ric. le Wyte, Ric. de Panes, 1319. Add. 26432.

———— Joh. de Romeneye, Walt. le Prentis, 1324. Add. 26433.

———— Roger. Plof, Hen. Babbecary, 1331. Harl. 47 G. 5.

———— Rob. Guyan, Walt. Prentiz, 1332. Harl. 47 C. 51.

———— Jac. Tylloye, Tho. de Welles, 1338. Harl. 53 D. 42.

Bristol, co. *Glouc.* (*continued*). *Vicecomes* (*continued*) (*nuper*). Tho. Whithead, Will. Pitts, 1615. Harl. 58 A. 15.

—— —— Matth. Warren, Will. Turner, 1618. Harl. 111 C. 55.

—— —— Rich. Lane, Joh. Knight,· 1681. Add. 7171.

—— *Camerarius.* Joh. Willi, 1553. Add. 26500.

—— *Clericus Villæ.* Ric. de Calne, [1285?]. Add. 25882;—c. 1302-5. Harl. 47 G. 32.

—— —— Rob. Martin, 1305. Add. 6517.

—— *Aldermun.* Joh. Whitson, 1603. Harl. 56 C. 41.

—— —— Tho. James, Will. Hicks, Will. Vawer, Chris. Kedgwin. Matth. Haviland. Joh. Butcher. Rob. Aldworth, 1617. Harl. 111 C. 54.

Bristowe. *v.* Burstow, *co. Surr.*

Bristwoldintona. *v.* Brightwalton, *co. Berks.*

Britford, *co. Wilts.* Grants, etc., in, *t.* Edw. I. Lansd. 683 (Britford):— 1315. Lansd. 684 (Brutford):—1334. Lansd. 685 (do.), 686;—1361. Lansd. 687 (Bruteford).

—— *Perpet. Vicarius.* Joh. Colembel, 1334. Lansd. 685.

*v. also* Longford, *in Britford, co. Wilts.*

Brithwalle. *v.* Brightwell, *co. Suff.*

Britreichsfeld. *v.* Brushfield, *co. Derb.*

Britton. *v.* Bretton, *in Eyam, co. Derb.*

Britwell Salome. *v.* Brightwell-Salome, *co. Oxon.*

Brixham, *co. Devon.* Brief for rebuilding the chapel, 1815. Ch. Br. B. lvi. 4.

Brixton, *co. Devon.* Power to give seisin in, 1478 (Bryghtricheston). Add. 26178.

Brixton, *I. of Wight.* Lease of Shut place in, 1565. Harl. 78 H. 49.

Brixton Hundred, *co. Surr.* Accompt of collector of taxes in, 1570-1. Add. 8143.

Brixworth, *co. Northt.* Grant, etc., in, 1307. Add. 21660 (Briclesworth); —1316. Add. 21661 (do.).

—— Foundation of chaplaincies in, 1349 (Briklesworth). Harl. 57 C. 27, 28.

Brixworth, *co. Northt.* (*continued*). *Vicarius.* Tho. Newbery, 1487. Add. 22506.

Brize, Norton. *v.* Norton Brize, *co. Oxon.*

Broadfield. *v. sub* Bodenham, *co. Heref.*

Broadfield, *co. Som.* Suit on a lease in, 1651 (Bradfeild). Add. 6228.

Broadfield *al.* Bradfield, *co. Wilts.* Sale of custody of the manor, 1620. Add. 18383.

Broadholm, *co. Nott.* Conff. of grants in, to Newhouse Abbey, [1150-60] (Brodholm). Harl. 43 H. 14-17;— [1156 or 7?]. Harl. 51 H. 1.

Broadlow Ash, *in Thorpe, co. Derb.* Power to take seisin of the manor, 1373 (Bredlowe). Woll. vi. 59.

Broadmead, *in Folkestone, co. Kent.* Covenant for keeping the sea-wall at, *t.* Hen. III. (Brademed). Harl. 47 E. 31.

Broadmoor, *nr. Talbenny, co. Pemb.* License to enclose lands in, 1306 (Brodmore). Add. 8063.

Broadwater. *v. sub* Wareslley, *co. Hunt.*

Broadwater (Bradewater, etc.), *co. Suss.* Grants in Offington (Offenton, etc.) in, to Waverley Abbey, 12-13 cent. Harl. 77 E. 43;—t. Edw. I. Harl. 79 E. 12.

—— Grants, etc., in Offington, etc., in, 1331. Harl. 76 F. 10;—1335. Add. 8830;— 1336. Add. 8823;—1355. Harl. 80 A. 22, 23;—1356. Harl. 76 F. 48;—1357. Harl. 80 A. 20, 80 H. 8;—1365. Add. 8837;—1371. Harl. 80 A. 25:—1398. Harl. 76 E. 44;— 1400. Add. 8855 (Lytyl Bradewatere); —1403. Add. 24665;—1436. Add. 8878 (Lytel Bradewater);—1455. Add. 8893;—1456. Add. 18753 (Brodewater);—1472. Add. 8901 (Bradwater);—1476. Add. 1007:—1549. Add. 18828;—1587. Add. 18866 (Gt. Brodwater);—1595. Add. 18879;— 1601. Harl. 76 A. 27;—1604. Add. 18897;—1680. Add. 15874.

—— Release, etc., of the manor, 1433. Add. 20055 (Bradwater);—1595. Add. 18880.

—— Lease in Offington in, by Waverley Abbey, 1500. Harl. 75 G. 14.

—— Release of Little Broadwater manor, 1583. Add. 18865.

43 G. 33;—1485. Harl. 50 I. 7;—
1500. Harl. 50 I. 8.

—— Conf. by Hen. II. of grants in,
to Newhouse Abbey, [1156 or 7?].
Harl. 51 H. 1 (Broclosebi).

—— Grant of a portion of All Saints'
church, etc., to Tupholme Abbey,
*ante* 1166. Harl. 58 H. 4 (Brokelosby)
(copy).

—— Fine in, with Newhouse Abbey,
1226. Harl. 49 G. 1.

—— Leases in, from Newhouse Abbey,
1271. Harl. 44 G. 57;—1434. Harl.
44 H. 32.

—— Grant in, to Newhouse Abbey
from Tupholme Abbey, *t.* Hen. III. or
Edw. I. Harl. 45 A. 15.

—— Grant in, *t.* Hen. III.-Edw. I.
Harl. 47 C. 27.

—— Dispute conc. tithes to the church,
*c.* 1304. Harl. 48 G. 35.

—— Inquisitions conc. the advowson,
1304. Harl. 54 A. 43 (Broclousby);—
1305. Harl. 43 H. 32;—1349. Harl.
43 H. 43 (Brokelesby).

—— Resignation of a sixth part of
the church by Will. Longspeye, 1305.
Harl. 43 H. 30.

—— Institution of G. de Kirnington
to a sixth of the church, with resignation, 1305. Harl. 43 H. 31-33.

—— Inquisition conc. bounds of Newhouse Abbey in, 1312. Harl. 58 G. 38.

—— Certificate of the Abp. of Canterbury conc. right of Newhouse Abbey to tithes in, 1319. Harl. 43 G. 29.

—— Covenant with Newhouse Abbey
for two chaplains in the church of, to
pray for Dom. W. Longespeye, 1324.
Harl. 44 H. 20.

—— Bond to Newhouse Abbey conc.
presentation to, 1331 (Broklesby).
Harl. 50 I. 43.

—— Grant, etc., of a sixth part of the
advowson by Tupholme Abbey to
Newhouse Abbey, 1348. Harl. 43
D. 44, 45 A. 17, 18, 20, 21, 54 C. 11.

—— Mandate conc. tithes in, to Newhouse Abbey, 1369. Harl. 45 A. 7.

—— Lease of a portion of the church,
etc., to Newhouse Abbey, 1434. Harl.
44 H. 32.

—— *Capellanus.* Gilbertus, early 13
cent. Harl. 52 D. 9.

—— —— David, early Hen. III.
Harl. 52 D. 14.

**Brocklesby** (Broclosbi, Broclesby,
Broclousbi, etc.), *co. Linc.* (*continued*).
*Capellanus* (*continued*). Johannes,
1271. Harl. 44 G. 57.

—— —— Willelmus, *t.* Hen. III.
or Edw. I. Harl. 46 F. 22, 47 C. 28,
54 C. 37.

—— *Clericus.* Henricus, [1155-66].
Harl. 47 C. 20.

—— *Custos Cantarie.* Dom. Will.
de Limbergia, 1376. Harl. 56 E. 6;
—1383. Harl. 52 G. 15, 16.

—— *Parciarius parochialis eccl.* Willelmus, 1311. Harl. 49 I. 40.

—— *Persona.* Willelmus, late 12
cent. Harl. 48 C. 12.

—— *Porcionarius eccl.* Dom. Ric. de
Brinkilhou *al.* Brinkelhou, 1331.
Cott. xxx. 18, Harl. 57 F. 4, 5;—1332.
Harl. 55 E. 21;—(as *persona*), 1346,
1347. Cott. v. 53, Harl. 53 B. 46-49.

—— *Presbyter.* Johannes, *c.* 1147.
Harl. 50 B. 12;—*c.* 1155-60. Harl.
44 G. 15, 46 B. 4, 47 C. 21;—[1157-
63]. Cott. xi. 26.

—— —— Johannes, end 12 cent.
Harl. 48 A. 19.

—— *Proporcionarius eccl.* Dom. Rad.
de Kyrnington, 1373. Harl. 55 F. 46;
—(as *proporc. tercie partis eccl.*), 1376.
Harl. 56 E. 2.

—— *Proporcioner.* Sire Will. Longespey, *c.* 1304. Harl. 48 G. 35;—(as
*Rector sexte partis eccl.*), 1305. Harl.
43 H. 30, 32.

—— *Rector eccl.* Dom. Ricardus, 1349.
Harl. 43 H. 43.

—— *Rector sexte partis eccl.* Mag.
Gocelin. de Kirnington, 1305. Harl.
43 H. 31-33.

—— —— (*ultimus*). Dom. Tho. de
Graynham, 1349. Harl. 43 H. 43.

—— —— Mag. Rob. de Skippewith,
1349. Harl. 43 H. 43.

—— —— Dom. Joh. Est, 1434.
Harl. 44 H. 32.

—— *Rector tercie partis eccl.* Dom.
Galf. de Neubald, *ante* 1376. Harl.
56 E. 6.

—— *Sacerdos.* Bovo, [1143 - 47].
Cott. xii. 18.

—— —— Johannes, *t.* Hen. III.
Harl. 46 F. 22.

*v. also* Newsham, *co. Linc.*

**Brocksham,** *nr. Westerham, co. Kent.*
Grants of wood in, 973. Cott. viii. 33
(Broccesham);—987. Cott. viii. 14
(Broccesham).

**Bromfield** (Brumfeld, Bromfeld, etc.), co. *Cumb.* (*continued*). Leases, etc., in, 1584. Add. 17164;—1625. Add. 17166;—1638. Add. 17167;—1667-8. Add. 17176-17179, 17181;—1671. Add. 17190;—1690. Add. 17180, 17183;—1695. Add. 17194.

—— Presentations to the vicarage by H. Thompson, 1648, 1663. Add. 17195, 17201.

—— Fines, etc., of the manor, 1654. Add. 17171-17173;—1668. Add. 17174, 17175.

—— Presentation to the rectory by Walt. Calverley and Frances, his wife, 1673. Add. 17202.

—— Sale of a chancel-seat in the church, 1680. Add. 17192.

—— *Capellanus.* Willelmus, 1322. Add. 17157.

—— *Rector* (late). Rich. Garth, 1673. Add. 17202.

—— —— (nominate). John Thomlinson, 1673. Add. 17202.

—— *Vicarius.* Radulfus, 1322. Add. 17157.

—— —— Will. Granger *al.* Grainger, 1648. Add. 17195, 17196;—1662. Add. 17197-17200.

—— —— Rich. Waugh, 1663. Add. 17201.

v. *also* Allonby, co. *Cumb.*
v. *also* Yearngill, co. *Cumb.*

**Bromfield,** co. *Salop.* Conf. by Hen. II. of lands in, etc., to Bromfield Priory, [1155] (Bromfeldehernesse). Cott. xvii. 4.

—— Sale in, 1574. Add. 23853.

—— *Presbyter.* Edricus, [1155]. Cott. xvii. 4.

—— *Rector.* Thomas, 1263 (Brumeffeld). Harl. 48 C. 31.

**Bromfield Hundred** (Dominium de Bromfeld), co. *Denb.* Grant in Burton, etc., in, 1495. Add. 8646.

—— Extract from an extent in 1391-2 of, *t.* Hen. VIII. Harl. 58 E. 32.

—— Excheq. acquittances for fines in, 1587, 1586. Add. 25739, 25742.

—— *Capitalis Forrstarius.* David ap Gron. ap Jor., *de Borton,* 1391. Add. 8633.

—— *Senescallus.* Petr. Salford, 1391. Add. 8633.

—— —— Joh. Wele, 1414. Add. 8637.

—— —— Joh. Shilston, *miles,* 1520. Add. 8647.

**Bromford.** v. Bramford, co. *Suff.*

**Bromgearde.** v. Bromyard, co. *Heref.*

**Bromgeheg.** v. *sub* Frindsbury, co. *Kent.*

**Bromhalle Manor.** v. *sub* Livermere Magna, co. *Suff.*

**Bromham,** co. *Bedf.* Compotus of rents in, 1457-8. Add. 657.

**Bromham,** co. *Wilts.* Grant of the manor, by Will. II., to Battle Abbey, [1087-92]. Cott. MS. Aug. ii. 53.

—— Conf. of, by Hen. I., to Battle Abbey, c. 1121. Campb. xvi. 13.

—— Conf. of tithes in (?), to Battle Abbey, [1121-5]. Cott. MS. Nero C. iii., f. 189.

—— Grants, etc., in, from Battle Abbey, t. Steph. Campb. xxii. 10;—t. Rich. I. Cott. MS. Nero C. iii., ff. 186, 187, 189, Campb. vii. 4;—1265. Campb. xxiii. 18.

**Bromhey.** v. *sub* Frindsbury, co. *Kent.*

**Bromholm,** co. *Norf.* A pension to be paid to the church of, from lands in, early 13 cent. Harl. 49 G. 21.

—— Grant in, 1334. Cott. xxix. 26.

**Bromkinsthorpe,** nr. *Leicester,* co. *Leic.* Bond on crops in, 1283 (Brunskynisthorp). Add. 26930.

**Bromle.** v. Bramley, co. *Southt.*

**Bromle** *al.* Chingley, *Den of.* v. *sub* Goudhurst, co. *Kent.*

**Bromle, Bromlegh.** v. Bramley, co. *Surr.*

**Bromley.** v. *sub* Standon, co. *Hertf.*

**Bromley,** co. *Kent.* Grant at, 862 (Bromleag). Cott. viii. 32.

—— Grant at, to the see of Rochester, 973 (æt Bromleage). Cott. viii. 33.

—— Grant in, 987 (Bromleg). Cott. viii. 14.

—— (Bromle, Bromlegh). Grants, etc., in, 1325-6. Harl. 111 E. 43;—1347. Harl. 112 A. 54;—1391. Harl. 111 D. 60;—1407. Harl. 111 D. 43;—1411. Harl. 112 E. 13;—1430. Harl. 112 A. 12;—1433. Harl. 111 G. 27;—1440. Harl. 111 G. 26;—1451. Harl. 112 F. 2.

—— *Rector* (?). Will. de Wyklewode, 1335. Harl. 58 C. 40.

**Bromley, Bagots,** co. *Staff.* Release in, 1388. Cott. xxviii. 104.

Roll K. 32;—*t.* Hen. VI. Harl. Roll A. 42.

—— Court-rolls, 1389-1499. Harl. Rolls B. 1, 11-14 (Brokeynde, Broke-yend).

Brookes, Hamelett de. *v. sub* Ips-wich, *co. Suff.*

Brookhouse (Brokhous), *co. York.* Grant, etc., in, 1329. Harl. 44 F. 22; —1377. Harl. 57 A. 10.

Brookland, *co. Kent.* Grant in, 1396 (Broklonde). Harl. 56 I. 5.

—— *Rector. Dom.* Rob. Paulyn, 1316. Add. 20155;—1322. Add. 20148, 20156.

Brooksby, *co. Leic.* Re-grant in, 1455 (Brokesby). Add. 21195.

Brookthrop *al.* Brockthrop, *co. Glouc.* Grant of the manor to the see of Gloucester, 1541 (Brokethorp). Cott. xiii. 34.

Brookyelchestre Manor. *v. sub* Ilchester, *co. Som.*

Broom (Broma), *co. Bedf.* Conf. of a grant in, to Wardon Abbey, 1257-8. Cott. MS. Nero C. iii., f. 230.

—— Conf. of grant in, to Chicksand Priory, *t.* Hen. III. Harl. 45 I. 18.

Broom, *co. Staff.* Brief for rebuilding the church, 1776. Ch. Br. B. xvi. 2.

Broom, King's, *nr.* Bidford, *co. Warw.* Re-grant in, 1305 (Kygges-brome). Cott. xxiii. 9.

Broome (Brom, Broom), *co. Norf.* Grants, etc., in, early Hen. III. Add. 22570;—1332. Add. 14564;—1383. Add. 14565;—1403. Cott. xxvii. 162; —1404. Harl. 54 A. 1;—1419. Harl. 51 E. 53;—1422. Harl. 50 F. 36;— 1425. Add. 14643;—1426. Add. 14644;—1455. Add. 14566;—1460. Add. 14646;—1462. Harl. 54 I. 19; —1517. Add. 14648;—1574. Add. 14652;—1582. Add. 14567;—1593. Add. 14653;—1623. Add. 14568.

—— *Rector.* Willelmus, *t.* Edw. I. Harl. 83 D. 45.

Broome, *co. Suff.* Release in, 1619. Add. 10482.

—— Extracts from Court-rolls of Broome Hall manor in, 1608. Add. 10502;—1686. Add. 10501.

—— Extract from Court-roll of Ling Hall manor in, 1656. Add. 10495.

Broome Hall Manor. *v. sub* Liver-mere Magna, *co. Suff.*

Broomfield. *v. sub* Boxford, *co. Suff.*

Broomfield (Bromfeld), *co. Essex.* Grant, etc., of the church to Holy Trinity Priory, Aldgate, *t.* Hen. II. Cott. xiii. 18 (17, 18) (*copies*).

—— Grant of a nativus in, 1334. Cott. v. 43.

—— Mem. of title in, *t.* Edw. III. Harl. 56 D. 25.

—— Grants, etc., in, 1349. Add. 18108;—1382. Add. 18110;—1394. Add. 18112;—1414. Add. 18116;— 1433. Add. 24197;—1438. Add. 18117;—1450. Add. 18118;—1511. Add. 18125-18127.

Broomfield, *co. Kent.* Crown lease in, 1584 (Bromefild). Add. 8629.

Broomham, [*in Guestling?*], *co. Suss.* Fine of the manor, 1507 (Bromeham). Add. 24909.

—— Covenant for settlement of the manor, 1583 (Bromhame). Add. 8792.

Broomhill (Prumhell, Promhull, Prom-hell), *cos. Suss. and Kent.* Grants in Pedling, etc., in, to Robertsbridge Abbey, late 12 cent. Campb. xxv. 20;—early 13 cent.-early Hen. III. Campb. xiv. 4, xvi. 6, xxv. 3, 4, 5, 7, 10, 12, 14, 15, 17, 21, 22, 25, xxvi. 2, 5, 7, 9, 10, 15, 16, xxvii. 1, 3. 5, 16, 18, 20, 22, 24, Eg. 383;—c. 1222. Campb. iii. 3;—1231. Campb. xxvi. 22;—c. 1231. Campb. xxvi. 23;—*t.* Hen. III. Campb. xxv. 1, 2, 8, 9, 13, 16, 24, xxvi. 1, 3, 4, 17, 18, xxvii. 7, 9, 14, 21, 26;—*t.* Edw. I. Campb. xxvii. 25;—1308-9. Campb. xxvi. 11, 12;— 1310. Campb. xxvii. 8, 23;—1312. Campb. xxv. 19;—1313. Campb. xxvii. 13;—1319-20. Campb. xxvii. 12;—1333. Campb. xxvi. 14;—1334. Campb. xxvi. 8, 13, 14*.

—— Ref. to lands impleaded in, by Robertsbridge Abbey, 12-13 cent. Campb. xxvii. 17.

—— Grant of a villein in, to Roberts-bridge Abbey, from Battle Abbey, 1212. Campb. xxvii. 6.

—— Covenant for enclosure in, betw. Battle and Robertsbridge Abbeys, 1222. Campb. xxvii. 2.

—— Grants, etc., in, early 13 cent. Campb. xvi. 15, xxvii. 4;—1235. Campb. xxvi. 21;—c. 1235. Campb. xxvi. 20.

—— Reservation of pasture in Bule-mers in, *t.* Hen. III. Eg. 383.

Brunsmhet, an. Dumfries, to. Dumfr. Conf. of a grant of, to Melrose Abbey, 1237. Cott. xviii. 11.

Brunskynethorp. v. Bromkinsthorpe, w. Leicester.

Branthorpe (Bonthorpe?), wr. Well, co. Linc. Grant "in Nouiendo de Brunterp," late 12 cent. Harl. 57 F. 42.

—— Conveyance of the manor, 1355. Harl. 57 G. 11.

—— Power to take seisin in, 1417. Harl. 57 G. 17.

—— Capellanus. Hugo, t. Hen. III. Harl. 46 D. 27.

Bruntingthorpe, co. Leic. Rob. f. dai. de Branthingcessorpe, a witness, a. 1240-6. Add. 21594.

—— Settlement in, 1510 (Brentyng-thorpe). Cott. v. 16.

—— Dominus. Willelmus, early Hen. III. (Branthgestorp). Add. 7534, 21271, 21275.

Brunufyston. v. Burnaston, in Etwall, co. Derb.

Bruselea. v. Brisley, co. Norf.

Bruses Manor. v. sub Tottenham, co. Midd.

Brushfield, co. Derb. Conf. of a covenant in, with Rufford Abbey, late 12 cent. (Bricthicesfel). Woll. ix. 3.

—— Grant in, early 13 cent. (Britseich-feld). Add. 19264.

Brustun. v. Burston, co. Norf.

Brutford. v. Britford, co. Wilts.

Bruton, co. Som. Certificate by men of, in a case of illegitimacy, late 15 cent. Harl. 50 F. 9.

Brutwell. v. Brightwell, co. Oxon.

Bryan's Maund Manor. v. sub Bodenham, co. Heref.

Bryanston, co. Dors. Settlement of the manor, 1661. Add. 5984.

Bryghtricheston. v. Brixton, co. Devon.

Brymbo, co. Denb. Fines in, 1595. Add. 8656;—1618. Add. 8657.

Brymmycham. v. Birmingham, co. Worc.

Brymore (Brummore), in Cannington, co. Som. Fine in, 1299. Add. 20222.

—— Grants in, 1318. Add. 20223;—1452. Add. 20226.

Bryn Eglwys, co. Denb. Brief for rebuilding the church, 1759. Ch. Br. A. vi. 3.

Bryncroes, co. Carnarv. Recovery in, 1699. Add. 25812.

Bryngwyn, co. Radnor. Grant in Abergavenny in the fee of, 1379. Harl. 85 F. 45.

—— Grant, etc., in, 1610. Add. 1039 (Bringwine);—1625. Add. 1040 (do.).

Brynhill. v. Brindle, co. Lanc.

Brynllys, co. Brecon. Grant of rents in, to Clifford Priory, [1222-31?] (Brenles, Branleis). Harl. 48 C. 29.

—— Constabularius. Res ab Meuric, 1251 (Brantleys). Campb. xviii. 2.

—— Capellanus. Philippus, 1263 (Brentles). Harl. 48 C. 31.

Brynnaldston. v. Burnaston, in Etwall, co. Derb.

Bryntangor, co. Denb. Lease in, 1451 (Brynntangour). Harl. 58 F. 36.

Brynyngham. v. Briningham, co. Norf.

Brytewell. v. Brightwell, co. Suff.

—— v. sub Burnham, co. Buck.

Bubbeherst, Den of. v. sub Frittenden, co. Kent.

Bubnell, in Bakewell, co. Derb. Bonds conc. lands in, 1485. Woll. iii. 72, 76.

Bucgan ora. v. Bognor, co. Suss.

Bucheham. v. Buckenham, Old, co. Norf.

Buchetona. v. Buckton, co. York.

Buckby, Long, co. Northt. Grants, etc., in, late 13 cent. Add. 21544 (Bockeby); — 1312. Add. 21664 (Buckeby);—1317. Add. 21665;—1358. Add. 21666 (Bukby);—1392. Add. 21667 (Bukkeby).

—— Order conc. privileges of the manor, as parcel of the Duchy of Lancaster, t. Chas. I. Add. 21668.

—— Persona. R—, [1203-6]. Harl. 84 D. 3.

—— Rad. le Blount, 1342. Add. 21596, 21597, 21600.

Buckden, co. Hunt. Grant of, by Earl Simon, [1141-53?] (Bogeton). Add. 11233 (5) (copy).

—— Brief conc. a fire at, 1770. Ch. Br. B. xi. 1.

Buckenelia, nr. Horstead Keynes (?), co. Suss. Exchange in, by Lewes Priory, t. Steph. Harl. 44 F. 21.

**Buckenham Ferry**, *co. Norf.* Feoffment of the manor and advowson, 1451 (Bokenham Ferye). Add. 7386.

**Buckenham, Little** (Bokeham), *co. Norf.* Grant in, with conf. to Sawtrey Abbey, *t.* Hen. II. Harl. 83 A. 46;— late 12 cent. Harl. 83 A. 54.

**Buckenham, New**, *co. Norf.* Grants, etc., in, 1343. Slo. xxxiii. 27 (Nova Bokenham); — 1398. Add. 14573 (Bokenham nova); — 1614. Add. 14575;—1636. Add. 14576;—1647. Add. 14577.

—— Money spent on defence, etc., of the castle, etc., by Sir W. Knyvet, 1477. Add. 815.

**Buckenham, Old**, *co. Norf.* Foundation of Buckenham Priory in the manor of, etc., [1151] (Buchcham). Harl. 83 D. 9.

—— Extent of the manor, *c.* 1300 (Bukeham). Add. 16534.

—— Defeasance of bond conc. land in, 1343 (Vetus Bokenham). Slo. xxxiii. 27.

—— Lease in the Priory manor in, 1470 (Bokynham Prioratus). Add. 14578.

—— The manor held by Sir W. Knyvet, 1477. Add. 815.

—— *Presbiter.* |Turstanus, [1151]. Harl. 83 D. 9.

**Buckenhill**, *in Woolhope, co. Heref.* Lease in, 1407 (Bokenhulle). Harl. 111 C. 33.

**Buckerweston.** *v.* Buckhorn Weston, *co. Dors.*

**Buckeswrda.** *v.* Buckworth, *co. Hunt.*

**Buckfast**, *co. Devon.* Brief conc. a fire in, 1825. Ch. Br. C. vi. 9.

**Buckfastleigh**, *co. Devon.* Grant in Scoriton (Scoriaton) nr., with a rent in Alre nr., due from Buckfastleigh Abbey, 1292 (Bugwastene). Add. 8446.

—— Defeasance of a grant in Coulaton in, 1400. Add. 7853.

—— Award in, 1499. Add. 5248.

—— Acquittance for homage for lands in Warmecombe in, held of Maynebowe manor, 1618. Add. 7890.

—— Grant in Bowdon and Cowlaton in, 1618. Add. 7891.

—— Grant in, 1624. Add. 7893.

*v. also* Bozedon, *co. Devon.*

**Buckholt.** *v. sub* Bexhill, *co. Suss.*

**Buckhorn Weston**, *co. Dors.* Grant of wardship in, [1550–53] (Buckerweston). Cott. MS. Vesp. F. xiii. art. 222.

**Buckhurst, Don of.** *v. sub* Frittenden, *co. Kent.*

**Buckhurst Wood.** *v. sub* Woodford, *co. Essex.*

**Buckingham, *County of.*** Grant of rent from lands of T. de Museenden in, 1350. Harl. 53 D. 48.

—— Extract from pipe roll conc. taxes due from Biddlesdon Abbey, 1487–8. Harl. 84 F. 18.

—— Gen. release in, to Joh. Yorke, 1510. Harl. 78 E. 30.

—— Grant by Marg., Cm. of Salisbury, of an annuity in, to Henry her son, 1527. Harl. 43 F. 10.

—— Appointment of R. Pekham as escheator for, 1545. Harl. 84 C. 27.

—— Warrant to collect subsidies in, 1558. Harl. 84 C. 34.

—— Money collected in, for Hammersmith Hospital, co. Midd., 1578. Harl. 86 B. 11.

—— Bond on behalf of Hen. Fleetwood, as Feodary of, 1595. Harl. 84 I. 5.

—— Acquittances to collectors of subsidies in, 1595, 1596. Add. 25568–25570.

—— Mortgage of lands in, 1603. Add. 23868, 23869.

—— *Vicecomes.* Assur (?), [1150–1]. Harl. 85 G. 48.

—— —— Will. de Holewell, 1245. Harl. 84 D. 35, 36;—[1242–9]. Harl. 85 F. 14.

—— —— *Sirs* Phelip de Aylesbury, 1331. Harl. 86 A. 27.

—— —— Petr. de Salford, 1365. Harl. 86 D. 44.

—— —— Rob. Peckham, *miles*, 1556. Harl. 84 C. 33.

—— —— Tho. Pycott, 1557. Harl. 84 C. 33.

—— —— Rob. Drury, *miles*, 1562. Harl. 75 H. 11.

—— —— Edw. Asshefeld, 1570. Harl. 75 H. 15.

—— —— *Sir* Geo. Peckham, 1573. Harl. 84 C. 37.

—— —— Ralph Astrey, 1574. Harl. 84 C. 38.

**Buckingham,** *County of (continued).*
*Vicecomes (continued).* Nich. Hackett,
1681. Add. 23871.

**Buckingham** (Bukingham, etc.), *co.
Buck.* Covenant with Biddlesdon
Abbey made in the church of St.
Peter at, [1199] (Buk.). Harl. 84 D.
14.

—— Grants, etc., in, to Biddlesdon
Abbey, early 13 cent.-late Hen. III.
Harl. 84 I 19, 42, 43, 85 C. 2, 20, 85
D. 13, 85 G. 36, 86 E. 13, 86 G. 19;—
1249. Harl. 84 D. 40–44 (Bokingham, etc.);—c. 1260. Harl. 85 B. 14;—
late 13 cent. Harl. 85 G. 61, 86 B. 1.

—— Rent in, reserved to the church
of St. Peter, early 13 cent. Harl. 84
I. 28.

—— "Totum portimotum" of, a witness, early 13 cent. Harl. 84 I. 28.

—— Grants, etc., in, early 13 cent.-
t. Hen. III. Harl. 84 I. 27, 28, 44;—
late 13 cent. Harl. 85 G. 13;—t.
Edw. I. Lansd. 562;—1324. Lansd.
563;—1325. Lansd. 564;—1329.
Lansd. 565;—1335. Harl. 47 B. 50
(Bukyngham);—1385. Lansd. 567;—
1398. Lansd. 568 (Bukkyngham);—
1403. Lansd. 569–571;—1425. Lansd.
573;—1454. Lansd. 574;—1486.
Lansd. 575;—1612. Add. 23870.

—— Surrender by Biddlesdon Abbey
of a lease of the chapel of, 1298. Harl.
84 E. 26.

—— Rental of J. Barton in the
vill and hundred of, 1423. Lansd.
572.

—— Rental of the borough, as held
by the Duke of Buckingham, [1441–
59?]. Add. 217.

—— Precipe on a covenant in, 1564.
Add. 24918.

—— *Ballivus.* Joh. Smyth, 1403.
Lansd. 569.

—— *Dominus.* Robertus, t. Hen. III.
Harl. 86 A. 17.

—— —— Walt. de Clifford, c. 1260.
Harl. 85 B. 14.

—— —— *Dom.* Joh. de Brewouse
al. Braosa, 1335. Harl. 47 B. 50.

—— *Capellanus.* Giffardus, t. Hen.
III. Harl. 86 E. 35, 36.

—— —— Ricardus, t. Hen. III.
Harl. 86 E. 35–37.

—— *Clericus.* Baldwinus, ante 1174.
Harl. 85 C. 23.

—— —— Willelmus, [1198–1207].
Harl. 85 A. 58.

**Buckingham's Lands.** *v. sub* Tonbridge, co. *Kent.*

**Buckland.** *v. sub* Luddesdown, co.
*Kent.*

**Buckland,** co. *Buck.* Grant, etc., in,
early 14 cent. Add. 5994 (Bokelond);
—1374. Harl. 84 F. 50 (Boklond).

**Buckland,** co. *Heref.* Grant in, 1654.
Add. 1953.

**Buckland** (Bokeland, etc.), *in Woodhall,* co. *Linc.* Grants, etc., in, to
Kirkstead Abbey, 1154. Harl. 57 F.
14 (Boclande):—late Hen. II. Cott.
xxix. 31 (Bokland);—early 13 cent.
Harl. 56 I. 23 (Bocland);—1262. Harl.
45 B. 5;—t. Hen. III. Cott. xxix. 91,
Harl. 51 B. 31;—1365. Harl. 58 C. 2.

—— Grants, etc., in, t. Hen. III.
Harl. 46 I. 54 (Bochlant);—t. Edw. I.
Harl. 45 A. 16;—1314. Harl. 46 F.
8;—1370. Harl. 56 B. 49;—1431.
Harl. 48 G. 44.

—— License for a grant in, to Greenfield Priory, 1392. Harl. 43 G. 53.

**Buckland,** co. *Surr.* Grant in Hartswood in, early Hen. III. Add. 24586.

—— Grant in, 1388 (Bokelond).
Add. 24553.

—— *Rector.* Will. Peyto, 1378. Add.
18665.

**Buckland Denham,** co. *Som.* Fine,
etc., of the manor, 1653. Harl. 86 I.
59;—1655. Harl. 111 E. 35 (B.
Dynham).

**Buckland, Egg,** co. *Devon.* Return
of yearly value of lands in, 1572
(Eke Bucklande). Cott. xvii. 22.

**Buckland Newton,** co. *Dors.* Crown
appointment of a steward of the manor,
1572. Harl. 75 E. 41.

**Buckland St. Mary,** co. *Som.* Fine
in, 1346 (Bokeland S. Marie). Add.
25876.

—— Grants, etc., in, 1364. Harl. 45 E.
66 (Seint Marie Bokelonde);—1370.
Cott. xxvii. 108. Harl. 47 D. 26;—
1371. Harl. 48 I. 9 (S. M. Boukelond),
49 F. 31 (S. M. Bokelound).

**Bucklebury,** co. *Berks.* Release of
the church to Reading Abbey, [1151–4]
(Burchildeberia). Add. 19590.

—— Covenant conc. the church, by
Reading Abbey. [1189–99] (Burkilleberi). Add. 19610.

—— Covenant conc. tithes in, betw.
Reading Abbey and the rector of Stanford, 1267 (Burghildebiri). Add. 19627.

Bulphan, *co. Essex (continued)*. Fine of Bulphan Hall manor, etc., in, 1654 (Bulfan *al.* Bulvan). Add. 15616.

Bulsford, *co. Devon* (?). Grant of, early 13 cent. (Budelesford). Add. 5953.

Bulstrode, *co. Buck*. Compotus-rolls of the manor, 1309-11 (Bolstrode, Bolestrode). Harl. Rolls A. 25-27.

Bulstrodes. *v. sub* Sonning, *co. Oxon.*

Bultham. *v.* Boultham, *co. Linc.*

Bulverhithe, *co. Suss*. Grants in, *t.* Edw. I. or II. Add. 20051 (Bulewarehethe);—1355. Add. 20052 (Bolewarheth).

Bulwell, *co. Nott*. Fines of the manor, etc., 1702. Woll. xi. 75, xii. 5.

—— Brief for rebuilding the church, 1768. Ch. Br. B. viii. 9.

Bulwick (Bolwyk, etc.), *co. Northt*. Grant in, to Fineshed Priory, c. 1300 (Bolewik). Add. 21545.

—— Covenant conc. descent of the manor, 1372 (Bolewyk). Add. 19979.

—— Grants, etc., in, 1377. Add. 21542 (Bullewyk);—1407. Add. 721 (Bulwyk);—1410. Add. 712;—1453. Add. 723 (Bullewyke);—1457. Add. 713;— 1467. Add. 7595;— 1468. Add. 7578;—1472. Add. 813, 7579;—1499. Add. 725 (Bulweke);—1506. Add. 726 (Bulwick);—1519. Add. 715, 716, 826, 828;—1520. Add. 825; 1533. Add. 727;—1555. Add. 7582 (Bulweck);—1571. Add. 728.

—— Mortgage, etc., of the manor, 1477. Add. 815, 816;—1596. Harl. 48 D. 44.

—— Fines in, 1539. Add. 837, 838;—1579. Add. 21669.

—— *Persona al. Rector*. Benedict de Foxley, 1318. Add. 16767;—1319. Add. 16768;—1320. Add. 16774;—1321. Add. 16771.

Bulyngtona. *v.* Bullington, *co. Linc.*

Bumpstead Helion, *co. Essex*. Exchequer order to seize lands in Hersham in, 1350. Cott. xiii. 5 (4).

—— Surrender for settlement in, 1433 (Bumsted). Add. 5253.

—— Brief for rebuilding the church, 1796. Ch. Br. B. xxxvi. 5.

Bumpstead, Steeple, *co. Essex*. Lease in, 1328 (Stepel Bumstede). Add. 15592.

Bumpstead, Steeple, *co. Essex (continued)*. Conveyance of the manor (?), 1347 (Bumsted). Add. 14761.

—— Precipe on a covenant conc. Walton's manor, etc., in, 1561 (Bumpsted ad turrim). Add. 24934.

Bunbury, *co. Chest*. Brief conc. a fire in, 1781. Ch. Br. B. xxi. 1.

Bunchesham, North. *v.* Bensham, *in* Croydon, *co. Surr.*

Buncton, *co. Suss*. Grant of freewarren in, 1285. Harl. 58 I. 37 (Bungeton).

Bungay (Bungey, etc.), *co. Suff*. Grants, etc., in, *t.* Hen. III. Harl. 46 D. 44;—1584. Add. 10577;—1594. Add. 10578 (Bongey);—1636. Add. 19397.

—— Extent of fees in, bel. to the Earls Marshal, c. 1400. Add. 19338.

—— Compotus of Joh. Snoryng, chaplain of St. Thomas's church, 1404-5. Add. 16563.

—— Precipes on covenants in, 1555. Add. 25279;—1561. Add. 25307;—1589. Add. 25397, 25398;—1592. Add. 25422, 25425.

—— Extract of Court-roll of, 1613. Add. 10580.

—— Fine in, 1645. Add. 10582.

Bungeton. *v.* Buncton, *co. Suss.*

Buntingford, *co. Hertf*. Court-roll, 1392 (Buntyngfford). Harl. Roll B. 16.

—— Compotus-rolls of the manor, 1470-1 (Bontyngford). Harl. Roll A. 15;—1471-2. Harl. Roll H. 13.

Bunynton. *v.* Binton, *co. Warw.*

Bur. *v.* Burgh in the Marsh, *co. Linc.*

Burbage (Burbach), *co. Leic*. Grants in, 1385. Add. 26928;—1477. Add. 26929.

Burbage Savage, *co. Wilts*. Compotus-rolls of, bel. to the Duke of Buckingham, 1499-1500, 1511-12. Add. 26873, 26874.

Burc. *v.* Burgh in the Marsh, *co. Linc.*

—— *v.* Burrough on the Hill, *co. Leic.*

Burcheley. *v.* Burley, *nr. Leeds, co. York.*

Burchildeberia. *v.* Bucklebury, *co. Berks.*

Burchore. *v.* Birchover, *in* Youlgreave, *co. Derb.*

**Burgh.** *v.* Brough in Hope, *co. Derb.*

**Burgh** *al.* **Burghlond,** *co. Devon.*
Fine in, 1305. Add. 12945.
—— Settlement of lands in, 1465.
Add. 13061–13064 (Burghlond).

**Burgh** *al.* **Burrough,** *nr. Aylsham,*
*co. Norf.* Grant, etc., in, 1350. Add.
14862;—1420. Add. 14806;—1484.
Add. 14807.
—— Sale of the manor and advowson,
1538 (Burghe *al.* Burghall). Harl.
55 H. 44.

**Burgh,** *in Holt Hund., co. Norf.* Recovery in, 1540 (Parva Burgh). Add.
14871.

**Burgh,** *in Carlford Hund., co. Suff.*
Grants, etc., in, *t.* Hen. III. (Burg).
Add. 15668;—1379 (Burgh). Add.
5512.
—— Precipe on a covenant conc. the
manor, etc., 1589. Add. 25399.
—— Admission to land in Burghall
manor in, 1646. Add. 10251.

**Burgh,** *in Lothingland Hund., co. Suff.*
Grants, etc., in, 1343 (Berwe). Add.
691 (2) (copy);—1423 (Berewe). Add.
8452.

**Burgh by Sands,** *co. Cumb. Capitalis
senescallus.* Joh. Appilby, 1484. Harl.
112 G. 29.
—— *Ballivus.* Will. Lydelle, 1484.
Harl. 112 G. 29.

**Burgh in the Marsh** (Burc, Burg,
etc.), *co. Linc.* Grants, etc., in, to
Bullington Priory, late Hen. II. Cott.
xxvii. 121, Harl. 47 E. 14;—12–13
cent. Harl. 44 A. 24, 52 G. 42;—*t.*
John or early 13 cent. Harl. 46 E.
15, 16, 47 C. 8, 47 E. 19, 21, 23, 50 B.
26, 54 A. 11, 12, 57 D. 26, 58 D. 11
(Bur.):—1230. Harl. 54 C. 19;—*t.* Hen.
III. Cott. xxviii. 11, Harl. 44 A. 37,
45 H. 11, 47 E. 24, 26, 29, 47 F. 10,
49 A. 14, 51 C. 22, 54 A. 14, 54 C. 20,
55 F. 47;—late 13 cent. Cott. xxvii.
181, Harl. 45 H. 20, 57 A. 31;—*c.*
1290. Harl. 57 F. 32;—1291. Harl.
57 F. 33;—*t.* Edw. I. or II. Harl. 52
H. 5;—*t.* Edw. II. Cott. xxvii. 4;—
1316. Harl. 45 H. 22, 23;—*c.* 1320.
Cott. xxviii. 78, Harl. 50 I. 28;—1321.
Harl. 49 H. 51, 52, 50 I. 23;—1322.
Harl. 50 I. 27, Cott. xxviii. 12;—*c.*
1322. Harl. 52 H. 27;—1324. Harl.
43 D. 23;—1334. Harl. 50 I. 26;—
1335. Harl. 47 E. 30 (Bourgh);—1381.
Harl. 44 B. 12.

**Burgh in the Marsh** (Burc, Burg,
etc.), *co. Linc.* (*continued*). Induction
of the canons of Bullington to St.
Peter's church at, [1173–81]. Harl.
43 C. 37.
—— Conf. of the church to the same,
by Galfr., Bp. elect of Lincoln, [1173–
81]. Harl. 43 C. 36.
—— Compos. of suit betw. Grimsby
Abbey and Bullington Priory conc.
churches in, 1193. Harl. 45 A. 6.
—— Lease in Newland in, by
Bullington Priory, *c.* 1200. Harl. 44
A. 30.
—— Grants, etc., of Aldideland *al.*
Aldezland *al.* Aldithland in, to Bul-
lington Priory, early 13 cent. Harl.
47 E. 21;—1230. Harl. 54 C. 19;—*t.*
Hen. III. Harl. 54 C. 20.
—— Grants, etc., in, to St. Peter's
church, early 13 cent.—*t.* Hen. III.
Harl. 47 E. 16, 18, 25.
—— Grants, etc., in, from Bullington
Priory, *c.* 1230. Cott. xii. 9;—*t.* Hen.
III. Harl. 44 A. 40, 42;—1360. Cott.
xxi. 4;—1383. Harl. 44 B. 10;—
1438. Harl. 44 B. 14.
—— Grants, etc., in, early 13 cent.—
*t.* Hen. III. Cott. xxvii. 183, 184,
Harl. 47 E. 3, 22, 27, 51 C. 28, 58
D. 10, 75 C. 53;—*t.* Edw. I. Harl.
54 H. 41;—1293. Harl. 50 G. 46;—*t.*
Edw. II. Harl. 54 H. 45;—1318.
Harl. 50 I. 24, 25, 54 H. 43;—*c.* 1318.
Harl. 54 H. 42;—1320. Cott. xxviii.
79;—*c.* 1320. Cott. xxviii. 77;—1321.
Harl. 54 H. 44;—1325. Harl. 50 E.
7;—1330. Harl. 54 H. 46;—1331.
Cott. xxiii. 5;—1345. Cott. xxvii. 3
(Burgh juxta Waynflet), Harl. 53 C.
36 (Bourgh juxta Waynflet);—1347.
Harl. 44 A. 8;—1349. Harl. 55 F. 4.
—— Release in (?), [1232–46]. Eg.
440.
—— Grant in, to St. Mary's church,
*t.* Hen. III. Harl. 47 H. 41.
—— Conf. of rent from a windmill at,
by the Master of Sempringham, to Bul-
lington Priory, 1235. Harl. 44 I. 14.
—— Release of rent in, for the ward
of Richmond, to Bullington Priory,
*t.* Hen. III. Harl. 54 A. 14.
—— Conf. of St. Peter's church with
St. Mary's chapel, etc., to Bullington
Priory, *c.* 1250. Cott. xxix. 89;—
1256. Harl. 52 H. 28.
—— Conf. of a rent from the church
of, by the Master of Sempringham, to
Bullington Priory, 1263. Harl. 44 I. 17.

Burgh in the Marsh (Burc, Burg, etc.), co. Linc. (continued). Fines in, 1302. Harl. 45 H. 18;—1634. Add. 25926.

—— Covenant and license for rent in, from Bardney Abbey to Greenfield Priory, 1347. Harl. 44 A. 8;—1348. Harl. 43 D. 43.

—— Certif. of Abp. of Canterbury, etc., of rights of Bullington Priory in the church, chapel, etc., 1389. Harl. 43 G. 32;—1399. Harl. 43 I. 3;— 1485. Harl. 43 I. 13.

—— Capellanus. Ascelinus, late 12 cent. Add. 21096.

—— —— Johannes, t. Rich. I.- John. Harl. 44 A. 24, 30, 47 E. 21;— early 13 cent.-t. Hen. III. Harl. 46 E. 15, 16, 47 E. 16, 17, 19, 23, 26, 50 B. 26, 54 E. 11, 57 D. 26, 58 D. 10, 11.

—— —— Symon, t. John. Harl. 44 A. 30, 47 E. 21;—early 13 cent.- t. Hen. III. Harl. 46 E. 15, 47 E. 16, 17, 19.

—— —— Robertus, early 13 cent. Harl. 46 E. 16, 50 B. 26, 54 E. 11;— 1230. Harl. 54 C. 19.

—— —— Alanus, 1230. Harl. 54 C. 19;—c. 1230. Cott. xii. 9;—t. Hen. III. Harl. 45 H. 11, 47. H. 41.

—— —— (?) Alan. Plant, t. Hen. III. Harl. 47 E. 25.

—— —— Rogerus, c. 1230. Cott. xii. 9.

—— —— Willelmus, al. Will. de Scegrena, t. Hen. III. Harl. 45 H. 11, 47 H. 41.

—— Clericus. Gillebertus, t. Hen. II. Harl. 47 E. 15.

—— —— Johannes, t. Hen. III. Harl. 47 E. 3.

—— Vicarius, Ricardus, t. Hen. III. Harl. 47 E. 25, 47 F. 10.

—— —— Alanus, al. Alan. Plant, t. Hen. III. Harl. 47 E. 3, 18;—c. 1250. Cott. xxix. 89.

Burgh St. Margaret and St. Mary, co. Norf. Persona. Johannes, t. Hen. III. Add. 14607.

—— Persona eccl. S. Margarete de Burgh Flegg al. Novele. Will. Manstan, 1391. Add. 14708.

Burgh St. Peter, co. Norf. Exemplif., in 1561, of suit conc. the manor and advowson, 1515 (Whettaker Borowgh). Harl. 51 H. 25

—— Fine of the manor, 1554 (Wheateacre Brugh). Harl. 51 E. 21.

Burgh, South (S. Bergh), co. Norf. Grants, etc., in, 1360. Harl. 49 G. 42; —1381. Add. 9184;—1384. Harl. 56 H. 48.

Burgh [Wallis?], co. York. Feoffment in, 1459 (Bergh). Add. 16951.

Burghardys Manor. v. sub Spexhall, co. Suff.

Burghasshe. v. Burwash, co. Suss.

Burghfield (Burghfeld, etc.), co. Berks. Grants, etc., in, 1343. Harl. 45 G. 69;—1361. Harl. 47 E. 44;—1407 (Burefeld). Harl. 52 D. 47;—1542. Add. 12668;—1618. Add. 19210, 19211.

—— Grant of the advowson, 1361. Harl. 47 E. 44.

—— Grants, etc., of the manor, etc., 1409 (Berefeld). Harl. 47 C. 4;— 1412 (Berefeld). Harl. 49 F. 35;— 1441 (Berfyld). Harl. 53 A. 22.

—— Power to give seisin of Nethercourt manor in, 1441 (Burghfelde Regis). Harl. 43 E. 49.

Burghildebiri. v. Bucklebury, co. Berks.

Burghill, co. Heref. Entail of lands in, 1459 (Burghull). Add. 4605.

—— Brief conc. a fire in, 1791. Ch. Br. B. xxxi. 6.

Burghlay. v. Burley, co. York.

Burghlond. v. Burgh, co. Devon.

Burghwere. v. Weare, Over (?), co. Som.

Burgotha. v. sub St. Stephen in Brannel, co. Cornw.

Burgtune. v. Bourton on the Water, co. Glouc.

Burgum. v. Brough in Hope, co. Derb.

—— v. Burrough on the Hill, co. Leic.

Burhheia. v. Burway (?), co. Salop.

Burlcroft, in Bicester, co. Oxon. Grant in, to Bicester Priory, early Hen. III. Add. 10612.

Buriton. v. Burrington, co. Heref.

Burkilleberi. v. Bucklebury, co. Berks.

Burkote. v. Burcot, in Wells, co. Som.

Burleia. v. Bearley, co. Warw.

Burleigh, in Knebworth, co. Hertf. Grant in, ante 1292 (Borueleye). Add. 24063.

Burleigh, co. Northt. Lease, etc., of the manor, 1379. Harl. 54 C. 7 (Burlee);—1430. Harl. 43 E. 19 (Burley); —1431. Harl. 45 I. 12, 50 H. 27, 28, 54 I. 15;—1435. Add. 2016.

**Burleigh, Little** (Petit Burlee), co. *Northt.* Lease of the manor, 1383. Harl. 54 C. 10.

—— Covenant conc. waste in, 1384. Harl. 54 C. 9.

**Burley.** *v.* Bearley, co. *Warw.*

**Burley,** co. *Southt.* Fine of the manor, 1569. Add. 8467.

**Burley** (Burlay *al.* Burghlay, etc., in Querfildale, Werfedalle, Querleclalle, etc.), *nr. Otley, in Wharfedale,* co. *York.* Grants, etc., in, *t.* Edw. I. or II. Add. 16757 (Burghlay in Quervesdale);—1318. Add. 16767;—1320. Add. 16774;—1362. Add. 16807;—1366. Add. 16806;—1402. Add. 16896;—1485. Add. 16966.

—— Acquittances to J. de Calverley as steward of the manor of, 1319. Add. 16768;—1321. Add. 16771.

—— Grant in, to Esholt Priory, 1349. Add. 16808.

—— Grants, etc., of the manor, 1371. Add. 16828;—1384. Add. 16840;—1389. Add. 16863;—1401. Add. 16887-16890, 16892-16895;—1423. Add. 16908;—1424. Add. 16909;—1427. Add. 16913;—1444. Add. 16935.

—— (?). Acquittance for crown rents in the manor, 1320 (Burghle). Add. 16772.

—— Inquest conc. breaking of Burley Hall, 154². Add. 17009.

**Burley** (Burghlay, etc.), *nr. Leeds,* co. *York.* Grants of the manor, *t.* Edw. I. or II. Add. 16750 (Burcheley);—1322. Add. 16792;—1323. Add. 16776, 16777, 16793.

—— Grant, etc., in, 1337. Add. 16695, 16696;—1572. Add. 17030.

**Burley on the Hill,** co. *Rutl.* Grant in, 1650. Add. 1800.

**Burlingham St. Andrew** *al.* **North B.** (Birlingham, Byrlyngham, etc.), co. *Norf.* Grants, etc., in, 1318. Add. 14579;—1427. Add. 14580;—1456. Add. 15194;—1470. Add. 14581, 14582;—1499. Add. 14585;—1550. Add. 14583.

—— Release of the manor, 1422. Add. 15768.

—— Inspex., in 1554, of feoffment of the advowson, 1422. Add. 17243.

—— Settlement of Dawbneys manor in, 1621. Add. 14584.

**Burlingham St. Peter,** co. *Norf.* Settlement in, 1621. Add. 14584.

**Burmarsh,** co. *Kent.* Settlement in, on divorce of Marg. de Valoignes, 1326 (Borewaremersh). Harl. 80 H. 4.

—— Grant in, 1376 (Berewaremersche). Harl. 80 C. 44.

—— Writ for an assize of Nov. Diss. in, 1486 (Bourghmersh). Harl. 53 F. 12.

—— Feoffment of the manor, 1606 (Boroughmarsh). Add. 20000.

—— Acquittance for fees from Tremeton manor in, for ward of Dover Castle, 1609-23. Add. 23751.

**Burminghelde.** *v. sub* Swanscombe, co. *Kent.*

**Burn, Burnes.** *v.* Beaksbourne, co. *Kent.*

**Burnan, aet.** *v.* Bishopsbourne, co. *Kent.*

**Burnaston** (Brunnaldeston, Brunnaldiston, etc.), *in Etwall,* co. *Derb.* Grants, etc., in, *t.* Hen. III. Woll. ix. 36 (Brunufyston);—late Hen. III. Woll. ix. 37;—1290, *c.* 1290. Woll. ix. 34, 35;—1316. Woll. ix. 38, 39;—1353 (Brunaldeston). Woll. ix. 40, 41;—1423. Woll. iv. 89 (Brynnaldston);—1476. Woll. ix. 42;—1495. Woll. xi. 48, xii. 133;—1502. Woll. xii. 103, 103.*

—— *Clericus.* Osbertus, 1290. Woll. ix. 34, 35.

**Burne.** *v.* Bourne, co. *Linc.*

**Burnecestria.** *v.* Bicester, co. *Oxon.*

**Burnshaghe.** *v. sub* Guiseley, co. *York.*

**Burnevile's Manor.** *v. sub* Levington, co. *Suf.*

**Burnham,** co. *Buck.* Grants, etc., in, 1345. Harl. 44 B. 40, Lansd. 113; —1410. Add. 5160;—1415. Add. 5161;—1416. Add. 5162;—1429. Lansd. 149;—1443. Lansd. 159;—1477. Harl. 76 G. 30;—1484. Harl. 75 G. 27;—1532. Lansd. 177;—1535. Lansd. 178;—1537. Harl. 86 G. 30, Lansd. 576;—1538. Lansd. 179;—1542. Harl. 78 H. 45, 46;—1553. Harl. 76 E. 12;—1561. Harl. 75 H. 24, Lansd. 577, 578;—1562. Harl. 75 H. 11 (Bournham);—1568. Add. 5163;—1594. Harl. 75 G. 49, 75 H. 28;—1610. Add. 26363;—1624. Harl. 75 H. 43;—1630. Add. 13704;—1634. Harl. 75 H. 49, 76 F. 43.

Buxted (Boostede, Boxstede, etc.), co.
Suss. Release of Pende in, t. Hen. III.
Harl. 80 B. 44.
—— Grant of "quatuor derratas"
yearly in, t. Hen. III. or Edw. I.
Harl. 78 A. 49.
—— Grants, etc., in, late 13 cent.
Harl. 79 C. 2, 3, 4 (Boksted) :—1310.
Harl. 76 C. 2:—1335. Harl. 79 C.
5-7:—1383. Add. 19147 (Bokstede);
—1511. Add. 19150 (Buxstod).
—— Grant of a fulling mill in, 1316.
Harl. 78 G. 35.
—— Award conc. a heriot in, 1567.
Add. 20084.

Buxton. v. sub Bentley, co. Suff.

Buxton, co. Derb. Settlement of Cowlow Buxtons (Coulowe Bukstones)
and other lands in, 1322. Woll. iv. 59.
—— Grant in, 1509. Woll. i. 90
(Buxstonys), vii. 14.
—— Sale of tithes of the mill at,
[1554-7] (Buxstan). Woll. iv. 65.
—— Sale of "the Talbot" Inn in,
1576 (Buxston). Woll. xii. 106.
—— Briefs for rebuilding the chapel,
1798, 1805. Ch. Br. B. xxxviii. 5,
xlvi. 2.

Buxton, co. Norf. Grants in, 1297.
Add. 19297 (Buxtune);—1398. Add.
14586.
—— Accompt of tithes of, 1673-1682.
Add. 14808.
—— Vicarius. Joh. Gough, 1673-
1682. Add. 14808.

Buyton. v. Byton, co. Heref.

Bwayecomb. v. sub Farway, co.
Devon.

Byastenouere. v. sub Pevensey, co.
Suss.

Bychamwelle. v. Beechamwell, co.
Norf.

Bycheuestoke. v. Chew Stoke, co. Som.

Bydictun. Charter of Ceolwulf of
Mercia dated at, 822. Cott. MS. Aug.
ii. 93.

Bydynden. v. Biddenden, co. Kent.

Byenstede. v. Binsted, co. Southt.

Byfield, co. Northt. Covenant of Biddlesdon Abbey conc. common of pasture in, 1260 (Bifeld). Harl. 84 D. 56.
—— Clericus. Philippus, late Hen.
II. Add. 19817 (Bifeldia);—early 13
cent. Harl. 85 B. 47 (Byfeld), 86 B.
40 (Biffeld).

Byfleet, co. Surr. Grant in, 1414. Add.
26645 (Byflete);—1462. Add. 26666
(Biflete).
—— Rector. Willelmus, late Hen.
III. Add. 26610.

Byford. v. Beeford, co. York.

Byford, co. Heref. Rector. Johannes,
1418. Harl. 112 F. 13.

Byggeden. v. sub Woolley, co. York.

Bygrave, co. Hertf. Grant in, t. Hen.
III. (Bigrave). Harl. 111 D. 28.

Bykenhull. v. Bickenhill, co. Warw.

Byker. v. Bicker, co. Linc.

Byker, co. Northumb. Grant by Edw.
III. of a third part of the manor and
advowson, 1355. Harl. 83 C. 14.

Bylaugh (Belhagh, etc.), co. Norf.
Feoffments, etc., of the manor, 1369.
Harl. 54 G. 50;—1386. Harl. 51 E.
25;—1404. Add. 15537 (Belhawe);
—1461. Add. 2007 (Bilhaghe).
—— Grant in, 1380 (Belhagh). Add.
15498.

Bylesbi. v. Bilsby, co. Linc.

Byliesdyne, Byliges dyne. v. Bildeston, co. Suff.

Byncheaham, N. v. Bensham, co. Surr.

Byncombe. v. Bincombe, co. Dors.

Bynedon. v. Bindon, Lit., co. Dors.

Bynfylde. v. Binfield, co. Berks.

Byngfeld. v. Bingfield, co. Northumb.

Byngham. v. Bingham, co. Nott.

Byntre. v. Bintree, co. Norf.

Byrestune, co. Essex. Bequest of
land at, post 991. Harl. 43 C. 4.

Byrcheover. v. Birchover, in Youlgreave, co. Derb.

Byrdenburye. v. Bredenbury, co.
Heref.

Byrille. v. Bierley, in Bradford, co.
York.

Byrlingahamme. v. Birlingham, co.
Worc.

Byrlyngham. v. Burlingham St.
Andrew, co. Norf.

Byrnyngham. v. Briningham, co. Norf.

Byrstal. v. Birstall, co. York.

Byrston. v. Burston, co. Norf.

Byrtchett. v. sub Dronfield, co. Derb.

Byrton. v. Burton, Kirk, co. York.

Byrydowne. v. Berry Down, nr. Combe Martin, co. Devon.

Byrystede. v. sub Horton, co. Northt.

Byscopthorpe. v. Biscathorpe, co. Linc.

Bysshe Court Manor. v. sub Horne, co. Surr.

Bysshopestthorp. v. Biscathorpe, co. Linc.

Bysshopeswode, Byswoode. v. Bushwood, co. Warw.

Byssopindenne. v. sub Chart, Great, co. Kent.

Bytham, Castle, co. Linc. Payment of rents to Ouston Abbey made at, 1362 (Bytham). Harl. 58 G. 47 (3) (copy).
—— Grant in, 1401 (Westbitham). Cott. xxvii. 79.
—— Dominus. Rob. Coleuille, miles, 1348 (Byham). Harl. 45 G. 36.
—— Domina. Alicia Basset, 1411. Lansd. 641.

Bytham, Little, co. Linc. Grant in, 1401 (Estbitham). Cott. xxvii. 79.

Bytlesbrok. v. Bisbrooke, co Rutl.

Bytlesden, etc. v. Biddlesdon, co. Buck.

Byton (Buyton), co. Heref. Grants, etc., in, 1386. Add. 6199;—1477. Cott. xxiii. 4;—1487. Cott. xxvi. 27.

Byworth, in Petworth, co. Suss. Sale of Sellescombe to be held of the manor of, 1539. Eg. 282.
—— Exchequer acquittance for a fine in, 1595. Add. 25674 a.

Byxlea. v. Bexley, co. Kent.

Byxpeche. v. sub Marden, co. Kent.

## C

Cabergh, co. Westm. Grant of free-warren in, 1335. Add. 7212.

Cabourn (Caburnia, Kaburnia, etc.), co. Linc. Grants, etc., in, to New-house Abbey, [1143-7]. Harl. 43 H. 10, 45 F. 18 (Catborna);—c. 1150. Harl. 45 F. 17, 19;—c. 1150-60. Harl. 43 H. 14-17;—[1156 or 7]. Harl. 51 H. 1;—c. 1160-66. Cott. v. 19;—t. Hen. III. Harl. 47 F. 31, 47 G. 51, 56 I. 39-41.
—— Covenant conc. pasture in, betw. Newhouse and Thornton Abbeys, c. 1200 (Kaburne). Harl. 45 A. 23.

Cabourn (Caburnia, Kaburnia, etc.), co. Linc. (continued). Release in Polrunthorndaile and Lingdaile in (?), to Newhouse Abbey, c. 1200. Harl. 56 I. 37.
—— Lease in, 1537 (Cayborne). Harl. 43 F. 36.
—— Declar. of trusts on a mortgage on the manor and advowson, 1702. Eg. 104.
—— Sacerdos. Osmundus, [1157-63]. Cott. xi. 26.

Cadbury (?), nr. Eaton Socon, co. Bedf. Conf. by King John of a grant in, 1208 (Cadebyri). Add. 6014.

Cadbury, co. Devon. Grant in, t. Hen. III. (Catteburgh). Lansd. 84.
—— Grant by Edw. I. of free-warren in, 1296 (Cadebury). Harl. 58 I. 40.

Cadbury, South, co. Som. Acquit-tance for homage for the manor of, t. Edw. II. Harl. 58 H. 10.

Caddington, co. Hertf. Grant of a site in, etc., to Merkyate Priory, 1145 (Cadeudona). Cott. xi. 6, 8.
—— Grants, etc., in, t. Edw. I. Harl. 58 D. 31 (Kadindon);—1329. Harl. 56 D. 11 (Cadindon);—1346. Harl. 55 E. 5 (West Cadyngdone);—1393. Add. 19956 (Cadyngdone); — 1435. Add. 23178 (West Cadyndone);—1448. Add. 9708 (Kadyngton).

Caddoxton juxta Neath, co. Glam. Capellanus. Mauricius, early 13 cent. (S. Caddocus). Harl. 75 C. 35.

Cadebrooke [Cattybrooke, nr. Almond-bury ?], co. Glouc. Fines, etc., in, 1556. Add. 15793, 15794; — 1565. Add. 15801;—1566. Add. 15802;—1570. Add. 15805, 15806; — 1600. Add. 15821, 15823;—1601. Add. 15824;— 1633. Add. 15832, 15833; — 1638. Add. 15834, 15836.

Cadeby [with Wyham], co. Linc. Covenant conc. pasture in, with Kirk-stead Abbey, c. 1162 (Catebi). Harl. 44 E. 53.

Cadebyri. v. Cadbury (?), co. Bedf.

Cadendona. v. Caddington, co. Hertf.

Cadeneye. v. Cadney, co. Linc.

Cadhay, co. Devon. Covenant for recovery of the manor, 1553. Add. 19190.

Calsthorpe, *nr. Elkington, co. Linc.*
Grant, etc., in, late t. Hen. II. Add.
20605 (Calctorp);—1274. Harl. 47 B.
27 (Kayllestorp).

Calswat. *v. Calceworth, co. Linc.*

Calthorn. *v. Cawthorne, co. York.*

Calthorpe, *co. Norf.* Grants, etc., in,
t. Hen. III. Add. 2002 (Kaletorp),
2003 (Calethorp), 14587 (do.), 14588
(d..);—1306. Add. 14589 (Calthorp);
—1578. Add. 14937 (Calthorpp).

—— Verdict of "libera conditio" in
the manor court, 1448. Add. 16543.

—— Commission of enquiry conc. the
living, 1659. Add. 14975.

—— *Persona.* Johannes, early Hen.
III. Add. 19275.

—— *Presbiter.* Rogerus, early Hen.
III. Add. 19275.

Calton, *in Bakewell, co. Derb.* Sale in,
1547. Woll. xi. 40.

Calton, *co. Staff.* Grant in, t. Hen. III.
Harl. 112 A. 26.

—— Brief for rebuilding the chapel,
1794. Ch. Br. B. xxxv. 4.

Caluore, Caluour. *v. Calver, in Bakewell, co. Derb.*

Calver (Caluore, etc.), *in Bakewell, co.
Derb.* Grants, etc., in, 1239. Lansd.
584 (Calfouer);—1365. Woll. vii. 53 ;
—1395. Woll. vii. 54 ;—1403. Woll.
vii. 58 ;—1409. Woll. i. 91 (Caluour),
vii. 59 (do.);—1439. Woll. vii. 57 ;—
1445. Woll. vii. 56 (Calfowr);—1490.
Woll. vii. 48.

Calverley (Kalverlay, Calverlay, etc.),
*co. York.* Marriage settlement in,
late 12 cent. Add. 16580 (Kalverlaia).

—— Conf. of a grant in Tyersall
(Tyrsale) in, to Woodkirk Priory,
early Hen. III. Add. 16584.

—— Grants, etc., in, early Hen. III.
-early 14 cent. Add. 16583, 16588,
16589, 16592, 16594, 16596, 16603,
16606 - 16618, 16632, 16634, 16636,
16641, 16643 - 16645, 16648, 16650,
16651, 16654, 16658 - 16661, 16668,
16703, 16704, 16707, 16708, 16710,
16711, 16714 - 16720, 16738, 16739,
16741, 16742, 16747, 16751, 16755,
16756, 16758 ;—1254. Add. 16624 ;—
1256. Add. 16622, 16625 ;— 1258.
Add. 16619, 16620 ; — 1259. Add.
16621, 16626 ;—1260. Add. 16627 ;—
1261. Add. 16638 ; — 1265. Add.
16639, 16640 ;—1284. Add. 16699 ;—
1291. Add. 16712, 16713 ; — 1307.

Add. 16761 ;—1308. Add. 16685 ;—
1310. Add. 16763 ; — 1319. Add.
16689 ;—1326. Add. 16783—16787 ;—
1335. Add. 16721 ; — 1345. Add.
16735 ;—1363. Add. 16822 ;—1397.
Add. 16868 ;—1398. Add. 16885 ;—
1437. Add. 16926 ;—1482. Add.
16962, 16963 ;—1498. Add. 16977,
16978 ;—1502. Add. 16992 ;—1559.
Add. 17026 ; — 1568. Add. 17029.

—— Grants, etc., in Tyersall (Tyrsale,
Tiresale) in, t. Hen. III.-early 14
cent. Add. 16586, 16598, 16601, 16678,
16681, 16744, 16745 ;—t. Edw. III.
Add. 16697 ;—1396. Add. 16877.

—— Fine in, 1293. Add. 16682,
16683.

—— Mem. of land held by Joh. Scot
in, t. Edw. I. or II. Add. 16701.

—— Grant in Ravenscliff in, t. Edw.
I. or II. Add. 16758.

—— Release of rent from the mill of,
1307. Add. 16795.

—— Grant to the tenants, etc., of
commonage in Bramley, 1311. Add.
16782.

—— Entail of the manor, 1349. Add.
16799.

—— Grants, etc., of the manor, 1371.
Add. 16828 ;—1384. Add. 16840 ;—
1396. Add. 16877 ; — 1401. Add.
16887 - 16890, 16892 - 16895 ;—1423.
Add. 16908 ;—1424. Add. 16909 ;—
1437. Add. 16913 ;—1444. Add.
16935 ;—1485. Add. 16965, 16966.

—— Grant of Milnewod, etc., in,
1377. Add. 16834.

—— Mem. of land in, held by Will.
Calverley, c. 1450. Add. 16954.

—— Extent of Sir W. Calverley's
lands in, 1500. Add. 16989.

—— Exchequer acquittance for farm
of land in, 1596. Add. 25717 a.

—— Brief conc. a fire at Calverley
Mills, 1822. Ch. Br. C. iii. 7.

—— *Persona.* Robertus, t. Hen. III.
Add. 16599, 16606, 16613, 16615,
16616 ;—1254. Add. 16624.

—— *Vicarius.* Henricus, 1254. Add.
16624 ;—1256. Add. 16625 ;—t. Hen.
III. Add. 16609, 16616, 16617.

—— —— Robertus, t. Hen. III. or
Edw. I. Add. 16646.

—— —— *al. Vic. perpetuus.* Rob.
Power, 1319. Add. 16689 ;—1345.
Add. 16735.

Candelent Manor. *v. sub* Trimley St. Mary, *co. Suff.*

Candlesby, *co. Linc. Persona.* Ricardus, 1346. Harl. 54 E. 14.

—— —— Joh. North, 1350. Harl. 54 E. 15;—1351. Harl. 56 G. 38.

Candover, Brown, and Preston C., *co. Southt.* Grant in, 1410 (Brouncandeuere, Prestone Candeuere). Harl. 57 G. 33.

Canengis. *v.* Cannings, Bishop's, *co. Wilts.*

Canewdon (Canewedon, etc.), *co. Essex.* Grants, etc., in, 1269. Harl. 55 B. 15, 55 C. 3;—1273. Harl. 48 G. 4;—1296. Harl. 47 H. 3 (Canowedun);—1369. Harl. 50 H. 18;—1407. Harl. 51 D. 13 (Canwedon), 57 A. 18;—1457. Harl. 45 G. 19.

—— Lease, etc., of "Godiebernelond" *al.* "Gydibernes" in, 1274. Harl. 45 D. 25;—1277-8. Harl. 49 H. 28.

—— Grant, etc., of Scottes manor in, 1407. Harl. 51 D. 13, 57 A. 18.

—— Conveyance, etc., of Lambourn Hall manor in, 1457. Harl. 45 G. 19, 20, 56 B. 29-31;—1462. Harl. 46 I. 43.

—— Fine in, 1541. Add. 15868.

—— *Vicarius.* Th[omas?], *t.* Hen. III. (Kanewedon). Harl. 49 B. 43.

Canfield, Little *al.* Childer, *co. Essex.* Grant of tithes of, to Lewes Priory, late 12 cent. (Kanefed). Cott. xi. 50.

—— Fines in, 1285 (Childeskanefeld). Harl. 83 D. 15, 16.

—— Court-rolls, 1400-1445. Add. 19108.

—— Precipe on a covenant in, 1593. Add. 25036.

—— *Capellanus.* Petrus, late 12 cent. Cott. xi. 50.

—— *Clericus.* Ricardus, late 12 cent. Cott. xi. 50.

Canford, Great, *co. Dors.* Compotus of the manor, 1553-4. Add. 664.

—— Brief conc. a fire at, 1758. Ch. Br. A. iv. 6.

Cannaligee, *co. Cornw.* Grant, etc., in, 1513 (Canalezy). Harl. 50 C. 41-43.

Cannings, Bishop's, *co. Wilts.* Papal conf. of the church to Salisbury chapter, [1161] (Canengis). Harl. 43 A. 23.

Cannington. *v. sub* Uplyme, *co. Devon.*

Cannington (Canyngton, etc.), *co. Som.* Conf. of a grant of "terra de Blakemora" in, early 13 cent. Add. 20418.

—— Grant in Peredham in, late Hen. III. Add. 26751.

—— Grant at Stoniland nr. (?), late 13 cent. Add. 20401.

—— Defeasance of grant of rents in, 1294. Add. 20224.

—— Settlement of Wodecrofte in, 1299. Add. 22551.

—— Fine in, 1299 (Canynton). Add. 20222.

—— Grants in Brymore (Brummore), etc., in, 1318. Add. 20223 (Canygton); —1404. Add. 20225;—1452. Add. 20226.

—— Assignment of a lease of three parts of the manor, rectory, etc., 1686. Harl. 111 H. 22.

Cannington Hundred. Order for an extent of, 1301. Add. 19302.

Cannock, *co. Staff.* Charter of Hen. III. dated in the camp at, 4 Oct., 1245. Harl. 58 I. 4 (Gannok).

—— Grant in, 1343 (Canokburi). Add. 20450.

Cannock Chace. Order to deliver three "foldes" in, 1401 (Cannok). Woll. v. 14 a.

Cannon Manor. *v. sub* Mitcham, *co. Surr.*

Canokburi. *v.* Cannock, *co. Staff.*

Canonbury Manor. *v. sub* Kingston, *co. Surr.*

Canon's *al.* Cannon's Manor. *v. sub* Parndon, Gt., *co. Essex.*

Canon's Court Manor. *v. sub* Newington, *co. Kent.*

Cantelay. *v.* Cantley, *co* York.

Cantele. *v.* Cantley, *co. Norf.*

Canteles Manor. *v. sub* Snape, *co. Suff.*

Cantelos. *v. sub* Hethersett, *co. Norf.*

Cantelowes Manor, *in Kentish Town. v. sub* London, St. Pancras parish.

Canterbury, *co. Kent.* Grants in, 811. Cott. MS. Aug. ii. 10 (Dorovernia); —823. Cott. MS. Aug. ii. 75 (Dorovern);—839. Cott. MS. Aug. ii. 28 (Dorovernia);—815. Cott. MS. Aug. ii. 60 (Dorovernia);—868 (?). Cott. MS. Aug ii. 17 (Dorobernia).

L

**Canterbury,** *co. Kent (continued).* Purchase in, " prope barram de Sco. Sepulchro," by Christ Church Priory, 1152. Camph. xxii. 2.

—— Grant in, "juxta Fismanne cheriche," by Ch. Ch. Priory, [1167-75]. Campb. iv. 8.

—— Grant of a corrody, by Ch. Ch. Priory, in exchange for lands in, " ante portam ecclesie," [1167-75]. Add. 917.

—— Bequests to religious houses, etc., in, by Dna. A. de Clifford, c. 1220. Harl. 48 C. 25.

—— Bequests to same, by G. de Hagnefelde, 1305. Harl. 78 E. 6.

—— Grants, etc., in, 1306. Add. 16342:—1358. Add. 16360:—1435. Harl. 79 C. 49:—1480. Harl. 78 F. 45;—1485. Harl. 78 C. 17;—1548. Harl. 75 E. 22, 75 H. 4. 76 H. 50:— 1551. Harl. 75 E. 28, 76 I. 7;—1554. Harl. 79 D. 18, Harl. Roll S. 36;— 1555. Harl. 79 D. 17;—1579. Harl. 76 D. 44, 78 B. 11.

—— Expenses of W. de Rupe on a journey to, 1324. Add. 8061.

—— Petition conc. the keepership " des Eschaunges de Londres et de Caunterbirs," c. 1331. Cott. xxix. 82.

—— Verdict conc. amount, in 1340, of the " Nonus denarius Catallorum " in the liberty of, 1342. Harl. 80 D. 52.

—— Covenant with Christ Church Priory conc. mills on the R. Stour, 1357. Cott. xxi. 10.

—— Note of evidences of lands of T. Arderne in, 1550. Harl. 58 H. 18.

—— Crown grant of lands in Wincheap, etc., in, late bel. to St. James's Hospital, 1551. Harl. 75 H. 6.

—— Award conc. dower of D. Hales in, 1556. Harl. 76 D. 38.

—— Sales in Wincheapfield nr. the walls of, 1574. Harl. 79 A. 23, 86 H. 36;—1577. Harl. 86 H. 6, 7.

—— Conveyance, etc., of Berton House and mills nr., 1580. Harl. 77 B. 2-4, 77 H. 43.

—— Assessment roll for a subsidy in, 1641. Harl. Roll T. 1.

—— Release in the precincts of the Blackfriars in, 1668. Add. 8464.

—— Suit in the Mayor's Court, 1678. Harl. 84 B. 42.

—— Covenant conc. profits from " the Black Boy " tavern, 1800. Add. 17837.

**Canterbury,** *co. Kent (continued).* *Prepositus.* Haimo, [1167-75]. Campb. iv. 8, Add. 917.

—— *Major.* Joh. Frennyngham, *ante* 1475. Harl. 79 B. 5.

—— —— Tho. Propchant, 1493. Harl. 76 F. 49, 78 F. 48.

—— —— Edw. Bolney, 1494. Harl. 78 C. 15.

—— —— Tho. atte Wodde, 1505. Harl. 79 B. 5.

—— —— Nic. Nicholson, 1678. Harl. 84 B. 42.

—— *Ballivi.* Rob. Polre, Joh. Bigges, [1258]. Harl. 76 A. 36.

—— —— Edm. Cokyn, Steph. de Sellynge, 1357. Cott. xxi. 10;—1358. Add. 16361.

—— —— Will. Cornewaill, Nic. de Ba, 1371. Add. 16363.

—— —— Will. Elys, Joh. Proude, 1400. Harl. 80 B. 21.

—— —— Joh. Perye, Rob. Coupere, 1402. Add. 15008.

—— —— Will. Emery, Will. Benet, 1417. Harl. 78 G. 26.

—— —— Rob. Bertelot, Will. Osbarn, 1430. Add. 16365.

—— —— Will. Osbarn, Will. Bonyngton, 1435. Harl. 79 C. 49.

—— —— Will. Byllynton, Will. atte Wode, 1439. Add. 16366.

—— *Aldermannus.* Johannes, [1167-75]. Campb. iv. 8.

—— —— Tho. Ikham, 1402. Add. 15008.

—— —— Joh. Huett, 1505. Harl. 79 B. 5.

—— —— Har. Gosebourne, 1535. Harl. 78 E. 34.

—— —— Will. Coppyn, 1554. Harl. 77 E. 32.

—— —— Rich. May, 1658, 1660. Harl. 112 B. 25-27.

—— PARISHES, ETC. :—

—— PAR. OF ST. ALPHEGE. Exchange in, 1395. Harl. 78 F. 29.

—— —— Gen. release in (?), to Ch. Ch. Priory, 1458. Add. 16367.

—— —— *Rector.* Hen. de Norton juxta Twycros, al. Norton, 1364, 1365. Harl. 80 D. 46, 47;—1369. Harl. 79 E. 2.

—— PAR. OF ST. GEORGE. Grants, etc., in, 1493. Harl. 76 F. 49, 78 F. 48;—1516. Harl. 78 F. 50 a, b.

Canterbury, *co. Kent (continued)*.

—— PARISHES, ETC. *(continued)*:—

—— PAR. OF ST. LAURENCE. Grants in, 1507 (S. Laurenc. juxta Natyndon). Harl. 79 B. 3;—1508. Harl. 78 E. 29.

—— PAR. OF ST. MARGARET. Grants, etc., in, 1463. Harl. 78 G. 9;—1478. Harl. 78 G. 10;—1548. Harl. 75 H. 4, 76 H. 50;—1551. Harl. 75 H. 6;—1678. Harl. 84 B. 42.

—— PAR. OF ST. MARTIN. Grants, etc., in, 1480. Harl. 80 G. 15;—1551. Harl. 75 H. 6.

—— PAR. OF ST. MARY. Fine in, 1559 (par. B. Marie). Harl. 77 G. 25, 80 H. 64.

—— PAR. OF ST. MARY BREDIN, WITH ST. EDMUND'S OF RIDING-GATE. Conveyance, etc., in, 1508. Harl. 78 E. 29;—1548. Add. 14043;—1551. Harl. 75 H. 6;—1577. Harl. 86 H. 38.

—— PAR. OF ST. MARY BREDMAN. Lease in, by Ch. Ch. Priory, 1371. Add. 16363.

—— —— Grant of "the Swan" in, 1479. Harl. 80 E. 48, 49.

—— Feoffment, etc., in, 1480. Harl. 80 G. 15;—1486. Harl. 78 I. 2; —1551. Harl. 75 H. 6;—1577. Harl. 86 H. 6, 7.

—— PAR. OF ST. MARY NORTHGATE. Grants, etc., in, 1402. Add. 15008; —1430. Add. 16365;—1439. Add. 16366;—1529. Add. 16370;—1558. Harl. 77 E. 55;—1559. Harl. 76 I. 44; —1580. Harl. 77 B. 4.

—— —— Grant at Borysende in, to St. Gregory's Priory, 1501. Harl. 78 I. 17.

—— PAR. OF ST. MILDRED, WITH ST. MARY CASTELL. Grants, etc., in, 1516. Harl. 80 E. 46;—1548. Harl. 75 H. 4, 76 H. 50;—1551. Harl. 75 H. 6;— 1577. Harl. 84 H. 6, 7, 86 H. 38.

—— PAR. OF ST. PAUL. Release in, 1464. Add. 16368.

—— PAR. OF ST. PETER. Grant in, 1417. Harl. 78 G. 26.

—— —— *Rector.* Steph. de Stone, 1298. Add. 16396.

—— PAR. OF ST. SEPULCHRE. Grant in, 1507. Harl. 79 B. 3;—1508. Harl. 78 E. 29.

—— PAR. OF HOLY CROSS, WESTGATE. Grants, etc., in, 1488. Harl. 76 F. 20; —1551. Harl. 75 H. 6;—1577. Harl. 78 H. 50.

Canterbury, *co. Kent (continued)*.

—— PARISHES, ETC. *(continued)*:—

—— PAR. OF WESTGATE WITHOUT THE WALLS. Grants of right of way in, to St. Gregory's Priory, c. 1215. Harl. 75 F. 22, 45.

—— —— Grants, etc., in, 1356. Harl. 78 A. 32;—1512. Harl. 76 D. 3;—1548. Harl. 75 H. 4, 76 H. 50.

—— —— *Ballivus.* Gilb. de Boniton, *t.* Hen. III. Harl. 78 H. 35.

Canterbury Castle. Roll of gaol-delivery, 1317. Harl. Roll I. 33.

—— Royal grant of the keepership of, to Sir Will. Haute, 1465. Harl. 75 E. 12.

—— Bond for safe keeping of prisoners in, 1465. Harl. 80 C. 7.

—— *Keeper (late).* Alex. Culpeper, 1515. Harl. 75 E. 16.

—— —— *(late).* Sir Geo. Harper, 1549. Harl. 75 E. 26.

—— —— Tho. Culpeper, 1549. Harl. 75 E. 25, 26.

Canter Selyph *al.* Canter Selyf, *co. Brecon.* Grants, etc., of lands, etc., in, to Dore Abbey, *ante* 1205 (?). Harl. 48 C. 26;—1257. Harl. 48 C. 27;— 1271. Harl. 43 A. 71.

—— Award conc. rights of Dore Abbey to pasture in, 1251. Campb. xviii. 2.

Cantletts Manor. *v. sub* Snape, *co. Suff.*

Cantley, *co. Norf. Persoun. Sire* Will. de Bergh, 1354 (Cautele). Harl. 45 F. 52.

Cantley, *co. York.* Grant in, nr. St. Wilfred's church, *t.* Hen. III. (Cantelay). Harl. 46 F. 38.

—— Petition for conf. of title in, 1633. Cott. xvi. 22.

—— *Capellanus.* Haco, *t.* Hen. III. Harl. 46 F. 38.

—— *Persona.* Jerem. de Rosington, *t.* Hen. III. Harl. 46 F. 38.

*v. also* Brampton, *in Cantley, co. York.*

Cantlow. *v. sub* Hethersett, *co. Norf.*

Canton, nr. *Cardiff, co. Glam.* Grant in, *t.* Hen. III. or Edw. I. (Kaneton). Add. 24300.

Cantreff, *co. Brecon.* Grant in, 1514 (par. S. Kenedri de Kantreff). Harl. 111 D. 3.

Canwedon. *v.* Canewdon, *co. Essex.*

L 2

**Canwick,** *co. Linc.* Grant in, *t.* Hen. III. Harl. 52 C. 49 (Kanuic), 55 D. 34 (Camwik).

—— *Vicarius.* Alanus, *t.* Hen. III. Harl. 52 C. 49.

**Canygton, Canyngton, etc.** *v.* Cannington, *co. Som.*

**Canyton.** *v. sub* Uplyme, *co. Devon.*

**Caos.** *v.* Caus, *co. Salop.*

**Capehegh,** *nr. Axminster, co. Devon.* Feoffment of, 1402. Harl. 57 B. 52.

**Capel** *al.* Caple, *co. Kent.* Grants, etc., in, 1382. Harl. 80 F. 43 :—1407. Harl. 76 G. 39;—1428. Harl. 77 E. 39;—1444. Harl. 76 G. 53:—1565. Harl. 77 A. 10 ;—1569. Harl. 77 A. 23.

**Capel St. Andrew** (Capele), *co. Suff.* Sale, etc., in, 1638. Add. 10289 ;— 1694. Add. 9797;—1700. Add. 10291.

**Capel St. Mary** (Capele, etc.), *co. Suff.* Grants, etc., in, late Hen. III. Add. 9491 (Capeles) ;—1318. Add. 9580 (Capell):—1331. Add. 9591-9595;—1336. Add. 9602 ;—1341. Add. 8374 ; —1353. Add. 9624 ; — 1366. Add. 9640 ;—1369. Add. 9643 ;—1396. Add. 9671 ;—1488. Add. 8385 :— 1464. Harl. 55 C. 43.

—— *Rector. Dom.* Tho. de Bello Campo, 1318. Add. 9580.

**Caple, King's,** *co. Heref.* Extract of court-roll, 1547. Add. 1351.

—— Grant in, 1625. Add. 1924.

**Car Colston.** *v.* Colston, Car, *co. Nott.*

**Car Dyke,** *co. Linc.* Grant in Graby, *co.* Linc., on banks of, 12-13 cent. (Karesdic). Add. 20737.

**Carbrooke,** *co. Norf.* Exemplif. of suit conc., the manor, 1709. Add. 15893.

**Cardeston.** *v.* Kerdistone, *co. Norf.*

**Cardiff,** *co. Glam.* Grant in (?), by the Earl of Gloucester to Margam Abbey, *ante* 1166. Harl. 75 A. 8.

—— Grant, by the same, of rent "de novo burgo . . . extra villam de Kard," to the Ch. of St. Tho. Martyr at, *c.* 1171-80. Add. 7715.

—— Papal conf. of burgages in, and "in novo burgo," to Margam Abbey, 1186 (Chairdif, Kairdif). Harl. 75 A. 1.

—— *Augustinus,* "Capellanus Sci. Johannis de Kaerdif," a witness, [1186-91 ?]. Harl. 75 D. 25.

**Cardiff,** *co. Glam. (continued).* Grants, etc., in or nr., to Margam Abbey, late 12 cent. Harl. 75 C. 44, 45 :—[1193-1218]. Harl. 75 A. 20, 22 :—*t.* Hen. III. Harl. 75 C. 23 (Kardif), 43 (Kaerdif).

—— The sheriff a surety for a grant to Margam Abbey, [1199] (Kaerdif). Harl. 75 C. 24.

—— Certificate of a recognition of majority "in pleno comitatu de Kaerdif," [1218?]. Harl. 75 B. 37.

—— Rent to be paid in Bonvilston, *co.* Glam., "ad custodiam de Kardif," early Hen. III. Harl. 75 C. 54.

—— Grants, etc., in or nr., *c.* 1230. Harl. 75 B. 7 (Kaerdif):—*t.* Hen. III.-*t.* Edw. I. Harl. 75 C. 1 (Kardif). Add. 24248 (do.), 24249 (Kardif), 24264, 24265 (Kairdif), 24301.

—— Suit betw. Margam and Gloucester Abbeys heard in the church of St. John at, 1262 (Kaerdif). Harl. 75 A. 40.

—— Suit on writ of the Earl of Gloucester "in comitatu de Kerdif," [1262-95]. Harl. 75 A. 36, 75 C. 38.

—— *Vicecomes.* Hamo de Valun[iis], [1186-91]. Harl. 75 D. 10.

—— —— David de Brahull, 1217. Harl. 75 D. 14.

—— —— Petr. Pincerna, *c.* 1230-40. Harl. 75 D. 12.

—— *Constabularius (late).* Joh. Nanfan, 1447. Harl. 84 C. 20.

**Cardiff Forest,** *co. Carmar.* Exchequer acquittance for rent from, 1623. Add. 25724.

**Cardigan,** *County of.* Sales of lead from mines in, 1638, 1641, 1646. Harl. 111 D. 6, 8, 10.

—— Assignment of leases of mines in, 1641. Harl. 111 H. 19.

**Cardigan Castle.** Garrison establishment, 1369. Harl. Roll E. 7.

—— Appointment of a deputy constable, 1564. Harl. 75 G. 16.

**Cardington,** *co. Bedf.* Compotus of rents in, 1457-8. Add. 657.

—— Mortgage in, 1568. Harl. 79 D. 44.

—— Covenant for recovery of the manor, etc., 1571. Add. 992 :—1591. Add. 993 :—1610. Add. 994, 996 ;— 1611. Add. 995.

*v. also* Cotton End, *co. Bedf.*

Castle Camps, co. Camb. Recovery, etc., in, 1438. Add. 9251 (Castell-campes);—1578. Add. 25869, 25968.

Castle Carrock, co. Cumb. Lease in, 1572. Harl. 77 H. 37.

Castle Church, co. Staff. Brief for rebuilding the church, 1793. Ch. Br. B. xxxii. 4.

Castle Donington. v. Donington, Castle, co. Leic.

Castle Eden. v. Eden, Castle, co. Durh.

Castle Frome. v. Frome, Castle, co. Heref.

Castle Hedingham. v. Hedingham, Castle, co. Essex.

Castle Martin, co. Pembr. Inspex., in 1448, of a re-feoffment in, 1347. Slo. xxxii. 5.

Castle Moubray. v. Moubray, Castle, in Ulster.

Castle Ongar. v. Ongar, Chipping, co. Essex.

Castle Rising. v. Rising, Castle, co. Norf.

Castle Toome. v. Toome, Castle, co. Antrim.

Castle Trematon. v. Trematon, Castle, co. Cornw.

Castleacre (Acra), co. Norf. Charter of Will., Count of Boulogne and Warren, dated at, [1154–5 ?]. Harl. 83 A. 25.

Castlecombe (Combe, Castelcombe, etc.), co. Wilts. Release from suits of court in, t. John (Cumbe). Add. 18208 (4), 18215 (copies).

—— Grants, etc., in, 1269. Add. 18212 (Cumba);—c. 1269. Add. 18213 (Combe):—1300. Add. 18216;—1339. Add. 18219;—1457. Add. 18237;—1514. Add. 18258;—1527. Add. 18271;—1540. Add. 18282;—1567. Add. 18300;—1568. Add. 18306;—1572. Add. 18339;—1577. Add. 18345;—1595. Add. 18347;—1600. Add. 18349;—1602. Add. 18351;—1603. Add. 18352;—1604. Add. 18355;—1616. Add. 18381;—1627. Add. 18387;—1630. Add. 18389;—1637. Add. 18394;—1647. Add. 18404;—1653. Add. 18416, 18417;—1662. Add. 18427;—1663. Add. 18433;—1688. Add. 18455;—1692. Add. 18457;—1696. Add. 18458;—1699. Add. 18461.

Castlecombe (Combe, Castelcombe, etc.), co. Wilts. (continued). Letter to his tenants of, from Sir Joh. Tippetot, 1352. Add. 18218 (2).

—— Conf. to his tenants of, by Sir R. Tipetot, 1368. Add. 18218 (1).

—— Court-rolls, 1344–1633. Add. 18307, 18466–18469, 18472, 18473, 18475, 18476, 18478, 18479, 18486–18489, 18491, 18494, 18496, 18500–18505, 18508–18512, 18515.

—— Rentals, t. Edw. III. Add. 18471; — 1447–8. Add. 18480; — 1507–8. Add. 18490;—16 cent. Add. 18492;—1531. Add. 18495;—1545. Add. 18497.

—— Fines, etc., of the manor, 1389–91. Add. 18220, 18221;—1467. Add. 18240, 18242–18245, 18247;—1481. Add. 18251, 18253; — 1602. Add. 18350.

—— Returns of knights fees held of the manor, 1402. Add. 18223;—1444. Add. 18228;—1446. Add. 18236;—1468. Add. 18248.

—— Compotus-rolls, 1411–12. Add. 18474;—1436–7. Add. 18555;—16 cent. Add. 18547.

—— Lease in, to found anniversaries for Sir J. Fastolf and others, 1433. Add. 18226.

—— Acquittances for rent from the manor, 1448. Add. 18230–18234.

—— Releases of tenants of the manor from expenses of members of parliament, 1451. Add. 18235;—1466. Add. 18241;—1519. Add. 18264, 18266;—1572. Add. 18338;—1608. Add. 18380.

—— "Capitagia garcionum" in, 1481. Add. 18250; —1527. Add. 18272.

—— Surrenders and admissions, etc., to lands in the manor, 1514. Add. 18258;—1527. Add. 18273;—1530. Add. 18276;—1539. Add. 18301;—1541. Add. 18283;—1542. Add. 18284;—1556. Add. 18302;—1559. Add. 18303;—1560. Add. 18295;—1561. Add. 18296, 18297;—1565. Add. 18304;—1567. Add. 18305;—1570. Add. 18307;—1607. Add. 18376; — 1635 – 1672. Add. 18393, 18395, 18399, 18402, 18405, 18407–18413, 18415, 18418 – 18426, 18428, 18429, 18432, 18435, 18437, 18438, 18440 – 18442; — 1652 – 1664. Add. 18519 (1–5).

Castlecombe (Combe, Castelcombe, etc.), co. *Wilts.* (*continued*). Evidence conc. possession of, by Sir Joh. Scrope, deceased, 1519. Add. 18262.

—— Inspex. of return to writ conc. the manor, as ancient domain of the Crown in Domesday, 1519 (Cumb.) Add. 18263.

—— — Precept for inquisition conc. title to the manor, 1521. Add. 18269.

—— Letters patent conc. descent of the manor, 1529. Add. 18275.

—— Fine for hunting in the park, 1534. Add. 18279.

—— Dispensation to J. Scrope to hold the rectory, 1760. Add. 18462.

—— *Rector.* *Dom.* Johannes, 1339. Add. 18219.

—— —— Joh. Grene, 1433. Add. 18226.

—— —— (as *Persona*). *Sir* Ingram Bedyl, 1508–1517. Add. 18493.

—— —— (as *Persona*). Geo. Pokley, 1527. Add 18271.

—— —— Tho. Knyght, 1574. Add. 18344.

—— —— John Scrope, *D.D.*, 1760. Add. 18462.

—— *Curate.* *Sir* Tho. Kelly, [1508–17]. Add. 18493.

*v. also* Colham, co. *Wilts.*

Castleford, co. *York.* Grant in, 1467 (Castelford). Add. 16959.

Castleton (Castelton, etc.), co. *Derb.* Fine in the court of John, Duke of Lancaster, at, 1376. Woll. ii. 75.

—— Grants, etc., in, 1400. Woll. vii. 46 (Castilton);—1424. Harl. 84 A. 49;—1485. Woll. iii. 72, 76;—1541. Woll. ii. 71.

—— *Balliri Curie Joh. Ducis Lancastrie.* Rob. de Nedham, Will. f. Radulphi, Tho. de Bradwall, Will. Dany, 1376. Woll. ii. 75.

—— *Receptor Denariorum Castri et Honoris.* Joh. Hublyn, 1376. Woll. ii. 75.

Castlewright, nr. *Church Stoke*, co. *Montgom.* Power to give seisin in, 1344 (Castelrwyk). Add. 20445.

Castlines Manor. *v. sub* Groton, co. *Suff.*

Caston, co. *Norf.* Inspex., in 1454, of a feoffment of the manor, 1422. Add. 17243.

—— Admission to lands in Caston Hall manor in, 1520. Add. 14596.

Caston, co. *Norf.* (*continued*). *Parson.* Tho. Pekke, 1448. Add. 14902.

Castor, co. *Northt.* *Rector.* Ric. de Leicestria, 1375. Add. 19917.

Castre. *v.* Caister, co. *Norf.*

Castre, Castria. *v.* Caistor, co. *Linc.*

Castrum Leonis, C. Leonum. *v. sub* Holt, co. *Denb.*

Caswell. *v. sub* Portbury, co. *Som.*

Catborna. *v.* Cabourn, co. *Linc.*

Catcliffe, in *Bakewell* (?). *v. sub* Bakewell, co. *Derb.*

Catcombe. *v. sub* Colyton, co. *Devon.*

Catebi. *v.* Oadeby, co. *Linc.*

Cateby, co. *York.* *Clericus.* Bertramus, *t.* Hen. III. Harl. 46 F. 38.

Catefeud. *v.* Catfield, co. *Norf.*

Cateford. *v. sub* Lewisham, co. *Kent.*

Caterham, co. *Surr.* Release of Casherste wood in, early Edw. I. Add. 20037.

—— Grants, etc., in, 1304. Campb. xvi. 14;—1319. Harl. 48 G. 19;—1339. Add. 24560;—1355. Add. 20038;—1482. Add. 18770;—1555. Add. 25503.

—— Vicar. Joh. Tattersall, 1609 (Cattheram). Harl. 75 H. 21.

Cateriz. *v.* Chatteris, co. *Camb.*

Catesby, co. *Northt.* Grants, etc., in, *t.* Hen. III. Harl. 49 H. 30 (Cateby), Add. 7534 (Katesbi);—1668. Add. 1982.

Cateshala, Cateshella, Est Catesselle. *v.* Catshill, in *Godalming*, co. *Surr.*

Catfield, co. *Norf.* Grant, etc., in, 1297. Add. 2001 (Catefeld);—1308. Add. 14731 (Catefeud);—1323. Add. 9915 (Catefeld).

Catford. *v. sub* Lewisham, co. *Kent.*

Cathadala. *v.* Cadwell, in *Tathwell*, co. *Linc.*

Cathegrava. *v.* Chedgrave, co. *Norf.*

Cathwayt, nr. *Sutton upon Derwent* (?), co. *York.* Grant of a nativus in, to Ellerton Priory, *t.* John. Add. 20553.

—— Grants of the manor, 1369. Harl. 51 E. 39, 54 C. 13.

Catrik. *v.* Catterick, co. *York.*

Catsfield, co. Suss. Grants, etc., in, 1344. Add. 20063 (Catteafeldo);— 1412. Add. 20064 (do.);—1484. Add. 20065 (do.).

—— Fine in, 1507. Add. 24909 (Cattysfeld).

—— Grant in, for an Easter taper in the church, 1533. Add. 26090 (Cattisfeld).

Catshill, in Godalming, co. Surr. Precept of Hen. I. to discharge men of G. Purcell from tolls in, c. 1131-3 (?) (Chatishille). Add. 19572.

—— Conf. in, from King Stephen to Reading Abbey, c. 1140 (Cateshala). Add. 19584.

—— Precept of King Stephen conc. lands of Reading Abbey in, [1140-7]. Add. 19583.

—— Conf. in, from the Empress Matilda to the same, [1141?] (Cateshella). Add. 19576.

—— Grant in, t. Edw. I. (Est Cateselle). Add. 17279.

—— Return to the Hundred Court, 1484. Add. 26892.

Cattdale. v. Cadwell, in Tathwell, co. Linc.

Catteburgh. v. Cadbury, co. Devon.

Catteclyf, in Bakewell (?). v. sub Bakewell, co. Derb.

Catterick, co. York. Court-roll, 1441 (Catrik). Harl. Roll G. 23.

Catterlin, co. Cumb. Lease in, 1572 (Carterlyne). Harl. 77 H. 37.

Cattheram. v. Caterham, co. Surr.

Catthorpe. v. Caythorpe, co. Linc.

Catthorpe, co. Leic. Settlement in, late Edw. III. Add. 26999.

Cattistock, co. Dors. Grant of reversion in, 1378 (Cattestoke). Eg. 253.

Cattiwade. v. sub Brantham, co. Suff.

Catton. v. Cayton, co. York.

Catton, co. Berks. Power to take seisin of the manor, 1368. Cott. xxiv. 11.

Catton, in Croxall, co. Derb. Exch. of the manor, etc., 1336. Cott. xxviii. 109.

—— Settlement in, 1581. Woll. xii. 139.

Catton, in Taverham Hundred, co. Norf. Grants of, to Norwich Priory, 1101. Cott. MS. Aug. ii. 103 (copy); —[1136-45] Cott. ii. 1.

Catton, in Taverham Hundred, co. Norf. (continued). Grant in, to Bromholm Priory, early Hen. III. Add. 14601 (copy).

Catworth, co. Hunt. Acquittances for fines for lands in, as of Molesworth manor, 1544. Harl. 53 F. 24;—1545. Harl. 53 G. 11;—1550. Harl. 53 G. 29.

—— License for conveyance in, as of Molesworth manor, 1545. Harl. 53 G. 8.

Caueneby. v. Caenby, co. Linc.

Caundle, Bishop's, co. Dors. Grant nr. Bishop's Down in, 1499. Add. 665.

Caundle Marsh, co. Dors. Grants, etc., in, 1499. Add. 665 (Mersbe), Campb. viii. 21 (do.);—15$^2$8. Add. 666 (Mersch).

Caundle Pyle, co. Dors. Fine in, 1335. Harl. 51 B. 1 (Caundel Pyle).

Caundle Stourton al. Haddon, co. Dors. Marriage settlement in, late Hen. III. (Kandel). Harl. 53 D. 25.

—— Exchange of rents in, 1280 (Caundel Haddone). Cott. xxvii. 12.

—— Releases, etc., in the manor, 1419. Harl. 57 G. 39 (Caundell Haddon);— 1425. Harl. 48 B. 7;—1433. Harl. Roll C. 32:—1439. Harl. 58 D. 42.

Caunton, co. Nott. Grant in, to Rufford Abbey, early 13 cent. (Calfnadtun). Harl. 112 H. 5.

—— Clericus. Ricardus, late 12 cent. (Kalnadatun). Harl. 83 D. 2.

—— Hugo, early Hen. III. (Kalnadton). Harl. 112 I. 14.

Caus, co. Salop. Grant of a market at, 1200 (Caos). Cott. xi. 72.

—— Covenant conc. re-settlement of the castle and barony, 1315. Add. 20437, 20438.

—— Power to give seisin in Wallop, co. Salop, to the constable of, 1353. Add. 20447.

—— Grants, etc., of Breidden (Breythyn) in, 1355. Add. 20435, 20436, 20439.

—— Acquittance for a rent from, 1373 (Caus). Add. 20140.

—— Accompts of the receiver of Anne, Duchess of Buckingham, for the lordship of, 1472-3. Add. 22644.

Causton, Cauxston. v. Cawston, co. Norf.

Caustons. v. sub Hadlow, co. Kent.

Cearn, co. Som. (?). Conf. of grant of salt-pans at, to the see of Winchester, 938. Cott. viii. 17.

Cedene. v. Cheddon Fitzpaine, co. Som.

Cefn Llys, co. Radnor. Lease of the castle and domain, c. 1433 (Knelles). Harl. 53 H. 17.

—— Court-roll, 1679 (Kevenlleece). Harl. 58 E. 44.

——· Sale of the manor, 1687 (Kevenllice). Add. 1781.

Cellyng. v. Sellinge, co. Kent.

Centinces triow, ev. Essex. A boundary-mark, 692-3. Cott. MS. Aug. ii. 20.

Ceolbolding tun. v. Chilbolton, co. Southt.

Ceolsige. v. Cholsey, co. Berks.

Ceolulfing tun, co. Kent. Grant in, 949. Cott. MS. Aug. ii. 57.

Ceorla gráf. v. Chalgrove, co. Oxon.

Ceorla tun, nr. Pagham, co. Suss. Grant at, 680. Cott. MS. Aug. ii. 86.

Ceorla tune. v. Charlton, co. Wilts.

Ceorles Weorþe, Wyrðe. v. Chelsworth, co. S̄ḡf.

Cercelle. v. Churchill, co. Oxon.

Cerne, in Marshwood Manor, co. Dors. Conf. of grant in, late Hen. III. Cott. xii. 38.

Cerne (?), co. Dors. Acquittance for rent of mills at, 1354 (Caern). Add. 15442.

Cerne Abbas, co. Dors. Crown appointment of a steward of the manor and hundred, late held by Cerne Abbey, 1571. Harl. 75 E. 40.

Cerne, Upper (Upcerne), co. Dors. Releases, etc., of the manor and advowson, 1379. Harl. 57 G. 36;—1425. Harl. 48 B. 7;—1433. Harl. Roll C. 32;—1439. Harl. 58 D. 42.

Cernecote. v. Sharncott, co. Wilts.

Cerney, North, co. Glouc. Release in, t. Hen. III. (Norhcern). Add. 20430.

Cerney, South, co. Glouc. Grant of the rectory to the see of Gloucester, 1541. Cott. xiii. 34.

Cerrig y Druidion, co. Denb. Rector. Dom. Ric. ap Gruff, 1528 (Kerricydrudyon). Add. 9266.

Cert. v. Chart, co. Kent.

Certeseya. v. Chertsey, co. Surr.

Cestirfeld, Cestrefeld. v. Chesterfield, co. Derb.

Cestre, Cestria. v. Chester.

Cestreford. v. Chesterford, co. Essex.

Cestrehunt. v. Cheshunt, co. Hertf.

Cestresham. v. Chesham, co. Buck.

Cestretuna. v. Chesterton, co. Hunt.

Cethyng. v. Seething, co. Norf.

Chackmore, in Radclive, co. Buck. Grant of a rent in, to Biddlesdon Abbey, t. Edw. I. (Chalkemor). Harl. 86 D. 28.

Chaddesden, co. Derb. Fine of the manor, etc., 1638. Woll. xi. 29;—1694. Woll. xi. 111 (Chadson).

Chaddleworth, co. Berks. Grant at, 960 (Ceadelanwyrð). Cott. MS. Aug. ii. 40.

—— Assignment of rent in, to Netley Abbey, from Lieu Dieu Abbey, 1240 (Chadelworth.). Add. 20234.

—— Recovery in, 1674. Add. 19229.

Chadlewich, co. Warw. Grant of, t. John (Chadeleswiz). Cott. xxii. 4.

Chadlington, in Charlbury, co. Oxon. Grants, etc., in, t. Edw. I. Harl. 47 H. 43 (Chadelinton):—1384. Harl. 48 C. 44 (Chadlinton).

—— Rental, early 14 cent. Harl. Roll B. 23.

—— Defeasance of bond, with Ensham Abbey, conc. offerings from, in Charlbury church, etc., 1388 (Chadlyngton). Harl. 44 D. 45.

—— Power for seisin in Chadlington East End and West End, 1439. Harl. 43 I. 36.

v. also Charlbury, co. Oxon.

Chadson. v. Chaddesden, co. Derb.

Chadstone, co. Northt. Grant of remainder in the castle and manor of, 1392 (Chadeston). Harl. 47 B. 11.

Chadwell, in Barking, co. Essex. Exchange in, post 1262 (Chaldewell). Harl. 57 C. 5.

—— Precipe on a covenant in, 1578 (Chawdwell). Add. 24963.

—— Exchequer acquittance for a fine in, 1596. Add. 25718 b.

Chaggeleye. v. Chailey, co. Suss.

Chaigley, in Milton, co. Lanc. Brief conc. a fire at, 1814. Ch. Br. B. liv. 6.

H. 45;—1362. Harl. 50 I. 20;—1393. Harl. 48 F. 32;—1394. Harl. 54 F. 44;—1395. Harl. 52 B. 49;—1417. Harl. 48 G. 10;—1420. Harl. 47 H. 26;—1441. Harl. 45 G. 71;—1442. Harl. 50 F. 35;—1458. Harl. 52 I. 53, 54;—1459. Harl. 52 I. 55;—1460. Harl. 54 E. 50, 51;—1480. Harl. 52 C. 23;—1486. Harl. 46 E. 12.

—— Grants, etc., of West Chalk manor, c. 1240. Harl. 54 B. 20;—1344. Harl. 48 E. 10;—1358. Harl. 48 F. 23.

—— Suit conc. the advowson betw. Norwich and Bermondsey Priories, 1279. Harl. 53 H. 13 (3).

—— Grant, etc., of Green manor in, 1338. Harl. 49 H. 44, 58 C. 22;—1340. Harl. 58 C. 23.

—— Grant of W. Chalk manor to Cobham chantry, 1363. Harl. 48 E. 19.

—— License for an exchange of rents in E. Chalk with the advowson, betw. Norwich Priory and Cobham College, 1369. Harl. 43 E. 4.

—— Acquittances to Norwich Priory for subsidies to the Crown on account of the church, 1371–1373. Harl. 44 I. 4–7.

—— Letter from Norwich Priory to Lord Cobham conc. the church, 1378. Harl. 43 B. 25.

—— Exchange of lands in, with the church, from Norwich Priory to Cobham College, 1380. Harl. 43 I. 23, 44 C. 33, 44 G. 16, 44 H. 39, 41.

—— Inquisition of theft, at W. Chalk, 1417. Harl. 58 E. 23.

—— Court-rolls of W. Chalk manor, 1418, 4489–90. Harl. Rolls N. 13, 14.

—— Acquittances to Cobham College for subsidies on account of the church, 1515–1519. Harl. 44 I. 9, 10, 13.

—— Brief conc. a fire at, 1759. Ch. Br. A. v. 5.

**Chalk Hundred,** co. *Wilts.* Court-rolls, 1283–4. Add. 6269.

**Chalk, Bower,** co. *Wilts.* Court-rolls of the manor, 1558–9, 1567. Add. 24440, 24441.

**Chalk, Broad,** co. *Wilts.* Power for seisin in (?), 1385 (Chalk). Harl. 56 A. 35.

—— Court-rolls of the manor, 1558–9, 1567. Add. 24440, 24441.

**Chalkemor.** *v.* Chackmore, *in Rad-clive,* co. *Buck.*

**Chalkhill,** *nr.* Kingsbury, *co.* **Midd.** Grant at, to Westminster Abbey, 1044–46 (æt Cealchylle). Cott. vii. 6.

**Challock,** co. *Kent.* Charges on land at, 835 (?) (et Cealflocan). Cott. MS. Aug. ii. 64.

—— Grant, etc., in, 1415. Harl. 76 B. 13 (Challok);—1434. Add. 20003 (do.).

**Challock,** co. *Northt.* Grant in, c. 1250 (?) (Chaldelacke). Cott. xxiv. 7.

**Challow, East,** co. *Berks.* Covenant for settlement of Woodhill manor, etc., in, 1581. Harl. 78 A. 48.

**Challow, West,** co. *Berks.* Covenant for settlement of Potwick manor, etc., in, 1581. Harl. 78 A. 48.

**Chalstern.** *v.* Chawston, *in Roxton,* co. *Bedf.*

**Chalton, Chalturn.** *v.* Charlton, *nr. Blunham,* co. *Bedf.*

**Chalton,** *in Toddington,* co. *Bedf.* Settlement and recovery of the manor, etc., 1604. Add. 18143;—1638. Add. 18186.

**Chaluedon.** *v.* Chaldon, co. *Dors.*

—— *v.* Chaldon, co. *Surr.*

**Chalvington,** co. *Suss.* Grant of tithes in, to Lewes Priory, *t.* Steph. (Calvinton). Cott. MS. Nero C. iii., f. 217.

—— Precipe on a covenant conc. land in, 1588. Add. 25534.

**Chanderhill.** *v. sub* Brampton, co. *Derb.*

**Chapel en le Frith,** co. *Derb.* Lease in Ford in, 1343. Woll. iii. 7.

—— Affidavit conc. land in, 1483. Woll. xii. 48, 74.

—— Grants, etc., in Bowdon (Bawdon, etc.) in, 1484. Woll. iii. 23;—1495. Woll. iii. 10;—1519. Woll. xii. 69;—1542. Woll. xii. 57;—1571. Woll. xii. 45;—1610. Woll. xii. 87;—1619. Woll. xii. 93;—1636. Woll. xii. 88.

—— Grants, etc., in Bradshaw Edge in, *t.* Hen. VII. Woll. viii. 2;—1542. Woll. xii. 57;—1543. Woll. xii. 67, 80;—1547. Woll. xii. 70;—1567. Woll. xii. 50;—1570. Woll. xii. 76;—1610. Woll. xii. 87;—1619. Woll. xii. 93;—1636. Woll. xii. 88.

—— Suit for trespass in Bowdon (Bawdon, Bowedon) in, 1498–1500. Woll. xii. 42, 53, 66, 75.

M

Chart, Little (Parva Chert, etc.), co.
Kent (continued). Ballirus. Ric. de
Wilmyngton, 1281-2, 1282-3. Add.
16392, 16393.

———— ———— Wydo de Truleghe, 1298.
Add. 16396.

———— Serviens. Joh. le Vynyter, 1314.
Add. 16397.

Chart Sutton, co. Kent. Grant nr.,
814 (Cart). Harl. 83 A. 1.

———— Brief conc. a fire in the church,
1779. Ch. Br. B. xx. 4.

Chartham (Chertham, etc.), co. Kent.
Grant and release of a mill pool, etc.,
in Howfield (Hugifeld, Hughefeld) in,
to St. Gregory's Priory, Canterbury,
early 13 cent. Harl. 80 D. 6;—1293.
Harl. 80 D. 5.

———— Ref. to Howfield (Huggifeld)
grange in, bel. to the same, c. 1215.
Harl. 75 F. 45.

———— Release by the men of Horton
in, to the same, early 13 cent. Harl.
78 H. 23.

———— Grants, etc., in Dengewood, Hun-
steadwood, etc., in, to Christ Church,
Canterbury, t. Hen. III. Add. 16405-
16412, 16417:—1232. Add. 16413:—
1267-8. Add. 16416 (Chertaham):—
1270. Add. 16418:—1275-6. Add.
16419.

———— Grant in, from the same, 1263-4.
Add. 16415 (Chertcham).

———— Exch. in Howfield (Huggefeld)
in, by St. Gregory's Priory, 1283-4
(Cheartham). Harl. 75 F. 57.

———— Grants, etc., in, 1235-6. Add.
16414 (Chertcham):—1292-3. Harl.
77 E. 8 (Cheartham):—1301. Harl.
80 A. 42:—1305. Harl. 80 H. 3:—
1320. Harl. 78 A. 18:—1324-5.
Harl. 80 A. 30:—1326. Harl. 78 D. 1:
—1333. Harl. 76 F. 9, 78 C. 33:—
1334. Harl. 76 F. 56, 80 A. 14:—
1340. Harl. 80 A. 41:—1342. Harl.
76 G. 21:—1344. Harl. 77 E. 10:—
1346. Add. 16420:—1348. Harl. 76
G. 23:—1349. Harl. 80 A. 31:—1350.
Harl. 78 B. 36:—1352. Harl. 80 G. 9,
80 I. 3:—1354. Harl. 80 G. 10:—
1355. Harl. 80 G. 11:—1358. Harl.
76 G. 26:—1359. Harl. 77 D. 42:—
1361. Harl. 75 G. 30, 76 G. 25, 79
C. 52:—1362. Harl. 75 G. 31, 77 G.
51, 52, 78 C. 53:—1364. Harl. 76
D. 23:—1369. Harl. 80 B. 32 a:—
1370. Harl. 80 B. 32 b:—1371. Harl.
78 D. 4, 80 I. 5:—1374. Harl. 80
I. 4:—1375. Harl. 80 B. 17:—1384.

Harl. 76 C. 53, 80 I. 8;—1387. Harl.
80 B. 15, 80 H. 32;—1388. Harl. 80
I. 9;—1393 (?). Harl. 79 B. 17:—
1393. Harl. 80 I. 2;—1396. Harl.
77 D. 55;—1397. Harl. 77 D. 37;—
1398. Harl. 76 A. 29, 78 H. 40;—1402.
Harl. 80 G. 34, 35, 80 H. 17;—1403.
Harl. 80 G. 41;—1405. Harl. 78 D.
5;—1408. Harl. 78 D. 6;— 1409.
Harl. 80 E. 18:—1411. Harl. 76 C.
39, 77 G. 43:—1413. Harl. 77 D. 38;
—1417. Harl. 80 A. 54;—1422.
Harl. 76 C. 36 (Scherthom):—1432.
Harl. 77 G. 14:—1434. Harl. 78
B. 25:—1439. Harl. 80 A. 26:—1441.
Harl. 80 E. 34:—1447. Harl. 78 B.
26, 78 D. 7;—1449. Harl. 80 H. 46;
—1457. Add. 16422;—1459. Add.
16423;—1469. Harl. 80 A. 21;—1472.
Harl. 80 H. 50;—1475. Harl. 80 D.
8;—1477. Harl. 80 H. 51;—1478.
Harl. 80 H. 52;—1485. Harl. 78 C. 4,
80 B. 9, 80 C. 46;—1487. Harl. 79
B. 56;—1494. Harl. 78 C. 15, 80
C. 45;—1495. Harl. 79 C. 40;—1496.
Harl. 78 H. 13;—1497. Add. 16424;—
1498. Harl. 80 H. 53;—1500. Harl.
78 G. 27;—1501. Harl. 78 I. 17, 18;
—1539. Harl. 80 D. 14;—1577. Harl.
77 A. 48;—1580. Harl. 77 B. 4.

———— Grants in, "in tenura de Swer-
lingge" al. "Swartlyngg," "Swerd-
linge," 1292-3. Harl. 77 E. 8;—1356.
Harl. 80 E. 36, 80 G. 58;—1361. Harl.
76 G. 25;—1362. Harl. 75 G. 31, 76
G. 27, 78 G. 53;—1364. Harl. 76 D.
23, 80 B. 13, 14;—1382. Harl. 80 I.
6, 7;—1397. Harl. 77 D. 37.

———— Grants in, " in Borgho de Sapindon" al. "Sapynton," 1301. Harl. 80
A. 42;—1339. Harl. 77 E. 9;—1356.
Harl. 80 E. 36, 80 G. 58;—1361. Harl.
75 G. 30;—1367. Harl. 80 G. 40.

———— Release, etc., in Underdown in,
1305. Harl. 80 H. 3;—1341. Harl.
76 G. 20;—1354. Harl. 80 G. 10;—
1355. Harl. 80 G. 11.

———— Grants in le Danehelde in, 1339.
Harl. 77 E. 9, 78 C. 12;—1351. Harl.
77 E. 12;—1355. Harl. 80 I. 23;—
1360. Harl. 79 C. 51;—1382. Harl.
80 I. 6, 7;—1393. Harl. 80 I. 2, 11.

———— Lease at Nympton in, 1384.
Harl. 80 I. 8.

———— Sale, etc., of Horton manor in,
1385. Harl. 79 E. 7, 8:—1393. Harl.
79 B. 16, 17;—1401. Harl. 80 D. 21.

———— Grant, etc., in Howfield (Hughefeld) in, 1390. Harl. 80 E. 33;—1419.
Harl. 80 I. 76.            •

M 2

**Chertsey** (Certoseya, etc.), *co. Surr.*
Royal grants of fairs and a market in,
to Chertsey Abbey, [1129–35?]. Harl.
58 H. 37 (*copy*);—1249. Harl. 58 I.
8 (*copy*);—1281. Harl. 58 I. 25 (*copy*).

—— Grants, etc., in, *t.* Edw. I. or II.
Land. 96;—1375. Add. 15507;—
1513. Harl. 47 D. 33 (Chertesey):—
1515. Harl. 47 D. 34;—1530. Harl.
47 D. 31.

—— Lease of Hardwich manor in. by
Chertsey Abbey, 1529. Add. 23416.

—— Settlement of Lynd place, etc.,
in, 1538. Cott. xxv. 27.

—— Lease in Botley's (Bodley)
manor in, 1555. Harl. 111 D. 40.

—— Fine, etc., in, 1585. Add. 25662;
—1601. Add. 17442.

—— *Vicarius.* Joh. Parker, 1375.
Add. 15507.

**Cherwell**, *River, co. Oxon.* Grant on
banks of, in Grimsbury, co. Northt.,
*t.* John (Charewelle). Harl. 45 E. 30.

—— Lease of a fishery in, in Hardwick manor nr. Banbury, 1496. Add.
567.

**Chesbury.** *v.* Chisenbury, *co. Wilts.*

**Cheselborneford**, *in Piddleton, co.
Dors.* Grant of tithes of, with conf.,
to Montacute Priory, *t.* Hen. I.
(Chiselburneford, Chileborneford).
Add. 24879 (3, 8) (*copies*);—*t.* Hen. II.
(Chiseborneford). Add. 24879 (7)
(*copy*).

**Chesfeld.** *v.* Chisfield, *co. Hertf.*

**Chesham** (Cestresham, etc.), *co. Buck.*
Grants in Whelpley (Welpeleie) in,
early 13 cent. Harl. 85 D. 50;—*t.*
Hen. III. Harl. 48 A. 33.

—— Release in Blakemere in, *t.* Hen.
III. Harl. 45 G. 28.

—— Covenant conc. warranty in Ashley (Esseleya) in, *t.* Hen. III. Harl.
46 F. 43.

—— Assignment of homage in, *t.*
Hen. III. Harl. 47 C. 17.

—— Grants, etc., in, *t.* Hen. III.
Harl. 51 D. 28, 54 G. 10;—*t.* Edw. I.
Harl. 46 F. 47, 52 A. 47;—1348.
Harl. 46 G. 10;—1425. Harl. 48 C.
7;—[1432?]. Harl. 58 C. 11;—1483.
Harl. 51 F. 35;—1524. Add. 14038;
—1535. Harl. 56 G. 10;—1549. Harl.
53 G. 24;—1557. Land. 185 (Chesham magna);—1581. Land. 188, 189.

—— Distress for rent in, at suit of
executors of W., Bp. of Coventry, 1327.
Harl. 46 G. 7.

**Chesham** (Cestresham, etc.), *co. Buck.*
(*continued*). Feoffment of the manor,
1466. Harl. 57 C. 14.

—— Conveyance in Ashley Green in,
1468. Harl. 58 E. 39.

—— Admission to lands in Ashley
Green manor in, 1521. Harl. 58 E. 4.

—— Acquittance for rents due to
Chesham Higham manor, 1526, 1528.
Harl. 53 F. 27, 48.

—— Suit in, 1539. Harl. 53 F. 57.

—— Maudalen's manor in. *v. sub*
Berkhampstead, Gt., *co. Hertf.*

**Cheshunt**, *co. Hertf.* Petition and
letters conc. claims of Fougères Abbey
to the church of, [1190–98](Chestreunt,
Cestrehont, Cestrehunt). Cott. xi. 40,
44, 45.

—— Grant of lands and villains in,
to the Hospital of St. Mary without
Bishopsgate, 1298 (Cestrehunte). Add.
10647 b.

—— Grant in, 1299. Add. 10647 a.

—— Lease of the rectory, etc., by
Westminster Abbey, 1537. Eg. 361.

—— [*Persona?*]. Mag. Osbertus,
[1190–98]. Cott. xi. 44.

**Chesseburia.** *v.* Chisenbury, *co. Wilts.*

**Chessell.** *v.* Chishall, Great, *co. Essex.*

**Chessington**, *co. Surr.* Sale by Merton Priory of timber from Gosborough
Wood in, 1537. Harl. 112 C. 28.

**Chester** (Cestria, Cestre), *County of.*
Release of a nativus "in pleno comitatu" of, *c.* 1244. Add. 28743.

—— Acquittance to the sheriff from
the chamberlain of, 1314. Add. 20484.

—— Fine-rolls, 1327–77. Add. 26593.

—— Attornment of the Seneschalship
of, to W., Earl of Salisbury, 1337.
Harl. 43 D. 26.

—— Inspex. of an exch. of the Seneschalship of, betw. Qu. Isabella and W.,
Earl of Salisbury, 1338. Cott. xi. 61.

—— Fees in Framingham, co. Norfolk,
bel. to the honour of, *c.* 1400. Add.
19338.

—— Appointment of collectors of a
subsidy in Eddisbury Hundred in, by
Edw., Pr. of Wales, 1475, with return.
Add. 26786.

—— Extracts of the subsidy-roll for,
1589. Add. 8489.

—— *Camerarius.* Bertram. [de Ver-
don], *t.* Hen. II. Harl. 83 F. 32.

11 (do.);—1314. Harl. 112 I. 19;—1315. Harl. 112 L. 20;—1321. Cott. xxviii. 6;—1323. Harl. 84 B. 8;—1331. Harl. 83 G. 34;—1343. Harl. 112 H. 46;—1350. Harl. 83 E. 12 (Chastrefeld);—1363. Harl. 112 H. 56 (do.);—1365. Woll. vi. 55 (do.);—1369. Harl. 112 H. 59;—1373. Harl. 83 F. 31;—1375. Harl. 84 A. 12;—1376. Woll. vii. 30;—1384. Harl. 86 H. 13 (Chestrefeld);—1393. Harl. 83 F. 1 (do.);—1409. Cott. xxviii. 91;—1419. Woll. i. 83;—1421. Harl. 112 G. 38;—1425. Harl. 112 I. 60;—1430. Woll. i. 82;—1485. Woll. iii. 72, 76;—1541. Woll. ii. 71;—1560. Woll. iii. 74 (Chasterfild);—1590. Woll. v. 38;—1607. Woll. ii. 85;—1640. Woll. iv. 37;—1704. Add. 18065.

—— Letter conc. the office of schoolmaster at, t. Hen. III. Woll. x. 69 (Cestrf.).

—— Grant in Boythorpe, co. Derb., to St. Mary's Guild in, 1337. Harl. 83 D. 33.

—— Ref. to lands bel. to the same in Boythorpe, 1385. Woll. i. 86.

—— Ref. to the mill of the Dean of Lincoln at, 1409. Cott. xxviii. 91.

—— Extract from court-roll, 1555. Woll. iii. 70, 71.

—— Exchequer acquittance for rent of guild-lands in, 1576. Add. 25581.

—— *Mayor.* Gabriel Wayne, 1658. Woll. iv. 42.

—— *Clericus.* Rogerus, t. Hen. III. Harl. 112 G. 35.

—— —— Henricus, t. Hen. III. Woll. vii. 11.

—— *Rector.* S——, t. Hen. III. Woll. x. 69.

*v. also* Calow, co. *Derb.*

*v. also* Newbold, co. *Derb.*

**Chesterfield**, *nr. Shenston,* co. *Staff.* Grant in, 1343 (Chasterfeld). Add. 20474.

**Chesterford**, co. *Essex.* Extent of fees in, bel. to the Earls Marshal, c. 1400 (Cestreford). Add. 19338.

—— Assignment of the manor in dower, 1477 (Chestirford). Add. 26598.

**Chesterford, Great,** *co. Essex.* Precipes conc. lands in, 1587 (Ch. magna). Add. 24975;—1592. Add. 25015.

**Chesterford, Little,** co. *Essex.* Court-roll, 1273-5 (Cestreford parva). Add. 681.

—— Precipe conc. the manor, 1592 (Ch. parva). Add. 25015.

**Chesterton,** co. *Hunt.* Papal conf. of the church, etc., to Royston Priory, 1184. Cott. MS. Aug. ii. 124 (Cestretuna);—1192. Cott. MS. Aug. ii. 130 (Cestretona).

**Chesterton,** co. *Warw.* Release in, 1337. Add. 7506.

**Chestham,** *in Henfield,* co. *Suss.* Precipe conc. land in, 1578. Add. 25532.

**Chestlett.** *v.* Chislett, co. *Kent.*

**Chestreunt.** *v.* Cheshunt, co. *Hertf.*

**Cheswardine,** co. *Salop.* Briefs for rebuilding the church, etc., 1798-1818. Ch. Br. xxxix. 2, xliv. 3, xlix. 2, l. 11, liii. 5, lviii. 2.

**Chesylhurst.** *v.* Chislehurst, co. *Kent.*

**Chetbury.** *v.* Chedburgh, co. *Suf.*

**Chetelbergia.** *v.* Kettleburgh, co. *Suf.*

**Chetelton.** *v.* Cheddleton, co. *Suf.*

**Chetham.** *v.* Chatham, co. *Kent.*

**Chetilhopp.** *v.* Chattlehope, co. *Northumb.*

**Chettisham,** co. *Camb.* Admission to lands in, held of Ely Barton manor, 1640. Harl. 80 I. 95.

**Chetton,** co. *Salop.* Brief for rebuilding the church, 1775. Ch. Br. B. xv. 1.

**Cheuesfeld.** *v.* Chisfield, co. *Hertf.*

**Cheuton.** *v.* Chewton Mendip, co. *Som.*

**Cheveley,** co. *Camb.* Bequest of land at, post 991 (Cæuele). Harl. 43 C. 4.

—— Grants, etc., in Saxton, etc., in, 1319. Harl. 48 C. 47 (Chevelee);—1402. Add. 15536;—1453. Add. 13548;—1454. Add. 13549;—1477. Add. 13553;—1517. Add. 13560.

—— Precipe conc. lands in Saxton, etc., in, 1555. Add. 24290.

—— Award conc. Benstede manor, etc., as held of the manor of, 1582. Add. 19259.

—— Sale of Benstede manor in, 1602. Add. 19261.

**Chevet,** *in Royston,* co. *York.* Reservation of the tithes to Royston vicarage, 1233 (Chyuet). Campb. viii. 14.

—— *Domina de Chyveth.* Elisabet, late Hen. III. Add. 8239.

Chillington, *in Stokenham, co. Devon.* Grants in, 1473. Harl. 85 D. 12 (Chedelyngton) ;—1478. Harl. 86 F. 23 (Chedlington).

Chillington, *in Brewood, co. Staff.* Precipe conc. land in, 1552. Add. 25255.

Chilmark, *co. Wilts.* Court - rolls, 1558-9. Add. 24440 ;—1567. Add. 24441 ;—1584. Add. 24718.

Chilson, *nr. Madley, co. Heref.* Power to give seisin in. 1440 (Chilston). Add. 4603 ;—1446 (Childeston). Harl. 111 E. 2.

Chilson, *in Charlbury. co. Oxon.* Compotus, 1447-48 (Childoston). Harl. Roll C. 2.

Chiltern [All Saints ?], *co. Wilts.* Feoffment of the manor and chapel, etc., late bel. to Bradenstoke Priory, 1548 (Chitterne). Add. 5698.

Chiltern All Saints, *co. Wilts.* Conveyance of the rectory, 1665, 1667. Add. 15140, 15141.

Chiltern Hills, *co. Oxon.* Assignment of a lease of tithes in. bel. to Pirton parsonage, 1659. Add. 19227.

Chiltern Woods. *v. sub* Boyton, *co. Wilts.*

Chiltington, *co. Suss.* Grant of free warren at, 1285 (Chiltinton). Harl. 58 I. 37.

Chiltle. *v. sub* Liphook, *co. Southt.*

Chilton, *co. Berks.* Grant in (?), 767 (Ciltinne). Cott. MS. Aug. ii. 26.

—— Release in, to New College, Oxford, 1384. Add. 24322.

—— Settlement, fines, etc., in, 1512. Add. 19181 ;—1515. Add. 19183-19185 ;—1552. Add. 19189 ;—1588. Add. 19193 ;—1601. Add. 19196 ;—1602. Add. 19197 ; — 1605. Add. 19198 ;—1650. Add. 19224.

—— Lease of Gainsford manor, etc., in, 1592, 1598. Add. 19194, 19195.

Chilton, *nr. Gt. Waldingfield, co. Suff.* Court-rolls, 1342-1378. Add. 1265-1273.

—— Power to give seisin of the manor and advowson, 1413. Harl. 49 D. 37 (Chylton) ;—1431. Harl. 52 A. 2.

—— Exemplif., in 1643, of a fine in, 1550. Slo. xxxii. 60.

—— Sale in, 1657. Add. 19265.

Chilton Foliatt, *co. Wilts.* Pipe-roll acquittance on account of the manor, 1536-7. Add. 18280.

Chilton, Great, *co. Durh.* Releases of the manor, 1430. Harl. 43 E. 19 ;—1431. Harl. 45 I. 12.

Chilverscoton, *co. Warw.* Grant of the church to Erdbury Priory, [1198-1208] (Chelverdecote). Add. 21422.

—— Grants, etc., in, late Hen. III. (Chelverescote). Add. 21423 ;—1302. Add. 21424 (do.). 21425 ;—1539 (Chylverscotton). Add. 5681.

—— Exchange in. with Erdbury Priory, 1320. Add. 21426, 21427 (Cheluerescote).

—— Assignment of mortgage on the manor, 1688. Add. 15164.

Chilwell, *co. Nott.* Covenant of Darley Abbey conc. a mill-dam in, 1314 (Chilewell). Woll. v. 22.

—— Lease in, 1535 (Chylwyll). Harl. 44 D. 18.

Chilworth, *co. Surr.* Grants in, 1462. Add. 26666 (S. Martha) ;—1497. Add. 26679 (do.).

Chilworth, Gt. and Lit., *co. Oxon.* Conveyance in, 1416 (Magna et parva Chelworth). Harl. 54 I. 34.

Chimileyes. *v.* Chinley, *in Glossop, co. Derb.*

Chimwell. *v.* Chumwell, *co. Devon.*

Chinctuna. *v.* Kington St. Michael, *co. Wilts.*

Chineleuurde. *v.* Kenilworth, *co. Warw.*

Chingeshil. *v.* Kingshill, *in Whitfield, co. Northt.*

Chingford, *co. Essex.* Grant, etc., in, 1410. Harl. 78 G. 34 (Chyngeford) ;—1420. Harl. 80 I. 56 ;—1651. Add. 982.

Chinit. *v.* Kennington, *co. Berks* (?).

Chinley, *in Glossop, co. Derb.* Grants, etc., in, 1606. Woll. xii. 73 (Chynley) ;—1636. Woll. xii. 59 (Chimileyes *al.* Chinleies) ;—1653. Woll. xii. 92.

—— Survey of bounds of, 1609. Woll. xii. 42.

—— Suit for trespass in, 1639. Woll. xii. 83.

Chinnock, *co. Som.* Soul-scot charged on (?), c. 995 (Cinnuc). Cott. viii. 38.

Chinnock, West, *co. Som.* Brief conc. a fire at, 1789. Ch. Br. B. xxix. 2.

Chinnor, *co. Oxon.* Grant in, 1241 (Chynhore). Cott. viii. 7.

—— Acquittance from Wallingford Priory for rents in, 1451 (Chynnore). Add. 20330.

Chintun. *v.* Kennington, *co. Kent.*

Chipley, *nr. Poslingford, co. Suff.* Grants, etc., in, 1291. Harl. 49 H. 34 (parochia de Chippeleye); — 1368. Harl. 51 B. 10 (villa de Chippeleygh); —1382. Harl. 48 D. 3, 4 (Chyppeleye);—1421. Harl. 48 D. 15 (Chippeleye); — 1539. Harl. 48 D. 33 (Chypley).

—— Roll of charters in, 1375–1414. Harl. Roll O. 27.

—— Release to the Crown of Chiplev al. Clopton Hall manor, etc., in, 1575. Harl. 48 D. 49.

Chipnall, *in Cheswardine, co. Salop.* Briefs conc. fires at, 1802, 1805. Ch. Br. B. xlii. 2, xlv. 6.

Chippenham, *co. Camb.* Grants in, to the Knights Hospitallers of, *t.* Hen. III. (Chyppenham). Harl. 48 B. 18.

—— Grant in, *t.* Hen. III. or Edw. I. (Chipeham). Cott. xxx. 5.

—— Presentation to the living of, 1554 (Chepenham). Harl. 76 D. 14.

—— *Vicar (deprived).* Rob. Abraham, 1554. Harl. 76 D. 14.

—— Will. Bretton, 1554. Harl. 76 D. 14.

Chippenham, *co. Wilts.* Grant in Manecrofte in, *t.* Hen. III. Harl. 48 F. 49.

—— Grant in Cockelnborough in, to Farley Priory, 1400. Campb. xiii. 14.

—— Grants, etc., in, 1417. Campb. xiii. 8, 9;—1432. Campb. vi. 12, xiii. 10;—1434. Add. 7069;—1671. Add. 18439;—1673. Add. 18444.

Chippenham Hundred, *co. Wilts.* Lrs. patent, etc., conc. lands in, *t.* Hen. VIII. Add. 15017.

—— Assessments for ship-money in, 1635. Add. 18516, 18518.

Chipping Campden. *v.* Campden, Chipping, *co. Glouc.*

Chipping Ongar. *v.* Ongar, Chipping, *co. Essex.*

Chipstead, *co. Surr.* Grant of the manor and advowson, by R., Earl of Gloucester, *c.* 1250–60 (Chepsted). Add. 20039.

—— Division of lands in, 1365 (Chepstede). Add. 23729.

—— Grants, etc., in, 1424. Add. 23174 (Shipstede); — 1429. Add. 23540 (Chipstede).

—— General release in, to Mercia Carew, 1440. Add. 23730.

—— Award in, 1451. Add. 23656.

—— Bequest of land in, 1479. Add. 23731.

Chirbury, *co. Salop.* Grants in or nr., *c.* 1240–50. Add. 8078 (Chirburia);— 1259. Add. 20442 (Chyrebury);—*t.* Edw. I. Add. 8118.

Chirchebi. *v.* Kirkby cum Osgodby, *co. Linc.*

Chirchehalum. *v.* Hallam, Kirk, *co. Derb.*

Chirk, *co. Denb.* Conf. of the chapel of, to Whalley Abbey, 1344 (Chirche). Add. 1060.

—— Demise in the lordship of, 1577. Add. 8487.

Chirningtun. *v.* Kirmington, *co. Linc.*

Chirokes. *v.* Shireoaks, *co. Nott.*

Chirstoke. *v.* Churchstoke, *co. Salop.*

Chiseborneford, Chiselburneford. *v.* Cheselborneford, *co. Dors.*

Chiselborough, *co. Som.* Bond of warranty for the manor, *c.* 1250 (Cisselberg). Add. 23840.

Chiselden, *co. Wilts.* Feoffment, to trustees, of charity lands in, 1677. Add. 17456.

Chisenbury, *co. Wilts.* Expenses of J. de Cobeham on taking seisin of the manor, 1279 (Chesæbury). Harl. Roll C. 28.

—— Compotus-rolls of the manor, 1285–86 (Chuseburia, Chessburia). Harl. Roll G. 33;—1307–8 (Chessebur.). Harl. Roll C. 13 a.

—— Record of a suit conc. the manor, 1288–89 (Chesseburia). Harl. Roll N. 35.

—— Title of Joh. de Cobeham, 1332 (Chissebery). Harl. Roll N. 34.

—— "Des Vales qui sount hors de la Singnurie," *t.* Edw. III. (Chussebur.). Harl. Roll C. 13 b.

Chivington, *in Bletchingley, co. Surr.* Grant in, 1318 (Chevygton). Add. 24548.

Chiwe. *v.* Chew Magna, *co. Som.*

Cholderton, *co. Wilts.* Papal conf. of the church to St. Neot's Priory, [1180?] (Cheldretona). Harl. 43 A. 21.

Cholleswyht. *v. sub* Cornwood, *co. Devon.*

Cholsey, *co. Berks.* Bequest of land at, late 10 cent. (æt Ceolsige). Harl. 43 C. 4.

—— Conff. of, etc., to Reading Abbey, *c.* 1125. Add. 19575 (Cenlseia):— [1157]. Add. 19591 (Chelseia), 19593 (Ceals.).

Cholwich. *v. sub* Cornwood, *co. Devon.*

Chopwell, *co. Durh.* Appointment of a steward of the manor, 1574. Harl. 111 B. 57, Cott. xxv. 18.

Chorlebury. *v.* Charlbury, *co. Oxon.*

Chorletun. *v. sub* Henbury, *co. Glouc.*

Chorley, *co. Lanc.* Power to take seisin of the manor, 1411. Add. 20515.

Chorley, *co. Staff.* Precipe conc. land in, 1520. Harl. 55 F. 19.

Chorley Moor, *co. Lanc.* Brief conc. a fire at, 1819. Ch. Br. B. lx. 5.

Chorlton with Hardy, *in Manchester, co. Lanc.* Brief for rebuilding the chapel, 1774. Ch. Br. B. xiv. 6.

Chorlwell. *v.* Churwell, *co. York.*

Chorsbure, *in Weston under Redcastle, co. Salop.* Grant of, 1228. Add. 20441.

Chotingdone, *in Gt. Chart, co. Kent.* Grant "in tenura de," 1312. Add. 19992.

Choulesbury, *co. Buck.* Sale in, 1561 (Chollesbury). Add. 5165.

Chriche. *v.* Crich, *co. Derb.*

Chrishall (Cristeshale, etc.), *co. Essex.* Settlement and fine of a manor in, *c.* 1280. Harl. 51 C. 16, 17;—1280. Harl. 50 C. 16.

—— Grants, etc., in, 1299. Harl. 55 A. 53;—1394. Add. 15192;—1406. Add. 14295;—1517. Add. 9370;— 1563. Add. 14233;—1577. Add. 14314 (Crisall);—1588. Add. 14316 (Crishull);—1625. Add. 14333;— 1627. Add. 14337;—1628. Add. 14339;—1631. Add. 14343.

Chrishall (Christeshale, etc.), *co. Essex* (*continued*). Acquittance for a fine on the manor of, 1358 (Creshale). Harl. 56 E. 26.

—— Compotus on sale of the manor, 1391. Harl. 48 E. 53.

—— Covenant, etc., conc. tenure of the reversion of the manor, 1403. Harl. 47 B. 15, Add. 15501 (Creshale).

—— Release, etc., of the manor, 1424. Harl. 48 F. 25 (Creshale);—1510. Harl. 46 H. 40 (Cressale).

—— Precipe conc. lands in, 1566 (Cristyshall). Add. 24942.

—— Precipe on a covenant conc. Chiswick Hall (Cheswykhall) manor, etc., in, 1592 (Creshall). Add. 25005.

—— *Vicarius.* Ric. Gynne, 1486. Add. 14304.

Christchurch, *co. Southt.* Lease in, 1674 (Christchurch Twynham). Add. 6205.

—— Brief conc. a fire at Knapp mill in, 1762. Ch. Br. B. ii. 1.

—— Brief conc. a fire at Stanpit in, 1784-5. Ch. Br. B. xxv. 5.

—— *v. also* Winkton, *in Christchurch, co. Southt.*

Christleton, *co. Chester. Rector.* Will. Pette, 1395 (Cristelton). Add. 15500.

Christon, *co. Som.* Grant in, with the advowson, 1381 (Cricheston). Harl. 48 A. 24.

Chroerst. *v.* Crowhurst, *co. Suss.*

Chryche. *v.* Crich, *co. Derb.*

Chudeham. *v.* Chidham, *co. Suss.*

Chudyngfold. *v.* Chiddingfold, *co. Surr.*

Chumwell, *in Bratton Fleming, co. Devon.* Lease of, 1672 (Barton of Chimwell). Harl. 112 F. 17.

Church Hall. *v. sub* Paglesham, *co. Essex.*

Church Kirk, *in Whalley, co. Lanc.* Inspex. of grant of the chapel to Whalley Abbey, 1344;(Chirche). Add. 1060.

—— Brief for rebuilding the chapel, 1805. Ch. Br. B. xlvi. 3.

Church Merrington. *v.* Merrington, Church, *co. Durh.*

Church Minshull. *v.* Minshull, Church, *co. Chest.*

Churchespene. *v.* Speen, Church, *co. Berks.*

Clænefelda. *v.* Clanfield, *co. Southt.*

Clakesbi. *v.* Claxby, *co. Linc.*

Claketorp. *v.* Claythorpe, *co. Linc.*

Claketun. *v.* Claxton, *co. Norf.*

Clane, *co. Kildare.* Petition from the portreeves, etc., of, conc. riots, 1454. Cott. iv. 35.

Claneboy, *in Ulster.* Grant in, 1571 (Claneybuy, Clandeboye). Add. 15574.

Clanefeld. *v. sub* Marcle, Much, *co. Heref.*

Clanfield, *co. Oxon.* Release in, [1225-6] (Clænefeld). Add. 26694.

Clanfield, *co. Southt.* A boundary mark, 909 (Clænefelda). Harl. 43 C. 1.

Clapcott, *nr. Wallingford, co. Berks.* Covenant for a fine of the manor, 1547. Harl. 79 G. 18.

Clapethorne. *v.* Glapthorn, *co. Northt.*

Clapham, *co. Surr.* (?). *Seignour de Clopham.* Tho. le Romeyn, [1303 ?]. Add. 23344.

Clapham, W. R., *co. York.* Grant of the church to St. Mary's Abbey, York, *t.* John. Add. 17153.

—— *Vicar.* Tho. Yedon, 1520. Harl. 112 B. 43.

Clapton, *co. Som.* Ref. to bequest of land in, 1674. Add. 15842.

Clarage, nuper nominata Hellowe. *v.* Belleau, *co. Linc.*

Clare (Clayore, etc.), *in Pirton, co. Oxon.* Grants, etc., in, *t.* Edw. I. (?). Add. 20331 (Cleore) (copy);—1349. Add. 20346 (Cleyore);—1382. Add. 20332 (Clayore), 20333;—1398. Add. 20334;—1421. Add. 20335;—1433. Add. 20336;—1437. Add. 20377;—1440. Add. 20337;—1457. Add. 20338, 20355;—1515. Add. 20339.

—— Precipe on a covenant conc. the manor, etc., 1593. Add. 25208.

Clare (Clara), *co. Suff.* Grants, etc., in, [1139-51]. Harl. 76 F. 35;—*t.* Hen. III. Harl. 46 E. 39.

—— Conf. of grant in Wenlauesdene nr. (?), [1173-98]. Harl. 78 A. 53.

—— Crown grant of St. Mary's chantry in, 1549. Add. 7060.

Clare, *Honour of.* Rentals, *t.* Edw. I., 1314-15. Add. 1263, 1264.

—— Compotus, *t.* Hen. IV. Add. 1275.

Clare, *Honour of (continued).* Court-rolls, 1410, 1427. Add. 16541 *a, b.*

—— Extracts from Court-rolls, 1501, 1587. Add. 15613;—1581. Add. 1278;—1582. Add. 1279.

Clareborough (Clareburgh, etc.), *co. Nott.* Reservation of rents in Hayton, *co.* Nott., to the poor of, late Hen. III. Lansd. 66 (Clauerborg).

—— Grant, etc., nr. and in Gringley (Gringelay, Grynley) in, *t.* Edw. I. Harl. 83 D. 27;—1375. Harl. 112 F. 60.

—— Grants, etc., in, 1286. Cott. xxvi. 16 (Clauerburge);—1302. Slo. xxxi. 11 (3);—1306. Add. 17128 (Clauerburgh);—1383. Add. 16838, 16856;—1393. Add. 16839;—1457. Add. 16948, 16949;—1514. Add. 17004;—1520. Add. 24168.

—— *Vicarius.* Dom. Adam f. Ran. de Lound, 1306. Add. 17128.

—— Thomas, 1383. Add. 16838.

—— *v. also* Welham and Welham Moorhouse, *co. Nott.*

Clarendon, *co. Wilts.* Rob. Bp. of Lincoln, Gilb. Bp. of London, and others present at [the Council of, 1164]. Harl. 43 H. 8.

—— Compotus of works at the royal palace of, 1364-7. Add. 26594.

—— Declaration conc. hay in the royal grange at, 1393. Add. 7379.

Clarendon Forest, *co. Wilts.* Extracts from Iter of, conc. Gt. Wishford manor, *co.* Wilts, 1355. Add. 15082, 15083.

Claret Hall. *v. sub* Ashen, *co. Essex.*

Clarkheton. *v.* Heaton, Clock, *co. York.*

Claskesbi. *v.* Claxby, *co. Linc.*

Classthorpe (Claxthorpe, etc.), *in Floore, co. Northt.* Grants, etc., in, late 13 cent. Add. 21674 (Claxthrop);—1336. Add. 22163;—1357. Add. 21675;—1386. Add. 22219.

—— Feoffments, etc., of the manor, 1371. Add. 21676;—1383, 1385. Add. 22213-22216;—1422. Add. 22263, 22264;—1464-5. Add. 22392;—1470. Add. 22295, 22296.

Clatford, *co. Wilts.* Recovery of the manor, 1562. Add. 7585.

Claydon (Cleydon), co. Suff. Grants, etc., in, 1332. Add. 9952;—1361. Add. 10012, 10013;— 1367. Add. 8378;— 1388. Add. 10317;— 1417. Add. 10061.

—— Power to take seisin of the manor, 1396. Harl. 43 E. 21.

Claydon, For of. Grant in, in Westleton, co. Suff., 1379. Add. 10377.

Claydon, East, co. Buck. Sale of tithe in, 1576 (East Cleidon). Eg. 294.

—— Fines in, 1577 (Est Claydon). Eg. 296, 297.

Claydon St. Botulph, co. Buck. Sale of tithes in, 1576 (Bottle Cleidon). Eg. 294.

—— Fines in, 1577 (Bottle Claydon). Eg. 296, 297.

Claydon, Steeple, co. Buck. Lease of the manor, c. 1433 (Stepulclaydon). Harl. 53 H. 17.

Claydon's Manor. v. sub Westleton, co. Suff.

Claygate, in Thames Ditton, co. Surr. Conf., by Edw. the Confessor, of a grant in, to Westminster Abbey, 1066 [ac. 1065] (Claeigate). Cott. vi. 2 (copy).

—— Court-rolls, 1539-1593 (Claygate). Harl. Roll T. 17.

Claygate, in Ash, co. Surr. Rental of the manor, 1547-1549 (Cleygate). Harl. Roll C. 12.

—— Precipe on a covenant conc. the manor, 1564. Add. 25508.

Clayhall. v. sub Barking, co. Essex.

Clayhanger (Cleyhangre), co. Devon. Grant, etc., in, 1408. Harl. 57 A. 27;—1501. Add. 13074.

Clayhanger, co. Staff. Grant of commonage in, to Oseney Abbey, t. Hen. III. (Cleyhungre). Harl. 55 F. 18.

Clayore. v. Clare, in Pirton, co. Oxon.

Claypole, co. Linc. Persona. W—, [1203–6] (Cleipol). Harl. 84 D. 3.

—— —— Joh. Wolde, 1393. Harl. 57 E. 22.

—— Rector. Dom. Tho. de S. Laudo, 1298. Add. 20652.

Claythorpe, co. Linc. Grant in, to Burwell Priory, late 12 cent. (Clacthorp). Harl. 51 D. 20.

—— Grant in, to Greenfield Priory, early 13 cent. (Clactorp). Harl. 50 I. 36, 58 G. 31 (copy).

Claythorpe, co. Linc. (continued). Grant in, early 13 cent. Harl. 48 B. 23 (Clakotorp).

—— Release to Greenfield Priory from suit of court in, post 1217 (Clactorp). Harl. 52 A. 16.

—— Capellanus. Walterus, early 13 cent. Harl. 48 B. 23, 50 I. 36.

—— Sacerdos. W—, early Hen. III. Harl. 54 B. 21.

Clayton, co. Staff. Suit against Trentham Priory for lands in, 1310. Campb. xxviii. 9.

—— Power to receive seisin in, 1338. Campb. xxviii. 2.

Clayton, co. Suss. Assignment of the manor to Edw. II., 1316 (Cleyton). Harl. 57 E. 33.

—— Feoffment, etc., in, 1474. Add. 18767;—1538. Add. 8111, 8112.

Clayton, nr. Bradford, co. York. Grant in, 1321. Add. 15650.

Clayton in the Clay, co. York. Grant in, 1389 (Claytone). Cott. xxviii. 92.

Clayton, West (?), co. York. Conff. of grants in, to Byland Abbey, post 1194. Add. 7477 (copy);—[1232–40]. Add. 7465 (copy);—ante 1298. Add. 7438.

Clayworth, co. Nott. Grant in, 1304 (Clowurde). Slo. xxxi. 11 (1) (copy).

—— Precipe on a covenant in, 1369 (Clanworth). Add. 25186.

Cleatham, co. Linc. Precipe on a covenant in, 1578 (Cletham). Add. 25085.

Cleck Heaton. v. Heaton, Cleck, co. York.

Clee, co. Linc. Fine in, 1323 (Clee juxta Grymesby). Add. 6253.

—— Vicarius. Tho. Luffe, 1407. Add. 19324.

Cleeton, co. Salop. Lease of the manor, c. 1433 (Cleoton). Harl. 53 H. 17.

Cleeve, co. Som. Lease in Lynegercote, etc., in the manor of, by Cleeve Abbey, 1367 (Clyva). Add. 11164.

—— Release in, 1438 (Clyve). Harl. 50 E. 6.

—— Vicarius. Laur. de Lomene, 1367. Add. 11165.

Cleeve, Bishop's, co. Glouc. Grant in, t. Hen. III. (Cliuia). Harl. 48 C. 45.

Clothall, *co. Hertf* Grants, *etc.*, in, *t.* Hen. III. Harl. 111 D. 24 (Cloball), 111 E. 44 (Clahall); —1300. Harl. 111 D. 57 (Clohale).

—— Release in le Brade in, 1440 (Clotbale). Harl. 112 F. 14.

—— Inquisition conc. manors in, 1522. Add. 7390.

—— *Domini feodi.* Heredes Laurenc. Scot, *t.* Hen. III. Harl. 111 D. 24.

—— *Dominus.* Simon, *t.* Hen. III. Harl. 111 E. 44.

—— *Rector. Dom.* Rob. de Hauvile, 1305. Harl. 112 A. 3.

Clovelly, *co. Devon.* Grant and release in Crosselond in the manor of, 1426 (Clovelye). Add. 13044, 13045.

Clowne, *co. Derb.* Award in suit of, with the Earl of Shrewsbury, 1578. Add. 13938.

Clownes, *in Hatfield Chase, co. York.* Grants nr., to St. Katharine's Hospital, Lincoln, [1189-99] (Clunes). Harl. 43 C. 14, 15.

Cloworde. *v.* Clayworth, *co. Nott.*

Clun, *co. Salop.* Brief for rebuilding the church, 1756. Ch. Br. A. ii. 3.

Clyde, *River, in Scotland.* Grant of a salmon net in, to Cupar Abbey, *c.* 1177-8 (Clyd). Cott. xviii. 24.

Clyff. *v.* Cliffe at Hoo, *co. Kent.*

Clyfton. *v.* Clifton.

Clyfware. *v.* Clewer, *co. Berks.*

Clyston, *in Black Auton, co. Devon.* Releases in, 1516, 1522. Add. 26184, 26186.

Clyve. *v.* Cleeve, *co. Som.*

—— *v.* Cliffe at Hoo, *co. Kent.*

Clyve, Edithe. *v. sub* Frome, *co. Som.*

Clyve, West. *v. sub* Cliffe at Hoo, *co. Kent.*

Clyvesende. *v. sub* St. Lawrence, *co. Kent.*

Clywere. *v.* Clewer, *co. Som.*

Cnichtebrugge. *v.* Knightsbridge, *co. Midd.*

Cnihttengilda, Soca de Anglica. *v.* London, Portsoken Ward.

Cnolla. *v.* Knowle, *in Waldron* (?), *co. Suss.*

Cnossainton, Cnossitonia. *v.* Knossington, *co. Leic.*

Cnottig. *v.* Knotting, *co. Bedf.*

Cnowles. *v. sub* Brenchley, *co. Kent.*

Cnwclas *al.* Knucklass, *co. Radnor.* Lease of the castle and demesne, *c.* 1433 (Knorlas). Harl. 53 H. 17.

Coal Aston. *v.* Aston, Coal, *co. Derb.*

Coates, *in Aslacoe Wap., co. Linc.* Conf. of covenants with Bullington Priory conc. lands in, *ante* 1191 (Cotes). Harl. 52 G. 43.

—— Grants in, *t.* Edw. I. Harl. 52 B. 24 (Cotes), 52 B. 38 (Cotes juxta Stowe B. Murie).

Coates, *in Rushbury, co. Salop.* Grant, etc., in, 1331. Add. 8076 (La Cote); —1340. Add. 8077 (do.).

Coates, *co. Suss.* Assignment of land in, 1501 (Cotes). Add. 18790.

Coates, Great, *co. Linc.* Settlement of Gt. Cotes and the Grose Manor, etc., [1613-15] (Cotes magna). Harl. 45 G. 5.

—— *Persona.* Galfridus, [1234]. Harl. 52 E. 47; —*t.* Hen. III. Harl. 47 A. 32, 54 B. 42.

Coates, Little, *co. Linc.* Grant in, [1613-15]. Harl. 45 G. 5.

Coates, North, *co. Linc.* Fine in, 1338 (Northcotes). Harl. 58 A. 47.

—— Fine of the manor, 1638 (Northcotes). Woll. xi. 29.

Coaxdon. *v. sub* Chardstock, *co. Dors.*

Cobdock. *v.* Copdock, *co. Suf.*

Cobele. *v.* Cubley, *co. Derb.*

Coberle. *v.* Cubberley, *co. Glouc.*

Cobham (Cobeham, *etc.*), *co. Kent.* Grants, etc., in, early 13 cent.-*t.* Hen. III. Harl. 49 A. 37, 49 B. 3, 50 A. 19, 51 F. 46 (Cubbeham), 55 E. 17 (do.); —1317. Harl. 56 G. 11; —1331. Harl. 53 C. 40; —1339. Harl. 54 F. 59; —1344. Harl. 56 C. 25; —1345. Harl. 45 C. 24; —1348. Harl. 48 F. 13; —1349. Harl. 53 D. 17; —1359. Harl. 48 E. 20; —1361. Harl. 45 L 3; —1363. Harl. 43 I. 30; —1370. Harl. 48 E. 26, 52 B. 3, 4, 53 A. 46, 47; —1371. Harl. 44 C. 31; —1372. Harl. 48 E. 28, 53 A. 48; —1375. Harl. 43 I. 31; —1380. Harl. 48 F. 14; —1384. Harl. 52 A. 6; —1389. Harl. 58 A. 21; —1392. Harl. 58 A. 22; —1395. Harl. 52 H. 53; —1401. Harl. 45 F. 36, 55 A. 40; —1402. Harl. 56 D. 39, 56 I. 10; —1409. Harl. 51 G. 33, 56 D. 40, 44; —1414. Harl. 45 H. 38; —

G. 40;—1316. Harl. 47 E. 7;—1318.
Harl. 54 C. 27;—1329. Add. 24655,
24656;—1583. Harl. 57 H. 18;—
1632. Harl. 56 I. 17, 18.

—— *Persona.* *Dom.* Adam de Haut-
boys, 1360. Harl. 49 G. 42;—1368.
Harl. 47 B. 2.

**Cocking,** *co. Suss.* Grant of free-
warren, markets, etc., in, 1285. Harl.
58 I. 37.

**Cocklebury.** *v. sub* Chippenham, *co.
Wilts.*

**Cockley Cley.** *v.* Cley, *co. Norf.*

**Cockthorpe,** *co. Oxon.* *Capellanus.*
Robertus, 1212-13 (Coctorp). Harl.
45 D. 18.

**Coore.** *v.* Coker, East, *co. Som.*

**Cocton.** *v.* Coughton, *nr. Ross, co.
Heref.*

**Coddenham** (Codenham, etc.), *co. Suff.*
Grant of St. Mary's church in, to
found a monastery at, early Hen. II.
(Codeneham). Cott. MS. Nero C. iii.,
f. 227.

—— Papal conf. of the church in,
to Royston Priory, 1184. Cott. MS.
Aug. ii. 124;—1192. Cott. MS. Aug. ii.
130 (Coddham).

—— Conf. of a grant in, to Leystone
Abbey, t. Hen. III. (Codehom). Add.
10294.

—— Grants, etc., in, 1294. Add.
9842 (Codeham);—1331. Add. 9942;
—1367. Add. 8378;—1384. Add.
10316;—1400. Add. 5513;—1464.
Add. 10068;—1474. Add. 10073;—
1476. Add. 10074;—1685. Add.
15005.

—— Grant of the manor, 1319. Harl.
50 A. 35.

*v. also* Crowfield, *co. Suff.*

**Coddenham Hall.** *v. sub* Boxford,
*co. Suff.*

**Codscombe Mohun.** *v.* Cutcombe,
*co. Som.*

**Codeham.** *v.* Coddenham, *co. Suff.*

—— *v.* Cudham, *co. Kent.*

**Codenouere, Codenore, Code-
noure.** *v.* Codnor, *co. Derb.*

**Codesford.** *v.* Cottisford, *co. Oxon.*

**Codestoke.** *v.* Cotterstock, *co. Northt.*

**Codford St. Mary,** *co. Wilts.* Award
in a suit in, 1550 (Est Codford). Add.
24436.

**Codford [St. Peter ?],** *co. Wilts.*
Conf. of grant of, to Farley Priory,
[1167 ?] (Cutiford). Harl. 43 C. 22.

**Codicote,** *co. Hertf.* Livery and extent in, 1541. Add. 18559 a, b.

**Codingale,** *co. Suss.* Freedom to Battle
Abbey from service for, [1100-1135].
Harl. 43 C. 12.

**Codinton Bouston.** *v.* Cuddington,
*co. Surr.*

**Codmanton.** *v. sub* Sholden, *co. Kent.*

**Codnor** (Codenoure, etc.), *co. Derb.*
Grants, etc., in, 1285. Woll. iv. 7;—
t. Edw. I. Woll. iv. 6 (Codenovere);—
1329. Woll. iv. 8, 9, 12;—1345. Woll.
iv. 11;—1349. Woll. iv. 16 (Codenore);
—1359. Woll. iv. 13 (do.);—1401.
Woll. iv. 18;—1429. Woll. iv. 17.—
1439. Woll. iv. 15;—1443. Woll. iv.
14;—1449. Woll. iv. 23 (Codnore).—
1450. Woll. iv. 26 (Codnour);—1460.
Woll. iv. 46 (do.);—1465. Woll. iv.
19;—1474. Woll. iv. 20, 21 (Codnore);
—1516. Woll. iv. 25 (Codnour);—1552.
Woll. iv. 29 (do.);—1640. Woll. iv. 37.

—— Audits of the collector of Lady
de Grey's dower in, 1448-1451. Woll.
iv. 32, 34.

—— Inspex. of a grant of the keepership of Codnor Park, 1459. Woll. iv. 31.

—— Order for salary to the keeper of
the park, 1459. Woll. iv. 31.

—— Sale of wood betw. Boterley and
Codnor Parks, 1474. Woll. iv. 22.

—— *Ballivus.* Joh. Nawden, 1450.
Woll. iv. 26.

—— *Seigneur.* Ric. de Grey, 1277.
Woll. iv. 5.

—— *Capellanus.* Radulfus, 1239.
Lansd. 584.

**Codrington,** *co. Glouc.* Grants in, to
Stanley Abbey, *co.* Wilts., [1189?]
(Cudelintona). Campb. xxiii. 20.

**Codsall,** *co. Staff.* Briefs for rebuilding
the church, 1803, 1806. Ch. Br. B.
xliii. 4, xlvii. 4.

**Codyngton.** *v.* Cuddington, *co. Surr.*

**Coffley.** *v. sub* Northaw, *co. Hertf.*

**Cofton,** *co. Worc.* Grant at, to Bredon
Monastery, 780 (æt Coftune). Cott.
MS. Aug. ii. 30.

**Cogan,** *co. Glam.* Grant in Coganes-
mur to Margam Abbey, t. Hen. III.
Harl. 75 D. 24.

—— Grants in the fee of, etc., t. Hen.
III.-t. Edw. I. Add. 24250-24252.

Colchester (Colocestria, Colecestre), co. *Essex* (*continued*). Conf. of tithes in, to the rectory of All Saints, 1544. Add. 15866.
—— Exchequer acquittance for a subsidy from, 1596. Add. 25587.
—— Conveyance in trust in, 1631. Add. 5142.
—— Court-rolls of Shawe's manor in, 1701-16. Add. 25790.
—— Petition of the borough for re-incorporation, 1740. Add. 156,7
—— Rental of Shawe's manor in, 1765. Add. 25791.
—— *Ballivi.* Saher le Parmenter, Rad. Sauar, 1306. Campb. ii. 5.
—— —— Will. de Hadleye, Rog. Belch, 1348. Campb. xxiii. 14.
—— —— Joh. Beche, Rob. Sylby, 1429. Campb. xxix. 10.
—— *Alderman.* Joh. Langley, *ante* 1658. Add. 1042.
—— —— Andr. Fromenteele, 1661. Add. 9795.
—— *Clericus.* Martinus, [1181-4]. Harl. 75 A. 13.

Colchitt Hundred. *v.* Coleshill Hundred, co. *Flint.*

Colcombe, *nr. Colyton, co. Devon.* Settlement of the manor, 1425 (Colecomb). Add. 13924.

Colcutt, co. *Wilts.* Release of the manor, 1272 (Colecote). Harl. 57 C. 32.

Cold Ashby. *v.* Ashby, Cold, *co. Northt.*

Cold Aston. *v.* Aston, Blank al. Cold, *co. Glouc.*
—— *v.* Aston, Coal, co. *Derb.*

Cold Eaton. *v.* Eaton, Cold, co. *Derb.*

Cold Hanworth. *v.* Hanworth, Cold, co. *Linc.*

Cold Newton. *v.* Newton, Cold, co. *Leic.*

Cold Norton. *v.* Norton, Cold, co. *Essex.*

Coldehall. *v. sub* Margaretting, co. *Essex.*

Colden, co. *York.* Grants, etc., in, early Hen. III. Add. 5723 (Nordcoldoua), 5724 (Coldon), 5725 (Coldon);—1326. Add. 5743 (North Coldon);—1345. Add. 5747 (Magna Coldon);—1539. Add. 5798 (do.).

Coldesseeby. *v.* Ashby, Cold, *co. Northt.*

Coldham, co. *Suff.* Grants of the manor, *t.* Edw. I., 1296, 1297. Harl. 48 G. 13, 15-17.

Coldred, co. *Kent.* Release in, *t.* Hen. III. (Colrede). Harl. 76 E. 41.

Coldrey (Colrithe), *nr. Froyle, co. Southt.* Grants, etc., in, 1323. Add. 10662;—1350. Add. 17413;—1489. Add. 17432.
—— Settlement of the manor, 1462. Add. 17600.
—— *Dominus.* Will. de Castro Radulphi, 1323. Add. 10662.
*v. also* Froyle, co. *Southt.*

Cole Orton. *v.* Orton, Cole, co. *Leic.*

Colebrok. *v.* Colnbrook, co. *Buck.*

Colecestria. *v.* Colchester, co. *Essex.*

Colecomb. *v.* Colcombe, *nr. Colyton, co. Devon.*

Coleford, *in Stogumber* (?), co. *Som.* Grant of "tota terra de," *t.* Hen. III. Add. 4889.

Colemore al. Colmer, co. *Southt.* Compotus of the manor, 1369-70. Harl. Roll D. 6.
—— Sale of Colmer farm in, 1625. Add. 6004.

Coleraine, co. *Londonderry.* Warrant for expenses of the warden of the castle, 1263 (Culrath). Add. 26515 (4).

Colesbourn, co. *Glouc.* Grant in, to Bruerne Abbey, early Hen. II. (Colesburna). Add. 20394.

Colesdon, *in Roxton, co. Bedf.* Lease in, 1441 (Collesden). Lansd. 157, 158.

Coleshill, co. *Berks.* Bequest of land at, *c.* 995 (æt Colles hylle). Cott. viii. 38.
—— Covenant for marriage settlement in, 1581. Harl. 78 A. 48.

Coleshill, co. *Warw.* Bequest of land, etc., at, 11 cent. (æt Cylles hale). Harl. 83 A. 2.
—— Grants, etc., in, 1329. Add. 21429 (Collishulle); — 1337. Add. 21430 (Colleshulle); — 1349. Add. 21431;—1350. Add. 21432;—1352. Add. 21433; — 1354. Add. 21434 (Coleshul);—1369. Add. 21435 (Coleshull);—1383. Add. 21436 (Colleshull);—1409. Add. 21439 (do.);—1420. Add. 21440 (Colahull);—1469. Add. 21441 (do.);—1540. Cott. ii. 15 (Colsell).
—— Grant in Blythefield in, 1360. Add. 21414.

# INDEX LOCORUM.

Coleshill, co. Warw. (continued). Conf. of the church to Markyate Priory, 1362 (Colshulle). Cott. iv. 60 (copy).

—— Bequests to the church of, 1401. Add. 21437.

—— Covenant for a corrody on a grant in, 1404 (Colleshull). Add. 21438.

—— Inventory of goods. etc., of Lady Ofaley at Coleshill Hall, 1628. Add. 18340.

—— Ballivus. Joh. Booher, 1409. Add. 21439.

—— Capellanus. Rogerus, late 12 cent. Cott. xxiv. 21.

Coleshill Hundred, co. Flint. Exchequer acquittance for farm of lead mines in, 1589 (Colchitt). Add. 25744.

Colestun. v. Colston Basset, co. Nott.

Coleton. v. Colton, in Bolton Percy, co. York.

Coleweye. v. sub Lyme Regis, co. Dors.

Colewrth. v. Culworth, co. Northt.

Coleys, in Halifax, co. York. Briefs for rebuilding the chapel, 1798, 1804. Ch. Br. B. xxxviii. 10, xlv. 2.

Colham, co. Midd. Grant near, 831 (Colanhomm). Cott. MS. Aug. ii. 94.

—— Grant of common of pasture on the moor of, 1313. Harl. 84 G. 50.

—— Fine in, 1403. Harl. 54 H. 1.

—— Rental, 1434 (Colnham). Harl. Roll D. 22.

Colham, in Castlecombe. co. Wilts. Surrenders and admissions to lands in, 1514. Add. 18258;—1530. Add. 18276;—1559. Add. 18303;—1567. Add. 18305;—1645. Add. 18397;— 1648. Add. 18407;—1649. Add. 18410;—1651. Add. 18412;—1657. Add. 18425;—1662. Add. 18428;— 1663. Add. 18432 - 18435;—1669. Add. 18437;—1670. Add. 18438;— 1671. Add. 18441.

—— Lease of free warren in, 1602. Add. 18351.

Coliford. v. Colyford, co. Devon.

Colinges. v. Cowling, co. Suff.

Colingthwaite Grange. v. sub Cuckney, co. Nott.

Colinton, [in Ticehurst?], co. Suss. Grant of, to Combwell Priory, t. Hen. III. Harl. 76 A. 5.

Colintona, Parva. v. Collington, Lit., co. Heref.

Colkirk, co. Norf. Grant of the manor to the see of Norwich, [1101]. Cott. MS. Aug. ii. 103 (copy).

Collan, Nether. v. Colan, co. Cornw.

Colleforde. v. sub Holne, co. Devon.

Collesden. v. Colesdon, in Roxton, co. Bedf.

Colles hylle. v. Coleshill, co. Berks.

Collevylles Manor. v. sub Stanton, Long, co. Camb.

Colley. v. Cowley, nr. Dronfield, co. Derb.

—— v. sub Harptree, East, co. Som.

Collian, co. Merion. Conff. of grants in 1414 in the commote of, 1436, 1442. Add. 26069, 26070.

Colliford. v. sub Holne, co. Devon.

Colling. v. Cooling, co. Kent.

Collingbourne, co. Wilts. Bequest at, c. 950 (æt Collinga burnan). Cott. viii. 16.

—— Brief conc. a fire at, 1764. Ch. Br. B. iv. 12.

Collingbourne Ducis, co. Wilts. Precipe conc. right of presentation to the church of, 1632. Harl. 86 G. 35.

Collingham, North, co. Nott. Release in, 1472 (Northcolyngham). Woll. i. 77.

Collington, Little, co. Heref. Grant of the domain, chapel, etc., of, late Hen. III. (Parva Colintona). Cott. xxv. 39.

Collingtree, co. Northt. Grant in, 1358 (Colyngtrow). Add. 21688.

Collom. v. Cowlam, co. York.

Collumpton, co. Devon. Release in, 1396 (Columpton). Add. 13032.

—— Grant of dower in Colbroke in, 1488. Harl. 48 I. 26.

—— Interrogatories in suit conc. the Barton of Colbrooke in, 1635. Add. 13184.

Collyweston, co. Northt. Evidences conc. title to the manor and advowson, 1441. Cott. iv. 55.

Colmer. v. Colemore, co. Southt.

Colmslie, co. Roxburgh. Conf. of a site for a "vaccaria," etc.. at, to Melrose Abbey, [1166-70?] (Cumbesleia). Cott. xviii. 13, 14.

Combe English, co. Som. Power to take seisin in, 1362 (Inglesuomb). Add. 5457.

Combe Florey, co. Som. General release at, 1367. Cott. xxvii. 102.

Combe, La [Pepperscombe ?], in Steyning, co. Suss. Grant of reversion of, with fine, 1355. Harl. 80 A. 22, 23.

Combe Martin, co. Devon. Lease in Berry Down nr., 1450. Add. 13059.

Combe octave Prebend, dioc. Bath. Conditions of filling up vacancy in, 1371. Harl. 48 A. 20.

Combe Pyne, co. Devon. Fine of the manor, etc., 1408. Harl. 58 G. 37.

Combe Rawleigh, co. Devon. Release in Alyshoys in, 1420. Add. 13039.

Combe Wakswell al. Thorneland, co. Devon. Court-rolls of the manor, 1586-7. Add. 9397;—1591. Add. 9408;—1592. Add. 9411;—1609-1614. Add. 9415-9417.

Combe Wyche. v. Combwich, in Cannington (?), co. Som.

Comberton, co. Worc. Conf. of land in, to Pershore Abbey, 972 (Cumbrincgtun). Cott. MS. Aug. ii. 6.

—— Settlement in, 1363 (Comburton, Comberton). Harl. 50 H. 26.

Comberton, Great, co. Worc. Feoffment of the manor, 1370. Add. 20422.

—— Grant, etc., in, 1444. Add. 24772 (Comberton Magna);—1514. Add. 24787 (do.).

Combs, in Chapel en le Frith, co. Der. Power for seisin in Alstonlegh in, 14— (Le Combs). Woll. iii. 23.

Combs, co. Suff. Bequest of goods i the manor of, by M. de Crek, 128— (Comb, Camb). Campb. iii. 1.

—— Grants of free warren in, 128 (Cambes). Harl. 58 L 37;—129 (Combes). Add. 6337.

—— Grants of rents out of the manor of, 1338 (Combes). Harl. 43 D. 35;—1431 (do.). Harl. 57 A. 1.

—— Grants, etc., of the manor and advowson, 1400. Harl. 54 H. 2;—1429. Harl. 58 B. 17;—1434. Harl. 47 C. 44;—1457. Harl. 43 E. 46;—1508. Harl. 51 H. 18;—1516. Harl. 52 B. 10 (Combys).

—— Grant in, 1612. Add. 10579.

—— Persona. Joh. de Teuelby, 1403. Harl. 46 D. 8 a, 49 G. 45;—1405. Harl. 58 B. 19.

—— Rector. Rogerus, 1282. Campb. iii. 1.

Combwell. v. sub Goudhurst, co. Kent.

Combwich, in Cannington (?), co. Som. Re-feoffment in, 1421 (Combe Wyche). Add. 15845.

Comcarvan. v. Cwmcarvan, co. Monm.

Comotoidre. v. Cwmdeuddwr, co. Radnor.

Compton, in Compton Hundred, co. Berks. Grant of, early Hen. II. (Cumtuu). Add. 21172.

Cookstown, co. Meath. Grant in, 1557 (Cookeston). Add. 7046.

Coole (Cowell), nr. Nantwich, co. Chest. Rental, 1391. Add. 5230.
—— Writ on a claim to lands in, 1420. Add 6278.

Cooling, co. Kent. A boundary mark, 774 (Colling). Cott. MS. Aug. ii. 99;
——778 (Culingagemere). Cott. viii. 34.
—— Grant at, 808 (Culingas). Cott. MS. Aug. ii. 98.
—— Acquittance for rent of the manor, 1300 (Culingg). Harl. 46 I. 34.
—— Conveyance of the manor, 1345 (Coulyng). Harl. 45 C. 24.
—— Grants, etc., in, 1370. Harl. 51 F. 16 (Culyng);—1467. Harl. 45 H. 24 (Coulling);—1470. Harl. 58 A. 5 (Este Coulling);—1471. Harl. 45 H. 25 (Cowling);—1495. Harl. 56 A. 29;—1496. Harl. 54 G. 35 a;—1511. Harl. 49 C. 14;—1526. Harl. 45 H. 26;—1534. Harl. 47 B. 28;—1536. Harl. 112 A. 60;—1540. Harl. 46 I. 20.
—— Payments, contracts, etc., for works at the castle, etc., 1381. Harl. 48 E. 37, 39, 41, 42, 44;—1382. Harl. 51 B. 47, 55 G. 34, 35;—1383. Harl. 48 E. 47;—1384. Harl. 55 G. 36;—1386. Harl. 55 G. 37;—1390. Harl. 46 D. 23.
—— Robbery of sheep in, 1417. Harl. 56 E. 23.
—— Acquittances for rent of the manor, 1429. Harl. 46 H. 8;—1431. Harl. 46 H. 11;—1433. Harl. 46 H. 15.
—— Lease of the parsonage, etc., 1536 (Colyng). Harl. 46 L 15 a, b.
—— Persona. Joh. de Sholdone, 1345. Harl. 45 C. 24.
—— —— Reginald de Cobham, 1363. Harl. 53 B. 45;—1364. Harl. 56 B. 21;—1367. Harl. 48 E. 24;—1369. Harl. 48 F. 8, 49 B. 5, 53 A. 45;—1370. Harl. 44 B. 46, 48 F. 9, 10, 51 F. 16, 53 A. 46, 47, 56 B. 19, 58 A. 33;—1371. Harl. 48 F. 11, 51 C. 24;—1372. Harl. 52 C. 14, 53 A. 48;—1380. Harl. 48 F. 14.
—— Rector. Benedict Grauntden, al. Sire Beneyt, persone, 1395. Harl. 52 B. 49;—1396. Harl. 51 A. 39.

Coombe. v. sub Whitley, co. Berks.

Coombe (Cumbe, Cumba), in Chipping Campden, co. Glouc. Grant of, to Bordesley Abbey, [1140-9]. Campb. xviii. 8.

Coombe (Cumbe, Cumba), in Chipping Campden, co. Glouc. (continued). Precept from the Exchequer conc. tenure of, by Bordesley Abbey, [1155?]. Cott. MS. Nero C. iii. f. 188.
—— Conf. of, by Hen. II., to Bordesley Abbey, [1157?]. Cott. MS. Nero C. iii. f. 176.

Coombe, in Enford, co. Wilts. Complaint of the prior of St. Swithyn, Winchester, conc. the manor, t. Hen. VI. Harl. Roll CC. 28.
—— Fine of the manor, 1627. Add. 15123.

Coombe Almer (?), in Sturminster Marshall, co. Dors. Recovery of a moiety of the manor, 1508 (Coombe). Add. 13556.

Coombe Bessett, in Sturminster Marshall, co. Dors. Settlement in, 1587. Add. 13576.

Coombs, co. Suss. Sale in, 1620. Add. 18927.

Copdock, co. Suff. Grants, etc., in, t. Hen. III. Add. 5904 (Coppedoo), 9477 (Copped.), 9488 (Coppedehoo);—1285. Add. 9833 (Coppedhok);—1287. Add. 9523 (Coppedoc);—1290. Add. 9525 (Coppedok), 9526;—1361. Add. 9632 (do.), 9633;—1375. Add. 9649 (Copedook);—1388. Add. 9664 (Copedoke), 9665 (do.);—1396. Add. 9671 (Coppedok);—1420. Add. 9693 (do.);—1450. Add. 9717 (Coppedook);—1662. Add. 10166.
—— Precipe on a covenant in, 1578. Add. 25349 (Cobdock).
—— Assignment of advowson of, 1721. Add. 9798 (Cobdock).

Copelowe, Grangia de. v. sub Babraham, co. Camb.

Copford, co. Essex. Conveyance in, 1453. Harl. 47 D. 24.
—— Precipe on a covenant in, 1592. Add. 24996.

Cople, co. Bedf. Grants in, to Chicksands Priory, c. 1150. Harl. 45 I. 7 (Cogopol);—t. Hen. III. Harl. 45 I. 18 (Cogepol).
—— Settlement in, 1347. Harl. 55 E. 36 (Coupol).
—— Compotus of rents in, 1457-58. Add. 657.

Copner, nr. Portsmouth, co. Southt. Grant in, by Quarr Abbey, late H n. II. (Copponore). Add. 15687.

Corscombe, co. Devs. (continued). Release, etc., in West Corscomb, 1396.
Add. 6089;—1403. Add. 6090.
v. also Halstock, co. Dors.

Corsham, co. Wilts. Grant of annuity
from the manor, by Anne, Queen of
Rich. II., 1394 (Cosham). Cott. xi. 71.

Corsalsry, Aqua de, nr. St. Ishmaels,
co. Pembr. Grant of eel fishery in,
[1234-41]. Add. 8412.

Corston, co. Salop. Warrant for a
grant of the manor, [1514-20]. Add.
30008.

Cortlingstock, co. Nott. Grant in, t.
Edw. I.-II. (Cortligstoke). Harl. 84
A. 3.

Corton, in Portisham, co. Dors. Grant
of tithes of, to Montacute Priory, t.
Hen. I. (Corftona). Add. 24879 (2)
(copy).

—— Grant of the manor, 1414 (Corfton). Harl. 48 I. 25.

Corton, co. Suff. Grants in, t. Edw. I.
Harl. 48 H. 13;—1440. Add. 19335.

Corton al. Cortington, in Boyton, co.
Wilts. Sale of woods in, 1639. Add.
15139.

Corwen, co. Merioneth. Brief for rebuilding the church, 1767. Ch. Br. B.
vii. 8.

Corxston. v. Croxton, co. Norf.

Cory, North. v. Curry, N., co. Som.

Cory Ryvel. v. Curry Rivell, co. Som.

Coryngdon. v. sub Corscombe, co.
Dors.

Cosford. v. sub Hadleigh, co. Suff.

Cosford, co. Warw. Covenant in, with
Pipewell Abbey, [1246-9] (Cosseford).
Add. 21479.

—— Warrant for inquisition on lands
of Pipewell Abbey in, 1278. Add.
21484.

Cosgrove (Couesgrave), co. Northt.
Grants, etc., in, to Biddlesdon Abbey,
t. Hen. III. Harl. 85 B. 8, 15, 16, 36
C. 3.

—— Grants in, t. Hen. III. Harl.
85 B. 30, 85 E. 2.

—— Release from Biddlesdon Abbey
of arrears of rent in, 1330. Harl. 84
E. 55.

—— Precipes on covenants in, 1555.
Add. 25148;—1593. Add. 25179.

—— Marriage settlements, etc., in,
1659. Add. 18032;—1660. Add.

18033;—1666. Add. 6074;—1695.
Add. 18055-18061.

—— Clericus. Henricus, t. Hen. III.
Harl. 85 B. 8, 15.

—— Persona. Willelmus, t. John.
Harl. 86 D. 4.

Cosham. v. Corsham, co. Wilts.

Cosham Wymering, co. Southt. Conveyance of the manor, 1649. Add.
18971.

Cosington. v. sub Aylesford, co. Kent.

—— v. sub Northfleet, co. Kent.

Coskirnny al. Coshirney, in the
Barony of Philipstown, Queen's County,
Ireland. Lease of the lands of, 1704.
Add. 24474.

Cosmerisblene al. Cosmus Bleane,
Cosmus et Damyan. v. Blean, co.
Kent.

Cossey, co. Norf. Grant of tithes in,
to Rumburgh Priory, [1121-37] (Cos-
tesseia). Campb. ix. 9 (7) (copy).

—— Grants, etc., of the manor, 1424.
Harl. 54 I. 8 (Costeseye);—1430.
Harl. 43 E. 19 (do.), 54 I. 13;—1431.
Harl. 45 I. 12, 50 H. 27, 28, 54 I. 15;
—1485. Add. 2016.

—— Sales, etc., in, 1555. Add. 14224-
14227;—1557. Add. 14228;—1609.
Add. 14280, 14281.

—— Vicarius. Dom. Robertus, 1329.
Add. 17737.

Cossington, co. Leic. License for a
grant in, to Ouston Abbey, 1344 (Cosyngton). Campb. xv. 6.

Coston al. Cosmeston, in Lavernock,
co. Glam. Crown lease in, 1526. Harl.
75 E. 19.

Coston, co. Leic. Persona. Hen. de
Bereford (?), 1327. Add. 26603.

—— —— Roger Gowteby, 1402.
Add. 21810, 21811.

Costowe, in Wroughton, co. Wilts. Release in, c. 1250 (Cotstowe). Add.
18214 (copy).

Cosyngton. v. Cossington, co. Leic.

Cosyngton Magna. v. sub Aylesford,
co. Kent.

Cosyngton parva juxta Ifeld. v.
sub Northfleet, co. Kent.

Cote. v. sub Charlbury, co. Oxon.

Cotenhall. v. sub Keddington, co. Suff.

Cotes. v. Coates, co. Linc.

—— v. Coates, co. Suss.

Cowlow Buxtons. *v. sub* Buxton, co. Derb.

Cowton, East (?), *nr. Richmond, co. York.* Conf. of grant in, to Rievaulx Abbey, early Hen. II. (Kutona). Add. 20564.

Cowton, North, *W. R., co. York.* Conf. of grant in, *c.* 1250 (North Outun). Cott. x. 9.

Cowyck. *v.* Cowick, co. *Devon.*

Cowyke. *v.* Cowick, co. York.

Coxden. *v. sub* Chardstock, co. *Dors.*

Coxhall. *v.* Coggeshall, co. *Essex.*

Coxwall, *in Brampton Bryan, co. Heref.* Grant in, 1524 (Cockeshall). Cott. xxiv. 35.

Coxwell, *cp. Berks.* Grant of the chapel, etc., with conf., to Beaulieu Abbey, 1205, 1268 (Cokeswell). Harl. 58 I. 25 (*copy*).

Coxwell, Great, *co. Berks.* Court-rolls, 1410, 1470. Add. 26814.

Coxwold, *co. York.* Grant of market, etc., in the manor of, 1304 (Cukewald). Harl. 58 I. 43.

—— Sale in, 1545 (Cookwold). Add. 13337.

—— License of L. Sterne to the curacy of, 1760. Add. 16166.

Craeft. Mercian council held at, 836. Cott. MS. Aug. ii. 9.

Craeft, *co. Berks* (?). Bequest of land at, *c.* 950. Cott. viii. 16.

Craega. *v.* Cray, co. *Kent.*

Craforde. *v.* Crawford, Gt., *in Spetisbury, co. Dors.*

Craft. *v.* Croft, co. *Leic.*

Craft, *co.* —— (?). Persona. Ricardus, [1246–57]. Campb. iii. 14.

Craie. *v.* Cray, St. Paul's, co. *Kent.*

Crail (Karel), *co. Fife.* Conf. of grant in, by Will., King of Scotland, *c.* 1200. Campb. xxx. 5.

—— Covenant conc. tithes in, betw. St. Andrew's Priory and the nuns of Haddington, 1245. Cott. xviii. 28.

Crailing, *co. Roxburgh.* Conf., by Edw. I., of the manor and advowson to the Bp. of Durham, 1301 (Craling). Harl. 43 D. 7.

Crailing, Nether, *co. Roxburgh.* Royal conf. of a grant of, 1441. Add. 19560

Craiselound, *in I. of Axholme, co. Lincoln.* Grant in, to Melwood Chapel afterwards Priory, early 13 cent. Harl. 45 I. 40.

—— Grant in, to Sulby Abbey, Hen. III. (Craslund). Add. 20700.

—— Release in, 1472 (Craslound). Woll. i. 77.

Craketheit *v. sub* Ailby, co. *Linc.*

Crakham. *v.* Crookham, co. *Berks.*

Craling. *v.* Crailing, co. *Roxburgh.*

Cranborne, *cos. Dors. and Wilts.* Lease of the manor, *c.* 1438 (?) (Cranburn). Harl. 53 H. 17.

—— Compotus, 1509 (Cranbourne). Harl. Roll D. 19.

Cranbrooke (Cranebroke, etc.), *co. Kent.* Grant in Hawkridge (Hocrede), etc., in, to Combwell Priory, *t.* Hen. III. Harl. 80 G. 31.

—— Grant in Hartley (Hertle) in, to Combwell Priory, 1260. Harl. 78 G. 37 b.

—— Grants, etc., in, late Hen. III.–*t.* Edw. I. Harl. 78 B. 20, 80 C. 43 (Cranebroc);—1285–6. Harl. 78 B. 16;—1300. Harl. 80 I. 53;—1303. Harl. 78 B. 18, 19;—1326. Harl. 78 B. 21;—1327. Harl. 77 D. 54;—1335. Harl. 80 I. 32;—1342. Harl. 77 D. 47–49, 78 B. 22;—1354. Harl. 79 D. 8;—1359. Harl. 77 G. 10;—1389. Harl. 76 B. 29;—1392. Harl. 78 D. 58;—1396. Harl. 76 B. 35, 76 E. 22;—1398. Harl. 76 B. 30–82;—1401. Add. 24509;—1411. Harl. 76 B. 36, 80 H. 39;—1412. Harl. 76 B. 37, 38, Add. 12642;—1422. Harl. 76 B. 41, 42;—1425. Add. 12645;—1426. Add. 24510;—1430. Add. 24511;—1444. Harl. 76 G. 15, 53;—1458. Harl. 76 G. 56, 57;—1460. Harl. 76 E. 13;—1482. Add. 24513;—1499. Add. 24514;—1516. Harl. 78 I. 42, 50, 51;—1521. Harl. 76 H. 16, 18;—1527. Harl. 76 H. 17;—1543. Harl. 76 H. 26, 44;—1548. Harl. 76 H. 51;—1551. Harl. 78 G. 31;—1559. Harl. 76 I. 44, 77 G. 24;—1601. Harl. 77 C. 58, 77 D. 1;—1609. Harl. 80 C. 16, 17;—1618. Harl. 77 D. 9, 10;—1624. Harl. 77 C. 55.

—— Grants, etc., of Ford Manor and lands in, 1282–3. Harl. 78 B. 17;—1396. Harl. 80 C. 33;—1406. Harl. 76 B. 33, 34;—1425. Harl. 80 C. 34;—1436. Harl. 80 C. 9, 10;—1437. Harl. 79 A. 18–21;—[1445?]. Harl.

Cransford (Cranesford), co. *Suff.* (continued). *Persona.* R——, 12 – 13 cent. Add. 15262 (copy).

—— *Rector. Dom.* Will. fil. Aubrici de Valines, late 13 cent. Harl. 51 G. 5.

Cransley, co. *Northt.* Release in, with the advowson, to St. Mary's College, Leicester, 1429. Add. 10652 (Cransle).

—— Lease in, 1528. Add. 10655 (Crannesley).

—— Precipe on a covenant in, 1593. Add. 25177.

—— *Persona.* Simon de Braybroc, 1342. Cott. xxiii. 27.

—— —— Simon le Forester, 1347. Add. 21766.

Cranwell, co. *Linc.* License for Sempringham Priory to acquire land in, 1329. Add. 21100.

Cranworth, co. *Norf.* Grants, etc., in, t. Hen. III. Harl. 49 H. 37 (Cranewrth); —1360. Harl. 49 G. 42 (Craneworth); —1384. Harl. 56 H. 48 (do.);—1429. Add. 14721 (do.).

—— Precipe on a covenant in, 1370. Add. 14003.

—— Suit conc. the manor, 1709. Add. 15893.

Crasalton. *v.* Carshalton, co. *Surr.*

Craslund. *v.* Craiselound, *in I. of Axholme*, co. *Linc.*

Cratela. *v. sub* Wellow, co. *Nott.*

Cratfield (Cratefeld, etc.), co. *Suff.* Conff. of the church to St. Neot's Priory, 1165. Add. 8517;—c. 1165–70. Add. 8521.

—— Grants in, early 13 cent. Add. 22576 (Crattefeld);—[1236–42]. Add. 5897.

—— Extent of fees in, bel. to the Earls Marshal, c. 1400. Add. 19338.

—— Inspex. in 1454 of a feoffment in, 1422. Add. 17243.

—— *Vicarius.* Tho. Yongge, 1378. Add. 19317.

Cratle. *v. sub* Wellow, co. *Nott.*

Crauden. *v.* Croydon, co. *Camb.*

Crauele. *v.* Crawley, N., co. *Buck.*

Crauenhurst, Magna et Parva. *v.* Gravenhurst, Upper and Lower, co. *Bedf.*

Craule, Magna. *v.* Crawley, N., co. *Buck.*

Craumareis. *v.* Crowmarsh, co. *Oxon.*

Cravens. *v. sub* Henham, co. *Suff.*

Crawford, Great, *in Spetisbury*, co. *Dors.* Release in, 1468 (Magna Craneford). Harl. 52 A. 41.

—— Appointment of Edm. Downing as steward of the manor, 1571 (Onforde). Harl. 75 E. 40.

Crawfurd Lindsay, co. *Lanark.* Precept for seisin of the lands of, 1539. Eg. 367.

Crawley, co. *Southt.* A boundary mark, 909 (Crawelesinga Mearc). Harl. 43 C. 1.

Crawley (Craule, etc.), co. *Suss.* Grants, etc., in, 1280. Add. 17267, 17268; —1310. Add. 17291;—1324. Add. 24672;—1345. Add. 17308;—1349. Add. 24673;—1352. Add. 24675;— 1357. Add. 24676;—1364. Add. 8094; —1554. Add. 5676.

—— Inquisition conc. Woolborough manor in, 1488. Add. 7388.

—— Award, etc., in, 1510. Add. 5673, 5674.

Crawley, North (Craule, Magna Craule, Crawle, etc.), co. *Buck.* Grants, etc., in, t. Hen. III.-t. Edw. I. Add. 23899 (Crawele), 23900, 23901 (Mag. Crawell.), 24090, 24164; — 1292. Add. 23898; — 1304. Add. 23902 (Mag. Croule);—1310. Add. 23903;—1318. Add. 23904; — 1322. Add. 23905 (Crauele);—1331. Add. 23906 (Crawele); — 1336. Add. 23907 (Krowlen);—1347. Add. 23908; — 1349. Add. 23909; — 1350. Add. 23910; —1352. Add. 23911;—1353. Add. 23912;—1355. Add. 23913 (Croules); —1356. Add. 23914;—1363. Add. 23915, 23916 (Crowle);—1365. Add. 23917;—1367. Add. 23918;—1370. Add. 23919;—1383. Add. 23920 (Mag. Crowlee); — 1399. Add. 23897;— 1403. Add. 23921 (Crawlee);—1421. Add. 23922 (do.);—1425. Add. 23923, 23924;—1429. Add. 23925 (Crawle Magna);—1436. Add. 23926 (do.);— 1438. Add. 5164;—1442. Add. 23927 (N. Crowle);—1463. Add. 23928;— 1508. Add. 23929 (N. Crowley);— 1509. Add. 23930, 23931;—1512. Add. 23932;—1537. Add. 23933 (N. Crowlay);—1542. Add. 23934 (N. Croley); —1580. Add. 23883;—1586. Add. 23935;—1587. Add. 23936;—1591. Add. 23884, 23885;—1593. Add. 23937;—1601. Add. 23938;—1602. Add. 23888–23890; — 1616. Add.

23940;—1618. Add. 23941;—1652.
Add. 23943;—1636. Add. 23944;—
1637. Add. 23945, 23946;—1642,
1643. Add. 23947-23952;—1645. Add.
23954;—1650. Add. 23960-23965;—
1659. Add. 23966-23968;—1662. Add.
23994;—1663. Add. 23995;—1668.
Add. 23996-23998;—1674. Add. 23955,
23999 a, b;—1675. Add. 23956;—
1676. Add. 23958;—1678. Add. 23959;
—1696. Add. 23962, 23963;—1699.
Add. 23964;—1712. Add. 23968;—
1715. Add. 23967;—1718. Add.
23970.

—— Terrier of lands of R. Lattimer
in, 1547. Add. 22651.

—— Sale of the advowson, etc., 1604.
Add. 23989.

—— Covenant by the inhabitants to
prevent strangers from becoming
chargeable on the parish rates, 1627.
Add. 23942.

—— Lands in, inherited by N. Carewe,
c. 1710. Add. 22704.

—— Covenant conc. marriage settlement of Eliz. Hackett in, 1710. Add.
23965, 23966.

Craxton. v. sub Barrowby, co. Linc.

Cray. v. sub Ramsden, co. Essex.

Cray, River, co. Kent. Grant on, 814
(Cræga). Cott. MS. Aug. ii. 77.

Cray, co. Kent. Title of land at, ante
966 (Cræga). Cott. viii. 20.

Cray, Foots, co. Kent. Institution of
J. de Clenchewarton to the church of,
1269 (Fottescreye). Harl. 43 I. 29.

—— Release in, 1590 (Fotyscray).
Add. 10588.

Cray, St. Paul's, co. Kent. Grant of
the manor and advowson to the Bp. of
Durham, 1293 (Paulinescreye). Harl.
49 A. 4.

—— Grant in (?), to Edw. I., 1305
(Craye). Harl. 43 D. 12.

Cray, St. Paul's (?), North (?), co.
Kent. Grant of Norhale grove in. t.
John (Craie). Harl. 112 C. 41.

—— Persona. Robertus, t. John. Harl.
112 C. 41.

Crayford, co. Kent. Grant of Howbury (Hobury) manor in, 1379. Slo.
xxxii. 45.

—— Note of the forces of the Duke
of York, etc., at, 1452. Cott. ii. 23
(18).

Creake, North, co. Norf. Bequest to
the church of, 1282 (Crek). Campb.
iii. 1.

—— Grant of custody of the manor,
1456 (Creyke). Add. 16557.

—— Vicarius. Eudo de Tylney, 1282
(Northcrek). Campb. iii. 1.

Creake al. Creyke, South, co. Norf.
Feoffment of Roseys manor in, 1451
(Southcreyk). Add. 7386.

Creaton, Great (Creton Magna). co.
Northt. Lease in, c. 1360. Cott.
xxvii. 118, Add. 21696.

—— Persona. Willelmus, early Edw.
I. Add. 21901.

—— —— Dom. Joh. Malesoures,
c. 1360. Cott. xxvii. 118, Add. 21696.

Crec. v. Crick, co. Northt.

Crediton (Criditon), co. Devon. Grant
of freedom from secular exactions to
the see of, 933. Cott. MS. Aug. ii. 31.

—— Marriage settlement, etc., in,
1383, 1384 (Novus burgus et vetus
villa). Add. 25988-25990.

—— Grants, etc., in, 1484. Add.
13070;—1490. Add. 13071.

—— Rental, 1637 (Crediton, al. Kirton). Harl. 83 H. 39.

—— Grant of the park, 1637. Harl.
83 H. 39.

Credlinge. v. Cridling, co. York.

Creech, co. Dors. Conveyance of the
manor, c. 1433 (?) (Crich). Harl. 53
H. 17.

Creed, co. Cornw. Grants, etc., in Bra-
silian and Nansclason, etc., nr., 1400-
1438. Add. 12974-12996 (S. Cryda,
S. Crede);—1427. Add. 13046.

Creedy, co. Devon. Grant in, [1018]
(Cridia). Cott. ii. 11 (4).

—— Grant of St. Martin's chapel,
etc., to Crediton church, 1217 [1227 ?]
(Cridia). Cott. ii. 11 (6, 7).

—— Grant of the perpetual vicarage
of the chapel, t. Hen. III. (Cria). Cott.
ii. 11 (8).

—— Release of the advowson of the
chapel to Crediton church, t. Hen. III.
(Cridia). Cott. ii. 11 (9).

—— Resignation of the chapel by
Rich. Culling, c. 1230-40 (do.). Cott.
ii. 11 (14).

—— Sacerdos. Samson, 1217 [1227 ?].
Cott. ii. 11 (7).

Creeting All Saints, co. Suff. Grants,
etc., in, 1400. Add. 5513 (Cretyngge);

—1472. Add: 10072 (Cretyng);—
1685. Add. 15005 (Creating).

**Creeting St. Mary's,** *co. Suff.* Grants,
etc., in. *t.* Edw. I. Add. 9829;—1400.
Add. 5513;—1472. Add. 10072;—
1685. Add. 15005.

**Creeting St. Olave's,** *co. Suff.* . Exemption of the manor from ecclesiastical taxation, 1372 (Cretyng). Harl.
Roll A A. 22.

—— Grant in, 1400. Add. 5513.

—— Grant of the manor and advowson, 1414. Cott. xxviii. 87.

—— Precipe on a covenant conc. lands
in, 1561 (St. Tolys Creting). Add.
25308.

—— Extract from court-roll of, 1705.
Add. 10115.

**Creeting St. Peter's** *al.* **West
Creeting,** *co. Suff.* Release in, 1396.
Add. 25922.

—— Inspex., in 1454, of a feoffment of
the manor (?), 1422. Add. 17243.

—— Precipe on a covenant in, 1593
(Weste Cretinge). Add. 25456.

—— *Persona. Dom.* Tho. de Wirling-
ham, 1331. Add. 9942.

—— Baldwinus, 1354. Add.
14767.

—— *Rector.* Edmundus, 1396. Add.
25922.

**Creeton** (Creton), *co. Linc.* Grants,
etc., of the manor, advowson, etc., 1396.
Harl. 52 F. 30;—1401. Cott. xii. 39,
xxvii. 79.

**Crekelade.** *v.* Cricklade, *co. Wilts.*

**Creke's Hall.** *v. sub* Helmingham,
*co. Suff.*

**Creshale.** *v.* Chrishall, *co. Essex.*

**Cresseners.** *v. sub* Gazeley, *co. Suff.*

**Cressingham, Great,** *co. Norf.* Grant
in, 1342. Harl. 45 D. 24.

—— Power to give seisin of the
manor, 1371 (Cresyngham Magna).
Harl. 45 D. 23.

**Cressy's.** *v. sub* Thelnetham, *co. Suff.*

**Creswell,** *co. Northumb.* Grant in,
*c.* 1300 (Cressewelle). Harl. 57 C. 38.

**Creswell,** *nr. Welbeck, co. Nott.* Covenant to convey lands in, 1571. Woll.
xi. 51.

**Cresyngham, Magna.** *v.* Cressingham, Gt., *co. Norf.*

**Cretingham** (Gretingham, etc.),
*Suff.* Conf. of a grant in, to Leyston
Abbey, *t.* Hen. III. Add. 10294.

—— Grants, etc., in, 1296. Add. 10297
—1301. Add. 10269;— 1307. Add.
10270 (Gretingham Parva);—1309.
Add. 10302 :—1311. Add. 10271;—
1314. Add. 10272, 10273 :—1323. Add.
10191 ;—1327. Add. 10304 ;—1332.
Add. 10305 ;—1333. Add. 10275
(Over Gretingham); — 1361. Add.
10199 ;—1376. Add. 10375; — 1418.
Add. 102×2 ;—1433. Add. 10337 ;—
1440. Add. 10205;—1615. Add.
10284.

—— Release of Cretingham Hall
manor in, 1476. Add. 10074.

**Creton.** *v.* Creeton, *co. Linc.*

**Cretyng.** *v.* Creeting, *co. Suff.*

**Crewe,** *co. Chest.* Release of all actions
as to the manor, 1346 (Crue). Campb.
xxviii. 3.

**Crewkerne,** *co. Som.* Settlement of
the manor, 1425 (Crukern). Add.
13924.

**Cria.** *v.* Creedy, *co. Devon.*

**Criccieth,** *co. Carnar.* Garrison establishment of the castle, 1369 (Crukyth).
Harl. Roll E. 7.

**Crich,** *co. Derb.* Conf. of a grant in,
12 or 13 cent. (Cruch). Woll. vi. 49
(copy).

—— Acquittance for payment for the
ward of the manor, 1270 (Cruch).
Harl. 86 G. 55.

—— Surrender of deeds relating to,
1293. Harl. 86 H. 20.

—— Acquittance for relief and rents
in. 1316 (Crouch). Woll. vi 50 (copy).

—— Grants in Plaistow (Plastowe)
in, 1315. Woll. vi. 51 ;—1320. Woll.
vi. 52 ;—1354. Woll vi. 53 ;—1357.
Woll. vi. 54 ;—1358. Woll. vi. 56 ;—
1381. Woll. vi. 57.

—— Lease of Lea (Le Lee) manor,
etc., in, 1357. Woll. vi. 54.

—— License to Thurgarton Priory to
endow a chaplaincy at, 1368 (Cruche).
Woll. iv. 58.

—— Lease of Nunne Feld in Borowcote in, from Derby Priory, 1514
(Cryche). Woll. iv. 51.

—— Rental of lands in, 1538 (Cruch).
Woll. xi. 19, 20.

—— Particulars of a crown-grant of
Nunneclose, etc., in, late bel. to Derby
Priory, 1546 (Chriche). Woll. x. 68

Crich, co. Derb. (continued). Grants,
etc., in Borowoote in, 1547. Woll.
iv. 52 (Cryche) ;—1588. Woll. iv.
53, 54 (Criche) ;—1590. Woll. iv. 55
(Chryche al. Cruche) ;—1604. Woll.
iv. 56 (do.).

—— Extract of court-roll of, t. Hen.
VIII. (Cruche). Woll. xi. 9*.

—— Dominus. Dom. Rad. de
Frecheuile, 1289. Harl. 86 I. 3.

—— Vicarius. Dom. Willelmus, 1320.
Woll. vi. 52.

—— —— Joh. Fessaut, 1405. Harl.
112 H. 29.

—— v. also Wakebridge, in Crich, co.
Derb.

Cricheston. v. Christon, co. Som.

Crick, co. Northt. Grant in, t. John
(Cree). Harl. 47 G. 16.

Cricklade (Crekelade), co. Wilts. Inspex. of grant of, 1276. Cott. xv. 10.

—— Bond to acquit for a rent to the
Crown from the manor, 1276. Harl.
50 D. 40.

—— Assignment, etc., of an annuity
on the manor, 1279. Cott. xxvii. 31,
32.

—— Crown-grant of church lands in,
1540. Add. 26022.

—— Lease in, 1650. Add. 13714.

Cricklade and Highworth Hundred, co. Wilts. License to endow
Fotheringhay College, co. Northt.,
with, 1415 (Criklade). Campb. x. 5.

Cricksea, co. Essex. Compotus of Berne-
mere Marsh nr., 1365-6. Lansd. 630.

—— Release, etc., of the manor, 1407
(Crykseth). Harl. 51 D. 13, 57 A. 18;
—1414 (Cryxhethe). Add. 19977.

Cridelistruhe, nr. Fordingbridge, co.
Southt. Release in, to Maiden Bradley
Priory, t. Hen. III. or Edw. I. Harl.
50 H. 14.

Cridia. v. Creedy, co. Devon.

Cridingges. v. sub Treeton, co. York.

Criditon. v. Crediton, co. Devon.

Cridling, in Darrington, co. York.
Precipes to keepers of the park, 1441-
49. Add. 17139-17151.

—— Fine of the manor, 1638 (Credlinge). Woll. xi. 29.

—— Parcarius. Hen. Vavasour, 1441-
49. Add. 17139-17151.

—— —— Joh. Skypwith, 1441-
1443. Add. 17139-17143.

Crigglestone, in Gt. Sandal, co. York.
Crown lease in, 1555 (Seregylston).
Harl. 84 C. 32.

Crikmede, [in Breamore?], co. Southt.
Bond for rent from, to Breamore
Priory, t. Hen. III. or Edw. I. Add.
15698.

Crimsham, in Pagham, co. Suss. Grant
at Crymesham, 680 (sic). Cott. MS.
Aug. ii. 86.

Cringleford, co. Norf. Conf. of the
church to St. Giles's Hospital, Norwich,
1251 (Cringelford). Add. 19278.

—— Grant in, to Horsham St. Faith
Priory, t. Hen. III. (Cringelford). Add.
14610.

—— Acquittance from Norwich
Priory for tithes in, 1525 (Cryngyl-
ford). Add. 14793.

—— Sales, etc., in, 1526-1552. Add.
14611-14620, 14622, 15720 ; — 1573.
Add. 14624 ;—1574. Add. 14623 ;—
1575. Add. 6299, 14625 ;—1577. Add.
14626 ;—1583. Add. 14627-14630.

—— Discharge of J. Pykarell from
the constableship of, 1604. Add.
17260.

Cringplegate. v. sub Worcester, co.
Worc.

Crisehage, in Aspall (?), co. Suff. Grant
in, late 12 cent. Harl. 50 H. 19.

Cristelton. v. Christleton, co. Chester.

Cristeshale. v. Chrishall, co. Essex.

Cristionyth Vechan, nr. Holt, co.
Denb. Admission to lands in, 1456.
Add. 8641.

Critchurch, nr. Carew, co. Pembr.
Grant of the manor, etc., 1441. Harl.
80 A. 15.

Crockenhulle. v. sub Newton St. Loe,
co. Som.

Crockerton, North, co. Wilts. Lease
in, 1467 (N. Crokerton). Add. 23839.

Crockwell, nr. Bicester, co. Oxon.
Grants in, to Bicester Abbey, c. 1200.
Add. 10598 (Crocwelle) ;—t. John.
Add. 10594 (Crockewelle) ;—c. 1245.
Add. 10610 (Croowell).

Crofeld, Croffeld, Croffild. v. Crowfield, co. Suff.

Croft, co. Heref. Bond for a lease of
the manor, 1547. Cott. xxiv. 48.

—— Exchequer acquittance for the
farm of the manor, 1595. Add. 25601.

P

Croft (Craft), co. Leic. Grants, etc., in,
to Sulby Abbey, 12–13 cent. Add.
21198 ;—t. Hen. III. Harl. 45 G. 27,
Add. 21690-21693.

—— Capellanus. Johannes, 12–13
cent. Add. 21198.

—— Persona. Willelmus, c. 1240–50.
Add. 21690, 21692.

Croft, nr. Burgh, co. Linc. Grant
of rents from the mill of, etc., to
Bullington Priory. c. 1150–60 (Croft).
Harl. 52 G. 18.

—— Grant of Cullecroft al. Culcroft
in or nr. (?), to the same, early 13 cent.
Harl. 55 G. 23 ;—1235. Harl. 44 I. 14.

—— Release, etc., in (?), early 13 cent.
Harl. 75 B. 43, 75 C. 27.

—— Capellanus. Osuerus, early 13
cent. Harl. 55 G. 23.

—— Clericus. Willelmus, early 13
cent. Harl. 52 B. 32 ;—t. Hen. III.
Harl. 45 H. 11.

Crofthole, in Sheviock, co. Cornw.
Lease, etc., in, 1461. Slo. xxxiii. 71
a, b, c ;—1602. Slo. xxxiii. 86.

Crofton. v. Croughton, co. Northt.

Crofton, co. Kent. Feoffment, etc., of
the manor, 1444. Harl. 78 G. 14 ;—
1480. Harl. 80 G. 15.

Crofton, in Aunsby (?), co. Linc. Grant
in, 1296 (Croktou). Harl. 83 A. 9.

Croftynhoke, nr. Cork, co. Cork.
Recovery in, 1563. Add. 8696.

Croghan, co. Roscommon. Grant in,
[1263 – 72] (Crohun in Cantredo de
Tirmany in Connacia). Harl. 45 D. 7.

Crogles. v. Crowle, co. Worc.

Croglin, co. Cumb. Lease in, 1572.
Harl. 77 H. 37.

Croherste. v. Crowhurst, co. Susx.

Crohum. v. Croom, co. York.

Crokemereale, nr. Wybunbury (?), co.
Chest. Grant in, t. Hen. III. Harl.
83 D. 19.

Crokesbi. v. Croxby, co. Linc.

Crokeston. v. Croxton, co. Linc.

Croketake. v. Crooked Oak, in Shotley, co. Northumb.

Crokham. v. Crookham, co. Berks.

Crokton. v. Crofton, in Aunsby (?), co.
Linc.

Crolton. v. Croughton, co. Northt.

Oromban, in. v. Croome d'Abitot, co.
Worc.

Crombury. v. sub Hadlow, co. Kent.

Cromer, co. Norf. Grant in, t. Hen.
III. or Edw. I. (Crowemere). Add.
14856.

—— Bequests to guilds, etc., in, 1523.
Add. 14203.

—— Brief for rebuilding the church,
1768. Ch. Br. B. viii. 6.

—— Vicarius. Symond Norman, 1445.
Add. 14525.

Cromford, co. Derb. Release, etc., in,
t. Hen. III. Woll viii. 16 (Crumford):
—1491. Woll. vii. 14 (Crumforth) :—
1595. Woll. xi. 90 ;—1613. Woll.
xi. 87.

Crondall, co. Southt. Power for seisin
in, 1447. Add. 17434.

—— Rector. Mag. Joh. Wykham,
1413, 1414. Add. 17596, 17597.

Cronkston, in Hartington, co. Derb.
Appointment of bailiffs for Merivale
Abbey in, 1543 (Crouxtone). Harl.
112 F. 27.

Crookdake, in Bromfield, co. Cumb.
Commutation of tithes in, 1639. Add.
17169, 17170.

Crooked Oak, in Shotley, co. Northumb.
Covenant to settle lands in, 1421
(Crnketake). Cott. xii. 41.

Crookham, nr. Newbury, co. Berks.
Grant of free warren "ad vulpem,
leporem et capreolum " in, 1228
(Croukham). Add. 24703.

—— Inspex. of charters conc. the
keepership of the park and warren of,
1475 (Crakham, Crokham). Harl. Roll
C. 11.

Crooks, in Ecclesall Bierlow, co. York.
Conf. of an entail in, 1536 (Crokes).
Harl. 112 G. 15.

Croom, co. York. Conf. of a grant in,
to Sulby Abbey, t. John (Crohum).
Add. 21697.

—— Fine in, 1527. Add. 17005.

Croome d'Abitot, co. Worc. Conf.
of grants in (?), to Pershore Abbey,
972 (in Cromban). Cott. MS. Aug.
ii. 6.

Cropil. v. Cropwell Bishop, co. Nott.

Cropsale, co. Buck. Lease in, 1529.
Add. 14040.

Crowle, *co. Worc.* Grant at,' 836 (Croglea). Cott. MS. Aug. ii. 9.

Crowlton. *v.* Croughton, *co. Northt.*

Crowmarsh (Craumareis). *co. Oxon.* Royal .conff. of the manor, etc., to Battle Abbey, [1082-7]. Cott, xvi. 28;—[1086-7]. Harl. 83 A. 12 (copy); —c. 1121. Campb. xvi. 13.

—— Rel. to the hospital at, 1220-1. Add. 19615.

Crownesthill. *v. sub* Ellington, *co. Hunt.*

Crows Hall. *v. sub* Debenham, *co. Suff.*

Crowstone, *in Halifax, co. York.* Marriage settlement of T. Ramsden in 1722. Add. 25920, 25921.

Crowthorne Hundred, *co. Glouc.* Grant of rent from, 1634 (Crothey). Add. 18391.

Crowthorpe, *in Barnwell St. Andrew's, co. Northt.* Release in, 1336 (Crouthorp). Add. 21534.

Croxall, *cos. Derb. and Staff.* Conveyance of the manor and advowson, 1581. Woll. xii. 139.

Croxby (Crokesbi), *co. Linc.* Grants. etc., in, to Newhouse Abbey, [1148-66]. Harl. 43 H. 16. 17;—[1156 or 7?]. Harl. 51 H. 1;—t. John. Harl. 44 G. 42;—c. 1270. Harl. 44 G. 54.

—— Covenant in, betw. Newhouse and Revesby Abbeys, 1154 (Croxebi). Harl. 44 I. 1.

Croxden, *co. Staff.* Assignment of lands in, 1607. Campb. xxvi. 25.

Croxebi. *v.* Croxby, *co. Linc.*

Croxehaga. *v. sub* Salcby, *co. Linc.*

Croxton, *co. Camb.* Covenant conc., and sale of, Westbury manor in, 1507. Harl. 55 H. 27;—1557. Harl. 45 D. 52.

—— Sales in, 1557. Harl. 45 D. 51, 53.

Croxton (Croxtun), *co. Linc.* Grants, etc., in, to Newhouse Abbey, [1148-66]. Harl. 43 H. 15, 16;—1238. Harl. 47 H. 17;—1240. Harl. 49 A. 27;— t. Hen. III. Harl. 47 H. 22, 49 A. 7, 23, 26, 28-32, 52 D. 11, 18;—1455. Harl. 55 E. 32.

—— Grant in, etc., from Newhouse Abbey, early 13 cent. Harl. 44 G. 28; —late 13 cent. Cott. xxvii. 169.

—— Grants in, t. Hen. III. Harl. 49 A. 35;—1433. Harl. 53 A. 4.

Croxton (Croxtun), *co. Linc.* (continued). *Capellanus.* Henricus, 1224. Harl. 49 A. 25.

—— *Clericus.* Galfridus, c. 1157-63. Cott. xxvii. 34.

—————— Gilbertus, t. Hen. II. Harl. 49 A. 30, 31.

—— *Persona. Sire* Edw. Fremund, early 14 cent. (Crokeston). Harl. 44 G. 37.

Croxton (Croxton, Cruxtun), *co. Norf.* Grants, etc., in, 1304. Add. 14631;— 1307. Add. 14632;—1316. Add. 14633;—1321. Add. 14634;—1329. Add. 15715 (Corxaton);—1330. Add. 14635;—1345. Add. 14636;—1404. Add. 15778.

—— Fine in, 1700. Add. 19104.

Croxton, South, *co. Leic.* Lease in, 1721. Add. 19050.

Croydon (Crandon), *co. Camb.* Conf. of grants in, to Sawtrey Abbey, late 13 cent. Harl. 83 B. 46.

—— Lease in, from Sawtrey Abbey, 1316. Harl. 83 A. 39.

Croydon, *co. Surr.* Grants in, from the Abp. of Canterbury, 1258. Add. 23435 (Croyndon); — 1261. Add. 23436, 23437 (Croydeue).

—— Grants, etc., in, and nr., late 13 cent. Add. 23439, 23440 (Croyndene); —1266. Add. 23614;—1294. Add. 23438 (Croyndon); — 1319. Add. 23442 (do.);—1323. Add. 23443 (Croindon);—1329. Add. 5941 (do.);—1346. Add. 23653;—1357. Add. 23444;— 1361. Add. 23445; — 1377. Add. 23440, 23446;—1379. Add. 6254;— 1383. Add. 23449; — 1398. Add. 23158;—1402. Add. 23165, 23166, 23449;—1410. Add. 23170;—1425. Add. 23450, 24616;— 1426. Add. 23451;—1427. Add. 24617;—1428. Add. 23452, 23453; — 1431. Add. 23176;—1435. Add. 23178;—1439. Add. 24618;—1444. Add. 24620;— 1447. Add. 23455-23457; — 1452. Add. 23458, 24571, 24624; — 1463. Add. 24576-24579; — 1466. Add. 23459;—1471. Add. 24615, 24625-24630;—1489. Add. 23461;—t. Hen. VII. Add. 23460 (copy); — 1503. Add. 23466;—1508. Add. 23463;— 1564. Add. 23470; — 1567. Add. 23473;—1585. Add. 23479;—1586. Add. 23480;—1589. Add. 23481;— 1592. Add. 23485-23487; — 1503. Add. 23488;—1597. Add. 23489;— 1599. Add. 23490; —1608-1627. Add.

Cyninton. *v.* Kington, *co. Heref.*

Cyrendene. *v.* Surrendea, *in Hullavington, co. Wilts.*

Cysel hyrst, *v.* Chislehurst, *co. Kent.*

Cysse stanes gemæro, Cystaninga mearo, *v.* Keston, *so. Kent.*

## D

Dachet, Dachetta. *v.* Datchet, *co. Buck.*

Dadelond, *nr. Checkley, co. Staff.* Grant in, 1340. Add. 4887.

Dadford. *v.* Dudford, *in Stowe, co. Buck.*

Dæcceuuyrthe. *v.* Datchworth, *co. Hertf.*

Dægeles forda. *v.* Daylesford, *co. Worc.*

Dagenham, *co. Essex.* Grant of, to Barking Abbey, 692–3 (Dæccanhaam). Cott. MS. Aug. ii. 29.

—— (Dakenham). Exchequer order to seize lands in, 1350. Cott. xiii. 5 (4).

—— Grants, etc., in, 1379. Add. 19972 :—1385. Add. 19973.

—— Precipe on a covenant in, 1578. Add. 24961.

—— Briefs for rebuilding the church, 1796, 1802. Ch. Br. B. xxxviii. 6, xlii. 16.

Dagworth, *co. Suff.* Grant, etc., in, 1479. Harl. 54 I. 22 ;—1647. Add. 10583.

—— Precipe on a covenant in, 1592. Add. 25439.

Dairsie, *co. Fife.* Church restored by the Papal Legate to St. Andrew's Priory, [1180] (Derveisin). Cott. xviii. 35.

—— *Persona.* Jocelinus, [1180]. Cott. xviii. 35.

Dalbury, *co. Derb.* Grant in (?), early 13 cent. (Dalebir.). Woll. x. 23.

—— Grant in (?), to Derby Priory, early 13 cent (Dalenburi). Woll. x. 24.

—— Assignment of lease in, 1612 (Dalbery). Woll. xii. 131.

Dalby, *co. Linc.* Feoffments of the manor, 1346. Harl. 54 E. 14 ;—1350. Harl. 54 E. 15 ;—1351. Harl. 56 G. 38.

Dalby, *co. Linc. (continued).* Clericus. Simon, early Hen. II. Harl. 45 B. 38, 39.

Dalby, Little, *co. Leic.* Grant, etc., of the church to Langley Priory, *t.* Hen. II. Cott. v. 62 (Dalbi) ;—1411. Add. 21201.

—— Attornment of the manor, 1411. Lansd. 641.

—— Exchequer acquittance to tenants in, 1418. Lansd. 642.

—— (?) *Capellanus.* Galfridus, [1241–64]. Cumpb. xv. 11 (Duleby).

Dalby on the Wolds, *co. Leic.* Grant in, 1491. Add. 7170.

Dalderby, *co. Linc.* Release in, 1472. Woll. i. 77.

Dale, *co. Derb.* Papal conf. of lands of, to Dale Abbey, 1224 (Depedale). Woll. x. 32.

Dalegate, [*in Hockerton?*], *co. Nott.* Grant in, to Rufford Abbey, early 13 cent. Harl. 83 F. 24.

Dalenburi. *v.* Dalbury, *co. Derb.*

Dalgerkirke. *v.* Algarkirk, *co. Linc.*

Dalham, *co. Suff.* Grant, etc., in, 1360. Harl. 48 C. 52 ;—1607. Add. 9275.

—— Grant of remainder of the manor and advowson, 1374. Harl. 47 B. 18.

Dalling, ——, *co. Norf.* Persona. Hugo, early Hen. III. (Dallinges). Add. 14704.

Dalling, Field, *co. Norf.* List of suitors to the Court of, 14 cent. Add. 19070 (1).

—— Court-rolls, 1377 - 1396. Add. 19070 ;—1422-1451. Add. 19076.

Dalling, Wood, *co. Norf.* Feoffment of Mounceux manor in, 1587. Add. 15721.

Dallinghoe, *co. Suff.* Grant in, *t.* Hen. III. (Dallingho). Harl. 45 I. 48.

—— Inspex. in 1454 of a feoffment of the manor, etc., 1422 (Dolaugho). Add. 17243.

—— *Clericus.* Stephanus, *t.* Hen. III. (Dalingho). Add. 5903.

Dallington, *co. Northt.* Conf. by King John of grant of the mill, 1208 ('Talinton). Add. 6014.

Dallington, *co. Suss.* Conf. of seisin of the Forest of, 1446, 1455. Add. 23801, 23802, 23803.

Dallington, co. *Suss.* (*continued*). Leases, etc., in, 1475. Add. 23800 ;—1480. Add. 23826 ;—1541. Add. 5675 ; —1601. Add. 914.

Dalmellington, co. *Ayr.* Conf. of a settlement in 1626 of the barony, etc., of, 1632. Add. 26691.

Dalton, *in Kirk Heaton*, co. *York.* Release in, *t.* Edw. I. Add. 20514.

Dalton, *wr. Rotherham*, co. York. Grants, etc., in, 1264. Add. 15659 ;—1366. Harl. 52 E. 15 ;—1402. Harl. 54 C. 14 ;—1727. Add. 18073 ;—1785. Add. 18086.

Dalton in Furness, co. *Lanc.* Papal conf. of the church to Furness Abbey, 1194. Harl. 83 A. 22.

—— Lease of three water-mills in, late bel. to Furness Abbey, 1590. Add. 19543.

Dalton, North, co. *York.* Grant in, to Beverley College, *t.* Edw. I. Lansd. 409.

—— Release in, to Watton Priory, 1322. Harl. 55 E. 23.

Dalton, South, co. *York.* Grant in Kipling Cotes (Killingcotes) in, to Beverley College, *t.* Hen. III. Lansd. 401.

Damerham, co. *Wilts.* Bequest at, to Glastonbury Abbey, late 10 cent. (æt Domar hamme). Harl. 43 C. 4.

—— Homage for land in, to Tewkesbury Abbey, 1430. Add. 7700.

Danbury, co. *Essex.* Sale, etc., in, 1555. Add. 5263 ;—1564. Harl. 79 G. 20.

—— Precipes on covenants in, 1587. Add. 24992 ;—1593. Add. 25042.

—— *Rector.* Gilbertus, 1309 (Danewober.). Harl. 50 G. 44.

Danby, N. R., co. *York.* Court-roll, 1440–41. Harl. Roll G. 23.

Danby Whisk, co. *York.* Settlement in marriage of the manor and advowson, late 13 cent. (Daneby super Wiske). Cott. xxviii. 5, Harl. 112 H. 41.

Dane. *v. sub* Elmstead, co. *Kent.*

Dane, La, Dane Court. *v. sub* Tilmanstone, co. *Kent.*

*cf.* Denncourt, co. *Kent.*

Danehelde, Le. *v. sub* Chartham, co. *Kent.*

Danhurst, co. *Surr.* Grant of life-interest in the manor, 1434. Add. 15726.

Danigawurde, co. *Suss.* Precipe for Battle Abbey to be free of service for, onto 1121. Harl. 43 C. 12.

Darenth, co. *Kent.* Grant at (?), 934 (æt Derantune). Cott. MS. Aug. ii. 65.

—— Grant in, 1345 (Darente). Harl. 45 C. 24.

—— Fine in, 1465. Slo. xxxii. 41.

Darenth, *River*, co. *Kent.* A boundary mark, 822 (Diorente). Cott. MS. Aug. ii. 93.

Darfield (Derfold), co. *York.* Fine for settlement of Woodhall manor in, with the advowson, 1302. Add. 17047 (2) (copy).

—— Release in Overwoodhall in, 1321. Harl. 112 G. 25.

—— Grant in Edderthorpe in, 1345. Add. 22610.

—— Covenant for settlement of Woodhall manor, etc., 1420. Add. 17046.

—— Marriage settlement of Rob. Drax, etc., in, 1435. Add. 17047 (3) ; —1460. Add. 17050.

—— Title to lands in, c. 1500. Add. 16988.

—— *Persona.* Hugo, 1212, c. 1212. Harl. 83 F. 15, 16.

—— —— *Dom.* Johannes, *t.* Hen. III. Harl. 83 E. 13.

—— —— *Dom.* Robertus, *t.* Hen. III.-Edw. I. Harl. 83 E. 13, Add. 8178.

—— *Rector Mediet. eccl.* Joh. Boswell, 1460. Add. 17050.

*v. also* Worsborough, co. *York.*

Dargavel, nr. *Dumfries*, co. *Dumfr.* Conf. of grant of, to Melrose Abbey, 1237 (Dergavel). Cott. xviii. 11.

Darlaston, co. *Staff.* Brief for rebuilding the church, 1807. Ch. Br. B. xlvii. 6.

Darleton, co. *Nott.* Precipe on a covenant in, 1578. Add. 25192.

Darley, co. *Derb.* Grants, etc., in, late 13 cent. Woll. i. 2 (Derl.) ;—1304. Woll. i. 1 (Derlegh) ;—1346. Woll. i. 3 (Derley) ;—1427. Woll. i. 4 (do.) ;—1599. Woll. xi. 41.

—— Sale of a moiety of the manor, 1547. Woll. xi. 40.

—— Fine in, 1604. Woll. xi. 44, 45 (Derley).

—— Release of Netherhall and Overhall, etc., manors in, 1654. Woll. xi. 82.

Debenham, *co. Suff.* (*continued*). *Vicarius.* Joh. Wynch, 1365. Add. 9639.

—— —— (*nuper*). Joh. Brasyere, 1433. Add. 10327.

Deccanhaam. *v.* Dagenham, *co. Essex.*

Decoot, Dechette. *v.* Datchet, *co. Buck.*

Dechyngham. *v.* Ditchingham, *co. Norf.*

Decies, *Barony of, co. Waterford.* Grant in, 1655. Add. 19264.

Dedanham. *v.* Denham, *co. Buck.*

Dedham, *co. Essex.* Grant of the manor, 1338. Harl. 43 D. 35.

—— Grant in, 1389. Cott. xxvii. 174.

Dedyngton, *co. Staff.* (?). Grant in, 1453. Harl. 111 G. 32.

Dee, *River, co Chest.* Grant of fishery in, *t.* Rich. I. (De). Harl. 52 A. 17.

Deene, *co. Northt.* Grant in, by Edw. the Confessor, to Westminster Abbey, 1066 [*sc.* 1065] (Den). Cott. vi. 2 (*copy*).

—— Grant in, "juxta crucem de Kyrkeby," *t.* Hen. III. (Den). Add. 5887.

—— (Deen, etc.). Grants, etc., in, 1348. Add. 710, 711, 720;—1378. Add. 852, 853;—1407. Add. 721:—1410. Add. 712:—1453. Add. 723; —1457. Add. 713; — 1467. Add. 7575;—1468. Add. 7578;—1472. Add. 813, 7579; — 1499. Add. 725 —1506. Add. 726;—1519. Add. 715, 716, 826, 828;—1520. Add. 825:—1533. Add. 727;—1555. Add. 7582; —1571. Add. 728.

—— Mortgage of the manor, 1477. Add. 815, 816.

—— Fine in, 1539. Add. 837, 838.

Deenethorpe (Deenthorp, etc.), *in Deene, co. Northt.* Grants, etc., of the manor, etc., 1410. Add. 712:—1453. Add. 825:—1457. Add. 713:—1467. Add. 7575;—1468. Add. 7578;—1472. Add. 813, 7579;—1476. Add. 814;—1477. Add. 815, 816;—1519. Add. 714, 715, 716.

—— Sales of timber in, 1523. Add. 830-833.

—— Fine in, 1539 (Dyngthorp). Add. 837, 838.

—— Leases in, 1545. Add. 717:—1560. Add. 741;—1563. Add. 827 (Dynthorp), 843 (do.).

Deepdale. *v. sub* Cayton, *co. York.*

Deeping Gate, *in Maxey, co. Northt.* Power to take seisin in, 1549. Add. 13561.

Deeping, Market, *co. Linc.* Power to take seisin in, 1549. Add. 13561.

Deeping St. James, *co. Linc.* Power to take seisin of the manor and rectory, 1549. Add. 13561.

Deerhurst, *co. Glouc.* Grant in, by Edw. the Confessor, to Westminster Abbey, 1066, [*sc.* 1065] (Deorhyrste). Cott. vi. 2 (*copy*).

Defford, *co. Worc.* Conf. of grants in, to Pershore Abbey, 972 (in Deopanforda). Cott. MS. Aug. ii. 6.

—— (?) Grant in, 1365. Cott. xxiv. 34.

Deghall. *v.* Diggle, *nr. Saddleworth, co. York.*

Deighton, *co. York. Persona.* Will. de Authorpe, 1402 (Dyghton). Harl. 112 A. 30.

Deighton, *co. York.* Grant of the manor by Rich. III., 1484 (Dighton). Harl. 83 C. 16.

Deingemareis. *v.* Dunge Marsh, *co. Kent.*

Delangho. *v.* Dallinghoe, *co. Suff.*

Delse, Great and Little. *v. sub* Rochester, *co. Kent.*

Delyngtone. *v.* Dillington, *co. Hunt.*

Dembleby, *co. Linc.* Release in, 1577. Add. 6480.

Demechirch. *v.* Dymchurch, *co. Kent.*

Dempford. *v.* Dumpford, *co. Suss.*

Den. *v.* Deene, *co. Northt.*

Denaby, *nr. Mexborough* (?), *co. York.* Power for seisin of Wetecroft and Tadecroft nr. (?), 1288 (Deneby). Harl. 83 F. 37.

Denardiston, *co. Suff.* Grants, etc., in, 1343. Harl. Roll Y. 5 (Denarston); —1539. Harl. 48 D. 33 (Denerdeston).

—— Fine in, 1393. Harl. 58 H. 9 (Denastone).

—— Releases of the manor, 1405. Harl. 78 D. 12 (Denarston), 80 H. 27 (Denherston).

Denbigh, *County of.* Grant by the Earl of Leicester of the stewardship of his manors in, 1566. Harl. 83 E. 26.

Denbigh, *co. Denb.* Garrison of the castle, 1369 (Dynbiegh). Harl. Roll E. 7.

**Denbigh**, *co. Denb.* (*continued*). Mortgage of Ystredeloc in, 1458. Add. 9256.

—— Exchequer acquittance for a fine for Ystrad mill nr., 1595. Add. 25741.

**Denby**, *co. Derb.* Grant in, " in parco de Bol," 1480. Woll. iv. 73.

—— Conveyance, etc., in, 1564. Woll. xii. 132 ;—1571. Woll. xii. 138.

**Denby** (Denebi, Deneby), *co. York.* Grants in or nr. Pilate Croft in, to Byland Abbey, *ante* 1186. Add. 7427, 7432 ;—end of 12 cent. Add. 7414, 7415.

—— Grants, etc., in or nr., to the same, end of 12 cent. Add. 7455 ;—[1192–5]. Add. 7416, 7448, 7450 ;—[1195–9]. Add. 7423, 7487, 7447 ;—*post* 1194. Add. 7477 (copy) ;—c. 1200. Add. 7480 ;—1203. Add. 7463 ;—c. 1203. Add. 7409, 7411, 7422, 7424, 7425 ;—[1205–9]. Add. 7410, 7417, 7441 ;—t. John. Add. 7418, 7433, 7435, 7439 ;—*post* 1211. Add. 7413 (copy), 7436, 7449 ;—c. 1220. Add. 7434 ; — early 13 cent.-t. Hen. III. Add. 7428, 7429, 7454, 7456, 7457 ;—[1232–40]. Add. 7465 (copy) ;—1259. Add. 7444 ;—late Hen. III. or late 13 cent. Add. 7421, 7443, 7458, 7464, 7467 ;—*ante* 1298. Add. 7438 ;—t. Edw. I.-II. Add. 7419, 7420, 7446, 7468–7474, 7478 ;—1383–1385. Add. 7460–7462, 7475, 7476, 7479.

—— Rent bond in, from Byland Abbey, t. John. Add. 7431.

—— Grant of villeins in, to Byland Abbey, early 13 cent. Add. 7459.

—— Settlement of disputes in, betw. W. de Denebi and Byland Abbey, 1220. Add. 7442.

—— Grant in Brudelay in, to Byland Abbey, 1269. Add. 7426.

**Denchworth**, *co. Berks.* Grant at, 956 (Deniceswyrð). Cott. MS. Aug. ii. 40.

—— Grants, etc., in Hyde. etc., in, 1301. Add. 6093 (Sutdencheswrthe) ;—1345. Add. 6095 (Southdenchesworthe) ;—1347. Lansd. 117 (Sethdenchesworthe) ;—1362. Harl. 58 D. 45 (Denchesworth) ; — 1420. Add. 6098 – 6100 (Suthdenchesworth) ;—1427. Harl. 49 C. 16 (South Dengesworth).

—— Settlement of Suchcote manor in, 1324 (Deynchesworth). Add. 6094.

—— Covenant conc. the manor and presentation to the living, 1350 (Denchesworth). Harl. 54 D. 28.

**Denchworth**, *co. Berks.* (*continued*). Release of the manor, 1367. Add. 6096 (Southdenchesworth) ; — 1399. Add. 6097 (do.).

—— Release of Hyde (La Hyde) manor in, 1399 (Northdenchesworthe). Add. 6097.

—— Fine in, 1655 (N. Denchworth). Cott. xxx. 36.

**Dencourt**. *v. Deancourt, co. Kent.*

**Dene**. *v. Dean, co. Glouc.*
*v. sub Elmstead, co. Kent.*

**Denebi, Deneby**. *v. Densby, co. York.*

—— *v. Deuby, co. York.*

**Deneham**. *v. Denham, co. Buck.*

**Denesdane**. *v. Dunsden, in Sonning, co. Oxon.*

**Deneshull Wood**, *co. Essex.* Sale of timber in, 1450. Harl. 45 G. 22.

**Dene tun**. *v. Denton, co. Kent.*

**Denford**, *co. Berks.* Bequest of land at, c. 950 (æt Den forda). Cott. viii. 16.

**Denford** (Deneford), *co. Northt.* Covenant conc. the upper and lower mills at, early 13 cent. Cott. xxviii. 74.

—— Release of lands in, to the church of H. Trinity of, 1219. Harl. 50 A. 41.

—— Grants, etc., in, early 13 cent.-t. Hen. III. Harl. 46 I. 33, 48 B. 24–26 ;—1358. Harl. 47 I. 27 ;—1365. Cott. xxviii. 105, 106 ;—1400. Add. 857 ;—1428. Harl. 47 I. 29.

—— Grant, etc., of the manor, 1371. Cott. xxiv. 8 ;—1397. Cott. xv. 13.

—— Precipe on a covenant conc. land in, 1593. Add. 25172.

—— *Persona*. Mag. T——, 1219. Harl. 50 A. 41.

—— —— P——, early Hen. III. Harl. 46 I. 33.

**Dengemersh**. *v. Dunge Marsh, co. Kent.*

**Dengesworth, South**. *v. Denchworth, co. Berks.*

**Dengewood**. *v. sub Chartham, co. Kent.*

**Dengey**, *co. Essex.* Rector. Nic. de Doncastr., 1354. Add. 6435.

**Denham**, *co. Buck.* Conf. by Edw. the Confessor of a grant in, to Westminster Abbey, 1066 [sc. 1065] (Daneham). Cott. vi. 2 (copy).

—— (Deneham, etc.). Grant of 30s. from the church of, for the High Altar

Denne Manor, co. Surr. (?). Lands of John Weston held of, by military service, 1484. Lansd. 677.

Dennesdene. v. Dunsden, in Sonning, co. Oxon.

Denny Strode Manor. v. sub Strood, co. Kent.

Dennington, co. Suff. Grants, etc., in, to Butley Priory, early 13 cent. Harl. 49 F. 13 (Dinnieuton), 14 (Dinnieuston), 15 (Dinieuetun), 57 F. 25 (Dinnieueton);—early Hen. III. Harl. 45 G. 64 (Dingneueton).

—— Grants, etc., in, 1323. Add. 9914 (Dynieton);—1425. Add. 15539 (Donyngton); —1470. Add. 15546 (do.);—1497. Add. 15551;—1591. Add. 7653;—1622. Add. 15563;—1642. Add. 15564.

—— Precipes on covenants in, 1593. Add. 25460 (Donyngton), 25463 (Dynnengton).

—— Fine in, 1649 (Dynnyngton). Add. 15566.

Dennome, Dennwme. v. Denholm, co. Roxb.

Dennstrue. v. sub Petham, co. Kent.

Denny, co. Glouc. Release of a rent in, 1274-5 (Dunye). Harl. 43 C. 44.

Denshanger, co. Northt. Grants, etc., in, t. Hen. III. Harl. 85 B. 10 (Dunshanger);—late 13 cent. Add. 17363 (Deneshanger);—1316-1332. Add. 17367-17371.

—— Clericus. Rogerus, early 13 cent. Harl. 83 B. 2.

Dent, co. York. Pledge to observe a settlement of the manor, 1348 (Dent in Lonesdale). Harl. 54 C. 12.

Denton, co. Kent. A boundary mark, 799 (Dene tun). Cott. MS. Aug. ii. 96.

—— Grants, etc., in, 1487. Harl. 46 E. 12;—1501. Harl. 54 C. 43;—1513. Harl. 58 F. 45;—1556. Add. 17822.

—— Fine in, 1548. Harl. 75 H. 4, . 76 H. 50.

—— Settlement by H. Oxenden of household stuff, etc., in, 1668. Add. 17828.

Denton, co. Norf. Grant, etc., in, 1439. Add. 14538;—1559. Add. 14544.

Denton, co. Suss. Fine in, 1389. Add. 24891.

—— Exchequer acquittance for farm of land in, 1595. Add. 25671.

Denton, co. York. Sale of the manor, 1637. Add. 1797.

Denys Powys. v. Dinas Powis, co. Glam.

Deopancumb, nr. Mangersbury, co. Glouc. A boundary, 949. Cott. viii. 6 (copy).

Deopanforda. v. Defford, co. Worc.

Deorham. v. Dyrham, co. Glouc.

Deorhyrste. v. Deerhurst, co. Glouc.

Deormodes ealdtune. v. Dormston, co. Worc.

Depden, co. Essex. Grant in. to Hatfield Peverel Priory, post 1227 (Depeden). Harl. 53 D. 1.

Depden, co. Suff. Fine in, 1893. Harl. 58 F. 9.

—— Court-rolls, 1629-57. Add. 26203.

Depedale. v. Burnham Deepdale, co. Norf.

—— v. Dale, co. Derb.

Depenale. v. Dippenhall, in Farnham, co. Surr.

Depers. v. sub Binfield, co. Berks.

Deptford, co. Kent. Contract for a dock at, 1517 (Depforde). Add. 6289.

—— Leases, etc., in, 1522. Harl. 58 H. 27 (Depford);—1655, 1662. Add. 17450-17453.

—— Sale of Cobham Marsh in Hatcham in, 1533. Add. 26105.

Deptford, in Wylye, co. Wilts. Grant in, 1362 (Depeford). Add. 24873.

Derantune, set. v. Darenth, co. Kent.

Derby, County of. "Totus comitatus" of, as witness, early Hen. II. (Derbeia). Woll. x. 1.

—— Inquest of knights' fees in Morleston and Litchurch Wapentakes, [1283-8?]. Woll xi. 1 (copy).

—— Feodary of the honour of Tutbury in, t. Edw. III. (?). Woll. xi. 1 (copy).

—— Payments by tenants of knights' fees in, 1445. Harl. Roll I. 10.

—— Grant of an annuity from land in, by Darley Abbey, 1536. Campb. xxix. 13.

—— Compotus of Sir T. Gresham's manors in, 1566-69. Add. 16336.

—— Lord Lieutenant. Will. Cavendish, Earl of Devonshire, 1626. Woll. xii. 100.

—— Nicholas Leke, Earl of Scarsdale, 1712. Woll. xi. 61.

—— Vicecomes. Ranu'fus, [1156-65]. Woll. x. 1.

Q

Devon, *County of* (*continued*). Accompts of manors, etc., in. [bel. to the Marquis of Exeter?], t. Hen. VIII. Add. 13907.

—— Writ against J. Latch and others in, 1623. Harl. 43 G. 8.

—— Petitions to the Exchequer conc. collection of Hearth-money in, c. 1667. Harl. 83 H. 47;—1674. Harl. 112 C. 48.

—— *Vicecomes.* Ric. fil. Baldwini, [1114–6?]. Cott. xvii. 7 (2);—[1123?]. Cott. vii. 2;—[1136–7?]. Cott. xvi. 34.

—— —— Joh. Cole, 1406. Harl. 46 G. 48.

—— —— Joh. Nanfan, 1458. Add. 6144.

Devon stream, *co. Nott.* Assignment of fishery in, nr. Newark, 1680. Harl. 111 H. 11.

Devynock, *co. Brecon.* Grant of the rectory to the see of Gloucester, 1541. Cott. xiii. 34.

Dewchurch, *co. Heref.* Conf. of grant of Scudemore, etc., in, to Acornbury Priory, 1275 (Deweschirche). Harl. 54 H. 53.

Dewchurch, Little, *co. Heref.* Leases, etc., in, 1583. Add. 1858;—1601. Add. 1882;—1622. Add. 1359;—1635. Add. 1937.

Dewchurch, Much, *co. Heref.* Grant of the manor and rectory to the see of Gloucester, 1541. Cott. xiii. 34.

Dewsall, *co. Heref.* Grant in, 1625 (Dewshall). Add. 1924.

Dewsbury, *co. York.* Fine in, 1671. Add. 12681.

—— Marriage settlement in, 1722. Add. 25020, 25921.

—— Brief for rebuilding the church, 1766. Ch. Br. B. vi. 3.

—— *Vicarius.* Dom. Joh. Gates, 1381. Add. 15660.

Dexthorpe, *co. Linc.* Grants in, t. Hen. III. Harl. 51 C. 33 (Drexthorpp); —1355. Harl. 57 G. 11 (Drexthorp).

Dichingham. *v.* Ditchingham, *co. Norf.*

Dickering [Wapentake], *co. York. Ballivus de Dikeringge.* Galfr. de Gedingges, [1216–22]. Harl. 55 F. 13.

Dickleburgh, *co. Norf.* Grant at Normedew in Semere in, t. Hen. III. Harl. 56 A. 45.

—— Grants, etc., in, t. Hen. III. Harl. 48 H. 9 (Dicleburch);—1373.

Harl. 47 G. 4 (Doslebugh) Add. 18827 (Dekylboroughe) Add. 15556 (Dиskilboroughe).

Diotuns. *v.* Ditton, Fenny, c

Didoot, *co. Berks.* Fine of th and advowson, 1334 (Dodcot Roll G. 17.

Didcot, *in Beckford, co. Glouc.* by Tewkesbury Abbey of t to Beckford church, 1177 (D Add. 7013.

Diddington, *co. Hunt. Vicari* Chapman, 1496. Harl. 56 H.

Diddlebury, *co. Salop. Cu* Ricardus, t. Hen. III. (D Harl. 83 E. 4.

Didington, *co. Warw.* Lease lease in, by Merkyate Priory 98]. Cott. xi. 36 (Didindona Hen. III. Cott. xxi. 5 (do.).

—— Covenant with Kenilwor conc. pasturage of, in Pa Prior's manor, co. Warw., 129 tona). Cott. viii. 5.

Didling, *co. Suss.* Release manor, 1433 (Dydlyngge). Ad

—— Settlement in, 1605. Ad

Didmarton, *co. Glouc.* Conf. at, to Pershore Abbey, 972 ( meretune). Cott. MS. Aug. l

Digaðeswrð, Digðeswrth Diseworth, *co. Leic.*

Diggle, *nr. Saddleworth, co. Yo* of the manor, 1638 (Deghall xi. 29.

Diggalands. *v. sub* Nackin *Kent.*

Dighton. *v.* Deighton, *co. Yo*

Dilhorne, *co. Staff.* Beques in, to the poor of Caversw (Dillorne). Camph. xi. 29.

—— *Perpet. Vicarius.* Hen. 1371. Add. 26922.

Diling tun. Grant at, by K. of Mercia, 674 (?). Add. 197

Dillington, *co. Hunt.* Coven descent of the manor, 1372 tone). Add. 19979.

Dilworth, *co. Lanc.* Brief co at, 1825. Ch. Br. C. vi. 5.

Dilwyn, *co. Heref.* Grant (Dilwin). Add. 1953.

Dinardank, *in St. Ive* (?), *co* Grant in, 1316. Add. 25913.

Ditcham, *in Harting, co. Suss.* Grant of rent in the manor of, by Dureford Abbey, 1583. Harl. 111 C. 62.

Ditchampton, *co. Wilts.* Court-rolls, 1559. Add. 24440; — 1567. Add. 24441; — 1584. Add. 24718.

Ditcheat, *co. Som.* Grant of Alhampton and Northover manors in, 1365. Harl. 111 F. 51.

Ditchelling, *co. Suss.* Assignment of the manor to Edw. II., 1316 (Dychenyng). Harl. 57 E. 33.

—— Brief conc. a hail-storm at, 1764. Ch. Br. B. iv. 8.

Ditchingham (Dechyngham, etc.), *co. Norf.* Grants, etc., in, 1321. Add. 14639 (Dychingham); — 1370. Add. 14640 (Dychyngham); — 1400. Add. 14641; — 1401. Add. 14642; — 1425. Add. 14643 (Dychyngham); — 1426. Add. 14644 (dn.); — 1460. Add. 14646; — 1490. Add. 14647; — 1517. Add. 14648; — 1556. Add. 14649; — 1558. Add. 14650, 14651; — 1574. Add. 14652; — 1582. Add. 14567 (Dichingham); — 1608. Add. 14654; — 1610. Add. 14655, 14656; — 1623. Add. 14568, 14657; — 1631. Add. 14658; — 1632. Add. 14659; — 1651. Add. 14661.

—— Extracts from court-rolls, 1443. Add. 14645 (Dycyngham); — 1639. Add. 14660.

Ditton, *nr. Stoke Poges, co. Buck.* Grants in (?), to Southwark Priory, t. Hen. III. Harl. 56 F. 2, Add. 7621.

—— Release in, t. Hen. III. (Dittone). Harl. 56 G. 31.

—— *Capellanus. Dom.* Hugo Harlecombe, 1485. Add. 5218.

Ditton, Fenny, *co. Camb.* Bequest at, to Ely Abbey, late 10 cent. (æt Dictunæ). Harl. 43 C. 4.

Ditton, Long, *co. Surr.* Grant in Talworth (Talewrthe) in, *post* 1228. Add. 23666.

—— Brief for rebuilding the church, 1776. Ch. Br. B. xvi. 6.

—— Brief conc. a fire at, 1798. Ch. Br. B. xxxviii. 3.

—— *Rector.* Rob. Pocock, *clerk*, 1689. Add. 24147.

Ditton, Wood, *co. Camb.* Fine in, 1305 (Ditton Valoynes). Add. 15526.

—— Release, etc., in, 1335. Add. 15529 (Ditton Valeyns); — 1402. Add. 15586 (Dytton); — 1547. Add. 13560 (Dytton Valence).

Ditton, Wood, *co. Camb. (continued).* Lease of a windmill in, 1490 (Ditton Valence). Add. 6210.

—— Power to take seisin of the manor, 1500 (Dytton Valaunce). Add. 6211.

—— Precipe on a covenant conc. lands in Dytton and Dytton Valence, 1555. Add. 24920.

—— Award conc. lands in, held of Cheveley manor, co. Camb., 1582 (Ditton Valence). Add. 19259.

—— Fine of Wood Ditton and Ditton Valence manors, 1630. Add. 13700.

Docacar. *v. sub* Launceston, co. Corn.

Doccynoge. *v.* Docking, co. Norf.

Docettes Manor. *v. sub* Rochford, co. Essex.

Dockedic. *v.* Dogdyke, co. Linc.

Docking, *co. Norf.* Directions for sale of land at, 1038 (?) (æt Doccynoge). Cott. MS. Aug. ii. 85.

—— Delivery of dower in, 1390 (Dockyng). Harl. 57 E. 5.

—— *Perpet. Vicarius.* Ric. Rayner, 1427. Cott. xxix. 62.

Doddafordung gemære, Doddanforda. *v.* Dodford, co. Northt.

Doddenham, *co. Worc.* Defeasance of a grant nr. Sandeford in, 1400 (Dodesham). Harl. 49 D. 25.

Doddershall, *co. Buck.* Release in, 1329. Add. 14001.

Doddington, *co. Camb.* Grant of Suthwode, etc., in, to Reading Abbey, c. 1275 (?). Harl. 54 D. 15.

—— Assignment to uses of rent from Suwode manor in, by Reading Abbey, 1284. Add. 19633.

—— Sale of church lands in, 1561. Harl. 80 H. 61.

Doddington, *co. Kent.* Brief for rebuilding the church, 1788. Ch. Br. B. xxviii. 6.

Doddington, *co. Northumb.* Assignment of a mortgage of the manor, 1682. Add. 13731.

Doddington, Great, *co. Northt.* Release of rent charge on [Barnard's] manor in, 1309 (Magna Dodington). Add. 21701, 21702.

—— Release in, 1344 (Dodyngton). Add. 22537.

—— Sales of lands in Barnard's and Turvill's manors in, etc., 1646. Add.

Draiton. v. Drayton, co. Southt.

Dranfeld. v. Dronfeld, co. Derb.

Drannock, co. Corno. Grants of the manor, t. Edw. I. (Draynec). Harl. 46 I. 47;—1306 (Draynek). Harl. 46 I. 49.

Draughton (Drauton, Drauthon, etc.), in Rothwell Hundred, co. North. Grants in, in the fee of the King of Scotland, c. 1170 (?). Harl. 43 B. 6 (Drachton), 45 B. 37 (Drahtona).

—— Grants, etc., in, [1170–74]. Add. 21708 (Drahtun), 21732 (copy);—ante 1248. Add. 21707, 21726 (Drawton); —1250-1. Add. 21704;—t. Hen. III.- t. Edw. II. Add. 21705, 21706, 21708— 21725, 21749;—1292. Add. 21727, 21728;—1298. Add. 21729;—1312. Add. 21735;—1816. Add. 21736 (Draugthon), 21737;—1817. Add. 21739;—1322. Add. 21741;—1324. Add. 21743 (Draghton), 21744 (do.), 21745 (Draughton), 21746 (do.), 21747;—1325. Add. 21748 (Drauc- tone);—1328. Add. 21733;—1329. Add. 21751;—1331. Add. 21752;— 1334. Add. 21754, 21755;—1337. Add. 21758;—1340. Add. 21759 (Drhauton);—1341. Add. 21761;— 1342. Add. 21762;—1343. Add. 21763, 21764;—1344. Add. 21765 (Drawton);— 1348. Add. 21767;— 1349. Add. 21768;—1353. Add. 21769; —1354. Add. 21770 (Drawton);— 1361. Add. 21730 (Draugthon), 21773. (Draghton), 22185, 22186;— 1364. Add. 21774, 21775;—1366. Add. 21776, 21778:—1367. Add. 21780-21782, 21784, 22189, 22190;— 1368. Add. 21783, 21785, 21786;— 1371. Add. 21787;—1375. Add. 21788, 21789;—1378. Add. 21790;—1380. Add. 21792;—1384. Add. 21793;— 1386. Add. 22219;—1392. Add. 21795, 21796;—1393. Add. 21797, 21798;—1394. Add. 21799, 21800;— 1396. Add. 21803, 22409;—1397. Add. 21804;—1399. Add. 21806;— 1400. Add. 21806, 21807;—1401. Add. 21808;—1406. Add. 21813, 21814;—1408. Add. 21815;—1410. Add. 21817;—1414. Add. 21819, 21823;—1415. Add. 21820, 21821, 22410;—1417. Add. 21826, 21827;— 1418. Add. 21828, 21829, 22411, 22412;—1422. Add. 21830-21832;— 1426. Add. 21833, 21834;—1430. Add. 21836;—1437. Add. 22272;— 1462. Add. 22289;—1475. Add. 21841;—1483. Add. 21845;—1484.

Add. 21843;—1485. Add. 21 1487. Add. 22301;—1488. 21847;—1494. Add. 21848; Add. 21849;—1526. Add. 21 1540. Add. 21851.

—— Fines in, 1228. Add. (Dragton);—1340. Add. 21 1347. Add. 21766.

—— Grants, etc., of the manor Add. 21788;—1352. Add. 21 1357. Add. 21771, 21772; Add. 21777, 21779;—1367. 21781;—1366. Add. 21794; Add. 21801;—1402. Add. 21 1414. Add. 21809, 21822; Add. 22263, 22264;—1429. 21835;—1430. Add. 22270; Add. 22274;—1447. Add. 21 1464–5. Add. 22292;—1465. 21840;—1470. Add. 22295, 22 1473. Add. 21837;—1483. 21844;—1528. Add. 22307; Add. 22309;—1537. Add. 223

—— Sale of crops in, 1323, 21742.

—— Descent of land in, to H. 1334, 1342. Add. 21756.

—— Covenant conc. bounds in Add. 22168.

—— Acquittance to the Ea on a payment in, 1374. Add. 2

—— Acquittance from the She a fine in, 1378. Add. 21791.

—— Fine of the manor, 1394. 21802.

—— Precept for surrender in Mallore, [1400?]. Add. 21750.

—— Suit in, [1402?]. Add. 2

—— Order conc. lands in, as to Anne, Cha. of Stafford, 1402. 19654.

—— Warrant to arrest J. Burn illegal possession in, 1405. Add:

—— Lease, etc., of Hedon's me 1410. Add. 21816;—1414. 21824, 21825.

—— Acquittance for the fa 1412. Add. 21818.

—— Affidavit conc. a title in, l Add. 22265.

—— Petition of J. Seyton co lands in, c. 1429. Add. 21842.

—— Petition of Tho. Seyton fc tution of the manor, 1440–44. 21535.

—— Grant of a rent from the to Pipewell Abbey, 1458. Add.

Drighlington, co. York. Lease of the manor, 1444 (Dryghtlyngton). Add. 16936.

Drihil, Drihehil. v. sub Ailby, co. Linc.

Driholm, wr. Saxelby, co. Linc. Grant in, to Newhouse Abbey, t. Hen. II. Harl. 45 B. 27.

Dringhouses, wr. York. Exchequer acquittance for a fine on the manor, 1567. Add. 25707.

Drinkstone, co. Suff. Plea conc. property of Dame M. de Lovayn in, c. 1275. Add. 8415.

—— Grant of the manor, 1389 (Drinxstone). Add. 7906.

—— Sale, etc., in, 1532. Add. 10533 (Drenkston); — 1587. Add. 10536 (Drinckstone);—1670. Add. 10538; —1703. Add. 10541.

—— Extract of court-roll of Timperley's manor in, 1563. Add. 10535.

—— Persons. Joh. Spenser, 1393 (Drenkston). Harl. 48 F. 55.

Drogheda, co. Louth. The seal of the "prepositura" of, attached to a grant in Mellor, co. Lanc., t. Edw. I. Add. 20506.

—— Inspex. in 1442 of a conf. from Rich. II. to the Earl of March of a rent from the town and castle, 1394. Harl. 43 E. 28.

Droiscourt. v. sub Brockworth, co. Glouc.

Droitwich, co. Worc. Conf. to Pershore Abbey of salt-works at Middelwic, etc., in (?), 972. Cott. MS. Aug. ii. 6.

—— Re-grant in, by Will. I., to Westminster Abbey, 1067 (Wic). Cott. vi. 3 (copy).

—— Grant, etc., of a "novus puteus" in, to Bordesley Abbey, [1138 ?]. Add. 20419 (Wich), Harl. 45 I. 30 (do.).

—— Conf. by Hen. II. of grants in, to Bordesley Abbey, [1157 ?] (Wich). Cott. MS. Nero C. iii., f. 176.

—— Grants, etc., in, 1870. Add. 9239 (Wych);—1545. Add. 1823, 1824; —1547. Add. 1352;—1610. Harl. 83 H. 28;—1629-30. Add. 1926.

Dronfield, co. Derb. Grant in the fee of, 1349 (Dronefeld). Harl. 112 H. 4.

—— Reversion of lands in Hope to the guild of St. Mary at, 1394 (Dronfeld). Woll. iii. 13.

Dronfield, co. Derb. (continued). Extract from court-roll of, 1489. Harl. 111 C. 41.

—— Appointment of a steward of the manor, 1469 (Dranfeld). Add. 20594.

—— Dues for burials, etc., for the use of the church of, 15 cent. Woll. viii. 18a.

—— Fine in Birchett (Byrtchett), Summerly, etc., in, 1541 (Draunfelde). Woll. ii. 71.

—— Covenant as to uses in, 1577. Woll. xii. 97.

—— Brief for rebuilding the church, 1818. Ch. Br. B. lix. 5.

—— Capellanus. Will. Hudsone, 1401. Woll. viii. 46.

—— Chantry priest. Sir John Blakwall, 1507. Woll. i. 15.

v. also Holmesfield, co. Derb.
—— Unston, co. Derb.

Drumcross, co. Linlithgow. Grant of the lands of, to J. Melville, by Queen Mary, 1565. Cott. xviii. 20.

Drumshallon, co. Louth. Exemplif. of license for alienation of, 1572. (Drumsalen). Add. 7041.

Drumtarsi. v. Killowen, co. Londonderry.

Drusselan. v. Dryslwyn, co. Carmar.

Drypool, co. York. Releases of the manor, 1430 (Drypole). Harl. 43 E. 19;—1431 (do.). Harl. 45 I. 12.

—— Brief for re-building the church, 1822. Ch. Br. C. iii. 4.

Dryslwyn, co. Carmar. Garrison of the castle, 1369 (Drusselan). Harl. Roll E. 7.

Dubbridge, Dubbrugge. v. Doveridge, co. Derb.

Dublin, co. Dubl. Rolls of Pleas held at, 1290. Add. 13598;—1330. Add. 13599;—14-15 cent. Add. 13600.

—— Grant in Scarletis Lane in, by the Corporation, 1297. Add. 26516.

—— Appointment of officers in the Mint in the Castle, 1550. Harl. 57 H. 4.

—— Leases in Cooke Street, 1628, 1634. Add. 7048, 7049.

Ducemanetun, Duchemanetun. v. Duckmanton, co. Derb.

Duckington, co. Chest. Grant in, early Hen. III. (Dukinton). Add. 21176.

Dunham, co. Norf. Delivery of dower in, 1390. Harl. 57 E. 5.

—— Clericus. Willelmus, [1174–80]. Toph. 15.

Dunham, co. Nott. Restoration of, by King John to Reg. de Danmartin, 1212 (Duneham). Add. 11239.

—— Grants, etc., in, t. Hen. III.—t. Edw. I. Add. 5380–5383; — 1331. Add. 5394; — 1340. Add. 5396; — 1342. Add. 5398; —1347. Add. 5403; —1350. Add. 5404; — 1352. Add. 5405; —'1357. Add. 5406; — 1360. Add. 5407; —1362. Add. 5408; —1364. Add. 5411; —1365. Add. 5412; —1369. Add. 5413; —c. 1370. Add. 5415; —1372. Add. 5401, 5402; —1378. Add. 5416; — 1412. Add. 15740; — 1427. Add. 5422.

—— Rob. le Taillour, "quond. mag. scolarum grammaticalium de," 1352. Add. 5405.

—— Bequest for the fabric and bells of the church, 1451. Add. 5426.

—— Brief for rebuilding the church, 1796. Ch. Br. B. xxxvi. 6.

—— v. also Whimpton, in Dunham, co. Nott.

Dunholme (Dunham), co. Linc. Conff. of grants in, to Kirkstead Abbey, c. 1150–60. Harl. 43 H. 20; —1187. Harl. 47 I. 9.

Dunhurst, nr. Petworth, co. Suss. Conf. of le More in Petworth to be held of the manor of, 1434. Campb. xxiii. 12.

Dunintona. v. Donington, Castle, co. Leic.

Dunitun. v. Donington, co. Linc.

Dunkyrke. v. Dunchurch, co. Warw.

Dunmeer, nr. Bodmin, co. Cornw. Award in suit in, 1434 (Dynmur). Harl. 57 A. 35.

Dunmore, co. Galway. Conveyance in, 1688. Add. 13601.

Dunmow, Great, co. Essex. Fine in (?), 1227 (Dunmawe). Harl. 50 B. 27.

—— Conf. of a grant, etc., in, 1273 (Magna Donmawe). Harl. 48 G. 4; — t. Edw. I. (Dunmawe). Lansd. 95.

—— Court-rolls of Marks manor in, 1377 - 1399. Add. 26817 - 26820; — 1559 - 1586. Add. 26821 - 26824; — 1614–1659. Add. 26825.

Dunmow, Great, co. Essex (continued). Release of warranty in, by Dunmow Priory, 1392 (Mag. Dunmowe). Cott. xxii. 9.

—— Fine in, 1425 (Mag. Dunmowe). Add. 6263.

—— Precipes on covenants conc. lands in, 1578 (Mag. Dunmowe). Add. 24952; — 1593 (do.). Add. 25031, 25037, 25038.

—— Fine of the manor, 1638 (Dunmowe). Woll. xi. 29.

—— Vicarius. Joh. Spicer, 1389. Add. 7906.

Dunmow, Little, co. Essex. Grant of oblations of the chapel of Walt. f. Roberti at (?), to Dunmow Priory, late t. Hen. II. (Dunmawe). Cott. xvi. 39.

—— Conf. of grant in (?), to the Priory, 1221 (Dunmawe). Cott. xxi. 15.

—— Court of the manor for adjudging the "Bacon of Dunmow," 1701. Lansd. Roll 25.

Dunnechete. v. Donyatt, co. Som.

Dunnino lande. v. Donyland, co. Essex.

Dunning, in Stratherne, co. Perth. Conf. of a grant of the meadow land of, 1381, 1382 (Donyne). Campb. xxx. 14, 19.

Dunnington, in Beeford, co. York. Exemplif. of fine in, 1687. Add. 800.

Dunningworth, co. Suff. Compotus of the manor, 1303–4 (Donigworth). Harl. Roll E. 1.

—— Extent of fees in, bel. to the Earls Marshal, c. 1400. Add. 19338.

Dunnintune. v. Donington, co. Salop.

Dunre. v. Dinedor (?), co. Heref.

Dunsby (Dunnesby, etc.), co. Linc. Grants, etc., in, t. Hen. III. Harl. 55 D. 34 (Dunesbi); —1378. Add. 20702; —1382. Add. 20703, 20887, 20888; — 1384. Add. 20889, 20890; — 1388. Add. 20704; — 1393. Add. 20705, 20706; —1421. Add. 21127; —1500. Add. 21129.

—— Fine in, 1350 (Dunesby). Harl. 58 G. 34.

Dunscore, in Nithsdale, co. Dumfries. Grant in, to Melrose Abbey, 1229 (Dunscor). Cott. xviii. 2.

—— Grant of the Loch, etc., to the same, 1236 (Lacus de Dunschor). Cott. xviii. 8.

R 2

Dymchurch, *co. Kent (continued).*
Grant in, 1347 (Demecherch). Add.
20177, 20178.

—— Writ for an assize of Nov. Diss. in,
1486 (Demechirch). Harl. 53 F. 12.

—— Lease of a marsh in, 1534 (Dym-
chirche). Harl. 50 C. 56.

—— Court of the King held at, 1622.
Harl. 75 D. 50.

Dymock, *co. Glouc.* Grant nr. Ketford
Bridge in, *t.* Hen. III. Add: 24752.

—— Lease of a mill in Ketford in,
1354 (Dymok). Add. 24762.

Dymuill, *nr. Holt, co. Denb.* Admission to lands in, 1456. Add. 8641.

Dynam, Dynham. *v.* Dinham, *co.
Cornw.*

Dynbiegh. *v.* Denbigh, *co. Denb.*

Dynelek, *co. Meath.* Release in the
manor, 1364. Add. 5828.

Dynes *al.* Deanes Manor. *v. sub*
Maplestead, *co. Essex.*

Dynevor, *co. Carmar.* Garrison of the
castle, 1369 (Dynnevor). Harl. Roll
E. 7.

Dyngthorp. *v.* Deenethorpe, *co. Northt.*

Dynham, Buckland. *v.* Buckland
Denham, *co. Som.*

Dynieton. *v.* Dennington, *co. Suff.*

Dynington. *v.* Dinnington, *co. York.*

Dynmur. *v.* Dunmeer, *co. Cornw.*

Dynnesdene. *v.* Dunsdon, *in Sonning,
co. Oxon.*

Dynneale. *v.* Dinsley, Temple, *co.
Hertf.*

Dynnevor. *v.* Dynevor, *co. Carmar.*

Dynnyngton. *v.* Dennington, *co. Suff.*

Dyrham, *co. Glouc.* Conf. of grants
at, to Pershore Abbey, 972 (Deorham).
Cott. MS. Aug. ii. 6.

—— Grants, etc., in, [1246-9]. Add.
7680 (Derham);—late 13 cent. Add.
7681 (Durham);—1303. Add. 7683
(Derham);—1304. Add. 7017, 7684,
7685;—1308. Add. 7709 (Durham);
—1344. Add. 7686;—1365. Add.
7687 (Durham), 7688 (do.); — 1385.
Add. 7690 (Derem);— 1435. Add.
7693, 7694;—1468. Add. 7695 (Durham);—1486. Add. 7696.

—— Extract from court-roll, 1545.
Add. 7697.

—— *Rector. Dom.* Rob. Burnell, 1468.
Add. 7695.

Dysse. *v.* Diss, *co. Norf.*

Dythisworth. *v.* Diseworth, *co. Leic.*

# E

Eabbincg wylle. Grant near, 854.
Cott. MS. Aug. ii. 46.

Eadbrihtincgtun. *v.* Abberton, *co.
Worc.*

Eadburgge byrig, *co. Wilts or Berks.*
Bequest of land at, *c.* 995. Cott.
viii. 38.

Eadelmeton. *v.* Edmonton, *co. Midd.*

Eadmunddes cote, *co. Worc.* (?).
Lease at, 1042. Add. 19799.

Eadulmest. *v.* Edlaston, *co. Derb.*

Eakring, *co. Nott.* Papal conf. of
grant of, to Rufford Abbey, 1156
(Eikeringe). Harl. 111 A. 2.

—— Grants, etc., in, to Rufford
Abbey, *t.* Hen. II. Harl. 112 H. 17
(Eicringe);—late 12 cent. Harl. 83 F.
17 (Eycring), 84 A. 24 (heykering),
27 (Eichring);—1236. Harl. 84 A.
29 (Eykringe);—early 13 cent.-*t.* Hen.
III. Harl. 84 A. 28 (Eykeryng), 30
(Eykering), 31 (Eycring), 112 G. 8,
112 H. 18-21, 23, 112 I. 7;—1259.
Harl. 112 F. 38 (Ekering);—early 14
cent. Cott. xxix. 1.

—— Grants, etc., in, late 12 cent.
Cott. xxvi. 18 (Eigring), Harl. 84 A.
25 (Aikering), 26 (do.), 112 H. 7 (do.);
—*t.* John. Harl. 112 G. 40 (Aikring);
—*t.* Hen. III.-Edw. I. Cott. xxvii.
175 (Aykring), 188 (do.), xxviii. 43
(Eykring), Harl. 112 G. 30 (do.), 112
H. 22 (do.);—1298. Harl. 112 I. 56
(Eykering);—1317. Harl. 112 I. 58
(Eykring);—1323. Harl. 112 G. 55,
56;—1327. Harl. 112 H. 11;—1336.
Harl. 112 H. 14;—1340. Cott. xxviii.
53;—1341. Harl. 112 G. 13;—1344.
Harl. 112 I. 61 (Aykering);—1347.
Harl. 112 I. 45;—1415. Harl. 112
F. 52.

—— Reservations of service for lands
in, of ½lb. of incense to St. Andrew's
church. *t.* John. Harl. 112 G. 40;—
*t.* Hen. III. Harl. 112 H. 22.

—— Papal conf. of a covenant in,
betw. the rector and Rufford Abbey,
1229 (Aikering). Harl. 111 A. 9.

—— Grants, etc., in, from Rufford
Abbey, *t.* Hen. III.-Edw. I. Harl.
112 F. 35, 39 (Eykering);—1330.
Harl. 112 F. 42 (Hekeringe);—1345-
1391. Cott. xxi. 30-39.

**Edale,** *in Castleton, co. Derb.* Release of a foresterahip in, 1428 (Eydale). Woll. iii. 12.

———— Briefs for rebuilding the chapel, 1794, 1809. Ch. Br. B. xxxv. 5, xlix. 7.

**Edburton,** *co. Suss.* Grants, etc., in, 1317 (Edburgheton). Add. 24651, 24657;—1434 (Edburghton). Add. 24658;—1673. Add. 19014;—*t.* Chas. II. Add. 8989.

**Edderthorpe,** *in Darfield, co. York.* Grant in, 1365 (Ederikthorpe). Add. 22610.

———— *Clericus.* Willelmus, *t.* Hen. III. (Edriport). Harl. 112 G. 58.

**Eddeston.** *v.* Edstone, Great (?), *co. York.*

**Eddinghall:** *v.* Edingale, *co. Staff.*

**Eddinglay.** *v.* Headingley, *co. York.*

**Eddisbury Hundred,** *co. Chest.* Appointment of collectors of a subsidy in, by Edw. Pr. of Wales, with assessments, 1475. Add. 26786.

**Eddlesborough,** *co. Buck.* Sales, etc., in Northall in, 1560. Add. 23972;— 1606. Add. 23975;—1613–1624. Add. 24005–24017;—1637. Add. 24022;— 1641. Add. 24023;— 1642. Add. 24024, 24025;—1668. Add. 24040– 24043.

———— Mortgages, etc., of Butler's manor in. 1610. Add. 23976–23978; —1613. Add. 24000, 24001;—1625.

Edricheshull, *in the New Forest, co.
Southt.* Grant in, by Hen. III., to
Breamore Priory, 1247. Add. 15696.

Edricheston, Edrichiston. *v.* Edstone, *co. Warw.*

Edrichey. *v. sub* Wirksworth, *co. Derb.*

Edriport. *v.* Edderthorpe, *in Darfield,
co. York.*

Edrom, *co. Berwick.* Lease of, by
Coldingham Priory, 1536 (Edram).
Eg. 366.

Edstone, *in Bearley, co. Warw.* Conf.
of a pension from the church of, to
Tewkesbury Abbey, [1193-5] (Edricheston). Add. 6708.

—— Conf. and release in, to Bordesley
Abbey, late Hen. III. (Edrichiston).
Add. 21428.

—— *Persona.* Johannes, *t.* Edw. I.
(Edrychstone). Add. 9215.

Edstone, Great (?), *co. York.* License
to distrain on lands of Hexham Priory
in, 1421 (Eddeston). Harl. 75 G. 6.

Edvin Loach, *co. Worc.* Grant
near (?), "in villa de Piro," *t.* Edw. I.
(Yedefenne Loges). Add. 8151. ¶

Edwalton, *co. Nott.* Covenant for a
settlement of the manor, 1437. Add.
20542.

Edwardestowe. *v.* Stowe on the
Wolds, *co. Glouc.*

Edwardstone (Edwardeston, etc.), *co.
Suff.* Grants, etc., in, *t.* Hen. III.
Harl. 49 G. 27;—1294. Harl. 53 D.
38;—1304. Harl. 49 F. 26 (Edwardys-
toun), 51 C. 57, 51 D. 1;—1305. Harl.
54 H. 14 (Edwardestoun);—1311.
Harl. 54 A. 5 (Edwardistone);—1353.
Harl. 45 E. 34;—1398. Add. 10571;
—1558. Add. 50 D. 29, 58 H. 33
(copy).

—— Precipe on a covenant in, 1592.
Add. 25429.

Edwinstowe, *co. Nott. Persona.*
Willelmus, *t.* Hen. III. (Edenestowe).
Harl. 112 F. 33.

Edworth, *co. Bedf.* Release of the
manor, 1355. Harl. 57 D. 1.

Edyndouyn. *v.* Edentown, *in Strath-
miglo, co. Fife.*

Edyngle. *v.* Edingley, *co. Nott.*

Edynsowre. *v.* Edensor, *co. Derb.*

Edythe Stoke. *v.* Stoke Edith, *co.
Heref.*

Eferdune. *v.* Everdon, *co. Northt.*

Effeton. *v. sub* Romney, Old, *co. Kent.*

Effingham (Effyngham, etc.), *co. Surr.*
Grant of the manor by R., Earl of
Gloucester, *a.* 1250-60 (Effingeham).
Add. 20039.

—— Suit conc. lands in, 1307. Add.
20036.

—— Grants, etc., in, 1322. Add.
5588, 5589;—1338. Add. 7607
(Effyngeham);—1385. Add. 5607;—
1388. Add. 5608;—1397. Add. 5610;
—1401. Add. 5611, 5613;—1445.
Add. 5619.

—— *Perpet. Vicarius. Dom. Johannes,*
1385, 1388. Add. 5607, 5608.

—— *Vicarius.* Joh. Tottesford, 1394.
Add. 5609.

Egefeld. *v.* Edgefield, *co. Norf.*

Egeleskeynwir. *v.* Llangeinor, *co.
Glam.*

Egemondon. *v.* Edgmond, *co. Salop.*

Egenton. *v.* Egginton, *co. Derb.*

Egerton, *co. Kent.* Grant in, 1495.
Add. 9739.

—— Crown grant of Field Farm
(Fylther) manor in, 1551. Harl. 75
H. 6.

Egesfeld. *v.* Edgefield, *co. Norf.*

Egeswere. *v.* Edgeware, *co. Midd.*

Egford (Eggeford), *in Frome, co. Som.*
Feoffment, etc., in 1470. Campb. i.
5;—1488. Harl. 80 G. 51.

Egg Buckland. *v.* Buckland, Egg,
*co. Devon.*

Eggdean, *co. Suss.* Sale in, 1539.
Eg. 282.

Egge Meere. *v.* Egmere, *co. Norf.*

Eggefeld, Eggesfeld. *v.* Edgefield,
*co. Norf.*

Egginton, *co. Derb.* Grant of power
of distraint in, *t.* Hen. III. (Egenton,
Woll. ix. 24.

—— Grant of Lappynghalugh in, 1337
(Egynton). Harl. 112 C. 40.

—— Grants in, 1404. Woll. x. 18
(do.);—1447. Woll. vi. 35 (do.).

—— Descent of the manor, 1511
(Eggyngton). Woll. xi. 21.

—— Commission of enquiry and order
conc. lands in (?), 1592. Woll. xii.
114;—1593. Woll. xii. 101 (Ekington
al. Eggington).

—— *Capellanus.* Robertus, *t.* Edw. II.
(Egintone). Woll. ix. 31.

**Ellingstring**, *co. York.* Grant in, 1369 (Ellyngstring). Add. 20555.

**Ellington**, *co. Hunt.* Release of Krowenesthill, etc., in, to Ramsey Abbey, [1216–30]. Add. 5949.

**Ellington**, *co. Northumb.* Covenant by Alnwick Abbey conc. purchases of lands in, 1269. Harl. 44 A. 4.

—— Grants, etc., in, late Hen. III.-*t.* Edw. I. Harl. 52 C. 15, Cott. xii. 10 (Ellinton);—1355. Harl. 48 I. 20 (Ellyngton);—1381. Harl. 57 G. 14 (Elyngton).

—— Grants, etc., of the manor, 1272. Harl. 57 C. 32 (Elington);—*c.* 1300. Harl. 57 C. 38 (do.);—1573. Add. 24166;—1575. Add. 24167.

—— Appointment of C. Elmer as steward of the manor, 1574. Harl. 111 B. 57.

—— Sale of the stewardship of, 1576. Cott. xxv. 18.

—— *Ballivus.* Will. Echewyk, late Hen. III. Harl. 52 C. 15.

**Ellington, High and Low,** *co. York.* Grant in, 1369 (Over, Nether Elington). Add. 20555.

**Ellinthorpe**, *co. York.* Release in, 1523 (Ellyngthorpe). Harl. 112 F. 53.

**Ellishays.** *v. sub* Combe Rawleigh, *co. Devon.*

**Ellough**, *co. Suff.* Grant in, early 14 cent. (Elech). Harl. 48 G. 13.

—— (?) *Rector de Helw.* Robertus, 1356. Harl. 83 C. 51.

**Elm**, *co. Som.* Feoffment, etc., in, 1470. Campb. i. 5.

—— *Rector.* Will. Harewode, 1431. Add. 5689.

**Elmdon** (Elmedon), *co. Essex.* Settlement of a manor in, etc., *c.* 1280. Harl. 51 C. 16, 17;—1298. Harl. 55 A. 52.

—— Title to the manor, 1417. Harl. 53 E. 1.

—— Precipe on a covenant conc. Pygotts manor in, 1555. Add. 24926.

**Elmdon**, *co. Warw.* Feoffment of the manor and advowson, 1375. Cott. xxx. 22.

—— *Dominus.* Ric. de Whitacre, 1375. Cott. xxx. 22.

—— *Persona.* Steph. de Overtone, 1375. Cott. xxx. 22.

**Elme.** *v.* Elham, *co. Kent.*

**Elmergate,** *in Middleton, co. Suss.* Grant of rent in, 1608. Add. 18906.

**Elmes Manor.** *v. sub* Ash, *nr. Sandwich, co. Kent.*

**Elmesall.** *v.* Elmsall, N. and S., *in S. Kirkby, co. York.*

**Elmesett.** *v.* Elmsett, *co. Suff.*

**Elmestede.** *v.* Elmstead, *co. Essex.*

—— *v.* Elmstead, *co. Kent.*

**Elmeston.** *v.* Elmstone, *co. Kent.*

**Elmham**, *co. Norf.* Bequest for the support of the priests at, 1038 (?) (Ælmham). Cott. MS. Aug. ii. 85.

**Elmham, North,** *co. Norf.* Conf. of the church, etc., to Norwich Priory, [1136–45] (Elmham). Cott. ii. 1, ii. 21 (9).

**Elmham, South,** *co. Suff.* Gift of the manor to the see of Norwich, [1103–6?] (Elmham). Cott. MS. Aug. ii. 103 (copy), Cott. ii. 21 (1).

—— Grant " coram soca Elmhamic," early 13 cent. Campb. i. 12.

—— Grant of rent in, to Flixton Priory, *t.* Edw. I. (Suthelmham). Campb. xii. 19.

—— Grant of a "nativa" in, 1329 (Suthelmham). Campb. xii. 7.

—— Compotus of the manor, 1398–99 (Southelmham). Harl. Roll L. 29.

**Elmham, S., All Saints** (?), *co. Suff.* Grant of rents in, 1337 (Suthelmham). Campb. i. 25.

**Elmham, S., St. Cross,** *co. Suff.* Grants, etc., in, early 13 cent. Campb. i. 12;—*t.* Hen. III. Campb. i. 14, 21–23 (Sancroft);—1301. Campb. i. 26 (Sandcroft).

—— (?) Release in, to Flixton Priory, *t.* Edw. I. Campb. vi. 7.

—— Settlement, by will, of the manor, 1437 (Sancroft). Campb. xii. 14 a.

—— Bequest for repairs of the church, 1437 (Sancroft). Campb. xii. 14 b.

—— Precipes on covenants in, 1564. Add. 25319 (Sancroft Southelmham), 25320 (Sandecrofte).

**Elmham, S., St. James,** *co. Suff.* Precipe on a covenant in, 1588. Add. 25385.

**Elmham, S., St. Michael,** *co. Suff.* Release in, to Flixton Priory, *t.* Edw. I. (Helmham, in parochia S. Micael.). Campb. vi. 6.

77 H. 5, 6;—1595. Harl. 77 B. 27, 77 H. 47;—1598. Harl. 77 B. 34, 77 C. 7, 79 F. 40;—1599. Harl. 77 C. 12, 57, 77 H. 48;—1601. Harl. 75 H. 19; —1602. Harl. 77 C. 32, 33, 77 D. 2, 3, 5, 78 D. 43;—1603. Harl. 77 C. 27, 77 H. 49, 79 F. 12.

—— Evidence and award conc. the manor, etc., c. 1574. Harl. Roll I. 22.

—— Certif. of leases of the manor in 1505 and 1538, by St. Swithin's Priory, Winchester, 1589-99. Harl. 111 C. 22.

—— Exemplif. of depositions conc. tenure of the manor, 1596. Harl. 111 H. 7.

—— Covenant conc. tithes from Chisenbury farm in, to the rectory, 1602. Harl. 78 D. 42.

—— Extr. of court-rolls, 1603. Harl. Roll X. 2.

—— Exchequer acquittance for homage for a mill in, 1610. Harl. 78 C. 34.

—— Lease in Littlecott in, 1629. Add. 15138.

—— Sale of fee-farm rents from the rectory, 1650. Add. 15168.

—— Vicar. John Powell, c. 1574. Harl. Roll I. 22;—1574. Harl. 78 B. 39.

Engeherst, Engherst. v. sub Marden, co. Kent.

Engelbi super Leuene. v. Ingleby, co. York.

Engelby, Engleby. v. Ingleby, co. Linc.

Engelcros, in E. Lound, in Isle of Axholme, co. Linc. Grants at, to Sulby Abbey, early 13 cent. Add. 20573, 20574.

Englefield (Englefeld), co. Berks. Grant of a hide of land in, late Hen. II. (Englefeldia). Add. 7200.

—— Grant of Middleham meadow in, late 12 cent. Add. 7201.

—— Grants, etc., in, t. John–t. Hen. III. Add. 7206, 18202, 19138-19140, 20250, 20269, 20596;—1335. Add. 20256;—1396. Add. 9243;—1536. Add. 19186;—1676. Add. 19230; —1728. Add. 19249.

—— Sale nr. Wick (Wyca) in (?), early Hen. III. Add. 19141.

—— Institution to the church of, 1232 (Engelfeld). Add. 20252.

Englefield (Englefeld), co. Berks. (continued). Release of the manor, by W. de Valence, 1277 (Englefeud). Add. 20253.

—— Grant of the manor, church and chapel, to R., Bp. of Coventry, 1277. Add. 20254.

—— Persona. Rad. de Englefeld, Clericus, 1232. Add. 20252.

Englisshes. v. sub Haveringland, co. Norf.

Enham, co. Southt. Grant of the manor, 1280. Add. 7735.

Enketon, nr. Killingholme, co. Linc. Covenant with Newhouse Abbey conc. right of way to, 1279. Harl. 44 H. 1.

Enmore, co. Som. Grant in Dorburghescombe nr., 1399 (Enemer). Cott. xxiii. 31.

Ennerdale, co. Cumb. Compotus-roll of the manor, 1514, 1515. Add. 24451.

Ensfield. v. sub Penshurst, co. Kent.

Ensham (Eynesham, etc.), co. Oxon. Court-rolls, etc., 1296. Harl. Roll E. 23;—1307-1316. Harl. Rolls E. 17-22;—1337-38. Harl. Roll E. 24;—1386-89. Harl. Roll E. 30;—1417-21. Harl. Roll F. 8;—1458-60. Harl. Roll F. 18;—1461. Harl. Roll F. 31;—1465. Harl. Roll F. 32;—1476. Harl. Roll F. 23;—1476-77. Harl. Roll G. 1;—1478-79. Harl. Rolls G. 3-5.

—— Compotus-rolls, 1337-38. Harl. Roll E. 27;—1357-58. Harl. Rolls E. 25, 26;—1376-77. Harl. Roll E. 28;—1384-85. Harl. Roll E. 29;—1389-90. Harl. Roll E. 31;—1392-94. Harl. Rolls E. 33, F. 1;—1400-1407. Harl. Rolls F. 3-6;—1414-15. Harl. Rolls F. 2, 7;—1418-19. Harl. Roll F. 10;—1426-27. Harl. Roll F. 11;—1437-38. Harl. Roll F. 12; —1440-42. Harl. Rolls F. 13, 14;—1442-43. Harl. Roll F. 24;—1445-46. Harl. Roll F. 15;—1453. Harl. Roll F. 16;—1456-57. Harl. Roll F. 17;—1460-61. Harl. Roll G. 6;—[1471-72 ?]. Harl. Rolls G. 10, 11;—1474-75. Harl. Roll G. 2;—1493-94. Harl. Roll G. 8;—15 cent. Harl. Rolls F. 22, 25;—1517-18. Harl. Roll G. 12;—1522-23. Harl. Roll G. 13.

—— Rentals of the manor, 1389. Harl. Roll E. 32;—t. Hen. VI. Harl. Roll F. 19;—1467. Harl. Roll F. 33.

—— Woodward's compotus, 1447-48. Harl. Roll G. 7.

Ensham (Eynesham, etc.), co. Oxon. (continued). Rolls of Portmote courts, 1453–54. Harl. Roll F. 21; — 1475–77. Harl. Roll F. 35.

—— Staller's and others' compotus, late 15 cent. Harl. Rolls F. 29, 30.

—— Fines paid at Portmote courts, 1518. Harl. Roll G. 9.

Enston, co. Oxon. Grant of the manor and advowson, 1540. Add. 17354.

—— Assignment of a lease of the "Rock or Grott" at, 1669. Harl. 111 E. 14.

Eofordunenga Gemære. v. Everdon, co. North.

Eosterege. v. Eastry, co. Kent.

Eowere. v. Ure, River, co. York.

Eowniglade. v. Evenlode, co. Worc.

Epperstone, co. Nott. Fine of the manor, 1319 (Eprestone). Harl. 53 H. 31.

Epping, co. Essex. Power to take seisin of Madles manor in, 1447. Harl. 45 G. 62.

—— Covenant on sale of Madalles manor in, etc., 1508 (Ippyng). Harl. 55 H. 28.

—— Rules conc. the deer in the Forest, t. Hen. VIII. Roy. Roll 14 B. xxxvi.

—— Recovery, etc., in, 1560. Harl. 77 F. 27;—1561. Harl. 75 E. 34, 36, 75 H. 8, 10, 79 F. 13, 80 C. 35, 36.

—— Sale of timber in Wintry Park in, 1565. Harl. 80 F. 24.

—— Assignment of mortgage of the manor, 1682. Add. 13731.

Eppynt Mountains, co. Brecon. Grant on, to Dore Abbey, ante 1205 (?) (Epint). Harl. 48 C. 26.

Epse. v. Apse, in Walton on Thames, co. Surr.

Epsom, co. Surr. Grants, etc., in Horton in, 1404. Slo. xxxii. 29 (Epsum);—1496. Harl. 111 E. 34 (Ebbesham);—1538. Harl. 112 B. 36.

—— Release of rent in, 1499–1500 (Ebsham). Harl. 84 B. 44.

—— Sales of timber in, 1560, 1561. Add. 23504, 23505 (Ebesham);—1574. Add. 23703 (Epposham).

—— Fine in, 1615. Add. 23718, 23719.

Epworth, in Isle of Axholme, co. Linc. Grant in, to Sulby Abbey, t. Hen. III. (Epewrthe). Add. 20730.

—— Admission to lands in Belton in the manor of, 1666. Harl. 111 C. 57.

—— Clericus. Radulfus, ante 1222. Add. 20615.

—— Persona. Will. fil. Sim. Wake, 1369. Add. 21256.

Equinton. v. Bakington, co. Derb.

Erbury. v. sub Stoke by Clare, co. Suff.

Ercall, Child's, co. Salop. Briefs for rebuilding the church, 1802, 1806, 1811. Ch. Br. B. xlii. 5, xlvi. 7, li. 10.

Ercall, High, co. Salop. Grant, etc., of Moortown (Mora) and in Osbaston (Obernestun, Osbernestun) in, early t. Steph. Harl. 54 G. 46;—late 12 cent. Harl. 55 B. 4.

—— Inspex. of a conf. in Osbaston (Hosbertonia) in, by Hen. II. [in 1181] to Wombridge Priory, 1319. Cott. iv. 36 (3).

Erceham. v. Hitcham, co. Norf.

Ercheafunt. v. Urchfont, co. Wilts.

Erdburghe. v. Burrough on the Hill, co. Leic.

Erdealaia, Erdesleie, etc. v. Ardsley, co. York.

Erdintona. v. Ardington, co. Berks.

Erdintune. v. Eardington, nr. Bridgwater, co. Salop.

Erdisdon. v. Earsdon, in Bothal, co. Northumb.

Erdislay, etc. v. Ardsley, co. York.

Erdley. v. Yardley, co. Hertf.

Eremua. v. Yarmouth, Isle of Wight.

Eresby, co. Linc. Fines, etc., of the manor, 1302. Harl. 45 H. 18;—1387. Harl. 53 C. 38;—1388. Harl. 58 B. 10.

Ereswell. v. Eriswell, co. Suff.

Erewash, River. Covenant by Darley Abbey conc. the pool of Chilwell mill, co. Nott., on, etc., 1314 (Irewys). Woll. v. 22.

Erghum. v. Arkholme, co. Lanc.

Eriswell, co. Suff. Grants in, early Hen. III. Add. 5913 (Ereswell);— 1301. Add. 5494.

**Eruemouthe.** *v.* Yarmouth, *I. of Wight.*

**Erwarton,** *co. Suff. Persona.* Rob. de Sheltone, 1331. Add. 14775 (Euirwartone).

—— Will. Newman *al.* Neweman, 1848. Add. 9610 (Euerwarton), 9611, 9613;—*(as nuper persona)* 1371. Add. 9645 (Euerwardton).

**Esbornhamme.** *v.* Ashburnham, *co. Suss.*

**Escheholt, Esscholt.** *v.* Esholt, *co. York.*

**Esclenggeabi.** *v.* Slingsby, *co. York.*

**Esclud Vwych y Clauth,** *in Bromfield Hundred, co. Denb.* Lease in, 1554. Add. 8652.

**Esclusham,** *co. Denb.* Sale in, 1554. Add. 8655.

**Eseborne.** *v.* Easebourne, *co. Suss.*

**Esedentone.** *v. sub* Binsted, *co. Southt.*

**Eselbergh, Eselborwe, Eselburght,** etc. *v.* Ellesborough, *co. Buck.*

**Esfeld.** *v.* Ashfield, Gr at, *co. Suff.*

**Esfordebi.** *v.* Ashfordby, *co. Leic.*

**Esgarton.** *v.* Garston, East, *co. Berks.*

**Esh,** *in Lanchester, co. Durh.* Grant in, late 12 cent. (Es). Add. 26729.

**Esham,** *nr. Weybread, co. Suff.* Grant in, to Butley Priory, 1240 (Hesham). Harl. 51 E. 40.

—— Grants, etc., in, 1379. Add. 19318;—1408. Harl. 54 I. 7;—1425. Add. 19330;—1430. Harl. 43 E. 19, 54 I. 10;—1431. Harl. 50 H. 27, 28, 54 I. 15;—1435. Add. 2016.

—— Lease in, from Wingfield College, 1536. Add. 19364.

**Esher (Essere),** *co. Surr.* Grant and conf. in, to Waverley Abbey, late 13 cent. Add. 5533;—1281. Add. 5534, 5535.

**Eshetisford.** *v.* Ashford, *co. Kent.*

**Esholt,** *in Yeadon, co. York.* Grants, etc., in, to Esholt Priory, etc., 1321. Add. 17066 (Nunescholt);—1324. Add. 16734 (Esscholt);—c. 1325. Add. 17108 (do.);—1327. Add. 16706 (Eeseholt);—1340. Add. 17076 (Esehould);—1348. Add. |17080, (Eeseholt);—1349. Add. 17081 '—1353. Add. 15647 (Escheholt);—1357.

Add. 17082 (Esholt), 17083 (do.); —1358. Add. 15656 (Eeshald);— 1361. Add. 15657 (Essholt);—1367. Add. 17098 (Esseholt). 17099 (do.);— 1368. Add. 17090 (Essholt), 17091 (do.);—1372. Add. 15776 (Eeseholt), 17100 (Esseholt), 17101;—1374. Add. 17102 (Essholt).

—— Livery of seisin of the manor, 1347 (Escholt). Add. 15654.

**Eshurst, Den of,** *nr. Staplehurst (?), co. Kent.* Grant on, to Combwell Priory, 1257. Harl. 78 A. 19.

**Esilbergh.** *v.* Ellesborough, *co. Buck.*

**Esingtone, Esintone.** *v.* Easington, *co. Suf.*

**Esintona.** *v.* Easington, *co. York.*

**Eske,** *in Beverley, co. York.* Release in, 1419. Lansd. 438.

**Eskhilby.** *v.* Asby, [Gt.?], *co. Westm.*

**Eskholm,** *in Brampton in Cantley, co. York.* Grants, etc., of and nr., to Newhouse Abbey, *t.* Hen. III. Harl. 46 D. 21;—1257. Harl. 43 A. 66 *a, b, c*;—c. 1260. Harl. 47 A. 39.

**Eslenggesbi.** *v.* Slingsby, *co. York.*

**Eslyng.** *v.* Eastling, *co. Kent.*

**Esneberia.** *v.* Eynesbury, *co. Hunt.*

**Esole al. St. Alban's Court Manor.** *v. sub* Nonington, *co. Kent.*

**Essch, Esse, Esshe.** *v.* Ash, *nr. Sandwich, co. Kent.*

**Esscholt, Esshald,** etc. *v.* Esholt, *co. York.*

**Esse.** *v.* Ash Priors, *co. Som.*

**Essebi, Essebia, Esseby.** *v.* Ashby.

**Essebroc.** *v.* Eastbrook, *nr. Sutton Coldfield, co. Warw.*

**Esseby, Davyd.** *v.* Ashby, Castle, *co. Northt.*

**Esseford.** *v.* Ashford, Upper (?), *co. Salop.*

**Essele.** *v.* Ashley, *co. Northt.*

**Esseley.** *v. sub* Chesham, *co. Buck.*

**Essen.** *v.* Ashton, *in Cleley Hundred, co. Northt.*

**Essendon.** *v.* Ashdon, *co. Essex.*

**Essendon (Essenden),** *co. Hertf.* Grant, etc., in, 1351. Add. 1988;— 1368. Add. 5291.

Estcote. *v.* Eastcote, co. *Northt.*

Estderham. *v.* Dereham, East, co. *Norf.*

Estebrok, *Hameletius de. v. sub* Hemel Hempstead, co. *Hertf.*

Esteluele. *v.* Ella Kirk, co. *York.*

Estenseton, Estestone. *v.* Easton Neston, co. *Northt.*

Estfeld. [*in Polstead ?*], co. *Suff.* Grant in, *t.* Hen. III. Harl. 50 G. 2.

Estgeyng. *v.* Ginge, East, *in West Hendred*, co. *Berks.*

Esthacche, Esthache. *v. sub* Tisbury, co. *Wilts.*

Esthall. *v.* Asthall, co. *Oxon.*

—— *v. sub* Paglesham, co. *Essex.*

—— *v. sub* Walcott, co. *Norf.*

Esthallingeleye, Esthallingeleies, Esthalluncgeleia, etc. *v.* Asthall Leigh, co. *Oxon.*

Estham. *v.* Merstham, co. *Surr.*

Esthamme. *v.* Ham, East, co. *Dors.*

—— *v.* Ham, East, co. *Essex.*

Estharpetre, Esthertre. *v.* Harptree, East, co. *Som.*

Esthathelsay, Esthauselsay. *v.* Haddlesey, East, co. *York.*

Esthattele. *v.* Hatley, East, co. *Camb.*

Esthrop, Esthroppe. *v.* Eastrop, *in Highworth*, co. *Wilts.*

Estington. *v.* Eastington, co. *Glouc.*

Estirkel, Estkele. *v.* Keal, East, co. *Linc.*

Estlavent, Estlovent. *v.* Lavant, East, co. *Suss.*

Estlech. *v.* Leach Martin, East, co. *Glouc.*

—— *v.* Leach Turville, East, co. *Glouc.*

Estleek. *v.* Leake, East, co. *Nott.*

Estlund. *v.* Lound, East, *in Hasey*, co. *Linc.*

Estmanton, [*in Sparsholt ?*], co. *Berks.* Lease in, 1585. Add. 13654.

Estmerdon. *v.* Marden, East, co. *Suss.*

Estnestone. *v.* Easton Neston, co. *Northt.*

Eston. *v.* Ashdon, co. *Essex.*

—— *v.* Aston, cos. *Hertf.,* etc.

—— *v.* Easton, cos. *Northt.,* etc.

Eston Gossebek. *v.* Gosbeck, co. *Suff.*

Estone, nr. *Oddham* (?), co. *Southt.* Grant "super Aleberwe" in, *t.* Edw. I. Add. 26618.

Estrahanent. *v.* Annandale, co. *Dumfries.*

Estrasen, Estrasne. *v.* Rasen, East, co. *Linc.*

Estre. *v.* Eastry, co. *Kent.*

Estrelawe, *Commote of,* [Usterley, co. *Carm?*]. Grant of reversion of, 1443. Harl. 51 H. 10.

Estrumenistre. *v.* Sturminster Marshall, co. *Dors.*

Estruston. *v.* Ruston, East, co. *Norf.*

Est Sutton. *v.* Sutton, East, co. *Kent.*

Estthorn. *v.* Thorne St. Margaret, co. *Som.*

Esttuderle. *v.* Tytherley, East, co. *Southt.*

Estudeham. *v.* Tuddenham, East, co. *Norf.*

Esturminstre Mareschal. *v.* Sturminster Marshall, co. *Dors.*

Estwaltham. *v.* Waltham, Cold, co. *Suss.*

Estwaltone. *v.* Walton, East, co. *Norf.*

Estwelle. *v.* Eastwell, co. *Kent.*

Estwhaite. *v.* Eastwood, co. *Nott.*

Estwik. *v.* Eastwick, co. *Hertf.*

Estwode. *v.* Astwood, co. *Buck.*

—— *v.* Eastwood, co. *Essex.*

—— *v. sub* Harptree, E., co. *Som.*

Estwordelham. *v.* Worldham, East, co. *Southt.*

Estwyghtryng. *v.* Wittering, East, co. *Suss.*

Estwyk. *v.* Astwick, co. *Bedf.*

—— *v. sub* Bookham, Great, co. *Surr.*

Estwyt. *v.* Eastwood, co. *Nott.*

Eswell. *v. sub* Wappenham, co. *Northt.*

Etchden. *v. sub* Bethersden, co. *Kent.*

Etchells. *v. sub* Northenden, co. *Chest.*

Etchingham, co. *Suss.* Grants, etc., in, *t.* Hen. III. Harl. 80 I. 34 (Echingeham);—1358. Add. 9233 (Echyngeham);—1548. Harl. 75 E. 23 (Echyngham), 85 H. 35, 36, 86 G. 59;—1562. Harl. 77 A. 6, 34.

**Evershaw** (Eversawe, etc.), co. *Buck.* (*continued*). *Vicarius.* Radulfus, *t.* Hen. III. Harl. 85 D. 22.

**Eversley**, co. *Southt.* Conf. by Will. I. of a grant in (?), to Westminster Abbey, 1067 (Thunreslea in Suthamtuneiscire). Cott. vi. 3 (*copy*).

—— Precipe on a covenant in, 1578. Add. 25222.

—— *Rector.* Nic. de Haweman, 1313 (Eversle). Add. 6713.

**Everton**, co. *Bedf.* Grants, etc., in, to Sawtrey Abbey, 12–13 cent. Harl. 83 B. 13;—*t.* John. Harl. 83 A. 48; —*t.* Hen. III. Harl. 83 B. 11.

—— Grants in, from St. Neot's Priory, [1218–23]. Harl. 83 A. 36;—[1226–35]. Harl. 83 A. 35.

—— Acquittance for a fine on account of the manor, 1355 (Everdone in com. Hunt.). Cott. xxvii. 152.

—— Compotus on sale of the reversion to the manor, 1391. Harl. 48 E. 53.

—— Covenant conc. an exchange of the manor, 1403. Harl. 47 B. 15.

—— Court-rolls, 1418–19. Harl. Roll E. 16.

—— Release of the manor, 1424. Harl. 48 F. 25.

—— Compotus of the manor, 1438–39. Harl. Roll K. 24.

—— Grant of annuity from the manor, 1570. Add. 6136.

—— *Capellanus.* Nicholaus, [1218–23]. Harl. 83 A. 36.

—— *Clericus.* Robertus, c. 1220–30. Harl. 83 A. 35, 36.

—— *Sacerdos.* Robertus, [1146–54]. Harl. 83 B. 4–6.

**Everton**, co. *Nott.* Grant in, 1304. Slo. xxxi. 11 (1) (*copy*).

**Evesbatch**, co. *Heref. Rector.* Joh. Copyn, 1365. Cott. xxiv. 34.

**Evington** (Avintona), co. *Leic.* Release of the church by Biddlesdon Abbey, to St. Mary de Pré Abbey, Leicester, c. 1150. Harl. 84 D. 12.

—— Grant, etc., in, c. 1160. Harl. 55 D. 8, Lansd. 691.

**Ewecote**, *in Bilsdale* (?), co. *York.* Grant of the manor, 1650 (Yewcott). Add. 1800.

**Ewegham.** *v.* Egham, co. *Surr.*

**Ewell**, nr. *Faversham*, co. *Kent.* Recovery, etc., of a share of, 1515. Add. 953;—1548. Harl. 76 A. 18;—1566. Harl. 76 I. 2.

**Ewell**, co. *Surr.* Conf. by Edw. the Confessor of a grant in, to Westminster Abbey, 1066 [sc. 1065] (Esunella). Cott. vi. 2 (*copy*).

—— "Totum Capitulum de Ewelle" as witness to charter of Southwark Priory, in Banstead, co. Surr., 1202. Campb. xvi. 2.

—— Grant in, by Merton Priory, 1311 (Ewelle). Harl. 111 D. 58.

—— Grant at Kingswood (Kyngeswode) in, 1327. Add. 9028.

—— Grants, etc., in, 1424. Add. 23174;—1482. Add. 18770;—1497. Harl. 112 E. 14;—1499–1500. Harl. 84 B. 44;—*t.* Eliz. Harl. 112 D. 10;—1597. Harl. 111 B. 58;—1615. Add. 23718, 23719.

**Ewelme**, co. *Oxon.* The Duke of Orleans a prisoner at, 1433. Add. 402.

—— Grant in, to the Earl and Cos. of Suffolk, 1440. Harl. 45 A. 26.

—— *Persona.* Will. de Mercah, 1323. Add. 9915.

**Ewerby**, co. *Linc.* Release in, 1280 (Ywarby). Harl. 52 I. 6, 7.

—— *Persona.* Joh. de Haburgh, 1376 (Iwardby). Harl. 57 D. 7, 8.

**Ewes, Le.** *v. sub* Cusworth, co. *York.*

**Ewhurst**, co. *Surr.* Grant in La Slefherst in, *t.* Hen. III. Add. 5564.

—— Grant nr. La Hoke in, *t.* Hen. III. Add. 7601.

—— Grants, etc., in, 1295. Add. 5572 (Ywhurst);—1298. Add. 5578 (do.);— c. 1300. Add. 5938 (Iwhurst);—*t.* Edw. I.–II. Add. 5565, 17281 (Ihurst), 18579 (Yuhurst);—*t.* Edw. II. Add. 5566 (Newhurst), 5567 (Iwhurst);— 1321. Add. 5587 (Ywhurst);—1325. Add. 17297 (do.);—1330. Add. 5592 (do.);—1339. Add. 5597, 5599;— 1340. Add. 5600;—1342. Add. 17306 (Ihurst);—1371. Add. 5605;—1427. Add. 5617;—1489. Harl. 45 E. 40 (Ewerst);—1596. Harl. 79 F. 38 a, b; —1609. Harl. 75 H. 41, 79 A. 16.

—— Precipe on a covenant in, 1592. Add. 25518.

—— Brief for rebuilding the church, 1770. Ch. Br. B. x. 7.

—— *Persona (quondam).* Robertus, *t.* Hen. III. Add. 18574.

**Ewhurst**, co. *Suss.* Grant of Badilande in, *t.* Hen. III. Eg. 388.

**Exton**, *co. Rutl.* License to St. Andrew's Priory, Northampton, to cultivate land in, [1124–36] (Extona). Cott. xviii. 41.

**Exton**, *co. Som.* Grants, etc., in N. and S. Quarum (Quarme, etc.) in, *t.* Edw. I. Add. 25896;—1305. Add. 25895;—1354. Add. 25897;—1355. Add. 25898;—1428. Add. 25899;—1470. Add. 25900.

**Exton**, *co. Southt.* Conf. of the church to St. Cross Hosp., Winchester, 1189. Harl. 43 C. 28.

**Exwick**, *nr. Exeter, co. Devon.* Release in, 1436. Add. 19256.

**Eyam** (Eyum, Eyom, etc.), *co. Derb.* Grants in, conditional on a lamp being kept burning at St. Helen's altar in the church of, *t.* Hen. III. Woll. vii. 37 (Eium), 38 (Aihum), 44 (Eyum).

—— Grants, etc., in, Riley, Eyam Cliff, etc., in, late 13 cent. Woll. vi. 39;—14 cent. Woll. ii. 76;—1329. Woll. viii. 6, 7;—1338. Woll. vii. 45;—1351. Woll. vii. 42;—1354. Woll. vii. 61;—1365. Woll. vii. 53;—1369. Woll. vii. 41, 43;—1400. Woll. vii. 46;—1403. Woll. vii. 58;—1405. Woll. vii. 52;—1409. Woll. i. 91, vii. 59;—1410. Woll. vii. 65;—1421. Woll. vii. 62, 63, 64;—1432. Woll. vii. 57;—1436. Woll. vii. 66 (Eyham); —1438. Woll. vii. 67;—1442. Woll. vii. 68;—1445. Woll. vii. 56, 69, 70; —1465. Woll. vii. 55, 60;—1490. Woll. vii. 48;—1520. Woll. vii. 49;—1570. Woll. vii. 50;—1576. Woll. xii. 46 (Eame);—1594. Woll. xii. 85; —1610. Woll. xii. 87;—1619. Woll. xii. 93;—1629. Woll. vii. 51;—1704. Add. 18065;—1710. Woll. xii. 68 (Eayme);—1716. Woll. xii. 89* (do.).

—— Grants, etc., in Bretton in, 1636. Woll. xii. 88;—1653. Woll. xii. 92.

—— *Dominus.* Roger de Morteyn, 1300. Woll. vii. 40.

—— *Rector.* Joh. Pope, 1410. Harl. 112 H. 1.

—— *Curate.* John Nedham, 1567. Woll. xii. 51.

—— *Parson.* Rob. Talbott, 1629. Woll. vii. 51.

*v. also* Foolow, *in Eyam, co. Derb.*

**Eycring.** *v.* Eakring, *co. Nott.*

**Eydale.** *v.* Edale, *in Castleton, co. Derb.*

**Eydon** (Eindona, etc.), *co. North. Sale,* etc., in, *t.* John (?). Harl. 84 I. 26, 33.

—— Exchange in, "citra Whetstones supra rubeum fontem," etc., *t.* John (?). Harl. 85 D. 11.

—— Release of the mill in, early 13 cent. (Heindon). Harl. 86 B. 6.

—— *Persona.* Philippus, late 12-early 13 cent. Cott. xxvii. 189, Add. 22320, Harl. 84 I. 26, 85 D. 11.

—— *Sacerdos.* Johannes, late Hen. II. Add. 19817.

**Eye**, *co. Heref.* Conf. of rights of burial to Brimfield chapel bel. to the church of, *c.* 1173–80 (Eia). Add. 19585.

**Eye** (Eya, etc.), *co. Suff.* Grant of the honour of, to Ranulf, Earl of Chester, [1153]. Cott. xvii. 2.

—— Conf. of the church to Eye Priory, *c.* 1150–60 (Eia). Harl. 43 G. 22.

—— Rents payable "ad wardam de," *t.* Hen. III. Harl. 49 B. 1, Add. 7539.

—— Grants, etc., in, *t.* Edw. I. Harl. 48 I. 34, 53 C. 7;—1336. Harl. 48 I. 36;—1350. Harl. 45 B. 2, 3;—1380-1395. Add. 5500–5506;—1510. Add. 5515;—1619. Add. 10482;—1650. Add. 10491;—1654. Add. 10472, 10493;—1681. Add. 19098;—1685. Add. 10500, 10540.

—— Letters of protection for the liberties of, from the Duke of Suffolk, 1478. Add. 16566.

—— Release by the Duke of Suffolk of a fee-farm for markets from, 1480 (?). Add. 16567.

—— Mortgage, etc., in Langton hamlet in, 1553. Add. 10475;—1648. Add. 10488;—1649. Add. 10489;—1650. Add. 10490;—1658. Add. 10496.

—— Precipe on a covenant in, 1561. Add. 25309.

—— Extracts from court-rolls of Eye Hall and Eye Sokemer manors in, 1559. Add. 19666;—1619. Add. 10483;—1621. Add. 10485;—1623. Add. 10486;—1649. Add. 10489;—1650. Add. 10492;—1655. Add. 10494;—1663. Add. 10497.

—— *Ballivi.* Ric. Grey, Galfr. Dunston, 1480 (?). Add. 16567.

—— *Senescallus.* Hubert. Gernegan, early *t.* Hen. III. Harl. 49 F. 15.

—— *Clericus.* Philippus, end of 12 cent. (?). Harl. 45 G. 70.

**Fairford,** *co. Glouc.* (?). *Rector. Dom.* Steph. Malorre, 1323. Add. 21742.

**Fairlee,** *I. of Wight.* Grant in, *t.* Hen. III. (Fayreleg). Cott. v. 67.

**Fairlight,** *co. Suss.* Conf. of lands in, to Robertsbridge Abbey, *t.* Rich. I. (Farleia). Eg. 373.

—— Release in Grikes, etc., in, to the same, early Hen. III. (Farleia). Eg. 384.

—— Mortgage of the manor (?), 1280 (Farle). Harl. 45 I. 19.

—— Covenant conc. lands "in tenura de Pratteys" in, etc., 1281. Add. 16208 (Farleg);—1410. Add. 20071 (Farlegh);—1484. Add. 20077 (do.).

—— Precipe on covenant conc. lands in, 1592 (Farlighe). Add. 15231.

**Fairsted,** *co. Essex.* License for alienation of the manor, 1602. Add. 5271.

**Fairwell,** *co. Staff. Capellani.* Bernardus, Paganus, *c.* 1170 (Faierwellia). Cott. xxviii. 56.

**Fakele.** *v.* Fackeley, *co. Northt.*

**Fakenham,** *co. Norf.* Grant of the manor, by Edw. III. to his son John, 1372 (Fakenhamdam). Cott. xv. 1.

—— Royal license for a grant in, 1582. Add. 14852.

**Fakenham** *al.* **Great Fakenham,** *co. Suff.* Grants, etc., in, late 13 cent. Add. 10520 (Fekeham), 10521;—1305-15. Add. 8361;—*t.* Edw. II. Add. 9818 (Fakynham Magna);—1323. Add. 10523;—1373. Add. 8379.

—— Compotus of the manor, 1329-30. Add. 9100.

—— Power to take seisin of Fakenham Aspes manor, 1470. Add. 10653.

—— *Dominus.* Edm. de Pakenham, 1329-30. Add. 9100.

—— *Persona.* Radulfus, 1371. Harl. 57 B. 11.

**Fakenham, Little,** *co. Suff.* Conf. of grant of the church to St. Denis Priory, Southampton, *t.* John (Parva Fageham). Harl. 57 E. 24.

—— *Persona.* Petr. Rolf, 1389. Add. 15749.

**Fakkeleya.** *v.* Fackeley Wood, *co. Northt.*

**Faldingworth** (Faldingword, Faldigword, etc.), *co. Linc.* Grants, etc., in, to Bullington Priory, *c.* 1150-60.

Harl. 52 G. 18, 21;—late Hen. II. 44 A. 21 (?), 45 H. 28, 51 B. 17, 52 G. 29;—*t.* Rich. I. Harl. 50 F. 3;—1256. Harl. 52 H. 28 (Faldingwurth);—*t.* Hen. III. or Edw. I. Harl. 54 B. 32.

—— Conff. of Aldefeld Grange in, to the same, *c.* 1150-60. Harl. 52 G. 21;—*t.* Edw. I.-II. Harl. 52 H. 5;—*c.* 1322. Harl. 52 H. 27.

—— Conf. by Hen. II. of grants in, to the same, [1155] (Faldigwrd). Harl. 43 C. 19.

—— Fine in, with the same, 1187 (Faldingwurthe). Harl. 44 A. 22.

—— Grants, etc., in, *c.* 1216 (?). Harl. 50 I. 4 (Faldigwrtbe);—late 18 cent. Harl. 49 I. 20, 50 I. 5, 54 B. 43.

—— Descent of land in, *t.* Edw. III. Harl. 58 H. 1.

—— Protection to possessions of Bullington Priory in, 1499. Harl. 43 I. 11.

—— *Persona.* Arnaldus, early *t.* Hen. III. Harl. 54 B. 15.

—— *Rector.* Ric. de Neuporth, *t.* Hen. III.-*t.* Edw. I. Harl. 54 B. 32.

**Faldo,** *co. Bedf.* Bond to assure rents in, 1813 (Faldho). Harl. 52 C. 53.

**Faleweale.** *v.* Fawsley, *co. Northt.*

**Falkenham,** *al.* **Faltenham,** *co. Suff.* Surrenders, etc., in, 1459. Add. 10215 (Falcenham);—1538. Add. 10225 (Feltnam);—1580. Add. 10234;—1602. Add. 15761;—1632. Add. 10249;—1662. Add. 10166.

—— *Vicarius.* Will. Lolt, de Whytingtons [Whitton], 1381 (Faltenham). Add. 9944.

**Falkirk,** *co. Stirling.* Grant of the church of, "que varia capella dicitur," to Holyrood Abbey, 1166 (Egglesbrec). Harl. 111 B. 14.

**Falley.** *v.* Fawley, *co. Buck.*

—— *v.* Fawley, *co. Southt.*

**Faluesle, Falweale.** *v.* Fawsley, *co. Northt.*

**Fambridge, North,** *co. Essex.* Precipes on covenants conc. lands in, 1555. Add. 24928;—1592. Add. 25009.

**Fambridge, South,** *co. Essex.* Precipe on a convenant conc. land in, 1592. Add. 25009.

**Fanard,** *co. Cork* (?). Grant of the vill of, 1406. Add. 8672.

I. 12 (Varlye):—1439. Harl. 86 I.
13 (Varle):—1480. Harl. 86 I. 5
(Farlye):—1485. Harl. 78 E. 48
(Fareleigh):—1499. Harl. 86 H. 22
(do.).
—— Sale of Iveden, etc., in, 1646.
Harl. 85 II. 60.

**Farley, Monkton,** co. *Wilts.* License
to Farley Priory to acquire land in,
1397 (Farleghe). Cott. ii. 22.
—— License to alienate, etc., in, 1544.
Add. 5699 (Farleigh), 5700 (do.);—
1556. Add. 5705 (do.).

**Farlighe.** v. Fairlight, co. *Suss.*

**Farlow,** co. *Salop.* Lease of the manor,
c. 1433 (Ferlowe). Harl. 53 H. 17.

**Farlsthorpe,** co. *Linc.* Conveyance
in, 1855 (Farlesthorp). Harl. 57 G. 11.
—— *Capellanus.* Robertus, early 13
cent. Harl. 45 B. 44 (Farlestorp).
—— —— Thomas, early Hen. III.
Harl. 47 E. 23 (Harlestorp), 56 D. 10,
11 (do.).
—— *Clericus.* Galfridus, early Hen.
III. (Farlestorp). Harl. 75 C. 53.

**Farmanby,** co. *York.* Grant, etc., in,
early Hen. III. Harl. 51 E. 32;—
t. Edw. I. Harl. 52 G. 10.

**Farmcote,** co. *Glouc.* Release in, 1362
(Farncote). Harl. 58 D. 45.
—— Covenant conc. settlement of the
manor, 1350 (do.). Harl. 54 D. 28.

**Farnborough,** co. *Kent.* Grants
bounded by, 862 (Fearnbiorginga
meare). Cott. viii. 32;—987 (Fearn
beorhginga mearc). Cott. viii. 14.
—— Royal grant of free warren in,
1317 (Farnbergh). Harl. 84 C. 14.

**Farnborough,** co. *Southt.* Extracts
from court-rolls of, 1612, 1631. Add.
17446-17448.

**Farnborough,** co. *Warw.* Grant of a
hen-rent in, t. Hen. III.–Edw. I.
(Farnberuhe). Add. 26417.

**Farncombe,** in *Godalming,* co. *Surr.*
Grant in, 1348 (Farncumbe). Toph. 18.

**Farndon,** in *Wardon Hundred,* co.
*Northt.* Feoffments, etc., of the manor,
1365, 1366 (Farndon juxta Byfeld).
Add. 21858-21862.
—— *Dominus.* Willelmus, early 13
cent. Harl. 84 I. 26.

**Farndon,** co. *Nott.* Lease of the
parsonage, 1543. Harl. 86 C. 15
(Farundon), 111 C. 35 (Farudon).

**Farndon,** co. *Nott.* (continued). Bond
for warranty in, 1586 (Faryngdon).
Add. 26012.
—— Exemplif. of writs for recovery
in, 1586-7. Add. 26014.
—— *Parson.* Rich. Benese, Canon of
Lincoln, 1543. Harl. 86 C. 15, 111 C. 35.
—— *Vicarius.* Rob. Bokour, 1292
(Farndon). Harl. 46 F. 17.

**Farndon Prebend,** *dioc. Linc., in co.
Nott.* Grant of next nomination to,
1546 (Farndon). Harl. 86 A. 47.

**Farnesfeld.** v. Farnsfield, co. *Nott.*

**Farnham,** co. *Dors.* Petitions for
restoration to lands in, with the ad-
vowson, c. 1833. Harl. 47 A. 26
(Ferneham), 27, 52 A. 48 (Fernham).
—— Exchange of dower in, 1356
(Fernham). Harl. 47 H. 3.
—— Covenant for pre-emption in,
1408 (Farnam). Add. 15446.

**Farnham,** co. *Essex.* Precipe on a
covenant in, 1592 (Farneham). Add.
25007.

**Farnham,** co. *Suff.* Grants, etc., in,
t. Hen. III. Harl. 49 B. 1 (Farham);
—1295. Harl. 49 I. 22-24 (Farenham);
—1366. Add. 26253;—1372, 1372 (?).
Add. 26256, 26261;—1383. Harl. 47
A. 28;—1391. Add. 26268;—1394.
Add. 26269;—1408. Harl. 54 I. 7;—
1417. Add. 26275;—1430. Harl. 43
E. 19, 54 I. 10;—1431. Harl. 50 H.
27, 28, 54 I. 15;—1435. Add. 2016;—
1442. Add. 26287;—1455. Add.
26290;—1460. Add. 26291;—1466.
Add. 26292;—1486. Add. 26296;—
1488. Add. 26309;—1497. Add.
26311;—1513. Add. 26326;—1542.
Add. 26325;—1584. Add. 26340;—
1576. Add. 26343, 26344;—1602.
Add. 26356-26358;—1603. Add.
26359;—1645. Add. 26379;—1678.
Add. 13727.
—— Sale of the manor, late bel. to
Butley Priory, 1557-8 (Forneham).
Harl. 80 A. 52.

**Farnham,** co. *Surr.* Papal conf. of K.
Stephen's grant of, to Waverley Abbey,
1147 (Ferneham). Lansd. 27.
—— Grants, etc., in, 1429. Add.
26648, 26649;—1430. Add. 26650;—
1477. Add. 26671;—1627. Add. 5678.
—— Petition conc. pasture in the
manor, 1495. Add. 26675.
—— Lease of Compton Hall al. Moor
Hall, etc., in, 1634. Harl. 76 F. 40.
—— *Capellanus.* Dom. Rob. Rother-
ham, 1430. Add. 26650.

Farnham, co. York. Manumission of
a nativus of, 1381. Campb. iii. 20.

—— Brief for rebuilding the church,
1770. Ch. Br. B. x. 2.

Farnham Royal al. Farnham
Verdon, co. Buck. Grants, etc., in,
t. Hen. III–t. Edw. I. Add. 9213
(Farnham), Lansd. 82 (Fernham), 83
(Farnham lee), 87 (Fernham);—1814.
Lansd. 101;—1318. Lansd. 104;—
1345. Lansd. 112;—1347. Lansd.
116;—1376. Lansd. 134 (Furnam);
—1415. Lansd. 139, 140; — 1429.
Lansd. 149;—1430. Lansd. 150, 151;
—1439. Lansd. 155;—1448. Lansd.
159;—1460. Lansd. 164, 165;—1532.
Lansd. 177 (Furnam Varden);—1535.
Lansd. 178 (Farnam Ryall);—1587.
Lansd. 576;—1554. Lansd. 184;—
1561. Lansd. 577, 578;—1590. Lansd.
190.

—— Fine in, 1564. Lansd. 579.

—— Appointment of a bailiff of the
manor, 1572 (Farneham Riall). Harl.
75 H. 16.

—— Writ for inquest on damage done
to adjoining lands by the mill, 1572.
Harl. 84 C. 38 b.

—— Crown lease in the manor of,
[1560] (Farneham Ryall). Add. 8462.

Farnhulle. v. sub Fonthill Giffard,
co. Wilts.

Farnhurst, co. Suss. Grant [of the
manor?], early Hen. III. (tota terra de
Farhurst). Add. 24659.

—— Grant in, 1414. Add. 24660.

—— Precipe on covenant conc. land
in, 1592. Add. 15228.

Farningham, co. Kent. Exemplif. of
fine of Farningham, with Charton,
Upper and Nether court manors, 1590.
Harl. 111 H. 5.

—— Lease of woods in, 1601. Add.
23782.

—— Perpet. Vicarius. Dom. Will. de
Kyngeston, 1301 (Frenigeham). Harl.
55 H. 23.

Farnleg. v. Farley, co. Surr.

Farnley, co. York. Precept for seisin
in, to Kirkstall Abbey, 1348 (Farne-
lay). Add. 17119.

Farnley Tyas, co. York. Capellanus.
Rogerus, t. Hen. III. (Farnl.) Lansd.
70.

Farnleya. v. Farley, in Darley, co.
Derb.

Farnsfield, co. Nott. License for a
grant in, to a chapel at Normanton,
1381 (Farnesfeld). Woll. v. 1.

Farren Iglashine, Kerryourrihy
Barony, co. Cork. Sale of, 1626. Add.
8781.

Farringdon, in Stoke Courcy (?), co.
Som. Bailiff's accompts, 1346–7 (Far-
andon, Faryngdon). Add. 7675.

—— Court-rolls, 1375–1377 (Ferndon,
Feryngdon). Add. 7676; — 1461
(Faryngdon Blwet). Add. 7671.

Farsley, co. York. Grants, etc., in,
t. Edw. I. Add. 16679 (Ferseley),
16726 (Ferslay);—1362. Add. 16820
(do.):—1396. Add. 16877 (Farselay);
—1437. Add. 16926 (Ferslay);—1485.
Add. 16966 (Fersley).

—— Mem. of land held by John Scot
in, t. Edw. I. or II. (Fersley). Add.
16701.

—— Fine in, 1504 (Ferley). Add.
16995.

Farwath. v. Firbeck, co. York.

Farway (Fareweye, etc.), co. Devon.
Grants of Appledore in, 1333. Add.
18019, 18020 ;—1398. Add. 13766.

—— Grants, etc., of the manor and
advowson, 1349. Add. 13915 ;—1396.
Add. 13921, 13922; — 1545. Add.
13793, 13796 ;—1548. Add. 13801 :—
1558. Add. 13806, 13807; — 1562.
Add. 13810 ;—1572. Add. 13813.

—— Grants, etc., in, 1373. Add.
13028 ;—1404. Add. 13011 ;—1415.
Add. 13012 ;—1559. Add. 13808 ;—
1560. Add. 13809 ;—1609–10. Add.
13851 ;—1611. Add. 13857 ;—1623.
Add. 13866.

—— Grants, etc., in Boycombe in,
1377. Add. 13008 ; — 1386. Add.
13009 ;—1399. Add. 13767, 13768 ;—
1401. Add. 13010, 13033, 13769 ;—
1421. Add. 13040 ;—1564. Add.
13811 (Bwayecomb) ;—1566. Add.
13812 ;—1590. Add. 13829 ;—1623.
Add. 13867.

—— Lease, etc., of Devenische in,
1381. Add. 13918 ;—1609–10. Add.
13852.

—— Grant, etc., in Knoll, Barrys,
etc., in, 1421. Add. 13040 ;—1564.
Add. 13811.

—— Extracts from court-rolls, 1501.
Add. 13778 ;—1528. Add. 13780 ;—
1532. Add. 13781 ; — 1558. Add.
13803, 13804 ;—1572–82. Add. 13805 ;

T 2

Fawley, co. Southt. Precipe on a covenant conc. land in, 1593 (Falley). Add. 25239.

Fawnsheallgate. v. Fanshawgate, in Holmesfield, co. Derb.

Fawsley, co. Northt. Grant in Braunstone, co. Northt., pertaining to the King's manor of, early 13 cent. (Faluesle). Harl. 48 C. 6.

—— License to convey the manor, 1337 (Falwesle). Harl. 43 E. 29.

—— Capellanus. Helyas, early 13 cent. (Falewesle). Harl. 84 D. 22.

—— Persona. Thomas, t. John (do.) Harl. 85 B. 18.

—— —— Willelmus, early 13 cent. (do.). Harl. 84 D. 22.

—— Perpet. Vicarius. Henricus, 1276 (do.). Harl. 84 F. 31.

Fawy. v. Fowey, co. Corns.

Faxton, co. Northt. Grant in, t. Hen. II. Harl. 49 F. 53.

—— Fine in, 1387. Add. 22402.

—— Powers to take seisin of the manor, 1417. Harl. 57 G. 17;—1447. Harl. 45 G. 62.

—— Bond conc. land in, 1504 (Faxaton). Add. 21206.

—— Sale of a ninth part of the manor, 1573, 1575. Add. 24166, 24167.

Fayrchyl. v. sub Hellesdon, co. Norf.

Fayreleg. v. Fairlee, I. of Wight.

Fearby, co. York. Grant of the manor, 1369 (Feyerby). Add. 20555.

—— Brief conc. a fire at, 1760. Ch. Br. A. vii. 3.

Fearn beorhginga Mearc. v. Farnborough, co. Kent.

Fearne. v. sub Bodenham, co. Heref.

Fearynda Hidery, co. Cork. Release in, 1566. Add. 8713.

Featherstone, co. York. Persona. Robertus, early 13 cent. (Fedherstan). Add. 7433.

—— Vicarius. Joh. de Cotes, 1411. Add. 20515.

Febresham. v. Faversham, co. Kent.

Fecchaam, Fecheam. v. Feckenham, co. Worc.

Fecham. v. Fetcham, co. Surr.

Feckelessole. v. sub Chelsham, co. Surr.

Feckenham, co. Worc. Grant of Holloway (Holeweia) grange in, with forest easements, etc., to Bordesley Abbey, [1138?] (Fecheam). Add. 20419.

—— Notif. of the above to S., Bp. of Worcester, c. 1138 (Fecchaam). Harl. 45 I. 30.

—— Conf. of the above by Hen. II., [1157?] (Feccheam). Cott. MS. Nero C. iii. f. 176.

—— Settlement of Astwood manor in, with the advowson, 1598. Harl. 79 F. 6.

Fedherstan. v. Featherstone, co. York.

Feering, co. Essex. Grant of the "mansio" of, by Will. I., to Westminster Abbey, 1067 (Feringes). Cott. vi. 3 (copy).

—— Rental, early Hen. III. (Ferynges). Add. 8139.

—— Covenant conc. descent of Preisted (Perstede) manor in, 1372. Add. 19979.

—— Conveyance in, 1453 (Feryng). Harl. 47 D. 24.

Fefres hám. v. Faversham, co. Kent.

Feham. v. Fetcham, co. Surr.

Fekeham. v. Fakenham, co. Suff.

Fekeleshole. v. sub Chelsham, co. Surr.

Felborough Hundred, co. Kent. Grant in, 1434. Harl. 78 B. 25.

Felbrigg, co. Norf. Grants, etc., in, 1379. Add. 14521;— 1409. Add. 19325;—1593. Add. 14264, 14265.

Feletby. v. Fulletby, co. Leic.

Feletorp. v. Felthorpe, co. Norf.

Felgham. v. Felpham, co. Suss.

Feliskirk, co. York. Assignment of the reversion of Ravensthorpe manor in, 1404. Add. 22391.

Felix Hall. v. sub Kelvedon, co. Essex.

Felixstowe, co. Suff. Conf. of a fine in, 1459 (Fylstowe). Add. 10215.

—— Precipes on covenants conc. lands in, 1589. Add. 25401, 25402;— 1593. Add. 25464.

Felkirk, co. York. Persona. Ricardus, early 13 cent. (Felekirke). Harl. 83 G. 22.

—— Vicarius. Hugo de Derfelde, 1389. Cott. xxviii. 92.

**Fell Beck Mill,** *in Ripon, co. York.*
Brief conc. a fire at, 1799. Ch. Br.
B. xxxix. 7.

**Felmingham** (Felmyngham), *co. Norf.*
Appropriation of the church to Hulme
St. Benet's Abbey, 1262. Cott. iv. 57
(5) (copy).

—— Grants in, *t.* Edw. I.-II. Add.
6314;—1451. Add. 7386.

—— Precipe on a covenant conc. lands
in, 1370. Add. 25145.

—— Power to give seisin, and covenant on conveyance of Brian's manor
in, 1378. Add. 14664;—1396. Add.
14665.

—— *Perpet. vicarius.* Alanus, 1378.
Add. 14664.

**Felolleshall.** v. *sub* Kelvedon, *co.
Essex.*

**Felpham,** *co. Suss.* Valor of lands in
the manor, 1574 (Feltham, Felgham).
Harl. Roll AA. 20.

**Felsham,** *co. Suf.* Lease, etc., of the
manor, 1388. Add. 18671;—1389.
Add. 7906.

—— Precipe on a covenant conc. land
in, 1578. Add. 25350.

**Felstead** (Felstede), *co. Essex.* Grant,
etc., in, 1332. Add. 15576;—1442.
Add. 6200.

—— *Vicarius.* Joh. Elford, 1421.
Add. 6180.

**Feltham.** v. Felpham, *co. Suss.*

—— v. Field Ham, *co. Buck.*

—— v. *sub* Frome, *co. Som.*

**Feltham,** *co. Midd.* Grant in, 1629.
Add. 6491.

—— Brief for rebuilding the church,
1801. Ch. Br. B. xli. 10.

**Felthorpe,** *co. Norf.* Grant in, to
Horsham Priory, late 12 cent. (Feletorp). Add. 15184.

—— Sales, etc., in, 1449. Add. 14148;
—1555. Add. 14224-14227;—1557.
Add. 14228;—1586. Add. 9396.

—— Sale of Russels Doole in, with
game of swans, bel. to Bardolfes *al.*
Whitefoots manor in, 1609. Add.
14666.

—— *Persona.* Willelmus, 1353. Toph.
25.

**Feltnam.** v. Falkenham, *co. Suf.*

**Felton,** *co. Heref.* Grants, etc., in,
1404. Add. 19414;—1419. Add.
19416, 19417;—1654. Add. 1953.

**Felton,** *co. Northumb.* Grant of Glant-
lees in, with estovers in the woods
of, etc., [1246-58]. Campb. iii. 14.

—— Conf. of a grant of Swarland in,
[1267-9]. Harl. 46 D. 15.

—— Covenant by Qu. Alienor conc.
the mills of, 1272. Harl. 43 C. 43.

—— Power to give seisin of the mills
to A. de Valence, 1280. Harl. 56 F. 40.

**Felton,** *nr. Bromfield, co. Salop.* Conf.
of land in, by Hen. II., to Bromfield Priory, [1155] (Feltuna). Cott.
xvii. 4.

—— *Presbyter.* Robertus, [1155]. Cott.
xvii. 4.

**Felton, West,** *co. Salop.* Brief for rebuilding the church, 1783. Ch. Br.
B. xxiii. 4.

**Feltwell,** *co. Norf.* Papal conf. of a
grant in, to Huntingdon Priory, 1147
(Fletuuella). Cott. MS. Aug. ii. 112.

—— Grants in, to Beaubec Abbey,
1162. Harl. 111 B. 48 (Fautewelle),
112 D. 57 (do.);—late 12 cent. Add.
19804 (do.).

—— Mortgage, etc., in, [1179]. Harl.
111 G. 50 (Feutewell), 112 D. 58
(Fautewell).

—— Grant of rents in, to Biddlesdon
Abbey, *co.* Buck., by Beaubec Abbey,
1272. Harl. 84 D. 11 (Feuteuuelle);
—c. 1272. Harl. 84 D. 10 (Feltewell).

—— Exchange of rents in, by Biddlesdon Abbey, 1272. Harl. 84 E. 3.

**Fen,** *nr. Boston, co. Linc.* Release in,
1387 (Fenn). Harl. 53 C. 38.

**Fenby,** *co. Linc.* Grant, etc., in, *c.* 1260.
Add. 15765 (Fenneby);—1338. Harl.
54 B. 36 (Feneby).

**Fencot,** *in Charlton, co. Oxon.* Precipe on a covenant conc. land in, 1561.
Add. 25206.

**Fenglesham.** v. Finglesham, *co. Kent.*

**Fenne.** v. *sub* Churchstowe, *co. Devon.*

**Fenneby.** v. Fenby, *co. Linc.*

**Fennikumton, Fenny Compton.**
v. Compton, Fenny, *co. Warw.*

**Fenny Sutton.** v. Sutton Veney, *co.
Wilts.*

**Fenton,** *co. Cumb.* Lease in, 1572.
Harl. 77 H. 37.

**Fenton,** *co. Linc.* Grants of the manor,
etc., [1153-67]. Harl. 50 F. 31;—

Feuteuuelle, Feutewell. *v.* Feltwell, *co. Norf.*

Feversham. *v.* Faversham, *co. Kent.*

Fewston, *co. York.* Brief conc. a hailstorm at, 1765. Ch. Br. B. v. 3.

—— Brief conc. inundations at, 1768. Ch. Br. B. viii. 10.

—— Briefs for rebuilding the church, 1807, 1811. Ch. Br. B. xlviii. 1, li. 8.

Feyarby. *v.* Fearby, *co. York.*

Feyerfelde, Feyrfeld. *v.* Fairfield, *co. Kent.*

Fickleshole. *v. sub* Chelsham, *co. Surr.*

Fiddington (Fydyngton), *co. Som.* Fine and release of the manor, 1433. Harl. Roll C. 32;—1439. Harl. 58 D. 42.

—— *Persona.* Joh. Taphot, 1401. Add. 13033.

Fidelton. *v.* Fittleton, *co. Wilts.*

Field Dalling. *v.* Dalling, Field, *co. Norf.*

Field Farm. *v. sub* Egerton, *co. Kent.*

Field Ham, *co. Buck.* Grant of the manor, 1370 (Feltham). Harl. 58 D. 47.

Fifehead Neville, *co. Dors.* Releases, etc., of the manor, 1379. Harl. 50 C. 18 (Fyfhide Nevyle), 57 G. 36 (Fifhide Nevile);—1415. Harl. 47 F. 7;—1425. Harl. 48 B. 7;—1439. Harl. 58 D. 42.

—— Fine of the manor, 1433 (Fyfhyde Nevylle). Harl. Roll C. 32.

Fifhed. *v.* Fivehead, *co. Som.*

Fifhide. *v.* Fyfield, *co. Essex.*

Fifhyde St. Quintyn. *v. sub* Ashmore, *co. Dors.*

Filby, *co. Norf.* Papal conf. of tithes in, to Horsham St. Faith Priory, 1163 (Filibbi). Cott. MS. Aug. ii. 136.

—— Grant in, to St. Paul's Hosp., Norwich, late 12 cent. (Filleby). Cott. ii. 19 (12) (copy).

—— Grant in, 1345. Add. 19313.

—— Feoffment, etc., of Holm Hall manor in, 1381. Add. 14667;—1391. Add. 14708.

—— *Clericus.* Willelmus, early 13 cent. (Fileby). Add. 7362.

Fileshent. *v.* Filsham, *nr. Hastings, co. Suss.*

Filey, *co. York.* Conf. of a grant of the church to Bridlington Priory, [1128–32] (Fiuelai). Cott. MS. Aug. ii. 56.

Filey, *co. York (continued).* Conf. of grants in, to the same, 1328 (Fivele). Add. 20557.

Filham, *in Ugborough, co. Devon.* Rental of lands in, 1605. Add. 26199.

Filingham. *v.* Fillingham, *co. Linc.*

Filkins, *nr. Broughton Pogis, co. Oxon.* Power for seisin of, 1383 (Nether fylkings). Cott. xxvii. 69.

Filletts, *co. Oxon.* Conveyance of the manor, 1614. Harl. 79 G. 5.

Fillingham (Filingham), *co. Linc.* Grants, etc., in, *t.* Hen. III.-*t.* Edw. I. Add. 8390, Harl. 52 B. 24;—1326. Harl. 52 B. 38.

—— *Clericus.* Antonius, *t.* Hen. III. Harl. 47 G. 27.

—— *Rector.* Dom. Will. de Broclesby, 1331. Cott. xxx. 18, Harl. 57 F. 45;—(*as nuper rector*), 1332. Harl. 55 E. 21.

—— —— Dom. Joh. de Reane, 1332. Harl. 47 C. 32, 33.

Fillongley, *co. Warw.* Evidence conc. appropriation of the church to Maxstoke Priory, 1345 (Filongley). Cott. iv. 8.

—— Lease of the farm of the rectory by Maxstoke Priory, 1525. Harl. 75 G. 8.

—— Sale of the manor, 1540 (Phillonglaye). Harl. 47 A. 53.

Filsham, *nr. Hastings, co. Suss.* Grant of rent from the mill to Robertsbridge Abbey, early 13 cent. (Fileshent). Camph. xxv. 6.

—— Court-rolls, 1444–1533. Add. 26894–26897.

—— Lands held of the manor of, in Westfield, co. Suss., 1534. Add. 24867.

Finborough, *co. Suff.* Grant in, *t.* Hen. III. (Fineberie). Add. 8366.

—— Grant of free warren in, 1293 (Magna Finbergh). Add. 6337.

—— Pardon on alienation of the manor, 1310 (Fynebergh). Add. 10644.

Fincham, *co. Norf.* Grants, etc., in, *t.* Hen. III.-*t.* Edw. I. or II. Harl. 47 D. 38 (Fyncham), 47 H. 52, 49 B. 7, 8, 25, 49 D. 14, 49 I. 53–55, 50 D. 48, 50 H. 22, 51 F. 47, 53 A. 38, 56 G. 45.

—— *Rector eccl. S. Martini.* R——, *t.* Hen. III. Harl. 51 F. 47.

Firbeck, *co. York.* Releases in, 1414. Harl. 112 I. 4 (Farwath);—1445. Harl. 112 I. 3 (Ferebach).

—— Court-rolls of, 1596-1600 (Firbeck). Add. 26910.

—— *Sacerdos.* Ernisius, [1171-9?] (Friebec). Harl. 112 B. 1.

Firle, West, *co. Suss.* Grant of tithes in Charlston (Cherlakestuua) nr., to Sulby Abbey, co. Northt., [1200-10]. Add. 21879.

Firmins Barton. *v. sub* Hackington, *co. Kent.*

Firsby, *co. Linc.* Covenant for rent in, to Greenfield Priory by Bardney Abbey, with license for same, 1347. Harl. 44 A. 8 (Frysby);—1348. Harl. 43 D. 43 (Frisby).

Fiscesburna, *co. Midd.* A boundary mark, 704. Cott. MS. Aug. ii. 82.

Fiscwille, *nr. Maugersbury, co. Glouc.* A boundary, 949. Cott. viii. 6 (*copy*).

Fishbourne, *co. Suss.* Conveyance in, 1451 (Fyshbourne). Harl. 54 A. 21.

Fisherton Anger, *co. Wilts.* Feoffments in, 1440. Harl. 53 C. 9 (Fissherton Aucher);—1523. Add. 5140 (F. Auchier).

—— Surrender of the gaol, 1547. Add. 18291.

Fisherton de la Mere, *co. Wilts.* Acquittance for rent from the manor, 1472 (Fyssherton). Harl. 55 A. 10.

—— *Rector. Dom.* Will. de Beloney, 1314 (Fysscherton). Add. 13014.

—— *Vicarius. Dom.* Willelmus, 1314. Add. 13014.

Fishlake, *co. York.* Order for a tithe of eels in, to Roche Abbey, t. Steph. (Fislake). Cott. xxx. 17 (*copy*).

—— License to endow Fotheringay College, co. Northt. with the manor, 1415 (Fysshlake). Camph. x. 5.

Fishtoft (Toft, etc.), *co. Linc.* Grant of the vill, 1183. Harl. 49 A. 3.

—— Fines in, 1349. Harl. 55 E. 24; —1371. Harl. 55 D. 37.

—— Conveyance in, 1362. Cott. v. 18.

—— Fines of the manor, 1364. Harl. 52 A. 38 (Toft juxta Freston);—1374. Harl. 56 F. 43, 44;—1378. Harl. 56 G. 26.

—— Precipe on a covenant conc. land in, 1555 (Tofte juxta Boston). Add. 25055.

Fishtoft (Toft, etc.), *co. Linc.* (*continued*). Grant, etc., of the advowson, 1365. Harl. 80 F. 25;—1568. Harl. 77 F. 54.

—— *Persona.* Joh. Deynes, 1371. Harl. 55 D. 37.

Fiskerton, *co. Nott.* Rent charge on the manor for chantries in Crich, co. Derb., and Normanton, co. Nott., 1368 (Wyakerton). Woll. iv. 58.

—— Exemplif. of writs for a recovery in, 1586-7. Add. 26014.

Fislake. *v.* Fishlake, *co. York.*

Fismanne Cheriche. *v. sub* Canterbury, *co. Kent.*

Fittleton, *co. Wilts.* Conveyance of the manor, 1394 (Fytelton). Add. 24701.

—— Complaint of the prior of St. Swithin's, Winchester, conc. the manor, t. Hen. VI. (Fidelton). Harl. Roll CC. 23.

Fittleworth, *co. Suss.* Assignment of land in, 1501 (Fetylworth). Add. 18790.

—— Precipe on a covenant conc. land in, 1592 (Fyttleworthe). Add. 15227.

Fitz Walters Manor. *v. sub* Shenfield, *co. Essex.*

Fitzwarren, Norton. *v.* Norton Fitzwarren, *co. Som.*

Fiuelai. *v.* Filey, *co. York.*

Fivehead, *co. Som.* Sale of the manor, etc., 1576 (Fifhed). Harl. 79 F. 14.

Fladbury, *co. Worc.* Feoffment in, 1374 (Fladebur.). Add. 14006.

Flaferth. *v.* Flyford, *co. Worc.*

Flagg, *in Chelmorton, co. Derb.* Grants, etc., in, 1284. Harl. 83 E. 17:—1327. Harl. 83 E. 10;—1345. Harl. 83 E. 31:—1346. Harl. 83 E. 16, 83 F. 39, 40;—134[6?]. Harl. 83 F. 38;— 1347. Harl. 83 E. 45, 83 F. 41;— [1554-7]. Woll. iv. 65;—1559. Woll. iv. 64, 66.

—— Appointment of bailiffs of Merivale Abbey in the manor of, 1543. Harl. 112 F. 27.

Flamborough, *co. York.* Conf. of grants of the church, etc., to Bridlington Priory, [1128-32] (Fleineburhc). Cott. MS. Aug. ii. 56.

—— Exchequer acquittance for rent in, 1623. Add. 25723.

Flixton, co. Suf. Bond conc. service in, to Rumburgh Priory, transferred from St. Mary's Abbey, York, early 13 cent. (Flixtan). Campb. i. 20.

—— License to found a priory in the fee of R. de Tateshale in, c. 1258. Campb. xii. 20.

—— Release of the manor and a moiety of the advowson to Flixton Priory, [1258-66]. Campb. iii. 7.

—— Conf. by Sir R. de Tateshale of a grant in his fee in, to Flixton Priory, [1258-72]. Campb. i. 4.

—— Acquittance for a fine on a grant in, to the same, [1258-72]. Campb. xii. 17.

—— Conff. of a moiety of the church of, to the same, 1268. Campb. vii. 7, 8.

—— Grants, etc., in, to the priory, t. Hen. III.-t. Edw. I. Campb. i. 6, ii. 4, 8, 9, v. 14, vi. 6, viii. 3, xii. 12, 15, 16;—1284. Campb. v. 15;—1293. Campb. iii. 16.

—— Covenant for maintenance on a grant in, late Hen. III. Campb. i. 28.

—— Taxation of a moiety of the church, 1274. Campb. xii. 18.

—— Exchange, by the priory with the see of Norwich, of a moiety of the advowson, 1321. Campb. xii. 13, Toph. 43.

—— Bequest of the manor, 1437. Campb. xii. 14.

—— Persona. Dom. Ranulphus, late Hen. III. Campb. i. 28 :—as Rector medietatis ecclesie, t. Hen. III.-t. Edw. I. Campb. iii. 7, xii. 19.

—— Perpet. Vicarius medietatis ecclesie. Reginald. de Hillington, 1274. Campb. xii. 18.

—— Vicarius. Walterus, 1284. Campb. v. 15.

Flockton, co. York. Grants, etc., in, to Byland Abbey, post 1194. Add. 7477 (copy); — t. John. Add. 7456 (Flocketon);—[1232-40]. Add. 7465 (copy); — t. Hen. III. Add. 7481 (Floketun);—ante 1298. Add. 7438 (Flocketon).

—— Exchange of Haukenisclif in, and lands nr. Syelington Wood, with Byland Abbey, t. John (Flokcton). Add. 7453.

—— Settlement of dispute in, with Byland Abbey, [1220] (Floketon). Add. 7442.

Flockton, co. York. (continued). Grants in, t. Hen. III.-t. Edw. I. Add. 7452 (Floketone), 7482 (do.) (copy).

Floketon. v. Flowton, co. Suf.

Floore (Flor, Flore). co. North. Conf. of tithes in, to St. Andrew's Priory, Northampton, early Hen. III. Cott. xxvii. 36.

—— Grants in, 1276. Add. 21863 ;— 1316. Add. 21864.

—— Bond conc. an estate in the manor of, 1320. Harl. 57 A. 54.

—— Terrier of lands in, bel. to St. Andrew's Priory, 14 cent. Campb. ix. 1.

—— Persona. Ricardus, 1371. Add. 21676.

v. also Classthorpe, co. North.

Flordon, co. Norf. Grant in, t. Edw. I. (Flordune). Add. 1381.

Flotemanton. v. Newton Flotman, co. Norf.

Flowton, co. Suf. Grants, etc., in, t. Hen. III. Harl. 85 G. 9 (Floketun); —1317. Add. 9896 (Floketon);— 1348. Add. 10000 (do.);—1503. Woll. v. 16 (Floweton);—1646. Add. 10111; —1653. Add. 10113.

—— Rector. Rob. fil. Galfr. Maukael, t. Hen. III. Harl. 85 G. 9.

—— Alex. de Sprowton, 1311. Add. 9875.

Flyford, co. Worc. Conf. of grants at, to Pershore Abbey, 972 (Flæferth). Cott. MS. Aug. ii. 6.

Foalow. v. Foolow, in Eyam, co. Derb.

Fobbing, co. Essex. Lease in, 1283. Add. 24074.

—— Release of a marsh in, 1360. Add. 19968.

Focgingabyra. v. Hockenbury, co. Kent.

Foddringeia. v. Fotheringay, co. North.

Foeloua. v. Foolow, in Eyam, co. Derb.

Foghay. v. sub St. Thomas, nr. Exeter, co. Devon.

Folbiry. v. Fowberry, in Chatton, co. Northumb.

Folces stane. v. Folkestone, co. Kent.

Folcwininglond, nr. Eastry, co. Kent. Grant at, 811. Cott. MS. Aug. ii. 47.

Folds, nr. Tickhill, co. York. Grant in, 1336 (Foldu). Harl. 45 E. 52.

U

**Freckenham** (Frekenham, etc.), **co.
Suff.** (continued). Grants, etc., in,
1325. Harl. 49 F. 44;—1326. Harl.
49 F. 45 (Frekynham);—1333. Harl.
57 E. 38;—1372. Harl. 54 C. 41;—
1379. Harl. 54 C. 42;—1424. Add.
9122;—1441. Add. 18737 (Frekynham);—1466. Add. 18763;—1476.
Add. 18768, 18769;—1514. Add.
18797.

—— Release of Bek manor in, 1349.
(Frakenham). Harl. 48 D. 9.

—— Roll of lands of J. Scarlet in,
1403-4. Add. 8996, 9118.

—— Precipe on a covenant conc. land
in, 1578. Add. 25351.

**Freiston.** v. Friston, co. Suff.

**Freiston,** co. Linc. Grants, etc., in
Old Scrane (Vetus Screinga, Scrainga),
W. Newland (West Neuland), etc., in,
to Kirkstead Abbey, ante 1158. Harl.
49 A. 2;—1158. Harl. 49 A. 1;—c.
1158 (?). Harl. 52 A. 34.

—— Grant in Windesland in or nr.,
to Kirkstead Abbey, [1174–93]. Harl.
51 B. 44.

—— Fines in, 1183. Harl. 49 A. 3
(Friston);—1349. Harl. 55 E. 24
(Freston).

—— List of deeds conc. lands of
Kirkstead Abbey in Old Scrane,
early 13 cent. Harl. Roll O. 5.

—— Grant in, 1362 (Frestone). Cott.
v. 18.

—— Fine of Hiptoft Hall (Hippetoft-
hull) manor in, 1371. Harl. 55 D. 37.

—— Precipe on a covenant conc.
lands in, 1555 (Freyston). Add.
25055.

—— Vicarius. Ric. Hargar, 1430.
Cott. xii. 22.

**Fremesfeld.** v. Framfield, co. Suss.

**Fremington,** co. Devon. Fine in,
1653. Harl. 86 I. 59.

—— Vicarius. Rog. Magott, t. Edw.
III. Harl. 45 E. 38.

**Fremington,** co. York. Pledge to
observe a settlement of the manor,
1348 (Fremyngton in Swaldale). Harl.
54 C. 12.

**Fremlyngham.** v. Framlingham, co.
Suff.

**Frend., Frendisbery, Frendisburi.**
v. Frindsbury, co. Kent.

**Frensham,** co. Surr. Grant of free-
warren in Pitfold in, 1285. Harl. 58 I.
37 (copy).

**Frensham,** co. Surr. (continued). Disposition of Frensham Beal manor,
1627. Add. 5678.

**Frense,** co. Norf. Conf. of grant of, to
Norwich Priory, [1136–45] (Frainges).
Cott. ii. 1.

—— Extract from court-roll, 1703.
Add. 19702.

—— Rector. Joh. de Knapeton, 1341
(Frengges). Add. 17221.

**Frerio burna,** co. Kent (?). Ch. of
Egcberht dated at, 838. Cott. viii. 30.

**Fresantun.** v. Freston, co. Suff.

**Freschenel.** v. Friskney, co. Linc.

**Freshford,** co. Som. Feoffment in,
1470. Campb. i. 5.

**Freshwater,** Isle of Wight. Suit conc.
tithes of, [1450–70]. Harl. 80 A. 44.

—— Compotus of the manor, 1488-9
(Fresshewater). Harl. Roll A. 38.

—— Exchequer acquittance for rent
in, 1623. Add. 25724.

—— Rector. Nic. Porter, [1450–70].
Harl. 80 A. 44.

**Freskena, Freskenay, Fresken-
eia,** etc. v. Friskney, co. Linc.

**Fressingfield,** co. Suff. Grant in
Chebenhale in, to Bungay Priory, a.
1230-40. Harl. 56 A. 33.

—— Grants, etc., in, late 13 cent.
Add. 5928 (Fresingfeud);—1289.
Add. 7522 (Fresingfeld);—1408.
Harl. 54 I. 7 (Fresyngefeld);—1427.
Add. 15889 (Fresyngfeld);—1430.
Harl. 43 E. 19, 54 I. 10;—1431. Harl.
50 H. 27, 28, 54 I. 15;—1435. Add.
2016.

—— Surrender of dower in Chebenhale manor in, 1393 (Fresyngfeld).
Harl. 84 B. 10.

—— Extract from court-roll, 1500
(Fresyngefeld). Add. 6554.

—— Precipe on a covenant conc.
Wittingham and Cuddons manors in,
etc., 1552. Add. 25273.

—— Precipe on a covenant conc. land
in, 1593. Add. 25466.

**Frestendene.** v. Frostenden, co. Suff.

**Fresthorp.** v. Fristhorpe, co. Linc.

**Freston.** v. Freiston, co. Linc.

—— v. Friston, co. Suff.

**Freston,** co. Suff. Bequest of land at,
post 991 (Fresantun). Harl. 43 C. 4.

—— Grants, etc., in, late 13 cent.
Harl. 56 H. 2;—1315-6. Harl. 58 G.

Friskney, co. *Linc.* (*continued*). Award in suit betw. Bullington and St. Katherine's, Lincoln, Priories and the parishioners of, 1390. Harl. 44 F. 29.

―― Precipe on a covenant conc. land in, 1555 (Fryssney). Add. 25054.

Fristhorpe, co. *Linc.* Conf. to Bullington Priory of right to tithes of Riddyng in, 1399 (Fresthorp). Harl. 43 I. 3.

―― *Sacerdos.* Lambertus, late 12 cent. (Frustorp). Cott. xii. 58.

Friston (Freston, etc.), co. *Suff.* Grants, etc., in, *t.* Hen. III. Add. 26218 (Freyston);―*t.* Edw. I. Add. 26220; ―1294. Add. 26223; ― 1206-1336. Add. 26226 - 26242; ― 1349. Add. 26247;―1365. Add. 26252;―1369. Add. 26254;―1372. Add. 26262;― 1382. Add. 26264; ― 1394. Add. 26269;―1408. Harl. 54 I. 7;―1411. Add. 26272;―1417. Add. 26274;― 1423. Add. 26278;―1430. Harl. 43 E. 19 (Freeston), 54 I. 10;―1431. Harl. 50 H. 27, 28, 54 I. 15;―1473. Add. 26293;―1478. Add. 26294;― 1486. Add. 26296; ― 1488. Add. 26309;―1497. Add. 26311;―1498. Add. 26312;―1503. Add. 26321;― 1510. Add. 26323; ― 1511. Add. 26324;―1513. Add. 26326; ― 1542. Add. 26325;―1564. Add. 26340;― 1576. Add. 26343, 26344; ― 1602, 1603. Add. 26356 - 26359; ― 1610. Add. 26367;―1612. Add. 26371;― 1645. Add. 26378, 26379; ― 1659. Add. 26383;―1660. Add. 26384;― 1661. Add. 13723 (Freiston), 13724 (do.);―1665. Add. 26386; ― 1678. Add. 13727;―1694. Add. 26391.

―― Release of Beklyng manor in, 1435. Add. 2016.

―― Covenant to resist encroachment on common lands at, 1651. Add. 26377.

―― Admission to land in, 1662. Add. 10517.

―― Appointment of a gamekeeper to the manor, 1711. Add. 13648.

Friston, co. *Suss.* Grants in, *t.* Edw. I. Lansd. 94 (Fristun); ― 1364. Add. 20159.

―― Grant of homage, etc., of tenants in Bechyngtone in, 1375. Lansd. 133.

―― Precipe on a covenant conc. land in, 1588. Add. 25534.

―― Assignment of a charge on the manor, 1664. Add. 18989.

Frith. *v. sub* Hendon, co. M[...]

Frith, co. *Derb.* Extract of [...] 1440 (Frythe). Woll. iii. 9.

Frith, North and South [...] Woods, etc. *v. sub* Tomb[...] Kent.

Frith, South, Wood. *v. s[...]* hurst, co. Kent.

Frithenden, Frithindenn, [...] *of. v. sub* Marden, co. Kent.

Frittenden, co. Kent. Gr[...] in, 1426. Add. 24510 (Fryt[...] ―1452. Add. 24539 (Frythi[...] 1482. Add. 24513 (Frithen[...]

―― Power to give seisin on [...] of Buckhurst, Bubhurst, etc. [...] Harl. 78 A. 10.

―― Power to receive seisin [...] Faversham Abbey, 1506 (Fr[...] Add. 24516.

Fritton (Freton, etc.), co. Nor[...] etc., in, *t.* Hen. III. Harl. [...] (Fretune), 51 C. 18, 57 D. 3[...] Harl. 51 E. 7;―1307. Harl. [...] ―1315. Harl. 45 F. 54;―13[...] 47 A. 12;―1384 (?). Harl. [...]

―― Fine in, 1340. Harl. 5[...]

―― *Persona.* Ricardus, 1[...] 14867.

Fritton (Freton), co. Suff. G[...] lease of the manor, etc., 1[...] Add. 17738, 17739.

―― Bequests to the chu[...] 1482. Add. 17253.

―― Grant in, 1588. Add. [...]

Frisinghall, in Bradford, [...] Brief conc. a fire at, 1764. [...] iv. 4.

Frodan. *v. sub* St. Enoder, [...]

Frodesley, co. Salop. Brief fo[...] ing the church, 1810. Ch. [...]

Frodley. *v.* Fradley, co. Sta[...]

Frogfeld, in I. of Sheppey, [...] Covenant conc. rent of lan[...] of Mere Court manor [in B[...] co. Kent, 1489. Harl. Roll [...]

Froggham, in St. Mabyn, [...] Grant in, 1331. Harl. 51 E[...]

Frognal, [in Wickham Br[...] Kent. Fine of the manor, 1[...] 75 H. 4, 76 H. 50.

Frognal, Little. *v. sub* To[...] Kent.

Froille. *v.* Froyle, co. South[...]

**Frome Vauchurch,** *co. Dors:* Grant of wardship in, [1550–53] (Fromvawchurche). Cott. MS. Vesp. F. xiii. art. 222.

**Frostenden,** *co. Suff.* Grants, etc., in, *t.* Edw. I., 1296, 1297 (Frestendene). Harl. 48 G. 13, 15–17.

—— Conveyance, etc., of the manor and advowson, 1349. Harl. 46 E. 8; —1384. Harl. 57 D. 2;—1396. Harl. 48 I. 39;—1413. Harl. 45 F. 44.

—— *Persona.* Rog. de Biskele, 1349. Harl. 46 E. 8.

—— —— Rog. de Gislam, 1363. Add. 14547.

**Frowick.** *v. sub* St. Osyth, *co. Essex.*

**Frowlesworth,** *co. Leic.* Grant of next presentation to the church, 1465. Add. 24224.

—— Brief for rebuilding the church, 1760. Ch. Br. A. vi. 7.

**Froxfield,** *co. Wilts.* Lease in, 1521 (Froxfyld). Harl. 46 H. 46.

**Froyle,** *co. Southt.* Compotus-rolls of the manor, held by St. Mary's Abbey, Winchester, [1236–65 ?]. Add. 17457–17478 ;—c. 1260. Add. 13338, 13339; —1363–1486. Add. 17479–17511 ;— 1504–1537. Add. 17513–17518.

—— Court-rolls, 1281–2, 1367, 1369, 1413–1514. Add. 17519–17553 ;— 1546–1657. Add. 17554–17581.

—— Grants, etc., in, *t.* Edw. I. Add. 17582 ;—1336. Add. 17583 ;—1382–1414. Add. 17585–17597 ;—1430. Add. 17599.

—— Rental of the manor, 1414–5 (Froille). Add. 17512.

—— Acquittance on sale of Hussey's manor in, 1416. Add. 17598.

—— Sale of the manor and advowson, 1531. Add. 17601.

—— Respite of payments on purchase of the manor, etc., 1543. Add. 17602.

—— Writ in suit in, 1715. Add. 17603.

—— *Vicarius.* Will. Polhampton, 1409. Add. 17591, 17592 ;—1413. Add. 17596 ;—1414. Add. 17597.

*v. also* Coldrey, *nr. Froyle, co. Southt.*

**Frustorp.** *v.* Fristhorpe, *co. Linc.*

**Frutsanant,** *River, co. Glam.* Grant on, in Llanwonno, to Margam Abbey, *t.* Hen. II. Harl. 75 B. 29.

**Frydelsham.** *v.* Frilsham, *co. Berks.*

**Fryndesbury.** *v.* Frindsbury, *co. Kent.*

**Frysby.** *v.* Firsby, *co. Linc.*

**Frysendens** *al.* **Fysendens Manor,** *co. Kent.* Fine of, 1548. Harl. 75 H. 4, 76 H. 50.

**Fryssney.** *v.* Friskney, *co. Linc.*

**Fryston, Water,** *in Ferry Fryston, co. York.* Crown lease in, 1555 (Fryston iuxta aquam). Harl. 84 C. 32.

**Frythe.** *v. sub* Hendon, *co. Midd.*

**Frythe,** *co. Staff.* Admission to lands according to custom of the manor of, 1440. Woll. iii. 9.

**Frythinden, Frythynden.** *v.* Frittenden, *co. Kent.*

**Frythinden, Frythyndenne,** *Den of.* *v. sub* Marden, *co. Kent.*

**Fugglestone,** *co. Wilts.* Court-rolls, 1559. Add. 24440 ;—1567. Add. 24441 ;—1584. Add. 24718.

**Fughelnesse.** *v.* Foulness, *co. Essex.*

**Fughelstuo.** *v.* Fulstow, *co. Linc.*

**Fuheldun.** *v.* Fouldon, *co. Norf.*

**Fulanpettæ,** *co. Essex.* Bequest of land at, *post* 991. Harl. 43 C. 4.

**Fulbourne** (Fulburn), *co. Camb.* Grants, etc., in, 1410. Add. 26642, 26643 ;—1439. Add. 26652 ;—1458. Add. 26662 ;—1472. Add. 26670 ;— 1496. Add. 26676, 26677.

—— *Clericus.* Galfridus, *t.* Hen. III. (Fulburn). Harl. 49 A. 5.

**Fulbrook,** *co. Oxon.* Release of Westhall and Fulbrook manors, 1355. Harl. 57 D. 1.

—— Compotus-rolls of same manors, 1402–3. Harl. Roll A. 37 ;—1441–2. Harl. Roll K. 33.

**Fulchersrede.** *v. sub* Hawkhurst, *co. Kent.*

**Fuldmerthorp,** *nr. Brocklesby* (?), *co. Linc.* Grant of, to Tupholme Abbey, *ante* 1166. Harl. 58 H. 4 (copy).

**Fuleford.** *v. sub* Itchinfield, *co. Suss.*

**Fuletheby.** *v.* Fulletby, *co. Linc.*

**Fulford,** *co. York.* Exchequer acquittance for a fine in, 1580. Add. 25709.

**Fulford Chapel,** *in Stone, co. Staff.* Briefs for rebuilding, 1818, 1823. Ch. Br. B. lix. 4, C. iv. 2.

**Fulham,** *co. Midd.* Grants, etc., in, 1498. Add. 5335 ;—1528. Harl. 75

**Fylingdales,** *co. York.* Briefs for rebuilding the church, 1818, 1822. Ch. Br. B. lix. 6, C. iii. 8.

**Fylstowe.** *v.* Felixstowe, *co. Suff.*

**Fylther.** *v. sub* Egerton, *co. Kent.*

**Fylyaheys,** *nr. Sidmouth, co. Devon.* Release in, 1420. Add. 13039.

**Fyncham.** *v.* Fincham, *co. Norf.*

**Fynchingfeld, Fynchyngfeld.** *v.* Finchingfield, *co. Essex.*

**Fynebergh, Magna.** *v.* Finborough, Gt., *co. Suff.*

**Fynemere.** *v.* Finmere, *co. Oxon.*

**Fyneton Malerbe.** *v.* Fincton, *co. Devon.*

**Fyning Wood.** *v. sub* Harting, W., *co. Suss.*

**Fynkslee** *al.* **Finkelee Forest,** *co. Southt.* Sales of timber in, to Winchester Priory, 1298-9. Add. 19292(3).

**Fynstok.** *v. sub* Charlbury, *co. Oxon.*

**Fyntengoys.** *v.* Fentongoose, *nr. Truro, co. Corniv.*

**Fyringford.** *v.* Fringford, *co. Oxon.*

**Fyrmyns Barton.** *v. sub* Hackington, *co. Kent.*

**Fyskerton.** *v.* Fiskerton, *co. Nott.*

**Fysscherton, Fyssherton.** *v.* Fisherton de la Mere, *co. Wilts.*

# G

**Gabul dene,** *co. Suff.* (?). Grant near, 854. Cott. MS. Aug. ii. 46.

**Gabwell,** *nr. Stoke in Teignhead, co. Devon.* Release in, 1420 (Gabbewyll). Add. 13039.

**Gaddesden, Little** (Parva Gatesden), *co. Hertf.* Grant, etc., in, *t.* Hen. III. Harl. 49 C. 49;—1452. Roy. Roll 14 B. lii.

—— *Perpetuus Vicarius.* Hernicus Gustard, 1452. Roy. Roll 14 B. lii.

**Gadeburgh Marsh.** *v. sub* Brede, *co. Suss.*

**Gadegrave.** *v.* Gedgrave, *co. Suff.*

**Gadisthorp.** *v.* Gasthorpe, *co. Norf.*

**Gæysætc.** *v.* Guist, *co. Norf.*

**Gaines.** *v. sub* Upminster, *co. Essex.*

**Gainford,** *co. Durh.* Grant of **the** church to St. Mary's Abbey, York, [1186-88]. Cott. v. 75.

**Gainsborough,** *co. Linc.* Grant in, *t.* Hen. III. (Gaynesburg). Harl. 56 G.44.

**Gainsford.** *v. sub* Chilton, *co. Berks.*

**Gainspark Hall.** *v. sub* Theydon Garnon, *co. Essex.*

**Gaitforthe.** *v.* Gateforth, *co. York.*

**Gaiton, etc.** *v.* Gayton.

**Gaiwde.** *v.* Gaywood, *co. Norf.*

**Gala Water,** *co. Roxburgh.* Conff. of lands, etc., betw. Gala and Leader Waters, to Melrose Abbey, 1236. Cott. xviii. 9 (Galwhe), 10 (Galwe).

**Galby,** *co. Leic.* Grants, etc., in, 1258. Add. 21208 (Galeby);—*c.* 1258. Add. 21209 (do.);—*t.* Edw. I.-*t.* Edw. II. Add. 21210-21225, 24204 (Gauby, etc.);—1286. Add. 21226 (Galbys), 21227 (Gauby);—1315-1370. Add. 21229-21257;—1361. Add. 21010;—1372(?). Add. 21207;—*c.* 1390. Add. 21261;—1415. Add. 26974;—1438. Add. 21263;—1448. Add. 21054;—1455. Add. 26977;—1544. Add. 21264.

—— Marriage settlement in, on M. de Norton, 1296. Add. 21228.

—— Grant, etc., of the manor, 1389. Add. 21259;—1394. Add. 21258, 21260.

—— Lease of a mill in, with covenant to rebuild, 1423. Add. 21262.

—— *Persona.* Joh. de Leycestria, 1318. Add. 21237.

—— *Rector.* Joh. de Rippley, *c.* 1390. Add. 21261.

**Galcote.** *v.* Gawcote, *in Buckingham, co. Buck.*

**Galklynt Wood,** *nr. Rushton, co. Northt.* (?). Release in, *t.* Hen. III. Harl. 83 E. 22.

**Gallow Hundred,** *co. Norf.* Lease of, from Eliz., Qu. of Edw. IV., 1467. Add. 17741.

—— Subsidy rolls, 1593, 1603. Add. 9410, 9414.

**Gallow Marsh,** *co. Norf.* Sale of, 1615 (Galley). Add. 15860.

**Galmetona.** *v.* Ganton, *co. York.*

**Galtegei.** *v.* Gamlingay, *co. Camb.*

**Galway, County of.** Petition from the Protestants of, on the Act of Resumption, 1702. Add. 19536.

Garton, *co. York (continued). Vicarius. Dom.* Joh. Collom, [1447 ?]. Lansd. 397.

Garton on the Wolds, *co. York.* Release in, to Watton Priory, 1322. Harl. 55 E. 23.

Garvestone, *co. Norf.* Grant in, *t.* Edw. I. (Geroluaston). Add. 14964.

Garw, *River, co. Glam.* Grants betw. Garw and Ogwr rivers, to Margam Abbey, late 12 cent. Harl. 75 C. 31; —*t.* John. Harl. 75 D. 20 ;—1234. Harl. 75 A. 25, 75 B. 40 ;—c. 1234. Harl. 75 B. 39 ;—1448. Harl. 75 A. 12.

Garwinton, Garwynton. *v. sub* Littlebourne, *co. Kent.*

Gasper, *co. Som.* Covenant in, 1411 (Gayspore). Add. 15301.

Gasthorpe, *co. Norf.* Release, etc., in, 1275. Add. 14673 (Gadisthorp) ;— 1404. Add. 14674.

Gataham. *v.* Gotham, *co. Nott.*

Gatcombe. *v. sub* Colyton, *co. Devon.*

Gate Burton. *v.* Burton, Gate, *co. Linc.*

Gateforth, *co. York.* Rentals of the manor, 1530-1533 (Gaitforthe, Gaytforthe). Harl. Rolls G. 18, 19.

Gategrave. *v.* Gedgrave, *co. Suff.*

Gately, *co. Norf.* Grant in, to Castle Acre Priory, late 12 cent. (Gathele). Harl. 83 G. 20.

—— *Presbiter.* Simon, late 12 cent. Harl. 83 G. 20.

Gatemerston, *in Lulworth, co. Dors.* Release in, late *t.* Hen. III. (Gatemorestone). Cott. xxv. 34.

Gateministre. *v.* Yetminster, *co. Dors.*

Gatewykmede, *co. Kent.* Feoffment of, 1407. Harl. 76 G. 39.

Gathampton, *co. Oxon.* Covenant for a fine of the manor, 1547. Harl. 79 G. 13.

Gatton, *co. Surr.* Grants, etc., in, 1327. Add. 9028 ; — 1365. Add. 23729 ;—1535. Add. 18818 ;—1698. Add. 23509.

Gaukeswelle, *v.* Gokewell, *in Broughton, co. Linc.*

Gaulden, *in Tolland, co. Som.* Compotus of, bel. to Taunton Priory, 1438-9 (Gaweldon). Add. 25873.

Gawcott, *in Buckingham, co. Buck.* Release in, 1486 (Galcote). Lansd. 575.

Gayhurst, *co. Buck.* Entail of the manor, 1584-5 (Gotehurst). Harl. 79 D. 20.

Gayles. *v. sub* Teddington, *co. Midd.*

Gaynessparkhall. *v. sub* Theydon Garnon, *co. Essex.*

Gayseham Hall. *v. sub* Barking, *co. Essex.*

Gayspore. *v.* Gasper, *co. Som.*

Gaytburtone. *v.* Burton, Gate, *co. Linc.*

Gayterig, *co. York.* Conf. of grants of a fishery in the Tees and lands at, to Byland Abbey, 1392. Add. 20569.

Gaytforthe. *v.* Gateforth, *co. York.*

Gayton, *co. Norf.* Conff. of St. Nicholas' Church to St. Stephen's Abbey, Caen, [1197-1205]. Harl. 43 G. 25 (Gaitona) ;—[1235-57]. Harl. 44 H. 38 (Gaitone, Geytone).

—— Ref. to resignation of the church of [late 12 cent.], by Mag. Ranulf de Bissacia, [1235-57]. Harl. 44 H. 38.

Gayton, *co. Northt.* Grants, etc., in, 1342. Add. 20733 ; — 1343. Add. 20734 ;—1345. Harl. 50 F. 51.

—— Homage in, 1346 (Gaytone). Cott. xxvii. 88.

—— Grant of rent out of the manor, 1570. Add. 6136.

—— Covenant for a fine in, 1603. Add. 6141.

Gayton, *co. Staff.* Release of a fifth part of the manor, 1824. Add. 20733.

Gayton le Marsh, *co. Linc.* Grant in, 1311. Harl. 45 D. 9.

—— Acquittance on payment of a rent from lands in, 1346 (Geyton). Harl. 57 G. 15.

—— Inq. p. m. of lands in, 1538 (Gaiton). Harl. Roll G. 20.

—— *Persona.* Ricardus, *t.* Hen. III. Harl. 50 F. 50.

Gayton le Wolds (Gaituna, etc.), *co. Linc.* Covenant on conveyance in, to Kirkstead Abbey from Bégard Abbey, *c.* 1150. Harl. 43 B. 45.

—— Grants of the church and lands in, with conff. to Kirkstead Abbey, *c.* 1150-54. Harl. 48 G. 40 ;—[1155 ?]. Harl. 43 C. 17 ;—*c.* 1160-70. Harl. 48 G. 41, 42 ;—[1166 ?]. Harl. 43 C.

Gernemothe, Gernemuta Parva.
*v.* Yarmouth, Lit., *co. Suff.*

Gerner. *v. sub* Wormingford, *co. Essex.*

Gerneshull, *nr. Blundleshay, co. Dors.*
Grants, etc., in, 1379. Harl. 48 F.
42 (Jerynshulle);—1396. Add. 15444
(Grynsattehille):—1409. Harl. 55 G.
44 (Gerynsattehull);—1410. Harl.
51 F. 40 (Gerynsathull), 41 (Geryns-
atte Hulle);—1448. Harl. 46 H. 23
(Gerens atte Hille);—1524. Harl. 46
H. 47 (Gerens).

Gerthom. *v.* Gardham, *in Etton, co.
York.*

Gerton, *co. Cumb.* (?). Grant in, 1467.
Add. 21174.

Gestingthorpe, *co. Essex.* Release of
Parkesgrave in, *t.* Hen. III. (Gestyn-
torpe). Harl. 52 B. 14.

Gestlinge, Gesteling. *v.* Guestling,
*co. Suss.*

Geynes. *v. sub* Upminster, *co. Essex.*

Geytone. *v.* Gayton, *co. Norf.*

Geywode. *v.* Gaywood, *co. Norf.*

Giberichisforde. *v.* Gilberts ford, *nr.
Reynoldston, co. Pembr.*

Gibwicum. *v.* Ipswich, *co. Suff.*

Gidding, Great, *co. Hunt.* Papal
conf. of the church, etc., to Huntingdon Priory, 1147 (Geddinga). Cott.
MS. Aug. ii. 112.

——— Covenant conc. descent of the
manor (?), 1372. Add. 19979.

Gidleigh *al.* Gidley, *co. Devon.* Bequest of soul-scot to, *c.* 995 (Gyfle).
Cott. viii. 38.

——— Deposition conc. tenure of the
manor, late Edw. I. (Gyddelegh).
Add. 20235.

Gifford's. *v. sub* Wickhambrook, *co.
Suff.*

Gihtslepe. *v.* Islip, *co. Oxon.*

Gilberdes Ruding. *v. sub* Longdon,
*co. Worc.*

Gilberts ford, *nr. Reynoldston, co.
Pembr.* Grants of mills, etc., at, *t.*
Edw. I. Add. 8058 (Giberichisforde),
8410 (vadum Gilberti).

Gildenwells, *co. York.* Grant in,
1499. Eg. 477.

Gildersome, *co. York.* Award conc.
land in, 1487. Add. 16967.

Gildesburc. *v.* Guilsborough, *co.
Northt.*

Gilling, *co. York.* Court-roll, 1441
(Gyllyng). Harl. Roll G. 23.

Gillingham, *co. Dors.* Settlement of
lands in, *c.* 1450. Add. 6268.

——— Grant of keepership of the forest,
manor, etc., to Lord Pembroke, 1602.
Eg. 418.

——— Surrender of the manor, etc.,
to Charles I., 1625. Eg. 419, 420.

——— Acquittance on purchase of the
manor, etc., 1661. Eg. 424.

Gillingham, *co. Kent.* Fine in, 1548
(Gyllyngham). Harl. 75 H. 4, 76 H. 50.

——— Grant of Brodehurst hermitage,
etc., in, 1549. Add. 4607.

Gillingham, *co. Norf.* Grants, etc.,
in, early 14 cent. Harl. 48 G. 13
(Giligham);—1375. Harl. 53 E. 45
(Gelyngham);—1386. Harl. 56 G.
21 (Gylyngham);—1422. Harl. 50
F. 36.

——— Release, etc., of the manor, 1361.
Harl. 52 B. 11 (Gylyngham);—1437.
Campb. xii. 14 (do.).

——— Fines in, 1419. Harl. 51 E. 53
(Gyllyngham);—1462. Harl. 54 I
19 (Gelyngham).

———*Clericus.* Robertus, 1275. Harl.
45 H. 44.

Gilly, *in Gwennap, co. Cornw.* Fines
in, 1582. Add. 15372;—1610. Add.
15378.

Gilstauyt, Giltweth. *v.* Guilthwaite,
*in Whiston, co. York.*

Gilston, *co. Hertf.* Feoffment in,
1607 (Gedellston). Add. 4825.

Gimingham, *co. Norf.* Acquittance
for an annuity from the manor, 1388
(Gymyngham). Harl. 49 H. 21.

——— Grant of a chantry in, 1402
(Gymyngham). Add. 14713 (*dors.*).

——— Fine of the manor, 1638 (Gym-
ingham). Woll. xi. 29.

———*Rector. Dom.* Rob. Stratton,
1417. Add. 10061.

Ginge, East, *in West Hendred, co.
Berks.* Covenant betw. Wallingford
Priory and Reading Abbey conc.
tithes of, *c.* 1225 (Estgeyng). Add.
19623.

Ginges, Gingjoyberd Laundry.
*v.* Buttsbury, *co. Essex.*

Gippewycum, etc. *v.* Ipswich, *co.
Suff.*

**Gloucester,** *Honour of.* Acquittance for payments to, in Warminster, co. Wilts., 1374 (Honor de Gloucestre). Add. 26716.

—— Acquittance for suit due to, at Bristol, 1556. Add. 6551.

**Glutintune,** *nr. Aloiston* (?), *co. Suss.* Conf. of tithes of, to Battle Abbey, [1121–5]. Cott. MS. Nero C. iii. f. 189.

**Gluvian,** *nr. St. Columb Major, co. Cornw.* Grants, etc., in, 1366. Harl. 50 C. 36 (Glyuyan mark);—1392. Harl. 50 C. 37 (Glyuyon Flamank);—1394. Harl. 51 E. 16 (Glyuyan Flamank);—1513. Harl. 50 C. 41.

**Glynn Collwn,** *co. Brecon.* Bond conc. the forest of, 1508 (Glyncolwyn). Harl. 111 B. 24.

**Gnareburg.** *v. Knaresborough, co. York.*

**Gnateshale, Gnatishale.** *v. Knattishall, co. Suff.*

**Gnatyngdon,** *co. Norf.* Conf. of grant of the manor to Norwich Priory, [1136–45] (Gnatingetune). Cott. ii. 1, ii. 21 (9) (copy).

**Gnolla.** *v. Knolle, co. Warw.*

**Gnosall,** *co. Staff.* Lease in, 1677. Campb. xi. 22 (covers).

—— Briefs conc. fires in, 1778, 1819. Ch. Br. B. xviii. 4, lix. 7.

**Goadby,** *co. Leic.* Covenant by Garendon Abbey conc. tithes of, 1182 (Goutebi). Add. 19815.

—— Feoffments, etc., of the manor, 1336. Add. 22163 (Gouteby);—1363. Add. 21266 (do.);—1383. Add. 22213, 22214 (do.);—1385. Add. 21267, 22215, 22216;—ante 1437. Add. 21265 (Gowdeby);—1441. Add. 22274 (do.);—1464–5. Add. 22292 (do.);—1470. Add. 22295, 22296.

—— Persona. Willelmus, 1182. Add. 19815.

**Goathill,** *co. Som.* The manor held by Will. de Monte Acuto [ob. 1270] (Godhulle). Add. 26754.

**Gobyons.** *v. sub Tilbury, East, co. Essex.*

**Godalming,** *co. Surr.* Indulgence for devotees at the church, 1270 (Godalmyng). Add. 19629.

—— Sales, etc., in, 1368. Add. 17328;—1502. Add. 13554;—1507. Add. 13557;—1587. Add. 13577.

**Godalming,** *co. Surr. (continued).* Præcipe on a covenant conc. land in, 1592. Add. 25510.

—— *Vicarius.* Dom. Joh. Chapman, 1378. Add. 18665.
   *v. also* Catshill, *co. Surr.*
   *v. also* Chiddingfold, *co. Surr.*

**Godalming Hundred,** *co. Surr.* Court-rolls, etc., 1483–4. Add. 26892.

—— Aid raised in, 1503–4. Add. 13555.

**Godenoch,** *in Kyle, co. Ayr.* Conf. of grant of, to Melrose Abbey, 1268. Cott. xviii. 3.

**Goderyngton.** *v. Goodrington, co. Devon.*

**Godford,** *nr. Payhembury, co. Devon.* Settlement in, 1465 (Godeford). Add. 13061–13064.

**Godhulle.** *v. Goathill, co. Som.*

**Godmanchester,** *co. Hunt.* Grant of, to Earl David, by Rich. I., 1194 (Gumcestria). Cott. MS. Nero C. iii. f. 191 (copy).

—— Conf. of, to Edm. Earl of Lancaster, 1285 (Gomecestria). Cott. MS. Aug. ii. 135 (5).

—— *Clericus.* Ricardus, [1146–54] (Gutmuncetre). Harl. 83 B. 4–6.

**Godmersham,** *co. Kent.* Grants, etc., in, t. Hen. III. Harl. 77 G. 21;—1415. Harl. 76 B. 13;—1699. Add. 958.

**Godmundesleah.** *v. Gumley, co. Leic.*

**Godney Island,** *in Glastonbury, co. Som.* Conf. of jurisdiction of the Abbat of Glastonbury in, 1344 (Godeneya). Campb. xiii. 19.

**Godshill,** *Isle of Wight.* Grant in Hale in, 1340 (Godeshull). Harl. 51 C. 45.

—— Lease, etc., in, 1518. Add. 18800 (Goddis hill);—t. Hen. VIII. Add. 9199 (Goodyshull);—1591. Add. 18871.

**Godstone,** *co. Surr.* Release of Lagham (Lageham) and Marden (Mereden) manors in, 1355. Harl. 55 G. 8.

—— Grant in, 1392 (Wolkstede). Add. 7618.

—— Sale of timber in, 1553. Harl. 79 F. 33.

—— Præcipe on a covenant conc. land in, with a moiety of the rectory, 1592 (Godstone al. Walkhampsted). Add. 25519.

uarby):—1615. Add. 6480 (Gonwarby);—1635. Add. 6481 (Gunwarbie).

Gonmares, Goonemaris, etc. v. sub St. Stephen's in Brannel, co. Cornw.

Gonnildesland. v. sub Eastwood, co. Essex.

Gonnildthweyt. v. Gunthwaite, co. York.

Gonvennou, Gonuenov, Gonvenow. v. Gunvenna, co. Cornw.

Gonwarby. v. Gonerby, co. Linc.

Goodestre. v. Easter, Good, co. Essex.

Goodherst. v. Goudhurst, co. Kent.

Goodleigh, co. Devon. Fine in, 1198 (Godelcia). Harl. 54 H. 32.

Goodmanham, co. York. Leases in, 1203 (Gudmundham). Add. 17388;—1697. Add. 1807.

—— Rector. Dom. Joh. Sutton, 1348. Harl. 44 D. 21.

Goodnestone, co. Kent. Grant, etc., in Rowling (Rollynge) in, 1341. Harl. 75 G. 18;—1533. Harl. 78 A. 12.

—— Grants, etc., in, 1508. Harl. 76 D. 35 (Goodnyston);—1509. Harl. 79 E. 30, 86 G. 29 (do.);—1515. Add. 953 (Godwynston);—1529. Harl. 78 E. 31;—1530. Harl. 78 A. 11 (Godeneston), 80 G. 59.

—— Fine in, 1548 (Goodeston). Harl. 75 H. 4, 76 H. 50.

Goodrich, co. Heref. Payment to the clerk of the castle, 1302 (Castrum godrici). Add. 20413.

—— Release of the castle, manor, etc., [1322-6] (Goderich). Harl. 48 G. 39.

Goodrington, co. Devon. Grant of the manor, 1414 (Gotheryngton). Harl. 48 I. 25.

—— Compotus-roll, 1414-15 (Goderyngton). Add. 13770.

Goodshaw, in Whalley, co. Lanc. Brief for rebuilding the chapel, 1783. Ch. Br, B. xxiii. 2.

Goodwick. v. sub Wyboston, co. Bedf.

Goodwood, co. Suss. Release of the park, etc., 1675. Add. 19016.

Goosey, in Stanford in the Vale, co. Berks. Terrier of the chapelry, 1608. Add. 25986.

Goostree, co. Chester. Brief for rebuilding the church, 1791. Ch. Br. B. xxxi. 8.

Gooswell, in Plymstock, co. Devon. Return of the value of the manor, 1572 (Gosewell). Cott. xvii. 22.

Gore. v. sub Upchurch, co. Kent.

Gore, in Shaftesbury, co. Dors. Fine in, for a chantry in Shaftesbury Abbey. 1282 (Gora). Add. 5250.

—— Sale of lands in Bradford, co. Wilts, late bel. to St. Anne's chantry in, 1551. Add. 5702.

Gore Gap. v. sub Barnham Broom, co. Norf.

Gorhale. v. sub Dodford, co. Buck.

Goring, co. Oxon. Grant in, t. Steph.(?) (Garingies). Harl. 83 A. 5.

—— Capellanus. Radulfus, late 12 cent. (Garinges). Harl. 47 H. 46.

Goring (Goryngg), co. Suss. Grants, etc., in, 1335-1411. Add. 24661-24668;—1441. Add. 24671;—1553. Add. 18835.

—— Sale of Goring Lee manor, 1657. Add. 18980, 18981.

—— Mortgage of rent from the same manor, 1658. Add. 18982, 18983.

Gorleston, co. Suff. Grants, etc., in, n. d., 1343. Add. 691 (1, 2) (copies); —1538. Add. 10225 (Garleston).

—— Record of suits with Yarmouth as to Port Right, t. Hen. VIII. Land. Roll 12.

—— Precipes on covenants conc. lands in, 1578. Add. 25355;—1589. Add. 25404;—1593. Add. 25451.

—— Release of the manor, 1606. Add. 14279.

Gornall, co. Staff. Grants, etc., in, t. Hen. III. Add. 6142 (Gornhal); —1375. Add. 6143 (Goronhale).

Gorrall. v. sub Dodford, co. Buck.

Gorsley wood, in Bridge, co. Kent. Grant of, 1541 (Gosley). Harl. 75 H. 3.

Gorwell. v. sub Tollesbury, co. Essex.

Gosbeck (Eston Gosebek, etc.), co. Suff. Grants, etc., in, 1300. Add. 9853;—1318. Add. 9904;—1320. Add. 9908, 9909;—1323. Add. 8370, 9916, 9918; —1332. Add. 9954;—1347. Add. 9994 (Gosebek), 9997;—1361. Add. 10011;—1413. Add. 10056 (Gosebac); —1476. Add. 10074.

—— Persona. Joh. de Hocham, 1361. Add. 10011.

—— Rector. Joh. de Okham, 1318. Add. 9904;—1323. Add. 8370, 9918.

Goodneston (?), co. Linc. Grant in, late 12 cent. (Gosheroburah). Harl. 52 G. 7.

—— Release in, to Sempringham Priory, late 13 cent. (Gowbeckiruhe). Add. ...

—— Conveyance of Doubledyke (Dubldyk) manor, etc., in, 1398 (Gebuldik). Harl. 57 E. 22.

—— Pledge on a covenant conc. land in, 1378 (Gosbertowne). Add. 25092.

—— Particulars of the Qu. Dowager's suit in, 1658. Add. 13562.

—— Power. Sire Rauf de Brok, 1332. Harl. 58 D. 32.

Goodford, Barzeya. v. sub Odcombe, co. Som.

Goodhope, Pastura de. v. sub ..., co. Kent.

Good... wude, nr. Faldingworth (?), co. Linc. Grant of tithe in, to Bul... ... Priory, early Hen. III. Harl. ...

Goodswell, v. Gocswell, in Plymstock, co. Devon.

Good...field, co. Hunt. Grants, etc., in, t. ... III. Harl. 79 D. 29 (Gosfeld);— ... Add. ...;—1535-1565. Add. ...

—— Grant of Morella, late Shardelowes (Shardelowes), manor in, etc., 1417. Add. 13645.

—— Assignment of mortgage of the manor, 1662. Add. 13731.

—— Vicarius. Dom. Johannes, 1340. Harl. 51 D. 6.

Goodford. v. sub Odcombe, co. Som.

Goodforth, co. Cumb. Compotus-roll of the manor, 1514, 1515 (Gosseford). Add. 24451.

Goodholm, nr. Newbold, co. Linc. Conf. of the water of, to Bullington Priory, t. John. Harl. 59 A. 18 (copy).

—— Lease of fishery, etc., of, to Barlings Abbey, by Bullington Priory, 1422. Harl. 44 B. 15.

Goodwood. v. sub Wotton, co. Surr.

Gotehurst. v. Gayhurst, co. Buck.

Gotham, co. Nott. Treaty conc. the castle betw. the Earls of Chester and Leicester, [1151-2] (Gataham). Cott. MS. Nero C. iii. f. 178.

Gotheryngton. v. Goodrington, co. Devon.

Gotton, nr. Taunton, [in W. Monkton?], co. Som. Grant in, 1403. Add. 17688.

Goudhurst, co. Kent. Grant at Bedgbury (Begoebyra) and Risden (?) (Hritsden) in, 814. Harl. 83 A. 1.

—— Grants, etc., in or nr., to Combwell Priory, 1231. Harl. 77 F. 23; —t. Edw. I. Harl. 76 B. 18, 19, 20, 23, 78 G. 46;—1330. Harl. 78 H. 8.

———— Grants, etc., in the den of Coombden (Cumden, etc.) in, 1278. Harl. 78 H. 6;—1307-8. Harl. 76 B. 24;—t. Edw. II. Harl. 77 D. 45;—1327. Harl. 77 D. 53;—1355. Harl. 76 B. 27;—1412. Harl. 76 B. 40.

—— Grants, etc., in the den of Bedgbury (Beggeberi, Beggere, etc.) in, 1278. Harl. 78 H. 6;—1281. Harl. 79 E. 47-49;—1282-3. Harl. 80 A. 28;—1297. Harl. 76 B. 25;—1307-8. Harl. 76 B. 24;—1322. Harl. 80 A. 45;—1326-7. Harl. 78 H. 7.

—— Grants, etc., in the den of Bromle al. Chingley in, 1281-2. Harl. 76 D. 43;—1413. Harl. 80 B. 25;—1420. Harl. 80 G. 55;—1423. Harl. 80 I. 88-90;—1437. Harl. 76 D. 7;—1446. Harl. 80 D. 30;—1461. Harl. 78 H. 9;—1474. Harl. 78 H. E. 9;—1479. Harl. 78 G. 36, 78 H. 10, 11, 78 I. 49;—1517. Harl. 76 H. 3, 9, 10;—1519. Harl. 80 D. 10;—1521. Harl. 78 I. 43, 44.

—— Grants, etc., in or near, t. Edw. I. Harl. 76 B. 21, 77 D. 44, 79 E. 53;—1283. Harl. 77 D. 43;—1307-8. Harl. 80 D. 45;—1313-4. Harl. 78 G. 42;—1315. Harl. 79 E. 18, 19;—1318-9. Harl. 77 D. 46;—1327. Harl. 77 D. 53, 54;—1328. Harl. 79 E. 54;—1334. Harl. 78 I. 29;—1354. Harl. 79 D. 8;—1359. Harl. 77 G. 10;—1367. Harl. 76 B. 28, 78 E. 40;—1380. Harl. 80 B. 23;—1386. Harl. 78 C. 35;—1389. Harl. 76 B. 29;—1392. Harl. 78 D. 58;—1393. Harl. 78 H. 32;—1396. Harl. 76 B. 35, 76 E. 22, 78 G. 43, 80 C. 33;—1397. Harl. 79 C. 26;—1398. Harl. 76 B. 30-32;—1399. Harl. 78 G. 25;—1401. Add. 24509;—1403. Harl. 79 E. 24;—1408. Harl. 80 B. 3;—1411. Harl. 76 B. 36, 78 G. 44;—1412. Harl. 76 B. 37, 38, 40;—1414. Harl. 76 B. 39, 76 C. 44;—1415. Harl. 77 G. 45, 46;—1417. Harl. 79 E. 25;—1419. Harl. 80 B. 46;—1422. Harl. 76 B. 41, 42;—1423. Harl. 76 B. 8;—1425. Harl. 80 C. 34;—1427. Harl. 78 D. 56, 80 E. 16;—1433. Harl. 80 D. 49, 50, 80

Greenfield, *in Wirksworth* (?), *co. Derb.* Covenant conc. title in, 1503 (Grenefeld). Woll. x. 15.

Greenfield (Grenefeld), *co. Linc.* Grants, etc., in, to Greenfield Priory, *c.* 1150. Harl. 50 I. 30 ;—late 12 cent. Harl. 50 I. 31 ;—*t.* Hen. III. Harl. 47 F. 42, 57 G. 5 ;—1474. Harl. 57 A. 29.

—— Lease in, by Greenfield Priory, 1340. Harl. 44 E. 5.

—— Release in, 1474. Harl. 50 O. 27.

Greenford, *co. Midd.* Conf. by Edw. the Confessor of a grant in, to Westminster Abbey, 1066 [*sc.* 1065] (Greneforde). Cott. vi. 2 (*copy*).

—— Customary roll of, bel. to Westminster Abbey, early Hen. III. (Greneford). Add. 8139.

—— Fines in, 1700, 1701, 1709. Add. 1653-1658.

—— Extracts of court-rolls of Greenford cum Hanwell manor, 1723, 1738. Add. 1678, 1679.

Greenham, *in Stawley, co. Som.* Exchequer acquittance for farm of two parts of the manor, etc., 1595 (Greneham). Add. 25650.

Greenhill. *v. sub* Harrow on the Hill, *co. Midd.*

Greenhill, *nr. Norton, co. Derb.* Grants, etc., in, 1495. Woll. i. 22-24 (Grenehill);—1536. Harl. 112 G. 15 (Grenylle).

—— Fine in, 1541 (Grenchyll). Woll. ii. 71.

Greenhill, *nr. Bingley, co. York.* Power to give seisin in, 1392 (Greynhill). Harl. 45 F. 28.

Greenhithe, *co. Kent.* Grants in, 1405. Harl. 58 C. 45 (Grenehethe);— 1407. Harl. 76 G. 39 (Grenerersh).

Greenhoe, North, Hundred, *co. Norf.* Grant of, by Edw. III., to Pr. John, his son, 1372. Cott. xv. 1.

—— Lease of, by Eliz., Queen of Edw. IV., 1467. Add. 17741.

Greenhow, *co. York.* Grants, etc., in, early 13 cent. Harl. 112 H. 58 (Grenehau);—*t.* Hen. III. Harl. 112 H. 42 (Greneh.);—late 13 cent. Harl. 112 G. 16 (Grenhowe), Lansd. 74 (Grenehou).

Greenlow. *v.* Grindlow, *co. Derb.*

Greens Norton. *v.* Norton, Greens, *co. North.*

Greensbury. *v. sub* Bolnhurst, *co. Bedf.*

Greenstead, *co. Essex.* Bequests of land at, late 10 cent. (Grenstyda, Grenstede). Harl. 43 C. 4.

Greenstead, *nr. Colchester, co. Essex.* Letters patent conc. a tenth assessed on, in 8 Edw. III., 1429 (Grensted). Campb. xxix. 10.

Greenstead, *in Ongar Hundred, co. Essex.* Grant in, 1314 (Grenestede). Cott. xii. 40.

—— Releases of the manor (?), 1334, 1347. Add. 19984, 19985.

Greenway, *in Lower Hardres* (?), *co. Kent.* Grant, etc., in, 1270-1. Harl. 80 I. 91 (Greneweye);—1280. Harl. 78 D. 36 (do.).

Greenwell, *co. Durham.* Power to give seisin in, 1366 (Grenwell). Harl. 45 I. 39.

Greenwich, *co. Kent.* Grant of rent in, late Hen. III. (Grenewic). Harl. 50 I. 41.

—— Grants, etc., in, 1291. Harl. 52 F. 27 (Estgrenewyc);—1341. Harl. 50 O. 35 (Estgrenewych);—1508. Add. 23780.

—— Fine in, 1511 (Estgrenewyche). Harl. 84 B. 43.

—— Sale in Bengeworth, *co. Worc.,* held of E. Greenwich manor, 1591. Harl. 76 E. 21.

—— License for enclosure in E. G. manor, 1699. Add. 4834.

Greet, *in Winchcombe, co. Glouc.* Grant in, early 13 cent. (Greta). Slo. xxxiii. 3.

Greetham, *co. Linc.* Release in, 1351 (Gretham parva). Campb. v. 13.

—— *Persona.* Tho. de Elsham, 1388 (Gretham). Cott. xxviii. 94.

Greibi. *v.* Graby, *co. Linc.*

Grempthorp. *v.* Grainthorpe, *co. Linc.*

Gren. *v.* Grain, Isle of, *co. Kent.*

Grenbourghe. *v.* Grandborough, *co. Warw.*

Grendale. *v.* Grindall, *co. York.*

Grendon, *co. North.* Release, etc., in, early Hen. III. Harl. 49 I. 18 (Grendune);—1362. Add. 21868.

—— Letters pat. for an assise of nov. diss. in, 1391. Add. 710.

Grendon, co. Northt. (continued). Precipe on a covenant conc. land in, 1578. Add. 25154.

Grendon, co. Warw. Persona. Willelmus, [1216-23]. Cott. xii. 54.

——— Johannes, [1236]. Add. 20463.

Grendon, Bishop's, co. Heref. Settlement in, 1585. Add. 7089.

Grendon Underwood, co. Buck. Power to take seisin, etc., of the manor, 1368. Cott. xxiv. 11 ;—1581. Harl. 55 F. 38.

——— Inquest on title to the manor, 1492. Harl. Roll G. 27.

Grene. v. sub Northfleet, co. Kent.
——— v. sub Shorne, co. Kent.

Grenebi. v. Granby, co. Nott.

Greneforde. v. Greenford, co. Midd.

Grenegh., Grenehau, etc. v. Greenhow, co. York.

Greneham. v. Greenham, in Stawley, co. Som.

Grenehill. v. Greenhill, nr. Norton, co. Derb.

Grenelawa, in Gamlingay, co. Camb. Grant in, to Sawtrey Abbey, [1154-5?]. Harl. 83 A. 25.

Grenestede. v. Greenstead, co. Essex.
——— v. Grinstead, E., co. Suss.

Grenewic. v. Greenwich, co. Kent.

Greneworth, co. Som. Appointment of a steward of the manor, 1571. Harl. 75 E. 40.

Grenewyke, co. Linc. Fine in, 1302. Harl. 45 H. 18.

Grenleghe. v. sub Boxford, co. Suff.

Grenloue. v. Grindlow, in Hope, co. Derb.

Grenwell. v. Greenwell, co. Durh.

Gresby. v. Grasby, co. Linc.

Gresford, co. Denb. Grants, etc., in, 1391. Add. 8633, 8635 ;—1450. Add. 8639 ; — 1464. Add. 8643 ; — 1551. Add. 8528.

——— Rector. Ebulo Lestraunge, 1396. Harl. 56 F. 25.

——— v. also Burton, in Gresford, co. Denb.

Gresham, co. Norf. Award conc. tithes of, [1244-8]. Add. 14676.

Gresham, co. Norf. (continued). Power to give seisin in, 1379. Add. 14521.

——— Lease of the manor, 1399. Add. 14677.

——— Petitions conc. a riot at, [1450]. Add. 17239, 17240.

——— Conf. to Thetford Priory of a rent from the church of, 1457. Add. 17245.

——— Bequests to the church, etc., 1482. Add. 17253.

Gresley. v. Greasley, co. Nott.

Gresley, co. Derb. Conveyance of Church Gresley and Castle Gresley manors, 1660 (Greysley). Add. 6084.

——— Brief for rebuilding the church, 1786. Ch. Br. B. xxvi. 6.

Gresseby. v. Grasby, co. Linc.

Gressingham, co. Lanc. Settlement of the manor, etc., 1670. Add. 19547.

Gresthorp. v. Grassthorpe, co. Nott.

Gresty, in Shavington, co. Chest. Lease, etc., of the manor, 1395. Campb. xxviii. 8 (Graysty) ;—1400. Campb. xxviii. 10 (Greysty).

Greta. v. Groet, in Winchcombe, co. Glouc.

Gretenerssh. v. Greenhithe, co. Kent.

Gretingham, Gretyngham. v. Cretingham, co. Suff.

Gretna, co. Dumfries. Conf. of grant of the church to Gisburne Priory, t. Edw. I. (Gretenhow). Cott. xi. 58, Harl. 43 B. 12.

Gretton, co. Northt. Grants, etc., in, 1349. Add. 21869 ; — 1381. Add. 21870 ;—1499. Add. 21873 ;—1555. Add. 7582 ;—1571. Add. 728.

——— Grant of the manor, 1430. Add. 21871.

——— Order to the woodward conc. rights in, 1461. Add. 21872.

——— Sale of timber in, 1517. Add. 21874.

——— Fine in, 1579. Add. 21669.

——— Vicarius. Henricus, 1349. Add. 21869.

Gretton, in Rushbury, co. Salop. Grant in, 1421 (Grootynton). Add. 24884.

Gretwood, nr. Stafford, co. Staff. Defeasance of bond for a recovery in, 1421 (Gretewode). Lansd. 144.

Grewis, Le, al. The Greaves. v. sub Beeley, co. Derb.

**Grove, Le,** *in Holton* (?), *co. Oxon.*
Grant of reversion to the manor, etc.,
1429. Harl. 53 A. 5.

**Grove, The.** *v. sub* Ellesborough, *co.
Buck.*

**Grove Hill,** *in Beverley, co. York.*
Grant of rent in, 1360 (Grovall).
Lansd. 313.

**Grove Place.** *v. sub* Chalfont St.
Giles, *co. Buck.*

**Groveley,** *Forest of.* *v.* Graveley,
*Forest of, co. Wilts.*

**Grundisburgh,** *co. Suff.* Grants,
etc., in, *t.* Edw. I. Add. 5492
(Grundesburch) ; — 1295. Add. 7269
(Grundesburg) ; — 1379. Add. 5512
(Grundesburgh) ;—1499. Add. 10222
(Groundesburgh).
—— Precipe on a covenant conc. land
in, 1589. Add. 25399.
—— *Persona.* Rob. Thurgarton, 1415.
Campb. i. 27.

**Grutteford.** *v.* Girtford, *co. Bedf.*

**Grykes Marsh,** *co. Suss.* Award conc.
bounds in, betw. Battle and Robertsbridge Abbeys, 1244. Eg. 375.

**Grymes.** *v. sub* Snetterton, *co. Norf.*

**Grymesbury.** *v. sub* Bolnhurst, *co.
Bedf.*

**Grymestone.** *v. sub* Trimley St.
Martin, *co. Suff.*

**Grymoldby.** *v.* Grimoldby, *co. Linc.*

**Grymson.** *v.* Grimston, *co. Leic.*

**Grynglay.** *v.* Gringley on the Hill,
*co. Nott.*

**Grynsattehille,** *v.* Garneshull, *nr.
Blundleshay, co. Dors.*

**Grynstede, East, West.** *v.* Grinstead,
E. and W., *co. Suss.*

**Grytelhale,** *co. Essex.* Acquittance
for a fine for the manor, 1355. Cott.
xxvii. 152.

**Guavos.** *v.* Gwavas, *nr. Grade, co.
Cornw.*

**Gudherst.** *v.* Goudhurst, *co. Kent.*

**Gudmundham.** *v.* Goodmanham, *co.
York.*

**Gudunburnell** *al.* **Gudeburnell,**
*co. Salop.* Warrant for a grant of the
manor, [1514-20]. Add. 22628.

**Guedwelle,** *nr. Canterbury, co. Kent.*
Grant in, to the Priory of the H.

Sepulchre, Canterbury, early 13 cent.
Harl. 78 A. 50.

**Guer.** *v.* Gower, *co. Glam.*

**Guernsey, Island of.** Restoration of
lands in, to O. de la Sale, 1323 (lisle de
Guernecie). Add. 19809.
—— Grant of the ward of Castle
Cornet (?) in, 1397 (Garnessy). Harl.
43 E. 37.
—— Order against the Receiver of
the Duke of Gloucester in, 1439.
Add. 19810.
—— Certificate of title to lands in
St. Peter's Port, 1479. Add. 19811.
—— License to Trinity of the Forest
par. in, to sell corn, etc., 1548. Add.
19812.
—— Order on the Receiver of, for
maintenance of N. Baudouin, 1563.
Add. 19813.
—— Bills of partition of inherited
lands in, 1585, 1594. Add. 26810-
26812.
—— Certificate of exchange of lands
in St. Sampson's and St. Peter's Port,
1612. Add. 19814.
—— *Gardein des Isles de Jeresey et
Garnesey.* Edw. Deuerwyk [sc. of
York], *Counte de Rutteland et de Cork,*
1397. Harl. 43 E. 37.
—— *Captain.* Francis Chamberleyn,
1563. Harl. 83 H. 2.
—— *Justice Errant.* Hen. Spigournel,
1323. Add. 19809.

**Guestling,** *co. Suss.* Grants, etc., in,
1281. Add. 16208 (Gestling) ;—1344.
Add. 20072 (Gestlinge) ;—1347. Add.
20077, 20078 ; — 1360. Add. 9236
(Gystlyng) ; — 1367. Add. 20057
(Gestlinge) ;—1424. Add. 20073, 20074
(Gestelyng) ; — 1499. Add. 24858
(Gestlynge).
—— Lands of the fee of, in Rye,
Peasemarsh, Beckley, etc., 1299-1300.
Add. 20153.
—— Grant in Pickham (Pykeham)
in, 1308. Add. 20150.
—— Precipe on a covenant conc. land
in, 1589. Add. 25536.
—— *Rector.* Steph. Breuetour *al.*
Breuetor, 1375. Harl. 78 A. 23 ;—
1378. Harl. 78 A. 24.
—— —— Pet. Dyst, 1419. Add.
972 ;—1424. Add. 20074.

**Guestling Hundred,** *co. Suss.* Grant
in, 1380 (Gestlinge). Add. 16211.

# H

Habberley, *in Kidderminster,* co.
Worc.(?). Grant in, *t.* Edw. I. (?) (Haburleygh). Add. 24706 (*copy*).

Habeton. *v.* Hapton, co. Norf.

Habrough (Haburc, Haburg, etc.), co.
*Linc.* Grants, etc., of St. Margaret's
church and lands in, to Newhouse
Abbey, *c.* 1150. Harl. 45 F. 17, 19,
50 H. 58;—*t.* Steph.–*t.* Hen. II. or late
12 cent. Harl. 45 E. 42, 46 B. 2-11,
47 C. 23, 49 C. 19-21, 50 I. 1, 54 B. 10,
16, 17;—early 13 cent. Harl. 46 A.
17, 46 B. 13-15, 49 A. 8, 50 I. 3, 51 A.
42, 52 D. 8, 54 B. 11, 18;—*t.* Hen. III.
Harl. 43 A. 65 *a, b,* 44 C. 57, 46 B. 16-
19, 21-26, 47 G. 17-19, 48 A. 38, 48 H.
30, 32, 33, 49 A. 23, 50 A. 12, 51 A. 46,
52 D. 18, 54 H. 30;—1269. Harl. 48
H. 31;—1271. Harl. 52 H. 45;—*t.* Edw.
I. Cott. xxvii. 30, Harl. 47 B. 41, 54
F. 31;—1303. Harl. 50 I. 2, 6;—
1307. Cott. v. 45;—*t.* Edw. II. Harl.
45 F. 61, 46 B. 31;—1320. Cott. xxiv.
1;—1336. Harl. 50 G. 45;—*t.* Edw.
III. Harl. 48 A. 39;—1363. Cott. v.
44;—1380. Harl. 46 D. 6.

—— Episcopal conff., etc., of the
church to Newhouse Abbey, [1143-7].
Harl. 43 H. 10;—*c.* 1150-60. Harl.
43 G. 19, 43 H. 14-17;—[1189-95].
Harl. 43 H. 38 *b;—c.* 1216. Harl. 43
H. 23;—1263. Harl. 44 F. 27;—
1287. Harl. 43 H. 27;—1307. Harl.
43 H. 34;—1319. Harl. 43 G. 29;—
1333. Harl. 43 H. 39, 40;—1344.
Harl. 43 H. 41;—1368. Harl. 43 H.
44;—1389. Harl. 43 G. 33;—1424.
Harl. 43 G. 35;—1485. Harl. 43 I. 7;
—1500. Harl. 43 I. 8.

—— Conf. of grants in, to the same, by
Hen. II., [1156-7?]. Harl. 51 H. 1.

—— Grant in, to the church of, late
Hen. II. Harl. 46 B. 12.

—— Grants, etc., in, *t.* Hen. II. Harl.
46 A. 55, 46 B. 1;—*t.* Hen. III.–*t.*
Edw. I. Harl. 48 A. 37, 50 D. 41;—
1314. Harl. 46 B. 29, 30;—*t.* Edw. II.
Harl. 46 B. 20 (Hauburg), 28;—1325.
Harl. 46 B. 33;—1537. Harl. 43 F. 36.

—— Grants, etc., in, to Nun Cotun
Priory, late 12 cent. Add. 20741;—*t.*
John. Add. 20740;—*c.* 1240-50. Add.
20742.

—— Covenant by H. de Neville and
his men of, conc. tithes to Newhouse
Abbey, early 13 cent. Harl. 44 I. 12.

Habrough (Haburc, Haburg, etc.), co.
*Linc.* (*continued*). Award in a suit for
tithes in, betw. Newhouse and Croxton
Abbeys, and Nun Cotun Priory, 1228.
Harl. 44 E. 20.

—— Grants, etc., in, from Newhouse
Abbey, early Hen. III. Harl. 58 G.
41;—*c.* 1260. Harl. 44 G. 46;—1327.
Harl. 44 H 21;—1345. Harl. 44 H. 27.

—— Taxation of the vicarage, [1239-
65]. Harl. 45 A. 24.

—— Conveyance of the manor (?) to
A. de Laci, 1270 (Hautebarge). Harl.
52 H. 43 *b.*

—— License to Newhouse Abbey to
make a bridge in, *t.* Edw. I. Harl. 49
C. 46, 47.

—— Certificates conc. tithes to Newhouse Abbey from the mill of, 1311.
Harl. 44 E. 13, 49 I. 40;—1312. Harl.
56 B. 34.

—— Service due from Newhouse
Abbey in, 1314. Harl. 46 B. 30.

—— Grant of the manor, 1326. Harl.
46 B. 34.

—— Licenses to grant the manor to
Newhouse Abbey, 1327. Harl. 43 D.
27, 52 H. 34.

—— Mandate by the Prior of Thornholme conc. tithes in, to Newhouse
Abbey, 1365. Harl. 45 A. 7.

—— Covenant by Newhouse Abbey
to maintain a chantry in St. Katharine's chapel in St. Margaret's church,
1373. Harl. 55 F. 46.

—— Deposition conc. wreckage seized
by Newhouse Abbey in the manor,
1506. Harl. 48 I. 30.

—— *Capellanus.* Matheus, late 12
cent. Harl. 46 B. 7, 12, 47 C. 29;—
early 13 cent. Harl. 46 B. 21.

—— —— Willelmus, early 13 cent.
Harl. 46 B. 13, 21, 54 B. 8;—*t.* Hen.
III. Harl. 54 B. 18.

—— —— Nicolaus, *t.* Hen. III.
Harl. 46 B. 26.

—— *Clericus.* Gervasius, [1143-7].
Cott. xii. 18;—early Hen. II. Harl.
46 A. 55, 46 B. 2, 3, 4.

—— —— Walterus, *t.* Hen. II.
Harl. 46 B. 4, 6, 10, 11, 12, 49 C. 19;—
early 13 cent. Harl. 46 A. 9.

—— —— Willelmus, late Hen. II.
Harl. 54 B. 16, 17.

—— —— Galfridus, *t.* Hen. III.
Harl. 46 B. 22, 27, 48 H. 32, 33, 49 C. 39.

—— —— Robertus, 1325. Harl. 46
B. 33;—1326. Harl. 46 B. 34;—1327.

Y

(Hacketorn):—1187. Harl. 44 A. 22
(Haketorn):—late 12 cent.-early 13
cent. Harl. 47 H. 7, 48 I. 50, 52, 50 D.
6, 7, 51 B. 13–16, 18, 21–24, 57 A. 32–34,
57 C. 20, 21, 57 D. 48, 57 E. 7, Cott.
xii. 15;—early Hen. III.-t. Edw. I.
Harl. 43 A. 57, 45 B. 25, 45 G. 42, 54,
55, 48 H. 10, 11, 48 I. 54, 55, 51 B. 26–
29, 32–34, 54 B. 19, 54 F. 24, 55 B.
35, 57 C. 22, 23, 27, 57 G. 29. 58 B. 39 ;
—1273. Harl. 44 I. 20 ;—1308. Harl.
45 B. 26 ;—1343. Harl. 51 B. 35 ;—
1349 Harl. 45 H. 35.

—— Conf. of covenant with Bullington Priory conc. the church, c. 1160 (?)
(Haketorn). Harl. 43 H. 21.

—— Grant of a moiety of the church
to Bullington Priory, with conf., t. Hen.
II. Harl. 54 E. 36 (Hack-torne):—
t. Hen. III. Harl. 52 I. 40 (Hakethorn).

—— Episcopal conff., etc., of rights
in the church of, to the same, [1175-
82]. Harl. 43 C. 36 (Hachetorn) ;—
1389. Harl. 43 G. 32 (Hakethorn);
—1399. Harl. 43 I. 3 ;—1485. Harl.
43 I. 13.

—— Lands held in dower in, [1185-
89] (Hacchet.). Harl. 51 B. 20.

—— Grants, etc., in, by Bullington
Priory, c. 1200. Harl. 44 A. 28
(Hachetorn);—t. Hen. III. Harl. 44
A. 47 (Hakethorn), 52 (do.);—1308.
Harl. 44 B. 1 (Hakthorne).

—— Conff. of lands in, with a moiety
of the church, to Bullington Priory
by P., W. and P. de Kyme, 1256. Harl.
52 H. 28 ;—t. Edw. I.–II. Harl. 52 H.
5 ;—post 1322. Harl. 52 H. 27.

—— Grants, etc., in, t. Hen. III.-t.
Edw. I. Harl. 45 B. 24 (Hackethorn),
46 D. 36 (Haketorn), 51 B. 19 (Hake-
thoren), 30 (Haketorn), Cott. xxx. 12
(Hactorn);—1347. Harl. 51 G. 52
(Hakthorn).

—— Grant of a rent from the manor,
1381 (Hakthorn). Harl. 56 G. 43.

—— Conf. of a bull of protection, etc.,
for lands in, to Bullington Priory,
1499. Harl. 43 I. 11.

—— Capellanus. Walterus, early 13
cent. Harl. 47 H. 47, 50 D. 6.

—— —— Willelmus, early 13 cent.
Harl. 48 I. 52, 51 B. 21.

—— —— Johannes, early 13 cent.
Harl. 51 B. 24.

—— Persona. Alanus, early 13 cent.
Harl. 50 D. 6, 51 B. 13, 16, 18, 22–25.

Hackthorn (Hakethorn, etc.), co. Linc.
(continued). Persona (continued). Robertus, early 13 cent.-t. Hen. III. Harl.
48 B. 44, 48 H. 11, 48 I. 54, 55, 51 B. 19,
57 A. 33, 34 ;—1242. Harl. 44 E. 49.

—— Rector. Dom. Robertus, t. Hen.
III. Cott. xxx. 12.

—— Sacerdos. Walterus, 12–13 cent.
Harl. 51 B. 18.

—— Vicarius. Robertus, t. Hen. III.
Harl. 48 B. 44.

Hacleah. v Oakley, in Higham, co. Kent.

Hactona. v. Aughton, in Aston, co. York.

Hacumby, Hacunby. v. Hacconby,
co. Linc.

Haddels. v. Hadley, co. Salop.

Haddenham, co. Buck. Grant of the
manor and church to Rochester Cathedral, [1088–9]' (Hedreham). Campb.
vii. 1.

—— Exchequer acquittance for farm
of the manor, 1615. Add. 25571.

—— Brief conc. a fire at, 1760. Ch.
Br. A. vii. 1.

Haddenham, co. Camb. Grants in,
t. Hen. III. Add. 15517 (Hadenham);
—1337. Lansd. 108 (do.).

Haddington, co. Hadd. Grants, by
King David and Earl Henry, of Clerk-
ington, with tithes, etc., to St. Mary's
church at, [1140–6] (Hadintune). Cott.
xviii. 12, 22.

—— Subordination of the church, by
King David, to St. Andrew's Priory,
[1140–6] (do.). Campb. xxx. 1.

—— Conff. of St. Mary's church to
St. Andrew's Priory, c. 1173–7. Cott.
xviii. 32 (Hadintunia);—1240. Cott.
xviii. 27 (Haddintune);—1281. Cott.
xviii. 29 (Hadigtun).

—— Papal conf. of the same to the
same, [1185] (Hadintona). Cott.
xviii. 31.

—— Assignment of tithes in, to the
vicar, ante 1233 (Hadinton). Cott.
xviii. 36.

—— Order to tax the vicarage, ante
1233 (Hadingtona). Cott. xviii. 37.

—— Affidavits conc. the vicar's portion
of the vicarage, ante 1233 (Hadingtona). Cott. xxi. 16.

—— Dispute conc. tithes in, betw.
St. Andrew's Priory and Haddington
Nunnery, [1245]. Cott. xviii. 30 ;—
1245. Cott. xviii. 28.

—— Acquittance to St. Andrew's

1345. Add. 15459 (Hadleye);—1564. Harl. 57 H. 14 (Hadlegh);—1599. Harl. 51 H. 32 (Hadleygh).

—— Power to take seisin of the castle and town, 1378 (Hadele). Harl. 57 C. 12.

—— Fines in, 1536. Harl. 58 H. 16 (Hadleyght);—1564. Harl. 48 D. 40, 58 D. 52;—1634. Harl. 45 G. 7.

Hadleigh, co. Suff. Grants, etc., in, 1334. Harl. 56 D. 18, 19 (Hadleye); —1334-5.· Harl. 58 G. 17 dors (copy); —1464. Harl. 55 C. 43 (Hadlegh);— 1578. Add. 24305;—1583. Harl. 86 H. 10;—1617. Add. 9784;—1653. Add. 10573.

—— Power to give seisin of Pond and Cosford manors, etc., in, 1398. Add. 10571.

—— Dispute as to title to Toppesfield manor in, t. Hen. VI. (Hadlye). Harl. Roll C. 14.

—— Precipes on covenants conc. lands in, 1593. Add. 25469, 25470.

—— Persona. Dom. Joh. Lyncolne, 1408. Harl. 56 H. 37.

—— Tho. Walbere, 1446. Add. 10145.

—— Rector. Joh. fil. Ric. Farewel, 1332. Harl. 49 I. 25.

—— John Still, D.D., 1578. Add. 24305.

Hadley, nr. Wellington, co. Salop. Covenant conc. settlement of the manor, etc., 1350. Harl. 54 D. 28 (Haddelee); —1380. Harl. 85 B. 40 (Haddele).

Hadley Monachorum al. Monken Hadley, co. Midd. Grants, etc., in, 1416. Add. 24830 (Hadlee);—1485. Add. 24831 (Hadley Monachorum);— 1525. Add. 24832;—1542. Add. 24833, 24834.

Hadlow, co. Kent. Grant of tithe from the mill, etc., to Combwell Priory, t. Hen. II. (Aslo). Harl. 77 E. 50.

—— Grants, etc., in, early 13 cent. Add. 20007 (Hadlo);—1316-7. Harl. 78 C. 32;—1324. Harl. 76 G. 38;— 1461. Harl. 79 D. 41;—1547. Harl. 57 B. 25;—1557. Harl. 78 F. 1;— 1558. Harl. 78 F. 3.

—— Fine in, 1380 (Hadlo). Add. 6260.

—— Court-rolls of Hadlow and Lomwood manors, 1478-1482. Add. 23788-23791.

·—— Court-rolls, etc., of Hadlow Place

manor, 1518, 1662-1772. Add. 25960, 25981.

—— Leases, etc., of Crombury and Caustons manors, etc., in, 1555. Harl. 75 E. 31;—1556. Harl. 75 H. 23;— 1574. Harl. 77 H. 35.

—— Warrant for deduction from rent due to the Crown for lease of the manor, [1559-60]. Harl. 86 G. 33.

—— Covenant conc. sale of the manor, 1560. Harl. 76 E. 40.

—— N. Frith park, etc., in. v. sub Tonbridge, co. Kent.

Hadnock, in Forest of Dean, co. Monm. Exchange of, betw. B. de Monemue and Monmouth Priory, c. 1150-60 (Hodenoc). Add. 20405.

—— Conf. of grant, etc., in, late Hen. II. Add. 7012 (Hodhenac);—late 13 cent. Add. 7706 (Hodenac).

—— Grants, etc., in, to Lanthony Priory, t. John. Add. 7705 (Hodenach);—1283. Add. 6709 (Hodenac); —t. Edw. I. Add. 7707 (Hodenak).

—— Court-roll, 1345 (Hademak). Add. 7698.

—— Leases in, by Lanthony Priory, 1447. Add. 7708 (Hodemak);—1466. Add. 7023 (Haddenock).

Hadres, Niper. v. Hardres, Nether al. Lower, co. Kent.

Haeccaham, co. Worc. (?). Accord conc. land at, 836. Cott. MS. Aug. ii. 9.

Haese. v. Hayes, co. Midd.

Hafingseota, co. Kent. Grant at, 798. Cott. MS. Aug. ii. 97.

Hafkherst. v. Hawkhurst, co. Kent.

Hafod y Porth, co. Glam. Claim to tithes in, by Margam Abbey, 1339 (Portbauoth). Harl. 75 A. 28.

—— Covenant of Margam Abbey not to molest tenants in fee of, 1470 (Havotporth). Harl. 75 A. 46.

Haga. v. Haugh, co. Linc.

Hagard, The, co. Louth. Release in the manor of, 1364. Add. 5828.

Hagborne, co. Berks. Suit conc. land in, 990-994 (æt Hacceburnan). Cott. MS. Aug. ii. 15.

Hagenes. v. Hawnes, co. Bedf.

Hagh. v. Haugh, co. Linc.

Hagham. v. Haugham, co. Linc.

Haghenedon, Mons de. v. sub Kenn, co. Devon.

Haghenifeld, Hagnefeld. *v. sub* Waltham, *co. Kent.*

Hagherthorpe. *v.* Hawthorpe, *in Iraham, co. Linc.*

Haghethorp. *v.* Authorpe, *co. Linc.*

Hagnaby, *co. Linc.* Precipe on a covenant conc. land in, 1578 (Hagnaby *al.* Hawnby). Add. 25074.

Hagnes. *v.* Hawnes, *co. Bedf.*

Hagworthingham, *co. Linc.* Release in, 1387. Harl. 53 C. 38.

——— Precipe on a covenant conc. the manor, 1555. Add. 25056.

Hahylle. *v.* Hethel, *co. Norf.*

Haisiariaia. *v.* Hatherley, *co. Glouc.*

Haidon. *v. sub* Rodbourne Cheyney, *co. Wilts.*

Hail Weston, *co. Hunt.* Grant in, t. Steph. (Weston = Hail Weston ?). Add. 11233 (5) (*copy*).

——— Papal conf. of the chapel to Huntingdon Priory, 1427 (Hayle Weston). Cott. MS. Aug. ii. 119.

Hailsham (Haylesham, etc.), *co. Suss.* Grants, etc., in. 1402. Add. 8095;—1450. Add. 8097;—1489. Add. 8101;—1507. Add. 8105;—1508. Add. 8106, 8107 (Haillesham);—1511. Add. 8108;—1517. Add. 8109;—1519. Add. 8110;—1541. Add. 8113.

——— Fine in, 1500. Add. 15215.

——— Precipes on covenants conc. lands in, etc., 1578. Add. 18095;—1593. Add. 18100.

——— *Vicarius (nuper)*. Tho. Altofte, 1507. Add. 8105.

*v. also* Mayham, *nr. Hailsham, co. Suss.*

Hainford, *co. Norf.* Compotus of the manor (?), 1363-4 (Heyneford). Add. 26060.

——— *Persona*. Rodbertus, late 12 cent. (Heinford). Add. 15186.

Hainton, *co. Linc.* Grants and fine of the manor, *c.* 1240. Harl. 52 B. 34 (Haynthon);—1250. Harl. 58 C. 27 (Heynton);—1393. Harl. 57 E. 22 (Haynton).

——— Grant in, *ante* 1285 (Hynton). Harl. 54 B. 25.

——— *Rector*. Dom. Bernard de Nevil, *ante* 1285. Harl. 54 B. 25.

Hainworth, *nr. Keighley, co. York.*

Feoffments in, 1547 (Haneworth). Add. 17010, 17011.

Hakebrig. *v. sub* Tetney, *co. Linc.*

Hakebrug. *v.* Hackbridge, *in Carshalton, co. Surr.*

Hakeleye. *v.* Hackley, *in Bodenham, co. Heref.*

Hakelinton. *v.* Hackleton, *co. Northt.*

Hakenestone. *v.* Haxton, *co. Wilts.*

Hakeney. *v.* Hackney, *co. Midd.*

Hakenton, Hakinton, Hakyngton, etc. *v.* Hackington, *co. Kent.*

Hakethorn, Hakethoren, Haketorn, etc. *v.* Hackthorn, *co. Linc.*

Hakewell. *v.* Hawkwell, *co. Essex.*

Halak. *v.* Allexton, *co. Leic.*

Halam, *nr. Southwell, co. Nott.* License for a grant in, to Normanton chapel, 1331 (Halum). Woll. v. 1.

——— Fine in, 1541 (Halom). Woll. ii. 71.

Halden. *v. sub* Rolvenden, *co. Kent.*

Halden, High, *co. Kent.* Grant in, 1392. Harl. 78 A. 20.

——— Fines in, 1548. Harl. 75 H. 4, 76 H. 50;—1559. Harl. 77 G. 24.

Haldenebi, Haldeneby. *v.* Holdenby, *co. Northt.*

Haldon, Great. *v. sub* Kenn, *co. Devon.*

Hale, *in Godshill, Isle of Wight.* Grant in, 1340 (Heyle). Harl. 51 C. 45.

Hale, Great (Magna Hale), *co. Linc.* Grants, etc., in, 1318. Eg. 459;—1412. Add. 20803;—1514. Eg. 479.

——— *Vicarius*. Will. de Saxilby, 1372. Add. 20768, 20769.

——— ——— Willelmus, 1382. Add. 20781.

——— ——— Hugo Croke, 1438. Add. 20823-20825.

Hale Holme, Haleholm. *v.* Holme Hale, *co. Norf.*

Hale, La. *v. sub* Hampton, Little, *co. Suss.*

Halebi. *v.* Ailby, *co. Linc.*

Halelod, *nr. Louth* (?), *co. Linc.* Sale "juxta pontem de," late 12 cent. Harl. 56 H. 43.

Hales, *co. Norf.* Abstracts of charters relating to, *t.* Edw. I. Add. 16533 *a, b.*

——— Grants in, 1359. Cott. xii. 1;—1386. Harl. 56 G. 21.

Hales, North. *v.* Covehithe, *co. Suff.*

Hales Owen, *cos. Salop and Worc.* Lease of Howley (Owley) Grange manor in Lapal in, by Hales Owen Abbey, 1533. Add. 7391.

Hales, Sheriff, *co. Staff.* Conf. of a sale of Brockton (Broctun) Grange in, to Buildwas Abbey, *c.* 1175. Harl. 50 A. 2.

—— Covenant betw. Buildwas and St. Evroul Abbeys conc. tithes from Brockton Grange to the church of, late 12 cent. (Hales). Harl. 44 A. 17.

Halesbi. *v.* Aylesby, *cn. Linc.*

Halesworth, *co. Suff.* Compotus-rolls of the manor. 1365–74. Add. 25971–25978 :—1366–7. Add. 25864 ; —1484–5. Add. 25865.

—— Releases in, 1404. Harl. 55 C. 5:—1454. Harl. 48 B. 51.

—— The steeple of Walberswick church to be modelled on that of, 1426. Add. 17634.

Haleuthton. *v.* Haughton, *co. Staff.*

Haley, *in Gt. Amwell, co. Hertf.* Grant of the manor, late Hen. I. (Heilet). Harl. 46 I. 30.

—— Rental, 1374 (?) (Heyle). Add. 26828.

Halfnaked. *v.* Halnaker, *co. Suss.*

Halford, *co. Salop.* Conf. of land in, by Hen. II., to Bromfield Priory, [1155] (Hanerford). Cott. xvii. 4.

Halford, Up and Nether. *v.* Halli-ford, *co. Midd.*

Halfyoke. *v. sub* Maidstone, *co. Kent.*

Halgavor, *nr. Bodmin, cn. Cornw.* Grant in, 1487. Add. 15364.

Halgestoke. *v.* Halstock, *co. Dors.*

Halghele, *co.* —— (?). Grant in Kedelesfeld nr. the mill of, 1284. Harl. 52 D. 2.

Halghton, Halgtone. *v.* Haughton, *nr. Shifnal, co. Salop.*

Halghwyll. *v.* Halwill, *co. Devon.*

Halhtuna. *v.* Halton, *co. Salop.*

Halifax, *co. York.* Fine in, 1371. Add. 18027.

—— Grants, etc., in S. Owram, Skir-cont, Siddal, etc., in, 1516–1608. Add. 26122–26129, 26131 ; — 1588. Add. 12674;—1637. Add. 26135; — 1671. Add. 18041, 18042.

—— Marriage settlements, etc., in,

1635. Add. 18075;—1636. Add. 18023, 18024; — 1722. Add. 25920, 25921.

—— Sales of woolshops in, 1675. Add. 18048 ;—1676. Add. 18051, 18052.

—— Brief for rebuilding St. Anne's chapel, 1817. Ch. Br. B. lvii. 9.

—— *Vicarius. Dom. Ric. de Heton,* 1370. Add. 15658; — 1381. Add. 15660, 15661 ;—1390. Add. 15718.

—— —— *(quondam).* Chris. Ashe-burne, *Clericus,* 1588. Add. 12674.

Halinctona. *v.* Hallington, *co. Linc.*

Halliwelle. *v.* Halliwell, *nr. Pontefract, co. York.*

Halliwelle, *nr. Castle Eden, co. Durh.* Grant of, to Gisburne Priory, late Hen. II. Add. 20516.

Halkin, *co. Flint.* Brief for rebuilding the church, 1761. Ch. Br. B. i. 4.

Hall. *v. sub* Hackington, *co. Kent.*

Hall Court. *v. sub* Harbledown, *co. Kent.*

Hallam, Kirk, *co. Derb.* Grants, etc., in, *t.* Hen. III. Lansd. 587 (Kyrke-halum), 588 (Chirchehalum), 589 (Kyrkehalum);—1282. Lansd. 590–592 (Chirchehalum);—*c.* 1290. Lansd. 593 (Chirkehalum);—1291. Lansd. 594 (Chirkehalum); — *t.* Edw. I. Lansd. 595 (Chyrchehalam);—1472. Woll. i. 77 (Kirkhalom).

—— Power to give seisin, etc., of the manor, 1450. Woll. i. 75 (Kirkhalom); —1628. Woll. xi. 33 (Kirkhallom).

—— Commission conc. a fine of Park Hall manor in, etc., 1596. Woll. xi. 108, xii. 111.

—— Brief for rebuilding the church, 1778. Ch. Br. B. xviii. 6.

—— *v. also* Mapperley, *in Kirk Hal-lam, co. Derb.*

Hallam, West, *co. Derb.* Grant of rents, etc., in, 1417 (Halum). Harl. 49 A. 44.

Hallamshire, *co. York.* Covenants conc. annuities charged on lands in, 1366. Woll. ix. 50 (Hallomshire);— 1367. Woll. v. 32 (Halumschir).

—— Acquittances for rents from, 1442, 1443 (Halomshire). Campb. xx. 1 a–c, e–g.

Hallaton, *cn. Leic.* Records in the Tower conc. the manor, 1274–1480. Add. 26934.

—— Grants, etc., in, late 13 cent.

Halton, East (Haltuna, Hauton, etc.), co. Linc. (continued). Grants in, to Ballington Priory, t. Hen. II. Harl. 52 G. 37;—1191. Harl. 52 G. 39;—[1191?]. Harl. 46 A. 7 (Halton super Humbriam).

—— Award, etc., to Newhouse Abbey, in suit with Elstow Abbey for St. Peter's church, 1177. Harl. 44 I. 33; —[1177-8]. Harl. 43 G. 23, 24.

—— Grants, etc., in, t. Hen. II. Harl. 51 C. 1;—1331. Cott. xxx. 18, Harl. 57 F. 4, 5;—1332. Harl. 55 E. 21.

—— Grant from Newhouse Abbey for masses in the chapel of SS. Stephen and Thomas in the church of, [1223-33]. Harl. 44 G. 30.

—— Taxation of the vicarage, [1239-65]. Harl. 45 A. 24.

—— Grant to Newhouse Abbey for masses in St. Stephen's chapel at, late Hen. III. (Haltan). Harl. 52 F. 1.

—— Erection of a chapel in the cemetery of St. Peter's church at, c. 1292. Harl. 58 A. 40.

—— Inspex. of a grant of the manor to Thornton Abbey, 1292. Campb. xxi. 4 (6).

—— Mandate by the prior of Thornholme conc. tithes in, to Newhouse Abbey, 1365. Harl. 45 A. 7.

—— Acquittances to Newhouse Abbey, from Elstow Abbey, for a pension from the church, [1414-18]. Harl. 44 D. 33-35.

—— Fine in, 1728. Add. 7408.

—— Capellanus. Simon, [1147-66]. Harl. 47 A. 34, 49 C. 23;—[1152-75]. Harl. 47 I. 23;—t. Hen. II. Harl. 55 F. 42.

—— —— Henricus, end of 12 cent.-t. John. Harl. 45 I. 53, 46 A. 1, 46 B. 13, 47 C. 29, 48 H. 35, 50 E. 50, 52 E. 43, 56 F. 28, 56 I. 12.

—— —— Walterus, early 13 cent. Harl. 52 E. 44, 45.

—— —— Gilbertus, early Hen. III. Harl. 45 H. 42, 50 E. 43, 56 I. 13.

—— —— Robertus, t. Hen. III. Harl. 46 C. 23.

—— Vicarius. Gilbertus, c. 1230-50. Harl. 52 E. 49;—t. Hen. III. Harl. 52 C. 12, 52 D. 28.

—— —— Joh. fil. Rob. de Halton, 1376. Harl. 56 E. 6;—c. 1383. Harl. 45 I. 40.

Halton Holegate (Halton juxta Stephing, H. juxta Spillesby, etc.), co. Linc. Grant, etc., in, late Hen. III. Harl. 56 E. 33;—1608. Harl. 112 C. 13.

—— Fines in, 1284. Harl. 51 C. 5; —1302. Harl. 45 H. 18;—1429. Harl. 56 I. 49.

—— Precipe on a covenant conc. land in, 1578. Add. 25088.

—— Rector. Walterus, late Hen. III. Harl. 56 E. 33.

Halugh Wood. v. sub Weldon, Gt., co. Northt.

Halughton. v. Haughton, co. Staff.

Halughton, Halugton, Haluton, etc. v. Hallaton, co. Leic.

Halum. v. Halam, nr. Southwell, co. Nott.

—— v. Hallam, West, co. Derb.

Halumschir. v. Hallamshire, co. York.

Haluton. v. Halloughton, nr. Nether Whitacre, co. Warw.

Halvergate, co. Norf. Extract from court-roll, 1528. Add. 14680.

Halwestoke. v. Halstock, co. Dors.

Halwestowe. v. Halstow, co. Kent.

Halwill, co. Devon. Settlement of lands in, 1465 (Halghwyll). Add. 13061-13064.

Halwynfeld. v. Wingfield, South (?), co. Derb.

Halyfeld. v. sub Waltham Holy Cross, co. Essex.

Halyngbury. v. Hallingbury, Great, co. Essex.

Halyok. v. Holyoaks, nr. Great Easton, co. Leic.

Ham. v. sub Angmering, co. Suss.

—— v. sub Sidlesham, co. Suss.

Ham, in Berkeley, co. Glouc. Grant of rent in, nr. Crockerespull, 1251 (Hamm). Add. 8445.

Ham, [in Upchurch ?], co. Kent. Grant at, 875. Cott. MS. Aug. ii. 89.

Ham, co. Kent or co. Suss. Bequest of land at, to Christ Church, Canterbury, late 10 cent. (æt Hamme). Harl. 43 C. 4.

Ham, nr. Sandwich, co. Kent. Grant in, 1349 (Hamme). Cott. xxvii. 27.

Ham, co. Surr. Warrant for a lease of the custody of the manor, [post 1522]. Add. 22631.

Ham, *nr. Shalbourn, co. Wilts.* Grant at, 931 (æt Hamme). Cott. viii. 16 *a*.

—— Bequest at, *c.* 950 (æt Hamme). Cott. viii. 16 *b*.

Ham, East, [*in Ham Preston ?*], co. *Dors.* Grant in, 1333 (Esthamme). Harl. 58 D. 17.

Ham, East, co. *Essex.* Conf. by Edw. the Confessor of a grant in, to Westminster Abbey, 1066 [*sc.* 1065] (Hamme). Cott. vi. 2 (*copy*).

—— Grant, etc., in, *c.* 1250. Cott. xxvii. 133 (Esthamme);—*ante* 1302. Lansd. 93 (do.).

—— Grant in. to Stratford Langthorne Abbey, 1336 (do.). Add. 8049.

—— Precipe on a covenant conc. lands in, 1561 (Eastham). Add. 24941.

—— *Curate. Sir* Tho. Griffyth, 1556. Harl. 43 I. 14.

Ham Street. *v. sub* Orlestone, co. *Kent.*

Ham, West, co. *Essex.* Grant of "totum dominium" of, etc., to Stratford Langthorne Abbey, [1130–35] (Hamma). Harl. 53 E. 15.

—— Conf. by Hen. II. of grant in, to the same, [1164?] (Hamma). Harl. 43 C. 20.

—— Conf. of the church to the same, [1186] (Westhamma). Harl. 43 G. 26.

—— Grant in S. Marsh of, to the same, late 12 cent. (?) (Hamma). Harl. 51 G. 41.

—— Grant in, *t.* Edw. I. (Westhamme). Harl. 50 B. 28.

—— Release in Woodford in, 1574. Add. 24872.

—— Precipes on covenants conc. lands in, 1578. Add. 24973;—1587. Add. 24993.

—— Crown lease in, [1580]. Add. 8462.

—— Conveyance in trust of an annuity in, 1682. Add. 13730.

Hambi, Hamby. *v.* Hanby, co. *Linc.*

Hamble le Rice, co. *Southt.* Grant of market and fair at, 1354 (Hamelhoke). Harl. 75 E. 8.

Hambleden, co. *Buck.* Bond to levy a fine in, 1538 (Hamelden). Add. 19913.

—— Exemplif. of suit conc. the manor, 1709. Add. 15893.

Hambledon, co. *Surr.* Return to the Hundred Court of, 1484. Add. 26842.

—— Mortgage in, 1487 (Hamelden). Add. 26787.

—— Marriage settlement of the manor, 1621, 1622. Harl. 57 H. 43, 44.

Hambleton, co. *Rutl.* Re-grant of the church to Westminster Abbey, by Will. I., 1067 (Hameloduna). Cott. vi. 3 (*copy*).

—— Court-roll, 1622. Add. 7177.

Hambur., Hambury. *v.* Hanbury, co. *Staff.*

Hamden, South, co. *Som.* Bond conc. wardship in, 1350 (South Hamedon). Harl. 57 B. 10.

Hameffolowe. *v.* Hamfallow, co. *Glouc.*

Hameleduna. *v.* Hambleton, co. *Rutl.*

Hamelegh. *v.* Himley, co. *Staff.*

Hamelhoke. *v.* Hamble le Rice, co. *Southt.*

Hamelonde, *nr. Bickleigh* (?), co. *Devon.* Grant in, 1336. Harl. 46 E. 4.

Hameringham, co. *Linc.* Conf., etc., of the church to Bullington Priory, early Hen. II. Harl. 52 G. 30 (Hamerigham);—[1175–81]. Harl. 43 C. 36 (Hamringham);—*c.* 1253. Harl. 45 H. 47 (Hameringham);—1256. Harl. 52 H. 28 (do.);—*t.* Edw. I.-II. Harl. 52 H. 5 (do.);—*c.* 1322. Harl. 52 H. 27 (do.);—1389. Harl. 43 G. 32 (Hameryngham).

—— Fine in, 1302 (Hameryngham). Harl. 45 H. 18.

—— *Clericus.* Gaufridus, 1158. Harl. 49 A. 1.

Hamerton, co. *Hunt.* Grant of, to A. de Dammartin, *c.* 1152–3 (?) (Hamertun). Add. 11233 (4) (*copy*).

Hamestede. *v.* Hamstead, *Isle of Wight.*

Hamfallow, co. *Glouc.* Grant in, 1425 (Hameffolowe). Add. 9248.

Hamme. *v.* Ham, cos. *Glouc., Kent, etc.*

—— *v.* Holme Lacy, co. *Heref.*

Hammersmith, co. *Midd.* Defeasance of conveyance of the "King's Arms," etc., in, 1642. Add. 4891.

Hammerton, Kirk, co. *York.* Brief for rebuilding the church, 1780. Ch. Br. B. xx. 8.

Hammes. *v.* Hamsey, co. *Suss.*

Hampton, Welsh, co. *Salop.* Fine in, 1379 (Hampton). Add. 6255.

Hamreden. *v.* Hamperden, co. *Essex.*

Hamringham. *v.* Hameringham, co. *Linc.*

Hamsey, co. *Suss.* Grant in, *t.* Hen. III.-Edw. I. (Hames). Harl. 80 C. 42 (copy).

—— Inq. conc. grant of a rent from the manor, 1510 (Hamsay *al.* Hammes). Harl. Roll Y. 9.

—— Power to give seisin of the manor, 1526. Harl. 77 G. 16.

—— Precipe on a covenant conc. land in, 1529. Add. 25523.

—— Royal grant of reversion of the manor, etc., 1561. Harl. 75 H. 9.

Hamstall Ridware. *v.* Ridware, Hamstall, co. *Staff.*

Hamstead, *nr. Yarmouth, Isle of Wight.* Grant of free warren in, to Quarr Abbey, 1284 (Hamestede). Add. 15701.

Hamstead, South. *v. sub* Dorking, co. *Surr.*

Hamsted. *v.* Hempstead. co. *Essex.*

Hamstede. *v.* Hempstead, *in Framfield* (?), co. *Suss.*

Hamstede Marshall. *v.* Hampstead Marshal, co. *Berks.*

Hamthwayt. *v.* Hampsthwaite, co. *York.*

Hamton, Ham tune, Hamtune. *v.* Southampton, co. *South.*

Hamwolde. *v. sub* Woodnesborough, co. *Kent.*

Hanai, Haneie. *v.* Hannah, co. *Linc.*

Hanborough, co. *Oxon.* Release to Reading Abbey, from the Bp. of Lincoln, for a pension from the church, 1403 (Hanneburgh). Add. 19647.

Hanbury, co. *Staff.* Grant in Needwood forest bounded by the Park of, *c.* 1265 (Hambur.). Add. 20459.

—— Release in, 1298 (do.). Campb. viii. 6.

—— *Persona. Sire* Ric. Passemer, 1343. Cott. xvi. 60.

—— —— Joh. Cheyne, 1365. Add. 4859;—1383. Woll. iii. 1 (Hambury).

Hanby, *in Welton,* co. *Linc.* Release of the chapel, etc., by Thornton Abbey, 1229 (Humbi). Harl. 45 A. 3.

Hanby, *in Welton,* co. *Linc.* (continued). Fine in, 1438 (Hamby). Harl. 5 F. 12.

Hancastre, Hanecastre. *v.* Ancaster, co. *Linc.*

Hanchemstede, co. *Essex.* A boundary mark, 692-3. Cott. MS. Aug. ii. 29.

Handerbi. *v.* Anderby, co. *Linc.*

Handford (Hanaford), *next Ipswich,* co. *Suff.* Grants, etc., in, 1331. Add. 8371;—1335. Add. 10124;—1337. Add. 10126, 10127;—1362. Add. 10133.

Handley, *in Staveley,* co. *Derb.* Grant in, 1469 (Handeley). Harl. 86 H. 15.

—— Fine in, 1541 (Hanley). Woll. ii. 71.

Handley, co. *Dors.* Sale of the manor, 1686. Add. 15166, 15167.

Handsacre, *in Armitage,* co. *Staff.* Lease in, 1540 (Handysacre). Add. 13558.

—— *Capellanus Hermitagii de Hendehakers.* Johannes, *t.* Hen. III.-Edw. I. Add. 24239.

Handsworth, co. *Staff. Persona.* Joh. Hide, 1399. Cott. xxvi. 5 (Honnysworthe);—1402. Cott. xxiii. 39, 40 (do.).

Handsworth, co. *York.* Conf. of grant in, to Kirkstead Abbey, late 12 cent. (Handeswrth). Harl. 50 E. 54.

—— Release of " terra de Camera " in, *t.* Hen. III. Harl. 112 H. 35.

—— Grants, etc., in Woodhouses (Wodehousia, etc.), in, *t.* Hen. III. Harl. 112 G. 34 ;—late 13 cent. Harl. 112 H. 63 ;—1305. Harl. 112 H. 2 ;— 1343. Harl. 112 H. 64 ;—1387. Harl. 112 G. 44 ;—1442. Woll. v. 29 ;—1465. Harl. 112 H. 29 :—1485. Woll. v. 28 (1) (copy) ;—1548. Harl. 112 I. 11.

—— Grant in Woodhouses in, by Wallingwells Priory, late 13 cent. (Handeswurthe Wodehuses). Harl. 112 F. 30.

—— Grant in le Boure, etc., in, 1366. Harl. 112 G. 28.

—— Covenant for annuity from lands in, 1367 (Hannesworth). Woll. v. 32.

—— Fine in Gleadless in, 1473 (Hannesworthe). Harl. 112 G. 2.

—— Grants, etc., in, 1483. Harl. 112 G. 3 (Handysworthe);—1612, 1613. Add. 18006-18008.

—— *Persona.* Eustacius, *t.* Hen. III. (Andeswrth). Add. 7492.

Handsworth, *co. York (continued).*
*Person.* Will. Cart, 1635. Add. 5146.

—— *Rector.* Joh. Chambirlayne, 1366.
Harl. 112 G. 28.

—— —— Tho. Tylney, 1465. Harl.
112 H. 29.

*s. also* Gleadless, *co. York.*

Hanefald. *v. sub* Waltham, *co. Kent.*

Haneksham. *v.* Hankham, *nr. Pevensey, co. Suss.*

Hanewell. *v.* Hanwell, *co. Midd.*

—— *v.* Hanwell, *co. Oxon.*

Hanewrde, Hanewurthe, etc. *v.*
Hanworth, Cold, *co. Linc.*

Hanfeld, South. *v.* Hanningfield, S.,
*co. Essex.*

Hanfelde. *v.* Henfield, *co. Suss.*

Hanford Bridge, *nr. Stoke upon Trent,
co. Staf.* Brief conc. an inundation at,
1796. Ch. Br. B. xxxvi. 3.

Hanham Abbots and West Hanham. *v. sub* Bitton, *co. Glouc.*

Hanigges, Haninges. *v.* Honing, *co.
Norf.*

Hanincton. *v.* Hannington, *co. Southt.*

Hankham, *nr. Pevensey, co. Suss.* Conf.
of tithes in, to Battle Abbey, [1121-5]
(Henam). Cott. MS. Nero C. iii. f. 189.

—— Grant in, *t.* Edw. I. (Hanekeham). Add. 26750.

Hanley. *v.* Handley, *in Staveley, co.
Derb.*

Hanley, *in Towcester, co. Northt.* Grant
in, *c.* 1250 (?) (Hanle crofd.). Cott.
xxiv. 7.

Hanley, *in Stoke upon Trent, co. Staf.*
Briefs for rebuilding the chapel, 1777,
1791. Ch. Br. B. xvii. 8, xxxi. 3.

—— Brief conc. a fire at, 1808. Ch.
Br. B. xlix. 6.

Hanley, Child, *in Eastham, co. Worc.*
Briefs for rebuilding the chapel, 1797,
1801. Ch. Br. B. xxxvii. 1, xli. 4.

Hanlith, *in Kirkby in Malhamdale, co.
York.* Lease of tithes in, 1662. Harl.
112 D. 7.

Hanmer, *co. Flint.* Brief conc. a fire
at, 1765. Ch. Br. B. v. 8.

Hannah, *co. Linc.* Grant in, late 13
cent. (Haneie). Harl. 56 G. 16.

—— *Clericus.* Willelmus, *t.* Hen. II.
(Hanai). Harl. 51 B. 4, 5.

Hannam Abbots. *v. sub* Bitton, *co.
Glouc.*

Hanneburgh. *v.* Hauborough, *co.
Oxon.*

Hannesworth. *v.* Handsworth, *co.
York.*

Hannesworth. *v.* Hanworth, Cold, *co.
Linc.*

Hanney, East, *co. Berks.* Fine of
Herles Court manor, etc., in, 1655.
Cott. xxx. 36.

Hanney, West, *co. Berks.* Fine in,
1655. Cott. xxx. 36.

Hanningfield, South, *co. Essex.*
Grants of Chasteleyns wood, etc., in,
1335. Harl. 76 C. 14 (Suthanyngfeld);—1383. Harl. 77 F. 47 (Southannyngefeld), 77 G. 50 (South Hanyngfeld), 78 H. 16 (do.), Add. 14868
(Southanyngfeld);—1394. Harl. 54
E. 26 (do.);—1402. Harl. 78 I. 15
(Southhanfeld), 80 E. 50 (do.);—1431.
Harl. 76 A. 54 (South Hanyngfeld).

Hannington, *co. Northt.* Settlement
of the manor, 1347 (Hanyngtone).
Cott. xxvi. 38.

Hannington, *co. Southt.* Grant of the
church to the Knts. Hospitallers, 1185
(Hanincton). Harl. 43 I. 38.

Hanslope, *co. Buck.* Precipe on a
covenant conc. lands in, 1564. Add.
24919.

—— Covenant to levy a fine in, 1650.
Add. 23983.

—— *Persona.* Turstan. Basset, early
Hen. III. Harl. 50 D. 5.

Hant. *v.* Hampton in Arden, *co. Warw.*

Hanton. *v.* Hampton, *co. Chest.*

Hanum. *v. sub* Bitton, *co. Glouc.*

Hanwell, *co. Midd.* Conf. by Edw. the
Confessor of a grant in, to Westminster
Abbey, 1066 [*sc.* 1065] (Hanauuelle).
Cott. vi. 2 (*copy*).

—— Conf. by Abp. Theobald of a
grant of liberties bel. to the church of,
to Westminster Abbey, [1150-54]
(Hanewell). Campb. xvi. 1.

—— Exemplif. of a recovery in, 1624.
Cott. xxx. 10.

—— Extracts of court-rolls of Greenford cum Hanwell manor, 1723, 1738.
Add. 1678, 1679.

—— Brief for rebuilding the church,
1781. Ch. Br. B. xxi. 4.

z 2

Harston, *co. Camb.* Lease, etc., in, 1221. Harl. 54 D. 36 (Herleston):— 1495. Add. 15550 (Hardeleston).

—— Court-rolls of Harston Tiptoft (Hardleston, Harleston Tybbatoft, etc.) manor, 1279-1281, 1359-1447. Add. 18521, 18523 - 18525, 18527, 18530, 18531, 18533 - 18538; — 1445 - 1461. Add. 18540;—(as Haiston Wygorn manor), 1465-1469. Add. 18540 (3-7).

—— Compotus-rolls of same manor, 1314-19. Add. 18522 (Harliston):— 1387-1399. Add. 18527-18529 18531.

—— Rental of Harston Newton (Hardleston Neuton) manor, [1342-3?]. Add. 18540 (1, 2).

—— Roll of capital pledges, with their decennaries, etc., in the manor, *t.* Hen. IV.-*t.* Hen. V. Add. 18526 (Hardeleton), 18532 (Hardleston, etc.).

—— Court-roll of Harston Botellers manor, 1423, 1424. Add. 18537 (26, 30).

—— Rental of Harston Tiptoft manor, late 15 cent. Add. 18541.

Harston, *nr. Matlock, co. Derb.* Extract of court-roll, 1538 (Herston). Woll. xi. 9.

Harston, *co. Leic.* Release of the manor, etc., 1472. Woll. i. 77.

Harswell, *co. York. Capellanus.* Hugo, *t.* John. Add. 21697.

Harsyng Great Marsh, *in Cliffe at Hoo, co. Kent.* Lease of, 1544. Harl. 46 I. 22 *a, b.*

Hart, *co. Durh.* Conf. of grant of the church to Gisburne Priory, *t.* Edw. I. (Hert). Cott. xi. 58, Harl. 43 B. 12.

—— *Presbiter.* Robertus, *c.* 1180. Add. 20570.

Hartburn, *co. Northumb.* Grant of Harwood Wood (*boscus de Harewuda*) in, by Hen. II., *c.* 1155. Campb. ii. 2.

Hartcliffe Hundred, *co. Som.* Grant of, *c.* 1148 (Harecliue). Add. 7760.

—— Quo warranto conc. tenure of, [1280] (Harecliue). Add. 7791.

Hartest, *co. Suff.* Grants, etc., in, 1351. Harl. 51 A. 37 (Herthurst):—1477. Add. 5514 (do.):—1516. Add. 5516 (Herthurst):—1530. Add. 5517 (do.); —1602. Add. 5520;—1616. Add. 5521.

Hartfield (Hortefeld), *co. Suss.* Grants, etc., in, to Combwell Priory, 1256.

Harl. 78 G. 38;—*t.* Hen. III. Harl. 76 A. 23;—1300. Harl. 78 G. 26.

—— Re-feoffment in, 1406. Add. 20049.

—— Precipe on a covenant conc. land in, 1588. Add. 25534.

Hartford, *co. Hunt.* Papal conf. of the manor, church and mill, to Huntingdon Priory, 1147 (Herford). Cott. MS. Aug. ii. 112.

Hartford, West, *co. Northumb.* Lease in, 1334 (Horford West). Harl. 5 B. 6.

Hartham, *co. Wilts. Dominus.* Johannes, *t.* Edw. I. Add. 1535.

Harthill, *in Bakewell, co. Derb.* Reference to a claim on the manor, 1448 (Herthyll). Woll. vi. 5.

Harting, *co. Suss.* Grant of the advowson, 1365 (Hertyngge). Add. 8830.

—— Compotus of the manor, 1399, 1400 (Hertynge). Add. 18558.

—— Settlement, leases, etc., of the manor, 1434. Add. 18726, 18727 (Hertyng); — 1440. Add. 8879 (do.):— 1453. Add. 18752 (do.);—1460. Add. 18758 (Hertynggus); — 1464. Add. 18762 (Hertynges); — 1521. Add. 18808:—1526. Add. 18810;—1555. Add. 18838, 18839;—1656. Add. 18977, 18978.

—— List of tenants, etc., *t.* Hen. VI. Add. 19060.

—— Grants, etc., in, 1460. Add. 18758;—1554. Add. 18837;—1559. Add. 18848;—1569. Add. 18854;— 1605. Add. 18899;—1609. Add. 18910;—1629. Add. 18937;—1635. Add. 18947;—1640. Add. 18957;— 1642. Add. 18959, 18961-18963;— 1659. Add. 18984 - 18986; — 1667. Add. 18994, 18996; — 1670. Add. 19002;—1686. Add. 19021;—1688. Add. 19022; — 1707. Add. 19038, 19040;—1758. Add. 19056;—1763. Add. 19057.

—— Inquisition p. m. conc. the manor, etc., 1471 (Hertynges). Add. 18765.

—— Fines in, 1522. Add. 18807:— 1559. Add. 18844; — 1601. Add. 18893;—1606. Add. 18902;—1673. Add. 19012, 19013; — 1707. Add. 19039.

—— Lease of Ladeholte in, 1528. Add. 18814.

—— Grants of next presentation to, and leases of the parsonage, etc., *c.* 1546. Add. 8937 (Hurtinge):—1549.

Hartshill, *in Mancester, co. Warw.*
Treaty betw. the Earls of Chester and
Leicester conc. the castle, [1151-2]
(Hardredeshella). Cott. MS. Nero C.
iii. f. 178.

—— Rental of the manor, *t.* Edw. II.
or III. (Hardreshull). Cott. iv. 52.

—— Court-roll, 1376 (Hardeshull).
Harl. Roll Y. 13.

—— Settlements of the manor, etc.,
1426. Harl. 76 G 45 (Hardeshull);
—1429. Harl. 76 G. 49 (Hardeshull);
—1434. Harl. 77 F. 14 (do.);—1536.
Harl. Roll V. 3 (Hardyshull);—1542.
Harl. 76 A. 31 (do.).

—— Bond and award conc. a lease of
Hardishall Leasues in, 1544. Harl. 76
H. 46, 79 A. 42.

Hartshorn, *co. Derb.* Sale of underwood nr. Southwood in, 1434(?)
(Horteshorne). Lansd. 643.

—— Grant in, 1495 (Herteshorne).
Add. 4878, 4879.

Hartswood, *in Buckland, co. Surr.*
Grant of Rudne field in, early Hen.
III. (Herteswode). Add. 24586.

Hartwell (Hertwell), *co. Northt.* Conveyance, etc., in, 1426. Harl. 76 G.
45;—1430. Harl. 76 G. 50;—1434.
Harl. 77 F. 14;—1437. Harl. 76 G. 52.

—— Power to give seisin of the manor
and advowson, 1489. Cott. xxx. 34.

—— Crown lease, etc., in, 1584-1684.
Add. 24149 - 24156;—1707. Add.
24148.

Harty, Isle of, *co. Kent.* Fine in,
1548. Harl. 75 H. 4, 76 H. 50.

—— Sale of lands in, 1555. Harl. 76
I. 23.

Harudon, Major et Minor. *v.*
Harrowden, Great and Little, *co.
Northt.*

Harvena. *v. sub* St. Enoder, *co. Cornw.*

Harvington, *co. Worc. Persona.* Joh.
de Braunsford, 1334 (Herforton).
Harl. 112 B. 20.

Harwardstokke. *v.* Stock, *co. Essex.*

Harwarton. *v. sub* Speldhurst, *co.
Kent.*

Harwe. *v.* Harrow, *co. Midd.*

Harwell, *co. Berks.* Release of the
manor, [1340-60] (Harewelle). Cott.
xxviii. 38.

Harwich, *co. Essex.* Letter conc. a
cargo of wine at, for Berwick on

Tweed, *t.* Edw. I. (Herewyz). Add.
6317a.

—— Assignment of the manor, in
dower, 1477. Add. 26598.

—— Precipes on covenants conc. land,
etc., in, 1592. Add. 25006 (Harwicum);
—1593. Add. 25040 (do.).

—— Court-rolls, 1612-16. Add. 25779.

—— Brief for rebuilding St. Nicholas
Chapel, 1779. Ch. Br. B. xix. 2.

Harwood, *in Hartburn, co. Northumb.*
Grant of the wood of, by Hen. II., c.
1155 (Harewuda). Campb. ii. 2.

Harwood Grange. *v. sub* Beeley,
*co. Derb.*

Harworth, *co. Nott.* Grant in Westfield in, *t.* Edw. I. Add. 20162.

Harygge. *v.* Hayridge Hundred, *co.
Devon.*

Haryng. *v. sub* Sellinge, *co. Kent.*

Hascebia, Hasebia. *v.* Aisby, *co.
Linc.*

Hascombe, *co. Surr.* Grant in, 1465.
Add. 7616.

—— Grant of life-interest in the
manor, etc., 1434. Add. 18726, 18727.

—— Arbitration in, 1494. Add. 7638.

Hasdebia. *v.* Haceby (?), nr. Haydor,
*co. Linc.*

Haseden. *v. sub* Tonbridge, *co. Kent.*

Haselbache in le Peake. *v. sub*
Hope, *co. Derb.*

Haselbeech, *co. Northt.* Grants, etc.,
in, 1328. Add. 22008 (Haselbech);—
1332. Add. 22342;—1335. Add.
22009 (Haselebich);—1390. Add.
21936 (Haselbech);—1486. Add.
21966, 21967 (Haselbych);—1499.
Add. 22010 (do.);—1511. Add. 21971.

Haselbury, *co. Som.* Fine in, 1346
(Hiseburc). Add. 25876.

—— Grants, etc., in, 1364. Harl. 45
E. 66 (Hisbere);—1370. Cott. xxvii.
108 (do.), Harl. 47 D. 26 (do.);—1371.
Harl. 48 I. 9 (Hysebeere), 49 F. 31
(Hysbure).

Haselbury Bryan (Haselbere in
Blakemor), *co. Dors.* Fine of the
manor and advowson, 1346. Add.
25876.

—— Release in, 1356. Cott. xxix. 37.

—— Release of the manor, 1366. Harl.
46 F. 33.

—— *Persona.* Ric. Bat, 1346. Add.
25876.

Haugh (Haga, etc.), co. *Linc.* (*continued*). *Vicarius Perpetuus.* Philippus, 1346. Harl. 52, I. 9.

—— Robertus, 1412. Harl. 52 D. 7.

Haugh, *nr. Rawmarsh, co. York.* Grant of a coal mine in, 1396 (Netherhalgh). Harl. 55 G. 39.

—— Exemplif. of suit in, with Southwell Chapter, 1409 (over Halk, nether Halk). Add. 15239.

Haugh, Little. *v. sub* Norton, co. *Suff.*

Haugh, The (?), co. *Durh.* Exchequer acquittance for farm of the manor, 1613 (Le Hughe). Add. 25632.

Haugham, co. *Linc.* Grant in the fee of, early 13 cent. (Hacham). Harl. 50 B. 8.

—— Sale in, reserving rent to St. Sever Abbey, early 13 cent. (Hagham). Harl. 51 B. 8.

—— *Rector.* Matheus, 1251. Harl. 44 F. 24.

Haughfield, *in Ashover, co. Derb.* Sale, etc., in, 1572. Woll. vii. 9, xi. 103.

Haughley, co. *Suff.* Appointment of Sir T. Tirell as keeper of the park, 1515. Add. 16573.

Haughton, *nr. Walesby, co. Nott.* Grant, etc., in, to Rufford Abbey, [1200–1203] (Hoctune). Harl. 83 G. 38.

—— Covenant on above grant in, c. 1200–1203 (Octon). Harl. 83 G. 37.

—— Grant in, 1375 (Hoghton). Harl. 83 G. 30.

—— *Capellanus.* Rogerus, [1200–1203]. Harl. 83 G. 38.

Haughton, *nr. Shiffnal, co. Salop.* Inspex., in 1319, of license from Edw. I. to Wombridge Priory to acquire a mill in, 1281 (Halghton). Cott. iv. 36 (4).

—— Grant in, 1384 (Halgtone). Cott. v. 8.

Haughton, co. *Staff.* Grant of free warren in, 1267 (Haleuthton). Add. 15773.

—— Defeasance of bond conc. recovery of the manor, 1421 (Halughton). Lansd. 144.

—— Briefs conc. a fire at, 1804, 1819. Ch. Br. B. xliv. 1, lix. 11.

Haukeherst, Haukherst. *v.* Hawkhurst, co. *Kent.*

Haukenioclif, *nr. Flockton, co. York.* Grant of, to Byland Abbey, t. Joh. Add. 7453.

Haulton juxta Scropton. *v.* Halton, *in Marston upon Dove, co. Derb.*

Hauot Porth. *v.* Hafod y Porth, co. *Glam.*

Haurich. *v.* Arlsey, co. *Bedf.*

Haurug, Haurugge. *v.* Hawridge, co. *Buck.*

Haurug at the Bowre. *v.* Havering at Bower, co. *Essex.*

Hauste. *v.* Aust, co. *Glouc.*

Haustone, co. —— (?). *Persona.* Ricardus, 1385. Add. 26216.

Haut Estre. *v.* Euster, High, co. *Essex.*

Haut Peck, Foresta de. *v.* Peak, The, co. *Derb.*

Hautbois, Great (Hauboys magna), co. *Norf.* Fines of the manor, etc., 1302. Harl. 45 G. 54, 55;—1312. Harl. 45 G. 57, 58;—1313. Harl. 45 F. 40.

—— Commission of enquiry conc. the living, 1659 (Hobis). Add. 14975.

Hautebarge. *v.* Habrough, co. *Linc.*

Hautecleve. *v.* Hutcliffe, co. *Linc.*

Hauteyn's Hall. *v. sub* Barnham Broom, co. *Norf.*

Hauthorp. *v.* Authorpe, co. *Linc.*

Hauton. *v.* Halton, East, co. *Linc.*

Hautsbourne. *v. sub* Bishopsbourne, co. *Kent.*

Hautville, Norton. *v.* Norton Hautville, co. *Som.*

Hauxton, co. *Camb.* Conff. in, by Bps. of Ely, to Ely Abbey, [1109–31, 1133–69] (Hauchestuna). Harl. 43 H. 4, 5 (*copies*).

Havant, co. *Southt.* Sales, etc., in, 1614–1679. Add. 9430–9441;—1680. Add. 9325;—1686. Add. 9442, 9443;—1693–1700. Add. 9446–9452;—1702–1719. Add. 9454–9458;—1722. Add. 8791;—1729. Add. 9460.

—— *Rector.* John Lardner, 1687, 1692. Add. 9444, 9445.

Haverah, *nr. Knaresborough, co. York.* Compotus for works at the Castle, 1335–6 (Huywra). Add. 26909.

—— Fine of the Park, 1638 (Hawera al. Havera). Woll. xi. 29.

Haverfordwest, *co. Pembr.* Garrison establishment of the castle, 1369. Harl. Roll E. 7.

—— License for a grant in, to the Friars Preachers, 1394. Campb. xxiv. 5.

—— Exemplif. of a fine at, 1430. Sio. xxxii. 8.

Haverhill, *co. Suff.* Homage in, *t.* Hen. III. (Hauerille). Harl. 47 G. 42.

—— Bond for constructing a windmill at, 1294 (Hauerhelle). Harl. 53 B. 4.

—— Sale in, 1664. Add. 10568.

Haverholme, *co. Linc.* Grant of a *nativus* in, late 13 cent. (Haverholm). Add. 20745.

Havering at Bower, *co. Essex.* Grants, etc., in, *t.* Hen. III. Harl. 57 F. 2 (Auerigge), Toph. 53 (Hauering); —1406. Harl. 49 I. 30 (Haurug at the Bowre).

—— Compotus of the manor, 1419–21 (Haverynge atte Bowr.). Harl. Roll G. 40.

—— Plan of the royal palace at, 1578. Lansd. Roll 18.

—— *Ballivus.* Joh. de Walda, *t.* Hen. III. Toph. 53.

—— —— Rad. Tyle, 1379. Add. 19972.

Haveringland, *co. Norf.* Papal conf., etc., in, to Horsham St. Faith Priory, 1163. Cott. MS. Aug. ii. 136 (Heueringlant);—late 12 cent. Add. 15186 (Haueringlond).

—— License to Mountjoy Priory to hold lands in, 1353 (Heueringlond). Toph. 25.

—— Compotus-rolls, etc., of the manor, 1356–1358. Add. 15199, 15200;— 1364–5. Add. 15201;—1376–7. Add. 15202; — 1413–1451. Add. 9327 – 9355;—1559-1566. Add. 9382-9385.

—— Fines in, 1370. Add. 14089 (Heuerynglond);—1570. Add. 14244; —1576. Add. 14248;—1587. Add. 9398-9401 (Heverland).

—— Court-rolls, 1381–1399. Add. 14092–14100, 14103–14106, 14108, 14110, 14112-14116, 14118-14121, 14123–14127; — 1485 - 1490. Add. 14168;—1485-1500. Add. 9359-9368.

—— Grants, sales, etc., in, 1414. Add. 14130 (Heuerynglond);—1430. Add. 14136, 14137 (do.); — 1437. Add. 14140 (do.); — 1449. Add. 14147, 14148;—1453. Add. 14151;—1458. Add. 14158;—1471. Add. 14159;— 1472. Add. 14160, 14161; — 1482.

Add. 14165;—1491. Add. 14174;— 1504. Add. 14187; — 1522. Add. 14202;—1531. Add. 14206;—1537. Add. 14208;—1551. Add. 14222;— 1557. Add. 14228;—1567, 1568. Add. 14236–14239;—1569. Add. 14242;— 1570. Add. 14244; — 1577. Add. 14249;—1579. Add. 14251, 14252:— 1584. Add. 9391-9393, 14253, 14255, 14256; — 1586. Add. 9395; — 1589. Add. 14260;—1591. Add. 14263;— 1607. Add. 14277.

—— Extracts from court-rolls of Haveringland, Ulvestons and Mountjoy manors, 1512–1667. Add. 14195, 14199, 14204, 14206, 14209 - 14213, 14223, 14229, 14232, 14234, 14235, 14240, 14241, 14257, 14261, 14267, 14269, 14271, 14278, 14282, 14289, 14291;—1614-1618. Add. 9418-9421.

—— Suit in, 1521 (Heuerlond). Add. 14200.

—— Sale of the manor, 1528. Add. 14205.

—— Sales, etc., in Mountjoy (Mungey, Mongey, etc.), in, 1555. Add. 14224-14227;—1557. Add. 14228;—1569. Add. 14242;—1579. Add. 14252.

—— Sale of the manor, with Inglowes *al.* Inglisshes *al.* Billneys *al.* Holvestons *al.* Holstons *al.* Ulstons manor, 1572. Add. 14245, 14246.

—— Extracts from court-rolls of Inglyshes *al.* Englisshes manor, 1576. Add. 14247 ;—1578. Add. 14250.

—— Rental of the manor, 1586. Add. 14258.

—— *Persona.* Joh. Fode, 1353 (Heueringlond). Toph. 25.

—— *Vicarius.* Jac. Bossowell, 1527. Add. 14214.

—— —— Tho. Howlett, 1613. Add. 14725.

Havermere, *in E. Walton, co. Norf.* Grant at, 1298. Harl. 47 F. 23.

Haw. *v. sub* Herne, *co. Kent.*

Hawardebi. *v.* Hawerby, *co. Linc.*

Hawarden, *co. Flint.* Attornment to the Earl of Salisbury for the castle and manor, 1387 (Huwardyn). Harl. 43 D. 26.

—— Inspex. of an exchange of the castle and manor betw. Qu. Isabella and the Earl, 1338 (Hawardyn). Cott. xi. 61.

—— Livery of, to Eliz., Css. of Salisbury, *c.* 1400. Add. 662.

**Hawarden,** *co. Flint (continued).* Grant in Ewloe in, 1500 (Hawrden). Add. 25992.

—— *Persona.* Will. Pette, 1380. Add. 15498.

**Hawe.** *v. sub* Hackington, *co. Kent.*

**Hawe, Lytel.** *v. sub* Norton, *co. Suff.*

**Hawera.** *v.* Haverah, *nr. Knaresborough, co. York.*

**Hawerby,** *co. Linc.* Grant and conf. of the church to Beauport Abbey, 1202. Harl. 45 B. 23 (Hawardabi); —1204. Add. 15238 (Hawardeby).

—— Grant in, *t.* Hen. III. (Hawordeby). Harl. 51 D. 19.

—— *Persona.* Michael, *t.* Hen. III. Harl. 51 D. 19.

**Hawkchurch,** *co. Dors. Persona.* Joh. Hawys, 1436. Harl. 53 D. 23.

**Hawkedon** *al.* Hardon, *co. Suff.* Fine in, 1393 (Haukedon). Harl. 58 H. 9.

—— Precipe on a covenant conc. land in, 1592. Add. 25430.

—— *Rector al. persona.* Thomas, 1367. Harl. 53 C. 32, 33 ;—1379. Harl. 48 D. 2 ;—1380. Harl. 43 E. 24*, 48 E. 35.

—— *Rector.* Rob. Chekle, 1542. Add. 10546.

**Hawkesbury,** *co. Glouc.* Covenant conc. Mirywood Park, etc., in, with Pershore Abbey, 1261 (Hauekesbur.). Harl. 44 H. 52.

—— Rents in, of Pershore Abbey, early 14 cent. (Hauekesbur.). Harl. Roll N. 24.

**Hawkesbury, Great,** *co. Buck.* Lease of woods, etc., so called, 1529. Add. 14040.

**Hawkhurst** (Haukherst, etc.), *co. Kent.* Grant of Fulchersrede [Fowlers?] in, *t.* Edw. I. or II. (Hafkherst). Add. 24187.

—— Grants, etc., in, 1342. Harl. 77 D. 48, 49 (Hauekherst), 78 B. 22 ;— 1389. Harl. 76 B. 29 ;—1392. Harl. 78 D. 58 ;—1394. Add. 16347 (Haucherst) ;—1396. Harl. 76 B. 35, 76 E. 22, 80 C. 33 ;—1401. Add. 24509 ;— 1411. Harl. 80 H. 39 ;—1412. Harl. 76 B. 37, 38 ;—1421. Harl. 76 A. 28 ;— 1422. Harl. 76 B. 41, 42 ;—1425. Harl. 80 C. 34, Add. 12645 (Haucherst); —1436. Harl. 80 C. 9, 10 ;—1437. Harl. 79 A. 18-21 ;—1444. Harl. 76 G. 15 ;—1458. Harl. 76 G. 56 ;—1491.

Harl. 80 C. 21 ;—1510. Harl. 76 H. 13 ;—1521. Harl. 76 H. 16, 18 ;— 1529. Harl. 76 H. 19, 20 ;—1530. Harl. 76 H. 12 ;—1543. Harl. 76 H. 26, 41, 44 ;—1548. Harl. 75 E. 22, 85 H. 35, 36, 86 G. 59 ;—1559. Harl. 76 I. 44 ;—1581. Harl. 76 E. 18 ;— 1583. Add. 8792 ;—1595. Harl. 77 B. 28, 29 ;—1640. Harl. 83 H. 44 ;— 1646. Harl. 85 H. 13 ;—1652. Harl. 77 D. 19.

—— Division of lands in, 1555 (Hauekherst). Harl. 76 B. 27.

—— Release of Blakeham in, on Weeverynghope den, 1416. Harl. 77 A. 22.

—— Lease of South Frith wood and forge in, 1561. Harl. 85 H. 6.

—— Fines in, 1562. Harl. 76 A. 40, 41 ;—1601. Harl. 77 C. 56, 77 D. 1 ;— 1609. Harl. 80 C. 16, 17 ;—1616. Harl. 77 C. 52 ;—1620. Harl. 77 E. 33.

—— Lease of a rabbit-warren, etc., in, 1607. Harl. 77 C. 44.

**Hawkley,** *co. Southt.* Precipes on covenants conc. lands in, 1593. Add. 25240, 25241.

**Hawkridge,** *in Cranbrooke, co. Kent.* Grant of rent from, to Cumbwell Priory, *t.* Hen. III. (Hocrede). Harl. 80 G. 31.

—— Grant in Farngate in, from Faversham Abbey, 1320 (Hokeregge). Add. 24507.

—— Grant in the den of, from the same, 1362 (do.). Add. 24508.

—— Power to receive seisin of the manor from Faversham Abbey, 1506. (do.). Add. 24516.

—— Grant, etc., in the den of, 1522. Add. 24517 (Hokregge), 24518.

**Hawkstone,** *nr. Weston, co. Salop.* Grant in Pershall, co. Staff., in the fee of, 1453. Harl. 111 G. 32.

**Hawksworth,** *co. York.* Grant in, *t.* Edw. I. (Heukeswrd). Add. 15703.

**Hawkwell,** *co. Essex.* Grant of rent from the manor, to Buckingham Hospital, 1455 (Hakewell). Add. 13551.

—— Fine of the manor, 1541 (do.). Add. 15868.

**Hawkwellsitch.** *v. sub* Longdon, *co. Staff.*

**Hawle.** *v. sub* Hackington, *co. Kent.*

**Hawnby.** *v.* Hagnaby, *co. Linc.*

**Hawnes,** *co. Bedf.* Grant and conf. of the church and lands in, to Chick-

Haydon (Heyden, etc.), *co. Essex* (*continued*). Precipe on a covenant conc. lands in, 1566. Add. 24942.

—— Extracts from court-rolls of Haydon Bury manor, 1617. Add. 14328, 14329;—1627. Add. 14338 ;—1663. Add. 14347.

—— *Rector.* Joh. Rydere, 1394. Add. 15192;—1406. Add. 14295.

—— —— Ricardus, 1406. Add. 14295.

—— —— Joh. Hicheman, 1477. Add. 14302.

Haydon, *co. Northumb.* Grant, etc., in, *c.* 1300. Harl. 57 C. 38 (Heydene); 1381. Harl. 57 G. 14 (Heydon).

Haydor (Heydur, Haydur, Haydour, etc.), *co. Linc.* Grants, etc., in, *t.* Hen. III. Add. 6373 :—*t.* Edw. I.-II. Add. 6374, 6375, 6378–6385 ;—1311-1615. Add. 6386, 6389, 6390-6395, 6397–6400, 6402, 6403, 6405, 6406, 6408, 6409, 6411, 6414, 6415, 6417, 6418, 6422, 6425 – 6429, 6431 – 6435, 6439, 6442, 6443, 6446, 6449, 6455.

—— Powers for seisin, etc., of the manor, 1345. Harl. 52 C. 11 :—1355. Add. 6436;—1376. Add. 6437; —1504. Add. 6419.

—— Fines in, 1534. Add. 6421 ;—1547. Add. 6424 ;—1564. Add. 6447; —1577. Add. 6450.

—— *Clericus.* Johannes, *t.* Hen. III. Add. 6373.

—— *Vicarius.* Tho. de Appelby, 1344. Add. 6433.

—— —— *Dom.* Rob. de Donyngton, 1374. Add. 6397.

—— —— *Perpetuus. Dom.* Tho. Percy, 1412. Add. 6401.

—— —— Joh. Gybson, 1436. Add. 6406 ; — (*nuper perpet. vic. eccl. prebendalis*), 1452. Add. 6405.

—— —— Hen. Wardrop, 1454. Add. 6440 ;—1458. Add. 6411.

—— —— Rich. Ward, 1493. Add. 6417.

—— —— *Dom.* Tho. Cley, *t.* Hen. VIII. Add. 6442.

Hayes (Hese, etc.), *co. Kent.* Grants, etc., in, 1391. Harl. 111 D. 60 ;—1407. Harl. 111 D. 43 (Heese) ;—1409. Harl. 112 B. 3 ;—1414. Harl. 111 G. 24, 25 ;—1430. Harl. 112 A. 12 ;—1433. Harl. 111 G. 27 ;—1439. Harl. 112 C. 38, 112 D. 33 ;—1451. Harl. 112 F. 2 ;—1452. Harl. 112 C. 39 ;—1458. Harl. 112 B. 22 ;—1462.

Harl. 111 G. 7 ;—1539. Harl. 112 A 24 (Hethes) ;—1575. Harl. 112 E. 17 (Heyes), 18 (Heyse), 19 (do.) ;—1596. Harl. 111 E. 23 ;—1600. Harl. 111 F. 15 (Hays) ;—1627. Harl. 112 F. 19 (Haies).

—— Grant of Pickhurst Farm in, 1580. Harl. 111 G. 1.

—— Grant in Pickhurst Green in, 1590. Harl. 111 G. 53.

—— Fine in, 1608 (Heese). Harl. 112 A. 42.

Hayes, *co. Midd.* Grant nr., 83 (Hese). Cott. MS. Aug. ii. 94.

—— Exemption by the Abp. of Canterbury of his tenants at, from stallage, etc., 1441 (Hese). Lansd. 180.

Hayes, Prebend of, *nr. Exeter, co. Devon.* Defeasance of bond conc. a messuage, etc., in, 1355 (Heghes). Harl. 45 C. 17,

Hayete Munfichet. *v.* Ayott St. Peter, *co. Hertf.*

Hayfield, *in Glossop, co. Derb.* Plan of pews in the chapel, 1638. Add. 17732 (copy).

—— Brief for rebuilding the chapel, 1813. Ch. Br. B. liv. 3.

Hayford. *v.* Heyford, Upper, *co. Oxon.*

Haygil banc. *v. sub* Skirwith, *co. Cumb.*

Hayle Weston. *v.* Hail Weston, *co. Hunt.*

Hayles, *co. Glouc.* Conf. of grant of the manor to Hayles Abbey, 1246 (Heyles). Harl. 58 I. 5 (copy).

Haylesham. *v. sub* Nonington, *co. Kent.*

Hayleale. *v.* Haseley, *co. Essex.*

Hayling, *co. Southt.* Award conc. tithes in, claimed by Jumièges Abbey, 1253 (Helynge). Harl. 83 C. 32.

—— *Rector.* Nic. de Rya, 1253. Harl. 83 C. 32.

Hayling, North, *co. Southt.* Brief conc. a fire at, 1757. Ch. Br. A. iv. 1.

Hayne, *nr. Bampton* (?), *co. Devon.* Fine in, 1432. Harl. 46 H. 21.

Haynthon, Haynton. *v.* Hainton, *co. Linc.*

Hayridge Hundred, *co. Devon.* Compotus of, 1495-6 (Harygge). Add. 13177.

Hayrminne. *v.* Armin, *in Snaith, co. York.*

Heese. *v.* Hayes, *co. Kent.*

Heffeld. *v.* Hatfield, *co. York.*

Hegeðonhyrs, *nr. Staplehurst, co. Kent.* Grant at, 814. Harl. 83 A. 1.

Hegfeld. *v.* Heckfield, *co. Southt.*

Hegham. *v.* Higham, *co. Kent.*

Hegham, Hegham Poter. *v.* Heigham Potter, *co. Norf.*

Hegham, Heghham. *v.* Higham, *co. Suff.*

Hegherdres. *v.* Hardres, Upper, *co. Kent.*

Heghes. *v.* Hayes, Prebend of, *nr. Exeter, co. Devon.*

Hegheygg, Heighedge. *v.* Heage, *in Duffield, co. Derb.*

Hezham. *v.* Higham, *co. Kent.*

Heghlyntone. *v.* Ripe *al.* Eckington, *co. Suss.*

Hegtham. *v.* Ightham, *co. Kent.*

Hegyðe ðorn. *v.* Eythorne, *co. Kent.*

Heham. *v.* Heigham, *in Norwich, co. Norf.*

Heh ham. *v.* Higham, *co. Kent.*

Hehham. *v.* Higham, *nr. Tonbridge, co. Kent.*

Heidune. *v.* Hydon, *nr. W. Harptree, co. Som.*

Heigham, *in Norwich, co. Norf.* Lease of the manor to Rich. Basset by Hulme Abbey, [1127–34] (Heham). Harl. 44 E. 19.

—— Judgment pronounced in St. Leonard's chapel in, on a case of compulsory monastic orders, 1447 (Heygham). Campb. xx. 3.

—— Release in, 1523. Add. 17746.

Heigham Potter, *co. Norf.* Appropriation of the church to Hulme Abbey, [1182] (Hegham, H. Pottere). Cott. iv. 57 (68, 69) (*copies*).

—— Grants, etc., in, 1297. Add. 2001 (Heyham);—1308. Add. 14731 (Hegham Poter); — 1323. Add. 9915 (Hegham);—1408. Add 14701 (Heigham Pottere).

Heighestre. *v.* Easter, High, *co. Essex.*

Heighnor. *v.* Heanor, *co. Derb.*

Heighton, South, *co. Sussex.* Fine in, 1387 (Southeytton). Add. 24891.

Heile, Grangia de. *v. sub* Hutley St. George, *co. Camb.*

Heilet. *v.* Haley, *in Great Amwell, Hertf.*

Heindon. *v.* Eydon, *co. Northt.*

Heinford. *v.* Hainford, *co. Norf.*

Heinthone. *v.* Hinton Waldridge, *co. Berks.* (?).

Heitcham. *v.* Ightham, *co. Kent.*

Heitfeld. *v.* Hatfield Chase, *co. York.*

Hekeringe. *v.* Eakring, *co. Nott.*

Helay. *v.* Heeley, *nr. Sheffield, co. York.*

Heldune. *v.* Eildon, *co. Roxb.*

Helelo, Helgelo. *v.* Belleau, *co. Linc.*

Helengeie. *v.* Hilgay, *co. Norf.*

Helford, *co. Som.* Settlement in, 1661. Add. 5984.

Helgeye, Helingeia. *v.* Hilgay, *co. Norf.*

Helgoti Castrum. *v.* Holgate Castle, *co. Salop.*

Helhelo. *v.* Belleau, *co. Linc.*

Helhoughton, *co. Norf.* Conf. of grant o', with the advowson, to Horsham St. Faith Priory, *c.* 1150 (Helgetun). Harl. 47 H. 44.

Helintonia. *v.* Elington, *co. Berks.*

Hellaithes Grange. *v. sub* Holbeach, *co. Linc.*

Hellawe, Hellowe. *v.* Belleau, *co. Linc.*

Helles, Curia de. *v. sub* Ash, *nr. Sandwich, co. Kent.*

Hellesdon, *co. Norf.* Conf. of grant in, to Horsham St. Faith Priory, 1301 (Heylesdone). Toph. 51.

—— Payments for stock, etc., in, and in Fairchild in, 1384 (Heyllesdon). Add. 19914.

—— Memorandum conc. rent in, on death of J. de Heylesdon, *c.* 1385 (Heylesdon). Add. 19915.

—— Accompt of building works at, 1434–85. Add. 17231.

Hellethroup. *v. sub* Ramsbury, *co. Wilts.*

Hellidon, *co. Northt.* Acquittance for rent of, 1388–9 (Helydene). Harl. 51 A. 36.

—— Power for seisin in, 1405 (Helidene). Cott. xii. 8.

—— Faculty for repair of the chapel 1575. Add. 1981.

2 A 2

Helmingham, *co. Suff.* (*continued*). Assignment of rent from, with reversion of the manor, 1292. Add. 9838.

—— Grant, by the See of Norwich to Flixton Priory, of the advowson of, in exchange for a moiety of Flixton, 1321. Campb. xii. 13, Toph. 48.

—— Court-rolls, 1395, 1407. Add. 10044;—1457. Add. 10065;—1481, 1490. Add. 9812;—1482-1485. Add. 10082.

—— Court-rolls of Bury Hall manor in, 1400, 1406. Add. 10044;—1410. Add. 10053;—1412. Add. 10055;—1481, 1490. Add. 9812.

—— Release of rent for Bernards in, due to Mounseux manor in Otley, 1441. Add. 10206.

—— Release of Creke's Hall manor in, 1476. Add. 10074.

—— Extract from court-roll of Bury Hall manor, 1481. Add. 10080.

—— Grant of Booking Hall (Bokynghalle) manor in, 1493. Add. 10068.

—— *Capellanus.* Tho. Hovere, *de Gretyngham*, 1292. Add. 9837.

—— *Capellanus parochialis.* Willelmus, 1374. Add. 10030.

—— *Persona. Dom.* Joh. Oliver, 1342. Add. 9981.

—— *Rector.* Johannes, 1282. Campb. iii. 1;—*t.* Edw. I. Campb. vi. 7.

—— —— Alexander, 1390. Add. 10042, 10318.

—— —— Joh. Playford, 1482, 1485. Add. 10082.

Helmsley, *co. York.* Grant of the manor, etc., 1650 (Helmesley). Add. 1800.

—— Brief conc. a fire at, 1767. Ch. Br. B. vii. 7.

Helmys. *v. sub* Ash, *nr. Sandwich, co. Kent.*

Helpringham, *co. Linc.* Grants, etc., in, *t.* Edw. I. Add. 20753;—1320-1482. Add. 20754-20830;—1489. Add. 6483;—1527. Add. 6484;—1590. Add. 6485.

—— *Capellanus B. Marie.* Rob. de Hekington, 1340. Add. 20759.

—— *Persona.* Joh. de S. Quintino, 1354. Add. 20762.

—— —— *Dom.* Tho. de Wyke, 1373. Add. 20772.

—— *Rector.* Joh. de Ragenhill, 1338. Add. 20757.

Helpringham, *co. Linc.* (*continued*) *Vicarius.* Tho. Smythy, 1441. Add. 20827.

—— —— Simon Coke, 1464. Add. 20828, 20829.

Helstanford. *v.* Athelstanford, *Haddington.*

Helston, *co. Cornw.* Conveyance in, 1518. Harl. 50 F. 45.

—— Extract of court-roll, 1555. Add. 15368.

Helton. *v.* Hilton, *co. Dors.*

Helton, *in Worfield, co. Salop.* Brief conc. a fire at, 1813. Ch. Br. B. liii. 11.

Helton, *co. Westm.* Brief conc. a fire at, 1814. Ch. Br. B. liv. 10.

Helw. *v.* Ellough, *co. Suff.*

Helydene. *v.* Hellidon, *co. Northt.*

Helygy Hall, *co. Montgom.* Lease of, 1638. Add. 1038.

Helynge. *v.* Hayling, *co. Southt.*

Hemblington, *co. Norf.* Settlement in, 1621. Add. 14584.

Hembury Down. *v. sub* Payhembury, *co. Devon.*

Hemel Hempstead, *co. Hertf.* Release "in hameletto de Estebrok" in, *t.* Hen. III. (Hemel Hampstude). Harl. 112 C. 23.

—— Extract of court-roll, 1586. Add. 1979.

Hemenhall. *v.* Hempnall, *co. Norf.*

Hemesby. *v.* Hemsby, *co. Norf.*

Hemeston. *v.* Hempston, *co. Devon.*

Hemhangere, [*in Dodford* ?], *co. Buck.* Release, etc., of, to Biddlesdon Abbey, early 13 cent. Harl. 85 C. 30;—1236. Harl. 85 E. 6.

Hemingbrough, *co. York.* Brief conc. a fire at, 1789. Ch. Br. B. xxix. 3.

Hemingby, *co. Linc.* Conff. of grants of the mill, etc., to Bullington Priory, *t.* Hen. II. Harl. 52 G. 34 (Hemmingebi);—1256. Harl. 52 H. 26 (Hemmingby);—*t.* Edw. I. or II. Harl. 52 H. 5 (Hemmyngby);—*c.* 1322. Harl. 52 H. 27.

—— Settlement in, on marriage of Matilda, daughter of Hugh, Earl of Chester. [1189] (Emmungeby). Cott. xxiv. 15.

—— Surrender in, from Bridlington Priory to Bullington Priory, 1327. Harl. 44 B. 22.

Hemyock, co. *Devon (continued)*. *Persona*. Will. Rothewell, 1404. Add. 780.

Henam. *v.* Hankham, co. *Suss.*

Henbury, *in Sturminster Marshall, co. Dors.* Grants in, late 13 cent. Add. 23841 (Hymburi), 23842 (Himburi).

—— Conveyance of the manor. 1352, 1353 (Hymbury). Add. 23843, 23844.

Henbury, co. *Glouc.* Lease in Saltmarsh (Salsus marisous) nr., 1248. Harl. 75 D. 13.

—— Conf. of grants in same, to Margam Abbey, *ante* 1264. Harl. 75 D. 19.

—— Grants, etc., in Wick (Wyke) in, 1293. Add. 7730;—1369. Add. 7731;—1421. Add. 7692, 7732;—1443 Add. 7722;—1444. Add. 7723;—1450-55. Add. 7725-7728;—1455. Add. 7734.

—— Grants, etc., in Charlton (Chereleton, Charleton, Charelton, Chorleton) in, 1369. Add. 7731;—1421. Add. 7692, 7732;—1432. Add. 7720;—1434. Add. 7721;—1447. Add. 7724.

—— Writs of assize of nov. diss. in Charlton and Wick in, 1409. Add. 7720, 7733.

—— Foundation of a chantry at, 1531. Add. 7024.

—— Extract from court-roll of Wick (Wyck) in, 1536. Add. 7729.

—— *Vicarius.* Rob. Beausaunte, 1453. Add. 7726;—1455. Add. 7734.

Hendale (Hennedula), *in Gt. Limber, co. Linc.* Grants, etc.. in, to Newhouse Abbey, [1147?]. Harl. 56 A. 9;—*c.* 1150-60. Harl. 43 H. 14-17, 56 A. 8.

Henderby. *v.* Enderby, Bag, co. *Linc.*

—— *v.* Enderby, Wood, co. *Linc.*

Hendford, co. *Som.* Crown appointment of a steward of the manor, 1574 (Hyndeford). Harl. 75 E. 42.

Hendley. *v.* Henley, co. *Suff.*

Hendon, co. *Midd.* Conf. by Edw. the Confessor of a grant in. to Westminster Abbey, 1066 [*sc.* 1065] (Hendune). Cott. vi. 2 (*copy*).

—— Grants, etc., in, *t.* Hen. III. Harl. 112 C. 47;—1285. Add. 5867;—1315. Add. 1010.

—— Grant in Hepeworthe Hyde in (?), 1315. Add. 19306.

—— Release of the manor, 1361. Add. 17683;—1395. Add. 17687.

—— Covenant conc. title deeds of the manor, 1391. Add. 17686.

Hendon, co. *Midd. (continued)* plaint of assault at, 1542. D. 12.

—— Sale of timber in Frith hall manor in, 1571. Harl. 7

—— Lease in trust in, 176 19271.

Hendre, *nr. St. Enoder* (?), co Grant in, 1321. Add. 15348.

Hendre, co. *Cornw.* Conveya 1518. Eg. 276.

Hendred, East, co. *Berks.* by Hen. II. to Reading Abbey (Henreda). Add. 19591.

Hendred, West, co. *Berks.* betw. Wallingford Priory and Abbey conc. tithes of E. *c.* 1225 (Hendred). Add. 196

Heneyanaweht, co. *Glam.* of, by Margam Abbey to Abbey, 1203. Harl. 75 A. 32

Henfield, co. *Suss.* Release ley (Wantele) in, to Lewes [1255-68] (Hanfeld). Cott. C. iii. f. 214.

—— Precipe on a covenant in, 1578 (Hendfeld). Add. 2

—— Sale, etc., in, 1584. H 13 (do.);—1605. Add. 18899

—— Fines in, *t.* Chas. II 8989;—1673. Add. 19014.

Hengestes heath, *nr. Acto* champ, co. *Worc.* A bounda 972. Cott. MS. Aug. ii. 6.

Hengham, Hengtham. *v.* H co. *Norf.*

Hengham Sibill. *v.* Hedingh co. *Essex.*

Hengyvran. *v. sub* St. Stop Brannel, co. *Cornw.*

Henham, co. *Essex.* Exempl recovery in, 1570. Eg. 290.

—— Lease of the manor, 162 9277.

—— *Persona.* Galfridus, ea III. Harl. 54 C. 22.

Henham (Heneham), co. *Suff.* etc., of Craven's manor in, 14 xxvii. 93;—1439. Cott. f 1441. Cott. xii. 42;—1473. F. 3.

—— Grant in, 1439. Cott. x

Henham Abbots, West H *v. sub* Bitton, co. *Glouc.*

Hert. *v.* Hart, *co. Essex.*

Hertefeld. *v.* Hartfield, *co. Suss.*

Herteley, Herteley Abye. *v.* Hartley, *co. Berks.*

Herterege. *v. sub* Cranbrooke, *co. Kent.*

Herterpoll. *v.* Hartlepool, *co. Durh.*

Herteshorne. *v.* Hartshorn, *co. Derb.*

Herteswode. *v.* Hartswood, *in Buckland, co. Surr.*

Hertford, *County of.* Grant notified to the thegns "on Heortford scire," [1057–65]. Cott. MS. Aug. ii. 81.

——— Papal conf. of covenant betw. St. Alban's Abbey and the see of Lincoln conc. "processiones" of, [1161 ?] (Hertford soira). Harl. 43 A. 24.

——— Compotus of the Duke of Norfolk's lands in, 1483–84. Add. 16559.

——— Pipe-roll acquittance to the Escheator of, 1484–5. Harl. 58 H. 2.

——— Grant by Marg., Css. of Salisbury, of an annuity in, to Henry her son, 1527. Harl. 43 F. 10.

——— Commission conc. church furniture in, 1553. Add. 1987.

——— Acquittance on delivery of church plate to the Treasury, 1553. Add. 1995.

——— Writ to receive oaths of Commissioners of Sewers in, 1572. Harl. 84 C. 36.

——— Warrant to the Escheator of, 1588. Cott. xvii. 24.

——— Exchequer acquittances for rents, etc., in, 1595, 1607, 1634. Add. 25606–25608.

——— Commission of peace and gaol delivery, 1685. Add. 26832.

——— *Vicecomes.* Mauricius, [1157–8]. Slo. xxxii. 64.

——— ——— Rich. de Perar, 1327. Harl. 46 G. 7.

——— ——— Tho. Periam, 1536. Harl. 53 B. 39.

——— *Sub-Vicecomes.* Will. Hemelhamsted, 1327. Harl. 46 G. 7.

Hertford, *co. Hertf.* Grant in St. Andrew's par., to Hertford Priory, 1258. Campb. vi. 1.

——— Grant in, 1368. Campb. viii. 16.

——— Leases in, by Hertford Priory, 1388. Campb. iv. 13;—1507. Harl. 75 G. 5;—1520. Campb. x. 13.

Hertford, *co. Hertf. (continued).* Subsidy - collectors' accompts, 1445–6. Campb. x. 15.

——— Order in a suit conc. repairs to the castle, 1615. Cott. xxiv. 55.

——— *Ballivus.* Thurstan de Wygan, 1368. Campb. viii. 16.

——— *Headborough.* Tho. Emysley, 1520. Campb. x. 13.

——— *Capellanus Herefordie.* Reginaldus, *t.* Hen. II. Campb. x. 12.

Hertfortbrygge, *in* Holton (?), *co. Oxon.* Grant of reversion to Le Grove manor nr., 1429. Harl. 53 A. 5.

Hertham *al.* Hurtham. *v. sub* Chard, *co. Som.*

Hertherst. *v.* Hartest, *co. Suff.*

Herthewik, Herwyk. *v.* Hardwick, *co. Linc.*

Herthyll. *v.* Harthill, *in Bakewell, co. Derb.*

Hertingfordbury, *co. Hertf.* Fine in, 1638. Woll. xi. 29.

Hertle. *v. sub* Cranbrooke, *co. Kent.*

Hertle Mawdit, Hertlye Maudut. *v.* Hartley Mauditt, *co. Southt.*

Hertleburne. *v.* Hartleyburn, *co. Northumb.*

Hertondon. *v.* Hartington, *co. Derb.*

Hertruge. *v.* Hawridge, *co. Buck.*

Hertwell. *v.* Hartwell, *co. Northt.*

Hertyng, Hertynggus, etc. *v.* Harting, *co. Suss.*

Hes. *v.* Campsey Ash, *co. Suff.*

Hesdene, West. *v. sub* Tonbridge, *co. Kent.*

Hese. *v.* Hayes, *co. Kent.*

Hese, *co. Kent.* Grant of swine pasture at, 838. Cott. viii. 30.

Hesel, etc. *v.* Hessle, *co. York.*

Heselay. *v.* Healey, *co. Nott.*

Heselden, Hesylden, Den of. *v. sub* Goudhurst, *co. Kent.*

Heselschoh, Heselchou, Hesilschogh. *v.* Hessleskew, *in Sancton, co. York.*

Heshite. *v.* Heyshott, *co. Suss.*

Hesilden, Monk, *co. Durh.* Grant nr., to Gisburne Priory, late Hen. II. (Heselden). Add. 20516.

Heskyn Gaynoc, *in the Cwmwd of Edernion, co. Merion.* Lease in, 1525. Add. 10654.

**Higham,** *in Bargh.* *co. York.* Grant in, *t.* Hen. III. or Edw. I. (Heyham). Add. 8178.

**Higham Ferrers,** *co. North.* Conditional grant of, by Hen., Duke of Normandy, to the Earl of Chester, [1153] (Hecham). Cott. xvii. 2.

—— Lease of rent in, to St. James's Abbey, Northampton, 1255 (do.). Harl. 56 F. 1.

—— Acquittance from the Earl of Derby for an aid for his ransom, to be paid at, 1272 (do.). Harl. 49 I. 41.

—— Release in Britwinscote in, late 13 cent. (Heccam Fereres). Harl. 111 D. 45.

—— Precipes on covenants conc. lands in, 1578. Add. 25157;—1593. Add. 25176.

—— Rental of the manor, 1691 Add. 13593.

—— *Vicarius (nuper).* Joh. Bynetheton, 1406. Add. 730.

**Higham Gobion,** *co. Bedf.* Bond conc. rents in, 1313 (Heyham). Harl. 52 C. 53.

**Higham in Gazeley,** *co. Suff.* Grant in, late (?) Hen. III. (Hechham). Add. 26744.

**Higham on the Hill,** *co. Leic.* Sales, etc., in, 1619. Harl. 85 H. 34;—1633. Harl. 85 H. 39;—1634. Harl. 85 H. 38;—1653. Harl. 85 H. 4;—1659. Harl. 86 I. 52.

**Highambury,** *co. Buck.* Extract from court-roll, 1468. Harl. 58 E. 39.

**Highester.** *v.* Easter, High, *co. Essex.*

**Highgate,** *co. Midd.* Bonds to account for money collected for the almshouse at, 1580. Harl. 84 H. 38;—1581. Harl. 86 E. 34.

—— *Gubernator Domus Eliemosinarum.* Will. Storie, 1581. Harl. 86 E. 34.

**Highworth,** *co. Wilts.* Grant in Esthorp in, *t.* Hen. III. or Edw. I. (Worthe). Cott. xxvii. 71.

—— Inspex. of a grant of, by I. de Fortibus, 1276 (Worth). Cott. xv. 10.

—— Bond to acquit for rent to the Crown for the manor, 1276 (Worth). Harl. 50 D. 40.

—— Grant, etc., of Westrop (Westhrope) manor in, 1410. Harl. 51 F. 40, 41;—1421. Harl. 56 H. 22.

—— Covenant with Marlborough Priory conc. a release in 1409 of Westrop manor, 1431. Harl. 46 H. 10.

**Highworth and Cricklade Hundred,** *co. Wilts.* License to endow Fotheringay College, *co.* North., with, 1415 (Hyworth et Criklade). Campb. x. 5.

**Higley,** *co. Salop.* Exemplif. of a Crown grant of forfeited lands in, 1610. Harl. 83 H. 28.

**Hikeling.** *v.* Hickling, *co. Norf.*

**Hiklyng.** *v.* Hickling, *co. Nott.*

**Hil,** *co.* —— (?). *Persona.* Rad. Crophill, 1375. Harl. 53 E. 45.

**Hilborough,** *co. Norf.* Grant in, to St. Margaret's chapel, *t.* Edw. I. (Hildeburwr.). Add. 14702.

—— Grant, etc., in, 1342. Harl. 45 D. 24 (Hildeburworthe);—1577. Add. 14703 (Hylboroughe).

—— *Capellanus S. Margarete.* Herv. de Brokediz, *t.* Edw. I. Add. 14702.

**Hilbupewrpe.** *v.* Hillborough, *co. Warw.*

**Hilcot,** *in N. Newington, co. Wilts.* Court-rolls, 1558-9, 1566-7 (Hulcoote). Add. 24440, 24441.

**Hildenborough,** *co. Kent.* Frith woods in. *v. sub* Toubridge, *co. Kent.*

**Hilderthorpe,** *nr. Bridlington, co. York.* Grant and conf. in, by Hen. I., to Bridlington Priory, [1123-32] (Hildertorp). Cott. MS. Aug. ii. 56.

—— Exchequer acquittance for a fine in, 1596. Add. 25719.

**Hildesdon.** *v.* Hillesden, *co. Buck.*

**Hildialai.** *v.* Ilsley, *co. Berks.*

**Hildolveston.** *v.* Hindolweston, *co. Norf.*

**Hildyke,** *nr. Boston, co. Linc.* Precips on a covenant conc. land in, 1555. Add. 25055.

**Hilgay,** *co. Norf.* Grant in, to Norwich Priory, [1103-6?] (Helingeia). Cott. MS. Aug. ii. 103, Cott. ii. 21 (1) (copies).

—— Grant of fisheries in Hilgay fen to W. Dereham Abbey, early Hen. III. (Helengeie). Add. 14704.

—— Precipe on a covenant conc. land in, 1381 (Helgeye). Add. 14009.

**Hilketelsh.** *v.* Ilketshall, *co. Suff.*

**Hill.** *v. sub* Odiham, *co. Southt.*

**Hill,** *nr. Fladbury, co. Worc.* Grant in, 1374 (Hull). Add. 14006.

**Hill,** *nr. Sheffield, co. York* (?). Release in, *t.* Edw. I. (Hulle). Add. 26752.

Hill Deverill. v. Deverill, Hill, co. Wilts.

Hill Hall (?), nr. High Offley, co. Staff. Grant of free warren in, 1267 (Hulle). Add. 15773.

Hillborough, nr. Bidford, co. Warw. Conf. by Hen. II. of a grant in, to Bordesley Abbey, [1157?] (Hilbubewyye). Cott. MS. Nero C. iii. f. 176.

Hilldrop. v. sub Ramsbury, co. Wilts.

Hills, La. v. sub Payhembury, co. Devon.

Hilleah. v. Hilsley, co. Glouc.

Hillesden, co. Buck. Exchange with Woburn Abbey for lands in. t. Rich. I.—John (Hildesdon). Add. 6026.

Hillesley, West. v. Ilsley, co. Berks.

Hillingdon, co. Midd. Rental, 1434 (Hyllyngdon). Harl. Roll D. 22.

—— Settlement of the rectory on Philadelphia Carre, 1641. Harl. 77 H. 13.

—— Vicarius. Martinus, 1252 (Hilindone). Add. 7551.

Hillington, nr. King's Lynn, co. Norf. Acquittance for a fine in, 1355. Cott. xxvii. 152.

Hilliscote, co. —— (?). Court-roll, 1490-1. Add. 13073.

Hills Court. v. sub Ash, nr. Sandwich, co. Kent.

Hilmarton, co. Wilts. Exchequer acquittance for rent of the rectory, 1576 (Hilmerton). Add. 25696.

Hilperton, co. Wilts. Feoffments of a moiety of the manor, with the advowson, 1405. Add. 5687, 5688 (Hulpryngton);—1431. Add. 5689 (do.).

—— Feoffment, etc., in, 1467 (Hilpryngton). Add. 5470, 5471.

Hilsley, co. Glouc. Conf. of grants at (?), to Pershore Abbey, 972 (Hilleah). Cott. MS. Aug. ii. 6.

Hilton, in Marston upon Dove, co. Derb. Grants, etc., in, 1404. Woll. x. 18 (Hulton);—1447. Woll. vi. 35 (Hylton);—1495. Woll. xi. 48 (do.), xii. 133;—1502. Woll. xii. 103, 103*;—1504. Woll. xii. 105.

Hilton, co. Dors. Particulars of the manor, late bel. to Abbotsbury Abbey, 1602 (Helton). Add. 663.

Hilton, co. Hunt. Grants in, 1375, 1377 (Hylton). Harl. Roll O. 27.

—— Sale of church lands in, 1561. Harl. 80 H. 61.

Hilton, in Worfield, co. Salop. Brief conc. a fire at, 1808. Ch. Br. B. xlviii. 8.

Himburi. v. Henbury, in Sturminster Marshall, co. Dors.

Himingehaim, Himmigham. v. Immingham, co. Linc.

Himley, co. Staff. Grant nr., ante 1211 (Hamelegh). Add. 7205.

—— Land held in, by A. de Englefeld, 1226 (Humelee). Add. 19276.

Hincham. v. Ingham, co. Linc.

Hinckley, co. Leic. Treaty conc. the castle betw. the Earls of Chester and Leicester, [1151-2] (Hinchelai). Cott. MS. Nero C. iii. f. 178.

—— Grant in, 1368 (Hynkleye). Add. 24211.

—— Grant nr. Stockwell head in, 1653. Harl. 85 H. 55.

—— Entailment of a share of the manor, 1656. Cott. xxiv. 45.

—— Covenant to produce trust-deeds conc. land in, 1659. Harl. 86 I. 52.

v. also Wykin, in Hinckley, co. Leic.

Hincsteworth. v. Hinxworth, co. Hertf.

Hindley (Hyndelegh, etc.), co. Lanc. Grants, etc., in, late t. Hen. III. Add. 17666 (Hindeleg), 17667 (Hyndeleigh) (copy);—1316. Add. 17668 (Hyndeleghe);—1324. Add. 17669 (do.);—1333. Add. 17673;—1334. Add. 17679;—1343. Add. 17677;—1354. Add. 17680;—1369. Add. 17684;—1404. Add. 17689;—1418. Add. 17690, 17691;—1420. Add. 17692;—1430. Add. 17694;—1432. Add. 17698;—1433. Add. 17699;—1438. Add. 17701;—1460. Add. 17705 (Hyndley);—1469. Add. 17706;—1485. Add. 17707;—1489. Add. 17709;—1504. Add. 17710, 17712, 17713;—1512. Add. 17715;—1555. Add. 17718-17720;—1611. Add. 17728, 17729;—1728. Add. 17733.

—— Grants, etc., of the manor, 1325. Add. 17670;—1334. Add. 17674;—1361. Add. 17683;—1395. Add. 17687.

—— Fines in, 1335. Add. 17676;—1557. Add. 17721;—1597. Add. 17727.

**Hindley** (Hyndelegh, etc.), *co. Lanc.* (*continued*). Award conc. turf-cutting in, 1509. Add. 17714.

—— List of persons liable for ditching in, 1572. Add. 17723.

—— Power in a suit in, 1587-8. Add. 17726.

—— Monthly assessment in the township, 1651. Add. 17730.

—— Petition to Parliament from tenants of [P.?] Langton in, 1654. Add. 17731.

—— Brief for rebuilding the chapel, 1763. Ch. Br. B. iii. 3.

—— Briefs conc. inundations in, 1794, 1802. Ch. Br. B. xxxv. 2, xlii. 9.

**Hindolweston,** *co. Norf.* Grants, etc., of, to Norwich Priory, [1103–6 ?], Cott. MS. Aug. ii. 103 (Hildolueston), Cott. ii. 21 (1) (*copies*); — [1136-45 ?]. Cott. ii. 1 (do.), 21 (9) (*copies*).

—— Grant in, 1635. Add. 19094.

**Hindon,** *co. Wilts.* Release in, 1401. Add. 26774 (Hyndon):—1422. Add. 26781.

—— Election of an M.P., 1678. Add. 15181.

—— Brief conc. a fire at, 1755. Ch. Br. A. i. 4.

—— Briefs for rebuilding the chapel, 1808, 1812, 1817. Ch. Br. B. xlviii. 9, liii. 3, lvii. 8.

—— *Bailiff.* Will. Hewes, 1679. Add. 15181.

**Hindringham,** *co. Norf.* Grant, etc., of, to Norwich Priory, [1103–67]. Cott. MS. ii. 103 (Hyndringham), Cott. ii. 21 (1) (*copies*):—[1136-45?]. Cott. ii. 1, 21 (9) (*copies*).

—— Conf. of the church to the same, c. 1180 (?). Cott. ii. 21 (10) (*copy*).

—— Court-rolls of Hindringham and Astleys al. Nowers manors, 1310-1722. Add. 19069, 19071-19075, 19077-19085.

—— Compotus-rolls of the manor, 1411-22. Add. 19073.

—— Rental of Astleys manor, 1520. Add. 19085 (14).

—— Compotus-rolls of Nowers manor, 1537-50. Add. 19085 (1-13).

—— *Clericus.* Alanus, late 12 cent. (?) (Hindrincham). Toph. 42.

**Hingeshale,** *nr. Ashperton,* *co. Heref.* (?). Grant in, late Hen. III. Add. 24749.

**Hingham,** *co. Norf.* Compotus of the prepositus of the manor, 1271-2 (Hengtham). Campb. ix. 8.

—— Surrender of Klynghamhalle manor in, etc., 1360 (Hengham). Harl. 49 G. 42.

—— Sale in, 1517 (Hengham). Add. 14663.

—— *Persona.* Joh. de Derlyngton, 1383. Add. 19320.

**Hingham.** *v.* Ingham, *co. Linc.*

—— *v.* Ingham, *co. Suf.*

**Hinkershill.** *v.* Inkersel, *co. Derb.*

**Hinkeston,** *co. Camb.* Grant of the manor, 1337 (Henkeston). Lansd. 106.

—— Grant for life in, 1343 (do.). Add. 22584.

—— *Capellanus.* Ricardus, early Hen. III. Add. 21158.

**Hinstock,** *co. Salop.* Briefs conc. fires at, 1804, 1813, 1817. Ch. Br. B. xliv. 6, liv. 5, lvii. 10.

**Hintewode.** *v.* Intwood, *co. Norf.*

**Hintlesham,** *co. Suf.* Grant of, a. 1140. Harl. 50 B. 25.

—— Grants, etc., in, t. Hen. III.-t. Edw. I. Harl. 85 E. 28, 85 F. 34, 85 G. 43, 44, 86 E. 19, 86 G. 9:—1286. Harl. 85 F. 61:—1287. Harl. 85 F. 62;—1293. Harl. 86 C. 13;—1296. Harl. 85 G. 45, 86 F. 16:—1304. Harl. 86 E. 40:—1306. Harl. 86 C. 8;—1307. Harl. 86 F. 35;—1308. Harl. 85 G. 46 ;—1334. Harl. 56 D. 18, 19;—1334-5. Harl. 58 G. 17 (*copy*):—1398. Add. 10571;—1503. Woll. v. 16 (Hyntelysham):—1583. Harl. 86 H. 10:—1629. Add. 9790;—1635. Add. 9791;—1646. Add. 10111.

—— Grant of Priory manor, etc., in, 1539. Add. 14999.

—— Precipe on a covenant conc. land in, 1589. Add. 25393.

—— *Persona.* Ric. Clerk, 1418. Harl. 58 D. 12;—1442. Cott. xxix. 30.

**Hinton,** *nr. Dyrham, co. Glouc.* Grants, etc., in, t. Hen. III. Add. 7016 (Heanton):—1266. Add. 7679 (Henton):—1284. Add. 7682 (Henton Russel):—1303. Add. 7683 (Hentone):—1304. Add. 7685 (do.):—1385. Add. 7690 (do.):—1404. Add. 7691 (Henton Russell):—1468. Add. 7695 (do.):—1486. Add. 7696 (Henton).

Hinton, co. Northt. Precipe on a covenant conc. land in, 1593 (Hynton). Add. 25175.

Hinton, in Mudford, co. Som. Grant of the manor, 1414 (Hynton). Harl. 48 I. 25.

Hinton Ampner (?), co. Southt. Conf. of the church to St. Cross Hosp., Winchester, 1189 (Henton). Harl. 43 C. 28.

Hinton Blewett, co. Som. Compotus of rents in, 1327 (Henton). Add. 6546.

—— Leases in, 1389. Add. 6547 (Henton Blewet);—1426. Add. 6537 (H. Bluwet).

—— Valor of the manor, 1433–34 (Henton Blewet). Harl. Roll L. 35.

Hinton, Broad, co. Wilts. Grant in, and in Sharpridge (Scheperige) in, to Reading Abbey, c. 1250 (Henton). Add. 19622.

—— Expenses of J. de Cobeham on taking seisin of the manor, 1279 (Henton). Harl. Roll C. 28.

—— Compotus of the manor, 1285–6. Harl. Roll G. 33.

—— Visus compoti of the manor, 1309–10. Harl. Roll G. 34.

—— Title of Joh. de Cobeham in, 1332. Harl. Roll N. 34;—c. 1350. Harl. Roll C. 17.

—— Settlement of the manor, etc., 1341. Harl. 48 I. 22.

—— Defeasance of bond conc. rent from the manor, 1362. Harl. 52 B. 40.

—— Pipe-roll acquittance on account of the manor, 1536–7. Add. 18280.

v. also Bincknoll, co. Wilts.

Hinton, Charterhouse, co. Som. Mortgage of a fulling-mill in, 1553 (Henton). Add. 5703.

—— Crown appointment of a steward of the manor, 1571 (do.). Harl. 75 E. 40.

Hinton, Cherry, co. Camb. Grants, etc., in, t. Hen. III.-t. Edw. I. Harl. 49 A. 5 (Hinton), 52 G.11 (Hynton).

—— (?) Mortgage in, [1262–3] (Hynton). Harl. 50 A. 15.

—— (?) Fine of the manor, 1496 (Hynton). Harl. 56 H. 27.

Hinton Waldridge, co. Berks. (?). Grant of rent from the church of, to Lieu Dieu Abbey, 1207 (Heinthone). Eg. 11.

—— Assignment of above rent, by Lieu Dieu Abbey, to Netley Abbey, 1240 (Henneton). Add. 20234.

Hinton Woodford, co. Northt. (?). Grant in, to Canons Ashby Priory, late Hen. II. Add. 19817.

Hints, co. Staff. Brief for rebuilding the church, 1767. Ch. Br. B. vii. 10.

Hinxhill, co. Kent. Release, etc., in, 1431. Add. 20012 (Henxhille);—1482. Add. 20013 (Henxhylle); — 1492. Add. 20015 (do.).

Hinxworth, co. Hertf. Release in, 1273 (Hincesteworth). Harl. 83 B. 32.

Hiptoft Hall. v. sub Freiston, co. Linc.

Hirebi. v. Irby upon Humber, co. Linc.

Hireford. v. Orford, co. Linc.

Hiringham. v. Hardham, co. Suss.

Hirlawe, co. Northumb. Settlement of the domain lands of, t. Edw. II. Harl. 58 G. 22.

Hirnam. v. Irnham, co. Linc.

Hirwaun Wrgan, nr. Aberdare, co. Glam. Settlement of suit conc. the common of, betw. Margam and Caerleon Abbeys, 1203. Harl. 75 A. 32 (Hyrwenunworgan); — 1253. Harl. 75 A. 6 (Hyrwenworgan); — 1256. Harl. 75 A. 37 (Hyrwenwurgan).

Hisbere. v. Haselbury, co. Som.

Histon, co. Camb. Compotus of the rectory, [1445–6] (Hyston). Harl. Roll H. 1.

Hitcham, co. Buck. Release, etc., in, 1311. Harl. 52 E. 7 (Hucham);— 1410. Add. 5160 (Hecham);—1415. Add. 5161;—1416. Add. 5162;—1607. Harl. 75 G. 54; — 1624. Harl. 75 H. 43.

—— Fines in, 1542. Harl. 75 G. 28, 29 (Hycham);—1571. Harl. 75 G. 44.

—— Recovery, etc., of the manor and advowson, 1553. Harl. 76 E. 12 (Hycham);—1561. Harl. 75 H. 24 (Hucham);—1562. Harl. 75 H. 11 (Hutcham);—1634. Harl. 75 H. 49, 76 F. 43;—1641. Harl. 77 H. 13.

—— Delivery of goods at, to trustees, 1634. Harl. 76 F. 41.

—— Inventories of furniture, etc., in Hitcham House, 1634. Harl. Rolls T. 20, Y. 25.

Hitcham, co. Norf. Conf. of grant in, to Lewes Priory, [1087–8] (Erceham). Cott. xvi. 32.

Hitcham, co. Suff. Grant in, 1324 (Hecham). Harl. 52 G. 1.

—— Extract from court-roll, 1652. Add. 26204.

2 B

Hitchin, *co. Hertf.* Sale in, 1303 (Hiche). Harl. 46 G. 3.

—— Livery and extent of land in, 1541 (Hechyn). Add. 13559 *a, b.*

—— Delivery of church plate in, to the Treasury, 1553. Add. 1995.

—— Crown grant in, 1555 (Parva Hichen). Add. 13099.

Hleobyri. *v.* Libbery, *in Grafton Flyford, co. Worc.*

Hnut Scillingc. *v.* Nutshalling, *co. Southt.*

Hnydding. *v.* Nedging, *co. Suff.*

Hoarwithy, *in Hentland, co. Heref.* Grant, etc., in, *t.* Edw. I. Add. 1309 (*la* Horewythy);—1519. Add. 1341 (Horewethye).

—— *v.* also Treyseck, *in Hoarwithy, co. Heref.*

Hoath, *co. Kent.* Court rolls of Shelvingford manor in, 1405. Harl. Roll CO. 27;—1457-96. Harl. Rolls BB. 2-11.

—— Grants, etc., of, and in, Ford *al.* Shelvingford manor in, 1419. Harl. 80 D. 39;—1444. Harl. 78 G. 14;—1473. Harl. 78 F. 44;—1480. Harl. 80 G. 13;—1484. Harl. 78 F. 47.

—— Bequest to the church of, 1422 (Hothe). Harl. 78 D. 21.

—— Rental of Shelvingford manor, 15 cent. Harl. Roll BB. 13.

—— Grant in,.1479. Harl. 79 E. 28.

—— Expenses of the bailiff(?) of Shelvingford manor, 1514. Harl. Roll BB. 12.

—— *Capellanus. Dom.* Joh. Wasseyl, 1422. Harl. 78 D. 21.

Hoathly, West, *co. Suss.* Sale, etc., in, 1572, 1578 (Westhoithligh, Westbothlcygh). Add. 23830-23833.

Hoaton, *co. Pembr.* Grant nr., [1234-41] (Hoton). Add. 8412.

Hober Marsh, *in Barnby, co. Suff.* Grant in, *t.* Edw. I. (Houberge). Harl. 51 D. 9.

Hoborough, *nr. Snodland, co. Kent.* Grant in, 838 (æt Holan beorge). Cott. viii. 30.

Hobury. *v. sub* Crayford, *co. Kent.*

Hocbere. *v. sub* Netherbury, *co. Dors.*

Hocgestorp. *v.* Hogsthorpe, *co. Linc.*

Hocham. *v.* Oakham, *co. Rutl.*

Hochecote. *v.* Edgcote, *co. Northt.*

Hochton. *v.* Houghton, Lit., *co. North*

—— *v.* Houghton, Stoney, *in Pleasley co. Derb.*

Hockenbury, *in Headcorn* (?), *co. Kent.* Grant at, 814 (Focgingabyra). Harl. 83 A. 1.

Hockenbury, *Dom. of. v. sub* Headcorn, *co. Kent.*

Hockerton, *co. Nott.* Papal conf. of Rahage Grange in, to Rufford Abbey, 1156. Harl. 111 A. 2;—1160. Harl. 111 A. 5;—[1171-80]. Harl. 111 A. 4.

—— Grants, etc., in, to Rufford Abbey, late 12 cent. Harl. 83 F. 23 (Hocretona);—*t.* John–*t.* Hen. III. Harl. 83 F. 25 (Hocret.), 26 (Hochretон), 27 (Hokerton), 28 (Hocret.), 112 I. 12 (Hokert.), 13 (Hocreton).

—— Grant in Dalegate in (?), to the same, *t.* John. Harl. 83 F. 24.

—— Release, etc., in Rahage Wodehouse in, to the same, early 13 cent. Harl. 83 D. 38, 39, 112 I. 14;—late 13 cent. Harl. 83 D. 37.

—— *Capellanus.* Hugo de Snella, *t.* John. Harl. 83 F. 46.

—— —— Johannes, early 13 cent. Harl. 83 F. 26.

—— *Persona.* Gaufridus, early 13 cent. Harl. 83 F. 25, 112 I. 12.

—— —— Ricardus, early 13 cent. Harl. 83 D. 38, 39.

Hockham, *co. Norf.* Release in, 1390 (Hokham). Add. 9183.

—— Manumission of villeins in Gt. Hockham manor, 1538. Add. 14705.

Hockham, Little, *co. Norf.* Grant in, 1561. Add. 14706.

—— Extract from court-roll, 1597. Add. 14707.

Hockley, *co. Essex.* Fine in, 1232 (Parva Huckeleghe). Harl. 47 D. 44.

—— Releases, etc., in, 1269. Harl. 55 B. 15 (parva Hockeie), 55 C. 3 (p. Hokkele);—1273. Harl. 48 G. 4 (p. Hoekele);—1280. Harl. 51 C. 15 (do.).

—— Precipe on a covenant conc. land in, 1593. Add. 25024.

Hockworthy, *co. Devon.* Power to take seisin in, 1501 (Hocworthy). Add. 13074.

Hocote. *v.* Hulcote, *nr. Aylesbury, co. Buck.*

Hocrede. *v. sub* Cranbrooke, *co. Kent.*

Hocret, Hocretona. v. Hockerton, co. Nott.

Hocris, ar. Waresley, co. Hunt. Conf. of grant in, to Sawtrey Abbey, early 13 cent. Harl. 83 C. 2.

Hocthon, Hooton, Hooton Magna, etc. v. Houghton, Gt. and Lit., co. Northt.

Hocotona. v. Houghton Regis, co. Bedf.

Hoctune. v. Haughton, co. Nott.

—— v. Houghton in the Dale, co. Norf.

Hoddesdon, co. Hertf. Exemplif. of fine in, 1608. Add. 13582.

Hoddington, co. Southt. Grant in, to the see of Winchester, 1046 (Hoddingatun). Cott. xii. 76 (copy).

Hode. v. sub Patrixbourne, co. Kent.

Hodenac, Hodenoc, etc. v. Hadnock, co. Monm.

Hodenhelle, [nr. Pluckley?], co. Kent. Grant in, t. Edw. I. Add. 8539.

Hodesdale. v. Woodsdale, nr. Watlington, co. Suss.

Hodgeston, co. Pembr. Conveyance of a fourth part of the manor, and of the advowson, 1441 (Oggeston). Harl. 80 A. 15.

Hodnell, ar. Southam, co. Warw. Power for seisin in, 1405 (Hodenhulle). Cott. xii. 8.

Hodnet, co. Salop. v. Weston under Redcastle, co. Salop.

Hogbere. v. sub Netherbury, co. Dors.

Hogeseeth, Hoggeset. v. Ockshot, co. Surr.

Hoggeston al. Hogston, co. Buck. Persona. William, 1342. Eg. 463.

Hogh. v. sub Tickhill, co. York.

Hoghton. v. Haughton, co. Nott.

—— v. Houghton, nr. Pontefract, co. York.

Hoxton, Mangna. v. Houghton, Gt., co. Northt.

Hoghwyk. v. Howick, in Penwortham, co. Lanc.

Hognaston, co. Derb. Grants, etc., in, 1446. Woll. i. 33 (Hokenaston);—1456. Woll. i. 34 (Hogginaston);—1499. Woll. i. 35 (Hoknaston);—1535. Woll. i. 36;—1539. Woll. i. 37 (do.);—1540. Woll. i. 38-40 (do.).

Hogshaw, co. Buck. Licenses for settlement, etc., of the manor, rectory, etc., 1573. Eg. 291;—1602. Eg. 303.

—— Fines of the manor, etc., 1577. Eg. 296, 297 (Hoggeshawe).

Hogsthorpe, co. Linc. Grants in Aldefen in, to Greenfield Priory, t. Hen. III. (Hoggestorp). Harl. 45 C. 29, 57 G. 3.

—— Conveyance, etc., in, 1328. Harl. 50 F. 2 (Hoggesthorpe);—1329. Harl. 57 G. 7 (do.);—1355. Harl. 57 G. 11 (Hogesthorp);—[1361-8]. Harl. 55 B. 24 (Hoggesthorp).

—— Precipes on covenants conc. lands in, 1578 (Hoggestropp). Add. 25063, 25069.

—— Capellanus. Alanus, [1173-82] (Hocgestorp). Harl. 43 C. 37.

—— Persona. Rob. de Hamby, 1338. Harl. 58 A. 47.

—— Rector. Dom. Rob. de Wylugby, t. Hen. III. Harl. 51 C. 33.

Hogthon. v. Houghton Regis, co. Bedf.

Hoheleswrdi. v. Ozleworth, co. Glouc.

Hoilande. v. Holland, co. Linc.

Hoithligh, West. v. Hoathly, W., co. Suss.

Hokbere. v. sub Netherbury, co. Dors.

Hoke, La, v. sub Ewhurst, co. Surr.

—— v. Hook, co. Surr.

Hoke, Boscus de La. v. sub Henley, in Worplesdon, co. Surr.

Hokefforde. v. Oakford, co. Devon.

Hokeregge. v. sub Cranbrooke, co. Kent.

Hokerton. v. Hockerton, co. Nott.

Hoketone, Hokyngton. v. Oakington, co. Camb.

Hokynbery. v. sub Headcorn, co. Kent.

Hokythorp. v. sub Cawthorne, co. York.

Holacotan gemære. v. Holcot, co. Bedf.

Holan beorge, æt. v. Hoborough, co. Kent.

Holand. v. Holland, co. Linc.

—— v. Hulland, in Ashbourne, co. Derb.

Holbeach, co. Linc. Fine of the advowson, etc., 1284 (Holebech). Harl. 43 I. 49.

—— Court-roll, 1365 (Holb.). Add. 24442.

—— Power from Greenfield Priory to take seisin in (?), 1398 (Holbech). Harl. 44 E. 10.

2 B 2

Holdenby (Haldenebi, Haldeneby, etc.), co. Northt. (continued). Manumission of a nativus in, 1416. Add. 21950.

—— Sale of Couell manor in, 1476. Add. 21960.

—— Covenants in, for marriage of Mary Holdenby with Will. Hatton, 1516, 1519. Add. 21975, 21977.

—— Inquest conc. lands in, 1524. Add. 19872.

—— Sale of the House, etc., to Ad. Baynes, 1651. Add. 12629.

—— Capellanus. Roger de Esseby, early Hen. III. Add. 21893.

—— Rector. Symon fil. Walteri, t. Hen. III. Harl. 48 I. 8.

—— —— Petr. de Lobenham, 1291. Add. 21903;—1333. Add. 21914.

—— —— Galfridus, 1343. Add. 21920.

—— —— Tho. Payntour, Clericus, 1456. Add. 21956.

Holderness, Lordship of, co. York. Accompts of the receiver of Anne, Duchess of Buckingham, for dower from, 1473–4. Add. 22645.

—— Valor of the Demesne, 1519–20. Roy. Roll 14 B. xl.

—— Dapifer de Hildernessa. Everard fil. Petri, [1128–32]. Cott. MS. Aug. ii. 56.

—— Vicecomes. Rannulfus, early Hen. III. Harl. 50 D. 39.

—— —— Hen. de Cesterhunt, 1251. Harl. 50 D. 38.

Holditch, in Thorncombe, co. Devon. Grants, etc., in, late 13 cent. Harl. 54 L 30 (Holedych);—1295. Harl. 46 F. 52 (Holedich);—1342. Add. 20232 (do.);—1356. Harl. 46 G. 12 (Holdich);—1362. Harl. 46 G. 14 (do.);—1396. Harl. 46 G. 29 (Holdech);—1530. Harl. 46 I. 7.

—— Release, etc., of the manor, c. 1348. Harl. 46 G. 9;—1421. Harl. 56 H. 22.

—— Grants in Bushay (Bessehegh, Bessbehey) in, 1356. Harl. 46 G. 11; —1438. Harl. 50 E. 6.

—— Court-rolls, 1378. Harl. Roll G. 35 (Holdych);—1502-3. Harl. Roll L 7 (do.).

—— Feoffment of Chepmanhegh, etc., in (?), 1402. Harl. 57 B. 52.

—— Assault on Lord Cobham at, by the Earl of Wiltshire, c. 1450-60. Harl. 46 H. 26.

Hole, co. Kent. Lease in, early Edw. I. (Hola). Add. 8537.

Hole, nr. Grimsby, co. Linc. Grant in, 1407. Add. 19324.

Hole, La. v. sub Odiham, co. Southt.

Holebrok. v. Holbrooke, co. Suff.
—— v. sub Pinxton, co. Derb.

Holeford, Feodum de. Grant in Crundale, co. Kent, in, t. Hen. III. Cott. xxvii. 98, Harl. 57 A. 47.

Holeg. v. Hooley, in Coulsdon (?), co. Surr.

Holehgmede. v. sub Stanton Lacy, co. Salop.

Holekote. v. Holcote, co. Northt.

Holemedwe, Montana de La, nr. Stormy (?), co. Glam. Conf. of, to Margam Abbey, late 12 cent. Harl. 75 B. 27.

Holeton, in Dinas Powis, co. Glam. Exchange of rents in, 1302. Harl. 75 B. 22.

Holetun. v. Holton, co. Suff.

Holeweia. v. Holloway, in Feckenham, co. Worc.

Holewell, Holewell Magna. v. Holwell, co. Bedf.

Holeweyes lond al. Holeweyes, co. Devon. Fine in, 1305. Add. 12945.

—— Settlement in, 1465. Add. 13061-13064.

Holgate, nr. Sudbury, co. Suff. Grants of shares in the mill of, early Hen. III. Harl. 56 H. 1 (Holegate);— 1349. Harl. 48 A. 17.

Holgate Castle, co. Salop. Charter of Hen. I. dated at, [1109] (Castrum Helgoti). Cott. x. 8.

Holgill, in Craven, co. York. Grant in, 1467. Add. 16959.

Holhurst al. Sudton. v. sub Shere, co. Surr.

Holibed. v. Hollybed, co. Worc.

Holinton. v. Hollington, in Longford, co. Derb.

Holkham, co. Norf. Grant in, to Walsingham Priory, t. Hen. III. or Edw. I. (Holcham). Harl. 51 F. 42.*

Holland. v. Hulland, in Ashbourne, co. Derb.

—— v. sub Petherwin, S., co. Cornw.

Holland, co. *Linc.* Grant in Donnington and Bicker in, to Ouston Abbey, early Hen. II. (Hoilande). Add. 6025.

—— Grant of "redditum salis" in, to Biddlesdon Abbey, early Hen. II. (do.). Harl. 86 C. 40.

—— Rental, 1367 (Hoyland). Harl. Roll G. 38.

—— Suit with Kirkstead Abbey conc. Wildemore Fen in, 1369 (Holand). Harl. 43 E. 15.

Holland, Great, co. *Essex.* Grant of a moiety of the manor, with the advowson, *ante* 1302 (Mangua Holaund). Lansd. 93.

—— Fine of the manor, 1541. Add. 15868.

Holland, Little, co. *Essex.* Grant of the manor, c. 1245-50 (Hoylaunde). Harl. 50 G. 39.

Hollanton, in *Holme Lacy,* co. *Heref.* Release in, 1501 (Hollampton). Add. 1335.

Hollerst of Downe. *v. sub* Shore, co. *Surr.*

Hollesley, co. *Suff.* Lease, etc., in, 1537. Add. 909 (Howsley);—1657. Add. 10561.

Holleth, in *Garstang,* co. *Lanc.* Brief conc. a fire at, 1812. Ch. Br. B. liii. 6.

Hollewellebury, in com. *Hertf.* v. Holwellbury, nr. *Shillington,* co. *Bedf.*

Hollingbourne, co. *Kent.* Grants in, 1318. Harl. 53 E. 3 (Holyngebourne); —1458. Add. 8571 (Holyngbourne).

—— Covenant betw. Christ Church, Canterbury, and Boxley Abbey conc. · land in the manor of, 1336 (Holingborne). Add. 20008.

—— Arbitration in, 1519. Add. 8599.

Hollingrove, in *Brightling,* co. *Suss.* Rentals, 15 cent. (Holyngrove). Add. 8140, 8141.

Hollington (Holinton), in *Longford,* co. *Derb.* Grants in, t. Hen. III. Woll. ix. 44, 45.

Holliwell Marsh. *v. sub* Burnham, co. *Essex.*

Hollm. *v.* Peel, *Isle of Man.*

Holloway, in *Orich,* co. *Derb.* Lease in, 1357 (Holoweyes). Woll. vi. 54.

Holloway, in *Feckenham,* co. *Worc.* Grant of, to Bordesley Abbey, [1138?] (Holeweia). Add. 20419.

Holloway, in *Feckenham,* co. *Worc.* (continued). Notification of above to S., Bp. of Worcester, a. 1196 (Helewei). Harl. 45 I. 30.

—— Conf. of above by Hen. II., [1157?] (Holeweia). Cott. MS. Nero C. iii. f. 176.

Hollowell, co. *Northt.* Settlement in, 1513. Add. 21972.

Hollybed, in *Morton, Castle,* co. *Worc.* Grant, etc., in, to Lit. Malvern Priory, early Hen. III. Harl. 83 B. 37 (Holibed);—late Hen. III. Harl. 83 B. 44.

Hollym, co. *York.* Release in, 1393 (Holaym). Lansd. 532.

—— Exemplif. of a recovery in, 1476 (Holyme in Holdernesse). Harl. 111 B. 54.

Holm Hall, in *Filby,* co. *Norf.* Conveyance of two parts of the manor, called Illere and Titeshale, 1391. Add. 14708.

Holme, nr. *Brampton,* co. *Derb.* Grant in, t. Hen. III. (Hulm). Harl. 112 G. 54.

Holme, in *Whitwell,* co. *Derb.* Crown grant in, of lands late bel. to Welbeck Abbey, 1612. Cott. xiii. 35.

Holme (Holna), co. *Dors.* Conf. of, by Hen. I., etc., to Montacute Priory, c. 1106. Add. 24879 (4);—t. Hen. I. Add. 24879 (3) (copies).

—— *Clericus.* Alexander, t. Hen. II. Add. 24879 (7).

Holme, in *Glatton,* co. *Hunt.* Grant of the manor, by Edw. III., to Pr. John, his son, 1372. Cott. xv. 1.

—— Rental and customary of the manor, 1374. Add. 26835.

—— Court-rolls, 1575-1602. Add. 26836.

Holme, nr. *Hunstanton,* co. *Norf.* Bequest at, to Bury St. Edmunds, 1088 (?). Cott. MS. Aug. ii. 85.

Holme, in *Morton* in *Babworth,* co. *Nott.* Grant in, to Rufford Abbey, c. 1200. Harl. 112 H. 34.

Holme, nr. *Newark,* co. *Nott.* Grant in, to Rufford Abbey, late 12 cent. (Olm). Harl. 83 E. 43.

—— Release in, 1472 (Holm iuxta Newerk). Woll. i. 77.

Holme, co. *York.* Grant in, to Beverley College, early 13 cent. (Holm). Lansd. 400.

Holme Hale, co. *Norf.* Grant in, 1342 (Haleholm). Harl. 45 D. 24.

Holme Hale, co. Norf. (continued). Sale of a third part of the manor, with the advowson of St. Andrew's church, Hale, 1527. Add. 5357.

Holme Lacy, co. Heref. Grant, etc., in early Hen. III. Add. 8055 (Hamme);—1501. Add. 1335 (Homlacy).

——— Accompt of waste in the manor, while leased to Dore Abbey, post 1264 (Hamme). Cott. MS. Nero C. iii. f. 193.

——— Vicarius. Will. Androw, capellanus, 1509 (Homelacy). Add. 1337.

Holme on Spalding Moor, co. York. Land held by Swine Abbey nr. the Hermitage of, late Hen. II. (Heremitorium de Spaldiggeholm). Add. 26108.

——— Exchequer acquittance for a fine on the rectory, 1567. Add. 25700.

Holme on the Wolds, co. York. Conff. of grant of the church, etc., to Nun Appleton Priory, c. 1150. Cott. xii. 46 (Houm);—c. 1150-60. Harl. 50 A. 37 (do.).

——— Capellanus parochialis. Dom. Joh. de Seton, 1371 (Howme). Add. 5756.

Holme Pierrepont, co. Nott. Covenant for conveyance in, 1571 (Holme Peyrpointe). Woll. xi. 51.

Holme, South, in Hovingham, co. York. Grant, etc., in, 1336. Harl. 111 D. 53 (Southolme);—1463. Harl. 48 H. 45 (Holme juxta Hovyngham).

——— Precipe to receive homage in, 1584 (Southolme). Harl. 47 D. 50.

Holmer, in Lit. Missenden, co. Buck. Persona. Thomas, c. 1245. Add. 10610.

Holmer, co. Heref. Fine in, 1592. Add. 1864.

——— Grants in, 1598. Add. 1873;—1608. Add. 1896.

Holmeriddyng. v. sub Gringley, in Clareborough, co. Nott.

Holmes. v. sub Shenley, co. Hertf.

Holmesfield, in Dronfield, co. Derb. Release of, [1156-65] (Holmesfeld). Woll. x. 1.

——— Grants in or nr., 1409. Harl. 112 A. 43;—1528. Woll. viii. 25;—1534. Woll. viii. 26.

——— Extracts from court-rolls, 1417. Woll. viii. 19 a;—1431. Woll. viii. 19, 20;—1436. Woll. viii. 20 a;—1443. Woll. viii. 22;—1452. Woll.

viii. 71;—1456. Woll. viii. 29 a;—1466. Woll. viii. 28;—1472. Woll. viii. 24;—1491. Woll. viii. 18;—1494. Woll. viii. 24a, 30;—1540. Woll. viii. 32;—1553. Woll. viii. 31, 33;—1595. Woll. viii. 34;—1599. Woll. viii. 28.

——— Surrender of rent for the support of the chaplain of St. Swithin in, 1491. Woll. viii. 18.

——— Warrant for a grant of the manor, [1514-20]. Add. 22628.

——— List of copyholders, 16 cent. (Homsfeld). Woll. viii. 35.

——— Breviat of the customs of the manor, 16 cent. Woll. xi. 30.

v. also Fanshawgate, co. Derb.

v. also Woodthorpe, co. Derb.

Holmeshurne. v. sub Arlsey, co. Bedf.

Holmfirth, in Kirk Burton and Almondbury, co. York. Brief for rebuilding the chapel, 1777. Ch. Br. B. xvii. 6.

Holmpton (Holmeton), co. York. Grant, etc., in, 1352. Lansd. 532;—1354. Lansd. 451;—1739. Add. 24197.

——— Rector Capelle. Alan de Kilnese, 1354. Lansd. 451.

——— Rector. Alan Bole, 1358. Lansd. 429, 543.

——— Petr. de Bylton al. Belton, 1375, 1376 (Holmton). Lansd. 533, 534.

Holna. v. Holme, co. Dors.

Holne, co. Devon. Grant in Bodeton in S. Holne manor, etc., 1318. Add. 9223.

——— Grants, etc., of a mill and lands at Rowderfold (?) (Rotherasford, Rotherneforde), Hosefenne, etc., nr., 1318. Add. 9223;—1343. Add. 9229;—1344. Add. 9231;—1347. Add. 7825;—1351. Add. 9232;—1624. Add. 7893.

——— Acquittance on a sale in Colleforde nr., 1344. Add. 7823.

v. also Bozedon, co. Devon.

Holnest, co. Dors. Rentals of the manor, 1599, 1620. Campb. xiii. 1, 2.

Holond. v. Hulland, in Ashbourne, co. Derb.

Holowei. v. Holloway, in Feckenham, co. Worc.

Holoweyes. v. Holloway, in Crich, co. Derb.

Holsworthy, *co. Devon.* Lease of Barton land with Tracy's mill in, by St. Mary Graces' Abbey, London, 1421 (Holdesworthy). Campb. xiv. 27.

Holt, *co. Denbigh.* Extracts from court-roll, 1456. Add. 8041.

—— Recovery in, 1551. Add. 8528.

—— *Constabularius Castri Leonis.* David de Eyton, 1391. Add. 8633.

Holt, *co. Norf.* Grant in Lotfal nr., late 12 cent. Harl. 50 B. 37.

—— Grants, etc., in, 1416. Add. 14820;—1417. Add. 14821;—1540. Add. 14871.

Holt, [*in Kingsclere*], *co. Southt.* Grant nr., *t.* Hen. III.-Edw. I. Add. 24693.

Holt Hundred, *co. Norf.* Subsidy-rolls, 1593, 1603. Add. 9410–9414.

Holthaim, Holtham, etc. *v.* Haltham upon Bain, *co. Linc.*

Holthorp. *v.* Howthorpe, *co. York.*

Holting moor, *in Denham, co. Buck.* Grant of, 1461. Harl. 85 D. 2.

Holton, *co. Oxon.* Grant of reversion to Le Grove manor in (?), etc., 1429 (Halton). Harl. 53 A. 5.

Holton (Holetun, etc.), *in Blything Hundred, co. Suf.* Conff. of the chapel to St. Mary's Abbey, York, [1175–1200?]. Campb. ix. 9 (1);—[1239–42?]. Campb. ix. 9 (3) (*copies*).

—— Bequest to the church, 1439. Cott. iv. 34.

Holton Beckering, *co. Linc.* Grants, etc., in, to Bullington Priory, late Hen. II. Harl. 45 H. 29 (Bekering):— early 13 cent. Harl. 45 H. 30, 31 (do.).

—— (?) *Clericus.* Gilbertus, *t.* Hen. II. (Autun). Harl. 44 A. 21.

—— *Sacerdos.* Radulfus, late Hen. II. (Houton). Harl. 54 I. 31.

Holton Bosnyves *al.* Bodsnives. *v. sub* Bodmin, *co. Cornw.*

Holton le Clay, *co. Linc.* Conf. in Tuafletes and Westengea in, to Greenfield Priory, *t.* Hen. II. (Hutun). Harl. 52 A. 45.

—— Lease in the same, by Greenfield Priory, *t.* Hen. II. (do.). Harl. 44 D. 52.

—— Precipe on a covenant conc. land in, 1555 (Howlton juxt. Waltham). Add. 25062.

Holton St. Mary, *co. Suf.* Grants, etc., in, *t.* Edw. I. Harl. 47 A. 45 (Holeton);—1338. Harl. 47 E. 9;— 1464. Harl. 55 C. 43.

Holwell, *co. Bedf.* Conf. by Edw. the Confessor of a grant in, to Westminster Abbey, 1066 [*sc.* 1065] (Holeuuelle). Cott. vi. 2 (*copy*).

—— Grants, etc., in, *t.* John. Cott. xxvii. 20 (Holewelle);—1349. Add. 17659 (Magna Holewell);— 1377. Harl. 45 F. 62 (Holewell).

—— Payment for fine and release of Gt. Holwell manor, 1241 (Holewell magna). Harl. 51 D. 14.

—— Court-roll of Gt. Holwell manor, 1389. Harl. Roll A. 4.

—— Grants, etc., of the manor and advowson, 1490. Harl. 54 H. 24 (Hollewell);—1527. Harl. 46 H. 49 (Haliwell);—1531. Harl. 55 F. 38 (Holewell);—1532. Harl. 55 H. 41 (Halywell).

Holwell, *co. Dors. Rector.* Will. Brounsop, 1532. Harl. 47 D. 11.

Holwell, *co. Leic.* Assignment of the manor, 1411. Lansd. 641.

—— Acquittance for escheats from, 1413 (Holewell). Lansd. 642.

Holwell, *co. Oxon.* Precipe on a covenant conc. land in, 1598 (Hollwell). Add. 25207.

Holwellbury, *nr. Shitlington, co. Bedf.* Settlement, etc., of the manor, 1420. Add. 17225 (Hollewellebury in com. Hertf.);—1553. Harl. 45 D. 49 (Holwelbury).

Holybourne, *co. Southt.* Precipe on a covenant conc. land in, 1578 (Hallyborne). Add. 25224.

Holyfield. *v. sub* Waltham H. Cross, *co. Essex.*

Holyme in Holderness. *v.* Hollym, *co. York.*

Holyngrove. *v.* Hollingrove, *in Brightling, co. Suss.*

Holyoaks, *nr. Great Easton, co. Leic.* Conveyance in, 1396 (Halyok). Add. 854, 855.

Holywell. *v. sub* Oxford, *co. Oxon.*

Hom, *nr. Ross, co. Heref.* Grant in, 1431 (Le Homme). Harl. 111 D. 37.

Homanton. *v.* Humington, *co. Wilts.*

Hoo, *in Kimpton, co. Bedf.* Feoffment, etc., of the manor, 1415. Add. 19566, 19567.

Hoo Hundred, *co. Kent.* Grant of marsh land at Tunstalle, etc., in, early Hen. III. (Hou). Harl. 49 B. 52.

Hoo Allhallows, *co. Kent.* Lease of possession in, 1677. Add. 6368.

Hoo St. Mary (S. *Maria in Hoo, etc.*), *co. Kent.* Feoffments in, 1367. Harl. 48 E. 24;—1381. Harl. 48 E. 36.

—— Release in, to Cobham Chantry, *c.* 1370. Harl. 48 E. 30.

—— Release and grant of a windmill in, 1370. Harl. 48 F. 9, 58 A. 33.

—— Fine in, 1375. Harl. 48 F. 12.

Hoo St. Werburgh, *co. Kent.* Grant of Sledemersh and Benerse in (?), *ante* 1225. Harl. 50 B. 10.

—— (S. Werburga in Hoo, etc.). Grant of reversion to marsh lands in, 1345. Harl. 45 C. 24.

—— Lease in Cranfeld in, 1367. Harl. 48 E. 27.

—— Grant at La Welle in or nr., 1372. Harl. 52 C. 14.

—— Rental of La Welle and Vyaundes in, late 14 cent. (Hoo). Harl. Roll G. 37.

—— Robbery of sheep in (?), 1417 (Hoo). Harl. 58 E. 23.

—— Power to give seisin of Hertyngrave in, 1435 (S. Werburge in Hoo). Harl. 47 H. 49.

—— Roll of court of (?), 1463 (Hoo). Harl. 58 F. 56.

—— Schedule of rents in (?), 1463-4 (Hoo). Harl. 55 H. 22.

—— Lease in (?), by Cobham College, 1476 (Howe). Harl. 44 C. 40.

—— Memorandum of rent in (?), paid to Cobham College, 1513 (Hoo). Harl. 58 F. 45.

Hooe, *co. Suss.* Grant of the manor to Battle Abbey, by Will. I., 1086-7 (Hov). Harl. 83 A. 12 (*copy*).

—— Conf. of, to the same, by Hen. I., *c.* 1121 (Hov). Campb. xvi. 13.

—— Release, etc., in, *t.* Edw. I. Add. 20080;—1344. Add. 20081.

Hook. *v. sub* Ewhurst, *co. Surr.*

Hook, *in —— (?), co. Surr.* Grant of custody of forfeited lands in, 1335 (La Hoke). Add. 24596.

Hook, *co. York.* Conf. from St. Mary's Abbey, York, of a grant in (?), to Newhouse Abbey, co. Linc., early 13 cent. (Huc). Harl. 44 D. 20.

—— Lease in, 1314 (Houke). Add. 20558.

Hook, North, Marsh, *in Hundred of Hoo* (?), *co. Kent.* Lease of, by Cobham College, 1406 (Northhokes). Harl. 44 C. 36.

Hook Wood. *v. sub* Henley, *in Worplesdon, co. Surr.*

Hook Wood, [*in Boughton under Blean*], *co. Kent.* Sale of, 1589. Harl. 77 H. 46.

—— *v. also* Boughton under Blean, *co. Kent.*

Hoole, Much (Magna Hole), *co. Lanc.* Grants, etc., in, 1296. Add. 26026; —1303. Add.; 26028;—1305. Add. 26031;—1307. Add. 26032;—1316. Add. 26035, 26036;—1336. Add. 26041.

Hooley, *in Couledon* (?), *co. Surr.* Grant in, early Edw. I. (villa de Holeg.). Add. 24165.

Hooton. *v. sub* Laughton en le Morthen, *co. York.*

Hooton Paynel, *co. York.* Release in Bilham (Bilam) in, 1246. Lansd. 71.

—— Grant in, *c.* 1240-50 (Hotone). Add. 21268.

—— Release of common of pasture in, to the Knts. Hospitallers of, 1261 (Hoton Paynel). Toph. 16.

—— Conf. of grant, etc., in Moorhouse (Morhouses, etc.) in, late Hen. III. Cott. xxviii. 37;—1395. Add. 17059, 17060, 17062.

—— Conveyance, etc., of the rectory, with tithes of Bilham, Moorhouse, etc., in, 1670-84 (Hutton Pannell). Add. 13709-13713.

—— *Vicarius.* Rob. Atte Welle, 1389. Cott. xxviii. 92.

—— —— Rob. Gregson, 1395 (Hoton). Add. 17059, 17060, 17062.

Hooton Roberts, *co. York.* Grant in, 1434 (Hoton Robert). Harl. 57 A. 17.

Hooton upon Darwen. *v.* Hutton, Low, *in Huttons Ambo, co. York.*

Hope, *co. Derb.* License for resettlement in, with the bailliage of two forestries in Hopedale, etc., 1322. Woll. iv. 59.

Hope, co. Derb. (continued). Grants, etc., in, 1394. Woll. iii. 13;—1409. Woll. ii. 78;—1424. Harl. 84 A. 49;—1428. Woll. iii. 12;—1471. Harl. 83 E. 32;—1485. Woll. iii. 72, 76;—1496. Woll. ii. 79;—1594. Woll. xii. 85;—1610. Woll. xii. 87, 89;—1619. Woll. xii. 93;—1636. Woll. xii. 88;—1687. Woll. xii. 123.

——— Lease in Offerton in, 1399. Woll. viii. 5.

——— Acquittance for rents in, due to Lichfield Chapter, 1438. Woll. iii. 24.

——— Settlement of a forestry, etc., in, 1496. Woll. ii. 79.

——— Fine in, 1541 (Hawpe). Woll. ii. 71.

——— Sale of tithes of Hazlebadge -selbache in le Peake) in, [1554–7]. Woll. iv. 65.

——— Judgment in suit conc. tithes of lead ore in, 1730. Woll. xii. 144.

——— Prepositus Decani et capituli Lich[feld] apud. Jac. le Eyer, 1438. Woll. iii. 24.

——— Vicarius. Ric. Forester, 1394. Woll. iii. 13.

v. also Abney, co. Derb.
Ashop, co. Derb.
Bradwell, co. Derb.
Brough, co. Derb.
Hucklow, Gt. and Lit., co. Derb.
Shatton, co. Derb.
Thornhill, co. Derb.

Hope, co. Durh. Power for seisin in, 1366. Harl. 45 I. 39.

Hope, [in Goudhurst], co. Kent. Grant nr., t. Edw. I. (Le Hope). Harl. 79 E. 53.

Hope, La, in Portbury, co. Som. Grant in, 1343. Add. 7822.

Hope Mansell, co. Heref. Grant of the manor to the see of Gloucester, 1541. Cott. xiii. 34.

Hope Solers, co. Heref. Grant in, 1341. Slo. xxxiii. 25.

Hopewolnyth. v. Woolhope, co. Heref.

Hopperton (Hoperton, etc.), co. York. Grants, etc., in, t. Hen. III.–t. Edw. I. Add. 1292–1298;—1314. Add. 1299;—1317. Add. 1300;—1321. Add. 1249;—1322. Add. 1301, 1302;—1343. Add. 1303.

——— Grant of rent charge on the manor, 1529. Add. 1304.

Hopperton (Hoperton, etc.), co. York. (continued). Award in a suit in, 1556. Add. 1350.

——— Power to pay money due on lands in, 1587. Add. 1306.

Hopsford, in Withybrook, co. Warw. Power to give seisin of the manor, 1405. Cott. xii. 8.

Hopton, co. Derb. Clericus. Hen. fil. Henrici, t. Edw. I. Woll. i. 30.

Hopton, nr. Stafford, co. Staff. Grant in, 1343. Add. 20450.

Hopton, co. Suff. Grant in, 1538 (Hapton). Add. 10225.

Hoqueruge. v. Hawridge, co. Buck.

Horbling, co. Linc. Covenant to levy a fine of the manor, 1552. Add. 13562.

Horbury, in Wakefield, co. York. Crown lease in, 1555 (Horreberre). Harl. 84 C. 32.

Hordlawe, nr. Wirksworth (?), co. Derb. Grant of, t. Edw. I. Harl. 111 E. 17 (copy).

Horebrugg, Le. v. Horrabridge, in Buckland Monachorum, co. Devon.

Horeburn. v. Harborne, co. Staff.

Horehurst, North, Den of. v. sub Marden, co. Kent.

Horemed, Magna. v. Hormead, Gt., co. Hertf.

Hores. v. sub Dorking, co. Surr.

Horestone, Le, in Brinsop, co. Heref. Grant at, t. Edw. I. Add. 4589.

Horewethye, La Horewythy. v. Hoarwithy, in Hentland, co. Heref.

Horham, co. Suff. Acquittances for rents in, 1380–1395 (Heham, Horram, etc.). Add. 5500–5508.

——— Settlement, etc., in, 1477. Harl. 57 B. 35;—1510. Add. 5515.

——— Extract from court-roll, 1505. Add. 7321.

——— Precipes on covenants conc. lands in, 1588. Add. 25388, 25389.

——— Plea conc. tithes in, 1681. Add. 15003.

——— Persona. Dom. Rob. Lumkyn, 1352. Add. 10006.

——— ——— Andr. Flamund, 1380. Add. 9652.

——— Rector. Tho. Ryst, 1415. Add. 10059.

——— ——— Joh. Starlyng, 1477. Harl. 57 B. 35.

——— ——— Joh. Clubb, 1618. Add. 15003.

**Horingforde.** *v.* Horringford, *Isle of Wight.*

**Horkaley, Great,** *co. Essex.* Releases in, 1433. Add. 5253 (Horkesley magna);—1460. Harl. 50 F. 7 (Horkesleigh).

—— Precipe on a covenant conc. lands in, 1546 (Horkesley magna). Add. 24924.

—— *Persona.* Hugo Meenge, 1418. Harl. 58 D. 12;—1442. Cott. xxix. 30.

**Horkesley, Little,** *co. Essex.* Grant of Le Hope meadow in (?), early Hen. III. Harl. 51 G. 21.

—— Grants, etc., in, 1298. Harl. 58 D. 25 (Horskeleye parva);—1307. Harl. 51 G. 23 (Horkesleye parva):—1361. Harl. 55 E. 4 (petite Horkesleye);—1433. Add. 5253.

**Horkstow,** *co. Linc. Persona.* Walterus, early Hen. III. (Horkestou). Harl. 44 L 12.

**Horley,** *co. Oxon.* Grant in, by the Archdeacon of Buckingham, *c.* 1190–1200 (Hornel.). Harl. 84 F. 30.

**Horley** (Horle, etc.), *co. Surr.* Grants of Sidlow mill (Sideluue melne), etc., in, late 12 cent. Add. 24634, 24635.

—— Grants of Horley mill, with fishery, etc., *t.* Hen. III.–*t.* Edw. I. (Horleia) Add. 24587, 24589.

—— Grants, etc., in, *t.* Hen. III.–*t.* Edw. I. Add. 23512, 24588, 24590 (Horlye);—1303. Add. 24591;—1304. Add. 24592;—1332. Add. 17300;—1362. Add. 24594;—1413. Add. 24593;—1424. Add. 24554;—1429. Add. 23540;—1467. Harl. 111 D. 23;—1479. Harl. 112 E. 24;—1511. Add. 23596;—1567. Add. 23513;—1588. Add. 23514;—1617. Harl. 80 B. 42;—1618. Harl. 80 B. 43;—1635. Add. 18944.

—— Fine in, 1333 (Horlee). Add. 23338.

—— Lease in, from Qu. Katharine, 1514. Add. 22629.

—— Precipe on a covenant conc. land in, 1564. Add. 25509.

—— Chancery order conc. lands in, as held of Beddington manor, 1598. Add. 23515.

**Hormead, Great and Little,** *co. Hertf.* Grant in, for a lamp in the church for the soul of L. de Sanford, *t.* Hen. III. (Magna Horemed). Harl. 50 C. 17.

**Hormead, Great and Little,** *co. Hertf.* (continued). Fine in Gt. and Lit. Hormead, 1313 (Hormede magna, H. parva). Add. 6246.

—— Court-rolls, *t.* Edw. IV., 1511 (Hormed parva). Harl. Roll N. 16.

**Hornby,** *co. Lanc.* Release of the castle and manor to Hen. Duke of Lancaster, 1358 (Horneby). Add. 20560.

—— Conveyance of the manor and castle, etc., 1657. Add. 18979–18981.

**Hornby** (1), *co. York.* Grant in, to St. Peter's Hospital, York, *t.* Hen. III. Add. 15645.

**Hornby** (2), *co. York.* Grant of Brokholme in, 1331. Harl. 47 D. 16.

**Horncastle** (Horncastre, etc.), *co. Linc.* Grant of fairs and market in the manor of, to the Bp. of Carlisle, 1230. Harl. 58 H. 42 (copies).

—— Grants, etc., in, 1328. Harl. 55 F. 22, 58 C. 1;—1370. Harl. 56 B. 49.

—— Conff. of grants, etc., in, to Kirkstead Abbey, 1331. Harl. 43 G. 52;—1365. Harl. 58 C. 2.

—— *Clericus.* Alexander, *t.* Hen. III. Harl. 48 C. 9.

—— *Persona.* Joh. de Rouceby, 1371. Harl. 55 E. 39.

—— *Presbiter.* Willelmus, *c.* 1155–66 (Hornekastra). Harl. 45 A. 30.

**Hornchurch,** *co. Essex.* Precipe on a covenant conc. Le Lyon manor in, 1561. Add. 24932.

—— Livery of lands in, 1594 (Hornechurch). Harl. 51 H. 30.

**Horndon on the Hill,** *co. Essex.* Grants, etc., in (?), early 13 cent. Harl. 48 A. 4 (Hornind.);—*t.* Hen. III. Harl. 45 I. 47 (Hornidone), 49 B. 47 (Hornindun);—late 13 cent. Harl. 48 G. 26 (Horndon), 57 B 27 (Horndun).

—— Grant of Radeles in, *t.* Hen. III. (Hornd.). Harl. 45 D. 8.

—— Grant, etc., of S. Bradewerde marsh in, *t.* Hen. III. or Edw. I. (Horndon). Harl. 48 G. 25, Add. 19967, 19976.

—— Reservation of right of market, etc., in, 1281 (Horningdon). Add. 5251.

—— Precipes on covenants conc. lands in, 1555. Add. 24925 (Hornedon);—1575. Add. 24943 (Horndon super montem).

Horseheath, *co. Camb.* Acquittance for farm of the manor, 1305 (Horseth). Harl. 45 E. 36.

—— Feoffment, etc., in, 1503. Add. 25868 (Horseth) ;—1578. Add. 25869, 25968 (do.).

—— Fine in, 1670. Add. 25870.

Horsemonden, *co. Kent.* Release of the manor and advowson, 1281 (Horsmunden). Harl. 51 D. 32, 33.

—— Grants, etc., in, 1452-1494. Add. 24521-24529 ;—1517. Harl. 76 H. 4 ;—1552. Add. 24530.

—— Sale of Sherenden wood, etc., in, parcel of Bockingfold manor, 1557. Harl. 76 L 30, 77 F. 18.

—— Fines in, 1559. Harl. 76 I. 44, 77 G. 24 ;—1562. Harl. 78 A. 40, 41 ;—1616. Harl. 77 C. 52 ;—1620. Harl. 77 E. 33.

—— Precipe on a covenant conc. land in, 1566. Add. 18093.

—— Leases, etc., in, 1640. Harl. 83 H. 44 ;—1648. Harl. 79 G. 14 ;—1652. Harl. 77 D. 19.

—— Bockingfold manor in. *v. sub* Brenchley, *co. Kent.*

Horsendon, *co. Buck.* Release of the manor, 1389 (Horssyngdon). Harl. 46 F. 35.

Horseth. *v.* Horseheath, *co. Camb.*

Horsewold, *in Crowfield, co. Suff.* Acquittance for castle ward due to Horsford manor, co. Norf., for, 1441. Campb. viii. 4.

—— A note of the tenure of, *t.* Hen. VI. Campb. viii. 5.

Horsey, *co. Norf.* Conf. of tithes in, to Hulme Abbey, *t.* Steph. (Horseye). Cott. iv. 57 (25-27) (*copies*).

—— Grants, etc., in, 1347. Harl. 48 C. 3 ;—1361. Harl. 52 B. 11 ;—1379. Add. 14954.

—— Surrender of the manor, 1370 (Horseye). Add. 14867.

Horsey, *nr. Eastbourne, co. Suss.* Exchange of, by Lewes Priory, *t.* Steph. (terra de Horsia). Harl. 44 F. 21.

—— Grant in, 1391 (Horse). Add. 13030.

Horsford, *co. Norf.* Papal conf. of the church to Horsham St. Faith's Priory, 1163. Cott. MS. Aug. ii. 136.

—— Acquittance for castle ward due to the manor, in Crowfield, co. Suff., 1441. Campb. viii. 4.

Horsham, *nr. Haverhill, co. Suss.* Exchequer order to seise lands in, 1350 (Horsham). Cott. xiii. 5 (4) (*copy*).

Horsham, *co. Norf.* Papal conf. of the vill, and of Alderford (Alrefords) mill in, to Horsham St. Faith's Priory, 1163. Cott. MS. Aug. ii. 136.

—— Conf. of Alderford mill in, to the same, 1320. Add. 15189, 15190.

Horsham, *co. Suss.* Grants, etc., in, *t.* Hen. III.-*t.* Edw. I. Add. 8796 (Horsam), 8797, 18565, 18568 ; — 1309. Lansd. 678 ;—1315. Add. 8812 ;—1324. Add. 17296 ;—1335. Add. 8093, 18631 ;—1337. Add. 8825 ;—1353. Add. 8831 ;—1354. Add. 8833 ;—1355. Add. 8832, 8834 ;—1357. Add. 18631 ;—1365. Add. 8836 ;—1380. Add. 17334 ;—1389. Add. 8847 ;—1391. Add. 8848 ;—1395. Add. 18683 ;—1399. Add. 8852 ;—1400. Add. 8854 ;—1410. Add. 8862 ;—1411. Add. 8863, 8864 ;—1421. Add. 8867 ;—1422. Add. 8869 ;—1427. Add. 8874, 18715 ;—1428. Add. 8896 ;—1429 (?). Add. 8993 ;—1431. Add. 18716 ;—1433. Add. 8875 ;—1441. Add. 18739 ;—1447. Add. 8894-8896 ;—1454. Add. 8895 ;—1456. Add. 18755 ;—1457. Add. 8897 ;—1458. Add. 18757 ;—1462. Add. 8899 ;—1472. Add. 18766 ;—1474. Add. 18767 ;—1476. Add. 1007 ;—1482. Add. 18772 ;—1483-4. Add. 18774 ;—1492. Add. 8909 ;—1493. Add. 8102 ;—1502. Add. 8915 ;—1503. Add. 8916 ;—1504. Add. 8917 ;—1509. Add. 8919, 18794 ;—1525-6. Add. 18809 ;—1534. Add. 18817 ;—1536. Add. 8934, 18820 ;—1538. Add. 8935 ;—1542. Add. 18824 ;—1550. Add. 8933 ;—1552. Add. 18834 ; — 1557. Add. 8942 ;—1562. Add. 18849 ;—1573. Add. 18855 ;—1578. Add. 8954, 18860 ;—1591. Add. 8963 ; — 1597. Add. 18892 ;—1599. Add. 18886-18889 ;—1606. Add. 8976 ;—1608. Add. 8977, 8978, 18908 ;—1609. Add. 18909, 18911 ;—1616. Add. 18920 ; — 1620. Add. 18924, 18925 ;—1635. Add. 18945 ;—1636. Add. 8995 ;—1642. Add. 18946 ;—1647. Add. 18966-18970 ; — 1656. Add. 18977, 18978 ;—1668. Add. 19000.

—— Grant at Shortsfield (?) (Srottesfeld) in, *t.* Hen. III. or Edw. I. Add. 18572.

—— Endowment of a chantry in Horsham chapel, 1308. Add. 18599.

—— Inq.p.m. on W. Burgeys, 1324. Add. 8818.

Horton, *in Epsom, co. Surr.* Grants, etc., in, 1404. Slo. xxxii. 29 (Hortone in par. de Epsam);—1496. Harl. 111 E. 34;—1538. Harl. 112 B. 36.

Horton, *in Hampton Lovett, co. Worc.* Conf. of salt-works at, to Pershore Abbey, 972 (Hortun). Cott. MS. Aug. ii. 6.

Horton, Great, *in Bradford, co. York.* Release in, 1585. Add. 26130.

Horton Kirby (Hortun, Horton, etc.), *co. Kent.* Grants in Pindeu (Pinidene), etc., in, to endow a chantry in St. Mary's church, *t.* Hen. III. Harl. 58 A. 2, Add. 16449-16451, 16454;— 1259. Add. 16453.

—— Grants in, *t.* Hen. III. Add. 16448, 16452.

—— Bond for mortgage of Darenth mill in, 1256. Cott. xxviii. 68.

—— Fines of the manor, *t.* Edw. II., 1362, 1373 (Horton juxta Derteford). Harl. Roll G. 17.

—— Grant in Hennefeld and nr. La Nassch in, 1360. Add. 23520.

—— Release in Oxendoune in, with the advowson, to Lord Cobham, 1377 (Horton juxta Derteford). Harl. 48 F. 13.

—— Appropriation of the church to Cobham College, 1378. Harl. 43 I. 32.

—— Acquittance to Lord Cobham for fruits of the parsonage, 1380 (Horton jouste Derteford). Harl. 48 E. 33.

—— Decision conc. fruits of the chantry, in suit with Cobham College, [1454-64]. Harl. 43 G. 38.

—— Acquittance to Cobham College for a subsidy assessed on the church of, 1515, 1519. Harl. 44 I. 9, 10, 13.

—— Lease of woods in, 1601. Add. 23782.

—— Covenant for a settlement of a moiety of the manor, etc., 1658. Add. 23783.

—— *Persona.* Robertus, *t.* John. Harl. 112 C. 41.

—— *Rector.* Franco al. Francus, *t.* Hen. III. Harl. 58 A. 2, Add. 16450.

—— —— *Dom.* John de S. Dionisio, late Hen. III. Add. 16454.

—— —— *Mag.* Ric. de Montibus, 1259. Add. 16453.

—— —— *Mag.* Hen. de Grofhurst, 1360. Add. 23520.

—— *Vicar.* Sir John Bache, 1502. Harl. 44 C. 47.

Houghton Regis, *co. Bedf.* Conf. by Hen. II. of land in, to Reading Abbey, [1157] (Hoctona). Add. 19591.

—— Assignment of rent in the manor, by Reading Abbey, 1284 (Hogthou). Add. 19633.

—— Grants, etc., in, 1290-1328. Add. 19933-19938 (Houton, Houthon, etc.); —1393. Add. 19956;—1693. Add. 13736-13738.

Houghton, Stoney, *in Pleasley, co. Derb.* Grants in, 1280. Harl. 45 G. 46 (Hoel.ton);—1310. Lansd. 599 (do.).

Houingeford. *v.* Horringford, *I. of Wight.*

Houm. *v.* Holme on the Wolds, *co. York.*

Hound, *co. Southt.* Mortgage of the manor. 1572. Add. 16153.

Houndean, *nr. Lewes, co. Suss.* Assignment of the manor to Edw. II., 1316 (Houndeden). Harl. 57 E. 33.

Houthon. *v.* Houghton next Harpley, *co. Norf.*

Houton. *v.* Holton Beckering, *co. Linc.*

—— *v.* Hoton, *in Prestwold, co. Leic.*

—— *v.* Houghton, Lit., *co. Northt.*

—— *v.* Houghton on the Hill, *co. Norf.*

—— *v.* Houghton Regis, *co. Bedf.*

Houwald. *v.* Haywold, *nr. Huggate (?), co. York.*

Hov. *v.* Hooe, *co. Suss.*

Hover Wistan. *v.* Whiston, *co. York.*

Hoveringham, *co. Nott.* Charge upon the manor for chantries in Crich, *co. Derb.,* and Normanton, *co. Nott.,* 1368 (Houryngham). Woll. iv. 58.

—— Lease in, 1559. Add. 8458.

Hoveton, *co. Norf.* Appropriation of churches in, to Hulme Abbey, [1146-74]. Cott. iv. 57 (17) (copy).

Hovingham, *co. York.* Power to give seisin in, 1366 (Hovyngham). Harl. 112 E. 11.

—— Grant of custody of the manor, 1405. Harl. 112 F. 26.

—— Award in, conc. rents, etc., 1516. Harl. 111 D. 31.

Howbury, *in Crayford, co. Kent.* Grant of the manor, 1379 (Hobury). Slo. xxxii. 45.

Howden (Houeden, etc.), *co. York.* Lands held near, by Swine Abbey, late Hen. II. (Ouedan). Add. 26106.

—— Grants, etc., in Bulkholme in, late Hen. III.-Edw. I. Add. 26109-26112;—1322-1854. Add. 26113-26121.

—— Rent to be paid "ad terminos in Houedenschyre statutos," *t.* Edw. I. Add. 26112.

—— Grant near the Cornmarket, sited in, 1429. Harl. 111 D. 34.

—— Grants in, 1473. Lansd. 453;—1519. Lansd. 456.

—— Lease in, by the "magistri sive gardiani" of the guild of . . . . . . in the charnel of the College of, 1506. Lansd. 454.

—— Extract from court-roll, 1721. Add. 7407.

Howe. *v.* Hoo St. Werburgh, *co. Kent.*

Howe, *co. Norf.* Papal conf. of tithes in, to Horsham St. Faith Priory, 1163 (Hoa). Cott. MS. Aug. ii. 136.

Howertorp. *v.* Hawthorpe, *in Irnham, co. Linc.*

Howes. *v. sub* Alderton, *co. Suff.*

Howeton iuxta Prestewald. *v.* Hoton, *in Prestwold, co. Leic.*

Howfield. *v. sub* Chartham, *co. Kent.*

Howick, *in Penwortham, co. Linc.* Settlement of lands in, 1317 (Hoghwyk). Add. 26037.

Howley Grange. *v. sub* Hales Owen, *cos. Salop and Worc.*

Howlton iuxta Waltham. *v.* Holton le Clay, *co. Linc.*

Howme. *v.* Holme on the Wolds, *co. York.*

Howsham (Husum), *co. Linc. Clericus.* Radulfus, *c.* 1150-60. Cott. xxvii. 34;—[1157-63]. Cott. xi. 26.

Howsley. *v.* Hollesley, *co. Suff.*

Howthorpe, *co. York.* Lease of the manor, 1357 (Holthorp). Harl. 111 G. 60.

—— Grant in, 1361 (do.). Harl. 111 G. 61.

Howton. *v.* Hoton, *in Prestwold, co. Leic.*

Howton, *co. Heref.* Grant in, to Llanthony Priory, *t.* Hen. III. (Huton). Add. 7014.

Huish Episcopi, *co. Som.* Decree
in suit with ——— Roceter, vicar of,
1534 (Huyshe). Harl. 58 G. 29.

Huish, South, *co. Devon.* Award
conc. the manor, 1499 (Suthhewishe).
Add. 5248.

Huklowe. *v.* Hucklow, Gt. and Lit.,
*in Hope, co. Derb.*

Huknall. *v.* Hucknall, Ault, *co. Derb.*

Hulcoote. *v.* Hilcot, *in N. Newington,
co. Wilts.*

Hulcote. *v.* Holcot, *co. Northt.*

Hulcote, *nr. Aylesbury, co. Buck.* Recovery in, 1497 (Hocote). Add. 13929.

Huleby. *v.* Ulceby, *co. Linc.*

Hull. *v.* Hill, *nr. Fladbury, co. Worc.*

Hull, Bishop's. *v.* Fydock, *in Bishop's
Hull, co. Som.*

Hull Bridge. *v. sub* Beverley, *co. York.*

Hull, La. *v. sub* Marshwood, *co. Dors.*

Hulland, *in Ashbourne, co. Derb.* Grants,
etc., in, 1262. Woll. vi. 48 (Huland);
—1345. Woll. vi. 33 (Holond).

——— Extract from court-roll, 1522
(Holand). Woll. i. 84.

——— Fine of the manor, 1638 (Holland). Woll. xi. 29.

Hullavington, *co. Wilts.* Settlements
of Surrenden (Cyrendene, Sorenden)
manor in, c. 1330-35. Add. 7740 ;—
—1567. Add. 7071.

Hulle. *v.* Hill, *nr. Sheffield, co. York* (?).

——— *v.* Hill Hall (?), *nr. High Offley,
co. Staff.*

Hulle, La Hulle. *v. sub* Odiham, *co.
Southt.*

Hulle, *co. Som.* Settlement in, 1414.
Harl. 48 I. 25.

Hullethroup. *v. sub* Ramsbury, *co.
Wilts.*

Hullewrthe. *v.* Elworthy, *co. Som.*

Hulm. *v.* Holme, *nr. Brampton, co.
Derb.*

Hulpryngton. *v.* Hilperton, *co. Wilts.*

Hulton. *v.* Hilton, *in Marston upon
Dove, co. Derb.*

Hulvistorpe. *v.* Owsthorpe, *co. York.*

Humber, *River.* Grants, etc., of
fisheries in, to Newhouse Abbey, co.
Linc., [1143-7]. Harl. 43 H. 10 ;—c.
1150. Harl. 43 H. 14-17, 45 F. 19, 50
H. 58 ;—[1156 or 7 ?]. Harl. 51 H. 1.

Humber, *River (continued).* Attornment for a ferry over, at Hessle, *co.*
York, 1340. Harl. 57 A. 26.

Humber, *co. Heref.* Grant in the
manor of, 1654. Add. 1953.

Humber, Little, *co. York.* Compotus
of the storer of the king's sheep at,
1349-50. Harl. Roll H. 5.

Humberston, *co. Linc.* Grant in, t.
Hen. II. (Humbrest.). Cott. xii. 21.

——— Precipe on a covenant conc. land
in, 1555. Add. 25062.

Humberstone, *co. Leic.* Covenant
betw. Biddlesdon Abbey and St. Mary
de Pré Abbey, Leicester, conc. the
church of, c. 1150 (Humberstan). Harl.
84 D. 12.

Humberton, *co. York.* Grant in, 1278
(Hundburton). Add. 6194.

Humbor ford, *co.* ——— (?). Grant *nr.*,
854. Cott. MS. Aug. ii. 46.

Humbresfeld. *v.* Homersfield, *co. Suf.*

Humby, *co. Linc.* Grants in, 1463,
1464. Add. 6458-6460.

——— Conveyance of the manor, 1477.
Add. 6461.

——— Power to take seisin in Gt. and
Lit. Humby, 1530. Add. 6462.

Humelee. *v.* Himley, *co. Staff.*

Humene, *Mariscus de. v. sub* Heckingham, *co. Norf.*

Humeresfeld, Humresfeld. *v.* Homersfield, *co. Suf.*

Humington *al.* Homanton, *in Maddington, co. Wilts.* Grant in, t. Hen.
III. (Hughemanton). Harl. 58 B 32.

Hundburton. *v.* Humberton, *co. York.*

Hundela. *v.* Oundle, *co. Northt.*

Hundesdon. *v. sub* Stanton Lacy, *co.
Salop.*

Hundeston. *v.* Hunston, *co. Suf.*

Hundigton, Hundinctune, Hund-
ingtonia. *v.* Honington, *co. Linc.*

Hundle, *nr. Tattershall* (?), *co. Linc.*
Conveyance in, 1290 (Hondel). Harl.
47 B. 24.

Hundleby, *co. Linc.* Grant, etc., in,
c. 1145. Harl. 55 E. 10 (Hundelbia);
—1362. Cott. v. 18 (Hundelby).

——— Fines in, 1302. Harl. 45 H. 18
(do.) ;—1355. Harl. 50 E. 27, 28 (do.).

——— *Vicarius.* Petrus, 1265. Eg. 452.

**Huntingdon,** *County of* (*continued*). Correspondence, etc., conc. assessments of ship money in, 1636-1637. Cott. i. 8, 9, 13, xxvi. 19.

—— Bond of Sir T. Cotton as sheriff, 1637. Cott. xxiv. 44.

—— Pipe-roll acquittance to the sheriff, 1638. Cott. xiv. 14.

—— *Vicecomes.* Paganus, *t.* Steph. (?). Harl. 50 B. 25.

—— —— Hugo de Babynton, 1295. Harl. 58 E. 40, 41.

—— —— Tho. Tyrrell, 1631. Add. 7403.

—— —— Sir Tho. Cotton, 1636-1637. Cott. i. 6, 8, 9, 13, xxiv. 43, 44, 60, xxvi. 19.

—— *Under Sheriff.* Godfr. Wildbore, 1636. Cott. xxiv. 43.

—— *Escaetor* (*nuper*). John Say, *de Brokesburn*, 1462. Cott. viii. 13.

—— —— Rob. Russell, 1587. Cott. xxix. 49.

**Huntingdon,** *co. Hunt.* Papal conf. of churches, the castle chapel, etc., in, to the Priory there, 1147 (Huntendonia). Cott. MS. Aug. ii. 112.

—— Grant to, of a fair in the town, with tolls of St. Ives, 1252. Harl. 58 I. 10 (*copy*).

—— Conf. of the "redditus villate" to Edm., Earl of Lancaster, 1285 (Huntindou). Cott. MS. Aug. ii. 135 (5).

—— Papal conf. of grants in, to Sawtrey Abbey, 1300 (Huntyngton). Cott. MS. Aug. ii. 114.

**Huntingdon,** *Honour of.* Charters addressed to the men of, by Malcolm and William, Kings of Scotland, and by Earl David, [1157?]. Cott. xv. 21;—[1159?]. Cott. xv. 20;—[1163?]. Cott. xv. 19;—[1165-71?]. Cott. xviii. 49;—[c. 1186?]. Cott. xii. 78;—late 12 cent. Add. 19909;—c. 1200. Add. 22612.

—— Conf. by Hen. II. of a grant of a "socca" in London bel. to, [1175?]. Harl. 43 C. 26.

—— Conf. by R. de Brus to Wardon Abbey of lands held of, in co. Bedf., 1257-8. Cott. MS. Nero C. iii. f. 230.

**Huntingfield** (Huntyngfeld), *co. Suff.* Grants, etc., in, 1375. Harl. 49 C. 7; —1404. Harl. 55 C. 5;—1454. Harl. 48 B. 51;—1520. Add. 10309;—1621. Add. 10432.

**Huntingfield** (Huntyngfeld), *co. Suff.* (*continued*). Grants, etc., of the manor and advowson, 1401. Harl. 57 E. 1;—1430. Harl. 43 E. 19;—1481. Harl. 45 I. 12;—1435. Add. 9414.

—— Precipe on covenant conc. land in, 1588. Add. 10420.

—— *Persona.* Tho. Horne, 1372. Add. 25945.

—— *Rector.* Joh. de Lynstede, 1363. Add. 22586.

**Huntington,** *co. Heref.* Exchequer acquittance for sale of timber on the manor, 1567 (Huntingdon Welsh). Add. 25600.

—— Order conc. arrears of rent crown lands in, 1621. Add. 1919.

**Huntley,** *co. Glouc.* Grant and release of Awbercis, etc., in, 1529. Campb. xviii. 14* (Hunteley), 15.

—— Fine in, 1600. Campb. xviii.

**Hunton,** *co. Kent.* Covenant for covery and fine in, 1559. Harl. F 44, 77 G. 24.

—— *Rector.* Mag. Ric. de Beltry, 1370 (Hontyngton). Add. 8841-3.

**Hunton,** *in Brompton Patrick, co. Y* Exchequer acquittance for fine 1585. Add. 25712.

**Huntshaw,** *co. Devon.* Fine, etc., the manor and advowson, 1655. Harl. 86 I. 59 (Hunshaw);—1655. Harl. 111 E. 35.

**Huntspill,** *co. Som.* Grants, etc., the manor, 1408. Harl. 43 E. 17, (Honyspill); — 1415. Harl. 55 B 2 (do.).

**Huntwick,** *in Wragby, co. York.* Crown lease in, 1555. Harl. 84 C.

**Huntys.** *v. sub* Springfield, *co. Ess.*

**Hunwethon.** *v.* Honington, *co. Suff.*

**Hunworth,** *co. Norf.* Sale in Aschel eleshirne, etc., in, late Hen. 1 (Hunow.). Harl. 45 F. 15.

—— Recovery in, 1540. Add. 1487

**Huoton.** *v.* Hoton, *co. Leic.*

**Huphalle.** *v. sub* Wheatacre, *co. Nor.*

**Hupshire.** *v. sub* Waltham H. Cros *co. Essex.*

**Huptona.** *v.* Upton, *co. Northt.*

**Hurleston,** *co. Chest.* Settlement of th manor, 1325 (Hurdlaston). Add. 627

—— Rental, 1391 (Herdleston). Add 5230.

Huttoft (Hotoft, etc.), *co. Linc. (continued)*. Grants, etc., in, to Greenfield Priory, early 13 cent.-*t.* Hen. III. Harl. 45 G. 23, 24, 47 F. 22, 51 G. 44, 56 F. 49;—1254. Harl. 46 D. 53.

—— Grant in, to Greenfield Priory, from Louth Park Abbey, early 13 cent. Harl. 44 H. 49.

—— Release to Greenfield Priory from suits of court in, due at Grantham, *post* 1217. Harl. 52 A. 16.

—— Covenants conc. pasture in, betw. Bullington Priory and Louth Park Abbey and Markby Priory, etc., 1235. Harl. 44 H. 48;—1236. Harl. 44 A. 51;—1239. Harl. 44 A. 35;—1242. Harl. 44 A. 38, 39;—1235-42. Harl. Roll A. 29.

—— Grant, etc., in, to Bullington Priory, from Markby Priory, *t.* Hen. III. Harl. 44 G. 6, 7.

—— Exchange of crops in, by Burwell Priory, *t.* Hen. III. Harl. 46 E. 1.

—— Lease in, by Greenfield Priory, 1344. Harl. 44 E. 7.

—— Conveyance in, 1355 (Hutoft). Harl. 57 G. 11.

—— Conveyance of the manor, 1376 (Hotoft). Harl. 56 E. 6.

—— Conveyance, etc., of the manor to Newhouse Abbey, 1383. Harl. 45 I. 40, 52 G. 15, 16.

—— Mandate for protection in, for Bullington Priory, 1499. Harl. 43 I. 11.

—— Valor of crown lands in, *t.* Hen. VIII. Harl. Roll R. 4.

—— *Capellanus.* Radulfus, *t.* Hen. II. Harl. 52 A. 45.

—— —— Robertus, early 13 cent. Harl. 51 G. 4.

—— —— Moyses, early Hen. III. Harl. 47 F. 22.

—— —— Henricus, *t.* Hen. III. Cott. xxvii. 185, Harl. 46 D. 55.

Hutton (Hutoune), *co. Berwick.* Royal conff. of a marriage settlement, etc., in, 1475. Add. 19561;—1478. Add. 19562.

Hutton, *in Penwortham, co. Lanc.* Grant in, 1346 (Hoton). Add. 26042.

Hutton, *co. Som.* Grant of wardship in, 1467. Add. 6548.

—— *Rector.* Joh. Wylton, 1484. Add. 5474.

Hutton Cranswick, *co. York.* in, 1387. Add. 15582 (Hoton-wyk):—1485. Add. 15540 (

—— *Perpet. vicarius.* Will. 1387. Add. 15532.

Hutton, Low, *in Huttons York.* Assignment of a in, 1579 (Hooton upon Harl. 80 I. 54.

Hutton Pannell. *v.* Hoot co. York.

Huttons Ambo, *co. York.* a fire at, 1780. Ch. Br. B.

Huttorp. *v.* Hothorpe, *co. N*

Hutun. *v.* Holton le Clay, *c*

Huussthamstede. *v.* Wb stead, *co. Hertf.*

Huuermidhope. *v.* Midho *co. York.*

Huyeswyndon. *v.* Swindo

Huyshe. *v.* Huish Episcop

Huyton, *co. Lanc.* Conf. of 1277, to Burscough Priory Land at Rudgate [Rudega fee of Tarbock [Torbok] Add. 20521

—— Release by the Priory land at Rudgate (Le Ridg Harl. 44 B. 21.

Hweton stede, *co. Kent.* swine-pasture so called, 88 viii. 30.

Hwettan staneswylle, *n* ford, *co. Worc.* A bound Cott. viii. 6 (copy).

Hwifersac, *co. Suff. (?).* Beq Stoke monastery, late 10 ce 43 C. 4.

Hwite celd, *co. Kent.* Gran at, 858. Cott. MS. Aug. ti.

Hwytefelda. *v.* Whitfield,

Hwyteflet Marsh. *v. sub* Suss.

Hwytene. *v.* Whitney, *co. J*

Hycham. *v.* Hitcham, *co. B*

—— *v.* Ickham, *co. Kent.*

Hyoling. *v.* Hickling, *co. N*

Hyde. *v. sub* Beaconsfield, *co.*

—— *v. sub* Denchworth, *co.*

Hyde, *nr. Purley* (?), *co. Ber* of the manor, 1454. Add. 2

Hyde, *in Steeple, co. Dors.* conc. settlement of, 1613.

Ifield, *co. Suss. (continued)*. Fine of the manor, 1507 (Iffeld). Add. 24907.

—— Award, etc., in, 1510. Add. 5673, 5674.

—— *Vicarius. Dom.* Joh. de Schyre, 1350. Add. 24674.

—— *(nuper). Dom.* Joh. att Stighele, 1352. Add. 17322.

—— *Perpet. Vicarius. Dom.* Rob. Cook *al.* Cok, 1360. Add. 24677;—1362. Add. 17327.

Ifold. *v. sub* Kirdford, *co. Suss.*

Iford, *in Freshford, co. Som.* Feoffment in, 1470. Campb. i. 5.

Iford, *co. Suss.* Power for assignment of the vill to Edw. II., 1316. Harl. 57 E. 33.

—— Re-feoffment in the manor, 1401. Add. 20087.

—— Sale of the rectory, etc., 1590. Add. 15163.

Iford, *co. Wilts.* Mortgage in, 1553. Add. 5703.

Iggeham. *v.* Ingham, *co. Suff.*

Ightham, *co. Kent.* Grants, etc., in, *t.* Hen. III. Add. 16441 (Heitcham) (*copy*);—1363. Add. 16473 (Hegtham):—1594. Add. 5980 (Eightham); —1598. Add. 24532.

—— Grants, etc., of Mote manor in, 1399. Harl. Roll V. 9;—1444. Harl. 78 G. 14.

—— Opinion in a suit in, 1745. Add. 24533.

Iham, Ihamme. *v.* Higham, *co. Suss.*

Ihurst. *v.* Ewhurst, *co. Surr.*

Ikeham, Ikham. *v.* Ickham, *co. Kent.*

Ikelesham. *v.* Icklesham, *co. Suss.*

Ikelyngham. *v.* Icklingham, *co. Suff.*

Iken, *co. Suff.* Liberties of the manor, as parcel of the Duchy of Lancaster, 1479 (Ekyn). Add. 16565.

—— Precipe on a covenant conc. the manor, etc., 1545 (Ikyn). Add. 25269.

—— *Rector.* Laurentius, *t.* Edw. I. Add. 22566.

Ikenylt, via que vocatur. *v.* Icknield Street.

Ikkellesaham, Iklesham, Ikylsham. *v.* Icklesham, *co. Suss.*

Ilbrewer, Ilbruwere, Ilebruere. *v.* Isle Brewers, *co. Som.*

Ilchester (Iuelcestria, etc.), *co. Som.* Grants, etc., in, *t.* Hen. III.–*t.* Edw. I. Harl. 46 F. 16, 48 B. 21, 22 (Iuylcestr.), 49 G. 26, 56 C. 21, 56 H. 42, Add. 25879;—1318. Harl. 56 H. 23.

—— Grant of chattels in Ilchester and Brooke (Brok iuxte Mountagu) manors, 1356. Harl. 46 G. 12.

—— Fee-farm rent to the crown from, 1408–9. Harl. Roll CC. 31.

—— Release of Brooke (Brookyelchestre) manor in, 1488. Harl. 50 E. 6.

—— Grant, etc., of Brooke Court manor in, 1481. Harl. 46 H. 32;—1518. Harl. 46 H. 43;—1589. Harl. 46 I. 6.

—— Covenant to repair Pill Bridge in, 1530. Harl. 46 I. 6.

Ilderton, *co. Northumb.* Sale of tithes in, 1629. Add. 17213.

Ilford, Great, *in Barking, co. Essex.* Precipe on a covenant conc. land in, 1575. Add. 24950.

Ilkeston, *co. Derb.* Release of the advowson to Dale Abbey, 1386. Add. 26216.

—— Lease in, 1628. Woll. xi. 33.

—— *Rector. Dom.* Willelmus, late Edw. I. (Ilkesdon). Woll. viii. 65.

Ilketshall, *co. Suff.* Grants of Palmereslond, Le Clynt, etc., in, *t.* Hen. III. Harl. 52 I. 46 (Ylketelesh.), 68 G. 13 (Hylkel.), 14 (Hilketelsh.);—1567. Add. 1386.

—— Precipe on a covenant conc. land in, 1593. Add. 25471.

Ilketshall St. Andrew's, *co. Suff.* Precipes on covenants conc. lands in, 1564. Add. 25329;—1588. Add. 25382.

—— *Rector.* Reginaldus, *t.* Edw. I. Harl. 83 D. 45.

Ilketshall St. John's, *co. Suff.* Precipe on a covenant conc. land in, 1588. Add. 25383.

Ilkley, *co. York.* Grant of the advowson, 1376. Harl. 57 D. 7.

—— *Vicarius.* Rob. Whyte, 1454. Harl. 16946.

Illanlege, set. *v.* Eleigh, Monks, *co. Suff.*

Illere. *v. sub* Holm Hall, *in Filby, co. Norf.*

Illey Combusta. *v.* Eleigh, Brent, *co. Suff.*

Illington co. *Norf.* Release in, 1390 (Illyngton). Add. 9183.

Illingworth, *in Halifax, co. York.* Brief for rebuilding the chapel, 1762. Ch. Br. B. ii. 4.

Ilmington. co. *Warw.* Feoffment of the manor and advowson, 1326 (Ilmyn-don). Add. 21452.

—— Acquittance for farm of the manor, etc., 1392 (do.). Add. 21453.

—— *Persona.* Will. Mountfort, 1392. Add. 21453.

—— *Rector.* Ric. Mountfort, 1450. Cott. xxvii. 179.

——, co. *Berks.* Conf. of the church to St. Mary de Pré Abbey, Leicester, Rich. I. (Hildislai). Slo. xxxii. 22.

—— Lease in, 1693. Add. 19234.

—— Ref. to sale in 1604 of W. Ilsley manor, 1624 (West Hillesley). Harl. 75 H. 43.

Ilston on the Hill (Ilueston, etc.). co. *Leic.* Grants, etc., in, late Hen. III. Add. 26957 (Iluiston)-26959;—1318-1343. Add. 26961-26963, 26965-26967.

—— Inquest, etc., conc. lands in, bel. to Creake Abbey, co. Norf., 1309. Add. 26960.

—— Court-rolls of the manor, bel. to Creake Abbey, 1336. Add. 26964.

—— Covenant betw. Creake Abbey and its tenants in, c. 1470 (?). Add. 26963.

Ilstree. *v.* Elstree, co. *Hertf.*

Ilsyngton. *v.* Islington, co. *Norf.*

Ilton, *nr. Salcombe,* co. *Devon.* Award conc. the manor, 1499 (Edilton *al.* Ethelton). Add. 5248.

Imber, co. *Wilts.* Brief conc. a fire at, 1770. Ch. Br. B. x. 1.

Immingham, co. *Linc.* Conff. of grants in, to Nun Appleton Priory, co. York, c. 1150. Cott. xii. 46 (Himinge-haim);—c. 1150–60. Harl. 50 A. 37 (Himmigham).

—— Grants in, to Newhouse Abbey, 1241 (Imyngham). Harl. 55 E. 49;—late 13 cent. Harl. 55 F. 1 (Imigham), 2 (Imyngham).

—— Covenant conc. tithes in Killing-holme, co. Linc., bel. to the church of St. Andrew of, 1272. Harl. 44 A. 5.

—— Power from H. de Percy to give seisin in, 1335. Harl. 54 G. 21.

—— Fine in, 1728. Add. 7498.

Imphey. *v. sub* Buttsbury, co. *Essex.*

Inardestone, Inarstone, Innar-ston. *v. sub* Redmarley Dabitot, co. *Worc.*

Ince, co. *Chest.* Brief for rebuilding the church, 1791. Ch. Br. B. xxxi. 9.

Ince (Ines, etc.), co. *Lanc.* Grants, etc., in, 1335. Add. 17675;—1395. Add. 17687;—1432. Add. 17698.

—— Briefs conc. fires at, 1795, 1804. Ch. Br. B. xxxv. 6, xliv. 2.

Inchelemore. *v. sub* Swinefleet, co. *York.*

Inewre, *River, in Ireland.* Lease of lands betw. the Boyse and the, 1559-60. Harl. 83 A. 14.

Ingaldesthorpe. *v.* Ingoldisthorpe, co. *Norf.*

Ingam, Ingamia, Ingeham. *v.* Ingham, co. *Linc.*

Ingate, co. *Suff.* Settlement in, *t.* Edw. I. (Eudegate). Harl. 48 G. 13.

Ingatestone, co. *Essex.* Extract from court-roll, 1504 (Gynge Abbatisse). Lansd. 171.

Inge penne, set. *v.* Inkpen, co. *Berks.*

Ingescourte. *v. sub* Milton, Gt., co. *Oxon.*

Ingestrie, co. *Staff.* Release in, 1323 (Ingestre). Add. 20458.

—— *Rector.* Hen. de Scwanbache, 1323. Add. 20458.

Ingewyrðe, co. *Worc.* (?). Bequest of land at, 11 cent. Harl. 83 A. 2.

Inggeneshamme, set. *v.* Inglesham, co. *Wilts.*

Ingham, co. *Linc.* Grant and conff. of the church to Bullington Priory, [1158–63]. Harl. 52 G. 20 (Hincham); —c. 1175. Harl. 52 G. 30 (Igham);—[1175–81]. Harl. 43 C. 36 (Ingam); —t. John. Cott. xii. 3;—early 13 cent. Harl. 52 B. 20, 32;—1256. Harl. 52 H. 28;—1294. Harl. 44 A. 51;—1310. Harl. 43 D. 15, 43 H. 35;—t. Edw. I.–II. Harl. 52 H. 5;—c. 1322. Harl. 52 H. 27.

—— Grants, etc., in, to Bullington Priory, t. Hen. II. Harl. 52 G. 23, 24, 54 I. 39;—post 1169. Harl. 52 G. 19; —late Hen. II. Harl. 50 B. 29, 52 G. 29;—ante 1191. Harl. 52 G. 43;—t. Rich. I. Harl. 48 C. 11, 12;—[1195-1214]. Harl. 52 B. 30, 54 E. 9;—early 13 cent. Harl. 51 C. 18 (*copy*),

52 B. 18, 31;—[1215–9]. Harl. 54 E.
11;—*t.* Hen. III. Cott. v. 26, 28, Harl.
47 G. 24, 25, 27, 31, 48 A. 6, 50 D. 9, 52
B. 22, 23, 29;—1256. Harl. 52 H. 28;
—*t.* Edw. I.-II. Harl. 52 H. 5;—
1317. Harl. 44 I. 22;—*c.* 1322. Harl.
52 H. 27.

—— Exchange in, with Bullington
Priory, *c.* 1190–1. Harl. 52 G. 40.

—— Grants, etc., in, [1195–1214?].
Harl. 49 G. 50 (Ingamia);—early 13
cent.—*t.* Edw. I. Harl. 47 G. 26
(Hingham), 50 D. 8, 50 E. 17, 52 B.
19, 21, 24 (Hingham), 26, 55 B. 18;—
1326. Harl. 52 B. 38;—1345. Cott.
v. 78;—1346. Cott. v. 79.

—— Fine in, with Bullington Priory,
1226 (Ingeham). Harl. 50 A. 46.

—— Covenant betw. Bullington Priory
and the Rector conc. tithes, 1242.
Harl. 44 E. 49.

—— Grant nr. Bradegat in, to Bullington Priory, *t.* Hen. III. Harl. 52
B. 23.

—— Lease in, from Bullington Priory,
late Hen. III. Harl. 44 B. 2.

—— Release in, of lands impleaded
against Barlings Abbey, late 13 cent.
(Hengham). Woll. iii. 89.

—— Ordinance conc. maintenance of
the vicar, 1310. Harl. 43 H. 36.

—— Conf. by P., Master of Sempringham, of payment of pensions by Bullington Priory from the church of,
1317. Harl. 44 I. 22.

—— Certificates of rights of Bullington Priory in All Saints' church in,
1389. Harl. 43 G. 32;—1399. Harl.
43 I. 3;—1485. Harl. 43 I. 13.

—— Mandate to protect possessions
of Bullington Priory in, 1499. Harl.
43 I. 11.

—— *Capellanus.* Reinfridus, *t.* Rich.
I. Harl. 48 C. 11, 12.

—— —— Simon, early 13 cent.
Harl. 52 B. 19.

—— —— Adam, *t.* Hen. III. Harl.
47 G. 6.

—— *Clericus.* Radulfus, *t.* Hen. III.
Harl. 47 G. 31.

—— *Persona. Mag.* Stephanus, *t.*
Hen. III. Cott. v. 26.

—— —— Willelmus, *t.* Hen. III.
Harl. 47 G. 25, 52 B. 23, 29.

—— *Rector.* Willelmus, 1242. Harl.
44 E. 49.

—— —— Will. de Louther, 1294.
Harl. 44 A. 54.

Ingoldmells, co. Linc. (continued). Precipe on covenants conc. lands in, 1578. Add. 25072, 25086.

—— Fine of the manor, 1638 (Ingoldsmeales). Woll. xi. 29.

—— Brief conc. a fire at, 1827. Ch. Br. C. viii. 3.

Ingoldsby (Ingoldeby), co. Linc. Grant, etc., in, t. Hen. III. Harl. 52 B. 28. 53 E. 41.

—— Capellanus. Robertus, end of 12 cent. Add. 20580.

—— Persona. Robertus, late Hen. III. Add. 20913.

Ingoldsthorpe Hall. v. sub Snettisham, co. Norf.

Ingeworth, co. Norf. Grants, etc., in, 1320. Add. 15188 (Inggeworth);— 1321. Add. 15191 (do.);—1409. Add. 15193;—1414. Add. 14131;—1425. Add. 15193;—1450. Add. 14150;— 1468. Add. 15195; — 1473. Add. 14162.

Inkberrow, co. Worc. Suit conc. land at, 1012 (?) (æt Intebyrgan). Cott. viii. 37.

—— Release of a wood in, 1315 (Parva Intebergh). Harl. 83 F. 35.

Inkersel, co. Derb. Grant in, [1282-98] (Hinkershill). Harl. 86 H. 51.

Inklemoors. v. sub Swineflest, co. York.

Inkpen, co. Berks. Bequest at, c. 950 (æt inge penne). Cott. viii. 16.

Innse Vaihisam, dioc. Clogher, Ireland. Papal mandate to induct a vicar of, 1576. Add. 12805.

Inshintarshiallig, co. Cork. Award conc. lands of, 1596. Add. 8757.

Insula. v. sub Sedgefield, co. Durh.

Intebergh, Parva, æt Intebyrgan. v. Inkberrow, co. Worc.

Intwood, co. Norf. Grants, etc., in, to Horsham St. Faith Priory, c. 1228. Harl. 47 G. 29 (Hintewode);—t. Hen. III. Harl. 57 A. 2 (Intewode);— 1257. Harl. 57 B. 38 (Yntewode);— late Hen. III. Add. 14716 (Intewod).

—— Fine in, 1228 (Intewde). Harl. 47 G. 28.

—— Grants, etc., in, t. Hen. III. Harl. 57 B. 39 (Intewud);—1280. Harl. 51 F. 11 (Intewod); — 1283. Harl. 48 C. 19 (do.);—1327 (?). Cott. " 122:—1575. Add. 6299, 14625.

Intwood, co. Norf. (continued). Annuity charged on the manor, 1272 (Intewode). Harl. 54 D. 4.

—— Conveyance of the manor and advowson, 1449 (Intewode). Harl. 53 E. 37.

Inwinesburg, co. Glouc. Boundary of a grant at or nr. Bourton on the Water, 779. Cott. Aug. ii. 4.

Inworth, co. Essex. Conveyance in, 1453 (Inneworth). Harl. 47 D. 24.

Inysnergh. v. sub St. Stephen's in Brannel, co. Cornw.

Iognes hom. Record of dispute conc. land at, 825. Cott. MS. Aug. ii. 78.

Johannisflet, nr. Freiston (?), co. Linc. License to Kirkstead Abbey for a mill on, t. Hen. II. Harl. 52 A. 35.

Johnston, in Eccleshall, co. Staff. Conf. of grant in, early 13 cent. (Jonestona). Add. 20455.

Jokeford. v. Yoxford, co. Suff.

Jon (?) Manor, co. Bedf. (?). Conveyance of, 1531. Harl. 55 F. 38.

Jor. v. Ure al. Yore, River, co. York.

Iorotlaforda. v. Hartleford, co. Glouc.

Joscefort, Joxford. v. Yoxford, co. Suff.

Joxale, Joxhale. v. Yoxall, co. Staff.

Iping, co. Suss. Settlement, etc., of the manor and advowson and lands in, 1434, 1435. Add. 18726, 18727;— 1625. Add. 6004;—1630. Add. 6005; 1631. Add. 6006, 6007, 6009;—1632. Add. 6010.

Ippenbury Manor, co. Kent. Fines of, 1548. Harl. 75 H. 4, 76 H. 50;— 1559. Harl. 76 I. 44, 77 G. 24.

Ipplepen, co. Devon. Award conc. the manor, 1532 (Ippelpen al. Iplepen). Harl. 46 I. 11.

Ippollitts, co. Hertf. Livery and extent in, 1541 (Polettes). Add. 13559 a, b.

Ippyng. v. Epping, co. Essex.

Ipsden, co. Oxon. Sale in, 1562 (Ippesden). Add. 20310.

Ipsley, co. Warw. Grant, etc., in, 1334. Add. 21455 (Ippesley);—t. Hen. V. Add. 21454 (do.).

—— Brief for rebuilding the church, 1782. Ch. Br. B. xxii. 9.

Ipstones, co. Staff. Briefs for rebuilding the church, 1776-1800. Ch. Br. B. xvi. 4, xxvii. 6, xxxii. 8, xl. 10.

Kadenal. v. Cadney, co. Linc.

Kadindon, Kadyngton. v. Caddington, co. Hertf.

Kaerdif, Kairdif. v. Cardiff, co. Glam.

Kagwrth. v. Kegworth, co. Leic.

Kaiham. v. Keyham al. Keame, co.
Leic.

Kailmers. v. Kelmarsh, co. Northt.

Kalalh. v. Calow, in Chesterfield, co.
Derb.

Kaldebek. v. Caldbeck Forest, co. Cumb.

Kaldecothes. v. Cargo Fleet (?), co.
York.

Kaletorp. v. Calthorpe, co. Norf.

Kalswardthorp. v. Culverthorpe, co.
Linc.

Kalewetun. v. sub Kirton, co. Suff.

Kalnadatun, Kalnadton. v. Caunton, co. Nott.

Kaltorph. v. Cawthorpe, co. Linc.

Kalverlaia, Kalverlay. v. Calverley, co. York.

Kameis. v. Kemeys, co. Monm.

Kamerhigham. v. Cammeringham,
co. Linc.

Kanefed. v. Canfield, Lit., co. Essex.

Kaneschase. v. sub Lewston, co. Dors.

Kaneston. v. Canton, nr. Cardiff, co.
Glam.

Kanewedon. v. Canewdon, co. Essex.

Kanuic. v. Canwick, co. Linc.

Kardif. v. Cardiff, co. Glam.

Kardoill. v. Carlisle, co. Cumb.

Karel. v. Crail, co. Fife.

Karelion. v. Caerleon, co. Monm.

Karesdic. v. Car Dyke, co. Linc.

Karleton. v. Carlton, co. Nott.
——— v. Carlton, nr. Skipton (?), co.
York.
——— v. Carlton Colville, co. Suff.
——— v. Carlton [le Moorland ?], co.
Linc.

Karlton. v. Carlton, co. Bedf.
——— v. Carleton, co. Lanc. (Addenda).

Karsey Marsh. v. sub Benfleet, S.,
co. Essex.

Kayham. v. Keyham al. Keame, co.
Leic.

Kayllestorp. v. Calsthorpe, co. Linc.

Kayngham. v. Keyingham marsh, co.
York.

Kaynel al. Kayner. v. sub Frome,
co. Som.

Kea, co. Cornw. Conveyance in Hew-
goys in (?), 1516. Add. 13078.
——— Sale of timber in Hewgoose Wood
in, 1616. Add. 15379.

Keal, East, co. Linc. Fine in, 1302
(Estkele). Harl. 45 H. 18.
——— Grant in, 1377 (Estirkel). Eg.
464.
——— Rector medietatis ecclesiæ. Dom.
Joh. Pavy, 1387 (Estrekele). Sloane
xxxii. 54.

Keal, West, co. Linc. Fine in, 1302
(Westkele). Harl. 45 H. 18.
——— Grant in, 1377 (Westirkel). Eg.
464.
——— Grant, etc., of the manor, 1367.
Harl. 53 C. 38 (Westirkele);—1435.
Harl. 49 I. 81 (Westerkeel).
——— Persona. Dom. Joh. de Grym-
by, 1366. Harl. 58 A. 49, 58 B. 1;—
1368. Harl. 58 D. 46.
——— ——— Dom. Rob. Styut, 1372.
Harl. 57 G. 16;—1379. Harl. 56 I.
8;—1381. Harl. 57 G. 14;—1390.
Harl. 49 G. 11, 56 F. 47.

Keblestone al. Meyforde. v. sub
Stone, co. Staff.

Kechenham. v. Kitchenham, nr.
Etchingham, co. Suss.

Kechenore. v. sub Peasmarsh, co. Suss.

Keching, Kechyngg. v. Kitchen, co.
Bedf.

Kectellesby. v. Ketsby, in S. Ormsby,
co. Linc.

Keddington (Kedington, Kedyngton),
co. Linc. Grants, etc., in, t. Edw. I.
Harl. 45 H. 13;—1274. Harl. 47 B.
27;—1295. Harl. 45 H. 19;—1297.
Harl. 45 H. 15 b, 16.
——— Fine in, 1302. Harl. 45 H. 18.

Kedeleafeld, co. ——— (?). Grant in,
1284. Harl. 52 D. 2.

Kilmaine, *Barony of, co. Mayo.* Claim to (?), 18 cent. Add. 986 b.

Kilmainham, *co. Dublin.* Grant of interest in the watermills and weirs of, 1576 (Kylmaynam). Harl. 86 G. 47.

Kilnaglory, *co. Cork. Vicar. Sir* Edm. Breuaghe, 1569. Add. 8732.

Kilnsea, *co. York.* Grants, etc., in, *t.* Hen. III. Lansd. 460 (Kylnese);— 1310 (?). Lansd. 461 (Kilnesse);— 1333. Lansd. 462 (Kilnese), 463 (Kylnese).

Kiluigholm, etc. v. Killingholme, *co. Linc.*

Kilve, *co. Som.* Settlement of land in, 1661. Add. 5984.

Kilvey, *co. Glam.* Joh. de Avene, Lord of, a witness, 1328 (Kyluey). Harl. 75 C. 25.

——— Power from the Duke of Norfolk to give seisin of the Lordship of, 1448. Add. 17740.

Kilvington, *co. Nott.* Bond for warranty in, 1586. Add. 26012.

Kilvington, S., *co. York.* Grant of, late 12 cent. (Kiluinton). Add. 19922.

——— Grant in, *t.* Hen. III. (Suth Kiluingtona). Harl. 112 I. 27.

——— *Persona.* Joh. de Uppesal, *t.* Hen. III. Harl. 112 I. 27.

Kilwatermoy, *co. Waterford.* Lease at Teroullen More in, 1594. Add. 17352.

Kilwingholm, Kilyngholm. v. Killingholme, *co. Linc.*

Kilworth, North, *co. Leic.* Grants, etc., in, early Hen. III. Lansd. 75 (Kiuilingwrth);—*t.* Hen. III.–*t.* Edw. I. Harl. 45 G. 68 (Nortkeueligworth), 55 B. 10 (North Keueligworth), Add. 21350 (Kiuelingwrth Rabuz), 21404 (Kivelingurd Rabaz);—1422. Harl. 50 E. 18 (N. Kyllyngworth).

——— Grants, etc., in, to Sulby Abbey, *t.* Hen. III.–*t.* Edw. I. Add. 21270 (Kyuilingwrth), 21281 (Kiu'llincwria), 21283 (Kyuillingwrth), 21285 (Kiuelingwr.), 21286 (Kiueligwrth), 21290-21292, 21294, 21303-21305, 21307, 21308, 21310 (Northkyuelingwrth), 21311 (North Kyuillingwrhte), 21312, 21314-21322, 21339, 21351 (Kyuelingwrth Rabaz), 21352 (do.).

——— Release of common land in, to the freeholders of, late Hen. III. (Norþ Kyuill.). Add. 21313.

Kilworth, North, co. Leic. (continued). Ballivus. Walt. de Haddon, late 13. cent. Add. 21310.

——— Clericus. Alanus, early Hen. III. Lansd. 75.

——— Persona. Mag. Hugo Burun, late Hen. III. Add. 21316.

——— Rector. Alanus, late Hen. III. Add. 21350.

Kilworth, South, co. Leic. Grants, etc., in, early 12 cent. Add. 2177 (Kiuilingwrth), Harl. 52 G. 6 (Kiuilingwur5);—t. Hen. III.–t. Edw. Add. 21274-21277 (Kywelingwrthe Kiueling., etc.), 21279 (Kiudiwrthe), 21280 (Kyuelingwrth), 21337 (Suth Kiuiligwrth), Harl. 52 D. 44 (Suthkeuelingworth), 52 E. 34 (Suth Kyuelyugwrth), 35 (Suth Kiuill.), 52 H. 40 (Suth Kyuellingwrd), 53 A. 28 (Kyuelingwrthe Rogeri), 54 F. 40 (Sut Kyuelingwrd);—1311. Harl. 52 E. 36 (Sutk-uelingworth);—1333. Harl. 46 D. 16 (Suth Kyuelingworth), 54 C. 34 (do.);—1336. Harl. 45 H. 46 (do.);—1344. Harl. 50 E. 10 (Southe Keuelingworth);—1359. Harl. 50 I. 33 (do.);—1385. Harl. 52 A. 19 (S. Kylleworth);—1422. Harl. 50 E 18 (S. Kyllyngworth);—1522. Harl. 47 H. 33 (S. Kylworth).

——— Covenants for exchange on Wakefield, etc., in, with Sulby Abbey, 1229. Add. 21273 (Kyuillingwrth);— t. Hen. III. Add. 20600 (Suth Kiuilingwrth).

——— Grant of rents in, to St. Mary's altar in the church of, early Hen. III. (Kiueling.). Add. 21271.

——— Suit for tithes in (?), betw. the Rector and Sulby Abbey, 1236 (Kyuillingeworth). Add. 21289.

——— Grant, etc., in, to Sulby Abbey, to support St. Mary's chapel, t. Hen. III. Add. 21284 (Kyuillingwrth), 21342 (Suthkyuilli.gwrth).

——— Grants, etc., in, to Sulby Abbey, t. Hen. III.–t. Edw. I. Add. 21199 (Kyuillinewrht), 21272 (Kyuillingwrthe), 21282 (do.), 21287 (Kiuillingwrthe), 21288 (Australis Kyuillingwrthe), 21293, 21295-21302, 21306, 21309, 21323-21331, 21333-21336, 21338-21341, 21343-21346, 21695;— 1288. Add. 21347; — 1326. Add. 21332.

——— Covenant by Sulby Abbey to maintain the chapel of St. Mary in the cemetery of the church of, 1311. Add. 21348.

2 E

Harl. 43 H. 27;—1307. Harl. 43 H.
34;—1319. Harl. 43 G. 29;—1333.
Harl. 43 H. 39, 40;—1344. Harl. 43
H. 41;—1368 (Kiryngton). Harl. 43
H. 44;—1389. Harl. 43 G. 33;—
1424. Harl. 43 G. 35;—1485. Harl.
43 I. 7;—1500. Harl. 43 I. 8.

—— Conff. of grants of the church,
etc., to Newhouse Abbey, by Hen. II.,
[1156 or 7?]. Harl. 43 C. 18, 51 H. 1;
—[1175–9?]. Harl. 43 C. 24.

—— Grants, etc., in, to Newhouse
Abbey, c. 1157–63 (Chirningtun).
Cott. xxvii. 34;—t. Rich. I. Harl. 54
B. 9;—early 13 cent. Harl. 54 B. 18;
—t. Hen. III. Harl. 47 H. 22, 23, 52
G. 13, 54 B. 24;—t. Edw. I. Harl. 54
E. 16;—1303. Harl. 51 D. 37;—1455.
Harl. 55 E. 32.

—— Grant, etc., in, to Elsham
Priory, early 13 cent. Harl. 54 B. 8;
—t. Hen. III. Harl. 54 B. 30.

· —— Covenant of H. de Nevill and his
men of, conc. tithes in, to Newhouse
Abbey, early 13 cent. Harl. 44 I. 12.

—— Taxation of the vicarage, [1239–
65]. Harl. 45 A. 24.

—— Grants in, from Newhouse Abbey,
t. Edw. I. Harl. 44 H. 5, 9.

—— Grants, etc., in, 1360. Harl. 53
C. 19;—1433. Harl. 53 A. 4.

—— Mandate conc. tithes to Newhouse Abbey in, 1365 (Kyrington).
Harl. 45 A. 7.

—— License to Elsham Priory to
distrain in, 1387. Harl. 45 B. 22.

—— Decree conc. a pension from the
vicar of, to Newhouse Abbey, 1415.
Harl. 43 I. 5.

Kirstead, co. Norf. Persona. Radulfus, t. Hen. III. (Kirksstede). Add.
14558.

Kirtling, co. Camb. Grant in, 1319
(Kertlyng). Harl. 48 C. 47.

Kirtlington, co. Oxon. Conf. of grant
in, by H. de Oilli, late Hen. II. Add.
20739.

—— Release, etc., in, to Bicester
Priory, t. Hen. III. Add. 10609
(Kertlynton), 10613 (Kertlington).

Kirton, in Holland, co. Linc. Grants
of the manor, t. Edw. I. Harl. 52 E.
31 (Kirketon);—1345. Harl. 83 G.
54 (Kirketon in Hoyland).

—— Livery, etc., of Blossom Hall
(Bozonhalle, Bosomhall) manor in,
1380. Add. 8400;—1461. Add. 8403.

—— Recovery in, 1514 (Kyrton in
Holand). Eg. 479.

—— Precipe on a covenant conc. land
in, 1578. Add. 25080.

Kirton (Kyrketon, Kirketon), co. Nott.
Grants, etc., in, to Rufford Abbey,
late 12 cent. Harl. 83 G. 17;—early
13 cent.-t. Edw. I. Harl. 83 D. 25,
54, 83 E. 49, 83 G. 3, 4, 9, 10, 11, 16,
84 A. 11, 32, 52, 54, 112 F. 33, 112 I.
59;—1329. Harl. 83 C. 47.

—— Grants, etc., in, [1203–4]. Harl.
83 G. 18, 112 G. 53;—early 13 cent.-
t. Edw. I. Harl. 83 D. 18, 51, 52, 53,
83 F. 20, 83 G. 2, 7, 8, 15, 35, 84 B.
29, 112 H. 38, 112 I. 41;—1330. Harl.
112 H. 9;—1338. Cott. xxviii. 49;—
1341. Harl. 112 G. 41;—1346. Harl.
112 G. 62;—1371. Harl. 112 G. 63;
—1443. Add. 10207;—1448. Harl.
112 H. 6

Knelles. *v.* Cefn Llys, *co. Radnor.*

Knepp. *v. sub* Shipley, *co. Suss.*

Knightley, *in Gnosall, co. Staff.* Covenant conc. boundaries of the Park in, 1308-9 (Knyhtesle). Campb. i. 8.

Knighton, [*in Compton Beauchamp?*], *co. Berks.* Exchequer acquittance for rent in, 1575. Add. 25564.

Knighton, *in Beer Hackett, co. Dors.* Lease, etc., in, 1348.. Campb. vi. 8 (Knygth.);—1438. Campb. viii. 12 (Knyghton).

Knighton, *in Durweston, co. Dors.* Lease in, 1583. Add. 10416.

Knighton, *co. Radnor.* Lease of the demesnes, *c.* 1433 (Knyghton). Harl. 53 H. 17.

Knightsbridge, *co. Midd.* Customary of, bel. to Westminster Abbey, early Hen. III. (Cnichtebrugge). Add. 8139.

—— Grant at La Hoke in, 1338 (Knyghtebregg). Harl. 49 D. 38.

—— Bonds conc. moneys received for the Hospital in, 1573. Harl. 85 E. 49; —1577. Harl. 84 I. 23.

Knipsho *al.* Baynard's Manor. *v. sub* Mayland, *co. Essex.*

Kniveton. *v.* Kneeton, *co. Nott.*

Kniveton, *co. Derb.* Grant of custody of the manor, 1358 (Knyveton). Woll. vi. 34.

—— Grant, etc., in, 14 cent. (do.). Woll. vi. 44, 45 (*copies*).

Knockin, *co. Salop.* Brief conc. a fire at, 1757. Ch. Br. A. iv. 2.

Knoclas. *v.* Cnwclas, *co. Radnor.*

Knodishall (Knoteshall, etc.), *co. Suff.* Grants, etc., in, 1408. Harl. 54 I. 7; —1430. Harl. 43 E. 19 (Knodcshale), 54 I. 10;—1431. Harl. 50 H. 27, 28, 54 I. 15;—1435. Add. 2016;—1665. Add. 26386.

—— Precipe on a covenant conc. land in, 1593. Add. 25462.'

Knokk, *Den of. v. sub* Staplehurst, *co. Kent.*

Knole (Knolle), *nr. Sevenoaks, co. Kent.* Leases in, reserving the house and park, 1555. Harl. 75 E. 31;—1556. Harl. 75 H. 23;—1574. Harl. 77 H. 35.

Knoll. *v. sub* Farway, *co. Devon.*

—— *v.* Knowle, *co. Som.*

Knollbury, *co. Monm.* Inspex. in 1330 of grant in, to Usk Priory, *c.* 1150 (Elnulphbury). Add. 5342.

Kynesbiry. *v.* Kingsbury, co. *Warw.*

Kynewardestone. *v.* Kynaston, nr. *Much Marcle*, co. *Heref.*

Kynewarton. *v.* Kinwarton, co. *Warw.*

Kynges byrig. *v.* Kingsbury, co. *Midd.*

Kyngesbir., parochia de. *v.* Kingsbury, nr. *St. Alban's*, co. *Hertf.*

Kyngesbrigg. *v.* Kingsbridge, co. *Devon.*

Kyngesbyre. *v.* Bere Regis, co. *Dors.*

Kyngesdon. *v.* Kingsdon, co. *Som.*

Kyngesshey. *v.* Kingsey, co. *Buck.*

Kyngestarwyll. *v.* Kinkerswell, co. *Devon.*

Kyngeston. *v.* Kingston, cos. *Camb., Kent, Surr.*

Kyngestone juxta Modeford Terry. *v.* Kingston, *in Yeovil*, co. *Som.*

Kyngeswode. *v.* Kingswood, co. *Warw.*

Kynggeston. *v.* Kingston, co. *Suff.*

Kyngton Maundevile. *v.* Keinton Mandeville, co. *Som.*

Kyngysbrygge. *v.* Kingsbridge, co. *Devon.*

Kyngyshylle. *v.* Kingshill, *in Whitfield*, co. *Northt.*

Kynleuedene. *v.* Kelvedon, co. *Essex.*

Kynnestan. *v.* Kingston on Soar, co. *Nott.*

Kynnesthorp, Kynsthorp. *v.* Kingsthorpe, *in Polebrook hundred*, co. *Northt.*

Kyntun. *v.* Kington, nr. *Leintwardine*, co. *Heref.*

Kynwaldemers. *v.* Killamarsh, co. *Derb.*

Kynwarston. *v.* Kynaston, nr. *Much Marcle*, co. *Heref.*

Kynyhanos. *v.* Kynance, co. *Cornw.*

Kyrchebi. *v.* Kirkby Underwood, co. *Linc.*

Kyrdeford. *v.* Kirdford, co. *Suss.*

Kyrington. *v.* Kirmington, co. *Linc.*

Kyrk Wyllne. *v.* Wilne, co. *Derb.*

Kyrkeby. *v.* Kirby, co. *Northt.*

—— *v.* Kirkby in Ashfield, co. *Nott.*

Kyrkeby juxta Bolyngbrek. *v.* Kirkby, East, co. *Linc.*

Kyrkeby super Beyne. *v.* Kirby on Bain, co. *Linc.*

Kyrkehalum. *v.* Hallam, Kirk, co. *Derb.*

Kyrkelongele. *v.* Langley, Kirk, co. *Derb.*

Kyrkepatric. *v.* Kirkpatrick Fleming, co. *Dumfr.*

Kyrkested. *v.* Kirkstead, co. *Linc.*

Kyrketon. *v.* Kirton, co. *Nott.*

—— *v.* Kirton, co. *Suff.*

Kyrkyreton. *v.* Ireton, Kirk, co. *Derb.*

Kyrmyngton, Kyrnigton, etc. *v.* Kirmington, co. *Linc.*

Kytebroke. *v.* Kidbrooke, co. *Kent.*

Kyuelingwrth, Suth Kyuelyngwrth, Kyuelingwrthe Rogeri, Kywelingwrhe, etc. *v.* Kilworth, South, co. *Leic.*

Kyuelingwrth, Kyuelingwrth Rabaz, etc. *v.* Kilworth, North, co. *Leic.*

## L

La Lande. *v.* Launds, co. *Essex.*

La Leigh. *v.* Thurleigh, co. *Bedf.*

La Nante. *v.* Lelant, co. *Cornw.*

La Nye. *v.* Neigh, co. *Som.*

La Stock. *v.* Stoke Mandeville, co. *Buck.*

Labrunion. *v.* Lambrenny (?), co. *Cornw.*

Laceby, co. *Linc.* Grants, etc., in, to Newhouse Abbey, *ante* 1239. Harl. 45 H. 41 (Leyseby):—1239. Harl. 45 H. 43 (Laysby), 54 B. 39 (do.).

—— Grant in, *t.* Hen. III. (Leimeby). Harl. 54 B. 37.

—— *Persona.* Johannes, 1239. Harl. 45 H. 43 (Layseby), 54 B. 39.

—— *Rector. Dom.* Walt. Power, 1361. Cott. xxviii. 96.

—— *Dom.* Johannes, 1363. Harl. 52 G. 15, 16.

—— *Sacerdos.* Walterus, *t.* Hen. II. (Laifsebi). Harl. 46 B. 6.

Lacedune. *v.* Latchingdon Barns, *in* Purleigh, co. *Essex.*

Lambourn, Chipping, and Upper, *co. Berks.* Grant of reversion in, 1427 (Chepyngelamburn, Uplamburn). Harl. 49 C. 16.

Lambourn Hall. *v. sub* Canewdon, *co. Essex.*

Lambourne, *co. Essex.* Conf. of tithes in, to Holy Trinity Priory, Aldgate, 1206. Cott. xiii. 18(22) (*copy*).

—— Precipe on a covenant conc. land in, 1587 (Lamborne). Add. 24995.

Lambrenny (?), *nr. Davidstowe, co. Cornw.* Grant in, early Hen. III. (Labrunion). Harl. 53 B. 42.

Lamburnanden, *co. Kent.* Grant of swine pasture in, 858. Cott. MS. Aug. ii. 66.

Lambwood, *co. Berks.* Release, etc., in. 1409. Harl. 47 C. 4 (Lambewode); —1412. Harl. 49 F. 35 (do.).

Lamcote, *in Radcliffe, co. Nott.* Grant in, from Shelford Priory, *t.* Hen. III. (Lambecote). Campb. xi. 1.

—— Covenant to convey in, 1571. Woll. xi. 51.

Lamhytha. *v.* Lambeth, *co. Surr.*

Lammas, *co. Norf.* Rental, 1455-56 (Lammesse). Add. 13944.

—— Comm. of enquiry conc. the living, 1659 (Lamys). Add. 14975.

Lammeuthin. *v. sub* Llancarvan, *co. Glam.*

Lampeter, *co. Card.* Garrison establishment of the castle. 1369 (Lampedern). Harl. Roll E. 7.

Lamport, *in Stowe, co. Buck.* Grant in, to Oseney Abbey, early Hen. III. Harl. 52 I. 23.

—— Lease, etc., in, 1311. Harl. 85 C. 53 (Langeport);—1417. Harl. 85 C. 52 (do.);—1439. Harl. 86 A. 44.

—— Lease, etc., of a moiety of the manor, 1447. Lansd. 581 (Langport); —1480. Lansd. 581 *dors.* (do.).

—— Assessment for fifteenths, in 1537-1540, paid by, *t.* Mary. Harl. 86 G. 25, 27 (do.).

Lamport, *co. Northt.* Lease, etc., in, 1361. Add. 22185, 22186 (Langporthe);—1383. Add. 19916 (do.).

—— *Persona.* Ricardus, early Hen. III. Harl. 57 A. 53.

—— —— Will. Mosse, 1414. Add. 21822.

Lanantha. *v.* Lelant, *co. Cornw.*

Lanark, *co. Lanark.* Grant in, Melrose Abbey, [1189-98] (Lanrec)- Cott. xviii. 16.

Lancarffe Holton. *v. sub* Bodmin, *co. Cornw.*

Lancaster, *County of.* Fine rolls, 1377. Add. 26596.

—— Engagement of adherents to the Commonwealth in, 1650-1. Add. 7180.

—— Assignment of a lease of mines royal in, 1658. Harl. 111 H. 21.

—— *Vicecomes.* Dom. Hen. de L——, 1277. Add. 20521.

—— —— (*quondam*). Dom. Rad. de Monjoye al. Mountjoye, 1299. Woll. ix. 10;—1316. Woll. ix. 80.

—— *Sub-vicecomes* (*quondam*). Hugo de Acouere, 1299. Woll. ix. 10.

Lancaster, *co. Lanc.* Reservation of service "ad wardam Loncastrie," in Riby, co. Linc., *t.* John. Cott. xxvii. 132.

—— Award in suit for tithes in the parish of, betw. Sées and Cockersand Abbeys, 1216 (parochia de Lancastr.). Add. 20512.

—— Award in suit in the parish of, betw. Lancaster Priory and Cockersand Abbey, 1256. Add. 19618.

—— Reservation of service "ad wardam de Langeastre" (al. Lanchaster, Lancastre), in Ingham, co. Suff., *t.* Hen. III. Harl. 53 C. 36-42.

—— Settlement of suit conc. tithes from Beaumont Grange in St. Mary's parish, betw. Furness Abbey and Lancaster Priory, 1292-1306. Harl. 83 A. 31.

—— Grant in, *t.* Rich. II. Add. 20517.

—— Exchequer acquittance for rent in, 1623. Add. 25724.

—— *Major.* Joh. Elslak, *t.* Rich. II. Add. 20517.

Lancaster, *Honour of.* Conf. of, by Edw. I. to Edm., Earl of Lancaster, his brother, 1285. Cott. MS. Aug. ii. 135(5).

Lancaster, *Duchy of.* Lease by Royal feoffees of, of a mill in Ashbourne, co. Derb., 1439. Woll. vi. 30.

—— Covenant conc. land held of the fee of, in Holdenby, co. Northt., 1456. Add. 21527, 21528.

# INDEX LOCORUM.

Lanford, Lanforth. *v.* Langford, co. *Nott.*

Lang. *v.* Longney, co. *Glouc.*

Langandune, in. *v.* Longdon, co. *Worc.*

Langar, co. *Nott.* Bond for a fine of the manor, 1286. Harl. 43 G. 50.

—— Grant in, 1347. Harl. 45 C. 27.

Langdon, *nr.* Wembury. co *Devon.* Grant in, 1322 (Oueralangadone). Add. 13015.

Langdon, co. *Essex.* Conveyance of the manor, 1466. Harl. 57 C. 14.

Langdon, *nr.* Solihull, co. *Warw.* Grant in, *t.* John (Langedona). Cott. xxvi. 37.

—— Release of the manor, late Hen. III. (Langedon). Cott. xxvi. 33.

Langdon Hills, co. *Essex.* Precipe on a covenant conc. lands in, 1578. Add. 24960.

Langebarwe. *v.* Longborough, *nr. Knowsley,* co. *Lanc.*

Langedon, etc. *v.* Longdon, co. *Worc.*

Langedun. *v.* Longdon, co. *Staff.*

Langeford. *v.* Longford, co. *Derb.*

Langele. *v.* Langley, cos. *Kent, Norf. and Surr.*

Langeleg. *v.* Langley, cos. *Devon and Glouc.*

Langelya. *v. sub* Heanor, co. *Derb.*

Langeneia, co. —— (?). Grant of "tota terra de," to Oseney Abbey, late Hen. I. Add. 20120.

Langenham. *v. sub* Chard, co. *Som.*

Langenho, *nr. Gt.* Barford, co. *Bedf.* Grant in, 1323. Harl. 47 G. 55.

Langeport. *v.* Lamport, *in Stowe,* co. *Buck.*

Langepyn. *v. sub* Weldon, Gt., co. *Northt.*

Langethwayt. *v.* Langthwaite, co. *York.*

Langeton, etc. *v.* Langton, cos. *Linc. and York.*

Langetune. *v.* Launton, co. *Oxon.*

Langford, co. *Bedf.* Grants in, 1311. Add. 17655;—1334. Add. 17656.

Langford, co. *Berks.* Grant in, with conf., to Beaulieu Abbey, 1205, 1268. Harl. 58 I. 25 (*copy*).

Langford (Langeford), co. *Buc.* Exch. in, by Bileigh Abbey, 1291. Cott. xxi. 8.

—— Conveyance, etc., of the manor, 1383. Add. 8052;—1390. Harl. 45 I. 52.

Langford, co. *Norf.* Grant of free warren in, 1293. Add. 6337.

Langford, co. *Nott.* Defeas. of grant for prayers for Joh. Gras and Barbara his wife, late Lady of, 1470 (Lanford). Harl. 83 D. 17.

—— Release of the manor, 1471 (Lanforth). Woll. i. 77.

—— Precipe on a covenant conc. lands in, 1555 (Landford). Add. 25157.

Langford, co. *Oxon.* Precipe on covenant conc. Grafton manor in, 1590. Add. 25210.

Langford, Steeple, co. *Wilts.* Grant in Bathampton in, 1362. Add. 24873.

—— Recovery in, 1582. Add. 15132.

—— Precept for livery of the manor etc., 1626. Add. 15157.

—— *Presb.* Sir. Tho. Parys, ante 1459. Add. 18239.

—— *Rector.* Rad. de Codeford, 1362. Add. 24873.

Langhale, co. *Norf.* Release, etc., of the manor, 1310. Add. 14717;—1315. Add. 14718.

—— Sale, etc., in, 1626. Add. 14719;—1632. Add. 14720.

Langham. *v. sub* Chard, co. *Som.*

Langham, co. *Essex.* Conveyance, etc., of the manor and advowson, 1371. Harl. 43 G. 31;—1379. Harl. 54 C. 7;—1383. Harl. 54 C. 10;—1384. Harl. 54 C. 9;—1435. Add. 2016.

—— Fine of the manor, 1638. Woll. xi. 29.

Langham, co. *Norf.* Grant of, to Norwich Priory, [1103–6?]. Cott. MS. Aug. ii. 103, Cott. ii. 21 (1) (*copies*).

—— Extracts from court-rolls of Langham cum Merston Manor, 1596. Add. 19069 (4);—1631. Add. 19090.

Langham, co. *Suff.* Inquest on conveyance in, to Ixworth Priory, 1351. Harl. Roll H. 3.

—— Grants, etc., in, 1387. Harl. 58 G. 43 a (*copy*);—1422. Harl. 51 F. 1;—1460. Add. 18759;—1517. Harl. 57 G. 31;—1554. Harl. 56 G. 48;—1602. Harl. 48 I. 3;—1613. Harl. 45 E. 26, 57 H. 28;—1615. Harl. 45 E. 27.

Langton (Langeton), *nr. Horncastle and Woodhall, co. Linc.* (*continued*). Grants, etc., in, 1328. Harl. 58 C. 1; —1331. Harl. 58 B. 48, 51;—1332. Harl. 58 B. 49, 50;—1351. Cott. xxx. 30;—1365. Harl. 58 C. 2;—1370. Harl. 56 B. 49.

—— Exemplif., in 1431, of suit in, 1364. Harl. 51 H. 6.

—— *Clericus.* Henricus, late Hen. II. (Langet.). Harl. 48 C. 10.

—— *Persona.* Thomas, *t.* Hen. II. Cott. v. 74.

—— —— Ric. de Rowell, early 13 cent. Harl. 44 I. 12, 55 E. 42.

—— —— Alanus, 1370 (Langton juxta wodehall). Harl. 44 F. 8.

Langton (Langeton), *nr. Spilsby, co. Linc.* Grants, etc., in, to Greenfield Priory, *t.* Hen. III.–*t.* Edw. I. Harl. 47 C. 5, 52 I. 27, 28, 55 B. 8.

—— Fine in, 1302. Harl. 45 H. 18.

—— Feoffment, etc., of the manor, 1361. Harl. 58 A. 48;—1387. Harl. 53 C. 38.

—— Precipe on a covenant conc. land in, 1555 (Langton juxta Perteney). Add. 25059.

Langton (Langeton), *nr. Wragby, co. Linc.* Conff. of the church, etc., to Bullington Priory, *c.* 1150. Harl. 52 G. 25;—*t.* Hen. II. Harl. 52 G. 30; —[1175–81]. Harl. 43 C. 36;—1256. Harl. 52 H. 28;—*t.* Edw. I.–II. Harl. 52 H. 5;—*c.* 1322. Harl. 52 H. 27.

—— Grants, etc., in, to the same, early Hen. III. Harl. 52 G. 46, 47;— *t.* Hen. III. Harl. 52 I. 30;—1343: Harl. 52 E. 32.

—— Covenant of Bullington Priory conc. tithes in, 1293. Harl. 44 A. 53.

—— Grant of wardship in, 1311 (Suth-langeton). Harl. 53 A. 42.

—— Conf. of grant of tithes in, to Bullington Priory, to the use of the church of, 133–. Harl. 51 F. 39.

—— Certiff. of rights of the same, to St. Giles's church in, 1389. Harl. 43 G. 32;—1399. Harl. 43 I. 3;— 1485. Harl. 43 I. 13.

—— *Capellanus.* Walwanus, [1214– 23]. Harl. 45 A. 52.

—— *Sacerdos.* Willelmus, *ante* 1191. Harl. 50 B. 29, 52 G. 41, 83 C. 49.

—— *Perpet. Vicarius.* Joh. de Marham, 1375. Cott. xxvii. 204.

Langton, *nr. Malton, co. York.* Grant of goods and chattels in the same, 1395 (Langeton). Harl. 57 C. 24.

—— Excheq. acquittance for a tax in, 1595. Add. 25715 a.

Langton, *co. York* (?). *Rector.* Dn. Joh. de Sandale, 1372. Add. 17099, 17100, 17101;—1374. Add. 17098.

Langton, Church, *co. Leic.* Covenant conc. the manor and advowson, 139 (Langetone). Flo. xxxii. 2.

—— Settlement of dower in, 1391. Add. 17694.

—— Petition to the Queen for appointment of Hugh Palmer to the rectory, *t.* Mary. Harl. 86 B. 4.

—— *Rector.* Joh. de Belegrave, 1362. Add. 21362.

Langton, East, *co. Leic.* Settlement of the manor, etc., 1426. Add. 6417 (Estlangton);—1430. Add. 17694.

Langton Herring, *co. Dors.* Grant of tithes of, to Montacute Priory, *t.* Hen. I. (Langtona juxta Abbotesbury). Add. 24879 (3) (copy).

Langton Matravers, *co. Dors.* Feoffment of the manor and advowson, 1338 (Langeton). Harl. 58 D. 26.

Langton, Thorpe, *co. Leic.* Settlement in, 1585. Add. 4831.

Langton, Tur, *co. Leic.* Release of the manor, 1395 (Tirleton). Add. 17687.

Langton Wallis, *co. Dors.* Extracts from court-rolls, 1519–1526 (Langton Walyshe). Harl. 58 E. 47–50.

—— Power to take seisin of Willwood chapel in, 1534 (Langton Walyshe). Harl. 53 F. 44.

Langton, West, *co. Leic.* Release of the manor, 1361. Add. 17682;—1395. Add. 17687.

—— Settlement in, etc., 1430. Add. 17694;—1440. Add. 19860.

Langton's Manor. *v. sub* Burstall, *co. Suff.*

Langtun. *v.* Launton, *co. Oxon.*

Langtre. *v.* Longtree Hundred, *co. Glouc.*

Languard, *I. of Wight.* Grants in, *t.* Edw. III. Harl. 58 H. 37 *dors.* (Langerud);—1397. Harl. 55 A. 34 (Langred).

Languarde, Mons de. *v.* Llwyn y gaer, *co. Monm.*

by, co. *Cumb.* Lease of
1572. Harl. 77 H. 37.

, Nether, *in Cuckney*, co.
venant for conveyance in,
ther Langwith). Woll. xi.51.

Wood, co. *York.* Precept
very of, to York Chapter,
as of charters conc., 1286
Langwath). Harl. 53 H.

h. *v.* Llangonoyd, co. *Glam.*

h., co. *Linc.* List of deeds
ds of Kirkstead Abbey in,
ent. (Langwath). Harl. Roll

n, *in St. Eve,* co. *Cornw.*
a conc. settlement of the
488 (Lanhaddron). Add.

*v.* Lavenham, co. *Suff.*

, co. *Cornw.* Grant of the
Hen. VI. (Lamheron). Add.

terra de, *nr. Pevensey,* co.
change of, by Lewes Priory,
Harl. 44 F. 21.

co. *Cornw.* Grant in, 1528.

. *v.* Lantwit (?), co. *Glam.*

, *in Gulval,* co. *Cornw.* Ex-
art-roll, 1564. Add. 15369.

co. *Cornw.* Crown grant in,
yvet). Add. 7060.

n. *v.* Llancarvan, co. *Glam.*

ier, *nr. Caerau,* co. *Glam.*
, with the advowson, *t.* Hen.
. I. Add. 24292.

in. *v. sub* Llancarvan,

Byghan, *nr. Landewed-*
co. *Cornw.* Grant in, 1361.
49.

rne. *v. sub* Sheviock, co.

co. *Cornw.* Grant in, 1516.
78.

an. *v.* Llanstephan, co.

, *v.* Nantallan, co. *Cornw.*

, co. *Monm.* Inspex. of grant
ralley to Lanthony Prima
376. Campb. vii. 13.

thin. *v. sub* Llancarvan, co.

Lantrissen. *v.* Llantrisaint, co. *Monm.*

Lanturnia, co. ——. Hoedlew, presbiter, a witness to charter of Ystrad
Marcel Abbey, 1228. Add. 10637.

Lantwit, co. *Glam.* Grants, etc., in,
1539. Add. 26492-26494.

—— Exemplif. of a recovery of the
manor, 1606. Add. 26508.

—— *Ballivus.* Tho. Nicholl, 1539.
Add. 26493.

—— *Prepositus.* Joh Stevyn, 1539.
Add. 26493.

—— *Sacerdos* (?). Thomas, early 13
cent. (Laniltwit). Harl. 75 C. 9.

Lantwit vairdre, co. *Glam.* Fine in,
1699. Add. 19102, 19103.

Lantyan, *in St. Sampson's,* co. *Cornw.*
Appointment of J. Hurt as steward of
the manor, 1395. Cott. xxiv. 22

—— *Lord.* Loys de Clyfford, 1395.
Cott. xxiv. 22.

Lan y Coed, *in Dorstone,* co. *Heref.*
Grant of tithes from, to Clifford Priory,
[1309-24] (Lanercoyt). Campb. xvi.
16.

Laodonia. *v.* Lothian, *in Scotland.*

Lapal, *in Hales Owen,* cos. *Salop and
Worc.* Lease of Howley (Owley)
Grange manor in, by Hales Owen
Abbey, 1533. Add. 7391.

Lapley, co. *Staff.* Brief for rebuilding
the church and chapel, 1771. Ch. Br.
B. xi. 6.

—— Brief conc. a fire at Stinking
Lake in, 1814. Ch. Br. B. lv. 6.

—— Brief conc. a fire at Ivetsey Bank
in, 1815. Ch. Br. B. lv. 11.

Lapworth, co. *Warw.* Grants, etc., in,
late 12 cent. Harl. 86 E. 27 (Lappe-
wrthe); — 1374. Add. 14006; — 1379.
Add. 13322; — 1486. Add. 13320,
13321.

—— Grants, etc., in Bushwood nr.,
1349-1404. Add. 13316-13319.

—— Conf. of a grant of an annuity on
the manor, 1370. Add. 21476.

—— Precipe on a covenant conc. land
in, 1592. Add. 25555.

—— *Persona.* Nicholaus, *t.* Edw. I.
(Lappewrþe). Campb. xviii. 7.

Larkbear, co. *Devon.* Covenant for
recovery in, 1553. Add. 19190.

Larkstoke, co. *Glouc.* Grant of reversion of the manor, 1374. Add.
14006.

Larling, co. *Norf.* Conveyance in, 1374 (Lerlynge). Harl. 49 C. 15.

Larport. *v. sub* Murdiford, co. *Heref.*

Larracke. *v. sub* Lezant, co. *Cornw.*

Lascawyne. *v. sub* Sheviock, co. *Cornw.*

Lashbrook. *v. sub* Shiplake, co. *Oxon.*

Lassington, co. *Glouc.* Grant of part of the manor to the see of Gloucester, 1541. Cott. xiii. 34.

Lassyns, co. *Cornw.* Grant in, 1392. Harl. 50 C. 37.

Latchingdon, co. *Essex.* Bequest of land at, and at Lawling (Lelling) in, *post* 991 (æt lissingtune). Harl. 43 C. 4.

—— Release, etc., in Lawling (Lelling) in, [1254–5]. Harl. 49 G. 5.

—— Award in suit betw. the rector of, and the hamlet of Lawling (Lallyng), conc. a chaplain, 1367 (Lachyndon). Add. 15462.

—— *Rector.* Will. att Fen, 1367. Add. 15462.

Latchingdon Barns, *in Purleigh, co. Essex.* Conf. by Edw. the Confessor of a grant in, to Westminster Abbey, 1066 [*sc.* 1065] (Lacedune). Cott. vi. 2 (copy).

Latchley. *v. sub* Lindsell, co. *Essex.*

Latham, co. *York. Rector. Dom.* Will. Calveby, 1378. Harl. 56 D. 49.

Lathbury, co. *Buck.* Grants, etc., in, t. Hen. III. Add. 8122 (Latebur.);— 1313. Add. 8123;—1366. Add. 8124.

—— Grant of the manor, 1286 (Lathebur.). Harl. 56 E. 9.

—— Entail in, 1584–5. Harl. 79 D. 20.

Lathgrym. *v.* Leagram, co. *Lanc.*

Latton, co. *Wilts.* Crown grant of the manor, rectory, etc., late belonging to Cirencester Abbey, 1540. Add. 26022.

Lauan Ham. *v.* Lavenham, co. *Suf.*

Laudun. *v.* Loudoun, co. *Ayr.*

Laueham. *v.* Lavenham, co. *Suf.*

Laufar Alta. *v.* Laver, High, co. *Essex.*

Laugharne, co. *Carm. Vicarius de Tallagharn.* Reynold Goger, 1391. Add. 19145.

Laughton, co. *Leic.* Marriage settlement in, [1223] (Leicton). Harl. 55 E. 5.

Laughton, *in Aveland Wapentake, Linc.* License for Sempringham Priory, to acquire land in, 1229 (Westhoughtone). Add. 21100.

Laughton, co. *York.* Fine of the manor, 1688. Woll. xi. 22.

Laughton en le Morthen, co. *York.* Grants in Hooton and Osm, etc., in, 1329. Harl. 44 F. 22 (Laghton in Murthing);—1577. Harl. 57 A. 16 (do.).

—— Terrier of lands in Newhall in, c. 1600. Add. 18064.

—— Court-rolls, 1600–1. Add. 18616.

Launceston, co. *Cornw.* Grant re establishment of the castle, 1250 (Launceton). Harl. Roll E. 7.

—— Settlement in, 1514. Eg. 275.

—— Conveyance in Dunheved burgh in, 1518. Eg. 276.

—— Excheq. acquittance for a fine for Launceston Land manor, 1567. Add. 25575.

—— Fine in Doxmore (Doxmere), Downehevett Bourroughe, etc., in, 1573 (Lanceston). Eg. 292.

Launditch Hundred, co. *Norf.* Subsidy-rolls, 1593 (Lawndich). Add. 9410;—1603. Add. 9414.

Launds, co. *Essex.* Release in, 1532 (La Lande). Harl. 47 D. 32.

Launton, co. *Oxon.* Grant in, by Edw. the Confessor, to Westminster Abbey, 1066 [*sc.* 1065] (Langtun). Cott. vi. 2 (copy).

—— Customary of, bel. to Westminster Abbey, early Hen. III. (Langetune). Add. 8139.

Laurton. *v.* Laverton, co. *Som.*

Lausele. *v.* Lawshall, co. *Suf.*

Lauton. *v.* Lawton, co. *Salop.*

Lavant, East, co. *Suss.* Valor of lands in, late 14 cent. (Estlovent, Estlavent). Add. 8994.

—— Conveyance in, 1457 (Estlavent). Add. 8897.

Lavedwen, *nr. Bodmin, co. Cornw.* Grant of the mill, etc., 1487. Add. 15364.

Lavelyn Moor *al.* Ruthern Moor, *nr. Bodmin, co. Cornw.* Award in suit in, with Bodmin Priory, 1518. Harl. 44 A. 20.

Lavenden, co. *Buck.* Grant of free warren in, 1269. Add. 12632.

Lawford, Church, *co. Warw.* (*continued*). Precipe on a covenant conc. land in, 1591. Add. 25545.

Lawford, Little, *co. Warw.* Grant of services in, 1350 (Parva Lalleforde). Add. 20511.

Lawford, Long, *co. Warw.* Grants, etc., in, to Pipewell Abbey, *t.* Hen. II. Add. 21458 (Lalleford), 21468 (do.), 21469 (do.):—late 12 cent. Add. 21463 (Longa Lallefordia):—early 13 cent. Add. 5877 (do.), 7514 (Lelleford), 21459 (Longa Lalleford), 21466 (do.), 21467, 21470, 21471, 21475:—*t.* Hen. III. Add. 5876, 7541, 21457, 21472-21474, 21479;—late 13 cent. Add. 21478.

—— Grants, etc., in, late 12 cent. Add. 21456 (Longa Lalefort):—early 13 cent. Cott. xi. 31 (L. Lallefort), 21460 - 21462 (L. Lallefordia):—*t.* Hen. III. Add. 21464 (Lalleford), Cott. xxviii. 39;—1285. Add. 7542.

—— Release in, by Pipewell Abbey, *c.* 1209-31 (Lallefordia). Add. 21465.

—— Grant [nr. Thirne Mill on the Avon] in, to Pipewell Abbey, [1210-20?]. Add. 22387.

Lawharne. *v. sub* St. Neot, *co. Cornw.*

Lawling. *v. sub* Latchingdon, *co. Essex.*

Lawndich. *v.* Launditch Hundred, *co. Norf.*

Lawshall, *co. Suff.* Grants, etc., in, *t.* Hen. III.-*t.* Edw. I. Harl. 52 A. 28 (Lausele), 52 B. 17 (do.); — 1329. Add. 24655, 24656 (do.).

—— Precipe on a covenant conc. land in, 1578 (Lawsell). Add. 25361.

Lawton, *co. Heref.* Settlement in, 1585. Add. 7039.

Lawton, *in Diddlebury, co. Salop.* Grant in, 1311 (Lauton). Add. 5275.

Lawton, Church, *co. Chester.* Briefs for rebuilding the church, 1798, 1803. Ch. Br. B. xxxviii. 7, xliii. 3.

Lawylheghen. *v. sub* Payhembury, *co. Devon.*

Laxfield (Laxfeld), *co. Suff.* Grants, etc., in, 1297. Harl. 56 B. 14;—1354. Add. 9625;—1433. Add. 10456:—1542. Add. 5518;—1545. Add. 5519;—1591. Add. 7653.

—— Grant of Stodawe manor in, 1375. Harl. 49 D. 33.

Laxton, *co. Norfk.* Grants, etc., in, with patronage of All Saints' church, to Fineshead Priory, *t.* Rich. I.-John. Harl. 49 G. 51;—post 1242. Add. 22060;—*c.* 1300. Add. 23061.

—— Grants in, 1307. Add. 21561;—1377. Add. 21542.

—— Covenant conc. descent of the manor, 1372. Add. 19979.

—— Conveyance of the rectory, 1381. Harl. 46 D. 44.

—— *Capellanus.* Reginaldus, *t.* Ric. I.-John. Harl. 49 G. 51.

Laxton, *co. Nott.* Release in, to Rufford Abbey, late 13 cent. (Laxinton). Harl. 83 E. 50.

—— Conveyance of a close called Lampelande in, 1549. Campb. xi. 1.

—— *Clericus.* Radulfus, *t.* Hen. III. Harl. 83 G. 15.

—— —— Ricardus, *t.* Hen. III. Harl. 83 G. 16.

—— *Vicarius.* Ricardus, *t.* Hen. III. Harl. 83 G. 15, 16, 84 A. 32.

—— —— Hugh Pullen, 1549. Campb. xi. 2.

Laxton, *in Howden, co. York.* Grant in, 1519. Lansd. 456.

—— Brief for rebuilding the chapel, 1769. Ch. Br. B. ix. 2.

Laxwerp, *in Upwell* (?), *coa. Norf. and Camb.* Grant of fishery betw. Narhale and, to W. Dereham Abbey, early Hen. III. Toph. 17.

Laycock, *co. Wilts.* Covenant betw. Stanley Abbey and the rector of, conc. tithes of Eland in or nr., *c.* 1210 (Lacoq). Campb. xxii. 13.

—— Grants in, 1252. Add. 7065 (Lakoc);—1458. Add. 1586 (do.).

—— *Rector.* Rob. de Gloucestr, *c.* 1210. Campb. xxii. 13.

Layer Breton, *co. Essex.* Grant in, 1375 (Leyre Breton). Harl. 54 A. 42.

—— *Persona.* Rich. Houy, 1375. Harl. 54 A. 42.

Layer de la Hay, *co. Essex.* Grant in, 1375 (Leyre dil hay). Harl. 54 A. 42.

Layer Marny, *co. Essex.* Grant in the moor (La More) nr. Ralph's bridge (Pons Radulfi) in, *t.* Hen. III. (Legra Mareny). Cott. xxvii. 46.

—— *Persona.* Will. Keeche, 1407. Harl. 111 D. 43.

Lee, La, nr. Berkhampstead (?), co. Hertf. Lease in, 1297. Harl. 46 G. 2.

Lee, Priors, in Shiffnal, co. Salop. Inspex., in 1319, of a charter of Hen. II. in, to Wombridge Priory, 1181. Cott. iv. 36 (3).

—— Crown grant of lands in, late bel. to Wombridge Priory, 1545. Add. 26023.

Leeds (Ledes), co. Kent. Grant, etc., in, to Leeds Priory, t. Edw. I. Add. 8540–8542.

—— Grants, etc., in, 1383. Add. 8548; — 1433. Add. 8561; — 1458. Add. 8571; —1472. Add 8576, 8578; —1473. Add. 8579; —1478. Add. 8580; —1490. Add. 8591; — 1501. Add. 8594; —1519. Add. 8599; — 1551. Add. 8618; —1584. Add. 8629; —1639. Add. 1774.

—— co. York. Conff., etc., of the Church to Holy Trinity Priory, York, t. Hen. I. Add. 11292 (1-5) (Leddes) (copies); —1310. Add. 7677 (Ledes), 20568 (do.).

—— Conf. by Hen. II. of a grant in, from Marmoutier Abbey, [1181-9] (Liedes). Campb. xxix. 1.

—— Acquittance for an annuity in, 1498 (Ledes). Harl. 48 G. 48.

—— Covenant for conveyance in, 1498 (Ledes). Add. 26789.

—— Sale by the Crown of the advowson, 1587. Harl. 75 H. 2.

—— Fine of the manor, 1638. Woll. xi. 29.

Leegh. v. Leigh, co. Staff.

Leek, co. Staff. Grant of the rectory, 1567. Add. 7061.

—— Vicarius. Nic. Seynpere, 1361. Add. 26917.

Leese, Terra de la, co. Kent. Grant of, t. Hen. III. Add. 16441 (copy).

Leet, E., W., N. and S. v. sub Lothingland Hundred, co. Suff.

Lefstanchirche, Lefstonchirche. v. Layston, co. Hertf.

Lefstanston. v. Leiston (?), co. Suff. (?).

Leftwich, co. Chest. Settlement of the manor, 1325. Add. 6278.

—— Rental, 1391. Add. 5230.

Leg Marsh, [nr. Broomhill ?], co. Kent. Grant in, to Robertsbridge Abbey, early 13 cent. Campb. xxv. 18.

Lega. v. Leigh, South (?), co. Oxon.

Legbourne, co. Linc. Grants, etc., in, 1334. Harl. 56 F. 37 (Lekeburn); —1335. Harl. 54 G. 21 (do.); — 1355. Harl. 57 G. 11 (Legeburne).

—— Persona. Dom. Rad. Hed, 1381. Harl. 57 G. 14.

—— Sacerdos. Ranulfus, ante 1175 (Leccheburn). Harl. 51 B. 4, 5.

Legh. v. Leigh, co. Chest.

—— v. Leigh, co. Som.

—— v. Leigh [Powlet?] Manor, co. Devon.

Legh, East. v. sub Lyminge, co. Kent.

Legh, La. v. Leigh, co. Kent.

—— v. Leigh, co. Surr.

Legha. v. Lea, co. Heref. (?)

Leghe. v. sub Iden, co. Suss.

—— v. Leigh, cos. Kent, Staff.

Leghe juxta Durhurste. v. Leigh, co. Glouc.

Leghes Magna. v. Leighs, Gt., co. Essex.

Legra Mareny. v. Layer Marny, co. Essex.

Leia. v. Leigh, co. Glouc.

Leicester, County of. Rolls of knights' fees, etc., of the Basset family in 12–15 cent. Slo. xxxi. 3–7.

—— Feodary of Tutbury honour in, t. Edw. III. (?). Woll. xi. 1 (copy).

—— Return of payments by tenants of knights' fees in, 1445. Harl. Roll I. 10.

—— Settlement of lands inherited from Sir R. Harcourt in, 1507. Harl. 111 F. 55.

—— Compotus of dues to the Crown from tenants in, 1543. Add. 15891.

—— Grant by the Earl of Leicester of the stewardship of his manors in, 1566. Harl. 83 E. 26.

—— Exemplif. of grant of forfeited lands of J. Litleton in, 1610. Harl. 83 H. 28.

—— Exchequer acquittance to the receiver general of, 1613. Add. 25728.

—— Exchequer acquittance to the sheriff of, 1673. Add. 25734.

—— Vicecomes. Will. Basset, [1168-70]. Harl. 84 D. 13, 84 H. 20, 86 E. 33.

—— —— Philip. de Accles, [1240-6]. Add. 21694.

—— —— Dom. Osbert. de Bereford, 1285. Add. 7542, Eg. 457.

Leinster, *in Ireland.* "*Senescallus*" *of the Earl of Pembroke in.* Dom. David Basset, [1241–45]. Harl. 83 B. 38.

Leinthall Starkes, *co. Heref.* Release of service in, "de brevibus portandis et nuntiis faciendis," late Hen. III. (Leinth. Sterk.) Cott. xxvii. 159.

—— Release, etc., in, late 13 cent. Cott. xxv. 17 (Leinthale Starkare); —1419. Cott. xxiii. 7 (Leynthale Starker).

—— Compotus of the manor, 1390–91 (Lenthall Starkere). Add. 24883.

—— Sale of the manor, etc., 1566. Harl. 79 G. 21.

Leintwardine, *co. Heref.* Grants in, *t.* Hen. III. Harl. 111 D. 42 (Lentword.); — 1330. Harl. 111 F. 22 (Leyntwardyn).

—— Foundation of a chantry in the church, 1375 (Lentwardyn). Campb. xviii. 5.

—— Extract from Halimote-roll of, for land in Whitton in, 1556. Cott. xxvi. 24.

Leircestria. *v.* Leicester, *co. Leic.*

Leire, *co. Leic.* Conf. of a grant in, to Biddlesdon Abbey, *co.* Buck., *ante* 1166. Harl. 84 D. 1.

—— Brief for rebuilding the church, 1772. Ch. Br. B. xii. 8.

Leisnes. *v. sub* Erith, *co. Kent.*

Leisseby. *v.* Laceby, *co. Linc.*

Leiston, *co. Suff.* Grant of Batesford land in (?), *t.* Hen. III. (Lefstanston). Add. 9826.

—— Grant of market, etc., in, 1312 (Leyston). Harl. 58 I. 50.

—— Bond for rent in, 1377 (do.). Add. 7563.

—— Precipes on covenants conc. lands in, 1555. Add. 25280;—1561. Add. 25290.

Leith, *co. Edinb.* Remission of rent for lands in, 1556 (Leyt.). Campb. xxx. 21.

Leišenhala Wood. *v. sub* Pakenham, *co. Suff.*

Leke. *v.* Leake, *co. Nott.*

Lekhamsted. *v.* Leckhampstead, *co. Berks.*

Lelant, *co. Cornw.* Grant of market and fair in the manor, with free warren in Trevethow (Trewython), etc., in, 1296 (La Nunte). Harl. 58 I. 40 (copy).

Lelant, *co. Cornw.* (*continued*). Grants, etc., in, 1331. Add. 13013 (Lananth); —1349. Add. 13026 (Lananta).

—— Lease, etc., of a pourparty of Trevethow in, 1606, 1636 (Uny Lelantt). Add. 15374.

Leles., Lelesey. *v.* Lindsey, *co. Suff.*

Lelleford. *v.* Lawford, Long, *co. Warw.*

Lelling [Lawling?, *co. Essex*?]. *v. sub* Latchingdon, *co. Essex.*

Lembaldes. *v. sub* Westleton, *co. Suff.*

Lementon. *v.* Leamington Hastings, *co. Warw.*

Lenborough, *nr. Buckingham, co. Buck.* Grant of manumission in, 1412 (Lemburgh). Harl. 84 H. 29.

Lenchestoche de feudo de Portesie [Portsea, *co. Southt.*]. Grant in, to Quarr Abbey, late Hen. II. Add. 15687.

Lenchwick, *co. Worc.* Conveyance of the manor, 1646. Add. 1799.

Lengeby. *v.* Slingsby, *co. York.*

Lenham, *co. Kent.* Grant of land subject to, 858 (Leanaham). Cott. MS. Aug. ii. 66.

—— Grants, etc., in, 1405. Harl. 51 E. 23;—1585. Harl. 55 A. 15;—1661. Add. 5984.

—— Bond conc. an annuity from Runham (Ronham) manor in, 1567. Harl. 55 A. 16.

Lenn. *v.* Lynn, *co. Norf.*

Lennerton, *in Sherburn, co. York.* Power to give seisin in, 1368 (Lenarton). Add. 26770.

Lente. *v.* Lynt, *co. Wilts.*

Lenton, *co. Nott.* Leases, etc., in, 1291. Lansd. 594;—1413. Harl. 55 F. 26; —1515. Harl. 58 B. 27.

Lentword. *v.* Leintwardine, *co. Heref.*

Leofshema, Leofsnhsema. *v.* Lewisham, *co. Kent.*

Leom. *v.* Leam, *nr. Eyam, co. Derb.*

Leominster, *co. Heref.* Conf. of liberties in, to Reading Abbey, *c.* 1125 (Leoministria). Add. 19575.

—— Release of "villula de Bradeford" in (?), to the Earl of Hereford, [1150–4]. Add. 19588.

—— Conf. of, with its churches, to Reading Abbey, 1157 (Lhministria). Add. 19591.

Lincoln, *co. Linc. (continued).* Release in same to Bullington Priory, *t.* John. Harl. 55 B. 14.

—— Grant in Newport (Neuport) in, by Kirkstead Abbey, *t.* John. Harl. 55 G. 28.

—— Lease in Newland (nova terra) in, by Newhouse Abbey, *t.* Hen. III. Harl. 44 A. 41.

—— Release in, nr. the Friars Preachers in Silvergate, to Bullington Priory, *t.* Hen. III. Harl. 47 D. 47.

—— Grants, etc., in, *t.* Hen. III. Harl. 48 I. 29;—1311. Harl. 53 A. 42;—1382. Lansd. 646.

—— Grant in Northgate (Northegat. in suburbio Linc.) in, late Hen. III. Harl. 49 I. 51.

—— Conveyance, etc., of same lands in Northgate to Bullington Priory, *c.* 1270. Harl. 52 B. 25;—1332. Harl. 47 H. 40.

—— Grant in Pottergate in, to Bullington Priory, late 13 cent. Harl. 47 G. 30.

—— Grant, etc., in Walkergate in, to Newhouse Abbey, 1311, *c.* 1311. Harl. 47 H. 30, 32, 49 D. 31.

—— *Aldermannus.* Adam, late 12 cent. Harl. 55 G. 16.

—— *Major.* Adam, early 13 cent. Harl. 47 C. 9.

—— Petr. de Ponte, *t.* Hen. III. Harl. 47 H. 39.

—— Will. de Holgate, late Hen. III. Harl. 43 A. 67 a.

—— Tho. Beufou, late Hen. III. Harl. 49 I. 51.

—— Roger fil Benedicti, *c.* 1270. Harl. 52 B. 25;—1275. Add. 21162.

—— Jac. de Ponte, early Edw. I. Add. 19990;—1277. Harl. 49 C. 41, 42.

—— Steph. de Stanham, 1304. Add. 5951.

—— Joh. de Bliton, *c.* 1311. Harl. 49 D. 31;—*t.* Edw. II. Harl. 47 H. 40.

—— Steph. de Stonham, 1313. Harl. 51 F. 23.

—— Ric. Blakenden, 1321. Harl. 44 B. 8.

—— Ric. de Kele, 1332. Cott. xii. 26.

—— —— Rog. de Tatcshale, 1360. Harl. 53 A. 29.

Lincoln, *co. Linc. (continued).* Joh. de Thorley, 1398. Eg. 467.

—— —— Joh. de Balderton, 1400. Eg. 471.

—— —— Will. Kent, 1562. R. 484.

—— *Ballivi al. Propositi.* Ask Cause. Andr. de Horknstowe, late Hen. III. Harl. 43 A. 67 a.

—— —— Hen. Gupyl, Greg. le Bulur, late Hen. III. Harl. 49 I. 51.

—— —— Petr. de Thoresby. Alan. fil. Roberti, *c.* 1270. Harl. 52 B. 25.

—— —— Alan. Biwestenstel, 1275. Add. 21162.

—— —— Joh. Scarlet, Rob. de Lenna, early Edw. I. Add. 19994.

—— —— Rad. de Wylingham, Nich. le Graunger, 1297. Harl. 44 B. 7.

—— —— Joh. le Blake, Gilb. de Leic[estria], *c.* 1311. Harl. 49 D. 31.

—— —— Hen. le Clerk, David le Taverner, 1313. Harl. 51 F. 23.

—— —— Joh. de Leycestria, Hugo de Edlington, *t.* Edw. II. Harl. 47 H. 40.

—— —— Hen. Stoille, Ad. de Misen, 1321. Harl. 44 B. 8.

—— —— Will. Bayonne, Rog. de Furnaye, 1360. Harl. 53 A. 29.

—— —— Joh. de Howghtwn, Nic. de Hodeleston, Ric. de Staynfeld, 1398. Eg. 467.

—— —— Hen. de Dyke, Will. de Ile, Tho. Russell, 1400. Eg. 471.

—— *Coronatores.* Jac. ad Pontem, Tho. fil. Roberti, Jordanus, clericus, *c.* 1270. Harl. 52 B. 25.

—— *Sacerdos de Nicol.* Willelmus, *t.* Hen. II. Harl. 55 D. 13.

—— PARISHES:—

—— PAR. OF ALL SAINTS. Grant in, *t.* Edw. I. (paroch. O. SS. in Ballio Lincoln.). Cott. xxiv. 23.

—— PAR. OF ALL SAINTS, HUNGATE. Release in, 1360 (O. SS. in Hundgate). Harl. 53 A. 29.

—— PAR. OF H. TRINITY IN BUTTESWICK. Release in, to Bullington Priory, *t.* Hen. III. (S. Trin. in Butewerk). Harl. 48 G. 7.

—— PAR. OF H. TRINITY IN WIGFORD. Consent to a grant in, to Bullington Priory, late 12 cent. (S. Trin. in Wikeford). Harl. 55 G. 16, 58 G. 58 b (copy).

1385 (Lyston). Harl. 56 A. 35.

—— *Rector.* Roger Prynce, 1421. Harl. 48 D. 15.

**Lisvane,** *co. Glam.* Fine in, 1738. Add. 19106, 19107.

**Litcham,** *co. Norf.* Fine of the manor, 1547 (Lycheham *al.* Luyobeham). Add. 14726.

**Litchborough,** *co. Northt.* Precipe on a covenant conc. land in, 1593 (Lichbarowe). Add. 25185.

—— Release of third turn of the advowson, 1698. Add. 6128.

**Litchurch,** *in Derby, co. Derb.* Leases, etc., in, 1353. Woll. x. 35 (Luitchirch):—1524. Woll. iv. 60 (Lutchurche):—1537. Woll. iv. 61 (do.).

—— Freeholders owing suit at the court of, early 16 cent. (do.). Woll. xi. 11.

**Litlehey, Boscus de,** *in Eaton Socon* (?), *co. Bedf.* Conf. by King John of a grant of, 1208. Add. 6014.

**Litlemere,** *in Gamlingay, co. Camb.* Grants, etc., in, to Sawtrey Abbey, *t.* Hen. II. Harl. 83 A. 51, 52, 83 B. 41.

**Litlepeada,** *in Gamlingay, co. Camb.* Grants, etc., in, to Sawtrey Abbey, *t.* Hen. II. Harl. 83 A. 51, 52, 83 B. 41.

**Litlewetekere.** *v. sub* Waltham, *co. Kent.*

**Litons.** *v. sub* Melford, Long, *co. Suff.*

**Littelhay.** *v. sub* Keele, *co. Staff.*

**Littilcot.** *v.* Littlecote, *co. Buck.*

1310, 1311. Harl. 79 E. 32, 33.

—— Grant in Wingate in, *t.* Edw. II. Harl. 79 B. 19.

—— Grants, etc., in, 1310–11. Harl. 80 I. 12 ;—1322. Harl. 78 A. 7 ;—1345. Harl. 51 G. 51 ;—1362. Harl. 78 B. 30, 80 C. 11 ;—1455. Harl. 76 E. 46.

—— Grants in Wolton in, 1320. Add. 9224 ;—1325. Add. 13999.

—— Release of Lokedale manor in (?), 1345. Harl. 51 G. 51.

—— License for alienation, fine, etc., of Wingate *al.* Lower Garwinton manor, etc., in, 1548. Harl. 75 E. 22, 75 H. 4, 76 H. 50 :—1551. Harl. 75 E. 23 ;—1555. Harl. 77 H. 22 ;—1577. Harl. 77 A. 47 ;—1578. Harl. 77 A. 48 ;—1580. Harl. 77 B. 4 ;—1584. Harl. 75 H. 18 ;—1600. Harl. 77 B. 38.

—— *Ballivus.* Rob. de Lukedale, 1264. Harl 76 G. 35.

**Littlebrook,** *nr. Dartford, co. Kent.* Title of land at, *ante* 988 (Lytel broc). Cott. viii. 20.

—— Grants, etc., in, *t.* Hen. III.-*t.* Edw. I. Harl. 48 C. 13 (Litelbroc), 53 A. 37, 56 H. 29 (Litlebrok).

—— Demise of goods in the manor of, 1275 (Litelbrok). Harl. 46 F. 45.

—— Grant of the manor, 1379 (Litlebroke). Slo. xxxii. 45.

—— Defeasance of bond conc. drainage in, 1445. Slo. xxxii. 43.

—— Fine of the manor, etc., 1465 (Litelbroke). Slo. xxxii. 41.

Littlebury, co. *Essex*. Lease of the manor, etc., 1295 (Lettlebery juxta Aungre). Harl. 54 A. 7.

—— Precipe on a covenant conc. lands in, 1575. Add. 24947.

—— *Rector*. Will. de Feriby, 1384 (Lytelbury). Land. 557.

Littlecherth. *v*. Chart, Little, co. *Kent*.

Littlecomb. *v*. *sub* Branscombe. co. *Devon*.

Littlecote, co. *Buck*. A rent to be paid in Thornborough, by Biddlesden Abbey, to support St. Giles's chapel in, late 13 cent. (Lyttilkot, Littilcot, Litlekote). Harl. 85 C. 39–41.

Littlefield Hundred, co. *Kent*. Leases of, etc., 1555. Harl. 75 E. 31;—1556. Harl. 75 H. 23 (Lytlefeld);—1574. Harl. 77 H. 35.

—— Acquittance for crown rents of, 1611. Harl. 75 D. 63.

Littleham, co. *Devon*. Conf. of grant in, [1246–59]. Add. 13969.

Littleton, co. *Midd*. Rental in, 1445–1448 (Lytlyngton). Harl. Roll A. 14.

Littleton, *in* Compton Dando, co. *Som*. Grant in, 1330 (Litleton juxta Somerton). Add. 5449.

Littleton, *nr*. Semington, co. *Wilts*. Bishop's award conc. services for, 1470 (Litilton). Add. 5691.

Littleton, High (?), co. *Som*. Value of the manor, 1433–4 (Lytelton). Harl. Roll L. 35.

Littleton, Stony, *in* Wellow, co. *Som*. Precipe for possession of the manor, 1605. Add. 5482.

Littlington, co. *Camb*. Grants, etc., in, *t*. Edw. I. Add. 25933 (Letlingeton):—1311–1324. Add. 25934-25938 (Litlyngton);—1376 - 1457. Add. 25940-25956;—1599. Add. 25958.

—— Feoffment of the manor, 1368 (Littelyngtone). Add. 22586.

—— *Vicarius*. Rob. Brygge, 1410. Add. 25950, 25952.

Litton, *in* Tideswell, co. *Derb*. Grants, etc., in, early Edw. I. Add. 26419;—1347. Add. 7824;—1375. Add. 7842.

—— License and grants in, for a chantry at Tideswell, 1383. Woll. iii. 15, xi. 27;—1392. Woll. xi. 26.

—— Lease of the manor, 1640. Woll. xi. 80.

Litton Cheney, co. *Dors*. Appointment of a supervisor of the manor, 1384 (Litton). Harl. 54 I. 5.

Liveden, *nr*. Benefield, co. *Northt*. Power to give seisin in, 1344 (Potteraslyvedene). Add. 20262.

—— Acquittance to the Crown on account of a payment demanded for the manor, 1392 (Lyveden). Harl. 49 D. 54.

Livermere, Great, co. *Suff*. Conf. of a grant in, with the advowson, end of 12 cent. (Liuremere). Add. 7209.

—— Court-rolls, 1275, 1309 (Lyueremer, Lyweremere). Add. 9096, 9097.

—— Record of presentation of N. de Thelnetham to the living in 1361, 1409 (Lyuermere). Harl. Roll O. 7 (*copy*).

—— Demise of Broome Hall manor, with the advowson, etc., 1394. Harl. 45 D. 27.

—— Recoveries, etc., in, 1396. Add. 18684:—1402. Add. 9117;—1447. Add. 9126;—1460. Add. 9130.

—— *Rector*. Walt. Coket, 1447, 1460. Add. 9126, 9130.

—— Ric. Florance, 1568. Harl. 46 F. 12.

Livermere, Little, co. *Suff*. Grants, etc., in, *t*. Hen. III. Harl. 57 F. 19 (Lyuermere Parva);—1310. Add. 18602;—1367. Add. 18659;—1394. Harl. 45 D. 27;—1402. Add. 9117.

Liverpool, co. *Lanc*. The bailiff of Burscough Priory at, to pay a toll for Ormskirk market, to Edm., Earl of Lancaster, 1286 (Liurepool). Add. 20518.

—— Grant for a chaplain for the chapel of the Virgin and St. Nicholas the Bishop in, 1529 (Lyverpole). Harl. 58 E. 28.

—— Brief conc. a fire in Dale Street, 1793. Ch. Br. B. xxxiii. 2.

Liversedge, co. *York*. Grant in, 1405 (Lyversege). Add. 8319.

Lisard, co. *Cornw*. Grant in, *t*. Edw. IV. (Lysard). Add. 15302.

Llai, *nr*. Gresford, co. *Denb*. Grant in, 1495 (Llay). Add. 8646.

[Llanafan, co. *Card*.?]. Bond in, 1548. Eg. 286.

Llanarth, co. *Monm*. Precipes on covenants conc. lands in, 1592. Add. 25116;—1593. Add. 25128.

—— *Rector. Dom.* Philip William, 1528 (Llangeby). Add. 1818.

—— —— (?) Tho. Forster, 1535 (Langvby in Gwentloude). Harl. 50 D. 25.

**Llangonoyd,** *co. Glam.* Suit conc. tithes of, betw. Margam Abbey and the Bp. of Llandaff, 1413 (Langwneth). Harl. 75 A. 3.

—— *Capellanus.* Gronu, *c.* 1234. Harl. 75 B. 39, 75 C. 52 (Langonet).

—— *Clerici.* Mauricius et Resns, frater ejus, *c.* 1234. Harl. 75 B. 39, 75 C. 52.

—— —— Resus, 1246. Harl. 75 C. 25.

**Llangoven,** *co. Monm.* Release in, 1508. Add. 7150.

**Llangunnoch,** *nr. Llangarran, co. Heref.* Fine in, 1599 (Llangonnooke). Add. 1875.

**Llangwnadle,** *co. Carnarv.* Recovery in, 1699. Add. 25812.

**Llangynog,** *co. Montgom.* Brief for rebuilding the church, 1785. Ch. Br. B. xxv. 4.

**Llanhamlach,** *co. Brecon.* Lease in, 1429. Harl. 111 B. 32, 33.

**Llanhyngate** *al.* Llan Yngatt [Dingestow ?], *co. Monm.* Grant, etc., in, in the domain of Trelleck, 1507. Add. 7149 ;—1524. Add. 7153.

**Llansantffraid,** *co. Monm.* Precipe on a covenant conc. land in, 1562. Add. 25116.

**Llansantfraid Glyn Ceiriog,** *co. Denb.* Brief for rebuilding the church, 1776. Ch. Br. B. xvi. 5.

**Llansantfread,** *co. Brecon.* Lease, etc., in, 1536. Harl. 111 B. 28 ;—1542. Harl. 111 B. 26.

**Llanstephan,** *co. Carm.* Grants in (?), 1309. Add. 19143 ;—1312. Add. 19144.

—— Garrison establishment of the castle, 1369 (Llanstephan). Harl. Roll E. 7.

—— Grant in the Barony of, etc., 1391. Add. 19145 (Baronia de Landestephan) ;—1402. Add. 18204.

—— Grant of reversion of the castle, etc., 1443 (Lanstephan). Harl. 51 H. 10.

**Llantharog.** *v.* Llanddarog, *co. Carm.*

**Llanthetty,** *co. Brecon.* Release in, 1543. Harl. 112 F. 25.

**Llanthewy,** *co. Monm.* Grants, etc., in, 1524. Add. 1817 ;—1528. Add. 1818 ;—1532. Add. 1345.

**Llanthewy Skirrid,** *co. Monm.* Fine of the manor, etc., 1717. Eg. 334.

**Llanthomas,** *nr. Dingestow, co. Monm.* Bond to abide award in (?), 1567. Add. 7159.

Lookington, co. *Leic.* Grants, etc.,
in, *t.* Edw. I.-*t.* Edw. II. Woll. v. 12,
13 (Lokinton);—1328. Woll. v. 10
(Lokynton);—1356. Woll. v. 9 (do.).

Lookington, co. *York.* Grants, etc.,
in, *t.* Hen. III. Add. 5727 (Lokinton);
—1521. Add. 5786-5791 ;—1524. Add.
5794-5796 ;—1535. Add. 26790.

Looko, Nether, co. *Derb.* Covenant
to convey in, 1521 (Netherlokhaw).
Woll. xii. 117, 118.

—— Covenant to convey the manor,
1553. Woll. xii. 119, 135.

Lockton, co. *York.* Power to give seisin
in, 1463 (Lokton). Harl. 48 H. 45.

Loddon, co. *Norf.* Grants, etc., in, *t.*
Edw. I.-*t.* Edw. II. Add. 14727
(Lodn.), 16533 *a, b,* Harl. 58 G. 8
(do.);—1302. Harl. 45 F. 33 (do.) :—
1359. Cott. xii. 1 (Lodene);—1450.
Add. 17238 (Lodne);—1623. Add.
14568.

—— Fines in, 1302. Harl. 45 G. 56
(Lodne) ;—1579. Add. 14728.

—— Grant of the manor, 1451. Add.
7386.

—— Extract from court-roll of Loddon Stubbys manor, 1522. Add.
14916.

—— Extract from court-roll of Loddon Inglose manor, 1638. Add. 2010.

Loddon Hundred, co. *Norf.* Release
in, 1361 (Lodene). Harl. 52 B. 11.

Loddon Bridge, Lodenebrugg. *v.
sub* Hurst, co. *Berks.*

Lodesdone. *v.* Luddesdown, co. *Kent.*

Lodham. *v.* Ludham, co. *Norf.*

Loes Hundred, co. *Suff.* Assignment
of, in dower, 1477. Add. 26598.

Lofherst. *v. sub* Staplehurst, co. *Kent.*

Lofthall. *v. sub* Orset, co. *Essex.*

Lofthouse, *in Harewood,* co. *York.*
Release, etc., in, 1297. Harl. 112 F.
9 (Lofthuse) ;—1314. Harl. 112 D.
52 (do.).

Lofthouse, *nr. Wakefield,* co. *York.*
Crown lease in, 1555. Harl. 84 C. 32.

Logan, co. *Dumfries.* Conf. of grant
of the chapel to Gisburne Priory, *t.*
Edw. I. Cott. xi. 58, Harl. 43 B. 12.

Loggeston. *v.* Luggeston, *nr. Up Ottery,*
co. *Devon.*

Logie, co. *Perth.* Conf. of grant of the
church to Mag. Will. Blesensis, end of
12 cent. (Login). Harl. 84 C. 1.

Logmaban. *v.* Lochmaben, co. *Dumfries.*

Lois Wedon. *v.* Weedon Pynkney,
co. *Northt.*

Loke ultra Kentishestreta. *v. sub*
Lambeth, co. *Surr.*

Lokedale. *v. sub* Littlebourne, co. *Kent.*

Lokeal. *v.* Loxley, co. *Warw.*

Loketon. *v.* Lufton, co. *Som.*

Lokinton, Lokynton. *v.* Lockington,
co. *Leic.*

—— *v.* Lockington, co. *York.*

Lokyngton. *v.* Luckington, co. *Wilts.*

Lolworth, co. *Camb.* Conveyance in,
1436 (Lolleworth). Add. 13547.

—— *Rector. Dom.* Joh. Statherne,
1387. Slo. xxxii. 54.

Lombard's *al.* Lumbarde Park, *nr.
Cork,* co. *Cork.* Bond on a mortgage
of, etc., 1564. Add. 8697 ;—1585. Add.
8698-8700.

—— Conf. and releases of, 1566. Add.
8716, 8718, 8719.

Londenestrate, *in Gamlingay,* co.
*Camb.* Ref. to, as a boundary, *t.* Hen.
II. Harl. 83 A. 51.

LONDON, *City of, with near suburbs
and Westminster.* Annals, with succession of mayors and sheriffs, to 1463.
Harl. Roll C. 8.

—— Names of mayors and sheriffs,
1250-1276. Add. 5153.

—— Grant of "unius navis vectigal"
in the port of, 734 (Lundonia), with
conf., *c.* 845-850. Cott. xvii. 1.

—— Mercian Council at, 811. Cott.
MS. Aug. ii. 10.

—— Bequest of a messuage in, to St.
Peter's church, [Cornhill ?], 1038 (?)
(Lunden). Cott. MS. Aug. ii. 85.

—— Conf. by Will. I. of grants in, by
citizens of, to Westminster Abbey,
1067 (Lundonia). Cott. vi. 3 (copy).

—— Conf. of privileges to the Abbey,
by Will. I., addressed to, 1081 (Civitas
Lundonia). Cott. MS. Aug. ii. 54.

—— Conf. by Will. I. of grants, etc.,
in, to the Abbey, [1081-2 ?] (Civitas
Lundonia). Cott. xvi. 30.

—— Belief "de opere pontis London.,"
by Hen. I. to Battle Abbey for Alciston
manor, co. *Suss., ante* 1121. Harl. 43
C. 12.

LONDON, *City of, with near suburbs and Westminster (continued)*. Acquittance on account of dower of Qu. Johanna charged on the little customs of the port of, 1433. Add. 7586.

—— Acquittance from Sir Joh. Cornewayll for a pension on the little customs of the port of, 1433. Add. 7587.

—— Order conc. bond in 1438 of Flemish merchants to customers of wool at, 1440. Add. 12072.

—— Certificate of survey of cottages on Tower Hill, 1443. Add. 26073.

—— Release for repairs to a hospice in Paternoster Row, bel. to St. Paul's, 1453. Lansd. 653.

—— Acquittance to the sheriffs for payment for a lamp before the tomb of Qu. Matilda in Westminster Abbey, 1455. Harl. 45 A. 34.

—— Catalogue of the library founded by W. Skiryngton at Pardonchirchehawe adjoining St. Paul's, 1458. Cott. xiii. 11.

—— Notes on admission of sheriffs, *t*. Edw. IV. Campb. xx. 4 (2).

—— Acquittance to the Treasury for a standard of weights and measures for, 1496. Add. 19540.

—— Compotus of crown rents in St. Lawrence Lane, Water Lane, Broken Wharf, and St. George's Field, 1496–98. Roy. Roll 14 B. xxiv.

—— Request to, from the City of Hamburg, for a loan, 1500. Harl. 75 E. 6.

—— Certificate of admission of Rob. Bryde as a freeman, in Cordwainer Street ward, 1506. Harl. 47 D. 35.

—— Rate of prices of wares for custom due from Merchant Adventurers, 1507, 1532. Add. 16577.

—— Rental of certain lands bel. to the chamber of London, 1518–9. Harl. Roll H. 30.

—— "The Banquetinge Howse" in Hyde Park made against the coming of the French ambassadors, by R. Trunckey, *t*. Hen. VIII. Add. 1262*.

—— Rental of tenantryes in, in Lady Cobham's hands, early 16 cent. Harl. Roll P. 17.

—— Rental of tenements in Bread Street, early 16 cent. Harl. Roll H. 34.

LONDON, *City of, with near suburbs and Westminster (continued)*. Exchequer acquittances to the subsidy collectors in the port of, 1539–154— Harl. Rolls Z. 9–12.

—— Compotus of the subsidy collectors in the port of, 1543–44. Harl. Roll Z. 13.

—— Sale to the crown of lands of Geo. Monox in, 1561. Harl. 75 39, 40, 42, 43.

—— Exchequer acquittances to the farmer of customs of the port of, 157— Add. 25622.

—— Certificates, returned in 1548, to obituary and other services in the several churches, 1577. Harl. Roll H. 32.

—— License to Merchant Adventurers to export bullion, 1581. Cott. xvii. 23 b.

—— Bond of merchants trading to Spain and Portugal conc. a loan to the Duke of Medina Sidonia, 1582. Add. 1058.

—— Lrs. patent for repayment of £30,000 to the corporation, 1588. Harl. 51 H. 28.

—— Crown rents in, 1589. Add. 9490.

—— Decree in suit conc. "the Starr" in Eastcheap, 1631. Add. 8662.

—— Lease of mooring chains in the Thames at London Bridge, 1639. Add. 17604.

—— Declaration by the Society of London for Mines Royal on a lease of mines in Beer Ferris, co. Devon, 1665. Harl. 77 H. 1.

—— Contract to build a ship for the Royal African Company, 1675. Add. 13678.

—— Articles for buildings in Portugal Row, Lincoln's Inn Fields, *t*. Chas. II. Cott. xxiv. 47.

—— Certificate of a marriage of Quakers at "the Bull and Mouth," nr. Aldersgate, 1682. Add. 19408.

—— Bill of lading of the ship "John and Christ" bound for Bilbao, 1692. Harl. 84 B. 54.

—— Grant of a water-course in Whitefriars by the New River Company, 1697. Lansd. 662.

—— List of prisoners in Newgate, 1726. Add. 16510.

—— Appointment of a colonel of the Red Regiment of Militia, 1784. Add. 12686.

**LONDON,** *City of, with ar. suburbs and Westminster (continued). MAYORS AND OTHER OFFICERS (continued). Vicecomites (continued).* Joh. Bosham, Tho. Cornwaleys, 1379. Harl. 55 C. 11, 12.

———— ———— Walt. Doget, Will. Knyghtcote, 1380. Harl. 56 G. 22.

———— ———— Joh. Sely, Ad. Bamme, 1383. Harl. 54 H. 29, 56 F. 18.

———— ———— Sim. Wynchcombe, Joh. More, 1383. Cott. xii. 43.

———— ———— Nic. de Exton, Joh. Frossh, 1385. Harl. 86 H. 25.

———— ———— Joh. Organ, Joh. Chircheman, 1385. Harl. 57 B. 51;—1386. Harl. 49 F. 19, 50 H. 48.

———— ———— Ad. Karlill *al.* Carlyll, Tho. Augustyn *al.* Austyn, 1389. Harl. 48 H. 14, 56 D. 47.

———— ———— Joh. Loueye, Joh. Walcote, 1389. Harl. 47 G. 13.

———— ———— Tho. Vyuent (?), Joh. Fraunceys, 1391. Add. 19710.

———— ———— Tho. Newenton *al.* Neuton, Gilb. Mauffeld *al.* Maufeld, Maghfeld, 1392. Harl. 48 B. 16, 53 H. 39, Add. 15624.

———— ———— Drugo Barantyn, Ric. Whityngton, 1393. Harl. 58 A. 6.

———— ———— Tho. Knolles, Will. Brampton, 1395. Harl. Roll O. 81.

———— ———— Will. Shiryngham, Rog. Elys, 1395. Harl. 57 E. 37;—1396. Harl. 76 D. 1.

———— ———— Tho. Wilford *al.* Welford, Will. Parker, 1397. Add. 7584, Harl. 53 H. 42.

———— ———— Will. Askham, Joh. Wodecok, 1398. Harl. 47 D. 2.

———— ———— Will. Euote, Joh. Wakelee, 1401. Harl. 55 H. 2.

———— ———— Rob. Chicchele, Ric. Merlowe, 1403. Harl. 112 B. 8.

———— ———— Nic. Wotton, Galf. Broke *al.* Brook, 1406. Add. 5314, 15626, Harl. 56 G. 1.

———— ———— Hen. Pountfrete, Hen. Halton, 1408. Harl. 47 B. 29, 48 B. 35.

———— ———— Joh. Lane, Will. Chicchele, 1409. Harl. 49 A. 19.

———— ———— Joh. Reynewell, Walt. Cotton, 1412. Harl. 55 A. 33.

———— ———— Rad. Lobenham, Will. Sevenok, 1413. Harl. 76 C. 32.

———— ———— Joh. Sutton, Joh. Micholl, 1414. Harl. Roll O. 31.

**LONDON,** *City of. with ar. suburbs and Westminster (continued). MAYORS AND OTHER OFFICERS (continued). Vicecomites (continued).* Joh. Gedney *al.* Gedeneye, Hen. Reds, 1417. Harl. 49 H. 56;—1418. Harl. 56 B. 44

———— ———— Rad. Barton, Joh. Perneys, 1419. Harl. 57 B. 14.

———— ———— Joh. Botillere, Joh. Welles, 1420. Slo. xxxii. 32.

———— ———— Ric. Gosselyn, Will. Weston, 1422. Harl. 45 F. 34.

———— ———— Will. Melreth, Joh. Brokke, 1426. Harl. 52 A. 29.

———— ———— Rob. Arnold, Joh. Hiham, 1427. Campb. xiv. 26.

———— ———— Joh. Abbot, Tho. Defhous, 1429. Harl. Roll H. 85.

———— ———— Rob. Large, Walt. Chertesey, 1431. Harl. 51 A. 8.

———— ———— Will. Hales, Will. Chapman, 1437. Harl. 55 B. 37.

———— ———— Steph. Forster, Hugo Wyche (late), 1447. Harl. 86 F. 22.

———— ———— Joh. Derby, Galfr. Feldyng, 1445. Add. 26074.

———— ———— Will. Taillour, Joh. Felde, 1454. Harl. 55 H. 19;—1455. Harl. 45 A. 34, 54 C. 36.

———— ———— Will. Edwards, Tho. Reyner, 1458. Harl. 79 B. 38, Slo. xxxii. 84.

———— ———— Joh. Lok, Geo. Irlond, 1462. Add. 26082.

———— ———— Tho. Muschamp, Rob. Basset, 1464. Add. 19711.

———— ———— Hen. Bryce, Tho. Stoghton, 1467. Campb. xx. 4 (2).

———— ———— Joh. Crosby, Joh. Warde, 1471. Add. 26085.

———— ———— Rob. Colwyche, Hugo Bryce, 1476. Add. 19713.

———— ———— Rob. Hardyng, Rob. Byfield, 1478. Harl. 78 B. 6, 7.

———— ———— Will. Bacon, Tho. Danyell, 1480. Harl. 80 B. 40.

———— ———— Rob. Tate, Ric. Chawry, 1482. Harl. 51 C. 26.

———— ———— Joh. Swan, Joh. Tate, 1486. Harl. 58 G. 26.

———— ———— Tho. Wode, Will. Browne, 1492. Harl. 49 A. 16.

———— ———— Will. Purchas, Will. Welbek, 1493. Harl. 79 E. 39.

———— ———— *Sir* Laur. Aylmer, Kut., 1502. Add. 23409.

LONDON, *City of, with nr. suburbs and Westminster (continued). MAYORS AND OTHER OFFICERS (continued). Aldermannus (continued).* Will. de Hereford, 1295. Harl. 112 I. 2.

—— —— Walt. de Finchingfeld *al.* Finchingfeud, [1297–8]. Harl. 57 F. 41;—1298. Harl. Roll O. 26;—[1300–1]. Add. 15621;—1305. Harl. 45 F. 38.

—— —— Will. de Beton, 1298. Harl. Roll O. 26.

—— —— Joh. le Blound, 1298. Harl. Roll O. 26;—1301. Harl. 53 H. 22, 57 C. 48;—1307. Harl. 47 H. 35.

—— —— Ric. de Glouc. *al.* Glovernia, 1298. Harl. Roll O. 26;—1313. Harl. 53 E. 5.

—— —— Rad. de Honylane, 1299. Harl. 84 I. 57.

—— —— Ad. de Rokesle, 1299. Harl. 49 B. 49.

—— —— Will. de Leyre, [1304]. Harl. 47 F. 1;—1309. Harl. 52 D. 32.

—— —— Will. Coumbe Martyn, 1306. Harl. 58 B. 41.

—— —— Hugo Pourte, 1306–7. Harl. 46 A. 15.

—— —— Nic. de Farendon, 1306. Harl. 53 E. 17;—1314. Harl. 56 A. 28;—[1324–5]. Harl. 54 F. 13;—1331. Harl. 48 A. 11;—1332. Cott. xxvii. 42.

—— —— Joh. de Wanegrave *al.* Wynegrave (as *Ald. Warde Fori*), [1308–9]. Harl. 46 D. 19;—1310. Harl. 51 A. 51.

—— —— Will. Basing, 1309. Add. 22663.

—— —— Galf. de Condustu *al.* Conductu, 1309. Add. 22663, Harl. 55 E. 3.

—— —— Nigel. Drury, 1309. Harl. 50 H. 4.

—— —— Hen. de Gloucestria, 1309. Harl. 50 H. 4.

—— —— Ric. de Refham, 1309. Harl. 50 H. 4.

—— —— Nic. Pycot, 1309. Harl. 57 F. 9.

—— —— Joh. de Wyndesore, 1311. Harl. 52 L 20;—1312. Harl. 56 F. 6.

—— —— Rog. de Frowik, 1313. Harl. 53 E. 5.

—— —— Steph. de Abyndon, 1314. Harl. 51 D. 11.

—— —— Joh. Lambyn, [1315. Harl. 50 D. 10.

LONDON, *City of, with nr. suburbs and Westminster (continued). MAYORS AND OTHER OFFICERS (continued). Aldermannus (continued).* Elias de Suff., *al.* Suthfolk, Suffolk, 1316. Harl. 48 I. 45;—1319. Harl. 33 A. 8;—1324. Harl. 47 A. 56.

—— —— Sim. Corp, 1318. Harl. 45 G. 60.

—— —— Hamo Goodchep *al.* Godchep, 1318. Harl. 45 G. 60;—1321 (as *Ald. Warde de Bredstrete*). Harl. 111 G. 51;—1323. Harl. 48 B. 20.

—— —— Hamo de Chigwelle *al.* Chigewelle, 1319. Harl. 111 D. 34; —(as *Ald. Warde. Ripe Regine*), 1321. Harl. 111 G. 51;—1324. Add. 19706, 19707.

—— —— Rog. le Paumer, 1322. Harl. 53 C. 35.

—— —— Bened. de Fulsham, 1328. Harl. 53 D. 53.

—— —— Tho. de Leyre, 1328. Harl. 56 I. 40.

—— —— Ric. de Bettoigne, 1329. Harl. 48 I. 16.

—— —— Ric. de Hakeneye *al.* Hakueye, 1332. Harl. 48 F. 34;—1333. Harl. 58 B. 28.

—— —— Reg. de Conductu, 1332. Harl. 47 F. 2;—1337. Harl. 51 C. 34.

—— —— Rob. le Brct, 1333. Harl. 53 H. 32.

—— —— Joh. de Oxon.,' 1333. Harl. 51 B. 12.

—— —— Anketin. de Gisors, 1335. Harl. 58 C. 40.

—— —— Joh. de Hingeston, 1335. Harl. 46 A. 35.

—— —— Joh. de Preston, 1335. Harl. 49 F. 38.

—— —— Ric. le Lacer, 1335. Harl. 47 F. 35;—1338. Add. 24489.

—— —— Walt. de Mordon, 1336. Harl. 52 E. 26.

—— —— Joh. de Granham, 1338. Harl. 57 E. 4.

—— —— Walt. Neel *al.* Nel, 1342. Harl. 58 G. 25;—1345. Harl. 54 C. 58.

—— —— Will. de Pontefracto, 1343. Harl. 48 I. 11.

—— —— Hen. Pycard, 1349. Harl. 48 B. 33.

—— —— Sim. Franceis, 1351. Harl. 50 D. 52.

—— —— Will. de Causton, 1352. Harl. 55 F. 28.

—— —— Rog. de Depham, 1352. Harl. 58 D. 6.

LONDON, *City of, with nr. suburbs and Westminster (continued). PARISHES (continued).* PAR. OF. ST. JAMES, GARLICKHITHE *(continued). Capellanus perpet. cantarie ad altare S. Joh. Bapt. in eccl. S. Jac. de Garlekhythe.* Tho. Preston, 1400. Harl. 44 F. 40.

—— PAR. OF ST. JOHN, WALBROOK. Conf. of grant of rents from "la coppedehalle" in, 1267 (S. Joh. de Walebroc). Harl. 50 G. 49.

—— —— Bequest in, for chantries in the Hosp. of St. Mary, Bishopsgate, and the church of St. Mary Bothawe, 1318 (S. Joh. de Walebrok). Harl. 44 F. 39.

—— —— Sales, etc., in, 1445. Add. 26074 (S. Joh. super Walbrook);— 1446. Add. 26075 (do.);—1462. Add. 26082 (do.);—1470. Add. 26084 (do.); —1595. Harl. 75 H. 29, 30 ("The Ship" in), 32 ("The Holie Lamb" in);—1608. Harl. 75 H. 40.

—— PAR. OF ST. JOHN ZACHARY. Release in, 1338 (S. Joh. Zacharias). Add. 24489.

—— —— Suit for non-payment of rents in, 1406. Harl. 75 D. 66.

—— PAR. OF ST. KATHARINE COLEMAN. Crown lease in Billiter lane in, 1567. Add. 14046.

—— —— *Persona.* Joh. Phelip, 1403. Harl. 54 H. 1.

—— PAR. OF ST. KATHARINE CREE. Release in, 1295 (B. Kath. prope Crist[chirche]). Harl. 112 I. 2.

—— —— Grant by Sibton Abbey, co. Suff., of reversion to a lease in, 1307 (S. Kat. iufra Alegate). Harl. 112 F. 45.

—— —— Lease, etc., in, 1555. Add. 22669; — 1599. Add. 22676, 22677;—1603. Add. 22678.

—— PAR. OF ST. KATHARINE NEAR THE TOWER (?). Releases in Smithfield nr. the Tower, 1355. Harl. 53 D. 40, 54 E. 44.

—— PAR. OF ST. LAURENCE JEWRY (S. Laur. in Judaysmo, Judeiamo). Grants, etc., in, 1292. Harl. 52 F. 14-17;—1295-6. Harl. 49 F. 55, 56; —1301. Harl. 53 H. 22, 57 C. 48; —1308-9. Harl. 46 D. 19;—1309. Harl. 52 D. 32;—1332. Harl. 47 F. 2, 5;—1335. Harl. 56 F. 7;—1337. Harl. 51 C. 34;—1349. Harl. 58 C. 31;—1350. Harl. 47 D. 1, 50 D. 53; —1351. Harl. 50 D. 52;—1355. Harl. 53 H. 34;—1392. Harl. 53 H. 39;— 1669. Add. 13726.

LONDON, *City of, with nr. suburbs and Westminster (continued). PARISHES (continued).* PAR. OF ST. MAGNUS MARTYR *(continued).* Grants, etc., in, early 13 cent. Harl. 50 B. 40 (ante hostium eccl. S. Mag. Martiris), 54 B. 13 (in Bruestrete);—1349. Harl. 58 A. 16 (S. Mag. London.);—1383. Harl. 54 H. 29 (S. Mag. apud pontem);—1386. Harl. 49 F. 19 (S. Mag. London.);— 1395. Harl. 75 G. 50, 80 G. 5;— 1601. Harl. 75 H. 36.

—— —— Acquittance from Southwark Priory for rent in, 1409. Harl. 44 I. 56.

—— —— *Capellanus.* Johannes, early 13 cent. Harl. 50 B. 40.

—— PAR. OF ST. MARGARET, LOTHBURY. Sales, etc., in, 1544. Add. 5317;—1557. Add. 5318, 5319;— 1578. Add. 5328, 5329, 5330;—1580. Add. 5331.

—— PAR. OF ST. MARGARET MOSES. Papal conf. of the church to Horsham St. Faith Priory, co. Norf., 1163 (Eccl. S. Margarite). Cott. MS. Aug. ii. 136.

—— —— Grant in, [1238-9] (S. Marg. Lond. apud Fridaistrate). Harl. 50 E. 32.

—— —— Grant in, to Nutley Abbey, 1298 (do.). Harl. Roll O. 26 (*copy*).

—— —— License for grant in, to St. Mary Graces Abbey, 1375 (S. Marg. Moisy). Harl. 43 E. 7.

—— —— Sale, etc., in, 1437. Harl. 55 B. 37 (S. Marg. Moisi);—1541. Harl. 112 D. 39.

—— —— Lease in, by St. Mary Graces Abbey, 1532. Harl. 111 C. 36.

—— PAR. OF ST. MARGARET, NEW FISH STREET. Grants, etc., in, early 13 cent. Harl. 54 H. 40 (S. Marg. versus pontem London.), Add. 7592 (do.);—[1272-3]. Harl. 56 D. 32 (St. Marg. de la Walle);—1333. Harl. 58 B. 28 (in Finches lane in);—1576. Add. 24493;—1634. Add. 19570.

—— —— Foundation of a chantry in the church, with rents in, t. Edw. I. (S. Marg. de Breggestrete). Harl. 45 G. 41.

—— —— License for Christ Church, Canterbury, to acquire lands in, 1394 (S. Marg. de Briggestrete). Add. 16364.

—— —— *Rector. Dom.* Rob. Sprotburgh, 1381. Harl. 55 E. 37;—1382. Harl. 46 F. 9;—1389. Harl. 56 D. 47;—t. Rich. II. Harl. 47 G. 18.

LONDON, *City of, with nr. suburbs and Westminster (continued). PARISHES (continued).* PAR. OF ST. MARGARET, NEW FISH STREET *(continued). Rector (continued).* Joh. Phelip, 1410. Harl. 86 B. 46.

—— PAR. OF ST. MARTIN, LUDGATE. Grants, etc., in, [1273-4]. Harl. 52 E. 24;—1324. Harl. 54 F. 13;—1331. Harl. 48 A. 11, 56 D. 35;—1335. Harl. 47 F. 35;—1344. Harl. 55 A. 5 (in Le Baillye extra Lodegate);— 1374. Harl. 56 F. 20;—1412. Harl. 55 A. 33;—1452. Slo. xxxii. 37;— 1458. Slo. xxxii. 34.

—— —— Grant in, by Jas. I., 1612. Cott. xiii. 35.

—— —— Lease in, by the Corporation, 1670. Add. 1683.

—— —— *Rector. Mag.* Laur. de Barnet, 1333. Harl. 80 D. 23.

—— PAR. OF ST. MARTIN ORGAR. Lease, etc., in, 1558. Add. 24835;— 1586. Add. 24836.

—— PAR. OF ST. MARTIN OUTWICH. Covenant on grant in, 1384 (S. M. Oteswich). Harl. 58 D. 30.

—— —— Royal conf. of title in, 1384. Harl. 43 E. 28.

—— PAR. OF ST. MARTIN, VINTRY. Grants, etc., in, c. 1222. Harl. 50 A. 29 (S. M. de Baremannechyrche), 30 (S. M. in Vinetria), 31 (S. M. de Barmannecherche);—[1241-2]. Harl. 48 F. 27 (S. M. de Bermancherch); —1267. Harl. 50 G. 49 (S. M. de Vinetria);—[1278-9]. Harl. 111 G. 59, 112 B. 41 (do.);—1383. Cott. xii. 43;—1489. Cott. xxx. 34;—1523. Harl. 111 F. 20.

—— —— Grant of quit rents in, by St. Mary's Hospital, Bishopsgate, 1400 (S. M. in Vinetria). Harl. 44 F. 40.

—— PAR. OF ST. MARY ABCHURCH. Covenant of the new Hospital of St. Mary without Bishopsgate conc. a house in, 1325 (B. M. de Abbechirche). Harl. 53 H. 28 (*copy*).

—— —— Grants, etc., in, 1338. Harl. 49 F. 46;—1352. Harl. 58 D. 6; —1399. Harl. 53 H. 15;—1561. Harl. 77 F. 51;—1597. Harl. 75 H. 35 ("The Golden Gate" in);—1604. Harl. 75 H. 38 ("The George" in).

—— —— Conveyance of tenements called the "Wellhous" and "Caponhors" in, 1373-99. Harl. Roll II. 27.

LONDON, *City of, with nr. suburbs and Westminster (continued)*. *PARISHES (continued)*. PAR. OF ST. MICHAEL PATERNOSTER *al.* ROYAL *(continued)*. Grants, etc., in, *ante* 1212. Harl. 50 A. 3 (S. Mich. que vocatur paternostercherche);—1335. Harl. 58 C. 40 (S. M. de Paternostercherche) ;—1365. Cott. xxvii. 55 (par. de Paternosterchurche apud le Reole).

—————— Grant to the parson of patronage of chantries in, 1368 (S. M. de Paternosterchirche in La Riole). Harl. 55 D. 9.

—————— *Persona. Dom.* Tho. de Beere, 1368. Harl. 55 D. 9.

—————— PAR. OF ST. MICHAEL, QUEEN-HITHE. Grants, etc., in, 1232. Lansd. 652 (S. Mich. versus Ripam Regine);—1324. Add. 19706, 19707 (S. M. de Ripa Regine);—1358. Harl. 44 I. 54 (S. M. ad Ripam Regine);—1368. Add. 19708 (do.);—1374. Add. 19709;—1391-1504. Add. 19710-19716;—1422. Harl. 58 A. 8;—1432. Harl. 49 G. 46;—1439. Harl. 45 D. 1;—1486. Harl. 54 F. 46;—1489. Harl. 50 D. 44.

—————— PAR. OF ST. MICHAEL QUEEN. Grant of rents in, to Bullington Priory, co. Linc., early 13 cent. (St. Mich. in . . . bladi). Harl. 47 A. 44.

—————— License for the corporation to hold lands in, 1282 (S. M. ad Bladum). Add. 10646.

—————— License for grant in, to St. Mary Graces Abbey, 1375 (S. Mich. atte Corne). Harl. 43 E. 7.

—————— PAR. OF ST. MICHAEL VINTRY. Partition of houses in, 1505. Add. 6145.

—————— PAR. OF ST. MICHAEL, WOOD STREET. Grants, etc., in, early 13 cent. Harl. 50 B. 41 (S Mich. de Wudestrata);—1274. Harl. 50 H. 40 (S. M. de Hoggene lane);—1288. Harl. 46 A. 14 (do.).

—————— PAR. OF ST. MILDRED, BREAD STREET. Grant in, to Nutley Abbey, co. Buck., 1298 (S. Mildr. de Bred strete). Harl. Roll O, 26.

—————— Grants, etc., in Basing lane in, 1318. Harl. 45 G. 60;—1319. Harl. 45 B. 34;—1323. Harl. 48 B. 20;—1329. Harl. 48 I. 16.

—————— Pardon on grant of rent in St. Lawrence Jewry par. to the church of, 1368. Harl. 43 E. 3.

LONDON, *City of, with nr. suburbs and Westminster (continued)*. *PARISHES (continued)*. PAR. OF ST. MILDRED, POULTRY. Covenant conc. the church, and the chapel of St. Mary Conyhop in, betw. Southwark and H. Trinity, Aldgate, Priories, *s.* 1175 (Eccl. S. Mildrithe et Capella S. Marie Loudonie). Cott. xi. 52.

—————— Re-grant by Edw. II. of a messuage in, to a chantry in the church of, 1321 (S. Mildr. in Poletria). Harl. 43 D. 37.

—————— *Rector (nuper)*. Walt. Froy, 1420. Harl. 54 E. 25.

—————— Joh. Rothewell, 1420. Harl. 54 E. 25.

—————— *Dom.* Joh. Sneynton, 1435. Harl. 50 F. 27.

—————— PAR. OF. ST. NICHOLAS ACON. Lease in Abchurch lane in, by Reigate Hospital, *c.* 1240-50 (?) (S. Nich. Hacun). Campb. xvi. 8.

—————— *Rector. Dom.* Joh. Claypole, 1391. Add. 1320, 1321, 1322.

—————— PAR. OF ST. NICHOLAS AT THE SHAMBLES. Grant in "retro macellum," [1259-60] (par. S. Nicholai). Add. 10661.

—————— PAR. OF ST. NICHOLAS COLE ABBEY. Grants, etc., in Distaff lane in, late 12 cent. Harl. 84 H. 31;—early Hen. III. Harl. 86 F. 14;—1237. Harl. 85 E. 32;—t. Hen. III. Harl. 84 I. 59, 85 D. 21, 85 E. 33, 86 F. 15 (par. S. Nicholai).

—————— Release in "Distafialane" to Biddlesdon Abbey, co. Buck., [1272-3] (S. Nich. retro Fihstrate). Harl. 85 E. 22.

—————— Lease in Distaff lane in, to the rector, by Biddlesdon Abbey, 1295 (S. Nich. in veteri piscaria). Harl. 84 E. 25.

—————— Bond to repay to Biddlesdon Abbey money lent for purchase of a house in "Dystaves lane," 1298. Harl. 84 H. 5.

—————— Lease in "Distavelane" to Biddlesdon Abbey, 1299 (S. Nich. de veteri piscario). Harl. 84 I. 57.

—————— Grants, etc., in, 1319. Harl. 111 D. 54 (S. N. Coldabbeye); —1321. Harl. 111 G. 51;—1373. Harl. 57 A. 10;—1377. Harl. 57 A. 11;—1403. Harl. 112 B. 8;—1437. Harl. 55 B. 37.

**Longford,** *co. Midd.* Assignment of crown lease of mills at, 1568. Harl. 80 F. 36.

**Longford,** *in Britford, co. Wilts.* Releases, etc., in, *t.* Edw. I. Lansd. 683 (Langeford);—1388. Lansd. 688, 689 (Langefford).

—— *Dominus. Dom.* Alan. de Plugenet, *t.* Edw. I. Lansd. 683.

**Longhirst,** *co. Northumb.* Attornment in, 1348 (Langhirst). Harl. 54 C. 12.

**Longhope,** *co. Glouc.* Brief for rebuilding the church, 1770. Ch. Br. B. xi. 4.

—— *Vicar.* Tho. Rudge, *t.* Hen. VIII. Campb. xviii. 15.

**Longisdon.** *v.* Longstone, *co. Derb.*

**Longney,** *co.* —— (?). Grant of, to Oseney Abbey, late Hen. I. (tota terra de Langeneia). Add. 20120.

**Longney,** *co. Glouc.* Conf. of grants at, to Pershore Abbey, 972 (in Longanego). Cott. MS. Aug. ii. 6.

—— Grant of the church and a fishery at, to Pershore Abbey, *c.* 1100 (Langancia). Harl. 50 B. 22.

—— Grant in, by Gt. Malvern Priory, [1287-1300?] (Lang.). Harl. 83 A. 34.

—— *Capellanus.* Johannes, [1287-1300?]. Harl. 83 A. 34.

—— *Vicarius (quondam).* Stephanus, [1287-1300?]. Harl. 83 A. 34.

**Longnor,** *co. Salop.* Grant of free warren in, 1267 (Longenhore). Add. 15773.

**Longnor,** *co. Staff.* Admission to Harding Booth (Hardynggesbothe) nr., according to custom of Frythe manor, 1440. Woll. iii. 9.

—— Briefs for rebuilding the chapel, 1774-1816. Ch. Br. B. xiv. 7, xxiii. 7, xl. 1, xlvii. 10, lvi. 8.

**Longrigg,** *co. Cumb.* Commutation of tithes in, 1695. Add. 17193.

**Longstock,** *co. Southt.* Reservation to the manor of estovers from Dunewode wood, 1273 (Langestok). Campb. v. 3.

**Longstone, Great and Little,** *in Bakewell, co. Derb.* Grants, etc., in, early Hen. III. Add. 19284 (Parva Longisdon);—1347. Harl. 83 F. 6 (Magna, Parva, Longesdon);—1362. Woll. iii. 14 (Longesdon Magna);— 1490. Woll. vii. 48 (Longisdon);— 1576. Woll. xii. 46 (Longesden);— 1619. Woll. xii. 93.

**Longton** (Longeton), *in Penwortham, co. Lanc.* Grants, etc., in, 1288. Add. 26025;—1301. Add. 26027;—1304. Add. 26029, 26030;—1307. Add. 26033;—1308. Add. 26034;—1317. Add. 26038;—1320. Add. 26039;— 1322. Add. 26040.

—— Brief for rebuilding the chapel, 1767. Ch. Br. B. vii. 11.

**Longtree Hundred,** *co. Glouc.* Grant of rent from, 1634 (Langtre). Add. 18391.

**Longwood,** *in Huddersfield, co. York.* Brief for rebuilding the chapel, 1825. Ch. Br. C. vi. 8.

**Longworth,** *co. Berks.* Grant in, 1458 (Langworth). Harl. 55 A. 39.

—— *Rector. Mag.* Joh. Goldsmyth, 1458. Harl. 55 A. 39.

**Lonsdale,** *co. Lanc.* Conf. of the forest of, to Edm., Earl of Lancaster, 1285 (Lonesdale). Cott. MS. Aug. ii. 135(5).

—— Marriage settlement in Slyne in, 1670. Add. 19547.

**Looe, East,** *co. Cornw.* Grant of a market and fair at, in Pendrym manor, 1237 (Lo). Harl. 58 H. 47 (copy).

**Looe, West,** *al.* **Portpighian,** *co. Cornw.* Certif. by T. Bawden, Mayor, of the election of A. Mildemay as M.P., 1640. Harl. 112 E. 16.

**Loose** (Lose), *co. Kent.* Lease in, by Christ Church, Canterbury, *t.* Rich. I. Add. 16447.

—— Grant, etc., in, 1271-2. Add. 16463;—*t.* Edw. I. Add. 16462;— 1519. Add. 6215.

—— Settlement of the manor, etc., 1411. Add. 16464.

—— Settlement of the mill in, 1556. Harl. 57 H. 11.

**Lopen,** *co. Som.* Release in, *t.* Rich. II. Harl. 57 G. 18.

**Lopham,** *co. Norf.* Assignment in dower of the manor, 1477. Add. 26598.

—— Feoffment, etc., in, 1506. Add. 14729 (Sowth Lopham);—1538. Add. 14730.

—— *Rector.* Galfr. Simund, 1396. Harl. 48 I. 39.

**Loppington,** *co. Salop.* Grant of the manor, 1444 (Lopyngton). Harl. 83 F. 3, 4.

**Lordington,** *co. Suss.* Descent of the manor, early 14 cent. (Lurdyngton). Harl. 45 C. 49.

**Lowbrook**, *in Okeford FitzPain* (?), *co. Dors.* Conveyance in, 1358 (Lullebrook). Harl. 47 H. 8.

**Loweslegh, Lowesley.** *v.* Loseley, *nr. Guildford, co. Surr.*

**Lowestoft**, *co. Suff.* Precipes on covenants conc. lands in, 1588. Add. 25384;—1592. Add. 25424.

—— Release of the manor, 1608. Add. 14279.

**Lowick** *al.* **Luffwick**, *co. Northt.* Grant in, [1230?] (Lufwic). Harl. 53 B. 51 *a, b.*

—— Composition for disafforestation in, 1640. Harl. 111 H. 32.

**Lowthorpe**, *co. York.* Evidence conc. tithes due to the rector from Braycefordmilnebolme in, *c.* 1340. Lansd. 288.

—— Conf. of grant of a moiety of the manor, *t.* Rich. II. Lansd. 446.

—— Grant and release in, *t.* Edw. IV. Lansd. 466 (*copy*).

—— *Parson.* Sir Rob. de Buckton, *t.* Rich. II. Lansd. 446.

**Loxhore**, *co. Devon.* Fine in, 1653 (Loxford *al.* Loxhore). Harl. 86 I. 59.

—— Conveyance of the manor, 1660. Harl. 85 H. 59, 111 E. 36.

—— Covenants not to disturb in possession in, 1664. Harl. 85 H. 30, 31, 50, 86 I. 45, 112 B. 28.

**Loxley**, *co. Staff.* Grant of custody of the manor, 1305 (Lockeslegh). Harl. 43 C. 45.

—— Livery in, 1323 (Magna Lockesle). Harl. 46 E. 9.

**Loxley**, *co. Warw.* Grant of the church to Stone Priory, *co.* Staff., [1151–8?] (Lochesl.). Cott. xiii. 6 (13) (*copy*).

—— Grant, etc., in, to Stoneleigh Abbey, *co.* Warw., *t.* Hen. III. Add. 7498 (Lockesle), 20238 (Lokesl.).

**Loyes Wedon.** *v.* Weedon Pinkeney, *co. Northt.*

**Lubbenham**, *co. Leic.* Restoration of the church to Daventry Priory, [1147?] (Lubeho). Add. 21204.

—— Conf. by King John of a grant in, 1208 (Lubenho). Add. 6014.

—— Grant in, to Sulby Abbey, *t.* Hen. III. (Lubbeho). Add. 21366.

—— Exemplif. in 1402 of a grant of the manor, *t.* Hen. III. (?) (Lubbenho). Add. 22371 (2).

**Lubbenham**, *co. Leic.* (*continued*). Defeasance of bond in, from the rector, to St. Albans Abbey, 1382 (Lubenham). Add. 21367.

—— Lease for lives in, 1393. Add. 24214.

—— Acquittances from Bishops and the Chapter of Lincoln to Sulby Abbey for pensions from the church, 1506–1522. Add. 21368-21376, 21379.

—— Acquittances from St. Albans Abbey to Sulby Abbey for pensions from the church, 1510, 1514, 1522. Add. 21377, 21378, 21380.

—— Order in suit of Sulby Abbey for trespass in, 1522. Add. 22459.

—— *Capellanus.* Radulfus, *t.* Hen. III. Add. 21366.

—— *Persona.* Tho. de Wolvardynton, 1345. Harl. Roll CC. 29.

—— *Rector. Dom.* Hugo de Benington, *t.* Hen. III. (?). Add. 22371 (2).

—— *Dom.* Ric. Wodeford, 1382. Add. 21367.

**Lubbesthorpe**, *co. Leic.* Grant in, 1482. Add. 26972.

**Luburg**, [*co.* Derb. (?), Loughborough, *co.* Leic. (?)]. *Clericus.* Willelmus, *t.* Hen. III. Harl. 112 I. 43.

**Luca.** *v.* Luke, *nr. Bexinton, co. Dors.*

**Lucan**, *co.* Dubl. "Officiarii de Lucane," 1520. Add. 7045.

**Luccombe**, *I. of Wight.* Grants in, to Quarr Abbey, *c.* 1155 (?). Harl. 55 D. 21 (Louecumba);—1284. Add. 15701 (do.).

**Luceys.** *v. sub* Tattersett, *co. Norf.*

**Luckington**, *co.* Wilts. Grant in, 1458 (Lokynyton). Add. 1536.

**Lucton.** *v.* Lufton, *co.* Som.

**Luda.** *v.* Louth, *co.* Linc.

**Ludborough**, *co.* Linc. Precipe on a covenant conc. the manor, 1552 (Ludborowe). Add. 25052.

**Luddeford.** *v.* Lydford, West, *co.* Som.

**Luddenden**, *co.* York. Briefs for rebuilding the chapel, 1805-1820. Ch. Br. B. xlvi. 5, li. 5, lvii. 7, O. i. 2.

**Luddesdown**, *co.* Kent. Grants, etc., in, *t.* Hen. III. Harl. 51 F. 46 (Ludesdune);—1367. Harl. 48 E. 24 (Lodesdon);—1380. Harl. 48 F. 14 (do.);—1381. Harl. 48 E. 36 (do.);—1382. Harl. 54 I. 42 (do.).

·Luddesdown, *co. Kent (continued).*
Feoffment in Buckland (Boklonde)
in, 1345. Harl. 45 C. 24.

—— Grants, etc., in, to Cobham College, 1369. Harl. 53 A. 45 (Loddesdon);—1370. Harl. 52 B. 4 (Lodesdone), 53 A. 46, 47 (do.).

—— Fine in, 1370 (Loddesdon). Harl.
52 B. 3.

—— Rental, 14–15 cent. (Lodesdone).
Harl. Roll D. 28.

—— Feoffment of Gt. and Lit. Buckland manors in, 1556. Harl. 57 H. 11.

Luddington, *in I. of Axholme, co. Linc.*
Rentals, 1510, 1512. Add. 24184 a, b.

—— Sale in, 1520. Add. 24168.

Luddington, *co. Northt.* Covenant
conc. tenure of the manor of Peterborough Abbey, 1304 (Ludington).
Cott. xv. 18.

Luddington, *co. Warw.* Lease at,
11 cent. (Ludintune). Harl. 83 A. 3.

Ludeford, Estludeford. *v.* Lydford,
E., and Lydford, W., *co. Som.*

·Ludesdune. *v.* Luddesdown, *co. Kent.*

Ludford, *co. Linc.* Surrender of the
manor, early 13 cent. (Lang Ludford).
Harl. 54 G. 14 (*copy*).

—— Power to give suisin in, etc.,
1335. Harl. 54 G. 21 (Ludeford), 57
G. 8 (Lotheforth).

Ludford, *co. Salop.* Grant of Sheet
(La Seete juxta Lodelawe) manor in,
1292. Campb. xxiii. 1.

Ludham, *co. Norf.* Appropriation of
the church to Hulme Abbey, 1220.
Cott. iv. 57 (*copy*).

—— Grants, etc., in, 1297. Add.
2001 (Lodham);—1308. Add. 14731;
—1323. Add. 9915.

Ludlow, *co. Salop.* Rent to be paid to
W. de Lacy "ad nundinas de Lude-
luwe," *t.* John. Add. 19282.

—— Lease of the castle, town and
manor, *c.* 1433 (?) (Ludlowe). Harl.
53 H. 17.

—— La Seete manor nr. *v. sub* Ludford, *co. Salop.*

—— *Constabularius.* Rob. de Stantun, *t.* Hen. III. Add. 8343.

—— —— Ric. de Momele, late 13
cent. Add. 8351.

Ludney, *co. Linc.* Exchequer acquittance for fine in, 1576. Add. 25615.

Luffenham, *co. Rutl.* Valor of crown
lands in, *t.* Hen. VIII. Harl. Roll Y. 1.

Lufton, *co. Som.* Grant of a pension
from the manor, 1340 (Luketon). Add.
25891.

—— Attornment and release of the
manor and advowson, 1417. Harl. 56
E. 27 (Loketon);—1438. Harl. 50 E.
6 (Lucton).

Luggeston, *nr. Up Ottery, co. Devon.*
Release in, 1420 (Loggeston). Add.
13039.

Lugwardine, *co. Heref.* Grants, etc.,
in, 1332. Harl. 112 A. 20 (Logwor-
dyn);—1373. Harl. 111 F. 49, Eg.
359;—1376. Harl. 112 B. 56;—1386.
Harl. 111 E. 32;—1482. Harl. 112 F.
8;—1632. Add. 1929.

—— Bond conc. the advowson, 1633.
Add. 1360.

—— Brief for rebuilding the church,
1812. Ch. Br. B. lii. 8.

—— *Vicarius.* Johannes, 1386. Harl.
111 E. 32.

—— *v. also* Longford, *in Lugwardine,
co. Heref.*

Luke, *nr. Bexinton, co. Dors.* Conf. of
grant in, to Bindon Abbey, 1234
(Luca). Harl. 58 H. 45 (*copy*).

Lukedale. *v. sub* Littlebourne, *co.
Kent.*

Luketon. *v.* Lufton, *co. Som.*

Luketone, [*nr. Goudhurst?*], *co. Kent.*
Reservation of rents of the free fief of,
1355. Harl. 76 B. 27.

Lulham, *co. Heref.* Release in, 1426.
Add. 4601.

Lullebrouk. *v.* Lowbrook, *in Okeford
Fitz Pain (?), co. Dors.*

Lulles beorg, *co. Som.* (?). A boundary
mark, 938. Cott. viii. 17;—961. Harl.
43 C. 2.

Lullesfordehiderande. *v. sub* Arlsey,
*co. Bedf.*

Lullington, *co. Derb. Dominus.* Will.
de Gresele, early Hen. III. Add.
21491.

—— *Persona.* Willelmus, early Hen.
III. Add. 21491.

Lullington, "*membrum Manerii de
Ludingtona,*" *co. Northt.* Covenant
conc. surrender of the manor to Peterborough Abbey, 1304. Cott. xv. 18.

Lulworth, *co. Dors.* Conf. of grant in,
to Bindon Abbey, 1234 (Lullewurth).
Harl. 58 H. 45 (*copy*).

Lulworth, co. Dors. (continued). Release in Gatemerston (Gatemorestone) in, late Hen. III. Cott. xxv. 34.

Lumbarde Park. v. Lombard's Park, nr. Cork, co. Cork.

Lumby, in Sherburn, co. York. Grant in, 1387. Add. 26771.

Lund. v. Lound, cos. Linc., Nott., etc.

Lund, co. York. Lease in, 1606. Add. 7397.

Lund on the Wolds, co. York. Release, etc., in, 1619. Add. 7399;— 1659. Add. 7401.

Lundertorp, Lundt. v. Londonthorpe, co. Linc.

Luntsford, nr. Ninfield, co. Suss. Grant in, to Robertsbridge Abbey, t. Hen. III. (Lundresford). Campb. xxvii. 15.

Luppitt, co. Devon. Conf. of a grant in, 1379 (Loueputt). Add. 25987.

—— Covenant for recovery in, 1553. Add. 19190.

Lurdyngton. v. Lordington, co. Suss.

Lurgashall, co. Suss. Lease in, 1471. Add. 24678.

Lurgybawen. v. Aughnacloy, co. Tyrone.

Luscombe, in Sherford, co. Devon. Lease in, 1575. Add. 13200.

Luss, co. Dumbarton. Presentation to the " chaplanrie of oure Lady altare " at, 1575. Add. 8084.

—— Presentation of D. Arrall to the kirk of, 1600. Add. 8082.

Luston, co. Heref. Grant of lands in the manor of, 1367. Add. 7035.

—— Grant in Eyton in the fee of, 1422. Cott. xxx. 39.

Lutchurche. v. Litchurch, in Derby, co. Derb.

Luteringtone. v. Lotherton, nr. Aberford, co. York.

Luterwrth. v. Lutterworth, co. Leic.

Lutlyngtone. v. Lidlington, co. Bedf.

Luton, co. Bedf. Council held at, 931 (Leowtun = Luton ?). Cott. viii. 16.

—— Release for service to tenants of H. de Chaury in, t. Hen. III. (Luiton). Add. 19565.

—— Grants, etc., in, t. Hen. III. Harl. 112 E. 9 (Luiton);—1257. Harl. 111 D. 10 (Luyton);—t. Edw. I.-II. Add. 15432, 15723 (Lvtone);—1385.

Add. 15724;—1388. Add. 15708;— 1390. Add. 15725;—1493. Add. 15727.

—— Grants, etc., in W. and E. Hyde in, t. Hen. III. Harl. 111 G. 10 (Luytona);—1289. Harl. 112 A. 5;— 1301. Harl. 112 C. 21;—1358. Harl. 112 F. 18:—1447. Add. 19568;—1551. Add. 19569.

—— Power from Dunstable Priory to give seisin of W. Hyde manor in, 1415 (Luyton). Harl. 111 C. 27.

—— Feoffment of lands in the Soke of, bel. to Hoo manor, 1415. Add. 19567.

—— Fines in, 1613, 1615. Add. 654, 655.

Luton, in Northwood, I. of Wight. Grant in, ante 1175 (?) (Leuitona). Harl. 112 C. 12.

Lutons. v. sub Melford, Long, co. Suf.

Lutryngton. v. Lotherton, co. York.

Luttaton. v. sub Cornwood, co. Devon.

Luttechirch. v. Litchurch, in Derby, co. Derb.

Luttecote. v. Lidcott, nr. Bodmin, co. Cornw.

Lutterworth, co. Leic. Grant in, to Sulby Abbey, late 13 cent. (Luttirworde). Add. 21387.

—— Lease of mills and fisheries in, 1274. Campb. vi. 4.

—— Exchange in, 1446. Add. 24220.

—— Brief for repairing the church and rebuilding the steeple, 1759. Ch. Br. A. v. 7.

—— Clericus. Petrus, t. Hen. III. (Luterwrth). Add. 5885.

—— Persona. Joh. Morehous, 1388. Campb. xxiii. 2.

Lutton. v. sub Cornwood, co. Devon.

Luuelegh, co. Devon. Conf. in, 1377. Harl. 49 A. 10.

Luueretune. v. sub Rockbeare, co. Devon.

Luycheham, Lycheham. v. Litcham, co. Norf.

Luyton. v. Luton, co. Bedf.

Lyd Court. v. sub Worth, co. Kent.

Lydd (Lyde, etc.), co. Kent. Grant in, by a canon of St. Mary's, Hastings, t. Rich. I. (Lide). Campb. xvi. 17.

—— Grants, etc., in, 1393. Add. 8549;—1431. Add. 8559;—1432. Add. 8560;—1435. Add. 8563;—1438. Add.

8433; — 1450. Add. 8567; — 1466.
Add. 8574;—1468. Add. 8572, 8573;
—1469. Add. 8575;—1479. Add.
8581;—1480. Add. 8582;—1486. Add.
8584; — 1487. Add. 8587; — 1489.
Add. 8589;—1499. Add. 8593;—1508.
Add. 8595;—1518. Add. 8597;—1521.
Add. 8600;—1522. Add. 8601, 8602;
—1523. Add. 8604; — 1524. Add.
8605; — 1534. Add. 8607; — 1537.
Harl. 77 G. 17, 80 I. 55;—1539. Add.
8609 (Lidde), 8611; — 1545. Add.
8613;—1546. Add. 8614 (Lide);—
1581. Add. 8627;—1595. Add. 8630;—
1596. Add. 8631;—1658, 1660. Harl.
112 B. 25-27;—1670. Harl. 111 C. 6;
—1671. Harl. 86 I. 37;—1746. Add.
17836.

—— Sale of sheep at Scotney in, 1539.
Harl. 78 G. 29.

—— *Ballivus.* Will. Benet, 1468.
Add. 8573.

—— —— Tho. Gros, 1479. Add.
8581.

—— —— Steph. Locok, 1480. Add.
8582.

—— —— Laur. Grose, 1486. Add.
8584;—1487. Add. 8587;—1489. Add.
8589.

—— —— Will. Adam, 1518. Add.
8597.

—— —— Rob. Horsele, 1522. Add.
8602.

Lydden, *co. Kent.* Grant in, 1349
(Lydene). Cott. xxvii. 27.

Lydelynche. *v.* Lydlinch, *co. Dors.*

Lydford, *co. Devon.* Extract from
court-roll, 1564. Add. 7887.

Lydford, East, *co. Som.* Conveyance
in, 1431 (Estludeford). Harl. 55 E. 8.

—— *Persona.* Rich. Bacwill, 1397
(Estludeford). Harl. 44 H. 46.

Lydford, West, *co. Som.* Power to
give seisin of the manor, advowson,
etc., *t.* Edw. III. (Ludeford). Harl.
45 E. 38.

—— Appointment of a supervisor
of the manor, 1384 (Luddeford).
Harl. 54 I. 5.

Lydgynge. *v.* Lidsing, *co. Kent.*

Lydiard, Bishop's, *co. Som.* Covenant
on suit conc. waste of the manor on
Quantock Hills, 1314 (Lidiard Episcopi). Add. 25875.

Lydiard St. Lawrence, *co. Som.*
Compotus of lands of Taunton Priory
in Westowe in, 1438-9. Add. 25873.

Lydlinch, *co. Dors.* Fines of the manor
and advowson, 1337. Harl. 51 B. 2
(Lidelynch);—1433. Harl. Roll C. 32
(Lydelynche).

—— Fine in Stock Crockerne in, 1346.
Add. 25876.

—— Releases of the manor and advowson, 1379. Harl. 57 G. 36;—1425.
Harl. 48 B. 7;—1439. Harl. 58 D. 42.

—— Releases of Lydlinch Baret manor,
1379. Harl. 57 G. 36;—1425. Harl.
48 B. 7.

—— Fine of L. Baret manor, 1433.
Harl. Roll C. 32.

Lye. *v.* Leigh, *cos. Essex, Kent, etc.*

Lyes Magna. *v.* Leighs, Gt., *co. Essex.*

Lyford, *co. Berks.* Release, etc., in,
1420. Add. 6098-6100.

Lygetun. *v.* Leyton, *co. Essex.*

Lygh. *v. sub* Iden, *co. Suss.*

Lyghes. *v.* Leighs, Lit., *co. Essex.*

Lylenstone Lovell *al.* Lyllyng-
stone Lovell. *v.* Lillingstone Lovell,
*co. Oxon.*

Lylleston, *co.* —— (?). Fine in, 1561.
Harl. 80 F. 17, 20.

Lymballs. *v. sub* Westleton, *co. Suff.*

Lymbergh, Limbergia, Magna,
Parva. *v.* Limber, Gt. and Lit., *co.
Linc.*

Lymborne, *in S. Elmham, co. Suff.*
Grant of a nativa and lands in, 1329
(Lynburne). Campb. xii. 7.

Lyme Regis, *co. Dors.* Grant of a
hyde in (?), to Farley Priory, [1174–91]
(Lim.). Campb. xiii. 12.

—— Grant, etc., "super la nasse" *al.*
"Le nasse" in, 1356. Add. 15443
(Lym.);—1398. Harl. 47 D. 5 (Lyme).

—— Grants, etc., in, 1382. Harl. 57
A. 46;—1407. Harl. 46 G. 47 (Lyme),
51 F. 28;—1426. Harl. 48 F. 44;—
1438. Harl. 50 E. 6;—1471. Harl.
46 H. 27;—1476. Harl. 46 H. 30.

—— Conveyance in Nether Lyme and
Coleweye in, 1396. Harl. 48 G. 9.

—— *Major.* Joh. Dorset, 1398. Harl.
47 D. 5.

Lyme, Up. *v.* Uplyme, *co. Devon.*

Lymenenstre. *v.* Leominster, *co. Suss.*

Lyminge, *co. Kent.* Grant at (?), 811
(et Liminum). Cott. MS. Aug. ii. 47.

—— Settlement in, on divorce of Marg.
de Valoignes, 1326. Harl. 80 H. 4.

**Lyminge,** *co. Kent (continued).* Grant in East Legh manor in, 1365. Add. 12640.

—— Grant and release of Le Gore in, 1541. Harl. 78 F. 58, 78 G. 1, 2.

**Lymington,** *co. Southt.* Precipe on a covenant conc. land in, 1578. Add. 25229.

—— Precipe on a covenant conc. the borough, manors, etc., of New and Old Lymington, 1601. Add. 25253.

**Lymm,** *co. Chester.* Grant of right of way to the manor, 1346. Add. 16318.

**Lympehoye.** *v.* Limpenhoe, *co. Norf.*

**Lympne** (Lymne, etc.), *co. Kent.* Feoffments, etc., of Otterpool (Oterpole, etc.) manor and lands in, 1419. Harl. 80 D. 39;—1444. Harl. 78 G. 14;—1480. Harl. 80 G. 13;—1526. Harl. 78 F. 53–55.

—— Writ for an assize of nov. diss. in, 1486. Harl. 53 F. 12.

—— Sale in, to the Crown, 1541. Harl. 75 H. 3.

**Lympston,** *co. Devon.* *Persona.* Joh. Holcote, 1421 (Limeston). Add. 13041.

**Lynaker.** *v.* Linacre, *co. Derb.*

**Lynberg.** *v.* Limber, Gt., *co. Linc.*

**Lyncelade.** *v.* Linslade, *co. Buck.*

**Lyncombe,** *nr. Ilfracombe(?), co. Devon.* Fine of a third part of, 1198 (Lincumba). Harl. 54 H. 32.

**Lyncombe,** *nr. Bath, co. Som.* Suit conc. land in, *t.* Rich. II. Add. 6267.

**Lyncroft.** *v. sub* Rushall, *co. Norf.*

**Lynd Place.** *v. sub* Chertsey, *co. Surr.*

**Lyndestede, Lyndisted.** *v.* Linstead, *co. Kent.*

**Lyndewode.** *v.* Linwood, *co. Linc.*

**Lyndon,** *nr. Bickenhill, co. Warw.* Conf. of the chapel to Merkyate Priory, 1362. Cott. iv. 60 (copy).

—— Grant, etc., in, 1370· Cott. xii. 30;—1374. Add. 14006.

**Lynford,** *co. Norf.* Grant of the advowson, 1342 (Lineford). Harl. 45 D. 24.

—— Grant in, 1597. Add. 13581.

**Lyng,** *co. Norf.* *Persona.* Olyverus, 1363. Add. 14547.

—— *Rectors.* Rob. Hullyard, *ob.* 1613. Tho. Howlett, *inst.* 1613 (Linge). Add. 14724, 14725.·

**Lyngfylde.** *v.* Lingfield, *co. Surr.*

**Lynleyse.** *v.* Lilley, *co. Hertf.*

**Lynn,** *nr. Newport, co. Salop.* Recovery in, 1706. Add. 1687.

**Lynn, King's,** *co. Norf.* Grant and conf. of the church to Norwich Priory. [1103–6?]. Cott. MS. Aug. ii. 103 (Lynna), Cott. ii. 21 (1) (copies):—[1136–45]. Cott. ii. 1 (Linna), 21 (9) (copy).

—— Conf. of the same, as St. Margaret's church, with its chapels of St. James and St. Nicholas, 1180. Cott. ii. 21 (6) (copy).

—— Rental of lands in, bel. to W. Dereham Abbey, *t.* Edw. I. (Lenne). Add. 689.

——· Grant, etc., in All Saints' parish, *t.* Edw. I. (Lenn). Add. 7910, 7911.

—— Release of rents in, 1291 (Lenn). Add. 7913.

—— Settlement of suits betw. the corporation and the Bp. of Norwich, 1309 (Lenn). Add. 2014.

—— Acquittance to burgesses of, from the Exchequer, 1315 (Lenne). Add. 8069.

—— Roll of tenants of the see of Norwich in, *post* 1382. Add. 692.

—— License from the Bishop of Norwich for a grant in, to the corporation, 1392 (Lenn Epi.). Add. 6703.

—— Customs-rolls of, 1405–6. Harl. Rolls H. 23, 24.

—— License for grant of land in, from Mullicourt Priory, *co. Norf.,* to Ely Priory, 1446 (Lenn). Campb. xxvii. 29.

—— Covenant for a marriage settlement in, 1457 (Lynne). Harl. 54 A. 3, 4.

—— Suit conc. lands in (?), 1488 (Old lynne). Add. 14733.

—— Charter of Hen. VIII. to, 1524 (Lenn Episcopi). Cott. xiii. 22 (copy).

—— Levy of rents of W. Kenete in, 1531–2. Add. 690.

—— Abstract of receipts of Lynn lands, 1639–1661. Add. 14759.

—— Commission to Col. G. Hollis as governor, 1644. Add. 2015.

—— *Major.* Ad. de S. Edmundo, *t.* Edw. I. Add. 7910.

—— —— Joh. de Yspania, 1291. Add. 7913.

—— —— Joh. de Brunham, 1392. Add. 6703.

—— *Aldermanni.* Petr. de Thrundene, 1291. Add. 7913.

**Mablethorpe,** *co. Linc. (continued).*
*Persona. Dom.* Thomas, late 13 cent.
Harl. 56 G. 16.

—— *Persona eccl. S. Petri.* Johannes,
1352 (Malberthorp). Harl. 55 E. 33.

**Macclesfield,** *co. Chest.* Grant in
Winchul in the forest of, to Comber-
mere Abbey, late 12 cent. (Maclesfeld).
Add. 15771 *(copy)*.

—— Settlement in, 1372. Add. 20492.

—— Grant in, by Anne, Qu. of Rich.
II., 1390. Add. 20396.

**Maching.** *v.* Matching, *co. Essex.*

**Mackley,** *in Sudbury, co. Derb.* Feoff-
ment, etc., in, 1438. Add. 4876 (Macley
Wodhouses); — 1439. Add. 4875
(Makley).

—— Covenant for entry into the
lordship of, 1470 (Macley). Woll.
ix. 22.

—— Award in, 1472 (Makkeley).
Woll. ix. 49.

**Mackworth,** *co. Derb.* Grant of es-
sart in Bikirwude in, *t.* Hen. III.
Woll. vi. 66.

—— *Clericus.* Nicholaus, *t.* Hen. III.
Woll. ix. 33.

—— *Persona.* Thomas Tochet, 1393,
1401. Woll. xi. 5.

**Macnade.** *v. sub* Preston next Faversham, *co. Kent.*

**Madalles.** *v. sub* Epping, *co. Essex.*

**Maddington,** *co. Wilts.* Grant in
Humington (Hughemanton) in, *t.* Hen.
III. Harl. 58 B. 32.

**Madeley,** *co. Salop.* Brief for rebuilding the church, 1790. Ch. Br. B.
xxx. 5.

**Madeley,** *co. Staff.* Notif. of grant of St.
Leonard's church in, to Stone Priory,
[1138–47] (Madel.). Cott. xiii. 6 (4)
*(copy)*.

—— Grant in Onneley nr., *t.* Hen.
III. (Madeleg.). Harl. 111 F. 47.

—— Brief for rebuilding the church,
1774. Ch. Br. B. xiv. 3.

**Madeley,** *nr. Crozden, co. Staff.* Grants
of the manor, *c.* 1120. Slo. xxxi. 4
(10) (Madeleye Alfou);—1402. Slo.
xxxi. 4 (78) *(copies)*.

**Madersham.** *v.* Methersham, *co.
Suss.*

**Madford.** *v. sub* Heavitree, *co. Devon.*

**Madingley,** *co. Camb.* Release in,
1506. Add. 15552.

**Madles.** *v. sub* Epping, *co. Essex.*

**Madley,** *co. Heref. Vicarius. Dom.*
Ric. Brugge, 1440. Add. 4603;—
1446. Harl. 111 E. 2.

**Maelienydd,** *co. Radn.* Lease of the
demesnes, *c.* 1433 (Myllenyth). Harl.
53 H. 17.

**Maenor Dewi,** *co. Pemb.* Grant in,
[1219–31] (Mainardeyvi). Add. 8411.

**Maes Gwyn,** *nr. Bronllys. co. Brecon.*
Grant of rent from, to Clifford Priory,
[1222–31 ?] (Albus Campus). Harl.
48 C. 29.

**Maester.** *v. sub* Ixworth, *co. Suf.*

**Maeswille,** *nr. Maugersbury. co. Glouc.*
A boundary, 949. Cott. viii. 6 *(copy)*.

**Maesyr Odyn,** *co. Denb.* Grant in,
1528. Add. 9266.

**Maepelgares byrig.** *v.* Maugersbury,
*co. Glouc.*

**Maewi.** *v.* Meavy, *co. Devon.*

**Magdalena, Magdaleyne.** *v. sub*
Berkhampstead, *co. Hertf.*

**Magesetae,** *co. Heref.* Ref. to exch.
of lands at Yarkhill "on Magonsæ-
tum," 811. Cott. MS. Aug. ii. 47.

**Magor,** *co. Monm.* Inspex., in 1330, of
a grant in, to Usk Priory, *c.* 1150.
Add. 5312.

—— Grant in, 1536. Add. 24882.

—— Precipe on a covenant conc. land
in, 1555. Add. 25115.

**Maiden Newton.** *v.* Newton, Maiden,
*co. Dors.*

**Maidencombe,** *nr. Stoke in Teignhead,
co. Devon.* Release in, 1420 (Medenecomb). Add. 13039.

**Maidencourt.** *v. sub* Garston, E., *co.
Berks. (Addenda).*

**Maidford,** *co. Northt.* Grant of view
of frankpledge in, *c.* 1241–50 (Maydeford). Add. 6126 *(copy)*.

**Maids' Morton.** *v.* Morton, Maids',
*co. Buck.*

**Maidstone,** *co. Kent.* Settlement in,
reserving Halfyoke manor, 1411
(Maideston). Add. 16464.

—— Extract of view of frankpledge
at, 1431 (Maydeston). Harl. Roll
Z. 14.

—— Grants, etc., in, 1458. Add.
8571 (Maidestone); — 1519. Add.
6215 (Maydston);—1530–1619. Add.
923-929.

**Maidwell,** *co. Northt. (continued).* Release of annuity from the manor, 1537. Add. 22310.

—— Lease of the parsonage of 88. Peter and Mary, 1551. Add. 22074.

—— *Dominus.* Alan. fil. G. Breton, *t.* Hen. II. Add. 22145 (*copy*).

—— *Clericus.* Willelmus. early Hen. III. Add. 22087, 22103, 22106, 22107, 22117, 22122, 22140, Lansd. 75.

—— *Persona.* Adam, *t.* John–*t.* Hen. III. Add. 22100, 22102, 22109, 22113, 22130.

—— *Persona eccl. S. Marie. Dom.* Joh. Dautree, 1385. Add. 21267.

—— —— Ric. Wystowe, 1417. Add. 22260.

—— *Rector eccl. S. Marie.* Hugo de Maydewell, early Hen. III. Add. 22101.

—— —— Joh. de Clipston, 1336. Add. 22163;—1337. Add. 22164;— 1342. Add. 21680.

—— —— *Dom.* Johannes, 1360. Add. 22180.

—— —— Will. Batesford *al.* Battisford, 1391. Add. 22231;—1392. Add. 22232;—1397. Add. 22236– 22238.

—— *Advocatus eccl. S. Petri.* Petr. fil. Ric. Rabaz, *t.* Hen. III. Add. 22089.

—— *Persona eccl. S. Petri.* Robertus, 1385. Add. 21267, 22222.

—— —— Ric. Forestere, 1414. Add. 21822.

—— *Rector eccl. S. Petri.* Petr. fil. Petr. Rabaz, *t.* Hen. III. Add. 22088, 22089, (as *persona*) 22110.

—— —— *Dom.* Rudulfus, 1294. Add. 22142;—1295. Add. 22143.

—— —— *Dom.* Ric. fil. dni. Steph. Rabaz, 1325. Add. 22153;—1326. Add. 22155;—1327. Add. 22156, 22157;—1329. Add. 22159, 22160;— 1337. Add. 22165;—1343. Add. 22167;—1344. Add. 22169, 22170.

—— —— *Dom.* Rad. Alday, 1360. Add. 22180.

—— —— *Dom.* Sim. Godbody, 1367. Add. 22190;—1373. Add. 22192;— 1375. Add. 22195, 22196;—(*sup r rector*). 1379. Add. 22208.

—— *Parson of SS. Peter's and Mary's.* John Chapman, *clerk,* 1554. Add. 22074.

**Maighfeld.** *v.* Mayfield, *co. Suss.*

**Main Stonfield.** *v. sub* Chinley, *in Glossop, co. Derb.*

**Mainardeyvi.** *v.* Maenor Dewi, *co. Pemb.*

**Mainham,** *co. Kildare.* Grant of interest in the rectory, 1576 (Maynan *al.* Mayne). Harl. 86 G. 47.

**Maisemore,** *co. Glouc.* Grant of the manor and rectory to the see of Gloucester, 1541 (Maysmore). Cott. xiii. 31.

**Makenhavede, Maknade.** *v. sub* Preston next Faversham, *co. Kent.*

**Maker,** *co. Cornw.* Bond to abide award in Millbrook in, 1539. Harl. 48 I. 27.

**Makeseye.** *v.* Maxey, *co. Northt.*

**Makkeley, Makley,** *v.* Mackley, *in Sudbury, co. Derb.*

**Makstocke.** *v.* Maxstoke, *co. Warw.*

**Malbertorp, Malbretorp, etc.** *v.* Mablethorpe, *co. Linc.*

**Malbus Enderby.** *v.* Enderby, Mavis, *co. Linc.*

**Malden, Maldon.** *v.* Maulden, *co. Bedf.*

**Malden,** *co. Surr.* Grant of the manor to Merton College, 1264 (Meaudon). Harl. 53 H. 12 (*copy*).

—— Brief conc. a fire at, 1797. Ch. Br. B. xxxvii. 7.

**Maldon,** *co. Essex.* Grant of, by Matilda the Empress to G. de Mandeville, [1141 ?] (Meldona). Cott. xvi. 27.

—— Ordinance conc. rights of the Carmelite Friars of, and Bileigh Abbey in, 1300 (Maldona). Cott. v. 33.

—— Leases, etc., in, 1341. Cott. xxvii. 7 (Magna Maldone);—1540. Add. 15608, 15609;—1551. Add. 15611;—1556. Add. 15618, 15619;— 1585. Add. 5982;—1616. Harl. 111 F. 33;—1618. Harl. 85 H. 22;— 1623. Harl. 49 E. 11;—1661. Add. 5984;—1662. Add. 5985, 5986.

—— Bequest to All Saints' church in, 1341. Cott. xxvii. 7.

—— Copies of deeds conc. the tenement called Selyhous, 1342–1427. Harl. Roll O. 32.

—— Lease of Portmanmershe *al.* Portmammershe in, from the corporation, 1502. Harl. 58 F. 3.

—— *Bailiffs.* Edw. Coker, Rich. Josua, 1562. Harl. 58 F. 3.

Manby (Manneby, etc.), co. Linc. Grants, etc., in, [1281-2?]. Harl. 50 F. 29;—1355. Harl. 57 G. 11:—1359. Harl. 57 G. 13;—1362. Harl. 53 C. 49.

—— Grants, etc., of the manor and advowson, 1359. Harl. 57 G. 12;—1362. Harl. 56 E. 28;—1447. Harl. 45 G. 62.

—— Precipe on a covenant conc. land in, 1378. Add. 25097.

—— Persona. Dom. Willelmus, 1359. Harl. 57 G. 12.

Manchester, co. Lanc. Acquittance for rent of the manor, 1331 (Mamcestre). Campb. ii. 20.

—— Persone. Sire Johan de Claidone, 1331. Campb. ii. 20;—1339. Harl. 57 E. 21.

Mandeviles. v. sub Sternfield, co. Suff.

Manecrofte. v. sub Chippenham, co. Wilts.

Manfield, co. York. Re-grant in, [1146-54?] (Manafeld). Harl. 48 G. 43.

Mangerton, co. Dors. Fine, etc., in, 1333. Harl. 49 H. 54 (Manggerton), 55;—1352. Harl. 54 D. 17;—1392. Harl. 56 E. 32;—1479. Harl. 46 H. 31.

—— Grants, etc., of the manor, 1350 (Mangertone). Harl. 57 A. 19;—1438. Harl. 50 E. 6;—1447. Harl. 56 F. 11-13;—1449. Harl. 46 H. 24, 25.

—— Court-roll, 1433. Harl. Roll I. 4.

Mangesford. v. Manningford, co. Wilts.

Mangreen, in Swardestone, co. Norf. Conveyance in, 1449 (Mangreue). Harl. 53 E. 37.

Manistya Fen. v. sub Connington, co. Hunt.

Manley Wapentake, co. Linc. Ballivus. Ric. Robard, 1385. Add. 22568.

Manningford, co. Wilts. Conf. of the chapel to Fontenelle Abbey, [1142-80] (Mangesford). Add. 8071 (6) (copy).

—— Release in, t. Edw. I. (Manigford). Harl. 54 G. 17.

—— Fine of the manor, 1638. Woll. xi. 29.

Manningham, co. York. Grant in, 1457. Add. 16948, 16949.

Manningtree, co. Essex. Lists of patrons of the chapel, late 14 cent. (Manyngtre). Harl. 58 F. 48.

—— Conveyance in Mistley, co. Essex, to the Guild of the H. Trinity, 1481 (Manytre). Add. 15604.

—— Precipe on a covenant conc. land in, 1592 (Mannyngtre). Add. 24998.

—— Rector. John Langham, 1481. Add. 15604.

Mansbridge. v. sub Stoneham, South, co. Southt.

Mansell Lacy, co. Heref. Lease of the demesnes, c. 1433 (Malmeshulle Lacy). Harl. 53 H. 17.

—— Bond of warranty in, 1599. Add. 26018.

Mansfield, co. Nott. Grant of, with its soke, to R., Earl of Chester, [1153] (Mammesfeld). Cott. xvii. 2.

—— Statutes of the Grammar School, 1564 (Mawnsfelde). Add. 13937.

—— Power for surrender in, from the Governors of the Grammar School, 1785. Add. 13940.

—— Vicar. John Durham, 1785. Add. 13940.

Manthorpe, nr. Witham on the Hill, co. Linc. Lease in, from Croyland Abbey, early 13 cent. (Mannethorp). Campb. iv. 4.

Manthorpe, nr. Grantham, co. Linc. Grant, etc., in, 1465. Add. 6473;—1468. Add. 6474;—1490. Add. 6476;—1492. Add. 6477;—1588. Add. 10419.

Mapeham. v. Meopham, co. Kent.

Mapelton. v. Mappleton, co. York.

Maperleigh, Maperley, etc. v. Mapperley, in Kirk Hallam, co. Derb.

Maplebeck, co. Nott. Grant in, late 13 cent. (Mapilbec). Add. 6173.

Mapledurham, co. Southt. Compotus rolls of the manor, 1424-7. Add. 26870, 26871;—1499-1500. Add. 26873;—1511-12. Add. 26874.

Mapledurham, West, co. Southt. Court-roll, 1625. Add. 24825.

Maplestead, Great and Little, co. Essex. Conf. by Edw. the Confessor of a grant in, to Westminster Abbey, 1066 [sc. 1065] (Mapulderstede). Cott. vi. 2 (copy).

**Marden**, *co. Heref.* Grants, etc., in, 1419. Harl. 112 B. 46 (Maurlyn);—1614. Add. 1906;—1654. Add. 1953.

—— Lease of the demesne of, *c.* 1433 (Mawardyn). Harl. 53 H. 17.

—— Leases of the manor, 1667 (Mawarden). Woll. xii. 121;—1679. Woll. xii. 130;—1687. Woll. xii. 120.

**Marden** (Merdenne, etc.), *co. Kent.* Grant in Shiphurst (Sipherste) in, to Combwell Priory, *t.* Hen. III. Harl. 77 F. 22.

—— Grants, etc., on the den of Frithenden *al.* Frithindenn, Fridynden, Frythyndenne, etc., in, 1282-3. Harl. 79 C. 54;—1301. Harl. 80 D. 53;—1314. Harl. 76 F. 4, 5;—1375. Harl. 79 C. 28;—1388. Harl. 79 C. 29;—1389. Harl. 79 C. 30;—1422. Harl. 80 B. 30;—1440. Harl. 77 F. 21;—1445. Harl. 79 C. 26;—1450. Harl. 78 H. 43;—1471. Harl. 80 E. 51;—1473. Harl. 79 B. 39, 40;—1474. Harl. 80 A. 38;—1490. Harl. 78 A. 25.

—— Grants on Elhurst den in, 1345. Harl. 80 I. 65;—1408. Harl. 78 H. 42;—1410. Harl. 80 I. 67;—1417. Harl. 80 B. 28;—1419. Harl. 77 E. 46;—1423. Harl. 80 I. 70;—1440. Harl. 77 E. 53;—1442. Harl. 76 D. 25, 80 B. 31, 80 D. 26;—1450. Harl. 78 H. 43;—1471. Harl. 80 E. 51;—1561. Harl. 77 A. 3.

—— Grants, etc., in, 1370. Harl. 80 B. 29;—1375. Harl. 79 C. 24;—1380. Add. 6260;—1386. Harl. 79 C. 25;—1388. Harl. 80 I. 66;—1390. Harl. 79 G. 3 (Meredenne);—1397. Harl. 79 E. 55;—1399. Harl. 79 E. 56;—*t.* Rich. II. Harl. 80 A. 16;—1406. Harl. 80 D. 17;—1409. Harl. 80 D. 55;—1418. Harl. 78 D. 54;—1419. Harl. 75 G. 82;—1422. Harl. 75 G. 21;—1430. Harl. 80 D. 29;—1432. Harl. 76 A. 8;—1433. Harl. 76 G. 51;—1437. Harl. 80 A. 18;—1441. Harl. 76 A. 9;—1443. Harl. 80 D. 56;—1465. Harl. 80 B. 27;—1466. Harl. 80 B. 26;—1476. Harl. 76 F. 13;—1479. Harl. 80 B. 18;—1481. Harl. 78 C. 36;—1492. Harl. 77 G. 31;—1497. Harl. 78 G. 40, 41;—*c.* 1498. Harl. 79 B. 41;—1558. Harl. 77 E. 55;—1559. Harl. 76 I. 43, 44, 77 G. 24;—1561. Harl. 77 A. 4.

—— Grants, etc., on Widehurst *al.* Wytherst den in, 1405. Harl. 80 H. 40;—1407. Harl. 80 C. 37;—1415. Harl. 78 G. 17;—1416. Harl. 78 G.

37 *a*;—1428. Harl. 78 A. 13;—1443. Harl. 76 G. 5;—1444. Harl. 79 B. 38;—1451. Harl. 79 D. 81;—1470. Harl. 79 D. 33, 34;—1477. Harl. 78 H. 32, 79 D. 32, 35;—1498. Harl. 80 B. 19.

—— Grants, etc., on Henhurst (Engeherst) den in, 1405. Harl. 76 F. 11;—1432. Harl. 80 B. 35;—1449. Harl. 76 G. 55;—1463. Harl. 79 C. 27, 79 E. 4;—1465. Harl. 79 E. 5.

—— Settlement of Read (Rede) manor in, 1411. Add. 16464.

—— Grant on Bugeherst den in, 1428. Harl. 79 E. 57.

—— Release on Lit. Ridden den in, 1445. Harl. 79 C. 26.

—— Grant on N. Horehurst den in, 1445. Harl. 80 I. 17.

—— Sale, etc., on Bishiche den in, 1451. Harl. 79 D. 31;—1477. Harl. 78 H. 32;—1561. Harl. 77 A. 3.

—— Grants, etc., on Wanses and Pageherst dens in, 1486. Harl. 76 E. 20, 25;—1489. Harl. 76 E. 19.

—— Lease of the rectory, 1569. Harl. 77 A. 26.

—— Rents of Lady Packington's manor of Read in, *c.* 1600. Cott. ix. 10 (1).

—— Survey of Lady Packington's lands in Read in, 1619. Cott. xxix. 51.

—— Bockingfold manor in. *v. sub* Brenchley, *co. Kent.*

——— *Capellanus.* Ricardus, *t.* Hen. III. Harl. 77 F. 22.

——— *Vicarius.* Pet. Gunthorp, 1416. Harl. 78 G. 37*a*;—1418. Harl. 78 D. 54.

**Marden Ash**, *co. Essex.* Grants, etc., in, 1314. Cott. xii. 40 (Marlene);—1334. Add. 19984;—1347. Add. 19985.

**Marden, East**, *co. Suss.* Fine in, by Boxgrave Priory, 1280 (Estmerdon). Add. 20067.

**Marden, West**, *co. Suss.* Acquittance in, 1474 (Westmerdon). Harl. 51 A. 28.

**Mardley Bury**, *co. Hertf.* Sale of timber in the manor of, 1363 (Mardeleebury). Harl. 49 F. 7.

**Marefield**, *in Tilton, co. Leic.* Conf. of the chapel, etc., to Ouston Abbey, 1343 (Mardefeld). Add. 21391.

—— Covenant for a flue in, 1608 (Murfield). Add. 5145.

**Marefield,** *in Tilton, co. Leic. (continued).* Summons to prove title in, 1610 (Southmarfeild). Harl. 75 F. 6.

—— Fine in, 1686 (Marfeld). Add. 23781.

**Mareham le Fen,** *co. Linc.* Grant in, 1362 (Marum juxta Revesby). Cott. v. 18.

—— License for grant in, to Greenfield Priory, 1392 (Marum). Harl. 43 G. 53.

—— *Persona. Dom.* Will. Hardegrey, late 13 cent. (do.). Harl. 56 H. 19.

—— *Sacerdos.* Robertus, late 12 cent. (do.). Harl. 48 C. 10.

**Mareham on the Hill** (?), *co. Linc. Presbyter de Maring.* Willelmus, late Hen. II. Harl. 45 B. 42;—(as *Sacerdos*), late 12 cent. Harl. 45 C. 1.

**Maresfield,** *co. Suss.* Grant of the church, free chapel and manor by Edw. III., to Prince John, his sou, 1372 (Marsfeld). Cott. xv. 1.

—— Grant in, 1547. Add. 1376.

**Marewe.** *v.* Merrow, *co. Surr.*

**Margam,** *co. Glam.* Grants, etc., in, to Margam Abbey, [1147-73]. Harl. 75 A. 9;—early 13 cent. Harl. 75 B. 32.

—— Marriage settlement in, early 13 cent. Harl. 75 D. 4.

—— Lease of Terris grange, etc., in (?), by Margam Abbey, 1470. Harl. 75 A. 46.

**Margaretting,** *co. Essex.* Grant of Coptfold (Cupefald) in, to Southwark Priory, [1138-49]. Cott. MS. Nero C. iii. f. 228.

—— Precipe on a covenant conc. Coptfoldhall *al.* Coldehall manor, etc., in, 1575 (Gyngemargerett *al.* Margettinge). Add. 24945.

—— Precipes on covenants conc. lands in, 1587 (Margaretinge). Add. 24983; —1592 (Ging Margrett). Add. 25012.

**Marham,** *co. Norf.* Grant with conf. in, to Rudham Priory, [1146-8]. Harl. 47 H. 45.

—— Grant of free tenants and villeins in, [1249-57]. Harl. 57 E. 31.

—— Grant of estate in the manor, 1419. Harl. 49 F. 23.

**Marhas Vyhan,** [*nr. Camborne?*], *co. Cornw.* Power to give seisin in, 1417. Add. 15354.

**Mariland, Marilont.** *v. sub* Syresham, *co. Northt.*

**Marisden.** *v.* Rendcombe, Over, *co. Glouc.*

**Markel Magna, Markele Major.** *v.* Marcle, Much, *co. Heref.*

**Markenfield,** *co. York. Dominus.* Tho. de Merkyngfeld, 1415. Add. 16900, 16901.

**Market Bosworth.** *v.* Bosworth, Market, *co. Leic.*

**Market Harborough.** *v.* Harborough, Market, *co. Leic.*

**Market Rasen.** *v.* Rasen, Market, *co. Linc.*

**Markfield,** *co. Leic. Capellanus.* Robertus, [1241-64] (Marcefeld). Campb. xv. 11.

—— *Clericus.* Simon, [1241 - 64]. Campb. xv. 11.

**Marks.** *v. sub* Dunmow, Great, *co. Essex.*

**Marks Tey.** *v.* Tey, Marks, *co. Essex.*

**Marksbury** (Merkesbury, etc.), *co. Som.* Grants, etc., in, 1279. Add. 5438 (Merkesbire)—5442;—*c.* 1280. Add. 5443 (Merkesbyre);—1308. Add. 5446; — 1310. Add. 5447; — 1313. Add. 5448; — 1336. Add. 5452;— 1359-1373. Add. 5456 (Marcusbury) —5465;—1445. Add. 5468;—1472. Add. 5473.

—— Suit conc. lands in, *t.* Rich. II. Add. 6267.

**Markshall,** *co. Essex.* Grants in, to Colne Priory, *t.* Hen. III.-*t.* Edw. I. (?). Add 26405 (2,3) (Markeshale, Merkeshale) (*copies*).

—— *Persona.* Walt. de Gosewold, 1338. Add. 6181.

**Marland,** *co. Lanc.* Grant of, to Stanlaw Abbey, [1194-1211] (Merlande). Harl. 52 H. 43 *a.*

**Marlborough,** *co. Wilts.* Conf. by Hen. II. of a grant in (?), to Reading Abbey, [1157] (Merleberg). Add. 19591.

—— Grants, etc., in, 1390. Add. 15264 (Marlebergh); — 1532. Add. 5695, 5696 (Marleburgh); — 1535. Add. 5697.

—— *Constabularius Castri.* Joh. de Rochiz, *miles,* 1390. Add. 15264.

—— *Major.* Rob. Warner (?), 1390. Add. 15264.

Marlborough, *co. Wilts (continued)*.
*Major (continued)*. Ric. Diconson,
1532. Add. 5695, 5696.

—— *Prepositi*. Joh. Jeuewynne, Tho.
Cripse, Walt. Joop, Joh. Brid, Ric.
Grymbald, Will. Garlic, 1390. Add.
15264.

Marledge, *nr. Cheriton, co. Pemb*.
Inspex. of records conc. lands in,
1387 (Merlinche). Slo. xxxii. 19.

Marles Hall. *v. sub* Milding, *co. Suff.*

Marlesford, *co. Suff.* Covenant for
recovery in, 1618. Add. 9786, 9787.

Marlingford, *co. Norf.* Grant in,
1338. Add. 19405.

Marloes, *co. Pemb.* Grants nr., [1234-
41]. Add. 8412 (Malros);—[1241-5].
Add. 8413.

Marlow, Great, *co. Buck.* Fines in,
1574. Add. 19191;—1631. Harl. 80
D. 9.

—— Covenant for repair of the lock,
1628. Add. 13703.

—— Conveyance, etc., in, 1631. Harl.
76 F. 37-39, 77 H. 12;—1634. Harl.
75 H. 49, 76 F. 43.

—— *Persona*. Edm. Strete, 1384.
Add. 23629.

Marlow, Little, *co. Buck.* Recovery,
etc., of Losemore manor in, 1553. Harl.
76 E. 12;—1561. Harl. 75 H. 24;—
1562. Harl. 75 H. 11;—1631. Harl.
76 F. 37-39, 77 H. 12, 80 D. 9;—
1634. Harl. 75 H. 49, 76 F. 48;—
1641. Harl. 77 H. 13.

Marnham, *co. Nott.* Grant in, 1412.
Add. 15740.

Marnhull, *co. Dors.* Fine in, for a
chantry, 1282. Add. 5250.

—— Conveyance, etc., of More manor,
etc., in, 1453. Harl. 53 A. 24, 54 D. 19.

—— Bond conc. judgment on the
issues of More manor, 1498. Harl.
53 C. 13.

—— Crown appointment of a steward
of the manor, 1572 (Marnehull). Harl.
75 E. 41.

—— *Rector*. Will. de Selton, 1314.
Add. 13014.

Marple, *co. Chest. (?)*. Release in,
1548 (Marpull). Woll. xii. 56.

Marscotes croft. *v. sub* Hartlip, *co.
Kent.*

Marsden. *v. sub* Huddersfield, *co. York.*

Marsden, *co. Lanc.* Brief for rebuilding the chapel, 1804. Ch. Br. B. xliv.
10.

Marsfeld. *v.* Maresfield, *co. Suss.*

Marsh, *co. Buck.* Exemption of the
manor from ecclesiastical taxation,
1372 (Mersh). Harl. Roll AA. 24.

Marsh Maund. *v. sub* Bodenham,
*co. Heref.*

Marsh Willoughby. *v.* Willoughby,
*co. Linc.*

Marshal, Earls, *Honour of*. Extent
of knights' fees bel. to, in cos. Norf.,
Suff. and Essex, *c.* 1400. Add. 19338.

Marsham, *co. Norf.* Grant of tithes
in, to St. Paul's Hosp., Norwich, [1121-
30]. Cott. ii. 19 (1) (*copy*).

—— Suit conc. tithes in, betw. the
rector and Norwich Priory, 1247.
Cott. ii. 19 (16) (*copy*).

—— Conveyance in, 1420. Add.
14806.

Marshfield, *co. Glouc.* Re-feoffment
in, 1452 (Merschefeld). Harl. 112
B. 9.

—— Grant of the manor. 1548 (Mershefeilde). Add. 13180.

Marshfield, *co. Monm.* Precipes on
covenants conc. lands in, 1592 (Merch-
fyld). Add. 25123;—1593. Add.
25136, 25137.

Marshland, *in Whitgift, co. York.*
Ref. to suit against St. Mary's Abbey,
York, for lands in, 1302 (Merslaudia).
Add. 17155, 17156.

Marshwood, *co. Dors.* Release of
rent "pro term de la Hull" in the
manor of, early Hen. III. (Merswode).
Add. 15436.

—— Grant in Purcombe (Piricume),
etc., held of the manor of, *t.* Hen. III.
Cott. xii. 38.

—— Grant, etc., of La Strete in the
manor of, *t.* Hen. III. Harl. 54 H. 37
(Mersuude);—1329. Harl. 47 H. 4
(Merschwode);—1411. Harl. 46 G. 55.

—— Grants at Stone in, 1307 (Merswode). Harl. 57 F. 29;—1338. Harl.
46 F. 26.

—— Fine in, 1340 (Mersschwode).
Harl. 47 H. 7.

—— Grants, etc., in, 1396. Add.
15444 (Merschwode);—1409. Harl.
55 G. 43, 44 (Mershwode);—1410.
Harl. 51 F. 40, 41 (Mershwode).

—— *Capellanus*. Will. Pcw, 1331.
Harl. 45 E. 68.

Marshwood Hundred, *co. Dors.*
Petition of Cerne Abbey conc. claims
for suit to, for Symondsbury manor,
[1377–81?] (Hundr. de Mershwode).
Campb. xiii. 4.

Marshwood Vale, *co. Dors.* Conveyance, etc., in Bluntshay and else-
where in, 1331. Harl. 45 E. 68
(Mershoudewalle);—1338. Harl. 46
F. 26 (Vallis de Merchewod);—1379.
Harl. 48 F. 42 (Merashwodevale);—
1414. Harl. 50 D. 12 (Mershwodevale);
—1438. Harl. 50 E. 6.

—— Acquittance for farm of, paid to
Henry, Prince of Wales, 1413. Add.
15449 (Merswodevale).

*v. also* Whitchurch Canonicorum,
*co. Dors.*

Marske, *in Lungbargh Wapentake, co.
York.* Grant, etc., in, 1321. Harl.
112 H. 36 (Merske);—1426. Harl.
112 F. 63 (Mersk in Cleveland).

Marston, *co. Bedf.* A boundary mark,
969 (Mercstuninga gemære). Add.
19793.

Marston, *co. Glouc.* Covenant conc.
settlement of the manor, 1350 (Mershton). Harl. 54 D. 28.

Marston, *co. Linc.* Conf. of grant in,
to Greenfield Priory, *ante* 1166 (Merstona). Harl. 51 D. 21.

—— Leases in, to Haverholme Priory,
by Greenfield Priory, late 12 cent.
(Merstun). Harl. 44 D. 53, 54.

—— Rent-bond in, from Haverholme
Priory to Greenfield Priory, *c.* 1200
(Merstona). Harl. 44 E. 18.

—— Grant in, to Haverholme Priory,
1401 (Mershton). Harl. 44 E. 6.

—— *Rector.* Humfridus Ferrore,
*t.* Hen. VIII. Add. 6442.

Marston, *co. Staff.* Brief for rebuilding the church, 1814. Ch. Br. B. lv. 1.

Marston, *in Bickenhill, co. Warw.*
Grant by Hen. III. of free warren in,
1257 (Waure Merston). Woll. v. 21.

—— Sale of the manor, 1573 (Waver-
merstone). Cott. xii. 32.

Marston, *in Bulkington, co. Warw.*
Covenant betw. Leicester and Combe
Abbeys conc. tithes, 1232 (Mcrston).
Harl. 83 A. 32.

Marston, *nr. Devizes, co. Wilts.* Release in, 1309 (Merstone). Add. 7066.

Marston Bigott, *co. Som.* Grants,
etc., in, late Hen. III. Harl. 80 C. 2
(Merstona);—1317. Harl. 80 E. 45;

—1348. Add. 7826–7828 (Merston
Bygod);—1349. Harl. 77 F. 19
(Mershton Bygod);—1361. Harl. 75
D. 59 *a, b* (Merston) (*copies*);—1382.
Harl. 76 E. 4;—1400. Harl. 80 E. 55
(Merschton);—1465. Harl. 78 I. 55
(Merasheton Bygotte).

—— Royal conf. to Witham Priory of
rent, etc., in Monksham (La Monekes-
ham in Selewod in paroch. de
Mershton) in, 1349. Campb. xiii. 18.

—— Lease at Monksham (La
Monekeshamme) in, from Witham
Priory. 1350. Campb. xiii. 16.

—— Declaration against claims of
tenants in Yarnfield, etc., co. Som.,
to common in the woods of, late 14
cent. (Merstonebygod). Harl. 79 B. 45.

Marston, Broad, *in Pebworth, co.
Glouc.* Manumission in, 1448 (Brode-
merston). Add. 24773.

Marston, Butlers, *co. Warw.* Grant
of the church to Alcester Abbey, *c.*
1140 (Mersetona). Add. 21494.

—— Precipe on a covenant conc. land
in, 1592. Add. 25547.

Marston Culey, *nr. Bickenhill, co.
Warw.* Precipe on a covenant conc.
land in, 1592. Add. 25551.

Marston, Fleet, *co. Buck.* Sale in,
1545. Add. 19541.

Marston, Lea. *v.* Lea Marston, *co.
Warw.*

Marston Maisey (?), *co. Wilts.* Royal
grant of the manor, etc., late bel. to
Farley Priory, 1510. Add. 26022.

Marston Montgomery, *co. Derb.*
Power to give seisin of two parts of
the manor, 1428 (Merston Mountgomery). Woll. ix. 51.

—— Award conc. lands in Waldley
in, and for a rent charge on the lordship of, 1472 (Merston Montgomere).
Woll. ix. 49.

—— Covenant for fine in, 1652. Woll.
xii. 102.

Marston Moretaine, *co. Bedf.*
Grant, etc., in, 1461. Add. 17384
(Merston Morteyn);—1605. Add. 1980.

—— *Persona.* Willelmus, 1358. Cott.
xxvii. 156.

—— —— Will. de Stokes, 1381.
Harl. 84 F. 6;—(as *Rector*), 1391.
Add. 15435.

Marston, North, *co. Buck.* Release
in, 1486 (Northmerston). Lansd. 575.

**Marston, Potters,** *co. Leic.* Grant in, to Sulby Abbey, *c.* 1240–50 (Merstona). Add. 21692;—*t.* Hen. III. Add. 22311.

**Marston, Priors,** *co. Warw.* Power to give seisin in, 1405 (Prioris Merston). Cott. xii. 8.

—— Precipe on a covenant. conc. the manor, 1558 (Priors Merston). Add. 25543.

**Marston St. Lawrence,** *co. Northt. Diaconus.* Willelmus, early 13 cent. (Merston). Harl. 86 B. 28.

**Marston Trussel,** *co. Northt.* Grant in, to St. Mary's chapel, early Hen. III. (Merston). Harl. 57 A. 53.

—— *Dominus.* Ric. Trussel, *t.* Hen. III. Add. 21366, 22433.

**Marston upon Dove,** *co. Derb.* Grant in, [1254–78] (Merston). Woll. ix. 67.

*v. also* Hatton, *co. Derb.*

*v. also* Hilton, *co. Derb.*

**Marsworth,** *co. Buck.* Release of Goldingtons manor in, 1575. Add. 24049.

**Martelbeche,** *in Upwell* (?). *cos. Camb. and Norf.* Grant nr., to W. Dereham Abbey, early 13 cent. Toph. 17.

**Martenesia, Insula de,** *nr. Glastonbury, co. Som.* Conf. of the jurisdiction of the Abbat of Glastonbury in, 1344. Campb. xiii. 19.

**Martham,** *co. Norf.* Grant and conf. in, to Norwich Priory, [1103–6?]. Cott. MS. Aug. ii. 103, Cott. ii. 21 (1) (*copies*);—[1136–45]. Cott. ii. 1, 21 (9) (*copy*).

—— Grant in, *t.* Edw. I. Add. 14763; —1379. Add. 14954.

—— Release of a moiety of the manor, 1361. Harl. 52 B. 11.

—— Grant of the manor to Cobham College, 1369 (Merthum). Harl. 48 F. 8.

—— License to Cobham College to exchange the manor with Norwich Priory, 1369 (Mertham). Harl. 43 E. 4.

—— License for grant in Scratby and Ormsby, parcel of the manor of, to Cobham College, 1372. Harl. 47 G. 3.

—— Compotus of the manor, 1376–79. Harl. 48 E. 31, 34.

—— Letter from the Prior of Norwich conc. the manor, 1378. Harl. 43 B. 25.

—— Exchange of the manor, 1380. Harl. 43 I. 23, 44 C. 33, 44 G. 16, 44 H. 39, 41.

**Martham,** *co. Norf.* (*continued*). Acquittance from the Prior of Norwich on sale of stock of the manor, 1382. Harl. 44 H. 40.

**Marthiltwy.** *v.* Martletwy, *co. Pembr.*

**Martin** (Marton, Martun), *nr. Horncastle, co. Linc.* Grants, etc., in, to Kirkstead Abbey, *c.* 1150–60. Harl. 50 B. 18;—early 13 cent. Cott. xxvii. 62;—1365. Harl. 58 C. 2;—1370. Harl. 44 F. 8, 49 A. 43;—1376. Harl. 47 H. 15.

—— Lease in, from Kirkstead Abbey, late 12 cent. Harl. 44 E. 57.

—— Grants, etc., in, *t.* John–*t.* Hen. III. Cott. xxvii. 63, Harl. 48 A. 36, 58 B. 45;—1302. Harl. 45 H. 18;— 1332. Harl. 58 B. 49, 50;—1351. Cott. xxx. 30;—1370. Harl. 56 B. 49.

—— Lease in, to Stainfield Priory, by Kirkstead Abbey, 1278. Harl. 44 F. 3.

—— Reservation of service in Woodhall, etc., co. Linc., to the Hospital of, 1331. Harl. 58 B. 49.

—— *Vicarius.* Johannes, *t.* Hen. III. Harl. 48 A. 36.

**Martin** (Marton, Martun), *in Timberland, co. Linc.* Grant in the marsh of, to Bullington Priory, *t.* Hen. III. Cott. xii. 51.

—— Grants, etc., in, to Kirkstead Abbey, *t.* Hen. III.-Edw. I. Cott. xii. 34, xxvii. 129, xxix. 79, Harl. 47 G. 52;—1294. Harl. 48 H. 18;—1307. Harl. 48 H. 19.

—— Inquisition on land in, bel. to Kirkstead Abbey, 1301. Harl. 44 F. 2.

—— Lease in, by Kirkstead Abbey, &c. 1307. Cott. xxi. 21.

—— Marriage settlement of "les passages de Martonedyk," 1343. Harl. 57 G. 9.

—— *Clericus.* Andreas, *t.* Edw. I. Harl. 46 A. 36.

**Martin,** *co. Nott.* Fine in, with conf., 1217. Cott. v. 24 (Marton.);—*t.* Hen. III. Harl. 51 G. 47 (Martun).

**Martin Husingtree,** *co. Worc.* Conf. of grants in, to Pershore Abbey, 972 (on Meretun). Cott. MS. Aug. ii. 6.

—— *Persona.* Walt. Hay, [1357–77] (Merton). Add. 9239.

**Martinsthorpe,** *co. Rutl.* Feoffment, etc., of the manor and advowson, 1383. Add. 22213, 22214; — 1385. Add. 22215, 22216;—1419. Add. 21186;—

1422. Add. 22263, 22264;— [ante 1437]. Add. 21265.

—— Defeasance of feoffment in, 1385 (Martynsthorpe). Add. 21185.

**Martlesham,** co. Suff. Grant, etc., in, 1328. Add. 10193;—1612. Add. 10244.

**Martletwy,** co. Pembr. Release in, 1332 (Marthiltwy). Add. 23850.

**Martley,** co. Worc. Grants in, in the manor of, etc., t. Edw. I.-II. Harl. 111 G. 37 (Marteleve);—1312. Harl. 111 E. 55 (Mertele):—1323. Harl. 111 G. 38 (Murteleye);—1583. Add. 15276.

—— Rector. Petrus dictus Fillol, 1323. Harl. 111 G. 38.

**Martock,** co. Som. Grant of rent charge on the church of, to St. Michael's Mount Abbey, [1192-1205] (Mertock). Add. 19065, 19066 (copies).

—— Covenant conc. the church of, 1226 (Mertok). Add. 19067 (copy).

—— Rector. Bartholomeus, Archidiaconus Winton., 1226. Add. 19067.

**Marton.** v. Martin, co. Linc.

—— v. Martin, co. Nott.

**Marton,** in Aylesburne, co. Suff. Feoffment of a moiety of the manor, 1444. Harl. 83 F. 3, 4.

**Marton,** co. Warw. Release in, to Studley Priory, 1338 (Merton). Harl. 58 E. 1.

**Marton,** in S. Damerham, co. Wilts. Conf. by Will. I. of a grant in, to Westminster Abbey, 1067 (Mertune). Cott. vi. 3 (copy).

—— Grant of a market and fair in the manor to Glastonbury Abbey, 1266 (Merton). Harl. 58 I. 22 (copy).

**Marton,** N. R., co. York. Grant at Swarthowflat, etc., in (?), early Hen. III. Add. 20597.

**Marton,** in Pickering Lathe, co. York. Release of a nativus in (?), to Ellerton Priory, t. Hen. III. Campb. iii. 18.

**Marton in the Forest,** co. York. Conf. of grant of, to Marton Priory, late Hen. III. (Marton). Cott. xi. 42.

—— Curate. Rich. Musgrave, 1738. Add. 16159.

**Marum.** v. Mareham le Fen, co. Linc.

**Marwood,** co. Devon. Power to give seisin in, 1311 (Merewode). Harl. 56 E. 16.

**Marystood Wood.** v. sub Worplesdon, co. Surr.

**Masbrough,** in Rotherham, co. York. Mortgage in, 1746. Add. 18077.

**Mashbury,** co. Essex. Evidence conc. seizure of the manor, 1341 (Maschobiry). Cott. xiii. 5 (5).

—— Release in, 1473 (Masshburye). Harl. 43 F. 5.

**Maskelsbury.** v. sub Roothing, White, co. Essex.

**Massingham, Little,** co. Norf. Persona. Joh. de Kalthorp, 1292. Add. 9838.

**Matching,** co. Essex. Grant in, t. Hen. III. (Maching). Harl. 55 D. 49.

**Matfield,** in Brenchley, co. Kent. Ref. to, as a boundary, [1227-35] (Mattefeld). Campb. xiv. 3.

**Matham.** v. sub Rolvenden, co. Kent.

**Mathefeild, Over.** v. Mayfield, Upper, co. Staff.

**Matherne,** co. Monm. Inspex., in 1330, of a grant of the church, etc., to Usk Priory, c. 1150 (Mathenny). Add. 5342.

**Matishale.** v. Mattishall, co. Norf.

**Matlask,** co. Norf. Grants, etc., in, 1344. Add. 14764 (Matelask);—1347. Add. 14761;—1370. Add. 14867;—1416. Add. 14820 (Madelask);—1417. Add. 14821.

—— Grant and lease of the manor, etc., 1434. Add. 17738;—1435. Add. 17739.

—— Bequests to the church, etc., 1482 (Matelask). Add. 17253.

**Matlock** (Matlok, etc.), co. Derb. Grants, etc.. 1325. Woll. i. 8;—1349. Woll. i. 6, 7;—1350. Woll. x. 13;—1452. Woll. i. 9;—1473. Woll. iii. 16;—1486. Woll. iii. 17;—1533. Woll. xi. 71 (Mattelocke); — 1534. Woll. xi. 69 (Mattlok);—1536. Woll. xi. 72;—1540. Woll. xi. 68, 70;—1541. Woll. ii. 71;—1543. Woll. iii. 18;—1595. Woll. xi. 90;—1597. Woll. xii. 4;—1599. Woll. xi. 4, 11 (copy);—1608. Woll. xi. 110;—1610. Woll. xi. 83;—1611. Woll. xi. 105;—1614. Woll. xii. 62;—1616. Woll. ii. 82;—1702. Woll. xi. 73.

—— Extracts from court-rolls, 1473. Woll. iii. 16;—1486. Woll. iii. 17;—1543. Woll. iii. 18.

**Matlock** (Matlok, etc.), *co. Derb.* (*continued*). Rentals in, 1485. Woll. xi. 15, 16;—1509. Woll. xi. 18.

—— Exemplif. of judgment in suit conc. seizure of cattle at, 1547 (Matlokke). Woll. xi. 32.

—— Fine of the manor, 1638. Woll. xi. 29.

—— *Senescallus.* Nic. Longford, *miles*, 1473. Woll. iii. 16.

—— —— Joh. Savage, *miles*, 1486. Woll. iii. 17.

—— —— Thurstan Wodcok, 1543. Woll. iii. 18.

• **Matravers Chylrye.** *v. sub* Childrey, *co. Berks.*

**Mattishall,** *co. Norf.* Grant in, *t.* Edw. I. (Matishale). Add. 6315.

**Mattishall Burgh,** *co. Norf.* Nomination of John Deen to the living, 1439 (Matyshale Bergh). Harl. 53 E. 38.

**Maubache.** *v.* Meerbach, *nr. Bredwardine, co. Heref.*

**Mauberthorp, Maubertorp.** *v.* Mablethorpe, *co. Linc.*

**Mauchline,** *in Kyle, co. Ayr.* Conf. of grant in, to Melrose Abbey, 1264. Campb. xxx. 8 (Mauhelyne);—1266. Cott. xviii. 3 (Mauchlyn).

**Maudalen's.** *v. sub* Berkhampstead, *co. Hertf.*

**Maugersbury,** *in Stow on the Wolds, co. Glouc.* Grant of lands nr., 949 (Mæpelgares byrig). Cott. viii. 6 (*copy*).

**Maulden,** *co. Bedf.* Feoffment, etc., in, 1430. Add. 26783 (Maldon);— 1568. Harl. 79 D. 44 (Malden).

**Mauncelhall** *al.* **Baynards manor.** *v. sub* St. Lawrence, *co. Essex.*

**Maund, Marsh** *al.* **Brian's, M. Rous and M. Whitechurch.** *v. sub* Bodenham, *co. Heref.*

**Maurdyn.** *v.* Marden, *co. Heref.*

**Mauricastona** [Aston by Sutton], *co. Ches.* Inspex. of grant in, to Whalley Abbey, 1344. Add. 1060.

**Mautby,** *co. Norf.* Grants, etc., in, late Hen. III. Add. 7366 (Mauteby); —1361. Harl. 52 B. 11;—1609. Add. 14762 (Mawtby).

—— Grant, etc., in, to Herringfleet Priory, *t.* Edw. I. Add. 17222 (Mautebi) (*copy*);—1361. Add. 17223.

**Mautby,** *co. Norf.* (*continued*). Release from Horsham Priory of arrears of salt in, 1292 (Malteby). Add. 19234.

—— Grant of the manor, 1347 (Mauteby). Add. 14761.

—— Conf. to Horsham Priory of a salt-rent in, [1481]. Add. 17252.

—— Bequests to the church, etc., 1482 (Mauteby). Add. 17253.

—— *Persona.* Robertus, early 13 cent. (Malteby). Add. 7362.

**Mavesyn Ridware.** *v.* Ridware, Mavesyn, *co. Staff.*

**Mawarden, Mawardyn.** *v.* Marden, *co. Heref.*

**Mawdelens, Mawdelyns, Mawdlens.** *v. sub* Berkhampstead, *co. Hertf.*

**Mawene Rous, and M. Wytechirche.** *v. sub* Bodenham, *co. Heref.*

**Mawgan in Meneage,** *co. Cornw.* Declaration conc. settlement of Carmenow manor in, 1488. Add. 15739.

—— Bond to pay tithes in, 1573. Add. 13083.

—— *Parson.* Rob. Fletcher, 1573. Add. 13083.

**Mawgan in Pyder,** *co. Cornw. Persona.* Will. Hendre, 1394. Harl. 51 E. 16.

**Mawnsfelde.** *v.* Mansfeld, *co. Nott.*

**Mawsley,** *co. Northt.* Grant in, *ante* 1185 (Mulesleia). Harl. 49 F. 53.

—— Fine in, 1387 (Malleslee). Add. 22402.

**Maxey,** *co. Northt.* Conf. of grant in, to the chapel, 1277 (Makeseyu). Harl. 43 G. 27.

—— License to found a chantry in St. Mary's chapel at, 1368 (Makeseye). Campb. v. 10.

—— Grant in Nunton, *co. Northt.*, to St. Mary's chapel, 1372 (Makeseye). Harl. 56 I. 32.

—— Grant, etc., in, 1387. Slo. xxxii. 54 (Makeseye);—1549. Add. 13561.

—— Jean, Comte d'Angoulême, imprisoned at, 1420. Add. 3532;—1423. Add. 312;—1427. Add. 336, 3610;— 1428. Add. 3626.

—— Precipe on a covenant conc. land in, 1578. Add. 25159.

—— *Vicar.* Will. Sherman, 1536. Cott. iv. 29.

**Maxstoke,** *co. Warw.* Inspex. of charter of W. de Clynton founding a chantry in the church, 1332. Cott. iv. 56.

—— Consent to appropriation of the church to Maxstoke Priory, 1336. Cott. iv. 7.

—— Sale of the manor, 1540 (Maxstocke). Harl. 47 A. 53.

—— Sale in, 1540 (Makstocke). Cott. ii. 15.

—— *Rector.* Dom. Johannes, 1332. Cott. iv. 56.

—— *Vicarius.* Willelmus, 1345. Cott. iv. 8.

—— —— Tho. Lucas, 1404. Add. 21420.

**Maydeford.** *v.* Maidford, *co. Northt.*

**Maydeston.** *v.* Maidstone, *co. Kent.*

**Maydeworthy.** *v. sub* Heavitree, *co. Devon.*

**Mayfield,** *co. Suss.* Conf. of seisin of Bevelham *al.* Bibleham manor in, 1446. Add. 23801, 23808 ; — 1455. Add. 23802.

—— Extent of the manor, 17 cent. (Maighfeld). Harl. Roll l. 5.

**Mayfield, Upper,** *co. Staff.* Lease in, 1597 (Over Mathefeild). Woll. xi. 58.

**Mayford,** *in Woking, co. Surr.* Grant, etc., in, *c.* 1214–30. Add. 26619 ;— 1308. Add. 26616.

**Mayham,** *nr. Hailsham, co. Suss.* Grant, etc., in, *t.* Edw. II. Add. 8091 (Megham) ;— 1321. Add. 8092 ;— 1402. Add. 8095 ;—1450. Add. 8097 ; — 1470. Add. 8098 ;—1474. Add. 8100 ;— 1507. Add. 8105 ; — 1508. Add. 8106, 8107 ;—1519. Add. 8110.

—— *v. also* Hailsham, *co. Suss.*

**Mayland,** *co. Essex.* Conveyance, etc., of Baynards *al.* Knipsho manor in, 1462. Harl. 53 D. 9, 56 E. 7.

—— Lease of Mayland Hall manor in, 1540. Harl. 77 F. 39.

**Maynan, Mayne.** *v.* Mainham, *co. Kildare.*

**Mayndencote,** [Maidencourt, *in E. Garston* ?], *co. Berks.* Power to give seisin of the manor, 1385. Harl. 56 A. 35.

**Maynebowe.** *v. sub* Buckfastleigh, *co. Devon.*

**Maynooth,** *co. Kildare.* Dispute conc. the manor, 1454. Cott. iv. 35.

**Maynor Weyno.** *v.* Vainor, *co. Brecon.*

**Maytham.** *v. sub* Rolvenden, *co. Kent.*

**Mayton.** *v. sub* Horstead, *co. Norf.*

**Meaford.** *v. sub* Stone, *co. Staff.*

**Meaphám.** *v.* Meopham, *co. Kent.*

**Meare,** *co. Som.* Conf. of the jurisdiction of the Abbat of Glastonbury in (?), 1344 (Insula de Ferramere). Campb. xiii. 19.

—— Conveyance of Stileway (Stiuelegh) manor in, 1413. Harl. 55 B. 20.

—— *Vicarius.* Joh. Elys, 1410 (Mere). Harl. 48 F. 47.

**Mearsætham.** *v.* Merstham, *co. Surr.*

**Meath,** *County of.* Escheats in, 1341–44. Add. 13597.

—— *Senescallus* [*Galfridi de Geynvill*] *de Mydia.* Hen. de Stratton, 1259. Harl. 50 G. 38.

**Meaudon.** *v.* Malden, *co. Surr.*

**Meaux,** *co. York.* Conf. of exchange of, for Bewick, *co.* York, [1163 or 4?] (Melsa). Cott. xi. 27.

**Meavy,** *co. Devon.* Grant in, 1031 (Mæwi). Cott. MS. Aug. ii. 69.

—— *Rector.* Joh. Cole, *Capellanus,* 1435. Add. 26164.

**Meavy,** —(?), *co. Devon.* Exemplif. of a fine of the manor, 1707. Eg. 331.

**Mecheham.** *v.* Mitcham, *co. Surr.*

**Medbourne,** *co. Leic.* Grant in, 1347 (Medburn). Add. 26973.

**Medbourne,** *in Liddington, co. Wilts.* Pipe-roll acquittance on account of the manor, 1536–7. Add. 18280.

**Medenecomb.** *v.* Maidencombe, *nr. Stoke in Teignhead, co. Devon.*

**Medewcourt,** *nr. Brinsop, co. Heref.* Entail in, 1459. Add. 4605.

**Medewella.** *v.* Maidwell, *co. Northt.*

**Medhurst,** *nr. Hever, co. Kent.* Release of a mill in, to Combwell Priory, late Hen. III. (Medehurst). Harl. 78 G. 48.

**Medilton.** *v.* Middleton, *co. Suff.*

**Medina, West, Hundred,** *Isle of Wight.* Reservation of suits and service to, in Chale and W. Appleford, late 13 cent. (Westmedeine). Harl. 112 A. 32.

**Medsted,** *co. Southt.* Fine in, 1569. Add. 8467.

—— Precipe on a covenant conc. land in, 1593. Add. 25242.

Meleton. *v.* Milton, *nr. Repton, co. Derb.*

Melford, Long, *co. Suff.* Grant of Kentwell manor, etc., in. by Hen. III., 1251. Harl. 58 H. 17 (*copy*).

—— Grants, etc., in, *t.* Edw. I. Harl. 55 G. 32 (Meleford);—1298. Harl. 58 B. 42;—1303. Cott xxv. 33;—1304. Harl. 49 F. 26, 51 C. 57, 51 D. 1;—1305. Harl. 54 H. 14;—1326. Harl. 46 A. 18;—1333. Harl. 53 D. 34;—1349. Harl. 48 A. 17;—1351. Harl. 51 A. 37;—1355. Harl. 49 I. 47;—1364. Harl. 53 C. 4, 5, Cott. xii. 45;—1365. Harl. 56 B. 45;—1367. Harl. 53 C. 32, 33;—1371. Harl. 51 D. 12;—1375, 1377, 1378. Harl. Roll O. 27;—1381. Harl. 53 C. 34 (Melforth);—1407. Harl. 48 D. 12, 54 A. 22;—1421. Harl. 48 D. 15;—1448. Harl. 49 I. 39;—1583. Harl. 57 H. 18 (Milford);—1584. Harl. 48 D. 48;—1589. Add. 25408;—1599. Add. 10548, Harl. 51 H. 32;—1626. Add. 10549;—1639. Harl. 57 H. 38;—1657. Add. 19265.

—— Court-rolls of Kentwell manor, 1313. Harl. Roll H. 7.

—— Extent of lands in co. Suff., etc., owing suit to Kentwell manor, 1325. Harl. 58 H. 19 (*copy*).

—— Conveyance, etc., of Kentwell manor and lands in, 1366. Harl. 43 E. 1;—1368. Harl. 56 G. 41, 42;—1373. Harl. 48 E. 29, 50 I. 14;—1376. Harl. 57 G. 43;—1377. Harl. 48 E. 32;—1379. Harl. 48 D. 2;—1380. Harl. 43 E. 24*, 48 E. 35;—1382. Harl. 48 D. 3, 4;—1480. Harl. 48 D. 22;—1498. Harl. 43 F. 21;—1589. Harl. 51 H. 20;—1590. Harl. 43 F. 45;—1591. Harl. 57 H. 19;—1634. Harl. 53 H. 9.

—— Fine of Kentwell manor, including homage of the Prior of St. John of Jerusalem and others, 1369, 1379. Harl. 50 I. 13.

—— Homage due to Kentwell manor, for land in Thelnetham, co. Suff., 1416. Harl. 58 H. 17.

—— Mem. conc. lands in Thelnetham held of Kentwell manor, late 15 cent. Harl. 58 F. 52.

—— Mem. from court-rolls of Kentwell manor, *t.* Hen. VII. Harl. 58 H. 17, Harl. Roll O. 34;—1539. Harl. Roll H. 8.

—— Release to tenants in Monks Melford manor from a fine to the

Abbat of Bury St. Edmunds, 1517. Cott. xxi. 7.

—— Fines for homage in Kentwell manor, 1530. Harl. 58 H. 3.

—— Grant, etc., in the hamlet of Cranmer in, 1538. Add. 10544;—1586. Add. I0547.

—— Grants, etc., of Lutons (Litons), Woodhouse, Woodfoule and Blake's manors in, 1539. Harl. 48 D. 32, 50 E. 12, 13.

—— Bond on purchase of Monks Melford (Munks) manor, 1540. Harl. 48 D. 31.

—— Acquittance for homage for same manor, 1552. Harl. 48 D. 38, 39;—1635. Harl. 49 E. 40.

—— Pardon on alienation, etc., of same manor, etc., 1589. Harl. 51 H. 29;—1634. Harl. 53 H. 9.

—— Covenant for fine of Lutons, Woodhouse and Woodfoule's manors in, 1591. Harl. 57 H. 19.

—— Grant of annuity from Monks Melford manor, 1599. Harl. 51 H. 32.

—— Fine of Kentwell, Monks Melford and Lutons' manors in, etc., 1634. Harl. 45 G. 7.

—— Statements of accompts conc. Kentwell manor, 1649. Cott. xvi. 17.

—— Extract from court-roll of Melford rectory manor, 1670. Add. 10552.

—— *Rector.* Will. Skerne, 1514. Harl. 51 D. 49.

Melham Marsh, *co. Kent.* Lease of, by Cobham College, 1406. Harl. 44 C. 36.

Meliden, *co. Flint.* Fine in, 1597 (Meledyne). Add. 8534.

Melis Grange, *nr. Aberafon, co. Glam.* Grant of pasture, etc., at, to Margam Abbey, *t.* Hen. III. Harl. 75 C. 21, 36.

—— License to same for divine service at, 1239. Harl. 75 A. 26.

Melksham, *co. Wilts.* Grant, etc., in, 1458. Add. 1536 (Milkesham);—1652. Add. 5716, 5717.

—— Sale of lands in the forest, 1607. Add. 5712.

—— *Perpetuus Vicarius.* Tho. Newton, 1458. Add. 1536.

Melkys *al.* Veyses. *v. sub* Eleigh, Brent, *co. Suff.*

Melling, *co. Lanc.* Release of the manor, 1358. Add. 20560.

**Melling**, *co. Lanc. (continued).* Lease, etc., of the rectory, 1657. Add. 18979; —1659. Add. 18980, 18981.

**Mellington**, *nr. Church Stoke, co. Montgom.* Power to give seisin in, 1344 (Mulintone). Add. 20445.

**Mellis**, *co. Suff.* Tithe-suit in, betw. Thetford and Belvoir Priories, [1156] (Melue). Harl. 43 A. 18.

—— Grants, etc., in, *t.* Hen. III. Harl. 47 B. 42 (Melles), 43, 49 I. 10, 50 C. 58, Add. 15503; —*t.* Edw. I. Harl. 47 B. 44, 47 D. 20; —1296. Harl. 51 D. 18; —1343. Harl. 51 G. 6; —1355. Cott. xxvii. 119; —1359. Harl. 50 G. 58; —1363. Harl. 49 H. 19; —1375. Harl. 56 A. 47; —1386. Harl. 56 H. 35; —1412. Harl. 51 E. 52; —1417. Cott. xxvii. 208, Harl. 51 E. 55; —1450. Harl. 57 E. 45.

—— *Clericus.* Hubertus, *t.* Hen. III. (Melles). Harl. 45 I. 15.

**Mellond.** *v. sub* Woodsdale, *co. Suss.*

**Mellor**, *co. Derb.* Briefs for rebuilding the chapel, 1815, 1819, 1823. Ch. Br. B. lvi. 2, lx. 3, C. iv. 7.

**Mellor**, *nr. Blackburn, co. Lanc.* Grant in, *t.* Edw. I. (Meluer). Add. 20506.

—— *Dominus.* Gilb. de Southworth, *t.* Edw. I. Add. 20506.

**Mells**, *nr. Blythford, co. Suff.* Grant in, *t.* Edw. I. (Melles). Cott. xxvii. 94.

—— Precipe on a covenant conc. land in, 1555. Add. 25284.

**Mellyng.** *v.* Milding, *co. Suff.*

**Melneford.** *v.* Milford, *nr. Lymington, co. Southt.*

**Melplash, East**, *co. Dors.* Fine, etc., in, 1333. Harl. 49 H. 54 (Est Meleplessch); —1392. Harl. 56 E. 32 (Est Melplassh); —1438. Harl. 51 G. 6 (Est Melepleesh); —1447. Harl. 56 F. 11–13 (Estmelplayssh); —1449. Harl. 46 H. 24 (Milplassh).

—— Lease, etc., of the manor, 1350. Harl. 57 A. 19 (Eyst Meleplaisch); —1449. Harl. 46 H. 25 (Est Milplaysh).

**Melrose**, *co. Roxb.* Conf. of, to Melrose Abbey, [1166–70?]. Cott. xviii. 13, 14.

**Melsa.** *v.* Meaux, *co. York.*

**Meltham**, *in Almondbury, co. York.* Brief for rebuilding the chapel, 1782. Ch. Br. B. xxii. 10.

**Melton**, *co. Norf.* Release in, 1523. Add. 17746.

**Melton**, *co. Suff.* Conff. in, by Bps. of Ely, to Ely Abbey, [1109–31]. Harl. 43 H. 4 (Meltuna); —[1133–69]. Harl. 43 H. 5 (*copies*).

—— Grant of "terra Burel" nr. (?), *t.* Hen. III. Add. 5490.

—— Feoffment in, 1485. Add. 10559.

**Melton**, *co. York.* Grant in, 1377. Harl. 57 A. 16.

**Melton, High**, *co. York.* Covenant for settlement of the manor, 1420. Add. 17046.

**Melton Mowbray**, *co. Leic.* Conf. of grants in the manor to Monks Kirby Priory, early Hen. II. (Meltune). Harl. 53 G. 55.

—— Covenant betw. Lewes Priory, patron of the church of, and Monks Kirby Priory, conc. tithes, etc., 1358. Add. 21388.

**Melton Ross**, *co. Linc.* Exchange in, betw. Thornton Abbey and Elsham Priory, 1269 (Melton). Harl. 45 A. 12.

—— *Presbiter.* Thomas, [1157–63]. Cott. xxvii. 34.

**Meltonby**, *co. York.* Grant in, [1256–1269] (Meltoneby). Toph. 27.

**Melue.** *v.* Mellis, *co. Suff.*

**Melverley**, *co. Salop.* Sale in, 1554. Add. 26568.

—— Briefs conc. inundations in, 1771, 1782. Ch. Br. B. xi. 7, xxii. 1.

**Melwood**, *in Isle of Axholme, co. Linc.* Grant of pasture in, to Sulby Abbey, *c.* 1180–90. Harl. 53 G. 56 (Methelwde), Add. 21088 (Methelwode).

**Mendham**, *co. Suff.* Grants, etc., in, *t.* Hen. III. Harl. 58 C. 29, Camph. i. 13; —1408. Harl. 54 I. 7; —1430. Harl. 43 E. 19, 54 I. 10; —1431. Harl. 50 H. 27, 28, 54 I. 15; —1435. Add. 2016; —1529. Add. 10399; —1675. Add. 10462.

—— Acquittance for farm of Walsham Hall manor in, 1391. Harl. 57 C. 13.

**Mendips, The**, *co. Som.* Fine conc. pasture on, bel. to Priddy and Harptree, for the men of Bleadon, 1236 (Menedype). Add. 6521 (*copy*).

—— Declaration of uses conc. land on, in Doulting, *co. Som*, 1576 (Myndippe). Add. 15781.

**Mendlesham**, *co. Suff.* Grants, etc., in, [1171–2]. Harl. 49 C. 1; —early 13 cent. Harl. 50 G. 19; —1293. Add. 5930; —1356. Add. 10465; —1396.

Meriden, co. *Warw.* Grant, etc., in, 1348. Add. 8398;—1441. Harl. 86 F. 25 (Myrydene);—1702. Add. 19750.

——— Precipe on a covenant conc. land in, 1592. Add. 25552.

Meriet. *v.* Merriott, *co. Som.*

Merigg. *v.* Merridge, *co. Som.*

Merile, *Den of, nr. Goudhurst* (?), *co. Kent.* Conf. of, to Combwell Priory, 1231. Harl. 77 F. 23.

Meringethorp. *v.* Morningthorpe, *co. Norf.*

Merioneth, *County of.* Ministers' accompts for, 1521. Add. 7199.

Merkelai. *v.* Marcle, Much, *co. Heref.*

Merkesbire. *v.* Marksbury, *co. Som.*

Merkhage. *v.* Merschaw, *co. York.*

Merkisburg. *v.* Mexborough, *co. York.*

Merlande. *v.* Marland, *co. Lanc.*

Marleberg. *v.* Marlborough, *co. Wilts.*

Merlege, *betw. Sedgley and Himley, co. Staff.* Grant in, *ante* 1211. Add. 7205.

Merlinche. *v.* Marledge, *nr. Cheriton, co. Pembr.*

Merlonde. *v. sub* Withycombe, *co. Som.*

Merridge, *co. Som.* Grants, etc., of the manor. 1363. Add. 25877 (Merigg);—1364. Harl. 45 E. 66;—1370. Harl. 47 D. 26, Cott. xxvii. 108;—1371. Harl. 48 I. 9 (Merygg), 49 F. 31.

Merrington, Church, *co. Durh.* Lands of the manor of, in Aycliffe, etc., co. Durh., 1650. Add. 12628.

Merriott, *co. Som.* Grants, etc., in, 1342. Harl. 47 B. 33 (Meriet);—1359. Harl. 45 F. 45 (Meryet), 45 G. 45 (Meriet);—*t.* Rich. II. Harl. 57 G. 18;—1438. Harl. 50 E. 6.

Merrow, *co. Surr.* Grant in, by the Knts. Hospitallers, 1185 (Marewe). Cott. MS. Nero C. iii. f. 199.

——— Order of Hen. III. conc. the manor, c. 1250-60 (Merwe). Cott. MS. Claud. A. vi. f. 102.

——— Rent due to the Templars of, in Artington, nr. Guildford, co. Surr., late Hen. III. (Morewe). Add. 24584.

Mersaham. *v.* Mersham, *co. Kent.*

Mersbaldyndone. *v.* Baldon, Marsh, *co. Oxon.*

Mersburghe. *v.* Mexborough, *co. York.*

Mersc tun. *v.* Merston, *co. Kent.*

Mersch, [*nr. Shorne*], *co. Kent.* Assessment of a fifteenth, 1464-65. Harl. Roll E. 8.

Merschaw *al.* Merkhage, *nr. Woolley, co. York.* Conff. of grants in, to Byland Abbey, *post* 1194. Add. 7477 (*copy*);—[1232-40]. Add. 7485 (*copy*); —*ante* 1298. Add. 7438;—1350. Add. 8307.

Merscroft, *co. Linc.* Grant of, to Bullington Priory, *ante* 1191. Harl. 50 B. 31.

Mersea, *co. Essex.* Bequest of land at, late 10 cent. (æt Myres íge, Myræsegæ). Harl. 43 C. 4.

Mersetona. *v.* Marston, Butlers, *co. Warw.*

Mersh. *v.* Marsh, *co. Buck.*

Mersham, *co. Kent.* Grant in exchange for land at, 858 (Mersaham). Cott. MS. Aug. ii. 66.

——— Grants, etc., in, 1551. Harl. 75 H. 6 (Merscham);—1571. Harl. 77 D. 30, 80 F. 8;—1574. Harl. 77 D. 31, 78 A. 5;—1597. Harl. 78 A. 1, 2; —1610. Harl. 80 C. 12;—1611. Harl. 80 B. 48, 49, 80 H. 68, 69;—1617. Harl. 76 D. 39-41;—1638. Harl. 80 G. 22, 23;—1641. Harl. 111 C. 66;— 1646. Harl. 80 G. 24, 25.

Mershe. *v.* Caundle Marsh, *co. Dors.*

Mershefeilde. *v.* Marshfield, *co. Glouc.*

Mershoudewalle. *v.* Marshwood Vale, *co. Dors.*

Mershton. *v.* Marston, *co. Linc.*

Mersk in Cleveland. *v.* Marske, *in Langbargh Wapentake, co. York.*

Mersklandia. *v.* Marshland, *in Whitgift, co. York.*

Mershwode. *v.* Marshwood, *co. Dors.*

Merstham, *co. Surr.* Grant at, 947 (Mearsæt ham). Cott. MS. Aug. ii. 83.

——— Grants, etc., in, 1375. Add. 23625 (Estham), 23626;—1379. Add. 23627 (Estham), 23628 (Mestham); — 1384. Add. 23629 (Merstham);—1390. Add. 23630 (Merstam);—1413. Add. 23510;—1420. Add. 23632, 23633;— 1421. Add. 23538, 23539;—1429. Add. 23540;—1456. Add. 23541;— 1698. Add. 23509.

——— Grant of the patronage of the church of, by the Abp. of Canterbury, 1544. Add. 24599.

Merston. *v.* Marston, co. *Linc.*

—— *v.* Marston, co. *Warw.*

—— *v.* Marston Bigott, co. *Som.*

—— *v.* Marston, Potters, co. *Leic.*

—— *v.* Marston Trussel, co. *Northt.*

—— *v.* Morston, co. *Norf.*

Merston, co. *Kent.* A boundary mark, 774 (Mersc tun). Cott. MS. Aug. ii. 99.

—— Grants, etc., in, 1309. Harl. 50 G. 44;—1440. Harl. 47 H. 27;—1469. Harl. 49 D. 17, 56 B. 12;—1470. Harl. 52 C. 18;—1476. Harl. 52 C. 24, 56 C. 35;—1480. Harl. 52 C. 23;—1511. Harl. 52 C. 28, 28*.

—— Fine of the manor, 1437. Harl. 54 E. 55.

—— Conveyance, etc., of the manor and advowson, 1450. Harl. 54 F. 16; —1452. Harl. 54 F. 17;—1453. Harl. 53 G. 52;—1464. Harl. 54 F. 18, 55 H. 21;—1465. Harl. 54 F. 19;— 1478. Harl. 47 C. 39;—1529. Harl. 48 D. 56;—1534. Harl. 48 E. 2, 57 B. 24.

—— Memorandum of taxation of, *t.* Edw. IV. Harl. 58 F. 4.

—— Grant of a rent charge on the manor, 1534. Harl. 48 E. 1.

—— *Rector (quondam).* Gilbertus, 1309. Harl. 50 G. 44.

—— —— Benedictus Grauntdene, 1362. Harl. 50 I. 20.

Merston, co. *Suss.* Demise in, 1457. Add. 8897.

—— Deeds conc. the mortgage of the manor, 1697. Add. 19034;—1698. Add. 19033.

Mersuude, Merswode. *v.* Marshwood, co. *Dors.*

Mertele. *v.* Martley, co. *Worc.*

Mertham. *v.* Martham, co. *Norf.*

Merton. *v.* Martin Husingtree, co. *Worc.*

—— *v.* Marton, co. *Warw.*

—— *v.* Marton, co. *Wilts.*

Merton, co. *Devon.* Court - rolls of Potheridge (Poderidge) manor in, 1609-1614. Add. 9415-9417.

Merton, co. *Dors.* Court-roll, 1502-3. Harl. Roll I. 7.

Merton, co. *Surr.* Privy council held at, 1432. Lansd. 559.

—— Rental of [the manor?], 1528-9. Add. 23542.

Merton, co. *Surr. (continued). Capellanus.* Ricardus, late Hen. III. Add. 22949.

Mertune. *v.* Marton, co. *Wilts.*

Meryet. *v.* Merriott, co. *Som.*

Mesden. *v.* Meesden, co. *Hertf.*

Meslingues. *v.* Malling, West, co. *Kent.*

Messenden Parva. *v.* Missenden, Lit., co. *Buck.*

Messing, co. *Essex.* Quittance for homage for Lindholt in (?), late *t.* Hen. II. Cott. xxvii. 112.

—— Grants, etc., in, 1296. Harl. 46 F. 53 (Messingg);—1397. Harl. 48 G. 1 (Mesyn);—1453. Harl. 47 D. 24 (Messyng).

—— Grants, etc., of the manor, 1383. Add. 8052 (Messyngge);—1390. Harl. 46 I. 52;—1453. Harl. 47 D. 24 (Messyng).

—— Precipe on covenant conc. lands in, 1592. Add. 25008.

Metfield, co. *Suff.* Precipe on covenant conc. land in, 1593. Add. 25473.

—— Grant of annuity from the manor, 1605. Add. 10458.

Methe. *v.* Meeth, co. *Devon.*

Methelwode, Methelwde. *v.* Melwood, *in Isle of Axholme,* co. *Linc.*

Methelwolde. *v.* Methwold, co. *Norf.*

Metheringham, co. *Linc.* Grant, etc., in, to Bullington Priory, 1256. Harl. 52 H. 28;—*t.* Edw. I. or II. Harl. 52 H. 5 (Methringham);—c. 1325. Harl. 52 H. 27.

—— Grant, etc., in, 1331. Harl. 52 H. 35;—1471. Eg. 475 (Metryngham).

—— Sale, etc., of Zouches and Talboys manors in, 1617. Harl. 75 H. 42, 79 G. 9.

—— *Clericus.* Philippus, *t.* Hen. III. Harl. 45 G. 30;—late 13 cent. Cott. xxvii. 129.

—— *Vicarius.* Osbertus, *t.* Hen. III. (Meþeringham). Harl. 46 E. 21.

Methersham, *nr. Beckley,* co. *Suss.* Conf. of grant in, to Robertsbridge Abbey, 1269 (Maderesham). Eg. 255.

Methley, co. *York.* Lease, etc., in, 1562. Add. 12669;—1671. Add. 12681.

Methuen, co. *Perth. Persona.* Robertus, *ante* 1233. Cott. xviii. 36;— 1240. Cott. xviii. 27.

2 L

**Methwold,** *co. Norf.* Grant of Otringhithe (Otrigeide) in, by Castle Acre Priory, 1203. Add. 19274.

—— Grants in, 1290. Add. 14765 (Methelwolde);—1321. Add. 14766.

**Mettingham,** *co. Suff.* Conf. of lease, etc., of "Benedicite" meadow in, *t.* Hen. III. or Edw. I. Harl. 45 G. 63 (Metingham), 47 F. 3 (do.), 56 B. 18 (do.).

—— Lease of the castle, 1381. Harl. 57 C. 41 (Metyngham).

—— Settlement, etc., of lands in, 1403. Cott. xxvii. 162 (do.);—1593. Add. 25474;—1619. Add. 10581.

—— Acquittance for homage in, 1404. Harl. 54 A. 1 (do.).

—— *Vicarius.* Henricus, *t.* Edw. I. (Metingham). Harl. 83 D. 45.

**Metton,** *co. Norf.* Grants, etc., of the manor and advowson, 1354. Add. 14767;—1422. Add. 17243 (copy);—1597. Add. 14266.

—— Grants in, 1501. Add. 14181;—1593. Add. 14264, 14265.

**Meuele.** *v.* Yeovil, *co. Som.*

**Meuse.** *v.* Moze with Beaumont, *co. Essex.*

**Mevenneth,** *co. Cardigan.* Sale of "custom wool" from the grange of, 1567. Harl. 80 F. 31.

**Mexborough,** *co. York.* Grants, etc., in, or near, *t.* Hen. III. or Edw. I. Add. 17944 (Merkisburg);— 1377. Harl. 57 A. 16 (Mekesburgh);—1430. Add. 20598 (Mersburghe).

**Meyes, Meys.** *v. sub* Cawston, *co. Norf.*

**Meyforde, Meythford.** *v. sub* Stone, *co. Staff.*

**Meythe.** *v.* Meeth, *co. Devon.*

**Meyton.** *v. sub* Horstead, *co. Norf.*

**Michaelstone,** *co. Glam.* Grant in, *t.* John (Michelestowe). Add. 24266.

—— Rents from Dinas Powis to be paid in the church of, to the Knts. Hospitallers, *t.* Hen. III.-Edw. I. Add. 24262.

—— Demise of the Duke of Suffolk's lands in, 1483 (Mighelstowe). Harl. 43 I. 51.

—— Inquest by Margam Abbey conc. boundaries of lands called Penhuddiwaelod (Pennyth waylod) in, 1519. Harl. 75 A. 49.

**Michaelstowe.** *v. sub* Ramsey, *co. Essex.*

**Micheland.** *v.* Muchland Manor, *in Furness, co. Lanc.*

**Michell Troye.** *v.* Mitchel Troy, *co. Monm.*

**Mickelhol,** *nr. Timberland, co. Linc.* Grant in, to Kirkstead Abbey, *t.* Edw. I. Harl. 46 A. 36.

**Mickfield,** *co. Suff.* Exemption of the manor from ecclesiastical taxation, 1372 (Mikelefeld). Harl. Roll AA. 22.

—— Conf. of grant of the manor, 1439 (Mekilfeld). Cott. iv. 34.

**Micklefield.** *v. sub* Rickmansworth, *co. Hertf.*

**Mickleham,** *co. Surr.* Grants at Burford (Burgforde, Burghforde, Burhgforde), etc., in, 1311. Add. 18604;— 1316. Add. 8814 (Mykelham), 9022;—1324. Add. 9026.

—— *Capellanus.* Dom. Joh. Huse, 1344. Add. 23093.

**Micklethwaite,** *co. York.* Power to give seisin in, 1392 (Mikelthwayt). Harl. 45 F. 28.

**Mickleton,** *co. Glouc.* Compotus of the manor, 1337-38 (Mukelton). Harl. Roll E. 27.

**Mickley,** *nr. Dronfield, co. Derb.* Grant in, 1409. Harl. 112 A. 43.

**Miclehale,** *nr. Newbold, co. Linc.* Conf. of grant in, to Bullington Priory, *c.* 1205. Harl. 52 A. 18 (copy).

**Middelham, pratum de.** *v. sub* Englefield, *co. Berks.*

**Middelheved, [in Marton?], co. York.** Grant in, early Hen. III. Add. 20597.

**Middelton.** *v.* Middleton on the Wolds, *co. York.*

—— *v.* Milton, *co. Cumb.*

—— *v.* Milton Hundred, *co. Kent.*

—— *v.* Milton next Sittingbourne, *co. Kent.*

**Middelwic.** *v. sub* Droitwich, *co. Worc.*

**Middilton.** *v.* Middleton, *co. Suff.*

—— *v.* Middleton, Stony, *co. Derb.*

**Middle,** *co. Salop.* Power to give seisin in, 1536. Add. 9372.

—— *Rector.* Phil. de la Lee, 1396. Harl. 56 F. 25.

**Middleham**, *co. York*. Grant of annuity from the manor, 1484 (Middelham). Harl. 83 C. 16.

**Middlesex**, *County of*. Grants notified to the thegns "on Middelsexan." [1044–46]. Cott. vii. 6 ;—[1050–65]. Cott. vii. 13.

—— Copies of deeds conc. lands in, 1363–1412. Harl. Roll I. 9.

—— Appointments of Deputy Lieutenants, 1702. Add. 13629 ;—1711. Add. 13641.

—— *Vicecomes*. Ric. Pounz, 1332. Add. 9228.

—— —— Hen. Heydon, 1531. Harl. 50 F. 30.

—— —— *Sir* Nath. Herne, *Sir* John Lethulier, 1675. Harl. 111 F. 7.

—— *Justiciarius ad pacem*. Rob. Chidley, 1549. Harl. 48 B. 9.

**Middlethorpe**, *co. York*. Sale in, 1637. Add. 1797.

**Middleton**, *co.* —— (?). Lease in, 1241 (Midelton). Harl. 57 D. 23.

**Middleton**, *in Marcham, co. Berks*. Grant at, 956 (æt Middeltune). Cott. MS. Aug. ii. 41.

**Middleton**, *by Wirksworth, co. Derb*. Covenant for conveyance in, etc., 1595. Woll. xi. 90 ; — 1613. Woll. xi. 87 (Mydleton).

—— Fine in, 1702. Woll. xi. 73.

**Middleton**, *in Youlgreave, co. Derb*. Power to give seisin, etc., of the manor, 1364. Cott. xxvi. 23 (Myddeltone) ; —1446. Woll. vi. 5 (Middelton).

**Middleton**, *in Teesdale, co. Durh*. Grant of the church, etc., to St. Mary's Abbey, York, [1186–8] (Mideltun). Cott. v. 75.

—— Grant in, by Jas. I., 1612. Cott. xiii. 35.

**Middleton**, *co. Essex*. Grants, etc., in, 1318. Harl. 47 C. 52 (Middelton) ;— 1333. Harl. 54 H. 20 ;—1335. Harl. 54 H. 21 ;—1587. Slo. xxxii. 62.

—— Conf. of Barbour's manor. etc., in, to Sudbury College, 1528 (Middelton). Add. 8405.

**Middleton**, *co. Lanc*. Signatures of adherents to the Commonwealth at, 1650. Add. 7180.

**Middleton**, *in Lonsdale, co. Lanc*. Settlement of the manor, etc., 1670. Add. 19547.

**Middleton**, *by Lynn, co. Norf*. Fine of the manor, 1350. Harl. 58 G. 34.

—— Lease of the manor, 1686. Add. 19165.

**Middleton**, *nr. Rockingham, co. Northt*. Conveyance in, 1349 (Middilton). Harl. 57 C. 27.

**Middleton**, *in Clotworthy* (?), *co. Som*. Compotus of lands of Taunton Priory in, 1438–9 (Middeldon). Add. 25873.

**Middleton**, *co. Suff*. Grant, etc., in, late Hen. III. Add. 7262 (Middilton) ;—1321. Add. 10366 (do.).

—— Grant, etc., of Brentfen (Brendfen) manor in, 1471 (Medilton). Harl. 45 F. 41, 42 ;—1476. Harl. 51 G. 13.

**Middleton**, *co. Suss*. Power for assignment of the manor to Edw. II., 1316. Harl. 57 E. 33.

—— Acquittance for deeds conc. the manor, 1347 (Middelton). Harl. 58 C. 36.

—— Grant in Elmergate in, 1608. Add. 18906.

**Middleton**, *co. Warw*. Grant in, 1330. Add. 26604.

**Middleton Cheney**, *co. Northt*. Conf. of release of suit in, c. 1245–50 (Midelthon). Harl. 53 B. 15.

—— Sale of goods and chattels bel. to the manor, 1310 (Middeltone). Add. 22316.

—— Release, etc., of the manor, 1374. Add. 22317 (Middeltone Cheinduyt) ;— 1399. Add. 22319 (Middelton Cheyne).

—— Release of the manor from the Charterhouse Priory, 1402 (Middelton Cheynduyt). Add. 22318.

**Middleton Malsor**, *co. Northt*. Exemplif. of grant of the manor, 1402 (Middiltone). Add. 22371 (1).

**Middleton on the Wolds**, *co. York*. Grants, etc., in, to Beverley College, late 12 cent. (Midelton). Lansd. 404, 406–408 ;—t. Hen. III. Lansd. 405 (Middelton).

—— Grant in, by St. Giles's Hospital, Beverley, early 13 cent. Add. 5720.

—— Grants, etc., in, early Hen. III. Add. 5721 (Midelton), 5722 (Midelt.) ; —1357. Add. 5751 ;—1514. Add. 5779 (Mydylton):—1515. Add. 5783 (Midylton);—1521. Add. 5785 ;— 1558. Add. 5804 (Myddelton).

—— Release in, to Watton Priory, 1322 (Midelton). Harl. 55 E. 23.

2 L 2

**Middleton Park.** *v. sub* Longford, *co. Derb.*

**Middleton Scriven,** *co. Salop.* Brief for rebuilding the church, 1802. Ch. Br. B. xlii. 7.

**Middleton, Stony,** *co. Derb.* Grant of common of pasture in the manor, 1347 (Middilton juxta Eyum). Woll. i. 17.

—— Grants, etc., in, 1395. Woll. vii. 54 (Midulton Cliff);—1445. Woll. vii. 56 (Midylton Clyf);—1465. Woll. vii. 55 (Middylton Clif), 60 (Mydelton Clyf);—1490. Woll. vii. 48 (Middilton);—1636. Woll. xii. 88;—1640. Harl. 112 O. 55.

**Middlewich,** *co. Chest.* Grant, etc., in Mugeshale *al.* Muggesale nr., 1310. Add. 19978;—1317. Harl. 45 I. 34.

—— Grant of the advowson, 1393 (Wicus medius). Woll. xi. 5 (copy).

—— Writ on claim to lands in, 1420. Add. 6278.

—— Briefs for rebuilding the church, 1807, 1818. Ch. Br. B. xlviii. 2, lix. 3.

**Middlezoy,** *co. Som.* Presentation of J. Gregory to the vicarage, 1540 (Myddelsoway). Add. 10656.

**Midehurst.** *v.* Midhurst, *co. Suss.*

**Midelholm,** *in Kirton* (?), *co. Nott.* Exchange in, with Rufford Abbey, *t.* Hen. III.-Edw. I. Harl. 83 G. 11.

**Midford.** *v.* Mitford, *co. Northumb.*

**Midgham,** *in Fordingbridge, co. Southt.* Exchequer acquittance for rent (?) of, 1634. Add. 25657.

**Midhope,** *in Bradfield, co. York.* Grants in, late 13 cent. Add. 8230 (Midhop);—1304. Add. 8280;—1367. Add. 8312.

**Midhope, Over,** *in Bradfield, co. York.* Grants in, *t.* Edw. I. Add. 8196 (Huvermidhope);—1497. Add. 8328 (Ouermedope)

**Midhurst,** *co. Suss.* Grant of rent from the mill of, to Waverley Abbey, *ante* 1219 (Midehurst). Harl. 46 F. 2.

—— Grant of annuity to Waverley Abbey to be paid at, early 13 cent. (Midehurst). Harl. 46 F. 1.

—— Grant, etc., of the manor, *c.* 1283–4. Harl. 46 F. 4;—1430. Add. 20114 (Mydhurst).

—— Release of a rent charge on the mill of, by Waverley Abbey, 1289. Harl. 45 A. 29.

**Midhurst,** *co. Suss.* (*continued*). Precipes on covenants conc. lands in, 1555. Add. 15237 (Mydhurst);—1561. Add. 25529.

**Midley,** *co. Kent.* Grants, etc., in, 1536. Add. 8608 (Mydley);—1540. Harl. 76 H. 34;—1541. Add. 8612;—1550. Add. 8616.

**Midsomeresnorton.** *v.* Norton, Midsomer, *co. Som.*

**Midulton Cliff, Midylton Clyf.** *v.* Middleton, Stony, *co. Derb.*

**Migheleschurch.** *v.* St. Michaelchurch, *co. Som.*

**Mighelstowe.** *v.* Michaelstone, *co. Glam.*

**Mikelefeld.** *v.* Mickfield, *co. Suff.*

**Mikelthwayt.** *v.* Micklethwaite, *co. York.*

**Milborne Deverel,** *al.* Cary, *in Milborne St. Andrew, co. Dors.* Grants, etc., in, *t.* Edw. I.–II. Harl. 49 D. 53 (Mullebourne);—1340. Harl. 47 H. 6 (Mulebourne);—1358. Harl. 47 H. 8 (do.).

—— Warrant for seisin of the manor, 1477 (Mileborne). Harl. 53 G. 49.

**Milborne Port,** *co. Som.* Grant of Kingsbury Regis in, late Hen. III. (Meleburne). Harl. 47 E. 36.

—— *Rector.* Nicholas Dernforde, 1359. Add. 17660·

**Milborne St. Andrew,** *co. Dors.* Grant in, *t.* Edw. I. Harl. 56 F. 5 (Mileburne Sci. Andree).

**Milborne Stileham,** *in Bere Regis, co. Dors.* Releases in, to Bec Abbey, 1326. Toph. 23 (Mulleborne Beek); —1340. Toph. 29 (Parva Melebourn).

**Milbourn,** *co. Wilts.* Bequest of soulscot to the church of (?), *c.* 995 (to Mylen burnan). Cott. viii. 38.

**Milbourne,** *co. Westm. Persona.* Adam, early Hen. III. (Milleburne). Harl. 49 H. 49.

**Milcombe,** *co. Oxon.* Compotus of the manor, 1422–23. Harl. Roll I. 18 (Myldecombe);—1437–38. Harl. Roll I. 17;—1474–75. Harl. Roll G. 2.

—— Release of the manor, 1441 (Myldecombe). Harl. 86 F. 25.

—— Court-rolls, 1451–57. Harl. Roll I. 19;—1540. Harl. Roll O. 40 (Mildecombe).

**Milnhay** *al.* **Millehay** Common. *v. sub* Alderwasley, *co. Derb.*

**Milnrow,** *in Rochdale, co. Lanc.* Brief for rebuilding the chapel, 1785. Ch. Br. B. xxv. 2.

**Milsted,** *co. Kent.* Lease in, 1335. Harl. 79 C. 8.

**Milston,** *co. Wilts.* Brief conc. a fire at Brigmerston in, 1769. Ch. Br. B. ix. 4.

**Milthorpe,** *in Great Sandal* (?), *co. York.* Grant in, 1389. Cott. xxviii. 92.

—— Crown lease in, 1555 (Mylnethorpe). Harl. 84 C. 32.

**Milton,** *co. Camb.* Feoffments of the manor and advowson. 1396. Harl. 49 G. 20 (Middelton), 56 F. 24.

**Milton,** *nr. Repton, co. Derb.* Grant in, 1413 (Meleton). Add. 1537.

**Milton,** *nr. Canterbury, co. Kent.* Covenant conc. land in, 1044 (Melentun). Cott. MS. Aug. ii. 70.

**Milton,** *nr. Carew, co. Pembr.* Conveyance of the manor, 1441. Harl. 80 A. 15.

**Milton,** *in Christchurch Hundred, co. Southt.* Precipe on a covenant conc. land in, 1593 (Mylton). Add. 25251.

—— Brief conc. a fire at, 1789. Ch. Br. B. xxix. 1.

**Milton Hundred,** *co. Kent.* Exchange of lands in, 1395 (Middelton). Harl. 78 F. 29.

—— Award on claims to lands in, 1505. Lansd. 172.

**Milton Abbot,** *co. Devon.* Lease of the advowson, 1584. Add. 11170.

**Milton, Great,** *co. Oxon.* Conveyance of Ingescourte manor, etc., in, 1416 (Myltone Magna). Harl. 54 I. 34.

—— Precipe on a covenant conc. Ascott manor, etc., in, 1593 (Magna Mylton). Add. 25217.

**Milton, Little,** *co. Oxon.* Conveyance in, 1416 (Mylton Purva). Harl. 54 I. 34.

**Milton next Gravesend,** *co. Kent.* Reference to covenant for remainder of the manor, 1376 (Melton). Harl. 56 G. 47.

—— Extract from court-roll of Parrock's manor in, 1391. Harl. 75 D. 49.

**Milton next Sittingbourne,** *co. Kent.* Grants, etc., in, 1298. Harl. 54 G. 6

(Middelton):—1361. Harl. 48 E. 21; —1413. Harl. 78 F. 49:—*post* 1439. Harl. 78 F. 40, 41;—1505. Lansd. 174 (Myddelton):—1512. Harl. 80 D. 31;—1523. Harl. 75 E. 18; —1626. Harl. 75 H. 22.

—— Marriage settlement of Northwood Sheppey manor in, 1372. Harl. 54 C. 56.

—— Fine of two watermills in, 1408 (Middelton). Add. 6265.

—— Bequest of a watermill called Wasshyngmelle in, 1457 (Middelton). Harl. 75 D. 55.

—— Grant in Chalkwell in, 1525 (Medylton iuxta Sithyngbourne). Harl. 76 F. 18.

—— Settlement of Colsall manor, etc., in, 1661. Add. 5984.

**Milverton,** *co. Som.* Grant in, 1367. Add. 11165.

—— Lease of the manor, [1426–36]. Harl. 53 H. 17.

—— Crown appointment of a steward over the burgh, 1574. Harl. 75 E. 42.

—— Sale of a lease of Preston Bowyer manor in, 1576. Harl. 79 F. 23.

**Milwich,** *co. Staff.* Brief for rebuilding the church, 1792. Ch. Br. B. xxxii. 2.

**Mimma, North,** *co. Hertf.* Release, etc., in, 1327. Harl. 54 E. 27 (North Mimmes);—1386. Add. 19906.

—— *Persona.* Tho. de Hortone, 1372. Cott. xxiv. 12.

**Mimma, South,** *co. Midd.* Grants, etc., in. 1386. Add. 19906;—1464. Add. 19907;—1612. Cott. xiii. 35 (Southemymmes);—1657. Add. 17814.

—— Lease in (?), 1464. Add. 19908.

—— Court-roll, 1475 (Southmymmes). Add. 8142.

**Minchen Court.** *v. sub* Shadoxhurst, *co. Kent.*

**Minchin Hampton.** *v.* Hampton, Minchin, *co. Glouc.*

**Mincombe,** *in Sidbury, co. Devon.* Release, etc., in, 1420. Add. 13039 (Myncomb);—1564. Add. 13811;— 1566. Add. 13812; — 1590. Add. 13829.

**Mindenale.** *v.* Mildenhall, *co. Suff.*

**Minety Hundred,** *co. Glouc.* Grant of rent from, 1634 (Myntye). Add. 18391.

Mixon, *co. Staff.* Grant of, to Hilton Abbey, c. 1233 (Mixsne). Cott. xi. 38.

Moat. *v. sub* Ightham, *co. Kent.*

Moat, *nr. Iden, co. Suss.* Release of the manor, 1458 (Mote). Add. 16156.

—— Grant of the chapel advowson, 1459 (La Legh *al.* La Mote). Add. 16325.

Mochelbodwhidek. *v.* Bowithick, in —— (?), *co. Cornw.*

Mockings. *v. sub* Tottenham, *co. Midd.*

Modeford Terry. *v.* Mudford, *co. Som.*

Modinga hema mearc. *v.* Mottingham, *co. Kent.*

Modynden. *v. sub* Headcorn, *co. Kent.*

Moerheb, *nr. Kidderminster, co. Worc.* Wood of, a boundary, 736. Cott. MS. Aug. ii. 3.

Moese. *v.* Moze with Beaumont, *co. Essex.*

Moggerhanger, *co. Bedf.* Covenant conc. possession in, 1351 (Mogerhanger). Harl. 48 H. 29.

—— Sale of the manor, 1507 (Mogerhanger). Add. 990, 991.

—— Fine, etc., in, 1520. Add. 997 (Mogerhanger);—1600. Add. 998;—1623. Add. 999;—1626. Harl. 112 E. 38;—1629. Add. 1000 (Mowgranger);—1630. Add. 1001 (Mogerhanger), 1002.

Moggyngton, Mogynton. *v.* Mugginton, *co. Derb.*

Mohaute. *v.* Mold, *co. Flint.*

Mokkynge. *v.* Mucking, *co. Essex.*

Molash, *co. Kent.* Grant, etc., in, 1415. Harl. 76 B. 13;—1451. Add. 16443 (Molysch).

Mold, *co. Flint.* Attornment of the castle and manor to the Earl of Salisbury, 1337 (Mohaut). Harl. 43 D. 26.

—— Inspex. by Edw. III. of an exchange of the castle and vill betw. Qu. Isabella and the Earl of Salisbury, 1338 (Mons altus). Cott. xi. 61.

—— Livery of, to Eliz., Countess of Salisbury, c. 1400 (Mohaute). Add. 662.

Molesey *al.* Moulsey, West, *co. Surr.* Precipe on a covenant conc. land in, 1592 (Westmolsey). Add. 25521.

Molesho. *v.* Moulsoe, *co. Buck.*

Molesworth, *co. Hunt.* Grants, etc., in, *t.* Hen. III. Harl. 48 H. 4;—1324. Cott. xxvii. 173 (Moulisworthe);—1367. Harl. 49 F. 52;—1439. Add. 15479 (Mullesworthe);—1444. Harl. 58 C. 25 (do.).

—— Conveyance of a moiety of the manor and advowson, 1393. Harl. 57 E. 22 (Mullesworth).

—— Release of Dulaies manor in, 1398. Harl. 47 H. 2.

—— Acquittances from Chicksands Priory for rents in, 1467. Harl. 44 C. 27 (Mowlesworth);—1475. Harl. 44 C. 28;—1477. Harl. 44 C. 29;—1482. Harl. 44 C. 26.

—— Extracts from court-rolls, 1520. Harl. 58 F. 5;—1522. Harl. 58 F. 6;—1523. Harl. 58 F. 7.

—— Bond for award conc. glebe land in, 1524. Harl. 54 D. 27.

—— Acquittances for fines for lands in the manor, 1534. Harl. 53 G. 7;—1544. Harl. 53 F. 24;—1545. Harl. 53 G. 9, 10, 11;—1550. Harl. 53 G. 29.

—— License for conveyance in Catworth, as of the manor of, 1545. Harl. 53 G. 8.

—— *Parson. Sir* Thruston Urmyston, 1484. Harl. 48 B. 15.

Molla. *v.* Mow, *co. Roxb.*

Mollington, *co. Oxon.* Grant in, *t.* Hen. III. (Mollinton). Harl. 57 E. 8.

—— Release of the manor, 1441 (Molyngton). Harl. 86 F. 25.

Molton, South, *co. Devon.* Institution to the rectory, 1527. Harl. 86 G. 17.

—— Fine in, 1653. Harl. 86 I. 59.

—— *Rectores. Mag.* Ric. Pace (*late*), Tho. Marshall, *M.A.*, 1527. Harl. 86 G. 17.

Monaghan, *County of.* Petition from the protestants of, on the Act of Resumption, 1702. Add. 19538.

Monceux. *v. sub* Dalling, Wood, *co. Norf.*

Mondefeld. *v.* Mountfield, *co. Suss.*

Mondenhall. *v. sub* Mundon, *co. Essex.*

Monekeshamme, La. *v. sub* Marston Bigott, *co. Som.*

Monewdon, *co. Suff.* Grants, etc., in, *t.* Hen. III. Lansd. 69 (Munehedene);—1309. Add. 10302 (Monegedene);—1314. Add. 10272 (Moneweden);—1418. Add. 10282;—1433. Add. 10327.

Monewode. *v. sub* Ansley, *co. Warw.*

Mongeham, *co. Kent.* Grant at, to Christ Church, Canterbury, 832 (?) (Mundlingham). Cott. MS. Aug. ii. 92.

Mongeham, Great, *co. Kent.* Power to take seisin in, etc., 1465. Harl. 80 I. 58 ;—1471. Harl. 80 I. 59 ;—1549. Harl. 112 A. 46.

—— Notif. for presentation to the rectory of, 1604 (Mongham Magna). Harl. 111 C. 26.

—— *Rector (late).* Will. Baily, 1604. Harl. 111 C. 26.

Mongeham, Little, *co. Kent.* Power to take seisin in, 1465. Harl. 80 I. 58 ; —1471. Harl. 80 I. 59.

Mongey. *v. sub* Haveringland, *co. Norf.*

Moniassch, Moniasse. *v.* Monyash, *co. Derb.*

Monikie, *co. Fife.* Grant of Hynd Castle in, 1633. Add. 6224.

Monington, *co. Heref. Rector.* Joh. Byford, 1440. Add. 4603.

Monkaton, *nr. Exeter, co. Devon.* Grant at, to Exeter Monastery, 938 (?) (Munoca tun). Add. 19516.

Monkeboth. *v. sub* Walkeringham, *co. Nott.*

Monkenhook, *in Alfold, co. Surr.* Mortgage nr., 1325 (La Monekenhok). Add. 26762.

Monkethorp. *v.* Monksthorpe, *co. Linc.*

Monkland, *co. Heref.* Settlement in, 1585. Add. 7039.

Monks Eleigh. *v.* Eleigh, Monks, *co. Suff.*

Monks Kirby. *v.* Kirby, Monks, *co. Warw.*

Monks Melford. *v. sub* Melford, Long, *co. Suff.*

Monks Risborough. *v.* Risborough, Monks, *co. Buck.*

Monksham. *v. sub* Marston Bigott, *co. Som.*

Monksilver, *co. Som.* Sale of a lease of the manor, 1567 (Muneksylver). Harl. 79 F. 23.

Monkspath, *co. Warw.* Lands in Tanworth, co. Warw., held of the fee of, 1304 (Munkespath). Add. 6011.

—— Court rolls, 1629-1641. Add. 17806-17811.

Monksthorpe, *in Great Steeping, co. Linc.* Covenant conc. rent from, betw. Bardney Abbey and Greenfield Priory, 1347 (Monkethorp). Harl. 44 A. 8.

Monkton, *co. Kent.* Church of, restored to Christ Church, Canterbury, 1365 (Monketone). Add. 16178.

—— Conf. to Christ Church of drainage rights in marshes in, 1418 (Monketon). Add. 16489.

—— Sale, etc., in, 1505. Harl. 79 B. 5 ;—1661. Add. 5984.

—— Assignment of lease of the manor, 1626 (Mouncton). Harl. 83 H. 48.

Monkton, *nr. Pembroke, co. Pembr.* Inspex., in 1459, of a fine in, 1442. Slo. xxxii. 20.

Monkton Farley. *v.* Farley, Monkton, *co. Wilts.*

Monkton, Nun, *co. York.* Feoffment, etc., in, 1429-30. Add. 1782 (Nunningtone) ;—1504. Add. 6196 (Nonmonkton).

—— Brief for rebuilding the church, 1770. Ch. Br. B. x. 5.

—— *Rector.* Simon de Chauncy, late Hen. III. (Munketon). Harl. 56 E. 33.

Monkton, West, *co. Som.* Grant in Tobrygge in, with a fishery in the Tone at, 1340 (West Munketon). Add. 25893.

—— Fine, etc., in, 1346. Add. 25876 (Monketon) ;—1381. Harl. 48 A. 24 ; —t. Ric. II. Harl. 57 G. 18.

—— Grant in Gotton (Gotton juxta Taunton) in (?), 1408. Add. 17688.

Monkwood, *nr. Bluntshay, in Whitchurch Canonicorum, co. Dors.* Release, etc., in, 1379. Harl. 48 F. 42 (Monkwode) ;—1409. Harl. 55 G. 44 (Munkewode) ;—1410. Harl. 51 F. 40, 41 (Monkewode).

Monmouth, *County of.* Valor of Crown lands in, 1518. Roy. Roll 14 B. xxxviii.

—— Precipes on covenants for lands in, 1555-1593. Add. 25111.

—— *Senescallus Inferioris Wencie.* Will. de Wilt[on ?], 1244. Campb. v. 7.

—— *Vicecomes de Wenllook [Wentloog Hundred].* Gilbert Denys, *miles,* 1418. Add. 20509.

Monmouth, *co. Monm.* Grant of three forges in, "supra ripam Waie," to Monmouth Priory, *c.* 1150-60. Add. 20405.

Monmouth, *co. Monm. (continued).* License to Clifford Priory to buy and sell without toll in, early Hen. III. (Monemuta). Campb. xviii. 4.

—— Precipe on a covenant conc. land in, 1555. Add. 25112.

Monmouth, Little, *co. Monm.* Court-roll, 1345 (Parva Monem.). Add. 7698.

—— Fine in, 1638. Woll. xi. 29.

Monnington, *co. Heref.* Bequest of land in, 1418 (Monynton supra Wyam). Harl. 112 F. 13.

—— *Persona.* Joh. Byford, *ante* 1450. Harl. 78 F. 5.

—— *Rector.* Johannes, 1418. Harl. 112 F. 13.

Mons Altus. *v.* Mold, *co. Flint.*

Monstrewith. *v.* Minsterworth, *co. Glouc.*

Montacute, *co. Som.* Release in, 1438 (Mountagu). Harl. 50 E. 6.

Montacute, *Honour of.* Sock Dennis, co. Som., held " per servicium feodi dimidii militis de parvis militibus de honore montis acuti," [1175–89]. Harl. 58 G. 6 (*copy*).

Montgomery, *County of.* Valor of Crown lands in, 1518. Roy. Roll 14 B. xxxviii.

—— Assignments of lease of mines in the mountains of Keieilioge *al.* Keverling [Cyfeiliog?] in, 1641. Harl. 111 H. 19;—1648. Harl. 111 H. 20.

—— Brief conc. an inundation, 1783. Ch. Br. B. xxiv. 2.

Montgomery, *co. Montgom.* Grants, etc., in, *c.* 1240-5. Add. 8078 (Mungummer.);—*t.* Edw. I. Add. 8079 (Mons Gomeri);—1323. Add. 8080 (Mons gomere);—1328. Add. 8081 (Mons Gomere).

—— Garrison establishment of the castle, 1369 (Mountgomery). Harl. Roll E. 7.

Monyash, *co. Derb.* Grants, etc., in, late 13 cent. Harl. 83 G. 32 (Moniasse);—1316. Harl. 83 G. 43 (Moniassche);—1323. Harl. 83 G. 44;—1338. Harl. 84 A. 1 (Moniash);—1361. Harl. 83 G. 31 (Moniusch);—1366. Harl. 84 B. 35 (Moniassch);—1367. Harl. 83 G. 1;—1371. Harl. 112 H. 26;—1375. Harl. 84 A. 38;—1376. Harl. 84 A. 36;—1407. Harl. 84 A. 7;—1428. Harl. 83 G. 40;—1437. Harl. 83 D. 13;—1542. Woll.

vii. 47;—1619. Woll. xii. 93 (Moniash);—1636. Woll. xi. 88.

Monymusk, *co. Aberdeen. Persona.* Robertus, 1240. Cott. xviii. 27.

Moor. *v. sub* Petherton, South, *co. Som.*

—— *v. sub* Stoke by Clare, *co. Suff.*

Moor Hall. *v. sub* Farnham, *co. Surr.*

Moorbath, *in Symondsbury, co. Dors.* Grants, etc., in, *t.* Edw. I.-II. Harl. 53 D. 30 (Hameletus de Mourbathe juxta Simondesburgh), 57 G. 35 (Morbath);—1311. Harl. 53 E. 20 (Morbathe);—1338. Harl. 46 F. 26;—1379. Harl. 48 F. 42;—1396. Add. 15444;—1409. Harl. 55 G. 43, 44;—1410. Harl. 51 F. 40, 41;—1411. Harl. 46 G. 57.

—— Grant in Bornetome, etc., in, 1333. Harl. 47 H. 5.

—— Court - roll, 1433 (Morebath). Harl. Roll I. 4.

Moorby, *co. Linc.* License for grants in, to Greenfield Priory, 1392 (Moreby). Harl. 43 G. 53.

—— Sale of the manor, 1584 (Moreby). Add. 9273.

Moore. *v. sub* Rickmansworth, *co. Hertf.*

Moore, *nr. Fladbury, co. Worc.* Grant in, 1374 (More). Add. 14006.

Moorhouse. *v. sub* Hooton Paynel, *co. York.*

Moorhouse, *in Laxton, co. Nott.* Grant in, 1549 (Morehouse). Campb. xi. 2.

Moorhouses. *v. sub* Woolley, *co. York.*

Moorrow, *in Kelsick, co. Cumb.* Sale in, 1695. Add. 17194.

Moortown (Mora), *in High Ercall, co. Salop.* Grant of, with re-grant, early Steph. Harl. 54 G. 46;—late 12 cent. Harl. 55 B. 4.

Moorwood. *v. sub* Ashover, *co. Derb.*

Mor, *nr. S. Burlingham, co. Norf.* Papal conf. of the church and tithes in, to Horsham St. Faith Priory, 1163. Cott. MS. Aug. ii. 136.

Moramwic. *v. sub* Snaith, *co. York.*

Moray, *in Scotland.* Warrant of Edw. I. conc. submission of, 1296. Harl. 43 B. 8.

Morden, Guilden, *co. Camb.* Grant of the church, mill, domain, etc. (?), early Steph. (Morduna). Harl. 54 G. 46.

**Morden, Guilden,** co. *Camb.* (continued). Re-grant of the same (?), late 12 cent. (Mordona). Harl. 55 B. 4.

—— Reservation of homage, etc., due from Hugh Despenser in, 1255-6 (Geldenemordon). Add. 6293.

—— Grant of free warren in, by Edw. II., 1317 (Guldene Mordon). Harl. 84 C. 14.

—— Release in, 1622 (Gilden Morden). Add. 5278.

—— *Clericus de Mordonia al. Morduna.* Walchelinus, [1152-3]. Harl. 83 A. 25, 53.

**Morden, Steeple,** co. *Camb.* Grants, etc., in, 1256. Harl. 47 D. 14 (Stepelmordon);—t. Hen. III. Harl. 57 B. 13, Add. 25929 (Steplemorden);—t. Edw. I. Add. 25930 (Steplemordan), 25931 (Stepelmordon), 25932 ;—t. Edw. I.-II. Add. 25928 ; — 1410. Add. 25952 (Stepilmordon), 25953 ;—1457. Add. 25956.

**Mordiford,** co. *Heref.* Re-grant in Frome and Sufton in, 1332. Harl. 112 A. 20.

—— Exchange, etc., in, 1489. Harl. 112 E. 27 b (Mordyford);—1554. Add. 1826.

—— Exemplif. of recovery of Larpotte manor, etc., in, 1525. Woll. xii. 129.

—— Brief for rebuilding the church, 1811. Ch. Br. B. lii. 2.

**Mordon,** co. *Surr.* Conf. by Edw. the Confessor of a grant in, to Westminster Abbey, 1066 [sc. 1065] (Mordune). Cott. vi. 2 (copy).

—— Grant of the church to the Knts. Hospitallers, 1185 (Morduna). Harl. 43 I. 38.

—— Rental, early Hen. III. (Mordune). Add. 8139.

—— Feoffment, etc., in, 1478. Add. 23405, 23406 ;—1629. Add. 23589.

—— Court-rolls, 1485-1502, 1507-9. Add. 19407.

—— Precipes on covenants conc. land in, 1546. Add. 25501 ;—1601. Add. 25522 (Moredowne).

**Mordone.** v. Moredon, co. *Wilts.*

**More.** v. *sub* Marnhull, co. *Dors.*

—— v. *sub* Petherton, South, co. *Som.*

—— v. *sub* Rickmansworth, co. *Hertf.*

**More, La.** v. *sub* Bodenham, co. *Heref.*

—— v. *sub* Layer Marny, co. *Essex.*

**Moreby.** v. Moorby, co. *Linc.*

**Moredon,** co. *Wilts.* Conf. of grant in, [1227] (Mordone). Add. 7512.

**Morehall.** v. *sub* Campsey Ash, co. *Suff.*

**Morehelde ende, Morellynde.** v. *sub* Redmarley Dabitot, co. *Worc.*

**Morells.** v. *sub* Gosfield, co. *Essex.*

**More's,** *in Sturminster Marshall* (?), co. *Dors.* Grant of, [1204 ?] (Moreis). Harl. 45 I. 29.

**Mores,** *in Waltham H. Cross,* co. *Essex.* Mortgage of, 1566. Harl. 79 G. 25.

**Mores,** *in Romney Marsh,* co. *Kent.* Power to give seisin of the manor, 1418. Add. 8558.

**Moresbur, Moresburghe.** v. Mosborough, co. *Derb.*

**Moresk,** co. *Perth.* Grant in, 1268. Harl. 52 B. 16.

**Moretoin.** v. Mortain, *Honour of.*

**Moreton,** co. *Essex.* Fine in, 1437 (Morton). Harl. 54 E. 55.

**Moreton,** *in Thornbury,* co. *Glouc.* Conf. of grant in, 1301 (Morton). Add. 7736.

**Moreton,** co. *Northumb.* Mortgage of coalpits in, 1697. Add. 26392.

**Moreton,** co. *Salop.* Grant in, late 13 cent. (Morton). Add. 4886.

—— *Clericus.* Robertus, late 13 cent. Add. 4886.

**Moreton Corbet,** co. *Salop.* Brief conc. a fire in, 1813. Ch. Br. B. liv. 4.

**Moreton, North,** co. *Berks.* Release in, to New College, Oxford, 1384. Add. 24822.

—— Lease in, 1463 (North Mortone). Add. 20261.

**Morgannok, Morganwg.** v. Glamorgan, *County of.*

**Morgate,** nr. *Sherborne* (?), co. *Dors.* Lease at, from Sherborne Abbey, early Hen. III. Add. 6079.

**Morhale,** nr. *Lichfield,* co. *Staff.* Grant in, to Fairwell Priory, c. 1170. Cott. xxviii. 56.

**Morhamwic.** v. *sub* Snaith, co. *York.*

**Morhouses.** v. *sub* Hooton Paynel. co. *York.*

**Morton,** *nr. Southwell, co. Nott.* License for grant in. to the chapel of St. John the Evangelist, Normanton, 1331. Woll. v. 1.

—— Charge upon the manor for chantries in Crich, co. Derb., and Normanton, co. Nott., 1368. Woll. iv. 58.

—— Brief for repair of the church, 1754. Ch. Br. A. i. 1.

**Morton,** *in Bingley, co. York.* Grant, etc., in, 1547. Add. 17010, 17011.

**Morton,** [*nr. Billingley (?), co. York.* Assignment of lease in, 1572. Harl. 77 H. 37.

**Morton, Birts,** *co. Worc.* Grant in, 1322 (Mortone Brut). Harl. 86 D. 33.

—— *Dominus.* Ric. de Ruyhale, 1322. Harl. 86 D. 33.

**Morton, Castle,** *al.* **Morton Folet,** (Morton, etc.), *co. Worc.* Grants, etc., in, [1219–21?]. Harl. 83 B. 18; —*t.* Hen. III. Harl. 83 B. 20, 22.

—— Grants in Holibed, etc., in, to Lit. Malvern Priory, *t.* Hen. III. Harl. 83 B. 37, 44 (Morton Folet).

—— Exchange in, by Lit. Malvern Priory, *t.* Hen. III. (Morton Folet). Harl. 83 A. 44.

—— *Capellanus.* Thomas, *t.* Hen. III. Harl. 83 B. 37.

**Morton Jefferies,** *co. Heref.* Petition conc. outrages of R. de Schulle in, *t.* Rich. II. Cott. xxix. 41.

**Morton, Maids,** *co. Buck.* Grants, etc., in, to Biddlesdon Abbey, *t.* Hen. III. Harl. 85 F. 17 (Morton), 86 A. 17–20 (do.).

—— Grants, etc., in, *t.* Hen. III. Add. 5993 (Morton):—late 13 cent. Harl. 85 G. 13;—1403. Lansd. 569–571;—1425. Lansd. 573;—1454. Lansd. 574.

—— Leases in, by Biddlesdon Abbey, 1325. Harl. 84 E. 52 (Murton):—1330. Harl. 84 E. 56.

—— *Capellanus.* Walterus, 1245. Harl. 86 A. 22.

—— *Clericus.* Rob. fil. Ric. de Morton, 1239. Harl. 86 A. 5.

—— —— Gilbertus, *t.* Hen. III. Harl. 85 G. 17.

—— —— Walterus, *t.* Edw. I. Harl. 85 E. 20.

—— *Persona.* Rogerus, *t.* Hen. III. Harl. 86 E. 35, 36, 37.

**Morton, Maids,** *co. Buck. (continued).*
*Persona (continued).* Robertus, 1240. Harl. 84 D. 33, 86 A. 6;—*t.* Hen. III. Harl. 84 D. 41, 85 B. 14, 85 C. 27, 49, 50, 85 E. 11–14, 17, 23, 86 A. 11–15, 86 C. 35, 86 G. 19.

**Morton, North,** *nr. Retford, co. Nott.* Lease in, by Rufford Abbey, 1382 (North Mortone). Harl. 112 F. 44.

**Morton Pinkney** (Mortona, Morthon, etc.), *co. Northt.* Grants in. to Canons Ashby Priory, c. 1200. Add. 22320;—early 13 cent. Add. 5882.

—— Grants, etc., in, to Biddlesdon Abbey, [1203–18]. Harl. 86 A. 21;—post 1209. Harl. 86 B. 53, 54;—post 1232. Harl. 86 B. 58;—*t.* Hen. III. Harl. 84 I. 25;—1288. Harl. 86 C. 1.

—— Marriage settlement in, *t.* early Hen. III. Add. 20257.

—— Precipe on a covenant conc. land in, 1593. Add. 25173.

—— *Clericus.* Willelmus, 1240. Harl. 84 D. 32;—c. 1260. Harl. 85 A. 47.

—— *Persona.* Robertus, c. 1200. Add. 22320;—[1203–18]. Harl. 86 A. 21.

—— —— Leodegarius, *t.* Hen. III. Add. 5885.

—— *Vicarius.* Johannes, early 13 cent. Add. 5882.

**Mortyvaux.** *v. sub* Ashdon, *co. Essex.*

**Morvies** *al.* **Morieux.** *v. sub* Waldingfield, Great, *co. Suff.*

**Morwde.** *v. sub* Ashover, *co. Derb.*

**Morwick,** *co. Northumb.* Attornment in, 1348 (Morwyke). Harl. 54 C. 12.

**Mosborough,** *co. Derb.* Grants, etc., in, *t.* Hen. III. Harl. 83 G. 46 (Morsbur.), 47, 48 (Moresbur.), 49 (Morisburick), 50 (Morysburg), 51;—*t.* Edw. I. Cott. xxvii. 146 (Morisburge):—1315. Cott. xxvii. 147 (Moresburghe)—1317. Cott. xxvii. 148 (Moresburge), 149, Harl. 112 F. 62 (Moresburghe):—1334. Cott. xxvii. 150 (Morisburge), 151;—1336. Lansd. 107 (Moresburugh).

—— *Clericus.* Robertus, late Hen. III. Harl. 83 G. 47.

**Mose.** *v.* Moze with Beaumont, *co. Essex.*

**Moseley,** *co. Worc.* Brief for rebuilding the chapel, 1780. Ch. Br. B. xx. 6.

**Mosewella.** *v.* Muswell, *co. Midd.*

Moston Hall. *v. sub* Trimley St. Martin, *co. Suff.*

Motcombe, *co. Dors.* Lease in, 1543. Harl. 80 G. 52.

Mote. *v. sub* Ightbam, *co. Kent.*

—— *v.* Moat, *nr. Iden, co. Suss.*

Mottingham, *co. Kent.* Grant bounded by, 862 (Modinga hema mearc). Cott. viii. 32.

—— Power to give seisin in, 1422 (Modyngham). Slo. xxxii. 51.

Mottisfont, *co. Southt.* Precipe on a covenant conc. land in, 1578 (Mottesfounte). Add. 25225.

Mottrum [Mottram, *co. Chest.* (?)]. Rector. Petr. Romanus, 1263. Add. 8268.

Mottynden. *v. sub* Headcorn, *co. Kent.*

Moubray, Castle, *in Ulster.* Crown grant in, 1571. Add. 15574.

Moulsham, *co. Essex.* Conf. by Edw. the Confessor of a grant in, to Westminster Abbey, 1066 [*sc.* 1065] (Mulesham). Cott. vi. 2 (*copy*).

Moulsoe, *co. Buck.* Grants, etc., in, *t.* Hen. III. Add. 19919 (Molesho); —late 13 cent. Harl. 54 H. 47;— 1319. Harl. 53 C. 14 (Mullesho);— 1344. Harl. 52 I. 45 (Mulsho).

—— Acquittance for rent in, from Elstow Abbey, 1371 (Mulsho). Campb. x. 9.

Moulton, *co. Linc.* Grant in, 1341 (Molton). Harl. 53 E. 8.

—— Rental in, 1699. Add. 13595.

—— *Perpet. Vicarius.* Will. Watkynson, 1461. Add. 8403.

Moulton, *co. Norf.* Bequest of land at, 1038 (?) (on Mulan tune). Cott. MS. Aug. ii. 85.

—— *Rector.* Rob. de Brundale, *t.* Edw. I. (Moutune). Add. 14722.

Moulton (Multon), *co. Northt.* Grant in, *ante* 1185. Harl. 49 F. 53.

—— Covenant conc. repairs, etc., to the park, 1393. Add. 6047.

—— Demise of the site of a mill nr., 1443. Harl. 44 H. 35.

—— Acquittance for a bequest to the church, 1495. Add. 24710.

Moulton, *co. Suff.* Grants in, *t.* Edw. I. Lansd. 89;—1319. Harl. 48 C. 47 (Multon).

Moulton, *co. Suff.* (*continued*). Precipes on covenants conc. lands in, early Hen. VI. (Multon). Add. 25265;— 1555. Add. 25283;—1592. Add. 25444, 25445.

Moulton, *co. York.* Court-roll, 1441 (Multon). Harl. Roll G. 23.

Moulton, Great, *al.* St. Michaels, *co. Norf.* Sale of the manor and advowson, 1563. Harl. 111 E. 51.

—— Feoffment of the free chapel at, 1569. Add. 874.

Moulton, Little, *al.* All Saints, *co. Norf.* Sale of the advowson, etc., 1563. Harl. 111 E. 51.

Mounceux Manor. *v. sub* Wood Dalling, *co. Norf.*

Mouncton. *v.* Monkton, *co. Kent.*

Moundevilles Manor. *v. sub* Sternfield, *co. Suff.*

Mounseux Manor. *v. sub* Otley, *co. Suff.*

Mount. *v. sub* Elham, *co. Kent.*

Mount Grace, *co. York.* Grant, etc., of the manor, 1567. Harl. 76 D. 51, 77 E. 56, 86 H. 1.

—— Suit in, 1574, 1575. Harl. 76 D. 52.

Mount Sorrel, *co. Leic.* Treaty conc. the castle betw. the Earls of Chester and Leicester, [1151-2] (Munt Sorel). Cott. MS. Nero C. iii. f. 178.

—— Lease, etc., in, 1423. Add. 7108 (Mountsorell);—1428. Add. 7229;— 1442. Add. 7111;—1466. Add. 7242 (Mountsorel);—1484. Add. 7123 (Mountsorrell);—1501. Add. 7131.

Mountarran *al.* Crosclogh *al.* Crosloe, *co. Carlow.* Lease of the town lands, etc., 1697. Add. 24472.

Mounterbirne *al.* Kinard, *in Aghaloo parish, co. Tyrone.* Decree conc. restoration of, to C. Bolton, 1663. Eg. 315.

Mountfield, *co. Suss.* Grant in Oppoland in, *t.* Hen. III. or Edw. I. Add. 5646.

—— Grants, etc., in, *t.* Hen. III.-Edw. I. Add. 5644 (Mundefeld), 5647 (do.);—1293-4. Add. 5648 (do.);— 1335. Add. 5651 (Mondefeld);— 1342. Add. 5653 (Mundefelde);— 1344. Add. 20158 (Mondefelda);— 1358. Add. 9233 (Mundifeld);—1429. Add. 5656 (Mundfeld);—1433. Add.

5658 ;—1440. Add. 5659 ;—1446. Add.
5660 ;—1451. Add. 5663 ;—1466. Add.
5669.

—— Grant of the advowson to Robertsbridge Abbey, c. 1307-8 (Mundefeld).
Eg. 398.

—— Conveyance, etc., of Ferne manor,
etc., in, 1466. Add. 5667 :—1468.
Add. 5668 ;—1471. Add. 5669 :—
1479. Add. 5299 ;—1541. Add. 5675.

Mountgomery. v. Montgomery, co.
Montgom.

Mountjoy. v. sub Haveringland, co.
Norf.

Moushole, co. Cornw. Grant in,
1518. Eg. 276.

Mow, co. Roxb. Covenant conc. bounds
in, betw. Melrose and Kelso Abbeys,
[1208 ?] (Molle). Cott. xviii. 17.

—— Grant of free forestry in, to
Melrose Abbey, 1236 (Molla). Cott.
xviii. 7.

Mowgranger. v. Moggerhanger, co.
Bedf.

Mowlesworth. v. Molesworth, co.
Hunt.

Mowthorpe, co. York. Alienation of
the grange, 1623. Add. 888.

Moze with Beaumont, co. Essex.
Payments to the rector, 1421-2. Add.
682 (Mose).

—— Persona. Will. de Thornton,
1329. Add. 9934 (Meuse).

—— Rector. Will. de Braunford,
1329. Add. 9932 (Moese).

—— —— Hugo Thyrs, 1421-2.
Add. 682.

Much Hadham. v. Hadham, Much,
co. Hertf.

Much Marcle. v. Marcle, Much, co.
Heref.

Mucham. v. Mitcham, co. Surr.

Muchland Manor, in Furness, co.
Lanc. Compotus-rolls, 1514, 1515
(Micheland). Add. 24451.

Mucking, co. Essex. Vicarius. Johannes, 1398 (Mokkynge). Harl. 84
B. 22.

Muckleston, cos. Staff. and Salop.
Briefs for rebuilding the church, 1786,
1790. Ch. Br. B. xxvi. 3, xxx. 10.

—— Briefs conc. fires at Pool Hall
in, 1798, 1803. Ch. Br. B. xxxviii.
3, xliii. 7.

—— Brief conc. a fire in, 1799. Ch
Br. B. xxxix. 1.

Muckton, co. Linc. Grants in, t. Edw.
II. (Mucton). Harl. 52 H. 26 ;—1322.
Harl. 52 H. 33 (Mukton) ;—1337.
Harl. 52 H. 37 (Mockton).

Mudford, co. Som. Grants, etc., in
Old Sock in, 1342. Harl. 47 B. 33
(Sok Malerbe) ;—1359. Harl. 45 F.
45 (Oldesok), 45 G. 45 (Oldesokk);
—1431. Harl. 46 H. 13 (Oldesok);
—1438. Add. 50 E. 6 (Sokke).

—— Release, etc., in Kingston
(Kyngeston juxta Modeforde Terry)
nr., 1342. Harl. 53 A. 2 ;—1403.
Harl. 48 B. 6 ;—1414. Harl. 48 I. 25.

—— Covenant to adjourn suit conc.
lands in Kingston (Kyngeston juxta
Modeford Terry) nr., 1404. Harl.
46 G. 40.

—— Grant of the manor, 1414 (Modeford). Harl. 48 I. 25.

Mugeshale al. Muggesale, nr. Middlewich, co. Chest. Grant, etc., in,
1310. Add. 19978 ;—1317. Harl.
45 I. 34.

Mugginton, co. Derb. Grant, etc., in,
1391. Woll. vi. 41 (Mogynton) ;—
1431. Woll. i. 85.

—— Claim of presentation to the
church, 1511 (Moggyngton). Woll.
xi. 21.

—— Persona. Tho. Eston, t. Edw. II.
Woll. xi. 21.

—— —— Joh. Whitehed, 1380.
Harl. 112 F. 32 (Mogyngton). Lansd.
135.

—— Rector. Johannes, 1256. Woll.
vi. 47.

—— Rector medietatis ecclesie. Ric.
Bec, 1431 (Mogynton). Woll. i. 85.

Mukelton. v. Mickleton, co. Glouc.

Mulan tune. v. Moulton, co. Norf.

Mulbarton, co. Norf. Mortgage in,
1384 (Mulkeberton). Add. 14592.

—— Release of the manor, 1614. Add.
14284.

Mulebourne, Mullebourne. v. Milborne Deverel, co. Dors.

Mulesham. v. Moulsham, co. Essex.

Mulintone. v. Mellington, nr. Church
Stoke, co. Montgom.

Mulkeberton. v. Mulbarton, co. Norf.

Mulleborne Beek. v. Milborne
Stileham, in Bere Regis, co. Dors.

Mullesworth. v. Molesworth, co.
Hunt.

2 M

Muskham, South, co. *Nott.* Precipe
on a covenant conc. lands in, 1578.
Add. 25199.

Musters Manor. *v. sub* Ashover, *co.
Derb.*

Muston, *co.* —— (?). *Clericus.* Ricardus, 1278 (Mustun). Woll. x. 41.

Muston [Winterborne Muston (?), *in
Bere Regis*], *co. Dors.* Grant of wardship in, [1550–53] (Musterton). Cott.
MS. Vesp. F. xiii. art. 222.

Muston, *co. Kent.* Grant in, 1512.
Harl. 80 D. 31.

Muswell, *co. Midd.* Conf. of grant of,
to Clerkenwell Nunnery, [1152–60 ?]
(Mosewella). Harl. 83 C. 26.

Mutford, *co. Suff.* Grants, etc., of the
manor, 1429. Harl. 43 I. 50 ;—1447.
Harl. 52 A. 26;—1606. Add. 14275 ;
—1607. Add. 14276;—1608. Add.
14279.

—— Demise of Fastolf's manor in,
1429. Harl. 43 H. 9.

—— Release in, 1435. Harl. 58 C. 14.

Mutford Hundred, *co. Suff.* Grant
of, 1429. Harl. 43 I. 50.

Muttenden. *v. sub* Headcorn, *co. Kent.*

Muttuncnikel, *in Forton, co. Lanc.*
Grant to Furness Abbey in exchange
for, *t.* Hen. III. Harl. 52 I. 1.

Muytone. *v.* Myton, *co. Warw.*

Myddelsoway. *v.* Middlezoy, *co. Som.*

Myddelton. *v.* Milton next Sittingbourne, *co. Kent.*

Mydleton next Wirkesworth. *v.*
Middleton, *by Wirksworth, co. Derb.*

Mydweyha. *v.* Medway, *River, co.
Kent.*

Myldecombe. *v.* Milcombe, *co. Oxon.*

Myldenhale. *v.* Mildenhall, *co. Suff.*

Myldyng. *v.* Milding, *co. Suff.*

Mylen burnan. *v.* Milbourn, *co.
Wilts.*

Mylentun, *nr. Kemsing, co. Kent.* Grant
at, 822. Cott. MS. Aug. ii. 93.

Mylland farm. *v. sub* Trotton, *co.
Suss.*

Myllenyth. *v.* Maelienydd, *co. Radn.*

Mynchencourte. *v. sub* Shadoxhurst,
*co. Kent.*

Myncomb. *v.* Mincombe, *in Sidbury,
co. Devon.*

Mynnysmere. *v. sub* Westleton, *co.
Suff.*

Mynstre. *v.* Minster, *in Thanet, co.
Kent.*

Myntye. *v.* Minety Hundred, *co. Glouc.*

Mynyddyalwyn, *co. Monm.* Precipe
on a covenant conc. land in, 1593
(Mynyddyscloyn). Add. 25138.

Myræsegæ, Myresi, Myres ige. *v.*
Mersea, *co. Essex.*

Myserder. *v.* Miserden, *co. Glouc.*

Mysyn. *v.* Misson, *co. Nott.*

Mytford. *v.* Mitford, *in Freshford, co.
Som.*

Mythingesby. *v.* Miningsby, *co. Linc.*

Myton, *nr. Warwick, co. Warw.* Release in, 1335 (Muytone). Cott. xxviii.
21.

Myton, *nr. Hull, co. York.* Releases,
etc., of the manor with lands called
Kyngesfee in, 1424. Harl. 54 I. 8;—
1430. Harl. 43 E. 19 (Miton), 54 I.
12 :—1431. Harl. 45 I. 12 (Mytton),
54 I. 15.

# N

Naas, *co. Kildare.* Pleas held at, 1330.
Add. 13599.

—— Petition from the Portreeves,
etc., conc. riots, 1454. Cott. iv. 35.

Naby *al.* Nateby, *in Ronald Kirk, co.
York.* Grant in, by Jas. I., 1612.
Cott. xiii. 35.

Nackington, *co. Kent.* Grants, etc.,
of Nackington (Natyndon, etc.) and
Sextrey manors in, 1507. Harl. 79
B. 3 ;—1541. Harl. 75 H. 3 ;—1564.
Harl. 76 F. 30;—1567. Harl. 77
H. 26, 79 G. 23;—1569. Harl. 77 H.
33, 34, 36;—1574. Harl. 77 A. 39.

—— Conf. of grant of rent charge on
the manor, 1508 (Natynden). Harl.
78 E. 29.

—— Valor of crown lands in the
manor, *t.* Hen. VIII. (Natyndon).
Harl. Roll S. 34.

—— Fine of Diggslands, etc., in, 1548.
Harl. 75 H. 4, 76 H. 50.

—— Conveyance in, 1557 (Natyndon).
Harl. 76 I. 27, 34.

—— Fine in, 1568. Harl. 77 A. 21.

—— Acquittance for homage for the
manor, 1572 (Natynglon *al.* Sextrye).
Harl. 77 A. 41.

Nacton, *co. Suff.* Suit conc. Sholond manor, etc., in, 1456. Add. 17244.

—— Grants, etc., in, 1473. Add. 10217 (Naketon), 10218;—1526. Add. 19360; —1538. Add. 10225 (Necton).

—— Covenant conc. title to lands in, 1713. Add. 10263 a.

Nafferton, *co. Northumb.* Exchequer acquittance for farm of the manor, 1613. Add. 25632.

Nafferton, *co. York.* Acquittances for tithes in, due from Meaux Abbey to Whitby Abbey, 1502–8 (Nafraton). Lansd. 550.

—— Warrant conc. a recovery of the manor, 1510. Cott. xv. 11.

—— Grant of annuity from the demesne of, 1536 (Naffreton). Harl. 54 G. 24.

—— Fines, etc., in, 1576. Add. 18858 ; —1594. Add. 18877, 18878 ;—1597. Add. 18874;—1598. Add. 18884;— 1606. Add. 18901 ; — 1616. Add. 18921;—1617. Add. 18922;—1624. Add. 18931.

—— Release of the manor, 1626. Add. 18932.

Nailsea, *co. Som.* Grants, etc., in, t. Edw. I.–t. Edw. II. Add. 5445 (Naylsy), 7779 (Naylesye);—1337. Add. 5453 (Naylesy), 5454 (Naillesy) ; — 1351. Add. 5455 (Nayleshey);—1405. Add. 5466 (Naylsy);—1484. Add. 5474 (Nailesey).

—— Grant of the manor, 1472 (Naylesey). Add. 5472.

Nailstone, *co. Leic.* Marriage settlement, etc., in, 1335. Add. 24208 (Nayliston);—1428. Add. 24218;— 1502. Add. 24229.

—— Power to take seisin of the manor, 1460. Add. 24222.

Nakingdon. *v.* Nackington, *co. Kent.*

Nancemear, *nr. Truro, co. Cornw.* Power to give seisin, etc., in, 1363. Add. 15350 (Nansmour);—1410. Add. 15353 (Nansmoghe).

Nanhurst (?). *v. sub* Cranley, *co. Surr.*

Nanscent, Nansynt. *v.* St. Issey, *co. Cornw.*

Nansclasen, Nansglasen, *nr. Creed, co. Cornw.* Grants, etc., in, 1400–1438. Add. 12974 - 12996 ; — 1427. Add. 13046.

Nantallan, *co. Cornw.* Grants, etc., in, 1392. Harl. 50 C. 37 (Nanstalen); —1394. Harl. 51 E. 16 (do.) ;—1412. Harl. 50 C. 40 (Lantalan);—1513. Harl. 50 C. 41 (Nanstalan);—1594. Harl. 50 C. 48 (Nanstallan).

Nantclokenig, *River, co. Glam.* Grant on, to Margam Abbey, *t.* Hen. II. Harl. 75 B. 29.

Nanteglus. *v.* Llaneglwys, *co. Brecon.*

Nantwich, *co. Chest.* Grants, etc., in, [1303–6]. Add. 20501 (Wycus Malbanc);—1309. Add. 20481 (Wich Malbank);—1321. Add. 20500 (Wycus Malbanus).

—— Settlement of the manor, 1325 (Wich Malbank). Add. 6278.

—— Leases, etc., in Willaston in, and of a Wychehous in, 1338. Campb. xxviii. 2 ;—1356. Campb. xxviii. 7 ; —1395. Campb. xxviii. 8 ; — 1400. Campb. xxviii. 10.

—— Inquisition conc. the manor, 1409 (Wicus Malbani). Woll. xi. 5.

—— Briefs for rebuilding the church, 1789. Ch. Br. B. xxix. 11;—1793. Ch. Br. B. xxxiii. 1.

Napton on the Hill, *co. Warw.* Grant of the manor and advowson, *t.* Edw. I. (Naptona). Cott. xxviii. 1.

—— Grant, etc., in, 1322. Cott. xxviii. 2;—1405. Cott. xii. 8.

—— *Persona.* Willelmus, late Hen. III. Add. 21477.

—— *Rector.* Mag. Walterus, *t.* Edw. I. Cott. xxviii. 1.

Narberth, *co. Pembr.* Compotus of the receiver of the manor, 1413–14 (Nerberth). Campb. xx. 2.

Narborough, *co. Leic.* Feoffment, etc., of the manor and town, 1444 (Northburghe). Harl. 83 F. 3, 4, 112 H. 47–51.

Narborow. *v.* Northborough, *co. Northt.*

Narford, *co. Norf.* Papal conff. of grants in, to Sawtrey Abbey, 1176. Cott. MS. Aug. ii. 125 (Nerfordia);— 1195. Cott. MS. Aug. ii. 111 (Nareford), 115 (Nerford).

Narteford, Nartesford. *v.* Snarford, *co. Linc.*

Naseby (Nauesbi, Nauesby, etc.), *co. Northt.* Grants, etc., in, to Sulby Abbey, late 12 cent.–t. John. Add. 22007, 22321 - 22328, 22332, 22333,

22339, 22424, 22433 ;—*t.* Hen. III.-
*t.* Edw. I. Add. 22320, 22330, 22331,
22334–22337, 24320 (Nauisby).

—— Grants, etc., in, *t.* John. Add.
22329 ;—late Hen. III. Add. 22340
(Nauisby) ;—1650. Add. 6127 :—1685.
Add. 5375, 5376.

—— *Persona.* Rob. Byset, early 13
cent. Add. 22433.

—— —— Robertus, *t.* John–*t.* Hen.
III. Add. 22333, 22336, 22337.

—— *Rector, quondam.* Dom. Joh.
Busshoptre, 1416. Harl. 47 F. 8.

**Nash, Lower,** *co. Pembr.* Conveyance
of the manor, 1441 (Netherasshe).
Harl. 80 A. 15.

**Nash, Upper,** *co. Pembr.* Conveyance
of the manor, 1441 (Overasshe). Harl.
80 A. 15.

**Nasing.** *v.* Nazeing, *co. Essex.*

**Nassaburgh Hundred.** *v.* Peterborough, *Liberty of, co. Northt.*

**Nassington,** *co. Northt.* Grant in, by
Rich. I., to Earl David, 1194 (Nas-
sintona). Cott. MS. Nero C. iii. f. 191
(*copy*).

—— License to endow Fotheringay
College with the manor, 1415 (Nos-
sington). Campb. x. 5.

—— Grant in, 1517 (Nasshyngton).
Harl. 55 G. 18.

—— Exchequer acquittance for a fine
in, 1567. Add. 25583.

**Nastoke.** *v.* Navestock, *co. Essex.*

**Natgrave.** *v.* Notgrove, *co. Glouc.*

**Natornan,** *in St. Columb Minor, co.
Cornw.* Lease, etc., in, 1558. Add.
13081 ;—1576. Add. 13084.

**Natynden, Natyndon.** *v.* Nackington, *co. Kent.*

**Nauesbi, Nauisby.** *v.* Naseby, *co.
Northt.*

**Naughton,** *co. Suff.* Grant, etc., in,
*t.* Edw. I. Harl. 57 F. 8 (Nauelton) ;
—1398. Add. 10571 (Nauuton).

—— Grant of the advowson, etc.,
1349 (Nauelton). Add. 10569.

—— *Persona.* Dom. Joh. de Bokenham. *c.* 1349 (Noulton). Harl. 57
C. 28.

**Naunton,** *co. Glouc.* Settlement in
Harford (Hertford) in, 1359. Slo.
xxxiii. 40.

—— —— Settlement in Aylworth (Eyle-
worthe) in, 1412. Slo. xxxiii. 59.

**Naunton,** *in Winchcombe, co. Glouc.*
Leases, etc., of the manor, 1551. Harl.
76 I. 9 ;—1569. Harl. 111 E. 58 ;—
1578. Harl. 77 A. 49, 85 H. 8 ;—1580.
Harl. 77 H. 44 ;—1587. Harl. 77 H. 45.

—— Petition of the escheator for discharge in respect of the manor, 1552.
Harl. Roll BB. 15.

**Naunton,** *co. Worc.* Conf. of grants
at, to Pershore Abbey, 972 (in Niwau-
tune). Cott. MS. Aug. ii. 6.

**Naunton Beauchamp,** *co. Worc.*
Feoffment of the manor, 1370 (Newenton Beauchamp). Add. 20422.

**Nauuton.** *v.* Naughton, *co. Suff.*

**Navestock,** *co. Essex.* Grants "apud
Tyam," etc., in, *t.* Hen. III. Lansd.
85 (Nastoke) ;—1296. Lansd. 97 (do.).

—— Licenses from the Dean and
Chapter of St. Paul's to fell timber in,
1436. Lansd. 37 (Nauestoke) ;—1440.
Lansd. 631.

—— Release by the "Firmarius" of St.
Paul's of actions on account of repairs
in the manor, 1458. Lansd. 653.

—— *Clericus.* Ricardus, *t.* Hen. III.
Lansd. 85.

—— *Vicarius.* Walterus, *t.* Hen. III.
Lansd. 85.

**Nawton.** *v. sub* Alderton, *co. Suff.*

**Nayland,** *co. Suff.* Grants, etc., in,
early 13 cent.–*t.* Edw. I. Harl. 45 C.
10 (Nyelonde), 47 I. 28 (Neyland), 50
B. 7 (Nielend). 54 H. 11 (Nelend) ;—
1433. Add. 5253 (Neyland).

—— Precipes on covenants conc. lands
in, 1546. Add. 25272 (Nayland) ;—
1561. Add. 25311 ;— 1592. Add.
25446.

**Naylesye, Naylsy.** *v.* Nailsea, *co.
Som.*

**Naseing** *al.* **Nasing,** *co. Essex.* Recovery, etc., in, 1560. Harl. 77 F. 27 ;
—1561. Harl. 75 E. 34, 36, 75 H. 8,
10, 79 F. 13.

—— Fine in, 1561. Harl. 80 C. 35, 36.

—— Release of the manor, 1561.
Harl. 80 F. 13.

—— Precipe on a covenant conc. lands
in, 1587. Add. 24978.

**Neath,** *River, co. Glam.* Suit conc.
land nr., betw. Caerleon and Margam
Abbeys, 1203 (Fluvius de Neht). Harl.
75 A. 32.

—— Conf. of fishery in, to Margam
Abbey, 1246 (Neth). Harl. 75 C. 25.

Neath, *River, co. Glam.* (*continued*). Verdict in suit of Neath Abbey conc. the course of, 1249 (Neth). Harl. 75 C. 42.

Neath, *co. Glam. Constabularius.* Ernaldus, early 13 cent. (Neth). Harl. 75 C. 35.

Neatham, *in Holybourne, co. Southt.* Papal conf. of grant of, from K. Stephen, to Waverley Abbey, 1147 (Nietham). Lansd. 27.

—— Precipe on a covenant conc. land in, 1578 (Neteham). Add. 25224.

Neatishead, *co. Norf.* Appropriation of the church to Hulme Abbey, *c.* 1150 (Neteshirde). Cott. iv. 57 (13) (*copy*).

Nebrunne. *v.* Newbourne, *co. Suff.*

Necton. *v.* Nacton, *co. Suff.*

Necton, *co. Norf.* Release in, *t.* Edw. I. or II. (Neketon). Add. 6192.

—— Release of Sparham (Sperham) manor in, 1380. Add. 8114.

Neddrum Island, *co. Down.* Roll of charters conc. foundation of Neddrum Priory in, late 13 cent. Cott. xiii. 21.

Nedging, *co. Suff.* Bequest of land at, *post* 991 (Huydding). Harl. 43 C. 4.

Nedrefelde. *v.* Netherfield, *nr. Battle, co. Suss.*

Needham, *co. Norf.* Grant, etc., in, 1353. Harl. 44 G. 10 (Nedham);—1430. Harl. 43 E. 19.

Needham Market, *co. Suff.* Precipes on covenants conc. lands in, 1589. Add. 25409;—1593. Add. 25475.

Needwood Forest, *co. Staff.* Grants, etc., in, 1248. Campb. xi. 5 (Nedwode);—1309. Campb. xi. 12 (do.); —1373. Woll. vi. 59 (do.).

—— License to hunt fox and hare in, 1262 (do.). Eg. 443.

—— Grant at Hanbury in, *c.* 1265 (Neydwode). Add. 20459.

—— Petitions of the borderers of, *t.* Chas. II. Add. 15884, 15885.

Neenton, *co. Salop.* Release in, 1316 (Nethere Neuton). Cott. xxiv. 13.

Neht, Fluvius de. *v.* Neath, *River, co. Glam.*

Neiche, Le. *v. sub* Wanborough, *co. Wilts.*

Neigh, *co. Som.* Release in, 1343 (La Nye). Harl. 54 D. 26.

—— Conveyance of the manor, 1384 (do.). Harl. 48 A. 28.

Neither Langwith. *v.* Langwith, Nether, *in Cuckney, co. Nott.*

Neketon. *v.* Necton, *co. Norf.*

Nelehampton. *v. sub* Speldhurst, *co. Kent.*

Nelend. *v.* Nayland, *co. Suff.*

Nelmes. *v. sub* Ash, *nr. Sandwich, co. Kent.*

Nenfeld. *v.* Ninfield, *co. Suss.*

Neobold. *v.* Newbold Saucey, *nr. Ouston, co. Leic.*

Neodemestan wic, [*nr. Droitwich, co. Worc.?*]. Conf. of salt-works at, to Pershore Abbey, 972. Cott. MS. Aug. ii. 6.

Nesbitt, *co. Durh.* Grant of the manor, 1407. Lansd. 353.

Ness, *in Stonegrave, co. York.* Grant in Waterholme near, *c.* 1295 (Nesse). Harl. 112 C. 6.

Nesse Mathew, *co. Devon.* Grant of markets and fairs in, 1286. Harl. 58 I. 38 (*copy*).

Neston, *co. Chest.* Attornment of the manor to the Earl of Salisbury, 1337. Harl. 43 D. 26.

—— Conf. by Edw. III. of an exchange of the manor with Qu. Isabella, 1338. Cott. xi. 61.

—— Livery of, to Eliz., Countess of Salisbury, *c.* 1400. Add. 662.

Neteham. *v.* Neatham, *co. Southt.*

Netelcombe. *v.* Nettlecombe, *co. Som.*

Netelton, Neteltun. *v.* Nettleton, *co. Linc.*

Neteshirde. *v.* Neatishead, *co. Norf.*

Neth. *v.* Neath, *River, co. Glam.*

Nether Hall. *v.* Netherhall.

Nether Lyme. *v. sub* Lyme Regis, *co. Dors.*

Nether Neuton. *v.* Neenton, *co. Salop.*

Nether Weld, The. *v.* Weld, The Nether, *nr. Colney Street, co. Hertf.*

Netheravon, *co. Wilts.* Fine of the manor, 1627. Add. 15123.

Netherbury, *co. Dors.* Grant in Hokbere [Oxbridge?] in, *t.* Hen. III. or Edw. I. Harl. 47 F. 20.

—— Fines, etc., in N. and S. Bowood, E. Melphash and Hocbere *al.* Hogbere in, 1333. Harl. 49 H. 54, 55;—

1392. Harl. 56 E. 32;—1438. Harl. 50 E. 6;—1447. Harl. 56 F. 11–13; —1449. Harl. 46 H. 24, 25;—1468. Harl. 52 A. 41.

**Nethercote,** *in Bourton on the Water,* co. *Glouc.* Settlement in, 1412. Slo. xxxiii. 59.

———— Grant of the manor by Jas. I., 1612. Cott. xiii. 35.

**Nethercote,** co. *Warw.* Release in, 1598. Add. 1011.

**Nethercourt.** *v. sub* Burghfield, co. *Berks.*

———— *v. sub* Farningham, co. *Kent.*

———— *v. sub* Faversham, co. *Kent.*

**Netherfield,** *nr. Battle,* co. *Suss.* Conf. of tithes in, to Battle Abbey, [1121–5] (Nedrefelde). Cott. MS. Nero C. iii. f. 189.

———— Covenants, etc., conc. the manor, 1343. Add. 20121 (Nedderfeld);— 1344. Add. 20122 (do.)—1345. Add. 20116 (do.);—1349. Add. 20117 (do.), 20118 (do.).

**Netherhalford.** *v.* Halliford, co. *Midd.*

**Netherhalgh.** *v.* Haugh, co. *York.*

**Netherhall, Nether Hall** *v. sub* Barningham, co. *Suff.*

———— *v. sub* Darley, co. *Derb.*

———— *v. sub* Fletching, co. *Suss.*

———— *v. sub* Lavenham, co. *Suff.*

———— *v. sub* Roydon, co. *Essex.*

———— *v. sub* Saxlingham, co. *Norf.*

———— *v. sub* Stoke by Nayland, co. *Suff.*

———— *v. sub* Waldingfield, Lit., co. *Suff.*

**Netherhards.** *v.* Hardres, Nether *al.* Lower, co. *Kent.*

**Netherlokhaw.** *v.* Locko, Nether, co. *Derb.*

**Netherstock,** *in Halstock,* co. *Dors.* Grant in, to Sherborne Abbey, [1246–59] (Netherstok). Add. 6078.

———— Mortgage of Bickebere wood in, 1253. Add. 5991.

———— Grant in, *t.* Hen. III. (Niperstok). Add. 6077.

———— Lease in, by Sherborne Abbey, 1347 (Netherstok). Add. 6082.

**Netherthorpe.** *v. sub* Staveley, co. *Derb.*

**Netherton,** co. *Worc.* Court-roll, 1644. Add. 26902.

**Nethertynton.** *v.* Toynton, Low, co. *Linc.*

**Netherwent.** *v. sub* Monmouth, County of.

**Netherwere.** *v.* Weare, Nether, co. *Som.*

**Netherwood,** co. *Heref.* Lease of the demesnes, c. 1433 (Netherwode). Harl. 53 H. 17.

**Nethir lippijate.** *v.* Lypiatt, Lower, *in Stroud,* co. *Glouc.*

**Nethurfrenescourt.** *v. sub* Sutton St. Nicholas, co. *Heref.*

**Nethurfylkyngs.** *v.* Filkins, *nr.* Broughton Pogis, co. *Oxon.*

**Netteswell,** co. *Essex.* Extract from court-roll, 1556. Add. 4818.

**Nettington.** *v.* Nottington, *in Broadway,* co. *Dors.*

**Nettlebed,** co. *Oxon.* Lease in, 1408 (Netylbed). Add. 20388.

**Nettlecombe,** co. *Som.* A rent in Watchet reserved to the lord of the fee of, 1381 (Nettlecoumb). Add. 11182.

———— *Persona.* Joh. Hywyssch, 1403 (Netelcombe). Add. 11189.

**Nettlestead,** co. *Suff.* Precipe on a covenant conc. land in, 1593. Add. 25476.

**Nettlestone,** *I. of Wight.* Release in, 1329 (Noteleston). Add. 22614.

**Nettleton,** co. *Linc.* Grants, etc., in. late 12 cent. Harl. 53 C. 41 (Neteltun);—early Hen. III. Cott. xxvii. 56 (do.), Harl. 54 A. 38, 39 (Neteltun).

———— Grants in, to the Knts. Hospitallers, late 12 cent. Harl. 53 C. 42;—early 13 cent. Harl. 53 C. 43 (Netelton).

———— (Nettleton, Netelton, etc.). Grants, etc., in, to Newhouse Abbey, early 13 cent. Harl. 53 C. 44, 57 C. 44;—1236. Harl. 43 A. 61 a;—1239. Cott. xvi. 44;—*t.* Hen. III. Cott. v. 68, 71, xxvi. 29, xxviii. 4, Harl. 51 E. 34, 54 A. 36, 37, 41, 58 A. 25–28;— 1262–3. Harl. 54 C. 48;—late Hen. III. Cott. v. 54, Harl. 54 A. 40:—*t.* Edw. I. Harl. 46 E. 17, 55 B. 17, 55 E. 46, 58 D. 18–20.

———— Releases in, to Newhouse Abbey, from Jews of Lincoln, 1236. Harl. 43 A. 61 b.;—c. 1236. Cott. xxvi. 29.

———— Exchanges in, betw. Newhouse Abbey and Sixhills Priory, 1242. Harl. 44 G. 48;—1245. Harl. 44 G. 49.

**Newark,** *co. Nott.* (*continued*). Grant in, from Bullington Priory, *t.* Edw. I. (Neuwerck). Harl. 44 B. 3.

—— Lease in, to the guild of St. Peter by Bullington Priory, 1308 (Newerk). Harl. 44 B. 5.

—— Defeasance of grant in, with the guild of H. Trinity of, 1470. Harl. 83 D. 17.

—— Precipe on a covenant conc. houses in, 1555. Add. 25189.

—— Lease of the Chauntrie, etc., in, 1628. Woll. xi. 33.

—— Assignment of life interest of Qu. Catharine of Braganza in the castle, etc., 1680. Harl. 111 H. 11.

—— *Constabularius.* Joh. Breton, *t.* Hen. III. Harl. 50 B. 1.

—— —— Hen. de Sibtorp, *t.* Hen. III. Harl. 55 C. 10.

—— *Rector.* Dom. Feutro Albertini, 1327 (Newerk). Add. 21105.

—— *Vicarius perpetuus.* Joh. Burton, 1470. Harl. 83 D. 17.

—— *Magister Scolarum.* Mag. Simon de Boteleaford, 1345 (Neuwerk). Woll. ii. 25.

**Newbald, North,** *co. York.* Appointment of L. Sterne to the prebend of, in succession to Rob. Hitch, 1742. Add. 16161.

**Newbiggin,** *in Woodhorn, co. Northumb.* Reservation of rent in, *c.* 1300 (Neubigging). Harl. 57 C. 38.

**Newbiggin,** *in Shotley, co. Northumb.* Covenant to settle lands in, on J. de Middylton, 1421 (Newbiggyng juxt Blancheland). Cott. xii. 41.

**Newbiggin,** *in Bishopdale, co. York.* Grant in, *c.* 1230-50 (Newbigginge in Biscoppedale). Add. 21179.

**Newbold** (Neubold, etc.), *in Chesterfield, co. Derb.* Grants, etc., "super Brocholcclif," in or nr., early 13 cent. Harl. 112 I. 42 ;—*t.* Hen. III. Harl. 112 G. 35, 112 I. 43, 44.

—— Grants, etc., in, *t.* Hen. III.-*t.* Edw. I. Harl. 84 A. 56, 112 G. 54 (Neubald), Woll. vii. 11 ;—1339. Cott. xxviii. 8.

—— Grant in, "apud Susane wolle," 1338. Harl. 83 E. 11.

—— Fines in, 1541. Woll. ii. 71 ;—1704. Add. 18065.

—— *Clericus.* Willelmus, *t.* Hen. III. Harl. 112 I. 43, 44.

—— —— W——, *t.* Edw. I. Woll. iii. 20.

**Newbold,** *in Breedon, co. Leic.* Grant in, 1356 (Neubolt). Lansd. 637.

**Newbold** (Neubele, Neubela), *co. Linc.* Grants, etc., in or nr., to Bullington Priory, *c.* 1175. Harl. 52 G. 28 ;—*c.* 1205. Harl. 52 A. 18 (*copy*) (Nubele), 54 A. 45 ;—late Hen. III. Cott. xxviii. 7, Harl. 50 D. 47, 57 E. 17.

—— —— Covenant betw. Bullington and Stainfield Priories conc. pasture in, etc., [1188 ?]. Harl. 44 A. 23.

—— Covenant betw. Barlings Abbey and Bullington Priory conc. wood and fishing in, 1242. Harl. 44 A. 9.

—— Lease in, to Barlings Abbey from Bullington Priory, 1452. Harl. 44 B. 15.

**Newbold,** *in Catesby, co. Northt.* Power to give seisin in, 1405. Cott. xii. 8.

**Newbold,** *in Clipston, co. Northt.* Grant, etc., in, *t.* Hen. III. Add. 21482 (Newbolt) :—1370. Add. 21682 ;—1435-6. Add. 21485.

**Newbold Pacey,** *co. Warw.* Release in, 1325. Add. 21486.

—— *Rector, quondam.* Dom. Ad. de Steingreve, 1325. Add. 21486.

**Newbold Pantolf.** *v.* Newbold upon Avon, *co. Warw.*

**Newbold Saucey,** *nr. Ouston, co. Leic.* Grant and mortgage of, *t.* Hen. II. (Neobold). Harl. 45 C. 40.

**Newbold upon Avon,** *co. Warw.* Conf. of the church to Monks Kirby Priory, [1198 - 1208] (Neuboldum). Add. 20862.

—— Grants, etc., in, *t.* Hen. III. Add. 21480 (Neubold), 21483 (do.), 21487 (Neubold Pantolf).

—— Grants, etc., in, to Pipewell Abbey, 1246. Add. 21481 (Neubolde) ;—[1246-9]. Add. 21479 (do.) ;—1273. Add. 5881 (Neubold Pantolf) ;—1275. Add. 21489, 21490.

—— Warrant for inquest on lands of Pipewell Abbey in, 1278 (Neubold). Add. 21484.

—— Power conc. rents of Pipewell Abbey in, late 13 cent. (Neubold Pantolf). Add. 21488.

—— *Persona.* Alardus, [1155-67]. Add. 20567.

—— —— Matheus, *t.* Hen. II. Add. 21458.

—— *Vicarius.* Alardus, [1198-1208]. Add. 20862.

**Newcastle upon Tyne**, co. *Northumb.* (*continued*). Assignment of lease, from the corporation, of a wharf, etc., in Byker, 1655. Add. 19428.

—— *Major.* Nic. Lescot, 1321. Add. 20535.

—— —— Ric. de Galeweye, 1344. Harl. 43 D. 41.

—— —— Will. de Actone, 1373. Harl. 47 I. 5.

—— —— Will. Dawson, 1650. Eg. 307.

—— *Ballivi.* Hen. Scot, Nic. de Carliolo, Tho. de Tyndale, Pet. le Graper, Will. de Ogghel, 1300. Cott. xxix. 64.

—— —— Tho. Daulyn, Will. de Burnetona, Gilb. Hankyn, Rob. de Angertona, 1321. Add. 20535.

—— —— Joh. de Howden, 1373. Harl. 47 I. 5.

—— *Vicarius.* Henry Aglionby al. Aglenby, 1546. Harl. 45 B. 15.

**Newchurch**, co. *Kent.* Grant in, 1510. Harl. 78 I. 22, 23.

**Newchurch**, co. *Monm.* Precipe on covenant conc. land in, 1592. Add. 25120;—1593. Add. 25142.

**Newdigate**, co. *Surr.* Order for Southwark Priory to enjoy the chapel of, late Hen. II. (Niudegate). Cott. MS. Nero C. iii. f. 188.

—— Power to sell timber at Schonderby in or nr. (?), 1282. Add. 17269.

—— Grants, etc., in, t. Edw. I.-II. Add. 17282 (Neudegate)—17288; — 1316. Add. 17293 (Nywedegate);—1325. Harl. 78 D. 19;—1333. Add. 17301;—1335. Add. 17303;—1346. Add. 24603 (Neudegate);—1348. Add. 17311–17313;—1350. Add. 17319;—1355. Add. 17323; — 1449. Add. 17338;—1462. Add. 17341;—1472. Add. 17343;—1485, 1504. Add. 17349; —1505. Add. 17350;—1529. Harl. 112 F. 23 (Nudegate);—1569. Add. 17351;—1618. Harl. 80 B. 43;—1635. Add. 18944.

—— Feoffment of the manor, 1370 (Neudegate). Add. 20422.

**Newehalle, Le.** *v. sub* Ashover, co. *Derb.*

**Newehus.** *v.* Newsham, co. *Linc.*

**Newelonde, La.** *v. sub* Roxwell, co. *Essex.*

**Newenden**, co. *Kent.* Evidence conc. tenure of, [1072] (Neuenden). Cott. MS. Aug. ii. 36.

**Newenden**, co. *Kent* (*continued*). Grant of land called the " Castel " nr., t. Hen. III. (Nywenden). Harl. 80 I. 34.

**Newendon** al. **Nevendon**, co. *Essex.* Precipe on a covenant conc. lands in, 1561 (Newyngdon). Add. 24937.

**Newenham.** *v.* Newnham, co. *Camb.*

—— *v.* Sutton Veney, co. *Wilts.*

**Newenham, Newenham Hall.** *v. sub* Ashdon, co. *Essex.*

**Newent**, co. *Glouc.* Grant, etc., in, 1810. Slo. xxxiii. 17 ;—1320. Add. 24755.

—— Grant in " Scawe " in the manor of, 1313. Add. 24754.

—— Grant in Compton, etc., in, 1361, 1379. Slo. xxxiii. 47 a–d.

—— *Vicarius.* Rob. Hoke, 1410. Slo. xxxiii. 57.

**Newenton.** *v.* Newton, co. *Suf.*

**Newenton Beauchamp.** *v.* Naunton Beauchamp, co. *Worc.*

**Newenton Juell, N. Jewell.** *v.* Newington, [South ?], co. *Oxon.*

**Newenton juxta Hethe.** *v.* Newington next Hythe, co. *Kent.*

**Newerk.** *v.* Newark, co. *Nott.*

**Neweton.** *v.* Newington Butts, co. *Surr.*

—— *v.* Newton, co. ——.

—— *v.* Newton St. Loe, co. *Som.*

**Neweton Sulney.** *v.* Newton Solney, co. *Derb.*

**Newetone**, co. —— (?). *Rector.* Mag. Will. de Ludeham, [1272–3]. Harl. 56 D. 32.

**Newgrange**, co. *Monm.* Appointment of a steward of the manor, 1691. Add. 5349.

**Newhall, New Hall.** *v. sub* Boreham, co. *Essex.*

—— *v. sub* Ousden, co. *Suf.*

—— *v. sub* Snetterton, co. *Norf.*

—— *v. sub* Ware, co. *Hertf.*

**Newhall** al. **Frith.** *v. sub* Hendon, co. *Midd.*

**Newhall**, co. *Chest.* Inquisition conc. the manor, 1409 (Newehall). Woll. xi. 5.

—— Writ on a claim to lands in, 1420. Add. 6278.

Newhall, *co. Warw.* Grant in, 1412. Add. 15740.

Newhall, *in Laughton en le Morthen, co. York.* Terrier of lands of R. Cosen in, *c.* 1600. Add. 18064.

Newhall, *in Wath upon Dearne, co. York.* Grant in, 1361 (Newale). Harl. 83 E. 23.

Newhall, East. *v. sub* Ramsay, *co. Essex.*

Newham, *co. Northumb.* Power to give seisin of the manor, 1411. Harl. 111 C. 61.

Newhaven, *co. Edinburgh.* Notif. of surrender of lands to the bailiff, 1514 (Portus domine nostre gratie). Add. 2017.

Newhaven *al.* Meeching, *co. Suss.* Power for assignment of the manor to Edw. II., 1316 (Meching). Harl. 57 E. 33.

—— Fine in, 1387 (Mechynge). Add. 24891.

—— Brief for rebuilding the church, 1792. Ch. Br. B. xxxii. 6.

—— *Persona.* Hen. de Bourne, 1411 (Mechyngge). Add. 16464.

Newhichyn, Newhuchons, *nr. North Petherton* (?), *co. Som.* Power to take seisin in, 1458. Add. 6144.

—— Lease in, 1458. Harl. 56 H. 7.

Newhouse. *v.* Newsham, *co. Linc.*

Newhurst. *v.* Ewhurst, *co. Surr.*

Newick, *co. Suss.* Precipe on covenant conc. lands in, 1593 (Newycke). Add. 15236.

Newington, *co. Oxon.* Precipe on a covenant conc. Holcombe manor, etc., in, 1593. Add. 25217.

Newington Butts, *co. Surr.* Grants, etc., in, early 13 cent. Add. 15504 (Niwetune); — *t.* Hen. III. Add. 23728 (Neutone); — 1389. Harl. 46 G. 19 (Newentone); — 1446. Add. 7648 (Nywenton); — 1449. Add. 7647 (Newenton); — 1457. Add. 7642, 7643, 7646; — 1461. Add. 7645; — 1478. Add. 7644.

—— Grant in, to Christ Church, Canterbury, 1276. Add. 15505 (Neweton).

*v. also* Walworth, *co. Surr.*

Newington next Hythe, *co. Kent.* Exemplif., in 1413, of a fine of the manor, 1202 (Neweton). Harl. 51 H. 7.

Newington next Hythe, *co. Kent (continued).* Held by the Css. of Kent, [1241-2] (Newinton). Cott. xiii. 28.

—— Grant of the manor, [1271] (Neuton extra Heithe). Harl. 58 G. 14 (*copy*).

—— Leases, etc., of Belhouse manor in, 1384. Harl. 52 F. 29; — 1469. Harl. 52 F. 47; — 1476. Harl. 52 F. 49; — 1522. Harl. 48 D. 30; — 1536. Harl. 57 H. 3.

—— Lease, etc., in, 1407. Harl. 52 F. 32 (Newynton juxta Hethe); — 1424. Harl. 54 I. 35 (Newenton juxta Hethe).

—— Bond for arbitration in, 1410 (Newenton). Harl. 54 I. 33.

—— Acquittance for a pension charged on the rectory by the Prior of Folkestone, 1470 (Newenton juxta Hethe). Harl. 45 A. 54.

—— Suit conc. title deeds of Newton Belhouse manor in, 1516-1529. Harl. Roll O. 16.

—— Fines for homage of Newton Belhouse manor, 1530. Harl. 58 H. 3.

—— Lease of Combe manor in, to the Crown from the Abp. of Canterbury, 1583. Cott. xxv. 41.

—— Exchequer acquittance for a fine in Blackose *al.* Canons Court manor in, 1595. Add. 25674 *b.*

—— *Sacerdos.* Jordanus, early 13 cent. (Niwenth.). Campb. xxv. 18.

Newington next Sittingbourne, *co. Kent.* Power to give seisin and bequest of Tracy's (Traseis, Tracyes) manor in, 1452. Harl. 48 O. 36; — 1457. Harl. 75 D. 55.

—— Fine in, 1548. Harl. 75 H. 4, 76 H. 50.

Newington, [North?], *co. Oxon.* Suit conc. the manor, 1710-12 (Newington *al.* Newton). Add. 5138, 5139.

Newington, North, *co. Wilts.* Court-rolls of, and of Hilcot (Hulcoote) in, 1558-9. Add. 24440 (N. Newton); — 1566-7. Add. 24441.

Newington, [South?], *co. Oxon.* Settlement, etc., in, 1422. Add. 22263 (Newenton Juell); — *ante* 1437. Add. 21265 (do.); — 1437. Add. 20303-20305 (do.); — 1464. Add. 20906 (Jewell).

Newington, South, *co. Oxon.* Compotus of the rectory bel. to Eynsham Abbey, 1441-42 (Newnton). Harl. Roll K. 33.

Newington, Stoke, co. *Midd.* Conf. of a grant in (?), to Clerkenwell Priory, [1152–60] (Neutona). Harl. 83 C. 26.

—— Extracts from court-rolls of, 1490. Harl. 75 D. 51 (Stoke Newnton);—1644. Harl. 111 C. 44.

—— Assignment of a lease of the prebend, manor, etc., 1590. Harl. 79 G. 16.

Newington Toney, co. *Wilts.* Feoffment of the manor, 1370. Add. 20422.

Newington, West, co. *Oxon.* Covenant for settlement in, 1464 (W. Newentone). Add. 20306.

Newland. *v. sub* Lincoln, co. *Line.*

Newland, co. *Glouc.* Release in, 1332 (Nova terra). Slo. xxxiii. 24.

Newland, co. *Kent.* Conveyance of, 1407. Harl. 76 G. 39.

Newland, *in Calne, co. Wilts.* Release in, 1563. Harl. 80 H. 37.

Newland, *in Collingham, co. York.* Releases of the manor, etc., 1430. Harl. 43 E. 19;—1431. Harl. 45 I. 12, 54 I. 15.

Newland, *in Normanton, co. York.* Crown lease in, of lands bel. to the Preceptory there, 1555. Harl. 84 C. 32.

Newland Squillers, co. *Hertf.* Extracts from court-rolls, 1582–1612, 1650. Add. 8505–8510.

Newland, West. *v. sub* Freiston, co. *Line.*

Newlands Manor, co. *Oxon.* Court-rolls, 1386–89, 1417–20 (Nova Terra). Harl. Rolls E. 30, F. 9.

*v. also* Ensham, co. *Oxon.*

Newlington *al.* Hewlington, co. *Denb.* Assignment of a crown lease in, 1625. Add. 5827.

Newlyn, co. *Cornw.* Petition conc. lands in, 1623 (Newlin). Harl. 45 D. 5.

Newmarket, co. *Camb.* Grants, etc., in, *t.* Hen. III.–late 13 cent. Add. 15518 (Novum Mercatum). Harl. 45 D. 13 (do ), 49 I. 59 (Novum Forum);—1402. Add. 15536 (Nov. Mercatum);—1555. Add. 24920, 25288.

—— Grant of "solarium lapideum quod se ext[e]ndit super Ykenildeweie" in, *t.* Hen. III. Add. 19286.

—— Compotus of the manor, 1403–4. Add. 25867.

Newnham. *v. sub* Sutton Veney, co. *Wilts.*

Newnham, *nr. Cambridge, co. Camb.* Release of rent in, *t.* Hen. III. (Newenham). Add. 15516.

Newnham, co. *Glouc.* Sale of " Aishrudge " in, 1594 (Newenham). Add. 24798.

Newnham, *I. of Wight.* Grant of free warren in, to Quarr Abbey, 1284 (Neuwenham). Add. 15701.

Newnham, co. *Kent.* Fine of the manor, 1548 (Newneham). Harl. 75 H. 4, 76 H. 50.

Newnham, co. *Northt.* Grant at, 1021–1023 (æt Niwanham). Cott. MS. Aug. ii. 24.

—— *Persona.* Mag. Thomas, 1229 (Neuha.). Harl. 86 B. 7.

Newnham, co. *Oxon.* Grant at (?), 966 (Niwanham). Harl. 43 C. 5.

—— Grant in, *ante* 1243 (Neuham). Add. 15430.

—— Compotus of the manor, 1296–97 (Nywenham). Harl. Roll K. 29.

Newnham, *in Aston Cantlow, co. Warw.* Conveyance in, 1460 (Newenham). Add. 8441.

—— Release in, to Studley Priory, 1482. Add. 8435.

Newnham Hall. *v. sub* Ashdon, co. *Essex.*

Newnham Murren, co. *Oxon.* Bequest in, to Reading Abbey, bordering on Grims Dyke (Grimesdich), 1220–1 (Niweham). Add. 19615.

—— Acquittance, made at English (Englys en le par. de Newenam) in (?), 1361. Harl. 49 H. 8.

Newnham Paddox, co. *Warw.* Writ of distraint in the manor, 1640. Cott. i. 10.

—— *Dominus.* Rogerus, early Hen. III. (Neuh.). Add. 21499.

Newnton. *v.* Newington, South, co. *Oxon.*

Newport. *v. sub* Lincoln, co. *Line.*

Newport, co. *Cornw.* Exchequer acquittance for a fine for the borough, 1567. Add. 25575.

Newport, *in Bishop's Tawton, co. Devon.* Fine in, 1653. Harl. 86 I. 59.

Newport, co. *Essex.* Grant of, by Matilda, the Empress, to G. de Mandeville, [1141] (Niweport). Cott. xvi. 27.

—— Bequests in, *t.* Hen. VII. (?). Harl. 80 H. 55.

**Newton,** *in Wisbeach Hundred, co. Camb.* Conff. in, by Bps. of Ely to Ely Abbey, [1103–31, 1133–69]. Harl. 43 H. 4 (Nowetuna), 5 (*copies*).

**Newton,** *in Manchester, co. Lanc.* Briefs for rebuilding the chapel, 1804, 1808. Ch. Br. B. xliv. 4, xlviii. 10.

**Newton,** *in Aveland Wapentake, co. Linc.* Grants, etc., in, 1441. Add. 21072;—1446. Add. 21074;—1505. Add. 21077;—1544. Add. 21081.

—— *Clericus.* Adam, *t.* Hen. II. Eg. 428.

**Newton,** *nr. Castleacre, co. Norf.* Statutes of the guild of St. John Baptist at, 1412 (Neweton juxta Castleacre). Cott. xiii. 1.

**Newton,** *co. Nott.* Grant in, *t.* Hen. III. (Neuton). Add. 5379.

—— Order conc. stipend of the curate, 1547. Add. 15274.

**Newton,** *nr. Blithefield, co. Staff.* Release in, 1388. Cott. xxviii. 104.

**Newton** (Neuton, etc.), *nr. Sudbury, co. Suff.* Grant in dower of Sayham *al.* Siam (Seihum) in, early 13 cent. Harl. 55 G. 6.

—— Grants, etc., in, *t.* Hen. III. Harl. 49 I. 48, 49;—1260. Harl. 47 A. 42 (Newenton);—*t.* Edw. I. Harl. 52 D. 34, 55 G. 7;—1297. Harl. 56 E. 44;—1299. Harl. 49 H. 25, 27, 49 I. 4;—1304. Harl. 51 C. 57 (Neweton), 51 D. 1;—1332. Harl. 54 H. 20;—1335. Harl. 54 H. 21;—1362. Harl. 58 D. 45;—1413. Harl. 49 D. 37;—1592. Add. 25442;—1657. Add. 19265;—1665. Slo. xxxii. 61.

—— Grant of goods in Sayham manor in, 1346. Harl. 54 H. 22.

—— Exemplif. in 1643 of a fine in, 1550-1. Slo. xxxii. 60.

**Newton,** *nr. Brown's Over, co. Warw.* Feoffment in, 1444. Cott. iv. 1.

**Newton,** *co. Wilts.* Interrogatories in a suit conc. the farm of, *t.* Eliz. Add. 24439.

**Newton,** *in Cottingham, co. York.* Grant, etc., in, *t.* Edw. I. Lansd. 467 (Neutona);—1362. Lansd. 693.

**Newton,** *nr. Leeds, co. York.* Acquittance for an annuity in, 1498. Harl. 48 G. 48.

**Newton,** *nr. Wintringham, co. York.* Grant in, *t.* Hen. III. Harl. 112 A. 19.

**Newton Abbot,** *co. Devon.* Grant of market and fair in the manor of, to Torre Abbey, 1270 (Shyreburn Neuton). Harl. 58 L. 27 (*copy*).

—— Power to give seisin in, 1354 (Nyweton Abbatis). Harl. 50 C. 59.

**Newton Belhouse.** *v. sub* Newington next Hythe, *co. Kent.*

**Newton Blossomville,** *co. Buck.* Fine in, 1575. Add. 23893, 23894.

**Newton by Toft,** *co. Linc.* Grants, etc., in, *t.* Hen. II. Harl. 52 G. 38 (Neutona); — late Hen. III. Cott. xxviii. 14 (do.);—1296. Cott. xxvii. 168.

—— Grants, etc., in, to Bullington Priory, *t.* Hen. II. Harl. 46 A. 54 (Neutun);—*post* 1169. Harl. 52 G. 19 (do.), 51 C. 18 (*copy*);—*c.* 1200. Cott. xii. 17 (do.);—*t.* Hen. III. Harl. 54 C. 25;—1256. Harl. 52 H. 28;—*t.* Edw. I.-II. Harl. 52 H. 5;—*c.* 1322. Harl. 52 H. 27.

—— *Persona* (?). Johannes, early Hen. III. (Neuton). Harl. 47 I. 46.

**Newton, Cold,** *co. Leic.* Release, etc., in, 1262. Add. 22341 (Neutona);—1361. Add. 21010; — 1394. Add. 21258;—1448. Add. 21054.

—— Grants, etc., of the manor, 1389. Add. 21259 (Neutone juxta Louseby);—1394. Add. 21260 (Neuton);—1442. Add. 21073 (Newetone).

—— Defeasance of a bond for rents in the manor, 1394 (Neutone). Add. 21258.

—— Pipe-roll acquittance to Lady Boswell, lady of the manor, 1629. Harl. 111 D. 46.

**Newton, East,** *in Aldbrough, co. York.* Grants, etc., in, 1413. Lansd. 440 (Estnewton);—1423 (?). Lansd. 441; —1436. Lansd. 442;—1461. Lansd. 443;—1462. Lansd. 444.

**Newton Flotman** (Flotemanton, etc.), *co. Norf.* Conveyances, etc., in, 1408. Harl. 54 I. 7;—1430. Harl. 43 E. 19 (Fleteman Newton), 54 I. 10;—1431. Harl. 50 H. 27, 28, 54 I. 15;—1435. Add. 2016.

—— Recovery of seisin of the manor, 1522. Add. 14698.

**Newton, Fuller.** *v.* Newton, West, *co. Norf.*

**Newton, King's,** *co. Derb.* Grant in, to Calke Priory, *t.* Hen. II. (Neutona). Add. 7213.

Newton, West (Neuton, etc.), co. Norf. (continued). Compotus - roll of the manor, 1294–5 (Westnewetone). Add. 9151.

—— Power to give seisin of the manor, 1385 (Fuller Neweton). Harl. 56 I. 1.

—— Rector. Ric. Tillyer, 1427. Cott. xxix. 62.

Newton, Wood, co. Northt. Conf. of grant of the manor to Fincshed Priory, c. 1300 (Wodeneutona). Add. 22081.

Newtown, co. Southt. Grant in, 1358 (Nova villa). Harl. 112 A. 35.

Newtown, Isle of Wight. Grants, etc., in, 1347. Add. 15887 (Fraunchevyle):—1444. Add. 15853 (Neweton), 15854 (Fraunchevyle);—1453. Add. 15856 (Newetown).

—— Major. Will. Wodnut, 1444. Add. 15853.

—— —— Will. Smyth, 1444. Add. 15854.

—— Ballivus. Galf. Symond, 1347. Add. 15887.

Newtown Ards, co. Down. Grant in, 1571. Harl. 15574.

Neydwode. v. Needwood Forest, co. Staff.

Neyerykynghale. v. Rickinghall Inferior, co. Suff.

Neylond. v. Nuyland, co. Suff.

Nibley, North, co. Glouc. Fine of the manor, 1581. Add. 15813.

Nidderdale, co. York. Covenant betw. R. de Mowbray and Fountains Abbey conc. the forest of, t. Hen. II. [c. 1185?] (Niderd.). Harl. 83 C. 38.

Nielend. v. Nayland, co. Suff.

Nietham. v Neatham, co. Southt.

Nigra Notele. v. Notley, Black, co. Essex.

Nigrit, Nemus de. v. sub Blean, co. Kent.

Ninfield, co. Suss. Feoffment in, 1475 (Nenfeld). Add. 23800.

—— Precipe on covenant conc. lands in, 1589 (do.). Add. 15226.

Niper Hadres. v. Hardres, Nether, co. Kent.

Niperstok. v. Netherstock, in Halstock, co. Dors.

Nithsdale, co. Dumfries. Ref. to bounds of, c. 1125 (Strunit). Cott. xviii. 45.

Nithsdale, co. Dumfries (continued). Grants in Dunscore, etc., in, to Melrose Abbey, 1229. Cott. xviii. 2 (Vallis de Nyth);—1236. Cott. xviii. 8 (do.).

Nitimbre. v. Newtimber, co. Suss.

Niton, Isle of Wight. Compotus of the manor, 1488–9 (Nyghton). Harl. Roll A. 38.

Niudegate. v. Newdigate, co. Surr.

Niwanham. v. Newnham, co. Northt.

—— v. Newnham, co. Oxon.

Niwantun. v. Naunton, co. Worc.

Niwebir. v. Newbury, co. Berks.

Niwecirce, in Lundonia. v. London. Par. of St. Mary le Bow.

Niweham. v. Newnham Murren, co. Oxon.

Niwenham. v. sub Sutton Veney, co. Wilts.

Niwenth. v. Newington next Hythe, co. Kent.

Niwenton. v. Newton Purcell, co. Oxon.

Niweport. v. Newport, co. Essex.

Niwetune. v. Newington Butts, co. Surr.

Nobottle, in Brington, co. Northt. Grant in, 1448. Add. 21602.

Nocton, co. Linc. Power to give seisin of a moiety of the manor, 1442. Add. 21075.

—— Vicarius. Dom. Rogerus, 1334 (Nocketon). Harl. 49 C. 49, 50.

Noke, co. Oxon. Lease in, 1422 (Oke). Harl. 76 C. 11.

Nokefelde [Nockholt?], co. Kent. Grant of land called "Tom at Halles" in the parish of, 1549. Add. 4607.

Noneford. v. sub Colyton, co. Devon.

Nonemanneslond. v. sub Staines, co. Midd.

Nonhampton [Northington?], co. Southt. Settlement in, 1410. Harl. 57 G. 33.

Nonington, co. Kent. Grant in Acol (Hacholte) in, t. Hen. III. Harl. 76 F. 51.

—— Grants, etc., in, late Hen. III. Harl. 78 A. 51;—1341. Harl. 75 G. 18 (Nonynton);—1417. Harl. 77 F. 8;—1417. Harl. 78 E. 27;—1454–5. Harl. 79 E. 3;—1529. Add. 8606;—1547. Add. 8615;—1548. Harl. 75 E. 22, 75 H. 4, 50;—1551. Harl. 75 E. 28,

Norfolk, *County of (continued)*. Acquittance by the Sheriff to Sir Will. de la Pole and his wife for fines, 1355. Cott. xxvii. 152.

—— Precipes on covenants conc. lands in, 1370. Add. 25145;—1514. Add. 25146.

—— Petition on forfeiture of Nic. Willy in, [1386-9]. Add. 14713.

—— Compotus of lands of the Earl Marshal in, 1401-4. Add. 16556.

—— Feodary of lands of Sir Edm. de Thorpe in, 1405-6. Add. 16540.

—— Compotus of lands of Dukes of Norfolk in, 1422-3. Add. 16555;—1483-4. Add. 16559.

—— Riots in, 1452. Add. 16545.

—— General pardon to J. Say, late Sheriff and Escheator, 1462. Cott. viii. 13.

—— Warrant for levy of a subsidy in, 1474. Add. 14973.

—— Compotus of Sir T. Gresham's manors in, 1566-69. Add. 16336.

—— Patent for Sir H. Bedingfield as seneschal of the Duchy of Lancaster in, 1608. Harl. 83 C. 18.

—— *Vicecomes.* Rob. [fil. Walteri], [1121-30]. Cott. ii. 19 (3).

—— —— Johannes, [1140?]. Add. 19584.

—— —— Will. fil. Roberti, [1157-63?]. Campb. xxiii. 5.

—— —— Joh. de Loudham, [1328-31]. Cott. iv. 23.

—— —— Will. de Middelton, 1352. Harl. 55 E. 33.

—— —— Tho. de Morieux, 1355. Cott. xxvii. 152.

—— —— Guido de Seyntcler, 1357. Add. 14972.

—— —— Joh. Say, *of Broxbourne,* co. *Hertf.,* [1449-50]. Cott. viii. 13.

—— —— Edm. Bedyngfeld, *miles,* 1529. Add. 17748.

Norhal. *v.* Covehithe, co. *Suff.*

Norham. *v.* Northam, co. *Southt.*

Norhamshire, co. *Northumb.* Grant of warren in, by Hugh, Bp. of Durham, *t.* Hen. II. (Norhamsyre). Campb. iv. 9.

Norhamton, Norhampton, Norhanthon. *v.* Northampton, co. *Northt.*

Norhoern. *v.* Cerney, North, co. *Glouc.*

Norholt, Boscus de. *v.* Northolt Wood, nr. *Arundel* (?), co. *Suss.*

Norhtstreton. *v.* Sturton, co. *Linc.*

Norlache. *v.* Leach, North, co. *Glouc.*

Normanby on the Wolds, co. *Linc.* Covenant in, betw. Newhouse and Revesby Abbeys, 1154 (Normannabi). Harl. 44 I. 1.

—— Grants, etc., in, to Newhouse Abbey, *c.* 1150-55. Harl. 47 A. 34;—early 13 cent. Cott. xxvii. 28, Harl. 48 B. 40, 49 B. 27, 29, 30, 35;—*t.* Hen. III. Harl. 46 A. 9, 47 A. 35, 48 A. 2, 18, 49 B. 36, 37;—late 13 cent. Harl. 49 B. 41.

—— Grant in, to Orford Priory, *c.* 1201-3. Harl. 54 C. 47.

—— Grant, etc., in, from Newhouse Abbey, early 13 cent. Harl. 44 G. 29;—*t.* Hen. III. Cott. xii. 19, Harl. 44 G. 37.

—— Grants in, early 13 cent. Harl. 49 B. 34;—1330. Cott. xxviii. 16.

—— *Capellanus.* Robertus, *t.* Hen. III. Cott. v. 69.

—— *Persona.* Johannes, early 13 cent. —*t.* Hen. III. Cott. v. 69, xxix. 34, Harl. 44 G. 29, 37, 46 A. 9, 12, 48 A. 2, 48 B. 39, 40, 43, 49 B. 27-30, 32, 33, 35, 38, 54 C. 48, 57 C. 44.

—— —— Joh. de Brayboue, 1242. Harl. 51 C. 39.

—— *Sacerdos.* Simon, early 13 cent. Harl. 54 I. 38.

Normancross Hundred, co. *Hunt.* Inquisition on owners of property in, 1295. Harl. 58 E. 41.

—— Court-rolls, 1628-33. Cott. iii. 14.

—— Suit of Sir T. Cotton and others conc. rents due to, from Yaxley manor, 1631. Cott. i. 2 (1-14).

Normannabi. *v.* Normanby on the Wolds, co. *Linc.*

Normanton, co. *Linc.* (?). *Persona.* Dom. Joh. Orston, 1396. Harl. 52 F. 30.

Normanton, *in Southwell,* co. *Nott.* Licenses for endowment, etc., of the chapel of St. John Evang. at, 1331. Woll. v. 1;—1368. Woll. iv. 58.

—— Rental of Will. de Wakebrugg in, [1444?]. Woll. xi. 2 a.

Normanton, *in Agbrigg Wap.,* co. *York.* Grants of Brakenhill [now Fernhill?] in, *t.* Edw. I.-II. Add.

16750:—1322. Add. 16792;—1323.
Add. 16776, 16777, 16793;—1359.
Add. 16819.

—— Lease in Snydall and Woodhouse in, by the Knts. Hospitallers,
1357. Campb. xiv. 25°.

—— Grants, etc., in Altofts in, 1359.
Add. 16819;—1485. Add. 16966.

—— Grants, etc., of Altofts manor in,
1401. Add. 16887-16890, 16892-16894;
—1423. Add. 16908;—1424. Add.
16909;—1427. Add. 16913.

—— Lands in Altofts in, held by Rob.
Calverley, c. 1450. Add. 16954.

—— Crown lease of site of Newland
Preceptory, with lands in Woodhouse,
Altofts, etc., in, 1555. Harl. 84 C. 32.

—— Fine in, 1657. Add. 12679.

—— Persona. Bernardus, early 13
cent. Add. 7433.

Normanton, South, co. Derb. Grant
of, early Hen. III. (Normantona).
Woll. x. 46.

—— Grants, etc., of Pinxton Normanton manor and advowson, 1356. Woll.
x. 47 (Pencaston et Normonston);—
1369. Woll. x. 48 (Penkeston cum
hamella de Normanton);—1391. Woll.
x. 52 (Penkeston et Normanton);—
1408. Woll. x. 57 (Pynkeston et Normanton);—1412. Woll. x. 54 (Penkeston Normanton);—1424. Woll. x. 56
(Pynkeston Normanton).

—— Grants of rents charged on above
manor, 1369. Woll. x. 51 (Penkeston
cum hamella de Normanton);—1431.
Woll. xi. 47 (Pynkeston Normanton).

—— Fine of a moiety of above manor,
1412. Woll. x. 53 (Penkeston Normanton).

—— Lease in, 1562. Woll. x. 61.

—— Fine of the manor, etc., 1567.
Woll. x. 60.

—— Persona. Tho. Chelaston, 1408.
Woll. x. 57.

Normanton, Temple, co. Derb. Surrenders, etc., in Bagthorpe and Brampton, of lands held of the manor, 1453.
Woll. iii. 67;—1477. Woll. iii. 58;—
1491. Woll. iii. 77;—1501. Woll. iii.
66;—1535. Woll. iii. 68, 69;—1552.
Woll. iii. 65;—1560. Woll. iii. 74.

Normanton Turville, co. Leic. Grant
of right of way in, to Sulby Abbey, t.
Hen. III. (Normanton). Harl. 45 G. 27.

—— Grant, etc., of Bassethouses manor
in, 1371. Add. 26922, 26923;—1444.
Add. 26924-26927.

Normanton upon Trent, co. Nott.
Grants, etc., of the manor, [1254-68].
Harl. 112 I. 55 (Normanthon);—1430.
Harl. 54 I. 12;—1431. Harl. 45 I. 12,
50 H. 27, 28, 54 I. 15:—1435. Add.
2016:—1436. Harl. 48 E. 19.

—— Grants, etc., in, late 13 cent.
Cott. xxviii. 17;—1412. Add. 15740;
—1424. Harl. 54 I. 8.

Normondi. v. sub Marcle, Much, co.
Heref.

Norridge, co. Wilts. Grant of reversion of the manor, 1440 (Norigge).
Harl. 53 C. 11.

Norstede. v. Nursted, co. Kent.

Nortadinton. v. Addington, Great,
co. Northt.

Nortbroc. v. Northbrook, nr. Steeple
Morden, co. Camb.

Nortcaldewellemor al. Norht-
caldewellemor, in Finmere, co.
Oxon. Lease, etc., of, to Biddlesdon
Abbey, t. Rich. I. or John. Harl. 84
D. 15, 86 C. 24.

North. v. Norton, King's, co. Leic.

North Allerton. v. Allerton, North,
co. York.

Northale, Northales. v. Covehithe,
co. Suff.

Northall v. sub Eddlesborough, co.
Buck.

—— v. sub Kelsey, N., co. Linc.

—— v. Northaw, co. Hertf.

—— v. Northolt, co. Midd.

Northall al. Corners Hall. v. sub
Finchingfield, co. Essex.

Northall al. Cornhall. v. sub Bures
St. Mary, cos. Suff. and Essex.

Northall, nr. Sleaford, co. Linc. Recovery of the manor, 1514. Eg. 479.

Northam, co. Southt. Grant in, to
St. Denis Priory, Southampton, 1151
(Norham). Harl. 50 A. 8.

Northampton, County of. Grant,
etc., of lands in, to J. de Stuteville, c.
1160. Lansd. 691, Harl. 55 D. 8.

—— Conf., by her next heir, of grants
in, made by Dna. Devorgilla Olifart,
1287. Add. 21505.

—— Pleas conc. privileges of the
Knights Hospitallers in, [1327 ?]. Slo.
xxxi. 13, 14.

—— Fine Rolls, 1327-1374. Add.
26589.

Northampton (Norhamton, etc.), co.
Northt. (continued). Major (continued).
Tho. Spriggy, 1390.   Add. 22368.

———— Ric. Spicer, 1392.  Add.
22369.

———— Hen. Caysho, 1396. Add.
21803.

———— ——— Joh. Loudham, 1402.
Add. 22371.

——— ——— Joh. Shrouesbury, 1406.
Add. 730, 731.

———— Hen. Caysho, 1410. Add.
21816.

———— ——— Joh. Spryng, 1415. Add.
22373.

———— ——— Tho. Sale, 1419. Add.
732 (1).

———— Hen. Stone, 1435. Add.
735.

———— ——— Will. Russheden, jun.,
1440. Add. 732.

———— ——— Ric. Wemmes, 1440.
Add. 6055 ;—1441. Add. 734.

———— ——— Will. Peryn, 1444. Add.
735.

———— ——— (nuper). Joh. Wattes,
1498. Add. 22375.

———— ——— (nuper). Tho. Wellys,
1512. Add. 21849.

———— Prepositi. Will. Walensis, Will.
fil. Rogeri, early Hen. III. Harl.
85 O. 1.

———— Luc. Parmentarius, Simon
de Houton, c. 1240–55. Add. 22351.

———— ——— Rob de Leycestria, jun.,
Rad. Passelewe, Mich. fil. Philippi,
c. 1240–55. Add. 22353.

———— ——— Rad. Passelewe, Ead-
mundus, c. 1240–55. Add. 22344.

———— Ballivi. Gilb. de Blichesworth,
Rog. de Arderne, late Hen. III. Add.
22347.

———— Hen. de Stormesworthe,
Ric. de S. Neoto, late Hen. III. Add.
22384.

———— Ric. de S. Neoto, Osb.
de Crouetrop, early Edw. I. Add.
22349.

———— ——— Ad. Le Hosiere, Rob. Le
Rous, 1277. Add. 22358.

———— ——— Hugo de Staunford, Joh.
de Catteworth, c. 1280–85. Add.
22346.

———— ——— Joh. Gerveys, Will. Mont,
c. 1280–85. Add. 22348.

———— ——— Will. Mount, Joh. fil. Ger-
vasii, c. 1280–85. Add. 22354.

Northampton (Norhamton, etc.), co.
Northt. (continued). Ballivi (con-
tinued). Pet. de Leye., Phil. le Rous,
Rob. fil. Henrici, Joh. de Longavilla,
Joh. de Estaunf., Jord. le Gaunter,
Will. Cappe, c. 1290. Cott. xxviii. 18.

———— ——— Will. le Mercer, Gilb. de
Somersete, t. Edw. I. Add. 22356.

———— ——— Pentecost de Kersbalton.
Simon Whyteneye, 1296. Add. 22357.

———— ——— Hugo de Middelton, Hen.
de la Leye, t. Edw. I.–II. Add. 22360.

———— ——— Hen. de Weston, Barth. de
Reyny, 1316. Add. 22361.

———— ——— Will. Elya, Joh. de Cage-
ho, 1321. Add. 22355.

———— ——— Joh. Caudroun, Rad. de
Cortenhale, 1334. Add. 22363.

———— ——— Tho. de Staunford, Pet.
de Boys, 1335. Add. 22364.

———— ——— Onorius Saucee, Phil. de
Pysford, 1337. Add. 729.

———— ——— Joh. Moigne, Rob. Toly,
1361. Add. 7574.

———— ——— Reg. Barker, Will. Shef-
ford, 1383. Add. 22366, 22367.

———— ——— Nic. Baude, Joh. Bucke-
brok, 1384. Add. 21793.

———— ——— Will. Nonecourt, Joh.
Toly, 1390. Add. 22368.

———— ——— Joh. Sywell, Joh. Warde,
1392. Add. 22369.

———— ——— Will. Wale, Joh. Wode-
ward, 1396. Add. 21803.

———— ——— Joh. Tiryngham, Joh.
Ryuell, 1406. Add. 730, 731.

———— ——— Joh. Hendele, Will. Pat,
1410. Add. 21816.

———— ——— Joh. Spriggy, Tho. Sale,
1415. Add. 22373.

———— ——— Will. Pirye, Draper, Joh.
Bernhill, 1419. Add. 732.

———— ——— Will. Russheden, Joh.
Reve, 1435. Add. 735.

———— ——— Joh. Clerk, Hen. Baltes-
well, 1441. Add. 734.

———— Coronatores. Rob. Sawce, Rob. de
Bedeford, Rob. de Cattewrth, Will. de
Stormeswrth, c. 1280–85. Add. 22354.

———— ——— Rob. de Bedeford, Rob.
de Catteworth, Phil. Le Rows, t. Edw.
I. Add. 22356.

———— ——— Rob. Sauce, Rob. de Bedeford, Rob. de Cateworth, Will. de
Stormisworth, 1296. Add. 22357.

Northibl. *v.* Norby, *co. York.*

Northie, *nr. Hastings, co. Suss.* Lease of the manor, 1281. Add. 16182.

Northington, *nr. Beaksbourne, co. Kent.* Grant, etc., in, 1338. Harl. 76 B. 45 (Northynton):—1340. Harl. 76 B. 48 (Northyton).

—— Suit in, *c.* 1390. Harl. 78 D. 20.

Northington (?), *co. Southt.* Settlement in, 1410 (Nonhampton). Harl. 57 G. 33.

Northkelleseie. *v.* Kelsey, North, *co. Linc.*

Northlegh. *v.* Leigh, North, *co. Devon.*

Northleu. *v.* Lew, North, *co. Devon.*

Northmortone. *v.* Morton, North, *nr. Retford, co. Nott.*

Northolm, *co.* —— (?). Bond for rent in, to N. de Yeland, early Hen. III. Harl. 112 B. 52.

Northolm, *in Eye, co. Northt.* Inspex., in 1314, of a grant of market and fair in the manor to Peterborough Abbey, [1305–6?]. Harl. 58 I. 52 (*copy*).

Northolt (Northall), *co. Midd.* Lease of the manor, 1339. Add. 7559.

—— Release of La Doune manor in, 1355. Add. 19895, 19896.

—— Release in, 1370. Add. 7558.

—— Extracts from court-rolls of Northolt and Downbarns manors, 1451. Add. 1607:—1460. Add. 1606;—1581–1622. Add. 1608–1610, 1612–1616;—1636. Add. 1626;—1641. Add. 1627;—1654. Add. 1630;—1655. Add. 1631;—1656. Add. 1635, 1636;—1668. Add. 1642;—1680. Add. 1647;—1700. Add. 1651.

—— Sales, etc., in, 1598. Add. 1611;—1629. Add. ;1617, 1618, 1619;—1635. Add. 1622–1625;—1656. Add. 1634;—1662. Add. 1637;—1667. Add. 1638, 1639;—1674. Add. 19464, 19465, 19469, 19470;—1675. Add. 19467;—1676. Add. 1645;—1681. Add. 1648, 1649;—1682. Add. 1650;—1700. Add. 1651–1656;—1709. Add. 1657, 1658.

—— Assignment in trust, etc., of the manor, 1647. Add. 1628, 1629;—1699. Add. 1652.

—— Bequest in, 1658. Add. 19455.

—— Fines of the manor, 1665. Add. 1640;—1670. Add. 1641;—1700. Add. 1653, 1654;—1701. Add. 1655, 1656.

Northolt Wood, *nr. Arundel* (?), *co. Suss.* Papal conf. of grant of, from Qu. Adeliza to Waverley Abbey, 1147 (Norholt). Lansd. 27.

Northop, *co. Flint.* Rental of Leadbrooke manor in, 1735. Add. 1009.

Northorpe (?), *co. Linc.* Grants in, to Newhouse Abbey, *ante* 1259. Harl. 52 F. 5 (Thorpe);—late Hen. III. Harl. 58 A. 37.

Northover. *v. sub* Ditcheat, *co. Som.*

Northrede, *co. Kent.* Grant in, 1358. Harl. 76 G. 26.

Norð tun. *v.* Norton, *co. Worc.*

Northumberland, *County of.* Precipe of Hen. II. to the Barons, etc., of, [1158?] (Northimberl.). Campb. ii. 2.

—— Conf. in 1285 of the grant of lands in J. le Vescunte's barony in, to Edm., Earl of Lancaster, 1269 (Northumbria). Cott. MS. Aug. ii. 13½ (1).

—— Mandate to the sheriff conc. manors of the Earl of Angus in, 1303. Harl. 43 D. 8.

—— Settlement of the above manors, *t.* Edw. II. Harl. 58 G. 22.

—— Fine-rolls, 1327–1371. Add. 26591.

—— Compotus of church lands, etc., in, 1578–79. Add. 26687;—1608–9. Add. 26688;—1618–9. Add. 26600.

—— Assignment of lease of mines royal in, 1658. Harl. 111 H. 21.

—— *Vicecomes.* Will. Hayrun, [1246–58]. Campb. iii. 14.

—— —— Gwychard. de Charron, [1267–69]. Harl. 45 D. 15.

—— —— Adam de Swyneborne, 1281. Harl. 111 G. 22.

—— —— Joh. de Fenwyk, *miles,* 1323. Cott. xxviii. 26–29.

—— —— *Dom.* Rob. Dareys, 1334. Harl. 58 B. 6.

—— —— Rob. de Isle, *miles,* 1407. Cott. xxix. 68.

—— —— Rob. de Ogle, *miles,* 1418. Add. 20531, 20532.

—— —— Rob. Collingwood, *arm.,* 1553. Harl. 111 B. 56.

Norð wic. *v.* Norwich, *co. Norf.*

Northwick, *in Claines, nr. Worcester, co. Worc.* Grant in, to St. Oswald's Hospital, 1350. Harl. 83 B. 31.

Northwood, *I. of Wight*. Grant in Luton (Luitona) in, *ante* 1175 (?). Harl. 112 C. 12.

—— Precipe on a covenant conc. land in, 1593. Add. 25252.

—— Brief conc. a fire at, 1805. Ch. Br. B. xlvi. 1.

Northwood Sheppey. *v. sub* Milton next Sittingbourne, *co. Kent.*

Northynton. *v.* Northington, *co. Kent.*

Nortkeueligworth, Northkyllyngworth, etc. *v.* Kilworth, North, *co. Leic.*

Nortkiluingholm. *v.* Halton, East, *co. Linc.*

Nortoft. *v. sub* Tilbury juxta Clare, *co. Essex.*

Nortoft, *nr. Guilsborough, co. Northt.* Grants in, to Sulby Abbey, late 12 cent. Harl. 49 F. 12;—*t.* John. Add. 21879.

—— Lease "super le dede quene furlong," etc., in, 1294. Harl. 112 B. 53.

—— Grant, etc., in, 1310. Harl. 112 B. 54;—1393. Harl. 57 E. 22 (Northtoft).

—— Conveyance of the manor, 1393 (Northtoft). Harl. 57 G. 22.

Norton, *co.* —— (?). Grant of the manor by Bp. Walt. de Langton, 1311. Add. 5485.

Norton, *co.* —— (?). Power to give seisin in, 1349. Harl. 52 A. 4.

Norton, *co. Derb.* Covenant for feoffment, etc., in, 1440. Woll. viii. 43;—1441. Woll. viii. 44;—1589. Woll. xii. 12.

—— Grants, etc., in Greenhill nr., 1495. Woll. i. 22-24;—1536. Harl. 112 G. 15.

—— Fine in Bradway, Greenhill, Norton Leys, etc., nr., 1541. Woll. ii. 71.

Norton, *co. Northt.* Grant, etc., in, late Hen. III. (Nortona). Add. 22385;—1586. Add. 16171.

Norton, *co. Oxon.* Restoration of, by K. John to Reg. de Dammartin, 1212. Add. 11239 (*copy*).

Norton, *co. Radn.* Lease of the demesnes, *c.* 1433. Harl. 53 H. 17.

—— Mortgage at Blackbanche in, 1535. Cott. xxx. 37.

—— Sale of the manor and parsonage, 1569. Harl. 79 G. 3.

Norton, *co. Radn. (continued).* Bond to pay annuities charged on the manor, 1569. Harl. 80 F. 38.

Norton, *co. Salop. v. sub* Tong with Norton, *co. Salop.*

Norton, *in Selborne, co. Southt.* Sale, etc., of the manor, 1572. Add. 16197;—1576. Add. 16198.

Norton, *co. Staff.* Grant in, 1287. Harl. 53 A. 50.

Norton, *co. Suff.* Royal conff., etc., of the manor to A. and R. de Dammartin, late Hen. I. Add. 11233(2);—*c.* 1183. Add. 11233 (3);—1212. Add. 11239 (*copies*).

—— Grants, etc., in, *t.* Hen. III. Harl. 52 D. 46 (Nortun), 54 D. 3;—1330. Harl. 51 E. 37;—1546. Harl. 56 C. 36;—1558. Harl. 45 D. 55;—1559. Harl. 45 D. 57;—1583. Harl. 45 D. 59;—1632. Harl. 56 I. 17, 18, 57 H. 37;—1663. Add. 10523;—1678. Add. 10529.

—— Process against the Abbat of Battle conc. the rectory, 1279. Cott. xiii. 23.

—— Exchange in, with Ixworth Priory, 1325. Harl. 44 E. 51.

—— License for grant of the manor to Ixworth Priory, 1371. Harl. 57 B. 11.

—— Grant of Lit. Haugh (Lytelhawe) manor in, 1382. Harl. 45 G. 61.

—— Suit conc. Lit. Haugh manor, 1392. Harl. 58 G. 12.

—— Conveyance of the manor, 1404. Add. 15537.

—— Acquittance for castle-ward in the manor to Bury St. Edmunds Abbey, 1448. Harl. 44 D. 30;—1454. Harl. 44 D. 29.

—— Arbitration conc. Lit. Haugh manor in, 1464. Harl. 49 F. 39.

—— Acquittance for homage in, 1545. Harl. 45 D. 48.

—— Sale of the manor, 1589. Add. 18867.

—— *Rector.* Petr. Sarracenus, *ante* 1279. Cott. xiii. 23.

—— —— Joh. de Batalia, 1279. Cott. xiii. 23.

Norton, *co. Worc.* Leases at, 1017-23 (Norð tun). Add. 19796;—1058 (Norð tun). Add. 19801.

Norton, *nr. Evesham, co. Worc.* Marriage settlement of the manor, 1646. Add. 1799.

Norton Beauchamp, *in Kew Stoke,* co. *Som.* Suit to the manor, in La Sonde, 1389. Harl. 46 G. 21.

Norton, Bishop's, co. *Linc.* Lease in, 1510. Add. 9264.

Norton Brize, co. *Oxon.* Court-roll, 1464–5 (Brimsnorton). Add. 872.

—— Compotus of the manor, 1474–75 (Broynesnorton). Harl. Roll G. 2.

Norton, Chipping, co. *Oxon.* Grant of the manor, 1466 (Chepyng Norton). Harl. 57 C. 14.

—— Grant of rents from the manor, 1598. Harl. 76 E. 50.

—— Brief for rebuilding the church, 1822. Ch. Br. C. iii. 6.

Norton, Cold *al.* Norton Hall, co. *Essex.* Precipe on covenant conc. the manor, etc., 1555. Add. 24928.

Norton Curlew, *in Budbrooks,* co. *Warw.* Covenant for fine, sale, etc., in, 1565. Add. 24172;—1599. Add. 24173, 24174;—1613. Add. 24176;— 1617. Add. 24175, 24177, 24178;— 1649. Add. 24179; — 1681. Add. 24181.

—— Suit conc. lands inherited from N. Langford in, 1670. Add. 24180.

Norton Davy. *v.* Norton, Green's, co. *North.*

Norton Disney, co. *Linc.* Grant of Raudemilne, with St. James's chapel, etc., in, to Newhouse Abbey, c. 1155 (Nortun). Harl. 50 B. 44.

—— Conff. of above grant of Rodemilne *al.* Routhemilne, etc., c. 1155. Harl. 43 H. 15–17;—[1156 or 7?]. Harl. 51 H. 1;—c. 1231. Harl. 52 C. 5.

—— Lease of Routhemilne in, from Newhouse Abbey, with covenant to maintain the chapel, 1230. Harl. 44 G. 19.

—— Descent of lands in, to R. Basset, *t.* Hen. III. Slo. xxxii. 11 (copy).

—— License to Newhouse Abbey to sell lands in, 1267. Harl. 44 F. 31.

—— Surrender, etc., of Rugesmolyn manor in, to Newhouse Abbey, 1299. Harl. 52 C. 6.

—— License to the Abbat of Newhouse for services in the oratory of Rouchemolyn manor in, 1344. Harl. 43 H. 42.

—— (?) *Persona.* Johannes, end of 12 cent. (Nortune). Add. 20580.

—— —— Johannes, c. 1231. Harl. 52 C. 5.

Norton, East, co. *Leic.* Conf. of the church, etc., to Ouston Abbey, 1343. Add. 21391.

Norton FitzWarren, co. *Som.* Release in, 1487 (Northtone). Add. 25991.

Norton Folgate, co. *Midd.* Release of actions on account of repairs in the manor by the "firmarius" of St. Paul's, London, 1453. Lansd. 653.

Norton Giffard, *in Weston sub Edge,* co. *Glouc.* (?). Grant of the tithes to Monmouth Priory, c. 1125. Campb. v. 5.

Norton, Green's, co. *North.* Covenant for a feoffment in, and in Duncote (Doncote) in, 1276 (Norton). Add. 22509.

—— Power from St. James's Abbey, Northampton, to give seisin of the chantry, 1524 (Norton Davy). Campb. x. 3.

—— Lease of the park, 1693. Add. 6076, 6151;—1698. Add. 6152.

—— *Persona.* Tho. de Useflete, 1345. Add. 6029.

Norton Hall. *v. sub* Finchingfield, co. *Essex.*

Norton Hautville, co. *Som.* Grant in, 1467. Add. 5470, 5471.

Norton in Hales, co. *Salop.* Briefs for rebuilding the church, 1801–1817. Ch. Br. B. xli. 6, xlv. 8, l. 7, liv. 8, lviii. 3.

Norton juxta Twycross, co. *Leic.* Grant and release in, to Polesworth Abbey, early Hen. III. (Nortona). Add. 21491.

—— Terrier of lands in, 15 cent. Slo. xxxi. 9.

Norton King's *al.* Norton by Galby, co. *Leic.* License for foundation of a chantry annexed to the church of, 1344 (Norton). Campb. xv. 6.

—— Memoranda of tithes bel. to, in Gt. Stretton, co. Leic., [1360–86] (do.). Cott. xvi. 65.

—— Grants, etc., in, 1415–1537. Add. 26974 – 26987; — 1511. Add. 21071 (West Nortton).

—— Power to give seisin in, to the New Hospital at Leicester, 1614. Add. 26989.

—— *Clericus.* Nicholaus (?), c. 1160 (North.). Lansd. 691.

—— *Vicarius.* Joh. Broughton, 1499. Add. 26982;—1517. Add. 26986.

Norwich, *co. Norf. (continued). Aldermanni (continued).* Gregory Clerk, Hen. atte Mere, 1511. Add. 14191.

—— —— Will. Hart, 1512. Add. 15553.

—— —— Joh. Rightwys *(deceased),* Rob. Brown, 1517 (?). Add. 14215.

—— —— Rob. Burgh *(deceased),* Joh. Marsham, 1523. Add. 17746.

—— —— Edw. Rede, 1526. Add. 14612 ;—1527. Add. 14611 ;—1541. Add. 14616, 14617.

—— —— Augustin. Styward, 1527. Add. 14611 ;—1528. Add. 14613.

—— —— Geffery Warde, 1557. Add. 14543.

—— —— Tho. Malby *(deceased),* 1559. Add. 14230.

—— —— Tho. Layour, 1574. Add. 14623.

—— —— Rob. Suckling, Rich. Bate, Christoph. Layer, Tho. Layer, 1577. Add. 14626.

—— —— Rich. Baker, 1584. Add. 14254.

—— —— *Cyrographarii Judaismi.* Symon le Paumere, Hubert. de Morlee, 1281. Lansd. 666–669.

—— —— Abraham de Euerwyk, Ysaac fil. Deuelcre, 1281. Lansd. 668, 669.

—— —— PARISHES.

—— PAR. OF ST. ANDREW. Feoffments, etc., in, 1467. Add. 15545 ;—1473. Add. 15547, 15548 ; — 1493. Add. 15549 ;—1512. Add. 15553.

—— PAR. OF ST. AUGUSTINE. Grant in, early 13 cent. Harl. 50 B. 14.

—— PAR. OF ST. BARTHOLOMEW BERSTREET. Feoffment in, 1430. Add. 14790.

—— PAR. OF ST EDMUND FISHERGATE. Grant, etc., in, 1342. Add. 19312 ;—1383. Add. 19320.

—— PAR. OF ST. JOHN BERSTREET. Release in, 1306. Add. 6704.

—— PAR. OF ST. MARTIN COSLANY. Grant in, by the corporation, 1327. Add. 14786.

—— PAR. OF ST. MARY THE LESS. Grant in, to Pentney Priory, *c.* 1270. Add. 14779 *(copy).*

—— PAR. OF ST. MICHAEL IN CONISFORD. Release in, 1322. Add. 17220.

—— PAR. OF ST. MICHAEL COSLANY. Grant, etc., in, 1296. Harl. 58 C. 20 ; —1302. Harl. 58 C. 21.

Norwich, *co. Norf. (continued).* PARISHES *(continued).* PAR. OF ST. PETER MANCROFT. License to a Jew to sell his houses in, 1280. Lansd. 665.

—— —— Grants, etc., in, 1281. Lansd. 666–669 ;—1294. Add. 14783 ; —1316. Harl. 55 D. 2 ;—1379. Add. 14789.

—— PAR. OF ST. SEPULCHRE. Grant in, from Haliwell Priory, Shoreditch, [1261]. Toph. 11.[3]

—— PAR. OF ST. STEPHEN. *Vicarius.* Ric. de Caystre, *ob.* 1419. Harl. 58 C. 14 *dors.*

—— PAR. OF ST. VEDAST. Release in, to Sibton Abbey, *t.* Edw. I. Harl. 84 A. 48.

—— —— Release in, 1484. Add. 2009.

Norwime. *v.* Witham, North, *co. Linc.*

Norwood, *co. Midd.* Brief conc. a fire at Southall Green in the Precinct of, 1799. Ch. Br. B. xxxix. 3.

Noseley, *co. Leic. Custos Capelle B. Marie.* Rad. Peek, 1369. Add. 26938.

Nosterfield, *in Shudy Camps, co. Camb.* Grant of (?), *t.* John (Nostrefeld). Harl. 52 I. 37.

—— Feoffment in, 1438 (Nostrefeld) Add. 9251.

Notasse. *v.* Nottage, *co. Glam.*

Noteham. *v.* Nutham, *co. Suss.*

—— *v. sub* Pauntley, *co. Glouc.*

Notehurst. *v.* Nuthurst, *co. Suss.*

Noteshulling. *v.* Nutshalling, *co. Southt.*

Notgrove, *co. Glouc.* Release in, 1349 (Nategrave). Harl. 49 H. 40.

—— Grant of the manor, 1359 (Natgrave). Slo. xxxiii. 40.

—— Admission of R. Scudamore to the rectory of, 1641. Add. 1362, 1363.

—— *Persona.* Thomas, 1359. Slo. xxxiii. 40.

Notha. *v.* Nottingham, *co. Nott.*

Notingeton. *v.* Nottington, *in Broadway, co. Dors.*

Notingham. *v.* Nottingham, *co. Nott.*

Notisworthy. *v. sub* Widecombe in the Moor, *co. Devon.*

Notley, Black, *co. Essex.* Grant in (?), *t.* John. Cott. xxvii. 23.

—— Release in, to Dunmow Priory, *t.* Hen. III. (Nigra Notele). Harl. 51 B. 46.

Nottingham, *co. Nott. (continued).*
*Prepositi in Burgo Francko.* Rob.
Bugge, Astin. Coffe, *t.* Hen. III.
Harl. 112 F. 37.

—— —— *in Burgo Ancglico.* Will.
Maynard, Nic. le Ferrur, *t.* Hen. III.
Harl. 112 F. 37.

—— —— *Ballivi.* Adam Le Palmer,
Mich. Le Orfeur, *t.* Edw. I. Harl. 45
C. 11.

—— —— *Mag.* Joh. de Rempes-
ton, Ric. de Lincoln., *t.* Edw. I. Harl.
45 C. 12.

—— —— Joh. Le Flemeng, Mich.
Le Orfeure, 1284. Harl. 45 C. 13.

—— —— Will. Jorden, Reg. de
Acre, 1286. Harl. 45 C. 14.

—— —— Will. de Crophill, Walt.
de Lincolnia, 1304. Harl. 47 D. 40, 41.

—— —— Will. Godmouth, Joh. Le
Colyer, 1320. Harl. 51 C. 32.

—— —— Will. Brian, Joh. de
Toumby, 1337. Add. 21181.

—— —— Will. de Depinge, Steph.
le Especer. [1353]. Harl. 112 F. 41.

—— —— Joh. de Chastre, 1360.
Harl. 48 G. 27 *dors.*

Nottirgton *al.* **Nettington,** *in
Broadway, co. Dors.* Conf. of a grant
in, to Bindon Abbey, 1234. Harl. 58
H. 45 (Notingeton) (*copy*).

Nottisworthye. *v. sub* Widecombe
in the Moor, *co. Devon.*

Nottyng. *v.* Knotting, *co. Bedf.*

Nova Terra. *v.* Newland, *co. Glouc.*

—— *v.* Newlands Manor, *co. Oxon.*

Nova Villa. *v.* Newton Nottage, *co.
Glam.*

—— *v.* Newton, Shire, *co. Monm.*

Novum Castrum. *v.* Newcastle, *co.
Glam., etc.*

Novum Castrum subtus Lymam.
*v.* Newcastle under Lyme, *co. Staff.*

Novum Mercatum. *v.* Newmarket,
*co. Camb.*

Novus Burgus. *v.* Cardiff, *co. Glam.*

—— *v.* Newport, *Isle of Wight.*

Nowers Manor. *v. sub* Hindringham, *co. Norf.*

Nowetuna. *v.* Newton, *co. Camb.*

Nowhethe, *nr. Wicken, co. Camb.*
Release in, 1405. Harl. 58 D. 48.

Nowton, *co. Suff.* Grant of rents in, to
St. Helen's Priory, Bishopsgate, 1417.
Toph. 39.

—— Precipes on covenants conc.
lands in, 1578. Add. 25363; —1593.
Add. 25477.

Nubele. *v.* Newbold, *co. Linc.*

Nudegate. *v.* Newdigate, *co. Surr.*

Nudegate Lands. *v. sub* Shalford,
*co. Surr.*

Nuffield, *co. Oxon.* Grants, etc., in,
1483. Add. 20380 (Tuffeld): —1440.
Harl. 45 A. 26; —1465. Add. 20357;
—1476. Add. 20358; —1483. Add.
20359.

Nuford. *v.* Nutford, *co. Dors.*

Nuneaton, *co. Warw.* Marriage settlement and grants in, 1483. Add.
24228; —1504. Add. 24230; —1508.
Add. 24231, 24232.

—— Presentation of J. Sledd as
vicar, [1580–1603]. Cott. xxi. 28.

—— *Vicarius.* Ric. Busvyle, 1483.
Add. 24228.

Nuneham Courtney, *co. Oxon.*
Evidence conc. alienation of the manor,
end of 15 cent. Add. 20356.

Nunford. *v. sub* Colyton, *co. Devon.*

Nunney, *co. Som.* Grants in, 1361
(Nony). Harl. 75 D. 59 *a, b* (*copies*);
—1382. Harl. 76 E. 4 (do.).

—— Acquittance for rent from the
manor, 1472 (Nony). Harl. 55 A. 10.

Nunton, *in Maxey, co. Northt.* License
to endow a chantry with lands in,
1368. Campb. v. 10.

—— Grant, etc., in, 1372. Harl. 56
I. 32; —1549. Add. 13561.

Nursling. *v.* Nutshalling, *co. Southt.*

Nursted, *co. Kent.* Grants, etc., in, *t.*
Hen. III. Harl. 55 F. 31 (Nutstede);
—1367. Harl. 48 E. 24 (do.); —1375.
Harl. 52 H. 51 (Nustede); —1381. Harl.
48 E. 36 (Nutstede); —1413. Harl.
47 I. 28 (Norstede).

—— *Rector.* Dom. Tho. Goldherst,
*ante* 1375. Harl. 52 H. 51.

Nutbourne, *co. Suss.* Livery of the
manor, 1554. Add. 18837.

Nuteleia. *v.* Notley, White, *co. Essex.*

Nutescheolua. *v. sub* Overton, *co.
Southt.*

Nutfield, *co. Surr.* Grants of a mill
and Widihorn wood in, late 12 cent.
Add. 24606 (Nutfeld). 24607.

—— Grants in, *t.* Hen. III. Add.
5933; —1316. Add. 24608 (Nutte-
felde); —1529. Harl. 112 F. 23.

Nutfield, co. Surr. (continued). Grant of Hale mill in, 1359 (Hale mulle in Notfeld). Add. 23615.

—— Grants, etc., of the manor and advowson, 1359-1390. Add. 23616, 23618-23630; — 1398. Add. 23785 (Notefeld):—1404. Add. 23632:—1420. Add. 23633; — 1456. Add. 23634, 23635.

Nutford, in Pimperne, co. Dors. Inspex., in 1280, of a conf. by King John of rents at, to Fontevrault Abbey, 1200 (Nuford). Harl. 58 I. 34 (copy).

—— Inspex., in 1231, of a Papal conf. of the same rents to the same, 1201 (Neudfort). Add. 17861.

Nuthall, co. Nott. Fine in, 1702. Woll. xi. 75, xii. 5.

Nutham. v. sub Pauntley, co. Glouc.

Nutham, nr.Horsham, co. Suss. Release, etc., in, 1357. Add. 18651 (Noteham); —1556. Add. 18977, 18978.

Nuthurst, co. Suss. Grants, etc., in, 1355. Add. 8852 (Noteherst);—1357. Add. 18651;—1408. Add. 1006 (Notehurst);— 1443. Add. 8881;—1476. Add. 1007;—1556. Add. 8940;—1631. Add. 18939;—1642. Add. 18964;—1647. Add. 18969.

—— Survey of timber in, 1598. Add. 18883.

Nuthurst, co. Warw. Grant of a moiety of the wood of, t. John (Nutehurst). Cott. xxiii. 15.

Nuthurstawey. v. Stowey, Nether, co. Som.

Nutshalling al. Nursling, co. Southt. Conf. of land at, to the see of Winchester, 909 (Hnut Scillingc). Harl. 43 C. 1.

—— Conf. of the church to St. Cross Hosp., Winchester, 1189 (Nutselling). Harl. 43 C. 28.

—— Grant of the manor, 1335 (Noteshulling). Add. 15466.

Nutshaw. v. sub Overton, co. Southt.

Nutstede. v. Nursted, co. Kent.

Nutsworthy. v. sub Widecombe in the Moor, co. Devon.

Nycols. v. sub Hunston, co. Suff.

Nye, La. v. sub Winscombe, co. Som.

Nyelende. v. Nayland, co. Suff.

Nyghton. v. Niton, I. of Wight.

Nyland, nr. Rodney Stoke, co. Som. Conf. of jurisdiction of the abbat of Glastonbury in, 1344 (Insula de Adredesia). Camp. xiii. 19.

Nympton. v. sub Chartham, co. Kent.

Nynehead Flory, co. Som. Suit conc. land in, 1519 (Nihed Florye). Harl. 57 F. 40.

Nyth, Vallis de. v. Nithsdale, co. Dumfries.

Nytherstaweye. v. Stowey, Nether, co. Som.

Nywedegate. v. Newdigate, co. Surr.

Nywenden. v. Newenden, co. Kent.

Nywenham. v. Newnham, co. Oxon.

—— v. sub Sutton Veney, co. Wilts.

Nyweton Abbatis. v. Newton Abbot, co. Devon.

## O

Oak Green, in Sudbury. co. Derb. Award conc. lands in, 1472 (Okkes). Woll. ix. 49.

Oakford, co. Devon. Accompts of the provost, 1377-8 (Hokafforde). Add. 7658.

Oakham, co. Rutl. Re-grant of the church, etc., by Will. I. to Westminster Abbey, 1067 (Ocham). Cott. vi. 3 (copy).

—— Treaty conc. the castle betw. the Earls of Chester and Leicester, [1151-2] (Hocham). Cott. MS. Nero C. iii. f. 178.

—— Warrant for expenses of works in the castle, 1386 (Okham). Add. 10650.

—— Court - rolls, 1622 (Okeham). Add. 15250.

—— Rolls of assize, 1693-1761. Add. 873 (1-30) (54-57).

Oakham, Barony of. Grant in Thorpe Satchville. co. Leic., held of, to Ouston Abbey, t. Edw. I. (Hocham). Campb. xv. 3.

Oakhurst. v. sub Sidlesham, co. Suss.

Oakhurst, nr. Colney Street, co. Hertf. Release, etc., in, 1256. Add. 18158 (Okerse):—1287. Add. 18186 (Okersh), 18189, 18190.

Oakington, co. Camb. Grant of the manor, 1361 (Hokyngton). Harl. 58 A. 48.

Oakington, co. Camb. (continued). Grants, etc., in, 1376. Harl. 58 B. 9 (Hokyngton);—1391. Add. 15533 (do.);—1401. Cott. xxvii. 6 (do.);—1439. Add. 22602 (Hoketone);—1481. Add. 22585.

Oakle, nr. Newent, co. Glouc. Release in, 1310. Add. 7215 (Acle);—1311. Add. 7216.

Oakley, co. Buck. Feoffments, etc., in, 1336. Add. 22163 (Occle in com. Oxon.);—1383. Add. 22213 (Okloe in Bernwod), 22214.

—— Covenant for a fine of the manor, etc., 1547 (Ocle, Ocley, Okley, Aclo). Harl. 79 G. 13.

Oakley, in Higham, co. Kent. A boundary-mark, 774 (Ac loah). Cott. MS. Aug. ii. 99.

—— Council held at, 805 (Hacleah). Cott. MS. Aug. ii. 87.

Oakley, nr. Chinnor, co. Oxon. Acquittance from Wallingford Priory for rents in, 1451 (Ocle). Add. 20330.

Oakley, in Crozall, co. Staff. Conveyance in, 1581 (Ockley). Woll. xii. 139.

Oakley, co. Suff. Admission to land in, held of Broome Hall manor, 1686. Add. 10501.

Oakley, Great, co. Essex. Grants, etc., in, 1308. Harl. 49 C. 17 (Magna Acle);—1318. Harl. 49 C. 18 (do.);—1392. Harl. 55 C. 38 (Magna Okelee).

—— Compotus of the manor, 1421-2 (Magna Ocle). Add. 682.

—— Precipes on covenants conc. lands in, 1587. Add. 24985 (Okeley magna), 24991.

Oakley, Great, co. Northt. Grant in, t. Hen. III. (Westacle). Add. 21183 (copy).

—— License to fold sheep on the demesne of, 1327. Harl. 112 B. 14.

Oakley, Little, co. Essex. Grants of the manor and advowson, 1343. Harl. 84 A. 53 (Okele Parva);—1398. Harl. 84 B. 22 (Parva Oclee).

—— Grants, etc., in, 1346. Lansd. 115 (Parva Okele);—1347. Lansd. 118;—1348. Lansd. 120 (Parva Oclee), 121;—1361. Harl. 84 A. 18 (Oklee parva).

Oakley, Little, co. Northt. Grant of Rodmeres Hawe wood in, t. John. Harl. 45 B. 9.

—— Rector. Edw. Clowes, 1530. Harl. 53 F. 33.

Oakwood. v. sub Wotton, co. Surr.

Oare, co. Berks. Release, etc., in, 1409. Add. 5159 (Oore);—1410. Add. 5160 (Ore);—1415. Add. 5161;—1416. Add. 5162.

Oatlands Park, co. Surr. Lease of a lodge in, 1715. Eg. 333.

Obbecumbe. v. sub Uplyme, co. Devon.

Obbethorp. v. Obthorpe, co. Linc.

Oberhall. v. sub Lavenham, co. Suff.

Obernestun. v. Osbaston, in High Ercall, co. Salop.

Obestona, Obestun. v. Ubbeston, co. Suff.

Obleygh. v. Ubley, co. Som.

Oborn. v. Wooburn, co. Buck.

Oborne, co. Dors. Inquest conc. charges on the manor incurred by Sherborne Abbey, 1386 (Woborne). Add. 6087.

—— Release, etc., in, 1425. Harl. 48 B. 7 (Wobourne);—1439. Harl. 58 D. 42 (Woborn).

Obston. v. Ubbeston, co. Suff.

Obthorpe, co. Linc. License for grant in, to St. Michael's Nunnery, Stamford, 1292 (Obbethorp). Harl. 43 D. 2.

Occasate. v. Ockshot, co. Surr.

Occingtun. v. Ossington, co. Nott.

Occle, in com. Oxon. v. Oakley, co. Buck.

Occlestone, co. Chest. Brief conc. a fire at, 1810. Ch. Br. B. l. 9.

Occold, co. Suff. Grant, etc., in, t. Hen. III. Harl. 50 C. 33 (Acholt);—1303. Harl. 47 A. 15 (Acholte).

—— Precipes on covenants conc. lands in, 1588. Add. 25390 (Occolte);—1593. Add. 25478.

—— Capellanus. Hugo, early 13 cent. Harl. 49 B. 21.

Ocfordskylling. v. Okeford, Shilling, co. Dors.

Ocham. v. Oakham, co. Rutl.

Ocham, co. Worc. (?). Rector (quondam). Joh. de Longeford, 1332. Harl. 112 A. 20.

Ockbrook, co. Derb. Papal conf. of land in, to Dale Abbey, 1224 (Okebro). Woll. x. 32.

Ockeborn. v. Ogbourne St. George, co. Wilts.

Ockefeld. v. Uckfield, co. Suss.

2 o

Ockehampton. v. Okehampton, co. Devon.

Ockendon, North, co. Essex. Grant of the vill, by Will. I. to Westminster Abbey, 1067 (Wokendune). Cott. vi. 3 (copy).

—— Grant in, 1424 (North Wokyndon). Harl. 55 A. 13.

—— Rector. Tho. Copto, 1424. Harl. 55 A. 13.

Ockendon, South, co. Essex. Suit conc. a partition of the manor, 1531 (South Wokyndon). Harl. Roll CC. 24.

—— Court-roll, 1569 (South Wokendon). Harl. Roll CC. 25.

—— Persona. Joh. Brondishe, 1365. Cott. xxvii. 55.

Ockendon Rokele, South, co. Essex. Covenant for recovery of the manor and advowson, 1528 (Southwokendon Rokele). Cott. v. 7.

Ockham, co. Surr. Grant of custody of lands of John Weston of, during minority, 1484 (Okham). Lansd. 677.

—— Disposition of land in, 1627. Add. 5678.

Ockley. v. Oakley, in Croxall, co. Staff.

Ockley, co. Surr. Grants, etc., in, t. Edw. I. Add. 9010 (Ockelee);—c. 1290. Add. 18580 (Ockele);—1309. Add. 9020 (Ockeley);—t. Edw. II. Add. 9014 (Ookely);—1323. Add. 1004 (Ockeley);—1325. Add. 17297; —1328. Add. 9029 (Ockelegh);—1334. Add. 9031;—1336. Add. 18633 (Ockelee);—1338. Add. 9032 (Ockelegh), 9033;—1339. Add. 9034, 9035;—1340. Add. 18635;—1345. Add. 9036;—1352. Add. 9040;—1355. Add. 9041;—1361. Add. 18652;—1363. Add. 18657 (Hockeley) —1368. Add. 1005 (Ockeleye);—1377. Add. 9050 (Ockelegh);—1383. Add. 9053;—1385. Add. 9054;—1388-9. Add. 18668;—1390. Add. 18675;—1397. Add. 9057;—1399. Add. 18687, 18688;—1400. Add. 18691 (Oklegh);—1406. Add. 18703 (Okkele);—1408. Add. 1006;—1414. Add. 18704;—1418. Add. 9064 (Okkelegh), 18699, 18700, 18702;—1434. Add. 9067 (Okkele);—1440. Add. 18735;—1442. Add. 18740-18742;—1476. Add. 1007;—1480. Add. 1008, 9071;—1507. Add. 18792 (Okeley); —1510. Add. 9077 (Okley), 9078, 18795;—1520. Add. 18803 (Ocley), 18804;—1529. Harl. 112 F. 23;—

1537. Add. 9085, 9086;—1544. Add. 18825, 18826;—1560. Add. 18846 :—1578. Add. 18861 ;—1621. Harl. 77 E. 16.

—— Power to give seisin of the manor and advowson, 1417 ( Oclee). Harl. 56 D. 26.

—— Award as to title to lands in, 1556 (Okley). Harl. 112 D. 9.

—— Persona. Nicholaus, t. Edw. II. Add. 5566, 5567.

v. also Rookham, in Ockley, co. Surr.

Ockahot, co. Surr. Grants, etc., in, to Waverley Abbey, t. John-late Hen. III. Add. 5528 (Occasate), 5529 (Occasat), 5530 (Oggeschate), 5533 (Hoggeset), 5536 (Hogeseth), 5536* (Ogsath, Ugsethe), 5537 (Oggesahte), 5538 (Oggesethe);—[1235]. Add. 5531 (Oggesset), 5532 ;—1281. Add. 5534 (Hoggesete), 5535.

—— Grants in, t. Hen. III. or Edw. I. Add. 5539 (Oxsete); — 1333. Add. 5595 (Ockschete).

Ocle. v. Oakley, co. Buck.

—— v. Oakley, nr. Chinnor, co. Oxon.

Ocle Magna. v. Oakley, Great, co. Essex.

Octeselue, Octeshelle, Oothesselua. v. Oxhill, co. Warw.

Octhebi. v. Otby, in Walesby, co. Linc.

Octon. v. Haughton, co. Nott.

Ocwode. v. sub Wotton, co. Surr.

Odcombe, co. Som. Grants, etc., of Gosford al. Barry Gosseford, Barreys Gosefor [l] in, t. Edw. I. Harl. 45 G. 14 ;—1386. Cott. xxvii. 43 (Odecombe);—1438. Harl. 50 E. 6 (do.).

—— Lease of the manor, c. 1433 (?) (do.). Harl. 53 H. 17.

Oddestun. v. Odstone, co. Leic.

Oddyng. v. sub Chalbury, co. Dors.

Odenebi. v. Owmby, co. Linc.

Odierda al. Wodehyerd. v. sub Denham, co. Buck.

Odiham (Odyham, etc.), co. Southt. Grant nr., "super Aleberwe in Estone," t. Edw. I. Add. 26618.

—— Grants, etc., at Hill (La Hulle, La Hole) in, 1333. Add. 26626 ;—1376. Add. 26636 ; — 1403. Add. 26640;—1436. Add. 26651.

Odiham (Odyham, etc.), *co. Southt.* (*continued*). Grants, etc., in, 1344. Add. 26629;—1360. Add. 26632;— 1411. Add. 26644;—1451-1456. Add. 26655-26660.

—— Grant in le Whitte downe in, 1446. Add. 26653.

—— Grants, etc., " infra decennam de Hulle " in, 1446. Add. 26654;—1459- 1460. Add. 26663 - 26665; — 1477. Add. 26672;—1490. Add. 26674.

—— Grant " in decenna de Rye " in, 1483. Add. 26673.

—— Grant of church lands, etc., in, 1549 (Odyam). Add. 4607.

—— Precipe on a covenant conc. lands in, 1578. Add. 25230.

—— *Rector.* Joh. Remes, 1442. Add. 26720.

Odiham, *Forest of, co. Southt.* Sale of timber in, to Winchester Priory, 1298- 9. Add. 19292 (3) (*copy*).

Odimere. *v.* Udimore, *co. Suss.*

Odstone, *co. Leic.* Grant of, late 12 cent. (Oddestun). Add. 21390.

Offa ham. *v.* Offham, *co. Kent.*

Offchurch, *co. Warw.* Precipe on a covenant conc. land in, 1558 (Of- churche bury). Add. 25543.

Offcote, *in Ashbourne, co. Derb.* Grants, etc., in, *t.* Hen. III. Woll. ix. 63 (Offidecot);—*t.* Edw. I. Woll x. 3;— 1468. Woll. vii. 15.

Offelowe. *v.* Offlow Hundred, *co. Staff.*

Offenham, *co. Worc.* Lease at, 1058 (on Afan hamme). Add. 19801.

Offerton, *in Hope, co. Derb.* Lease in, 1399. Woll. viii. 5.

Offham. *v. sub* Stoke, South, *co. Suss.*

Offham, *co. Kent.* Purchase of land at, 1014-48 (Offa ham). Cott. MS. Aug. ii. 35.

Offidecot. *v.* Offcote, *in Ashbourne, co. Derb.*

Offlega. *v.* Offley, High, *co. Staff.*

Offington, *in Broadwater, co. Suss.* Grants in La Hamme field, etc., in, to Waverley Abbey, 12-13 cent. Harl. 77 E. 43 (Offentun);—*t.* Edw. I. Harl. 79 E. 12 (Offenton).

—— Grants, etc., in, *t.* Hen. III. Harl. 80 H. 11 (Offyntun);—1285. Add. 17271 (Offintone), Harl. 76 F. 53-55; —1331. Harl. 76 F. 10, 78 A. 44;—

1355. Harl. 80 A. 22, 23;—1356. Harl. 76 F. 48;—1357. Harl. 80 A. 20, 80 H. 8;—1371. Harl. 80 A. 25; —1398. Harl. 79 E. 44 :—1425. Harl. 77 G. 20;—1494. Harl. 76 E. 51;— 1527. Harl. 80 A. 55.

—— Power to give seisin of the manor, 1381. Harl. 78 B. 2.

—— Court-rolls, 1386-1553 (Offyng- ton, etc.). Harl. Rolls AA. 1-11.

—— Compotus of the manor, 1454-55 (Offyngton). Harl. Roll AA. 12.

—— Lease in, nr. the Priests way, by Waverley Abbey, 1500. Harl. 75 G. 14.

—— Extract from court-roll, 1515 (Offyngton). Harl. 75 D. 48.

—— Conf. of title in the manor, etc., 1601. Harl. 76 A. 27.

*v. also* Broadwater, *co. Suss.*

Offley, Great, *co. Hertf.* Grants, etc., in, early Hen. III. Add. 24064 (Offe- leia). 24068;—*ante* 1292. Add. 24065 (Offell.);—1368. Add. 24066 (Offe- leye);—1435. Add. 23178;—1555. Add. 13099.

—— Grant of Welles *al.* Wellbury manor, etc., in, 1555. Add. 13099.

—— *Vicarius* (*quondam*). Johannes, *ante* 1292. Add. 24065.

—— *Perpet. Vicarius. Dom.* Willel- mus, *ante* 1292. Add. 24065.

Offley, High, *co. Staff.* Grant of free warren in, 1267 (Offilega). Add. 15773.

—— Fine, in 1340, and recovery of the manor, 1421 (Hieoffeleie). Lansd. 144.

—— Brief for rebuilding the church, 1765. Ch. Br. B. v. 10.

—— *Vicarius.* Tho. Andrewe, 1395 (Offyley). Campb. xxviii. 8.

Offley, Little, *co. Hertf.* Grant in, 1553. Add. 13099.

Offlow Hundred, *co. Staff.* Tenure roll, [1254-72] (Offelowe). Harl. Roll K. 10.

Offord, *in Wootton Wawen, co. Warw.* Power to give seisin of the manor, 1366. Add. 21492.

—— Grant in, 1460. Add. 8441.

Offord Darcy, *co. Hunt.* Papal conf. of a grant in (?), to Sawtrey Abbey, 1195 (Uppeford). Cott. MS. Aug. ii. 115.

—— Sale of church lands in, 1561. Harl. 80 H. 61.

**Oneston, Oniston.** *v.* Unstone, *co. Derb.*

**Ongar Hundred,** *co. Essex.* Grant of, to R. de Luci, [1174?] (Angr.). Cott. xi. 5.

—— Appointment of a bailiff, *t.* Edw. I. (Aungre). Harl. 55 D. 27.

—— Grant of, to Lord Stafford, 1348 (Aungre). Add. 19965.

—— Release of, 1359 (do.). Harl. 55 D. 31.

—— Subsidy assessment, 1589 (Onger). Harl. Roll X. 23.

**Ongar, Chipping,** *co. Essex.* Exchange for lands in, 1308 (Aungre ad castrum). Add. 19964.

—— Release of the manor, 1359 (Castel Aungre). Harl. 55 D. 31.

—— Precipe on a covenant conc. the manor, etc., 1593 (Chepinge onger *al.* Onger ad Castrum). Add. 25048.

—— *Dominus. Dom.* Joh. de Ripariis, *t.* Edw. I. (Aungre). Lansd. 79.

**Ongar, High,** *co. Essex.* Grants, etc., in, *t.* Hen. III. or Edw. I. (Alta Angre). Harl. 85 D. 26;—1308. Add. 19964 (Alta Aungre).

**Ongar Park.** *v. sub* Stanford Rivers, *co. Essex.*

**Onnanduun,** *co. Glouc.* or *co. Worc.* Boundary of grant " æt Onnanforda," 759. Add. 19789.

**Onnanford,** *co. Glouc.* or *co. Worc.* Grant at, 759. Add. 19789.

**Onnesbye.** *v.* Aunsby, *co. Linc.*

**Onston, Onuston.** *v.* Unstone, *co. Derb.*

**Onysacker.** *v. sub* Bradfield, *co. York.*

**Ophireche.** *v.* Upchurch, *co. Kent.*

**Openshaw,** *co. Lanc.* Briefs conc. fires at, 1803. Ch. Br. B. xliii. 2;—1808. Ch. Br. B. xlix. 6.

**Opotery.** *v.* Ottery, Up, *co. Devon.*

**Orby,** *co. Linc.* Fine of the advowson to Thornholm Priory, 1202 (Orreby). Harl. 54 E. 13.

—— License from Thornholm Priory for an oratory in the manor, etc., 1208 (Orreby). Harl. 45 A. 1, 2.

—— Grants, etc., in, 1355. Harl. 57 G. 11;—1369. Woll. x. 48;—1438. Harl. 57 F. 12.

—— Release of the manor, 1387 (Orreby). Harl. 53 C. 38.

**Orchardleigh,** *co. Som.* Grants in Frome, nr. the mill of, *t.* Edw. I. Harl. 80 A. 51 (Orcherdleg);—*t.* Edw. III. Harl. 75 D. 59 c (Orcherleygh) (copy).

—— Grant of a moiety of the manor and advowson, 1431 (Orcherleghe). Eg. 264.

**Orcheston,** *co. Wilts.* Compotus rolls of, bel. to the Duke of Buckingham, 1499–1500. Add. 26873;—1511–12. Add. 26874.

**Ordsall,** *co. Nott.* Grant in, 1375 (Ordsale). Harl. 112 F. 60.

**Ore,** *co. Suss.* Conf. of tithes in, to Battle Abbey, [1121–5] (Ora). Cott. MS. Nero C. iii. f. 189.

**Orepittes, Le.** *v. sub* Sheffield, *co. York.*

**Ores** *al.* **Greys Manor.** *v. sub* Chislett, *co. Kent.*

**Orestone,** *in Plymouth, co. Devon.* Certificate of the health of the port of, 1610. Harl. 83 A. 17.

**Orford,** *in Binbrook, co. Linc.* Episcopal conff., etc., of St. Michael's church in, etc., to Newhouse Abbey, *c.* 1150–55. Harl. 43 G. 19 (Hireford), 43 H. 14–17 (Irefordia, Hireford);—1319. Harl. 43 G. 29 (Ireford);—1333. Harl. 43 H. 39 (Irford), 40;—1344. Harl. 43 H. 41;—1368. Harl. 43 H. 44;—1389. Harl. 43 G. 33.

—— Grant, etc., in, to the same, [c. 1150–55] (Hyreforth). Harl. 50 A. 6;—[1203–23] (Ireford). Harl. 52 C. 2.

—— Covenant in, betw. Newhouse and Revesby Abbeys, 1154 (Hireford). Harl. 44 I. 1.

—— Conf. of grants in, to Newhouse Abbey, by Hen. II., [1156 or 7]. Harl. 51 H. 1.

—— Grant in, from Newhouse Abbey, *t.* John. Harl. 44 G. 42.

—— *Presbiter.* Hugo, [c. 1150–55]. Harl. 50 A. 6.

**Orford** (Oreford, etc.), *co. Suff.* Grants, etc., in, *t.* Hen. III.-Edw. I. Harl. 49 F. 21;—1305. Harl. 46 E. 14;—1315. Harl. 48 C. 23;—1346. Harl. 54 H. 50;—1364. Harl. 51 F. 12;—1431. Harl. 58 B. 16;—1438. Harl. 58 B.18.

—— Inquiry conc. seizure of kiddles at, from Sibton Abbey, 1280 (Oreford). Harl. 54 D. 39.

Ormsby, South (Ormesby, etc.), *co. Linc.* (*continued*). *Persona* (*continued*). Thomas, *t.* Hen. III.–*t.* Edw. I. Harl. 44 D. 56, 52 E. 10, 54 D. 42, 46.

—— *Rector. Dom.* Rob. de Staueleya *al.* Stalay, *t.* Hen. III. Harl. 50 A. 20, 54 A. 33, 54 D. 48.

—— —— Joh. Hawlay, [1209–84]. Campb. xxi. 4.

*v. also* Ketsby, *in S. Ormsby, co. Linc.*

Ormskirk, *co. Lanc.* Grant of free market at, to Burscough Priory, 1286 (Ormiskyrke). Add. 20518.

Orpington, *co. Kent.* Release in, to H. Trinity Priory, Canterbury, *t.* Hen. III. (Orpintune). Add. 16468.

—— Feoffment in, 1433. Harl. 111 G. 27.

—— Brief for rebuilding the church, 1809. Ch. Br. B. l. 2.

Orreby. *v.* Orby, *co. Linc.*

Orresbi. *v.* Owersby, *co. Linc.*

Orrices den. *v.* Orkesden, *co. Kent.*

Orset, *co. Essex.* Endowment of a chantry in a chapel in the Bp. of London's palace nr. St. Paul's with Lofthall manor in, 1408. Harl. 55 H. 3.

—— Bond conc. rent from the manor, 1515. Harl. 52 A. 44.

—— Grant of next presentation to the church of, 1544. Add. 24499.

—— Precipes on covenants conc. lands in, 1555. Add. 24925 ;—1587. Add. 24976.

—— Lease in, 1557. Harl. 43 I. 15.

Ortbury, *in Bache, co. Salop.* Grant of, late 13 cent. Add. 8330.

Orton, Cole, *co. Leic.* Grant of twenty loads of sea coal in the manor of, 1571 (Cole Orton). Add. 21197.

—— *Persone. Sire* Will. Davy, 1343 (Ouerton). Cott. xvi. 60.

Orton Longville, *co. Hunt.* Fines of the manor and advowson, 1350. Harl. 58 G. 34 (Overton Longeville) ;—1433. Add. 16471 (Overton Longevyle).

—— Grants, etc., of the manor, 1422. Harl. 47 B. 17 (Overton Longville) ;— 1527. Harl. 46 H. 49 (Overton Langffeld) ;—1532. Harl. 55 A. 41 (Overton Longtield).

—— Court-roll, 1461–64 (Overton Longvile). Harl. Roll K. 14.

—— *Rector.* Joh. Rokesdon, 1391. Add. 15435.

Orton on the Hill, *co. Leic.* Brief for repairing the church, 1760. Ch. Br. A. vi. 10.

—— *Rector.* Joh. de Hyngham, 1330 (Ouerton sub Ardena). Campb. viii. 25, 26.

Orton, Over. *v.* Worton, Upper, *co. Oxon.*

Orton, Water, *co. Warw.* Release in, *t.* Edw. I. (Overton). Cott. xxiii. 35.

Orton Waterville, *co. Hunt.* Lease in, late 13 cent. (Overton wautervile). Cott. xxx. 3.

Osbaldwick, *co. York:* Bond for payment of the first fruits of the prebend of, 1545 (Osbaldwyke). Harl. 58 C. 18.

Osbaston, *in High Ercall, co. Salop.* Grant, with re-grant, in, early Steph. (Obernestun). Harl. 54 G. 46 ;—late 12 cent. (Osbernestun). Harl. 55 B. 4.

—— Inspex., in 1319, of a conf. in, by Hen. II. to Wombridge Priory, [1181] (Hosbertonia). Cott. iv. 36 (3).

Osberstown, *co. Kildare.* Petition against disorders at, 1454. Cott. iv. 35.

Osbournby, *co. Linc.* Grants, etc., in, 1446. Add. 21076 (Osbernby) ;—1505. Add. 21077 (Osburneby) ;—1520. Add. 21079 ;—1521. Add. 21078 ;—1532. Add. 21080 ;—1544. Add. 21081 ;— 1577. Add. 6430.

—— *Vicarius.* Edw. Pratt, 1544. Add. 21081.

Oseby, *co. Linc.* Grants, etc., in, early 14 cent. Add. 6378, 6380, 6381, 6383, 6385 ;—1310 (?). Add. 6393 ;—1311. Add. 6386 ;—1318. Add. 6389 ;—1323. Add. 6391 ;—1329. Add. 6392 ;—1343. Add. 6431 ;—1345. Add. 6394 ;—1366. Add. 6395 ;—1374. Add. 6397 ;—1377. Add. 6398 ;—1412. Add. 6401 ;— 1421. Add. 6402 ;—1424. Add. 6403 ; —1436. Add. 6406 ;—1438. Add. 6408 ;—1483. Add. 6414 ;—1487. Add. 6415 ;—1490. Add. 6416 ;— 1493. Add. 6417 ;—1503. Add. 6418 ;—1504. Add. 6419 ;—1540–41. Add. 6422 ;—1546. Add. 6423 ;—1560. Add. 6425, 6446 ;—1562. Add. 6426 ; —1563. Add. 6427 ;—1564. Add. 6447 ;—1566. Add. 6428 ;—1568. Add. 6429 ;—1577. Add. 6450.

—— Grant of custody, etc., of the manor, 1438. Add. 6407 ;—1447. Add. 6409 ;—1451. Add. 6410 ;—1472. Add. 6412 ;—1475. Add. 6413 ;—1500. Add. 6425 (Ooseby) ;—1564. Add. 6446.

**Oseby,** *co. Linc. (continued).* Fines of the manor, 1534. Add. 6421;—1547. Add. 6424 (Oosbye).

**Osemeresleia.** *v. sub* Alvechurch, *co. Worc.*

**Oseney, North,** *co. Oxon.* Release to Biddlesdon Abbey from suits of court at, 1275 (Northoseneye). Harl. 84 C. 9.

**Osgathorpe,** *co. Leic.* Fine in, *c.* 1200 (Angodestorp). Add. 5235.

**Osgodby,** *in Beltisloe Wapentake, co. Linc.* Grants, etc., in, 1347. Add. 20996;—1348. Add. 21000;—1447. Add. 21083;—1457. Add. 21084, 21085;—1463. Add. 21086.

—— *Dominus.* Nic. de S. Marcho, *t.* Edw. I. Add. 20917.

**Osgodby,** *in Walshcroft Wapentake, co. Linc.* Grant in, to Bardney Abbey, [1266–79] (Osgoteby). Harl. 44 A. 7, 53 D. 50.

**Osgodby,** *co. Linc.* (?) Settlement, etc., of the manor, 1353. Add. 22177 (Oscoteby);—1360. Add. 22180.

—— Feoffments in, 1359 (Oscoteby). Add. 22179;—1361. Add. 22185, 22186.

**Osgodby,** *in Hemingbrough, co. York.* Grant in, to Temple Hurst Preceptory, *t.* Hen. III. (Osgoteby). Toph. 40.

**Osleston,** *in Sutton on the Hill, co. Derb.* Sale in, 1530 (Oslaston). Woll. xii. 107.

**Osmaston,** *co. Derb.* Brief for rebuilding the church, 1791. Ch. Br. B. xxxi. 10.

**Osmondeston,** *co. Norf.* Release, etc., of the manor, 1619. Add. 14849 (Osmondeston);—1635. Add. 14850 (Osmondeston).

**Osmonds manor.** *v. sub* Sutton, *co. Suff.*

**Osmondthorpe,** *co. Nott.* License for a grant in, to the chapel of St. John the Evangelist at Normanton, 1331 (Osmundthorp). Woll. v. 1.

**Osolueston.** *v.* Ouston, *co. Leic.*

**Ospringe,** *co. Kent.* Conf. of grant of the advowson to St. Mary's Hospital, Dover, 1231 (Osprenge). Add. 920.

—— Release in, to the same, 1290. Add. 16181.

—— Release in, 1393 (Osprenge). Harl. 79 B 16.

**Ospringe,** *co. Kent (continued).* Sale, etc., of Plumford manor and lands in, late bel. to Mottenden Priory, 1544. Harl. 83 H. 25;—1548. Harl. 75 E. 24. 76 A. 18;—1550. Harl. 76 I. 1, 77 H. 17.

—— Fine in, 1555. Add. 17823.

—— *Perpet. Vicarius.* Ricardus, 1290. Add. 16181.

**Ossington,** *co. Nott.* Conf. of a grant of, to the Knts. Hospitallers, early Hen. III. (Occingtun). Toph. 14.

—— *Capellanus.* Ricardus, early Hen. III. Toph. 14.

**Ostenhanger,** *co. Kent.* Conveyance, etc., in, 1526. Harl. 78 F. 53–55 (Ostynhanger);—1541. Harl. 75 H. 3 (do.).

—— Inventory of Viscount Strangford's house, 1635. Harl. Roll BB. 17.

—— Order to stay proceedings for tithes from Westenhanger Park claimed by the rector, Tho. Eaton, 1637. Harl. 75 F. 14.

**Oston.** *v.* Oxton, *co. Nott.*

**Oswald, Kirk,** *co. Cumb.* Conveyance in, 1572 (Kurkeswoild). Harl. 77 H. 37.

**Oswalding tune,** *co. Kent* (?). Grant at, 940. Cott. MS. Aug. ii. 62.

**Oswaldkirk,** *co. York.* Grant of the advowson, etc., 1441. Harl. 55 A. 43.

—— *Rector.* Will. Lovell, 1381. Harl. 75 G. 4.

**Oswardebec,** *co. Nott.* Grant of the Wapentac to the Earl of Chester, by Henry, Duke of Normandy, [1153]. Cott. xvii. 2.

—— Grant of the stewardship of, to Rob. Strelley, 1444 (Oswaldbek). Harl. 112 B. 50.

**Oswestry,** *co. Salop.* Bond conc. land in, 1565. Harl. 80 I. 78.

—— Briefs conc. a fire at Llwynymaen mill in, 1814, 1819. Ch. Br. B. liv. 9, lix. 11.

**Otby,** *in Walesby, co. Linc.* Covenant in, betw. Revesby and Newhouse Abbeys, 1154 (Octhebi). Harl. 44 I. 41.

—— Grant in, from Revesby Abbey, *t.* Edw. I. (Ottheby). Add. 5305.

**Oterburn.** *v.* Otterburn, *co. Northumb.*

**Oterpole.** *v. sub* Lympne, *co. Kent.*

**Otford,** *co. Kent.* Grant, etc., in, 1407. Harl. 76 G. 39;—1569. Harl. 77 A. 22.

Otford, co. *Kent (continued).* Appointment of Visct. Rochford as bailiff of the manor, 1528. Add. 23786.

—— Lease of lands in Sevenoaks, parcel of the honour of, 1558 (Oteforde). Harl. 78 F. 2.

—— Recovery of the manor, etc., 1628. Add. 1530.

—— *Ballivus.* Joh. de Westwik, 1296 (Otteford). Add. 16508.

Otham, *co. Kent.* Grant in, 1314 (Otteham). Add. 16470.

—— Settlement of the manor and advowson, 1411 (Oteham). Add. 16464.

Otherton, *co. Staff.* Grant in, 1287. Harl. 53 A. 50.

Othery, *co. Som.* Grant in, 1363. Cott. v. 29.

Otley (Otteleye, Oteleye, etc.), *co. Suff.* Grants, etc., in, late 13 cent. Add. 10176;—1283. Add. 10181;—1296. Add. 10297;—1300. Add. 10188 (Ottele);—1301. Add. 10268;—1304. Add. 10189;—1309. Add. 10302;—1322. Add. 10190;—1323. Add. 10191, 10192;—1330. Add. 9937 (Ottelee);—1331. Add. 9942;—1332. Add. 10305;—1334. Add. 10306;—1335. Add. 10194;—1347. Add. 10278;—1356. Add. 10009 (Ottileighe);—1359. Add. 10198;—1361. Add. 10199;—1363. Add. 10200;—1394. Add. 8381;—1440. Add. 10205;—1452. Add. 19339;—1476. Add. 10074;—1539. Harl. 48 D. 33;—1577. Add. 10233, 19376;—1599. Add. 10241.

—— Release of rents in Helmingham, co. Suff., due to Mounseux manor in, 1441. Add. 10206.

—— Extracts from court-rolls, 1483. Add. 10219;—1553. Add. 10227.

—— *Persona. Dom.* Rob. de Cleydon, 1315. Harl. 48 C. 23;—1322. Add. 10190, 10192;—1327. Add. 10304.

—— Ric. Deneys, 1415. Campb. i. 27.

—— Will. Arderne, 1440. Add. 10205;—1441. Add. 10206;—1442. Add. 10062.

Otley, *co. York.* Grant in Pool (Pouele) in, *t.* Hen. II. (Ottbel.). Cott. xxviii. 93.

—— Grant, etc., in, 1459. Add. 16050 (Otteley);—1505. Add. 16996.

—— Monition conc. the non-payment of Peter's pence in the deanery of, 1479 (Ottclay). Add. 17137.

Otley, *co. York (continued).* Suit conc. tithes in, 1576 (Ottley). Add. 17033.

—— *Ballivus.* Helias, *t.* Edw. I. (Ottelay). Add. 15703.

—— *Vicarius. Dom.* Ricardus, 1422. Add. 17129.

—— *Perpet. Vicarius.* Will. Tailyour, 1479. Add. 17137.

Otrigeide, Otringhithe. *v. sub* Methwold, *co. Norf.*

Otteham. *v.* Otham, *co. Kent.*

Otterburn, *co. Northumb.* Mandate to give seisin of the manor, 1303 (Oterburn). Harl. 43 D. 8.

—— Settlement of the manor, *t.* Edw. II. (Otreburn). Harl. 58 G. 22.

Otterden, *co. Kent.* Declaration of trust in the manor, etc., 1588. Add. 5983;—1661. Add. 5984.

Otterpool. *v. sub* Lympne, *co. Kent.*

Otterton, *co. Devon. Vicarius.* Walterus, 1397. Harl. 44 H. 46.

Ottery St. Mary, *co. Devon.* Foundation of the college, 1338. Add. 15453.

—— Accompts of the treasurers of the church, 1382-83. Add. 13973.

—— Bailiffs' accompts of the manor, 1448-9. Add. 13974;—1452-3. Add. 13975.

—— Covenant for a recovery in, 1553. Add. 19190.

—— Inq. post mortem at, 1586. Add. 13984.

Ottery, Up (Opotery), *co. Devon.* Grants, etc., in, 1330-1335. Add. 7018-7020.

Ottewrth. *v. sub* Cranley, *co. Surr.*

Ottheby. *v.* Otby, *in Walesby, co. Linc.*

Otthel. *v.* Otley, *co. York.*

Ottringham, *co. York.* Grants, etc., in, 1281-1404. Lansd. 474 (Otringhame)-517, 519-521, 523-527.

—— Lease in, from Meaux Abbey, 1391. Lansd. 522.

—— *Clericus.* Willelmus, 1294. Lansd. 479.

Oucketon. *v.* Upton, *co. Pembr.*

Ouedan. *v.* Howden, *co. York.*

Ouenston. *v.* Unstone, *co. Derb.*

Ouerahsforde. *v.* Ashford Jones, *co. Heref.*

Oueralangadone. *v.* Langdon, *nr. Wembury, co. Devon.*

Overdene, co. *Devon.* Acquittance from Plympton Priory for homage in, 1475. Add. 5249.

Overgorther, *in Caus, co. Salop.* Reservation of, 1355. Add. 20439.

Overgravenest. *v.* Gravenhurst, Upper. *co. Bedf.*

Overhall, Over Hall. *v. sub* Darley, co. *Derb.*

—— *v. sub* Lavenham, co. *Suff.*

—— *v. sub* Maidwell, co. *Northt.*

Overland. *v. sub* Ash, nr. *Sandwich,* co. *Kent.*

Overorton. *v.* Worton, Upper, co. *Oxon.*

Overseley, co. *Warw.* Grant of a moiety of the mills at, and the chapel in the castle, to Alcester Abbey, c. 1140 (Ouresleia). Add. 21494.

Overton. *v.* Orton, Cole, co. *Leic.*

—— *v.* Orton, Water, co. *Warw.*

Overton, co. *Bedf.* (?). Release of the manor, 1532. Harl. 55 H. 41.

[Overton, co. *Southt.*]. Papal conf. of grants of Nutshaw (?) (Nutescheolua) and Poolhampton (Polementona) in or nr., to Waverley Abbey, 1147. Lansd. 27.

Overton, nr. *Kennett,* co. *Wilts.* Grant at, 939 (Uferan tun). Cott. viii. 22.

Overton, co. *York.* Exchequer acquittance for farm of, late bel. to St. Mary's Abbey, York, 1595. Add. 25601 b.

Overton, East, co. *Wilts.* Court-rolls, 1559. Add. 24440;—1567. Add. 24441.

Overton Langffeld, O. Longeville. *v.* Orton Longville, co. *Hunt.*

Overton Wauterville. *v.* Orton Waterville, co. *Hunt.*

Overton, West, co. *Wilts.* Court-rolls, 1559. Add. 24440;—1567. Add. 24441.

Oving, co. *Suss.* Grants, etc., in, 1501. Add. 18790;—1558. Add. 8941;—1560. Add. 8946 (Ovynge);—1599. Add. 18891;—1600. Add. 18892;—1610. Add. 8980, 8982, 18913, 18915.

—— Survey of Drayton farm in, 1637. Add. 18949.

—— Lease of the same, 1642. Add. 18960.

Ovingdean, co. *Suss.* Battle Abbey freed from services for, [1100–23] (Ouingedene). Harl. 43 C. 12.

Ovingham, co. *Northumb.* Covenant conc. repairs of the "stagnum" and fishery at, [1222–45]. Harl. 57 D. 6.

—— —— Attornment for rent from the mill, 1310 (Oveneham). Harl. 57 A. 26.

—— —— *Persona.* Joh. de Pikworth, 1376. Harl. 43 E. 8, 57 D. 7, 8.

Ovington, co. *Essex.* Grants in, 1313. Harl. 46 A. 23 (Ovitone), 51 A. 40 (do.);—1320. Harl. 46 A. 24 (Ovytone).

Ovington, co. *Southt.* Conf. of the church to St. Cross Hosp., Winchester, 1189 (Ovinton). Harl. 43 C. 28.

Owenstewne co. *Monm.* Extract from court-roll, 1559. Add. 7156.

Owersby, co. *Linc.* Conff. of grant in, to Elsham Priory, [1163–5 (?), 1203–5] (Ouresbi). Harl. 45 A. 4, 45 C. 32, 33.

—— Papal conf. of the church to Royston Priory, 1192 (Orresbi). Cott. MS. Aug. ii. 130.

Owley Grange. *v. sub* Hales Owen, cos. *Salop and Worc.*

Owmby, co. *Linc.* Conff. of grants in, to Newhouse Abbey, [c. 1150–55]. Harl. 43 H. 14 (Odenebi), 15 (Outhenbi), 16 (Outhenebi).

—— Grant in, to Elsham Priory, c. 1250 (Oupeneby). Harl. 54 G. 15.

—— Conf. of grant in, to Thornton Abbey, [1249–53] (Authenby). Harl. 54 G. 16.

—— Power from H. de Percy to give seisin in, 1335 (Outhenby). Harl. 54 G. 21.

—— *Persona.* Dom. Petrus, t. Hen. III. Harl. 112 B. 55.

Owram, North, co. *York.* Grants, etc., in, 1358. Add. 15649 (Northowrom);—1370. Add. 15658;—1381. Add. 15660, 15661;—1390. Add. 15718;—1594. Add. 15666 (Ourome).

Owram, South, co. *York.* Grants, etc., in, 1508. Add. 26124 (Southourme);—1533. Add. 26125 (Southourome);—1544. Add. 26127 (Southourom);—1555. Add. 26128;—1560. Add. 26129;—1608. Add. 26131;—1635. Add. 18075;—1636. Add. 18023, 18024;—1671. Add. 18041.

—— Brief for rebuilding St. Anne's chapel, 1783. Ch. Br. B. xxiii. 8.

Owsthorpe, co. *York.* Grants in, early 13 cent. (Ulvisthorpe, Hulvistorpe). Add. 16581, 16596, 16604, 16605.

Owston. *v.* Ouston, *co. Leic.*

Owston (Ouston, Oustun), *in Isle of Axholme, co. Linc.* Grants, etc., in, to Sulby Abbey, *c.* 1180–90. Harl. 53 G. 56, Add. 21088;—*t.* Hen. III. Add. 21089;—1322. Add. 21090;—1342. Add. 20611;—1348. Harl. 43 D. 45.

—— Grant in, by Sulby Abbey, *c.* 1240–55. Add. 21865.

—— Grant in. *t.* Hen. III. or Edw. I. (Oustona). Add. 20852.

—— *Prepositus.* Reinaldus, *t.* Hen. II. Add. 5870.

—— *Capellanus.* Jocelinus *al.* Gocelinus, early 13 cent.-*t.* Hen. III. Add. 20575, 21877.

—— *Clericus.* Heuricus, *t.* Hen. III. Add. 20686.

Owstwick, *co. York.* Grant in, by Nun Keeling Priory, *t.* Hen. III. (Ouistwic). Harl. 44 E. 56.

Owthethorp, *nr. Wakefield, co. York.* Crown-lease in, 1555. Harl. 84 C. 32.

Oxana ford. *v.* Oxford, *co. Oxon.*

Oxburgh, *co. Norf.* Grants, etc., in, 1351. Add. 5350 (Oxeburgh);—1399. Add. 5652;—1488. Add. 5355;—1493. Add. 5356.

Oxcombe, *co. Linc.* Grant of the church to Bullington Priory, *t.* Hen. II. (Oxecub.). Harl. 52 G. 30.

—— Conf. of above grant, [1175–81] (Oxecumba). Harl. 43 C. 36.

—— Conff. of grants in, to the same, 1256. Harl. 52 H. 28 (Oxecumbe);—*t.* Edw. I.-II. Harl. 52 H. 5;—*c.* 1322. Harl. 52 H. 27.

—— Mandate for protection of lands of Bullington Priory in, 1499. Harl. 43 I. 11.

Oxcroft, *in Bolsover, co. Derb.* Covenant to convey land in, 1571. Woll. xi. 51.

Oxena gehæg. *v.* Oxney, *co. Kent.*

Oxenbridge, *nr. Rye, co. Suss.* Release in (?), 1350. Add. 20010.

Oxendon, Great, *co. Northt.* Grant, etc., in (?), 1312. Add. 6115 (Oxendon);—1320. Add. 6116 (Oxindon).

—— Grant in, 1376 (Oxendone Magna). Add. 22386.

—— Suit relating to the manor, *c.* 1620. Add. 6124.

Oxendon, Little, *co. Northt.* Feoffment in, 1353 (Oxyndone parva). Add. 22177.

Oxendoune, [*in Horton Kirby* ?], *co. Kent.* Release in, 1377. Harl. 48 F. 13.

Oxeneforda. *v. sub* Witley, *co. Surr.*

Oxenhall, *co. Glouc.* Grant in, 1353 (Oxenhale). Harl. 111 G. 36.

Oxenton *al.* Oxmanton, *co. Glouc.* Compotus-rolls of the manor, 1346. Add. 18542 (Oxendon);—1435–6. Add. 18555;—1452-3. Add. 18543.

—— Fines of the manor, 1389–90, 1391 (Oxendon). Add. 18220, 18221 (*copies*).

—— Grants, etc., of the manor, 1467. Add. 18240, 18242–18245;—1481. Add. 18252, 18254;—1532. Add. 18277, 18278;—1602. Add. 18330.

—— Grants in, 1482. Add. 18255 (Oxindon);—1558. Add. 18294.

—— Compotus of extortions by the receiver of the manor, *t.* Hen. VII.-VIII. (Oxendon). Add. 18549.

—— Court-rolls, 1513. Add. 18257;—1586, 1590. Add. 18545;—1594. Add. 18546;—1605. Add. 18548.

—— Inspex. of return to writ conc. the manor, as ancient domain of the Crown in Domesday, 1519 (Oxmanton, Oxendon). Add. 18263.

—— Release to tenants from Crown taxes, 1519 (Oxmanton). Add. 18227, 18265.

—— Extracts from court-rolls conc. lands in Ashton under Hill, etc., 1543. Add. 18285;—1571. Add. 18308;—1574. Add. 18343;—*t.* Chas. I. Add. 18400;—1635. Add. 18392;—1645. Add. 18398, 18401;—1648. Add. 18406;—1652. Add. 18414.

—— Rental of the manor, 1550. Add. 18544.

—— Terrier of lands in Ashton under Hill in the manor of, 1585. Add. 18506.

—— Covenant for fine of the manor, 1677. Add. 18446, 18447.

Oxenwood, *in Shalbourn, co. Berks.* Grant and conf. in, to St. Nicholas Hospital, Salisbury, *c.* 1220–38 (Oxenewde). Harl. 50 I. 46, 54 E. 35.

—— Grant in. [1245–8] (Oxenewode). Harl. 56 H. 16.

Oxford, *County of.* Rolls of lands of R. Basset in, etc., 12–15 cent. Slo. xxxi. 3–7.

—— Compotus-rolls of scutage of Henry of Lancaster in, 1315. Harl. Roll K. 13;—1318–24. Harl. Roll H. 20.

**Oxford,** *County of (continued).* Acquittances for annuities granted by the Crown to be paid by the sheriff of, 1356, 1357. Harl. 49 H. 5–7, 57 C. 45–47.

—— Power from Gerard Braybroke to give seisin of manors in, etc., 1421. Add. 20288.

—— Settlement of lands in, inherited from Sir R. Harcourt, 1507. Harl. 111 F. 55.

—— Grant of an annuity from lands in, by W. Lendall of Reading, 1509. Harl. 53 A. 6.

—— General release in, to J. Yorke, of Hilldrop, co. Wilts, 1510. Harl. 78 E. 30.

—— Compotus of lands of the Duke of Norfolk in, 1517–18. Add. 16547.

—— Precipes on covenants conc. lands in, 1561–1598. Add. 25206–25217.

—— Exchequer acquittances for a fifteenth, etc., in, 1567. Add. 25640;—1596. Add. 25642.

—— Appointments of deputy lieutenants, 1712. Add. 13643;—1715. Add. 13644.

—— Patent of the Duke of Marlborough as Lord Lieutenant, 1739. Add. 6311.

—— *Vicecomes.* Rob. de Witefeld *al.* Wytfeld, [1182]. Add. 10593, 10595, 10616.

—— —— Rob. de la Haye, [1226–32]. Add. 10608.

—— —— Alan de Fernham, [1245–8]. Harl. 56 H. 16.

—— —— Joh. Laundela, 1356, 1357. Harl. 49 H. 5–7, 57 C. 45–47.

**Oxford,** *co. Oxon.* K. Harold at, 1038 (Oxana ford). Cott. MS. Aug. ii. 90.

—— Grant of St. George's church (eccl. S. Georgii in castello Oxenef.) to Oseney Abbey, c. 1149–50. Add. 20361.

—— Robertus, presbiter de Sco. Martino [*al.* Carfax], a witness in, c. 1149–50. Add. 20361.

—— Grant of the share of the honour of J. de St. John in, bel. to St. George's church, to Oseney Abbey, c. 1149–50. Add. 20360.

—— Fine in, with Oseney Abbey, [1176] (Oxeuef.). Cott. xi. 72.

—— Ricardus, presbiter Sci. Georgii, a witness in, early Hen. III. Add. 20268.

**Oxford,** *co. Oxon (continued).* Willelmus, Rector Sci. Budoci, a witness in, [1232–8]. Cott. xi. 67, Add. 20469.

—— Award of tithes in Wolvercote, co. Oxon., to Robert, Vicar, and the church of St. Peter in the East (eccl. B. Petri ad orientem Oxon.), 1239. Add. 10639.

—— Bond for loan at, 1258. Harl. 47 A. 43.

—— Reference to the church "B. Petri Orientalis Oxon.," 1274. Harl. 50 H. 41.

—— Grant in, by the Knights Hospitallers, 1284. Cott. iv. 6 (2) (*copy*).

—— Grant in "Stocwelle strete," etc., to the Priory of SS. John and Benedict, c. 1284. Cott. iv. 6 (1, 3) (*copies*).

—— Appointment of justices for gaol-delivery at, 1296. Harl. 43 D. 4.

—— Settlement of suit conc. tithes bel. to St. George's church, 1300. Add. 10629.

—— Lease, etc., in, 1377 (Oxon.). Harl. 49 G. 37;—1419. Add. 19327.

—— Suit betw. Biddlesdon and Oseney Abbeys to be tried in the church of St. Peter in the East, 1391. Lansd. 692.

—— Defeasance of a bond of warranty in All Saints' parish, 1398. Add. 20362.

—— Lease of land in Holywell in, by Merton College, 1670. Add. 1965.

—— Petition from the mayor, etc., to the H. of Lords against the removal of Roman Catholic disabilities, 1812. Add. 6343.

—— Brief for rebuilding St. Ebbe's church in, 1814. Ch. Br. B. lv. 3.

—— *Major (quondam).* Joh. de Dekelyntona, 1310. Add. 22535.

—— —— Walt. Bowne, 1398. Add. 20362.

—— —— Rob. atte Wode, 1457. Add. 20355.

—— *Ballivi.* Mich. Salesbury, Will. Douk, 1398. Add. 20362.

—— *Clericus de villa Oxon.* Thomas, 1274. Harl. 50 H. 41.

—— *Serviens Oxon.* Will. Brunstar., 1274. Harl. 50 H. 41.

**Oxhey,** *co. Hertf.* "Transgressiones" of Steph. Elienore "de Oxey" in the manor, t. Edw. II. Add. 5290.

**Oxhey Walround** *al.* **Wiggenhall.** *v. sub* Watford, co. Hertf.

**Padstow,** *co. Cornw.* Release, etc., in, 1513. Harl. 50 C. 41 (Puddistaw), 42 (Padstaw), 43.

—— Crown appointment of a bailiff, etc., in, 1571 (Padstocke). Harl. 75 E. 38.

**Padworth,** *co. Berks.* Release in, 1396 (Padeworthe). Add. 9243.

—— Brief conc. a hail-storm at, 1762. Ch. Br. B. ii. 2.

**Pæccingas.** *v.* Patching, *co. Suss.*

**Pagehurst.** *v. sub* Marden, *co. Kent.*

**Pagham,** *co. Suss.* Grant at, to Bp. Wilfrid, 680 (?) (Pecgan ham). Cott. MS. Aug. ii. 86.

—— Fine in, 1457 (Pageham). Add. 24902.

—— Assignment of lands in, 1501. Add. 18790.

**Paglesham,** *co. Essex.* Conf. by Edw. the Confessor of a grant in, to Westminster Abbey, 1066 [*sc.* 1065] (Paclesham). Cott. vi. 2 (*copy*).

—— Conf. of tithes in, to Dunmow Priory, 1221 (Paclesham). Cott. xxi. 15.

—— Grant, etc., in, 1266. Harl. 50 F. 20 (Pakelisham);—1207. Harl. 49 F. 18 (Pakelsham).

—— Fine of Paglesham, Easthall and Southall manors, 1541 (Pakelsham). Add. 15868.

—— Precipe on a covenant conc. Church Hall manor, etc., in, 1578. Add. 24971.

**Paignton,** *co. Devon.* Grant of Goodrington (Gotheryngton) manor in, 1414. Harl. 48 I. 25.

—— Compotus-roll of Goodrington (Goderyngton) manor, 1414-5. Add. 13770.

**Pailton,** *co. Warw.* Grants, etc., in, early Hen. III. Add. 21495 (Pallint.); —*t.* Hen. III. Cott. iv. 21 (Pailintona);—1302. Cott. xxix. 90 (Paylintona);—1328. Harl. 48 A. 14 (Paylington).

**Painswick,** *co. Glouc.* Order to pay expenses of an assise of the manor, 1302 (Peyneswick). Add. 20413.

**Pakelisham, Pakelsham.** *v.* Paglesham, *co. Essex.*

**Pakenham,** *co. Suff.* Grant nr. Leišenhala wood in, by Bury St. Edmund's Abbey, *ante* 1180 (Pachenham). Harl. 44 D. 22.

**Pakenham,** *co. Suff. (continued).* Grants, etc., in, *t.* Hen. III.-*t.* Edw. I. Cott. xxvii. 41, Harl. 52 C. 33 (Pakeham), Add. 5905-5907;— 1331. Harl. 50 E. 40;—1334. Harl. 51 F. 6;—1335. Harl. 46 F. 54;— 1342. Harl. 54 D. 21;—1345. Harl. 52 F. 19;—1355. Harl. 54 F. 4;— 1362. Harl. 57 D. 42:—1390. Harl. 58 G. 43 *b* (*copy*);—1423. Harl. 45 D. 33 (Pakynham);—1546. Harl. 56 C. 36;—1600. Harl. 55 A. 26;—1632. Harl. 56 H. 17, 18, 57 H. 37;—1637. Harl. 49 E. 44;—1639. Harl. 49 E. 50.

—— Court-rolls of Malkins Hall manor in, 1316-1393, 1596-1667. Harl. Rolls K. 15-21.

—— Accompts of the collector of rents in, 1393-4. Add. 868.

—— Accompts of sheep breeding, etc., in, 1557-1561. Add. 16576.

—— Extract from court-roll of New Hall *al.* Malkins Hall manor, 1559. Harl. 58 F. 10.

—— Acquittances for homage for the same manor, 1623. Harl. 49 F. 41;— 1624. Harl. 49 E. 14, 49 F. 42;— 1628. Harl. 49 E. 19;—1632. Harl. 49 E. 35;—1633. Harl. 49 E. 37;— 1634. Harl. 49 E. 38;—1636. Harl. 49 E. 46;—1638. Harl. 49 E. 48.

—— Bill of expenses in suit for Malkins Hall manor, 1624. Harl. 58 H. 30.

—— Lease, etc., of same manor, 1637. Harl. 49 E. 44;—1639. Harl. 49 E. 50.

**Pakenham's Hall.** *v. sub* Garboldisham, *co. Norf.*

**Paknage.** *v. sub* Brampton, *co. Derb.*

**Palgrave,** *co. Suff.* Grants in, *t.* Hen. III. Harl. 48 F. 28 (Palegraue);— 1444. Add. 19060.

**Palgrave, Great and Little,** *in Sporle, co. Norf.* Assignment of dower in, 1390 (Pagrave magna, P. parva). Harl. 57 E. 5.

**Pallethorpe,** *co. York.* Attornment of the manor, 1340 (Paddokthorp). Harl. 57 A. 26.

**Palling,** *co. Norf.* Brief conc. a fire at, 1779. Ch. Br. B. xx. 2.

**Pallint.** *v.* Pailton, *co. Warw.*

**Palmereslond.** *v. sub* Ilketshall, *co. Suff.*

**Palstre.** *v. sub* Wittersham, *co. Kent.*

Parndon, Great, co. Essex. Conf. of a grant in, to Southwark Priory, [1138-48] (Perenduna). Cott. MS. Nero C. iii. f. 228.

—— Grant in, by Southwark Priory, c. 1200 (Perendona). Harl. 44 I. 52.

—— Grant in, 1480 (Peryngdon magna). Harl. 77 G. 22.

—— Sale of interest in Cannons manor in, 1548 (Peringdon magna). Harl. 79 E. 50.

—— Precipe on a covenant conc. Cannons manor, etc., 1587 (Paringdon magna). Add. 24989.

Parris al. Parrishes. v. sub Snetterton, co. Norf.

Parrocks. v. sub Milton next Gravesend, co. Kent.

Parrok, in Marshwood Vale, co. Dors. Releases in, 1414. Harl. 50 D. 12 (La Parrok);—1438. Harl. 50 E. 6 (Lytil Parrok).

Partemue. v. Portsmouth, co. Southt.

Parthesin, co. Forfar (?). Covenant by Cupar Abbey conc. tithes in, c. 1210. Cott. xviii. 33, 34.

Partney, co. Linc. Fines in, 1302. Harl. 45 H. 18 (Parteney);—1319. Harl. 58 D. 4, 5 (Partenaye);—1348. Harl. 50 E. 22–26.

—— Grant in, 1355 (Partenay). Harl. 57 G. 11.

—— Precipe on a covenant conc. land in, 1578. Add. 25100.

Parwich, co. Derb. Grants in, to Garendon Abbey, co. Leic., t. Hen. III. Campb. xv. 13 (Peuerwich), Eg. 454 (Pewerwich).

—— Covenant for a fine in, 1608 (Parwidge). Woll. xi. 34.

—— Release of the manor, 1612. Woll. xi. 87.

—— Fine in, 1638 (Perwich). Woll. xi. 29.

Passefeld, co. Essex. Conf. of tithes in, to Dunmow Priory, 1221. Cott. xxi. 15.

Passelowes. v. sub Gazeley, co. Suff.

Passenham, co. Northt. Power to give seisin in, 1411. Add. 17383.

—— Power to give seisin of the manor and advowson, 1489. Cott. xxx. 34.

—— Persona. Willelmus, t. Hen. III. (Passaham). Harl. 85 D. 47.

Paston (Pastun, etc.), co. Norf. Grants, etc., in, t. Hen. III.—t. Edw. I. Add. 2004, 14810–14815, 17217–17219;—1382. Add. 14816, 14817;—1386. Add. 14818;—1444. Add. 14571.

—— Grant in Pastune hawe, t. Edw. I. Add. 14511.

—— Lease of Woodmyll in, 1446. Add. 14819.

—— Vicarius. Joh. Pertrik al. Pertryk, 1444. Add. 14571, 17235.

—— Perpet. Vicarius. Will. Pope, 1447. Add. 17235.

Paston, co. Northt. Grant nr., by Peterborough Abbey, c. 1200 (Pastune). Add. 5360.

—— Grant of next presentation to, by Peterborough Abbey, 1538. Eg. 482.

Pastons Magna. v. Paxton, Gt., co. Hunt.

Patching, co. Suss. Grant at, 960 (Pæccinga). Cott. MS. Aug. ii. 40.

—— Grants, etc., in, 1364. Add. 24679 (Pacchyngge);—1413. Add. 24669;—1460. Add. 24680, 24681.

Pateshull, co. Northt. Grant, etc., of a moiety of the church to Godstowe Abbey, t. Hen. II. Cott. v. 20 (Pateshille);—1217. Cott. xi. 32.

—— Mortgage, etc., in, 1277. Harl. 57 F. 24;—1593. Add. 7920.

—— Perpet. vicarius medietatis ecclesie. Joh. de Mildecumb, 1217. Cott. xi. 32.

—— Vicarius. Dom. Walterus, 1277. Harl. 57 F. 24.

Pathelesworthe. v. Paddlesworth, co. Kent.

Patheneburga, Insula de. v. Panborough, co. Som.

Pathlow Hundred, co. Warw. Release from suits of court in, post 1257 (Pathelowe). Cott. xxix. 55.

Patleshull. v. Patteshull, co. Staff.

Patney, co. Wilts. Court-rolls, 1558-9. Add. 24440;—1566. Add. 24441.

Patribrompton. v. Brompton, Patrick, co. York.

Patricesseia, Patricheseia. v. Battersea, co. Surr.

Patrington, co. York. Grant in Colsweynthorpe nr., 1358. Lansd. 429.

—— Bond for feoffment in, etc., 1457. Harl. 112 F. 24;—1466. Lansd. 580;—1484. Lansd. 581.

**Payhembury,** co. *Devon* (*continued*).
Grants in N. Charlton (Northere
Churleton, N. Churletone) in or nr.,
t. Edw. I. Add. 12939;—1302. Add.
12997.

—— Grants, etc., in Hill in Upton
and on Hembury down, etc., in, 1302-
1491. Add. 12997-13004 : — 1465.
Add. 13061-13064 :;—1491. Add.
13072.

—— Fine in Lawylheghen, La Hille,
Swynisheghen and North Charlton
(Northchurlleton) in or nr., 1302.
Add. 12944.

—— Fine in Broad Charlton (Brode-
charleton) in, 1305. Add. 12945.

—— Conveyances in Rull al. Rill
(Ryll) in, 1579, 1591, 1616. Add.
13181.

—— Rector. Johannes, 1236. Add.
13970.

—— Vicarius. Joh. Prodhomme,
1334. Add. 12998.

—— Ric. Laueransz, 1400.
Add. 13001.

**Paylington, Paylintona.** v. Pailton, co. Warw.

**Paynge.** v. Penge, co. Surr.

**Paynshay.** v. sub Yarcombe, co. Devon.

**Peabimbery.** v. Pembury, co. Kent.

**Peak, The,** co. Derb. Service due at
the castle of (Castrum de Pecco), for
Eyam manor, 1300. Woll. vii. 40.

—— Power to receive rents in, 1345
(de Pecco). Woll. ii. 25.

—— License for a deputy forester,
1345 (Foresta de Haut Peck). Lansd.
114.

—— Grant of the castle, manor, etc.,
with free chace in the forest, by Edw.
III. to John, his son, 1372 (de Alto
Pecco). Cott. xv. 1.

—— Inquest of the forest, 1471 (de
Alto Pecco). Woll. x. 66.

—— Rent payable from the revenues
of the Lordship, 1482 (de Alto Pecco).
Woll. viii. 15.

—— Fine in, 1638 (de Alto Pecco).
Woll. xi. 29.

—— Ballivus. Clem. de la Ford,
1305 (de Pecco). Woll. iii. 11.

—— Tho. de Wombwell, 1376.
Woll. ii. 75.

—— Receptor Denariorum Castri et
Honoris. Joh. Hublyn, 1376. Woll.
ii. 75.

**Peak, The,** co. Derb. (*continued*).
Seneschal and Master of the Foresters.
Hen. Vernon, 1471. Woll. x. 66.

**Peakirk,** co. North. Persona. Ric.
Wulf, 1405 (Peykyrke). Add. 858.

**Peampymburi, Peapyngeberi.** v.
Pembury, co. Kent.

**Peasenhall,** co. Suff. Conf. of a sale
in, etc., to Sibton Abbey, early Hen.
II. Campb. xxiii. 5 (Pesenhala):—
late 12 cent. Harl. 84 A. 10 (Pesehale).

—— Grants, etc., in, t. Hen. III.-
t. Edw. I. Add. 8365 (Pesenhalle),
Harl. 83 E. 33;—1313. Harl. 83 E.
34;—1610. Add. 10429.

—— License for Sibton Abbey to acquire the manor, t. Edw. I. (Pesenhale). Harl. 83 D. 41.

—— Conf. of a grant in, to Campsey
Priory, 1321 (do.). Cott. v. 5.

—— Extent of fees in, bel. to the
Earls Marshal, c. 1400. Add. 19338.

—— Court-rolls, 1568. Add. 10418
(Peasynhall) ; — 1592-1599. Add.
10421-10423.

—— Lease in, from St. James's Hosp.,
Dunwich, 1642. Add. 19398.

—— Clericus. Bodbertus, early 13
cent. (Pisehale). Harl. 83 F. 19.

**Peasmarsh,** co. Suss. Grant in or nr.,
service being paid at the court of
Kitchenour (Kechonore), early 13
cent. Add. 20078.

—— Grants, etc., in, t. Edw. I. Add.
20123-20126 (Pesemers, Pesemersch);
—1299-1300. Add. 20153 (Pesa-
mersse); — 1314-1428 Add. 20127
(Pesemerse) — 20133, 20135-20140,
20143-20146;—1347. Add. 20151;—
1458. Add. 16156;—1507. Add.
24910;—1530. Harl. 76 H. 12.

—— Release "in villa de Wyucle-
regge in parochia de Pesemersh,"
1344. Add. 20134.

**Peatling, Great,** co. Leic. Grant in,
1396 (Magna Petelyng). Add. 21392.

**Peatting tune.** v. Patton, co. Salop.

**Peatton.** v. Petton, co. Devon.

**Pebidiog,** Cantref of, al. Dewisland
Hundred, co. Pemb. Senescallus de
Penbidiauc. Will. de Bruera, t. Edw.
I. Add. 8410.

**Pebmarsh,** co. Essex. Precipe on a
covenant conc. land in, 1593 (Peb-
mershe al. Pedmershe). Add. 25044.

Pebworth, *co. Glouc.* Grant in, to Alcester Abbey, *c.* 1140 (Pebewrda). Add. 21494.

—— Conf. of a grant in, *t.* Edw. I. Add. 24751.

—— Covenant conc. settlement of the manor, etc., 1350. Harl. 54 D. 28 (Pebbeworth) ;—1362. Harl. 58 D. 45.

Pecclinton. *v.* Peckleton, *co. Leic.*

Pecgan ham. *v.* Pagham, *co. Suss.*

Peches Manor. *v. sub* Alderton, *co. Suff.*

Peckham, *co. Surr.* Settlement in, 1620. Add. 23636.

Peckham, *co. Suss.* Power for assignment of the manor to Edw. II., 1316 (Pechham). Harl. 57 E. 33.

Peckham, East (?), West (?), *co. Kent.* Lease in, by Christ Church, Canterbury, *t.* Rich. I. (Pecham). Add. 16447.

Peckham, East, *co. Kent.* Fine in, 1380 (Est Pekham). Add. 6260.

—— Release in, 1547 (Eastpekham). Harl. 57 B. 25.

Peckham, West, *co. Kent.* Grant of a fourth part of Bigemille in, *t.* Hen. III. (Westpecham). Harl. 112 F. 12.

—— License for a grant in, to Cobham Chantry, 1369 (Parva Pekham). Harl. 49 B. 5.

—— Leases in, from Cobham College, 1459. Harl. 44 C. 38 (Parva Pekham) ; —1503. Harl. 44 C. 46 ;—1528. Harl. 44 C. 51.

—— Release in, 1547 (Westpekham). Harl. 57 B. 25.

Peckleton, *co. Leic.* Grant of right of way in, through Tuoley (Tolawe) Park, to Sulby Abbey, *t.* Hen. III. (Pecclinton). Harl. 45 G. 27.

Pedinton. *v.* Piddington, *co. Oxon.*

Pedling. *v. sub* Broomhill, *cos. Suss. and Kent.*

Pednesham. *v.* Pensham, *co. Worc.*

Pedwardine, Upper and Lower (Pedwardyn, etc.), *in Brampton Bryan, co. Heref.* Grants, etc., in, 1339. Cott. xxv. 1 ;—1340. Cott. xxviii. 42 ;—1342. Cott. xxix. 85 ;—1345. Cott. xxiv. 26 ; —1346. Cott. xxx. 26 ;—1348. Cott. xxviii. 64 ;—1370. Cott. xxviii. 65 ;— 1393-4. Cott. xxx. 21 ;—1448. Cott. xxv. 30 ;—1466. Cott. xxvi. 32 ;— 1475. Cott. xxv. 8 ;—1493 (Peddwardyne). Cott. xxv. 9.

Pedwardine, Upper and Lower (Pedwardyn, etc.), *in Brampton Bryan, co. Heref. (continued).* Lease of the manor, 1432. Cott. xxviii. 63.

—— Grant in, by the Knts. Hospitallers of Dinmore, 1462 (Pedwardyne). Cott. xxv. 2.

*v. also* Brampton Bryan, *co. Heref.*

Peebles, *co. Peebles.* Reference to a fine at, betw. David, King of Scots, and the Archdeacon of Lothian, [1140–46] (Pebles). Cott. xviii. 12, Campb. xxx. 1.

Peel, *Isle of Man.* Petition for restoration of the castle to S. le Scrop, early 15 cent. Add. 18267.

—— *Vicarius de Hollm.* Moricius, 1408. Add. 8482.

Pegdes setl. Grant near, 854. Cott. MS. Aug. ii. 46.

Pekes. *v. sub* Whaplode, *co. Linc.*

Pekham, Lytyl *al.* Parva. *v.* Peckham, West, *co. Kent.*

Peldon, *co. Essex.* Bequests of land at, late 10 cent. (æt Peltandune). Harl. 43 C. 4.

—— Grant in, 1326. Add. 19309.

—— Covenant conc. waste in the manor, 1384. Harl. 54 C. 9.

—— Precipes on covenants conc. lands in, 1555. Add. 24927 ;—1561. Add. 24930.

Pelecoc. *v.* Thornham Magna, *co. Suff.*

Pelham Furneux, *co. Hertf.* Fine in, 1313. Add. 6246.

Pelhams Wood, *co. Essex.* Conveyance of, 1510. Add. 15607.

Peling. *v.* Wootton Pillinge, *co. Bedf.*

Pelsall, *co. Staff.* Brief for rebuilding the church, 1797. Ch. Br. B. xxxvii. 9.

Peltandun. *v.* Peldon, *co. Essex.*

Pelynt, *co. Cornw.* Crown appointment of a bailiff of Trelawne manor and of lands in Cartowl (Cruoketole) in, 1571. Harl. 75 E. 38.

Pembridge, *co. Heref.* Lease of the demesne, *c.* 1433 (Pembrugge). Harl. 53 H. 17.

—— *Clericus.* Paganus, late 12 cent. (Penebrigia). Add. 5288.

Pembroke, *County of.* Inspex. conc. heritage of T. Crispyn in, 1383. Slo. xxxii. 19.

—— Sheriff's compotus, *post* 1634. Harl. Roll DD. 2.

**Pembroke,** *County of (continued).* *Vicecomes.* Rob. de Syrburne, 1299. Slo. xxxii. 14.

—— —— Steph. Jacob, 1347. Slo. xxxii. 5.

—— —— Joh. Wydlok, 1383. Slo. xxxii. 19.

—— —— Tho. Wyryet, 1442. Slo. xxxii. 20.

—— —— Joh. Scurfeild, *post* 1634. Harl. Roll DD. 2.

—— *Cancellarius et Thesaurarius.* Will. Payneswike, 1448. Slo. xxxii. 5.

**Pembroke,** *co. Pembr.* Conf. of a grant in, nr. St. Mary's church, *t.* Hen. III. Add. 19130.

—— Service of the garrison in the castle, 1377. Harl. 56 B. 6.

—— Grant of reversion of the castle and domain, etc., to the Earl of Suffolk, 1433. Harl. 51 H. 10.

—— *Prepositi.* Joh. fil. David, Nic. Methelan, *t.* Hen. III. Add. 19136.

—— *Senescallus.* Joh. Beneger, *t.* Edw. I. Add. 8410.

—— —— Joh. de Neuborch, 1299. Slo. xxxii. 14.

—— —— *Dom.* Will. de Castro Martini, *t.* Edw. I.-II. Add. 8409.

—— —— Guydo de Bryane, 1340. Add. 6027.

—— —— Joh. Wydlok, 1383. Slo. xxxii. 19.

—— —— Hen. W——n, *Miles,* 1442. Slo. xxxii. 20;—1448. Slo. xxxii. 5.

**Pembrokes.** *v. sub* Tottenham, co. Midd.

**Pembury,** *co. Kent.* Suit conc. the mill, etc., at Bayhall (La Beyhalle) in, *t.* Edw. I.-II. (Peapyngbery). Harl. Roll AA. 16.

—— Grants, etc., of lands at Bayhall (Boghalle, La Baihalle, Le Beyhalle), etc., in, 1308-9. Harl. 78 A. 14 (Peapyngeberi);—1309. Harl. 76 B. 1 (Peapingbery);—1311-12. Harl. 80 B. 10 (Pepingbery);—1312-3. Harl. 76 A. 33 (Peappingbury), 76 B. 2 (Pepingebury), 79 D. 45 (Pepingbery); —1313-4. Harl. 76 B. 4 (Pepingebury);—1314. Harl. 77 F. 20 (Pepynbery);—1314-5. Harl. 76 A. 50 (Peping-bery), 78 I. 14 (Pepingebury); —1315-6. Harl. 77 F. 43 (Pepingehere);—1316-7. Harl. 76 A. 51, 52, 79 D. 46, 47;—1317. Harl. 76 C. 3;— 1317-8. Harl. 77 E. 52;—1318. Harl. 76 A. 53;—1320. Harl. 80 F. 45, 46

(Peabimbery);—1391. Harl. 80 I. 93; —1399. Harl. 80 A. 34;—1419. Harl. 51 F. 18;—1444. Harl. 76 G. 53 (Pepyngbery);—1569. Harl. 77 A. 23 (Pepingebury).

—— Grant in the fee of Rankham (Banecombe) in, 1315-6. Harl. 77 F. 43.

—— Inquest, etc., conc. lands of Tho. Colepeper in, 1324-5 (Pepyngbury, Peampymburi, etc.). Harl. Roll T. 21.

—— Grant in Ashden (Assedene) in, *t.* Edw. II. (Pepingebur.). Add. 18586.

—— Grant, etc., of the manor, 1407. Harl. 76 G. 39;—1430. Harl. 76 H. 1.

—— Bond for wainscot for Lord Cobham's house at, 1534 (Pepenbury). Harl. 47 I. 31.

**Penally,** *co. Pembr.* Obligation of Aconbury Priory to maintain a chaplain in the church, 1301 (Peunaly). Harl. 45 G. 13.

**Penarth,** *co. Glam.* Grant in, *t.* Hen. III. or Edw. I. (Pennard). Add. 24295.

**Penbidiauc.** *v.* Pebidiog, *Cantref of, co. Pembr.*

**Pencaitland,** *co. Haddington. Persona.* Johannes, *ante* 1233. Cott. xviii. 36.

**Penceat Wood,** *in Battersea manor, co. Surr.* Grant of the "venatio" of, by Will. I., to Westminster Abbey, 1067. Cott. vi. 3 (copy).

**Penchistona.** *v.* Pinxton, *co. Derb.*

**Penckhull.** *v.* Penkhull, *in Stoke upon Trent, co. Staff.*

**Penclau, Penclauthe.** *v.* Pen y Clawdd, *co. Monm.*

**Pencric.** *v.* Penkridge, *co. Staff.*

**Pencuke,** *nr. St. Gennys (?), co. Cornw.* Power to give seisin of, etc., 1426. Add. 13043 (Penkyvok infra Hundredum de Lesnywyth);—1433. Add. 13053 (do.).

**Pendeley.** *v. sub* Aldbury, *co. Hertf.*

**Penderyn,** *co. Brecon.* Grant in, 1468. Harl. 111 B. 40.

**Pendewey,** *nr. Bodmin, co. Cornw.* Conveyance of watercourse at, 1563 (Penduy). Harl. 50 C. 45.

**Pendhill,** *in Bletchingley, co. Surr.* Re-feoffment of the manor, 1329 (Pendell). Harl. 112 F. 23.

**Pendlebury,** *co. Lanc.* Brief conc. a fire at, 1794. Ch. Br. B. xxxv. 3.

**Pendock,** *co. Worc. Persona.* Joh. Berston, 1419. Add. 24770.

Pendrym, *in St. Martin's by Looe, co. Cornw.* Grant of a market and fair at E. Looe in the manor of, 1237 (Pendrem). Harl. 58 H. 47 (*copy*).

Pendyfig, *co. Cornw.* Grant in exchange for land in, 949. Cott. MS. Aug. ii. 57.

Penebrigia. *v.* Pembridge, *co. Heref.*

Penenden Heath, *nr. Boxley, co. Kent.* Return of evidence at the trial at, [1072]. Cott. MS. Aug. ii. 36.

Peneuesel. *c.* Pevensey, *co. Suss.*

Penferu, *co. Cornw.* Power to give seisin in, 1417. Add. 15354.

Penfin. *v.* Pinvin, *co. Worc.*

Penge, *co. Surr.* Rental of, as bel. to Westminster Abbey, early Hen. III. (Paenge). Add. 8139.

—— Grant nr., "a bosco quod vocatur Pange usque ad foveam que appellatur Marc de Cancia," *t.* Hen. III. Harl. 111 G. 46.

—— Grants, etc., in, *t.* Hen. III. Harl. 111 D. 44 (Penge in parochia de Badricheseye);—1308. Harl. 111 G. 23 (Peenge);—1334. Harl. 111 F. 53;—1370. Harl. 111 G. 47;—1387. Harl. 111 F. 10 (Pinge);—1396. Harl. 112 F. 11 (Paynge);—1411. Harl. 112 A. 36.

—— Acquittance by Westminster Abbey for rents in, 1454. Harl. 111 C. 39.

Pengelly. *v. sub* St. Erme, *co. Cornw.*

Penhale. *v. sub* St. Enoder, *co. Cornw.*

Penhale, [*nr. St. Breock?*], *co. Cornw.* Marriage settlement in, *t.* Edw. I. Harl. 57 A. 36.

Penhale, *co. Cornw.* Conveyance in, 1516. Add. 13078.

Penhall, *co. Cornw.* Entailment in, 1518. Eg. 276.

Penhow, *co. Monm.* Precipe on a covenant conc. land in, 1593. Add. 25140.

Penhurst, *co. Suss.* Grants, etc., in, 1412. Add. 20064 (Penherst);—1446. Add. 17703, 17704;—1479. Add. 17708;—1562. Add. 17722.

Pen hydd, *co. Glam.* Claim to tithes in, by Margam Abbey, 1339 (Pennath Superior et Inferior). Harl. 75 A. 28.

Pen hydd waelod, *co. Glam.* Inquest by Margam Abbey conc. boundaries in, 1519 (Pen nyth waylod). Harl. 75 A. 49.

Peningsale, *nr. Penistone (?), co. York.* Release of the manor, 1301. Harl. 112 I. 62.

Penistone, *co. York.* Covenant conc. Hunshelf (Hunesself) mill, etc., nr., 1227. Add. 8066.

—— *Persona.* Ric. de Roderham, 1331. Harl. 112 G. 22, 23;—1332. Harl. 112 G. 24.

—— *Rector.* Will. de Staynton, 1350. Add. 8299.

Penkeston. *v.* Pinxton, *co. Derb.*

Penkhull, *in Stoke upon Trent, co. Staff.* Fine in, 1638 (Penckhull). Woll. xi. 29.

Penkoun, Penkun, Penkeyne. *v.* Penquain, *nr. St. Breock (?), co. Cornw.*

Penkridge, *co. Staff.* Bequest to [the church of], 11 cent. (Pencric). Harl. 83 A. 2.

Penkyvok, *infra Hundredum de Lesnywyth. v.* Pencake, *nr. St. Gennys (?), co. Cornw.*

Penllech, *co. Carnarv.* Recovery in, 1699. Add. 25812.

Penllyn, *Commote of, co. Merioneth.* Lease in, by Ystrad Marchell Abbey, 1525. Add. 10654.

Penllyne, *nr. Cowbridge, co. Glam.* Suit conc. tithes of, betw. Margam Abbey and the Bp. of Llandaff, 1413 (Penthlyn). Harl. 75 A. 3.

Penmaen, *co. Glam.* Grant nr., to Neath Abbey, early 13 cent. (Penmain). Harl. 75 B. 5 b.

Penmark, *co. Glam.* Grant in, 1339. Add. 24296.

—— Plea for lands in, 1339. Add. 24297.

Penmene. *v. sub* St. Enoder, *co. Cornw.*

Penn, *co. Buck.* Compotus of the manor, 1371-72. Add. 659, 660.

Penn, *co. Staff.* Brief for rebuilding the church, 1764. Ch. Br. B. iv. 10.

Pennal, *co. Merion.* Brief for rebuilding the church, 1761. Ch. Br. B. i. 5.

Pennalth, *co. Cornw.* Conveyance in, 1479. Add. 13067-13069.

Pennaly. *v.* Penally, *co. Pembr.*

Pennard, East, *co. Som.* Grant in Stone in, early Hen. III. Add. 21149.

Pennarthe, *co. Cornw.* Entailment in, 1518. Eg. 276.

Penne. *v.* Penselwood, *co. Som.*

**Penneth,** *co. Card.* Sale of "custom wool" from the grange of, 1567. Harl. 80 F. 31.

**Pennington,** *co. Southt.* Precipe on a covenant conc. the manor, etc., 1578 (Penyton). Add. 25229.

**Pennuth.** *v.* Pen hydd, *co. Glam.*

**Pennycrosse.** *v.* Weston Peverell, *co. Devon.*

**Pen nyth waylod.** *v.* Pen hydd waelod, *co. Glam.*

**Penpoll,** [*in Kea ?*], *co. Cornw.* Grant in, 1516. Add. 13078.

**Penpons,** *co. Cornw.* Fine in, 1661, 1662. Add. 15387.

**Penquain,** *nr. St. Breock (?), co. Cornw.* Grants in, *t.* Edw. I. Harl. 57 A. 36 (Penkoun):—*t.* Edw. I.-II. Harl. 57 A. 37 (Penkun);—1513. Harl. 50 C. 41 (Penkeyne).

**Penrith,** *co. Cumb.* Grant of the manor, 1290 (Penreth). Campb. xxx. 9.

—— Petition of Dame M. Howard for dower charged on the rectory of, 1664. Cott. iii. 8.

**Penros,** *nr. St. Enoder (?), co. Cornw.* Grant in, 1321. Add. 15348.

**Pensaunce.** *v.* Penzance, *co. Cornw.*

**Penselwood,** *co. Som.* Lease, etc., of the manor, 1419. Harl. 78 F. 31 (Penne);—1427. Harl. 78 F. 33 (do.).

**Pensham,** *co. Worc.* Conf. of land in, to Pershore Abbey, 972 (Pednesham). Cott. MS. Aug. ii. 6.

**Penshurst** (Pensherst), *co. Kent.* Evidence conc. the tenure of, [1072]. Cott. MS. Aug. ii. 36.

—— Power to take seisin, etc., of Enafeld (zenesfeld, Yensfeld) manor in, 1341. Add. 15729;—1371. Add. 15748.

—— Grant for lives at Doubleton (Dubbylton) in, 1405. Add. 15730.

—— Conveyance, etc., in, 1407. Harl. 76 G. 39;—1559. Harl. 76 I. 48.

—— Grant, etc., in, "super iugum de Estchestede," 1437, 1438. Add. 24534, 24535.

—— Arbitration conc. a water course in, 1464. Add. 15731.

—— Claims to the manor, and to Enafield *al.* Yensfeld manor in, etc., [1551-2]. Harl. 83 H. 36.

**Pensthorp.** *v. sub* Welwick, *co. York.*

**Penthlyn.** *v.* Penllyne, *co. Glam.*

**Pentire,** *co. Cornw.* Settlement in, 1439 (Penteyrwartha, Penteyrwoloys, Penteyrvorgan). Add. 15357.

**Pentlow,** *co. Essex.* Grants, etc., in, *t.* Edw. I. Add. 15006 (Pentelawe): —1341. Add. 15595 (Pentelowe);— 1387. Harl. 47 D. 27;—1400. Harl. 46 F. 7.

—— Grant of view of frank pledge in, 1344 (Pentelowe). Add. 7076.

—— Precipes on covenants conc. land in, 1593. Add. 25026, 25039.

**Penton Grafton.** *v.* Weyhill, *co. Southt.*

**Penton Mewsey,** *co. Southt.* Fine of the manor, 1342 (Penytou Meysy). Harl. Roll G. 17.

—— Brief conc. a fire at, 1754. Ch. Br. A. i. 3.

—— Rector *al. Persona.* Rob. Foxtone, 1393. Add. 20384;—1396. Add. 20386.

**Penvel.** *v.* Pen y fai, *nr. Newcastle, co. Glam.*

**Penventon,** *nr. Gwennap (?), co. Cornw.* Fine in, 1608. Add. 15376.

**Penwortham,** *co. Lanc.* Grant in Longton, *co. Lanc.*, for a yearly payment to the church of St. Mary at, 1304. Add. 26030.

—— *v. also* Longton, *in Penwortham, co. Lanc.*

**Penyard,** *co. Heref.* Grant in, *t.* Hen. III. (Penjar). Eg. 341.

**Pen y Clawdd,** *co. Monm.* Inspex. in 1330 of a grant in (?), to Usk Priory, *c.* 1150 (Penclau). Add. 5342.

—— Release in, 1508 (Penclauthe). Add. 7130.

—— Fine of the manor, etc., 1717. Eg. 334.

**Pen y fai,** *nr. Newcastle, co. Glam.* Grants, etc., in, with mining rights, to Margam Abbey, *c.* 1200. Harl. 75 C. 39 (Penvei):—1261. Harl. 75 C. 40 (Penvey). 49, 50, 51.

**Penystorp, Penythorpp.** *v. sub* Welwick, *co. York.*

**Penyton Meysy.** *v.* Penton Mewsey, *co. Southt.*

**Penzance,** *co. Cornw.* Grant in, 1552 (Pensaunce). Harl. 77 G. 12.

Peopleton, *co. Worc.* Conf. of grants at, to Pershore Abbey, 972 (in Piplincgtune). Cott. MS. Aug. ii. 6.

—— *Capellanus.* Robertus, early 13 cent. (Piplint.). Add. 20427.

Pepenbury, Pepingebur, Pepyngbery, etc. *v.* Pembury, *co. Kent.*

Peperharow, *co. Surr.* Papal conf. of Rye hill (Riehulla) in, to Waverley Abbey, 1147. Lansd. 27.

—— Rental of lands of R. Pexhall in, 1549. Add. 26560.

Perbald. *v.* Parbold, *co. Lanc.*

Peredham, [*in Cannington*], *co. Som.* Grant in, late Hen. III. Add. 26751.

Perefricth. *v.* Pirbright, *co. Surr.*

Pereham. *v.* Parham, *co. Suss.*

Ferenduna. *v.* Parndon, Gt., *co. Essex.*

Perham. *v.* Parham, *co. Suff.*

Periton. *v.* Pirton, *co. Worc.*

Perland [Park]. *v. sub* Windsor, *co. Berks.*

Perlethorpe, *in Edwinstowe, co. Nott.* Grant in, 1421 (Perlthorppe juxta Eddynstowe). Campb. xi. 7.

Pernhowe. *v.* Pirnhow, *co. Norf.*

Perpounds and Poynyngs manor. *v. sub* Henstead, *co. Suff.*

Perrie. *v.* Paulerspury, *co. Northt.*

Perris *al.* Perrishes manor. *v. sub* Snetterton, *co. Norf.*

Perry. *v. sub* Shorne, *co. Kent.*

Perry, *nr. Bickleigh, co. Devon.* Grant in, 1336 (Pirie). Harl. 46 E. 4.

Perry, *nr. Graffham, co. Hunt.* Grant of, late Steph. (Pir.). Add. 11233 (5) (copy).

Perry Mill, *nr. Bathealton* (?), *co. Som.* Grant of reversion in, 1408 (Peremulle). Harl. 57 A. 27.

Perry, Wild (?), *nr. Edvin Loach, co. Worc.* Grant in, *t.* Edw. I. (villa de Piro). Add. 8151.

Pershall, *in Eccleshall, co. Staff.* Grant in, " in feodo de Hawketone," co. Salop, 1453 (Peeshale). Harl. 111 G. 32.

Pershore, *co. Worc.* Grant of, by Edw. the Confessor, to Westminster Abbey, " post mortem Eadgithe regine conjugis mee," 1066 [*sc.* 1065] (Perscoran). Cott. vi. 2 (copy).

Pershore, *co. Worc. (continued).* Grant in, late 12 cent. (Persora). Add. 20423.

—— Grant, etc., of rents in, to Pershore Abbey, early 13 cent. (Persora). Add. 20426, 20427.

—— Rents in, of Pershore Abbey, early 14 cent. (Perschora). Harl. Roll N. 24.

Perstede. *v. sub* Feering, *co. Essex.*

Pertenhall, *co. Bedf.* Valor of Hardwick's manor in, 1542. Harl. 75 E. 21.

Perton, *co. Staff.* Grant in, by Edw. the Confessor, to Westminster Abbey, 1066 [*sc.* 1065]. Cott. vi. 2 (copy).

Perwich. *v.* Parwich, *co. Derb.*

Pery, West Pery. *v.* Paulerspury, *co. Northt.*

Peryngdon Magna. *v.* Parndon, Gt., *co. Essex.*

Pesecroft. *v. sub* Thorington, *co. Suff.*

Peshale, Pesenhale. *v.* Peasenhall, *co. Suff.*

Pesemers, Pesemersch, etc. *v.* Peasmarsh, *co. Suss.*

Peterborough, *co. Northt.* Grants in or nr., by the Abbey, *t.* John. Add. 5360, 5869.

—— Release in, 1353 (Burgus S. Petri). Add. 15716.

—— Chas. Duke of Orleans imprisoned at, 1428. Add. 3628.

—— Precipes on covenants conc. lands in, 1578 (Burgus S. Petri). Add. 25153, 25161, 25162.

—— Fine in, 1609. Harl. 75 G. 55.

Peterborough, *Liberty of.* Conf. by Hen. III. of a grant of de-afforestation of, to Peterborough Abbey, 1227 (Nassus burgi). Cott. viii. 8.

Peterchurch, *co. Heref.* Grant in Lignehales in, 1476. Add. 4606.

Petersfield, *co. Southt.* Compotus-rolls of the borough, 1425-8. Add. 26870, 26871.

—— Compotus-rolls of, bel. to the Duke of Buckingham, 1499-1500. Add. 26873.

—— Rentals of borough lands, etc., 1592-1756. Add. 19752-19787.

—— *Prepositus Burgi.* Joh. atte Brygge, 1425-6. Add. 26870.

—— —— Tho. Strode, 1427-8. Add. 26871.

Petersfield, co. Southt. (continued).
Mayor. Joh. Hall, 1592. Add. 19752.
—— —— Hen. Smith, 1646–47.
Add. 19754.
—— —— Rob. Parker, 1648–49.
Add. 19786.
—— —— Joh. Reeues, 1682–83.
Add. 19773.
—— —— Nioh. Allen, 1690–91.
Add. 19775.
—— —— Barth. Starr, 1695–96.
Add. 19777.
—— —— Ralph Bucknall, 1696–97.
Add. 19779.
—— —— Edw. Hunt, 1708–9.
Add. 19784.

Petersham, co. Surr. Warrant for a
lease of custody of the manor, [post
1522]. Add. 22631.

Pethaghe. v. Pettaugh, co. Suf.

Petham, co. Kent. Grant at Bockholt
(Bocholt) in, 805. Cott. MS. Aug. ii. 87.
—— Grants, etc., in, t. Hen. III.
Harl. 77 G. 21, 32, 78 E. 2 ;—c. 1282–3.
Harl. 78 B. 27, 28 ;—1297. Harl. 80 G.
39 ;—1309–10. Harl. 79 E. 11 :—1331.
Harl. 79 A. 28 ;—1334. Harl. 80 A.
14 ;—1344. Harl. 80 E. 26 :—1349.
Harl. 76 G. 24, 80 E. 10 :—1352.
Harl. 80 I. 3 ;—1354. Harl. 78 E. 19 ;
—1374. Harl. 80 I. 4 ;—1415. Harl.
76 B. 13 ;—1425. Harl. 78 G. 8 ;—
1479. Harl. 80 E. 48, 49 ;—1485.
Harl. 80 C. 46 :—1486. Harl. 78 I.
2 ;—t. Hen. VII. Harl. 78 B. 52 ;—
1500. Harl. 78 G. 27 ;—1529. Harl.
76 D. 26 ;—1548. Harl. 75 H. 4, 76
H. 50 ;—1589. Harl. 77 H. 46.
—— Grants, etc., in Dwnsterue al.
Dunesterne, Dunsterne, Dennstrue
in, t. Hen. III. Harl. 78 B. 27, 28 ;—
1249–50. Harl. 78 I. 38 ;—1252. Harl.
80 I. 46 ;—1272–3. Harl. 76 D. 19 :—
1280–1. Harl. 76 D. 20 ;—1318–9.
Harl. 76 A. 24 ;—1323. Harl. 80 I. 48.
—— Grant of a wood at Fulling in,
1257–8. Harl. 79 C. 43.
—— Grant in Kenfield in, 1285. Harl.
80 C. 31.
—— Surrenders, etc., of Swarling
(Swerdling) manor in, 1421. Harl.
78 F. 30, 78 G. 7 ;—1495. Harl.
78 F. 51.
—— Grant in Chartham " in dominio
manerii de Swarlyng " in, 1494. Harl.
78 C. 15.
—— Fine, etc., of Kenfield manor in,
1548. Harl. 75 H. 4, 76 H. 50 ;—1554.
Harl. 79 G. 2.

Petham, co. Kent (continued). Ballivus.
Will. Grac, t. Hen. III. Harl. 77 G. 32.
—— —— Tho. Burgeis, c. 1260.
Harl. 77 G. 21, 78 E. 11.
—— —— Tho. Pender, 1262 – 3.
Harl. 79 B. 1.
—— —— Hen. de Sirwell, late
Hen. III. Harl. 77 G. 35.
—— —— Mag. Joh. de Dovoria,
1292–3. Harl. 77 E. 8.
—— Sacerdos. Martinus, late 12
cent. Harl. 75 F. 56.

Pethaye. v. Pettaugh, co. Suf.

Petherton, North, co. Som. Vicarius.
Joh. Coleforde, 1396. Harl. 48 G. 9.

Petherton, South, co. Som. Defeasance of a grant of Moor (More) in, etc.,
1324. Add. 15704 ;—1349. Harl. 48
I. 23.
—— Grant of custody of Wigborough
(Wyggebeare) manor in, 1408. Harl.
43 E. 17, 18.
—— Conveyance of a third part of
Wigborough (Wiggebere) manor in,
1415. Harl. 53 B. 2.
v. also Compton Durvill, co. Som.

Petherwin, North, co. Devon. Grant
of an annuity in Weston in, 1579.
Eg. 299.

Petherwin, South, co. Cornw. En-
tailment in Treguddick, etc., in, 1518.
Eg. 276.
—— Entailment in, 1544. Eg. 283.
—— Grant of an annuity in Holland
in, 1579. Eg. 299.

Pethlleny, co. Monm. Inspex. in 1330
of grant in, to Usk Priory, c. 1150
(Pethlenny). Add. 5342.

Petistre. v. Petlistree, co. Suf.

Petistres Manor. v. sub Sutton, co.
Suf.

Petmady. v. sub Strathern, co. Perth.

Petsoe, co. Buck. The manor given as
surety to J. de Pabeham, 1327 (Pet-
tisso). Cott. xxviii. 40.

Pett, co. Suss. Precipe on a covenant
conc. lands in, 1592. Add. 15231.

Pettaugh, co. Suf. Conf. of a grant
in, to Leystone Abbey, t. Hen. III.
(Pethaye). Add. 10294.
—— Grants, etc., in, 1307. Add.
10300 (Pethaghe) :—1384. Harl. 57
D. 2 ;—1476. Add. 10074 ;—1477.
Add. 10076 (Pottehawe) :—1577. Add.
10233, 19376.

Pickering, *co. York.* Conf. of the manor, castle, etc., to Edm., Earl of Lancaster, 1285 (Pykeringe). Cott. MS. Aug. ii. 135 (5) (*copy*).

—— Power to give seisin in, 1463 (Pykering). Harl. 48 H. 45.

—— Sale of the honour, castle, etc., 1652. Add. 12630.

Pickham. *v. sub* Guestling, *co. Suss.*

Pickhill, *co. York.* Grant of the advowson. etc., to St. Leonard's Hospital, York, 1308. Add. 7466.

Pickhurst Green. *v. sub* Hayes, *co. Kent.*

Pickwell, *co. Leic.* Sentence in suit conc. burials in, 1241 (Pikewelle). Cott. MS. Nero C. iii. f. 199.

—— *Rector.* Theobaldus, 1241. Cott. MS. Nero C. iii. f. 199.

Pickworth, *co. Linc.* Grant in, late 13 cent. (Pykeworth) Add. 17389.

—— Grant of an annuity from the manor, 1383. Add. 17422.

—— *Capellanus.* Osbertus, *t.* Hen. III. (Pichewort). Add. 6370.

—— *Persona* (*quondam*). Joh. Saperton, *clericus*, 1407. Add. 6399.

—— Joh. Scherman, 1438. Add. 21052.

—— *Rector.* Ricardus, *t.* Hen. III. (Pikeword). Add. 6371.

Pickworth, *co. Rutl.* Valor of crown lands in, *t.* Hen. VIII. (Pyckworthe). Harl. Roll Y. 1.

Picoumbe. *v.* Pyecombe, *co. Suss.*

Picteale. *v.* Pitchley, *co. Northt.*

Picton, *co. Chest.* Settlement of the manor, 1325 (Pycton). Add. 6278.

—— Rental, 1391. Add. 5230.

Piddinghoe, *co. Suss.* Power for assignment of the vill to Edw. II., 1316 (Pidinghowe). Harl. 57 E. 33.

—— Lease in, *t.* Eliz.-Jas. I. Add. 23815.

Piddington, *co. Northt.* Conveyance in, 1349 (Pydyngton). Harl. 57 C. 27.

Piddington, *co. Oxon.* Restoration of, by King John to R. de Dammartin, 1212 (Pedinton). Add. 11239 (*copy*).

Piddle, *co. Worc.* Grant, etc., in, 1216. Harl. 83 H. 33 (Pidele):—1430. Add. 20432 (Pedulle).

Piddle, *co. Worc.* (*continued*). Feoffment, etc., of the manor, 1370. Add. 20422 (Pydele):—1448. Add. 17740 (Northpydill).

Piddle Trenthide, *co. Dors.* Grant in, 1323-4 (Pudele Trentehyde). Harl. 49 G. 47.

Piddletown, *co. Dors.* Conf. in, to Quarr Abbey, *t.* Hen. II. (Pidcltona). Harl. 55 D. 22.

—— Court-rolls, 1359-60, 1383, 1393, 1395, 1399, 1400, 1405, 1412, 1459, *n. d.* (Pudeleton, Pudeltoune). Add. 667-680.

Pidelynchope, *nr. Wigmore* (?), *co. Heref.* Grant nr., *post* 1247. Add. 7499.

Pidley, *co. Hunt.* Assessment of poor-rates in, 1635. Cott. i. 14, f. 3.

Pidseburton. *v.* Burton Pidsea, *co. York.*

Pilardinthon. *v.* Pillerton, *co. Warw.*

Pilatecroft. *v. sub* Denby, *co. York.*

Pilateshul. *v. sub* Trusley, *co. Derb.*

Pilcock *al.* Thornham Pilcock. *v.* Thornham, Great, *co. Suf.*

Pilehund Croft, *in Aspall, co. Suf.* Grant in, late 12 cent. (Crofta Pilehund). Harl. 50 H. 19.

Piletta. *v. sub* Welton in the Marsh, *co. Linc.*

Pill, *in Steynton, co. Pembr.* Grant at Rhodal (Pulla Rodifal), nr. (?), *t.* Edw. I.-II. Add. 8409.

Pill Bridge. *v. sub* Ilchester, *co. Som.*

Pillary, The, Farm. *v. sub* Goudhurst, *co. Kent.*

Pillerton, *co. Warw.* Release in, 1301 (Pilardinthon). Cott. xxix. 57.

Pillerton Hercy, *co. Warw. Dominus.* Tho. Wandac, 1332. Cott. iv. 14 (2).

Pillesyate. *v. sub* Barnack, *co. Northt.*

Pilleth, *co. Radn.* Lease of the demesnes, *c.* 1433 (Pullith). Harl. 53 H. 17.

Pilsbury, *in Hartington, co. Derb.* Appointment of bailiffs in, for Merivale Abbey, 1543 (Pillesbury). Harl. 112 F. 27.

Pilsgate. *v. sub* Barnack, *co. Northt.*

Pilsley, *in Edensor, co. Derb.* Sale in, 1547. Woll. xi. 40.

Plumpton, *nr. Canons Ashby, co. Northt.* Grant of the chapel to Wedon Pinkney Priory, late Hen. II. (Plumton). Cott. v. 34.

Plumpton, *co. Suss.* Grants, etc., in, to Battle Abbey, *t.* Edw. I.-*t.* Edw. II. (Plumton). Campb. xvi. 11 (*copies*).

—— Lease in, 1503 (Plompton). Add. 8104.

—— Covenant to levy a fine of Plumpton Bustage and P. Piddinghoe manors, 1593. Add. 23816.

Plumpton Pery. *v. sub* Paulerspury, *co. Northt.*

Plumpton, Wood, *nr. Preston, co. Lanc.* Lease of Lower Bartle Hay (Nezerbartaileaheye) in, 1287 (Plumton). Add. 20149.

—— *Dominus.* Ric. de Stokeport, 1287. Add. 20149.

Plumstead, *co. Kent.* Conf. of a grant of a hermitage in, to Southwark Priory, *ante* 1207 (Plumstede). Harl. 55 E. 18.

—— Grants, etc., in, 1269. Harl. 55 C. 4 (Plumstode);—1273. Harl. 48 G. 4 (Plumstede);—1592. Add. 12675;—1626. Harl. 112 D. 29;—1658. Harl. 112 B. 26, 27;—1660. Harl. 112 B. 25.

—— Order in court conc. rents in, 1670. Harl. 111 C. 6.

—— *Capellanus.* Johannes, *ante* 1207. Harl. 55 E. 18.

Plumstead, *in N. Erpingham Hundred, co. Norf.* Grants, etc., in, 1370. Add. 14867 (Plumstedu);—1408. Harl. 52 C. 16 (do.), 17 (Plumpstede);—1416. Add. 14820 (Plumstede);—1417. Add. 14821 (do.).

—— *Rector.* Will. Howlyn, 1408. Harl. 52 C. 16, 17.

Plumstead, Great (Plumstode, etc.), *co. Norf.* Grants, etc., in (?), by Bps. of Norwich to Norwich Priory, [1103-6?]. Cott. MS. Aug. ii. 103, Cott. ii. 21 (1) (*copies*);—[1121-35?]. Cott. ii. 21 (8) (*copy*);—[1136-45?]. Cott. ii. 1, 21 (9) (*copies*).

—— Release in, 1347 (Plumstede Magna). Harl. 48 C. 3.

Plumstead, Little, *co. Norf.* Exchange in, by John, Bp. of Norwich, 1310 (Parva Plumstede). Add. 14822.

Plumtree, *co. Nott.* Release in, 1445 (Plumtre). Harl. 112 I. 3.

Plumtree, Little, *co. Nott.* Acquittance from Blith Priory for rents in, 1460 (Parvus Plomptre). Add. 7387.

Plungar, *co. Leic.* Grant of rents in, on a fine, 1285 (Plungarl). Harl. 45 H. 48.

—— Decree against Belvoir Priory for augmentation of the vicarage, 1449 (Plumgarth). Harl. 111 C. 14.

—— *Vicarius perpetuus.* Rob. Knotte, 1449. Harl. 111 C. 14.

Plusshenden, *co. Kent.* Sale, etc., of the manor and lands in, late bel. to Mottenden Priory, 1544. Harl. 83 H. 25;—1548. Harl. 75 E. 24, 76 A. 18;—1551. Harl. 76 I. 6.

Plymouth, *co. Devon.* Order of Council for a writ to the Mayor and Bailiffs to make arrests, 1432 (Plymouth). Lansd. 559.

—— Exemplif. of fine in, 1560. Add. 13963.

—— Rental of land of A. Cholwich in, 1605 (Plimmouthe al. Sutton Priour). Add. 26199.

Plympton, *co. Devon.* Grant in, *t.* Edw. I. Add. 5247.

—— *Prepositus.* Job. Kena, *t.* Edw. I. Add. 5247.

Plympton Hundred, *co. Devon.* Compotus, 1495-6. Add. 13177.

Plymstock, *co. Devon.* Return of value of Gooswell (Gooewoll) manor in, 1572. Cott. xvii. 22.

Pockley, *co. York.* Grant of the manor, 1650. Add. 1800.

Pocklington, *co. York.* Grant, etc., in, by the Css. of Albemarle, [1260-62] (Pokellugton). Toph. 27.

—— Grant of market and free warren in the manor of, 1299 (do.). Harl. 58 I. 42 (*copy*).

Pockthorpe, *co. York.* Fines, etc., in, 1576. Add. 18858;—1594. Add. 18877, 18878;—1597. Add. 18874;—1598. Add. 18884;—1606. Add. 18901;—1616. Add. 18921;—1617. Add. 18922;—1624. Add. 18931.

—— Release of the manor, 1626. Add. 18932.

Pocknedge. *v. sub* Brampton, *co. Derb.*

Poolesherse, *nr. Fairlight* (?), *co. Suss.* Conf. of, to Robertsbridge Abbey, [1180-1204]. Eg. 373.

Poderidge. *r.* Potheridge, *in Merton, co. Devon.*

Podesey, Podusay, etc. v. Pudsey, co. York.

Podmore, co. Staff. Grant in, 1453. Harl. 111 G. 32.

Poinegwic. v. Powick, co. Worc.

Pointon, co. Linc. Grant of custody of lands in, 1438 (Poynton). Add. 6407.

—— Covenant for a fine of the manor, 1552. Add. 13562.

—— Precipe on a covenant conc. land in, 1578. Add. 25064.

—— Clericus. Hugo, early Hen. II. (Pointun). Add. 20624.

—— Toraldus, late Hen. II. Add. 20627.

Pokebrok. v. Polebrook, co. Northt.

Pokel. v. Puxley, co. Northt.

Pokelonde, in Cannington, co. Som. Grant in, t. Edw. I.–II. Add. 19980.

Pokemilne, co. Linc. Grant of rent from the mill of, to Sempringham Priory, end of 12 cent. Add. 20580.

Pokesle, Pokesleia. v. Puxley, co. Northt.

Pola. v. Welshpool, co. Montgom.

Poldre. v. sub Woodnesborough, co. Kent.

Pole. v. Poole, co. Dors.

—— v. Poole Keynes, co. Wilts.

—— v. sub Southfleet, co. Kent.

Pole manor, co. Berks. Release of, 1396. Add. 9243.

Pole, La. v. sub Stanton Lacy, co. Salop.

Poleanthony, co. Devon. Lands in Tiverton held of the manor of, 1546. Harl. 112 E. 27 a.

Polebrook, co. Northt. Grants, etc., in, t. Hen. III. Harl. 45 E. 62 (Pokebrok), 64 (Pokebroc), 45 I. 49, 50; —1424, 1437. Add. 738 a, b.

—— Bond from Armston Hospital on a purchase of lands in, 1277 (Pokebrok). Harl. 44 A. 6.

—— Grant in, to Armston Hospital, 1279 (do.). Cott. xxvii. 1.

Poleghelegh. v. sub Wormingford, co. Essex.

Polementona. v. Poolhampton, nr. Overton, co. Southt.

Polesworth, co. Warw. Lease of a mill at, by Polesworth Abbey, 1530 (Pollesworth). Cott. xi. 9.

Polettes. v. Ippollitta, co. Hertf.

Poling, co. Suss. Precipe on a covenant conc. land in, 1593 (Pulynge). Add. 15233.

—— Note of a lease in, 1614. Add. 8963.

Polla. v. Welshpool, co. Montgom.

Polruan, co. Cornw. Grants, etc., in, t. Edw. I. Add. 12956, 12957;—1321. Add. 12959;—1454. Add. 12960.

Polrunthorndaile. v. sub Cabourn, co. Linc.

Polstead, co. Suff. Bequests of land at, late 10 cent. (æt Polsteda, etc.). Harl. 43 C. 4.

—— Grants, etc., in Ernefeld, etc., in, early 13 cent.–t. Hen. III. (Polsted, etc.). Harl. 50 F. 53, 54, 50 G. 1, 2, 4;—1257. Harl. 50 G. 3.

—— Grant of rent in Sunfeld in, on a marriage, early Hen. III. (Polsted). Harl. 50 C. 60.

—— Grants, etc., in, late Hen. III. Harl. 50 G. 7;—1301. Harl. 57 E. 15;—1337. Harl. 56 H. 34;—1376. Harl. 47 H. 48;—1658. Add. 1042.

—— Precipes on covenants conc. land in, 1555. Add. 25278 (Poulsted);— 1561. Add. 25302.

—— Persona. Michael, t. Hen. III. Harl. 54 D. 23, 54 G. 32.

—— Joh. Brook, 1403. Harl. 47 A. 29.

Pond. v. sub Hadleigh, co. Suff.

Pondall. v. sub Linstead, Gt., co. Suff.

Ponsksyre, nr. Grampound, co. Cornw. Releases in, 1430. Add. 12990;— 1431. Add. 12994.

Ponte, de, [Bridgend?] nr. Neath, co. Glam. Capellanus. Henricus, early 13 cent. Harl. 75 C. 35.

Pontefract, co. York. A yearly payment due to the castle of, late Hen. III. (Castrum Pontefracti). Add. 8252.

—— Grant for life in, by Ant. Bek, Bp. of Durham, a. 1300 (villa de Pontefracto). Harl. 43 I. 48.

—— Grants in, 1324. Add. 16691 (de Pontefracto);—1374. Add. 16831 (Pontffrayt); — 1467. Add. 16959 (Pountfrett).

—— Crown lease in, 1555 (Pountfryt). Harl. 84 C. 32.

—— Brief conc. a fire at Park Lodge, 1767. Ch. Br. B. vii. 2.

2 Q

II. Add. 7771, 7773;—t. Edw. III. Add. 7798;—1340. Add. 7816.

—— Grants, etc., of the manor, early 14 cent. Add. 7790;—1337. Add. 7183; — 1455. Add. 7191; — 1468. Add. 7872, 7873, 7192;—1485. Add. 7845.

—— Lease of Failand (Foyland) in the manor of, 1336. Add. 7812.

—— Grant in La Hope in, 1343. Add. 7822.

—— Grant of a market at, 1348. Add. 7184.

—— Grant of profits of "Laghedaies," etc., in, 1353. Add. 7833.

—— Chantry at, for the Berkeley family, 1354. Add. 7834;—1370. Add. 7840.

—— Vicarius al. Perpet. Vicarius. Dom. Adam, late Hen III.-t. Edw. I. or II. Add. 7767, 7769, 7771, 7773; —1289. Add. 7775;—1292. Add. 7776;—1293. Add. 7780.

—— —— Will. Godwyne, early 14 cent. Add. 7789; — 1327. Add. 7799; — 1340. Add. 7817; — 1341 (quondam). Add. 7819.

—— —— Sire Johan Waltres, 1370. Add. 7840.

Portbury Hundred, co. Som. Grant of, c. 1148 (Portbure). Add. 7760.

—— Quo warranto conc. the tenure of, [1280]. Add. 7791.

—— Feoffment in, 1470. Campb. i. 5.

Portesdona. v. Portsdown, co. Southt.

Portesheved. v. Portishead, co. Som.

Portesmues. v. Portsmouth, co. Southt.

Porteswald, Terra de, co. Southt. Conf. of, to Quarr Abbey, late Hen. II. Add. 15687.

Porthauoth. v. Hafod y porth, co. Glam.

Porthedre, Portheedreth, etc. v. Prothether, nr. Lit. Dewchurch, co. Heref.

Portisham, co. Dors. Grant of tithes of Corton (Corftona) in, to Montacute Priory, t. Hen. I. Add. 24879 (3) (copy).

—— Grant of Corton (Corfton) manor in, 1414. Harl. 48 I. 25.

Portishead, co. Som. Grants, etc., in, late 13 cent. Campb. i. 7 (Poresheuede), vi. 14 (Porteshed);—1308. Add. 7793 (Porteshcued); — 1321. Add. 7796, 7797;—1337. Add. 7183;

—1340. Add. 7818 (Portesheued in Gordene);—1349. Add. 7830;—1377. Add. 7838, 7843;—1383. Add. 7187; —1386. Add. 7847 (Porteshed);— 1412. Add. 7189, 7856–7858;—1470. Campb. i. 5 (Portyshed).

—— Exchange in Capenor in, 1336. Add. 7811.

—— Grant in the manor of, 1354 (Portesheved). Add. 26438; — 1357. Add. 9234.

Portland, co. Dors. Lease of the manor, c. 1433 (?). Harl. 53 H. 17.

Portlemouth, co. Devon. Persona. Joh. de Malston, 1340. Harl. 53 C. 47.

Portlester Castle, co. Meath. Inventory of goods, etc., of Lady Offaley at, 1628. Add. 13340.

Portmanmersh al. Pontmanmersh, nr. Maldon, co. Essex. Lease of, by the corporation of Maldon, 1562. Harl. 58 F. 3.

Porton, co. Wilts. (?). Certif. of descent of lands in, 1375. Harl. 45 A. 37.

Portpighian. v. Looe, West, co. Cornw.

Portraine, co. Dubl. Grant of interest in the rectory of, 1576 (Portravan al. Protrarne, Portrahen). Harl. 86 G. 47.

Portscuett, co. Monm. Grant in, 1443 (Porscuet). Add. 5343.

Portsdown, co. Southt. Grant of " terra de ultra Portesdona que dicitur Frendestapele" to Quarr Abbey, t. Hen. II. Harl. 46 E. 55.

Portsea, co. Southt. Exchange of land at Lenchestoche of the fee of, with Quarr Abbey, for land at Copnor (Copponore), t. Hen. II. (Portesin). Add. 15687.

Portslade, nr. New Shoreham, co. Suss. Grant in, 1293 (Porteslade). Add. 26756, 26757.

Portsmouth, co. Southt. Inspex., in 1280, of a conf. by King John of two mills at, to Fontevrault Abbey, 1200 (Portesmues). Harl. 58 I. 34 (copy).

—— Inspex., in 1231, of a papal conf. of above mills to the same, 1201 (Partemue). Add. 17861.

—— Grant, etc., in, 1450. Add. 15855; —1461. Add. 15857;—1463. Add. 15858.

—— Precipes on covenants in, 1578 (Portesmouthe). Add. 25226;—1593. Add. 25245.

2 Q 2

**Portsmouth**, *co. Southt. (continued).* *Ballivus.* Joh. Fynsy, 1450. Add. 15855.

—— —— Rob. Foule, 1463. Add. 15858.

—— *Constabularii.* Joh. More, Joh. Coleyn, 1450. Add. 15855.

—— *Servientes.* Rob. Abraham, Rob. Fawle, Ric. Bounde, Joh. Berne, Joh. Whytop, Joh. Boveled, 1450. Add. 15855.

**Portus domine nostre gratie.** *v.* Newhaven, *co. Edinburgh.*

**Poseney Park**, *co. Denb.* Exchequer acquittance for a fine for, 1595. Add. 25740.

**Poslingford**, *co. Suff.* Grants, etc., in, 1294. Harl. 49 H. 34 (Poselingwrth);—1312. Harl. 56 F. 16 (Posselyngworth); — 1320. Harl. 55 A. 2 (Poselyngford);—1375-1414. Harl. Roll O. 27;—1382. Harl. 48 D. 3, 4 (Poselyngworth);—1421. Harl. 48 D. 15 (Poselyngford);—1575. Harl. 48 D. 49.

—— Precipe on a covenant conc. land in, 1578. Add. 25364.

—— *Capellanus.* Martinus, [1139-51] (Poseligwrdia). Harl. 76 F. 35.

**Possewyke.** *v.* Postwick, *co. Norf.*

**Postern.** *v. sub* Tonbridge, *co. Kent.*

**Postern**, *in Duffield, co. Derb.* Grant of the custody of the Park, 1523. Woll. iii. 95.

**Postling**, *co. Kent.* Grants, etc., in or nr., early Hen. III. Add. 8536 (Potelinge);—1306. Add. 16342 (Postlyng); —1389. Harl. 58 B. 35.

**Postridge**, *in Spaxton, co. Som.* Conf. of a grant of, to Plympton Priory, [1136-66] (terra de Posterigge). Harl. 49 B. 23.

—— Conf. of a grant in, by Plympton Priory, 1280 (Postrigge). Add. 20230.

**Postwick**, *co. Norf.* Release in, 1347 (Possewyk). Harl. 48 C. 3.

—— Petition conc. a riot at, [1452] (Possewyke). Add. 17241.

**Potbury.** *v. sub* Eastwell, *co. Kent.*

**Potenhull.** *v.* Putnell, *nr. Cannington, co. Som.*

**Potesterf.** *v. sub* Brede, *co. Suss.*

**Potheridge**, *in Merton, co. Devon.* Court-rolls, 1609-1614 (Poderidge). Add. 9415-9417.

**Potheriggebury.** *v. sub* Lilley, *co. Hertf.*

**Potinton.** *v.* Puddington, *co. Devon.*

**Potlock.** *v. sub* Willington, *co. Derb.*

**Potten, Great, Fen**, *co. Essex.* Release of, [1259-62] (Mariscus de magna Potting). Add. 19981.

**Pottereslyvedene.** *v.* Liveden, *co. Northt.*

**Potterne**, *co. Wilts.* Release in, 1309 (Poterne). Add. 7066.

**Potters Somersall.** *v. sub* Somersall Herbert, *co. Derb.*

**Potterspury**, *co. Northt.* Power to give seisin in, etc., 1411. Add. 17383 (Potterspyrie);—1659. Add. 18032; —1666. Add. 6074.

**Potterton**, *in Barwick in Elmett, co. York.* Lease of the hall, etc., 1572. Harl. 77 H. 37.

**Potting, Magna.** *v.* Potten, Gt., Fen, *co. Essex.*

**Potto**, *in Whorlton, co. York.* Grant in, late 13 cent. (Potthou). Harl. 112 F. 56.

**Potton**, *co. Bedf.* Acquittance for a fine to the Crown in, 1355. Cott. xxvii. 152.

—— Conf. of feoffment of the church, etc., to the Nuns Minoresses without Aldgate, London, 1394. Add. 19951.

—— Compotus-rolls, 1402-3. Harl. Roll A. 57;—1438-39. Harl. Roll K. 24.

—— Grant of rent from the manor, 1570. Add. 6136.

—— *Capellanus.* Simon, early 13 cent. Harl. 54 I. 45.

**Pouhier, Fee of.** Grant in Waltham H. Cross, *co. Essex,* of land held of, *t.* Edw. I. Harl. 76 D. 31.

**Poukheldebrok, Aqua de,** *in Brightling, co. Suss.* Grant of, to Robertsbridge Abbey, 1315. Eg. 399.

**Poulton**, *co. Chest.* Grant in, to found an abbey, *c.* 1150 (Puntona). Cott. MS. Nero C. iii. f. 215.

**Poulton**, *in Lonsdale, co. Lanc.* Marriage settlement in, 1670. Add. 19547.

**Poulton in the Fylde**, *co. Lanc.* Award in a suit in, betw. Séez and Cokersand Abbeys, 1216 (Pultona). Add. 20512.

Preston upon the Weald Moor, *co.
Salop.* Grant of lands in the manor
of, 1384 (Prestono juxta Wylde Mor).
Cott. v. 8.

Preston upon Wye, *co. Heref.* Power
to give seisin in, etc., 1417. Add.
19415; — 1440. Add. 4603; — 1446.
Harl. 111 E. 2;—1544. Add. 19418;—
1558. Add. 19420; — 1650. Add.
19425 ;—1653. Add. 19427.

—— Extract of court-roll, 1653. Add.
19426.

Preston, West. *v.* Preston Capes, *co.
Northt.*

Preston with Uppingham, *co. Rutl.*
Court-roll, 1735-6. Add. 25984.

Preston [Wynne ?], *co. Heref.* Entail
in, 1459. Add. 4605.

Prestwat. *v.* Prestwold, *co. Leic.*

Prestwick, *co. Lanc.* Brief conc. a
fire at, 1798. Ch. Br. B. xxxviii. 8.

—— *Parson.* Tho. Longley, 1509.
Add. 17714.

Prestwold (Prestewald, etc.), *co. Leic.*
Grant and conff. of St. Andrew's
church with its chapels of Hoton and
Cotes to Bullington Priory, *t.* Hen. II.
Harl. 52 G. 30, 31 (Presteswad) ;—
[1175-81]. Harl. 43 C. 36;—*t.* John.
Harl. 55 A. 21, 22 ;—*c.* 1253. Harl.
45 H. 47;—1256. Harl. 52 H. 28 ;—
*t.* Edw. I.-II. Harl. 52 H. 5;—*c.* 1322.
Harl. 52 H. 27.

—— Grants, etc., in, to Bullington
Priory, *t.* Hen. II. Harl. 52 G. 32
(Prestewald);—*t.* John. Harl. 46 A.
37, 54 I. 28, 55 A. 24;—early 13
cent.–*t.* Edw. I. Harl. 47 D. 22, 47 I.
48, 48 H. 36, 49 H. 35, 50 I. 32, 55 A.
12, 23.

—— "Paccatio" betw. St. Andrew's
church and Cotes chapel, late Hen. II.
Harl. 44 H. 53 (Prestewald) ;—Conf.
of above, [1217]. Harl. 45 A. 25.

—— Grant in Burton, *co.* Leic., to the
church of, *t.* John. Harl. 46 A. 37.

—— Decree for the chaplain of, to
serve Burton chapel, etc., *t.* John.
Harl. 44 H. 47.

—— Covenant, etc., betw. the parson
of, and Bullington Priory, conc. tithes
of Hoton, *t.* John. Harl. 44 A. 31
(Prestwat), 45 C. 39.

—— Lease in, from Bullington Priory,
*t.* John (Prestwald). Harl. 44 A. 33.

—— Certificate of presentation by
Bullington Priory to the church of,
early 13 cent. Harl. 46 E. 32.

Prestwold (Prestewald, etc.), *co. Leic.*
(*continued*). Suit of Bullington Priory
with Garendon Abbey conc. tithes,
1251 (Prestewald). Harl. 44 D. 47,
53 A. 23.

—— Release of claims on the church
of, by Rob., Treasurer of Besançon,
*c.* 1253 (Prestewold). Harl. 45 H. 47.

—— Payment by Bullington Priory
on a fine in, 1254. Harl. 55 A. 11.

—— Exchanges in, by Bullington
Priory, *t.* Hen. III.–*t.* Edw. I. Cott.
v. 56, xxviii. 95, Harl. 48 H. 34, 49 F.
50, 55 A. 25.

—— Fine, etc., of the advowson to
Bullington Priory, 1287. Harl. 58 G.
9 ;—late 13 cent. Harl. 55 A. 38.

—— Conff. of rights of Bullington
Priory in St. Andrew's church, 1389.
Harl. 43 G. 32 ;—1399. Harl. 43 I.
3 ;—1485. Harl. 43 I. 13.

—— *Advocatus ecclesie.* Phil. de
Kima, late Hen. II. Harl. 44 H. 53.

—— *Capellanus.* Hanctinus *al.* Au-
ketillus, *t.* John. Harl. 46 A. 37, 55
A. 21, 22 ;—early 13 cent. Harl. 44
F. 19.

—— —— Martinus, *t.* John. Harl.
44 A. 31, 45 C. 39, 47 I. 48, 55 A. 22.

—— —— Robertus, *t.* John. Harl.
44 A. 31-34, 45 C. 39, 54 I. 28.

—— —— Walkelinus, early 13 cent.
Harl. 46 E. 32.

—— —— Radulphus, early 13 cent.
Harl. 46 E. 32;—*t.* Hen. III. Cott.
xxviii. 107.

—— *Persona.* Ric. de S. Petro, late
Hen. II. Harl. 44 H. 53.

—— —— Anketinus *al.* Anketillus,
*t.* John. Harl. 44 A. 31-34, 45 C. 39,
54 I. 28 ;—early 13 cent. Harl. 46 E.
32 ;—(as *Rector*), 1217. Harl. 45 A. 25.

—— —— Godefridus, early 13 cent.
Harl. 46 E. 32, Cott. v. 80.

*v. also* Cotes, *co. Leic.*

*v. also* Hoton, *co. Leic.*

Prestwood, *co. Staff.* Exemplif. of
Crown grant of the manor, 1610. Harl.
83 H. 28.

Priddleton, *nr. Docklow, co. Heref.*
Grant in, 1654 (Prittleton). Add. 1953.

Priddy, *co. Som.* Grant in, to Farley
Priory, [1174-91] (Pridi). Campb.
xiii. 12.

—— Grant in, to Bruerne Abbey, *c.*
1180-90 (Pridia). Harl. 51 E. 29.

**Priddy,** *co. Som. (continued).* Fine with St. Swithin's Priory, Winchester, conc. common of pasture in, 1236 (Pridie). Add. 6521 (*copy*).

—— License to alienate and assignment of Crown lease in, 1567. Lansd. 675 (Prydye al. Predye);—1572. Harl. 79 F. 31 (Prodie).

**Priestcliffe,** *co. Derb.* Grant in, *t.* Edw. II. (Presteclove). Add. 8073.

**Priesthorpe,** *nr. Calverley, co. York.* Grants, etc., in, *t.* Edw. I. Add. 16728 (Presthorp), 16740; — 1310. Add. 16763;—1392. Harl. 45 F. 28;—1398. Add. 16885.

—— Award in, 1487 (Presthorp). Add. 16967.

**Priests way, The.** *v. sub* Offington, *in Broadwater, co. Suss.*

**Princes Risborough.** *v.* Risborough, Princes, *co. Buck.*

**Prioris Heredwyk.** *v.* Hardwick, Priors, *co. Warw.*

**Prioris Marston.** *v.* Marston, Priors, *co. Warw.*

**Priors Dean.** *v.* Dean, Priors, *co. Southt.*

**Priors Lee.** *v.* Lee, Priors, *co. Salop.*

**Priors, Newton.** *v.* Newton Priors, *co. Devon.*

**Priory Manor.** *v. sub* Hintlesham, *co. Suff.*

**Priston,** *co. Som.* Fine, etc., of Wilmington (Wylmyndon, Wilmyngdon) manor in, 1329. Eg. 260;—1363. Eg. 286.

—— Grant of next presentation to the rectory, 1530 (Preston). Add. 5478.

—— Extract from halimote court-roll of the manor, bel. to Bath Abbey, 1533 (Prysheton). Add. 5477.

—— Crown-lease of the site of the manor, etc., 1551 (Preston). Add. 5480.

—— Presentation of David Appowell, as Rector, 1554. Add. 5479.

—— Extract from roll of court-baron of, bel. to R. Longe, 1614. Add. 5484.

**Prittleton.** *v.* Priddleton, *nr. Docklow, co. Heref.*

**Prittlewell,** *co. Essex.* Grants, etc., in, 1260–1. Harl. 48 I. 47 (Pritelewell);—1287–8. Harl. 57 E. 29 (Pritewell); — 1345. Add. 15459 (Pritelwell);—1385. Cott. xxviii. 96; —1564. Harl. 79 G. 20.

**Prittlewell,** *co. Essex (continued).* Compotus of the manor, 1515 [Pirtewelle]. Add. 215.

—— Precipes on covenants conc. lands in, 1561. Add. 24931 (Pryklewell), 24989 (Prytwell);—1587. Add. 24988.

**Promhell, Promhull.** *v.* Broomhill, *cos. Kent and Suss.*

**Prothether,** *nr. Llanddewi Velfrey, co. Heref.* Grants, etc., in, 1409. Add. 1323 (Portheadreth);—1411. Add. 1325 (Porthedre);—1419. Add. 1326, 1327 (do.);—1534. Add. 1346 (Portheder);—1548. Add. 1353 (Porthether);—1565. Add. 1831 (Portheder).

**Protrarne.** *v.* Portraine, *co. Dubl.*

**Provender,** *co. Suss.* Settlement in, 1605. Add. 18899.

**Prudhoe,** *co. Northumb.* Lease in Hedley, in return for a day's reaping at, etc., [1222–45] (Prudh.). Harl. 57 D. 6.

—— Grant of the constableship of the castle to Sir R. Ogle, 1461. Cott. xvii. 17.

**Pryorsden.** *v.* Dean, Priors, *co. Southt.*

**Publow,** *co. Som.* Conveyance in Woollard (Wolwade) in, 1405. Harl. 46 G. 43.

**Puckeridge,** *in Braughin, co. Hertf.* Bond for rent in, 1343 (Pokerich). Harl. 46 F. 14.

**Puddington** *al.* **Podington,** *co. Devon.* Order for an extent of the manor, 1301 (Potinton). Add. 19302.

**Puddlestone,** *co. Heref.* Brief for rebuilding the church, 1809. Ch. Br. B. l. 1.

**Pudegesaia.** *v.* Pudsey, *co. York.*

**Pudele Trentehyde.** *v.* Piddle Trenthide, *co. Dors.*

**Pudeleton.** *v.* Piddletown, *co. Dors.*

**Pudlicot,** *nr. Charlbury, co. Oxon.* Compotus, 1447–8 (Pudlecote). Harl. Roll C. 2.

**Pudsey,** *nr. Ashingdon, co. Essex.* Grant in, *t.* Hen. III. (Pudesheia). Harl. 54 H. 54.

**Pudsey,** *co. York.* Grants in Barcroft (Berecroft, Bercroft) in, early 13 cent. Add. 16582, 16585;—*t.* Edw. I. Add. 16698;—1372. Add. 16829.

**Purley,** *co. Berks.* Covenant for warranty of lands in Lit. Purley, 1315 (Petit Purle, *on back*). Add. 20850.

—— Suit for Gt. Purley manor, etc., 1398. Add. 23785; — 1451. Add. 23864 ;—1454. Add. 23865 ;—1455. Add. 23866.

—— Power for seisin of Lit. Purley manor, etc., 1424. Add. 20270 ;—1451. Add. 20317.

—— Valor of N. Carrew's manor of, [1440]. Add. 23023.

—— Settlement of the manor, 1514. Add. 23411, 23412.

**Purley,** *in Sanderstead, co. Surr.* Grant in, 1373. Add. 24614.

—— Feoffments, etc., of W. Purley (Westpirley, Westpurle, etc.), 1445. Add. 24621-24623; — 1452. Add. 24624 ;—1471. Add. 24615, 24625-24630 ;—1472. Add. 24631 ;—1537. Add. 24632 ; — 1555, 1558. Add. 24633 a, b.

—— Lease of E. Purley (Est Pirle) manor, 1447. Add. 23654.

—— Inspex. of proceedings in a suit for W. Purley, 1472. Add. 24631.

**Purton.** *v.* Pirton, *co. Oxon.*

**Purton,** *co. Wilts.* Grant of the manor, 1299 (Pyrryton). Harl. 52 C. 54, 55.

—— Expenses of the churchwardens in a law suit, 1674. Harl. Roll AA. 24.

**Purye.** *v. sub* Bentley, *co. Southt.*

**Pushull.** *v.* Pishill, *co. Oxon.*

**Pusterves.** *v. sub* Brede, *co. Suss.*

**Putfold.** *v.* Pitfold, *in Frensham, co. Surr.*

**[Putford, East,** *co. Devon].* Settlement in Wedfield (Wydefyld) in (?), 1430. Add. 13052.

**Putley,** *co. Heref. Rector.* Will. de la Hulle, 1373. Harl. 111 F. 49 ;—1376. Harl. 112 B. 56.

**Putnell,** *nr. Cannington, co. Som.* Refeoffment in, 1421 (Potenhall). Add. 15845.

**Puttelesfeld.** *v. sub* Addington, *co. Surr.*

**Putteneye, Putteneye Lorty, Putteneye et Werne.** *v.* Pitney, *co. Som.*

**Puttenham,** *co. Surr.* Lease of wardship of Puttenham Bury, P. Prior and Sholand manors, etc., 1567. Harl. 111 E. 25.

**Putteridge Bury.** *v. sub* Lilley, *co. Hertf.*

**Putteworth.** *v.* Petworth, *co. Suss.*

**Puttukes Herdewik.** *v.* Hardwick, Puttocks, *co. Hunt.*

**Puxley,** *co. Northt.* Grants in, early 13 cent. Slo. xxxii. 17 (Pokel.), Harl. 85 B. 9 (Pokesleia), 86 D. 4 (Pokeslo).

**Pychelesthorne, Pychesthorne.** *v.* Pitstone, *co. Buck.*

**Pyckworthe.** *v.* Pickworth, *co. Rutl.*

**Pyecombe,** *co. Suss.* Power for assignment of the manor to Edw. II., 1316 (Picoumbe). Harl. 57 E. 33.

**Pyenest, The,** *in Upshire.* *v. sub* Waltham H. Cross, *co. Essex.*

**Pyghtesle, Pyghteslay.** *v.* Pitchley, *co. Northt.*

**Pygotts.** *v. sub* Elmdon, *co. Essex.*

**Pykeham.** *v. sub* Guestling, *co. Suss.*

**Pykenham, North, Suth.** *v.* Pickenham, N. and S., *co. Norf.*

**Pykeworth.** *v.* Pickworth, *co. Linc.*

**Pyleooc.** *v.* Thornham Magna, *co. Suff.*

**Pylkynton.** *v.* Pilton, *co. Northt.*

**Pympre.** *v.* Pimperne, *co. Dors.*

**Pynessonestede.** *v. sub* Bilney, *co. Norf.*

**Pynhay.** *v.* Pinhay, *co. Devon.*

**Pynkenes.** *v. sub* Tattersett, *co. Norf.*

**Pynkeston, Pynxston.** *v.* Pinxton, *co. Derb.*

**Pynmore,** *co. Northumb.* Attornment in, 1348. Harl. 54 C. 12.

**Pynnore.** *v.* Pinner, *co. Midd.*

**Pyrcombe.** *v.* Purcombe, *nr. Whitchurch Canonicorum, co. Dors.*

**Pyrford,** *co. Surr.* Grant of the "fundus" of, by Will. I. to Westminster Abbey, 1067 (Piriford). Cott. vi. 3 (*copy*).

—— Grants, etc., in, late Hen. III. Add. 26610 (Piriford) ;—1305. Add. 26614 (Puriford) ;—1353. Add. 26631 ;—1361. Add. 26633 (Pyriford) ;—1362. Add. 26634 ;—1414. Add. 26645 (Puryford) ; —1452. Add. 26666 ;—1472. Add. 26669 ; — 1497. Add. 26679 ;—1498. Add. 26680.

**Pyriae.** *v.* Pirie, *co. Worc.*

**Pyritune, Pyrton.** *v.* Pirton, *co. Worc.*

Pyrton, Pyryton. *v.* Pirton, *co. Hertf.*

Pyrye. *v. sub* Shorne, *co. Kent.*

Pyryton. *v.* Purton, *co. Wilts.*

Pytlond. *v.* Pitland, *in Whitchurch Hundred, co. Dors.*

Pytte. *v. sub* Whitchurch Canonicorum, *co. Dors.*

Pytteney, Pytteney Lorti, Pytteney Werne. *v.* Pitney, *co. Som.*

Pyvintone. *v.* Pevington, *co. Kent.*


## Q

Quadring, *co. Linc.* Conveyance in, 1393 (Quadryng). Harl. 57 E. 22.

—— Precipe on a covenant conc. lands in, 1578. Add. 25070.

Quainton, *co. Buck.* Conf. by Hen. II., to Notley Abbey, of the hermitage of Fiuemere nr., etc., [1179?]. Harl. Roll O. 26 (3).

—— Fine in, 1252 (Queinton). Harl. 46 F. 44.

Qualmstowe. *v. sub* Stowmarket, *co. Suff.*

Quantock, *co. Som.* Grant in, 1311 (Cantok). Add. 25874.

Quantock Hills, *co. Som.* Covenant on a suit for waste on, as bel. to W. Bagborough or Bps. Lydiard manors, 1314 (Mons de Cantok). Add. 25875.

Quarley, *co. Southt.* Conf. of lands in, to Bec Herlewin Abbey, 1219 (Cornel.). Toph. 45.

—— *Persona.* Johannes, 1219. Toph. 45.

Quarndon, *co. Derb.* Defeasance of grant in, 1384 (Quarundon). Add. 5241.

Quarnford, *co. Staff.* Briefs for rebuilding the chapel, 1794, 1812. Ch. Br. B. xxxv. 1, liii. 9.

Quarum, North and South, *in Exton, co. Som.* Grants, etc., in, *t.* Edw. I. Add. 25896 (N. Quarme, Suth Quarme);—1305. Add. 25895 (N. Quarme);—1354. Add. 25897 (N. Quarme Mounciaux);—1355. Add. 25898 (do.);—1428. Add. 25899 (Quarme); — 1470. Add. 25900 (Quaram Frome).

Quatcote. *v.* Whatcote, *co. Warw.*

Quatford. *v. sub* Redmarley Dabitot, *co. Worc.*

Quatford, *co. Salop.* Grant in, by James I., 1612. Cott. xiii. 35.

—— *Capellanus.* Willelmus, 1349. Add. 7916.

Quedgley, *co. Glouc.* Grant in Woolstrope (Woluestrop) in, late Hen. III. Harl. 79 A. 32.

Queen Hoo, *in or nr. Tewin, co. Hertf.* Fine in, 1313 (Qwenhawe). Add. 6245.

Queenborough, *co. Kent.* Accompts for stores for, 1548. Lansd. Roll 14.

Queenhill, *co. Worc.* Leases in, 1543. Add. 15272;—1546. Add. 15273;—1580. Add. 15275.

Queen's County, *Ireland.* Lease in, by the Company for making Hollow Sword Blades, 1704. Add. 24474.

Queinton. *v.* Quainton, *co. Buck.*

Queinton, *co. Glouc. Rector.* Tho. de la Morehall, *t.* Rich. II. Add. 20424.

Querdon. *v.* Quorndon, *co. Leic.*

Querendon, Queryndon. *v. sub* Corscombe, *co. Dors.*

Querle. *v. sub* Woodham Walter, *co. Essex.*

Querondon, Queryndon. *v.* Quorndon, *co. Leic.*

Querstede. *v.* Wherstead, *co. Suff.*

Quiddenham, *co. Norf.* Grant in, to Reading Abbey, *c.* 1180. Add. 19603, 19604.

—— Grants, etc., in, 1362. Add. 14515 (Quydenham);—1374. Harl. 49 C. 15 (Quidenham);—1578. Add. 18862.

—— *Capellanus.* Nigellus, 1253 (Quydeham). Campb. ix. 9 (11) (*copy*).

Quidhampton, *co. Wilts.* Fines of the manor, etc., 1585. Add. 15150;—1586. Add. 15154;—1612. Add. 15152;—1613. Add. 15155.

Quineberge. *v.* Whinbergh, *co. Norf.*

Quinton, *co. Northt.* Conf. of the church to St. Andrew's Priory, Northampton, [1148–66] (Quentona). Harl. 48 H. 11.

—— Conveyance, etc., in, 1349. Harl. 57 C. 27 (Quenton);—1438. Add. 22564.

—— Agreement on sale of the manor, 1649. Add. 739.

—— *Persona.* Henricus, 1353. Add. 22177.

Rand, co. *Linc.* (*continued*). Grant of advowson of St. Oswald's church to Bullington Priory, 1461 (Raudde). Harl. 58 B. 22.

—— - *Sacerdos.* Willelmus, 1165. Cott. xxvii. 195 ;—*t.* Hen. II. Harl. 44 A. 21, 54 I. 31.

Randby, co. *Linc.* Grant of Halimilhne mill in, to Tupholme Abbey, *ante* 1166 (Randeby). Harl. 58 H. 4 (*copy*).

Randes Marsh, *nr. Barking,* co. *Essex.* Sale in, 1583. Harl. 79 O. 47.

Randistone. *v.* Thrandeston, co. *Suff.*

Ranecombe, Rankham. *v. sub* Pembury, co. *Kent.*

Ranfeld. *v.* Ravenfield, co. *York.*

Ranglas. *v.* Ravenglas, co. *Cumb.*

Rankedich. *v. sub* Arlsey, co. *Bedf.*

Ranscombe. *v. sub* Sherford, co. *Devon.*

Ranton. *v.* Ronton, co. *Staff.*

Rapetun. *v. sub* Ashford, co. *Kent.*

Rapsgate Hundred, co. *Glouc.* Grant of rent from, 1634 (Respegate). Add. 18391.

Rapton, co. *Suff.* Grant, etc., in, to Sibton Abbey, [1157–63 ?]. Campb. xxiii. 5 (Wrabet.);—late 12 cent. Harl. 84 A. 10 (Wrabetun).

Rasen, East *al.* Market, co. *Linc.* Grants of the church to H. Trinity Priory, York, *c.* 1150. Add. 11292 (6) (Rasa), (7) (Magna Rasna).

—— Grants in (?), early 13 cent. Harl. 54 B. 28 (Rasa), 54 E. 54 (do.).

—— Fine of the manor, 1250 (Estrasne). Harl. 58 C. 27.

—— Lease, etc., in, 1340. Add. 8391 (Estrasen) ;—1371. Harl. 57 B. 82 (Estrasyn) ;—1396. Harl. Roll G. 28 (Est Rasyn) ;—1478. Harl. 57 G. 34 (do.) ;—1576. Harl. 79 F. 37.

—— Inquisition conc. liberties of the manor, 1386 (Estrasyn). Harl. 58 F. 14.

—— *Clericus.* Thomas, early 13 cent. (Rasen). Harl. 51 B. 21.

—— (?) *Presbiter.* Willelmus, late Hen. II. (Rasne). Harl. 50 C. 23.

Rasen, Middle, co. *Linc.* Lease, etc., in, 1242. Harl. 51 C. 39 (Media Rasen); — 1371. Harl. 57 B. 32 (Media Rasyn) ; — 1529. Eg. 481 (Midill Rasyn).

Rasen, Middle, co. *Linc.* (*continued*). Papal conf. of the church to Drax Priory, 1251 (Media Rasne). Add. 21095.

Raskelf, *in Easingwold par.,* co. *York.* Grant of, 1318 (Clausum de Raschelf). Harl. 112 B. 49.

Ratby, co. *Leic.* Brief for rebuilding the church, 1764. Ch. Br. B. iv. 2.

Ratcliffe Culey, co. *Leic.* Grants, etc., in, 1426. Harl. 76 G. 45 (Radeclyf juxta Wetherley);—1434. Harl. 77 F. 14;—1544. Harl. 76 H. 46, 79 A. 42;—1549. Harl. 76 H. 53.

Ratcliffe on Trent, co. *Nott.* Grant of a rent-charge on the rectory to Shelford Priory, *c.* 1224–40 (Radeclive). Campb. xi. 3, 4.

—— Exchequer acquittance for farm of the site of the manor, 1596. Add. 25636.

—— Covenant for recovery of the manor and rectory, 1624. Add. 26019; —1641. Add. 26021.

—— *Rector.* Gerardus, *c.* 1224–40. Campb. xi. 3, 4.

Ratcliffe upon Soar, co. *Nott.* Conf. of the church to Norton Priory, *t.* Rich. I. (Radcelive super Soram). Cott. MS. Nero C. iii. f. 174.

Rathcoffy Castle, co. *Kildare.* Petition conc. abduction of Anne Wogan from, 1454. Cott. iv. 35.

Rathcore, co. *Meath.* Grant of interest in the town of, 1576 (Rathcourt). Harl. 86 G. 47.

Rathduffe, co. *Carlow.* Lease of the lands, etc., of, 1697. Add. 24472.

Ratheby. *v.* Raithby, co. *Linc.*

Ratheram. *v.* Rotherham, co. *York.*

Rathmore, co. *Kildare.* Dispute conc. the manor, 1454. Cott. iv. 35.

Ratley, co. *Warw.* Grant in, to Stoneleigh Abbey, *t.* Hen. II. (Rotteleia). Harl. 45 C. 47.

Rattlesden, co. *Suff.* Grant in Aldwick in, *t.* Hen. III. Harl. 45 G. 12.

—— Grant in, 1393 (Ratlesden). Harl. 48 F. 55.

Rauceby, North, co. *Linc.* Release in, 1530. Add. 6488 (N. Rausby), 6495 (N. Rawsby).

—— (?) *Clericus.* Willelmus, *t.* Rich. I. (Roucebi). Add. 20625.

Raynaldtorp. *v. sub* Thorpe Salvin, co. York.

Rayne, co. *Essex.* Conf. by Edw. the Confessor of a grant in, to Westminster Abbey, 1066 [sc. 1065] (Reine). Cott. vi. 2 (copy).

—— Grant of, by Hen. II., [1174 ?] (Reines). Add. 15577.

—— Settlement of the manor and advowson, etc., 1338. Add. 6181 (Parva Reynes) ;—1417. Add. 6183 (Parva Reygne).

—— Grants, etc., in, 1378. Add. 6182 ; — 1446. Add. 6185 (Parva Reynes) :—1474. Add. 6186 ;—1526. Add. 6187 ;—1548. Add. 6188 ;—1549. Add. 6189.

—— Power to give seisin of Old Hall manor in, 1435. Add. 6184.

Rayneham. *v.* Rainham, co. *Kent.*

Raynham. *v.* Rainham, co. *Essex.*

Raynpatric. *v.* Redpatrick, co. *Dumfries.*

Read. *v. sub* Marden, co. *Kent.*

Reada beorg. Grant near a tumulus called, 755–757. Cott. viii. 3.

Reading, co. *Berks.* Bequest of land at, late 10 cent. (at Readingan). Harl. 43 C. 4.

—— Grant of the church of, by Will. I. to Battle Abbey, [1086-7] (de Radingia). Harl. 83 A. 12.

—— Grant, by Hen. I., of Appledram, co. Suss., to Battle Abbey in exchange for, c. 1121 (Rading.). Campb. xvi. 13.

—— Charters of Matilda the Empress dated at, [1140-1 ?] (do.). Add. 19578 ; —[1141 ?]. Add. 19576 (do.).

—— Charter of King Stephen dated at, c. 1140-50 (do.). Add. 19582.

—— General conf. of, by Hen. II., with its churches to Reading Abbey, [1157 ?] (Radingia). Add. 19591.

—— Grants in, by the Abbot of Reading, [1173–80] (Rading.). Add. 19601, 19602.

—— Grant of the profits of St. Laurence's chapel to St. Laurence's hospital in, [1190-93] (do.). Add. 19611.

—— Grants, etc., in, c. 1230. Add. 20250 (Rading.) ;—1350. Cott. xxvii. 117 (Radyng.) ;—1379. Harl. 48 I. 17 (Radyng.) ;—1396. Harl. 56 I. 15 (Redyng.) :—1403. Add. 24697 (do.) ; —1405. Harl. 45 G. 44, Add. 26407 ; —1433, 1434. Add. 26408 ;—1465. Add. 26410 ;—1470. Add. 26083 :—

1478. Add. 26411 ; — 1483. Add. 26087 ;—1493. Harl. 44 H. 55 ;— 1506. Add. 26412 ; — 1510. Add. 26413, 26414 ;—1693. Add. 19285.

—— Certif. of proceedings in chancery with Reading Abbey, 1390. Add. 19644.

—— License for services in the oratory of the new hospice in London Street, 1410. Add. 19648.

—— Fines in, 1635. Add. 19217 ;— 1636. Add. 19218 ;—1649. Add. 19222 ; —1695. Add. 19237 ;—1742. Add. 19251 :—1764. Add. 19254.

—— Roll of rents payable for charities in, 1656. Add. 25982.

—— Recital of covenants conc. loans to the trustees of highways nr., 1731. Add. 19250.

—— *Prepositi* (?). Warinus, Walterus, [1172-80]. Add. 19602.

—— *Major.* Petr. Croft, 1350. Cott. xxvii. 117.

—— —— Tho. Smyth, 1379. Harl. 48 I. 17.

—— —— (*nuper*). David Hacche, 1387. Add. 19644.

—— —— Will. Skariere, 1396. Harl. 56 I. 15.

—— —— Ric. Clover al. Glover, 1405. Harl. 45 G. 44, Add. 26407.

—— —— Rob. Morys, 1433. Add. 26408.

—— —— Tho. Swayne, 1434. Add. 26409.

—— —— Tho. Clerke, 1465. Add. 26410.

—— —— Will. Rede, 1470. Add. 26083.

—— —— Will. Lynacre, 1478. Add. 26411.

—— — —— Steph. Dunstere, 1483. Add. 26087.

—— —— Rich. Allright, 1656. Add. 25982.

—— *Ballivi.* Joh. Heued, Rob. Warde, 1379. Harl. 48 I. 17.

—— —— Nic. Barbour, Ric. Farle, 1433, 1434. Add. 26408, 26409.

—— —— Will. Blewett, Joh. Brode, 1465. Add. 26410 ; — 1470. Add. 26083.

—— —— Joh. Derlyng, Hen. Justice, 1478. Add. 26411.

—— *Constabularii.* Joh. Upstone, Hen. Kyng, 1465. Add. 26410.

2 R 2

**Redgrave,** *co. Suff. (continued).* *Persona.* Will. de la Rokele, 1361. Harl. 55 E. 4.

**Redham.** *v.* Reedham. *co. Norf.*

**Redisham,** *co. Suff.* Grant, etc., in, early 14 cent. Harl. 48 G. 13 (Redesham);—1476. Add. 10074.

—— Grant, etc., of the manor, 1435. Cott. v. 3, 22 (Redesham);—1496. Harl. 50 F. 37, 38 (do.).

—— Precipe on a covenant conc. land in, 1564 (Redsham). Add. 25318.

**Redisham, Little,** *co. Suff.* Release of the manor, 1395. Add. 15752.

**Redisl., Redisleye.** *v.* Rodaley, *in Longford, co. Derb.*

**Redlees,** *nr. Alwinton, co. Northumb.* Grant in, *t.* Edw. II. (Reddeleys). Harl. 58 G. 22.

**Redleye.** *v.* Rodley, *co. Glouc.*

**Redlingfield,** *co. Suff.* Acquittances for rent in, 1380-95 (Rydlingfeld, etc.). Add. 5500-5508.

—— Settlement in, 1510. Add. 5515.

**Redmarley D'Abitot,** *co. Worc.* Grants, etc., in, early Hen. III. Slo. xxxiii. 6 (Rudmerlee);—1322. Add. 24756 (Rudmarleye);—1323. Add. 24757 (Bydmereleye), Slo. xxxiii. 20 (Rudmarleye);— 1324. Slo. xxxiii. 21;—1327. Add. 24760 (Rodmerleye); —1330. Slo. xxxiii. 22;—1331. Slo. xxxiii. 12;—1335. Add. 24761;— 1345. Slo. xxxiii. 28 (Rudemarley Dabitot), 29 ;—1346. Slo. xxxiii. 30 ;— 1347. Slo. xxxiii. 32;— 1348 (?). Slo. xxxiii. 87 *b*;—1348-9. Slo. xxxiii. 35;—1349. Slo. xxxiii. 33, 34;—1352. Slo. xxxiii. 37;—1357. Slo. xxxiii. 39;—1359. Add. 24764;—1365. Slo. xxxiii. 41;—1378. Slo. xxxiii. 44;— 1382. Add. 24766;—1385. Slo. xxxiii. 87 *a*;—1389. Slo. xxxiii. 49;—1392. Add. 24768;—1403. Slo. xxxiii. 53; —1405. Slo. xxxiii. 54, 55;—1410. Slo. xxxiii. 57;—1412. Slo. xxxiii. 58;— 1418. Slo. xxxiii. 62, 63;— 1419. Add. 24770;—1457. Slo. xxxiii. 70;— 1479. Add. 24780;— 1497. Add. 24783, 24784;— 1502. Add. 24785, 24786;—1530. Slo. xxxiii. 81; —1568. Add. 24793;—1593. Add. 24795, 24796, 24797;—1613. Add. 24799;—1645. Add. 24800;—1688. Add. 23856-23858.

—— Grant nr. Quatford in, 1302. Add. 24753.

**Redmarley D'Abitot,** *co. Worc. (continued).* Grant of Assedene in, 1325. Add. 24758.

—— Lease in Haselden, etc., in, 1356. Add. 24763.

—— Grant, etc., in Inardestone *al.* Inarstone, Innarston in, 1380. Slo. xxxiii. 48 ;—1426. Slo. xxxiii. 64 ;— 1433. Add. 24771.

—— Grant in Payford in, 1413. Add. 24769.

—— Release, etc., in Morehelde *ende al.* Morellynde in, 1459. Add. 24775 ;— 1502. Add. 24785, 24786.

—— Writ to bind over to keep the peace in, 1518. Add. 24788.

—— Sale, etc., of Thurbach mill in, 1549. Add. 24789, 24790; — 1556. Add. 24791, 24792; — 1568. Add. 24794.

—— *Persona.* Will. Hoke, 1431. Slo. xxxiii. 65.

—— *Rector.* Rob. Amyas, 1365. Slo. xxxiii. 41.

—— —— Geo. Savage, 1502. Add. 24786.

**Rednall,** *co. Worc.* Grant at, to Bredon monastery, 780 (æt Wreodanhale). Cott. MS. Aug. ii. 30.

**Redpatrick,** *co. Dumfr.* Conf. of grant of the church to Gisburne Priory, *t.* Edw. I. (Raynpatric). Cott. xi. 58, Harl. 43 B. 12.

**Redwalls** [Fagwyr Goch, *in Morvill* ?], *co. Pembr.* Grant in, *t.* Hen. III. (Reddewalles). Add. 8408.

**Redwick,** *co. Monm.* Release, etc., in, 1581. Add. 9389 ;—1597. Add. 9413.

**Redyng.** *v.* Reading, *co. Berks.*

**Reedham,** *co. Norf.* Grant in or nr., *t.* Rich. I.-John. Harl. 51 D. 50 (Redham);—*t.* Hen. III. Add. 14824.

—— Compotus-rolls of the manor, 1377-95, 1444-5. Add. 26852-26863 ; —1461-1471. Add. 26864.

- —— Bequest to the church, 1482 (Redham). Add. 17253.

—— Settlement to uses of the manor, advowson, etc., 1646. Add. 19160.

**Reedinges.** *v.* Reading Street, *in Ebony, co. Kent.*

**Reedness,** *in Whitgift, co. York.* Inspex. of covenants with Selby Abbey conc. tithes, etc., in, 1293 (Redneswe). Harl. 111 C. 21.

**Richmond,** *Honour of.* Conf. by P. de Sabaudia, as "Dominus Honoris," of a grant in co. Suff. to Rumburgh Priory, 1242. Campb. ix. 9 (5, 6) (*copies*).

**Richmonds.** *v. sub* Thaxted, *co. Essex.*

**Richmond's lands.** *v. sub* Dartford, *co. Kent.*

**Richtona.** *v.* Reighton, *co. York.*

**Ricingahaam,** *co. Essex.* Grant of, to Barking Abbey, 692–3. Cott. MS. Aug. ii. 29.

**Rickinghall Inferior,** *co. Suff.* Grant of a marsh, etc., in, by Bury St. Edmunds Abbey. [1257–79] (Rikinghale). Add. 7211.

—— Grants, etc., in, *t.* Hen. III. Harl. 50 E. 39 (Rikinghale Inferior);—1339. Harl. 51 F. 21 (Rykynghale Inf.);—1378. Harl. 46 A. 19 (Neyerykynghale);—1387. Harl. 51 D. 52 (Rikynghale Inf.);—1407. Harl. 58 D.. 22 (do.);—1416. Add. 9692 (Netherrekynghal).

**Rickinghall Superior,** *co. Suff.* Grant in, nr. Ashcroft (Aciescroft), etc., late Hen. III. (Rikinghal). Harl. 52 I. 39.

—— (Rikingehall, Rykynghale, Over-Rykinghale, etc.). Grants, etc., in, *t.* Hen. III. Harl. 50 C. 54;—1316–7. Harl. 49 B. 51;—1328. Harl. 48 C. 22;—1346. Harl. 57 F. 42;—1352. Harl. 51 D. 51;—1361. Harl. 51 F. 13;—1378. Harl. 46 A. 19;—1385. Harl. 51 F. 37;—1387. Harl. 51 D. 52;—1391. Harl. 53 D. 22;—1407. Harl. 58 D. 22, 43;—1412. Harl. 56 B. 41;—1444. Harl. 46 A. 20.

—— Covenant conc. Facon's Hall manor in, 1501. Add. 16570, 16571.

**Rickmansworth,** *co. Hertf.* Grants, etc., in, *t.* Edw. I. Add. 17362 (Rykamereswrthe);—1425. Harl. 56 B. 9 (Rikmansworth);—1439–40. Harl. 85 E. 45 (Rikmeresworth).

—— Rental of Micklefield (Mukelfeld) manor in, bel. to St. Albans Abbey, 1350. Add. 26831.

—— Extracts from court-roll of Moore (More) manor in, 1459. Add. 7166, 7167.

—— *Capellanus.* Adam, *t.* John (Rikemereswrth). Harl. 86 A. 56.

**Ridden, Little.** *v. sub* Marden, *co. Kent.*

**Ridel,** *Fee of.* *v. sub* St. Osyth, *co. Essex.*

**Ridelestun.** *v.* Redelestun, *co. Devon* (?).

**Ridge,** *in Chilmark, co. Wilts.* Courtrolls, 1558–9, 1567. Add. 24440, 24441.

**Ridgwell,** *co. Essex.* Release in, 1322 (Radeswell). Harl. 47 D. 52.

—— Appointment of a steward of the manor, 1371 (Rodeswell). Lansd. 1³².

**Ridinghurst.** *v. sub* Cranley, *co. Surr.*

**Ridley,** *co. Kent.* Lease, etc., of the advowson by St. Mary Graces Abbey, London, 1536. Toph. 2; — 1543. Campb. xxiv. 1 (Redley).

**Ridlington,** *co. Norf.* Grants, etc., in, early 13 cent. Harl. 49 G. 21 (Redelingtun); — 1335. Cott. xxix. 27 (Rydlingtone);—1403. Harl. 49 G. 45 (Redlyngton);—1405. Harl. 58 B. 19;—1554. Harl. 51 E. 21.

—— Extent of the lands of Tho. Roscelyn in, 1352 (Redelyngton). Harl. 55 E. 33.

**Ridware, Hamstall,** *co. Staff.* Grant of annuity on the manor, 1341 (Rideware Hamstall). Add. 20460.

**Ridware, Mavesyn,** *co. Staff.* Brief for rebuilding the church, 1780. Ch. Br. B. xx. 9.

**Riehul.** *v. sub* Charnwood Forest, *co. Leic.*

**Riehulla.** *v. sub* Peperharow, *co. Surr.*

**Rievaulx,** *co. York.* Grant of the manor, 1650. Add. 1800.

**Righton.** *v.* Reighton, *co. York.*

**Rigsby** (Riggesbi, etc.), *co. Linc.* Grants, with conf., of Wlfrichag, etc., in, to Greenfield Priory, c. 1150. Harl. 55 D. 11;—c. 1155. Harl. 43 G. 21, 43 H. 19;—t. Hen. II. Harl. 45 B. 41 (Rigesbi), 45 C. 3 (Righesbi), 5, 55 D. 12 (Riggbesbia), 13; — [1175?]. Harl. 43 C. 21;—late 12 cent. Harl. 45 C. 6;—[1189–95]. Harl. 43 H. 22; —[1203–6]. Harl. 43 H. 25;— early 13 cent. Cott. xxvii. 51, Harl. 55 D. 14;—t. Hen. III. Harl. 55 D. 15;—1392. Cott. xxvii. 5 (Riggesby), Harl. 43 E. 36, 43 I. 47.

—— Settlement of tithes from lands in the fee of, 1220 (Riggesbi). Harl. 57 F. 51.

—— Grants in, late Hen. III. (Rigesby). Harl. 56 C. 22, 23.

Rigsby (Riggesbi, etc.), co. Linc. (continued). Homage of Prioresses of Greenfield in, 1327, 1332 (Ryggesby). Hurl. Roll K. 36.

—— Conveyance in, [1361–8] (do.). Harl. 55 B. 24.

—— Sacerdos. Julianus, late Hen. II. Harl. 54 B. 23.

Rigton, co. York. Sale of the manor, 1637. Add. 1797.

Rihale. v. Ryhall, co. Rutl.

Rikinghale, etc. v. Rickinghall, Inferior and Superior, co. Suff.

Rikmersworth, Rikmansworth. v. Rickmansworth, co. Hertf.

Riley. v. sub Eyam, co. Derb.

Rill. v. sub Payhembury, co. Devon.

Rimecuda [Ringwood, co. Southt.?]. Grant at, by K. Eadgar to Abingdon Monastery, 961. Cott. MS. Aug. ii. 39.

Rimswell, co. York. Grant of a "nativus" of, to Beverley College, late Hen. II. (Rimeswell). Lansd. 410.

—— Release, etc., of the manor, 1430. Harl. 43 E. 19 (Rymeswell);—1431. Harl. 45 I. 12. 50 H. 27, 28, 54 I. 15;—1435. Add. 2016.

Rindburna, co. Glouc. or Worc. Boundary of a grant "æt Onnanforda," 759, Add. 19789.

Rindecumbe, Vuere. v. Rendcomb, Over, co. Glouc.

Ringham, Fee of, co. Berks. Release to Alan. de Englefeld of lands bel. to, early Hen. III. Add. 19142.

Ringhouses, co. York. Grant of the manor, 1510 (Rynghowses). Roy. Roll 14 B. xviii.

Ringmer, co. Suss. Fines in, 1412 (Ryngmere). Add. 24895;—1457. Add. 24903.

Ringmore (?), co. Devon. Notif. of grant of knts. fees, called "feoda de Rydmore," 1333. Harl. 46 A. 13.

Ringsfield, co. Suff. Grants, etc., in, early 14 cent. Harl. 48 G. 13 (Ringgesfeld);—1386. Harl. 56 G. 21 (Ryngesfeld);—1396. Harl. 48 I. 39 (Ryngefeld);—1422. Harl. 50 F. 36.

—— Rector. Mich. de Culesle, late Hen. III. Harl. 56 B. 18;—(as Dom. Michael), t. Edw. I. Harl. 47 F. 3.

Ringshall, co. Suff. Grant of goods in the manor, 1394 (Ryngesell). Harl. 51 E. 11.

Ringshall, co. Suff. (continued). Extracts from court-rolls, 1545–1553. Add. 10098.

—— Lease, etc., in, 1632. Add. 10108;—1636. Add. 10110.

—— Persona. Willelmus, 1355 (Renggeselle). Harl. 54 G. 49.

Ringstone, in Rippingale, co. Linc. Grants, etc., in, t. Hen. III.–Edw. I. Harl. 55 D. 34 (Ringedon), Add. 21116 (Bingesdon), 21120 (Ringisdone);—1284. Add. 21121 (Ringesdoun);—1295. Add. 21122 (Ryngesdona);—1327. Add. 21105 (Ringesdona), 21106;—1382. Add. 20703 (Ryngesdone), 20887, 20888;—1384. Add. 20889, 20890;—1421. Add. 21127;—1429. Add. 20892;—1438. Add. 6407;—1439. Add. 20894;—[1443?]. Add. 21128;—1447. Add. 6409;—1448. Add. 21054;—1500. Add. 21129;—1512, 1513. Add. 21111, 21130–21132.

—— Grants, etc., in, to Sempringham Priory, late Hen. III. Add. 21117 (Ryngesdun), 21119, 21138 (Ringesdund);—1328. Add. 20870;—1329. Add. 21100.

—— Defeasance of bond, etc., for the manor, 1400. Add. 21123, 21124;—1415. Add. 21035;—1416. Add. 21126.

—— Acquittance for a relief to the Bp. of Lincoln in, 1403. Add. 21125.

—— Acquittance by Bourne Abbey for rent in, 1525. Add. 21133.

Ringwood, co. Southt. Grant at (?), by K. Eadgar to Abingdon Monastery, 961 (Rimecuda). Cott. MS. Aug. ii. 39.

—— Grant in Kingston (Kyngeston) in, t. Hen. III. Harl. 112 B. 32.

—— Release in St. Ives (villa de Yvetis) nr., late 13 cent. Add. 15465.

Ringwould, co. Kent. Grant in, 1441 (Ryngewelde). Add. 951.

Ripe al. Eckington, co. Suss. Grant, etc., of the manor, 1359 (Heghlyntone, Heyghyntone). Add. 20053, 20054.

Ripesley. v. sub Trotton, co. Suss.

Ripley, co. Derb. Brief for rebuilding the chapel, 1819. Ch. Br. B. lx. 2.

Ripley, co. Surr. License from Merton Priory to Newark Priory for a chapel in, [1249–52] (Roppelegh). Cott. xxi. 25.

Riplingham, co. York. Exchequer acquittance for farm of lands in, 1596. Add. 25717 b.

Riplingham, co. York (continued). Lease of recusants' lands in, 1635. Add. 6273.

Ripon, co. York. Ballivus. Will. de Thornton, t. Edw. I. Add. 13997.

Ripp, co. Kent. Grant bounded by the wood of, 740. Cott. MS. Aug. ii. 101.

Rippingale, co. Linc. Grants, etc., in, to Sempringham Priory, late Hen. II. (?). Add. 21096 (Repingale), 21097 (Repinghale);—1328. Add. 20870 (do.);—1329. Add. 21100 (Repynghale).

—— Grants, etc., in, t. Hen. III.–t. Edw. I. Harl. 55 D. 34 (Repingehale), Add. 21098, 21099, 21115; — 1310. Add. 21101;—1316. Add. 21102;— 1322. Add. 21103;—1323. Add. 21104;—1327. Add. 21105, 21106;— 1341. Add. 21107; — 1349. Add. 21108 (Repynghale);—1382. Add. 20703;—1421. Add. 21127;—1438. Add. 6407;—c. 1443. Add. 21109;— 1447. Add. 6409;—1485. Add. 21110; —1500. Add. 21129;—1513. Add. 21111;—1549. Add. 21114.

—— Grant by Spalding Priory of two presentations to a chantry in, 1525 (Repynghale). Add. 21112.

—— Inquest conc. trespass by E. Marmyon, 1534. Add. 21113.

—— Capellanus. Ricardus, late Hen. II. (?). Add. 21096.

—— Persona duarum partium ecclesie. Ric. Gobaud, 1349. Add. 21108.

—— Persona. Will. de Wylughby, 1365. Harl. 58 B. 8.

—— Rector. Tho. Ramerigge, 1362. Add. 21868.

—— —— (quondam). Mag. Rob. Edenham, 1497. Add. 20727.

　v. also Ringstone, in Rippingale, co. Linc.

Ripple, co. Kent. Powers to take seisin in, 1465. Harl. 80 I. 58;—1471. Harl. 80 I. 59.

Ripton. v. sub Ashford, co. Kent.

Ripton, Abbots, co. Hunt. Court-roll, 1311. Harl. Roll G. 32.

Risborough, Monks, co. Buck. Exemption from stallage, etc., to tenants of the Abp. of Canterbury in, 1441 (Rusburgh). Lansd. 180.

—— Manumission in, by Christ Church, Canterbury, 1452 (Risbergh Manochorum). Campb. xxii. 7.

Risborough, Monks, co. Buck. (continued). Marriage settlement, etc., in, 1609. Harl. 112 ;A. 21 ;—1631, 1632. Harl. 85 H. 19–21.

—— Fine in, 1631. Harl. 85 H. 19 b.

—— Settlement of Saunderton manor in, 1631. Harl. 85 H. 19 c.

—— Grant of a mill-close at Brokende in, 1598 (Risboroughe Monachorum). Harl. 86 H. 33.

Risborough, Princes, co. Buck. Release nr. Horsyndonebroke in, 1315 (Magna Risembergh). Campb. x. 6.

—— Grant of free-warren in, 1317 (Rysebergh). Harl. 84 C. 14.

Risbridge, [in Goudhurst], co. Kent. Grant nr., t. Edw. I. (Risbregge). Harl. 79 E. 53.

Risbury, co. Heref. Grant of the manor, 1654. Add. 1953.

Risby, in Walesby, co. Linc. Covenant in, betw. Newhouse and Revesby Abbeys, 1154 (Risebi). Harl. 44 I. 1.

—— Grant in, 1589 (Resby). Add. 5311.

Risby, co. Suff. Covenant conc. the manor betw. Bury St. Edmunds Abbey and Dom. R. de Houel, 1261 (Riseby). Add. 5488.

Risby, in Rowley, co. York. Grant, etc., in, 1354. Lansd. 437 (Rysceby); —1356. Lansd. 424 (do.); — 1363. Lansd. 411 (Resceby).

—— Lease of recusants' lands in, 1635. Add. 6273.

Risca, co. Monm. Precipes on covenants conc. land in, 1593. Add. 25141, 25144.

Risden, Den of. v. sub Goudhurst, co. Kent.

Risden (?), in Goudhurst, co. Kent. Grant at, 814 (Hris den). Harl. 83 A. 1.

Riseholme, co. Linc. Brief conc. a fire at, 1809. Ch. Br. B. l. 6.

Riseley, co. Bedf. Grant, etc., in, 1357. Add. 5154 (Rislegh);—1445. Add. 24105;—[1458 ?]. Add. 24106.

Rishangles, co. Suff. Conveyance of wardship in, 1317 (Rishanghel). Harl. 57 G. 41.

—— Bond for feoffment in, etc., 1346. Harl. 55 F. 44 (Risshangell);—1511. Harl. 51 H. 20.

—— Capellanus. Jurdanus, early 13 cent. (Rishangre). Harl. 49 B. 21.

Rooh, co. *Pembr.* Leases in, 1353.
Add. 8059 (de Rupe);—1356. Add.
8074 (La Roche);—1367. Add. 8060.

—— Covenant to repair the castle,
1367 (de Rupe). Add. 8060.

Rochalanda. *v.* Ruckland, *co. Linc.*

Roohb. *v.* Roxburgh, *co. Roxburgh.*

Rochebi. *v.* Rugby, *co. Warw.*

Rochester, *co. Kent.* Grant in, to the
see of Rochester, 781 (Hrofi). Cott.
vi. 4 (copy).

—— Grant at Borstal nr., 811 (Hrofes-
cester). Cott. viii. 31.

—— Grants at, 838 (Hroui civitas).
Cott. viii. 30; — 860-862 (Civitas
hrobi). Cott. viii. 29.

—— Grants, etc., in, *t.* Hen. III. Harl.
50 A. 26 (Roffa);—1364. Harl. 53
A. 43 (Roucestre);—1365. Harl. 57
D. 30;—1366. Harl. 57 C. 50 (Roffa),
58 A. 18;—1368. Harl. 53 A. 44;—
1393. Harl. 45 C. 18;—1398. Harl.
46 A. 25;—1408. Harl. 49 A. 36;—
1417. Harl. 49 F. 16;—1431. Harl.
55 E. 40.

—— Dispute betw. Joh. and Tho. de
Cobham conc. custody of the castle,
c. 1340(?) (Roucestre). Harl. Roll C. 27.

—— Petition, etc., conc. repairs of
the bridge, 1360. Harl. 58 F. 18;—
1381. Harl. 43 E. 32;—1383. Harl.
43 E. 27, 58 F. 17, 19, 20;—1387.
Harl. 58 H. 23;—1391. Harl. 43 B.
26, 27;—*t.* Rich. II. Harl. Roll K. 34.

—— Grant "in tenura de Borstalle"
in, 1370. Harl. 55 A. 4.

—— Power to give seisin of Gt. Delce
[Magna Dels] manor in, 1385. Harl.
56 A. 35.

—— Note of a chantry founded in, by
John, Lord Cobham, c. 1395 (?). Harl.
44 I. 8.

—— Conveyance of Lit. Delce [Lyt-
eledelse] manor in, 1397-8. Harl.
78 F. 28.

—— Leases in, from Denny Abbey,
1404. Harl. 44 D. 15 (Rouchestre);
—1431. Harl. 44 D. 16 a, b;—1487.
Harl. 44 D. 17.

—— Names of persons indicted for
treason at, 1451. Cott. ii. 23 (13).

—— "Rochester rents" due from
Speldhurst and other manors, co.
Kent, 1539. Add. 211.

—— *Constable of the Castle. Mons.*
Hen. de Cobeham, 1326 (Roucestre).
Harl. 55 G. 4.

Rochester, *co. Kent (continued). Constable of the Castle (continued). Sire*
Joh. Neweton, [1383]. Harl. 58 F. 19.

PARISHES :—

—— PAR. OF ST. CLEMENT. Grants,
etc., in, 1382. Harl. 51 E. 38;—1394.
Harl. 50 G. 47;—1407. Harl. 53
A. 49;—1427. Harl. 55 F. 34.

—— —— *Rector. Dom.* Joh. Aleyn,
1382. Harl. 51 E. 38.

—— —— *Rector perpetuus.* Joh.
Ticciour, *de Lambhyth,* [1389-1400].
Harl. 44 I. 8.

—— PAR. OF ST. MARGARET. Grants,
etc., in, 1380. Harl. 48 F. 14;—1408.
Harl. 55 E. 40;—1437. Harl. 49
A. 49;—1448. Harl. 44 C. 37;—1536.
Harl. 44 C. 52.

—— —— Grant of St. William's
chapel in, 1549. Add. 4607.

—— PAR. OF ST. NICHOLAS. Grant,
etc., in, 1350. Harl. 53 C. 48;—1529.
Harl. 78 I. 46.

Rochford, *co. Essex.* Grants, etc., in,
1232-3. Harl. 49 D. 46 (Rocheford);—
*t.* Hen. III. Harl. 49 B. 43 (Roches-
furd);— 1273. Harl. 48 G. 4;—
1296. Harl. 56 I. 11;—*t.* Edw. I.
Harl. 54 G. 28.

—— Grant in Upphall in, *ante* 1310.
Harl. 45 C. 43.

—— Arrears of the bailiffs of the
manor, 1426. Add. 15865.

—— Fine of Doggetts (Docettes,
Dogettys), Upwick (Upwyke) and
Combes manors in, 1541. Add. 15868.

Rochford, *co. Heref.* [*now co. Worc.*].
Grant at, 1323 (Racheford). Add.
4592.

Rochford Hundred, *co. Essex.* Sale,
etc., in, *t.* Hen. III. Harl. 45 E. 29;
—1342. Add. 15458.

—— *Ballivus.* Andr. de Vautort,
*t.* Edw. I. Harl. 51 C. 16, 17.

Rochintona. *v.* Rowington, *co. Warw.*

Rook, *co. Worc.* Grant in, 1326 (Rok).
Add. 20428.

—— Verdict in suit for trespass at,
1582. Woll. xii. 128.

Rockbeare, *co. Devon.* Release in
Luueretune in or nr., 1260 (Rokeber).
Add. 12929.

—— Grant of free-warren in, 1296
(Rokebere). Harl. 58 I. 40.

—— Compotus of the prepositus, 1377-8
(Rokebere). Add. 7657.

Rodmell, co. *Suss.* Power for assignment of the manor to Edw. II., 1316 (Radomeld). Harl. 57 E. 32.

—— Exchequer acquittance for a fine in, 1585 (Rednell). Add. 25669.

Rodmeres Hawe Wood. *v. sub* Oakley, Lit., co. *Northt.*

Rodmersham, co. *Kent.* Recovery in, 1572. Add. 912.

Rodsley, co. *Derb.* Grants, etc., in, 1269. Woll. ix. 19 (Redislg.);—1277. Woll. viii. 55 (Redisleye);—t. Hen. III.-t. Edw. I. Woll. viii. 56 (Roddisley), 57 (Redisl.), 58, 70 (Roddeale), ix. 18, 21, 43 (Rodealeg), 77 (Reddisles), 78, 79;—1314. Woll. viii. 59 (Roddesleye).

—— Grant of the manor, 1470 (Roddesley). Woll. ix. 22.

Roeginga hám. *v.* Rainham, co. *Kent.*

Roelay. *v.* Rothley, co. *Leic.*

Roffa. *v.* Rochester, co. *Kent.*

Rofford, *in Chalgrove,* co. *Oxon.* Grants, etc., in, 1394. Add. 20311 (Rufford): —1463. Add. 20322;—1656. Add. 19226.

—— Power to give seisin of the manor, 1408 (Rufford). Add. 20312.

—— Bond on security of rent from the manor, etc., 1451. Add. 20317 (do.);—1487. Add. 20328 (do.).

—— Acquittance on sale of the manor, 1498. Add. 20329.

Rogate, co. *Suss.* Settlement, etc., of Wenham (Weneham, Weenham, Weyneham) manor in, 1434. Add. 18796, 18727;—1453. Add. 18752;— 1460. Add. 18758 (Rowgate);—1569. Add. 18853.

—— Inq. p. m. conc. Wenham manor, 1471. Add. 18765.

—— Grants, etc., in, 1526. Add. 18810;—1554. Add. 18837;—1559. Add. 18841, 18843, 18844;—1592. Add. 18872, 18873;—1605. Add. 18899;—1617. Add. 18923;—1656. Add. 18977, 18978.

—— Lease of Ryland manor in, 1569. Add. 18853.

—— Division of lands in, [1582]. Add. 18864.

—— Assignment of lease of Combeland, etc., in, 1631. Add. 6008.

—— Fees to the steward of the manor, etc., 1651. Add. 19058.

—— Rent-roll of the manor, 1685. Add. 19020.

Rogerthorpe, *in Badsworth,* co. *York.* Covenant to acquit for services in, 1345. Add. 20520.

Roghoombe. *v. sub* Tisbury, co. *Wilts.*

Rogheye, La. *v. sub* Horsham, co. *Suss.*

Roing. *v.* Roothing Aythorp, co. *Essex.*

Rok. *v.* Rock, co. *Worc.*

Roke. *v. sub* Coulsdon, co. *Surr.*

Roke, co. *Oxon.* Attornment for a tenement in, c. 1252 (Rokes). Harl. 52 B. 35.

Roke, *in Romsey,* co. *Southt.* Grants in, 1443. Add. 17433 (villa de Ook):— 1478. Add. 17435;—1529. Add. 17440.

Roksbere. *v.* Rockbeare, co. *Devon.*

Rokeby. *v.* Rugby, co. *Warw.*

Rokeford. *v.* Ruxford, *in Sandford,* co. *Devon.*

Rokelond. *v.* Rockland, co. *Linc.*

Rokelond Seynt Andrew. *v.* Rockland, co. *Norf.*

Rokenham. *v.* Rookham, co. *Surr.*

Rokesburgh. *v.* Roxburgh, co. *Roxburgh.*

Rokintun. *v.* Rowington, co. *Warw.*

Rokyng. *v.* Rucking, co. *Kent.*

Rokyngham. *v.* Rockingham, co. *Northt.*

Roland. *v.* Rowland, *in Bakewell,* co. *Derb.*

Rolandryght, Rollenderith, etc. *v.* Rollright, co. *Oxon.*

Roleya. *v.* Rothley, co. *Leic.*

Rollesby, co. *Norf.* Conf. of a grant in, to St. Giles's Hosp., Norwich, 1279. Add. 14784.

—— Release in, 1361. Harl. 52 B. 11.

—— Court-rolls, 1599-1601. Add. 14847.

Rollesley, Mechell. *v.* Rowsley, *in Bakewell,* co. *Derb.*

Rolleston. *v.* Rowlston, co. *York.*

Rolleston, co. *Leic. Capellanus. Dom.* Joh. Williamson, 1517. Add. 26966.

Rolleston, co. *Nott.* Fine in, 1541 (Rolston). Woll. ii. 71.

—— *Clericus.* Willelmus, late 12 cent. (Rollestun). Harl. 84 A. 41.

**Romsey,** co. *Southt.* Grants, etc., in Stanbridge in, 1342. Add. 17407:—1364. Add. 17415; — 1367. Add. 17417; — 1374. Add. 17419;—1385. Add. 17421, 17423; — 1403. Add. 17425; — 1410. Add. 17426, 17427; —1426. Add. 17430:—1443. Add. 17433;—1478. Add. 17435; — 1529. Add. 17440.

—— Grant in, 1381 (Romesye). Add. 17420.

—— Grants in Roke (Ook, etc.) in, 1443. Add. 17433 :—1478. Add. 17435; —1529. Add. 17440.

**Roncomb.** *v. sub* Sidbury, co. *Devon.*

**Rongeton.** *v.* Runcton, co. *Suss.*

**Ronham.** *v.* Runham, co. *Norf.*

**Ronton,** co. *Staff.* Brief conc. a fire at Extoll in, 1790 (Ranton). Ch. Br. B. xxx. 8.

—— Brief for rebuilding the church, 1806. Ch. Br. B. xlvi. 9.

**Roohawe,** nr. *Southwell,* co. *Nott.* Covenant for settlement of the manor, 1437. Add. 20542.

**Rookham,** *in Ockley and Wotton, co. Surr.* Grants, etc., in, t. Hen. III.–t. Edw. I. Add. 18570 (Rokenham in par. de Okeleye), 18574 (Rukenham); —1332. Add. 18625 (Rukenham in villa de Ockelegh); — 1362. Add. 18654 (Rokenham), 18655 (do.); — 1373. Add. 9048 (Rokenham in Wodgton);—1374. Add. 9049 (Rokenham in par. de Wodeton);—1396. Add. 9055 (R. in par. de Wodyton);—1397. Add. 9057 (R. in par. de Wodyngton et Ocklegh);—1399. Add. 18687 (R. in par. de Ockelegh et Wodyton), 18688 (do.);—1418. Add. 9063 (R. in par. de Wodyton et Okkelegh), 18702.

—— Surrender of the manor, 1560 (Rookenham). Add. 18846.

**Rookwood.** *v. sub* Acton, co. *Suff.*

**Roothing Aythorp,** co. *Essex.* Service of two knights owed for, by S. de Roing, late 12 cent. (Roing). Harl. 83 A. 7.

—— Bond conc. descent of the manor, 1338 (Rothynges Aytrop). Add. 8053.

—— Grant of the manor, etc., 1389 (Rothing Aytrop). Add. 7906.

—— *Capellanus.* Willelmus, late 12 cent. Harl. 83 A. 7.

**Roothing, Berners,** *al.* **Bernish Roding,** co. *Essex.* Fine of the manor, 1452 (Rothyng Bernera). Lansd. 161.

—— Precipe on a covenant conc. land in, 1593 (Barners Rothing al. Barnish Roothinge). Add. 25047.

**Roothing, High,** co. *Essex.* Fine of the manor, 1541 (Rothyng). Add. 15868.

**Roothing, White,** co. *Essex.* Grant of a rent from Maskerellesburi manor in, 1351 (alba Rothyngg). Add. 15460.

—— Defeasance of bonds on a conveyance of [Maskelsbury] manor in, 1359 (Rothyngg). Harl. 46 G. 13.

**Roppelegh.** *v.* Ripley, co. *Surr.*

**Ropsley,** co. *Leic.* Grant, etc., in, 1463. Add. 6458 (Roppesley), 6459;—1464. Add. 6460.

—— Conveyance, etc., of the manor, 1477. Add. 6461 (Roppesley);—1530. Add. 6462 (do.).

**Roreston.** *v.* Royston, co. *York.*

**Rosavallan.** *v. sub* St. Stephen's in Brannel, co. *Cornw.*

**Rosboya,** nr. *Davidstowe,* co. *Cornw.* Grant in, early Hen. III. Harl. 53 B. 42.

**Rosdew,** *in the barony of Luss, co. Dumbarton.* Presentation to the chaplainry of, 1575. Add. 8084.

**Rose Court.** *v. sub* Grain, co. *Kent.*

**Rosethet,** nr. *Davidstowe,* co. *Cornw.* Grant in, early Hen. III. Harl. 53 B. 42.

**Rosevillen,** [nr. *Lanivet?*], co. *Cornw.* Grants, etc., in, 1392. Harl. 50 C. 37 (Reyseuelyn);—1394. Harl. 51 E. 16 (Ruscenelyn);—1513. Harl. 50 C. 41 (Rosavylyn);—1594. Harl. 50 C. 48.

**Rosewin,** *in St. Minver,* co. *Cornw.* Grants, etc., in, t. Edw. I.-II. Harl. 57 A. 37 (Roswyn);—1392. Harl. 50 C. 37 (Ryswyn);—1394. Harl. 51 E. 16 (Reswyn);—1513. Harl. 50 C. 41 (Rosewyn).

—— Suit, etc., conc. land in, with the vicar of St. Minver, 1427. Harl. 56 G. 50 (Reswyn);—1447. Harl. 43 E. 44 (Roswyn).

**Roseys.** *v. sub* Creake, S., co. *Norf.*

**Roshowelin.** *v.* Resolven, co. *Glam.*

**Rosliston,** co. *Derb.* Brief for rebuilding the church, 1818. Ch. Br. B. lix. 2.

**Rosmanaher,** co. *Clare* (?). Mortgage, etc., at, 1548. Eg. 98, 99.

**Rosmaroh,** nr. *Davidstowe,* co. *Cornw.* Grant in, early Hen. III. Harl. 53 B. 42.

Rosminawet, *nr. Davidstowe, co. Cornw.* Grant in, early Hen. III. Harl. 53 B. 42.

Rosogou. *v. sub* St. Stephen in Brannel, *co. Cornw.*

Rospeygh, [*nr. Camborne?*], *co. Cornw.* Power to give seisin in, 1417. Add. 15354.

Ross, *co. Heref.* Grants, etc., in or near, *t.* Hen. III.-*t.* Edw. I. Harl. 11² C. 1 (Ro°), Eg. 350 (do.);—1431. Harl. 111 D. 37 (Rosseffor.); — 1492. Harl. 112 C. 11 (Rosse);—1563. Add. 1829 ; — 1568. Add. 1832 ; — 1569. Add. 1833 :—1574. Add. 1838, 1839 ; —1581. Add. 1852 ; — 1585. Add. 1857 ; — 1597. Add. 1872 ; — 1605. Add. 1889 ; — 1609. Add. 1895 ; — 1663. Add. 1962 ;—1721. Add. 13610.

—— Grant in the fee of Wilton near, *t.* Edw. I. Eg. 350.

—— Conveyance of the domain and manor, 1591 (Rosse forreinn). Harl. 79 F. 39.

—— Grant, etc., of the rectory, 1606. Add. 1890 ; — 1612. Add. 1902 ;— 1642. Add. 1947.

—— *Ballivus* Roger. de Fonte, *t.* Edw. I. Eg. 350.

—— *Rector.* Griffith Williams, 1554. Add. 1832, 1833.

—— —— Hen. Hackett, *Prebendary of Over Preston,* 1636. Add. 1941.

—— —— Rowland Scudamore, 1642. Add. 1947.

Rossall, *nr. Shrewsbury, co. Salop.* Crown lease in, 1576. Harl. 75 E. 45.

Rossaulin, Rossoulyn. *v.* Resolven, *co. Glam.*

Rosse, New, *co. Wexford.* Grant of freedom of the borough, 1719. Add. 26724.

Rosseffor. *v.* Ross, *co. Heref.*

Rosshebrook. *v.* Rushbrook, *co. Suff.*

Rosshemere. *v.* Rushmere, *nr. Mutford, co. Suff.*

Rossington, Rossynton. *v.* Roston, *co. Derb.*

Rossington, *co. York.* Grants, etc., in Brancroft in, 1316. Harl. 83 D. 43; —1336. Harl. 83 E. 3;—1381. Harl. 83 D. 28 ;—1382. Harl. 84 A. 16;— 1389. Lansd. 137;—1391. Harl. 84 A. 13 ;—1407. Harl. 83 D. 22 ;— 1408. Harl. 112. G. 6.

Rossuchet. *v. sub* Chapel of Garioch, *co. Aberdeen.*

Rostherne, *co. Chest. Persona.* Rog. Venables, 1431 (Rowstorne). Woll. xi. 47.

Roston, *co. Derb.* Grants, etc., in, *t.* Hen. III. Woll. viii. 53 (Rossynton); —1349. Woll. ix. 69 (Rotyngton);— 1404. Woll. x. 18 (Rossington).

Rostormel. *v.* Restormel, *co. Cornw.*

Rosvanallen. *v. sub* St. Stephen in Brannel, *co. Cornw.*

Roswyn. *v.* Rosewin, *co. Cornw.*

Roteland. *v.* Rutland, *County of.*

Rothbury, *co. Northumb.* Grant of the constableship of the castle to Sir R. Ogle, 1461. Cott. xvii. 17.

Rothelan. *v.* Rhuddlan, *co. Flint.*

Rothelaye. *v.* Rodley, *in Calverley, co. York.*

Rothemerche. *v.* Rawmarsh, *co. York.*

Rothen. *v.* Ruthern, *nr. Bodmin, co. Cornw.*

Rotheraford, Rotherneforde, etc. *v. sub* Holne, *co. Devon.*

Rotherfield, *co. Suss.* Extracts from court-rolls, 1488. Harl. 111 C. 42;— 1546. Harl. 111 C. 43.

—— Fine in, 1491. Add. 15214.

—— Award conc. a heriot in, 1567. Add. 20084.

Rotherfield Peppard, *co. Oxon.* Grants, etc., in, *t.* Edw. I. Add. 20367 (Rutherfeld Pyppard);—1457. Add. 20297-20800 (Retherfeld Pipperd, Ritherfeld Pipard).

Rotherham, *co. York.* Papal conf. of the rectory to R. de Lexinton, 1228 (Roderham). Harl. 111 A. 8.

—— Bulls conc. patronage of the rectory, etc., 1256. Harl. 111 A. 22 (Roderham) :—1259. Harl. 111 A. 23 (Raderham).

—— Bull to Clairvaux Abbey to alienate a moiety of the church, 1288 (Roderham). Harl. 111 A. 27.

—— Grants, etc., in, 1300. Add. 9218;—1371. Add. 18027 ; — 1423. Harl. 83 G. 6 (Roderham) ; — 1439. Harl. 112 G. 7 ;—1483. Harl. 112 G. 3; —1541. Woll. ii. 71 (Ratheram);— 1588. Add. 17975 ;— 1617. Add. 18050 ;—1656. Add. 18030, 18031 ;— 1776. Add. 18081.

2 s

**Rotherham,** *co. York (continued).* Papal conf. of a moiety of the church to Rufford Abbey, 1380. Harl. 111 A. 32.

—— Lease in Greaseborough (Greasebrooke) in, 1761. Add. 18080.

—— Lease of the Brecks in Dalton in, 1782. Add. 18084;—1785. Add. 18086.

—— *Vicarius.* Henricus, *t.* Hen. III. Harl. 83 G. 15, 16, 84 A. 32.

**Rotherhithe,** *co. Surr.* Covenant conc. debts and lands in, 1268 (Rutherheth.). Cott. MS. Nero C. iii, f. 213.

—— Grant of an annuity in, 1580 (Roderythe). Harl. 112 E. 50.

**Rothersthorpe,** *co. Northt.* Precipe on a covenant conc. land in, 1593 (Rothers Thruppe). Add. 25175.

—— Conveyance of the manor, 1674. Add. 24157.

—— *Vicarius.* Hen. Brikhull, 1362 (Throp). Slo. xxxii. 12.

**Rotherwick,** *co. Southt.* Sale in, 1513. Add. 19182.

**Rothley,** *co. Leic.* Grant of, with its soke, by Hen., Duke of Normandy, to the Earl of Chester, 1153 (Roelay). Cott. xvii. 2.

—— Grants, etc., in, *t.* Hen. III.–*t.* Edw. I. Add. 7086 (Rol.), 7087 (Rotheleya), 7088 (Rotheleya), 7089 (Roleya), 7090, 7091 (Rothele), 7092 (Roleya), 7220-7222;—1285. Add. 7093 (Rothele); — 1293-4. Add. 7094;—1295. Add. 7223; — 1317. Add. 7095; — 1324. Add. 7096; — 1327. Add. 7224; — 1335. Add. 7097; — 1344. Add. 7225;—1353. Add. 7098; — 1355. Add. 7226 (Rothelee) ; — 1358. Add. 7099; — 1373. Add. 7100; — 1376. Add. 7101; — 1395. Add. 7102;—1414. Add. 7103 (Rotheley); — 1417. Add. 7104; — 1418. Add. 7105; — 1419. Add. 7227; — 1423. Add. 7107, 7108;—1426. Add. 7106, 7109;—1428. Add. 7229;— 1431. Add. 7231;—1432. Add. 7230;— 1436. Add. 7232;—1437. Add. 7234; — 1438. Add. 7233;—1441. Add. 7235; — 1442. Add. 7111; — 1444. Add. 7236; — 1454. Add. 7237;— 1455. Add. 7112;—1456. Add. 7113;— 1461. Add. 7238, 7239;—1464. Add. 7240; — 1465. Add. 7241; — 1466. Add. 7114, 7242;—1467. Add. 7115; —1468. Add. 7243;—1470. Add. 7244; — 1473. Add. 7116; — 1475. Add. 7117; — 1478. Add. 7118; — 1479. Add. 7119 ;—1480. Add. 7246 ;

—1481. Add. 7245 ; — 1482. Add. 7121, 7122;—1484. Add. 7123, 7124 ; —1488. Add. 7125;—1496. Add. 7126, 7127, 7128;—1499. Add. 7129;— 1501. Add. 7131 ;—1502. Add. 7130; —1504. Add. 7133, 7134;—1506. Add. 7136, 7138, 7172;—1521. Add. 7139, 7249;—1534. Add. 7140, 7250.

—— Extract from court-roll of the manor, bel. to the Knts. Hospitallers, 1495. Add. 7247.

—— Grant in the fee of the soke of, 1537. Add. 9267.

—— Debt to the Crown charged on land in, 1546. Add. 7251.

—— Summons to prove title to land in, late bel. to the Knts. Hospitallers, 1610. Harl. 75 F. 6.

—— *Presbiter.* Willelmus, *t.* Hen II. Cott. v. 62.

—— *Vicarius perpetuus.* Joh. de Stoke, 1376. Add. 7101.

—— *Vicarius.* Joh. Derby, 1441. Add. 7235;—1461. Add. 7239.

—— —— Joh. Parsons, 1480 (as *vic. perpetuus*). Add. 7246;—1481. Add. 7245;—1502. Add. 7130;—1504. Add. 7133, 7134 ;—1506. Add. 7136, 7137.

**Rothwell** (Rowell, etc.), *co. Linc.* Grants, etc., in, to Newhouse Abbey, *c.* 1150-55. Harl. 43 H. 14-17 (Rodewelle), 55 E. 41 (Rodeuuell);—[1156 or 7]. Harl. 51 H. 1 (Rothewelle);—late Hen. II. Cott. v. 74;—*t.* Hen. III. Harl. 55 E. 44 ;—*t.* Edw. I. Harl. 55 E. 45 (Rouwelle);—1304. Harl. 45 D. 20, 21.

—— Covenant betw. Newhouse and Revesby Abbeys conc. lands in, 1154 (Rodewelle). Harl. 44 I. 1.

—— Conff. of grants in, to Elsham Priory, [1163-5 ?, 1203-5 ?] (Rowella, Rowellia). Harl. 45 A. 4, 45 C. 32, 33.

—— Covenant in, betw. Newhouse Abbey and Will. fil. Alani de Rowell, early 13 cent. Harl. 55 E. 42.

—— Lease in, from Newhouse Abbey, 1315. Cott. v. 36.

—— *Capellanus.* Robertus, late Hen. II. Cott. v. 74.

—— *Clericus.* Robertus, *c.* 1150-55. Harl. 55 E. 41.

**Rothwell,** *co. Northt.* Conf. by King John of grants in, 1208 (Rowell). Add. 6014.

Rothwell, *co. Northt.* (*continued*). Grant of "domum que vocatur hospitale cum curia" in, early Edw. I. (Rowell). Add. 20398.

—— Release of dower in, 1280 (Rowelle). Add. 20399.

—— Lease, etc., in, 1335. Add. 22401 (Rothewelle);—1377. Harl. 52 I. 43;—1421. Add. 21612.

—— Acquittance for a relief to the lord of, in Kelmarsh, co. Northt., 1362. Add. 22051.

—— Fines in, 1387. Add. 22402;—1418. Add. 6266.

—— Order conc. the manor, etc., assigned to the Css. of Stafford, 1402. Add. 19854.

—— Draughton manor, co. Northt., held as of the manor of, 1429. Add. 21835.

—— Precipe on a covenant conc. the manor, 1555. Add. 25149.

—— Inquisition conc. the manor, 1627. Add. 6073.

—— *Capellanus.* Willelmus, early 13 cent. Add. 20524.

Rothwell, *co. York.* Fines of the manor, etc., 1671. Add. 12681.

Rothyng. *v.* Roothing, High, *co. Essex.*

Rotsea, *in Hutton Cranswick, co. York.* Grant in, to Beverley College, *t.* Hen. III. (Rottese). Lansd. 413.

—— Release in, to Gisburne Priory, 1408 (Rotse). Add. 20586.

Rotteleia. *v.* Ratley, *co. Warw.*

Rottingdean, *co. Suss.* Power for assignment of the manor to Edw. II., 1316 (Rottyngden). Harl. 57 E. 33.

—— Refeoffment of the reversion to the manor, 1401 (Radyngdene). Add. 20087.

—— Fine in, 1457 (Rottyngdene). Add. 24904.

Rotyngton. *v.* Roston, *co. Derb.*

Rouberghe. *v.* Rowberrow, *co. Som.*

Roubury. *v. sub* Bodenham, *co. Heref.*

Roucebi. *v.* Rauceby, North, *co. Linc.*

Roucestre. *v.* Rochester, *co. Kent.*

Rouchemolyn, Routhemilne manor. *v. sub* Norton Disney, *co. Linc.*

Roudun. *v.* Rawden, *co. York.*

Rougham, *co. Norf.* Grant in, *t.* Edw. I. (Rucham). Harl. 56 F. 22.

Rougham, *co. Suff.* Sale in, 1566. Add. 19257.

Roughcombe. *v. sub* Tisbury, *co. Wilts.*

Roughey. *v. sub* Horsham, *co. Suss.*

Roughmere, *in Brockhall* (?), *co. Northt.* Release in, 1586. Add. 16171.

Roughsparre. *v.* Rusper, *co. Suss.*

Roughton (Ructon, Rugton, Ruchtun, etc.), *co. Linc.* Grants, etc., in, to Kirkstead Abbey, late 12 cent. Harl. 47 H. 43–48, 53 H. 11, 55 F. 5, 6, 58 B. 43;—[1196–8]. Harl. 58 B. 44;—early 13 cent. Harl. 55 F. 8–11;—late 13 cent. Harl. 54 G. 33;—1331. Harl. 43 G. 52.

—— Grant of Dunnesdaile in, to the same, late 12 cent. Cott. xii. 52.

—— Grants, etc., in, late 12 cent. Harl. 55 F. 7;—*t.* John. Harl. 50 A. 4;—*t.* Hen. III. Cott. xxix. 33, Harl. 56 A. 4, 5, 56 I. 3, 4;—late 13 cent. Harl. 52 B. 44, 45, 53 C. 1, 56 A. 6;—1315. Harl. 55 F. 12;—early 14 cent. Cott. xxviii. 46;—1342. Harl. 54 F. 29.

—— Rent of wax for St. Margaret's altar in the church of, early Hen. III. Harl. 56 I. 3.

—— Grant of a spring on the moor to Kirkstead Abbey, 1265. Harl. 53 D. 4.

—— Exemplif. in 1431 of a suit in, 1364. Harl. 51 H. 6.

—— License to alienate the manor, 1564. Add. 15798.

—— Precipe on a covenant conc. lands in, 1578. Add. 25102.

—— *Clericus.* Robertus, 1158 (Ruct.). Harl. 49 A. 1.

—— *Persona.* Petrus, *t.* Hen. II. Harl. 56 A. 19;—late 12 cent. Harl. 55 F. 6, 7;—*t.* John or Hen. III. Cott. xxvii. 62.

—— Petr. fil. Roberti, late 13 cent. Harl. 54 G. 33.

—— *Rector. Mag.* Pet. Meuerel, *t.* Hen. III. Harl. 56 A. 5;—(*as* Petrus), late 13 cent. Harl. 53 C. 1.

—— Rob. de Wyshawe, late 13 cent. Harl. 52 B. 45.

Roughton, *co. Norf.* Powers to give seisin, etc., of the manor, 1400. Harl. 54 H. 2;—1429. Harl. 58 B. 17;—1431. Harl. 58 B. 16;—1434. Harl. 47 C. 44.

—— Grant in, 1431. Harl. 57 A. 1.

2 s 2

17270;—1535. Add. 18632;—1349. Add. 8829;—1372. Add. 18664;— 1380. Add. 8845; — 1388. Add. 18669;—1397. Add. 8850, 8851;— 1427. Add. 8874 (Ruggewyke), 18715 (do.);—1431. Add. 18729;— 1440. Add. 18735;—1442 Add. 18740-18742;—1485. Add. 20075;— 1516. Add. 18799;—1519. Add. 8930; — 1527. Add. 18812; — 1553. Add. 6232, 18835; — 1606. Add. 18950.

—— Grant, etc., in Hornshill (Hornes-elle) in, 1379 (Regwicke). Add. 8841-8843.

—— Inq. post mortem conc. lands in, 1488 (Ruggewyk). Add. 7388.

—— Survey of timber in, 1598 (Rydgeweeke). Add. 18883.

—— Vicarius. Alexander, 1349. Add. 8829;—1370. Add. 8841-8843.

Mudham, co. Norf. Conf. of E. and W. Rudham churches, with lands in, to Coxford Priory, [1148?] (Rudeham). Harl. 47 H. 45.

—— Papal conf. of [West?] Rudham to Horsham St. Faith's Priory, 1163 (terra de Ruddaham). Cott. MS. Aug. ii. 136.

—— Terrier of lands in E. and W. Rudham bel. to Coxford Priory, 1410-11. Campb. xxi. 8.

—— Presentation of Ant. Burrall as vicar of W. Rudham in succ. to Nicodemus Paulett, 1652. Add. 14848.

—— Presbyteri. Bruno, Willelmus, [1148?]. Harl. 47 H. 45.

Ruding, La. v. sub Missenden, Little, co. Buck.

Rudmarleye, Rudmerlee. v. Red-marley D'Abitot, co. Worc.

Rueberge. v. Roborough, co. Devon.

Ruelowe. v. sub Finmere, co. Oxon.

Ruerdean, co. Glouc. Grant in, 1405 (Ruardyn). Eg. 360.

Rufford. v. Rofford, in Chalgrove, co. Oxon.

Rufford, co. Nott. Papal conf. of grants in, to Rufford Abbey, 1156. Harl. 111 A. 2;—1160. Harl. 111 A. 5.

—— Release, etc., in, to Bufford Abbey, t. Hen. II. Harl. 112 H. 17 (Ruford):—late 12 cent. Harl. 84 A. 24 (Rufordia).

Rugby (Rokeby), co. Warw. Release in, to Monks Kirby Priory, t. Edw. I. Add. 20584.

—— Grant of custody of the church, etc., 1296. Cott. xxiii. 3.

—— Release, etc., of the manor, 1350. Cott. xxiv. 9, Add. 20585.

—— Acquittance to the Earl of Stafford on a payment for the manor, 1384. Cott. xxv. 35.

—— Ballivus. Joh. Huet, 1445. Cott. xxx. 33.

—— Sacerdos. Simon, t. Hen. II. (Rochebi). Add. 21458.

—— Vicarius. Dom. Robertus, t. Edw. I. Cott. xxviii. 1.

Rugeley, co. Staff. Grant in the fee of, 1402. Add. 24242.

—— Lease, etc., in, 1540. Add. 13558 (Rygoley); — 1612. Campb. xxviii. 1 (Ridgley).

—— Brief for rebuilding the church, 1819. Ch. Br. B. lx. 1.

Rugesmolyn. v. sub Norton Disney, co. Linc.

Ruggewyk, Rugwyk, etc. v. Rudg-wick, co. Suss.

Rughton. v. Roughton, co. Linc.

Rugley, co. Northumb. Attornment in, 1348 (Rouclay). Harl. 54 C. 12.

Ruhelav. v. sub Finmere, co. Oxon.

Ruholm, co. Linc. Grant with conff. of, to Newhouse Abbey, c. 1150-55. Cott. xxvii. 26, Harl. 43 H. 17 (Rug-holm juxta Ascolne):—[1156 or 7]. Harl. 51 H. 1; — [1157-63]. Cott. xi. 26.

Ruislip, co. Midd. Extracts of court-rolls, 1608-1725. Add. 1659-1677.

—— Sale, etc., in, 1627. Add. 19453; —1650. Add. 1663.

—— Fine in, 1701 (Rislipp al. Islipp). Add. 1655, 1656.

Ruiton. v. Ryton on Dunsmore, co. Warw.

Rukenham. v. Rookham, co. Surr.

Rumbolds Wyke, co. Suss. Royal grant of free-warren in, 1317 (Rum-baldeswyk). Harl. 84 C. 14.

—— Assignment of lands in, 1501 (Rumbaldeswyke). Add. 18790.

Rumburgh, co. Suf. Conf. of the church to St. Mary's Abbey, York, t. Rich. I. or John, [1239-42]. Campb. ix. 9 (1, 3) (Romburg) (copies).

St. Neot, *co. Cornw.* Bond to abide award in Lewarne [Lawharne?] in, 1539 (Seynt Nyett). Harl. 48 I. 27.

—— Exchequer acquittance for rent of the rectory, 1576. Add. 25576.

St. Nicholas, *nr. Cardiff, co. Glam.* Conf. of grant in, to Margam Abbey, [1185–91?] (S. Nicholaus). Harl. 75 D. 10.

—— Fine in, 1676. Add. 19097.

St. Nicholas at Wade, *Isle of Thanet, co. Kent.* Acquittance on payment to the executors of the Earl of Huntingdon for goods, etc., in the manor, 1357 (Seint Nicholas in Thanet). Harl. 76 F. 28.

—— Covenant by tenants of Wade (Le Warde) marsh in, with Christ Church, Canterbury, conc. dykes, 1418. Add. 16489.

St. Osyth, *co. Essex.* Conf. of a grant [in Frowick?] in(?), early 13 cent. Harl. 55 D. 7.

—— Release of arrears of rents in Chircheridel "de feodo Ridel" in, 1323. Harl. 49 I. 42.

—— Feoffment of Frowick (Frothewik) manor in, etc., 1363 (S. Ositha). Harl. 76 E. 45.

—— Account of irruptions of the sea in, [1381–92?]. Cott. iv. 3.

St. Pancras, *co. Midd.* Appointment of Fulcherius the priest as perpet. vicar of, by W. de Belmeis, canon of St. Paul's, *c.* 1183 (eccl. S. Pancratii). Add. 1045.

—— Award in dispute of the church of, with St. Giles in the Fields church, *t* Rich. I. (eccl. S. Pancratii). Add. 5865.

—— Lease in, [1226?] (par. S. Pancratii extra London.). Add. 7593.

—— Conveyance, etc., of Copthall nr. Tottenham Court in, 1552. Harl. 76 D. 22;—1554. Harl. 78 B. 14;—1561. Harl. 77 G. 48, 49.

—— Lease, etc., in the manor of Cantelowe's in Kentish Town, 1642. Harl. 112 E. 42;—1656. Harl. 111 G. 57;—1657. Harl. 111 G. 33;—1658. Harl. 111 G. 58.

—— Extract from court-roll of Cantelowe's manor in, 1650. Harl. 112 E. 42 *b.*

—— Brief for rebuilding the chapel in Kentish Town, 1779. Ch. Br. B. xx. 5.

St. Patrick's Isle, *off Peel, Isle of Man.* Inspex., in 1423, of a conf. in 1329 of a grant of, to the Bps. of Man, [1253–65]. Add. 8483.

St. Peter's *al.* Alverd's Manor. *v. sub* Ipswich, *co. Suff.*

St Pierre, *co. Monm.* Covenant for a division of Landrest wood in, 1244. Campb. v. 7.

St. Sampson *al.* Golant, *co. Cornw.* Appointment of a steward of Lantyan manor in, 1395. Cott. xxiv. 22.

—— Power to give seisin in, 1421 (Golleuant). Add. 15355.

St. Stephen. *v.* Hackington, *co. Kent.*

St. Stephen in Brannel, *co. Cornw.* Grant in Trevi-coe (Truviskermur) in, 1318. Add. 12958.

—— Grants, fines, etc., in Trethosa (Trewytoda, Trewythosa), Burgotha (Bargoythou), Kernick, Meledor (Menledor), Eglosellans, Inysuergh and other lands in, *t.* Edw. III. Add. 19479, 19480;— 1329–1349. Add. 19481–19503;—1347. Add. 13023–13025;—1372–1396. Add. 19504–19510;—1432. Add. 19511;—1441. Add. 19512.

—— Conveyance, etc., of Trethosa manor with lands in above places, 1465. Add. 19514;—1466. Add. 19515, 22615;—1471. Add. 19513.

—— *Vicarius.* Baldewinus, *t.* Edw. III. Add. 19480;—1332. Add. 19485;—1336. Add. 19486;—1342. Add. 19494.

—— —— Joh. Chywarton, 1422. Add. 12976, 12977;—1425. Add. 12980–12982.

St. Stephen in Neuland parish. *v. sub* Lincoln, *co. Linc.*

St. Thomas, *nr. Exeter, co. Devon.* Lease of Foghay (Fogghey) in, 1575. Add. 11167.

St. Tolys Creting. *v.* Creeting St. Olave's, *co. Suff.*

St. Veep, *co. Cornw.* Release, etc., in, "in villa de la Combe," 1407 (Seint Vep). Add. 13035, 13036.

St. Wenn *co. Cornw.* Grant, etc., in, 1513 (Ween). Harl. 50 C. 41, 42.

St. Weonards, *co. Heref.* Grant in, 1654 (St. Waynards). Add. 1953.

St. Werburgh, co. Kent. Charters
dated at, 823 (Werburging wic). Cott.
MS. Aug. ii. 75;—845-850 (Werburge-
wic). Cott. xvii. 1.

— v. Hoo St. Werburgh, co. Kent.

St. Winner. v. Gwinnear, co. Cornw.

Sainthill. v. sub Kentisbeare, co. Devon.

Salbourne. v. sub Standon, co. Hertf.

Salbrigge. v. Sawbridge, in Wolfhamcote, co. Warw.

Salchewilla, in England(?), in Nor-
mandy(?). Release of the mill of,
by A. de S. Martino, 1161. Eg. 371.

Salcombe, co. Devon. Award conc. the
manor, 1499 (Saltcumbe). Add. 5248.

Salcott, co. Essex. Grant of Wlfsies-
land and Aldeberi in, t. John (Salt-
cot). Harl. 45 F. 13.

—— Persona. Robertus, t. John.
Harl. 45 F. 13.

Saleby, co. Linc. Grants, etc., of
Oroxehaga al. Croshaga wood, and in
Aiureker, etc., in, to Greenfield Priory,
c. 1150. Harl. 50 I. 30;—c. 1150-60.
Harl. 43 G. 21, 43 H. 19;—late Hen.
II. Harl. 56 F. 32 (Salebi);—[1189-
95]. Harl. 43 H. 22.

—— Grants, etc., in, early Hen. II.
Add. 20591 (Salebeia);—early 14 cent.
Harl. 78 F. 17;—1368. Harl. 78 E. 47.

—— Grants, etc., in or nr., to Greenfield Priory, late 12 cent. Harl. 54 B.
23;—early 13 cent. Harl. 54 B. 21;—
t. Hen. III. Harl. 43 A. 69.

—— Compotus of the manor, 1358-
59 (Saylby). Harl. Roll AA. 31.

—— Grant, etc., of the manor, 1367.
Harl. 76 E. 26;—1396. Harl. 76 D.
42;—1427. Harl. 76 G. 46;—c. 1434.
Harl. 77 F. 13;—1560. Harl. 75 D. 70.

—— Court-rolls, 1406-7. Harl. Roll
AA. 33;—1410-11. Harl. Roll AA. 35.

—— Rental of the manor, 14.5. Harl.
Roll AA. 32.

—— Appointment of administrators of
the manor, 1429. Harl. 76 G. 49.

—— Mem. conc. tenure of the manor
in 1396 by Tho. Colepeper, and
descent in his family, 15 cent. Harl.
Roll AA. 34.

—— Covenant to levy a fine of the
manor, 1560. Harl. 79 F. 35.

—— Senescallus. Odo, early Hen. III.
Cott. xxix. 72.

—— Capellanus. Eudo, late 12 cent.
Harl. 48 D. 24-26, 50 I. 31;—c.
1200 (?). Harl. 45 E. 41.

Saleby, co. Linc. (continued). Capellanus
(continued). Radulfus, ante 1217.
Harl. 52 D. 31.

—— Clericus. Thomas, early Hen.
III. Harl. 47 I. 19.

—— Presbiter. Eudo, late Hen. II.
Harl. 45 B. 42.

— — Sacerdos. Eudo, ante 1175. Harl.
51 B. 4 (Salesbi), 5;—t. Hen. II. Harl.
45 B. 42, 43, 47 I. 34, 58 C. 10.

——— Rogerus, ante 1190. Harl.
56 F. 32.

——— Radulfus, early 13 cent.
or early Hen. III. Cott. xxvii. 51,
Harl. 47 I. 19, 56 I. 34.

—— Vicarius. Robertus. 1368. Harl.
78 E. 47.

Salehurst (Salhurst, etc.), co. Suss.
Decree in favour of Robertsbridge
Abbey conc. tithes in, [1205-16?]
(Salhirst). Eg. 382.

—— Grants, etc., in, t. Hen. III. Harl.
80 I. 33;—1344. Add. 20158;—1432.
Harl. 78 E. 50;—1446. Add. 5660;—
1451. Add. 5663;—1466. Add. 5667;
—1468. Add. 5668;—1471. Add.
5669;—1474. Add. 17345;—1536.
Add. 24859;—1541. Add. 5675;—
1562. Harl. 77 A. 6, 34;—1650. Add.
6556.

—— Grant in Wigsell (Wygesell) in,
1304. Harl. 77 E. 44.

—— Grant of the advowson, etc., to
Robertsbridge Abbey, c. 1307-8 (Sal-
herst). Eg. 398.

—— Release in, to Robertsbridge
Abbey, 1319 (do.). Eg. 400.

—— Lrs. patent confirming tenure of
the prebend of, etc., to Robertsbridge
Abbey, 1333 (Salhirst). Eg. 401.

—— Grant in Glottenham (Glotynge-
ham) nr., 1358 (Salhurst). Add. 9233.

—— Power to give seisin of Wigsell
(Wyggeshull) manor in, 1407. Harl.
76 G. 40, 41.

—— Compotus-rolls of Wigsell manor
in, 1450-51. Harl. Roll CC. 26;—
1462-63. Harl. Roll CC. 27.

—— Award and covenant conc. Bugshill (Bekwesill, Bekwesell) and Wigsell (Wygsell) manors in, 1529. Harl.
79 G. 24;—1530. Harl. 76 H. 12.

— — Covenant for a recovery and fine
in Bugshill (Beckotwesell) in, 1559.
Harl. 76 I. 44, 77 G. 24.

——— Precipes on covenants conc. lands
in, 1578. Add. 15223;—1592. Add.
15230.

Salehurst (Salhurst, etc.), co. Suss. (continued). Capellanus. Robertus, t. Hen. III. Campb. xxvii. 15.

—— Rector. Mag. Thomas, [1205-16?]. Eg. 382.

Salfletby, etc. v. Saltfleetby, co. Linc.

Salflethaven. v. Saltfleet Haven, co. Linc.

Salford, co. Bedf. Grants, etc., in, 1573. Add. 24108, 24109 ; — 1587. Add. 24110 ;—1591. Add. 24111 ;— 1592. Add. 24112 ; — 1599. Add. 24114 ;—1606. Add. 24115, 24116 ;— 1608. Add. 24118 ; — 1722. Add. 24126.

· —— Sale, etc., of the rectory, 1597. Add. 24113 ;—1664. Add. 24125.

·—— Mortgage of the manor farm, etc., 1661. Add. 24080, 24123.

—— Decree in suit conc. lands inherited from N. Langford in, 1670. Add. 24180.

Salford, co. Oxon. Precipe on a covenant conc. land in, 1593 (Salforde al. Sawforde). Add. 25214.

Salhouse, co. Norf. Grant in, 1451. Add. 7386.

Salhurst. v. Salehurst, co. Suss.

Saling, co. Essex. Conf. of the church to Dunmow Priory, 1221. Cott. xxi. 15.

—— Grants, etc., in, t. Hen. III. Add. 5946 ;—t. Edw. I. Add. 6178 ;— 1296. Add. 15575 (Salynges) :—1406. Add. 6179 ;—1421. Add. 6180.

Saling, Little, co. Essex. Grant in, 1321 (Berdefeld Sulyngg). Harl. 46 A. 28.

—— Precipe on a covenant conc. lands in. 1529 (Berdfeld Salyng). Add. 24923.

Salisbury (Nova Sar.), co. Wilts. Grant of liberties, etc., to, by Hen. III., 1227 ; with conf., [1263-70]. Harl. 58 H. 38, 39 (copies).

—— Grants, etc., in or nr., t. Hen. III. Lansd. 682 ;—1397. Add. 17424 ; —1427. Harl. 76 D. 6 ;—1440. Harl. 53 C. 9 ;—1472. Add. 17344.

—— Joh. de Wilton, persona eccl. Sci. Thome de Nova Sar., comptroller of works at Clarendon, 1364-7. Add. 26594.

—— Compotus, 1489. Add. 14363.

—— Briefs for repairing and rebuilding Trinity Hospital, 1803, 1809. Ch. Br. B. xliii. 6, xlix. 8.

Salisbury (Nova Sar.), co. Wilts. (continued). Major. Ric. Spencer, 1397. Add. 17424.

—— —— Joh. Sarisbury, 1403. Campb. viii. 8.

—— · —— Joh. Bremle, 1427. Harl. 76 D. 6.

—— —— Joh. Halle, 1465. Harl. 78 I. 55.

—— —— Will. Maynard, 1489. Add. 14363.

—— Prepositi. Joh. Leucesham, Walt. Naudre, 1397. Add. 17424.

—— —— Joh. Hayne, Steph. Couper, 1427. Harl. 76 D. 6.

—— Ballivus. Joh. Gowayn, 1403. Campb. viii. 8.

—— Coronatores. Ric. Juwel, 1397. Add. 17424.

—— —— Will. Cokkys, Ric. Gate, 1427. Harl. 76 D. 6.

—— Clericus. Guillermus, early 13 cent. (Saresbyr.). Harl. 86 C. 23.

Salley, co. Wilts. Acquittance for dues from the manor, 1536-7. Add. 18280.

Sallowe. v. Sawley, co. Derb.

Salmanmor. v. sub Panmure, co. Forfar.

Salmonsbury, [now Bourton on the Water?], co. Glouc. Grant of land bel. to, 799 (Sulmonnes burg). Cott. MS. Aug. ii. 4.

Salop, County of. Precipe to the sheriff to enforce payment of "le cherchambre" to Buildwas Abbey, [1163-6]. Campb. xxix. 6.

—— Precipe to the sheriff for inquisition conc. tenants of Wenlock Priory, 1247. Harl. 45 A. 33.

—— Valor of Crown lands in, 1518. Roy. Roll 14 B. xxxviii.

—— Grant by the Earl of Leicester of the stewardship of his manors in, 1566. Harl. 83 E. 26.

—— Exemplif. of Crown grant of forfeited lands of J. Litleton in, 1610. Harl. 83 H. 28.

—— Commission conc. fines of recusants in, 1687. Harl. 111 H. 12.

—— Vicecomes (nuper). Will. Bagod, 1280. Woll. v. 20.

Salopesbiria. v. Shrewsbury, co. Salop.

Salsus Mariscus, Saltmarsh. v. sub Almondsbury, co. Glouc.

**Salt**, *nr. Stafford, co. Staff.* Grant in, 1343. Add. 20450.

**Saltcoot.** *v. Salcott, co. Essex.*

**Saltcumbe.** *v. Salcombe, co. Devon.*

**Saltereia, Saltreia, etc.** *v. Sawtrey, co. Hunt.*

**Salterhaga**, *co. Linc.* Grant in, by Hub. de Gant, late 12 cent. Harl. 50 F. 33.

**Saltersich.** *v. sub* Willaston, *co. Chest.*

**Saltfleet Haven**, *co. Linc.* Conf. in, to Louth Park Abbey, 1295 (Salflethauen). Harl. 45 H. 19.

—— Conveyance, etc., of the manor, 1361 (Saltflethaven). Harl. 58 A. 48; —1387. Harl. 53 C. 38.

—— Fine in, 1429. Harl. 56 I. 49.

—— Deed conc. Gayton enrolled in the court of the Cas. of Richmond at, 1502 (Saltflethaven). Harl. 48 G. 41.

**Saltfleetby**, *co. Linc.* Grants, etc., in, 1293. Harl. 50 G. 46 (Saltfletuby);— 1359. Harl. 57 G. 13 (Saltfletby); 1362. Harl. 53 C. 49, 56 E. 28;— 1425. Harl. 52 G. 8.

—— Conf. in, to Louth Park Abbey, 1295 (Salfletby). Harl. 45 H. 19.

—— Fine in, 1302 (Salfleteby). Harl. 45 H. 18.

—— Precipe on a covenant conc. lands in, 1555 (Saltfletby Omnium Sanctorum). Add. 25061.

—— Crown lease in, of lands late bel. to Louth Park Abbey, 1562 (Saltefletby). Harl. 75 E. 35.

**Saltwood**, *co. Kent.* Grant of, to Christ Church, Canterbury, 1026 (Saltuuda). Cott. x. 11.

—— Evidence conc. tenure of, by Hugo de Muntfort, [1072] (Saltuda). Cott. MS. Aug. ii. 36.

—— Acquittance for the compotus of the manor, 1496-7. Harl. 53 G. 43.

—— Lands in Hythe, co. Kent, held by St. Bartholomew's Hospital at, 1574. Add. 26002;—1618. Add. 26008.

**Salueya.** *v. Sawley, co. Derb.*

**Salvington**, *co. Suss.* Lease in, 1357. Harl. 80 H. 8.

**Salwarp,** *co. Worc.* A boundary mark, 1038 (innan Salewearpan). Add. 19798.

—— Exemplif. of Crown grant of forfeited lands in, 1610. Harl. 83 H. 28.

**Salynges.** *v. Saling, co. Essex.*

**Samford, co.** —— (?). *Clericus.* Tomas, as witness, nr. Watford, co. Hertf., early 13 cent. Harl. 86 A. 56.

**Samford Hundred**, *co. Suff.* Grant made " coram capitulo de hundredo de Sanford." [1175–1200]. Cott. MS. Nero C. iii. f. 191.

—— Subsidy-roll, 1563–4. Add. 9764.

—— *Ballivus de Saunford.* Rad. de Alneto, 1256. Add. 9486.

**Sampford.** *v. Sandford, co. Oxon.*

**Sampford Brett**, *co. Som.* Grants, etc., in, 1329. Add. 11176 (Sandforde Bret);—1384. Add. 11185 (do.);— 1393. Add. 11186 (Saundford Bryt);— 1403. Add. 11189 (do.);—1404. Add. 11190-11192 (Samford Brit, etc.);— 1415. Add. 11195 (Saunford Brytle).

**Sampford, Great and Little**, *co. Essex.* Reservation of rights to the church of Great S. over Hempstead chapel, [1218–35] (Samf rd). Add. 20076.

—— Release, etc., of the manor, 1343. Harl. 56 H. 6 (Saunford);—1388. Harl. 48 E. 52.

—— Precipe on a covenant conc. lands in, 1592 (S. Magna, S. Parva). Add. 25016.

—— *Rector eccl. de Sampford parva.* Ric. Cayli al. Caily, 1350. Harl. 48 C. 50;—1355. Harl. 54 G. 49;—1364. Harl. 48 C. 53;—1368. Harl. 47 G. 1.

**Sampton**, *in W. Hythe, co. Kent.* Grants at, to Lyminge monastery, 732 (Sand tun). Cott. MS. Aug. ii. 91;— 833 (Sand tun). Cott. MS. Aug. ii. 102.

**Sanager,** *co. Glouc.* Grant, etc., in, 1331. Add. 7737 (Swonhungre);— 1332. Add. 7738.

**S. Augustini parochia.** *v. sub* Norwich, *co. Norf.*

**S. Botulphus.** *v.* Boston, *co. Linc.*

**S. Breuell.** *v.* St. Briavels, *co. Glouc.*

**S. Brigidi ecclesia.** *v.* Bride, *Isle of Man.*

**S. Caddocus.** *v.* Caddoxton juxta Neath, *co. Glam.*

**SS. Cosme et Damiani parochia.** *v.* Blean, *co. Kent.*

**S. Cryda, S. Crede.** *v.* Creed, *co. Cornw.*

**S. Edalberti parochia.** *v. sub* Mendlesham, *co. Suff.*

S. Elene ecclesia. *v. sub* London, Par. of St. Helen, Bishopsgate.

S. Georgii ecclesia. *v. sub* Oxford, *co. Oxon.*

S. Gunlei de Novo burgo ecclesia. *v.* Newport, *co. Monm.*

S. Gwynoci parochia. *v.* Vainor, *co. Brecon.*

SS. Ide et Lidi parochia. *v.* St. Issey, *co. Cornw.*

S. Julita, *co. Glam.* (?). *Sacerdos.* Willelmus, early 13 cent. Harl. 75 B. 28.

S. Kehinwehir capella. *v.* Llangeinor, *co. Glam.*

S. Kenedri de Kantreff parochia. *v.* Cantreff, *co. Brecon.*

S. Kierani ecclesia, [*in Exeter?*], *co. Devon. Persona.* Tho. Cook, 1426, 1427. Harl. 85 B. 33.

S. Maria in Hoo. *v.* Hoo St. Mary, *co. Kent.*

S. Marie ecclesia, *co. Linc. Vicarius.* Adam, *t.* Hen. II. Add. 20503.

S. Martha, parochia vocata. *v.* Chilworth, *co. Surr.*

S. Martino, [ecclesia] de. *v. sub* Oxford, *co. Oxon.*

S. Nicholao, capella de. *v. sub* Tickhill, *co. York.*

S. Padoci ecclesia. *v.* Llanbaddock, *co. Monm.*

Sancton, *co. York.* Re-grant in, *t.* Steph.–Hen. II. (Santoua). Add. 20507.

—— Grant of Hesleskew (Heselchon) in, to Watton Priory, early Hen. II. (Sautun). Add. 21134.

—— Release of a moiety of the church, etc., to Watton Priory, late 13 cent. Add. 22569 (Santon);—1339. Harl. 53 G. 58 (do.).

Sand, *in Kewstoke* (?), *co. Som.* Lease in, saving suit to Norton Beauchamp manor, 1389 (La Sonde). Harl. 46 G. 21.

Sandal, Great, *co. York.* Rent in West Bretton due to the church of, *t.* Edw. I. Add. 8207.

—— Grant in, 1315 (Sandale). Harl. 54 G. 43.

—— Crown lease in Crigglestone (Seregylston), etc., in, 1555. Harl. 84 C. 32.

Sandal, Great, *co. York* (*continued*). *Persons.* Robertus, early 13 cent. Add. 7433.

—— *Rector. Dom.* Jacobus de Langgetoft, 1292. Add. 8276.

—— *Vicarius.* Will. Bulle, 1353. Add. 20603.

Sandal, Kirk, *co. York.* Grant in, 1375 (Sandall). Harl. 50 G. 8.

Sandbach, *co. Chest.* Settlement in, 1331 (Soubache). Add. 20487.

—— *Vicarius.* Philippus, 1331. Add. 20487.

Sandcroft. *v.* Elmham, S., St. Cross, *co. Suff.*

Sanderstead (Sandirsted, etc.), *co. Surr.* Conf. by Hyde Abbey of a grant in, *t.* Rich. I. (?) (Sandestuda). Add. 24613.

—— Suit conc. common of pasture in, 1307. Add. 15851.

—— Grants, etc., in, 1346. Add. 23658;—1377. Add. 23446;—1425. Add. 23450, 24616;—1426. Add. 23451;—1427. Add. 24617;—1428. Add. 23452, 23453;—1429. Add. 23540;—1439. Add. 24618;—1444. Add. 24620;—1447. Add. 23455-23457;—1451. Add. 23656;—1489. Add. 23461;—1508. Add. 23463;—1522. Add. 23655.

—— Grant in Purley in, 1373. Add. 24614.

—— General release in, to Mercia Carew, 1440. Add. 23730.

—— Feoffments, etc., of W. Purley (Westpirley, Westpurle, etc.) in, 1445. Add. 24621-24623;—1452. Add. 24624;—1471. Add. 24615, 24625-24630;—1537. Add. 24632;—1555, 1558. Add. 24633 *a, b.*

—— Lease of E. Purley (Est Pirle) manor in, 1447. Add. 23654.

—— Inspex. of proceedings in a suit for W. Purley in, 1472. Add. 24631.

Sandford, *nr.* Sonning (?), *co. Berks.* Brief conc. a fire at the mills, 1759. Ch. Br. A. vi. 2.

Sandford, *in Doddenham, co. Dors.* Defeasance of grant of "le place apud le Hille" nr., 1400 (Sandeford). Harl. 42 D. 25.

Sandford, *in Bullington Hundred, co. Oxon.* Precipe on a covenant conc. the manor, etc., 1593 (Sampford *al.* Sunford). Add. 25216.

2 T

Sandford, co. *Oxon.* Brief conc. a fire at, 1768. Ch. Rr. B. viii. 11.

Sandford, *in Winscomb, co. Som.* Lease, etc., in, 1340. Harl. 54 D. 24 (S. juxta Banewell); –1343. Harl. 54 D. 26.

Sandforde Bret. *v.* Sampford Brett, co. *Som.*

Sandherst, terra de. *v. sub* Tonbridge, co. *Kent.*

Sandhurst, co. *Glouc.* Grant, etc., in Wulsworth in, 1343. Add. 6028;— 1369. Add. 5276.

Sandhurst, co. *Kent.* Grant on the den of Feryngeherst in (?), 1316. Harl. 80 C. 55.

—— Release of land called Bourneton, etc., in, 1408. Harl. 77 G. 44.

—— Conveyance, etc., in, 1444. Harl. 76 G. 53;—1551. Cott xv. 34.

—— *Rector.* Joh. Vergieu, 1365. Add. 16178.

Sandhurst Wood, [*nr. Ashford ?*], co. *Kent.* Grant of swine pasture in, 858 (Sandhyrst). Cott. MS. Aug. ii. 66.

Sandiacre, co. *Derb.* Conf. of grant in, to Dale Abbey, co. Derb., early 13 cent. Woll. vi. 1.

—— Grants, etc., in, *t.* Edw. I. Lansd. 600, 601 (Sandiakyr);—1328. Lansd. 602.

—— Power to give seisin, etc., of the manor, 1450. Woll. i. 75;—1472. Woll. i. 77;—1628. Woll. xi. 33.

Sandlake. *v. sub* Battle, co. *Suss.*

Sandleford, co. *Berks.* Grant of a fair at, to the Priory, 1234 (Sandelford). Harl. 58 H. 46 (*copy*).

Sandon, co. *Essex.* Release, etc., in, 1555. Add. 5263;—1561. Harl. 80 F. 16, 19.

—— Sale of the manor, etc., 1564. Harl. 79 G. 20.

—— Precipe on a covenant conc. land in, 1593. Add. 25042.

Sandon, co. *Hertf.* Fine in, 1314. Add. 6248.

Sandridge, co. *Hertf.* Power to give seisin in, 1372 (Sandrugge). Add. 22609.

Sand tun. *v.* Sampton, *in W. Hythe,* co. *Kent.*

Sandwell. *v. sub* Bromwich, West, co. *Staf.*

Sandwich, co. *Kent.* Grant of the port and town to the church of Canterbury, [972 or 973?] (Sanduuich). Cott. MS. Aug. ii. 67 (*copy*).

—— Dispute as to the title to, 1038 (Sandwic). Cott. MS. Aug. ii. 90.

—— Grant of a marsh nr., to Boxley Abbey, early 13 cent. Harl. 45 E. 23.

—— Grants, etc., in, 1301. Harl. 80 C. 26;—1344. Harl. 80 C. 27;—1345. Harl. 80 C. 28, 29;—1418. Harl. 78 D. 9.

—— Grant of land in Ash late bel. to the "Jesus Masse Brotherhede" at, 1549. Add. 4607.

—— Release, etc., to the grammar school, of woodlands in Hackington, co. Kent, 1568. Harl 75 F. 44, 78 C. 21.

—— Exchequer acquittance to the farmer of the customs of the port of, 1576. Add. 25622.

—— *Major.* Omerus, *t.* Hen. III. Add. 16457.

—— *Prepositus.* Joh. de Cliveshende, *t.* Hen. III. Add. 16457.

—— *Rector eccl. S. Petri.* Stephanus, 1351. Campb. xiv. 2.

—— *Sacerdotes.* Jacobus, Willelmus, early 13 cent. Harl. 45 E. 33.

Sandwith, co. *York.* Sale in, 1637. Add. 1797.

Sandy, co. *Bedf.* Covenant conc. descent of the manor, 1372 (Sondeye). Add. 19979.

—— Sale, etc., in, 1507. Add. 990 (Sonday), 991;—1626. Harl. 112 E. 38;—1629. Add. 1000;—1631. Harl. 112 E. 39.

—— Grant of the advowson, 1525. Harl. 83 A. 29.

—— *Capellanus.* Robertus, *t.* Hen. III. Harl. 83 B. 43.

Sanford. *v.* Samford Hundred, co. *Suff.*

Saninghelle, *nr. Harbledown* (?), co. *Kent.* Grant in, to H. Sepulchre Priory, Canterbury, early 13 cent. Harl. 78 A. 50.

Sankey, co. *Lanc.* Brief for rebuilding the chapel, 1765. Ch. Br. B. v. 1.

Santersdune. *v.* Saunderton, co. *Buck.*

Santon, Santun. *v.* Sancton, co. *York.*

Santon (?), *nr. Harrold,* co. *Bedf.* (?). Covenant conc. land in, betw. Harrold Priory and Biddlesdon Abbey, 1251 (Suonton, Swonton). Harl. 84 F. 34.

Sapcote, co. Leic. Grant of a pension from the manor, 1309. Add. 21393.

Sapey Pritchard, co. Worc. Grant in, 1519 (Sapy Pychar). Harl. 55 F. 29.

Sapindon, Sapynton. v. sub Chartham, co. Kent.

Sapiston, co. Suff. Grant, etc., in, early Hen. III. Harl. 55 G. 19 (Sapestune);—1442. Harl. 51 F. 1 (Sapston).
—— Clericus. Johannes, late 13 cent. Add. 10521.

Sapperton, co. Linc. Power to take seisin in, 1530 (Sapurton). Add. 6462.

Sapy Pychar. v. Sapey Pritchard, co. Worc.

Sardeloua. v. Shardlow, co. Derb.

Saredon, Great, co. Staff. Brief conc. a fire at, 1794. Ch. Br. B. xxxiv. 6.

Sarnebr. v. Shernborne, co. Norf.

Sarneford. v. Sharnford, co. Leic.

Sarratt, co. Hertf. Grant, etc., in, 1441. Harl. 47 L 30 (Sarret);—1592. Add. 8461.

Sarsden, co. Oxon. Precipe on a covenant conc. land in, 1593. Add. 25215.

Sarum, New. v. Salisbury, co. Wilts.

Sarum, Old, co. Wilts. Feoffment in, 1523. Add. 5140.

Saughall, Great, co. Flint. Rental of the manor, 1735. Add. 1009.

Saunderton, co. Buck. Grant of woodlands in, to Thame Abbey, late Hen. II. (Santersdune). Add. 20375, 20376.
—— Grant of free-warren in, 1317 (Saundreton). Harl. 84 C. 14.
—— Release of the manor, 1389 (Saundreston). Harl. 46 F. 35.
—— Clericus. Johannes, late Hen. II. Add. 20375, 20376.

Saunderton Manor. v. sub Risborough, Monks, co. Buck.

Saundford Bryt, Saunford Brytte. v. Sampford Brett, co. Som.

Saunford. v. Samford Hundred, co. Suff.
—— v. Sampford, Great and Little, co. Essex.

Sausthorpe, co. Linc. Grant in, t. Hen. III. (Sauzthorp). Harl. 48 G. 2.

Sausthorpe, co. Linc. (continued). Power to give seisin of the manor, 1395. Harl. 58 B. 11.

Sawbridge, in Wolfhamcote, co. Warw. Feoffment in, 1444 (Salbrigge). Cott. iv. 1.
—— Release of the manor, 1598 (Salbridge). Add. 1011.

Sawbridgeworth, co. Hertf. Conf. of grant in, in the fee of the Earl of Essex, [1157-8] (Sabristeswrda). Slo. xxxii. 64.
—— Grant of a combe of corn yearly in, to Southwark Priory, c. 1158 (?) (Sabricusteswurthe). Harl. 50 A. 89.
—— Conf. of a grant of the church to Westminster Abbey, c. 1170 (Sabrihteswrõe). Cott. x. i.
—— Grant in, to Latton Priory, co. Essex, early 13 cent. (Sabrichteswrth). Harl. 50 G. 18.
—— Grants, etc., in, early 13 cent.-t. Edw. I. Add. 4718-4747 (Sabricteswrth, etc.);—1285. Add. 4748;—1302. Cott. xxvii. 33;—1304-1544. Add. 4749-4813;—1598. Add. 4822;—1607. Add. 4825.
—— Extracts of court-rolls, 1493. Add. 4806 (Sabrysford);—1538. Add. 4810;—1539. Add. 4811;—1559. Add. 4819.
—— Memoranda of conveyances in, 1516-1597. Add. 4823.
—— Exchequer acquittance for rent of Pishoe al. Pishoebury manor in, 1607. Add. 25607.
—— Acquittance for a charge on land in, 1634. Add. 4827.

Sawforde. v. Salford, co. Oxon.

Sawley, co. Derb. "Duo cupones in Mayo" to be rendered at (?), t. Edw. I. (Salueya). Harl. 111 E. 17 (copy).
—— Will proved in the prebendal church of, 1502 (Sallow). Woll. i. 81.
—— Vicarius. Will. Beke, 1391 (Sallowe). Woll. vi. 41, 46.

Sawston, co. Camb. Exemption of Dernford manor in or nr., from ecclesiastical taxation, 1372. Harl. Roll AA. 22.
—— Fine of the rectory, 1609. Harl. 75 G. 55.

Sawtrey, co. Hunt. Grants, etc., o', to Sawtrey Abbey, [1147-8?]. Cott. vii. 3 (Salterein);—[1157-8]. Cott. xv. 21 (Salterein);—[1186?]. Cott. xii. 79 (Salteruis);—[1184-9]. Cott. xii. 78 (Sauteria).

**Sawtrey**, *co. Hunt. (continued)*. Papal conff. of above, etc., 1164. Cott. MS. Aug. ii. 116;—1176. Cott. MS. Aug. ii. 125;—1195. Cott. MS. Aug. ii. 111;—1205. Cott. MS. Aug. ii. 121.

**Saxby**, *in Aslacoe Wapentake, co. Linc. Persona,* Johannes, 1242. Harl. 44 E. 49.

**Saxby on Humber** (Saxebi, Saxeby), *co. Linc.* Grant in, to Aulnay Abbey, early 13 cent. Harl. 52 A. 23.

—— Grant, etc., in, *c.* 1201-3. Harl. 55 G. 25;—1329. Add. 8448.

—— Grants, etc., in, to Newhouse Abbey, early 13 cent. Harl. 45 H. 4;— *t.* Hen. III. Hail. 53 C. 21; —*c.* 1260. Harl. 44 A. 2, 3;—late Hen. III. Harl. 51 G. 25;—*t.* Edw. I. Cott. xxvii. 48, 49, Harl. 55 F. 26;—1305. Harl. 48 B. 52.

—— Plea in, against Newhouse Abbey, 1288. Harl. 48 D. 55.

—— *Clericus.* Robertus, early 13 cent. Harl. 52 A. 23.

—— —— Walterus, late Hen. III. Harl. 51 G. 25.

—— *Persona (quondam).* Radulphus, *t.* Edw. I. Harl. 55 F. 26.

—— *Rector (quondam).* Joh. de Manneby, 1329. Add. 8448.

**Saxelby**, *co. Linc.* Conff., etc., of St. Botulph's church and lands in, to Newhouse Abbey, [1143-7]. Harl. 43 H. 10 (Saxelebi);—*c.* 1150-55. Harl. 43 G. 19 (Saxolebi), 43 H. 14 (Saxebia), 15 (Saxlebi), 16, 17 (Saxclebi); —[1156 or 7]. Harl. 51 H. 1 (Saxelbi);—early Hen. II. Harl. 45 B. 27 (Saxolebi);—[1182-3 ?]. Harl. 43 A. 25 (Saxelebi); — [1190-95]. Harl. 43 H. 38 *b* (Saxelbi);—*c.* 1195-6. Harl. 43 H. 23 (Saxolebi);—1263. Harl. 44 F. 27 (Saexelby);—1287. Harl. 43 H. 27;—1307. Harl. 43 H. 34;—1319. Harl. 43 G. 29;—1333. Harl. 43 H. 39, 40; — 1344. Harl. 43 H. 41;—1368. Harl. 43 H. 44;— 1389. Harl. 43 G. 33;—1424. Harl. 43 G. 35;—1485. Harl. 43 I. 7;—1500. Harl. 43 I. 8.

—— Tithe of hay paid to the church of, [1223] (Saxelbi). Harl. 44 F. 25.

—— Taxation of the vicarage, with rights of Newhouse Abbey in the same, [1239-65] (Saxelby). Harl. 45 A. 24.

—— Grant of homage, etc., in, to Thornton Abbey, [1249-53] (Saxeleby iuxta Linc.]. Harl. 54 G. 16.

**Saxelby**, *co. Linc. (continued)*. Covenants, etc., conc. tithes, etc., in, with Newhouse Abbey. *t.* Hen. III. Harl. 44 G. 34, 40;—1288. Cott. xxviii. 9; —1314. Harl. 44 H. 18; — 1365. Harl. 45 A. 7.

—— Bond to Newhouse Abbey conc. presentation to, 1331. Harl. 50 I. 43.

—— Power to give seisin in, 1335. Harl. 54 G. 21.

—— Enquiry conc. a lease of the church by Newhouse Abbey, 1361. Harl. 44 H. 31.

—— Suits betw. Newhouse Abbey and Broadholm Priory conc. tithes in, *t.* Edw. III. Harl. 58 G. 39.

—— *Capellanus.* Matthew, early Hen. III. Harl. 53 D. 43.

—— *Vicarius.* Dom. Tho. de Cavo, 1311. Harl. 47 H. 32.

**Saxham**, *co. Suff.* Release in, *t.* Edw. I. (Sexton). Harl. 52 I. 49.

**Saxham, Little**, *co. Suff.* Precipe on a covenant conc. lands in, 1565. Add. 25330.

**Saxlingham**, *in Henstead Hundred, co. Norf.* Papal conf. of tithes of, to Horsham St. Faith Priory, 1163 (Saxlingaham). Cott. MS. Aug. ii. 136.

—— Feoffments, etc., of Netherhall manor, etc., in, 1408. Harl. 54 I. 7 (Saxlyngham);—1430. Harl. 43 E. 19, 54 I. 10;—1431. Harl. 45 I. 12, 50 H. 27, 28, 54 I. 15;—1435. Add. 2016.

—— *Clericus.* Radulfus, [1146-7?]. Harl. 47 H. 45.

**Saxmundham**, *co. Suff.* Grants, etc., in, *t.* Hen. III. Harl. 49 B. 1, Add. 5899, 5900.

—— Feoffments, etc., of Hurtes and Swans manors, etc., in, 1384. Cott. xxviii. 85;—1408. Harl. 54 I. 7;—1430. Harl. 43 E. 19, 54 I. 10; —1431. Harl. 45 I. 12, 50 H. 27, 28, 54 I. 15;—1435. Add. 2016.

—— Crown grant of Swans (Swannes) manor in, 1508. Harl. 51 H. 18.

—— Crown grant of a fair and market at, with the advowson, 1511. Harl. 51 H. 20.

—— Precipe on a covenant conc. land in, 1593. Add. 25480.

**Saxondale**, *in Shelford, co. Nott.* Release of the manor, 1472 (Saxendale). Woll. i. 77.

—— Order conc. stipend of the curate, 1547. Add. 15274.

**Saxstead,** *co. Suff.* Extract of court-roll, 1575. Add. 10457.

—— Precipe on a covenant conc. land in, 1593. Add. 25460.

**Saxthorpe,** *co. Norf. Sacerdos.* Radulfus, [1146–7?] (Saxtorpe). Harl. 47 H. 45.

**Saxton** *al.* **Saxon.** *v. sub* Cheveley, *co. Camb.*

**Saxton,** *co. York.* Grant in, 1394–5. Add. 26773.

—— Sale of Lead Grange manor in, 1575. Harl. 111 D. 41.

**Sayham.** *v. sub* Newton, *co. Suff.*

**Saylby.** *v.* Saleby, *co. Linc.*

**Scacresden.** *v. sub* Gamlingay, *co. Camb.*

**Scaga,** *in Frindsbury* (?), *co. Kent.* Grant of the marsh of, to the Bp. of Rochester, 778. Cott. viii. 34.

**Scagglethorpe,** *co. York.* Feoffment of the manor, 1441 (Scagilthorpe). Harl. 83 F. 3, 4.

**Scal.** *v.* Skellow, *in Owston, co. York.*

**Scalby.** *v.* Scawby, *co. Linc.*

**Scalby,** *co. York.* Conf. of the manor to Edm., Earl of Lancaster, 1285. Cott. MS. Aug. ii. 135 (5).

—— Sale of the manor, 1652. Add. 12630.

**Scaldwell,** *co. Northt.* Grant of rent in, to a chapel in Marston Trussel church, early Hen. III. (Scaudewell). Harl. 57 A. 53.

—— Grant of land in, to build a wind-mill on, late Hen. III. (Scaudewell). Add. 22406.

—— Grants of same, with the mill, late Hen. III. (Scaudewelle). Add. 22404, 22405.

—— Grants, etc., in, *t.* Edw. I. Add. 22407 (Scaudewell); — 1307. Add. 21660 (Scaldewell); — 1348. Add. 21767; — 1360. Add. 22408; — 1393. Add. 21797; — 1396. Add. 21803, 22409; — 1400. Add. 21806, 21807; — 1415. Add. 22410; — 1418. Add. 22411, 22412; — 1422. Add. 22263, 22264; — 1437. Add. 22272; — 1487. Add. 22301.

—— Grant of a nativus of, to the Earl of Devon, 1384 (Schaldewell). Harl. 49 G. 54.

**Scaldwell,** *co. Northt. (continued).* Feoffment, etc., of the manor, 1464–5. Add. 22292; — 1470. Add. 22293, 22296; — 1473. Add. 22413; — 1528. Add. 22307; — 1535. Add. 22309.

—— Precipe on a covenant conc. land in, 1578. Add. 25164.

—— *Rector.* Joh. Wright, 1406. Add. 21813.

**Scalford,** *co. Leic.* Conf. of a mill, etc., at, to St. Andrew's Priory, Northampton, [1124–36] (Scaldeford). Cott. xviii. 41.

—— Restoration of the church to Daventry Priory, [1147?] (Scaldofort). Add. 21204.

—— Settlement in marriage of a mill, etc., in, late 12 cent. (Scaldiford). Harl. 111 D. 22.

—— *Persona.* Willelmus, late 12 cent. Add. 10597.

**Scalndeburne.** *v.* Shalbourn, *co. Berks.*

**Scalteby.** *v.* Scawby, *co. Linc.*

**Scamblesby,** *co. Linc. Clericus.* Hugo, late Hen. II. (Scamelcsbi). Harl. 47 F. 48.

—— *Diaconus.* Laurencius, late Hen. II. (Scamelbi). Harl. 47 F. 48.

**Scampton** (Scamton, Scamtun, etc.), *co. Linc.* Grants, etc., in, to Kirkstead Abbey, [1155?]. Harl. 43 C. 17 (Scamtuna); — c. 1156 (?). Harl. 50 F. 32 (do.), Cott. xvi. 37 (Schamtun); — *t.* Hen. II. Harl. 45 B. 28; — late 12 cent. Harl. 47 I. 14 (Scant.), 15 (Scantona), 16, 54 G. 2; — *t.* John. Harl. 47 I. 17, 18, 55 G. 27, 28; — c. 1270–4. Harl. 52 F. 20, 21, 25; — 1271. Harl. 52 F. 22, 23; — 1273. Harl. 52 E. 16, 52 F. 24; — 1274. Harl. 52 G. 4; — 1336. Harl. 45 I. 35, 36, 46 A. 33; — 1353. Harl. 57 D. 21; — 1392. Harl. 46 F. 17.

—— Lease in, to Kirkstead Abbey, from Norwich Priory, with conf., c. 1175 (?). Harl. 44 H. 36; — [1175–1200]. Harl. 43 I. 17.

—— Freedom from sheriff's aid for above lands, late 12 cent. Harl. 44 H. 37.

—— Grants, etc., in, *t.* Hen. II. Harl. 55 E. 13 (Scamtonia); — late 13 cent. Harl. 47 F. 33, 48 E. 5.

—— Leases, etc., in, from Kirkstead Abbey, late Hen. II. Harl. 44 E. 54; — *post* 1274. Harl. 44 F. 4, 5.

Schadwell, *in Rushford*, co. *Norf.* Release in, *t.* Edw. I. (Schadewelle). Add. 22566.

Schakerlonde. *v. sub* Badwell, co. *Suff.*

Schalford. *v.* Shalford, co. *Surr.*

Schalthorp. *v.* Scawthorpe, co. *York.*

Schamtun. *v.* Scampton, co. *Linc.*

Schapeheye, Schapeye. *v.* Sheppey, Isle of, co. *Kent.*

Scharneburne, etc. *v.* Shernborne, co. *Norf.*

Scharpishame. *v. sub* Woodsdale, co. *Suss.*

Scharvisdal. *v.* Scarsdale, co. *Derb.*

Scharwelton. *v.* Charwelton, co. *Northt.*

Scharynden. *v. sub* Staplehurst, co. *Kent.*

Schaston. Burgus. *v.* Shaftesbury, co. *Dors.*

Schaudefeld. *v.* Shadingfield, co. *Suff.*

Schawe, La. *v.* Shawe, The, *nr. Kingsley*, co. *Staff.* (?).

—— *v. sub* Tonge, co. *Salop.*

Schebbedon. *v.* Shebdon, co. *Staff.*

Scheffeld. *v.* Sheffield, co. *York.*

Scheftintona. *v.* Skeffington, co. *Leic.*

Schegenes. *v.* Skegness, co. *Linc.*

Scheilmardon. *v.* Chelmorton, co. *Derb.*

Schelfangre. *v.* Sholfanger, co. *Norf.*

Schelfhull. *v.* Shelfield, co. *Warw.*

Schelton. *v.* Shelton, co. *Norf.*

—— *v.* Shelton, co. *Nott.*

Schendelby. *v.* Skendleby, co. *Linc.*

Schenefeld. *v.* Shenfield, co. *Essex.*

Schenindon. *v.* Shenington, co. *Oxon,* formerly co. *Glouc.*

Schepedham. *v.* Shipdham, co. *Norf.*

Schepereth. *v.* Shepreth, co. *Camb.*

Scheperige. *v. sub* Hinton, Broad, co. *Wilts.*

Scherdelowes. *v. sub* Gosfield, co. *Essex.*

Scherthom. *v.* Chartham, co. *Kent.*

Scheufeud. *v. sub* Theale, co. *Berks.*

Schevyok. *v.* Sheviock, co. *Cornw.*

Scheyle, Ouer. *v. sub* Seal, co. *Leic.*

Schiddinchou. *v. sub* Mistley, co. *Essex.*

Schifford. *v.* Shifford, co. *Oxon.*

Schilington. *v.* Skillington, co. *Linc.*

Schipden. *v.* Shipden, co. *Norf.*

Schipden, Over. *v.* Shibden, Over, *in N. Owram*, co. *York.*

Schipmedwe. *v.* Shipmeadow, co. *Suff.*

Schipstale, *nr. Grampound*, co. *Cornw.* Releases in, 1430. Add. 12990 ;—1431 Add. 12994.

Schirborne. *v.* Sherborne, co. *Dors.*

—— *v.* Shirburn, co. *Oxon.*

Schireford. *v.* Sherford, co. *Devon.*

Schirefrede, [*nr. Calverley?*], co. *York.* Release in, *t.* Hen. III. Add. 16595.

Schiremannemad. *v. sub* Waltham H. Cross, co. *Essex.*

Schirley. *v.* Shirley, co. *Derb.*

Schirlington. *v.* Skirlington, co. *York.*

Schirwolde. *v. sub* Harptree, East, co. *Som.*

Schirwyt. *v.* Skirwith, co. *Cumb.*

Schitere. *v.* Skittur, co. *Linc.*

Scholdene. *v.* Sholden, co. *Kent.*

Scholes, *in Barwick in Elmett*, co. *York.* Grant in, early 14 cent. (Scoles). Add. 16702.

—— Fine of the manor, 1638 (Scoles). Woll. xi. 29.

Scholes, *nr. Cleckheaton*, co. *York.* Power to give seisin in, 1413 (Scoles). Add. 8321.

Schonderley, *nr. Newdigate* (?), co. *Surr.* Power to sell timber at, 1282. Add. 17269.

Schorne. *v.* Shorne, co. *Kent.*

Schotesham. *v.* Shottesham, co. *Norf.*

Schroffold. *v. sub* Lee, co. *Kent.*

Schropham. *v.* Shropham, co. *Norf.*

Schudy Campes. *v.* Shudy Camps, co. *Camb.*

Schukburgh. *v.* Shuckburgh, co. *Warw.*

Schulton. *v.* Shilton, co. *Berks.*

Schyfford. *v.* Shifford, co. *Oxon.*

Schymplyngge, etc. *v.* Shimpling, co. *Suff.*

Schyngham. *v.* Shingham, *co. Norf.*

Schypedham. *v.* Shipdham, *co. Norf.*

Schypelee. *v.* Shipley, *co. Suss.*

Schypmedwe. *v.* Shipmeadow, *co. Suf.*

Scihtre, Scithre, Scitra. *v.* Skitter, *co. Linc.*

Sciligton. *v.* Skillington, *co. Linc.*

Scipleag, *co. Southt.* A boundary mark, 909. Harl. 43 C. 1.

Scirsham. *v.* Syresham, *co. Northt.*

Scleholm, *nr. Beesby* (?), *co. Linc. Clericus.* Willelmus, *t.* Hen. III. Harl. 46 D. 28.

Sclengesby. *v.* Slingsby, *co. York.*

Scnytirton. *v.* Snetterton, *co. Norf.*

Scogholm. *v.* Skokholm, Island of, *co. Pembr.*

Scohesby. *v.* Skewsby, *co. York.*

Scoles. *v:* Scholes, *co. York.*

Scopers, *nr. Goudhurst, co. Kent.* Fine and recovery of, 1559. Harl. 76 I. 44, 77 G. 24.

Scopwick, *co. Linc.* Grant in, to Sempringham Priory, *t.* Hen. II. (Scapewic). Add. 20863.
——— *Clericus.* Robertus, late Hen. II. Harl. 51 G. 15 (Scapwic), 56 C. 46 (do.).
——— *Sacerdos.* Ricardus, *t.* Hen. II. Add. 20863.

Scoreby, *co. York.* Grants, etc., of the manor, 1276. Cott. xii. 31 (Skorreby); —1299. Cott. v. 47 (Scorresby);—*c.* 1300. Harl. 43 I. 48;—1369. Harl. 51 E. 39, 54 C. 13.
——— Order for rents in, to be paid to Ant. Bek, 1279 (Scorreby). Cott. xxviii. 69.

Scorenes. *v.* Shorne, *co. Kent.*

Scorham. *v.* Shoreham, *co. Kent.*

Scoriaton, Scoriton. *v. sub* Buckfastleigh, *co. Devon.*

Scotney. *v. sub* Lydd, *co. Kent.*

Scottlethorpe, *nr. Grimsthorpe, co. Linc.* Grants in, *t.* John. Cott. xxvii. 186 (Scotlathorp);—late 13 cent. Add. 20590 (Scotilthorp).

Scottnetts. *v. sub* Debenham, *co. Suf.*

Scotton, *in Lindsey, co. Linc. Persona. Dom.* Ric. de Nevill, 1337. Add. 21594;—(as *Rector*), 1346. Add. 21631.

Scotton, *co. York.* Grant in, *c.* 1295 (Scottona juxta Richemund). Harl. 112 C. 6.

Scottow, *co. Norf.* Appropriation of the church to Hulme Abbey, 1232. Cott. iv. 57 (*copy*).
——— Fine in, 1313 (Scothowe). Harl. 45 F. 40.
——— Rental, 1455-6 (Skothow). Add. 13944.
——— Commission of enquiry conc. the living, 1659. Add. 14975.

Scoulton, *co. Norf.* Surrender in, 1360 (Sculton). Harl. 49 G. 42.

Scouueswelle, *co. Suss.* Battle Abbey freed from services for, by Hen. I., [1100-23]. Harl. 43 C. 12.

Scouyngton. *v. sub* Tong, *co. Kent.*

Scowesbi. *v.* Skewsby, *co. York.*

Scragard. *v. sub* Waltham, *co. Kent.*

Scrane *al.* Crane, Old, *in Freiston, co. Linc.* Grants, etc., in, to Kirkstead Abbey, *ante* 1158. Harl. 49 A. 2 (Vetus Screinga);—1158. Harl. 49 A. 1;—*c.* 1158 (?). Harl. 52 A. 34 (V. Scrainga);—*t.* Hen. II. Harl. 51 B. 44.
——— List of deeds conc. lands of Kirkstead Abbey in, early 13 cent. (Scrahingh). Harl. Roll O. 5.

Scraptoft, *co. Leic. Vicar.* Nich. Fisher, 1605. Woll. iv. 63.

Scratby, *co. Norf.* Release, etc., in, 1300. Add. 14851 (Scrouteby);— 1347. Harl. 48 C. 3;—1361. Harl. 52 B. 11.
——— License for a grant in, to Cobham College, *co. Kent*, 1372 (Skrouteby). Harl. 47 G. 3.

Scremby, *co. Linc.* Release of rents in, 1293 (Scrymby). Harl. 50 G. 46.

Scremby Hall. *v. sub* Kirkby on Bain, *co. Linc.*

Screveton, *co. Nott.* Grants, etc., in, *t.* Hen. III. Add. 5389;—1325. Add. 5396; — 1340. Add. 5397; — 1365. Harl. 58 B. 8.
——— Precipe on a covenant conc. lands in, 1578. Add. 25200.

Scrifenan hamme. *v.* Shrivenham, *co. Berks.*

Scrin, *in Panmure, co. Forfar.* Inquest conc. the pasture of Falmanmor in, 1286 (Scrin, Scryn). Harl. 43 B. 9.

**Seamer,** *in Cleveland, co. York.* Grant in, 1346 (Semere in Clyvelund). Harl. 83 C. 29.

—— *Capellanus.* Walterus, *c.* 1225. Add. 20587.

**Searby,** *co. Linc.* Grant in, to Newhouse Abbey, early Hen. III. (Seuerby). Harl. 50 D. 54.

—— *Presbiter.* Willelmus, *c.* 1150-55 (Seuerbi). Cott. xxvii. 34.

**Searnægles** ford [Shawford?], *co. Southt.* A boundary mark, 909. Harl. 43 C. 1.

**Seasalter,** *co. Kent.* Sales, etc., in, 1548. Harl. 75 E. 22, 75 H. 4, 76 H. 50;—1551. Harl. 75 E. 38;—1555. Harl. 76 I. 23;—1579. Harl. 78 B. 11;—1580. Harl. 77 B. 2–4, 77 H. 43.

—— *Rector.* Dom. Henricus, *c.* 1230 (Sesaltre). Add. 16350.

**Seaton,** *co. Devon.* Court-roll, 1537. Add. 13786.

**Seaton** (Seyton, etc.), *co. Rull.* Grants, etc., in, [1277]. Add. 21187;—1421. Add. 792;—1566. Add. 848;—1571. Add. 728.

—— Inquest conc. tenure of, 1302 (Scitone). Add. 7371.

—— Feoffments, etc., of the manor, 1383. Add. 22213, 22214;—1385. Add. 22215, 22216;—1422. Add. 22263, 22264;—*ante* 1437. Add. 21265;—1441. Add. 22274;—1464-5. Add. 22292;—1470. Add. 22295, 22296.

—— *Persona.* Nic. Greneham, 1414. Add. 21822.

—— *Rector.* Mag. Rogerus, [1277]. Add. 21187.

**Seaton,** *E.R., co. York.* Grant in, 1369. Add. 5754, 5755.

**Seatons.** *v. sub* Boughton Aluph, *co. Kent.*

**Seavington,** *co. Som.* Grant of goods, etc., in Sevenhampton Vaus manor in, 1346. Add. 17317.

**Seche, Sechithe.** *v.* Setchey, *co. Norf.*

**Sedbergh,** *co. York.* Pledge to observe a settlement in, 1348 (Sadbery in Lonesdale). Harl. 51 C. 12.

—— Lease of the rectory to Sir T. Cotton by Trinity College, Cambridge, 1637. Cott. xxiv. 27.

—— *Rector.* Dom. Hugo de Uppesal, *t.* Hen. III. (Soddeberg). Harl. 112 I. 27.

**Sedgefield,** *co. Durh.* Releases of the Isle (Insula) manor in, 1430. Harl. 43 E. 19;—1431. Harl. 45 I. 12.

**Sedgeford,** *co. Norf.* Conf. of a grant of the church to Norwich Priory, [1136-45] (Secheeforde). Cott. ii. 1.

**Sedgewick,** *in Horsham, co. Suss.* Lease in, 1590-1 (Sedgwick). Add. 8960.

**Sedgley,** *co. Staff.* Grant nr., *ante* 1211 (Seggeslegh). Add. 7205.

**Sedgrave.** *v.* Segrave, *co. Leic.*

**Sedlescombe,** *co. Suss.* Inhibition to the chaplain of, from taking tithes from the lands of Robertsbridge Abbey in, [1205-16?] (Sedelescumbe). Eg. 382.

—— Settlement of suit in, with Robertsbridge Abbey, [1255] (Sedelescombe). Eg. 390.

—— Release, etc., in, 1331. Add. 5650 (Sedlescumbe);—1344. Add. 20158 (Sedlescoumbe);—1530. Harl. 76 H. 12 (Setlescombe).

—— Precipe on a covenant conc. land in, 1592 (Sedelscombe). Add. 15232.

—— *Capellanus.* Johannes, [1205-16?]. Eg. 382.

**Sedsall,** *co. Derb.* Grants, etc., in, 1329. Add. 4883 (Soxgesale);—1356. Add. 4884 (Segosale);—1392. Woll. x. 27 (Seddissall).

—— Power to distrain on the manor, 1381 (Seggeshale). Woll. ix. 68.

**Seele, La.** *v.* Seal, *co. Kent.*

**Seete, La.** *v. sub* Ludford, *co. Salop.*

**Seeth.** *v.* Setchey, *co. Norf.*

**Seething,** *co. Norf.* Conf., etc., of moieties of the advowson and lands in, to St. Giles's Hospital, Norwich, *post* 1257. Toph. 31 (Senges), 34 (do.), 41 (do.), 44 (do.).

—— Exchange in, by St. Giles's Hospital, late Hen. III. (Senges). Campb. xii. 11.

—— Grants of Stradeseeto, etc., in, to the same, 1276. Toph. 56 (Senges);—*c.* 1276. Toph. 37 (do.).

—— Grants, etc., in, *t.* Hen. III.-Edw. I. Add. 14853 (Senges), 15491 (Seenges), 15714 (Senges);—1295. Add. 16475 (do.);—1321. Add. 16476 (do.);—1331. Add. 14775 (Sythyngge);—1450. Add. 17238 (Sethyng);—1451. Add. 7386.

**Settrington,** *co. York.* Grant in R. Bigod's manor in, [1232-4] (Seteringtone). Add. 17735.

—— Grants, etc., in, *c.* 1290. Add. 5736, 5737;—1291. Add. 5735;—1294. Add. 5738.

—— *Dominus.* Joh. Bigot, *chiv.*, 1401. Add. 16887-16890, 16892-16894; — 1423-4. Add. 16908, 16909.

**Seueburgh.** *v.* Seaborough, *co. Som.*

**Seuerby.** *v.* Searby, *co. Linc.*

**Seuewell.** *v.* Showell, *in Great Tew, co. Oxon.*

**Seuredeswelle,** *co. Suss.* Freedom to Battle Abbey from services for, [1100-20]. Harl. 43 C. 12.

**Seutherton.** *v.* Sotherton, *co. Suff.*

**Sevenhampton,** *co. Wilts.* Inspex. of a grant of the manor by the Countess of Albemarle, 1276 (Sevenht.). Cott. xv. 10.

—— Bond to acquit for a rent to the Crown from the manor, 1276 (Sevehampton). Harl. 50 D. 40.

—— License to endow Fotheringay College, *co. Northt.*, with the manor, 1415. Campb. x. 5.

**Sevenhampton Vaus.** *v. sub* Seavington, *co. Som.*

**Sevenoaks,** *co. Kent.* Conveyances, etc., in, and in Panthurst (Paunthurst) in, 1407. Harl. 76 G. 39 (Sevenok); —1555. Harl. 75 E. 31, 75 H. 23;—1569. Harl. 77 A. 22;—1574. Harl. 77 H. 35.

—— Claim to lands in, [1551-2]. Harl. 83 H. 36.

—— Lease of lands in St. John's par., parcel of the honour of Otford, 1558. Harl. 78 F. 2.

—— Lease of Bridgers in, 1559. Harl. 76 I. 48.

—— Grant of the next presentation to the rectory, 1560. Harl. 76 I. 51.

—— Warrant conc. rent due to the Crown for a lease of the manor, *t.* Eliz. Harl. 86 G. 33.

**Severnstoke,** *co. Worc.* Conf. of grants in (?), to Pershore Abbey, 972 (in Stoce). Cott. MS. Aug. ii. 6.

**Sevington,** *co. Kent.* Releases in, 1482. Add. 20013;—1492. Add. 20015.

**Sewardstone.** *v. sub* Waltham Holy Cross, *co. Essex.*

**Sewardswick.** *v. sub* Compton Dundo, *co. Som.*

**Sewer,** *nr. Salcombe, co. Devon.* Award conc. the manor, 1499 (Soure). Add. 5248.

**Sewerby,** *co. York.* Grant of a [nativus] in (?), to Bridlington Priory, by Will. de Siwardebi, *t.* Hen. II. Add. 20551.

**Sewingshields.** *v. sub* Warden, *co. Northumb.*

**Sexton.** *v.* Saxham, *co. Suff.*

**Sextrey, Sextrye.** *v. sub* Nuckington, *co. Kent.*

**Seymer.** *v.* Soamer, *nr. Scarborough, co. York.*

**Seynclere.** *v.* St. Clear, *co. Carmarth.*

**Seynthill, Seyntylmede.** *v. sub* Kentisbeare, *co. Devon.*

**Seyton.** *v.* Seaton, *co. Rutl.*

**Shabbington,** *co. Buck.* Settlement, etc., of the manor, 1542. Harl. 79 G. 30 (Shobyndon), 80 I. 35 (Shobingdon);—1552. Harl. 79 G. 29;—1561. Harl. 75 H. 24;—1570. Harl. 75 H. 15, 76 F. 45, 77 G. 11, 79 E. 40, 80 I. 40;—1625. Add. 24020, 24021;—1641. Harl. 77 H. 13.

—— Grant of annuity from Peppershill in the manor, 1634. Harl. 77 H. 14, 15.

**Shackerstone,** *co. Leic.* Brief for rebuilding the church, 1764. Ch. Br. B. iv. 1.

**Shadingfield,** *co. Suff.* Grants, etc., in, *t.* Edw. I. Harl. 48 G. 13 (Schadenfeld), Add. 15743 (Schadenefeld); —1296. Harl. 48 G. 16 (Shadenefeld);—1297. Harl. 48 G. 15, 17 (do);—1396. Harl. 48 I. 39 (Schaudefeld); — 1400. Add. 10576 (Shadyngfeld);—1476. Add. 10074.

—— *Rector (nuper).* Rob. Sawnburne, 1409 (Schadyngfeld). Add. 10383.

**Shadoxhurst,** *co. Kent.* Grants, etc., in, [1271]. Harl. 58 G. 14 (Shattokeshert) (*copy*); — 1376. Add. 8545 (Shaddokkesherst).

—— Crown grant of Fryryngcourte *al.* Mynchencourte, etc., in, late bel. to Thanington Hospital, 1551 (Shadokesherst). Harl. 75 H. 6.

**Shadwell,** *co. Norf.* Grant in, 1307 (Shadewell). Harl. 57 G. 20.

**Shaftesbury,** *co. Dors.* Conf. of Blintosfield (Blingesfolda) in, with the church of St. James, to Alcester Abbey, t. Steph. Add. 21494.

—— Fine in, and in Gore (Gora) in, for a chautry in the Abbey, 1282 (Shafton.). Add. 5250.

—— Grant, etc., in, 1426. Harl. 76 C. 16 (Burgus Shastonie);— 1433. Harl. 53 A. 24, 54 D. 19.

—— Appointment by the corporation of a bailiff of Bishopstrow, co. Wilts, 1434. Harl. 80 D. 51.

—— Sale of lands in Bradford, co. Wilts, late bel. to the chantry of St. Anne "de la Gore" in, 1551. Add. 5702.

—— *Major.* Edw. Loawte, 1375. Harl. 76 B. 15.

—— —— Rob. Pope, 1388. Harl. 76 F. 33, 79 B. 24.

—— —— Joh. Vynemere, 1407. Harl. 79 C. 19.

—— —— Tho. Hatte, 1410. Harl. 79 B. 8, 25;—1417. Harl. 78 D. 16.

—— —— Joh. Bien, 1426. Harl. 80 D. 22;—1427. Harl. 79 E. 51.

—— —— Joh. Squyer, 1434. Harl. 80 D. 51.

—— —— Will. Mathew, 1493. Harl. 78 B. 4, 80 A. 36, 37.

—— —— Joh. Mathew, 1516. Harl. 79 A. 39.

—— —— Rob. Boure, 1518. Harl. 78 H. 53, 54.

—— *Ballivus.* Joh. Cerne, 1375. Harl. 76 B. 15.

—— —— Tho. Herwy, 1388. Harl. 76 F. 33, 79 B. 24.

—— —— Will. Holyer, 1407. Harl. 79 C. 19.

—— —— Joh. Swayn, 1410. Harl. 79 B. 8, 25.

—— —— Tho. Hatte, Tho. Haselmere, Will. Cole, Joh. Taylor al. Mercer, 1426. Harl. 80 D. 22;—1427. Harl. 79 E. 51.

—— —— Ric. Reede (*vicem gerens ballivi dni. Regis*), 1493. Harl. 80 A. 36, 37.

—— *Constabularii.* Will. Carnage al. Cronyeh, Edw. Pety, 1493. Harl. 78 B. 4, 80 A. 36, 37.

—— *Custodes et Camerarii communis redditus burgi.* Will. Cole, Joh. Sillegh, 1434. Harl. 80 D. 51.

**Shaftesbury,** *co. Dors. (continued).*
PARISHES:—

—— PAR. OF H. TRINITY. Grants, etc., in, 1388. Harl. 76 F. 33;—1417. Harl. 78 D. 16;—1426. Harl. 80 D. 22;—1427. Harl. 79 E. 51;—1524. Harl. 78 H. 20.

—— PAR. OF ST. JAMES. Grant in, 1359. Add. 17660;— 1517. Harl. 80 A. 3.

—— PAR. OF ST. JOHN. Grant in, 1518. Harl. 78 H. 53, 54.

—— PAR. OF ST. MARTIN. Grant in, 1516. Harl. 79 A. 39, 40.

—— PAR. OF ST. MARY. Grants, etc., in, 1375. Harl. 76 B. 15;—1388. Harl. 79 B. 24;—1410. Harl. 79 B. 8;—1416. Harl. 79 E. 43.

—— —— Grants of Wiltonysplace in. 1407. Harl. 79 C. 19 (Burgus Shafton.);—1410. Ha l. 79 B. 25 (do.).

—— PAR. OF ST. PETER. Grants, etc., in, 1478. Harl. 80 G. 50;—1481. Harl. 78 B. 3;—1493. Harl. 78 B. 4, 80 A. 36, 37;—1504. Harl. 80 I. 77;—1516. Harl. 79 A. 39, 40.

**Shalbourn,** *co. Berks.* Grant, etc., in Oxenwood (Oxenowde) in, to St. Nicholas' Hospital, Salisbury, c. 1220-38. Harl. 50 I. 46 (Scaludelurne), 54 E. 35.

—— Grant in Oxenwood (Oxenewode) in, [1245-8]. Harl. 56 H. 16.

**Shalcomb,** *Isle of Wight.* Grant of free warren in, to Quarr Abbey, 1284 (Shaldecumbe). Add. 15701.

**Shalfleet,** *Isle of Wight.* Grant in, to Quarr Abbey, t. Edw. I. (Scaudefluet). Add. 15699.

—— Precipe on a covenant conc. lands in, 1593. Add. 25234.

—— *Vicarius.* Joh. Reynold, 1444 (Shaldeflet). Add. 15854.

**Shalford,** *co. Essex.* Precipe on a covenant conc. lands in, 1529. Add. 24923.

**Shalford,** *co. Surr.* Grants, etc., in, t. Edw. I. Add. 18573 (West Scaudeford);—1344. Add. 5942 (Shaldeford);—1462. Add. 17341 (Schalford), 26666 (Westshalforde);—1497. Add. 26679 (Westeshaldeforde).

—— Grant in dower of lands called "Nudegate," "Reynoldeslond," "Chynthurst," etc., in, 1452 (Shaldeford). Harl. 56 B. 25.

**Shalfount.** v. Chalfont St. Peter, co. Buck.

2 U

2 U 2

**Sherford** (Schireford, Shyrford), *co. Devon* (*continued*). Order for court to be proclaimed " in the open church," after morning prayers, *t.* Eliz. Add. 13132.

—— Decrees of court for discharge of debts on the manor, 1616. Add. 13145 ;—1621. Add. 13151.

—— Suit in, *c.* 1625–30. Add. 13283.

—— Action of ejectment in the manor, early Chas. I. Add. 13159.

**Sheriff Hales.** *v.* Hales, Sheriff, *co. Staff.*

**Sherlande Marsh,** *in Cowling, co. Kent.* Lease of, 1540. Harl. 46 I. 20.

**Shermanbury,** *co. Sus.* Sale in, 1584. Harl. 80 I. 13.

—— Fine in, 1673. Add. 8989, 19014.

**Shernborne,** *co. Norf.* Grants, etc., in, *t.* Hen. III. Add. 14864 (Sarnebr.); —132.. Add. 19307 (Scharneburn);— 1419. Add. 15538 (Scharnborn), 19326 (copy) ;—1427. Cott. xxix. 62 (Sharneburne), Add. 19332 ; — 1466. Add. 19340 ;—1483. Add. 19344 ;—1492- 1512. Add. 19348–19351, 19353, 19354, 19356 - 19358 ; — 1527 - 1567. Add. 19361, 19363, 19365–19370, 19372– 19375 ; — 1593-1607. Add. 19378- 19384 ; — 1614 - 1624. Add. 19387, 19390–19392 ;—1633. Add. 19396 ;— 1662. Add. 19400 ; — 1675. Add. 19403.

—— *Vicar.* Tho. Rogerson, 1562. Add. 19373.

**Sherrick Green** (?), *in Willesden, co. Midd.* Grant in, by Walt. Map, *ante* 1196 (Sericheafeld). Cott. xvi. 40.

**Sherringham,** *co. Norf.* Power to give seisin in, 1379 (Shyringham). Add. 14521.

—— Grant of a water mill, etc., in, 1409 (Sheryngham). Add. 19325.

**Sherrington,** *co. Buck.* Lease, etc., in, 1639. Add. 24051 ;—1650. Add. 23963.

**Sherrington,** *co. Wilts.* Grant in, 1413. Add. 26777.

—— Dispensation to Rich. Scrope, D.D., to hold the rectory, 1772. Add. 18463.

**Sherston,** *co. Wilts.* Transfer of the church from Fontenelle Abbey to the see of Salisbury, etc., *c.* 1207 (Sorestane). Add. 8071.

—— Grant in Wilsley (Wyuelesleye) in, 1308. Cott. xxiii. 28.

**Sherston,** *co. Wilts.* (*continued*). Demise in, 1458. Add. 1536.

—— Fine in Silkwood, etc., in, 1663 (Gt. Sherston). Add. 18430, 18431.

**Sherte.** *v. sub* Hackington, *co. Kent.*

**Sherwill,** *co. Devon.* Fine, etc., of the hundred, manor and advowson, 1653. Harl. 86 I. 59 ;—1655. Harl. 111 E. 35 (Shirwell);—1660. Harl. 85 H. 50, 111 E. 36.

—— Grants, etc., in, 1667. Harl. 85 H. 46, 86 I. 48, 112 B. 31 ;—1674. Harl. 83 H. 24 *a*, 37.

**Sherwood Forest,** *co. Nott.* Assize conc. trespass in, 14 cent. (Shirwod). Woll. xii. 109.

—— Roll of Regard, 1393 (Shyrewode). Add. 10659.

—— Conf. of the appointments of the Count of Mortaigne and Lord Cromwell as keepers, 1437. Cott. MS. Vesp. F. xiii. art. 72.

—— Perambulation, 1538. Roy. Roll 14 B. xlviii.

—— Lease in, 1596. Woll. xi. 77.

**Shete,** *in Brixton* (?), *Isle of Wight.* Grant of free-warren in, to Quarr Abbey, 1284. Add. 15701.

**Sheviock,** *co. Cornw.* Grants, etc., in Lescawne (Lanscawyn, Lascawyn, Lanscawen) in, *t.* Edw. II. Slo. xxxiii. 13 ;—1461. Slo. xxxiii. 71 *a*, *b*, *c* ;—1488. Slo. xxxiii. 75 *a* (Schevyok), *b.*

—— Grant of Tredis (Tredehyst) in, 1460 (Shevyok). Add. 13060.

—— Grants in Crofthole (Burgagium de Crofthole) in, 1461. Slo. xxxiii. 71 *a*, *b*, *c* ;—1602. Slo. xxxiii. 86.

—— Extract from court-roll for land in Vellond in, 1528. Slo. xxxiii. 80.

**Sheyle.** *v.* Seal, *co. Leic.*

**Shibbrok.** *v.* Shipbrook, *co. Chest.*

**Shibden, Over,** *in North Owram, co. York.* Grants, etc., in, 1381. Add. 15660 (Ouerahypden) ;—1390. Add. 15718 (Ouerschipden).

—— Fine in, 1381 (Ouerahipden). Add. 15661.

**Shiffeld.** *v. sub* Theale, *co. Berks.*

**Shiffnal,** *co. Salop.* Grant of rent charge on Stanton in the domain of, 1493 (Idsall *al.* Shuffenall). Add. 18783.

**Shiffnal**, *co. Salop* (*continued*). Royal grant of mills, etc., in, late bel. to Wombridge Priory, 1545 (Shuffenall infra dominium de Idsall). Add. 26023.

—— Standard bushel for the market of, 1696 (Shiffenhale). Add. 6230.

—— Brief conc. a fire at, 1816. Ch. Br. B. lvii. 6.

**Shifford** (Schifford, Schyfford, Shyfford), *co. Oxon.* Compotus-rolls of the manor, 1380–81. Harl. Roll K. 41;—1391-2, 1397-8, 1402-3, 1405-6, 1422-3, 1427-8, 1433-4. Harl. Rolls L. 1-7;——1436-7. Harl. Roll L. 10;—1474-5. Harl. Roll G. 2.

—— Inquiry conc. repairs of the ferry-barge, 1426. Harl. Roll O. 20.

—— Court-rolls, 1434. Harl. Roll L. 8;—1437. Harl. Roll L. 9;—1441. Harl. Roll L. 11;—1458. Harl. Roll L. 12;—1459. Harl. Roll L. 13;—1460. Harl. Roll L. 14;—1473-4. Harl. Roll L. 15;—1524-5. Harl. Rolls L. 16, 17.

**Shilbottle**, *co. Northumb.* Declaration conc. a settlement in, etc., 1617, 1618. Harl. 79 G. 8, 9.

**Shilling Okeford.** *v.* Okeford, Shilling, *co. Dors.*

**Shilton**, *co. Berks.* Grant, with conf., of the church, etc., to Beaulieu Abbey, 1205, 1268 (Soulton). Harl. 58 I. 25 (copy).

—— Court-rolls, 1346, 1360, 1410, 1470 (Schulton, Shulton). Add. 26814.

**Shilton, Earl.** *v.* Shelton, Earl, *co. Leic.*

**Shilvington**, *in Morpeth, co. Northumb.* Grant of free-warren in, 1341 (Shilvyngton). Cott. xvii. 13.

**Shimpling**, *co. Norf.* Grant in, late 12 cent. Harl. 50 C. 14 (Simpling); —1373. Harl. 47 G. 4 (Shymplyngge).

**Shimpling**, *co. Suff.* Grants, etc., in, t. Hen. II. Harl. 50 B. 30 (Simpeling);—1316. Harl. 47 E. 7 (Schymplyngge);—1318. Harl. 54 C. 27 (Shymplinggc);—1351. Harl. 51 A. 37;—1364. Cott. xii. 45 (Schymplyng), Harl. 53 C. 4, 5;—1367. Harl. 53 C. 32, 33 (Nchimplyngge);—1371. Harl. 51 D. 12 (Chymplynge);—1375. Harl. 50 H. 30 (Shymplynge);—1381. Harl. 53 C. 34 (Schymplynge);—1382. Harl. 48 D. 3, 4 (Schymplyngg);—1407. Harl. 48 D. 12, 54 A. 22

(Schymplyngg);—1421. Harl. 48 D. 15 (Shymplynge);—1517. Add. 10543;—1542. Add. 10545, 10546:—1583. Harl. 57 H. 18;—1634. Harl. 45 G. 7.

—— Appointment of a bailiff of the manor, 1438 (Shymplyng). Harl. 48 F. 24.

—— Grant of the manor, 1470 (do.). Harl. 50 C. 13.

—— Precipe on a covenant conc. land in, 1593. Add. 25481.

—— Assignment of life interest of Qu. Catharine of Braganza in the park at, 1680. Harl. 111 H. 11.

—— *Persona.* Joh. de Willingham 1351. Harl. 51 A. 37.

**Shinfield**, *co. Berks.* Grants, etc., in, [1190-1?]. Harl. 83 A. 4 (Soenexofeld);—1365. Add. 20239 (Shynyngfeld.

—— Brief conc. a hail-storm at, 1765. Ch. Br. B. v. 2.

**Shingham**, *co. Norf.* Inquisition in, 1276–77 (Shengham). Harl. Roll K. 6.

—— Grant in, 1377 (Schyngham). Harl. 52 B. 43.

—— Rental in, t. Hen. IV. (?) (Shyngham). Harl. Roll A. 10.

**Shipborne**, *co. Kent.* Grant of free-warren, market, etc., in, 1285. Harl. 58 I. 37.

—— Reference to a grant in, 1566. Harl. 77 A. 14.

**Shipbrook**, *co. Chest.* Settlement of the manor, 1325 (Shibbrok). Add. 6278.

—— Rental, 1391 (Shybbrok). Add. 5230.

**Shipden**, *co. Norf.* Grant in, t. Hen. III. or Edw. I. (Shypedon). Add. 14856.

—— Decree in dispute for the rectory, 1380 (Schipden). Add. 19851.

—— Bequest to the Guild of St. George, 1448. Add. 14145.

—— *Rector.* Joh. Stalham, 1380. Add. 19851.

**Shipdham**, *co. Norf.* Release, etc., in, 1384. Harl. 56 H. 48 (Schcpedham); —1502. Add. 1383.

—— Inspex. in 1454 of a feoffment of the manor, 1422 (Schypedham). Add. 17243.

**Shipherst, Shiphurst.** *v. sub* Marden, *co. Kent.*

**Shiplake**, *co. Oxon.* Grant in Lashbrook (Lechebroc) in, to Reading Abbey. *t.* Rich. I. Add. 19612.

—— Suit with Missenden Abbey conc. services in W. de Engelfeld's chapel in, 1240–1251 (Sipplake). Add. 20370–20373.

—— Grants, etc., of Colyns in Binfeld (Benefeld), etc., in, 1457. Add. 20297–20300.

—— *Vicarius.* Simon, *t.* Rich. I. Add. 19612.

———— Simon, [1242]. Add. 20370.

—— — Joh. Westgrave, 1409. Add. 20249.

**Shipley**, *co. Suss.* Land in Henfield, co. Suss., held by Lewes Priory, "faciendo parcagium de la Kneppe" in, [1255–66]. Cott. MS. Nero C. iii. f. 214.

—— Grants, etc., in, 1355. Add. 8832 (Schypeke);—1423. Add. 8870 (Shepele);—1562. Add. 18849 (Chipley);—1614. Add. 18918;—1663. Add. 18991;—1666. Add. 18993.

—— License for alienation of the manor, rectory and vicarage, 1578. Add. 8955.

—— Deeds conc. Knepp al. Knapp manor in, 1657. Add. 18979–18981; —1658. Add. 18982, 18983.

—— Rental of R. Caryll at Knepp in, late 17 cent. Add. 19061.

**Shipmeadow**, *co. Suff.* Grants, etc., in, 1375. Harl. 53 E. 45 (Shipmedwe); —1306. Harl. 48 I. 39 (Shepmedwe); —1403. Cott. xxvii. 162 (Shipmedwe); —1422. Harl. 50 F. 36.

—— Acquittance for homage in, 1404 (Schypmedwe). Harl. 54 A. 1.

—— *Rector.* Joh. de Redenhale, 1313 (Schipmedwe). Harl. 88 E. 34.

**Shipstede.** *v.* Chipstead, *co. Surr.*

**Shipton**, *co. Southt.* Grant in, to Newark Priory, early Hen. III. (Shepton). Cott. xxvii. 64.

—— Fine in, 1342. Harl. Roll G. 17 (15).

**Shipton George**, *co. Dors.* Grant in, 1515 (Shypton). Harl. 86 A. 43.

**Shipton Montagu.** *v.* Shepton Montague, *co. Som.*

**Shipton upon Cherwell**, *co. Oxon.* Covenant as to descent of the manor and advowson, 1496. Add. 5684.

—— Recovery of same, 1500. Add. 5685 c.

**Shirborne.** *v.* Sherborne, *co. Dors.*

**Shirbourne.** *v. sub* Harptree, E., *co. Som.*

**Shirburn**, *co. Oxon.* Grant in, 1361 (Schirborne). Add. 26368.

—— *Vicarius.* Adam de Stratforde, 1386. Add. 19906.

**Shire Newton.** *v.* Newton, Shire, *co. Monm.*

**Shirebrook**, *in Pleasley, co. Derb.* Covenant for conveyance in, 1571 (Sherbroke). Woll. xi. 51.

**Shirehead**, *co. Lanc.* Briefs for rebuilding the chapel. 1802. Ch. Br. B. xlii. 7;—1807. Ch. Br. B. xlvii. 11.

**Shireoaks**, *co. Nott.* Release in, *t.* Edw. I. Harl. 83 E. 14.

**Shirewold**, **Shirwall.** *v. sub* Harptree, E., *co. Som.*

**Shirford.** *v. sub* Fineton, *co. Devon.*

**Shirley**, *co. Derb.* Exchange in, 1311 (Schirley). Woll. ix. 20.

—— *v. also* Yeaveley, *in Shirley, co. Derb.*

**Shitelhanger.** *v.* Shuttlehanger, *co. Northt.*

**Shiteyham.** *v. sub* Arlsey, *co. Bedf.*

**Shitlington**, *co. Bedf.* Settlement, etc., of Holwollbury (Hollewellsbury, Holwelbury) manor nr., 1420. Add. 17225;—1553. Harl. 45 D. 49.

**[Shobdon]**, *co. Heref.* Conf. by Wigmore Abbey of a grant in, 1281. Cott. xxi. 43.

**Shobingdon, etc.** *v.* Shabbington, *co. Buck.*

**Shoebury, North,** *co. Essex.* Release, etc., in, 1260–1. Harl. 48 I. 47 (Parva Roberia);—1345. Add. 15459 (Northshobery).

**Shoebury, South,** *co. Essex.* Lease of the manor, 1516 (Showbury magna). Harl. 77 F. 39.

**Sholand.** *v. sub* Puttenham, *co. Surr.*

**Sholden**, *co. Kent.* Grant in, 1349 (Scholdene). Cott. xxvii. 27.

—— Recovery of Codmanton al. Cotington manor, etc., in, 1628. Add. 1530.

**Sholond.** *v. sub* Nacton, *co. Suff.*

**Shoort.** *v. sub* Hackington, *co. Kent.*

Shortcombe, co. Som. Grant in, 1401 (decenus de Shortecombe infra hundr. de Brompton Regis). Add. 25890.

Shorthampton, co. Oxon. Compotus, 1447-48. Harl. Roll E. 2.

Shortsfield. v. sub Horsham, co. Suss.

Shostoke. v. Shustoke, co. Warw.

Shotley, co. Northumb. Covenant to settle lands at Crooked Oak (Croketake), etc., in, 1421. Cott. xii. 41.

Shotley, co. Suff. Grant of a rent in Kirkton (Kyrketon) in, 1429. Add. 9699.

—— Conveyance, etc., in, 1537. Add. 9758 (Shotteley);—1738. Add. 9799 (S. al. Kirkton).

Shotover Forest, co. Oxon. Covenant for a fine of the keepership, etc., of, 1547. Harl. 79 G. 13.

—— Exchequer acquittance for rent of herbage, etc., in, 1576. Add. 25641.

Shotswell, co. Warw. Grant in, to Polesworth Abbey, [1216-23] (Sotuwell). Cott. xii. 54.

—— Rector. Rob. Wandac, 1332. Cott. iv. 14 (2).

Shottesbrook, co. Berks. Release, etc., in, 1332. Harl. 50 H. 32 (Sottesbrok); —1381. Harl. 56 C. 20 (Sotesbrok);— 1434. Harl. 56 C. 18 (Shottesbrok); —1606. Harl. 83 H. 20 (Shasbrooke).

Shottesham, co. Norf. Papal conf. of tithes in, to Horsham St. Faith Priory, 1163 (Sotesham). Cott. MS. Aug. ii. 136.

—— Grant in, t. Hen. III. (Schotesham). Harl. 83 F. 22.

Shottington. v. sub Westwell, co. Kent.

Shouldham Thorpe, co. Norf. Grant, etc., in, t. Hen. III. Harl. 46 D. 17 (Torpe), 48 A. 40 (Thorp).

Showbery Magna. v. Shoebury, South, co. Essex.

Showell, in Gt. Tew, co. Oxon. Mortgage at, to Reading Abbey, 1220 (Seuewell). Add. 19613.

Shrawardine, co. Salop. Brief conc. an inundation at, 1771. Ch. Br. B. xi. 7.

Shrewsbury, co. Salop. Ch. dated at, 901 (Scrobbensis civitas). Cott. viii. 17.

—— Ch. of King Stephen dated at, 1139 (apud Salopesbiriam in obsidione). Cott. MS. Nero C. iii. f. 177.

Shrewsbury, co. Salop (continued). Exchequer acquittance for farm of land in, 1616. Add. 25646.

—— Brief for rebuilding St. Chad's church, 1789. Ch. Br. B. xxix. 4.

—— Brief for rebuilding St. Alkmund's church, 1793. Ch. Br. B. xxxiii. 8.

Shripney, nr. Bersted, co. Suss. Grant at, 580 (Scrippan eg). Cott. MS. Aug. ii. 86.

Shrivenham, co. Berks. Bequest of soul scot to, c. 995 (to Scrifenan hamme). Cott. viii. 38.

Shrofield. v. sub Lee, co. Kent.

Shropham, co. Norf. Covenant with the tenants of, 1286 (Scropham). Add. 14857.

—— Grant, etc., in, 1307. Add. 14858 (Sropham);—1330. Harl. 49 D. 24;—1374. Harl. 49 C. 15 (Schropham);—1578. Add. 18262.

—— Grant of the advowson, etc., 1375. Add. 14859.

—— Grant of Bradcar hall manor in, with the advowson, to Thompson College, 1397. Add. 14860.

—— Sale of above manor and advowson, 1548. Add. 14861.

—— Capellani. Willelmus, Galfridus, 1253. Campb. ix. 9 (11).

—— Vicarius. Joh. Lalle, 1446. Add. 14672.

Shrowle. v. sub Harptree, E., co. Som.

Shuckburgh, Upper and Lower, co. Warw. Power to give seisin in, 1405 (over, nether, Schokburghe). Cott. xii. 8.

Shuckthorn, in Crich, co. Derb. Conf. of a grant in, t. Rich. I.-John (Sachkethorn). Woll. vi. 49 (copy).

—— Grant in Plaistow in the fee of, 1354 (Shukthorne). Woll. vi. 53.

Shudy Camps, co. Camb. Grant of Nosterfield (Nostrefeld) in, t. John. Harl. 52 I. 37.

—— Feoffment, etc., in, 1438. Add. 9251 (Schudy Campes);—1503. Add. 25868;—1578. Add. 25860, 25968; —1670. Add. 25870;—1673. Add. 25871.

Shulton. v. Shelton, Earl, co. Leic.

Shurdington, co. Glouc. Inspex. in 1330 of a grant of the chapel to Usk Priory, c. 1150 (Surditona). Add. 5342.

Silston, co. Northt. Brief for rebuilding the church, 1779. Ch. Br. B. xix. 5.

Silton, co. Dors. Lease in, 1314 (Selton). Add. 13014.

Silton, Nether, in Leake, co. York. Grant in, t. Edw. I. or II. (Silton Paynel). Harl. 112 I. 47.

Silverley, co. Camb. Grants, etc., in, late 13 cent. Cott. xxii. 7 (Seluerl.), Harl. 52 E. 4, 5 (Seluerleye), 6 (Siluerleye);—1319. Harl. 48 C. 47 a (Seluerleye);—1360. Harl. 48 C. 52 (Seluerleigh);—1539. Harl. 48 D. 33 (Syluersley).

—— Release in, to the Knts. Hospitallers, 1303 (Seluerle). Harl. 53 D. 41.

—— Conveyance of the manor, c. 1320 (?). Harl. 48 C. 47 b (copy).

—— Persona. Willelmus, t. Hen. III. Harl. 53 E. 2.

Silverton, co. Devon. Conveyance in Butterleigh (Boterlegh) in, 1479 (Sylferton). Add. 13067-13069.

Silveston, co. Northt. Royal grants of woods in, 1612. Cott. xiii. 35.

—— Clericus. Henricus, late 12 cent. Harl. 85 A. 54 (Silvest.);—[1198-9?]. Harl. 85 A. 58 (Selvestone);—early 13 cent. Harl. 86 A. 21, 86 B. 57.

—— —— Ricardus, t. Edw. I. (Sulveston). Harl. 85 E. 20.

Simpeling. v. Shimpling, co. Suff.

Sindlesham, nr. Arborfield, co. Berks. Exchequer acquittance for rent in, 1576 (Syndelsham). Add. 25565.

Singleton, Little, co. Lanc. Settlement, etc., in, 1372 (parva Syngletoue). Add. 20511, 20522.

Sinker, nr. Roughton, co. Linc. Release of the conduit, mill, etc., of, to Kirkstead Abbey, [1196-8]. Harl. 58 B. 44.

Sintclers Manor. v. sub Barningham, co. Suff.

Sipherste. v. sub Marden, co. Kent.

Sipplake. v. Shiplake, co. Oxon.

Sireford. v. Shelford, co. Warw.

Siresham, Sirsam. v. Syresham, co. Northt.

Sirewateres. v. sub Walcott, co. Norf.

Siselaunde, Sislonde. v. Sizeland, co. Norf.

Sissinghurst. v. sub Cranbrooke, co. Kent.

Sisterne. v. Syderstone, co. Norf.

Siston. v. Syston, co. Linc.

Siston, co. Glouc. Order for an extent of the manor, 1301 (Cistone). Add. 19302.

Sitelhangre. v. Shuttlehanger, co. Northt.

Sittingbourne, co. Kent. Grants, etc., in, t. Hen. III. Harl. 46 E. 47 (Sidingeborne);—1361. Harl. 48 E. 21 (Sidyngbourne);—1512. Harl. 80 D. 31;—1572. Add. 912.

—— Suit in, 1626. Harl. 75 H. 22.

—— Brief conc. a fire at, 1763. Ch. Br. B. iii. 1.

—— Vicarius. Dom. Hen. Willy, 1383. Add. 8548.

Siwardestune. v. sub Waltham H. Cross, co. Essex.

Sixhills, co. Linc. Acquittance for deeds relating to the manor, 1347 (Sixhull). Harl. 56 C. 36.

Sixteendale. v. Thixendale, co. York.

Sizeland, co. Norf. Grants, etc., in, 1301. Add. 14910 (Sislonde);—1331. Add. 14775 (Syslonde);—early 14 cent. Harl. 58 G. 8 (Siselaunde);—1359. Cott. xii. 1 (Siselonde);—1450. Add. 17238;—1451. Add. 7386;—1579. Add. 14728 (Syseland).

—— Rector. Joh. de Gales, 1329. Add. 14774.

Sizewell, in Leiston, co. Suff. Precipe on a covenant conc. land in, 1561. Add. 25290.

Skampton. v. Scampton, co. Linc.

Skarnyng. v. Scarning, co. Norf.

Skaynes, nr. Pevensey (?), co. Suss. Precipe on covenant conc. the manor, 1589. Add. 15226.

Skeffington, co. Leic. Grant of, c. 1160 (Scheftintona). Lansd. 691.

—— Clericus. Robertus, t. Hen. II. (Ceceftitun). Add. 1048.

Skegby, co. Nott. Fine in, 1541. Woll. ii. 71.

—— Grant of custody of the manor, 1545. Add. 22633.

Skegness, co. Linc. Grants, etc., in, to Bullington Priory, t. Hen. II. Harl. 50 B. 35 (Sche genes);—1256. Harl. 52 H. 28 (Skegenes);—t. Edw. I.-II. Harl. 52 H. 5;—c. 1322. Harl. 52 H. 27;—1324. Harl. 43 D. 23;—late Edw. II. Cott. xxvii. 30 (Skegnesse).

Snetterton, co. *Norf.* (*continued*). Lease of New Hall manor in, 1573. Add. 18862.

—— Sale of Perris *al.* Perrishes *al.* Parris *al.* Parrishes *al.* Grymes manor in, 1634. Add. 14863.

—— *Persona eccl. Omnium Sanctorum.* Roger. Dauney, 1374. Harl. 49 C. 15; —1385. Harl. 56 I. 1.

—— —— Tho. Boscvyll, 1428. Add. 14837.

—— *Rector eccl. Omnium Sanctorum.* Joh. de Bokenham, 1325. Harl. 46 F. 10.

—— *Persona eccl. S. Andrea.* Thomas, 1428. Add. 14837.

Snettisham, co. *Norf.* Grants in, from Castleacre Priory, *t.* Hen. II. Add. 15508 ;—*c.* 1174–80. Toph. 15.

—— Grant in, from Wymondham Priory, late 12 cent. (Snetesham). Toph. 5.

—— Grants, etc., in, *t.* Hen. III. Add. 14864 (Snetesham); — 1427. Cott. xxix. 62 ;—1510. Add. 19357 (Snetisham);—1530. Add. 19362 ; — 1567 (Snettysham). Eg. 289;—1603. Add. 19381;—1607. Add. 19382;—1619. Add. 19390, 19391 ; — 1624. Add. 19392.

—— Grant of the manor by Edw. III. to Pr. John, his son, 1372 (Snetesham). Cott. xv. 1.

—— Extract from court-roll of Ingoldsthorpe Hall manor in, 1662. Add. 19400.

—— *Perpet. Vicarius.* Nich. Walter, 1427. Cott. xxix. 62.

Sneylewell. *v.* Snailwall, co. *Camb.*

Sneynton. *v.* Snainton, co. *York.*

—— *v.* Sneinton, co. *Nott.*

Sneyth. *v.* Snaith, co. *York.*

Sniterton. *v.* Snetterton, co. *Norf.*

Snitterfield, co. *Warw.* Conf. by Hen. II. of Suthongre in, to Bordesley Abbey, [1157?]. Cott. MS. Nero C. iii. f. 176.

Snitterton, *in* Darley, co. *Derb.* Grants, etc., in, *t.* Hen. III. Woll. x. 4 (Snuterton) :—1319. Woll. i. 1 a (Snyterton):—1330. Woll. x. 64 a ;—*t.* Edw. II. Woll. x. 9 (Sniterton);—1350. Woll. x. 13.

Snoddesbyri. *v.* Snodsbury, co. *Worc.*

Snodding land. *v.* Snodland, co. *Kent.*

Snodhill, co. *Heref.* Conf. of a covenant in, with Dore Abbey, *post* 1220 (Snodehull). Harl. 47 G. 35.

Snodland, co. *Kent.* Grant in, 838 (Snodding land). Cott. viii. 30.

—— Fine in, 1539. Harl. 46 I. 18, 19.

Snodsbury, co. *Worc.* Conf. of grants at, to Pershore Abbey, 972 (in Snoddesbyri). Cott. MS. Aug. ii. 6.

Snoring, Great, co. *Norf.* Power to give seisin of the manor and advowson, 1454 (Magna Snoryng). Add. 14866.

—— Conveyance in (?), 1477 (Snoryng). Add. 7586.

—— Grant of rent from the manor, 1559 (Snoryng). Add. 14855.

Snoring, Little, co. *Norf.* Fine of the manor, 1388 (Parva Snoryng). Harl. 49 I. 29.

Snorscomb, *in* Everdon, co. *Northt.* Release, etc., in, *t.* Edw. I. (Snotescomb). Harl. 46 I. 36 ;—1324 (Snottescumbe). Harl. 58 G. 45 (*copy*).

—— Copies of deeds conc. the manor, 15 cent. Harl. Roll O. 11.

Snouwedon. *v. sub* Yeovil, co. *Som.*

Snowford, co. *Warw.* A boundary mark, 1001 (Saaw forda). Cott. MS. Aug. ii. 22.

Snuterton, Snyterton. *v.* Snitterton, *in* Darley, co. *Derb.*

Snydale, *in* Normanton, co. *York.* Lease in, from the Knights Hospitallers, 1357 (Snytale). Campb. xiv. 25*.

—— Crown lease in, 1555 (Snytall). Harl. 84 C. 32.

Snyterton. *v.* Snetterton, co. *Norf.*

Soaflet. *v.* Swayfield (?), co. *Linc.*

Sobeford. *v.* Sibford, *nr.* Hook Norton, co. *Oxon.*

Soberia, Parva. *v.* Shoebury, North, co. *Essex.*

Soberton, co. *Southt.* Release, etc., in, by Durford Abbey, *t.* Hen. III. (Subertune). Cott. MS. Vesp. E. xxiii. ff. 2, 4.

—— Bond for rent in, to Beaulieu Abbey, *t.* Hen. III. (Subertune). Cott. MS. Vesp. E. xxiii. f. 3.

Soborne. *v.* Sudbourne, co. *Suff.*

Soca de Anglica Cnihttengilda. *v. sub* London, *City of.*

**Sock Dennis** [illegible]

—— [illegible]

—— [illegible] Harl. [illegible]

—— [illegible] Harl. [illegible]

—— [illegible] Harl. [illegible]

**Sock, Old.** v. sub Mudford, co. Som.

**Sockburn** [illegible] Lansd. [illegible]

**Sockenersh.** v. sub Brightling, co. Suss.

**Sogenhoe,** co. Suff. [illegible] Harl. [illegible]

—— [illegible] Harl. [illegible]

**Soham,** co. Camb. [illegible] Harl. [illegible]

—— [illegible] Harl. [illegible]

—— Grant of the manor by Edw. III. [illegible]

—— [illegible] Lansd. [illegible]

**Soham, Monk,** co. Suff. [illegible] Add. [illegible]

—— Compotus-rolls of the manor, bel. to Bury St. Edmunds Abbey, [illegible] Add. [illegible]

—— Court-rolls. 1391. 1394. Add. [illegible]

**Sok.** v. Sock Dennis, co. Som.

**Sok Malerbe** al. **Oldesokk, Sokke.** v. sub Mudford, co. Som.

**Sokburn iuxta Dedinsale.** v. Sockburn, nr. Dinsdale, co. Durh.

**Sokenersh.** v. sub Brightling, co. Suss.

**Sokono.** v. Sogenhoe, co. Suff.

**Sole, La.** v. sub Selling, co. Kent.

**Solebi, Soleby.** v. Welford, co. Northt.

**Solegreue.** v. Sulgrave, co. Northt.

**Soleton.** v. Sutton, co. Salop.

**Solihull,** co. Warw. [illegible] Solihulle [illegible] Solihull [illegible]

—— [illegible]

—— Court-rolls. [illegible] Add. [illegible]

—— Rentals of the town and manor. [illegible] Add. [illegible]

—— Survey of the manor. [illegible] Add. [illegible]

—— Roll of suitors in the manor, [illegible] Add. [illegible]

**Sollers.** v. sub Remenham, co. Berks.

**Solney, Newton.** v. Newton Solney, co. Derb.

**Solymere.** v. sub Frome, co. Som.

**Somborne, King's,** co. Southt. Crown lease of the manor, 1537 (Somborne). Add. [illegible]

—— Precepts re covenants conc. lands in, 1581. Add. [illegible] (Somborne), [illegible] (Kyngessomborne).

—— Fine of the manor, 1535 (Somborne). Woll. x. 29.

**Somborne, King's, Hundred,** co. Southt. Court-rolls. 1498-99, 1501-2, 1512-13, 1514-15 (Somborne Regis). Harl. Rolls L. 21, 22, 24, 25.

—— Rental. 1509. Harl. Roll L. 23.

**Somerby,** co. Leic. Grant, etc., of the church, etc., to Langley Priory, t. Hen. II. (Sumerdebi). Cott. v. 62;—1411. Add. 21391.

—— Assignment of the manor, 1411. Lansd. 641.

—— Acquittance for escheats in, 1413. Lansd. 642.

—— Grant in, 1457. Add. 24221.

—— Vicarius. Will. Baly, 1457. Add. 24221.

**Somerby,** nr. Caistor, co. Linc. Power to give seisin in, 1335. Harl. 54 G. 21.

2 x 2

Somerset al. Mumby. v. sub Mumby, co. Linc.

Somersham, co. Hunt. Conf. in, by Bps. of Ely, to Ely Abbey, [1103-31, 1133-69] (Sumeresham). Harl. 43 H. 4, 5 (copies).

Somerton. v. sub Boothby Graffo, co. Linc.

Somerton, co. Oxon. Sale of goods in the manor, 1275 (Sumertone). Harl. 46 F. 45.

Somerton, co. Som. The castle and domain held of Hen. IV. by Sir R. de Rochefort, 1412. Add. 12652.

——— Lease of a water mill called Somersy myln in, etc., 1437 (dominium de Somerton). Harl. 56 D. 14.

——— Grant of rent from the manor, 1514. Harl. 43 F. 8.

Somerton, co. Suff. Precipes on covenants in, 1578. Add. 25365;—1589. Add. 25394;—1592. Add. 25432.

Somerton, East and West, co. Norf. Covenant conc. right of way in, 1278 (Somertone). Add. 14953.

——— Suits of the Crown against Butley Priory conc. W. Somerton manor, 1290-1300. Harl. Roll N. 20.

——— Conveyance, etc., of the manor, 1347. Add. 14761 (Somerton);—1370. Add. 14867 (do.).

——— Release in, 1347 (West Somerton, Est Somerton). Harl. 48 C. 3.

Somerton, North and South, co. Norf. Grant of rent charge on Fleghalle manor in, 1379 (Somertone). Add. 14954.

Sompting, co. Suss. Grants, etc., in, 1365. Add. 8838 (Suntyng);—1400 Add. 8855 (Sunntynge); — 1436. Add. 8878 (Sountynge);—1455. Add. 8893 (Sounptyng);—1456. Add. 18753 (Sountyng);—1472. Add. 8901 (Somtyng);—1549. Add. 18828;—1578. Add. 8955; — 1587. Add. 18866 (Sountinge);—1595. Add. 18879;—1604. Add. 18897.

——— Lease in, by Waverley Abbey, 1500 (Sountyng). Harl. 75 G. 14.

——— Grant of the advowson, rectory, etc., 1545. Add. 18827;—1562. Add. 18850;—1680. Add. 15874 (Sounting).

——— Vicarius. Joh. Shipbourne, 1350 (Suntynge). Lansd. 124.

Sonbache. v. Sandbach, co. Chest.

Sonday, Sondeys. v. Sandy, co. Bedf.

Sonde. v. Sound, co. Chest.

Sonde, La. v. Sand, co. Som.

Sonning, co. Berks and Oxon. Grants, etc., in Dunsden (Denesdene, Dynnesdene) in, 1368. Add. 20247, 20248;—1457. Add. 20297-20299.

——— Grant of Bulstrodes in Dunsden (Denesdene) in, 1409. Add. 20249.

——— Sale, etc., in, 1608. Add. 19297;—1609. Add. 13606;—1612. Add. 19208;—1623. Add. 13701.

——— Vicarius. Stephanus, 1385. Harl. 56 A. 35.

——— Rad. Haswell, 1437. Harl. 54 E. 31.

Sookholme, in Warsop, co. Nott. Crown grant of the manor, late bel. to Newstall Priory, 1558 (Sockholme). Harl. 51 H. 22.

Soothill, in Dewsbury, co. York. Leases of moieties of Soothill Hall, etc., 1637. Harl. 112 D. 5;—1658. Harl. 112 D. 3.

Soperhurst, [w. Hampton in Arden?], co. Warw. Marriage settlement of "tota terra de," c. 1200(?). Cott. xxii. 4.

Sorenden. v. Surrenden, co. Wilts.

Sorestane. v. Sherston, co. Wilts.

Sorham, Nova. v. Shoreham, New, co. Suss.

Sotby, co. Linc. Conf. of grant in, to Bullington Priory, [1155] (Sottebi). Harl. 43 C. 19.

——— Grant in, t. Hen. II. (Soltebi). Harl. 52 G. 38.

——— License for feoffment of the manor, 1334. Harl. 43 D. 31.

——— Capellanus. Willelmus, t. Hen. II. (Soteby). Harl. 48 I. 36.

——— Clericus. Johannes, c. 1200, Cott. xii. 17.

Sotesbrok. v. Shottesbrook, co. Berks.

Sotesham. v. Shottesham, co. Norf.

Sotherton. v. sub Willesborough, co. Kent.

Sotherton, co. Suff. Grant of the manor and advowson, 1381 (Scutherton). Add. 10378.

——— Grants, etc., in, 1424. Cott. xxvii. 93 (Sothirtone);—1441. Cott. xii. 42;—1473. Harl. 51 F. 3.

Soton in Dal. v. Sutton Scarsdale al. Sutton in the Dale, co. Derb.

Southampton, co. *Southt.* (*continued*). Grant "in vico anglico" in St. Laurence parish, to St. Denis Priory, a. 1270 (do.). Add. 15689.

—— Grant in Rockesdon nr. (?), to St. Denis Priory, *t.* Edw. II. Add. 15691.

—— Lease of "La Westhalle" "in vico francisco" in, 1314 (do.). Add. 685.

—— Custom dues to be paid to the port of, from Hamble le Rice, 1354. Harl. 75 E. 8.

—— Petition of Qu. Margaret to Hen. VI. on behalf of the customs officers of, 1455. Cott. xvi. 72.

—— Payment for repairs of the castle, 1518. Add. 13305.

—— Lease in St. Cross [Holyrood] par., 1545. Add. 7219.

—— Exchequer acquittance for dues from the port of, 1595. Add. 25653.

—— Rent-roll of 'town lands, 1637. Add. 17449.

—— Recovery in, 1662. Add. 18987.

—— *Constabularius.* Osbertus, 1151 (Hamtona). Harl. 50 A. 8.

—— *Custos.* Ad. de Letford, [1267-79]. Add. 15697.

—— *Major.* Tho. Lyster, 1545. Add. 7219.

—— *Ballivi.* Hen. le Flameng, Jac. Ysenberd, c. 1270. Add. 15689.

—— —— Joh. Baluayr, Ric. Bagge, 1314. Add. 685.

—— *Aldermannus.* Joh. le Flemyng, 1314. Add. 685.

Southanyngfeld. *v.* Hanningfield, S., co. *Essex.*

Southborough. *v. sub* Tonbridge, co. *Kent.*

Southchurch, co. *Essex.* Grant in, 1322 (Suthcherche). Add. 15455.

—— Release, etc., of the manor, 1345. Add. 15459;—1354. Add. 15461.

—— *Persona.* Tho. de Walton, 1372. Cott. xxiv. 12.

Southcott, co. *Buck.* Sale of goods in the manor, 1275 (Suthcote). Harl. 46 F. 45.

—— Release in, 1285 (Suthcot). Harl. 46 G. 1.

Southcott, co. *Devon.* Settlement of the manor, 1483. Harl. Roll L. 28.

Southcourt. *v. sub* Tilmanstone, co. *Kent.*

Southease, co. *Suss.* Sale of the advowson, 1590. Add. 15163.

Southegh, Southeys. *v. sub* Binsted, co. *Southt.*

Southey Soake, co. *Suss.* Leases in, 1671. Add. 5964;—1687. Add. 5965.

Southfleet, co. *Kent.* Grants, etc., in, *t.* Edw. I. Harl. 45 I. 2 (Suthfleto); —1295-6. Add. 19296;—1389. Harl. 55 F. 28.

—— Acquittance for rents in, and from Pole in, 1340 (Suthflete). Harl. 48 E. 8.

—— Covenant for settlement of Pole manor in, 1341. Harl. 48 I. 22.

—— *Persona.* Tho. de Alkham, 1345. Harl. 45 C. 24.

—— *Rector.* Robertus, 1295-6. Add. 19296.

—— —— *Mag.* Rob. Bourne, 1378. Harl. 43 I. 32.

Southhanyngfeld. *v.* Hanningfield, S., co. *Essex.*

Southill, co. *Bedf.* Conf. of a grant in, to Chicksands Priory, *t.* Hen. III. (Sugyuel). Harl. 45 I. 18.

—— Conf. of a grant in, to Wardon Abbey, 1257-8 (Sutgiuele). Cott. MS. Nero C. iii. f. 230.

—— *Vicarius.* Simon Tyrel, 1370, 1372 (Southyeuel, Sthuchyeuell). Harl. Roll K. 23.

Southill, co. *Cornw.* Fine of Manaton Hamett manor, etc., in, 1550. Eg. 284.

—— Exemplif. of a fine at Manaton, etc., in, 1679. Eg. 321.

Southle, Southley. *v. sub* Datchet, co. *Buck.*

Southmarfeild. *v.* Marcfield, *in Tilton*, co. *Leic.*

Southmills, nr. *Blunham*, co. *Bedf.* Fine, etc., in, 1520. Add. 997;—1626. Harl. 112 E. 38.

Southminster, co. *Essex.* Release of Cages manor in, 1414. Add. 19977.

—— Precipe on a covenant conc. lands in, 1575. Add. 24949.

Southmore, co. *Nott.* Release of "tota aqua et piscaria de," 1445. Harl. 112 I. 3.

Southmymmes. *v.* Mimms, South, co. *Midd.*

Southoe, co. *Hunt.* Grant of, late St. Ph. (Sudham). Add. 11233 (5) (copy).

Southoe, co. Hunt. (continued). Papal conf. of grants in, to Huntingdon Priory, 1147 (Sudham). Cott. MS. Aug. ii. 112.

—— Papal conf. of the church to the same, 1427 (Southo). Cott. MS. Aug. ii. 119.

—— Persona. Will. Lovetot, 1365. Add. 19847.

Southolme. v. Holme, S., in Hovingham, co. York.

Southorpe (Suthorpe, etc.), nr. Edenham, co. Linc. Fines of the manor, 1183. Harl. 49 A. 3;—1364. Harl. 52 A. 88.

—— Grants, etc., in, c. 1290. Add. 20709;—1295. Add. 20711, 20712;—c. 1295. Add. 20710;—1311. Add. 20713;—1317. Add. 20714;—1325. Add. 20715;—1341. Add. 20716;—1407. Add. 20719; — 1487. Add. 20721-20724, 20726; — 1497. Add. 20727, 20728;—1498. Add. 20725, 20729.

Southorpe, nr. Gayton le Wolds, co. Linc. Grants, etc., in, to Kirkstead Abbey, c. 1150-60. Harl. 54 H. 4 (Suthorp);—ante 1170. Harl. 48 G. 41 (Suthorp juxta Gayton);—c. 1295. Harl. 45 H. 14.

Southorpe, nr. Kirton in Lindsey, co. Linc. Grant of the manor, 1375. Add. 20718.

Southorpe, co. Northt. License for grant of Southorpe Hall manor in, 1553. Add. 5366.

—— Sale in, 1579. Add. 9272.

Southorpe, nr. Hornsea, co. York. Grant in, 1453. Add. 5765;—1465. Add. 5768.

Southourme, Southourome. v. Owram, S., co. York.

Southover, co. Suss. Fine in, 1342 (Southenover juxta Lewes). Add. 24889.

—— Precipe on a covenant conc. lands in, 1598. Add. 15234.

Southrop, co. Glouc. Conf. of a grant in, to E. Leach church, by Great Malvern Priory, [1139 - 47] (Sudthropa). Campb. xviii. 11*.

Southry, co. Linc. Grants, etc., in, to Bullington Priory, t. Hen. III. Harl. 52 H. 2 (Sutheraye), 57 B. 3 (Sureya); —1256. Harl. 52 H. 28 (do.);—t. Edw. I.-II. (Sutheroya). Harl. 52 H. 5;—c. 1322. Harl. 52 H. 27.

Southry, co. Linc. (continued). Grant of a hospice in, to the order of Sempringham, t. Hen. III. (Suthreya). Harl. 56 E. 39.

Southwark, co. Surr. Mortgage in, "versus Tamisiam." [1166] (Sudwerk). Cott. MS. Nero C. iii. f. 200.

—— Grant in, "in westrate, de feudo monachorum de Beremundesei," to Southwark Priory, late Hen. II. (Sutwerc). Harl. 56 H. 40.

—— Grant in the marsh of, t. Rich. I.-John (Suwerch). Harl. 83 D 30.

—— Grant of rent from the "Selda de Winton juxta Stodmerbreg" in, to Southwark Priory, t. John (Suwerk). Harl. 47 I. 7.

—— License by H. de Burgo to dispose of a house in, [1200-15] (Sudwerk). Campb. xxiii. 8.

—— Release of a garden in the marsh of, nr. the "wala puellarum," etc., early Hen. III. (Suwerk). Harl. 48 F. 40.

—— Grants, etc., in, 1326. Harl. 52 B. 41;—1333. Harl. 80 E. 52;—1347. Harl. 52 B. 42;—1389. Harl. 46 G. 19;—1475. Add. 7630;—1481. Harl. 112 E. 85.

—— Acquittance in, from Merton Priory, to St. Thomas's Hosp., 1359. Add. 22869.

—— Inventory of furniture, fetters, etc., in the Marshalsea, 1483. Add. 5835.

—— Marriage at the Quakers' meeting place at Horsleydown in, 1677. Add. 7405.

—— Inquest upon a prisoner in the Marshalsea, 1688. Add. 6555.

—— Appointment of a bailiff of his manor of Southwark by the Bp. of Winchester, 1745. Add. 5975.

—— Ballivus. Will. Vinitarius, early Hen. III. Harl. 48 F. 10.

—— Ad. le Chaundelier, 1314. Add. 23657.

—— Ballivus dni. Regis. Ric. Clymppin, 1276-7. Add. 15505.

—— Parishes:—

—— Par. of St. George. Grant, etc., in, 1400. Add. 1813;—1449. Add. 7647;—1462. Add. 17600.

—— —— Rector (nuper). Will. Brook, 1457. Add. 7642, 7643, 7616.

**Southwark**, *co. Surr.* (*continued*). PAR. OF ST. MARGARET. Grants, etc., in, *t.* Edw. I. Add. 9001;—1337. Add. 1313; — 1360. Add. 1314;—1373. Add. 1317;—1391. Add. 1320–1322;—1392. Cott. xxviii. 41;—1400. Add. 1313;—1433. Add. 1315;—1438. Harl. 50 D. 43;—1529. Harl. 112 F. 23 ("The Three Crownes").

—— PAR. OF ST. MARY MAGDALENE. Grants, etc., in, 1326. Add. 23658, 23659;—1349. Add. 23660.

—— PAR. OF ST. OLAVE. Release, etc., in, 1314. Add. 23657;—1349. Add. 23660;—1652. Harl. 57 H. 40.

—— —— Precipe on a covenant conc. lands in, 1555. Add. 25502.

—— —— *Rector.* Hen. Boghebay *al.* Bogbay, 1396. Harl. 76 C. 50;—1400. Harl. 78 B. 50.

—— PAR. OF ST. SAVIOUR. Bequest of the "Green Dragon" inn, 1544. Add. 6290.

—— —— Precipe on a covenant conc. land in, 1555. Add. 25502.

—— —— Lease of the "Green Man" in, 1692. Add. 1976.

—— —— Lease in Clink Street in, 1778. Add. 5978.

—— PAR. OF ST. THOMAS. Lease in, 1678. Cott. xxviii. 110.

**Southwell**, *co. Nott.* Grant in, by Thurstan, Abp. of York, to St. Clement's Priory, *c.* 1130 (Sudwelle). Cott. xi. 66.

—— License for a grant in, for a chaplain in Normanton church, 1331 (Suthewell). Woll. v. 1.

—— Covenant for settlement of Roohawe manor nr., 1437. Add. 20542.

—— Rental of Will. de Wakebrugg in, [1444?]. Woll. xi. 2 a.

—— *Clericus.* Rogerus, early 13 cent. Harl. 83 F. 27.

**Southwick**, *co. Northt.* Papal conf. of the church, etc., to Huntingdon Priory, 1147 (Suduic). Cott. MS. Aug. ii. 112.

—— Lease of mills, etc., in, 1658. Harl. 111 H. 18.

**Southwick**, *co. Southt.* Court-rolls, 1475–1477. Add. 13299, 13300.

**Southwick**, *in North Bradley, co. Wilts.* Grant at Langham (Longeham) Mill in, *t.* Hen. III. Add. 19137.

**Southwick**, *in North Bradley, co. Wilts.* (*continued*). Recovery of the manor, 1556. Add. 5704.

—— Grant of annuity from the manor, 1560. Add. 5706.

—— Extent of the manor, 1568. Add. 5709.

**Southwold**, *co. Suff.* Sale in, 1685. Add. 10443.

**Southwood.** *v. sub* Doddington, *co. Camb.*

—— *v. sub* Duffield, *co. Derb.*

**Southwood Park**, *nr. Denham, co. Suff.* Release of, 1607. Add. 9275.

**Southworth**, *co. Lanc.* Fine of the manor, 1652. Add. 5303.

**Southyevel.** *v.* Southill, *co. Bedf.*

**Sowe**, *co. Warw.* Release, etc., in, late Hen. III. Add. 17359;—1304. Add. 21497.

—— Precipe on a covenant conc. land in, 1592. Add. 25554.

**Sowerby**, *co. York.* Fine in, 1594. Add. 15666.

**Sowerby Bridge**, *co. York.* Briefs for rebuilding the chapel, 1818, 1821. Ch. Br. B. lviii. 7, C. ii. 3.

**Sowrton.** *v.* Sourton, *co. Devon.*

**Sowthlay.** *v. sub* Datchet, *co. Buck.*

**Spaceston.** *v.* Spaxton, *co. Som.*

**Spaldiggeholm, Heremitorium de.** *v. sub* Holme on Spalding Moor, *co. York.*

**Spalding**, *co. Linc.* Grants in, 1341 (Spaldyng). Harl. 53 E. 8;—1393. Harl. 57 E. 22.

—— Court-roll, 1487–8. Add. 24449.

—— Precipe on covenants conc. land in, 1578. Add. 25084, 25089.

—— Particulars of rents and rental of the Qu. Dowager's lands in, 1688. Add. 13592;—1699. Add. 13595.

—— *Capellanus.* Galfridus, [1261–2]. Harl. 49 I. 56, Cott. xxvii. 142.

**Spaldington**, *co. York.* Grant in, to Swine Abbey, late Hen. II. (Spaldiggetun). Add. 26108.

**Spaldwick**, *co. Hunt.* Transfer of, from Ely Abbey to the see of Lincoln, 1109 (Spalduic). Harl. 43 C. 11.

**Sparham.** *v. sub* Necton, *co. Norf.*

**Stamford,** *co. Linc. (continued).* Valor of Crown lands formerly bel. to religious houses in, *t.* Eliz. (?). Harl. Roll Y. 21.

—— Precipe on a covenant in, 1578. Add. 25083.

—— *Aldermannus.* Rob. Stolam, 1396. Add. 6092.

—— *Persona.* Herbertus, *ante* 1264 (Standeford). Campb. xv. 11.

—— *Parson of St. George's.* David Smyth, 1536. Cott. iv. 29.

**Stamford,** *co. Northumb.* Mortgage of the manor, 1272 (Estaneford). Harl. 43 C. 43.

**Stamford Baron,** *co. Northt.* Sale in, 1579. Add. 9272.

**Stamford Bridge,** *co. York.* Grant of the manor, 1369. Harl. 51 E. 39 (Staumfordbrig), 54 C. 13 (Staynforth-brig).

**Stampforde manor,** [*in Gt. Walding-field?*], *co. Suff.* Release of, to the Crown, 1575. Harl. 48 D. 49.

**Stamvileham.** *v. sub* Charlwood, *co. Surr.*

**Stan.** *v.* Stone, *in E. Pennard, co. Som.*

—— *v.* Stonehouse, *co. Glouc.*

**Stana, Stáne.** *v.* Staines, *co. Midd.*

**Stanbrege Parva.** *v.* Stambridge, Lit., *co. Essex.*

**Stanbridge,** *co. Bedf.* Settlement in, 1349. Add. 19947, 19948.

**Stanbridge,** *in Romsey, co. Southt.* Grants, etc., in, 1342 (Stanbrygge). Add. 17407;—1364. Add. 17415;—1367. Add. 17417;—1374. Add. 17419;—1385. Add. 17421, 17423;—1403. Add. 17425;—1410. Add. 17426, 17427;—1443. Add. 17433;—1478. Add. 17435;—1529. Add. 17440.

—— Grant in Balnham in, 1426. Add. 17430.

**Stancil,** *in Tickhill, co. York.* Grant in Hogh in or nr., 1355. Harl. 49 H. 38.

**Stancliffe,** *in Darley, co. Derb.* Grant of Godesmedue in, 1304 (Stanclif). Woll. i. 1.

**Stancomb Dauney.** *v. sub* Sherford, *co. Devon.*

**Standeford.** *v.* Stamford, *co. Linc.*

**Standen,** *co. Wilts.* Covenant conc. and grant of the manor, 1435. Add. 18726, 18727;—1451. Add. 18748.

**Standish,** *co. Glouc.* Grant of the rectory to the see of Gloucester, 1541 (Standyshe). Cott. xiii. 34.

**Standish,** *co. Lanc.* Bequest for a free school at, 1604. Add. 8498.

—— *Persona.* Gilbertus, 1367. Add. 8493.

—— Rog. Standish, *ante* 1480. Harl. 78 I. 47.

—— William Legh, 1604. Add. 8498.

**Standish with Langtree,** *co. Lanc.* Brief conc. a fire at, 1814. Ch. Br. B. liv. 11.

**Standlake (Stanlake),** *co. Oxon.* Power to give seisin, etc., of the manor and advowson, 1333. Cott. xxvii. 69;—1350. Harl. 54 D. 28;—1362. Harl. 58 D. 45.

**Standlinch,** *nr. Downton, co. Wilts.* Release, etc., of, 1361 (Stallynch iouste Dounton). Lansd. 687;—1388 (Stanlynch). Lansd. 688, 689.

**Standon.** *v. sub* Hursley, *co. Southt.*

—— *v.* Stondon, *co. Bedf.*

**Standon,** *co. Hertf.* Grants, etc., in, *t.* Hen. III. Harl. 45 G. 11 (Stondon), 57 G. 21;—1317. Add. 625 (Staundon);—1355. Harl. 53 E. 43;—1356. Harl. 51 C. 55 (Staundon), Add. 15745;—1364. Harl. 49 H. 41 (Staundon);—1379. Harl. 48 F. 35;—1471. Harl. 56 C. 42, 43;—1470–1514. Harl. 44 C. 59–64, 44 D. 1–12.

—— Sale of Rennesley (Reneslegh) manor in, 1342 (Stanbrygge).

—— Sale of Rennesley (Reneslegh) manor in, to Bp. Ant. Bek, [1283-9] (Stondone). Harl. 48 I. 48.

—— Power to give seisin of "le Quarters" in, 1337. Harl. 47 E. 40.

—— Extract from court-roll of Rennesley (Renealee) manor, 1417. Harl. 58 F. 15.

—— Release of Bromley (Bromeleys) in, 1456. Harl. 45 G. 3.

—— Acquittance for homage for Bromley (Bromeley) in, 1462. Add. 15476.

—— Acquittances from Stoke by Clare College for rent of Salbourne *al.* Sabborne chapel in, 1472–1516. Harl. 44 I. 30-50.

—— Grant of the bailiffship, 1477. Add. 15478.

Stanion, co. *North.* Grant in Rod-
mereshawe wood near, *t.* John (Sta-
nerna). Harl. 45 B. 9.

—— Power to give seisin in, etc., 1421.
Add. 792 (Stanerne):—1607. Add.
871 (Staunyerne).

—— *Capellanus.* Radulfus, *t.* John.
Harl. 45 B. 9.

**Stanis.** *v.* Stean, co. *North.*

**Stanleia juxta Coventreiam.** *v.*
Stoneleigh, co. *Warw.*

**Stanley,** co. *Derb.* Papal conf. in, to
Dale Abbey, 1224 (Stanle). Woll. x. 32.

—— Lease in, 1326 (Stanle). Woll.
iv. 1.

—— *Persona.* Rogerus, 1349. Woll.
ix. 69.

**Stanley,** *in Weardale Forest,* co. *Durh.*
Consent by Durham Priory to a grant
in, by the Bp. of Durham, [1217-26].
Woll. v. 2.

—— License to celebrate service at
an oratory in, 1241 (Stanlegh). Woll.
v. 3.

—— License to enclose the wood of,
in Weardale Forest, 1449. Woll. v. 6.

**Stanley,** *in Wakefield,* co. *York.* Crown
lease in, 1555. Harl. 84 C. 32.

**Stanley, King's,** co. *Glouc.* Grant in
Leya in, *t.* Hen. III. (Stanleya Regis).
Slo. xxxiii. 8.

**Stanlow.** *v. sub* Stickford, co. *Linc.*

**Stanmore,** co. *Berks.* Grant at, 960
(Stanmere). Cott. MS. Aug. ii. 40.

**Stanmore,** co. *Midd.* Inspex. in 1580
of a grant in, by Abp. Cranmer to the
Crown, 1542. Add. 7490.

**Stanney,** co. *Chest.* Ref. to grant in, to
Stanlaw Abbey, 1344. Add. 1060.

**Stanningfield,** co. *Suff.* Grants in, *t.*
Edw. II. Add. 24500 (Stanefeud):—
1329. Add. 24655 (Stanesfeld), 24656;
—1507. Add. 24503.

**Stanpete.** *v. sub* Sheppey, Isle of, co.
*Kent.*

**Stanpette.** *v. sub* Seal, co. *Kent.*

**Stanpit.** *v. sub* Christchurch, co.
*Southt.*

**Stansfield,** co. *Suff.* Grants, etc., in,
[1139-51]. Harl. 76 F. 35 (Stanes-
feldia);—*t.* Hen. III. Harl. 45 O. 46
(Stanesfeld), 48 C. 46;—1375-1414.
Harl. Roll O. 27;—1382. Harl.
48 D. 8 (Stansfeld), 4;—1393. Harl.

58 H. 9;—1421. Harl. 48 D. 15;—
1539. Harl. 48 D. 33;—1575. Harl.
48 D. 49.

**Stanstead.** *v. sub* Halstead, co. *Essex.*

**Stanstead,** co. *Hertf.* Exemplif. of
fine in, 1608. Add. 13582.

**Stanstead,** co. *Kent.* Grant at, to
Christ Church, Canterbury, [805-810]
(Stanhamstede). Cott. MS. Aug. ii. 79.

**Stanstead,** co. *Suff.* Lease in, 1351
(Stansted). Harl. 51 A. 37.

—— Lease of the manor, 1419 (Stansted). Harl. 54 H. 31.

—— Depositions taken in the church,
*t.* Hen. VI. Harl. Roll C. 14.

—— Abstract of the bye-laws of Overhall and Netherhall manors in, 1503-
1570. Add. 26072.

—— Fine in, 1634. Harl. 45 G. 7.

—— *Persona.* Joh. de Multon, 1351.
Harl. 51 A. 37;—1361. Cott. xxvii. 131.

—— *Rector.* Joh. de Multone, 1365.
Harl. 56 B. 45;—1367. Harl. 53 C. 32.

**Stanstead,** co. *Suss.* Acquittance, with
defeasance of bond on an award in,
1474 (Stanstede). Harl. 51 A. 28.

**Stanstead St. Margaret's,** co. *Hertf.*
Conf. of appropr. of the church to
Thele College, 1316. Cott. xxix. 44;
—1318. Cott. v. 46.

**Stansted [Mountfitchet],** co. *Essex.*
Grant of reversion in, *ante* 1302.
Lansd. 93.

**Stansty,** co. *Denb.* Sale in, 1554
(Stansti Vcha). Add. 8654.

—— Precipe for livery of lands in,
1625. Add. 8659.

**Stanthorne,** co. *Chest.* Writ on a fine
in, 1420 (Stanthurl). Add. 6278.

**Stanton.** *v.* Staunton, co. *Worc.*

**Stanton,** co. *Derb.* or co. *Salop.* Grant
in exch. for land at, 901 (Stan tun).
Cott. viii. 27.

**Stanton** (Staunton, etc.), **with Stanton Woodhouse,** *in Youlgreave,* co.
*Derb.* Grants, etc., in, *t.* Hen. III.
Woll. ii. 3 (Stantona Leys et Wodehuses), 16 (copy);—1294. Woll. ii. 20;
—*t.* Edw. I.-II. Woll. ii. 6, 7, 13
(Stauntone Leyes), 18 (St. Wode-
houses);—1302. Woll. ii. 8, 21 (copy);
—1314. Woll. ii. 14;—1316. Woll. ii.
19;—1345. Woll. ii. 64;—1351. Woll.
ii. 17;—1372. Woll. ii. 22 (Stanton
in Alto Pecco) (copy);—1442. Woll.

2 Y

**Stanton Lacy** (Stantun, etc.), co. Salop (continued). Clericus (continued). Robertus, late 13 cent. Add. 8339.

—— Vicarius. Adam, 1387. Add. 8356, 8357.

**Stanton Leys**, in Stanton in Youlgreave, co. Derb. Grants, etc., in, t. Hen. III. Woll. ii. 3 (Leys), 4 (Stantonleys), 16 (Leeys) (copy);—1277. Woll. ii. 15 (Stantonleyes);—1284. Woll. ii. 10 (Stantonleg);—1300. Woll. ii. 12 (Stantoneleyes);—1375. Woll. ii. 23 (Stanton legbes).

—— Certificate conc. title to lands in, 1487. Woll. ii. 35.

**Stanton, Long**, co. Camb. Grants, etc., in, early 13 cent. Add. 21394;— t. Edw. I. Add. 22587;—1316. Add. 22589;—1323. Add. 22590;—1359. Add. 22592, 22598;— 1361. Add. 22594 (Longa Stantona);—1364. Add. 22595;—1401. Add. 22596;—1420. Add. 22599;—1423. Add. 22600;— 1434. Add. 22601;— 1445. Add. 22603;—1562. Add. 22605;—1597. Add. 22606;—1629. Add. 22607.

—— Grant of rents in, etc., to All Saints' church in, t. Hen. III. (Stantona). Add. 21395-21399, 22579;— 1331. Add. 22591.

—— Inquest conc. patronage of St. Michael's church in, etc., 1359. Add. 22588.

—— Feoffment of Cheynes and Collouylles manors in, 1406 (Longestanton). Add. 22597, 22598.

—— Grant of the manor, 1439. Add. 22602.

—— Bond to King's College, Cambridge, conc. the manor, 1580. Add. 22604.

—— Persona. Johannes, early 13 cent. Add. 21394.

—— Persona eccl. Omnium Sanctorum. Mag. Laurentius, t. Hen. III. Add. 21396, 21397.

—— Persona eccl. S. Michaelis. Herbertus, t. Hen. III. Add. 21397, 22579.

—— Rectores eccl. S. Michaelis. Joh. de Scardeburg [ob. 1359], Petr. Le Vavesour, clericus, 1359. Add. 22588.

**Stanton, Long**, co. Salop. Bond conc. a sale in, 1559 (Staunton). Harl. 78 G. 18.

**Stanton Prior**, co. Som. Exchange in Chermescumbe nr., late Hen. III. Add. 5444.

**Stanton Prior**, co. Som. (continued). (Staunton Priour, etc.). Grants, etc., in, 1362. Add. 5457-5459;—1366. Add. 5460;—1372. Add. 5462 (Staunton Priour), 5463-5465;—1445. Add. 5468;—1472. Add. 5473.

—— Suit in, t. Rich. II. Add. 6267.

—— Persona. Will. Wythek, 1465. Harl. 53 A. 9.

**Stanton** [St. Bernard ?], co. Wilts. Court-rolls, 1556-2, 1566-7. Add. 24440 (Staunton), 24441 (do.).

**Stanton St. Quintin**, co. Wilts. Compotus-roll's of, bel. to the Duke of Buckingham, 1499-1500, 1511-12. Add. 26873, 26874.

**Stanton, Stoney**, co. Leic. Grant, etc., of, c. 1160 (Stantona). Harl. 55 D. 8, Lansd. 601.

—— Grant of a pension from the manor, 1309 (Staunstone). Add. 21303.

—— Grant in, 1363 (Stonystaunton). Lansd. 606.

**Stanway**, co. Essex. Bequest of land at, post 991 (at Stanwægun). Harl. 43 C. 4.

—— Grant in, 1328 (Staneweye Magna). Harl. 52 C. 8.

—— Sale of Shrebb wood in, 1370. Harl. 45 L 41.

—— Grant of rent from Olivers manor in, to Bocking Hospital, 1455. Add. 13551.

—— Release to the Crown of a moiety of the manor, with the advowson, 1575. Harl. 48 D. 49.

—— Persona. Johan, 1359 (Staneweye). Lansd. 123.

**Stanwell**, co. Midd. Release in, to Newark Priory, 1281 (Stanewell). Harl. 50 F. 47.

—— Sale at Newes Bridge in, 1589. Add. 24838.

—— Rector. Dom. Ric. de Thorp, 1378. Harl. 56 D. 49.

**Stanwick**, co. Norfht. Compotus of the manor, 1281 (Stanewygg). Add. 737.

—— Precipe on a covenant conc. land in, 1593. Add. 25184.

**Stanwick**, co. York. Covenant conc. payment for the manor, 1460 (Estanwik). Add. 10216.

**Stanyggod.** v. Stenigot, co. Linc.

**Stisted,** *co. Essex (continued).* Grants, etc., in, *t.* Hen. III. Harl. 112 B. 7; —1291. Harl. 111 G. 17; — 1299. Harl. 54 H. 26;—1631. Add. 5142.

—— Lease of the manor, 1341. Add. 15456, 15457.

**Stitenache, Stithensæce, Stiveneth,** etc. *v.* Stevenage, *co. Hertf.*

**Stithians,** *co. Cornw.* Declaration conc. settlement of Kennal (Kynell) manor in, 1488. Add. 15739.

**Stiueclai, Stiuecle, Magna.** *v.* Stukeley, Great, *co. Hunt.*

**Stiuekeye, Stuuekeye.** *v.* Stiffkey, *co. Norf.*

**Stiuelegh.** *v.* Stileway, *in Meare, co. Som.*

**Stiuentona.** *v.* Stevington, *co. Bedf.*

**Stiuentonia.** *v.* Steventon, *co. Southt.*

**Stiuiceswrde.** *v.* Stetchworth, *co. Camb.*

**Stivichal,** *co. Warw.* Briefs for rebuilding the church, 1804-1816. Ch. Br. B. xlv. 4, L 10, lvi. 9.

**Stixwould,** *co. Linc.* Release in, 1365 (Stykeswold). Harl. 58 C. 2.

—— Release of Halstead (Hellestede) manor, etc., in, 1425 (Stykeswold). Harl. 52 G. 8.

**Stoake, East.** *v.* Stoke, East, *co. Nott.*

**Stoce.** *v.* Severnstoke, *co. Worc.*

**Stocfaston.** *v.* Stockerston, *co. Leic.*

**Stocha.** *v.* Stoke, *co. Suff.*

**Stoches.** *v.* Stoke Rochford, *co. Linc.*

**Stock,** *co. Essex.* Grants, etc., in, *t.* Hen. III. Harl. 49 A. 39;—1316. Campb. v. 11 (Hereward Stokke):— 1364. Harl. 54 E. 53 (Herewardistok):—1390. Harl. 55 A. 54 (Herewardstokke):—1423. Harl. 45 I. 41; —1424. Harl. 45 I. 42;—1456. Harl. 55 B. 38 (Herwardstok);—1470. Harl. 55 B 39;—1474. Harl. 46 D. 3 (Harwardstokke), 4;—1494. Harl. 53 C. 31 (Herferdstok);—1506. Harl. 55 B. 26, 27;—1507. Harl. 54 H. 20.

**Stock Crockerne.** *v. sub* Lydlinch, *co. Dors.*

**Stock Gayland,** *co. Dors.* Grant in Ramsbury (Remmesberi) in, *t.* Hen. III. Harl. 53 D. 25.

—— Fine in, 1335 (Stokk Coillard). Harl. 51 B. 1.

**Stock Gayland,** *co. Dors. (continued).* Release, etc., of Ramsbury (Remmesbere, Rammesbere) manor in, 1425. Harl. 48 B. 7, 8;—1433. Harl. Roll O. 32;—1439. Harl. 58 D. 42.

**Stock Turberville,** *co. Dors.* Fine in, 1346. Add. 25876.

**Stockbridge,** *co. York.* Grant in, 1412 (Stokbrige). Harl. 112 H. 44.

**Stockbury,** *co. Kent.* Bequest of Guildsted (Ylstede) manor in, 1457. Harl. 75 D. 55.

—— Fine in, 1548 (Stokberye). Harl. 75 H. 4, 76 H. 50.

**Stockeleye.** *v. sub* Rolleston, *co. Staff.*

**Stockerston,** *co. Leic.* Grant in, 1288 (Storfaston). Add. 21401.

**Stockholt,** *co. Buck.* Release, etc., of the manor, 1345 (Stocholt). Add. 6029;—1347. Add. 6030.

**Stockland,** *co. Devon. Vicarius.* Will. Combe, *ante* 1402. Harl. 57 B. 52.

**Stockleigh,** *co. Devon.* Grant of freewarren in, 1296 (Stokelegh). Harl. 58 I. 40.

**Stockley Park.** *v. sub* Rolleston, *co. Staff.*

**Stockport,** *co. Chest.* Settlement in, 1372 (Stopport). Add. 20492.

**Stockshill.** *v. sub* Brenchley, *co. Kent.*

**Stockton** (Stocton, Stokton), *co. Norf.* Grants, etc., of the manor, etc., 1225. Harl. 46 D. 38;—[1241-5]. Harl. 46 D. 41;—1338. Harl. 57 E. 35;—1340. Harl. 53 A. 20, 57 E. 36;—1375. Harl. 53 E. 43;—1388. Cott. xxiii. 42, Harl. 46 D. 46;—1403. Cott. xxvii. 163, 164;—1404. Cott. v. 31, Harl. 46 D. 47, 48, 53 E. 47;—1419. Harl. 51 E. 53;—1422. Harl. 50 F. 36;— 1435. Cott. v. 3, 22;—1436. Harl. 50 F. 37, 38;—1437. Harl. 50 F. 39;— 1446. Harl. 50 F. 40;—1462. Harl. 54 I. 19.

—— Grants, etc., in, 1275. Harl. 45 H. 44;—1361. Harl. 52 B. 11;— 1386. Harl. 56 G. 21.

—— Recital of documents in a suit conc. the manor, 1462 (Stokton). Harl. 51 H. 13.

**Stockton,** *co. Wilts.* Conf. of the church to St. Cross Hosp., Winchester, 1189 (Stocton). Harl. 43 C. 28.

**Stoke Atram** al. Atram, nr. Whit-church Canonicorum, co. Dors. (con-tinued). Fine in, 1340 (Atreham). Harl. 47 H. 7.

**Stoke Bardolph**, co. Nott. Lands in Hawton, co. Nott., held of the King's manor of, 1540. Add. 24169.

**Stoke Bishop**, nr. Bristol, co. Glouc. Fine in, 1677. Add. 15843.

**Stoke Bliss**, co. Heref. Release in Hyde in, 1459 (Stoke Blice). Add. 24774.

**Stoke Bruerne**, co. Northt. Award in suit betw. the parson of, and St. James's Abbey, Northampton, for tithes, c. 1200 (?) (Stokes). Add. 6109.

—— Grants, etc., in, [1215-25]. Harl. 57 E. 28 (Stokes);—1393. Harl. 57 E. 22 (Stokebruere).

—— Release in, to St. James's Abbey, c. 1230 (Stokes). Add. 6110.

—— Persona. W. de Roverio, c. 1200. Add. 6109.

—— —— Dom. Joh. Harwedon, 1324. Add. 22004.

—— Rector. Adam, c. 1230. Add. 6110.

**Stoke by Clare** (Stoke), co. Suff. Grants, etc., in Woodfield, Moor, etc., in, 1313. Harl. 46 A. 23, 51 A. 40;— 1322. Harl. 47 D. 52.

—— Compotus of Erbury manor in, 1407-8. Harl. Roll E. 13.

—— Extracts from court-rolls of Stoke cum Chilton manor in, 1581-1638. Add. 1278, 1279, 1282-1289.

—— Extracts from court-rolls of Stoke juxta Clare manor, 1582. Add. 1284; —1595. Add. 1286;—1610. Add. 10565;—1632. Add. 10567.

—— Precipe on a covenant conc. the manor, 1592 (Stoke). Add. 25015.

—— Inq. conc. site of the college, etc., 1627. Add. 6073.

**Stoke by Nayland**, co. Suff. Lease in Leuenhey in, by St. Osyth Priory, early 13 cent. (Stokes). Harl. 44 C. 16.

—— Grants, etc., in, early Hen. III. Harl. 54 H. 9 (Stokes);—1286. Harl. 44 C. 17 (Stoke Neylond);—t. Edw. I. Harl. 47 D. 15;—1324. Add. 9583;— 1337. Harl. 56 H. 34 (Stoke atte Neilond);—1361. Harl. 45 F. 27;— 1413. Harl. 56 H. 38.

—— Bequests to the church of, 1403. Harl. 56 H. 37.

**Stoke by Nayland**, co. Suff. (con-tinued). Acquittance by Prittlewell Priory for rent of the rectory, 1420. Cott. xxi. 27.

—— Compotus of the manor, 1515. Add. 215.

—— Precipes on covenants conc. land in, 1578. Add. 25372;—1592. Add. 25446.

—— Warranty in, 1581 (Stoke iuxta Neylond). Harl. 86 G. 49.

—— Precipe on a covenant conc. Levenhey al. Netherhall manor in, 1593. Add. 25482.

—— Rector (?). Phil. Mannoke, 1420. Cott. xxi. 27.

—— Vicarius. Hen. Tompstone al. Thameston, 1390. Harl. 56 H. 36;— 1403. Harl. 56 H. 37;—(as perpet. vicarius), 1403. Harl. 47 A. 29.

—— —— Dom. Phil. de Stokeney-lond, 1410. Add. 10052.

—— Vicarius Perpetuus. Hen. Heryng, 1413. Harl. 56 H. 38.

**Stoke [Canon ?]**, co. Devon (?). Com-potus of the manor, 1285-6 (Stok). Add. 4836.

**Stoke Climsland**, co. Cornw. Grant of tenants in the manor, [1217-20?] (Climeslande). Add. 13927.

**Stoke Courcy** al. Stogursey, co. Som. Conditional grant in the manor, 1241 (Stoke Curcy). Cott. viii. 7.

—— Order for an extent of the manor, 1301. Add. 19302.

—— Bond. conc. Week Fitz Paine (Wik) manor in, 1316. Harl. 50 B. 16.

—— Grant in la Wildemersche in, for a corrody, 1318. Add. 26760.

—— Grant in, t. Edw. II. Add. 26761. v. also Farringdon, in Stoke Courcy (?), co. Som.

**Stoke cum Chilton.** v. sub Stoke by Clare, co. Suff.

**Stoke D'Abernon**, co. Surr. Grants in, to Waverley Abbey, [1235-6] (Stok). Add. 5531, 5532.

—— Grants, etc., in, [1235-6]. Add. 5541;—t. Hen. III.-t. Edw. I. Add. 5539 (Stokes de Abernon), 5540, 5542, 5544 (Stokes);—1333. Add. 5594, 5595;—1351. Add. 5603;—1353. Add. 5604.

—— Conf. of grant in, to Newark Priory, late Hen. III. (Stokes). Add. 5543.

**Stoke Poges**, co. *Buck.* (*continued*). Release in Ditton, *t.* Hen. III. Harl. 56 G. 31.

—— Grants, etc., in, *t.* Edw. I. Harl. 56 E. 43 (Stok);—1429. Lansd. 149 (S. Pogeys);—1448. Lansd. 150;—1532. Lansd. 177 (S. Bogeys);—1535. Lansd. 178;—1537. Lansd. 576;—1561. Lansd. 577, 578;—1564. Lansd. 579.

—— Release in, from Southwark Priory, 1346 (Stok Puigeys). Harl. 44 I. 53.

—— Lease in, to Southwark Priory, from the Bp. of Winchester, 1383 (Stokepugeys). Harl. 43 I. 43.

—— *Vicarius perpetuus.* Will. de Medebourn, *c.* 1340. Harl. 44 I. 53.

—— *Vicarius.* Johannes, 1399. Add. 14677.

—— *Capellanus de Dytton in.* Dom. Hugo Harlocombe, 1435. Add. 5218.

**Stoke Rivers**, co. *Devon.* Fine, etc., of the manor and advowson, 1653. Harl. 86 I. 59;—1655. Harl. 111 E. 35.

—— Covenants not to disturb in possession in, 1664. Harl. 85 H. 47, 48, 52, 112 B. 29;—1666. Harl. 112 K. 30.

**Stoke Rochford**, co. *Linc. Clericus.* Robertus, 1172 (Stoches). Eg. 432, 433.

**Stoke Rodney** *al.* S. Giffard, co. *Som.* Conf. of jurisdiction of the Abbat of Glastonbury in Nyland (Adredesia) in, 1314. Campb. xiii. 19.

**Stoke St. Milburgh**, co. *Salop.* Excheq. acquittance for the farm of the manor. 1595 (Stooke Mylburne). Add. 25646.

**Stoke Say.** *v.* Stokesay, co. *Salop.*

**Stoke, South**, co. *Oxon.* Compotus, 1474-5 (Stoke Abbatis). Harl. Roll G. 2.

—— *Rector.* Dom. Walterus (?), 1242 (Stokes). Add. 20372.

**Stoke, South**, co. *Suss.* Grant of Offham (Offam) in, *c.* 1200. Harl. 45 B. 29.

—— Lease of fishery in, by Arundel College, 1451. Lansd. 160.

—— Fine in, and in Offham (Offam) in, 1487. Add. 15213.

**Stoke Talmage**, co. *Oxon.* Brief for rebuilding the church, 1758. Ch. Br. A. iv. 8.

**Stoke Wallis**, *nr. Whitchurch Cancellorum*, co. *Dors.* Grants, etc., in, *t.* Edw. I. Harl. 47 G. 57 (Stoke Walays), 56 F. 5 (S. Waleis);—1338. Harl. 46 F. 26 (S. Waleys);—1344. Harl. 47 H. 1 (S. Waleis in hundr. de Wytechurche);—1396. Add. 15444 (S. Waleys);—1409. Harl. 55 G. 43, 44 (do.);—1410. Harl. 51 F. 40, 41 (do.);—1411. Harl. 46 G. 56 (Stokeways).

—— Fine in, 1340. Harl. 47 H. 7.

—— Court-roll, 1433. Harl. Roll I. 4.

**Stokegommer.** *v.* Stogumber, co. *Som.*

**Stokeham**, co. *Nott.* Grant in, 1412 (Stokum). Add. 15740.

**Stokeleigh.** *v.* Stockleigh, co. *Devon.*

**Stokenchurch**, co. *Oxon.* Feoffments in, 1406. Add. 20351, 20352 (Stokyngchurche);—1414. Add. 20353, 20354 (do.).

**Stokenham**, co. *Devon.* Grants in Chillington (Chedelyngton, Chedlington) in, 1473. Harl. 85 D. 12;—1478. Harl. 86 F. 23.

**Stokes.** *v.* Stoke, co. *Kent.*

—— *v.* Stoke Bruerne, co. *Northt.*

—— *v.* Stoke by Nayland, co. *Suff.*

—— *v.* Stoke Golding, co. *Leic.*

**Stokesay**, co. *Salop.* Release in, reserving pasture in Seldenhale and Flaxforde in, *c.* 1260 (Stoke Say). Add. 8331.

—— Grant in Wettleton (Wetlinton) in, *t.* Hen. III. Add. 8334.

—— Release from suit to H. de Say's court at, on a grant in Wettleton, *t.* Hen. III (Stoke). Add. 8067.

—— *Dominus.* Dom. Job. de Verdun, *c.* 1260. Add. 8331.

—— *Vicarius.* Dom. Adam, *c.* 1260 (Stokes). Add. 8331.

**Stokesby**, co. *Norf.* Grants, etc., in, 1384. Add. 14873; — 1457. Add. 14874 (Stokysby);—1492. Add. 14875; —1517. Add. 14876, 14877;—1519. Add. 14878, 14879; — 1528. Add. 14880;—1531. Add. 14881;—1533. Add. 14882;—1552. Add. 14883;—1553. Add. 14884; — 1556. Add. 14885, 14886;—1557. Add. 14887;—1560. Add. 14888, 14889; — 1563. Add. 14890; — 1566. Add. 14893, 14894;—1567. Add. 14892;—1571. Add. 14895;—1573. Add. 14896;—1601. Add. 14898 (Stoxsbie);—1623. Add. 14900;—1630. Add. 14901.

**Stonehouse,** *co. Glouc.* Papal mandate conc. the church of, 1236 (Stan.). Harl. 43 A. 36.

—— Grant in Hawyatesfeld in, 1342 (Stonhouse). Slo. xxxiii. 26.

—— Settlement in Ebley (Ebballsie) in, 1359 (do.). Slo. xxxiii. 40.

**Stoneleigh,** *co. Warw.* Grant of, with its snke, to R., Earl of Chester, [1153] (Stauleia juxta Coventreiam). Cott. xvii. 2.

—— Fine in, 1554 (Stoneley). Harl. 54 E. 20.

**Stonepit.** *v sub* Seul, *co. Kent.*

—— *v. sub* Sheppey, Isle of, *co. Kent.*

**Stonesfield,** *co. Oxon.* Compotus-rolls, 1393-1431 (Stuntesfeld, etc.). Harl. Rolls B. 35, 38, 41, 42.

**Stonhale.** *v.* Stonall, *co. Staff.*

**Stonham,** *co. Suff.* Conf. in, to Leiston Abbey, *t.* Hen. III. (Stanham). Add. 10294.

**Stonham Aspall,** *co. Suff. Persona.* Will. de Aspale, 1334 (Stanham Antegan). Add. 9942.

—— —— Will. de Hengham, *t.* Edw. III. Harl. 51 E. 10.

—— —— Will. Broun, 1375 (Stonham). Harl. 51 E. 10.

**Stonham, Earl,** *co. Suff.* Annuity charged on the manor, 1442 (Stonham). Add. 17234.

—— Lease in, 1577 (Erle Stonham). Add. 19272.

—— *Persona. Dom.* Rob. de Bockyng ol. Bokkyngg, 1379. Harl. 48 D. 2;—1381. Harl. 53 C. 34;—(as *Rector*), 1380. Harl. 48 E. 35.

**Stonham, Little,** *co. Suff.* Release in, 1456 (Stonham Jernegan). Add. 10469.

—— Sale of Stonham Jernegan manor, 1565. Add. 15759.

—— Precipes on covenants conc. lands in, 1578. Add. 25332, 25373;—1589. Add. 25411.

—— *Rector.* Alex. Baroun, *de Whitingtone* [*Whitton*], 1273 (Stanham Gernegan). Add. 9830.

**Stoniland,** *nr. Cannington, co. Som.* (?). Grant of, late 13 cent. Add. 20401.

**Stonistratford.** *v.* Stratford, Stony, *co. Buck.*

**Stonlake.** *v. sub* Chiddingstone, *co. Kent.*

**Stonton.** *v.* Stanton, *co. Salop.*

**Stonyeston.** *v.* Easton, Stone, *co. Som.*

**Stonystaunton.** *v.* Stanton, Stoney, *co. Leic.*

**Stoondon.** *v.* Standon, *co. Hertf.*

**Stopport.** *v.* Stockport, *co. Chest.*

**Stormsworth,** *co. Leic.* Covenant conc. rents in, 1357. Add. 21772.

**Stormy (Sturmi, etc.),** *co. Glam.* Grants, etc., in or nr., to Margam Abbey, *t.* Hen. II.-late 12 cent. Harl. 75 A. 9, 75 B. 26, 75 D. 1, 2, 3;—1234. Harl. 75 B. 8 (Sturmiestun), 9 (do.); —c. 1230-40. Harl. 75 B. 6;—4. Hen. III. Harl. 75 D. 6.

—— Report and covenant conc. the church of, *t.* Hen. II. Harl. 75 B. 3; —*t.* John. Harl. 75 A. 34.

—— Conf. of "montana de la holemedwe" nr. (?), to Margam Abbey, late 12 cent. Harl. 75 B. 27.

—— *Capellanus ville Sturmi.* Thomas, *t.* Hen. II. Harl. 75 D. 2.

—— *Presbiter (quondam).* Thomas, *t.* Hen. II. Harl. 75 B. 3.

**Storrs,** *in Bradfield, co. York.* Lands bel. to G. Shaw in, 1748. Add. 18078.

**Stortford, Bishop's,** *co. Hertf.* Lands in Layer Marney held "ad wardam de Storteford," *t.* Hen. III. Cott. xxvii. 46.

—— Grants, etc., in, 1299. Add. 6197; —1441. Add. 5294 (Storteford);— 1481. Add. 5296;—1452-1634. Add. 19110-19125;—1656. Add. 19132.

—— License to erect a building in, 1439 (Storteford). Add. 5293.

—— Grant of a stall "in Bocheria," 1458. Add. 5295.

—— Lease in, by the charity tr.-offees, 1725. Add. 19133.

—— *Custodes bonorum ecclesie.* Will. Barbour, Joh. Cotiller, 1452. Add. 19110.

—— —— Joh. Algore, Joh. Sturdy, 1478. Add. 19111, 19112.

—— —— Joh. Jardevill, Joh. Grace, 1484. Add. 19113.

—— —— Joh. Grace, Joh. Busshe, 1491. Add. 19114.

—— —— Ric. Jardefeld, Joh. Smyth, 1538. Add. 19116.

—— —— Tho. Snowe, Tho. Crabbe, 1556. Add. 19118.

—— —— Edw. Gybson, Will. Brett, 1575. Add. 19119.

Stortford, Bishop's, *co. Hertf. (con-tinued). Custodes bonorum ecclesie (continued).* Will. Snowe, Geo. Jacobbe, 1595. Add. 19121, 19122.

—— —— Rob. Bowyere, Rob. Colte, 1614. Add. 19123.

—— —— Geo. Denyson, Rob. Bow-yere, 1634. Add. 19125.

—— —— Leonard Knight, Will. Reade, *Jun.*, 1656. Add. 19132.

—— *Yconimi ecclesie.* Joh. Maryon, Joh. Setcole, 1491. Add. 19114.

Storthwaite, *co. York.* Grant of the manor, 1369. Harl. 54 C. 13.

Stortone. *v.* Staughton, *co. Bedf.*

Stotesbur. *v.* Stutsbury, *co. Northt.*

Stotfold, *co. Bedf.* Grant in Arlsey to Waltham Abbey " contra aquam que venit de Stotfaud," early 13 cent. Eg. 407.

—— Conf. of the church, etc., to Chicksands Priory, *t.* Hen. III. (Stot-falde). Harl. 45 I. 18.

—— Grant, etc., in or nr., 1388. Add. 17661 ;—1406. Harl. 57 F. 38.

Stotton. *v.* Stoughton, *co. Suss.*

—— *v.* Stutton, *co. Suff.*

Stoughton, *co. Leic.* Papal conf. of a grant in, to Ulvescroft Priory, 1174 (Stoctona). Harl. 111 A. 6 (*copy*).

Stoughton, *co. Suss.* Compotus of the manor, 1282-3. Add. 26683 (Stotton).

Stour, *River, co. Kent.* Grant nr., 811 (Sture). Cott. MS. Aug. ii. 10.

—— Covenant conc. mills on, dredging, etc., at Canterbury, 1357. Cott. xxi. 10.

Stour, *River, co. Worc.* Grant for a monastery at " Husmerae " near, 736 (Stur). Cott. MS. Aug. ii. 3.

Stour (?), *co. Worc.* Conf. of grant in, to Pershore Abbey, 972 (in Sture). Cott. MS. Aug. ii. 6.

Stour, East. *v. sub* Ashford, *co. Kent.*

Stour Paine, *co. Dors.* Grant of ward-ship in, [1550-53] (Stowerpayne). Cott. MS. Vesp. F. xiii. art. 222.

Stourmouth, *co. Kent.* Grant, etc., in, 1349. Cott. xxvii. 27 ;—1664. Add. 18993.

Stourton, *co. Staff.* Conveyance of the manor by Tewkesbury Abbey, 1495. Harl. 44 I. 59.

Stouting, *co. Kent.* Covenant conc. land in, 1044 (Stuting). Cott. MS. Aug. ii. 70.

—— Covenant conc. pasture in the manor, 1326 (Stoutyng). Harl. 79 E. 59.

—— Bond as bailiff in, 1467. Harl. 79 B. 50.

—— Covenant for recovery in, 1543. Harl. 76 H. 41.

—— Fine in, 1641 (Stowtingo). Harl. 111 C. 66.

—— *Ballivus.* Tho. Morston, *yoman, de Sybertinveld [Silbertewould],* 1467. Harl. 79 B. 50.

Stouwe. *v.* Stow, *co. Linc.*

Stouwey. *v.* Stowey, *co. Som.*

Stoven, *co. Suff.* Grants, etc., in, *t.* Hen. III. Harl. 51 A. 18, 19 ;— *t.* Edw. I. Harl. 48 G. 13 ;—1296. Harl. 48 G. 16 :—1297. Harl. 48 G. 15, 17 ;—1329. Harl. 48 A. 10 ;—1396. Harl. 48 I. 39 ;—1476. Add. 10074.

—— Precipe on a covenant conc. land in, 1592. Add. 25424.

Stovorde. *v.* Stoford, *in S. Newton, co. Wilts.*

Stow, *in Threckingham, co. Linc.* Grant in, 1493. Add. 21154.

Stow, *in Well Wapentake, co. Linc.* Conveyance in, 1290. Harl. 47 B. 24.

Stow, *nr. Market Deeping, co. Linc.* Grants, etc., in, 1335. Add. 6457 ;— 1348. Add. 6466 (Stouwe) ;—1482. Add. 6467 ;—1491. Add. 6468 ;— 1577. Add. 6469.

—— Covenant for a fine of the manor, 1552. Add. 18562.

—— *Persona.* Tho. de Paxton, 1347. Harl. 47 C. 27.

Stow, *co. Staff.* Appropriation of the church to St. Thomas's Priory, Staf-ford, [1258-79] (Stowya). Add. 878-880.

—— *Rector.* Rob. de Braydeshale, [1258-79]. Add. 878-880.

Stow Bedon, *co. Norf.* Fine of the manor, 1316 (Stowe Bidoun). Add. 22613.

—— Sale in, 1580 (Stowe Bydon). Add. 14903.

Stow on the Wold, *co. Glouc.* Grant of lands at Maugersbury (Mæpelgares byrig) in, 949. Cott. viii. 6 (*copy*).

Streatley, *co. Berks.* Lease, etc., of the rectory, 1543. Add. 13650;— 1544. Add. 13651.

Stred ford. *v.* Stratford, *co. Suff.*

Street, *nr. Bromyard, co. Heref.* Settlement of the manor, 1585 (Streate). Add. 7039.

Street, *nr. Glastonbury, co. Som.* Re-feoffment in, 1330 (Strete juxta Glastone). Add. 5449.

—— Re-feoffment, etc., of Iveythorn manor, etc., in, 1421. Add. 15845;—1635. Add. 15846;—1684. Add. 15848.

—— Fine in Iveythorn in, 1712. Add. 15850.

Street Aston. *v.* Aston, Street, *co. Warw.*

Streethall, *co. Essex.* Release of the manor and advowson, 1403 (Strathale). Harl. 56 D. 3.

Streethay, *nr. Lichfield, co. Staff.* Lease in, 1586 (Stretehay). Add. 13573.

Strensham, *co. Worc.* Conf. of grants in, to Pershore Abbey, 972 (in Strengesbo). Cott. MS. Aug. ii. 6.

—— Grant in, to Pershore Abbey, [1249–62] (Strengesham). Campb. xviii. 6.

Streteham. *v.* Streatham, *co. Surr.*

Stretelonde, *in Marshwood Vale, co. Dors.* Grant in, 1338. Harl. 46 F. 26.

Stretfeld. *v.* Stratfield Mortimer, *cos. Berks and Southt.*

Stretford, *co. Heref.* Settlement in, 1585. Add. 7039.

Stretford Hundred, *co. Heref.* Subscribers in, to a loan to the king, 1627 (Streatford). Add. 9210.

Stretham. *v.* Streatham, *co. Surr.*

Stretham, *co. Camb.* Conf. in, by H., Bp. of Ely, to Ely Abbey, [1103–31] (Stratham). Harl. 43 H. 4 (copy).

—— Mortgage, etc., in, [1199]. Harl. 45 C. 9 (Estreham);—1337. Lansd. 108.

Stretleg, *co. Kent.* A boundary, 697. Cott. MS. Aug. ii. 88.

Stretton. *v.* Stratton, *co. Bedf.*

—— *v.* Stretton under Fosse, *co. Warw.*

—— *v.* Sturton, Gt., *co. Linc.*

—— *v.* Sturton le Steeple, *co. Nott.*

Stretton, *in N. Wingfield, co. Derb.* Grant in, from Dale Abbey, [1204–35]. Woll. vii. 1, 2.

Stretton, *co. Rutl.* Suit for enclosures in, 1636. Cott. ii. 25 (1–7).

Stretton Baskerville, *co. Warw.* Entailment of the manor and advowson, 1381 (Strettone). Harl. 112 E. 21.

—— (?) *Persona.* Galterus, late Hen. II. (Strettona). Cott. xi. 30.

—— (?) —— Hugo, 1232. Harl. 83 A. 32.

Stretton en le Fields, *cos. Derb. and Leic.* Conf. of a grant in, 1325 (Stretton). Add. 24206.

—— *Rector.* Willelmus, *t.* Hen. III. (do.). Add. 5992.

—— —— Willelmus, 1325. Add. 24206.

Stretton Grandison, *co. Heref.* Draft for a lease of forfeited lands in, *t.* Hen. VIII. (Stretton). Cott. xv. 33.

—— (?) *Persona.* Gilebertus, *c.* 1180 (Strettona). Campb. v. 8.

Stretton, Great, *co. Leic.* Mem. of tithes in, bel. to King's Norton, [1360–85] (Stretton Magna). Cott. xvi. 65.

—— Reference to a fine, in 1283, in, 1435. Harl. 44 H. 45.

Stretton in the Clay. *v.* Sturton le Steeple, *co. Nott.*

Stretton, Little, *in King's Norton, co. Leic.* License for a grant for a chantry in, to Ouston Abbey, *co. Leic.,* 1344 (Parva Stretton). Campb. xv. 6.

Stretton, Magna. *v.* Sturton, Gt., *co. Linc.*

Stretton on Dunsmore, *co. Warw.* Lease of a mill in, from Hagmond Abbey, [1180–1204] (Strettona). Harl. 111 C. 29.

—— Foundation of a chantry at, 1345 (Stretton super Donnesmor). Harl. Roll CC. 29.

—— Defeasance of bond for a marriage settlement in, 1409 (Stretton super Dunesmore). Add. 24216.

Stretton on the Fosse, *co. Warw.* Conf. of a grant in, *c.* 1170 (Strattona). Harl. 50 A. 45.

—— (?) Grant in, early 13 cent. (Streton). Campb. i. 9.

Stretton Sugwas, *co. Heref.* Grant at Wear (La Were juxta Sugwas) in, 1450. Harl. 78 F. 5.

—— (?) Lease of Bishop's Court in, 1565. Add. 1830.

Strumpshaw, co. *Norf.* Court-rolls,
1307-1350. Add. 25979 a ; — 1384-
1493. Add. 26865.

—— Inspex., in 1454. of feoffment of
the advowson, 1422 (Strumpeshagh).
Add. 17243.

—— Settlement of the manor, etc.,
1646. Add. 19160.

Stubbing Edge, Nether Stubbing,
Stubbyng. *v. sub* Ashover, co. *Derb.*

Stubbs, *nr. Hampole,* co. *York.* Mortgage in, 1395. Add. 17061, 17062.

Stucle. *v.* Stukeley, Great, co. *Hunt.*

Studebur. *v.* Stutsbury, co. *Northt.*

Studhagh. *v. sub* Laxfield, co. *Suff.*

Studham, co. *Bedf.* Grant in, 1392
(Stodham). Add. 19956.

—— Release of tithes from timber in,
by Dunstable Priory, 1406 (do.). Add.
19953.

—— Feoffment of the manor, 1435.
Add. 23178.

—— Sale of timber in, 1481. Add.
24137.

Studland, co. *Dors. Parsm.* Will.
Lillyngton, c. 1500 (?). Roy. Roll 14
B. xxi.

Studley, co. *Warw.* Grant of la Wyn-
yarde in, to Studley Priory, c. 1250-
60 (Stodleg). Cott. xi. 28.

—— Grants in Hardwick (Herdewik, Herdewyk) in, *t.* Edw. I. Cott.
xxvi. 20 (Stodleg) ; —1323. Cott. xv.
26 (Stodlegh).

—— Release in, to Studley Priory,
1338 (Stodlegh). Harl. 58 E. 1.

—— Grant in, 1376 (Stodleie). Cott.
xi. 70.

—— Inquest conc. descent of, 1412.
Cott. xxiii. 12.

Studley, North, co. *York.* Grant in,
1442 (N. Stodley). Add. 16930.

Studmore. *v. sub* Brenchley, co. *Kent.*

Stukehalle. *v. sub* Sparham, co. *Norf.*

Stukeley. *v.* Stewkley, co. *Buck.*

Stukeley, Great, co. *Hunt.* Papal
conf. of the church, etc., to Huntingdon Priory, 1147 (Stiueclai = Great
S.?). Cott. MS. Aug. ii. 112.

—— Grant of the manor by Earl
David, c. 1200 (Magna Steuecle).
Add. 22612.

—— Fine of the manor, 1316 (Magna
Stiuecle). Add. 22613.

Stukeley, Great, co. *Hunt.* (continued).
Compotus of the manor, 1342-3 (Magna
Styuecle). Add. 26685.

—— Release of the manor (?), 1433
(Stucle). Add. 20055.

Stukeley, Little, co. *Hunt.* Crown
rents of the manor, late bel. to Ramsey
Abbey, 1589 (Stewkley Parva). Add.
8490.

Stuntesfeld. *v.* Stonesfield, co. *Oxon.*

Stuntney, co. *Camb.* Conff. of, with an
eel fishery, to Ely Abbey, by Bps. of
Ely, [1103-31, 1133-69] (Stunteneia).
Harl. 43 H. 4, 5 (copies).

Stuple. *v.* Steeple, co. *Dors.*

Stur. *v.* Stour, *River,* co. *Worc.*

Sture. *v.* Stour, *River,* co. *Kent.*

—— *v.* Stour (?), co. *Worc.*

Sturia. *v.* Sturry, co. *Kent.*

Sturmere, co. *Essex.* Grant of the
manor, 1336. Harl. 50 H. 36.

—— Precipe on a covenant in, 1561.
Add. 24934.

Sturmi. *v.* Stormy, co. *Glam.*

Sturminster Marshall, co. *Dors.*
Grant of the manor, [1204 ?] (Estrumenistre). Harl. 45 I. 29.

—— Grants in Henbury (Hymburi,
Himburi) in, late 13 cent. (Stur-
minstre Marishal). Add. 23841, 23842.

—— Grant of a purparty of, 1327
(Esturminstre Mareschal). Harl. 53
E. 4.

—— Conveyance of Henbury (Hymbury) manor, etc., in, 1352. Add.
23843 ; —1353. Add. 23844.

—— Recovery of a moiety of Coombe
[Almer ?] (Combe) manor, etc., in,
1508. Add. 13556.

—— Settlement in Coombe Bassett,
etc., in, 1587. Add. 13576.

Sturry, co. *Kent.* Grant in, 679
(Sturia). Cott. MS. Aug. ii. 2.

—— Grants "in tenura de," "in
borgha de Hothe," 1317. Harl. 80 B.
38 (Stureye) : —1335. Harl. 76 D. 34
(do.) : —1347. Harl. 76 E. 7 (do.).

—— (?) Grant in, "in Bergha de
Sturaete," 1356. Harl. 78 A. 32.

—— Grants, etc., in, 1362. Harl. 78
B. 32 ; —1389. Harl. 79 E. 37 ; —1485.
Harl. 78 C. 17 : —1505. Harl. 79 B.
5 ; —1548. Harl. 75 H. 4, 76 H. 50 ; —
1554. Harl. 76 I. 18 ; —1559. Harl.
78 F. 6 ; —1567. Harl. 76 A. 34, 35,

Sulhampstead Abbotts, co. *Berks.* Release, etc., in, 1396. Add. 9243 (Syllamstede Abbots);—1536. Add. 19186.

—— Brief conc. a hail storm at, 1762. Ch. Br. B. ii. 2.

Sulhampstead Banister, co. *Berks.* Grants, etc., in, *t.* John(?). Add. 20267 (Silhamsted):—early Hen. III. Add. 20250 (do.);—1396. Add. 9243 (Syllams'ede Banastre):— (?) 1542. Add. 12668;—1711. Add. 19239.

—— *Rector. Dom.* Joh. Mundy, 1405. Harl. 45 G. 44.

Sullington (Sullyngton), co. *Suss.* Grant, etc., in, 1364. Add. 24679;—1427. Add. 8874, 18715.

—— Valor of lands, etc., in, late 14 cent. Add. 8994.

Sully, co. *Glam.* Lease in, 1526. Harl. 75 E. 19.

—— *Dominus.* Joh. de Auene, 1328. Harl. 75 C. 25.

Sulmonnes burg. *v.* Salmonsbury, co. *Glouc.*

Sultherun. *v.* Souldern, co. *Oxon.*

Sulveston. *v.* Silveston, co. *Northt.*

Sumerdebi. *v.* Somerby, co. *Leic.*

Sumeresfeld. *v. sub* Banstead, co. *Surr.*

Sumeresham. *v.* Someraham, co. *Hunt.*

Sumerhebi. *v.* Somersby, co. *Linc.*

Sumerhetti, [*nr. Wyberton*], co. *Linc.* Grant in, to be held of Wyberton church, early 13 cent. Harl. 50 C. 51.

Sumertone. *v.* Somerton, co. *Oxon.*

Sunbury, co. *Midd.* Conf. by Edw. the Confessor of a grant in, to Westminster Abbey, 1066 [*sc.* 1065] (Sunnebyri). Cott. vi. 2 (*copy*).

Sunderlandwick, *in Hutton Cranswick,* co. *York.* Release in, to Watton Priory, 1322 (Sunderlandwik). Harl. 55 E. 23.

—— Release in, 1387 (Sundrelandwik). Add. 15532.

Sundridge, co. *Kent.* Grants of a den at, 862 (Sænget bryg). Cott. viii. 32;—987 (Sænget hryc). Cott. viii. 14.

—— Evidence conc. tenure of, [1072] (Sunderhirse). Cott. MS. Aug. ii. 36.

Suneford. *v.* Swinford, co. *Leic.*

Sunetorp, Sunnetorp. *v.* Swinethorpe, *in Snelland,* co. *Linc.*

Sunnewis, *in* Aby, co. *Linc.* Covenant conc. pasture "ver'ans crucem de bosco de," 1219. Harl. 52 C. 46.

Sunntynge, Suntyng. *v.* Sompting, co. *Suss.*

Sunthorpe, *nr. Kilnsea,* co. *York.* Grants in, 1356–1359. Lansd. 542, 543.

Surbiton, co. *Surr.* Grants, etc., in, 1294. Add. 17272 (Surbeton);— 1296. Add. 17273;—1323. Add. 9025;—1348. Add. 23528.

Surditona. *v.* Shurdington, co. *Glouc.*

Sureya. *v.* Southry, co. *Linc.*

Surfleet, co. *Linc.* Grant in, late 13 cent. (Surflet). Harl. 52 G. 7.

—— Particulars of the Qu. Dowager's rents in, 1688. Add. 13592.

Surlingham, co. *Norf.* Grant in, to Bungay Priory, *t.* Hen. III. (Surrlingham). Harl. 83 F. 22.

—— *Clericus.* Vincentius, *t.* Rich. I.- John. Harl. 84 B. 7.

Surrenden, *in Hullavington,* co. *Wilts.* Settlements of the manor, c. 1390–35. Add. 7740 (Cyrendene);—1567. Add. 7071 (Sorenden).

Surrey, *County of.* Precipe to the sheriff conc. lands in Banstead, [1199?]. Cott. MS. Nero C. iii. f. 197.

—— Compotus of the bailiff of the Earl of Stafford for an aid, etc., in, 1376–7. Add. 22705.

—— Grants, etc., in, 1377. Add. 22707;—1400. Harl. 86 I. 14;—1439. Harl. 86 I. 12, 13.

—— Precipes on covenants conc. lands in, 1432–1601. Add. 25499–25522.

—— Commission of array in, 1496. Add. 5640.

—— Pensions to members of dissolved monasteries in, 1540–41. Harl. Roll I. 11.

—— Exchequer acquittances to sheriffs, 1576. Add. 25661;—1615. Add. 25666.

—— Patent of the Earl of Nottingham as Lord Lieutenant, 1608. Add. 5642.

—— Commissions to dep. lieutenants, 1613. Add. 5643;—1620–1642. Add. 22695–22701.

—— List of clergy in, appointed to provide arms, 1623. Add. 22634.

716

Suthburhe. v. Sudborough, co. Northt.

Suthcherche. v. Southchurch, co. Essex.

Suthcote. v. Southcott, co. Buck.

Sutheraye, Suthereya. v. Southry, co. Linc.

Suthessohe. v. Ash, nr. Wrotham, co. Kent.

Suthewell. v. Southwell, co. Nott.

Suthfeld. v. Suffield, co. Norf.

Suthferibi, etc. v. Ferriby, South, co. Linc.

Suthflete. v. Southfleet, co. Kent.

Suthgarstun. v. sub Bitton (Oldland in), co. Glouc.

Suthhewishe. v. Huish, South, co. Devon.

Suthkenelingworth, etc. v. Kilworth, South, co. Leic.

Suthkyluingholm. v. Killingholme, co. Linc.

Suthmaresfelde, etc. v. sub Banstead, co. Surr.

——. v. sub Snitterfield, co. Warw.

Suthongre.

Suthorp. v. Southorpe, co. Linc.

Suthreya. v. Southry, co. Linc.

Suthstede. v. Busted, co. Norf.

Suthstoc, co. Worc.(?). Conf. of grants in, to Pershore Abbey, 972. Cott. MS. Aug. ii. 6.

Suð tun. v. Sutton Valence, co. Kent.

Suthwode. v. sub Doddington, co. Camb.

Suthwyme. v. Witham, South, co. Linc.

Sutterton, co. Linc. Power to give seisin in, 1380 (Sotyrton). Add. 8400.

——. Precipe on a covenant conc. land in, 1578. Add. 25095.

Suttinghurst. v. sub Chiddingfold, co. Surr.

Sutton. v. sub Shere, co. Surr.

Sutton, co. Bedf. Exchange of a moiety of the advowson, 1311 (Sutton juxta Bicleswade). Add. 19954.

——. Grant in, 1311. Harl. 84 A. 50.

——. Capellanus. Robertus, early 13 cent. (Suttun). Harl. 54 I. 45.

Sutton, in Isle of Ely, co. Camb. Conff. of, by Bps. of Ely, to Ely Abbey, [1109-31, 1133-69] (Suttuna). Harl. 43 H. 4, 5 (copies).

Sutton, co. Essex. Conveyance in, 1295 (Magna Suttone). Harl. 54 G. 37.

——. Conveyances of Fleet Hall (Flethall, Fletehall) manor in, 1425. Harl. 55 D. 16;—1477. Harl. 51 F. 4.

Sutton, co. Glouc. Brief conc. a hall storm at, 1768. Ch. Br. B. viii. 3.

Sutton, in Amberley, co. Heref. Lease in, 1679. Add. 1968.

Sutton, co. Kent. Grants in Goodhurst "de tenura de," al. "de feodo de," t. Hen. III.-4. Edw. I. Harl. 76 B. 17, 18, 19, 78 G. 46;—c. 1283. Harl. 77 D. 44;—1307-8. Harl. 80 D. 45;—1320. Harl. 80 G. 54.

Sutton, co. Lanc. Briefs conc. fires at Sutton mill, 1807, 1817. Ch. Br. B. xlviii. 4, lviii. 5.

Sutton, co. Norf. Extract from courtroll of Outaoken manor, 1677. Add. 14600.

Sutton, co. Nott. Clericus. Turstanus, [1171-79] (Suttuna). Harl. 112 B. 1.

——. Adam, c. 1200. Harl. 83 G. 36.

——. Vicarius. Dom. Johannes, early Edw. I. Cott. xxviii. 102.

Sutton, co. Suff. Lease in, 1537. Add. 909.

——. Precipe on a covenant conc. Osmonds and Petistres manors, etc., in, 1589. Add. 25412.

Sutton, in Woking, co. Surr. License to Newark Priory, from Merton Priory, for a chapel in, [1249-52] (Suttun). Cott. xxi. 25.

Sutton, in Wallington Hundred, co. Surr. Grants, etc., in, 1388. Add. 23174;—1429. 23398;—1424. Add. 23178;—1478. Add. 23540;—1485. Add. 23405, 23406;—1504. Add. 23665;—1615. Add. 23718, 23719.

——. Rental of the manor, bel. to Chertsey Abbey, with boundaries, 1496. Add. 24636.

——. Lease, etc., of the manor and advowson, 1588. Add. 23663, 23664.

——. Brief for rebuilding the church, 1788. Ch. Br. B. xxviii. 4.

Sutton, nr. Petworth, co. Suss. Fine in, 1418. Add. 24897.

Sutton, nr. Seaford, co. Suss. Conf. o a grant of the manor to Robertsbridg Abbey, [1202-8] (Sutton iuxta fordia). Campb. iv. 3.

**Sydenham,** *co. Oxon.* Covenant in, with Thame Abbey, [1232–43 ?] (Sydeham). Harl. 55 B. 6.

—— Covenant for marriage settlement in, 1241 (do.). Cott. viii. 7.

**Syderstone,** *co. Norf.* Admission of G. Hall to the rectory, 1605 (Sisterne). Add. 14909.

**Sydolesmere.** *v. sub* Whelnetham, Great and Lit., *co. Suff.*

**Syerston,** *co. Nott.* Exemplif. of writs for a recovery in, 1586–7. Add. 26014.

**Sygresham.** *v.* Syresham, *co. Northt.*

**Sylderburthge,** *in or nr. Sidbury. co. Devon.* Release of, 1262. Add. 12926.

**Syleham,** *co. Suff.* Tithe suit in, betw. Thetford and Belvoir Prioiies, [1156 ?] (Seleham). Harl. 43 A. 18.

—— Grants, etc., in, 1337. Harl. 84 A. 22 (Silham);—1408. Harl. 54 I. 7 (Sylham);—1430. Harl. 48 E. 19, 45 I. 12, 54 I. 10 ;—1431. Harl. 50 H. 27, 28, 54 I. 15 :—1435. Add. 2016 ;— 1512. Add. 19359.

—— Acquittances for rent in, 1380– 1395 (Silham). Add. 5500–5508.

—— Extents of Monkhall (S. Monachorum) manor bel. to Thetford Priory, 1379–80. Add. 16561 ;—1433. Add. 16562.

—— Grant in Esham in, 1425. Add. 19330.

—— Precipe on a covenant conc. Monks Syleham manor, etc., 1564. Add. 25327.

**Sylferton.** *v.* Silverton, *co. Devon.*

**Syllamstede Abbots.** *v.* Sulhampstead Abbotts, *co. Berks.*

**Syllamstede Banastre.** *v.* Sulhampstead Banister, *co. Berks.*

**Sylversley.** *v.* Silverley, *co. Camb.*

**Symondsbury,** *co. Dors.* Grants, etc., in Moorbath in, *t.* Edw. I.–II. Harl. 53 D. 30 (Simondesburgh), 57 G. 35 (Symondes buregh);—1311. Harl. 53 E. 20 :—1343. Add. 15440 (Symondesbergh);—1396. Add. 15444 ;—1409. Harl. 55 G. 43, 44 ;—1410. Harl. 51 F. 40, 41.

—— Fine in, 1340 (Simondesbergh). Harl. 47 H. 7.

—— Petition of Cerne Abbey conc. exactions from the manor, [1377–81 ?] (Symondesbergh). Campb. xiii. 4.

**Symston.** *v.* Selmeston, *co. Suss.*

**Syndelsham.** *v.* Sindlesham, *nr. Arborfield* (?), *co. Berks.*

**Synsesy** *al.* **St. Jidgey,** *in St. Issey, co. Cornw.* Grants, etc., in, 1486. Harl. 52 I. 35 ;—1513. Harl. 50 C. 41–43 (Zensesy, Zonzenzy).

—— Grants, etc., in Synzysy Woles *al.* Zenzysy Woles, 1542. Harl. 50 H. 6–9.

**Sypfeld.** *v. sub* Fletching, *co. Suss.*

**Syppenham.** *v.* Cippenham, *co. Buck.*

**Syresfelde.** *v. sub* Watlington, *co. Oxon.*

**Syresham** (Siresham, etc.), *co. Northt.* Grants, etc., of Murieland, Westcote, etc., in, to Biddlesdon Abbey, *c.* 1147. Harl. 84 H. 46 (Sigresham) ;—c. 1150. Harl. 86 B. 49 (Siresham) ;—[1150–1]. Harl. 84 C. 2 (Sigeresham), 85 G. 48 (Sigrisham) ;—1151. Harl. 84 C. 47, 48 ;—[1151 ?]. Harl. 84 C. 41 ;— [1153 ?]. Harl. 84 C. 3 (Sigeresham); —[1155 ?]. Harl. 84 C. 4 (Sigresham), 5 (*copy*) ;—*ante* 1166. Harl. 84 D. 1 ;— *t.* Hen. II. Harl. 86 E. 25 ;—late 12 cent. Harl. 84 H. 52, 86 B. 50, 51, 86 E. 26 (Siresham) ; — early 13 cent. or early Hen. III. Harl. 85 A. 13–19, 86 B. 53, 54, 56, 86 E. 50 ;—*t.* Hen. III. Harl. 84 G. 14, 15, 54, 56 ;— 1251. Harl. 84 D. 6 ;—1265–6. Harl. 84 C. 40 (Sygresham) ;—1273–4. Harl. 84 G. 57 ;—1278. Harl. 84 G. 23 ;— [1272–96]. Harl. 84 C. 10 ;—late Hen. III. or *t.* Edw. I. Harl. 84 G. 16–18, 35, 36, 38, 39, 41, 42, 45, 46, 84 I. 58, 85 B. 13, 85 G. 40, 86 A. 28–30, 86 D. 10–12 ;—1292. Harl. 84 C. 15 ;—1293. Harl. 84 G. 33 ;—1294. Harl 84 G. 34, 37, 40 ;—1314. Harl. 86 F. 37 ;— 1331. Harl. 85 B. 21 :—1354. Harl. 86 B. 8 ;—1355. Harl. 86 B. 9, 10 ;— *c.* 1370. Harl. 84 C. 16 ;—1469. Harl. 85 G. 59 ;—1475. Harl. 85 G. 60.

—— Covenants conc. tithes in, betw. Biddlesdon and St. Mary de Pré Abbeys, *c.* 1150–58. Harl. 84 D. 12 (Sigreham) ;—1209. Harl. 84 D. 19 (Siresham) ;—1382. Harl. 84 F. 7 (Sigresham).

—— Conf. of a grant of the church to St. Mary de Pré Abbey, Leicester, [1190– 1204] (Sigresham). Slo. xxxii. 22.

—— Fine in, to Biddlesdon Abbey, 1220. Harl. 86 B. 52.

—— Grants, etc., in, from Biddlesdon Abbey early 13 cent. Harl. 84 D. 24 (Sirsam) :—c. 1230–35. Harl. 84 D. 25, 26 ;—c. 1255–9. Harl. 84 E. 17 ;

3 A 2

**Swindon,** *co. Wilts.* Grant in Huyeswyndon and Westewyndon, 1394. Harl. 83 F. 18.

—— Pipe-roll acquittance on account of lands in, 1536–7 (Swynton). Add. 18280.

**Swindon,** *in Penistone, co. York.* Release in, 1301 (Swyndene). Harl. 112 I. 62.

**Swine,** *co. York.* Compotus-rolls of the manor, 1447–48, 1453–54 (Swyne). Harl. Rolls M. 41, 42.

—— Exemplif. of a fine in, 1687. Add. 890.

**Swinefleet,** *co. York.* Grants, etc., in Inklemoors (Inchelemore, Inkelesmore) in, to Newhouse Abbey, co. Linc., *t.* Hen. II. (Swinefleth). Harl. 52 A. 10; —1303. Harl. 43 D. 9.

—— Release nr. (?), to Newhouse Abbey, *t.* Edw. I. Harl. 47 C. 50.

—— Covenant between Selby and Newhouse Abbeys conc. tithes in, 1282 (Swyneflet). Harl. 44 I. 16.

**Swineshead,** *co. Hunt.* Descent of the manor, 1542 (Swanneshed). Harl. 75 E. 21.

—— *Persona.* Joh. Carpenter, 1367. Harl. 49 F. 52;—1398. Harl. 47 H. 2.

**Swineshead,** *co. Linc. Persona.* Nic. Motte, 1411. Add. 18090.

**Swinethorpe** (Sunetorp, Sunnetorp), *in Snelland, co. Linc.* Grants, etc., in, to Kirkstead Abbey, *c.* 1150–60. Harl. 43 H. 20;—1160. Harl. 47 I. 8;— late 12 cent. Harl. 47 I. 10, 51 G. 16, 58 A. 24, Cott. xii. 53, xxi. 22.

—— Conf. of covenant conc. tithes in, to the same, late 12 cent. Harl. 56 C. 45.

—— Power to give seisin in, 1404 (Sounttborp). Harl. 46 D. 31.

**Swinfen.** *v. sub* Weeford, *co. Staff.*

**Swinford,** *co. Leic.* Grants, etc., in, *t.* John. Harl. 47 G. 16 (Suneford); —1357. Add. 21772 (Swyneford); —1445. Cott. xxx. 33 (Swynford).

—— *Clericus.* Alanus, *c.* 1240 (Swyneford). Add. 21342.

—— *Persona.* Willelmus, early 13 cent. (Suineford). Add. 21475.

**Swinford, King's,** *co. Staff.* Exemplif. of Crown grant of forfeited lands in, 1610. Harl. 83 H. 28.

**Swingfield,** *co. Kent.* Power to give seisin of Northcourt (Halcourte) manor in, 1488. Harl. 76 F. 20.

—— Fine in, 1548 (Swynfyelde). Harl. 75 H. 4, 76 H. 50.

**Swinhope,** *co. Linc.* Licenses to alienate the manor, 1569. Add. 13602 (Swinope);—1577. Add. 13603 (Swynope).

**Swinnerton,** *co. Staff.* Conf. of the church to Stone Priory, with sentence in suit for same, *c.* 1155–60 (Suuinwrton, Swinurtona). Cott. xiii. 6 (21, 22) (*copies*).

—— *Clerici.* Osbertus et alter Osbertus, *c.* 1155–60. Cott. xiii. 6 (21, 22).

**Swinton,** *co. York.* Exchequer acquittance for a fine in, 1567. Add. 25702.

**Swithland,** *co. Leic.* Grants in, 1575. Add. 7253 (Swythlande);—1584. Add. 7254.

**Swonhungre.** *v.* Sanager, *co. Glouc.*

**Swonton.** *v.* Santon (?), *co. Bedf.* (?).

**Swordlinge.** *v. sub* Chartham, *co. Kent.*

**Swyftelyng,** etc. *v.* Swefling, *co. Suff.*

**Swyndene.** *v.* Swindon, *co. York.*

**Swynham,** *nr. Battle* (?), *co. Suss.* Release in, late 13 cent. Add. 20160.

**Swynisheghen.** *v. sub* Payhembury, *co. Devon.*

**Swynlonde.** *v.* Swilland, *co. Suff.*

**Swynope.** *v.* Swinhope, *co. Linc.*

**Swynton.** *v.* Swindon, *co. Wilts.*

**Swyre,** *co. Dors.* Conveyance, etc., of the manor, *c.* 1395. Harl. Roll M. 40.

—— Delivery of title deeds of the manor, etc., 1522. Harl. 53 G. 50;— 1523. Harl. 53 C. 27.

**Swyrygge.** *v.* Surridge, *in Bathealton* (?), *co. Som.*

**Sybertoft.** *v.* Sibbertoft, *co. Northt.*

**Sybeton,** etc. *v.* Sibton, *co. Suff.*

**Sybson, Sybston.** *v. sub* Stibbington, *co. Hunt.*

**Syclington, Boscus de.** *v. sub* Flockton, *co. York.*

**Sydcot.** *v. sub* Winscombe, *co. Som.*

**Syde, Aqua de.** *v.* Sid, *River, co. Devon.*

**Sydebiri,** etc. *v.* Sidbury, *co. Devon.*

**Thames**, *River*. Covenant to repair "wallam contra Thamisiam" in Erith, co. Kent, [1223-48]. Campb. xiv. 23;—early Hen. III. Add. 5950.

—— Petition conc. piracy by the Dutch in, *t.* Hen. VI. Cott. xxvii. 130.

**Thanet, Isle of**, *co. Kent*. Grants in, 679 (Tenid). Cott. MS. Aug. ii. 2;— 949 (Tænett). Cott. MS. Aug. ii. 57.

—— Covenant betw. the Abbat of St. Augustine's, Canterbury, and the men of, 1176. Campb. vi. 5,

—— Conf. to Christ Church, Canterbury, of drainage rights in marshes in, 1418. Add. 16489.

—— *Vicecomes*. Arnoldus, 1176. Campb. vi. 5.

**Thanington**, *co. Kent*. Grant by S., Abp. of Canterbury, of Tonford thicket (brochum de Tuniford) in, etc., to St. Gregory's Priory, Canterbury, with conf., c. 1215. Harl. 75 F. 22 (Tanintune), 45.

—— Grant in, to the same, [1258] (Taniton). Harl. 76 A. 36.

—— Grants, etc., in, *t.* Edw. II. Harl. 76 A. 15 (Tanynton);—1355. Harl. 76 D. 4 (Tenynton);—1361. Harl. 76 A. 55 (Tenyngton), 79 D. 86 (Tenenton);—1363. Harl. 77 E. 14 (Tanynton);—1375. Harl. 78 A. 47 (Tanenynton);— 1379. Harl 76 A. 16 (Tauyngton), 76 C. 21 ('Tanynton); —1397. Harl. 78 H. 5 (Tanyngton);— 1420. Harl. 76 C. 17;—1485. Harl. 78 C. 17;—1548. Harl. 75 E. 22;— 1551. Harl. 75 E. 28.

—— Lease in, by St. Gregory's Priory, 1458. Harl. 75 F. 59.

—— Fine, etc., of Tonford *al.* Tunford manor in, 1548. Harl. 75 H. 4, 76 H. 50;—1554. Harl. 79 F. 9, 79 G. 2;—1579. Harl. 77 H. 42;—1582. Harl. 75 F. 1;—1589. Harl. 77 H. 46.

**Tharlesthorpe**. *v.* Harlesthorpe, *nr. Elmton, co. Derb.*

**Thaseburg**. *v.* Tasburgh, *co. Norf.*

**Thatcham**, *co. Berks*. Conf. of liberties in, by Rog., Bp. of Salisbury, to Reading Abbey, c. 1125 (Thacheham). Add. 19575.

—— Conf. of, with the church, by Hen. II., to the same, [1157?] (Tacheham). Add. 19591.

—— Claim by Reading Abbey that the tithes of E. Ginge, co. Berks, belong to the rectory of, c. 1225 (Tacacheham). Add. 19623.

**Thatcham**, *co. Berks (continued)*. Ordinance conc. dues from the rector of, to Reading Abbey, 1239 (Thacham). Add. 19620.

—— Conf. of an appropriation of the church by Reading Abbey, 1317 (Taccham). Add. 19639.

—— View of frankpledge in, 1357. Add. 19642.

—— Grants, etc., in, 1409. Add. 5159 (Thacham);—1410. Add. 5160;— 1415. Add. 5161;—1416. Add. 5162.

—— *Rector*. Rob. de Taccheham, c. 1225. Add. 19623.

—— *Mag.* Gilb. de Byham, 1239. Add. 19620.

—— Anth. de Bradeneye, 1315. Add. 19638.

**Thateshale**. *v.* Tattershall, *co. Linc.*

**Thatingestun**. *v.* Tattingstone, *co. Suff.*

**Thawell**. *v.* Tathwell, *co. Linc.*

**Thawite**. *v.* Thwaite St. Mary, *co. Norf.*

**Thawthwyk**. *v.* Swathwick (?), *co. Derb.*

**Thawton, Sut.** *v.* Tawton, South, *co. Devon.*

**Thaxted**, *co. Essex*. Release in, late 13 cent. (Taxstede). Add. 15585.

—— Lease of the manor, c. 1433 (?) (Thaxstede). Harl. 53 H. 17.

—— Royal license to found a guild at, 1480 (Thaxstede). Add. 8453.

—— Precipes on covenants conc. lands in, 1578. Add. 24969; — 1587. Add. 24977, 24994;—1593. Add. 25028.

—— Extract from court-roll of Richmonds manor in, 1630. Add. 8145.

**Thaydon**. *v.* Theydon, *co. Essex.*

**Theale**, *co. Berks*. Sale of three nativi, sons of the miller of Sheffield (Seofeld) in, c. 1202. Add. 20592.

—— Grants in Sheffield (Suefeld, Scoefeld, Seoofeld) in, [1202?]. Add. 7203, 7204, 20593;—c. 1202. Add. 20595.

—— Grants, etc., in or nr., *t.* John. Add. 7206, 7363;—c. 1230. Add. 20269 (Thele);—1424. Add. 20270; —1608. Add. 19203-19206;—1721. Add. 19247.

—— Release of Sheffield Mill, etc., in, *t.* Hen. III. Add. 20594.

—— Assignment of rents in Sheffield (Scheufeud) in, "ad pietanciam," by Reading Abbey, 1284. Add. 19633.

**Thenford**, *co. Northt.* Power to receive seisin of the manor, 1449. Add. 7569.

**Denglesham.** *v.* Finglesham, *co. Kent.*

**Theodninge**, *a stream W. of the Windrush, co. Glouc.* Grant on either side of, 779. Cott. MS. Aug. ii. 4.

**Therfield**, *co. Hertf.* Fine in, 1314 (Therfeld). Add. 6248.

**Therneby.** *v.* Thornby, *co. Northt.*

**Thetford.** *v.* Tetford, *co. Linc.*

**Thetford**, *Isle of Ely, co. Camb.* Grant of the manor, 1337 (Theford). Lansd. 108.

**Thetford**, *co. Norf.* Grant of a fair in, to the Hospital of St. John Baptist, 1232 (Teford). Harl. 58 H. 44 (*copy*).

—— "Le Office le Meyr et de la Meyraute," 1313. Add. 17207.

—— Conf. of grants in, to the Priory of the H. Sepulchre, 1315 (Theford). Harl. 57 E. 32.

—— Grant in St. Nicholas' parish, from the Priory, 1467. Add. 26785.

—— Patent for a sword-bearer to precede, and not follow, the mayor, 1532. Add. 16575.

—— Release in, to the Corporation, 1551. Add. 15555.

—— Foundation of an annual sermon at, 1567. Add. 26723.

—— Certificate of freedom of, to Will. Gawdy, 1662. Add. 24245.

—— *Persona eccl. S. Etheldrede.* Ad. Foxle, 1389. Add. 15749;—1391. Add. 15751.

—— *Rector eccl. S. Petri.* Will. Balles, 1467. Add. 26785.

**Thetilthorp, Thetylthorp.** *v.* Theddlethorpe, *co. Linc.*

**Thettewrth.** *v.* Tetworth, *co. Hunt.*

**Theydon Bois**, *co. Essex.* Covenant conc. a sale in, 1508 (Theydon Boys). Harl. 55 H. 28.

**Theydon Garnon**, *co. Essex.* Power to take seisin of Park Hall and Hemnales manors in, 1447. Harl. 45 G. 62 (Thedon Garnon).

—— Grant in, 1452. Add. 9255.

—— Covenant conc. sale of Gaynes Park Hall and Hemnales manors in, 1508. Harl. 55 H. 28.

—— Precipe on a covenant conc. land in, 1592 (Theydon Garnon). Add. 25000.

**Theydon Mount**, *co. Essex.* Covenant conc. a sale in, 1508. Harl. 55 H. 28.

—— Precipe on a covenant conc. land in, 1592 (Thaydon Mount). Add. 25014.

**Thickthorns**, *near Chicheley, co. Buck.* Conf. of view of frankpledge, etc., in, to Tickford Priory, 1310. Add. 11224.

**Thieso.** *v.* Tysoe, *co. Warw.*

**Thimbleby**, *co. Linc.* Grants, etc., in, to Kirkstead Abbey, 1154. Harl. 57 F. 14 (Timlebi);—*t.* John. Harl. 56 I. 23 (Timelbi);—1331. Harl. 43 G. 52 (Thymelby);—1340. Harl. 50 D. 36 (Thimelby);—1365. Harl. 58 C. 2.

—— List of deeds conc. lands of Kirkstead Abbey in, early 13 cent. (Thimelby). Harl. Roll O. 5.

—— Grants, etc., in, 1332. Harl. 58 B. 49 (Thymelby), 50;—1335. Harl. 48 E. 7;—1338. Harl. 56 F. 42 (Thymelby);—1370. Harl. 56 B. 49.

—— *Capellanus.* Acardus, early 13 cent. (Thymeleby). Cott. xxvii. 62.

—— —— Hugo, *t.* Hen. III. Harl. 52 I. 25.

—— *Persona.* Alan. Heued, 1370 (Thymelby). Harl. 44 F. 8.

**Thimilthorp.** *v.* Themelthorpe, *co. Norf.*

**Thinden, Thingden,** etc. *v.* Finedon *al.* Thingdon, *co. Northt.*

**Thingstede**, *nr. Authorpe, co. Linc.* Grant in, to Burwell Priory, late 12 cent. Harl. 51 D. 20.

**Thirkleby**, *co. York.* Exemplif. of fine in, 1687. Add. 890.

**Thirlby**, *co. York.* Assignment in, 1404. Add. 22391.

**Thirling**, *nr. Upwell, cos. Camb. and Norf.* Sale of lands in, late bel. to Ixworth Priory, 1589. Add. 18867.

**Thirlowe.** *v.* Thurlow, Great, *co. Suff.*

**Thirlye.** *v.* Thurleigh, *co. Bedf.*

**Thirneby.** *v.* Thornby, *co. Northt.*

—— *v.* Thurnby, *co. Leic.*

**Thirneschogh, Thirnsco.** *v.* Thurnscoe, *co. York.*

**Thirnyng.** *v.* Thurning, *co. Hunt.*

**Thirsk**, *co. York.* Covenant conc. services in St. Nicholas' Chapel at, *t.* John (Tresc). Cott. v. 13.

—— Grant in, with Norby (Northibi) mill, *t.* John (Treske). Harl. 83 G. 53.

Thornton, *in Manerio de Ken. v. sub* Kenn, *co. Devon.*

Thornton, *co. Buck.* Grant of the advowson of the chantry, 1530. Harl. 86 F. 12.

Thornton, *in Marnhull, co. Dors.* Fine in, for a chantry, 1282. Add. 5250.

Thornton, *co. Leic.* Grants, etc., in, *t.* Hen. III. Harl. 46 F. 27 :—1278. Harl. 57 E. 11, 13 ;—1280. Harl. 46 F. 28 ;—*c.* 1280. Harl. 46 F. 27, 57 E. 12.

Thornton, *on. Linc.* Power to take seisin in, 1335 (Thorneton). Harl. 54 G. 21.

Thornton, *nr. Hardcastle, co. Linc.* Release, etc., in, 1351. Cott. xxx. 30 ; —1370. Harl. 56 B. 49 ;—1435. Harl. 49 I. 31.

—— Grants in, to Kirkstead Abbey, 1365. Harl. 58 C. 2 ;—1370. Harl. 44 F. 8.

—— *Capellanus.* Robertus, early 13 cent. Harl. 55 F. 10.

Thornton *al.* Temple Thornton, *co. Northumb.* Sale of the chapel, etc., 1574-5. Harl. 79 F. 22.

Thornton, *in Camrhôs, co. Pembr.* Grant in, *t.* Hen. III. (Villa Thoner). Add. 8272.

Thornton, *in Bradford, co. York.* Release, etc., in, *t.* Edw. I.-II. Add. 16655 (Thornetona), 16656, 16657 ;— 1394. Add. 16876 (Thorneton in Braddefordale);—1396. Add. 16877.

—— Brief for rebuilding the chapel, 1818. Ch. Br. B. lix. 1.

Thornton Hough, *in Wirrall, co. Chest.* Release in, 1465 (Thornton in Wirehale). Add. 8527.

Thornton Watlass, *co. York. Rector.* Will. de Plungar, 1395. Harl. 112 D. 13.

Thoroswaie. *v.* Thoresway, *co. Linc.*

Thoroton, *co. Nott.* Grant in, 1363 (Thurnerton). Harl. 58 B. 7.

Thoroudeby. *v.* Thoraldby, *in Bishopdale, co. York.*

Thorp. *v.* Kettleby Thorpe, *co. Linc.*

Thorp Arch, *co. York.* Grant in, to Nun Monketon Priory, 1278 (Thorp barthes). Add. 17962 (1).

—— Feoffment, etc., in, 1429 - 30 (Thorpparche). Add. 1782 ; — 1439. Add. 1783.

Thorp Edmer. *v.* Edmond Thorpe, *co. Leic.*

Thorpacre, *co. Leic.* Papal conf. of a grant in, to Ulvescroft Priory, 1174 (Torp). Harl. 111 A. 6 (*copy*).

—— Grants, etc., in, 1319. Add. 26990 (Thorp Haueker), 26991 ;— 1323. Add. 26992, 26993 ; — 1369. Add. 26994, 26995 ; — 1372. Add. 26996 ;—1435. Add. 26997 ;—1439. Add. 26998.

Thorpe. *v.* Ashweltborpe, *co. Norf.*

—— *v.* Barkby Thorpe, *co. Leic.*

—— *v.* Culverthorpe, *co. Linc.*

—— *v. sub* Hasketon, *co. Suf.*

—— *v.* Healey Thorpe, *co. York.*

—— *v.* Morningthorpe, *co. Norf.*

Thorpe, *in Hathersage, co. Derb.* Grant in, 1512. Add. 7193.

Thorpe, *nr. Easington, co. Durh.* Sale in, 1622. Add. 7400.

Thorpe, *co. Essex* (?). Grant of the chapel, tithes, etc., to Southwark Priory, [1138-48] (Torp). Cott. MS. Nero C. iii. f. 228.

Thorpe, *in Southchurch, co. Essex.* Grant in, late Hen. III. Add. 8392 ; —1345. Add. 15459.

Thorpe, *co. Linc.* Power to give seisin in, 1335 (Thorpe juxta Louth). Harl. 54 G. 21.

Thorpe, *in Cossey, co. Norf.* Grant of tithes in, to Rumburgh Priory, *co.* Suff., [1121-37]. Campb. ix. 9 (7) (*copy*).

Thorpe [Gayton Thorpe, *co. Norf.* ?]. Grant in, *t.* Hen. III. or Edw. I. (Torp). Harl. 56 I. 27.

Thorpe, *by Newark, co. Nott.* Grant in, to Rufford Abbey, [1147-53] (Torp). Harl. 83 G. 55.

—— Sale, etc., in, 1586. Add. 26010, 26012 ;—1586-7. Add. 26014 ;—1628. Woll. xi. 33.

Thorpe, *co. Suf.* (?). Bequest of land at, late 10 cent. (æt þorpæ). Harl. 43 C. 4.

Thorpe, *nr. Heveningham, co. Suf.* Grant, etc., in, to Sibton Abbey, early 13 cent.-*t.* Hen. III. Harl. 83 F. 19 (Thorph), 84 A. 57 (Torp).

Thorpe, *co. Surr.* Sale, etc., in, 1513 · Harl. 47 D. 33 ;—1538. Cott. xxv. 27

3 в 2

Thorpe Salvin, co. York. Grants,
etc., in Raynaldtorp in, late 13 cent.
Harl. 112 G. 48-50;—1297. Harl. 112
H. 16:—1303. Harl. 112 G. 51;—
1412. Harl. 112 I. 9.

Thorpe Satchville, co. Leic. Grant
of, c. 1160 (Torp). Lansd. 691.
—— Grant in, to Ouston Abbey, t.
Edw. I. (Torp Sechvill). Campb. xv. 3.
—— Assignment of a lease of monastic
lands in, 1567. Add. 27000.

Thorpe, Shouldham. v. Shouldham
Thorpe, co. Norf.

Thorpe, Tattershall. v. Tattershall
Thorpe, co. Linc.

Thorpe Waterville, co. Northt. Covenant conc. the castle and manor of,
1314. Harl. 43 C. 46.

Thorpeland, co. Norf. Grant in, t.
Rich. I. (Torpelandia). Harl. 57 A. 12.

Thorpthewles, in Grindon, co. Durh.
Release of the manor to Bishop Bek,
1308 (Thorptheules). Cott. xii. 48.

Thorrington, co. Essex. Defeasance
of a bond to levy a fine in, 1605 (Ter-
ington). Add. 19969.

Thotenham. v. Tottenham, co. Midd.

Thotham, Magna. v. Totham, Great,
co. Essex.

Thoutheby, Thovteby. v. Tothby,
nr. Alford, co. Linc.

Thoydon Bois, etc. v. Theydon
Bois, etc., co. Essex.

Thoyntona. v. Toynton, co. Linc.

Thrandeston, co. Suff. Grants, etc.,
in, 1296. Harl. 51 D. 18 (Randistone);
—1329. Harl. 49 G. 38;—1412. Harl.
51 E. 52;—1417. Cott. xxvii. 208,
Harl. 51 E. 55;—1668. Harl. 79 G. 32.
—— Release of a fee-farm for a market
at, 1480 (?). Add. 16567.

Thrapston, co. Northt. Grant of a
fair in the manor, 1245. Harl. 58 I. 4
(copy).
—— Covenant conc. ownership of the
River Nen betw. Denford and, t. Hen.
III. (Trapeston). Cott. xxviii. 74.
—— Grant in, 1400. Add. 857.
—— Persona. Hen. Petlyng. 1400.
Add. 857;—(nuper persona), 1414. Add.
783, 7565.
—— Rector. Dom. Symon, t. Hen. III.
(Trapston). Harl. 45 E. 35.

Thrasterstone. v. Thirston, in Felton,
co. Northumb.

Threckingham, co. Linc. Release in,
1577 (Threkingham). Add. 6430.
—— Vicarius. Rob. Baxtter, 1521.
Add. 21078.

Three Castles, Fee of the, co.
Monm. Surrender of lands, in the
court of Grosmount by men of, 1249-50
(Feodum Trium Castrorum). Add.
20414.

Thremowe, nr. Mildenhall (?), co. Suff.
Grant in, 1359. Add. 9110.

Threak. v. Thirsk, co. York.

Thribergh, co. York. Power to give
seisin of the manor, 1430 (Thrybergh).
Add. 20598.

Thrigby, co. Norf. Grants, etc., in,
1517. Add. 14876 (Thyrkeby);—
1528. Add. 14880 (Thrikby):—1556.
Add. 14885 (Thyrkby), 14886:—1563.
Add. 14890 (Thryuby):—1566. Add.
14893 (Thrygby), 14894:—1567. Add.
14892;—1573. Add. 14896.

Thrillowe, Magna et Parva. v.
Thurlow, Great and Little, co. Suff.

Thringston, co. Leic. Fine for heritage
in, c. 1200 (Trengeston). Add. 5235.

Throapham, nr. Tickhill, co. York.
Grant in, t. Edw. II. (Thropon). Harl.
47 I. 25.

Throcking, co. Hertf. Fine in, 1314
(Throkkynge). Add. 6248.

Thrompton. v. Thrumpton, co. Nott.

Throp. v. Rothersthorpe, co. Northt.

Thrope. v. sub Stroud, co. Glouc.

Thropp. v. sub Kidlington, co. Oxon.

Throwle, co. Surr. Demise of the
manor, 1409. Add. 7633, 7635.

Throwley (?), co. Kent. Bond for
arbitration in, 1478. Harl. 80 H. 22.

Thrufeld, nr. Tilney and Walpole, co.
Norf. Grant in, t. Hen. III. Harl.
51 F. 14.

Thrumpton, co. Nott. Grant, etc., in,
1495 (Thrompton). Woll. i. 22-24.
—— Precipe on a covenant conc. land
in, 1578. Add. 25204.

Thrupp. v. sub Kidlington, co. Oxon.
—— v. Rothersthorpe, co. Northt.
—— v. sub Stroud, co. Glouc.

Thrussington, co. Leic. Grant in, to
Monks Kirby Priory, t. Rich. I.–John
(Tursteinestau). Add. 21498.
—— Suit conc. the manor, 1344-6
(Thurstington). Add. 14002.

Thurlton, *co. Norf.* Grant in, early Hen. III. Add. 22570 (Thurvertun); —1384. Add. 14920 (Thurwetou).

—— Lease by Rob. de Rollesby, as "rector medietatis ecclesie de Thuruertou," 1329. Add. 14774.

—— Institution of Rob. de Rollesby, presbiter, as rector of "medietas eccl. de Thuruerton," 1335. Add. 10648.

Thurmaston, *co. Leic.* Conf. of a grant in, to Leicester Abbey, [1190–1204] (Turmodesthon). Slo. xxxii. 22.

—— Marriage settlement in, [1223] (Thurmodesthon). Harl. 55 B. 5.

—— License for a grant in, to Kirkby Bellars chapel, 1325 (Thornaston). Harl. 43 D. 25.

Thurn. *v.* Thorn, *co. Oxon.*

Thurnby, *co. Leic.* Covenant betw. Creeke Abbey and its tenants in, *c.* 1470 (?) (Thirneby). Add. 26968.

Thurne. *v.* Thearne, *co. York.*

Thurnham. *v.* Thornham, *co. Kent.*

Thurning, *co. Hunt.* Grants, etc., in, 1410. Add. 7567 (Thyrnynge); — 1426. Add. 699 (Thirnyng);—1467. Add. 7575;—1468. Add. 7578 (Thyrnyng);—1472. Add. 813 (Thirnyng), 7579;—1485. Add. 700 (Thernyng); —1519. Add. 715, 716, 826, 828;— 1520. Add. 825;—1539. Add. 837, 838;—1563. Add. 701, 702, 703.

—— Sale, etc., of the manor, 1476. Add. 814 (Thirnyng);—1477. Add. 815 (Thyrnyng), 816;—1577. Add. 704, 705.

Thurnscoe, *co. York.* Grant, etc., in, *t.* Edw. III. Harl. 45 G. 10 (Thirneschogh);—1407. Add. 19324 (Thirnsco).

—— *Rector.* Rad. Hancok, 1395. Add. 17059, 17060, 17062.

Thurnton. *v.* Thurton, *co. Norf.*

Thurrock, Grays, *co. Essex.* Grant in, 1375 (Thurrok Grey). Harl. 52 B. 27.

Thurrock, West, *co. Essex.* Grant in, 1407 (Westhurrok). Harl. 51 D. 13, 57 A. 18.

—— Compotus of the manor, 1503–4 (Westhurrok). Harl. Roll N. 12.

—— Pipe-roll acquittance for a fine conc. the mill in, 1665–6. Add. 17613.

Thursfield, *co. Staff.* Brief for rebuilding the chapel, 1766. Ch. Br. B. vi. 10.

Thursford, *co. Norf.* Court-roll, 1416–1422. Add. 19075.

—— Power to give seisin of Shelton's manor in, and of the advowson, 1454. Add. 14866.

—— Rental, 1520. Add. 19085.

—— Grant of rent from the manor, 1559. Add. 14855.

Thursley, *co. Surr.* Precipe on a covenant conc. land in, 1555. Add. 25506.

Thurstaston, *co. Chest.* Plea of recovery of the manor, 1420 (Thurstaneston). Woll. xii. 3.

Thurstington. *v.* Thrussington, *co. Leic.*

Thurston. *v.* Thuxton, *co. Norf.*

Thurston, *co. Suff.* Grants, etc., in, 1328. Harl. 53 A. 7;—1495. Add. 1382;—1558. Harl. 45 D. 55;—1583. Harl. 45 D. 59.

—— License for a grant in, to Ixworth Priory, 1371. Harl. 57 B. 11.

—— Precipe on a covenant conc. land in, 1561. Add. 25305.

—— *Persona.* Rob. de Fordham, 1401. Harl. 51 E. 6.

Thurton, *co. Norf.* Grants, etc., in, 1302. Harl. 45 F. 33, 45 G. 56 (Thurnton); — early 14 cont. Harl. 58 G. 8.

Thuruerton. *v.* Thoroton, *co. Notts.*

—— *v.* Thurlton, *co. Norf.*

Thurvaston, *co. Derb.* Grant, etc., in, 1392. Woll. x. 27; — 1530. Woll. xii. 107.

Thurvaston, Nether, *in Longford, co. Derb.* Covenant, etc., in, 1331. Woll. ix. 75;—1634. Woll. xi. 91.

Thurweton. *v.* Thurlton, *co. Norf.*

Thushul. *v. sub* Bickmarsh, *co. Warw.*

Thuxton, *co. Norf.* Release in Wodalsfeld "apud Fridaysmere" in, 1365 (Thurston). Add. 14914.

Thwaite, *co. York.* Lease of coal mines in, 1671. Add. 1803.

Thwaite All Saints, *co. Norf.* Release in, 1347 (Thweyt). Harl. 48 C. 3.

Thwaite St. George, *co. Suff.* Grants, etc., in, *t.* Hen. III. Harl. 57 D. 14 (Thueyt); — 1302. Harl. 47 A. 20 (Tweyt).

Tilbury, East, *co. Essex (continued).*
*Aquebaiulus.* Joh. Salman, *clericus,*
1390. Harl. 44 C. 35.
—— *Persona.* Joh. de Laufar, 1248.
Harl. 58 G. 49.
—— —— *Sire* Tho. Naldres, *t.*
Rich. II. Harl. 58 F. 23.
—— *Vicarius.* Rogerus, 1248. Harl.
58 G. 49 c.
—— —— *Sire* Joh. Haneper (?),
[*c.* 1366]. Harl. 58 F. 23.
—— —— *Sire* Joh. Bartelot, early
Rich. II. Harl. 58 F. 23.
—— —— *Sire* Henry, early Rich.
II. Harl. 58 F. 23.
—— —— *Sire* Joh. Golde, [*ante*
1385]. Harl. 58 F. 23.
—— —— *Sire* Rog. Willy *al. Dom.*
Rog. Wyle, [*c.* 1385]. Harl. 58 F.
23;—1390. Harl. 44 C. 35.

Tilbury juxta Clare, *co. Essex.* Exchequer order to seize lands in, 1350
(Tillebury). Cott. xiii. 5 (4).
—— Survey of the manor, with Scathes
*al.* Skeyts and Nortofts manors in,
1598. Lansd. Roll 19.
—— Rentals of the same manors,
1615. Add. 19475;—1690. Add. 19476.
—— Extract from court-roll of same
manors, 1729. Add. 19477.

Tilderessag, Tilderessaleye, Til-
dresle. *v.* Yeldersley, *in Ashbourne,*
*co. Derb.*

Tile *al.* Tyler Hill. *v. sub* Blean,
*co. Kent.*
—— *v. sub* Hackington, *co. Kent.*

Tiled Hall. *v. sub* Ramsden Cray, *co.*
*Essex.*

Tilehurst, *co. Berks.* Brief for rebuilding the church, 1771. Ch. Br.
B. xi. 10.

Tillebyr. *v.* Tilbury, East, *co. Essex.*

Tilles, Parva. *v.* Tylse, Little, *nr.*
*Arksey, co. York.*

Tillingdon, *in Tandridge, co. Surr.*
License to Sir N. Carewe to cut oaks
in, 1525. Add. 22630.

Tillingham, *co. Essex.* Fine in, 1545
(Tyllyngham). Add. 15610.

Tillingham, *in Peasemarsh, co. Suss.*
Grant in, 1428. Add. 20146.

Tillington, *co. Suss.* Grant at, 960
(Tullingtun). Cott. MS. Aug. ii. 40.
—— *Rector. Dom.* Joh. Wilcok, 1359
(Tolinton). Lans i. 124.

Tilmanstone, *co. Kent.* Evidence
conc. tenure in, by Osbernus, [1072]
(Tilemannestun). Cott. MS. Aug. ii. 36.
—— Compotus of Dane *al.* La Dane
in, [1309–10]. Harl. Roll D. 23.
—— Grant of La Dane manor in,
1349 (Tilmannistone). Cott. xxvii. 27.
—— Appointment of trustees for Dane
Court and South Court manors in,
1606. Harl. 79 E. 9.
—— *Curatus. Dom.* Joh. Browne,
1504. Harl. 78 H. 2, 3.
*cf. also* Deancourt, *co. Kent.*

Tilney, *co. Norf.* Rental in, of W.
Dereham Abbey, *t.* Edw. I. (Tylne).
Add. 689.
—— Grants, etc., in, 1431. Add. 9187
(Tylneye), 18718;—1440. Add. 9193;
—1475. Add. 9190;—1613. Add.
14742 (Tilnye).

Tils, Parva. *v.* Tylse, Lit., *nr. Arksey,*
*co. York.*

Tilsworth, *co. Bedf.* Acquittance for a
pension from the manor, 1405 (Tylles-
worthe). Cott. xxvii. 155.

Tilton, *co. Leic.* Covenant for a fine in,
1608. Add. 5145.
—— Fine in, 1686. Add. 23781.
*v. also* Marefield, *in Tilton, co.*
*Leic.*

Timberden, *in St. Peter's, near Worcester, co. Worc.* Release in, 1334
(Tymberden). Harl. 112 B. 20.

Timberland, *co. Linc.* Conf. of grant
in, by Hen. II. to Kirkstead Abbey,
[1155?] (Timberlund). Harl. 43 C. 17.
—— Grant in Mickelhol in, to the
same, *t.* Edw. I. (Tymberlund). Harl.
46 A. 36.
—— Lease of the rectory by Thur-
garton Priory, 1454. Harl. 45 A. 10.
—— *Clericus.* Galfridus, *t.* Edw. I.
Harl. 46 A. 36.
—— *Presbiter.* Radulfus, 1154. Harl.
57 F. 14;—1158. Harl. 49 A. 1.
—— *Vicarius.* Willelmus, *t.* Hen.
III. Cott. xii. 51.
—— —— *Dom.* Galfridus, late 13
cent. Cott. xii. 34.

Timberscombe, *co. Som.* Grant in,
1384 (Tymbercome). Harl. 49 G. 6.

Timlebi. *v.* Thimbleby, *co. Linc.*

Timolin, *Barony of, co. Kildare.* Grant
in, 1330 (Tughmelyng). Harl. 47 B. 31.

Toft, West, co. *Norf.* Grant of status in Toftes manor, 1419 (Toftes). Harl. 49 F. 23.

—— Inspex., in 1454, of a feoffment of the manor, etc., 1422 (Westoftys). Add. 17243.

—— Grant of Bigott's manor in, 1597. Add. 13581.

—— *Rector.* Johannes, 1375. Add. 14859.

Toftes juxta Rokeloundtoftes. *v.* Rockland *al.* Rockland Tofts, co. *Norf.*

Tokinton. *v.* Tookington, co. *Glouc.*

Tolawe, Parous de. *v. sub* Peckleton, co. *Leic.*

Tolesberi. *v.* Tollesbury, co. *Essex.*

Tolinton. *v.* Tillington, co. *Suss.*

Tolland, co. *Som.* Compotus of Gaulden (Gaweldon) in, bel. to Taunton Priory, 1438-9. Add. 25873.

Tollerton, co. *Nott.* Covenant to convey land in, 1571 (Torlaston). Woll. xi. 51.

—— Precipes on covenants conc. lands in, 1578 (Torlarton, Thorlaston). Add. 25202, 25203.

Tollerton, co. *York.* Brief conc. a fire at, 1767. Ch. Br. B. vii. 7.

Tollesbury, co. *Essex.* Grant in, by Barking Abbey, early 13 cent. (Tolesberi). Add. 15584.

—— Grant in, early 13 cent. (Tolesb.). Harl. 50 A. 11.

—— Fine in, with Newark Priory, co. Surr., 1235 (Tollebir.). Harl. 51. F. 43.

—— Release in, to Newark Priory, *t.* Hen. III. (Tollebur.). Harl. 57 A. 5.

—— Purchase in Gorwell in, by Bileigh Abbey, 1253. Campb. viii. 22.

—— *Capellanus. Dom.* Rogerus, *t.* Hen. III. Harl. 57 A. 5.

Tolleshunt, co. *Essex.* Grant of the manor by the Count of Guisnes, 1240 (Toleshonte). Harl. 48 B. 40.

—— Re-grant of the manor to the Bp. of London, *c.* 1245-50 (Toleshunt). Harl. 50 G. 39.

Tolleshunt d'Arcy, co. *Essex.* Exchange in, by Bileigh Abbey, 1331 (Toleshunte Tregos). Cott. xxi. 8.

Tolleshunt Knights, co. *Essex.* Precipe on a covenant conc. land in, 1587. Add. 24987.

Tolney, *in E. Stoke*, co. *Nott.* Assignment of life interest of Qu. Catharine of Braganza in the warren, etc., of, 1680. Harl. 111 H. 11.

Tome, Castle. *v.* Toome, Castle, co. *Antrim.*

Tomeworðig. *v.* Tamworth, cos. *Warw. and Staff.*

Tomlyns. *v. sub* Amersham, co. *Buck.*

Tomlyns Park. *v. sub* Seal, co. *Kent.*

Tonbridge, co. *Kent.* Grant of Sandhurst (terra de Sandherst) and Higham (Hehham) in or nr., [1173-1218] (Tunebrg.). Harl. 111 E. 45.

—— Grants, etc., in, 1310-11. Harl. 76 C. 55 (Thonebregge); — 1367. Harl. 48 E. 24; —1473. Harl. 79 D. 30.

—— Grant at Bromelaregg in, 1318 (Thonebregg). Harl. 80 C. 25.

—— Inquest, etc., conc. forfeited lands of Tho. Colepeper in, 1324-5 (Thonebregge, etc.). Harl. Roll T. 21.

—— Conveyance of rent in W. Haysden (Westhesdene), etc., in or nr., 1407. Harl. 76 G. 39.

—— Names of those slain there during Jack Cade's rebellion, 1450-1. Cott. ii. 23 (14).

—— Award in, 1464 (Tonbrigge). Add. 15731.

—— Court-rolls of Tonbridge Port, T. Southborough and T. Hilden manors, 1478-82. Add. 23788-23791.

—— Petition for lands in, [1551-2]. Harl. 83 H. 36.

—— Sale of tithes of corn and hay in, 1552. Harl. 78 A. 37.

—— Deeds relating to Buckingham's, Cage, N. and S. Frith and other lands in and nr., 1552. Harl. 77 G. 18; —1553. Harl. 78 E. 53; —1555. Harl. 75 E. 31; —1556. Harl. 75 H. 23, 78 E. 54; —1557. Harl. 76 C. 40, 76 I. 32, 33, 78 E. 55, 80 C. 18, 19; —1558. Harl. 78 A. 38, 78 I. 39; —1559. Harl. 76 I. 45, 80 I. 50; —1561. Harl. 76 C. 41, 76 I. 53, 54, 77 A. 1, 7, 15, 78 A. 28, 79 A. 9, 26, 85 H. 6; —1564. Add. 5979; —1565. Harl. 77 A. 10; —1566. Harl. 77 A. 14; —1573. Harl. 77 A. 35, 36; —1574. Harl. 77 H. 35; —1576. Harl. 77 B. 42; —1579. Harl. 77 B. 46.

—— Appointment of a keeper of a walk in N. Frith park nr., 1564. Harl. 75 E. 29.

Towcester, *co. Northt.* Recital of a grant of the church by Will. I. to Fontenelle Abbey, *c.* 1207 (Touecestre). Add. 8071.

—— Grants, etc., in, 1301. Add. 6112 (Toucestre); — 1505. Add. 6145; — 1545. Add. 13931.

—— Expenses conc. Archdeacon Sponne's chantry, 1449-51. Harl. Roll B. 21.

—— Precipe on a covenant conc. land in, 1578. Add. 25150.

—— *Capellanus et Rector. Dom.* Johannes, *t.* Hen. III. Harl. 86·D. 45.

—— *Persona.* J——, early Hen. III. Harl. 86 B. 57.

Towthorpe, *co. York.* Partition of lands in, 1599. Add. 5143, 5144.

Towton, *in Saxton, co. York.* Power to take seizin in, 1339 (Toveton). Add. 26764.

Toynton, *co. Linc.* Grants, etc., in, *c.* 1145. Harl. 55 E. 10 (Totin.); — *t.* Hen. III. Harl. 55 E. 14 (Totinton).

—— Fine of the manor, with a moiety of the advowson, 1302 (Toynton). Harl. 45 H. 18.

—— Grant in Nethertynton, 1355. Harl. 57 G. 11.

—— Release of the manor, 1387 (Toynton). Harl. 53 C. 38.

—— Fine of Overtoynton and Nethirtoynton manors, with a moiety of the advowson of the latter, 1429. Harl. 56 I. 49.

—— *Clericus.* Johannes, *t.* Hen. III. Cott. v. 61.

—— Willelmus, *t.* Hen. III. (Thoyntona). Harl. 48 G. 2.

—— *Persona.* Johannes, 1217 (Tingtun). Harl. 46 A. 4.

—— *Sacerdos.* David, *t.* Hen. II. Harl. 55 E. 14.

Tr . . . hach, *co.* —— (?). Rental, 16 cent. Harl. Roll CC. 7.

Tracey, Newton. *v.* Newton Tracey, *co. Devon.*

Tracys. *v. sub* Newington next Sittingbourne, *co. Kent.*

—— *v. sub* Stanford Rivers, *co. Essex.*

Tradyntona. *v.* Trotton, *co. Suss.*

Trallong Prebend, *co. Brecon.* Lease of, 1573. Add. 1837.

Tranby (Traneby), *co. York.* Grant in, by Gisburne Priory to Watton Priory, saving the advowson of the vicarage, etc., 1227. Add. 1050.

—— Grants in, 1338. Lansd. 449; — 1366. Lansd. 450.

—— Release in, to Watton Priory, 1339. Harl. 53 G. 58.

Trapeston, Trapston. *v.* Thrapston, *co. Northt.*

Traquair, *co. Peebles.* Conf. of the forest of, to Melrose Abbey. [1166-70?] (Treuequair). Cott. xviii. 13, 14.

Trattons. *v.* Trotton, *co. Suss.*

Traytourdowne, *nr. Grampound, co. Cornw.* Releases in, 1430. Add. 12990; —1431. Add. 12994.

Treaddow, *in Hentland, co. Heref.* Grants, etc., in, *t.* Edw. I. Add. 1309 (Treradou); —1519. Add. 1341 (Treradow); —1534. Add. 1346 (Trerado); —1625. Add. 1924.

Treburrick, *co. Cornw.* Grant, etc., in, 1394. Harl. 51 E. 16 (Treburthek); —1513. Harl. 50 C. 41 (Treburthook).

Trecarell, *in Lezant, co. Cornw.* Entail in, 1544. Eg. 283.

Trecrogan, *co. Cornw.* Grant in, 1518. Eg. 276.

Tredington, *co. Worc.* Sale in Longdon Travers in, 1600. Add. 19423.

Tredis, Tredehyst. *v. sub* Sheviock, *co. Cornw.*

Tredryn, *co. Cornw.* Crown appointment of a bailiff, etc., in, 1571. Harl. 75 E. 38.

Tredunnoch, *in Llangarran, co. Heref.* Fine in, 1599. Add. 1875.

Tredunnock, *co. Monm.* Release, etc., in, in the fee of Edlogan, 1451. Add. 1816 (Tredenock); —1513. Add. 1389 (Treredonock).

—— Release, etc., in, 1534. Add. 1821 • (Trerydenoc); — 1598. Add. 1874 (Tredonock); —1607. Add. 1893 (do.); —1620. Add. 1917.

—— Bond conc. the rectory of, 1575 (Trerdonock). Add. 1841.

—— Precipes on covenants conc. lands in, 1592. Add. 25121 (Tredonocke); —1593. Add. 25143 (Tredenock).

—— Crown acquittance to tenants of a recusant in, 1612 (Tredenocke). Add. 1905.

Treeton, *co. York*. Grants, etc., in, *t.* Hen. III. Cott. xxviii. 24 (Tretun); —1295. Harl. 83 G. 29 (Treton);— 1564. Add. 17966 – 17968 ; — 1603. Add. 18003, 18004 ; — 1612. Add. 18006, 18007 ;—1613. Add. 18008 ;— 1667. Add. 18040.

—— Grant in Cridingges and Ravenswartriding nr., *t.* Edw. I. (Treton). Woll. viii. 38.

—— Fine in, 1604. Add. 18009.

—— Covenant to grind corn at the mill, 1651. Add. 18035.

—— *Clericus.* Adam, 1316. Harl. 83 D. 8.

—— *Rector.* Philippus, *t.* Hen. III. Harl. 83 D. 12.

—— *Dom.* Rog. Stedman, 1436 (Tryton). Add. 7385.

—— *Vicar.* Rob. Foster, 1741. Woll. xii. 94 (1).

Tre Evan, *in Llangarran, co. Heref.* Fine in, 1599 (Treyevan *al.* Treevan). Add. 1875.

—— Release, etc., in, 1599. Add. 1878 (do.) ;—1619. Add. 1916 (do.).

Treevyn. *v. sub* Wembury, co. *Devon.*

Trefeld, *nr. Poulton in the Fylde* (?), *co. Lanc.* Award in suit conc. the grange of, betw. Lancaster Priory and Cockersand Abbey, 1256. Add. 19818.

Trefnant, *nr. Welshpool, co. Montgom.* Grant of the manor, *t.* Edw. I. (Trevenant). Cott. xxviii. 51.

Trefuen. *v.* Treven (?), *co. Cornw.*

Tregameer, [*in St. Columb Major?*], *co. Cornw.* Crown appointment of a bailiff, etc., in, 1571 (Truckmere). Harl. 75 E. 38.

Tregaminion, [*nr. St. Keverne*], *co. Cornw.* Settlement in, *t.* Edw. IV. Add. 15362 (Tregemynion).

Tregaminion, *co. Cornw.* [*the same?*]. Power to take seisin in, 1481 (Tregomynyon juxta Lysard). Add. 15363.

Tregayre, *co. Cornw.* Grant in, 1518. Eg. 276.

Tregeen, *nr. Davidstowe, co. Cornw.* Grant in, early Hen. III. (Treguen). Harl. 53 B. 42.

Tregelest, *nr. Davidstowe, co. Cornw.* Grant in, early Hen. III. Harl. 53 B. 42.

Tregelest, *co. Cornw.* Grant in, 1518. Eg. 276.

Tregennowe, *co. Cornw.* Grant in, 1518. Eg. 276.

Tregerean *al.* Tregerean Vean, [*nr. Padstow?*], *co. Cornw.* Settlement of the manor, 1622. Add. 7058.

Tregew, *in Feock, co. Cornw.* Sale, etc., in, 1649, 1651 (Tregye). Add. 15383–15385.

Treglasta, *in Davidstowe, co. Cornw.* Grant in, early Hen. III. (Treglastan). Harl. 53 B. 42.

Treglyne (Treglotenhou *al.* Tregluthnou, Treglothnowe, etc.), *in St. Minver, co. Cornw.* Grants, etc., in, *t.* Edw. I. or II. Harl. 57 A. 37 ;—1392. Harl. 50 C. 37 ;—1394. Harl. 51 E. 16 ;— 1513. Harl. 50 C. 41 ;—1576. Harl. 50 C. 46.

Treglynneck, *co. Cornw.* Grants, etc., in, 1366. Harl. 50 C. 36 (Tregillenek) ; —1392. Harl. 50 C. 37 (Tregglenek), 38, 39 (Treglynnek);—1394. Harl. 51 E. 16 (do.);—1513. Harl. 50 C. 41.

Tregonan, [*nr. St. Columb Major?*], *co. Cornw.* Release in, 1383. Add. 15351.

Tregonger (?), *nr. Davidstowe, co. Cornw.* Grant in, early Hen. III. (Treurengi). Harl. 53 B. 42.

Tregonhov, Tregonow. *v.* Tregunna, *in St. Breock, co. Cornw.*

Tregonnan, *co. Cornw.* Grant in, 1516. Add. 13078.

Tregony, *co. Cornw.* Grants, etc., in, 1345. Add. 13022 (Tregony Marche) ; —1422. Add. 12976, 12977 ;—1425. Add. 12980 – 12982 ; — 1430. Add. 12990 ;—1431. Add. 12994 ;—1513. Harl. 50 C. 41–43 (Tregonyburgh).

Tregors, *co. Cornw.* Warranty in, 1341. Harl. 57 A. 41.

Tregoyt Nithera. *v.* Trequites, *co. Cornw.*

Tregreg, *in Llangibby, co. Monm.* Release, etc., in the domain of, 1523. Add. 1344 (Tregruge) ; - 1524. Add. 1817 (Treirgruge) ;—1528. Add. 1818 (Tregruge) ;—1532. Add. 1345 (do.); —1537. Add. 1822.

Tregrygeowe, *co. Cornw.* Grant in, 1487. Add. 15364.

Treguddick, [*in S. Petherwin*], *co. Cornw.* Conveyance in, 1518 (Tregodek). Eg. 276.

Treguen. *v.* Tregeen, *co. Cornw.*

3 c 2

**Tregunna,** *in St. Breock, co. Cornw.*
Grants, etc., in, 1302. Harl. 57 A.
39 (Tregonow);—*t.* Edw. I. or II.
Harl. 57 A. 37 (Tregonhow);—1392.
Harl. 50 C. 37, 38, 39;—1513. Harl.
50 C. 41.

**Trehane,** *nr. Davidstowe. co. Cornw.*
Grant in, early Hen. III. (Treiaan).
Harl. 53 B. 42.

**Trehelig.** *co. Montgom.* Lease in, 1614.
Add. 1037.

**Treirgruge.** *v.* Tregreg, *co. Monm.*

**Trelawne,** [*in Polynt*], *co. Cornw.*
Crown-appointment of a bailiff of the
manor, 1571. Harl. 75 E. 38.

**Trelay,** *nr. Davidstowe, co. Cornw.*
Grant in, early Hen. III. Harl. 53
B. 42.

**Trelegharkettus,** [*nr. Llanarthney?*],
*co. Carmarth.* Exemplif. of fine in,
1618. Add. 979.

**Trelleck,** *co. Monm.* Grants, etc., in
the domain or fee of, 1507. Add.
7149 (Trelleke);—1509. Add. 7151
(Trillec);—1518. Add. 7152 (Trellek);
—1524. Add. 7153 (Trelegek);—1525.
Add. 7154 (Treleo).

—— Precipe on a covenant conc. land
in, 1592 (Trilleg). Add. 25119.

**Trematon,** *in St. Stephen, co. Cornw.*
Garrison establishment of the castle,
1369 (Treynaton). Harl. Roll E. 7.

—— Bond to abide award in, 1539
(Castell Tremyton). Harl. 48 I. 27.

**Trembeth** [Trembleath, *in St. Ervan?*],
*co. Cornw.* Grants, etc., in, 1366. Harl.
50 C. 36;—1392. Harl. 50 C. 37, 38,
39;—1394. Harl. 51 E. 16;—1513.
Harl. 50 C. 41.

**Tremley,** *co. Kent.* Grant in Hoch,
etc., in (?), to Combwell Priory, *t.* Hen.
III. Harl. 80 G. 31.

**Tremll, Tremley S. Martini.** *v.*
Trimley St. Martin, *co. Suff.*

**Tremodret,** *in Roche, co. Cornw.* Grant
of annuity from the manor, 1521.
Add. 23846.

**Tremston.** *v. sub* Burmarsh, *co. Kent.*

**Tremure.** *v.* Trevear, *in St. Issey, co.
Cornw.*

**Trenance,** [*nr. St. Keverne*], *co. Cornw.*
Grant in, *t.* Edw. IV. (Trenans). Add.
15362.

**Trendhurst,** *co. Kent.* Grant of wood
in, 973 (Trind hyrst). Cott. viii. 33.

[**Treneglos**], *co. Cornw.* Grant of
Downeckney (?) (Donethley) in, early
Hen. III. Add. 24263.

**Trengale,** *co. Cornw.* Grant in, 1518.
Eg. 276.

**Trengeston.** *v.* Thringston, *co. Leic.*

**Trenithon,** *in St. Keverne, co. Cornw.*
Grant in, *t.* Edw. IV. (Trenython).
Add. 15362.

**Trenowith,** *in St. Columb Major, co.
Cornw.* Suit conc. the manor, 1492.
Harl. Roll V. 10.

**Trent,** *River.* Papal conf. of 30 acres
of meadow on, in co. Nott., to Rufford
Abbey, 1156 (Trente). Harl. 111 A. 2.

—— Conff. of grants of mills on, to
Elsham Priory, co. Linc., [1163-5].
Harl. 45 A. 4, 45 C. 33.

—— Grant of a fishery in, nr. Yoxall,
co. Staff., early 13 cent. Campb. xi. 6.

—— Grant of a fishery in, at Kelfield,
in I. of Axholme, co. Linc., by Sulby
Abbey, *t.* Hen. III. Add. 20691.

—— Grant in Alrewas, co. Staff., of
land enclosed by, and the R. Tame,
*t.* Edw. I. (Trente). Campb. xi. 8.

**Trentesic.** *v. sub* Ailby, *co. Linc.*

**Trenysek** (?), *co. Cornw.* Grant in,
1518. Eg. 276.

**Trequites,** *nr. Helligan, in St. Mabyn,
co. Cornw.* Conveyance in, 1331 (Tregoyt Nithera). Harl. 51 E. 2.

**Treradow.** *v.* Treaddow, *co. Heref.*

**Treredonock, Trerrydenoc, etc.** *v.*
Tredunnock, *co. Monm.*

**Tresauec.** *v.* Trescake, *co. Cornw.*

**Tresavean,** *in Gwennap, co. Cornw.*
Fines, etc., in, 1588. Add. 15373
(Trusuevean *al.* Trewseuvean);—1608.
Add. 15375 (Trusoevean *al.* Trewseu-
vean), 15376 (Trusevean);—1623. Add.
15380;—1656. Add. 15367 (Trusa *al.*
Trysavean).

**Tresc, Treske.** *v.* Thirsk, *co. York.*

**Treseock, Treshacke, etc.** *v.* Treyseck, *in Hoarwithy, co. Heref.*

**Tresham,** *co. Glouc.* Conf. of grants
at (?), to Pershore Abbey, 972. Cott.
MS. Aug. ii. 6.

**Treskewes,** [*nr. St. Keverne*], *co. Cornw.*
Grant in, *t.* Edw. IV. (Tresckewys).
Add. 15362.

**Tresloget,** *in St. Mabyn, co. Cornw.*
Conveyance in, 1331. Harl. 51 E. 2.

Trewythosa. v. sub St. Stephen in Brannel, co. Cornw.

Trewythou. v. Trevelhow, in Lelant, co. Cornw.

Treyevan. v. Tre Evan, in Llangarran, co. Heref.

Treyford, co. Suss. Settlement in, 1605 (Treford). Add. 18899.

Treynaton. v. Trematon, co. Cornw.

Treyne, Commote of, in S. Wales. Grant of reversion of, 1443. Harl. 51 H. 10.

Treynthell, Treynthell parva, co. Cornw. Grant in, 1518. Eg. 276.

Treyseck, in Hoarwithy, co. Heref. Grants, etc., in, 1419. Add. 1326 (Treysac), 1327 (do.):—1474. Add. 1331 (Treysacke), 1332 (Treisack):—1534. Add. 1346 (Tresseck):—1546. Add. 1349 (Treshacke):—1548. Add. 1353 (Treseck):—1565. Add. 1831.

Tricombe, nr. Northleigh, co. Devon. Release in, 1420 (Trycomb). Add. 13039.

Trill, in Axminster, co. Devon. Lease in, 1636. Add. 13985.

Trillec, Trilleg. v. Trelleck, co. Monm.

Trilwardyn, in Shiffnal, co. Salop. Grant in, 1384. Cott. v. 8.

Trim, co Meath. Grant of the advowson of St. Patrick's church at, saving the vicarage, to Beaubec Abbey, t. John (Trum). Add. 19803.

—— Vicecomes [Galfridi de Geynvill] de Trum. Hugo de Portes, 1259. Harl. 50 G. 38.

Trimley St. Martin, co. Suff. Acquittance for fines for Grimston Hall manor in, and for the advowson, 1355 (Tremll.). Cott. xxvii. 152.

—— Conf. of status in Grimston and Moston Hall manors in, 1459 (Tremley S. Martini). Add. 10215.

—— Grant of Stratton Hall manor, etc., in, 1538 (Trymeley). Add. 10225.

—— Defeasance of bond on sale of Grimston, Moston and Stratton Hall manors in, 1597 (Trymley S. Martyn). Add. 10238.

—— Sales, etc., in, 1605. Add. 10242; —1618. Add. 10245;—1627. Add. 10247;—1654. Add. 10256;—1657. Add. 10258;—1729. Add. 10264.

Trimley St. Mary, co. Suff. Conf. of status in Blofeld manor, etc., in, 1459 (Tremley S. Marie). Add. 10215.

—— Sales, etc., in, 1495. Add. 10220 (Tremley); — 1503. Add. 10223 ; — 1538. Add. 10225; — 1563. Add. 10230;—1605. Add. 10242;—1609. Add. 10243;—1618. Add. 10245;—1627. Add. 10247; — 1654. Add. 10256;—1655. Add. 10257;—1673. Add. 10258.

—— Feoffment of Blofeld manor in, 1503. Add. 10223.

—— Sale of Candelent manor, etc., in, 1564. Add. 10231, 10232.

Trimley, Walton cum, Manor. v. sub Walton, co. Suff.

Trind hyrst. v. Trondhurst, co. Kent.

Tring, co. Hertf. Exemption to tenants of the Abp. of Canterbury in, from stallage, etc., 1441 (Trynge). Lansd. 180.

—— Release to executors of the late rector for dilapidations, 1468 (Tryng). Harl. 45 A. 9.

—— Rector (nuper). Mag. Joh. Stokys, 1468. Harl. 45 A. 9.

—— —— Tho. Wynterburn, clericus, 1468. Harl. 45 A. 9.

Trippleton, in Leintwardine, co. Heref. Grant in, 1358 (Turpletone). Harl. 112 E. 20.

Trithwall al. Trithall, co. Cornw. Fine in, 1656. Add. 15367.

Trium Castrorum, Feodum, co. Monm. Surrender of lands in the court of Grosmount by men of, 1249-50. Add. 20414.

Troan. v. sub St. Enoder, co. Cornw.

Trobrigge. v. Trowbridge, co. Wilts.

Troholm, [in Tumby], co. Linc. Grant of a fishery at, to Kirkstead Abbey, t. Hen. II. Harl. 57 B. 7.

Troll. v. Trowle, in Trowbridge, co. Wilts.

Tromkewull. v. Trunkwell, co. Berks.

Tropynden, Den of. v. sub Goudhurst, co. Kent.

Troston, co. Suff. Grants, etc., in, early 13 cent. Harl. 45 G. 18 (Trostun):—t. Hen. III. Add. 9142 (do.); —t. Edw. I. Harl. 50 C. 50:—1303. Harl. 57 C. 24:—1331. Harl. 56 H. 47:—1337. Harl. 54 D. 1;—1342. Harl. 52 D. 45;—1396. Add. 18684.

Troston, *co. Suff. (continued).* Appointment of a bailiff in, 1332. Harl. 57 G. 27.

—— Acquittances for castle-ward in, due to Bury St. Edmund's Abbey, 1448, 1454. Harl. 44 D. 29, 30.

—— Suit in, 1569. Add. 18852.

—— *Rector.* Joh. Moor, 1402. Add. 9117.

Trostrey, *co. Monm.* Inspex., in 1330, of grant in, nr. the Hermitage, to Usk Priory, c. 1150 (Trostrai). Add. 5342.

Trotton, *co. Suss.* Fine of the manor, 1288 (Tradyntona). Add. 20404.

—— Release of the manor, 1433 (Trattone). Add. 20055.

—— Settlement in, 1605. Add. 18899.

—— Sale, etc., of Milland farm and other lands in, 1625. Add. 6004;—1631. Add. 6008 (Tratton), 6009.

—— *Persona.* Willelmus, 1416. Harl. 54 I. 34.

Trouowan. *v. sub* St. Enoder, *co. Cornw.*

Trowbridge, *co. Wilts.* The castle and manor held for life by John, Earl of Surrey, with reversion to Will., Earl of Salisbury, 1338. Cott. xi. 61.

—— Grant in trust of the constableship of, 1523 (Trobrigge). Add. 5140.

—— Recovery in, 1556. Add. 5704.

—— Whaddon manor held of the manor, c. 1560-70. Add. 5711.

—— Release in Stodley in, 1563. Harl. 80 H. 37.

Trowe, *in Berwick St. John, co. Wilts.* Grant in, 1333. Add. 17302.

Trowle, *in Trowbridge, co. Wilts.* Lease in, 1349 (Troll). Campb. xviii. 1.

Trowse with Newton, *co. Norf.* Conff. of grants of Newton to Norwich Priory, [1103-6?]. Cott. MS. Aug. ii. 103, Cott. ii. 21 (1) (*copies*); —[1107-8?]. Cott. ii. 2;—[1136-45]. Cott. ii. 1.

—— Grants, etc., in Newton to St. Giles's Hospital, Norwich, *t.* Hen. III. Toph. 12 *a, b.*

—— Grant in Trowse (Treus), abutting on Trowse Millgate, *t.* Hen. III. or Edw. I. Add. 19287.

—— Grant in Trowse, 1355. Add. 14928.

Troy. *v.* Mitchel Troy, *co. Monm.*

Truckmere. *v.* Tregameer, [*in St. Columb Major?*], *co. Cornw.*

Trum. *v.* Trim, *co. Meath.*

Trumpington (Trumpeton), *co. Camb.* Grants in, *ante* 1275. Harl. 47 B. 45, 51 D. 27;—1328. Harl. 46 G. 6.

Trunch, *co. Norf.* Lease in, 1446. Add. 19336.

Trunkwell, *nr. Stratfield Mortimer, co. Berks.* Grant in, 1190-1 (Tromkewull). Harl. 83 A. 4.

Truro, *co. Cornw.* Grant, etc., in, 1363. Add. 15350;—1410. Add. 15353.

Trusevean, Trusoevean. *v.* Tresavean, *in Gwennap, co. Cornw.*

Trusley, *co. Derb.* Grant in, to the Knts. Hospitallers, late 12 cent. (Trusseleia). Woll. x. 21.

—— Conf. of a grant in Turmundel nr., of the fee of, late 12 cent. (Trusseleie). Woll. x. 20.

—— Release of Pilateshul, etc., in, by Derby Priory, end of 12 cent. (Trussele). Woll. x. 22.

—— Exchange in, by the same, early 13 cent. Woll. viii. 51.

—— Grant nr., to the same, early 13 cent. (Trusselega). Woll. x. 24.

—— Grant of Ermite medewe in, 1303 (Trusseleye). Woll. ix. 29.

—— Grants, etc., in, 1303. Woll. ix. 30 (do.);—1308. Woll. x. 25 (do.);—1317. Woll. x. 26;—1440-1. Woll. x. 28;—1447. Woll. x. 30;—1466. Woll. viii. 54;—1495. Woll. xi. 48, xii. 133;—1502. Woll. xii. 103, 103*;—1504. Woll. xii. 105;—1530. Woll. xii. 107.

—— Grants of the manor, 1422-44. Woll. x. 29 —1509. Woll. x. 31.

—— Induction of Nic. Brandewodde to the rectory on death of Tho. Steynton, 1475. Woll. x. 36.

—— Descent of the manor, 1583. Woll. xi. 35.

Trusthorpe, *co. Linc.* Release in, 1354. Harl. 51 B. 7.

—— Lease of the manor, 1355. Harl. 57 G. 11.

—— Sale of a ninth part of the manor, 1573. Add. 24166;—1575. Add. 24167.

—— *Persona.* Rob. de Cokewald *al.* Cokewold, 1347. Harl. 44 A. 8, 58 C. 36.

Trycomb. *v.* Tricombe, *nr. Northleigh, co. Devon.*

Trymeley. *v.* Trimley St. Martin, *co. Suff.*

**Tysoe,** *co. Warw. (continued).* Grants in, to Bordesley Abbey, [1183–9]. Harl. 56 D. 50 (Thieso, Tyeso), 56 E. 1 (Tyeso);—*c.* 1250. Cott. xxix. 54 (Tyaho).

—— Conf. of grant in Westcote in, to Stoneleigh Abbey, *t.* Hen. III. Add. 7498.

—— Grant, etc., in, late Hen. III. Cott. xxix. 55 (Thysho);—1301. Cott. xxix. 57 (Tysho).

—— Acquittance of suits in the court of, *t.* Hen. III. Add. 7498.

**Tyssebury.** *v.* Tisbury, co. Wilts.

**Tyssinton.** *v.* Tissington, co. Derb.

**Tytenesovere.** *v.* Tittensor, *in Stone,* co. Staff.

**Tythegston,** *co. Glam.* Exchange in, by Margam Abbey, 1292 (Tudekistowe). Harl. 75 A. 42.

—— Decree on behalf of Margam Abbey conc. tithes of the chapel, leased from Tewkesbury Abbey, 1332 (Tegestowe). Harl. 75 A. 27.

**Tytherleigh,** *in Chardstock, co. Dors.* Feoffment in, 1247 (Tyderlegh). Harl. 56 D. 22, 23.

**Tytherley,** *co. Southt.* Title of J. de Hastings to E. Tytherley (Esttuderle) manor, 1332. Harl. Roll N. 34.

—— Sale of wardship, etc., in, 1534. Cott. xxvi. 40.

**Tythrop,** *nr. Thame, co. Oxon.* Conveyance of the manor, 1416. Harl. 54 I. 34.

**Tyuerington.** *v.* Terrington, co. York.

**Tywa, magna.** *v.* Tew, Great, co. Oxon.

## U V

**Vadum Gilberti.** *v. sub* Rhinderston, *in Haycastle, co. Pembr.*

**Vahnge.** *v.* Vange, co. Essex.

**Vainor** *al.* **Faenor,** *co. Brecon.* Grants, etc., in, 1388. Harl. 111 B. 43 (Gwinaw);—1481. Harl. 111 B. 29 (par. S. Gwynoci);—1524. Harl. 111 B. 21 (Maynor Weyno).

**Valans** *al.* **Valeins** manor. *v. sub* Westleton, co. Suff.

**Valde, The,** *al.* **Vale.** *v.* Vauld, The, *in Marden, co. Heref.*

**Vange,** *co. Essex.* Assignment of rent of marsh land in, to Waltham H. Cross Abbey, *t.* Hen. III. (Vahnge). Harl. 48 D. 51.

—— Release of the manor, 1402 (Fanges). Add. 16446.

—— Precipe on a covenant conc. lands in, 1561 (Fange). Add. 24937.

**Varia Capella.** *v.* Egglesbreo, co. Stirling.

**Varle, Varlye.** *v.* Farley, co. Surr.

**Vauendane.** *v.* Wavendon, co. Buck.

**Vauld, The,** *in Marden, co. Heref.* Lease, etc., in, 1614. Add. 1906 (the Valde);—1654. Add. 1953 (Vale).

**Vaysies.** *v. sub* Milding, co. Suff.

**Ubbeston,** *co. Suff.* Grant and conf. of the church to St. Neot's Priory, 1165. Add. 8517 (Obostona);—*c.* 1165–70. Add. 8521 (do.).

—— Grants, etc., in, to the same, *t.* Hen. II. Add. 8518 (Ubbestun), 8519 (Obestun), 8520 (Ubestunia);—*c.* 1270. Add. 8522 (Obston);—1332. Add. 8524.

—— Release of the advowson of St. Peter's church to the same, 1272 (Obiston). Add. 8523.

—— Release of the manor, 1404. Harl. 45 D. 15.

—— Lease of the manor by St. Neot's Priory, 1476 (Obston). Add. 8525.

—— Precipe on a covenant conc. lands in, 1588 (Ubston). Add. 10420.

—— Dispensation for Sim. Sumpter to hold the perpet. vicarage of, 1640. Add. 5524, 5525.

—— *Capellanus.* Radulfus, *t.* Hen. III. Harl. 84 A. 57.

**Ubley,** *co. Som.* Grant, etc., in, 1385. Harl. 46 G. 15 (Uble);—1404. Harl. 46 G. 44 (Ubble).

—— License for entail of the manor, 1528 (Obleygh). Add. 6031.

**Ucha,** *in Berriew* (?), *co. Montgom.* Lease in, 1638. Add. 1038.

**Ucing ford,** *co. Som.* (?). A boundary mark, 938. Cott. viii. 17; — 961. Harl. 43 C. 2.

**Uckfield,** *co. Suss.* Grants, etc., in, 1306. Harl. 79 C. 57 (Uckefelde);—*c.* 1306. Harl. 79 C. 56 (Ockefeld);—1320. Harl. 78 A. 17 (Ukkefeld);—1332. Add. 23817 (Ukkefeud);—1418. Add. 23818 (Ukfeld);—1431. Add. 23793.

Uckfield, co. Suss. (continued). Bond for an award in, 1474 (Ukkefeld). Add. 23819.

Uckington, in Elmstone Hardwick, co. Glouc. Grant in, 1320 (Okynton). Slo. xxxiii. 19.

Uddyng. v. sub Chalbury, co. Dors.

Udimore, co. Suss. Grant of the advowson to Robertsbridge Abbey, c. 1307–8 (Odimere). Eg. 398.

—— Fines in, 1405. Add. 24892 (Udymer) ;—1507. Add. 24910 (do.).

—— Grant, etc., in, 1419. Add. 972 (Udymer) ;—1450. Add. 973 (Udemer).

—— Precipe on a covenant conc. lands in, 1592 (Udymer). Add. 15232.

—— Vicarius. Simon, early Hen. III. (Udlmer). Eg. 385.

Udlington, nr. Shrewsbury, co. Salop. Crown lease in, 1576. Harl. 75 E. 45.

Uedring mutha. v. Wittering, co. Suss.

Veises. v. sub Stratford St. Mary, co. Suff.

Vellow, in Stogumber, co. Som. Fine of the manor, etc., 1346 (Ayly). Add. 25876.

Venables [Pishill Venables?], co. Oxon. Fine of the manor, 1334. Harl. Roll G. 17.

Venn. v. sub Churchstowe, co. Devon.

Venn, The, in Marden, co. Heref. Lease in, 1614. Add. 1906.

Venny Sutton. v. Sutton Veney, co. Wilts.

Verence. v. sub Swanscombe, co. Kent.

Verlays manor. v. sub Sternfield, co. Suff.

Vernham, East, in Hurstborne Tarrant, co. Southt. Precipe on a covenant conc. land in, 1578 (Est Ferneham). Add. 25223.

Veseys. v. sub Stratford St. Mary, co. Suff.

Vestleveton. v. Westleton, co. Suff.

Veyses al. Melkys. v. sub Eleigh, Brent, co. Suff.

Ufethona. v. Upton, co. Northt.

Uferan tun. v. Overton, co. Wilts.

Uffoulme, co. Devon. Extract conc. inquest and seizure of the manor, 1410 (Uffecolme). Harl. 48 F. 47.

Uffoulme, co. Devon (continued). Grants, etc., of the manor, 1408. Harl. 43 E. 17, 18 (Ufeolme) ;—1415. Harl. 53 B. 2 (Uffecolmp).

Uffeton Richard, U. Robert. v. Ufton, co. Berks.

Uffington, co. Berks. Covenant conc. settlement of the manor, 1350 (Uffyntona). Harl. 54 D. 28.

—— Release, etc., in, 1362. Harl. 58 D. 45 (Offynton) ;—1620. Add. 6148.

Ufford, co. Northt. Sale, etc., in, 1482. Add. 6467 ;—1579. Add. 9272.

Ufford, co. Suff. Grants, etc., in, 1316. Harl. 84 B. 45 ;—1361. Add. 10014 ; —1391. Add. 10555 ;—1405. Add. 19322 ;—1408. Add. 10556 ;—1447. Add. 8386 ;—1460. Add. 10557 ;— 1470. Add. 10558 ;—1485. Add. 10559 ;—1487. Add. 10087 ;—1615. Add. 19688.

—— License for waste in the manor, 1400. Harl. 55 H. 1.

—— Conveyance, etc., of the manor, 1417. Harl. 58 B. 13 ;—1429. Harl. 58 B. 17 ;—1516. Harl. 52 B. 10.

—— Grant of rent charge on the manor, 1431. Harl. 57 A. 1.

—— License for grant of the advowson, 1439. Harl. 43 E. 43.

Ufton. v. sub Tunstall, co. Kent.

Ufton, co. Berks. Release in, 1396 (Uffeton Robert, U. Richard). Add. 9243.

—— Feoffment, etc., in, 1618. Add. 19210, 19211.

—— Brief conc. a hail-storm at, 1762. Ch. Br. B. ii. 2.

—— Clericus. Willelmus, t. Hen. III. Add. 20596.

Ufton, in S. Wingfield, co. Derb. Grants, etc., of the manor, 1292, 1293. Harl. 112 I. 18 a, b (Huftona) ;—1378. Harl. 112 I. 54 ;—1380. Harl. 112 F. 32, Lansd. 185.

Ufton al. Oloughton Prebend, cos. Warw. and Staff. Grant by the chapter of Coventry of next presentation to a moiety of the church, 1586. Cott. v. 27.

—— Royal grant of the advowson, 1559. Add. 26024.

Ugford, in S. Newton, co. Wilts. Court-rolls, 1559. Add. 24440 ;—1567. Add. 24441 ;—1584. Add. 24718.

Upledecumbe [? Letcombe Basset].
v. Letcombe —— (?), co. Berks.

Uplyme, co. Devon. Grant in Cannington (Canyton) and Obbecumbe in
the manor of, 1282 (Up Lym). Harl.
52 A. 12.

—— Persona. Philip Lowys, 1436.
Harl. 53 D. 23.

Upmantone. v. sub Selling, co. Kent.

Upminster, co. Essex. Livery in
Gaines (Geynes) manor, etc., in, 1594.
Harl. 51 H. 30.

—— Court-roll of Upminster Hall
manor in, 1652. Add. 683.

Up Ottery. v. Ottery, Up, co. Devon.

Uppatun, nr. Davidstowe, co. Cornw.
Grant in, early Hen. III. Harl. 53
B. 42.

Uppeford. v. Offord Darcy, co. Hunt.

Upperbourne. v. sub Bishopsbourne,
co. Kent.

Uppercourt. v. sub Farningham, co.
Kent.

Uppeton Prodhumme. v. sub Payhembury, co. Devon.

Upphall. v. sub Rochford, co. Essex.

Uppingham, co. Rutl. Re-grant of
the church, etc., by Will. I. to Westminster Abbey, 1067 (Yppingeham).
Cott. vi. 3 (copy).

—— Court-roll of Preston with Uppingham manor, 1735-6. Add. 25984.

Uppington. v. sub Withypoole, co.
Som.

Uppington, co. Wilts. Covenant, etc.,
in, 1411. Add. 15301;—1559. Add.
15106.

Uppledecoume [? Letcombe Basset].
v. Letcombe —— (?), co. Berks.

Upsall, co. York. Grant in, late 12
cent. (Upsale). Add. 19922.

Upshire. v. sub Waltham H. Cross,
co. Essex.

Upthrop, [nr. Eatington], co. Worc.
Grant at (?), 869. Cott. MS. Aug.
ii. 76.

Upton. v. sub Payhembury, co. Devon.

Upton, co. Buck. Exchequer acquittance for a fine in, 1567. Add. 25895.

—— Sale in Chalvey in (?), 1586.
Lansd. 582.

—— Receipt of court-rolls of, 1599.
Harl. Roll CC. 10.

Upton, co. Chest. Brief conc. a fire at,
1820. Ch. Br. C. i. 5.

Upton, co. Essex. Conveyance in, 1496
(Uptoun). Harl. 49 C. 13.

Upton, in Hawkesbury, co. Glouc. Conf.
of grants at, to Pershore Abbey, 972
(Upton). Cott. MS. Aug. ii. 6.

—— Covenant in, with Pershore
Abbey, 1261. Harl. 44 H. 52.

Upton, co. Hunt. Power to give seisin
in, 1372. Add. 22609.

Upton, co. Linc. Grant in, 1303. Harl.
57 D. 12.

—— Perpet. Vicarius. Robertus, 1303.
Harl. 57 D. 12.

Upton, co. Norf. (?). Vicarius. Radulfus, 1408. Harl. 58 C. 32.

Upton, co. Northt. Grant of, by Hen.
II., with conf. by Rich. I., [1175?].
Add. 22486 (Uppetona juxta Nordh.);
—1190. Harl. 43 C. 27 (Ufethona
juxta Norhanth.).

—— Grant of the chapel by St.
Andrew's Priory, Northampton, t.
John (Huptona). Harl. 44 H. 34.

—— Grants, etc., in, 1325-1487. Add.
22487-22506;—1365. Add. 8131.

—— Dominus. Nic. de Cancellis,
1325, 1326, 1345. Add. 22487-22491,
22495.

Upton, [nr. Peterborough, co. Northt.?].
Grant of a moiety of the chapel to St.
Michael's Nunnery, Stamford, ante
1227. Add. 21153.

Upton, nr. Southwell, co. Nott. Sale of
a third share in the water-mill at,
1561. Woll. xi. 120.

Upton, co. Pembr. Conveyance of the
manor, 1441 (Oncketon). Harl. 80
A. 15.

Upton, in Badsworth, co. York. Grant
in, 1350. Lansd. 465.

Upton, co. York [the same?]. Grant
of, by Hen. VIII., 1510. Roy. Roll 14
B. xviii.

Upton Bishop, co. Heref. Grants,
etc., in, 1459. Harl. 112 D. 28 (Op-
ton Episcopi);—1494. Harl. 111 G.
42;—1628. Campb. xviii. 3;—1654.
Add. 1953.

—— Vicarius. Ric. Spyne, 1494.
Harl. 111 G. 42.

Upton Cheney, in Bitton, co. Glouc.
Fine in, 1626 (Upton). Add. 15831.

Upton on Severn, *co. Worc.* Grant, etc., in, late 13 cent. Slo. xxxiii. 9; —1476. Add. 24779.

—— *Ballivus.* Joh. Knottesford, 1502. Add. 24786.

—— *Rector.* Ric. Norys, 1411. Harl. 111 C. 20.

—————— Geo. Savage, 1502. Add. 24786.

Upton St. Leonard's, *co. Glouc.* Grant of the rectory to the See of Gloucester, 1541. Cott. xiii. 34.

Upton Warren, *co. Worc.* Briefs for rebuilding the church, 1782, 1789. Ch. Br. B. xxii. 4, xxix. 5.

Up Waltham. *v.* Waltham, Up, *co. Suss.*

Upway, *co. Dors. Rector.* Tho. Samson, 1465. Add. 19514.

Upwell, *cos. Camb. and Norf.* Papal conf. of a grant of eels in (?), to Huntingdon Priory, 1147 (Wella). Cott. MS. Aug. ii. 112.

—— Grant in, to West Dereham Abbey, early 13 cent. Add. 15519.

—— Grant of fishery betw. Laxwerp and Nordhale in a meadow at Wevinge in (?), etc., to W. Dereham Abbey, early 13 cent. Toph. 17.

—— Conf. in, by Qu. Alienora, to William, Bp. of Ely, [1255–6]. Cott. xvii. 6.

—— Leases in, by Ixworth Priory, 1355. Add. 18650; —1469. Add. 18761; —1479. Add. 9191.

—— Lease in, 1431. Add. 18717.

—— License for a grant in, from Mullicourt Priory to Ely Priory, 1446. Campb. xxvii. 29.

—— Sale in, of lands late bel. to Ixworth Priory, 1589. Add. 18867.

Vpwere. *v.* Weare, *co. Som.*

Upwick. *v. sub* Rochford, *co. Essex.*

Urchfont (Erchesfont, etc.), *co. Wilts.* Court-rolls of, bel. to St. Mary's Abbey, Winchester, 1378–1399. Add. 26906–26908; — 1498–1500. Add. 19724, 19725; —1516. Add. 19728; —1517. Add. 19727.

—— Compotus-rolls of, bel. to the same, *c.* 1450–60. Add. 19718; — 1460–1. Add. 19717; —1463–4. Add. 19719; —1464–5. Add. 19720; —1469– 70. Add. 19721; —1499–1500. Add. 19722; —*c.* 1500. Add. 19723; —1509–

10. Add. 19726; —1519. Add. 19729; —*c.* 1520–5. Add. 19730; —1531. Add. 19731.

—— Court-rolls of, bel. to Lord Hertford, 1546–1548. Add. 19732–19735 (Erchefount); —1588–9. Add. 19736, 19737.

Ure *al.* Yore, *River, co. York.* Grant on banks of, nr Masham, *co.* York, late Hen. II. (Jor.) Add. 7491.

—— Grant on banks of (in campo de Eowere), nr. Boroughbridge (?), *t.* Hen. III. Harl. 57 E. I.

Urlewik, Urlewyk, nr. *Yeldersley* (?), *co. Derb.* Release, etc., in, *t.* Edw. I. Woll. ix. 14; —1317. Woll. ix. 81.

Urnegill. *v.* Yearngill, *in Bromfield, co. Cumb.*

Urswick, *co. Lanc.* Papal conf. of the church to Furness Abbey, 1194 (Ursewic). Harl. 83 A. 22.

Vrtligburg. *v.* Irthlingborough, *co. Northt.*

Ury, *River, co. Aberdeen.* Grant on banks of, [1200–14] (Hury). Cott. xvi.i. 23.

Use, Aqua de. *v.* Ouse, *River.*

Usk, *co. Monm.* Inspex., in 1330, of a grant of St. Mary's church, etc., in, to Usk Priory, *c.* 1150 (Uska, Usca). Add. 5342.

—— Grants, etc., in, 1432. Add. 7148; —1458. Add. 5345; —1524. Add. 1817; —1528. Add. 1818; — 1529. Add. 1819, 1820; —1532. Add. 1345, 1821; —1537. Add. 1822.

—— Valor of Usk and Caerleon (Usko, Kerljon) manors, 1531–32. Harl. Roll N. 9.

—— Precipe on a covenant conc. land in, 1593. Add. 25129.

—— Grant of land in "Newe Market streete" to the provost, etc., of, 1598. Add. 5348.

—— Appointment of J. Williams as steward of the manor, 1691. Add. 5349.

—— *Senescallus.* Will. Herbert, *miles*; —*Magister Serviens.* Joh. ap Jankyn ap Madocke; —*Ballivus.* Hugo ap Jankyn; —*Aldremen.* Will. ap Johan., Grono a Gwelym Catchepol, David ap Gwatkyn, Hugo ap Greff. ap Ythell; —*Clericus.* Joh. Clerke, 1458. Add. 5345.

3 D

Waith (Wathe), co. Linc. Grant, etc., in, c. 1260. Add. 15765;—1338. Harl. 54 B. 36;—1348. Laud. 119.

—— Persona. Rog. Gayton, 1393. Harl. 57 E. 22.

Wakebridge, in Crich, co. Derb. Extents of the manor, 1350. Woll. xi. 13 (Wakebrugge);—1538. Woll. xi. 20 (Wakbrugg).

—— Court-roll, 1444. Woll. xi. 2 a, b.

—— Rentals of the manor, etc., t. Edw. IV. Woll. xi. 14 (Wakbrydgg); —1485. Woll. xi. 15 (Wakbrug), 16 (Wakbrygg);—1509. Woll. xi. 18 (do.).

—— Attestation of payment of chief rent to lords of the manor, 1544 (Whakebreg). Woll. xi. 8.

—— Grant of remainder of lease of the manor, 1594 (Wackbrige al. Wakbrige). Woll. xi. 54.

Wakefield al. Grange Wakefield. v. sub Kilworth, S., co. Leic.

Wakefield, co. York. Grant in, 1303 (Wakefeud). Add. 16671.

—— Charters witnessed by "toto Wapentaco de Wakefeld," t. Edw. II. Add. 7470, 7474.

—— Appropriation of the church to the chapter of York, 1348 (Wakefeld). Harl. 44 D. 21.

—— Crown lease in and around, 1555. Harl. 84 C. 32.

—— Court-roll, 1624. Add. 26132.

—— Release of fulling-mills on the Calder nr., 1630. Add. 19262.

—— Mortgage of water-mills in, 1647. Add. 19263.

—— Fine in, 1671. Add. 12681.

—— Briefs conc. fires at, 1762, 1770. Ch. Br. B. ii. 1. x. 1.

—— Rector. Dom. Will. Custance, 1348. Harl. 44 D. 21.

Wakering, Great and Little, co. Essex. Release of a rent charge in, late 13 cent. (Magna Wakeringe). Harl. 54 B. 22.

—— Fine of the manor, etc., 1541 (Wakeryngys). Add. 15868.

Wakerley, co. Northt. Conf. in, to Fineshade Priory, t. Rich. I.-John (Wakerl.). Harl. 49 G. 51.

—— Persona. Willelmus, t. Rich. I.-John. Harl. 49 G. 51.

Waketon. v. Wacton, co. Norf.

Walberswick, co. Suff. Covenant to build a steeple for the church, 1426. Add. 17631.

—— Will of Joh. Wulward of, 1486. Add. 17635.

—— Precipe on a covenant conc. the manor, 1592. Add. 25440.

Walcot. v. sub Barnack, co. Northt.

Walcot, nr. Folkingham, co. Linc. Grants, etc., in, [1153–6]. Harl. 50 F. 31 (Walcota);—1348. Add. 21158; —1577. Add. 6430.

Walcot, co. Oxon. Compotus, 1447–8. Harl. Roll C. 2.

Walcot, nr. Pershore, co. Worc. Clericus. Willelmus, early 13 cent. Add. 20427.

Walcote (Walcorte), co. Leic. Grants, etc., in, to Sulby Abbey, co. Northt., t. Hen. III. Add. 21839, 22507, 22508.

Walcote, in Granborough, co. Warw. Feoffment in, 1444. Cott. vi. 1.

Walcote, nr. Swindon, co. Wilts. Grant in, 1394. Harl. 83 F. 18.

Walcott (Walcote, etc.), co. Norf. Grants, etc., in, late 12 cent. Harl. 49 G. 22 (Wallekote);—t. Edw. I. Cott. xxx. 7 (Walcote);—1308. Cott. xxix. 25 (Walcotes);—1334. Cott. xxix. 26 (Walkote);—1335. Cott. xxix. 27, 28.

—— Covenant at, betw. Lecia de Thurkelbi and Langley Abbey, conc. dower, 1260. Cott. v. 52.

—— Grants, etc., of the manor, 1333. Harl. 47 I. 40;—1336. Harl. 47 I. 39, 57 D. 31, 32;—1337. Harl. 58 A. 46; —1344. Harl. 46 F. 11;—1366. Harl. 58 A. 49, 58 B. 1;—1387. Harl. 53 C. 38.

—— Extent of lands of T. Roscelyne in, 1352. Harl. 55 E. 33.

—— Fines of the manor, etc., 1381. Harl. 54 C. 28, 56 B. 35;—1382. Harl. 49 G. 43, 44;—1388. Harl. 49 I. 29.

—— Release of Syrewateres manor in, 1403. Harl. 46 D. 8 a, 49 G. 45.

—— Fine of same manor, 1405. Harl. 58 B. 19.

—— Grant of Walcott Easthall manor, 1423. Harl. 58 B. 14.

—— Conveyance, etc., of Walcott Westhall manor, 1429. Harl. 58 B. 17;—1431. Harl. 58 B. 16;—1434. Harl. 47 C. 44.

—— Grant of rent charge on Westhall manor, 1431. Harl. 57 A. 1.

Add. 23694;—1327. Add. 23695;—1329. Add. 23696; — 1335. Add. 23697;—1336. Add. 23698; — 1347. Add. 23699;—1351. Add. 23120;—1352. Add. 23700;—1357. Add. 23701;—1359. Add. 23702;—1363. Add. 23389; — 1364. Add. 23130 - 23132; — 1376. Add. 23189;—1387. Add. 23154; — 1455. Add. 22881, 22882;—1461. Add. 23190;—1478. Add. 23405, 23406; — 1502. Add. 24558, 24559;—1534. Add. 23205;—1556. Add. 23212; — 1591. Add. 23414, 23415.

—— Grants, etc., in, to St. Thomas's Hospital, Southwark, t. Hen. III. Add. 23652, 23673, 23674, 23679, 23681, 23682.

—— Assignment to Merton Priory of rents in, due from St. Thomas's Hospital, Southwark, post 1228. Add. 23012.

—— Bequest, lease, etc., of the manor, 1437. Add. 23177;—1540. Harl. 112 D. 41;—1593. Add. 23232; — 1597. Add. 23234.

—— Lease in, nr. the chapel of "our blessed Lady of the more" in, 1502. Add. 23409.

—— Transfer of lease of Wallington Place, 1607. Add. 23238.

—— Acquittances for fines for the manor, 1613-1642. Add. 23242-23268.

v. also Beddington, co. Surr.

v. also Carshalton, co. Surr.

**Wallington Hundred**, co. Surr. Accompt of collector of taxes in, 1570-1. Add. 8143.

—— Acquittance for composition money for provisions for the King's Household due from, 1623. Add. 23670.

**Wallingwella**, co. Nott. Grant in, late 13 cent. (Wallandewelles). Add. 21575.

—— Exchequer acquittance for the farm of, 1575. Add. 25634.

**Wallop**, nr. Caus, co. Salop. Grant, etc., in, 1323. Add. 20446;—1353. Add. 20447 (Walope).

—— Accompts of the receiver of the Duchess of Buckingham, 1472-3. Add. 22644.

**Wallop**, co. Southt. Inspex. in 1231 of a Papal conf. of a grant of the manor by Hen. II. to Fontevrauld Abbey, 1201. Add. 17861.

**Wallop, Nether,** co. Southt. Mortgage of the manor, 1572. Add. 16153.

—— Brief conc. a fire at, 1786. Ch. Br. B. xxvi. 4.

**Wallsbatch,** nr. Eardington, co. Salop. Grant in, 1391 (Walkesbache). Add. 8119.

**Walltun.** v. Walton on the Wolds, co. Leic.

**Walmesgate** (Walmesgare), co. Linc. Grant of the manor, c. 1292. Harl. 51 D. 31.

—— Grant in, to the Knts. Hospitallers, t. Edw. I. Harl. 52 E. 11.

—— Grants, etc., in, [1293-1309?]. Add. 21159;—c. 1314. Harl. 46 F. 36;—1316. Harl. 52 H. 15;—ante 1322. Harl. 52 H. 5, 6;—1325. Harl. 52 E. 12.

—— Conf. of grant in, to Barlings Abbey, 1310. Harl. 52 H. 13.

—— Capellanus. Willelmus, t. Hen. III. Harl. 44 D. 56, 54 D. 46.

—— Rector. Gulfridus, t. Hen. III. Harl. 50 F. 50, Cott. v. 35.

**Walmestone.** v. sub Wingham, co. Kent.

**Walpole,** co. Suff. Grants in, to Sibton Abbey, early 13 cent. Harl. 83 G. 33 (Walepol);—t. Edw. I. Harl. 84 B. 12 (do.).

—— Grants, etc., in, 1311. Harl. 55 F. 21 (Walpol);—1332. Harl. 48 A. 34 (Walepol);—1375. Harl. 49 C. 7, 83 G. 41;—1387. Harl. 55 E. 34 (Walpool);—1404. Harl. 55 C. 5;—1454. Harl. 48 B. 51 (Walpool).

—— Extract from court-roll, 1502. Add. 17259.

**Walpole [St. Andrew?],** co. Norf. Persons. Tho. de Lewes, 1340. Harl. 53 A. 20.

**Walpole [St. Peter?],** co. Norf. Grants in, t. Hen. III. Harl. 57 D. 50, 57 E. 46.

**Walsall,** co. Staff. Grant in, t. Edw. II. (Walsale). Cott. xxvii. 154.

—— Brief conc. a fire at, 1815. Ch. Br. B. lvi. 5.

—— Brief for rebuilding the church, 1820. Ch. Br. C. i. 6.

—— Perpet. Vicarius. Walterus, 1272 (Waleshale). Harl. 53 E. 49, 50.

**Walshall Isle,** [in N. Cave?], co. York. Bond on sale of the manor, 1593. Harl. 77 F. 30.

**Warley,** *co. York.* Fine in, 1594. Add. 15666.

**Warley, Little,** *co. Essex.* Grant in, 1592 (Warley Senelles *al.* parva). Add. 26580.

**Warlingham,** *co. Surr.* Grants, etc., in, 1339. Add. 24560 ;—1355. Add. 20038 ;—1440. Add. 23730 ;—1451. Add. 23656 ; — 1485. Add. 24565, Harl. 78 E. 48 ;—1499. Harl. 86 H. 22.

**Warmecombe,** *in Buckfastleigh, co. Devon.* Acquittance for homage for lands in, held of Maynebowe manor, 1618. Add. 7890.

**Warmingham,** *co. Chest.* Briefs for rebuilding the church, 1787, 1794. Ch. Br. B. xxvii. 5, xxxiv. 2.

——*Persona.* Rich. Longespey, 1337 (Wermyncham). Cott. xxix. 87.

**Warmington,** *co. Northt.* Discharge for Crown dues in, 1392 (Wermyngton). Harl. 49 D. 54.

—— Grants in, 1424, 1437 (do.). Add. 738 *a, b.*

**Warmington,** *co. Warw.* Suit in, against Preaux Abbey, in Normandy, 1284, 1285 (Warmynton). Cott. iv. 14 (3, 4) *(copies.)*

**Warminster,** *co. Wilts.* Grants, etc., in, [1291–2?]. Add. 26695 (Weremenistr.) *(copy)* ;—1295. Add. 26696 (Weremenystre) ;—1296. Add. 26697 (do.) ;—*t.* Edw. I. Add. 26699–26702, 26709 (Wereministre, etc.); — 1305. Add. 26705 (Wermenstr.); — 1356. Add. 26712 (do.) ;—1410. Add. 26717 (do.) ;—1418. Add. 26718 (do.) ;— 1440. Add. 26719 ;—1471. Harl. 76 A. 41 (Warmester).

—— Grants in Bugley (Bugelighe, Bogelegh, Bokele) in, *t.* Edw. I. Add. 26708 ;—1326. Add. 26710 ;—1359. Add. 26713 ;—1362. Add. 26714 ;— 1369. Add. 26715.

—— Grant in Smallbrook in, 1327. Add. 26711.

—— Acquittance for payments in, to the Honour of Gloucester, 1374. Add. 26716.

—— Feoffment, etc., of Smallbrook manor in, 1442. Add. 26720 ;—1585. Eg. 300 ;—1592. Eg. 301.

—— Acquittance for payments for Smallbrook manor, 1471. Add. 26721.

—— *Vicar.* John Carpynter, 1471. Harl. 76 A. 41.

**Warmscombe,** *nr. Watlington, co. Oxon.* Fine of the manor, 1334 (Warmodescoumbe). Harl. Roll G. 17 (4).

**Warmsworth,** *co. York.* Marriage settlement in, 1698. Add. 18059, 18060.

**Warmwell,** *co. Dors.* Grant of St. Mary's church to Holme Priory, *t.* Steph. (Warmewelle). Add. 24879 (9) *(copy).*

—— *Persona.* Robertus, *Diaconus, t.* Steph. Add. 24879 (9).

**Warnborough, North,** *in Odiham, co. Southt.* Precipe on a covenant conc. land in, 1578. Add. 25230.

**Warnborough, South,** *co. Southt.* Fine of the manor, 1183 (Warneburne). Harl. 49 A. 3.

—— *Rector.* Tho. Hathy, 1442. Add. 26720.

**Warnham** (Wernham, etc.), *co. Suss.* Grants, etc., in, *t.* Edw. I. Add. 8795, 18562, 18583 (Warenham); — 1299. Add. 8809 ; — 1302. Add. 8810 ;— 1309. Lansd. 678 ; — 1315. Add. 8815 ;—1317. Add. 8817, 8819 (Woruham), 18607 ;—1332. Add. 18626 ;— 1333. Add. 8821 ;—1335. Add. 8822 ; —1336. Add. 8824 ;—1345. Add. 8828 ;—1346. Add. 18638–18640 ;— 1362. Add. 8835 ;—1369. Add. 18660 ; —1381. Add. 18608 ;—1388. Add. 18669 (Werham) ;—1391. Add. 8848, 18674 ;—1395. Add. 8849, 18682 ;— *t.* Hen. IV. Add. 18661 ;—1402. Add. 8856 ; — 1404. Add. 8857, 8859 ;— 1405. Add. 8858, 18692 ;—1408. Add. 8860 ;—1410. Add. 8861 ;—1418. Add. 9064 ;—1419. Add. 18704 (Warnaham); — 1421. Add. 8867 ; — 1425. Add. 8871 ;—1426. Add. 8872, 8873, 18711 – 18714 ; — 1427. Add. 8874, 18715 ; — 1434. Add. 8876, 9067, 18721 ;—1440. Add. 18735 ;—1442. Add. 18740, 18742 ; — 1450. Add. 8887, 18747 ;—1452. Add. 8888–8890, 18750, 18751 ;—1453. Add. 8891 ;— 1456. Add. 8896 ;—1457. Add. 8897 ; —1459. Add. 8898 ;—*t.* Edw. IV. Add. 8900 ;—1473. Add. 8902 ;— 1474. Add. 18767 ; — 1475. Add. 8905 ; — 1476. Add. 1007 ; — 1482. Add. 18771 ; — 1484. Add. 18773 – 18776 ;—1489. Add. 18778, 18779 ;— 1490. Add. 8908 ;—1491. Add. 18782 ; —1492. Add. 8909 ;—1494. Add. 18784, 18785 ;—1495. Add. 18786 ;— 1497. Add. 8911, 8912, 18787 ;—1498. Add. 8913 ; — 1499. Add. 18788,

3 E

3 E 2

Watelaund. *v. sub* Boxford, *co. Suf.*

Watelesfeld. *v.* Wattisfield, *co. Suf.*

Wateley. *v.* Wheatley, *co. Southt.*

Water Eaton. *v. sub* Bletchley, *co. Buck.*

—— *v. sub* Kidlington, *co. Oxon.*

Water Fryston. *v.* Fryston, Water, *co. York.*

Water Hastings. *v.* Eaton Hastings, *co. Berks.*

Water Newton. *v.* Newton, Water, *co. Hunt.*

Watercumbe. *v.* Whatcombe, *in Winterborne Whitchurch, co. Dors.*

Waterfall, *co. Staf.* Briefs for rebuilding the church, 1777, 1789. Ch. Br. B. xvii. 1, xxix. 6.

Waterford, *County of.* Compotus of W. de Rupella, as sheriff, 1261-2. Add. 26515 (1).

—— Escheats in, 1341-1344. Add. 13597.

—— Grant in the Barony of Decies, 1655. Add. 19264.

—— Petitions from Protestants of, on the Act of Resumption, 1702. Add. 19528, 19531.

Waterford, *co. Waterford.* Grant of, to H. de Valoniis, 1193 (Waterfordia). Lansd. 33.

—— Rolls of pleas at, 1290, 1330. Add. 13598, 13599.

Waterhall. *v. sub* Brayfield, Cold, *co. Buck.*

Waterholme, *in Stonegrave, co. York.* Grant in, *c.* 1295 (Waterholme prope Nesse). Harl. 112 C. 6.

Waterlynge. *v.* Wartling, *co. Suss.*

Waterperry, *co. Oxon.* Grant of the manor, with lands in Ledehale in, 1409 (Waterpury). Add. 6101.

Watersfield. *v. sub* Waltham, Cold, *co. Suss.*

Waterside House, *in Barton, co. Westm.* Brief conc. a fire at, 1813. Ch. Br. B. liii. 10.

Waterthorpe, *in Beighton, co. Derb.* Lease, etc., in, 1328. Camp. viii. 17 (Walterthorpe);—1330. Campb. i. 1 (do.).

Waterton, *nr. Garthorpe, in Isle of Axholme. co. Linc.* Rentals, 1510, 1512. Add. 24184 a, b.

—— Sale of a third part of the manor, 1520. Add. 24168.

Wateviles Manor. *v. sub* Chelsham, *co. Surr.*

Watfeld. *v.* Whatfield, *co. Suf.*

Watford, *co. Hertf.* Marriage settlement of rents from Brightwell (Bretewell) mill and lands in, early 13 cent. Harl. 86 A. 56.

—— Grant in, 1465. Add. 24494.

—— Bond for rent of woods at Wiggenhall in, 1583. Harl. 78 H. 17.

—— Court-rolls of Wiggenhall *al.* Oxhey Walround manor, 1647. Add. 18141;—1664. Add. 18144.

Watford, *co. Northt.* Conf. of grants in, to Sulby Abbey, early Hen. III. (Wathforde). Add. 22510.

—— Grants, etc., in, *t.* Hen. III. Cott. xxx. 19;—1408. Add. 15877;—1415. Add. 22511;—1416. Harl. 47 F. 8, Add. 22512;—1439. Add. 22513.

—— Acquittance for service at Newcastle for land in, 1322. Add. 21506.

—— *Persona.* Willelmus, end of 12 cent. Add. 22473 (Wathford);—early Hen. III. Add. 22510 (do.).

—— *Vicarius. Dom.* Reginald Boneton, 1416. Harl. 47 F. 8.

Wath upon Dearne (Wath, Wath super Dyrne), *co. York.* Grants in Brampton Bierlaw, Newhall, etc., in, 1319. Harl. 83 D. 48;—1358. Harl. 83 E. 56;—1361. Harl. 83 E. 23;—1363. Harl. 84 B. 30;—1364. Harl. 84 B. 34;—1365. Harl. 83 E. 55;—1375. Harl. 83 D. 4.

—— Covenant for a settlement of Thornhill Hall manor, etc., in, 1420. Add. 17046.

—— *Vicarius.* Tho. Whytby, 1479. Harl. 57 B. 34.

Wathall cum Houghton, [*nr. Tetney?*], *co. Linc.* Fine of the manor, 1638. Woll. xi. 29.

Wathamstede. *v.* Wheathampstead, *co. Hertf.*

Wathe. *v. sub* Cove, North, *co. Suf.*

—— *v.* Waith, *co. Linc.*

Watingdon. *v. sub* Coulsdon, *co. Surr.*

Watlas. *v.* Thornton Watlass, *co. York.*

Watling Street. A boundary mark in *co.* Northt., 944 (Wæclinga stræt). Cott. MS. Aug. ii. 63.

—— Foundation of Markyate Priory. *co.* Bedf., adjoining, [1145] (Wallingbestret). Cott. xi. 6.

Wealthæminga mearc. *v.* Waltham, Bishop's, *co. Southt.*

Wear. *v. sub* Chislett, *co. Kent.*

—— *v. sub* Stretton Sugwas, *co. Heref.*

Weardale, *co. Durh.* Power to give seisin of lands on banks of River Wear (Were) in, betw. Harperley Burn and Stanhope Park, 1423 (Wardale). Lansd. 624.

—— License for enclosure in the forest of, 1449 (Werdale). Woll. v. 6.

Weare, *co. Som.* Grants, etc., in, 1346. Add. 6502 (Netherwere);—1347. Add. 6503 (burgus de Were);—1390. Add. 6534 (Burghwere);—1524. Add. 6363 (Weer), 6544 (do.).

—— Bond conc. Upper Weare (Upwere) manor, 1458. Add. 5469.

—— Court-rolls, 1603-4 (Weere burgus). Add. 26507.

Wearne. *v. sub* Pitney, *co. Som.*

Webton (Webbeton), *co. Heref.* Lease, etc., of the manor, 1342. Add. 4594; —1440. Add. 4603;—1446. Harl. 111 E. 2.

—— Grants in, 1348. Add. 4597, 4598;—1407. Add. 4600.

Wechet. *v.* Watchet, *co. Som.*

Wedale, *Forest of, co. Roxb.* Conf. of pasture in, to Melrose Abbey, with declaration of bounds, [1174 ?] (Wedal). Cott. xviii. 18 (*copy*).

Wedenesberwe. *v.* Woodnesborough, *co. Kent.*

Wedenhala. *v. sub* Waltham, *co. Kent.*

Wedfield, *in E. Putford* (?), *co. Devon.* Settlement in, 1430 (Wydefyld). Add. 13052.

Wedhampton, *nr. Urchfont, co. Wilts.* Court-rolls of, bel. to St. Mary's Abbey, Winchester, 1500. Add. 19725;— 1517. Add. 19727.

—— Court-rolls of, bel. to Lord Hertford, 1546-1548. Add. 19732-19735.

Wedmore, *co. Som.* Kalendar of lands in, *t.* Edw. III. Add. 6550.

Wednesley. *v.* Wensley, *in Darley, co. Derb.*

Wedyngton. *v.* Waddington, *co. Linc.* (?).

Weedon, *co. Buck.* Conf., by Edw. the Confessor, of a grant in, to Westminster Abbey, 1066 [*sc.* 1065] (Weodune). Cott. vi. 2 (*copy*).

Weedon, *co. Northt.* Grant of rent in, to St. Andrew's Priory, Northampton, *t.* Hen. III. (Wedon). Harl. 54 C. 52.

Weedon Pinkeney *al.* **Weedon** Loes, *co. Northt.* Lease in, by Biddlesdon Abbey, 1535 (Wedon Pynkeney *al.* Loyeswedon). Harl. 84 F. 23.

—— Bond conc. the manor and parsonage, 1575 (Wedon Pynkeney *al.* Luis Wedon). Harl. 86 B. 3.

—— *Vicarius.* Willelmus, late Hen. II. Cott. v. 34.

Weeford, *co. Staff.* Marriage settlement of two parts of Swinfen, etc., in, *t.* Rich. I. Cott. xxiii. 24.

—— Grant in Swinfen (Swynefen), 1343. Add. 20474.

—— Briefs for rebuilding the church, 1767, 1802. Ch. Br. B. vii. 10, xlii. 6.

Week *al.* Wyck, *in Binsted, co. Southt.* Lease, etc., in, 1333. Add. 26625 (Wyke juxta Bynstede);—1357. Add. 17414 (Le Wyke).

Week *al.* Wick Fitz Paine. *v. sub* Stoke Courcy, *co. Som.*

Weeks (Wykes, etc.), *co. Essex.* Grants, etc., in, 1336. Harl. 55 C. 29;—*t.* Edw. III. Harl. 55 C. 40 (Wykys);— 1392. Harl. 55 C. 37, 41, 42;—1468. Harl. 55 C. 44.

Weel, *co. York.* Lease in, 1573 (Wele). Add. 886.

Weeley, *co. Essex.* Suit conc. tithes in, *c.* 1680. Add. 15871.

—— *Rector.* Rich. Cook, *c.* 1673. Add. 15871.

Ween. *v.* St. Wenn, *co. Cornw.*

Weenham. *v. sub* Rogate, *co. Suss.*

Weer. *v.* Weare, *co. Som.*

Weethley, *co. Warw.* Release of the manor to Evesham Abbey, 1350 (Wytheleye). Cott. xxvii. 193.

Weeting, *co. Norf. Rector.* Joh. Smyth, 1421 (Wetyng). Harl. 48 D. 15.

Weeton, *in Harewood, co. York.* Grants, etc., in, 1343. Harl. 112 B. 38 (Wytheton);—1344. Harl. 111 G. 19 (do.);— 1395. Harl. 112 D. 13 (Wheton);— 1488. Harl. 112 A. 62 (Weton).

Weetslade, North, *co. Northumb.* Grant in, 1284 (Northewydalade). Add. 7368.

Weeverynghope, *Den of.* *v. sub* Hawkhurst, *co. Kent.*

**Weldon, Great, with Little Weldon** (Weledon, Weledun, Magna Weledon, etc.), *co. Northt (continued). Persona (continued).* Joh. Lucas, 1414. Add. 7565.

—— *Rector.* Willelmus, late 13 cent. Add. 743 ;—(as *persona*). Add. 7523, 7533.

—— —— Will Morley *al.* Morlee, 1402, 1403. Add. 776–779 ;—(as *persona*), 1404. Harl. 48 H. 3.

—— —— Arnald Ymberd, 1455. Add. 864.

—— —— Joh. Stumble, 1472. Add. 813, 7579.

**Wele.** *v* Weel, *co. York.*

**Welewe.** *v.* Wellow, *co. Som.*

**Welford,** *co. Berks.* Grant at, 949 (Welig forda). Cott. MS. Aug. ii. 44.

**Welford,** *cos. Glouc. and Warw.* Power to give seisin of rent-charge on the manor, 1315 (Welneford). Add. 21421.

—— Grant of the rectory to the see of Gloucester, 1541. · Cott. xiii. 34.

—— Recovery in, 1608. Add. 7040.

**Welford, with Sulby,** *co. Northt.* Grants, etc., in, to Sulby Abbey, [1156–70]. Add. 22514 (Welleford) :—*t.* Hen. II. Add. 22519 (do.) :—late 12 cent. Add. 22420 (Sulebi), 22421 (do.) ;—*t.* John. Add. 22518 (Welleford), 22520 (do.) ;—early Hen. III. Add. 7546 (do.) ;—*t.* Hen. III. Add. 5875 (Welleford), 7515 (do.), 7530 (do.), 7532 (Sulcby), 22515 – 22517 (Welleford), 22521 (do.) ;—late Hen. III.–*t.* Edw. I. Add. 21671 (Suleby), 21673 (do.), 22426 (do.), 22429 (do.), 22431 (do.), 22432 (do.), 22435 (do.), 22436 (do.), 22441 (do.) ;—*c.* 1320. Add. 22403 (Welleford) ;—1327. Add. 22442 (do.) ;—1348. Harl. 43 D. 45 (do.), 58 C. 35 (Suleby) ;—1437. Add. 22445 (do.).

—— Release of Welford church, etc., to Sulby Abbey, *t.* Hen. II. (Welleford). Add. 22519.

—— Covenant to acquit the vill of Sulby (Sulebi) from knight's service, etc., *t.* John. Add. 22438.

—— Covenant with Sulby Abbey conc. pasturage in, 1225 (Welleford). Add. 22522.

—— Grants, etc., in, early Hen. III. Add. 22439 (Soleby) :—*t.* Hen. III.–*t.* Edw I. Add. 21672 (Suleby), 22077 (Welleford), 22425 (Soleby), 22440

(Suleby) ; —[1436?]. Add. 22415 (do.) :—1593. Add. 22461 (Sulbye) : —1650. Add. 6127 (Welford) ; — 1685. Add. 5375, 5376.

—— —— Land held in Sulby (Soleby) by Sulby church and Sulby Abbey, *t.* Hen. III. Add. 22425.

—— —— Bond by Sulby Abbey conc. distraint by Westminster Abbey on Sulby manor, 1257. Add. 22423.

—— —— Bond of warranty to Sulby Abbey for Sulby manor, 1258. Add. 22422.

—— —— Moneys paid by Sulby Abbey on purchase of same manor, [1258]. Add. 22431.

—— —— Grant in Sulby, etc., by Sulby Abbey, [1276 –c. 1280]. Add. 22430.

—— —— Covenant of Sulby Abbey conc. a pension to Monks Kirby Priory from Welford manor, 1336 (Welleford). Add. 22523.

—— —— License to Sulby Abbey to appropriate Sulby church, 1360. Add. 24321.

—— —— Release of Welford manor, 1364. Harl. 112 A. 11.

—— —— Descent of land in, 1447. Add. 5998, 5999.

—— —— Acquittances to Sulby Abbey from Westminster Abbey for rent of Sulby manor, 1509–1527. Add. 22447–22456 ;—1537. Add. 6065.

—— —— Extract conc. suit of Sulby Abbey in, 1522. Add. 22460.

—— —— Licenses to alienate lands in, 1560. Add. 5367 ;—1565. Add. 5368; —1570. Add. 5369 ;—1604. Add. 5373.

—— —— Livery in, 1595. Add. 5371, 5372.

—— —— *Persona de Sulebi.* Henricus, *t.* John. Add. 22007.

—— —— —— *de Suleby.* Helias, early Hen. III. Add. 5871.

—— —— —— *de Soleby.* Ricardus, *t.* Hen. III. Add. 21355, 22439.

—— —— *Rector de Suleby. Dom.* Walterus, *t.* Hen. III.–Edw. I. Add. 22441.

—— —— *Sacerdos de Sulebi.* Robertus, late 12 cent. Add. 22420.

—— —— *Vicarius de Welleford.* Eraaldus, *Capellanus,* late 13 cent. Add. 22077.

—— —— —— *Dom.* Philippus, late 13 cent. Add. 22082, 22334.

—— —— —— Joh. Stormesworthe, 1377. Add. 22524.

**Welgby.** *v.* Willoughby, *co. Linc.*

**Welham,** *co. Leic.* Grant, etc., in, 1376. Add. 26940;—1445. Add. 804.

**Welham,** *in Clareborough,* co *Nott.* Grants, etc., in, 1276. Harl. 84 B. 27 (Wellum);—1286. Cott. xxvi. 16;—1457. Add. 16948, 16949 (Wellum); —1514. Add. 17004 (Wellom);—1520. Add. 24168 (do.).

**Welham Moorhouse,** *in Clareborough, co. Nott.* Grants, etc., in, 1361. Cott. xxviii. 96 (Wellum Morhous);—1383. Add. 16838 (Wellum Morehowses), 16856 (do.).

**Welhous, Le.** *v. sub* London. Par. of St. Mary Abchurch.

**Welig forda.** *v.* Welford, *co. Berks.*

**Welintona.** *v.* Wellington, *co. Salop.*

**Well,** *in Ickham, co. Kent.* Feoffment, etc., in, 1345. Harl. 51 G. 51;—1403. Add. 20004;—1548. Harl. 75 E. 22; —1551. Harl. 75 E. 28.

—— Grants, etc., in Ailsham (Elisham, Eylesham, Aylysham, etc.) woods in or nr., 1367. Harl. 80 A. 12;—1405. Harl. 80 G. 56;—1418. Harl. 77 F. 11;—1445. Harl. 79 C. 59, 60.

—— Fine in, 1548. Harl. 75 H. 4, 76 H. 50.

**Well,** *co. Linc.* Grant in, late 12 cent. (Wellia). Harl. 57 F. 48. ·

—— Covenant with St. Katharine's Priory, Lincoln, conc. tithes due to the chapel of, 1220 (Welle). Harl. 57 F. 51.

—— Conveyance, etc., of the manor and advowson, 1355. Harl. 57 G. 11; —[1361-8]. Harl. 55 B. 24.

—— *Clericus.* Willielmus, *t.* John. Harl. 45 E. 41, 50 A. 28.

—— *Persona.* Symon, early Hen. III. Harl. 48 A. 3.

—— —— Willelmus, 1232. Harl. 44 D. 55.

—— *Rector Capelle.* Willelmus, *Capellanus,* 1220. Harl. 57 F. 51.

—— —— *Dom.* Walterus, late 13 cent. Harl. 52 A. 25.

**Wella.** *v.* Upwell, *cos. Camb. and Norf.*

**Wellbury.** *v. sub* Offley, Gt., *co. Hertf.*

**Welle.** *v. sub* Itchinfield, *co. Suss.*

**Welle, La.** *v. sub* Hoo St. Werburgh, *co. Kent.*

**Welle Park.** *v. sub* Skendleby, *co. Linc.*

**Welleburnia.** *v.* Welbourne, *co. Linc.*

**Welledun.** *v.* Weldon, *co. Northt.*

**Welleford.** *v.* Welford, *co. Northt.*

**Welles.** *v. sub* Offley, Gt., *co. Hertf.*

**Wellesbourne Hastings,** *co. Warw.* Sales in, 1591. Harl. 79 F. 18, 19.

**Wellesbourne Mountford,** *co. Warw.* Covenant as to descent of the manor, and recovery of same, 1496. Add. 5684;—1500. Add. 5685 a.

**Welletone,** etc. *v.* Welton in the Marsh, *co. Linc.*

—— *v.* Welton le Wold, *co. Linc.*

**Welleues.** *v.* Welwyn, *co. Hertf.*

**Wellhous, Le.** *v. sub* London. Par. of St. Mary Abchurch.

**Wellingborough,** *co. Northt.* Release in, 1344 (Wendlingburghe). Add. 22587.

—— License from Croyland Abbey to assign lands in, to the Guild of St. Mary, 1392 (Wendlyngburgh). Harl. 44 C. 58.

—— *Vicarius. Dom.* Ric. Quenton, 1360. Add. 22180.

**Wellingore,** *co. Linc. Sacerdos.* Willelmus, *t.* Hen. II. (Wellinghoure). Harl. 54 D. 31, 56 C. 47.

**Wellington,** *co. Heref.* Lease, etc., in, 1593. Add. 1867;—1600. Add. 1879.

**Wellington,** *co. Salop.* Inspex. in 1319 of a grant in, by Hen. II. to Wombridge Priory, [1181]. (Waletona). Cott. iv. 36 (3).

—— Grant of the manor in dower, c. 1222 (Welintona). Cott. xxiv. 17.

—— Grant in, 1384 (Welyntone) Cott. v. 8.

—— Exchequer acquittance for tenths in, 1595. Add. 25688.

—— *Vicar.* John Jordan, 1595. Add. 25688.

**Wellom, Wellum.** *v.* Welham, *in Clareborough, co. Nott.*

**Wellow,** *in Shalfleet (?), Isle of Wight. Clericus.* Robertus, *t.* Hen. II. (Wailie). Harl. 112 E. 15.

Widepole. *v.* Withypoole, *co. Som.*

Widheme, Nortwidhem. *v.* Witham, North, *co. Linc.*

Widkehale. *v.* Witbcall, *co. Linc.*

Widma, Widme, Aqua de. *v.* Witham, *River, co. Linc.*

Widma, Nord. *v.* Witham, North, *co. Linc.*

Widmerpool, *co. Nott.* Covenant for conveyance in, 1571 (Widmerepole). Woll. xi. 51.

Widnes, *co. Lanc.* Release of dower in, 1270 (Wydnes). Harl. 52 H. 43 *b.*

—— Claims of Hen., Duke of Lancaster, to the Lordship of, 1351-60. Add. 26838 (*copy*).

Wield *al.* Weald, *co. South.* License for Newark Priory to celebrate in their oratory at, 1248-9. Cott. xvi. 46.

—— Decree in suit betw. Newark Priory and the rector, 1283 (Walda). Cott. MS. Nero C. iii. f. 218.

—— Resignation of the rector, 1291 (Walda). Harl. 45 C. 48.

—— Crown grant of the rectory, etc., late bel. to Newark Priory, 1549 (Weld Episcopi). Add. 4607.

—— Fine of the manor, 1591 (Welde). Add. 8467.

—— *Rector. Mag.* Ricardus, *c.* 1200. Cott. MS. Nero C. iii. f. 218.

—— —— *Dom.* Joh. de Arundel, 1283. Cott. MS. Nero C. iii. f. 218;—1291. Harl. 45 C. 48.

Wieme, Nordwiema. *v.* Witham, North, *co. Linc.*

Wiernia. *v.* Withern, *co. Linc.*

Wierton. *v. sub* Boughton Monchelsea, *co. Kent.*

Wifærmersc, *nr.* Polstead, *co. Suff.* Bequest of land at, *post* 991. Harl. 43 C. 4.

Wigan, *co. Lanc.* Covenant conc. title deeds of the advowson, 1394. Add. 17686.

—— Grant in, 1499. Add. 17711.

—— Signatures of adherents to the Commonwealth at, 1650. Add. 7180.

—— Briefs conc. fires at, 1797, 1802. Ch. Br. B. xxxvii. 8, xlii. 4.

—— *Major.* Hugo del Mersh, 1418. Add. 17690, 17691.

—— —— Joh. Pemberton, 1499. Add. 17711.

Wigan, *co. Lanc. (continued).* *Persona.* Walt. de Cuumpedoue, 1365. Add. 4859.

—— —— Joh. Langton *al.* Longton, 1485. Add. 17707.

Wigborough. *v. sub* Petherton, South, *co. Som.*

Wigborough, Lit., *co. Essex.* Precipe on a covenant conc. lands in, 1555. Add. 24927.

Wigenholte, Wighenholt, *co.*——(?). *Clericus.* Johannes, [1202?]. Add. 7203, 7204, 20593.

Wigera ceastre scire. *n.* Worcester, *County of.*

Wigestana. *v.* Wigston, Lit., *co. Leic.*

Wigford. *v. sub* Lincoln, *co. Linc.*

Wiggangeat, *co. Worc.* (?). Conf. of grants at, to Pershore Abbey, 972. Cott. MS. Aug. ii. 6.

Wiggebeare, Wiggebere. *v. sub* Petherton, South, *co. Som.*

Wiggelee, Wiggeley. *v.* Wigley, *in* Brampton, *co. Derb.*

Wiggen. *v. sub* Bardwell, *co. Suff.*

Wiggenhall *al.* Oxhey Walround. *v. sub* Watford, *co. Herif.*

Wiggenhall ——(?), *co. Norf.* License for a grant of Towts in, from Mullicourt Priory to Ely Priory, 1446 (Wygnale). Campb. xxvii. 29.

Wiggenhall St. Germans, *co. Norf.* Conf. of St. German's church to Norwich Priory, *c.* 1180. Cott. ii. 21 (7) (*copy*).

—— Rent bond in, to West Dereham Abbey, *c.* 1240 (par. S. Germani de Wygehale). Toph. 9.

—— Grant of lands betw. Setchy and, *t.* Hen. III (Wygehale). Add. 8389.

—— Rental in, of W. Dereham Abbey, *t.* Edw. I. (par. S. Germani). Add. 689.

—— Covenant on a marriage settlement in, 1457 (Wyginall). Harl. 54 A. 3, 4.

—— Recovery in, 15 cent. Harl. 58 G. 17 (*dors*).

Wiggenhall St. Mary Magdalen, *co. Norf.* Rental in, of W. Dereham Abbey, *t.* Edw. I. (par. S. M. Magdalene). Add. 689.

Wilmarston, co. Heref. Conf. of a grant in, nr. Alrenemor. etc., early 13 cent. Add. 20416 (Wilmeston);— 1326. Add. 1312 (Wylmeston).

Wilmerisley. v. Womersley, co. York.

Wilmington, co. Kent. Recovery of Grandisons manor, etc., in, 1628. Add. 1530.

Wilmington, in Priston, co. Som. Fine, etc., of the manor, 1329. Eg. 260 (Wylmyndon);—1363. Eg. 336 (Wilmyngton).

Wilmington, co. Suss. Royal grant of the bailiwick of Endelenewyk in, 1872. Cott. xv. 1.

Wilmslow, co. Chest. Bond in, 1594. Harl. 111 F. 29.

Wilne, co. Derb. Fine for heritage in, c. 1200. Add. 5235.

—— Bequest to the church, 1502 (Kyrk Wyllne). Woll. i. 81.

Wilnecote (Wylmyncote), co. Warw. Grants in, 1356. Add. 21444;—1412. Add. 15740.

—— Brief for rebuilding the chapel, 1821. Ch. Br. O. ii. 6.

Wilrincga werpa. v. Worlingworth, co. Suff.

Wilsden, nr. Bradford, co. York. Conff. of grants in, to Byland Abbey, post 1194. Add. 7477 (Wlsiden) (copy);— [1232-40]. Add. 7465 (Wlsynden) (copy);—ante 1298. Add. 7438 (Wlsiden).

—— Lease in, 1306 (Willsidene). Add. 8282.

Wilsdon. v. Willesden, co. Midd.

Wilsford, co. Linc. Rector. Dom. Stpph. le Eyr, 1332 (Wilford). Harl. 47 C. 32, 33.

—— Persona. Tho. Baudewyn, 1408. Add. 21032.

Wilsford, co. Wilts. Transfer of lands and tithes in, from Fontenelle Abbey to the see of Salisbury, c. 1207 (Wiuelesford). Add. 8071.

—— Compotus-rolls of, bel. to the Duke of Buckingham, 1499 - 1500, 1511-12. Add. 26873, 26874.

Wilsley, in Great Sherston, co. Wilts. Grant in, 1308 (Wyuelesleye). Cott. xxiii. 28.

Wilson, co. Leic. Grant in, to Langley Priory, early Hen. II. (Wiueles-tunia). Harl. 111 F. 59.

—— Clericus. Johannes, 1345 (Weueleston). Lansd. 636.

Wilsthorpe, co. Derb. Mortgage (?) of the manor, 1647 (Wilstrupp). Harl. 111 F. 46.

Wilsthorpe, co. Linc. Grant in, 1491 (Willesthorp). Add. 6468.

Wiltesden. v. Wilden, co. Bedf.

Wilting, nr. Hollington, co. Suss. Exchequer acquittance for farm of the manor, 1595. Add. 25672.

Wilton, nr. Ross, co. Heref. Grants, etc., in the fee or domain of, t. Edw. I. Eg. 350;—1431. Harl. 111 D. 37;— 1492. Harl. 112 C. 11.

—— Constabularius. Nicholsus, clericus, post 1220. Harl. 47 G. 35.

—— Senescallus. [Will.?] de Parco, post 1220. Harl. 47 G. 35.

Wilton, co. Som. Compotus of lands of Taunton Priory in, 1438-9 (Fons Georgii). Add. 25873.

Wilton, co. Wilts. Council held at, 838-9 (Uuiltun). Cott. MS. Aug. ii. 20, 3ᵈ.

—— Ch. of Æthelwulf dated at, 854 (Uuiltun). Cott. MS. Aug. ii. 46.

—— Power to give seisin in, 1385 (Wylton). Harl. 56 A. 35.

—— Extract from court-roll, 1533. Harl. 58 F. 28.

—— Rental of the manor, 1544. Harl. Roll N. 25.

—— Fine in, 1615. Add. 15153.

—— Major. Hen. Haveresham, 1375. Harl. 45 A. 37.

—— Coronatores. Joh. Cole, Nic. Vyniter. Tho. Wysdom, Hen. Bount(?), 1375. Harl. 45 A. 37.

—— Clericus. Rogerus, early Hen. II. Add. 18208 (1, 2), 18215 (copies).

—— Rector eccl. B. Marie in Bredstreet de. Ric. Marten, 1515. Harl. 53 D. 11.

Wiltonysplace. v. sub Shaftesbury, co. Dors.

Wilts, County of. Inquis. post mortem of Alured de Lincoln in, 1264. Add. 24879 (1) (copy).

—— Compotus-rolls of scutage of Hen. of Lancaster in, 1315. Harl. Roll K. 13;—1318-24. Harl. Roll H. 20.

—— Order conc. lands of Sir Joh. de Lortie in, 1340. Harl. 43 D. 39.

—— Bequests to churches in, by Nic. de Bonham, 1386. Add. 15174.

Winchelsea, *co. Suss. (continued).*
*Major (continued).* Tho. Thonder, *jun.*,
1420-1. Add. 20206.

—— —— Joh. Silton *al.* Sylton,
1463. Add. 20209; — 1468. Add.
24869.

—— —— Hen. Fissh, 1476. Add.
24871.

—— *Bullivus.* Tho. Alard, 1297-1306.
Add. 8813.

—— —— Joh. Glynde, 1342. Add.
20174.

—— —— Steph. de Pudihamme,
1346. Add. 20175; — 1347. Add.
20177.

—— —— Vincent. Finch, 1364.
Add. 16209, 20187; — 1365. Add.
16210.

—— —— Will. Wille, 1379. Add.
20194.

—— —— Sim. Colred, 1385. Add.
20195.

—— —— Rob. Fyshlake *al.* Fysch-
lake, 1407-1410. Add. 20202-20204.

—— —— Joh. Copuldyk *al.* Copuldyk, 1463. Add. 20209; — 1468. Add.
24869.

Winchester, *co. Southt.* Synodal council held at, 993 (Wintonia). Cott. MS.
Aug. ii. 38.

—— Ch. dated "eodem anno quo
Hen. Rex fil. Henrici Regis et Regina
sua fuerunt apud Wintoniam coro-
nati," [1172]. Eg. 432.

—— Conf. by Rich. I. of rents in, to
St. Cross Hospital, 1189. Harl. 43
C. 28.

—— Exchange by Durford Abbey
for a tenement at St. Giles's fair, *ante*
1258-9 (Wintonia). Cott. MS. Vesp.
E. xxiii., f. 4.

—— Release in Hyde Street, 1350.
Add. 19315.

—— Precipe on a covenant conc.
lands in, Hyde Street, etc., 1593.
Add. 25249.

—— Precipe on a covenant conc. land
in St. Laurence parish, 1593. Add.
25250.

—— Petition for conf. of charters of
Qu. Eliz. to, conc. trade, customs, etc.,
*n. d.* Add. 15702 (*draft*, 18 cent.).

—— Grant in, by Jas. I., 1612. Cott.
xiii. 35.

—— *Major.* Joh. Edgar, *c.* 1240.
Add. 15690.

Winchester's Manor. *v. sub* Mendlesham, *co. Suff.*

Winchfield, *co. Southt.* Grant of
reversion of the manor to St. Stephen's
Chapel, Westminster, 1382. Harl.
43 E. 16.

Winchul. *v. sub* Macclesfield, *co.*
*Chest.*

Wincle, *in Prestbury, co. Chester.*
Briefs for rebuilding the chapel,
1788, 1815. Ch. Br. B. xxviii. 5,
lvi. 1.

Windale, *co. Norf.* Grants, etc., in,
1361. Harl. 52 B. 11 (Wyndhull);—
1375. Harl. 53 E. 45 (Wyndele);—
1386. Harl. 56 G. 21 (do.);—1422.
Harl. 50 F. 36 (do.).

—— Fines in, 1419. Harl. 51 G.
53 (do.); — 1462. Harl. 54 I. 19
(Windele).

Windeford Brook, *co. Staff.* Brief
conc. a fire at, 1817. Ch. Br. B. lvii. 11.

Windervile le Kay. *v. sub* Bredfield, *co. Suff.*

Windesland, [*in or nr. Freiston*], *co.*
*Linc.* Grant in, to Kirkstead Abbey,
[1174-93]. Harl. 51 B. 44.

Windham, Burnham. *v.* Burnham
Thorpe, *co. Norf.*

Windhill. *v. sub* Woolley, *in Royston,*
*co. York.*

Windlesham, *co. Surr.* Grant in, to
Newark Priory, 1256. Harl. 55 B. 41.

—— Conveyance, etc., in, 1513. Harl.
56 I. 6 (Wynsham); —1538. Cott.
xxv. 27 (Wyndelesham).

Windlesóra. *v.* Windsor, *co. Berks.*

Windley, *in Duffield, co. Derb.* Conveyance in, 1431 (Wyneley). Woll.
i. 85.

Windmill Down. *v. sub* Goudhurst,
*co. Kent.*

Windrush, *River, co. Glouc.* Boundary
of grants in Bourton on the Water,
779 (Wenriso). Cott. MS. Aug. ii. 4;
—949 (Wenris). Cott. viii. 6 (*copy*).

Windsor, *co. Berks.* Grant of, to
Westminster Abbey, 1050-65 (Windlesóra). Cott. vii. 13.

—— Grant in, by Edw. the Confessor,
to Westminster Abbey, 1066 [*sc.* 1065]
(Windlesore). Cott. vi. 2 (*copy*).

—— Grant in, by King Stephen, to
Reading Abbey, [1140?] (terra de
Windesoris). Add. 19584.

Wittenham, West, co. Berks. (continued). Release of Gt. Wittenham manor, etc., to New College, 1384. Add. 24322.

—— Power to give seisin of the manor, as held of New College, 1392. Add. 20284.

—— Rector. Robertus, [1219–31]. Add. 21165.

—— Vicarius. Joh. More, 1402. Add. 20245.

Wittering, co. Suss. Grant of Tangmere to the church of St. Andrew "super ripam orient. portus qui dicitur uedringmutha," 680 (?). Cott. MS. Aug. ii. 87.

Wittering, East, co. Suss. Assignment of lands in, 1501 (Estwyghtryng). Add. 18790.

Wittering, West, co. Suss. Fine in, 1337 (?) (Westwyctring). Add. 24887.

—— Assignment of lands in, 1501 (Westwyghtryng). Add. 18790.

—— Award in, 1579. Eg. 298.

Wittersham, co. Kent. Evidence conc. tenure of, [1072] (Witriscesham). Cott. MS. Aug. ii. 36.

—— Release in Palstre manor in, 1308. Campb. xxvii. 28.

—— Grants, etc., in, 1347. Add. 20177 (Wijtresham);—1375. Add. 20016 (Wytheryshame);—1383. Add. 20017 (Whittrishame);—1384. Add. 20018 (Wyghtersbame);—1414. Add. 20019 (Wyghtryshame);—1434. Add. 20020 (Wightersham);—1584. Harl. 85 H. 9;—1603. Harl. 80 H. 38;—1652. Harl. 77 D. 19.

—— Lease of the manor by Maidstone College, 1543. Harl. 86 G. 45.

—— Sub-lease, etc., of the manor, 1545. Harl. 86 H. 46;—1566. Harl. 86 H. 43;—1588. Harl. 85 H. 27, 86 H. 45;—1620. Harl. 86 I. 21.

—— Fines in, 1545. Harl. 78 B. 38; —1552. Harl. 78 E. 52;—1616. Harl. 77 C. 52;—1620. Harl. 77 E. 33.

Witthcal. v. Withcall, co. Linc.

Witthele, Wittheleie. v. Whitley, co. York.

Witthesmara. v. Whittlesey Mere, co. Hunt.

Wittingham. v. sub Fressingfield, co. Suff.

Witton. v. Whitton, in Leintwardine, co. Heref.

Witton, co. Hunt. Sale of church lands in, 1561. Harl. 80 H. 61.

Witton, in Blofield Hundred, co. Norf. Release in, 1347 (Wytton). Harl. 48 C. 3.

—— Inspex., in 1454, of a feoffment of the advowson, 1422 (do.). Add. 17243.

Witton, in Tunstead Hundred, co. Norf. Release, etc., in, 1330. Add. 14709 (Wyttone);—1403. Harl. 49 G. 45 (do.).

—— Fines in, 1381. Harl. 54 C. 28, 56 B. 35;—1405. Harl. 58 B. 19.

—— Surrender in, to Bromholm Priory, 1444 (Wytton). Add. 14571.

—— Capellanus. Nicholaus, early 13 cent. Harl. 49 G. 21, Add. 14932.

Witton, in Droitwich, co. Worc. Conf. of salt works in, to Pershore Abbey, 972 (on Wictune). Cott. MS. Aug. ii. 6.

Witton le Wear, co. Durh. Covenant for repayment of a loan at, 1416 (Wotton in Weredall). Lansd. 627.

Witton, Long, co. Northumb. Grants, etc., in, t. Edw. I. Cott. xxvii. 194 (Wotton);—1314. Harl. 112 C. 46 (do.);—1323. Cott. xxviii. 26–29 (Wttona).

Wiuelesford. v. Wilsford, co. Wilts.

Wiuelestunia. v. Wilson, co. Leic.

Wiuerdeston. v. Wyverston, co. Suff.

Wiuesleya, nr. Headington, co. Oxon. Release of rent from the mill of, by Bicester Priory, c. 1245. Add. 10610.

Wiuma. v. Witham, North, co. Linc.

Wiungua. v. Wing, co. Buck.

Wiuueho. v. Wivenhoe, co. Essex.

Wivelsfield, co. Suss. Grants, etc., in, 1328. Add. 24684 (Wyuelesfeld);—1377. Add. 24685 (do.);—1381. Add. 24686 (do.);—1404. Add. 24687, 24688 (Wevelesfeld);—1429. Add. 24683 (Weveliaf-ld);—1441. Add. 24689;—1485. Add. 24690 (Wyvelesfeld).

—— Brief conc. a hail-storm at, 1764. Ch. Br. B. iv. 8.

Wivenhoe, co. Essex. Rent to be paid to the Lord of, for Tendring, co. Essex, late 12 cent. (Wiuueho). Harl. 45 G. 39.

—— Precipe on a covenant conc. land in, 1587. Add. 24979.

Wood Rising. *v.* Rising, Wood, *co. Norf.*

Wood Walton. *v.* Walton, Wood, *co. Hunt.*

Woodborough, *in Winscombe. co. Som.* Lease in, 1385 (Wodebergh). Harl. 46 G. 16.

Woodbridge, *co. Suff.* Lease of tithes of the mill to Woodbridge Priory by Butley Priory, *c.* 1205 (?) (Wudebreg). Add. 7494.

—— Grant of marshland in, *t.* John (Wdebruge). Harl. 50 A. 1.

—— Covenant betw. the Priory, as rector, and the tenants of Rob. de Ufford in, and in Kingston in, conc. repairs to the "campanarium" of the parish church, etc., 1286 (Wodebrigg). Harl. 45 A. 50.

—— Grants, etc., in, 1415. Campb. i. 27 (Wodebregge);—1431. Harl. 57 A. 1 (Wodebrigge);—1439. Harl. 43 E. 43 (Wodbrigge).

—— Grant in, "super stratam usque gonucicrœs," by Woodbridge Priory, 1457 (Wodebregge). Cott. xxi. 44.

—— Conveyance of the manor, 1516 (Woodbryge). Harl. 52 B. 10.

—— Precipe on a covenant conc. the manor, etc., 1552 (Wodbridge). Add. 25273.

Woodbury, *co. Devon.* Brief conc. a fire at, 1804. Ch. Br. B. xlv. 1.

Woodbury, *in Bredwardine, co. Heref.* Grant, on marriage, of a hide in, late Hen. II. (Wdebiri). Add. 20408.

Woodchurch, *co. Chest.* Release of actions conc. Landican manor in, 1346. Campb. xxviii. 3.

Woodchurch, *co. Kent.* Grant of Cotesland in (?), early Hen. III. Add. 8536.

—— Grants, etc., in, 1376. Add. 8545 (Wodecherche);—1392. Harl. 78 A. 20 (Wodcherche);—1410. Add. 8553 (Wodecherche);—1494. Add. 8592 (do.);—1551. Harl. 78 G. 31;—1573. Add. 8625;—1575. Harl. 76 G. 37;— 1576. Harl. 78 A. 26, 27, 80 H. 65, 66;—1580. Harl. 79 C. 11;—1587. Harl. 75 G. 37;—1588. Harl. 75 G. 34, 35.

—— Fines in, 1588. Harl. 79 B. 11; —1635. Harl. 80 G. 17.

—— Suit and recovery in, 1626. Harl. 75 H. 22;—1631. Harl. 75 F. 12.

Woodcote, *co. Heref.* (?). Grant in, 1357 (Wodecote). Add. 7036.

Woodcote, *nr. Newbury, co. Salop.* Recovery of the manor, 1706. Add. 1687.

Woodcote, *in Beddington, co. Surr.* Grant, etc., in, to St. Thomas's Hospital, Southwark, *post* 1228. Add. 23020, 23021.

—— Grants, etc., in, *c.* 1250–60. Add. 22939, 22940, 22942;—*ante* 1262. Add. 22949, 22955;—1265. Add. 22923;— late Hen. III. Add. 22944, 22945, 22958;—*c.* 1270. Add. 22937, 22938, 22956;—1272. Add. 22953;—1276. Add. 22926;—*t.* Edw. I. Add. 22911, 22943, 22916–22948, 22950, 22951, 22954, 23005;—1812. Add. 23038;— 1314. Add. 23043;—1315. Add. 23015, 23048;—1816. Add. 23051;— 1318. Add. 23057;—1320. Add. 23058, 23059;—1322. Add. 23062, 23064–23066;—1323. Add. 23067, 23693;—1330. Add. 23074;—1332. Add. 23077;—1334. Add. 23078, 23079;—1344. Add. 23092, 23095;— 1347. Add. 23097, 23098;—1348. Add. 23103–23106;—1349. Add. 23111;—1353. Add. 23123;—1355. Add. 23125;—1357. Add. 23126;— 1375. Add. 23137;—1385. Add. 23150;—1386. Add. 23151, 23152;— 1388. Add. 23153;—1552. Add. 23209;—1567. Add. 23598;—1576. Add. 23227.

—— Lease of game of "conyse and rabettes" in, 1459. Add. 23189;— 1465. Add. 23193.

*v. also* Beddington, *co. Surr.*

Woodcote, *in Leek Wootton, co. Warw.* Power to give seisin in, 1333. Cott. xxvii. 69.

—— Entail of the manor, 1656. Cott. xxiv. 45.

Woodcott, *co. Chest.* Complaint of St. Evroul Abbey conc. the chapel of, 1205 (Wodecot). Woll. v. 27.

Woodcroft, *nr. Luton, co. Bedf.* Scire facias conc. the manor, with descent, 1426 (Wodecroft). Add. 656.

[Woodcroft, *co. Nortbt.*]. Bond in, with defeasance, 1430. Add. 22552, 22553.

Woode den. *v. sub* Staplehurst, *co. Kent.*

Wooden, *in Lesbury, co. Northumb.* Covenant conc. the manor, 1314 (Wuluedon). Add. 20540.

3 H 2

Woodend, *in Northolt, co. Midd.* Mortgage in, 1674. Add. 19464, 19465, 19469.

Woodfield. *v. sub* Stoke by Clare, *co. Suf.*

Woodford, *co. Essex.* Grant of Buckhurst (Bocherst) wood in, to Stratford Langthorne Abbey, *c.* 1135. Harl. 53 E. 15.

—— Release, etc., in, 1574. Add. 24872;—1584–1605. Harl. 57 H. 39.

Woodford, *nr. Denford, co. Northt.* Covenant conc. the River Nen and mills at, early Hen. III. (Wdeford). Cott. xxviii. 74.

—— Grant in, to light the Virgin in Gt. Addington church, *t.* Hen. III. (Wodeford). Harl. 50 D. 49.

Woodford, *in Chew Stoke, co. Som.* Lease of, 1421. Harl. 112 D. 54.

Woodfoule. *v. sub* Melford, Long, *co. Suf.*

Woodhall. *v. sub* Darfield, *co. York.*

Woodhall, *in Killamarsh, co. Derb.* Fine in, 1541. Woll. ii. 71.

Woodhall, *co. Hertf.* Extract from court-roll, 1563. Add. 5297.

Woodhall, *co. Linc.* Releases in Slatoft and Daw wood (Duuewd, Dufwudde) in, to Kirkstead Abbey, late Hen. II. Cott. v. 76;—[1196–8]. Harl. 58 B. 44.

—— Grants, etc., in, to Kirkstead Abbey, early 13 cent.–*t.* Edw. I. Cott. v. 61 (Wdehall), Harl. 48 C. 9 (Wudhall), 52 H. 41 (Wdhall), 52 I. 24–26 (Wdehall), 58 B. 46 (Wudehall);—1258. Harl. 58 D. 3 (Wdhal);—1274. Harl. 51 G. 42 (Wodhalle);—1370. Harl. 44 F. 8 (Wodehall).

—— Grants, etc., in, 1304. Harl. 58 B. 47 (Wodhalle);—1351. Cott. xxx. 30 (Wodehall);—1370, Harl. 56 B. 49 (Wodhall);—1431. Harl. 48 G. 44 (Wodehall).

—— Grants, etc., of the manor and advowson, *t.* Edw. I.–II. Cott. xxx. 27, 28;—1328. Harl. 58 C. 1;–1332. Harl. 47 C. 32, 33, 58 B. 49, 50, Cott. xxx. 29;—1335. Harl. 48 E. 7;—1338. Harl. 56 F. 42.

—— Covenant with Kirkstead Abbey conc. right of way in, 1325. Harl. 44 F. 6.

—— Grant, etc., of the manor to Kirkstead Abbey, 1332. Harl. 50 D. 34, 35;—1365. Harl. 58 C. 2.

Woodhall, *co. Linc.* (*continued*). Grant, etc., of the advowson to Kirkstead Abbey, 1340. Harl. 50 D. 36;—1393. Harl. 43 I. 2.

—— Exemplif. in 1431 of a suit in, 1364 (Wodehalle). Harl. 51 H. 6.

—— *Persona.* Johannes, late 12 cent. Harl. 56 C. 45.

—— —— Alanus, *t.* Hen. III.–*t.* Edw. I. Cott. v. 61, Harl. 52 H. 41, 52 I. 24, 25.

—— —— Ricardus, 1325. Harl. 44 F. 6.

—— —— Ric. de Forthygton *al.* Forthyngton, 1332. Harl. 50 D. 34, 35;—1333. Harl. 47 I. 26;—1335. Harl. 48 E. 7;—1338. Harl. 56 F. 42;—1340. Harl. 50 D. 36;—(*nuper persona*), 1365. Harl. 58 C. 2.

—— —— Will. de Kirkeby, 1370. Harl. 44 F. 8, 49 A. 43;—1371. Harl. 55 E. 39.

Woodhall, *in Calverley, co. York.* Grants, etc., in, early Hen. III.–*t.* Edw. I.–II. Add. 16587 (Wdehalle), 16589 (Wudehal), 16646 (Wodhalle), 16647 (Wdehall), 16648 (Wodhal), 16740, 16742, 16756, 16758, 16759;—1310. Add. 16763;—1357. Add. 16804, 16805;—1459. Add. 16950;—1506. Add. 16998–17000.

—— Award in, 1487 (Wodhall). Add. 16967.

—— *Clericus.* Hugo, early Hen. III. Add. 16587.

Woodhall, *co. York.* Exemplif. of fine in, 1604. Add. 908.

Woodham, *in Waddesdon, co. Buck.* Grant for life in, 1370 (Wodehamme). Harl. 58 D. 47.

Woodham, *co. Essex.* Bequests of land at, late 10 cent. (*at Wuda ham, etc.*). Harl. 43 C. 4.

Woodham Ferris, *co. Essex.* Rector. Joh. Watforde, 1438. Harl. 57 F. 16.

Woodham Walter, *co. Essex.* Grant of deer from the park of, to Christ Church, Canterbury, late 12 cent. (Wdeham). Add. 918.

—— Grant in Querle in, etc., *t.* Edw. I. (Wodeham). Harl. 46 I. 46.

—— Conveyance, etc., in, 1348 or 9. Harl. 52 I. 51 (Wodeham Walter);—1359. Harl. 49 I. 14 (Wodeham Water).

—— Grant of rent from the manor, 1623. Add. 15615.

—— *Capellanus.* Johannes, late 12 cent. Add. 918.

Wrotham (Wrotcham), *co. Kent.* Grant of E. Yaldham (East Audeham) manor in, 1275. Add. 16183, 16505.

—— Fine in E. Yaldham (E. Aldbam) in, 1275. Add. 16184.

—— Grants, etc., in, *t.* Edw. I.–*t.* Edw. II. Add. 16494–16502;—1285-6. Add. 16506;—1296. Add. 16508; —1547. Harl. 57 B. 25.

—— Grant in Yaldham (Aldeham) in, 1290. Add. 16507.

—— Grants, etc., of Bastead (Bersteile) and Lit. Yaldham (Lytelildham, Lityll Eldham) manors in, 1397, 1399. Harl. Roll V. 9;—1420. Harl. 80 D. 39;—1444. Harl. 78 G. 14.

—— *Vicarius.* Gilbertus, [1275?]. Add. 16505.

—— —— Johannes, 1282. Add. 16503.

Wrotlyng. *v.* Wartling, *co. Suss.*

Wrottesley, *co. Staff.* Bequest of land at, 11 cent. (Wrotteslea). Harl. 83 A. 2.

Wroughton *al.* Elingdon, *co. Wilts.* *Rector eccl. de Elindone, Sarr. dioc. Dom.* Rob. de Harewedone, 1304. Campb. vii. 12.

Wroxale, Wroxhale. *v.* Wraxall, *co. Som.*

Wroxall, *Isle of Wight.* Grant in, to Quarr Abbey, [1184-5?] (Wrokeshale). Add. 15688.

—— Lease of the manor, 1368. Add. 17418.

—— Compotus of the manor, 1488-9 (Wraxhall). Harl. Roll A. 38.

—— Brief conc. a fire at, 1811. Ch. Br. B. li. 11.

Wroxeter, *co. Salop.* Brief for rebuilding the church, 1759. Ch. Br. A. vi. 5.

Wroxhall, *co. Warw.* Papal conf. of, to Wroxhall Priory, 1163 (Wrocheshala). Harl. 83 A. 21.

Wrtham. *v.* Wortham, *co. Suff.*

Wrthested, etc. *v.* Worstead, *co. Norf.*

Wrydlyngton. *v.* Worlington, *co. Suff.*

Wrynggeworthi. *v. sub* Worthyvale, nr. *Camelford, co. Cornw.*

Wryngeton, Wrynston. *v.* Wrinstone, *co. Glam.*

Wrytell, Wryttyll, etc. *v.* Writtle, *co. Essex.*

Wttona. *v.* Witton, Long, *co. Northumb.*

—— *v.* Wootton, *co. Linc.*

—— *v.* Wootton Wawen, *co. Warw.*

Wuda ham. *v.* Woodham, *co. Essex.*

Wudebreg. *v.* Woodbridge, *co. Suff.*

Wudebroc. *v. sub* Richard's Castle, *co. Heref.*

Wudedole. *v. sub* Blythburgh, *co. Suff.*

Wudehall, Wudhall. *v.* Woodhall, *co. Linc.*

Wudemaresth. *v.* Woodmausterne, *co. Surr.*

Wudestort. *v.* Woodstreet, *co. Dors.*

Wudthorp. *v.* Woodthorpe, *co. Derb.*

Wudu tun. *v.* Wootton, *co. Kent.*

Wulda ham. *v.* Wouldham, *co. Kent.*

Wulfa mere. "Gemot" held at, *c.* 992. Cott. MS. Aug. ii. 15.

Wulfeia. *v.* Wolvey, *co. Warw.*

Wulfholm *al.* Wlfholm, *in Redbourne, co. Linc.* Grants, etc., in, *to* Bullington Priory, *t.* Steph. Harl. 48 I. 49;—*t.* Hen. II. Harl. 57 D. 20, 48 L. 51, 53.

Wulfrenton. *v.* Wolverton, *co. Buck.*

Wullafes wælle, *nr. Rchington, co. Warw.* A boundary mark, 1001. Cott. MS. Aug. ii. 22.

Wullauestonia. *v.* Wollaston, *co. Northt.*

Wullingham. *v.* Willingham, [South?], *co. Linc.*

Wulmyngton. *v.* Woolmington, *in Chardstock, co. Dors.*

Wuluardley. *v.* Woolverley, *co. Salop.*

Wuluedon. *v.* Wooden, *co. Northumb.*

Wuluelay, W. Morehoses. *v.* Woolley, *co. York.*

Wulusle. *v.* Woolley, *in White Waltham, co. Berks.*

Wuluenewich. *v.* Willian, *co. Hertf.*

Wuluyston. *v.* Wolverstone, *nr. Payhembury, co. Devon.*

Wumbaldelegh. *v.* Wimboldsley, *co. Chest.*

Wunfrod. *v.* Winford (?), *co. Som.*

Wurmeleá. *v.* Wormley, *co. Hertf.*

Wurplesdon. *v.* Worplesdon, *co. Surr.*

Wurtinge. *v.* Worting, *co. Southt.*

**Wutton.** *v.* Woodton, *co. Norf.*

—— *v.* Wootton Basset, *co. Wilts.*

**Wyaston,** *in Edlaston, co. Derb.* Fine with Tutbury Priory, reserving pasture to the men of, *t.* Hen. III. (Wiardest.). Woll. viii. 68.

—— Lease, etc., in, 1352. Woll. ix. 66 (Wyardeston);—1363. Lansd. 606 (do.).

**Wybaldeston, Wybaudiston, etc.** *v.* Wyboston, *co. Bedf.*

**Wyberton** (Wiberton, etc.), *co. Linc.* Grants in, to Greenfield Priory, early 13 cent. (?). Harl. 45 F. 5 ;—*t.* Hen. III. Harl. 58 C. 30.

—— Grant in Sumerhetti nr., to be held of the church of St. Leodegerius of, early 13 cent. Harl. 50 C. 51.

—— Grants, etc., in, early 13 cent.- *t.* Hen. III. Harl. 45 F. 4, 50 A. 42, 50 G. 17, 55 F. 14, 15 ;—1306. Harl. 55 G. 2.

—— Grant in Titton in, *t.* Hen. III. Cott. xxvii. 77.

—— Lease, etc., in, by Greenfield Priory, *t.* Hen. III. Harl. 58 A. 23 ; —1260. Harl. 44 D. 60 (Wyb.);— *c.* 1260. Harl. 46 A. 50.

—— Fine in, 1306. Harl. 52 A. 7.

—— Feoffment, etc., of the manor, 1355. Harl. 57 G. 11 ;—1447. Harl. 45 G. 62 (Wyburton).

—— *Capellanus.* Tho. de Bicra, early 13 cent. Harl. 45 F. 5.

**Wybesnade.** *v.* Whipsnade, *co. Bedf.*

**Wyboston** (Wyboldeston, etc.), *in Eaton Socon, co. Bedf.* Conf. by King John of a grant in, 1208 (Wibaudeston). Add. 6014.

—— Release of dower in Goodwick (Godynewyk) in, *t.* Edw. I. Harl. 46 I. 35.

—— Grants, etc., in, *t.* Edw. I. Harl. 48 H. 20 (Wybaudiston); — 1316. Harl. 48 A. 13 ;—1351. Harl. 48 H. 29 (Wybolteston);—1359. Harl. 54 E. 39, 40 ;—1366. Harl. 46 F. 34, 46 I. 55 ;—1369. Harl. 47 I. 43 ;—1374. Harl. 46 I. 56, 57.

—— Feoffment of the manor, 1444 (Wybaldeston). Harl. 83 F. 3, 4.

—— Exemplif. of fine in, 1589. Add. 5156.

**Wybunbury,** *co. Chest.* Grant in, *t.* Hen. III. (Wibenbury). Harl. 83 D. 19.

—— Lease, etc., of Batherton and Gresty manors in Shavington in, 1395. Campb. xxviii. 8 ;—1400. Campb. xxviii. 10.

—— Briefs for rebuilding the church, 1791, 1794. Ch. Br. B. xxxi. 5, xxxiv. 1.

—— *Persona.* Thomas, *t.* Hen. III. Harl. 83 D. 19.

—— *Vicarius.* Tho. de Copenhale, 1395. Campb. xxviii. 8.

**Wyca.** *v. sub* Englefield, *co. Berks.*

**Wycam, Est.** *v.* Wykeham, E., *co. Linc.*

**Wych.** *v.* Droitwich, *co. Worc.*

**Wycham.** *v.* Wickham Market, *co. Suff.*

—— *v.* Witcham, *co. Camb.*

—— *v.* Wykeham, *nr. Nettleton, co. Linc.*

**Wycham Breus.** *v.* Wickham Breux, *co. Kent.*

**Wychambrok.** *v.* Wickhambrook, *co. Suff.*

**Wychampton.** *v.* Witchampton, *co. Dors.*

**Wychbold,** *nr. Droitwich, co. Worc.* Charter of Wiglaf of Mercia dated at, 831 (Wicbold). Cott. MS. Aug. ii. 94.

—— Release in, 1370 (Wychebaud). Add. 9239.

**Wycheford Magna.** *v.* Wishford, Gt., *co. Wilts.*

**Wychenouere.** *v.* Wichnor, *co. Staff.*

**Wychford.** *v.* Witchford, *in Isle of Ely, co. Camb.*

**Wychiswode.** *v. sub* Cobham, *co. Kent.*

**Wyck.** *v. sub* Henbury, *co. Glouc.*

—— *v.* Week, *in Binsted, co. Southt.*

**Wyckerslay.** *v.* Wickersley, *co. York.*

**Wyckhambreux.** *v.* Wickham Breux, *co. Kent.*

**Wyckyn** *al.* **W. Bonant.** *v.* Wicken Bonant, *co. Essex.*

**Wycombe, High,** *co. Buck.* Release by fine of a nativus in, 1286 (Wycumb). Harl. 84 H. 39 (copy).

3 ı

**Wymondham,** *co. Norf. (continued).*
Extract from court-roll of Grishagh
manor in, 1634. Add. 14952.

—— Terrier of the vicarage glebe,
1678. Add. 15861.

—— *Preacher of God's Word at.* Joh.
Money, 1659. Add. 19266.

**Wymondley,** *co. Hertf.* Livery and
extent of Gt. and Lit. Wymondley
manors, 1541. Add. 13559 *a, b.*

**Wympton.** *v.* Whimpton, *co. Nott.*

**Wynberye.** *v.* Wembury, *co. Devon.*

**Wyncalton, Wyncaulton.** *v.* Wincanton, *co. Som.*

**Wyncgfeud,** etc. *v.* Wingfield, *co.
Suff.*

**Wynchefeld.** *v.* Winchfield, *co. Southt.*

**Wynchestrys.** *v. sub* Mendlesham,
*co. Suff.*

**Wyndele, Wyndhull.** *v.* Windale,
*co. Norf.*

**Wyndervile, Wyndirvile le Kay.**
*v. sub* Bredfield, *co. Suff.*

**Wyndesborough.** *v.* Woodnesborough, *co. Kent.*

**Wyndeston.** *v.* Winston, *co. Norf.*

**Wyndfrith.** *v.* Winford (?), *co. Som.*

**Wyndhill.** *v. sub* Woolley, *co. York.*

**Wyneberge.** *v.* Whinbergh, *co. Norf.*

**Wyneketone.** *v.* Winkton, *co. Southt.*

**Wyneley.** *v.* Windley, *co. Derb.*

**Wynescomb.** *v.* Winscombe, *co. Som.*

**Wynesford, Wynesford Ryvers.**
*v.* Winsford, *co. Som.*

**Wyneston, Wynestune,** etc. *v.*
Winston, *co. Suff.*

**Wynetorp.** *v.* Winthorpe, *co. Linc.*

**Wynewyk,** etc. *v.* Winwick, *co.
Northt.*

**Wynfeld.** *v.* Wingfield, South, *co. Derb.*

—— *v.* Winkfield, *co. Wilts.*

**Wynferthyng.** *v.* Winfarthing, *co.
Norf.*

**Wyngarworth, Wyngerworth,
Wyngreworth.** *v.* Wingerworth,
*co. Derb.*

**Wynggefeld, Wyngefeld,** etc. *v.*
Wingfield, *co. Suff*

**Wynghalton.** *v.* Wincanton, *co. Som.*

**Wynhale,** *nr. Chinnor* (?), *co. Oxon.*
Acquittance from Wallingford Priory
for rents in, 1451. Add. 20330.

**Wynhamford,** *in Brightling, co. Suss.*
Grant to Robertsbridge Abbey of
water rights for its mills at, 1315.
Eg. 399.

**Wynnefeld.** *v.* Wingfield, North, *co.
Derb.*

**Wynnesborough.** *v.* Woodnesborough, *co. Kent.*

**Wynpole.** *v.* Wimpole, *co. Camb.*

**Wynsecoumbe.** *v.* Winscombe, *co.
Som.*

**Wynselowe.** *v.* Winslow, *co. Buck.*

**Wynsham.** *v.* Windlesham, *co. Surr.*

**Wynston.** *v.* Winston, *co. Norf.*

—— *v.* Winston, *co. Suff.*

—— *v.* Winstone, *co. Glouc.*

**Wyntewrth.** *v.* Wentworth, *co. Camb.*

**Wyntrum.** *v.* Winscombe, *co. Som.*

**Wyppelygh.** *v. sub* Bramley, *co. Surr.*

**Wypsnade.** *v.* Whipsnade, *co. Bedf.*

**Wyrcuswerth,** etc. *v.* Wirksworth,
*co. Derb.*

**Wyresdale,** *co. Lanc.* Royal conf. of
the forest of, to Edm., Earl of Lon-
caster, 1285. Cott. MS. Aug. ii.
135 (5).

**Wyresdale, Lower.** Brief conc. a
fire at, 1812. Ch. Br. B. lii. 6.

**Wyreswall.** *v.* Wirswall, *in Whitchurch, co. Chest.*

**Wyrhale.** *v. sub* Bradfield, *co. York.*

**Wyrk., Wyrkesworth,** etc. *v.* Wirksworth, *co. Derb.*

**Wyrmondford.** *v.* Wormingford, *co.
Essex.*

**Wyrnthorp.** *v.* Wrenthorpe, *nr.
Wakefield, co. York.*

**Wyrtingas.** *v.* Worthing, *co. Suss.*

**Wysall,** *co. Nott.* Certif. of publication
of banns at, 1476 (Vyssow, Wysow).
Add. 20417.

—— *Vicarius.* Ric. Rosigton, 1476.
Add. 20417.

**Wysbargh, Wysbergh.** *v.* Wis-
borough Green, *co. Suss.*

**Wysbyche, Wysebech.** *v.* Wisbeach, *co. Camb.*

**Wyset, Wyseth, Wysseth.** *v.* Wis-
sett, *co. Suff.*

**Wysshawe.** *v.* Wishaw, *co. Warw.*

**Yalding**, *co. Kent. (continued).* Rental of lands in, bel. to Bookingfold manor, 1626. Cott. xv. 50.

—— Sale of farm-stock in, 1649. Harl. 78 I. 30.

—— *Vicarius.* Will. Sybthorp, 1411 (Ealdyngge). Add. 16464.

**Yale Hundred,** *co. Denb.* Extract from an extent in 1391-2 of, *t.* Hen. VIII (Dominium de Yale). Harl. 58 E. 22.

—— Exchequer acquittances for fines in, 1567, 1586 (do.). Add. 25739, 25742.

—— *Capitalis Forestarius.* David ap Gron. up Jor., *de Borton,* 1391. Add. 8633.

—— *Seneschallus.* Petr. Salford, 1391. Add. 8633.

—— —— Joh. Wele, 1414. Add. 8637.

—— —— Joh. Shilston, *miles,* 1520. Add. 8647.

**Yale Raglia,** *co. Denb.* Extract from court-roll, 1451. Harl. 58 F. 36.

**Yalecross.** *v. sub* Trotton, *co. Suss.*

**Yambrigge.** *v.* Yeolmbridge, *nr. Werrington, co. Devon.*

**Yanworth,** *co. Glouc.* Inquisition of the manor, 1551. Harl. Roll T. 24.

—— Suit conc. the manor, 1554. Harl. 76 I. 16, 22.

—— Leases, etc , of the manor, 1558. Harl. 76 I. 36;—1568. Harl. 77 B. 18, 19;—1569. Harl. 111 E. 58;—1580. Harl. 77 H. 44;—1595. Harl. 77 B. 27, 77 H. 47;—1603. Harl. 77 H. 49;—1610. Harl. 77 C. 49;—1611. Harl. 75 D. 58.

—— Leases of timber in, 1562. Harl. 77 A. 8;—1568. Harl. 77 A. 16, 20.

—— Sale of fee farm rents in, 1650. Add. 15168.

**Yapton,** *co. Suss.* Grant of rent in Bilsham (Bullsham) in, 1608. Add. 18906.

**Yarborough,** *co. Linc.* Conf. of a grant in, to Kirkstead Abbey, [1160-70?] (Yerburg). Harl. 48 G. 41.

—— *Clericus.* Hamelinus, late Hen. II. (Jerdeburch). Harl. 48 C. 10.

**Yarcombe,** *co. Devon.* Release in Paynshay in, 1420. Add. 13039.

**Yard.** *v. sub* Rampisham, *co. Dors.*

**Yard,** *nr. Wroxall* (?), *Isle of Wight.* Grant of free warren in, to Quarr Abbey, 1284 (La Yerde). Add. 15701.

**Yardbury,** *in Colyton, co. Devon.* Release in, 1420 (Yurdebury). Add. 13039.

—— Rental of, late bel. to the Marquis of Exeter, 1539 (Decenna de Yeardebury). Add. 13187.

**Yardley,** *co. Hertf.* Release of actions on account of repairs in the manor by the "firmarius" of St. Paul's, 1453 (Erdley). Lansd. 653.

**Yardley,** *co. Worc.* Conf. of grants at, to Pershore Abbey, 972 (Gyrdleah). Cott. MS. Aug. ii. 6.

—— Petition for conf. of grant of patronage of the church of, to Catesby Priory, *c.* 1300 (Yerdeleye). Add. 20433.

—— Sale of parsonage, 1540 (Yardeley). Harl. 47 A. 53.

—— *Rector.* Rad. de Haugham, *c.* 1300. Add. 20433.

**Yardley Gobion,** *co. Northt.* Sale. etc., in, 1659. Add. 18032;—1666. Add. 6074.

—— Fine, etc., in, 1695. Add. 18055—18058.

**Yarkhill,** *co. Heref.* Ref. to exchange of lands at, 811 (æt Geardcylle). Cott. MS. Aug. ii. 47.

**Yarlington,** *co. Som.* Manor held by Will. de Monte Acuto [*ob.* 1270], late 13 cent. (Jerlinton). Add. 26754.

**Yarm,** *co. York.* Grant of wreck of the sea between Runswick and, 1327 (Jarum). Add. 20581.

**Yarmouth,** *Isle of Wight.* Charter of King John dated at, 1206 (Eremua). Cott. viii. 25.

—— Computus of the manor, 1488-9 (Eruemouthe). Harl. Roll A. 38.

—— Precipe on a covenant conc. land in, 1593 (Yearmouth). Add. 25234.

**Yarmouth, Great,** *co. Norf.* Grant and conf. of St. Nicholas' church to Norwich Priory, [1103-6]. Cott. MS. Aug. ii. 103 (Jernemuta), Cott. ii. 21 (1);—[1136-45]. Cott. ii. 1 (Geruemutha), 21 (9).

—— Papal conf. of land in, to Horsham St. Faith Priory, 1163 (Geruemuta). Cott. MS. Aug. ii. 136.

—— Royal grant of the revenues of, to J. and D. de Baliol, [1227]. Cott. ii. 14 (*copy*).

**Yarmouth, Great,** *co. Norf. (continued).* Sales in, "in prædio phishussorum" nr. the New Hospital, *t.* Hen. III. Harl. 84 H. 12 (Gernem.), 85 F. 52.

—— Grants of the same lands to Biddlesdon Abbey, *t.* Hen. III. Harl. 85 A. 4 (Gernem.), 86 D. 32.

—— List of townsmen qualified to elect the bailiffs, *t.* Edw. I. Add. 6317.

—— Letter from the bailiffs conc. a cargo of wine for Berwick, *t.* Edw. I. (Gern.). Add. 6317 *a.*

—— Grants, etc., in, 1295. Harl. 46 E. 30 (Mag. Gernem.);—1353. Harl. 46 D. 33 (Mag. Jernemuth.);—1365. Add. 14965 (do.);—*t.* Rich. II. Add. 691;—1385. Harl. 56 G. 32 (do.);—1396. Add. 2006 (Weston Jernemuth); —1420. Harl. 45 D. 29 (Mag. Jernomewth), 30 (M. Jernomoth);—1421. Harl. 45 D. 31;—1424-1464. Harl. 45 D. 34-39;—1520. Harl. 58 D. 13; —1554. Add. 14968;—1567. Add. 14969;—1607. Add. 14971.

—— Extract from roll of pleas at York conc. land in, 1304 (M. Jernemuth). Add. 6318.

—— Accompts of collectors of murage at, 1336-1345. Add. 14976-14986.

—— Order for a fleet from, with particulars, 1340 (Mag. Jernemuth). Add. 8397 *a, b.*

—— License to endow a chaplain in the chapel called Le Charnell in, 1390 (do.). Add. 12641.

—— License to grant lands in, to the Corporation, for the poor, 1392 (do.). Add. 14966.

—— Bail to the bailiff of, for Utrecht merchants, 1401. Harl. 111 B. 4.

—— Commission of gaol delivery at, 1435. Add. 6320.

—— Bond for arbitration in, 1464 (Mag. Yarmouth). Harl. 49 F. 39.

—— Request to lepers at, 1482. Add. 17253.

—— Grant in, by the Corporation, 1522. Add. 14967.

— - — Record of suits with Gorleston conc. port rights, *t.* Hen. VIII. Lansd. Roll 12.

- - —— Action in the bailiffs court at, 1673-4. Harl. 83 H. 31.

—— *Ballivi.* Alex. fil. Alani, Joh. Beneyt, Galfr. Whit, Will. Rose, Will. Hamerose, *t.* Hen. III. Harl. 85 A. 4.

**Yarmouth, Great,** *co. Norf. (continued). Ballivi (continued).* Tho. Fastolf, Eust. Bataille, Will. de Carletone, Laur. de Moneslee, [1295]. Harl. 46 E. 30.

—— —— Galfr. Elys, Petr. Cressy, Galfr. de Drayton, Galfr. de Fordele, 1353. Harl. 46 D. 33.

—— —— Alex. de Beverle, Hugo Fastolf, Joh. de Wykes, Joh. de Halle, 1365. Add. 14965.

· —— —— Rad. Ramsey, Nich. Drayton, Warin Lucas, Ad. Heyron, 1385. Harl. 56 G. 32.

—— —— Tho. Concheyth, Will. atte Garre, Rich. Elys, Tho. Qwyte, 1424. Harl. 45 D. 34.

—— —— Tho. Engayn, Tho. Qwhyte, 1428. Harl. 45 D. 35.

—— —— Tho. Fenne, Joh. Pynne, 1457-8. Toph. 1.

—— —— Joh. Layle, Joh. Dobylday, 1522. Add. 14967.

—— —— Chris. Sylles, Bened. Cubytt, 1567. Add. 14969.

—— *Alderman.* Geo. England, 1657. Add. 14971.

**Yarmouth, Little,** *al.* **South Town,** *co. Suff.* Grant in, to Robertsbridge and Boxley Abbeys, late Edw. I. (Parva Gernemothe). Eg. 396.

—— Grants, etc., in, *t.* Edw. I. Harl. 52 E. 23 (Parva Gernemuta);—1421. Harl. 45 D. 32 (P. Jernomuth);—1445. Harl. 45 D. 37, 38 (le Southtoun);— 1464. Harl. 45 D. 39 (do.), 49 F. 39 (Southtun);—1520. Harl. 58 D. 13 (do.);—1538. Add. 10225 (do.).

**Yarmouth, Old,** *co. Suff.* Grant in, 1538. (Olde Yermouth). Add. 10225.

**Yarnfield,** *in Maiden Bradley, co. Som.* Grants, etc., in Aldefelde in, *t.* Hen. III. (Gernefeld). Harl. 55 F. 23-25.

—— Declaration against claims of tenants in, to common in Marston Bigod wood, co. Som., late 14 cent. (Yarnefeld). Harl. 79 B. 45.

**Yarwell,** *co. Northt.* Grant in, to Earl David, by Rich. I., 1194 (Jarewelle). Cott. MS. Nero C. iii. f. 191 (*copy*).

—— License to endow Fotheringay College with the manor, 1415. Campb. x. 5.

**Yatesbury,** *co. Wilts.* Order for an extent of the manor, 1301. Add. 19302.

—— Mortgage of the prebend and manor, 1600. Add. 15133.

—— *Prebendary.* Rich. Mulcaster, 1592. Add. 15133.

**Yelderaley**, *in Ashbourne, co. Derb.* Grants, etc., in or nr., late 12 cent. Woll. ix. 7 (Yldrealee);—early 13 cent. Woll. vi. 43 (Tilderesseg, Tildiresaleye, Til-Ireal-) (*copy*):—*t.* Hen. III. Woll. ix. 9 (Yhildrialeye);—*t.* Edw. I. Woll. ix. 12 (Yldrisleye), 14 (Yldirisle);— 1273. Woll. ix. 11 (do.); —1317. Woll. ix. 16 (Yeldrealeye), 81 (Yhildereale).

—— Grant nr., by Derby Priory, early 13 cent. (Yeldcris). Woll. viii. 51.

—— Grant nr. the wood of, by Tutbury Priory, c. 1230 (Thyldresleg). Woll. ix. 76.

—— Assignment of dower in, 1435 (Yeldursley). Woll. ix. 70.

**Yelling**, *co. Hunt.* Sale of Ashfield manor, etc., in, 1545 (Gellyng *al.* Yellinge). Harl. 53 B. 53.

**Yelvertoft**, *co. Northt.* Release in, 1445. Cott. xxx. 33.

**Yensfield**. *v. sub* Penshurst, *co. Kent.*

**Yeo**, *nr. Crediton, co. Devon.* Bond for services in the chapel, *t.* Hen. III. (Iwe). Cott. ii. 11 (11) (*copy*).

**Yeolmbridge**, *nr. Werrington, co. Devon.* Grant of, *t.* Hen. III. (Yambrigge). Harl. 48 G. 6.

**Yeovil**, *co. Som.* Release, etc., in Kingston (Kyngestoue) in, 1342. Harl. 53 A. 2;—1414. Harl. 48 I. 25 (Yeuele).

—— Grant of Snouwedon in la Merssh in, and within the demesne of Kingston (Kyngeston) in, 1403 (Meuele). Harl. 48 B. 6.

—— Covenant to adjourn suit conc. lands in Kingston (Kyngestone) in, 1404. Harl. 46 G. 40.

—— Crown appointment of a steward of the manor, 1574 (Yevell). Harl. 75 E. 42.

**Yerde, Le Yerde.** *v. sub* Rampisham, *co. Dors.*

**Yerde, La.** *v.* Yard, *Isle of Wight.*

**Yerdeleye.** *v.* Yardley, *co. Worc.*

**Yesilham.** *v.* Isleham, *co. Camb.*

**Yetminster**, *co. Dors.* Conveyance of Wydihouk manor with lands called La Baillie in, 1351 (Yatemynstre). Harl. 48 B. 37.

—— Grant, etc., in, 1414. Campb. iii. 17* (Yatmynstre);—1473. Add. 15764 (Yatemestre).

—— *Vicarius.* Ricardus, 1243 (Gateministre). Harl. 53 D. 36.

**Yetminster Prima** *al.* **Upbury Prebend**, *co. Dors.* Customary roll of the manor, 1576. Add. 26815.

**Yeuherst, Yewherst.** *v.* Ewhurst, *co. Suss.*

**Yevelchestre.** *v.* Ilchester, *co. Som.*

**Yeveley.** *v.* Yeaveley, *in Shirley, co. Derb.*

**Yevell.** *v.* Yeovil, *co. Som.*

**Yewcott.** *v.* Ewecote, *in Bilsdale* (?), *co. York.*

**Yfeld.** *v.* Ifield, *co. Suss.*

**Yhildereale, Yhildrialeye, Yldtirisle, etc.** *v.* Yelderaley, *in Ashbourne, co. Derb.*

**Yhurst.** *v.* Ewhurst, *co. Surr.*

**Ykenildeweie.** *v.* Icknield Street.

**Yklyngham.** *v.* Icklingham, *co. Suff.*

**Ylig.** *v.* Ely, *co. Camb.*

**Ylleg, Ylley combusta.** *v.* Eleigh, Brent, *co. Suff.*

**Ylmessston, set.** *v.* Elmsett, *co. Suff.*

**Ylstede.** *v. sub* Stockbury, *co. Kent.*

**Ynyagollen** (?), *nr. Neath, co. Glam.* Verdicts in suit conc., with Neath Abbey, 1249 (Eneagaueln). Harl. 75 C. 42.

**Yoleg., Yolegrave, Yolgreyva, etc.** *v.* Youlgrave, *co. Derb.*

**Yore, *River.*** *v.* Ure, *River, co. York.*

**York, *County of.*** Inspex. in 1232 of conf. by Rich. I. of lands in, to Roche Abbey, 1199. Harl. 58 H. 43 (*copy*).

—— General release of lands inherited from J. de Aseby in, *t.* Edw. I. Add. 6377.

—— Fine-rolls, 1327-1377. Add. 26590.

—— Escheator's accompts, 1341-1342. Add. 18197.

—— Defeasance of grant of rents in, by J. Flynton of Flinton, 1422. Lansd. 537.

—— Covenant for the ferm of Ulnage in, to be paid to Lord Welles, 1456. Add. 16947.

—— Crown rents in, 1492. Harl. Roll E. 3.

—— Rental of Crown lands late bel. to colleges, chantries, etc., in the North Riding, *t.* Edw. VI. Harl. Roll E. 4.

**Yoxall,** *co. Staff. (continued).* Writ for arrears of rent against tenants of chantry lands in, 1677 (Yoxhall). Campb. vi. 20.

**Yoxford,** *co. Suff.* Papal commission to decide suit betw. Thetford and Belvoir Priories for tithes of, [1156] (Joscefort). Harl. 43 A. 18.

—— Grants in Stikinclond, Stykynglod, etc., in, to Sibton Abbey, *t.* Hen. III. Harl. 83 D. 11, 112 H. 57 (Jokesford), 112 I. 22 (Jokeford).

—— Bequest of goods in the manor of, by M. de Crek, 1282 (Jokeford). Campb. iii. 1.

—— Conveyance of Yoxford with Stikland and Muryels manors, 1471. Harl. 45 F. 41, 42.

—— Precipes on covenants conc. lands in, 1589. Add. 25418;—1593. Add. 25497.

—— *Vicarius.* Nicholaus, 1356 (Joxford). Harl. 83 C. 51.

**Yppewrth.** *v.* Hepworth, *co. Suff.*

**Yppingeham.** *v.* Uppingham, *co. Rutl.*

**Yrde, La.** *v. sub* Rampisham, *co. Dors.*

**Yreby.** *v.* Irby upon Humber, *co. Linc.*

**Yrton.** *v.* Ireton, Kirk, *co. Derb.*

**Yselham, Yslham.** *v.* Isleham, *co. Camb.*

**Ystede.** *v.* Isted, *in Weybread, co. Suff.*

**Ystrad,** *nr. Denbigh, co. Denb.* Exchequer acquittance for fine for the the mill of, 1595 (Astrat). Add. 25741.

**Ystradvelltey,** *co. Brecon.* Grants in, 1502. Harl. 111 B. 22 (Stradvellte); —1531. Harl. 111 B. 27 (do.);—1536. Harl. 111 B. 18 (Estradvellte).

**Ystredeloc,** *nr. Denbigh, co. Denb.* Mortgage in, 1453. Add. 9256.

**Yuecherche, Yuechirch.** *v.* Ivychurch, *co. Kent.*

**Yuelee, Yueleye.** *v.* Yeaveley, *co. Derb.*

**Yuherst.** *v.* Ewhurst, *co. Suss.*

**Yuhurst.** *v.* Ewhurst, *co. Surr.*

**Yulesworth,** *co.* —— (?). Grant of a mill-pool in, *t.* Hen. III. Add. 12924.

**Yurdebury.** *v.* Yardbury, *co. Devon.*

**Yvetis, Villa de.** *v.* St. Ives (?), *nr. Ringwood, co. Southt.*

**Yvingeho.** *v.* Ivinghoe, *co. Buck.*

**Ywade.** *v.* Iwade, *co. Kent.*

**Ywarby.** *v.* Ewerby, *co. Linc.*

**Yweherste.** *v.* Ewhurst, *co. Suss.*

**Ywhurst.** *v.* Ewhurst, *co. Surr.*

**Ywode, Ywode Blwet.** *v. sub* Congresbury, *co. Som.*

**Yxning.** *v.* Exning, *co. Suff.*

## Z

**Zealing.** *v.* Ealing, *co. Midd.*

**Zele.** *v.* Seal, *co. Kent.*

**Zensesy, Zenzysy, etc.** *v.* Synsesy, *in St. Issey, co. Corn.*

**Zevereswyke.** *v. sub* Compton Dando, *co. Som.*

**Zolgreff.** *v.* Youlgreave, *co. Derb.*

**Zouches.** *v. sub* Metheringham, *co. Linc.*

# COUNTY INDEX.

3 K

**CORNWALL**—*cont.*—
Whitley
Willsworthy
Woon
Worthyvale
Wrynggeworthi
Wyllond

**CUMBERLAND**—
Aikton
Ainstable
Allerdale
Allonby
Aspatric
Baron Wood
Blackhall *al.* Blackwell
Brigham
Bromfield
Burgh by Sands
Caldbeck
Caldbeck Forest
Camerton
Carlatton
Carlisle
Castle Carrock
Catterlin
Cockermouth
Corby, Little
Coupland
Croglin
Crookdake
Culgaith
Cumwhitton
Drigg
Dundraw
Egremont
Ennerdale
Fenton
Gamblesby
Gosforth
Harrington
Haygil bane
Hayton
Heads Nook
Kelsick
Kelton
Kirk Andrews upon Eske
Kirland
Langrigg
Langwathby
Longrigg
Moorrow
Muncaster
Newton Regny
Oswald, Kirk
Penrith
Plumpton
Ravenglas
Ruckcroft
Skirwith
Stainton

**CUMBERLAND** —*cont.*
Ulcoats Mill
Westward
Wigton
Workington
Yearngill

**DENBIGH**—
Acton
Allington
Allmer
Bache
Benston (?)
Bersham
Bromfield Hundred
Broughton
Brymbo
Bryn Eglwys
Bryntangor
Castrum Leonis
Cerrig y Druidion
Chirk
Cristionyth Veohan
Denbigh
Dymuill
Eglwysfach
Esclud Vwych y Clauth
Esclusham
Gresford
Hewlington *al.* Newling-
ton
Holt
Is y coed
Llai
Llandegla
Llandysilio
Llanferras
Llanrwst
Llansannan
Llansantfraid Glyn Cei-
riog
Llanynys
Maesyr Odyn
Poseney Park
Stansty
Trevor Issa
Wrexham
Yale Hundred
Yale Raglia
Ystrad
Ystredeloc

**DERBY**—
Abney
Alderoar Park
Alderwasley
Aldwark
Alestre
Alfreton
Alkmonton
Alport

**DERBY**—*cont.*—
Alsop le Dale
Alstonlegh
Alvaston
Apperknowl
Appleby
Appletree Hundred
Ashbourne
Ashford
Ashleyhay
Ashop
Ashover
Aston
Aston, Coal
Bagthorpe
Bakewell
Ballidon
Bamford
Barlborough
Barlow *al.* Barley
Barlow Woodseats
Barton Blount *al.* B.
Bakepuz
Baslow
Bawdon
Bearwardcote
Beeley
Beighton
Belper
Bentley, Fenny *al.* Hun-
gry
Biggin Manor
Bikirwude in Macwrh
Birchett
Birchill
Birchover
Blackbrook Manor
Blackwell
Bolsover
Bonsall
Borowcote
Boulton
Bowdon
Boylstone
Boythorpe
Brackenfield
Bradborne
Bradley
Bradshaw Edge
Bradway
Bradwell
Brailsford
Brampton
Brassington
Breadsall
Breaston
Breeley (?)
Bretby
Bretton
Brimington
Broadlow Ash

**3 K 2**

3 L

3 N 2

# ADDENDA ET CORRIGENDA.

*Add* **Abbot's Manor.** *v. sub* Darsham, co *Suff.*

*Sub* **Acreholes,** *co. Linc. In par. 2, line 2, read c.* 1150-55. Harl. 43 H. 14-17, 47 A. 34;—[1156 or 7?]. Harl. 51 H. 1;—etc.

*Sub* **Adlingfleet,** *co. York. Add* Inspex. of covenants, etc., betw. the clerk and rector of, and Selby Abbey conc. tithes, 1293 (Adelingfleoth, Adelingflet). Harl. 111 C. 21.

*Add* **Adredesia, Insula de.** *v.* Nyland, *nr. Rodney Stoke, co. Som.*

*Dele* **Aishe juxta Campessye.** *v.* Campsey Ash, *co. Suff.*

*Add* **Alderford,** *co. Norf.* Papal conf. of lands in, to Horsham St. Faith Priory, 1163 (Halraforda). Cott. MS. Aug. ii. 136.

*Dele* **Aldredesey Island.**

*Sub* **Amber,** *River. Add* Grant on banks of, in Duffield Forest, [1191-9] (Ambre). Eg. 437.

*Add* **Anglica Cnihttengilda, Soca de.** *v. sub* London.

*Add* **Anvil Green.** *v. sub* Waltham, *co. Kent.*

*Sub* **Arthingworth,** *co. Northt. In par. 4 after* 13 *cent. add* (Herningwrd). *Read at end*
v. also Ardingworth.

*Sub* **Arundel,** *Honour of. Add* Inquest conc. lands in Rudgwick, co. Suss., held of, 1488. Add. 7388.

*Sub* **Ash,** *nr. Sandwich, co. Kent. In par.* 1 *after* 1280 *add* (Esse). *In par.* 7 *after* 77 G. 15 *add* (Eesch).

*Sub* **Ash,** *co. Surr. Add* Rental of Claygate (Cleygate) manor in, 1547-49. Harl. Roll C. 12.

*Add* **Ashton,** *nr. Stodday, in Lancaster parish, co. Lanc.* Award in suit conc. the grange of, betw. Lancaster Priory and Cockersand Abbey, 1256 (Estona). Add. 19818.

*Sub* **Ashton,** *in Cleley Hundred, co. Northt. Add* Compotus-rolls, 1489-1498 (Asshen). Harl. Rolls A A. 17-19.

*Sub* **Ashton, Steeple,** *co. Wilts. Add* Livery of Overcourt manor, as held of the manor of, 1613. Add. 5714.

*Add* **Aston by Sutton,** *co. Chest.* Inspex. of grant in, to Whalley Abbey, 1344 (Mauricastona). Add. 1060.

*Sub* **Avon, Nether,** *co. Wilts. Add* v. also Netheravon.

*Sub* **Aylestone,** *co. Leic. Add* v. also Aylstone.

*Sub* **Aylsham,** *co. Norf. Add* Conveyance in, 1420 (Aylesham). Add. 14806.

*Sub* **Ballingham,** *co. Heref. Add* v. also Carey, *nr. Ballingham, co. Heref.*

*Add* **Banaselek.** *v. sub* St. Enoder, *co. Cornw.*

*Sub* **Bargh al. Barugh,** *co. York. Add* Gr. in Higham (Hoyham) in, *t.* Hen. III. or Edw. I. Add. 8178.

*Svb* **Barwick in Elmett,** *co. York. Add* Lease of Potterton Hall, etc., in, 1572. Harl. 77 H. 37.

*Sub* **Bawdeswell,** *co. Norf. Add* Papal conf. of the mill to Horsham St. Faith Priory, 1163 (Baldrusella). Cott. MS. Aug. ii. 136.

3 o

*Add* Brightwell, *cv. Berks.* Fines in, 1350, 1364. Harl. Roll G. 17.

*Sub* Brill, *co. Buck. Add* Protection from Hen. II. to Notley Abbey in the forest of, [1179?] (Brihull). Harl. Roll O. 26 (3).

*Sub* Brixton, *Isle of Wight. Add* Reservation of the advowson of the chapel to the Bp. of Winchester, 1284 (Briccheston). Harl. Roll CO. 21.

*Add* Bromefield, Upper. *v. sub* Seal, *co. Kent.*

*Sub* Bromfield, *co. Cumb. Add* Commutation of tithes in Crookdake in, 1639. Add. 17169, 17170.

*Add* Brunstead, *co. Norf.* Conff. of tithes in, to Hulme Abbey, *t.* Steph. (Brunstede). Cott. iv. 57 (25-27) (*copies*).

*Sub* Buckingham, *County of. Add* Computus-rolls of lands in, bel. to St. Andrew's Priory, Northampton, 1455-56. Harl. Roll K. 7;—*t.* Hen. VII. Harl. Roll K. 8.

*Add* Bullocks Manor. *v. sub* Bray, *co. Berks* (*Addenda*).

*Add* Bury St. Edmunds, *Honour of.* Grant of knts. fees held of, to Alberic, Count of Guines, *c.* 1139-44. Cott. xxi. 6.

*Add* Calbourne, *Isle of Wight.* Quitclaim of Swainstone (Sweyneston) manor in, to the Crown, reserving the advowson, by the Bp. of Winchester, 1284 (Cauburn). Harl. Roll CO. 21.

——— Court-rolls of Swainstone manor in, 1485-1497. Harl. Rolls M. 31-39.

*Add* Caldecote, *co. Kent.* Grant of rent of, *t.* Hen. III. (Chaldecote). Add. 16441 (*copy*).

*Add* Caldey, *co. Chest.* Renunciation of a claim "de nayvitate" in (?), *c.* 1244. Add. 26743.

*Sub* Calton, *co. Staff. Add v. also* Caldon.

*Sub* Cambridge, *County of. Add* Crown grant of chantry lands in, to Dr. Tho. Wendye, 1549. Add. 7060.

*Sub* Cannington, *co. Som. Add* Grant in Pokelond in, *t.* Edw. I-II. Add. 19980.

——— Re-feoffment in Combwich (Combewyche) and Putnell (Potenhull) nr., 1421. Add. 15845.

*Add* Capwell, *nr. Charlbury* (?), *co. Oxon.* Rental, early 14 cent. Harl. Roll B. 23.

*Add* Carbonels. *v. sub* Whelnetham, Great and Little, *co. Suff.*

*Add* Carleton, *nr. Poulton in the Fylde, co. Lanc.* Award in suit conc. the grange of, betw. Lancaster Priory and Cockersand Abbey, 1256 (Karlton). Add. 19818.

*Add* Chalkwell. *v. sub* Milton next Sittingbourne, *co. Kent.*

*Sub* Chardstock, *co. Dors. Add* Feoffment in Wolmington in, 1377. Harl. 53 C. 10.

——— Court-roll of Wulmyngton in, 1502-3. Harl. Roll I. 7.

*Add* Charlton Musgrave, *co. Som.* Covenant conc. household stuff, etc., in Roundhill (Rounhull) in (?), 1411. Add. 15301.

*Sub* Chelsham, *co. Surr.* In par. 1, *for* 1490 *read* 1499.

*Sub* Chent. *v.* Kennet, *co. Wilts.* For Kennet *read* Chute, *co. Wilts.* (*Addenda*).

*Sub* Chilverscoton, *co. Warw. Add* Grant in, 1287 (Cotis). Add. 20453.

*Sub* Chisenbury. *co. Wilts.* For *heading read* Chisbury, *nr. Lit. Bedwyn, co. Wilts.* (*except for last entry*).

*Add* Chute, *co. Wilts.* Title of Joh. de Cobeham in, 1332 (Chent). Harl. Roll N. 34.

*Add* Chynthurst. *v. sub* Shalford, *co. Surr.*

*Sub* Colsall Manor. *For* Milton *read* Milton next Sittingbourne.

*Add* Combe, Villa de la. *v. sub* St. Veep, *co. Cornw.*

*For* Compton, [East, *co. Dors.*?]. *Read* Compton, *co. Suss.*

*Add* Cote *al.* Cotes, *nr. Chadlington, co. Oxon.* Rental, early 14 cent. Harl. Roll B. 23.

——— Compotus-rolls, 1372—1431. Harl. Rolls B. 31, 35, 36, 38, 41, 42.

*Sub* **Garston, East,** *co. Berks.* *Add*
Power for seisin of Maidencourt
(Mayndencote) manor in (?), 1385.
Harl. 56 A. 35.

*Add* **Garstun, Suth.** *v. sub* Bitton
(Oldland in), *co. Glouc.*

*Sub* **Gaytonthorpe,** *co. Norf.* *Add*
Grant in (?), *t.* Hen. III. or Edw. I.
(Torp). Harl. 56 I. 27.

*Add* **Geardcylle.** *v.* Yarkhill, *co.*
*Heref.*

*Sub* **Gilbertsford,** *nr. Reynoldston, co.*
*Pembr.* *For* Reynoldston *read*
Hayscastle.

*Add* **Glaston,** *co. Rutl.* Inquest conc.
tenure of, 1302 (Glacstone). Add.
7371.

*Sub* **Grikes,** *co. Suss.* *Add*
*v. also* Grykes.

*Add* **Grove Mill.** *v. sub* Haddenham,
*co. Buck. (Addenda).*

*Sub* **Haddenham,** *co. Buck.* *Add*
Lease of Grove mill in (?), 1518.
Add. 18802.

*Add* **Halcourte.** *v. sub* Swingfield,
*co. Kent.*

*Add* **Haldenby,** *nr. Adlingfleet, co.*
*York.* Inspex. of covenants with
Selby Abbey conc. tithes, etc., in,
1293 (Haldaneby). Harl. 111 C. 21.

*Add* **Hamons.** *v. sub* Stapleford
Abbots, *co. Essex.*

*Sub* **Hartwell,** *co. Northt.* *Add* Conveyance in Bozenham (Ouerbosenho
in Com. Buk.) in, 1430 (Hertwell).
Harl. 76 G. 50.

*Sub* **Hatherden,** *in Foxcot, co. Southt.*
*Add* Fine in, 1342 (Hetherdoue).
Harl. Roll G. 17 (15).

*Sub* **Haverholme,** *co. Linc. for* late 13
cent. *read* early Hen. III.

*Add* **Hayscastle,** *co. Pembr.* Grant,
etc., of mills, etc., at Gilbertsford in
Rhinderston (villa Raynori) in, *t.*
Edw. I. Add. 8058, 8410.

*Sub* **Heacham,** *co. Norf.* *Add* *v. also*
Hitcham, *co. Norf.*

*Sub* **Heckingham,** *co. Norf.* *Add*
Papal conf. of grant in, to Horsham
St. Faith Priory, 1163 (Huchinga-
ham). Cott. MS. Aug. ii. 136.

*Sub* **Henbury,** *co. Glouc.* *Add* Fine in,
1334 (Hembury in Salso Marisco).
Harl. Roll G. 17 (3).

*Sub* **Hertford,** *co. Hertf.* *Add* Grant
in, or near (?), by Rowney Priory,
*t.* Hen. III. Campb. iv. 2.

*Sub* **Heybridge,** *co. Essex.* *Add* Bequest of land at, to St. Paul's
Church, London, 991 (Tidwolding-
tun). Harl. 43 C. 4.

*Sub* **Hilton,** *co. Salop.* *Add*
*v. also* Helton.

*For* **Hitcham,** *co. Norf. read* Heacham,
*co. Norf. (q. v.)*

*Add* **Holdisworth.** *v.* Holsworthy, *co.*
*Devon.*

*Add* **Hollands Broughton.** *v. sub*
Weston Turville, *co. Buck.*

*Sub* **Holsworthy,** *co. Devon.* *Add*
Power to give seisin of the manor
and advowson, *t.* Edw. III. (Holdisworth). Harl. 45 E. 38.

*Sub* **Honeydon,** *co. Bedf.* *Add*
*v. also* Honydon.

*Sub* **Hoo St. Werburgh,** *co. Kent.*
*Add* Charters dated at, 823. Cott.
MS. Aug. ii. 75 (Werburging wic);—
845-850. Cott. xvii. 1 (Werburge-
wic).

*Sub* **Hutton Cranswick,** *co. York.*
*Add* Release in Sunderlundwick in,
to Watton Priory, 1322. Harl. 55
E. 23.

*Sub* **Ickenham,** *co. Midd.* *Add* Rental
of lands of R. Pexhall in Swakeley
(Swalclyff) manor in, 1549. Add.
26560.

——— Power to give seisin of a
twelfth part of Swakeley manor in,
1607. Harl. 84 II. 14.

*Add* **Ireland.** Charter dated "eo anno
quo verbum factum est de Hibernia
conquirenda." 1154 [*i.e.* Sept. 1155].
Harl. 83 C. 25.

——— Exchange of lands in Con-
naught held of Pr. Edward, for
manors in co. Essex, [1263-72].
Harl. 45 D. 7.

——— Letter conc. a lease of his
lands in, by Sir J. Bygod, 1285.
Harl. 43 B. 18.

——— Rolls of pleas at Dublin,
Waterford, etc., 1290. Add. 13598;
—1330. Add. 13599;—14-15 centt.
Add. 13600.

——— Petition from prelates of, to
Edw. I. (?), *n. d.* Cott. MS. Aug. ii.
104.

*Add* Ireland (*continued.*) *Thesaurarius et Camerarius de Scaccario.* Tho. Strange, *miles*, 1480. Harl. 57 A. 8;—1431. Harl. 52 E. 14.

—— *Treasurer.* Giles Thorndon, [1443]. Harl. 111 B. 12.

—— *Justiciarius Hibernie.* Joh. Darcy, *le Cosyn*, 1330. Add. 13599.

—— *Locum tenens Justiciarii Hibernie.* Fr. Rog. Outlawe, *Prior Hosp. S. Joh. Jerl. in Hibernia*, 1330. Add. 13599.

—— *Justiciarii de Banco.* Rob. Bagod, *Mag.* Tho. de Chaddesworth, Joh. de Hacche, 1290. Add. 13598.

*Add* **Karlton.** *v.* Carleton, *co. Lanc.* (*Addenda*).

*Sub* **Keddington,** *co. Linc. Add* Grant of the church to Daventry Priory, late Hen. II. (Chedintune, Kedintune). Cott. **xxv.** 23.

*Sub* **Kedington,** *co. Suff. Dele par.* 2.

*Sub* **Kettleby Thorpe,** *co. Linc. Add* Grants in, to Newhouse Abbey, *ante* 1259. Harl. 52 F. 5 (Thorp) :—late Hen. III. Harl. 58 A. 37 (do.).

*Add* **Kirklington,** *co. Nott.* Covenant for settlement of Roohawe manor in (?) or nr., 1437. Add. 20542.

*Sub* **Langrigg,** *co. Cumb. Add v. also* Longrigg.

*Sub* **Leicester,** *County of. Add* Compotus-rolls of lands in, bel. to St. Andrew's Priory, Northampton, 1455-56. Harl. Roll K. 7;— *t.* Hen. VII. Harl. Roll K. 8.

*For* **Letcombe** —— (?), *co. Berks. read* Letcombe Basset.

*Sub* **Lewes,** *co. Suss. Dele par.* 7. *Add*

—— *Vicecomes* (?). Petrus, *t.* Steph. Cott. MS. Nero C. iii. f. 217.

*Add* **Leya.** *v. sub* Stanley, King's, *co. Glouc.*

*Sub* **Lincoln,** *County of. Add* Compotus-rolls of lands in, bel. to St. Andrew's Priory, Northampton, 1455-56. Harl. Roll K. 7;— *t.* Hen. VII. Harl. Roll K. 8.

*Add* **Linton,** *co. Heref.* Sale in, 1654. Add. 1953.

*Sub* **London,** *City of. Add* Bond to the late Sheriffs from a merchant of Genoa, 1447. Harl. 50 F. 23.

*Sub* **London** (*continued*). *Add* Release on account of repairs in the manor of Norton Folgate (Norton) by the "firmarius" of St. Paul's, 1453. Lansd. 653.

*Add* **Lorties Manor.** *v. sub* Sutton Veney, *co. Wilts.*

*Add* **Luffenham, North,** *co. Rutl.* Inquest conc. tenure of, 1302 (Nortluftenham). Add. 7371.

*Sub* **Maugersbury,** *co. Glouc. Add* Conveyance of the manor, 1604. Add. 15157, 15158.

*Sub* **Meole Brace,** *co. Salop. Add* Briefs for rebuilding the church, 1799. Ch. Br. B. xxxix. 5;—1810. Ch. Br. B. l. 8.

*For* **Michaelstone,** *co. Glam. read* Michaelston le Pit, *co. Glam.*

*Sub* **Michaelstone,** *co. Glam. Dele par.* 4.

—— *Add v. also* Wrinstone, *co. Glam.*

*Add* **Midloe,** *co. Hunt.* Conf. of Sterth and Molesho in, to Wardon Abbey, 1257-8. Cott. MS. Nero C. iii. f. 230.

*Sub* **Monkton, West,** *co. Som. Add* Compotus of lands of Taunton Priory in Tonbrugge in, 1438-9. Add. 25873.

*Add* **Morcott,** *co. Rutl.* Inquest conc. tenure of, 1302 (Morcotu). Add. 7371.

*For* **More's,** *in Sturminster Marshall* (?), *co. Dors. read* Moreis [Moorhayes *in Collumpton, co. Devon* ?].

*Add* [**Morvill,** *co. Pembr.*]. Grant in Redwalls (Reddewalles) [*al.* Fagwyr Goch] in (?), *t.* Hen. III. Add. 8408.

*Add* [**Munden Great,** *co. Hertf.*]. Grant in or nr. (?), by Rowney Priory, *t.* Hen. III. Campb. iv. 2.

*Sub* **Murston,** *co. Kent. Add v. also* Murton.

*Sub* **Netheravon,** *co. Wilts. Add v. also* Avon, Nether.

*Add* **Netherhall.** *v. sub* Stanstead, *co. Suff.*

*Add* **Newland.** *v. sub* Roxwell, *co. Essex.*

*Add* **Nighs, The.** *v. sub* Wanborough, *co. Wilts.*

*Sub* **Norton Giffard,** *in Weston sub Edge, co. Glouc.* Dele (?). *And for c.* 1125 *read t.* Steph.

9 780331 482058